COLLINS
PAPERBACK
LATIN
DICTIONARY

LATIN ▶ ENGLISH   ENGLISH ▶ LATIN

GW00647405

HarperCollins*Publishers*

First published in this edition 1995

© **HarperCollins Publishers 1995**

ISBN 0 00 470687-0

Based on the Collins Latin Gem © 1957 by
Professor D A Kidd
Canterbury University

editorial coordinator
Joyce Littlejohn

Latin consultants
Ian Brookes
Denis Bruce   Michael D Igoe

supplements
Mary Wade

*Typeset by Tradespools Ltd.,
Somerset*

*Printed in Great Britain by
HarperCollins Manufacturing, Glasgow*

CONTENTS

Abbreviations used in this dictionary	iv
How to use the dictionary	v
Latin Alphabet, Spelling	vii
Pronunciation, Accent	viii
Grammar	xiii
LATIN-ENGLISH	1–236
Roman Life and Culture	1–25
Latin Verse	1–9
ENGLISH-LATIN	1–192
Latin phrases in English today	1–15

ABBREVIATIONS

adj	adjective	*MED*	medicine
abl	ablative	*MIL*	military
acc	accusative	*mod*	modern
adv	adverb	*n*	noun
AGR	agriculture	*NAUT*	nautical
ARCH	architecture	*neg*	negative
art	article	*nom*	nominative
ASTR	astronomy	*nt*	neuter
AUG	augury	*num*	numeral
COMM	business	*occ*	occasionally
CIRCS	circumstances	*p*	participle
compar	comparative	*pass*	passive
conj	conjunction	*perf*	perfect
cpd	compound	*perh*	perhaps
dat	dative	*pers*	person
defec	defective	*PHILOS*	philosophy
ECCL	ecclesiastical	*pl*	plural
esp	especially	*POL*	politics
excl	exclamatory	*ppa*	perfect participle active
f	feminine	*ppp*	perfect participle passive
fig	figurative	*prep*	preposition
fut	future	*pres*	present
gen	genitive	*pron*	pronoun
GEOG	geography	*prop*	properly
GRAM	grammar	*PROV*	proverb
impers	impersonal	*relat*	relative
imperf	imperfect	*RHET*	rhetoric
impv	imperative	*sg*	singular
indecl	indeclinable	*sim*	similarly
indic	indicative	*subj*	subjunctive
inf	informal	*superl*	superlative
infin	infinitive	*THEAT*	theatre
interj	interjection	*UNIV*	university
interrog	interrogative	*usu*	usually
LIT	literature	*vi*	intransitive verb
loc	locative	*voc*	vocative
m	masculine	*vt*	transitive verb
MATH	mathematics		

INTRODUCTION

Whether you are learning Latin for the first time or wish to "brush up" what you learned some time ago, this dictionary is designed to help you understand Latin and to express yourself in Latin, if you so wish.

HOW TO USE THE DICTIONARY

Entries are laid out as follows:

Headword

This is shown in **bold type**. On the Latin-English side all long vowels are shown by placing a ‾ above them. Latin nouns show the genitive singular form in bold. Latin verbs show the first person singular of the present indicative as the headword, followed by the infinitive, the first person singular of the perfect indicative and usually the past participle, all in bold type:

elegīa, -ae
elementum, -ī
ēlevō, āre
ēmātūrēscō, -ēscere, -uī

Part of Speech

Next comes the part of speech (noun, verb, adjective etc), shown in *italics*. Part of speech abbreviations used in the dictionary are shown in the abbreviations list (*p iv*). Where a word has more than one part of speech, each new part of speech is preceded by a black lozenge (♦). If a Latin headword is a preposition, the case taken by the preposition comes immediately after the part of speech, in *italics* and in brackets.

era, -ae *f*
ticklish *adj*
thunder *n* tonitrus *m* ♦ *vi* tonare, intonare.
ērgā *prep* (*with acc*) towards; against.

Meanings

Where a word or a part of speech has only one meaning, the translation comes immediately after the part of speech. However, many words have more than one meaning. Where the context is likely to show which translation is correct, variations in meaning are simply separated by a semi-colon. But usually there will also be an "indicator" in *italics* and in brackets. Some meanings relate to specific subject areas, for example religion, politics, military matters etc –

these indicators are in small italic capitals.

ēnsiger, -ī *adj* with his sword.
toy *n* crepundia *ntpl* ♦ *vi* ludere.
toll collector *n* exactor *m*; portitor *m*.
eō, -īre, īvī *and* **iī, itum** *vi* to go; (*MIL*) to march; (*time*) to pass; (*event*) to proceed, turn out.

Translations

Most words can be translated directly. On the English-Latin side, translations of nouns include the gender of the Latin noun in *italics*. However, sometimes a phrase is needed to show how a word is used, but in some cases a direct translation of a phrase would be meaningless: the symbol ~ in front of a translation shows that the translation is natural English, but does not mean word for word what the Latin means. Sometimes, even an approximate translation would not be very helpful (for place names, for example) – in these cases, an explanation in *italics* is given instead. In other cases, the user will need more information than simply the translation; in these cases, "indicators" are included in the translation(s), giving, for instance, the case required by a Latin verb or preposition or further details about a place or person.

thumb *n* pollex *m*; **have under one's ~** in potestate sua habere.
elephantomacha, -ae *m fighter mounted on an elephant.*
Erymanthus, -i *m* mountain range in Arcadia (*where Hercules killed the bear*).
thwart *vt* obstare (*dat*), officere (*dat*).

Pronunciation

Since Latin pronunciation is regular, once the basic rules have been learned (*see pp viii, ix*), the dictionary does not show phonetic transcriptions against each headword, but does show all long vowels.

Other Information

The dictionary also includes:

- a basic grammar section
- information about life in Roman times:
  – how government and the army were organized – how numbers and dates were calculated and expressed – family relationships – geographical names – major Roman authors – key events in Roman history – (*important historical and mythological characters and events are listed within the body of the main text*).
- a section on Latin poetry and scansion
- a list of Latin expressions commonly used in English today

LATIN ALPHABET

The Latin alphabet is the one which has been almost universally adopted by the modern languages of Europe and America. In the Classical period it had 23 letters, namely the English alphabet without letters **j**, **v** and **w**.

Letter *v*
The symbol **v** was the capital form of the letter **u**, but in a later age the small **v** came into use to represent the consonantal **u**, and as it is commonly so employed in modern editions of Latin authors, it has been retained as a distinct letter in this dictionary for convenience.

Letter *j*
The symbol **j** came to be used as the consonantal **i**, and is found in older editions of the Classics, but as it has been almost entirely discarded in modern texts, it is not used in this dictionary, and words found spelt with a **j** must therefore be looked up under **i**.

Letters *w, y, z*
The letter **w** may be seen in the Latinized forms of some modern names, *e.g.* **Westmonasterium**, Westminster. The letters **y** and **z** occur only in words of Greek origin.

ORTHOGRAPHY

Many Latin words which begin with a prefix can be spelled in two ways. The prefix can retain its original spelling, or it can be assimilated, changing a letter depending on the letter which follows it. Compare the following:

ad before **g, l, r** and **p**:

adpropinquare	appropinquare
adgredi	aggredi
adloquor	alloquor
adrogans	arrogans

ad is also often assimilated before **f** and **n**:

adfectus	affectus
adnexus	annexus

and **ad** is often shortened to **a** before **sc**:

adscendere	ascendere

in changes to **il** before **l**, to **im** before **m** or **p** and to **ir** before **r**.

con becomes **cor** when followed by another **r** and **col** when followed by **l**.

We have provided cross-references in the text to draw your attention to the alternative forms of words. Thus, although **arrogantia** does not appear in the Latin-English section, the cross-reference at **arr-** will point you to the entry for **adrogantia**, where the translation is given.

PRONUNCIATION

The ancient pronunciation of Latin has been established with a fair degree of certainty from the evidence of ancient authorities and inscriptions and inferences from the modern Romance languages. It is not possible, of course, to recapture the precise nuances of Classical Latin speech, but what follows is now generally accepted and generally understood as a reasonably accurate guide to the sounds of Latin as spoken by educated Romans during the two centuries from Cicero to Quintilian.

ACCENT

The Latin accent in the Classical period was a weak stress, perhaps with an element of pitch in it. It falls, as in English, on the second last syllable of the word, if that syllable is long, and on the third last syllable if the second last is short. Disyllabic words take the accent on the first syllable, unless they have already lost a final syllable, *e.g.* illīc(e).

Inflected words are commonly learned with the accent wrongly placed on the last syllable, for convenience in memorizing the inflexions. But it is advisable to get the accent as well as the ending right.

The correct accent of other words can easily be found by noting carefully the quantity of the second last syllable and then accenting the word as in English, according to the rule given above. Thus **fuērunt** is accented on the second last syllable because the **e** is long, whereas **fuerant** is accented on the third last, because the **e** is short.

VOWELS

Vowels are pure and should not be diphthongized as in certain sounds of Southern English. They may be long or short. Throughout this Dictionary all vowels known or believed by the best authorities to be long are marked with a line above them; those unmarked are either known to be short or of uncertain quantity.

	Short		*Long*	
agricol*a*	r*a*t	r*ā*mus	r*a*ther
heder*ā*	p*e*n	av*ē*	p*ay*
*ī*taque	k*i*n	c*ī*vis	k*ee*n
favor	r*o*b	ampli*ō*	r*o*be
neb*u*la	f*u*ll	l*ū*na	f*oo*l

y is a Greek sound and is pronounced (both short and long) as **u** in French *ie* r*u*e.

DIPHTHONGS

_ae_stas	tr_y_	
_au_diō	to_wn_	
h_ei_	p_ayee_	
m_eus_	_ay-oo_	with the accent on first sound
m_oe_cha	to_y_	
t_ui_tus	L_ou_is	

CONSONANTS

_b_alneae	_b_aby	
a_b_stēmius	a_p_se	
su_b_tractus	a_pt_	
_c_astra	_c_ar	
_ch_orda	sepul_ch_re	
inter_d_o	_d_og	
cōn_f_lō	_f_ortune	
in_g_redior	_g_o	
_h_abeō	_h_and	(_but faintly_)
_i_aceo	_y_es	(_consonantal i = j_)
_K_alendae	oa_k_	
conge_l_ō	_l_et	
co_m_es	_m_an	(_final m was hardly sounded and may have simply nasalized the preceding vowel_)
pā_n_is	_n_o	
pa_n_go	fi_n_ger	
stu_p_eō	a_p_t	
ra_ph_anus	_p_ill	
exse_qu_or	_qu_ite	
su_pr_ēmus	_br_ae	(_Scottish_)
mā_gn_u_s_	_s_ister	(_never as in ro_s_e_)
lae_t_us	_s_top	
_th_eātrum	_t_ake	
_v_apor _(and consonantal u)_	_w_in	
de_x_tra	si_x_	(_ks, not gs_)
_z_ōna	_z_ero	

Double consonants lengthen the sound of the consonant.

Latin Grammar

DECLENSIONS OF NOUNS

1st Declension

	mainly f		*m*	
SING				
Nom.	terra	crambē	Aenēās	Anchīsēs
Voc.	terra	crambē	Aenēā	Anchīsā, -ē
Acc.	terram	crambēn	Aenēam, -ān	Anchīsam, -ēn
Gen.	terrae	crambes	Aenēae	Anchīsae
Dat.	terrae	crambae	Aenēae	Anchīsae
Abl.	terra	cramba	Aenēā	Anchīsā

PLURAL		
Nom.	terrae	crambae
Voc.	terrae	crambae
Acc.	terrās	crambās
Gen.	terrārum	crambārum
Dat.	terrīs	crambīs
Abl.	terrīs	crambīs

2nd Declension

			mainly m		
SING					
Nom.	modus	Lūcius	Dēlos (*f*)	puer	liber
Voc.	mode	Lūcī	Dēle	puer	liber
Acc.	modum	Lūcium	Dēlon	puerum	librum
Gen.	modī	Lūcī	Dēlī	puerī	librī
Dat.	modō	Lūciō	Dēlō	puerō	librō
Abl.	modō	Lūciō	Dēlō	puerō	librō

PLURAL				
Nom.	modī		puerī	librī
Voc.	modī		puerī	librī
Acc.	modōs		puerōs	librōs
Gen.	modōrum		puerōrum	librōrum
Dat.	modīs		puerīs	librīs
Abl.	modīs		puerīs	librīs

SING	
Nom.	dōnum
Voc.	dōnum
Acc.	dōnum
Gen.	dōnī
Dat.	dōnō
Abl.	dōnō

PLURAL	
Nom.	dōna
Voc.	dōna
Acc.	dōna
Gen.	dōnōrum
Dat.	dōnīs
Abl.	dōnīs

3rd Declension

Group I: *Vowel stems, with gen pl in* **-ium**

SING	*m and f*		*nt*	
Nom.	clādēs	nāvis	rēte	animal
Voc.	clādēs	nāvis	rēte	animal
Acc.	clādem	nāvem, -im	rēte	animal
Gen.	clādis	nāvis	rētis	animālīs
Dat.	clādī	nāvī	rētī	animālī
Abl.	clāde	nāve, -ī	rētī	animālī
PLURAL				
Nom.	clādēs	nāvēs	rētia	animālia
Voc.	clādēs	nāvēs	rētia	animālia
Acc.	clādēs, -īs	nāvēs, -īs	rētia	animālia
Gen.	clādium	nāvium	rētium	animālium
Dat.	clādibus	nāvibus	rētibus	animālibus
Abl.	clādibus	nāvibus	rētibus	animālibus

Group II: *Consonant stems, some with gen pl in* **-ium**, *some in* **-um** *and some in either. Monosyllabic nouns ending in two consonants (e.g.* **urbs** *below) regularly have* **-ium**.

SING	*m and f*			*f*	*nt*
Nom.	urbs	amāns	laus	aetās	os
Voc.	urbs	amāns	laus	aetās	os
Acc.	urbem	amantem	laudem	aetātem	os
Gen.	urbis	amantis	laudis	aetātis	ossis
Dat.	urbī	amantī	laudī	aetātī	ossī
Abl.	urbe	amante	laude	aetāte	osse
PLURAL					
Nom.	urbēs	amantēs	laudēs	aetātēs	ossa
Voc.	urbēs	amantēs	laudēs	aetātēs	ossa

Acc.	urbēs	amantēs	laudēs	aetātēs	ossa
Gen.	urbium	amantium, -um	laudum, -ium	aetātum, -ium	ossium
Dat.	urbibus	amantibus	laudibus	aetātibus	ossibus
Abl.	urbibus	amantibus	laudibus	aetātibus	ossibus

Group III: *Consonant stems, with gen pl in* -um

	m and f			*nt*	
SING					
Nom.	mōs	ratiō	pater	nōmen	opus
Voc.	mōs	ratiō	pater	nōmen	opus
Acc.	mōrem	ratiōnem	patrem	nōmen	opus
Gen.	mōris	ratiōnis	patris	nōminis	operis
Dat.	mōrī	ratiōnī	patrī	nōminī	operī
Abl.	mōre	ratiōne	patre	nōmine	opere
PLURAL					
Nom.	mōrēs	ratiōnēs	patrēs	nōmina	opera
Voc.	mōrēs	ratiōnēs	patrēs	nōmina	opera
Acc.	mōrēs	ratiōnēs	patrēs	nōmina	opera
Gen.	mōrum	ratiōnum	patrum	nōminum	operum
Dat.	mōribus	ratiōnibus	patribus	nōminibus	operibus
Abl.	mōribus	ratiōnibus	patribus	nōminibus	operibus

Group IV: *Greek nouns*

	m		*f*		*nt*
SING					
Nom.	āēr	hērōs	Periclēs	Naias	poēma
Voc.	āēr	hērōs	Periclē	Naias	poēma
Acc.	āera	hērōa	Periclem, Periclea	Naiada	poēma
Gen.	āeris	hērōis	Periclis, -ī	Naiadis, -os	poēmatis
Dat.	āerī	hērōī	Periclī	Naiadī	poēmatī
Abl.	āere	hērōe	Periclē	Naiade	poēmate
PLURAL					
Nom.	āeres	hērōes		Naiades	poēmata
Voc.	āeres	hērōes		Naiades	poēmata
Acc.	āeras	hērōas		Naiadas	poēmata
Gen.	āerum	hērōum		Naiadum	poēmatōrum
Dat.	āeribus	hērōibus		Naiadibus	poēmatīs
Abl.	āeribus	hērōibus		Naiadibus	poēmatīs

	4th Declension		**5th Declension**	
	mainly m	*nt*	*mainly f*	
SING				
Nom.	portus	genū	diēs	rēs
Voc.	portus	genū	diēs	rēs
Acc.	portum	genū	diem	rem
Gen.	portūs	genūs	diēī	reī
Dat.	portuī	genū	diēī	reī
Abl.	portū	genū	diē	rē
PLURAL				
Nom.	portūs	genua	diēs	rēs
Voc.	portūs	genua	diēs	rēs
Acc.	portūs	genua	diēs	rēs
Gen.	portuum	genuum	diērum	rērum
Dat.	portibus, -ubus	genibus, -ubus	diēbus	rēbus
Abl.	portibus, -ubus	genibus, -ubus	diēbus	rēbus

CONJUGATIONS OF VERBS

ACTIVE

PRESENT TENSE

	First	**Second**	**Third**	**Fourth**
	parāre	**habēre**	**sūmere**	**audīre**
	prepare	*have*	*take*	*hear*

Indicative

	First	Second	Third	Fourth
SING				
1st pers	parō	habeō	sūmō	audiō
2nd pers	parās	habēs	sūmis	audīs
3rd pers	parat	habet	sūmit	audit
PLURAL				
1st pers	parāmus	habēmus	sūmimus	audīmus
2nd pers	parātis	habētis	sūmitis	audītīs
3rd pers	parant	habent	sūmunt	audiunt

Subjunctive

	First	Second	Third	Fourth
SING				
1st pers	parem	habeam	sūmam	audiam
2nd pers	parēs	habeās	sūmās	audiās
3rd pers	paret	habeat	sūmat	audiat
PLURAL				
1st pers	parēmus	habeāmus	sūmāmus	audiāmus
2nd pers	parētis	habeātis	sūmātis	audiātis
3rd pers	parent	habeant	sūmant	audiant

IMPERFECT TENSE
Indicative

SING				
1st pers	parābam	habēbam	sūmēbam	audiēbam
2nd pers	parābās	habēbās	sūmēbās	audiēbās
3rd pers	parābat	habēbat	sūmēbat	audiēbat
PLURAL				
1st pers	parābāmus	habēbāmus	sūmēbāmus	audiēbāmus
2nd pers	parābātis	habēbātis	sūmēbātis	audiēbātis
3rd pers	parābant	habēbant	sūmēbant	audiēbant

Subjunctive

SING				
1st pers	parārem	habērem	sūmerem	audīrem
2nd pers	parārēs	habērēs	sūmerēs	audīrēs
3rd pers	parāret	habēret	sūmeret	audīret
PLURAL				
1st pers	parārēmus	habērēmus	sūmerēmus	audīrēmus
2nd pers	parārētis	habērētis	sūmerētis	audīrētis
3rd pers	parārent	habērent	sūmerent	audīrent

FUTURE TENSE
Indicative

SING				
1st pers	parābō	habēbō	sūmam	audiam
2nd pers	parābis	habēbis	sūmēs	audiēs
3rd pers	parābit	habēbit	sūmet	audiet
PLURAL				
1st pers	parābimus	habēbimus	sūmēmus	audiēmus
2nd pers	parābitis	habēbitis	sūmētis	audiētis
3rd pers	parābunt	habēbunt	sūment	audient

Subjunctive

SING			
parātūrus, -a, -um	sim	*or*	essem
habitūrus, -a, -um	sīs		essēs
sūmptūrus, -a, -um	sit		esset
audītūrus, -a, -um			
PLURAL			
parātūrī, -ae, -a	simus	*or*	essēmus
habitūrī, -ae, -a	sītis		essētis
sūmptūrī, -ae, -a	sint		essent
audītūrī, -ae, -a			

PERFECT TENSE
Indicative

SING				
1st pers	parāvī	habuī	sūmpsī	audīvī
2nd pers	parāvistī	habuistī	sūmpsistī	audīvistī
3rd pers	parāvit	habuit	sūmpsit	audīvit

PLURAL				
1st pers	parāvimus	habuimus	sūmpsimus	audīvimus
2nd pers	parāvistis	habuistis	sūmpsistis	audīvistis
3rd pers	parāvērunt, -e	habuērunt, -e	sūmpsērunt, -e	audīvērunt, -e

Subjunctive

SING				
1st pers	parāverim	habuerim	sūmpserim	audīverim
2nd pers	parāveris	habueris	sūmpseris	audīveris
3rd pers	parāverit	habuerit	sūmpserit	audīverit

PLURAL				
1st pers	parāverimus	habuerimus	sūmpserimus	audīverimus
2nd pers	parāveritis	habueritis	sūmpseritis	audīveritis
3rd pers	parāverint	habuerint	sūmpserint	audīverint

PLUPERFECT TENSE
Indicative

SING				
1st pers	parāveram	habueram	sūmpseram	audīveram
2nd pers	parāverās	habuerās	sūmpserās	audīverās
3rd pers	parāverat	habuerat	sūmpserat	audīverat

PLURAL				
1st pers	parāverāmus	habuerāmus	sūmpserāmus	audīverāmus
2nd pers	parāverātis	habuerātis	sūmpserātis	audīverātis
3rd pers	parāverant	habuerant	sūmpserant	audīverant

Subjunctive

SING				
1st pers	parāvissem	habuissem	sūmpsissem	audīvissem
2nd pers	parāvissēs	habuissēs	sūmpsissēs	audīvissēs
3rd pers	parāvisset	habuisset	sūmpsisset	audīvisset

PLURAL				
1st pers	parāvissēmus	habuissēmus	sūmpsissēmus	audīvissēmus
2nd pers	parāvissētis	habuissētis	sūmpsissētis	audīvissētis
3rd pers	parāvissent	habuissent	sūmpsissent	audīvissent

FUTURE PERFECT TENSE
Indicative

SING				
1st pers	parāverō	habuerō	sūmpserō	audīverō
2nd pers	parāveris	habueris	sūmpseris	audīveris
3rd pers	parāverit	habuerit	sūmpserit	audīverit
PLURAL				
1st pers	parāverimus	habuerimus	sūmpserimus	audīverimus
2nd pers	parāveritis	habueritis	sūmpseritis	audīveritis
3rd pers	parāverint	habuerint	sūmpserint	audīverint

IMPERATIVE
Present

SING	parā	habē	sūme	audī
PLURAL	parāte	habēte	sūmite	audīte

Future

SING				
2nd pers	parātō	habētō	sūmitō	audītō
3rd pers	parātō	habētō	sūmitō	audītō
PLURAL				
2nd pers	parātōte	habētōte	sūmitōte	audītōte
3rd pers	parantō	habentō	sūmuntō	audiuntō

INFINITIVE
Present

parāre	habēre	sūmere	audīre

Perfect

parāvisse	habuisse	sūmpsisse	audīvisse

Future

parātūrus,	-a, -um, esse
habitūrus,	-a, -um, esse
sūmptūrus,	-a, -um, esse
audītūrus,	-a, -um, esse

PASSIVE

PRESENT TENSE
Indicative

SING			
1st pers	paror	habeor	sūmor	audior
2nd pers	parāris	habēris	sūmeris	audīris
3rd pers	parātur	habētur	sūmitur	audītur
PLURAL			
1st pers	parāmur	habēmur	sūmimur	audīmur
2nd pers	parāminī	habēminī	sūmiminī	audīminī
3rd pers	parantur	habentur	sūmuntur	audiuntur

Subjunctive

SING			
1st pers	parer	habear	sūmar	audiar
2nd pers	parēris	habeāris	sūmāris	audiāris
3rd pers	parētur	habeātur	sūmātur	audiātur
PLURAL			
1st pers	parēmur	habeāmur	sūmāmur	audiāmur
2nd pers	parēminī	habeāminī	sūmāminī	audiāminī
3rd pers	parentur	habeantur	sūmantur	audiantur

IMPERFECT TENSE
Indicative

SING			
1st pers	parābar	habēbar	sūmēbar	audiēbar
2nd pers	parābāris	habēbāris	sūmēbāris	audiēbāris
3rd pers	parābātur	habēbātur	sūmēbātur	audiēbātur
PLURAL			
1st pers	parābāmur	habēbāmur	sūmēbāmur	audiēbāmur
2nd pers	parābāmini	habēbāmini	sūmēbāminī	audiēbāminī
3rd pers	parābāntur	habēbantur	sūmēbantur	audiēbantur

Subjunctive

SING			
1st pers	parārer	habērer	sūmerer	audīrer
2nd pers	parārēris	habērēris	sūmerēris	audīrēris
3rd pers	parārētur	habērētur	sūmerētur	audīrētur

PLURAL				
1st pers	pararēmur	habērēmur	sūmerēmur	audīrēmur
2nd pers	pararēminī	habērēminī	sūmerēminī	audīrēminī
3rd pers	pararentur	habērentur	sūmerentur	audīrentur

FUTURE TENSE

Indicative

SING				
1st pers	parābor	habēbor	sūmar	audiar
2nd pers	parāberis	habēberis	sūmēris	audiēris
3rd pers	parābitur	habēbitur	sūmētur	audiētur

PLURAL				
1st pers	parābimur	habēbimur	sūmēmur	audiēmur
2nd pers	parābimini	habēbimini	sūmēminī	audiēminī
3rd pers	parābuntur	habēbuntur	sūmentur	audientur

PERFECT TENSE

Indicative

SING		PLURAL	
parātus, -a, -um	sum/es/est	parātī, -ae, -a	sumus/estis/sunt
habitus, -a, -um	sum/es/est	habītī, -ae, -a	sumus/estis/sunt
sūmptus, -a, -um	sum/es/est	sūmptī, -ae, -a	sumus/estis/sunt
audītus, -a, -um	sum/es/est	audītī, -ae, -a	sumus/estis/sunt

Subjunctive

SING		PLURAL	
parātus, -a, -um	sim/sīs/sit	parātī, -ae, -a	sīmus/sītis/sint
habitus, -a, -um	sim/sīs/sit	habītī, -ae, -a	sīmus/sītis/sint
sūmptus, -a, -um	sim/sīs/sit	sūmptī, -ae, -a	sīmus/sītis/sint
audītus, -a, -um	sim/sīs/sit	audītī, -ae, -a	sīmus/sītis/sint

PLUPERFECT TENSE

Indicative

SING		PLURAL	
parātus, -a, -um	eram/eras/erat	parātī, -ae, -a	eramus/eratis/erant
habitus, -a, -um	eram/eras/erat	habitī, -ae, -a	eramus/eratis/erant
sūmptus, -a, -um	eram/eras/erat	sūmptī, -ae, -a	eramus/eratis/erant
audītus, -a, -um	eram/eras/erat	audītī, -ae, -a	eramus/eratis/erant

Subjunctive

SING		PLURAL	
parātus, -a, -um	essem/essēs/esset	parātī, -ae, -a	essēmus/essētis/essent
habitus, -a, -um	essem/essēs/esset	habītī, -ae, -a	essēmus/essētis/essent
sūmptus, -a, -um	essem/essēs/esset	sūmptī, -ae, -a	essēmus/essētis/essent
audītus, -a, -um	essem/essēs/esset	audītī, -ae, -a	essēmus/essētis/essent

FUTURE PERFECT TENSE

Indicative

SING		PLURAL	
parātus, -a, -um	erō/eris/erit	parātī, -ae, -a	erimus/eritis/erunt
habitus, -a, -um	erō/eris/erit	habītī, -ae, -a	erimus/eritis/erunt
sūmptus, -a, -um	erō/eris/erit	sūmptī, -ae, -a	erimus/eritis/erunt
audītus, -a, -um	erō/eris/erit	audītī, -ae, -a	erimus/eritis/erunt

IMPERATIVE

Present

SING	parāre	habēre	sūmere	audīre
PLURAL	parāminī	habēminī	sūmiminī	audīminī

Future

SING				
2nd pers	parātor	habētor	sūmitor	audītor
3rd pers	parātor	habētor	sūmitor	audītor
PLURAL				
3rd pers	parantor	habentor	sūmuntor	audiuntor

INFINITIVE

Present

parārī	habērī	sūmī	audīrī

Perfect

parātus -a, -um, esse	habitus -a, -um, esse	sūmptus -a, -um, esse	audītus, -a, -um, esse

Future

parātum īrī	habitum īrī	sūmptum īrī	audītum īrī

VERBAL NOUNS AND ADJECTIVES

Present Participle Active

parāns	habēns	sūmēns	audiēns

Perfect Participle Passive

parātus	habitus	sūmptus	audītus

Future Participle Active

parātūrus	habitūrus	sūmptūrus	audītūrus

Gerund
(acc, gen, dat and abl)

parandum, -ī, -ō	habendum, -ī, -ō	sūmendum, -ī, -ō	audiendum, -ī, -ō

Gerundive

parandus	habendus	sūmendus	audiendus

Supines

1st	parātum	habitum	sūmptum	audītum
2nd	parātū	habitū	sūmptū	audītū

Note. *Some verbs of the 3rd conjugation have the present indicative ending in* **-io**; *e.g.* **capio**, *I capture.*

PRESENT TENSE

INDICATIVE		SUBJUNCTIVE	
Active	**Passive**	**Active**	**Passive**
capio	capior	capiam	capiar
capis	caperis	capias	capiāris
capit	capitur	capiat	capiātur
capimus	capimur	capiāmus	capiāmur
capitis	capiminī	capiātis	capiāminī
capiunt	capiuntur	capiant	capiantur

IMPERFECT TENSE

capiēbam *etc.*	capiēbar *etc.*	caperem *etc.*	caperer *etc.*

FUTURE TENSE

capiam	capiar
capiēs *etc.*	capiēris *etc.*

INFINITIVE MOOD

Present Active	capere
Present Passive	capī

PRESENT IMPERATIVE

	Active		Passive	
cape	capite	capere		capiminī

	PARTICIPLE	*GERUND*	*GERUNDIVE*
Pres.	capiēns	capiendum	capiendus, -a, um

In all other tenses and moods **capere** *is similar to* **sumere**.

IRREGULAR VERBS

	Esse *be*	**Posse** *be able*	**Velle** *wish*	**Ire** *go*

Present Indicative

SING				
1st Pers	sum	possum	volō	eō
2nd Pers	es	potes	vīs	īs
3rd Pers	est	potest	vult, volt	it
PLURAL				
1st Pers	sumus	possumus	volumus	īmus
2nd Pers	estis	potestis	vultis, voltis	ītis
3rd Pers	sunt	possunt	volunt	eunt

Present Subjunctive

SING				
1st Pers	sim	possim	velim	eam
2nd Pers	sīs	possīs	velīs	eās
3rd Pers	sit	possit	velit	eat
PLURAL				
1st Pers	sīmus	possīmus	velīmus	eāmus
2nd Pers	sītis	possītis	velītis	eātis
3rd Pers	sint	possint	velint	eant

Imperfect Indicative

1st Pers	eram	poteram	volēbam	ībam

Imperfect Subjunctive

1st Pers	essem	possem	vellem	īrem

Future Indicative

1st Pers	erō	poterō	volam	ībō

Future Subjunctive

1st Pers	futūrus, -a, -um sim *or* essem	—	—	itūrus, -a, -um sim *or* essem

Perfect Indicative

1st Pers	fuī	potuī	voluī	īvī, iī

Perfect Subjunctive

1st Pers	fuerim	potuerim	voluerim	īverim, ierim

Pluperfect Indicative

1st Pers	fueram	potueram	volueram	īveram, ieram

Pluperfect Subjunctive

1st Pers	fuissem	potuissem	voluissem	īvissem, iissem

Future Perfect Indicative

1st Pers	fuerō	potuerō	voluerō	īverō, ierō

Present Imperative

SING	es	—	—	ī
PLURAL	este	—	—	īte

Future Imperative

SING	estō	—	—	ītō
PLURAL	estōte	—	—	ītōte

Infinitives

PRES	esse	posse	velle	īre
PERF	fuisse	potuisse	voluisse	īvisse, iisse
FUT	futūrus, -a, -um, esse	—	—	itūrus, -a, -um, esse

Participles

PRES	—	—	—	iēns, euntis
FUT	futūrus	—	—	itūrus

Gerund and Supine

GERUND	—	—	—	eundum
SUPINE	—	—	—	itum

Latin-English

A, a

ā *prep (with abl)* from; after, since; by, in respect of; **ab epistulīs, ā manū** secretary; **ab hāc parte** on this side; **ab integrō** afresh; **ā nōbīs** on our side; **ā tergō** in the rear; **cōpiōsus ā frūmentō** rich in corn; **usque ab** ever since.

ā *interj* ah!

ab *prep see* **ā.**

abāctus *ppp of* **abigō.**

abacus, -ī *m* tray; sideboard; gaming board; panel; counting table.

abaliēnō, -āre, -āvī, -ātum *vt* to dispose of; to remove, estrange.

Abantiadēs *m* Acrisius *or* Perseus.

Abās, -antis *m a king of Argos.*

abavus, -ī *m* great-great-grandfather.

abbās, -ātis *m* abbot.

abbātia *f* abbey.

abbātissa *f* abbess.

Abdēra, -ōrum *or* **-ae** *ntpl or fs a town in Thrace.*

Abdērītānus *adj see n.*

Abdērītēs *m* Democritus *or* Protagoras.

abdicātiō, -ōnis *f* disowning, abdication.

abdicō, -āre, -āvī, -ātum *vt* to disown; to resign; **sē ~** abdicate.

abdīcō, -īcere, -īxī, -ictum *vt* (AUG) to be unfavourable to.

abditus *ppp of* **abdō.**

abdō, -ere, -idī, -itum *vt* to hide; to remove.

abdōmen, -inis *nt* paunch, belly; gluttony.

abdūcō, -ūcere, -ūxī, -uctum *vt* to lead away, take away; to seduce.

abductus *ppp of* **abdūcō.**

abecedārium, -iī *nt* alphabet.

abēgī *perf of* **abigō.**

abeō, -īre, -iī, -itum *vi* to go away, depart; to pass away; to be changed; to retire (*from an office*); **sīc ~** turn out like this.

abequitō, -āre, -āvī, -ātum *vi* to ride away.

aberrātiō, -ōnis *f* relief (*from trouble*).

aberrō, -āre, -āvī, -ātum *vi* to stray; to deviate; to have respite.

abfore *fut infin of* **absum.**

abfuī *perf of* **absum.**

abfutūrus *fut p of* **absum.**

abhinc *adv* since, ago.

abhorreō, -ēre, -uī *vi* to shrink from; to differ; to be inconsistent.

abiciō, -icere, -iēcī, -iectum *vt* to throw away, throw down; to abandon, degrade.

abiectus *ppp of* **abiciō ♦** *adj* despondent; contemptible.

abiēgnus *adj* of fir.

abiēns, -euntis *pres p of* **abeō.**

abiēs, -etis *f* fir; ship.

abigō, -igere, -ēgī, -āctum *vt* to drive away.

abitus, -ūs *m* departure; exit.

abiūdicō, -āre, -āvī, -ātum *vt* to take away (*by judicial award*).

abiūnctus *ppp of* **abiungō.**

abiungō, -ungere, -ūnxī, -ūnctum *vt* to unyoke; to detach.

abiūrō, -āre, -āvī, -ātum *vt* to deny on oath.

ablātus *ppp of* **auferō.**

ablēgātiō, -ōnis *f* sending away.

ablēgō, -āre, -āvī, -ātum *vt* to send out of the way.

abligurriō, -īre, -īvī, -ītum *vt* to spend extravagantly.

ablocō, -āre, -āvī, -ātum *vt* to let (a house).

ablūdō, -dere, -sī, -sum *vi* to be unlike.

abluō, -uere, -uī, -ūtum *vt* to wash clean; to remove.

abnegō, -āre, -āvī, -ātum *vt* to refuse.

abnepōs, -ōtis *m* great-great-grandson.

abneptis *f* great-great-granddaughter.

abnoctō, -āre *vi* to stay out all night.

abnōrmis *adj* unorthodox.

abnuō, -uere, -uī, -ūtum *vt* to refuse; to deny.

aboleō, -ēre, -ēvī, -itum *vt* to abolish.

abolēscō, -ēscere, -ēvī *vi* to vanish.

abolitiō, -ōnis *f* cancelling.

abolla, -ae *f* greatcoat.

abōminātus *adj* accursed.

abōminor, -ārī, -ātus *vt* to deprecate; to detest.

Aborīginēs, -um *mpl* original inhabitants.

aborior, -īrī, -tus *vi* to miscarry.

abortiō, -ōnis *f* miscarriage.

abortīvus *adj* born prematurely.

abortus, -ūs *m* miscarriage.

abrādō, -dere, -sī, -sum *vt* to scrape off, shave.

abrāsus *ppp of* **abrādō.**

abreptus *ppp of* **abripiō.**

abripiō, -ipere, -ipuī, -eptum *vt* to drag away, carry off.

Noun declensions and verb conjugations are shown on pp xiii to xxv. The present infinitive ending of a verb shows to which conjugation it belongs: **-āre** = 1st; **-ēre** = 2nd; **-ere** = 3rd and **-īre** = 4th. Irregular verbs are shown on p xxvi

abrogātiō, -ōnis *f* repeal.
abrogō, -āre, -āvī, -ātum *vt* to annul.
abrotonum, -ī *nt* southernwood.
abrumpō, -umpere, -ūpī, -uptum *vt* to break off.
abruptus *ppp of* **abrumpō** ♦ *adj* steep; abrupt, disconnected.
abs *etc see* **ā.**
abscēdō, -ēdere, -essi, -essum *vi* to depart, withdraw; to cease.
abscīdō, -dere, -dī, -sum *vt* to cut off.
abscindō, -ndere, -dī, -ssum *vt* to tear off, cut off.
abscissus *ppp of* **abscindō.**
abscīsus *ppp of* **abscīdō** ♦ *adj* steep; abrupt.
abscondō, -ere, -ī *and* **idī, -itum** *vt* to conceal; to leave behind.
absēns, -entis *pres p of* **absum** ♦ *adj* absent.
absentia, -ae *f* absence.
absiliō, -īre, -iī *and* **uī** *vi* to spring away.
absimilis *adj* unlike.
absinthium, -ī *and* **iī** *nt* wormwood.
absis, -īdis *f* vault; (*ECCL*) chancel.
absistō, -istere, -titī *vi* to come away; to desist.
absolūte *adv* fully, unrestrictedly.
absolūtiō, -ōnis *f* acquittal; perfection.
absolūtus *ppp of* **absolvō** ♦ *adj* complete; (*RHET*) unqualified.
absolvō, -vere, -vī, -ūtum *vt* to release, set free; (*law*) to acquit; to bring to completion, finish off; to pay off, discharge.
absonus *adj* unmusical; incongruous; ~ **ab** not in keeping with.
absorbeō, -bēre, -buī, -ptum *vt* to swallow up; to monopolize.
absp- *etc see* **asp-.**
absque *prep* (*with abl*) without, but for.
abstēmius *adj* temperate.
abstergeō, -gēre, -sī, -sum *vt* to wipe away; (*fig*) to banish.
absterreō, -ēre, -ui, -itum *vt* to scare away, deter.
abstinēns, -entis *adj* continent.
abstinenter *adv* with restraint.
abstinentia, -ae *f* restraint, self-control; fasting.
abstineō, -inēre, -inuī, -entum *vt* to withhold, keep off ♦ *vi* to abstain, refrain; **sē** ~ refrain.
abstitī *perf of* **absistō.**
abstō, -āre *vi* to stand aloof.
abstractus *ppp of* **abstrahō.**
abstrahō, -here, -xī, -ctum *vt* to drag away, remove; to divert.
abstrūdō, -dere, -sī, -sum *vt* to conceal.
abstrūsus *ppp of* **abstrūdō** ♦ *adj* deep, abstruse; reserved.
abstulī *perf of* **auferō.**
absum, abesse, āfuī *vi* to be away, absent, distant; to keep clear of; to be different; to be missing, fail to assist; **tantum abest ut** so far from; **haud multum āfuit quīn** I was (they

were *etc*) within an ace of.
absūmō, -ere, -psī, -ptum *vt* to consume; to ruin, kill; (*time*) to spend.
absurdē *adv* out of tune; absurdly.
absurdus *adj* unmusical; senseless, absurd.
Absyrtus, -ī *m* brother of Medea.
abundāns, -antis *adj* overflowing; abundant; rich; abounding in.
abundanter *adv* copiously.
abundantia, -ae *f* abundance, plenty; wealth.
abundē *adv* abundantly, more than enough.
abundō, -āre, -āvī, -ātum *vi* to overflow; to abound, be rich in.
abūsiō, -ōnis *f* (*RHET*) catachresis.
abusque *prep* (*with abl*) all the way from.
abūtor, -tī, -sus *vi* (*with abl*) to use up; to misuse.
Abydēnus *adj see n.*
Abȳdos, Abȳdus, -ī *m* a town on Dardanelles.
ac *etc see* **atque.**
Acadēmia, -ae *f* Plato's Academy at Athens; Plato's philosophy; Cicero's villa.
Acadēmica *ntpl* Cicero's book on the Academic philosophy.
Acadēmus, -ī *m* an Athenian hero.
acalanthis, -dis *f* thistlefinch.
acanthus, -ī *m* bear's-breech.
Acarnānes, -um *mpl* the Acarnanians.
Acarnānia, -iae *f* a district of N.W. Greece.
Acarnānicus *adj see n.*
Acca Larentia, -ae, -ae *f* Roman goddess.
accēdō, -ēdere, -essī, -essum *vi* to come, go to, approach; to attack; to be added; to agree with; (*duty*) to take up; **ad rem pūblicam** ~ to enter politics; **prope** ~ **ad** to resemble; ~**ēdit quod, hūc** ~**ēdit ut** moreover.
accelerō, -āre, -āvī, -ātum *vt, vi* to hasten.
accendō, -endere, -endī, -ēnsum *vt* to set on fire, light; to illuminate; (*fig*) to inflame, incite.
accēnseō, -ēre, -uī, -um *vt* to assign.
accēnsī *mpl* (*MIL*) supernumeraries.
accēnsus *ppp of* **accendō** *and* **accēnseō.**
accēnsus, -ī *m* officer attending a magistrate.
accentus, -ūs *m* accent.
accēpī *perf of* **accipiō.**
acceptiō, -ōnis *f* receiving.
acceptum *nt* credit side (of ledger); **in** ~ **referre** place to one's credit.
acceptus *ppp of* **accipiō** ♦ *adj* acceptable.
accersō *etc see* **arcessō.**
accessiō, -ōnis *f* coming, visiting; attack; increase, addition.
accessus, -ūs *m* approach, visit; flood tide; admittance, entrance.
Acciānus *adj see* **Accius.**
accīdō, -dere, -dī, -sum *vt* to fell, cut into; to eat up, impair.
accidō, -ere, -ī *vi* to fall (at, on); (*senses*) to strike; (*usu misfortune*) to befall, happen.
accingō, -gere, -xī, -ctum *vt* to gird on, arm; (*fig*) to make ready.
acciō, -īre, -īvī, -ītum *vt* to summon; to

procure.

accipiō, -ipere, -ēpī, -eptum *vt* to take, receive, accept; (*guest*) to treat; (*information*) to hear; to interpret, take as; to suffer; to approve.

accipiter, -ris *m* hawk.

accīsus *ppp of* **accīdō**.

accītus *ppp of* **acciō**.

accītus, -ūs *m* summons.

Accius, -ī *m Roman tragic poet.*

acclāmātiō, -ōnis *f* shout (*of approval or disapproval*).

acclāmō, -āre, -āvī, -ātum *vi* to cry out against; to hail.

acclārō, -āre, -āvī, -ātum *vt* to make known.

acclīnātus *adj* sloping.

acclīnis *adj* leaning against; inclined.

acclīnō, -āre, -āvī, -ātum *vt* to lean against; **sē ~** incline towards.

acclīvis *adj* uphill.

acclīvitās, -ātis *f* gradient.

accola, -ae *m* neighbour.

accolō, -olere, -oluī, -ultum *vt* to live near.

accommodātē *adv* suitably.

accommodātiō, -ōnis *f* fitting together; compliance.

accommodātus *adj* suited.

accommodō, -āre, -āvī, -ātum *vt* to fit, put on; to adjust, adapt, bring to; to apply; **sē ~** devote oneself.

accommodus *adj* suitable.

accrēdō, -ere, -idī, -itum *vi* to believe.

accrēscō, -ēscere, -ēvī, -ētum *vi* to increase, be added.

accrētiō, -ōnis *f* increasing.

accubitiō, -ōnis *f* reclining (*at meals*).

accubō, -āre *vi* to lie near; to recline (*at meals*).

accumbō, -mbere, -buī, -bitum *vi* to recline at table; **in sinū ~** sit next to.

accumulātē *adv* copiously.

accumulō, -āre, -āvī, -ātum *vt* to pile up, amass; to load.

accūrātē *adv* painstakingly.

accūrātiō, -ōnis *f* exactness.

accūrātus *adj* studied.

accūrō, -āre, -āvī, -ātum *vt* to attend to.

accurrō, -rrere, -currī *and* **rrī, -rsum** *vi* to hurry to.

accursus, -ūs *m* hurrying.

accūsābilis *adj* reprehensible.

accūsātiō, -ōnis *f* accusation.

accūsātor, -ōris *m* accuser, prosecutor.

accūsātōriē *adv* like an accuser.

accūsātōrius *adj* of the accuser.

accūsō, -āre, -āvī, -ātum *vt* to accuse, prosecute; to reproach; **ambitūs ~** prosecute for bribery.

acer, -is *nt* maple.

ācer, -ris *adj* sharp; (*sensation*) keen, pungent; (*emotion*) violent; (*mind*) shrewd; (*conduct*) eager, brave; hasty, fierce; (*circumstances*) severe.

acerbē *adv see* **acerbus**.

acerbitās, -ātis *f* bitterness; (*fig*) harshness, severity; sorrow.

acerbō, -āre, -āvī, -ātum *vt* to aggravate.

acerbus *adj* bitter, sour; harsh; (*fig*) premature; (*person*) rough, morose, violent; (*things*) troublesome, sad.

acernus *adj* of maple.

acerra, -ae *f* incense box.

acervātim *adv* in heaps.

acervō, -āre, -āvī, -ātum *vt* to pile up.

acervus, -ī *m* heap.

acēscō, -ere, acuī *vt* to turn sour.

Acestēs, -ae *m a mythical Sicilian.*

acētum, -ī *nt* vinegar; (*fig*) wit.

Achaemenēs, -is *m first Persian king; type of Oriental wealth.*

Achaeus *adj* Greek.

Achāia, -ae *f a district in W. Greece; Greece; Roman province.*

Achāicus *adj see n.*

Achātēs, -ae *m companion of Aeneas.*

Achelōius *adj see n.*

Achelōus, -ī *m river in N.W. Greece; river god.*

Acherōn, -ontis *m river in Hades.*

Acherūsius *adj see* **Acherōn**.

Achillēs, -is *m Greek epic hero.*

Achillēus *adj see n.*

Achīvus *adj* Greek.

Acidālia, -ae *f* Venus.

Acidālius *adj see n.*

acidus *adj* sour, tart; (*fig*) disagreeable.

aciēs, -ēī *f* sharp edge or point; (*eye*) sight, keen glance, pupil; (*mind*) power, apprehension; (*MIL*) line of troops, battle order, army, battle; (*fig*) debate; **prīma ~** van; **novissima ~** rearguard.

acīnacēs, -is *m* scimitar.

acinum, -ī *nt* berry, grape; fruit seed.

acinus, -ī *m* berry, grape; fruit seed.

acipēnser, -eris *m* sturgeon.

acipēnsis, -is *m* sturgeon.

aclys, -dis *f* javelin.

aconītum, -ī *nt* monkshood; poison.

acor, -ōris *m* sour taste.

acquiēscō, -ēscere, -ēvī, -ētum *vi* to rest, die; to find pleasure (in); to acquiesce.

acquīrō, -rere, -sīvī, -sītum *vt* to get in addition, acquire.

Acragās, -antis *m see* **Agrigentum**.

acrātophorum, -ī *nt* wine jar.

acrēdula, -ae *f* a bird (*unidentified*).

ācriculus *adj* peevish.

ācrimōnia, -ae *f* pungent taste; (*speech, action*) briskness, go.

Acrisiōniadēs, -ae *m* Perseus.

Acrisius, -ī *m father of Danae.*

Noun declensions and verb conjugations are shown on pp xiii to xxv. The present infinitive ending of a verb shows to which conjugation it belongs: **-āre** = 1st; **-ēre** = 2nd; **-ere** = 3rd and **-īre** = 4th. Irregular verbs are shown on p xxvi

ācriter *adv see* **ācer.**
ācroāma, -tis *nt* entertainment, entertainer.
ācroāsis, -is *f* public lecture.
Ācroceraunia, -ōrum *ntpl a promontory in*
  N.W. Greece.
Ācrocorinthus, -ī *f fortress of Corinth.*
acta, -ae *f* beach.
ācta, -ōrum *ntpl* public records, proceedings;
  ~ **diurna,** ~ **pūblica** daily gazette.
Actaeus *adj* Athenian.
āctiō, -ōnis *f* action, doing; official duties,
  negotiations; (*law*) action, suit, indictment,
  pleading, case, trial; (*RHET*) delivery; (*drama*)
  plot; ~ **grātiārum** expression of thanks;
  ~**ōnem intendere, īnstituere** bring an action.
āctitō, -āre, -āvī, -ātum *vt* to plead, act often.
Actium, -ī *and* **iī** *nt a town in N.W. Greece;*
  Augustus's great victory.
Actius, -iacus *adj see n.*
āctivus *adj* of action, practical.
āctor, -ōris *m* driver, performer; (*law*)
  plaintiff, pleader; (*COMM*) agent; (*RHET*) orator;
  (*drama*) actor; ~ **pūblicus** manager of public
  property; ~ **summārum** cashier.
āctuāria *f* pinnace.
āctuāriolum, -ī *m* small barge.
āctuārius *adj* fast (ship).
āctuōsē *adv* actively.
āctuōsus *adj* very active.
āctus *ppp of* **agō.**
āctus, -ūs *m* moving, driving; right of way for
  cattle *or* vehicles; performance; (*drama*)
  playing a part, recital, act of a play.
āctūtum *adv* immediately.
acuī *perf of* **acēscō;** *perf of* **acuō.**
acula, -ae *f* small stream.
aculeātus *adj* prickly; (*words*) stinging;
  quibbling.
aculeus, -ī *m* sting, prickle barb; (*fig*) sting.
acūmen, -inis *nt* point, sting; (*fig*)
  shrewdness, ingenuity; trickery.
acuō, -uere, -uī, -ūtum *vt* to sharpen; to
  exercise; (*the mind*) to stimulate; to rouse (to
  action).
acus, -ūs *f* needle, pin; **acū pingere**
  embroider; **rem acū tangere** ≈ hit the nail on
  the head.
acūtē *adv see* **acūtus.**
acūtulus *adj* rather subtle.
acūtus *adj* sharp, pointed; (*senses*) keen;
  (*sound*) high-pitched; severe; intelligent.
ad *prep* (*with acc*) to, towards, against; near, at;
  until; (*num*) about; with regard to, according
  to; for the purpose of, for; compared with;
  besides; **ad Castoris** to the temple of Castor;
  ad dextram on the right; **ad hōc** besides; **ad**
  locum on the spot; **ad manum** at hand; **ad**
  rem to the point; **ad summam** in short; **ad**
  tempus in time; **ad ūnum omnes** all without
  exception; **ad urbem esse** wait outside the
  city gates; **ad verbum** literally; **nīl ad**
  nothing to do with; **usque ad** right up to.
adāctiō, -ōnis *f* enforcing.

adāctus *ppp of* **adigō.**
adāctus, -ūs *m* snapping (*of teeth*).
adaequē *adv* equally.
adaequō, -āre, -āvī, -ātum *vt* to make equal,
  level; to equal, match ♦ *vi* to be equal.
adamantēus, adamantinus *adj see* **adamās.**
adamās, -antis *m* adamant, steel; diamond.
adamō, -āre, -āvī, -ātum *vt* to fall in love
  with.
adaperiō, -īre, -uī, -tum *vt* to throw open.
adapertilis *adj* openable.
adaquō, -āre, -āvī, -ātum *vt* (*plants, animals*)
  to water.
adaquor *vi* to fetch water.
adauctus, -ūs *m* growing.
adaugeō, -gēre, -xī, -ctum *vt* to aggravate;
  (*sacrifice*) to consecrate.
adaugēscō, -ere *vi* to grow bigger.
adbibō, -ere, -ī *vt* to drink; (*fig*) to drink in.
adbītō, -ere *vi* to come near.
adc- *etc see* **acc-.**
addecet, -ēre *vt* it becomes.
addēnseō, -ēre *vt* to close (ranks).
addīcō, -īcere, -īxī, -ictum *vi* (*AUG*) to be
  favourable ♦ *vt* (*law*) to award; (*auction*) to
  knock down; (*fig*) to sacrifice, devote.
addictiō, -ōnis *f* award (*at law*).
addictus *ppp of* **addīcō** ♦ *m* bondsman.
addiscō, -scere, -dicī *vt* to learn more.
additāmentum, -ī *nt* increase.
additus *ppp of* **addō.**
addō, -ere, -idī, -itum *vt* to add, put to, bring
  to; to impart; to increase; ~ **gradum** quicken
  pace; ~**e quod** besides.
addoceō, -ēre, -uī, -tum *vt* to teach new.
addubitō, -āre, -āvī, -ātum *vi* to be in doubt
  ♦ *vt* to question.
addūcō, -ūcere, -ūxī, -uctum *vt* to take,
  bring to; to draw together, pull taut,
  wrinkle; (*fig*) to induce; (*pass*) to be led to
  believe.
adductus *ppp of* **addūcō** ♦ *adj* contracted; (*fig*)
  severe.
adedō, -edere, -ēdī, -ēsum *vt* to begin to eat;
  to eat up; to use up; to wear away.
adēmī *perf of* **adimō.**
ademptiō, -ōnis *f* taking away.
ademptus *ppp of* **adimō.**
adeō, -īre, -iī, -itum *vt, vi* to go to, approach;
  to address; to undertake, submit to, enter
  upon.
adeō *adv* so; (*after pron*) just; (*after conj, adv,*
  adj: for emphasis) indeed, very; (*adding an*
  explanation) for, in fact, thus; or rather; ~
  nōn ... ut so far from; **atque** ~, **sīve** ~ or
  rather; **usque** ~ so far, so long, so much.
adeps, -ipis *m/f* fat; corpulence.
adeptiō, -ōnis *f* attainment.
adeptus *ppa of* **adipīscor.**
adequitō, -āre, -āvī, -ātum *vi* to ride up (to).
adesdum come here!
adesse *infin of* **adsum.**
adēsus *ppp of* **adedō.**

adfābilis *adj* easy to talk to.

adfābilitās, -ātis *f* courtesy.

adfabrē *adv* ingeniously.

adfatim *adv* to one's satisfaction, enough, ad nauseam.

adfātur, -rī, -tus *vt (defec)* to speak to.

adfātus *ppa of* **adfātur**.

adfātus, -ūs *m* speaking to.

adfectātiō, -ōnis *f* aspiring; (*RHET*) affectation.

adfectātus *adj (RHET)* studied.

adfectiō, -ōnis *f* frame of mind, mood; disposition; goodwill; (*ASTRO*) relative position.

adfectō, -āre, -āvī, -ātum *vt* to aspire to, aim at; to try to win over; to make pretence of; **viam ~ ad** try to get to.

adfectus *ppp of* **adficiō ♦** *adj* affected with, experienced (*abl*); (*person*) disposed; (*things*) weakened; (*undertakings*) well-advanced.

adfectus, -ūs *m* disposition, mood; fondness; (*pl*) loved ones.

adferō, adferre, attulī, adlātum *and* **allātum** *vt* to bring, carry to; to bring to bear, use against; to bring news; (*explanation*) to bring forward; to contribute (*something useful*).

adficiō, -icere, -ēcī, -ectum *vt* to affect; to endow, afflict with (*abl*); **exsiliō ~** banish; **honōre ~** honour; *also used with other nouns to express the corresponding verbs.*

adfictus *ppp of* **adfingō**.

adfīgō, -gere, -xī, -xum *vt* to fasten, attach; to impress (*on the mind*).

adfingō, -ngere, -nxī, -ctum *vt* to make, form (as part of); to invent.

adfīnis, -is *m/f* neighbour; relation (*by marriage*) **♦** *adj* neighbouring; associated with (*dat or gen*).

adfīnitās, -ātis *f* relationship (*by marriage*).

adfirmātē *adv* with assurance.

adfirmātiō, -ōnis *f* declaration.

adfirmō, -āre, -āvī, -ātum *vt* to declare; to confirm.

adfīxus *ppp of* **adfīgō**.

adflātus, -ūs *m* breath, exhalation; (*fig*) inspiration.

adfleō, -ēre *vi* to weep (at).

adflīctātiō, -ōnis *f* suffering.

adflīctō, -āre, -āvī, -ātum *vt* to harass, distress.

adflīctor, -ōris *m* destroyer.

adflīctus *ppp of* **adflīgō ♦** *adj* distressed, ruined; dejected; depraved.

adflīgō, -īgere, -īxī, -ictum *vt* to dash against, throw down; (*fig*) to impair, crush.

adflō, -āre, -āvī, -ātum *vt, vi* to blow on, breathe upon.

adfluēns, -entis *adj* rich (in).

adfluenter *adv* copiously.

adfluentia, -ae *f* abundance.

adfluō, -ere, -xī, -xum *vi* to flow; (*fig*) to flock in, abound in.

adfore *fut infin of* **adsum**.

adforem *imperf subj of* **adsum**.

adfuī *perf of* **adsum**.

adfulgeō, -gēre, -sī *vi* to shine on; to appear.

adfundō, -undere, -ūdī, -ūsum *vt* to pour in; to rush (troops) to.

adfūsus *adj* prostrate.

adfutūrus *fut p of* **adsum**.

adgemō, -ere *vi* to groan at.

adglomerō, -āre *vt* to add on.

adglūtinō, -āre *vt* to stick on.

adgravēscō, -ere *vi* to become worse.

adgravō, -āre, -āvī, -ātum *vt* to aggravate.

adgredior, -dī, -ssus *vt* to approach, accost; to attack; (*a task*) to undertake, take up.

adgregō, -āre, -āvī, -ātum *vt* to add, attach.

adgressiō, -ōnis *f* introductory remarks.

adgressus *ppa of* **adgredior**.

adhaereō, -rēre, -sī, -sum *vi* to stick to; (*fig*) to cling to, keep close to.

adhaerēscō, -ere *vi* to stick to or in; (*speech*) to falter.

adhaesiō, -ōnis *f* clinging.

adhaesus, -ūs *m* adhering.

adhibeō, -ēre, -uī, -itum *vt* to bring, put, add; to summon, consult, treat; to use, apply (*for some purpose*).

adhinniō, -īre, -īvī, -ītum *vi* to neigh to; (*fig*) to go into raptures over.

adhortātiō, -ōnis *f* exhortation.

adhortātor, -ōris *m* encourager.

adhortor, -ārī, -ātus *vt* to encourage, urge.

adhūc *adv* so far; as yet, till now; still ~ **nōn** not yet.

adiaceō, -ēre, -uī *vi* to lie near, border on.

adiciō, -icere, -iēcī, -iectum *vt* to throw to; to add; to turn (mind, eyes) towards.

adiectiō, -ōnis *f* addition.

adiectus *ppp of* **adiciō**.

adiectus, -ūs *m* bringing close.

adigō, -igere, -ēgī, -āctum *vt* to drive (to); to compel; **iūs iūrandum ~** put on oath; **in verba** ~ force to owe allegiance.

adimō, -imere, -ēmī, -emptum *vt* to take away (from *dat*).

adipātum *nt* pastry.

adipātus *adj* fatty; (*fig*) florid.

adipīscor, -ipīscī, -eptus *vt* to overtake; to attain, acquire.

aditus, -ūs *m* approach, access (*to a person*); entrance; (*fig*) avenue.

adiūdicō, -āre, -āvī, -ātum *vt* to award (*in arbitration*); to ascribe.

adiūmentum, -ī *nt* aid, means of support.

adiūncta *ntpl* collateral circumstances.

adiūnctiō, -ōnis *f* uniting; addition; (*RHET*) proviso; repetition.

Noun declensions and verb conjugations are shown on pp xiii to xxv. The present infinitive ending of a verb shows to which conjugation it belongs: **-āre** = 1st; **-ēre** = 2nd; **-ere** = 3rd and **-īre** = 4th. Irregular verbs are shown on p xxvi

adiūnctus *ppp of* **adiungō ♦** *adj* connected.
adiungō, -ungere, -ūnxī, -ūnctum *vt* to yoke; to attach; (*suspicion etc*) to direct; (*remark*) to add.
adiūrō, -āre, -āvī, -ātum *vt*, *vi* to swear, swear by.
adiūtō, -āre, -āvī, -ātum *vt* to help.
adiūtor, -ōris *m* helper; (*MIL*) adjutant; (*POL*) official; (*THEAT*) supporting cast.
adiūtrīx, -rīcis *f see* **adiūtor.**
adiūtus *ppp of* **adiuvō.**
adiuvō, -uvāre, -ūvī, -ūtum *vt* to help; to encourage.
adj- *etc see* **adi-.**
adlābor, -bī, -psus *vi* to fall, move towards, come to.
adlabōrō, -āre, -āvī, -ātum *vi* to work hard; to improve by taking trouble.
adlacrimō, -āre, -āvī, -ātum *vi* to shed tears.
adlāpsus *ppa of* **adlābor.**
adlāpsus, -ūs *m* stealthy approach.
adlātrō, -āre, -āvī, -ātum *vt* to bark at; (*fig*) to revile.
adlātus *ppp of* **adferō.**
adlaudō, -āre, -āvī, -ātum *vt* to praise highly.
adlectō, -āre, -āvī, -ātum *vt* to entice.
adlēctus *ppp of* **adlegō.**
adlectus *ppp of* **adliciō.**
adlēgātī *mpl* deputies.
adlēgātiō, -ōnis *f* mission.
adlēgō, -āre, -āvī, -ātum *vt* to despatch, commission; to mention.
adlegō, -egere, -ēgī, -ēctum *vt* to elect.
adlevāmentum, -ī *nt* relief.
adlevātiō, -ōnis *f* easing.
adlevō, -āre, -āvī, -ātum *vt* to lift up; to comfort; to weaken.
adliciō, -icere, -exī, -ectum *vt* to attract.
adlīdō, -dere, -sī, -sum *vt* to dash (against); (*fig*) to hurt.
adligō, -āre, -āvī, -ātum *vt* to tie up; bandage; (*fig*) to bind, lay under an obligation.
adlinō, -inere, -ēvī, -itum *vt* to smear; (*fig*) to attach.
adlīsus *ppp of* **adlīdō.**
adlocūtiō, -ōnis *f* address; comforting words.
adlocūtus *ppa of* **adloquor.**
adloquium, -ī *and* **iī** *nt* talk; encouragement.
adloquor, -quī, -cūtus *vt* to speak to, address.
adlūdiō, -āre, -āvī, -ātum *vi* to play (with).
adlūdō, -dere, -sī, -sum *vi* to joke, play.
adluō, -ere, -ī *vt* to wash.
adluviēs, -ēī *f* pool left by flood water.
adluviō, -ōnis *f* alluvial land.
admātūrō, -āre, -āvī, -atum *vt* to hurry on.
admētior, -tīrī, -nsus *vt* to measure out.
adminiculor, -ārī, -ātus *vt* to prop.
adminiculum, -ī *nt* (*AGR*) stake; (*fig*) support.
administer, -rī *m* assistant.

administrātiō, -ōnis *f* services; management.
administrātor, -ōris *m* manager.
administrō, -āre, -āvī, -ātum *vt* to manage, govern.
admīrābilis *adj* wonderful, surprising.
admīrābilitās, -ātis *f* wonderfulness.
admīrābiliter *adv* admirably; paradoxically.
admīrātiō, -ōnis *f* wonder, surprise, admiration.
admīror, -ārī, -ātus *vt* to wonder at, admire; to be surprised at.
admisceō, -scēre, -scuī, -xtum *vt* to mix in with, add to; (*fig*) to involve; **sē ~** interfere.
admissārius, -ī *and* **iī** *m* stallion.
admissum, -ī *nt* crime.
admissus *ppp of* **admittō.**
admittō, -ittere, -īsī, -issum *vt* to let in, admit; to set at a gallop; to allow; to commit (a crime); **equō ~issō** charging.
admixtiō, -ōnis *f* admixture.
admixtus *ppp of* **admisceō.**
admoderātē *adv* suitably.
admoderor, -ārī, -ātus *vt* to restrain.
admodum *adv* very, quite; fully; yes; (*with neg*) at all.
admoneō, -ēre, -uī, -itum *vt* to remind, suggest, advise, warn.
admonitiō, -ōnis *f* reminder, suggestion, admonition.
admonitor, -ōris *m* admonisher (*male*).
admonitrīx, -rīcis *f* admonisher (*female*).
admonitū at the suggestion, instance.
admordeō, -dēre, -sum *vt* to bite into; (*fig*) to cheat.
admorsus *ppp of* **admordeō.**
admōtiō, -ōnis *f* applying.
admōtus *ppp of* **admoveō.**
admoveo, -ovēre, -ōvī, -ōtum *vt* to move, bring up, apply; to lend (an ear), direct (the mind).
admurmurātiō, -ōnis *f* murmuring.
admurmurō, -āre, -āvī, -ātum *vi* to murmur (*of a crowd approving or disapproving*).
admutilō, -āre, -āvī, -ātum *vt* to clip close; (*fig*) to cheat.
adnectō, -ctere, -xuī, -xum *vt* to connect, tie.
adnexus, -ūs *m* connection.
adnīsus *ppp of* **adnītor.**
adnītor, -tī, -sus *and* **-xus** *vi* to lean on; to exert oneself.
adnīxus *ppp of* **adnītor.**
adnō, -āre *vt*, *vi* to swim to.
adnotō, -āre, -āvī, -ātum *vt* to comment on.
adnumerō, -āre, -āvī, -ātum *vt* to pay out; to reckon along with.
adnuō, -uere, -uī, -ūtum *vi* to nod; to assent, promise; to indicate.
adoleō, -olēre, -oluī, -ultum *vt* to burn; to pile with gifts.
adolēscen- *etc see* **adulēscen-.**
adolēscō, -ēscere, -ēvī *vi* to grow up, increase; to burn.

Adōnis, -is *and* **idis** *m a beautiful youth loved by Venus.*
adopertus *adj* covered.
adoptātiō, -ōnis *f* adopting.
adoptiō, -ōnis *f* adoption.
adoptīvus *adj* by adoption.
adoptō, -āre, -āvī, -ātum *vt* to choose; to adopt.
ador, -ōris *and* **oris** *nt* spelt.
adōreus *adj see n.*
adōrea *f* glory.
adorior, -īrī, -tus *vt* to accost; to attack; to set about.
adōrnō, -āre, -āvī, -ātum *vt* to get ready.
adōrō, -āre, -āvī, -ātum *vt* to entreat; to worship, revere.
adortus *ppa of* **adorior.**
adp- *etc see* **app-.**
adrādō, -dere, -sī, -sum *vt* to shave close.
Adrastus, -ī *m a king of Argos.*
adrāsus *ppp of* **adrādō.**
adrēctus *ppp of* **adrigō ♦** *adj* steep.
adrēpō, -ere, -sī, -tum *vi* to creep, steal into.
adreptus *ppp of* **adripiō.**
Adria *etc see* **Hadria** *etc.*
adrīdeō, -dēre, -sī, -sum *vt, vi* to laugh, smile at; to please.
adrigō, -igere, -ēxī, -ēctum *vt* to raise; (*fig*) to rouse.
adripiō, -ipere, -ipuī, -eptum *vt* to seize; to appropriate; to take hold of; to learn quickly; (*law*) to arrest; to satirize.
adrōdō, -dere, -sī, -sum *vt* to gnaw, nibble at.
adrogāns, -antis *adj* arrogant, insolent.
adroganter *adv see* **adrogāns.**
adrogantia, -ae *f* arrogance, presumption, haughtiness.
adrogātiō, -ōnis *f* adoption.
adrogō, -āre, -āvī, -ātum *vt* to ask; to associate; to claim, assume; (*fig*) to award.
adsc- *etc see* **asc-.**
adsecla *etc see* **adsecula.**
adsectātiō, -ōnis *f* attendance.
adsectātor, -ōris *m* follower.
adsector, -ārī, -ātus *vt* to attend on, follow (*esp a candidate*).
adsecula, -ae *m* follower (*derogatory*).
adsēdī *perf of* **adsideō;** *perf of* **adsīdō.**
adsēnsiō, -ōnis *f* assent, applause; (*PHILOS*) acceptance of the evidence of the senses.
adsēnsor, -ōris *m* one in agreement.
adsēnsus *ppa of* **adsentior.**
adsēnsus, -ūs *m* assent, approval; echo; (*PHILOS*) acceptance of the evidence of the senses.
adsentātiō, -ōnis *f* flattery.
adsentātiuncula *f* trivial compliments.
adsentātor, -ōris *m* flatterer (*male*).
adsentātōriē *adv* ingratiatingly.

adsentātrīx, -rīcis *f* flatterer (*female*).
adsentiō, -entīre, -ēnsī, -ēnsum; -entior, -entīrī, -ēnsus *vi* to agree, approve.
adsentor, -ārī, -ātus *vi* to agree, flatter.
adsequor, -quī, -cūtus *vt* to overtake; to attain; to grasp (*by understanding*).
adserō, -ere, -uī, -tum *vt* (*law*) to declare free (*usu with* **manū**), liberate (a slave); to lay claim to, appropriate; ~ **in servitūtem** claim as a slave.
adserō, -erere, -ēvī, -itum *vt* to plant near.
adsertiō, -ōnis *f* declaration of status.
adsertor, -ōris *m* champion.
adserviō, -īre *vi* to assist.
adservō, -āre, -āvī, -ātum *vt* to watch carefully; to keep, preserve.
adsessiō, -ōnis *f* sitting beside.
adsessor, -ōris *m* counsellor.
adsessus, -ūs *m* sitting beside.
adsevēranter *adv* emphatically.
adsevērātiō, -ōnis *f* assertion; earnestness.
adsevērō, -āre, -āvī, -ātum *vt* to do in earnest; to assert strongly.
adsideō, -idēre, -ēdī, -essum *vi* to sit by; to attend, assist; to besiege; to resemble.
adsīdō, -īdere, -ēdī *vi* to sit down.
adsiduē *adv* continually.
adsiduitās, -ātis *f* constant attendance; continuance, frequent recurrence.
adsiduō *adv* continually.
adsiduus *adj* constantly in attendance, busy; continual, incessant.
adsiduus, -ī *m* taxpayer.
adsignātiō, -ōnis *f* allotment (of land).
adsignō, -āre, -āvī, -ātum *vt* to allot (*esp land*); to assign; to impute, attribute; to consign.
adsiliō, -īlīre, -iluī, -ultum *vi* to leap at *or* on to.
adsimilis *adj* like.
adsimiliter *adv* similarly.
adsimulātus *adj* similar; counterfeit.
adsimulō, -āre, -āvī, -ātum *vt, vi* to compare; to pretend, imitate.
adsistō, -istere, -titī *vi* to stand (by); to defend.
adsitus *ppp of* **adserō.**
adsoleō, -ēre *vi* to be usual.
adsonō, -āre *vi* to respond.
adsp- *etc see* **asp-.**
adsternō, -ere *vt* to prostrate.
adstipulātor, -ōris *m* supporter.
adstipulor, -ārī, -ātus *vi* to agree with.
adstitī *perf of* **adsistō;** *perf of* **adstō.**
adstō, -āre, -itī *vi* to stand near, stand up; to assist.
adstrepō, -ere *vi* to roar.
adstrictē *adv* concisely.
adstrictus *ppp of* **adstringō ♦** *adj* tight, narrow; concise; stingy.

Noun declensions and verb conjugations are shown on pp xiii to xxv. The present infinitive ending of a verb shows to which conjugation it belongs: **-āre** = 1st; **-ēre** = 2nd; **-ere** = 3rd and **-īre** = 4th. Irregular verbs are shown on p xxvi

adstringō, -ngere, -nxī, -ctum _vt_ to draw close, tighten; to bind, oblige; to abridge.

adstruō, -ere, -xī, -ctum _vt_ to build on; to add.

adstupeō, -ēre _vi_ to be astonished.

adsuēfaciō, -acere, -ēcī, -actum _vt_ to accustom, train.

adsuēscō, -scere, -vī, -tum _vi_ to accustom, train.

adsuētūdō, -inis _f_ habit.

adsuētus _ppp of_ **adsuēscō** ♦ _adj_ customary.

adsultō, -āre, -āvī, -ātum _vi_ to jump; to attack.

adsultus, -ūs _m_ attack.

adsum, -esse, -fuī _vi_ to be present; to support, assist (_esp at law_); to come; to appear before (a tribunal); **animō ~** pay attention; **iam aderō** I'll be back soon.

adsūmō, -ere, -psī, -ptum _vt_ to take for oneself, receive; to take also.

adsūmptiō, -ōnis _f_ taking up; (_logic_) minor premise.

adsūmptīvus _adj_ (_law_) which takes its defence from extraneous circumstances.

adsūmptum, -ī _nt_ epithet.

adsūmptus _ppp of_ **adsūmō**.

adsuō, -ere _vt_ to sew on.

adsurgō, -gere, -rēxī, -rēctum _vi_ to rise, stand up; to swell, increase.

adt- _etc see_ **att-**.

adulātiō, -ōnis _f_ (_dogs_) fawning; servility.

adulātor, -ōris _m_ sycophant.

adulātōrius _adj_ flattering.

adulēscēns, -entis _m/f_ young man _or_ woman (_usu from 15 to 30 years_).

adulēscentia, -ae _f_ youth (_age 15 to 30_).

adulēscentula, -ae _f_ girl.

adulēscentulus, -ī _m_ quite a young man.

adulō, -āre, -āvī, -ātum; adulor, -ārī, -ātus _vt, vi_ to fawn upon, flatter, kowtow.

adulter, -ī _m_, **-a, -ae** _f_ adulterer, adulteress ♦ _adj_ adulterous.

adulterīnus _adj_ forged.

adulterium, -ī _and_ **iī** _nt_ adultery.

adulterō, -āre, -āvī, -ātum _vt, vi_ to commit adultery; to falsify.

adultus _ppp of_ **adolēscō** ♦ _adj_ adult, mature.

adumbrātim _adv_ in outline.

adumbrātiō, -ōnis _f_ sketch; semblance.

adumbrātus _adj_ false.

adumbrō, -āre, -āvī, -ātum _vt_ to sketch; to represent, copy.

aduncitās, -ātis _f_ curvature.

aduncus _adj_ hooked, curved.

adurgeō, -ēre _vt_ to pursue closely.

adūrō, -rere, -ssī, -stum _vt_ to burn; to freeze; (_fig_) to fire.

adusque _prep_ (_with acc_) right up to ♦ _adv_ entirely.

adūstus _ppp of_ **adūrō** ♦ _adj_ brown.

advectīcius _adj_ imported.

advectō, -āre _vt_ to carry frequently.

advectus _ppp of_ **advehō**.

advectus, -ūs _m_ bringing.

advehō, -here, -xī, -ctum _vt_ to carry, convey; (_pass_) to ride.

advēlō, -āre _vt_ to crown.

advena, -ae _m/f_ stranger ♦ _adj_ foreign.

adveniō, -enīre, -ēnī, -entum _vi_ to arrive, come.

adventīcius _adj_ foreign, extraneous; unearned.

adventō, -āre, -āvī, -ātum _vi_ to come nearer and nearer, advance rapidly.

adventor, -ōris _m_ visitor.

adventus, -ūs _m_ arrival, approach.

adversāria _ntpl_ daybook.

adversārius, -ī _and_ **iī** _m_ opponent ♦ _adj_ opposing.

adversātrīx, -īcis _f_ antagonist.

adversiō, -ōnis _f_ turning (the attention).

adversor, -ārī, -ātus _vi_ to oppose, resist.

adversum, -ī _nt_ opposite; misfortune ♦ _prep_ (_+ acc_) towards, against ♦ _adv_ to meet.

adversus _ppp of_ **advertō** ♦ _adj_ opposite, in front; hostile; **~ō flūmine** upstream; **~ae rēs** misfortune ♦ _prep_ (_+ acc_) towards, against ♦ _adv_ to meet.

advertō, -tere, -tī, -sum _vt_ to turn, direct towards; to call attention; **animum ~** notice, perceive; (_with_ **ad**) to attend to; (_with_ **in**) to punish.

advesperāscit, -scere, -vit _vi_ it is getting dark.

advigilō, -āre _vi_ to keep watch.

advocātiō, -ōnis _f_ legal assistance, counsel.

advocātus, -ī _m_ supporter in a lawsuit; advocate, counsel.

advocō, -āre, -āvī, -ātum _vt_ to summon; (_law_) to call in the assistance of.

advolō, -āre, -āvī, -ātum _vi_ to fly to, swoop down upon.

advolvō, -vere, -vī, -ūtum _vt_ to roll to; to prostrate.

advor- _etc see_ **adver-**.

adytum, -ī _nt_ sanctuary.

Aeacidēs, -idae _m_ Achilles; Pyrrhus.

Aeacus, -ī _m_ father of Peleus, and judge of the dead.

Aeaea, -ae _f_ Circe's island.

Aeaeus _adj_ of Circe.

aedēs, -is _f_ temple; (_pl_) house.

aedicula, -ae _f_ shrine; small house, room.

aedificātiō, -ōnis _f_ building.

aedificātiuncula, -ae _f_ little house.

aedificātor, -ōris _m_ builder.

aedificium, -ī _and_ **iī** _nt_ building.

aedificō, -āre, -āvī, -ātum _vt_ to build, construct.

aedīliclus _adj_ aedile's ♦ _m_ ex-aedile.

aedīlis, -is _m_ aedile.

aedīlitās, -ātis _f_ aedileship.

aedis, -is _see_ **aedēs**.

aeditumus, aedituus, -ī _m_ temple-keeper.

Aeduī, -ōrum _mpl_ a tribe of central Gaul.

Aeētēs, -ae _m_ father of Medea.

Aegaeus *adj* Aegean ♦ *nt* Aegean Sea.
Aegātēs, -um *fpl* islands off Sicily.
aeger, -rī *adj* ill, sick; sorrowful; weak.
Aegīna, -ae *f* a Greek island.
Aegīnēta, -ae *m* inhabitant of Aegina.
aegis, -dis *f* shield of Jupiter or Athena, aegis.
Aegisthus, -ī *m* paramour of Clytemnestra.
aegocerōs, -ōtis *m* Capricorn.
aegrē *adv* painfully; with displeasure; with difficulty; hardly; ~ **ferre** be annoyed.
aegrēscō, -ere *vi* to become ill; to be aggravated.
aegrimōnia, -ae *f* distress of mind.
aegritūdō, -inis *f* sickness; sorrow.
aegror, -ōris *m* illness.
aegrōtātiō, -ōnis *f* illness, disease.
aegrōtō, -āre, -āvī, -ātum *vi* to be ill.
aegrōtus *adj* ill, sick.
Aegyptius *adj see n.*
Aegyptus, -ī *f* Egypt ♦ *m* brother of Danaus.
aelinos, -ī *m* dirge.
Aemiliānus *adj esp* Scipio, destroyer of Carthage.
Aemilius, -ī Roman family name; **Via ~ia** road in N. Italy.
aemulātiō, -ōnis *f* rivalry (good or bad); jealousy.
aemulātor, -ōris *m* zealous imitator.
aemulor, -ārī, -ātus *vt* to rival, copy; to be jealous.
aemulus, -ī *m* rival ♦ *adj* rivalling; jealous.
Aeneadēs, -ae *m* Trojan; Roman.
Aenēās, -ae *m* Trojan leader and hero of Virgil's epic.
Aenēis, -idis *and* **idos** *f* Aeneid.
Aenēius *adj see n.*
aēneus *adj* of bronze.
aenigma, -tis *nt* riddle, mystery.
aēnum, -ī *nt* bronze vessel.
aēnus *adj* of bronze.
Aeolēs, -um *mpl* the Aeolians.
Aeolia *f* Lipari Island.
Aeolidēs *m* a descendant of Aeolus.
Aeolis, -idis *f* Aeolia (N.W. of Asia Minor).
Aeolis, -idis *f* daughter of Aeolus.
Aeolius *adj see n.*
Aeolus, -ī *m* king of the winds.
aequābilis *adj* equal; consistent, even; impartial.
aequābilitās, -ātis *f* uniformity; impartiality.
aequābiliter *adv* uniformly.
aequaevus *adj* of the same age.
aequālis *adj* equal, like; of the same age, contemporary; uniform.
aequālitās, -ātis *f* evenness; (in politics, age) equality, similarity.
aequāliter *adv* evenly.
aequanimitās, -ātis *f* goodwill; calmness.
aequātiō, -ōnis *f* equal distribution.
aequē *adv* equally; just as (with ac, atque, et, quam); justly.
Aequī, -ōrum *mpl* a people of central Italy.

Aequicus, Aequiculus *adj see n.*
Aequimaelium, -ī *and* **ī ī** *nt* an open space in Rome.
aequinoctiālis *adj see n.*
aequinoctium, -ī *and* **ī ī** *nt* equinox.
aequiperābilis *adj* comparable.
aequiperō, -āre, -āvī, -ātum *vt* to compare; to equal.
aequitās, -ātis *f* uniformity; fair dealing, equity; calmness of mind.
aequō, -āre, -āvī, -ātum *vt* to make equal, level; to compare; to equal; **solō ~** raze to the ground.
aequor, -is *nt* a level surface, sea.
aequoreus *adj* of the sea.
aequum, -ī *nt* plain; justice.
aequus *adj* level, equal; favourable, friendly, fair, just; calm; **~ō animō** patiently; **~ō Marte** without deciding the issue; **~um est** it is reasonable; **ex ~ō** equally.
āēr, āeris *m* air, weather; mist.
aerāria *f* mine.
aerārium *nt* treasury.
aerārius *adj* of bronze; of money ♦ *m* a citizen of the lowest class at Rome; **tribūnī ~ī** paymasters; a wealthy middle class at Rome.
aerātus *adj* of bronze.
aereus *adj* of copper or bronze.
aerifer, -ī *adj* carrying cymbals.
aeripēs, -edis *adj* bronze-footed.
āerius *adj* of the air; lofty.
aerūgō, -inis *f* rust; (fig) envy, avarice.
aerumna, -ae *f* trouble, hardship.
aerumnōsus *adj* wretched.
aes, aeris *nt* copper, bronze; money; (pl) objects made of copper or bronze (esp statues, instruments, vessels; soldiers' pay); **~ aliēnum** debt; **~ circumforāneum** borrowed money; **~ grave** Roman coin, as.
Aeschylus, -ī *m* Greek tragic poet.
Aesculāpius, -ī *m* god of medicine.
aesculētum, -ī *nt* oak forest.
aesculeus *adj see* **aesculus.**
aesculus, -ī *f* durmast oak.
Aesōn, -onis *m* father of Jason.
Aesonidēs, -ae *m* Jason.
Aesōpius *adj see n.*
Aesōpus, -ī *m* Greek writer of fables.
aestās, -ātis *f* summer.
aestifer, -ī *adj* heat-bringing.
aestimātiō, -ōnis *f* valuation, assessment; **lītis ~** assessment of damages.
aestimātor, -ōris *m* valuer.
aestimō, -āre, -āvī, -ātum *vt* to value, estimate the value of; **māgnī ~** think highly of.
aestīva, -ōrum *ntpl* summer camp, campaign.
aestīvus *adj* summer.
aestuārium, -ī *and* **ī ī** *nt* tidal waters, estuary.
aestuō, -āre, -āvī, -ātum *vi* to boil, burn;

Noun declensions and verb conjugations are shown on pp xiii to xxv. The present infinitive ending of a verb shows to which conjugation it belongs: **-āre** = 1st; **-ēre** = 2nd; **-ere** = 3rd and **-īre** = 4th. Irregular verbs are shown on p xxvi

(*movement*) to heave, toss; (*fig*) to be excited; to waver.

aestuōsus *adj* very hot; agitated.

aestus, -ūs *m* heat; surge of the sea; tide; (*fig*) passion; hesitation.

aetās, -ātis *f* age, life; time.

aetātem *adv* for life.

aetātula, -ae *f* tender age.

aeternitās, -ātis *f* eternity.

aeternō, -āre *vt* to immortalize.

aeternus *adj* eternal, immortal; lasting; **in ~um** for ever.

aethēr, -eris *m* sky, heaven; air.

aetherius *adj* ethereal, heavenly; of air.

Aethiops, -is *adj* Ethiopian; (*fig*) stupid.

aethra, -ae *f* sky.

Aetna, -ae *f* Etna (*in Sicily*).

Aetnaeus, Aetnēnsis *adj see n.*

Aetōlia, -iae *f* a district of N. Greece.

Aetōlus, -icus *adj see n.*

aevitās, -ātis old form of **aetās.**

aevum, -ī *nt* age, lifetime; eternity; **in ~** for ever.

Āfer, -rī *adj* African.

āfore *fut infin of* **absum.**

Āfrānius, -ī *m* Latin comic poet.

Africa, -ae *f* Roman province (*now* Tunisia).

Āfricānae *fpl* panthers.

Āfricānus *adj* name of two Scipios.

Āfricus *adj* African ♦ *m* south-west wind.

āfuī, āfutūrus *perf, fut p of* **absum.**

Agamēmnōn, -onis *m* leader of Greeks against Troy.

Agamēmnonius *adj see n.*

Aganippē, -ēs *f* a spring on Helicon.

agāsō, -ōnis *m* ostler, footman.

age, agedum come on!, well then.

agellus, -ī *m* plot of land.

Agēnōr, -oris *m* father of Europa.

Agēnoreus *adj see n.*

Agēnoridēs, -ae *m* Cadmus; Perseus.

agēns, -entis *adj* (*RHET*) effective.

ager, -rī *m* land, field; countryside; territory.

agg- *etc see* **adg-.**

agger, -is *m* rampart; mound, embankment, any built-up mass.

aggerō, -āre, -āvī, -ātum *vt* to pile up; to increase.

aggerō, -rere, -ssi, -stum *vt* to carry, bring.

aggestus, -ūs *m* accumulation.

agilis *adj* mobile; nimble, busy.

agilitās, -ātis *f* mobility.

agitābilis *adj* light.

agitātiō, -ōnis *f* movement, activity.

agitātor, -ōris *m* driver, charioteer.

agitō, -āre, -āvī, -ātum *vt* (*animals*) to drive; to move, chase, agitate; (*fig*) to excite (to action); to persecute, ridicule; to keep (*a ceremony*) ♦ *vi* to live; to deliberate.

agmen, -inis *nt* forward movement, procession, train; army on the march; **~ claudere** bring up the rear; **novissimum ~** rearguard; **prīmum ~** van.

agna, -ae *f* ewe lamb; lamb (flesh).

agnāscor, -scī, -tus *vi* to be born after.

agnātus, -ī *m* relation (*by blood on father's side*).

agnellus, -ī *m* little lamb.

agnīnus *adj* of lamb.

agnitiō, -ōnis *f* recognition, knowledge.

agnitus *ppp of* **agnōscō.**

agnōmen, -inis *nt* an extra surname (*eg Africanus*).

agnōscō, -ōscere, -ōvī, -itum *vt* to recognize; to acknowledge, allow; to understand.

agnus, -ī *m* lamb.

agō, agere, ēgī, āctum *vt* to drive, lead; to plunder; to push forward, put forth; (*fig*) to move, rouse, persecute; to do, act, perform; (*time*) to pass, spend; (*undertakings*) to manage, wage; (*public speaking*) to plead, discuss; to negotiate, treat; (*THEAT*) to play, act the part of; **~ cum populō** address the people; **age** come on!, well then; **age age** all right!; **āctum est dē** it is all up with; **aliud ~** not attend; **animam ~** expire; **annum quartum ~** be three years old; **causam ~** plead a cause; **hōc age** pay attention; **id ~ ut** aim at; **lēge ~** go to law; **nīl agis** it's no use; **quid agis?** how are you?; **rēs agitur** interests are at stake; **sē ~** go, come.

agrāriī *mpl* the land reform party.

agrārius *adj* of public land; **lēx ~a** land law.

agrestis *adj* rustic; boorish, wild, barbarous ♦ *m* countryman.

agricola, -ae *m* countryman, farmer.

Agricola, -ae *m* a Roman governor of Britain; his biography by Tacitus.

Agrigentīnus *adj see n.*

Agrigentum, -ī *nt* a town in Sicily.

agripeta, -ae *m* landgrabber.

Agrippa, -ae *m* Roman surname (*esp Augustus's minister*).

Agrippīna, -ae *f* mother of Nero; **Colōnia ~a** or **~ēnsis** Cologne.

Agyīeus, -eī *and* **eos** *m* Apollo.

āh *interj* ah! (*in sorrow or joy*).

aha *interj* expressing reproof *or* laughter.

ahēn- *etc see* **aēn-.**

Āiāx, -ācis *m* Ajax (*name of two Greek heroes at Troy*).

āiō *vt* (*defec*) to say, speak; **ain tū?/ain vērō?** really?; **quid ais?** I say!

āla, -ae *f* wing; armpit; (*MIL*) wing of army.

alabaster, -rī *m* perfume box.

alacer, -ris *adj* brisk, cheerful.

alacritās, -ātis *f* promptness, liveliness; joy, rapture.

alapa, -ae *f* slap on the face; a slave's freedom.

ālāriī *mpl* allied troops.

ālārius *adj* (*MIL*) on the wing.

ālātus *adj* winged.

alauda, -ae *f* lark; name of a legion of Caesar's.

alāzōn, -onis *m* braggart.

Alba Longa, -ae, -ae *f* a Latin town (*precursor of Rome*).
Albānus *adj* Alban; **Lacus ~, Mōns ~** *lake and mountain near Alba Longa*.
albātus *adj* dressed in white.
albeō, -ēre *vi* to be white; to dawn.
albēscō, -ere *vi* to become white; to dawn.
albicō, -āre *vi* to be white.
albidus *adj* white.
Albiōn, -ōnis *f* ancient name for Britain.
albitūdō, -inis *f* whiteness.
Albula, -ae *f* old name for the Tiber.
albulus *adj* whitish.
album, -ī *nt* white; records.
Albunea, -ae *f* a spring at Tibur; a sulphur spring near Alban Lake.
albus *adj* white, bright.
Alcaeus, -ī *m* Greek lyric poet.
alcēdō, -inis *f* kingfisher.
alcēdōnia *ntpl* halcyon days.
alcēs, -is *f* elk.
Alcibiadēs, -is *m* brilliant Athenian politician.
Alcīdēs, -ae *m* Hercules.
Alcinous, -ī *m* king of Phaeacians in the Odyssey.
ālea, -ae *f* gambling, dice; (*fig*) chance, hazard; **iacta ~ est** the die is cast; **in ~am dare** to risk.
āleātor, -ōris *m* gambler.
āleātōrius *adj* in gambling.
ālēc *etc see* **allēc**.
āleō, -ōnis *m* gambler.
āles, -itis *adj* winged; swift ♦ *m/f* bird; omen.
alēscō, -ere *vi* to grow up.
Alexander, -rī *m* a Greek name; Paris (*prince of Troy*); Alexander the Great (*king of Macedon*).
Alexandrēa (*later* -**īa**), **-ēae** *f* Alexandria in Egypt.
alga, -ae *f* seaweed.
algeō, -gēre, -sī *vi* to feel cold; (*fig*) to be neglected.
algēscō, -ere *vi* to catch cold.
Algidus, -ī *m* mountain in Latium.
algidus *adj* cold.
algor, -ōris *m* cold.
algū *abl sg m* with cold.
aliā *adv* in another way.
aliās *adv* at another time; at one time ... at another.
alibī *adv* elsewhere; otherwise; in one place ... in another.
alicubī *adv* somewhere.
alicunde *adv* from somewhere.
alid *old form of* **aliud**.
aliēnātiō, -ōnis *f* transfer; estrangement.
aliēnigena, -ae *m* foreigner.
aliēnigenus *adj* foreign; heterogeneous.
aliēnō, -āre, -āvī, -ātum *vt* to transfer (property by sale); to alienate, estrange; (*mind*) to derange.

aliēnus *adj* of another, of others; alien, strange; (*with abl or* **ab**) unsuited to, different from; hostile ♦ *m* stranger.
āliger, -ī *adj* winged.
alimentārius *adj* about food.
alimentum, -ī *nt* nourishment, food; obligation of children to parents; (*fig*) support.
alimōnium, -i *and* **iī** *nt* nourishment.
aliō *adv* in another direction, elsewhere; one way ... another way.
aliōquī, aliōquin *adv* otherwise, else; besides.
aliōrsum *adv* in another direction; differently.
ālipēs, -edis *adj* wing-footed; fleet.
alīptēs, -ae *m* sports trainer.
aliquā *adv* some way or other.
aliquam *adv:* **~ diū** for sometime; **~ multī** a considerable number.
aliquandō *adv* sometime, ever; sometimes; once, for once; now at last.
aliquantisper *adv* for a time.
aliquantō *adv* (*with comp*) somewhat.
aliquantulum *nt* a very little ♦ *adv* somewhat.
aliquantulus *adj* quite small.
aliquantum *adj* a good deal ♦ *adv* somewhat.
aliquantus *adj* considerable.
aliquātenus *adv* to some extent.
aliquī, -qua, -quod *adj* some, any; some other.
aliquid *adv* at all.
aliquis, -quid *pron* somebody, something; someone *or* something important.
aliquō *adv* to some place, somewhere else.
aliquot *adj* (*indecl*) some.
aliquotiēns *adv* several times.
aliter *adv* otherwise, differently; in one way ... in another.
alitus *ppp of* **alō**.
ālium, -i *and* **iī** *nt* garlic.
aliunde *adv* from somewhere else.
alius, alia, aliud *adj* other, another; different; **alius ... alius** some ... others; **alius ex aliō** one after the other; **in alia omnia īre** oppose a measure; **nihil aliud quam** only.
all- *etc see* **adl-**.
allēc, -is *nt* fish pickle.
allex, -icis *m* big toe.
Allia, -ae *f* tributary of the Tiber (*scene of a great Roman defeat*).
Alliēnsis *adj see* **Allia**.
Allobrogēs, -um *mpl* a people of S.E. Gaul.
Allobrogicus *adj see n.*
almus *adj* nourishing; kindly.
alnus, -ī *f* alder.
alō, -ere, -uī, -tum *and* **-itum** *vt* to nourish, rear; to increase, promote.
Alpēs, -ium *fpl* Alps.
Alphēus, -ī *m* river of Olympia in S.W. Greece.
Alpīnus *adj see n.*

Noun declensions and verb conjugations are shown on pp xiii to xxv. The present infinitive ending of a verb shows to which conjugation it belongs: **-āre** = 1st; **-ēre** = 2nd; **-ere** = 3rd and **-īre** = 4th. Irregular verbs are shown on p xxvi

alsī *perf of* **algeō**.

alsius, alsus *adj* cold.

altāria, -ium *ntpl* altars, altar; altar top.

altē *adv* on high, from above; deep; from afar.

alter, -īus *adj* the one, the other (*of two*); second, the next; fellow man; different; ~ ego, ~ īdem a second self; ~um tantum twice as much; ūnus et ~ one or two.

altercātiō, -ōnis *f* dispute, debate.

altercor, -ārī, -ātus *vi* to wrangle, dispute; to cross-examine.

alternīs *adv* alternately.

alternō, -āre, -āvī, -ātum *vt* to do by turns, alternate.

alternus *adj* one after the other, alternate; elegiac (*verses*).

alteruter, -īusutrīus *adj* one or the other.

altilis *adj* fat (*esp fowls*).

altisonus *adj* sounding on high.

altitonāns, -antis *adj* thundering on high.

altitūdō, -inis *f* height, depth; (*fig*) sublimity, (*mind*) secrecy.

altivolāns, -antis *adj* soaring on high.

altor, -ōris *m* foster father.

altrīnsecus *adv* on the other side.

altrīx, -īcis *f* nourisher, foster mother.

altum, -ī *nt* heaven; sea (*usu out of sight of land*); **ex ~ō repetītus** far-fetched.

altus *adj* high, deep; (*fig*) noble; profound.

ālūcinor, -ārī, -ātus *vi* to talk wildly; (*mind*) to wander.

aluī *perf of* **alō**.

alumnus, -ī *m/f* foster child; pupil.

alūta, -ae *f* soft leather; shoe, purse, face patch.

alveārium, -ī *and* **iī** *nt* beehive.

alveolus, -ī *m* basin.

alveus, -eī *m* hollow; trough; (*ship*) hold; bath tub; riverbed.

alvus, -ī *f* bowels; womb; stomach.

amābilis *adj* lovely, lovable.

amābilitās, -ātis *f* charm.

amābiliter *adv see* **amābilis**.

Amalthēa, -ae *f* nymph or she-goat; **cornū ~ae** horn of plenty.

Amalthēum, -ī *nt* Atticus's library.

āmandātiō *f* sending away.

āmandō, -āre, -āvī, -ātum *vt* to send away.

amāns, -antis *adj* fond ♦ *m* lover.

amanter *adv* affectionately.

āmanuēnsis, -is *m* secretary.

amāracinum, -inī *nt* marjoram ointment.

amāracum, -ī *nt, m/f,* **amāracus, -ī** sweet marjoram.

amārē *adv see* **amārus**.

amāritiēs, -ēī *f,* **amāritūdō, -inis** *f,* **amāror, -ōris** *m* bitterness.

amārus *adj* bitter; (*fig*) sad; ill-natured.

amāsius, -ī *and* **iī** *m* lover.

Amathūs, -ūntis *f* town in Cyprus.

Amathūsia *f* Venus.

amātiō, -ōnis *f* lovemaking.

amātor, -ōris *m* lover, paramour.

amātorculus *m* poor lover.

amatōriē *adv* amorously.

amatōrius *adj* of love, erotic.

amātrīx, -rīcis *f* mistress.

Amāzōn, -onis *f* Amazon, warrior woman.

Amāzonidēs *fpl* Amazons.

Amāzonius *adj see* n.

ambāctus, -ī *m* vassal.

ambāgēs, -is *f* windings; (*speech*) circumlocution, quibbling; enigma.

ambedō, -edere, -ēdī, -ēsum *vt* to consume.

ambēsus *ppp of* **ambedō**.

ambigō, -ere *vt, vi* to wander about; to be in doubt; to argue; to wrangle.

ambiguē *adv* doubtfully.

ambiguitās, -ātis *f* ambiguity.

ambiguus *adj* changeable, doubtful, unreliable; ambiguous.

ambiō, -īre, -īī, -ītum *vt* to go round, encircle; (*POL*) to canvass for votes; (*fig*) to court (for a favour).

ambitiō, -ōnis *f* canvassing for votes; currying favour; ambition.

ambitiōsē *adv* ostentatiously.

ambitiōsus *adj* winding; ostentatious, ambitious.

ambītus *ppp of* **ambiō**.

ambitus, -ūs *m* circuit, circumference; circumlocution; canvassing, bribery; **lēx de ~ū** a law against bribery.

ambō, ambae, ambō *num* both, two.

Ambracia, -ae *f* district of N.W. Greece.

Ambraciēnsis, -us *adj see* n.

ambrosia, -ae *f* food of the gods.

ambrosius *adj* divine.

ambūbāia, -ae *f* Syrian flute-girl.

ambulācrum, -ī *nt* avenue.

ambulātiō, -ōnis *f* walk, walking; walk (*place*).

ambulātiuncula *f* short walk.

ambulō, -āre, -āvī, -ātum *vi* to walk, go; to travel.

ambūrō, -rere, -ssī, -stum *vt* to burn up; to make frostbitten; (*fig*) to ruin.

ambūstus *ppp of* **ambūrō**.

amellus, -ī *m* Michaelmas daisy.

āmēns, -entis *adj* mad, frantic; stupid.

āmentia, -ae *f* madness; stupidity.

āmentum, -ī *nt* strap (for throwing javelin).

ames, -itis *m* fowler's pole.

amfr- *etc see* **anfr-**.

amīca, -ae *f* friend; mistress.

amiciō, -īre, -tus *vt* to clothe, cover.

amīciter, -ē *adv see* **amīcus**.

amīcitia, -ae *f* friendship; alliance.

amictus *ppp of* **amiciō**.

amictus, -us *m* (manner of) dress; clothing.

amiculum, -ī *nt* cloak.

amīculus, -ī *m* dear friend.

amīcus, -ī *m* friend ♦ *adj* friendly, fond.

āmissiō, -ōnis *f* loss.

āmissus *ppp of* **āmittō**.

amita, -ae *f* aunt (*on father's side*).

āmittō, -ittere, -īsī, -issum *vt* to let go, lose.
Ammōn, -is *m Egyptian god identified with Jupiter.*
Ammōniacus *adj see n.*
amnicola, -ae *m/f* sth growing by a river.
amniculus *m* brook.
amnicus *adj see n.*
amnis, -is *m* river.
amō, -āre, -āvī, -ātum *vt* to love, like; (*colloq*) to be obliged to; **ita mē dī ament!** ≈ *bless my soul!*; **amābō** please!
amoenitās, -ātis *f* delightfulness (*esp of scenery*).
amoenus *adj* delightful.
āmōlior, -īrī, -ītus *vt* to remove.
amōmum, -ī *nt* cardamom.
amor, -ōris *m* love; (*fig*) strong desire; term of endearment; Cupid; (*pl*) love affairs.
āmōtiō, -ōnis *f* removal.
āmōtus *ppp of* **āmoveō.**
āmoveō, -ovēre, -ōvī, -ōtum *vt* to remove; to banish.
amphibolia, -ae *f* ambiguity.
Amphīōn, -onis *m musician and builder of Thebes.*
Amphīonius *adj see n.*
amphitheātrum, -ī *nt* amphitheatre.
Amphitrītē, -ēs *f sea goddess;* the sea.
Amphitryō, -ōnis *m husband of Alcmena.*
Amphitryōniadēs *m Hercules.*
amphora, -ae *f* a two-handled jar; liquid measure; (*NAUT*) measure of tonnage.
Amphrȳsius *adj of Apollo.*
Amphrȳsus, -ī *m river in Thessaly.*
ample *adv see* **amplūs.**
amplector, -ctī, -xus *vt* to embrace, encircle; (*mind*) to grasp; (*speech*) to deal with; (*fig*) to cherish.
amplexor, -ārī, -ātus *vt* to embrace, love.
amplexus *ppa of* **amplector.**
amplexus, -ūs *m* embrace, encircling.
amplificātiō, -ōnis *f* enlargement; (*RHET*) a passage elaborated for effect.
amplificē *adv* splendidly.
amplificō, -āre, -āvī, -ātum *vt* to increase, enlarge; (*RHET*) to enlarge upon.
ampliō, -āre, -āvī, -ātum *vt* to enlarge; (*law*) to adjourn.
ampliter *adv see* **amplūs.**
amplitūdō, -inis *f* size; (*fig*) distinction; (*RHET*) fullness.
amplius *adv* more (*esp amount or number*), further, longer; ~ **ducentī** more than 200; ~ **nōn petere** take no further legal action; ~ **prōnūntiāre** adjourn a case.
amplūs *adj* large, spacious; great, abundant; powerful, splendid, eminent; (*sup*) distinguished.
ampulla, -ae *f* a two-handled flask; (*fig*) high-flown language.

ampullārius, -ārī *m* flask-maker.
ampullor, -ārī *vi* to use high-flown language.
amputātiō, -ōnis *f* pruning.
amputatus *adj* (*RHET*) disconnected.
amputō, -āre, -āvī, -ātum *vt* to cut off, prune; (*fig*) to lop off.
Amūlius, -ī *m king of Alba Longa, grand-uncle of Romulus.*
amurca, -ae *f* lees of olive oil.
amussitātus *adj* nicely adjusted.
Amȳclae, -ārum *fpl town in S. Greece.*
Amȳclaeus *adj see n.*
amygdalum, -ī *nt* almond.
amystis, -dis *f* emptying a cup at a draught.
an *conj* or; perhaps; (*with single question*) surely not; **haud sciō** ~ I feel sure.
Anacreōn, -ontis *m Greek lyric poet.*
anadēma, -tis *nt* headband.
anagnōstēs, -ae *m* reader.
anapaestum, -ī *nt* poem in anapaests.
anapaestus *adj*: ~ **pēs** anapaest.
anas, -tis *f* duck.
anaticula *f* duckling.
anatīnus *adj see n.*
anatocismus, -ī *m* compound interest.
Anaxagorās, -ae *m early Greek philosopher.*
Anaximander, -rī *m early Greek philosopher.*
anceps, -ipitis *adj* two-headed; double; wavering, doubtful; dangerous ♦ *nt* danger.
Anchīsēs, -ae *m father of Aeneas.*
Anchīsēus *adj* Aeneas.
Anchīsiadēs *m* Aeneas.
ancīle, -is *nt* oval shield (*esp one said to have fallen from heaven in Numa's reign*).
ancilla, -ae *f* servant.
ancillāris *adj* of a young servant.
ancillula *f* young servant.
ancīsus *adj* cut round.
ancora, -ae *f* anchor.
ancorārius *adj see n.*
ancorāle, -is *nt* cable.
Ancus Marcius, -ī, -ī *m 4th king of Rome.*
Ancȳra, -ae *f* Ankara (*capital of Galatia*).
andabata, -ae *m* blindfold gladiator.
Andrius *adj see* **Andros.**
androgynē, -ēs *f* hermaphrodite.
androgynus, -ī *m* hermaphrodite.
Andromachē, -ēs *f wife of Hector.*
Andromeda, -ae *f wife of Perseus;* a constellation.
Andronicus, -ī *m Livius (earliest Latin poet).*
Andros (-us), -ī *m Aegean island.*
ānellus, -ī *m* little ring.
anēthum, -ī *nt* fennel.
ānfrāctus, -ūs *m* bend, orbit; roundabout way; (*words*) digression, prolixity.
angelus, -ī *m* angel.
angina, -ae *f* quinsy.
angiportum, -ī *nt* alley.
angiportus, -ūs *m* alley.

Noun declensions and verb conjugations are shown on pp xiii to xxv. The present infinitive ending of a verb shows to which conjugation it belongs: **-āre** = 1st; **-ēre** = 2nd; **-ere** = 3rd and **-īre** = 4th. Irregular verbs are shown on p xxvi

angō, -ere *vt* to throttle; (*fig*) to distress, torment.
angor, -ōris *m* suffocation; (*fig*) anguish, torment.
anguicomus *adj* with snakes for hair.
anguiculus, -ī *m* small snake.
anguifer, -ī *adj* snake-carrying.
anguigena, -ae *m* one born of serpents; Theban.
anguīlla, -ae *f* eel.
anguimanus *adj* with a trunk.
anguipēs, -edis *adj* serpent-footed.
anguis, -is *m/f* snake, serpent; (*constellation*) Draco.
Anguitenēns, -entis *m* Ophiuchus.
angulātus *adj* angular.
angulus, -ī *m* angle, corner; out-of-the-way place; **ad parēs ~ōs** at right angles.
angustē *adv* close, within narrow limits; concisely.
angustiae, -ārum *fpl* defile, strait; (*time*) shortness; (*means*) want; (*CIRCS*) difficulty; (*mind*) narrowness; (*words*) subtleties.
angusticlāvius *adj* wearing a narrow purple stripe.
angustō, -āre *vt* to make narrow.
angustum, -ī *nt* narrowness; danger.
angustus *adj* narrow, close; (*time*) short; (*means*) scanty; (*mind*) mean; (*argument*) subtle; (*CIRCS*) difficult.
anhēlitus, -ūs *m* panting; breath, exhalation.
anhēlō, -āre, -āvī, -ātum *vi* to breathe hard, pant; to exhale.
anhēlus *adj* panting.
anicula, -ae *f* poor old woman.
Aniēnsis, Aniēnus *adj* of the river Anio.
Aniēnus *m* Anio.
anīlis *adj* of an old woman.
anīlitās, -tātis *f* old age.
anīliter *adv* like an old woman.
anima, -ae *f* wind, air; breath; life; soul, mind; ghost, spirit; **~am agere, efflāre** expire; **~am comprimere** hold one's breath.
animadversiō, -ōnis *f* observation; censure, punishment.
animadversor, -ōris *m* observer.
animadvertō, -tere, -tī, -sum *vt* to pay attention to, notice; to realise; to censure, punish; **~ in** punish.
animal, -ālis *nt* animal; living creature.
animālis *adj* of air; animate.
animāns, -antis *m/f/nt* living creature; animal.
animātiō, -ōnis *f* being.
animātus *adj* disposed, in a certain frame of mind; courageous.
animō, -āre, -āvī, -ātum *vt* to animate; to give a certain temperament to.
animōsē *adv* boldly, eagerly.
animōsus *adj* airy; lifelike; courageous, proud.
animula, -ae *f* little soul.
animulus, -ī *m* darling.
animus, -ī *m* mind, soul; consciousness;

reason, thought, opinion, imagination; heart, feelings, disposition; courage, spirit, pride, passion; will, purpose; term of endearment; **~ī** in mind, in heart; **~ī causā** for amusement; **~ō fingere** imagine; **~ō male est** I am fainting; **aequō ~ō esse** be patient, calm; **bonō ~ō esse** take courage; be well-disposed; **ex ~ō** sincerely; **ex ~ō effluere** be forgotten; **in ~ō habēre** purpose; **meō ~ō** in my opinion.
Aniō, -ēnis *m* tributary of the Tiber.
Anna Perenna, -ae, -ae *f* Roman popular goddess.
annālēs, -ium *mpl* annals, chronicle.
annālis *adj* of a year; **lēx ~** law prescribing ages for public offices.
anne *etc see* **an.**
anniculus *adj* a year old.
anniversārius *adj* annual.
annōn or not.
annōna, -ae *f* year's produce; grain; price of corn; the market.
annōsus *adj* aged.
annōtinus *adj* last year's.
annus, -ī *m* year; **~ māgnus** astronomical great year; **~ solidus** a full year.
annuus *adj* a year's; annual.
anquīrō, -rere, -sīvī, -sītum *vt* to search for; to make inquiries; (*law*) to institute an inquiry (*dē*) *or* prosecution (*abl or gen*).
ānsa, -ae *f* handle; (*fig*) opportunity.
ānsātus *adj* with a handle; (*comedy*) with arms akimbo.
ānser, -is *m* goose.
ānserīnus *adj see* **n.**
ante *prep* (*with acc*) before (*in time, place, comparison*) ♦ *adv* (*place*) in front; (*time*) before.
anteā *adv* before, formerly.
antecapiō, -apere, -ēpī, -eptum *vt* to take beforehand, anticipate.
antecēdō, -ēdere, -essī, -essum *vt* to precede; to surpass.
antecellō, -ere *vi* to excel, be superior.
anteceptus *ppp of* **antecapiō.**
antecessiō, -ōnis *f* preceding; antecedent cause.
antecessor, -ōris *m* forerunner.
antecursor, -ōris *m* forerunner, pioneer.
anteeō, -īre, -īī *vi* to precede, surpass.
anteferō, -ferre, -tulī, -lātum *vt* to carry before; to prefer; to anticipate.
antefīxus *adj* attached (in front) ♦ *ntpl* ornaments on roofs of buildings.
antegredior, -dī, -ssus *vt* to precede.
antehabeō, -ēre *vt* to prefer.
antehāc *adv* formerly, previously.
antelātus *ppp of* **anteferō.**
antelūcānus *adj* before dawn.
antemerīdiānus *adj* before noon.
antemittō, -ittere, -īsī, -issum *vt* to send on in front.
antenna, -ae *f* yardarm.

antepīlānī, -ōrum *mpl (MIL)* the front ranks.
antepōnō, -ōnere, -osuī, -ositum *vt* to set before; to prefer.
antequam *conj* before.
Anterōs, -ōtis *m* avenger of slighted love.
antēs, -ium *mpl* rows.
antesignānus, -ī *m (MIL)* leader; *(pl)* defenders of the standards.
antestō, antistō, -āre, -ētī *vi* to excel, distinguish oneself.
antestor, -ārī, -ātus *vi* to call a witness.
anteveniō, -enīre, -ēnī, -entum *vt, vi* to anticipate; to surpass.
antevertō, -tere, -tī, -sum *vt* to precede; to anticipate; to prefer.
anticipātiō, -ōnis *f* foreknowledge.
anticipō, -āre, -āvī, -ātum *vt* to take before, anticipate.
antīcus *adj* in front.
Antigonē, -ēs *f* daughter of Oedipus.
Antigonus, -ī *m* name of Macedonian kings.
Antiochēnsis *adj see n.*
Antiochīa, -īae *f* Antioch *(capital of Syria).*
Antiochus, -ī *m* name of kings of Syria.
antīquārius, -ī *and* **iī** *m* antiquary.
antīquē *adv* in the old style.
antīquitās, -ātis *f* antiquity, the ancients; integrity.
antīquitus *adv* long ago, from ancient times.
antīquō, -āre, -āvī, -ātum *vt* to vote against (a bill).
antīquus *adj* ancient, former, old; good old-fashioned, honest, illustrious; **antīquior** more important; **antīquissimus** most important.
antistēs, -itis *m/f* high priest, chief priestess; *(fig)* master *(in any art).*
Antisthenēs, -is *and* **ae** *m* founder of Cynic philosophy.
antistita, -ae *f* chief priestess.
antistō *etc see* **antestō.**
antitheton, -ī *nt (RHET)* antithesis.
Antōnīnus, -ī *m* name of Roman emperors *(esp Pius and Marcus Aurelius).*
Antōnius, -ī *m* Roman name *(esp the famous orator, and Mark Antony).*
antrum, -ī *nt* cave, hollow.
ānulārius, -ī *m* ringmaker.
ānulātus *adj* with rings on.
ānulus, -ī *m* ring; equestrian rank.
ānus, -ī *m* rectum; ring.
anus, -ūs *f* old woman ♦ *adj* old.
ānxiē *adv see* **anxius.**
ānxietās, -ātis *f* anxiety, trouble *(of the mind).*
ānxifer, -ī *adj* disquieting.
ānxitūdō, -inis *f* anxiety.
ānxius *adj (mind)* troubled; disquieting.
Āones, -um *adj* Boeotian.
Āonia *f* part of Boeotia.
Āonius *adj* of Boeotia, of Helicon.

Aornos, -ī *m* lake Avernus.
apage *interj* away with!, go away!
apēliōtēs, -ae *m* east wind.
Apellēs, -is *m* Greek painter.
aper, -rī *m* boar.
aperiō, -īre, -uī, -tum *vt* to uncover, disclose, open; *(country)* to open up; *(fig)* to unfold, explain, reveal.
apertē *adv* clearly, openly.
apertum, -ī *nt* open space; **in ~ō esse** be well known; be easy.
apertus *ppp of* **aperiō** ♦ *adj* open, exposed; clear, manifest; *(person)* frank.
aperuī *perf of* **aperiō.**
apex, -icis *m* summit; crown, priest's cap; *(fig)* crown.
aphractus, -ī *f* a long open boat.
apiārius, -ī *and* **iī** *m* beekeeper.
Apīcius, -ī *m* Roman epicure.
apicula, -ae *f* little bee.
apis, -is *f* bee.
apīscor, -īscī, -tus *vt* to catch, get, attain.
apium, -ī *and* **iī** *nt* celery.
aplustre, -is *nt* decorated stern of a ship.
apoclētī, -ōrum *mpl* committee of the Aetolian League.
apodytērium, -ī *and* **iī** *nt* dressing room.
Apollināris, -ineus *adj:* **lūdī ~inārēs** Roman games in July.
Apollō, -inis *m* Greek god of music, archery, prophecy, flocks and herds, and often identified with the sun.
apologus, -ī *m* narrative, fable.
apophorēta, -ōrum *ntpl* presents for guests to take home.
apoproēgmena, -ōrum *ntpl (PHILOS)* what is rejected.
apostolicus *adj see n.*
apostolus, -ī *m (ECCL)* apostle.
apothēca, -ae *f* storehouse, wine store.
apparātē *adv see* **apparātus.**
apparātiō, -ōnis *f* preparation.
apparātus *adj* ready, well-supplied, sumptuous.
apparātus, -ūs *m* preparation; equipment; munitions; pomp, ostentation.
appāreō, -ēre, -uī, -itum *vi* to come in sight, appear; to be seen, show oneself; to wait upon *(an official);* **~et** it is obvious.
appāritiō, -ōnis *f* service; domestic servants.
appāritor, -ōris *m* attendant.
apparō, -āre, -āvī, -ātum *vt* to prepare, provide.
appellātiō, -ōnis *f* accosting, appeal; title; pronunciation.
appellātor, -ōris *m* appellant.
appellitātus *adj* usually called.
appellō, -āre, -āvī, -ātum *vt* to speak to; to appeal to; *(for money)* to dun; *(law)* to sue; to call, name; to pronounce.

Noun declensions and verb conjugations are shown on pp xiii to xxv. The present infinitive ending of a verb shows to which conjugation it belongs: **-āre** = 1st; **-ēre** = 2nd; **-ere** = 3rd and **-īre** = 4th. Irregular verbs are shown on p xxvi

appellō, -ellere, -ulī, -ulsum _vt_ to drive, bring (to); (_NAUT_) to bring to land.
appendicula, -ae _f_ small addition.
appendix, -icis _f_ supplement.
appendō, -endere, -endī, -ensum _vt_ to weigh, pay.
appetēns, -entis _adj_ eager; greedy.
appetenter _adv see_ **appetēns.**
appetentia, -ae _f_ craving.
appetītiō, -ōnis _f_ grasping, craving.
appetītus _ppp of_ **appetō.**
appetītus, -ūs _m_ craving; natural desire (_as opposed to reason_).
appetō, -ere, -īvī, -ītum _vt_ to grasp, try to get at; to attack; to desire ♦ _vi_ to approach.
appingō, -ere _vt_ to paint (in); (_colloq_) to write more.
Appius, -ī _m_ Roman first name; **Via ~ia** _main road from Rome to Capua and Brundisium._
applaudō, -dere, -sī, -sum _vt_ to strike, clap ♦ _vi_ to applaud.
applicātiō, -ōnis _f_ applying (_of the mind_); **iūs ~ōnis** _the right of a patron to inherit a client's effects._
applicātus _and_ **itus** _ppp of_ **applicō.**
applicō, -āre, -āvī _and_ **uī, -ātum** _and_ **itum** _vt_ to attach, place close (to); (_NAUT_) to steer, bring to land; **sē, animum ~** devote self, attention (to).
applōrō, -āre _vt_ to deplore.
appōnō, -ōnere, -osuī, -ositum _vt_ to put (to, beside); (_meal_) to serve; to add, appoint; to reckon.
apporrēctus _adj_ stretched nearby.
apportō, -āre, -āvī, -ātum _vt_ to bring, carry (to).
apposcō, -ere _vt_ to demand also.
appositē _adv_ suitably.
appositus _ppp of_ **appōnō** ♦ _adj_ situated near; (_fig_) bordering on; suitable.
apposuī _perf of_ **appōnō.**
appōtus _adj_ drunk.
apprecor, -ārī, -ātus _vt_ to pray to.
apprehendō, -endere, -endī, -ēnsum _vt_ to take hold of; (_MIL_) to occupy; (_argument_) to bring forward.
apprīmē _adv_ especially.
apprimō, -imere, -essī, -essum _vt_ to press close.
approbātiō, -ōnis _f_ acquiescence; proof.
approbātor, -ōris _m_ approve.
approbē _adv_ very well.
approbō, -āre, -āvī, -ātum _vt_ to approve; to prove; to perform to someone's satisfaction.
apprōmittō, -ere _vt_ to promise also.
approperō, -āre, -āvī, -ātum _vt_ to hasten ♦ _vi_ to hurry up.
appropinquātiō, -ōnis _f_ approach.
appropinquō, -āre, -āvī, -ātum _vi_ to approach.
appugnō, -āre _vt_ to attack.
appulsus _ppp of_ **appellō.**
appulsus, -ūs _m_ landing; approach.

aprīcātiō, -ōnis _f_ basking.
aprīcor, -ārī _vi_ to bask.
aprīcus _adj_ sunny; basking; **in ~um prōferre** bring to light.
Aprīlis _adj_ April, of April.
aprūgnus _adj_ of the wild boar.
aps- _etc see_ **abs-.**
aptē _adv_ closely; suitably, rightly.
aptō, -āre, -āvī, -ātum _vt_ to fit, put on; (_fig_) to adapt; to prepare, equip.
aptus _adj_ attached, joined together, fitted (with); suitable.
apud _prep_ (_with acc_) **1.** (_with persons_) beside, by, with, at the house of, among, in the time of; (_speaking_) in the presence of, to; (_judgment_) in the opinion of; (_influence_) with; (_faith_) in; (_authors_) in. **2.** (_with places_) near, at, in; **est ~ mē** I have; **sum ~ mē** I am in my senses.
Āpūlia, -iae _f_ district of S.E. Italy.
Āpūlus _adj see n._
aput _prep see_ **apud.**
aqua, -ae _f_ water; **~ mihī haeret** I am in a fix; **intercus** dropsy; **~m adspergere** revive; **~m praebēre** entertain; **~m et terram petere** demand submission; **~ā et ignī interdīcere** outlaw.
aquae _fpl_ medicinal waters, spa.
aquaeductus, -ūs _m_ aqueduct; right of leading water.
aquāliculus _m_ belly.
aquālis, -is _m/f_ washbasin.
aquārius _adj_ of water ♦ _m_ water carrier, water inspector; a constellation.
aquāticus _adj_ aquatic; humid.
aquātilis _adj_ aquatic.
aquātiō, -ōnis _f_ fetching water; watering place.
aquātor, -ōris _m_ water carrier.
aquila, -ae _f_ eagle; standard of a legion; (_ARCH_) gable; a constellation; **~ae senectūs** a vigorous old age.
Aquileia, -ae _f_ town in N. Italy.
Aquileiēnsis _adj see n._
aquilifer, -ī _m_ chief standard-bearer.
aquilīnus _adj_ eagle's.
aquilō, -ōnis _m_ north wind; north.
aquilōnius _adj_ northerly.
aquilus _adj_ swarthy.
Aquīnās, ātis _adj see n._
Aquīnum, -ī _nt_ town in Latium.
Aquītānia, -iae _f_ district of S.W. Gaul.
Aquītānus _adj see n._
aquor, -ārī, -ātus _vi_ to fetch water.
aquōsus _adj_ humid, rainy.
aquula, -ae _f_ little stream.
āra, -ae _f_ altar; (_fig_) refuge; a constellation; **~ae et focī** hearth and home.
arabarchēs, -ae _m_ customs officer in Egypt.
Arabia, -iae _f_ Arabia.
Arabicē _adv_ with all the perfumes of Arabia.
Arabicus, Arabicius, Arabus _adj see n._
Arachnē, -s _f_ Lydian woman changed into a spider.

arānea, -ae *f* spider; cobweb.
arāneola *f*, **-olus** *m* small spider.
arāneōsus *adj* full of spiders' webs.
arāneum, -ī *nt* spider's web.
arāneus, -i *m* spider ♦ *adj* of spiders.
Arar, -is *m* river Saône.
Arātēus *adj see* **Arātus.**
arātiō, -ōnis *f* ploughing, farming; arable land.
arātiuncula *f* small plot.
arātor -ōris *m* ploughman, farmer; (*pl*) cultivators of public land.
arātrum, -ī *nt* plough.
Arātus, -ī *m* Greek astronomical poet.
Araxēs, -is *m* river in Armenia.
arbiter, -rī *m* witness; arbiter, judge, umpire; controller; ~ **bibendī** president of a drinking party.
arbitra, -ae *f* witness.
arbitrāriō *adv* with some uncertainty.
arbitrārius *adj* uncertain.
arbitrātus, -ūs *m* decision; **meō ~ū** in my judgment.
arbitrium, -ī *and* **iī** *nt* decision (*of an arbitrator*), judgment; mastery, control.
arbitror, -ārī, -ātus *vt, vi* to be a witness of; to testify; to think, suppose.
arbor, (arbōs), -oris *f* tree; ship, mast, oar; ~ **īnfēlīx** gallows.
arboreus *adj* of trees, like a tree.
arbustum, -ī *nt* plantation, orchard; (*pl*) trees.
arbustus *adj* wooded.
arbuteus *adj* of the strawberry tree.
arbutum, -ī *nt* fruit of strawberry tree.
arbutus, -ī *f* strawberry tree.
arca, -ae *f* box; moneybox, purse; coffin; prison cell; **ex ~ā absolvere** pay cash.
Arcades, -um *mpl* Arcadians.
Arcadia, -iae *f* district of S. Greece.
Arcadicus, -ius *adj see* **Arcadia.**
arcānō *adv* privately.
arcānum, -ī *nt* secret, mystery.
arcānus *adj* secret; able to keep secrets.
arceō, -ēre, -uī, -tum *vt* to enclose; to keep off, prevent.
accessītū *abl sg m* at the summons.
accessītus *ppp of* **accessō** ♦ *adj* far-fetched.
accessō, -ere, -īvī, -ītum *vt* to send for, fetch; (*law*) to summon, accuse; (*fig*) to derive.
archetypus, -ī *m* original.
Archilochus, -ī *m* Greek iambic and elegiac poet.
archimagīrus, -i *m* chief cook.
Archimēdēs, -is *m* famous mathematician of Syracuse.
archipīrāta, -ae *m* pirate chief.
architectōn, -onis *m* master builder; master in cunning.
architector, -ārī, -ātus *vt* to construct; (*fig*) to devise.
architectūra, -ae *f* architecture.

architectus, -ī *m* architect; (*fig*) author.
archōn, -ontis *m* Athenian magistrate.
Archytās, -ae *m* Pythagorean philosopher of Tarentum.
arcitenēns, -entis *adj* holding a bow ♦ *m* Apollo.
Arctophylax, -cis *m* (*constellation*) Bootes.
arctos, -ī *f* Great Bear, Little Bear; north, north wind; night.
Arctūrus, -ī *m* brightest star in Boötes.
arctus *etc see* **artus** *etc.*
arcuī *perf of* **arceō.**
arcula, -ae *f* casket; (*RHET*) ornament.
arcuō, -āre, -āvī, -ātum *vt* to curve.
arcus, -ūs *m* bow; rainbow; arch, curve; (*MATH*) arc.
ardea, -ae *f* heron.
Ardea, -ae *f* town in Latium.
ardeliō, -ōnis *m* busybody.
ārdēns, -entis *adj* hot, glowing, fiery; (*fig*) eager, ardent.
ārdenter *adv* passionately.
ārdeō, -dēre, -sī, -sum *vi* to be on fire, burn, shine; (*fig*) to be fired, burn.
ārdēscō, -ere *vi* to catch fire, gleam; (*fig*) to become inflamed, wax hotter.
ārdor, -ōris *m* heat, brightness; (*fig*) ardour, passion.
arduum, -ī *nt* steep slope; difficulty.
arduus *adj* steep, high; difficult, troublesome.
ārea, -ae *f* vacant site, open space, playground; threshing-floor; (*fig*) scope (*for effort*).
ārefaciō, -acere, -ēcī, -actum *vt* to dry.
arēna *etc see* **harēna.**
ārēns, -entis *adj* arid; thirsty.
āreō, -ēre *vi* to be dry.
āreola, -ae *f* small open space.
Arēopagītēs *m* member of the court.
Arēopagus, -ī *m* Mars' Hill in Athens; a criminal court.
Arēs, -is *m* Greek god of war.
ārēscō, -ere *vi* to dry, dry up.
Arestoridēs, -ae *m* Argus.
aretālogus, -ī *m* braggart.
Arethūsa, -ae *f* spring near Syracuse.
Arethūsis *adj* Syracusan.
Argēī, -ōrum *mpl* sacred places in Rome; effigies thrown annually into the Tiber.
argentāria, -ae *f* bank, banking; silver mine.
argentārius *adj* of silver, of money ♦ *m* banker.
argentātus *adj* silver-plated; backed with money.
argenteus *adj* of silver, adorned with silver; silvery (*in colour*); of the silver age.
argentum, -ī *nt* silver, silver plate; money.
Argēus, -īvus, -olicus *adj* Argive; Greek.
Argīlētānus *adj see n.*
Argīlētum, -ī *nt* part of Rome (*noted for*

bookshops).
argilla, -ae *f* clay.
Argō, -ūs *f* Jason's ship.
Argolis, -olidis *f district about Argos.*
Argonautae, -ārum *mpl* Argonauts.
Argonauticus *adj see n.*
Argos *nt*, -**ī**, -**ōrum** *mpl town in S.E. Greece.*
Argōus *adj see* **Argō**.
argūmentātiō, -ōnis *f* adducing proofs.
argūmentor, -ārī, -ātus *vt*, *vi* to prove,
    adduce as proof; to conclude.
argūmentum, -ī *nt* evidence, proof; (*LIT*)
    subject matter, theme, plot (*of a play*); (*art*)
    subject, motif.
arguō, -uere, -uī, -ūtum *vt* to prove, make
    known; to accuse, blame, denounce.
Argus, -ī *m monster with many eyes.*
argūtē *adv* subtly.
argūtiae, -ārum *fpl* nimbleness, liveliness;
    wit, subtlety, slyness.
argūtor, -ārī, -ātus *vi* to chatter.
argūtulus *adj* rather subtle.
argūtus *adj* (*sight*) clear, distinct, graceful;
    (*sound*) clear, melodious, noisy; (*mind*)
    acute, witty, sly.
argyraspis, -dis *adj* silver-shielded.
Ariadna, -ae *f daughter of Minos of Crete.*
Ariadnaeus *adj see n.*
āridulus *adj* rather dry.
āridum, -ī *nt* dry land.
āridus *adj* dry, withered; meagre; (*style*) flat.
ariēs, -etis *m* ram; 1st sign of Zodiac;
    battering ram; beam used as a breakwater.
arietō, -āre *vt*, *vi* to butt, strike hard.
Ariōn, -onis *m early Greek poet and musician.*
Ariōnius *adj see n.*
arista, -ae *f ear of corn.*
Aristaeus, -ī *m legendary founder of beekeeping.*
Aristarchus, -ī *m Alexandrian scholar; a severe
    critic.*
Aristīdēs, -is *m Athenian statesman noted for
    integrity.*
Aristippēus *adj see n.*
Aristippus, -ī *m Greek hedonist philosopher.*
aristolochia, -ae *f birthwort.*
Aristophanēs, -is *m Greek comic poet.*
Aristophanēus, and īus *adj see n.*
Aristotelēs, -is *m* Aristotle (*founder of
    Peripatetic school of philosophy*).
Aristotelēus, and īus *adj see n.*
arithmētica, -ōrum *ntpl* arithmetic.
āritūdō, -inis *f dryness.*
Ariūsius *adj* of Ariusia in Chios.
arma, -ōrum *ntpl* armour, shield; arms,
    weapons (*of close combat only*); warfare,
    troops; (*fig*) defence, protection;
    implements, ship's gear.
armāmenta, -ōrum *ntpl* implements, ship's
    gear.
armāmentārium, -ī and iī *nt* arsenal.
armāriolum, -ī *nt* small chest.
armārium, -ī and iī *nt* chest, safe.
armātū *m abl* armour; **gravī ~** with heavy-

armed troops.
armatūra, -ae *f* armour, equipment; **levis ~**
    light-armed troops.
armatus *adj* armed.
Armenia, -ae *f* Armenia.
Armeniaca, -acae *f* apricot tree.
Armeniacum, -acī *nt* apricot.
Armenius *adj see* **Armenia**.
armentālis *adj* of the herd.
armentārius, -ī and iī *m* cattle herd.
armentum, -ī *nt* cattle (*for ploughing*), herd
    (*cattle etc*).
armifer, -ī *adj* armed.
armiger, -ī *m* armour-bearer ♦ *adj* armed;
    productive of warriors.
armilla, -ae *f* bracelet.
armillātus *adj* wearing a bracelet.
armipotēns, -entis *adj* strong in battle.
armisonus *adj* resounding with arms.
armō, -āre, -āvī, -ātum *vt* to arm, equip; to
    rouse to arms (against).
armus, -ī *m* shoulder (*esp of animals*).
Arniēnsis *adj see* **Arnus**.
Arnus, -ī *m* river Arno.
arō, -āre, -āvī, -ātum *vt* to plough, cultivate;
    to live by farming; (*fig: sea, brow*) to furrow.
Arpīnās, -ātis *adj see n.*
Arpīnum, -ī *nt town in Latium (birthplace of
    Cicero).*
arquātus *adj* jaundiced.
arr- *etc see* **adr-**.
arrabō, -ōnis *m* earnest money.
ars, artis *f* skill (*in any craft*); the art (*of any
    profession*); science, theory; handbook; work
    of art; moral quality, virtue; artifice, fraud.
ārsī *perf of* **ārdeō**.
ārsus *ppp of* **ārdeō**.
artē *adv* closely, soundly, briefly.
artēria, -ae *f* windpipe; artery.
artēria, -ōrum *ntpl* trachea.
arthrīticus *adj* gouty.
articulātim *adv* joint by joint; (*speech*)
    distinctly.
articulō, -āre, -āvī, -ātum *vt* to articulate.
articulōsus *adj* minutely subdivided.
articulus, -ī *m* joint, knuckle; limb; (*words*)
    clause; (*time*) point, turning point; **in ipsō ~ō
    temporis** in the nick of time.
artifex, -icis *m* artist, craftsman, master; (*fig*)
    maker, author ♦ *adj* ingenious, artistic,
    artificial.
artificiōsē *adv* skilfully.
artificiōsus *adj* ingenious, artistic, artificial.
artificium, -ī and iī *nt* skill, workmanship; art,
    craft; theory, rule of an art; ingenuity,
    cunning.
artō, -āre *vt* to compress, curtail.
artolaganus, -ī *m kind of cake.*
artopta, -ae *m* baker; baking tin.
artus *adj* close, narrow, tight; (*sleep*) deep;
    (*fig*) strict, straitened.
artus, -ūs *m* joint; (*pl*) limbs, body; (*fig*)
    strength.

ārula, -ae f small altar.
arundō etc see **harundō** etc.
arvīna, -ae f grease.
arvum, -ī nt field; land, country, plain.
arvus adj ploughed.
arx, arcis f fortress, castle; height, summit; (fig) bulwark, stronghold; **arcem facere ē cloācā** make a mountain out of a molehill.
ās, assis m (weight) pound; (coin) bronze unit, of low value; (inheritance) the whole (subdivided into 12 parts); **ad assem** to the last farthing; **hērēs ex asse** sole heir.
Ascānius, -ī m son of Aeneas.
ascendō, -endere, -endī, -ēnsum vt, vi to go up, climb, embark; (fig) to rise.
ascēnsiō, -ōnis f ascent; (fig) sublimity.
ascēnsus, -ūs m ascent, rising; way up.
ascia, -ae f axe; mason's trowel.
asciō, -īre vt to admit.
ascīscō, -īscere, -īvī, -ītum vt to receive with approval; to admit (to some kind of association); to appropriate, adopt (esp customs); to arrogate to oneself.
ascītus adj acquired, alien.
Ascra, -ae f birthplace of Hesiod in Boeotia.
Ascraeus adj of Ascra; of Hesiod; of Helicon.
ascrībō, -bere, -psī, -ptum vt to add (in writing); to attribute, ascribe; to apply (an illustration); to enrol, include.
ascrīptīcius adj enrolled.
ascrīptiō, -ōnis f addition (in writing).
ascrīptīvus adj (MIL) supernumerary.
ascrīptor, -ōris m supporter.
ascrīptus ppp of **ascrībō**.
asella, -ae f young ass.
asellus, -ī m young ass.
Asia, -ae f Roman province; Asia Minor; Asia.
asīlus, -ī m gad fly.
asinus, -ī m ass; fool.
Asis, -dis f Asia.
Āsius (Āsiānus, Āsiāticus) adj see n.
Āsōpus, -ī m river in Boeotia.
asōtus, -ī m libertine.
asparagus, -ī m asparagus.
aspargō etc see **aspergō**.
aspectābilis adj visible.
aspectō, -āre vt to look at, gaze at; to pay heed to; (places) to face.
aspectus ppp of **aspiciō**.
aspectus, -ūs m look, sight; glance, sense of sight; aspect, appearance.
aspellō, -ere vt to drive away.
asper, -ī adj rough; (taste) bitter; (sound) harsh; (weather) severe; (style) rugged; (person) violent, exasperated, unkind, austere; (animal) savage; (CIRCS) difficult.
asperē adv see adj.
aspergō, -gere, -sī, -sum vt to scatter, sprinkle; to bespatter, besprinkle; **aquam ~** revive.
aspergō, -inis f sprinkling; spray.

asperitās, -ātis f roughness, unevenness, harshness, severity; (fig) ruggedness, fierceness; trouble, difficulty.
aspernātiō, -ōnis f disdain.
aspernor, -ārī, -ātus vt to reject, disdain.
asperō, -āre, -āvī, -ātum vt to roughen, sharpen; to exasperate.
aspersiō, -ōnis f sprinkling.
aspersus ppp of **aspergō**.
aspiciō, -icere, -exī, -ectum vt to catch sight of, look at; (places) to face; (fig) to examine, consider.
aspīrātiō, -ōnis f breathing (on); evaporation; pronouncing with an aspirate.
aspīrō, -āre, -āvī, -ātum vi to breathe, blow; to favour; to aspire, attain (to) ♦ vt to blow, instil.
aspis, -dis f asp.
asportātiō, -ōnis f removal.
asportō, -āre vt to carry off.
asprēta, -ōrum ntpl rough country.
ass- etc see **ads-**.
Assaracus, -ī m Trojan ancestor of Aeneas.
asser, -is m pole, stake.
assula, -ae f splinter.
assulātim adv in splinters.
āssum, -ī nt roast; (pl) sweating-bath.
āssus adj roasted.
Assyria, -ae f country in W. Asia.
Assyrius adj Assyrian; oriental.
ast conj (laws) and then; (vows) then; (strong contrast) and yet.
ast- etc see **adst-**.
Astraea, -ae f goddess of Justice.
Astraeus, -ī m father of winds; **~ī frātrēs** the winds.
astrologia, -ae f astronomy.
astrologus, -ī m astronomer; astrologer.
astrum, -ī nt star, heavenly body, constellation; a great height; heaven, immortality, glory.
astu nt (indecl) city (esp Athens).
astus, -ūs m cleverness, cunning.
astūtē adv cleverly.
astūtia, -ae f slyness, cunning.
astūtus adj artful, sly.
Astyanax, -ctis m son of Hector and Andromache.
asȳlum, -ī nt sanctuary.
asymbolus adj with no contribution.
at conj (adversative) but, on the other hand; (objecting) but it may be said; (limiting) at least, but at least; (continuing) then, thereupon; (transitional) now; (with passionate appeals) but oh!, look now!; **~ enim** yes, but; **~ tamen** nevertheless.
Atābulus, -ī m sirocco.
atat interj (expressing fright, pain, surprise) oh!
atavus, -ī m great-great-great-grandfather; ancestor.

Noun declensions and verb conjugations are shown on pp xiii to xxv. The present infinitive ending of a verb shows to which conjugation it belongs: **-āre** = 1st; **-ēre** = 2nd; **-ere** = 3rd and **-īre** = 4th. Irregular verbs are shown on p xxvi

Atella, -ae *f Oscan town in Campania.*
Ātellānicus, Ātellānius *adj see n.*
Ātellānus *adj:* **fābula ~āna** *kind of comic show popular in Rome.*
āter, -rī *adj* black, dark; gloomy, dismal; malicious; **diēs ~rī** unlucky days.
Athamantēus *adj see* **Athamās.**
Athamantiadēs *m* Palaemon.
Athamantis *f* Helle.
Athamās, -antis *m* king of Thessaly (*who went mad*).
Athēnae, -ārum *fpl* Athens.
Athēnaeus, -iēnsis *adj see n.*
atheos, -ī *m* atheist.
athlēta, -ae *m* wrestler, athlete.
athlēticē *adv* athletically.
Athos (*dat* -ō, *acc* -ō, -on, -ōnem) *m* mount *Athos in Macedonia.*
Atlanticus *adj:* **mare ~anticum** Atlantic Ocean.
Atlantiadēs *m* Mercury.
Atlantis *f* lost Atlantic island; a Pleiad.
Atlās, -antis *m giant supporting the sky;* Atlas *mountains.*
atomus, -ī *m* atom.
atque (*before consonants* **ac**) *conj* (*connecting words*) and, and in fact; (*connecting clauses*) and moreover, and then, and so, and yet; (*in comparison*) as, than, to, from; **~ adeō** and that too; or rather; **~ nōn** and not rather; **~ sī** as if; **alius ~** different from; **contrā ~** opposite to; **īdem ~** same as; **plūs ~** more than.
atquī *conj* (*adversative*) and yet, nevertheless, yes but; (*confirming*) by all means; (*minor premise*) now; **~ sī** if now.
ātrāmentum, -ī *nt* ink; blacking.
ātrātus *adj* in mourning.
Atreus, -eī *m* son of Pelops (*king of Argos*).
Atrīdēs *m* Agamemnon; Menelaus.
ātriēnsis, -is *m* steward, major-domo.
ātriolum, -ī *nt* anteroom.
ātrium, -ī *and* **iī** *nt* hall, *open central room in Roman house; forecourt of a temple;* hall (*in other buildings*).
atrōcitās, -ātis *f* hideousness; (*mind*) brutality; (*PHILOS*) severity.
atrōciter *adv* savagely.
Atropos, -ī *f* one of the Fates.
atrōx, -ōcis *adj* hideous, dreadful; fierce, brutal, unyielding.
attāctus *ppp of* **attingō.**
attāctus, -ūs *m* contact.
attagēn, -is *m* heathcock.
Attalica *ntpl garments of woven gold.*
Attalicus *adj* of Attalus; of Pergamum; ornamented with gold cloth.
Attalus, -ī *m* king of Pergamum (*who bequeathed his kingdom to Rome*).
attamen *conj* nevertheless.
attat *etc see* **atat.**
attegia, -ae *f* hut.
attemperātē *adv* opportunely.
attemptō *etc see* **attentō.**

attendō, -dere, -dī, -tum *vt* to direct (*the attention*); to attend to, notice.
attenē *adv* carefully.
attentiō, -ōnis *f* attentiveness.
attentō, -āre, -āvī, -ātum *vt* to test, try; (*loyalty*) to tamper with; to attack.
attentus *ppp of* **attendō** ♦ *adj* attentive, intent; businesslike, careful (*esp about money*).
attentus *ppp of* **attineō.**
attenuātē *adv* simply.
attenuātus *adj* weak; (*style*) brief; refined; plain.
attenuō, -āre, -āvī, -ātum *vt* to weaken, reduce; to diminish; to humble.
atterō, -erere, -rīvī, -rītum *vt* to rub; to wear away; (*fig*) to impair, exhaust.
attestor, -ārī, -ātus *vt* to confirm.
attexō, -ere, -uī, -tum *vt* to weave on; (*fig*) to add on.
Atthis, -dis *f* Attica.
Attiānus *adj see* **Attius.**
Attica, -ae *f district of Greece about Athens.*
Atticē *adv* in the Athenian manner.
Atticissō *vi* to speak in the Athenian manner.
Atticus *adj* Attic, Athenian; (*RHET*) of a plain and direct style.
attigī *perf of* **attingō.**
attigō *see* **attingō.**
attineō, -inēre, -inuī, -entum *vt* to hold fast, detain; to guard; to reach for ♦ *vi* to concern, pertain, be of importance, avail.
attingō, -ingere, -igī, -āctum *vt* to touch; to strike, assault; to arrive at; to border on; to affect; to mention; to undertake; to concern, resemble.
Attis, -dis *m* Phrygian priest of Cybele.
Attius, -ī *m* Latin tragic poet.
attollō, -ere *vt* to lift up, erect; (*fig*) to exalt, extol.
attondeō, -ondēre, -ondī, -ōnsum *vt* to shear, prune, crop; (*fig*) to diminish; (*comedy*) to fleece.
attonitus *adj* thunderstruck, terrified, astonished; inspired.
attonō, -āre, -uī, -itum *vt* to stupefy.
attōnsus *ppp of* **attondeō.**
attorqueō, -ēre *vt* to hurl upwards.
attractus *ppp of* **attrahō.**
attrahō, -here, -xī, -ctum *vt* to drag by force, attract; (*fig*) to draw, incite.
attrectō, -āre *vt* to touch, handle; to appropriate.
attrepidō, -āre *vi* to hobble along.
attribuō, -uere, -uī, -ūtum *vt* to assign, bestow; to add; to impute, attribute; to lay as a tax.
attribūtiō, -ōnis *f* (*money*) assignment; (*GRAM*) predicate.
attribūtum, -ī *nt* (*GRAM*) predicate.
attribūtus *ppp of* **attribuō** ♦ *adj* subject.
attrītus *ppp of* **atterō** ♦ *adj* worn; bruised; (*fig*) impudent.
attulī *perf of* **adferō.**

au *interj* (*expressing pain, surprise*) oh!
auceps, -upis *m* fowler; (*fig*) eavesdropper; a pedantic critic.
auctārium, -ī *and* **iī** *nt* extra.
auctificus *adj* increasing.
auctiō, -ōnis *f* increase; auction sale.
auctiōnārius *adj* auction; **tabulae ~ae** catalogues.
auctiōnor, -ārī, -ātus *vi* to hold an auction.
auctitō, -āre *vt* to greatly increase.
auctō, -āre *vt* to increase.
auctor, -ōris *m/f* 1. (*originator: of families*) progenitor; (: *of buildings*) founder; (: *of deeds*) doer. 2. (*composer: of writings*) author, historian; (: *of knowledge*) investigator, teacher; (: *of news*) informant. 3. (*instigator: of action*) adviser; (: *of measures*) promoter; (: *of laws*) proposer, supporter; ratifier. 4. (*person of influence: in public life*) leader; (: *of conduct*) model; (: *of guarantees*) witness, bail; (: *of property*) seller; (: *of women and minors*) guardian; (: *of others' welfare*) champion; **mē ~ōre** at my suggestion.
auctōrāmentum, -ī *nt* contract; wages.
auctōrātus *adj* bound (*by a pledge*); hired out (*for wages*).
auctōritās, -ātis *f* 1. source; lead, responsibility. 2. judgment; opinion; advice, support; bidding, guidance; (*of senate*) decree; (*of people*) will. 3. power; (*person*) influence, authority, prestige; (*things*) importance, worth; (*conduct*) example; (*knowledge*) warrant, document, authority; (*property*) right of possession.
auctumn- *etc see* **autumn-**.
auctus *ppp of* **augeō** ♦ *adj* enlarged, great.
auctus, -ūs *m* growth, increase.
aucupium, -ī *and* **iī** *nt* fowling; birds caught; (*fig*) hunting (after), quibbling.
aucupō, -āre *vt* to watch for.
aucupor, -ārī, -ātus *vi* to go fowling ♦ *vt* to chase; (*fig*) to try to catch.
audācia, -ae *f* daring, courage; audacity, impudence; (*pl*) deeds of daring.
audācter, audāciter *adv see* **audāx**.
audāx, -ācis *adj* bold, daring; rash, audacious; proud.
audēns, -entis *adj* bold, brave.
audenter *adv see* **audēns**.
audentia, -ae *f* boldness, courage.
audeō, -dēre, -sus *vt, vi* to dare, venture; to be brave.
audiēns, -entis *m* hearer ♦ *adj* obedient.
audientia, -ae *f* hearing; **~m facere** gain a hearing.
audiō, -īre, -īvī *and* **iī, -ītum** *vt* to hear; to learn, be told; to be called; to listen, attend to, study under (a teacher); to examine a case; to agree with; to obey, heed; **bene/male ~** have a good/bad reputation.

audītiō, -ōnis *f* listening; hearsay, news.
audītor, -ōris *m* hearer; pupil.
audītōrium, -i *and* **iī** *nt* lecture room, law court; audience.
audītus, -ūs *m* (sense of) hearing; a hearing; rumour.
auferō, auferre, abstulī, ablātum *vt* to take away, carry away; to mislead, lead into a digression; to take by force, steal; to win, obtain (*as the result of effort*); **aufer** away with!
Aufidus, -ō *m* river in Apulia.
aufugiō, -ugere, -ūgī *vi* to run away ♦ *vt* to flee from.
Augēās, -ae *m* king of Elis (*whose stables Hercules cleaned*).
augeō, -gēre, -xī, -ctum *vt* to increase; to enrich, bless (with); to praise, worship ♦ *vi* to increase.
augēscō, -ere *vi* to begin to grow, increase.
augmen, -inis *nt* growth.
augur, -is *m/f* augur; prophet, interpreter.
augurāle, -is *nt* part of camp where auspices were taken.
augurālis *adj* augur's.
augurātiō, -ōnis *f* soothsaying.
augurātō *adv* after taking auspices.
augurātus, -ūs *m* office of augur.
augurium, -ī *and* **iī** *nt* augury; an omen; prophecy, interpretation; presentiment.
augurius *adj* of augurs.
augurō, -āre *vt, vi* to take auguries; to consecrate by auguries; to forebode.
auguror, -ārī, -ātus *vt, vi* to take auguries; to foretell by omens; to predict, conjecture.
Augusta, -ae *f* title of the emperor's wife, mother, daughter or sister.
Augustālis *adj* of Augustus; **lūdī ~ēs** games in October; **praefectus ~is** governor of Egypt; **sodālēs ~ēs** priests of deified Augustus.
augustē *adv see* **augustus**.
augustus *adj* venerable, august, majestic.
Augustus, -ī *m* title given to C Octavius, first Roman emperor, and so to his successors ♦ *adj* imperial; (*month*) August, of August.
aula, -ae *f* courtyard of a Greek house; hall of a Roman house; palace, royal court; courtiers; royal power.
aula *etc see* **olla**.
aulaeum, -ī *nt* embroidered hangings, canopy, covering; (*THEAT*) curtain.
aulicī, -ōrum *mpl* courtiers.
aulicus *adj* of the court.
Aulis, -idis *and* **is** *f* port in Boeotia from which the Greeks sailed for Troy.
auloedus, -ī *m* singer accompanied by flute.
aura, -ae *f* breath of air, breeze, wind; air, upper world; vapour, odour, sound, gleam; (*fig*) winds (*of public favour*), breeze (*of prosperity*), air (*of freedom*), daylight (*of*

Noun declensions and verb conjugations are shown on pp xiii to xxv. The present infinitive ending of a verb shows to which conjugation it belongs: **-āre** = 1st; **-ēre** = 2nd; **-ere** = 3rd and **-īre** = 4th. Irregular verbs are shown on p xxvi

publicity).
aurāria, -ae *f* gold mine.
aurārius *adj* of gold.
aurātus *adj* gilt, ornamented with gold; gold.
Aurēlius, -ī *m* Roman name; **lēx ~ia** *law on the composition of juries*; **via ~ia** *main road running NW from Rome.*
aureolus *adj* gold; beautiful, splendid.
aureus *adj* gold, golden; gilded; (*fig*) beautiful splendid ♦ *m* gold coin.
aurichalcum, -ī *nt* a precious metal.
auricomus *adj* golden-leaved.
auricula, -ae *f* the external ear; ear.
aurifer, -ī *adj* gold-producing.
aurifex, -icis *m* goldsmith.
aurīga, -ae *m* charioteer, driver; groom; helmsman; a constellation.
aurigena, -ae *adj* gold-begotten.
auriger, -ī *adj* gilded.
aurīgō, -āre *vi* to compete in the chariot race.
auris, -is *f* ear; (*RHET*) judgment; (*AGR*) earthboard (*of a plough*); **ad ~em admonēre** whisper; **in utramvis ~em dormīre** sleep soundly.
aurītulus, -ī *m* "Long-Ears".
aurītus *adj* long-eared; attentive.
aurōra, -ae *f* dawn, morning; *goddess of dawn*; the East.
aurum, -ī *nt* gold; gold plate, jewellery, bit, fleece *etc*; money; lustre; the Golden Age.
auscultātiō, -ōnis *f* obedience.
auscultātor, -ōris *m* listener.
auscultō, -āre, -āvī, -ātum *vt* to listen to; to overhear ♦ *vi* (*of servants*) to wait at the door; to obey.
ausim *subj of* **audeō.**
Ausones, -um *mpl indigenous people of central Italy.*
Ausonia *f* Italy.
Ausonidae *mpl* Italians.
Ausonius, -is *adj* Italian.
auspex, -icis *m* augur, soothsayer; patron, commander; witness of a marriage contract.
auspicātō *adv* after taking auspices; at a lucky moment.
auspicātus *adj* consecrated; auspicious, lucky.
auspicium, -ī *and* **iī** *nt* augury, auspices; right of taking auspices; power, command; omen; **~ facere** give a sign.
auspicō, -āre *vi* to take the auspices.
auspicor, -ārī, -ātus *vi* to take the auspices; to make a beginning ♦ *vt* to begin, enter upon.
auster, -rī *m* south wind; south.
austērē *adv see* **austērus.**
austēritās, -ātis *f* severity.
austērus *adj* severe, serious; gloomy, irksome.
austrālis *adj* southern.
austrīnus *adj* from the south.
ausum, -ī *nt* enterprise.

ausus *ppa of* **audeō.**
aut *conj* or; either ... or; or else *or* at least, or rather.
autem *conj* (*adversative*) but, on the other hand; (*in transitions, parentheses*) moreover, now, and; (*in dialogue*) indeed.
authepsa, -ae *f* stove.
autographus *adj* written with his own hand.
Autolycus, -ī *m* a robber.
automaton, -ī *nt* automaton.
automatus *adj* spontaneous.
Automedōn, -ontis *m* a charioteer.
autumnālis *adj* autumn, autumnal.
autumnus, -ī *m* autumn ♦ *adj* autumnal.
autumō, -āre *vt* to assert.
auxī *perf of* **augeō.**
auxilia, -iōrum *ntpl* auxiliary troops; military force.
auxiliāris *adj* helping, auxiliary; of the auxiliaries ♦ *mpl* auxiliary troops.
auxiliārius *adj* helping; auxiliary.
auxiliātor, -ōris *m* helper.
auxiliātus, -ūs *m* aid.
auxilior, -ārī, -ātus *vi* to aid, support.
auxilium, -ī *and* **iī** *nt* help, assistance.
avārē, avāiter *adv see* **avārus.**
avāritia, -ae *f* greed, selfishness.
avāritiēs, -ēī *f* avarice.
avārus *adj* greedy, covetous; eager.
avē, avēte, avētō *impv* hail!, farewell!
āvehō, -here, -xī, -ctum *vt* to carry away; (*pass*) to ride away.
āvellō, -ellere, -ellī *and* **ulsī (-olsī), -ulsum (-olsum)** *vt* to pull away, tear off; to take away (by force), remove.
avēna, -ae *f* oats; (*music*) reed, shepherd's pipe.
Aventīnum, -ī *nt* Aventine hill.
Aventīnus, -ī *m* Aventine hill in Rome ♦ *adj* of Aventine.
avēns, -entis *adj* eager.
aveō, -ēre *vt* to desire, long for.
Avernālis *adj* of lake Avernus.
Avernus, -ī *m* lake near Cumae (*said to be an entrance to the lower world*); the lower world ♦ *adj* birdless; of Avernus; infernal.
āverruncō, -āre *vt* to avert.
āversābilis *adj* abominable.
āversor, -ārī, -ātus *vi* to turn away ♦ *vt* to repulse, decline.
āversor, -ōris *m* embezzler.
āversum, -ī *nt* back.
āversus *ppp of* **āvertō** ♦ *adj* in the rear, behind, backwards; hostile, averse.
āvertō, -tere, -tī, -sum *vt* to turn aside, avert; to divert; to embezzle; to estrange ♦ *vi* to withdraw.
avia, -ae *f* grandmother.
avia, -ōrum *ntpl* wilderness.
aviārium, -ī *nt* aviary, haunt of birds.
aviārius *adj* of birds.
avidē *adv see* **avidus.**
aviditās, -ātis *f* eagerness, longing; avarice.

avidus *adj* eager, covetous; avaricious, greedy; hungry; vast.
avis, -is *f* bird; omen; ~ **alba** a rarity.
avītus *adj* of a grandfather; ancestral.
āvius *adj* out of the way, lonely, untrodden; wandering, astray.
āvocāmentum, -ī *nt* relaxation.
āvocātiō, -ōnis *f* diversion.
āvocō, -āre *vt* to call off; to divert, distract; to amuse.
āvolō, -āre *vi* to fly away, hurry away; to depart, vanish.
āvolsus, avulsus *ppp of* **avellō**.
avunculus, -ī *m* uncle (*on mother's side*); ~ **māgnus** great-uncle.
avus, -ī *m* grandfather; ancestor.
Axenus, -ī *m* Black Sea.
axicia, axitia, -ae *f* scissors.
āxilla -ae *f* armpit.
axis, -is *m* axle, chariot; axis, pole, sky, clime; plank.
azȳmus *adj* unleavened.

B, b

babae *interj* (*expressing wonder or joy*) oho!
Babylōn, -ōnis *f* ancient city on the Euphrates.
Babylōnia *f* the country under Babylon.
Babylōnicus, (-)ōniēnsis *adj see n.*
Babylōnius *adj* Babylonian; Chaldaean, versed in astrology.
bāca, -ae *f* berry; olive; fruit; pearl.
bācātus *adj* of pearls.
bacca *etc see* **bāca**.
baccar, -is *nt* cyclamen.
Baccha, -ae *f* Bacchante.
Bacchānal, -ālis *nt place consecrated to Bacchus*; (*pl*) *festival of Bacchus*.
bacchātiō, -ōnis *f* revel.
Bacchēus, -icus, -ius *adj see n.*
Bacchiadae, -ārum *mpl* kings of Corinth (*founders of Syracuse*).
bacchor, -ārī, -ātus *vi to celebrate the festival of Bacchus*; to revel, rave; to rage.
Bacchus, -ī *m god of wine, vegetation, poetry, and religious ecstasy*; vine, wine.
bācifer, -ī *adj* olive-bearing.
bacillum, -ī *nt* stick, lictor's staff.
Bactra, -ōrum *ntpl capital of Bactria in central Asia* (*now* Balkh).
Bactriāna *f* Bactria.
Bactriānus *and* **ius** *adj* Bactrian.

baculum, -ī *nt*, **-us, -ī** *m* stick, staff.
Baetica *f* Roman province (*now* Andalusia).
Baeticus *adj see* **Baetis**.
Baetis, -is *m* river in Spain (*now* Guadalquivir).
Bagrada, -ae *m* river in Africa (*now* Mejerdah).
Bāiae, -ārum *fpl Roman spa on Bay of Naples.*
Bāiānus *adj see n.*
bāiulō, -āre *vt* to carry (*something heavy*).
bāiulus, -ī *m* porter.
bālaena, -ae *f* whale.
balanus, -ī *f* balsam (*from an Arabian nut*); a shellfish.
balatrō, -ōnis *m* jester.
bālātus, -ūs *m* bleating.
balbus *adj* stammering.
balbūtiō, -īre *vt, vi* to stammer, speak indistinctly; (*fig*) to speak obscurely.
Baliārēs, -ium *fpl* Balearic islands.
Baliāris, Baliāricus *adj see n.*
balineum *etc see* **balneum** *etc.*
ballista, -ae *f* (MIL) *catapult for shooting stones and other missiles*; (*fig*) weapon.
ballistārium, -ī *and* **i ī** *nt* catapult.
balneae, -ārum *fpl* bath, baths.
balneāria, -ōrum *ntpl* bathroom.
balneārius *adj* of the baths.
balneātor, -ōris *m* bath superintendent.
balneolum, -ī *nt* small bath.
balneum, -ī *nt* bath.
bālō, -āre *vi* to bleat.
balsamum, -ī *nt* balsam, balsam tree.
baltea, -ōrum *ntpl* belt (*esp swordbelt; woman's girdle; strapping*).
balteus, -ī *m* belt (*esp swordbelt; woman's girdle; strapping*).
Bandusia, -ae *f* spring near Horace's birthplace.
baptisma, -tis *nt* baptism.
baptizō, -āre *vt* (ECCL) to baptize.
barathrum, -ī *nt* abyss; the lower world; (*fig*) a greedy person.
barba, -ae *f* beard.
barbarē *adv* in a foreign language, in Latin; in an uncivilized way; roughly, cruelly.
barbaria, -ae, -ēs *acc, and* **-em** *f* a foreign country (*outside Greece or Italy*); (*words*) barbarism; (*manners*) rudeness, stupidity.
barbaricus *adj* foreign, outlandish; Italian.
barbarus *adj* foreign, barbarous; (*to a Greek*) Italian; rude, uncivilized; savage, barbarous ♦ *m* foreigner, barbarian.
barbātulus *adj* with a little beard.
barbātus *adj* bearded, adult; ancient (Romans); of philosophers.
barbiger, -ī *adj* bearded.
barbitos (*acc* **-on**) *m* lyre, lute.
barbula, -ae *f* little beard.
Barcās, -ae *m ancestor of Hannibal.*

Noun declensions and verb conjugations are shown on pp xiii to xxv. The present infinitive ending of a verb shows to which conjugation it belongs: **-āre** = 1st; **-ēre** = 2nd; **-ere** = 3rd and **-īre** = 4th. Irregular verbs are shown on p xxvi

Barcīnus *adj see n.*
bardus *adj* dull, stupid.
bardus, -ī *m* Gallic minstrel.
bārō, -ōnis *m* dunce.
barrus, -ī *m* elephant.
bascauda, -ae *f* basket (*for the table*).
bāsiātiō, -ōnis *f* kiss.
basilica, -ae *f* public building used as exchange and law court.
basilicē *adv* royally, in magnificent style.
basilicum, -ī *nt* regal robe.
basilicus *adj* royal, magnificent ♦ *m* highest throw at dice.
bāsiō, -āre *vt* to kiss.
basis, -is *f* pedestal, base.
bāsium, -ī *and* **iī** *nt* kiss.
Bassareus, -eī *m* Bacchus.
Batāvī, -ōrum *mpl* people of Batavia (*now Holland*).
batillum, -ī *nt* firepan.
Battiadēs, -ae *m* Callimachus.
bātuō, -ere, -ī *vt* to beat.
baubor, -ārī *vi* (*of dogs*) to howl.
Baucis, -idis *f* wife of Philemon.
beātē *adv see* **beātus.**
beātitās, -ātis *f* happiness.
beātitūdō, -inis *f* happiness.
beātulus, -ī *m* the blessed man.
beātus *adj* happy; prosperous, well-off; rich, abundant.
Bēdriacēnsis *adj see n.*
Bēdriācum, -ī *nt* village in N. Italy.
Belgae, -ārum *mpl* people of N. Gaul (*now Belgium*).
Bēlīdēs, -īdae *m* Danaus, Aegyptus, Lynceus.
Bēlides, -um *fpl* Danaids.
bellāria, -ōrum *ntpl* dessert, confectionery.
bellātor, -ōris *m* warrior, fighter ♦ *adj* warlike.
bellātōrius *adj* aggressive.
bellātrīx, -īcis *f* warrioress ♦ *adj* warlike.
bellē *adv* well, nicely; ~ **habēre** be well (in health).
Bellerophōn, -ontis *m* slayer of Chimaera, rider of Pegasus.
Bellerophontēus *adj see n.*
bellicōsus *adj* warlike.
bellicus *adj* of war, military; ~**um canere** give the signal for marching or attack.
belliger, -ī *adj* martial.
belligerō, -āre, -āvī, -ātum *vi* to wage war.
bellipotēns, -entis *adj* strong in war.
bellō, -āre, -āvī, -ātum *vi* to fight, wage war.
Bellōna, -ae *f* goddess of war.
bellor, -ārī *vi* to fight.
bellulus *adj* pretty.
bellum, -ī *nt* war, warfare; battle; ~ **gerere** wage war; ~**ī** in war.
bellus *adj* pretty, handsome; pleasant, nice.
bēlua, -ae *f* beast, monster (*esp large and fierce*); any animal; (*fig*) brute; ~ **Gaetula** India elephant.
bēluātus *adj* embroidered with animals.

bēluōsus *adj* full of monsters.
Bēlus, -ī *m* Baal; an oriental king.
Bēnācus, -ī *m* lake in N. Italy (*now* Garda).
bene *adv* (*compar* **melius**, *superl* **optimē**) well; correctly; profitably; very ♦ *interj* bravo!, good!; ~ **dīcere** speak well; speak well of, praise; ~ **emere** buy cheap; ~ **est tibi** you are well off; ~ **facere** do well; do good to; ~ **facis** thank you; **rem** ~ **gerere** be successful; ~ **sē habēre** have a good time; ~ **habet** all is well, it's all right; ~ **merērī dē** do a service to; ~ **partum** honestly acquired; ~ **tē**! your health!; ~ **vēndere** sell at a high price; ~ **vīvere** live a happy life.
benedīco, -īcere, -īxī, -ictum *vt* to speak well of, praise; (*ECCL*) to bless.
benedictiō, -ōnis *f* (*ECCL*) blessing.
beneficentia, -ae *f* kindness.
beneficiāriī, -ōrum *mpl* privileged soldiers.
beneficium, -ī *and* **iī** *nt* benefit, favour; (*POL, MIL*) promotion; ~**ō tuō** thanks to you.
beneficus *adj* generous, obliging.
Beneventānus *adj see n.*
Beneventum, -ī *nt* town in S. Italy (*now* Benevento).
benevolē *adv see* **benevolus.**
benevolēns, -entis *adj* kind-hearted.
benevolentia, -ae *f* goodwill, friendliness.
benevolus *adj* kindly, friendly; (*of servants*) devoted.
benīgnē *adv* willingly, courteously; generously; (*colloq*) no thank you; ~ **facere** do a favour.
benīgnitās, -ātis *f* kindness; liberality, bounty.
benīgnus *adj* kind, friendly; favourable; liberal, lavish; fruitful, bounteous.
beō, -āre, -āvī, -ātum *vt* to gladden, bless, enrich.
Berecyntia *f* Cybele.
Berecyntius *adj* of Berecyntus; of Cybele.
Berecyntus, -ī *m* mountain in Phrygia sacred to Cybele.
Berenīcē, -ēs *f* a queen of Egypt; **coma ~ēs** a constellation.
bēryllus, -ī *m* beryl.
bēs, bessis *m* two-thirds of the *as*; two-thirds.
bēstia, -ae *f* beast; wild animal for the arena.
bēstiārius *adj* of beasts ♦ *m* beast fighter in the arena.
bēstiola, -ae *f* small animal.
bēta, -ae *f* beet.
bēta *nt indecl* Greek letter beta.
bibī *perf of* **bibō.**
bibliopōla, -ae *m* bookseller.
bibliothēca, -ae, -ē, -ēs *f* library.
bibō, -ere, -ī *vt* to drink; to live on the banks of (*a river*); to drink in, absorb; (*fig*) to listen attentively, be imbued; ~ **aquas** be drowned; **Graecō mōre** ~ drink to one's health.
bibulus *adj* fond of drink, thirsty; (*things*) thirsty.
Bibulus, -ī *m* consul with Caesar in 59 BC.

biceps, -ipitis *adj* two-headed.
biclīnium, -ī *and* **iī** *nt* dining couch for two.
bicolor, -ōris *adj* two-coloured.
bicorniger, -ī *adj* two-horned.
bicornis *adj* two-horned, two-pronged; (*rivers*) two-mouthed.
bicorpor, -is *adj* two-bodied.
bidēns, -entis *adj* with two teeth *or* prongs ♦ *m* hoe ♦ *f* sheep (*or other sacrificial animal*).
bidental, -ālis *nt* a place struck by lightning.
biduum, -ī *nt* two days.
biennium -ī *and* **iī** *nt* two years.
bifāriam *adv* in two parts, twice.
bifer, -ī *adj* flowering twice a year.
bifidus *adj* split in two.
biforis *adj* double-doored; double.
bifōrmātus, bifōrmis *adj* with two forms.
bifrōns, -ontis *adj* two-headed.
bifurcus *adj* two-pronged, forked.
bīgae, -ārum *fpl* chariot and pair.
bīgātus *adj* stamped with a chariot and pair.
biiugī, -ōrum *mpl* two horses yoked abreast; chariot with two horses.
biiugis, biiugus *adj* yoked.
bilībra, -ae *f* two pounds.
bilībris *adj* holding two pounds.
bilinguis *adj* double-tongued; bilingual; deceitful.
bīlis, -is *f* bile, gall; (*fig*) anger, displeasure; ~ ātra, nigra melancholy; madness.
bilīx, -īcis *adj* double-stranded.
bilūstris *adj* ten years.
bimaris *adj* between two seas.
bimarītus, -ī *m* bigamist.
bimāter, -ris *adj* having two mothers.
bimembris *adj* half man, half beast; (*pl*) Centaurs.
bimēstris *adj* of two months, two months old.
bīmulus *adj* only two years old.
bīmus *adj* two years old, for two years.
bīnī, bīnae, bīna *num* two each, two by two; a pair; (*with pl nouns having a meaning*) two.
binoctium, -ī *and* **iī** *nt* two nights.
binōminis *adj* with two names.
Biōn, -ōnis *m* satirical philosopher.
Biōnēus *adj* satirical.
bipalmis *adj* two spans long.
bipartītō *adv* in two parts, in two directions.
bipartītus *adj* divided in two.
bipatēns, -entis *adj* double-opening.
bipedālis *adj* two feet long broad *or* thick.
bipennifer, -ī *adj* wielding a battle-axe.
bipennis *adj* two-edged ♦ *f* battle-axe.
bipertītō *etc see* **bipartītō.**
bipēs, -edis *adj* two-footed ♦ *m* biped.
birēmis *adj* two-oared; with two banks of oars ♦ *f* two-oared skiff; galley with two banks of oars.
bis *adv* twice, double; ~ ad eundem make the same mistake twice; ~ diē, in diē twice a day;

~ tantō, tantum twice as much; ~ terque frequently; ~ terve seldom.
bissextus, -ī *m* intercalary day after 24th Feb.
Bistones, -um *mpl people of Thrace.*
Bistonis *f* Thracian woman, Bacchante.
Bistonius *adj* Thracian.
bisulcilingua, -ae *adj* fork-tongued, deceitful.
bisulcus *adj* cloven.
Bīthȳnia, -iae *f province of Asia Minor.*
Bīthȳnicus, Bīthȳnius, -us *adj see* **Bīthȳnia.**
bītō, -ere *vi* to go.
bitūmen, -inis *nt* bitumen, a kind of pitch.
bitūmineus *adj see* **bitūmen.**
bivium *nt* two ways.
bivius *adj* two-way.
blaesus *adj* lisping, indistinct.
blandē *adv see* **blandus.**
blandidicus *adj* fair-spoken.
blandiloquentia, -ae *f* attractive language.
blandiloquus, -entulus *adj* fair-spoken.
blandīmentum, -ī *nt* compliment, allurement.
blandior, -īrī, -ītus *vi* to coax, caress; to flatter, pay compliments; (*things*) to please, entice.
blanditia, -ae *f* caress, flattery; charm, allurement.
blandītim *adv* caressingly.
blandus *adj* smooth-tongued, flattering, fawning; charming, winsome.
blaterō, -āre *vi* to babble.
blatiō, -īre *vt* to babble.
blatta, -ae *f* cockroach.
blennus, -ī *m* idiot.
bliteus *adj* silly.
blitum, -ī *nt* kind of spinach.
boārius *adj* of cattle; **forum -um** *cattle market in Rome.*
Bodotria, -ae *f* Firth of Forth.
Boeōtarchēs *m chief magistrate of Boeotia.*
Boeōtia, -iae *f district of central Greece.*
Boeōtius, -us *adj see* n.
boiae, -ārum *fpl* collar.
Boiī, -ōrum *mpl people of S.E. Gaul.*
Boiohaemī, -ōrum *mpl* Bohemians.
bōlētus, -ī *m* mushroom.
bolus, -ī *m* (*dice*) throw; (*net*) cast; (*fig*) haul, piece of good luck; titbit.
bombus, -ī *m* booming, humming, buzzing.
bombȳcinus *adj* of silk.
bombȳx, -ȳcis *m* silkworm; silk.
Bona Dea, -ae, -ae *f goddess worshipped by women.*
bonitās, -ātis *f* goodness; honesty, integrity; kindness, affability.
Bonōnia, -ae *f* town in N. Italy (*now* Bologna).
Bonōniēnsis *adj see* n.
bonum, -ī *nt* a moral good; advantage, blessing; (*pl*) property; **cuī ~ō?** who was the

gainer?

bonus *adj* (*compar* **melior**, *superl* **optimus**) good; kind; brave; loyal; beneficial; lucky ♦ *mpl* upper class party, conservatives; ~**a aetās** prime of life; ~**ō animō** of good cheer; well-disposed; ~**ae artēs** integrity; culture, liberal education; ~ **a dicta** witticisms; ~**a fidēs** good faith; ~**ī mōrēs** morality; ~**ī nummī** genuine money; ~**a pars** large part; conservative party; ~**ae rēs** comforts, luxuries; prosperity; morality; ~**ā veniā** with kind permission; ~**a verba** words of good omen; well-chosen diction; ~**a vōx** loud voice.

boō, -āre *vi* to cry aloud.

Boōtēs, -ae *nt constellation containing Arcturus.*

Boreās, -ae *m* north wind; north.

Boreus *adj see n.*

Borysthenēs, -is *m* river Dnieper.

Borysthenidae *mpl dwellers near the Dnieper.*

Borysthenius *adj see* **Borysthenidae.**

bōs, bovis *m/f* ox, cow; kind of turbot; ~ **Lūca** elephant; **bovī clitellās impōnere** ≈ *put a round peg in a square hole.*

Bosporānus *adj see n.*

Bosporius *adj:* ~ **Cimmerius** *strait from Sea of Azov to Black Sea.*

Bosporus, -ī *m strait from Black Sea to Sea of Marmora.*

Boudicca, -ae *f* British queen (*falsely called Boadicea*).

bovārius *etc see* **boārius.**

Bovillae, -ārum *fpl ancient Latin town.*

Bovillānus *adj see n.*

bovillus *adj* of oxen.

brācae, -ārum *fpl* trousers.

brācātus *adj* trousered; barbarian (*esp of tribes beyond the Alps*).

bracchiālis *adj* of the arm.

bracchiolum, -ī *nt* dainty arm.

bracchium, -ī *and* **iī** *nt* arm, forearm; (*shellfish*) claw; (*tree*) branch; (*sea*) arm; (NAUT) yardarm; (MIL) outwork, mole; **levī, mollī bracchiō** casually.

bractea *etc see* **brattea.**

brassica, -ae *f* cabbage.

brattea, -ae *f* gold leaf.

bratteola, -ae *f* very fine gold leaf.

Brennus, -ī *m Gallic chief who defeated the Romans.*

brevī *adv* shortly, soon; briefly, in a few words.

brevia, -ium *ntpl* shoals.

breviārium, -ī *and* **iī** *nt* summary, statistical survey, official report.

breviculus *adj* shortish.

breviloquēns, -ēntis *adj* brief.

brevis *adj* short, small, shallow; brief, short-lived; concise.

brevitās, -ātis *f* shortness, smallness; brevity, conciseness.

breviter *adv* concisely.

Brigantēs, -um *mpl British tribe in N. England.*

Briganticus *adj see n.*

Brisēis, -idos *f captive of Achilles.*

Britannia, -iae *f* Britain; the British Isles.

Britannicus *m son of emperor Claudius.*

Britannus, (-icus) *adj see n.*

Bromius, -ī *and* **iī** *m* Bacchus.

brūma, -ae *f* winter solstice, midwinter; winter.

brūmālis *adj* of the winter solstice; wintry; ~ **flexus** tropic of Capricorn.

Brundisīnus *adj see n.*

Brundisium, -ī *and* **iī** *nt* port in S.E. Italy (*now Brindisi*).

Bruttiī, -ōrum *mpl people of the toe of Italy.*

Bruttius *adj see n.*

brūtus *adj* heavy, unwieldy; stupid, irrational.

Brūtus, -ī *m liberator of Rome from kings; murderer of Caesar.*

bubīle, -is *nt* stall.

būbo, -ōnis *m/f* owl.

būbula, -ae *f* beef.

bubulcitor, -ārī *vi* to drive oxen.

bubulcus, -ī *m* ploughman.

būbulus *adj* of cattle.

būcaeda, -ae *m* flogged slave.

bucca, -ae *f* cheek; mouth; ranter.

buccō, -ōnis *m* babbler.

buccula, -ae *f* visor.

bucculentus *adj* fat-cheeked.

būcerus *adj* horned.

būcina, -ae *f* shepherd's horn; military trumpet; night watch.

būcinātor, -ōris *m* trumpeter.

būcolica, -ōrum *ntpl* pastoral poetry.

būcula, -ae *f* young cow.

būfō, -ōnis *m* toad.

bulbus, -ī *m* bulb; onion.

būlē, -es *f* Greek senate.

būleuta *m* senator.

būleutērium *nt* senate house.

bulla, -ae *f* bubble; knob, stud; gold charm worn round the neck by children of noblemen.

bullātus *adj* wearing the bulla; still a child.

būmastus, -ī *f* kind of vine.

būris, -is *m* plough-beam.

Burrus old form of **Pyrrhus.**

Busīris, -idis *m Egyptian king killed by Hercules.*

bustirapus, -ī *m* graverobber.

bustuārius *adj* at a funeral.

bustum, -ī *nt* funeral place; tomb, grave.

buxifer, -ī *adj* famed for its box trees.

buxum, -ī *nt* boxwood; flute, top, comb, tablet.

buxus, -ī *f* box tree; flute.

Byzantium, -ī *and* **iī** *nt* city on Bosporus (*later Constantinople, now Istanbul*).

Byzantius *adj see n.*

C, c

caballīnus *adj* horse's.
caballus, -ī *m* horse.
cacātus *adj* impure.
cachinnātiō, -ōnis *f* loud laughter.
cachinnō, -āre *vi* to laugh, guffaw.
cachinnō, -ōnis *m* scoffer.
cachinnus, -ī *m* laugh, derisive laughter;
   (*waves*) splashing.
cacō, -āre *vi* to evacuate the bowels.
cacoëthes, -is *nt* (*fig*) itch.
cacula, -ae *m* soldier's slave.
cacūmen, -inis *nt* extremity, point, summit,
   treetop; (*fig*) height, limit.
cacūminō, -āre *vt* to make pointed.
Cācus, -ī *m giant robber, son of Vulcan.*
cadāver, -is *nt* corpse, carcass.
cadāverōsus *adj* ghastly.
Cadmēa, -ēae *f fortress of Thebes.*
Cadmēis, -ēidis *f Agave; Ino; Semele.*
Cadmēus, (-ēius) *adj of Cadmus; Theban.*
Cadmus, -ī *m founder of Thebes.*
cadō, -ere, cecidī, cāsum *vi* to fall; to droop,
   die, be killed; (*ASTRO*) to set; (*dice*) to be
   thrown; (*events*) to happen, turn out; (*money*)
   to be due; (*strength, speech, courage*) to
   diminish, cease, fail; (*wind, rage*) to subside;
   (*words*) to end; ~ **in** suit, agree with; come
   under; ~ **sub** be exposed to; **animīs** ~ be
   disheartened; **causā** ~ lose one's case.
cādūceātor, -ōris *m* officer with flag of truce.
cādūceus, -ī *m* herald's staff; Mercury's
   wand.
cādūcifer, -ī *adj* with herald's staff.
cadūcus *adj* falling, fallen; (*fig*) perishable,
   fleeting, vain; (*law*) without an heir ♦ *nt*
   property without an heir.
Cadurcī, -ōrum *mpl Gallic tribe.*
Cadurcum, -ī *nt* linen coverlet.
cadus, -ī *m* jar, flask (*esp for wine*); urn.
caecigenus *adj* born blind.
Caeciliānus *adj see n.*
Caecilius, -ī *m Roman name (esp early Latin
   comic poet).*
caecitās, -ātis *f* blindness.
caecō, -āre, -āvī, -ātum *vt* to blind; to make
   obscure.
Caecubum, -ī *nt choice wine from the Ager
   Caecubus in S. Latium.*
caecus *adj* blind; invisible, secret; dark,
   obscure; (*fig*) aimless, unknown, uncertain;
   appāret ~ō ≈ it's as clear as daylight; **domus ~a**
   a house with no windows; **~ā diē emere** buy

on credit; **~um corpus** the back.
caedēs, -is *f* murder, massacre; gore; the
   slain.
caedō, -ere, cecīdī, caesum *vt* to cut; to
   strike; to kill, cut to pieces; (*animals*) to
   sacrifice.
caelāmen, -inis *nt* engraved work.
caelātor, -ōris *m* engraver.
caelātūra, -ae *f* engraving in bas-relief.
caelebs, -ibis *adj* unmarried (bachelor *or*
   widower); (*trees*) with no vine trained on.
caeles, -itis *adj* celestial ♦ *mpl* the gods.
caelestis, -is *adj* of the sky, heavenly; divine;
   glorious ♦ *mpl* the gods ♦ *ntpl* the heavenly
   bodies.
Caeliānus *adj see n.*
caelibātus, -ūs *m* celibacy.
caelicola, -ae *m* god.
caelifer, -ī *adj* supporting the sky.
Caelius, -ī *m Roman name; Roman hill.*
caelō, -āre, -āvī, -ātum *vt* to engrave (*in relief
   on metals*), carve (*on wood*); (*fig*) to compose.
caelum, -ī *nt* engraver's chisel.
caelum, -ī *nt* sky, heaven; air, climate,
   weather; (*fig*) height of success, glory; **~um
   ac terrās miscēre** create chaos; **ad ~um ferre**
   extol; **dē ~ō dēlāpsus** a messiah; **dē ~ō
   servāre** watch for omens; **dē ~ō tangī** be
   struck by lightning; **digitō ~um attingere** ≈
   be in the seventh heaven; **in ~ō esse** be
   overjoyed.
caementum, -ī *nt* quarrystone, rubble.
caenōsus *adj* muddy.
caenum, -ī *nt* mud, filth.
caepa, -ae *f*, **caepe, -is** *nt* onion.
Caere *nt indecl* (*gen* -**itis**, *abl* -**ēte**) *f ancient
   Etruscan town.*
Caeres, -itis *and* **ētis** *adj:* ~**ite cērā dignī** like
   the disfranchised masses.
caerimōnia, -ae *f* sanctity; veneration (*for
   gods*); religious usage, ritual.
caeruleus, caerulus *adj* blue, dark blue, dark
   green, dusky ♦ *ntpl* the sea.
Caesar, -is *m Julius (great Roman soldier,
   statesman, author); Augustus; the emperor.*
Caesareus, *and* **iānus,** *and* **īnus** *adj see n.*
caesariātus *adj* bushy-haired.
caesariēs, -ēī *f* hair.
caesīcius *adj* bluish.
caesim *adv* with the edge of the sword; (*RHET*)
   in short clauses.
caesius *adj* bluish grey, blue-eyed.
caespes, -itis *m* sod, turf; mass of roots.
caestus, -ūs *m* boxing glove.
caesus *ppp of* **caedō.**
caetra, -ae *f* targe.
caetrātus *adj* armed with a targe.
Caīcus, -ī *m river in Asia Minor.*
Cāiēta, -ae, -ē, -ēs *f town in Latium.*
Cāius *etc see* **Gaius.**

Noun declensions and verb conjugations are shown on pp xiii to xxv. The present infinitive ending of a verb shows
to which conjugation it belongs: **-āre** = 1st; **-ēre** = 2nd; **-ere** = 3rd and **-īre** = 4th. Irregular verbs are shown on p xxvi

Calaber, -rī *adj* Calabrian.
Calabria *f S.E. peninsula of Italy.*
Calamis, -idis *m Greek sculptor.*
calamister, -rī *m,* **-rum, -rī** *nt* curling iron; (*RHET*) flourish.
calamistrātus *adj* curled; foppish.
calamitās, -ātis *f* disaster; (*MIL*) defeat; (*AGR*) damage, failure.
calamitōsē *adv see* **calamitōsus.**
calamitōsus *adj* disastrous, ruinous; blighted, unfortunate.
calamus, -ī *m* reed; stalk; pen, pipe, arrow, fishing rod.
calathiscus, -ī *m* small basket.
calathus, -ī *m* wicker basket; bowl, cup.
calātor, -ōris *m* servant.
calcāneum, -ī *nt* heel.
calcar, -āris *nt* spur.
calceāmentum, -ī *nt* shoe.
calceātus *ppp* shod.
calceolārius, -ī *and* **iī** *m* shoemaker.
calceolus, -ī *m* small shoe.
calceus, -ī *m* shoe.
Calchās, -antis *m Greek prophet at Troy.*
calcitrō, -āre *vi* to kick; (*fig*) to resist.
calcō, -āre, -āvī, -ātum *vt* to tread, trample on; (*fig*) to spurn.
calculus, -ī *m* pebble, stone; draughtsman, counting stone, reckoning, voting stone; **~um redūcere** take back a move; **~ōs subdūcere** compute; **ad ~ōs vocāre** subject to a reckoning.
caldārius *adj* with warm water.
caldus *etc see* **calidus.**
Calēdonia, -ae *f* the Scottish Highlands.
Calēdonius *adj see n.*
calefaciō, (calfaciō), -facere, -fēcī, -factum *vt* to warm, heat; (*fig*) to provoke, excite.
calefactō, -āre *vt* to warm.
Calendae *see* **Kalendae.**
Calēnus *adj of Cales* ♦ *nt wine of Cales.*
caleō, -ēre *vi* to be warm, be hot, glow; (*mind*) to be inflamed; (*things*) to be pursued with enthusiasm; to be fresh.
Calēs, -ium *fpl town in Campania.*
calēscō, -ere, -uī *vi* to get hot; (*fig*) to become inflamed.
calidē *adv* promptly.
calidus *adj* warm, hot; (*fig*) fiery, eager; hasty; prompt ♦ *f* warm water ♦ *nt* warm drink.
caliendrum, -ī *nt* headdress of hair.
caliga, -ae *f* soldier's boot.
caligātus *adj* heavily shod.
cālīginōsus *adj* misty, obscure.
cālīgō, -inis *f* mist, fog; dimness, darkness; (*mind*) obtuseness; (*CIRCS*) trouble.
cālīgō, -āre *vi* to be misty, be dim; to cause dizziness.
Caligula, -ae *m emperor Gaius.*
calix, -cis *m* wine cup; cooking pot.
calleō, -ēre *vi* to be thick-skinned; (*fig*) to be unfeeling; to be wise, be skilful ♦ *vt* to know, understand.

callidē *adv see* **callidus.**
calliditās, -ātis *f* skill; cunning.
callidus *adj* skilful, clever; crafty.
Callimachus, -ī *m Greek poet of Alexandria.*
Calliopē, -ēs, *and* **ēa, -ēae** *f Muse of epic poetry.*
callis, -is *m* footpath, mountain track; pass; hill pastures.
Callistō, -ūs *f daughter of Lycaon;* (*constellation*) Great Bear.
callōsus *adj* hard-skinned; solid.
callum, -ī *nt* hard *or* thick skin; firm flesh; (*fig*) callousness.
calō, -āre, -āvī, -ātum *vt* to convoke.
cālō, -ōnis *m* soldier's servant; drudge.
calor, -ōris *m* warmth, heat; (*fig*) passion, love.
Calpē, -ēs *f* Rock of Gibraltar.
Calpurniānus *adj see n.*
Calpurnius, -ī *m Roman name.*
caltha, -ae *f* marigold.
calthula, -ae *f* yellow dress.
caluī *perf of* **calēscō.**
calumnia, -ae *f* chicanery, sharp practice; subterfuge; misrepresentation; (*law*) dishonest accusation, blackmail; being convicted of malicious prosecution; **~am iūrāre** swear that an action is brought in good faith.
calumniātor, -ōris *m* legal trickster, slanderer.
calumnior, -ārī, -ātus *vt* to misrepresent, slander; (*law*) to bring an action in bad faith; **sē ~** deprecate oneself.
calva, -ae *f* bald head.
calvitium, -ī *and* **iī** *nt* baldness.
calvor, -ārī *vt* to deceive.
calvus *adj* bald.
calx, -cis *f* heel; foot; **~ce petere, ferīre** kick; **adversus stimulum ~cēs** ≈ *kicking against the pricks.*
calx, -cis *f* pebble; lime, chalk; finishing line, end; **ad carceres ā ~ce revocārī** have to begin all over again.
Calydōn, -ōnis *f town in Aetolia.*
Calydōnis *adj* Calydonian.
Calydōnius *f* Deianira; **~ōnius amnis** Achelous; **~ hērōs** Meleager; **~ōnia rēgna** Daunia in S. Italy.
Calypsō, -ūs (*acc* **-ō**) *f nymph who detained Ulysses in Ogygia.*
camēlīnus *adj* camel's.
camella, -ae *f* wine cup.
camēlus, -ī *m* camel.
Camēna, -ae *f* Muse; poetry.
camera, -ae *f* arched roof.
Camerīnum, -ī *nt town in Umbria.*
Camers, -tis, *and* **tīnus** *adj* of Camerinum.
Camillus, -ī *m Roman hero* (*who saved Rome from the Gauls*).
camīnus, -ī *m* furnace, fire; forge; **oleum addere ~ō** ≈ *add fuel to the flames.*
cammarus, -ī *m* lobster.

Campānia, -iae *f district of W. Italy.*
Campānicus, *and* **ius,** *and* **us** *adj* Campanian, Capuan.
campē, -ēs *f* evasion.
campester, -ris *adj* of the plain; of the Campus Martius ♦ *nt* loincloth ♦ *ntpl* level ground.
campus, -ī *m* plain; sports field; any level surface; (*fig*) theatre, arena (*of action, debate*); ~ **Martius** level ground by the Tiber (*used for assemblies, sports, military drills*).
Camulodūnum, -ī *nt* town of Trinobantes (*now* Colchester).
camur, -ī *adj* crooked.
canālis, -is *m* pipe, conduit, canal.
cancellī, -ōrum *mpl* grating, enclosure; barrier (*in public places*), bar of law court.
cancer, -rī *m* crab; (*constellation*) Cancer; south, tropical heat; (*MED*) cancer.
candefaciō, -ere *vt* to make dazzlingly white.
candēla, -ae *f* taper, tallow candle; waxed cord; ~**am appōnere valvīs** set the house on fire.
candēlābrum, -ī *nt* candlestick, chandelier, lampstand.
candēns, -entis *adj* dazzling white; white-hot.
candeō, -ēre *vi* to shine, be white; to be white-hot.
candēscō, -ere *vi* to become white; to grow white-hot.
candidātōrius *adj* of a candidate.
candidātus *adj* dressed in white ♦ *m* candidate for office.
candidē *adv* in white; sincerely.
candidulus *adj* pretty white.
candidus *adj* white, bright; radiant, beautiful; clothed in white; (*style*) clear; (*mind*) candid, frank; (*CIRCS*) happy; ~**a sententia** acquittal.
candor, -ōris *m* whiteness, brightness, beauty; (*fig*) brilliance, sincerity.
cānēns, -entis *adj* white.
cāneō, -ēre, -uī *vi* to be grey, be white.
cānescō, -ere *vi* to grow white; to grow old.
canīcula, -ae *f* bitch; Dog Star, Sirius.
canīnus *adj* dog's, canine; snarling, spiteful; ~ **littera** letter R.
canis, -is *m/f* dog, bitch; (*fig*) shameless *or* angry person; hanger-on; (*dice*) lowest throw; (*ASTRO*) Canis Major, Canis Minor; (*myth*) Cerberus.
canistrum, -ī *nt* wicker basket.
cānitiēs, -ēī *f* greyness; grey hair; old age.
canna, -ae *f* reed; pipe; gondola.
cannabis, -is *f* hemp.
Cannae, -ārum *fpl* village in Apulia (*scene of great Roman defeat by Hannibal*).
Cannēnsis *adj see n.*
canō, canere, cecinī *vt, vi* to sing; to play; to sing about, recite, celebrate; to prophesy; (*MIL*) to sound; (*birds*) to sing, crow.

canor, -ōris *m* song, tune, sound.
canōrus *adj* musical, melodious; singsong ♦ *nt* melodiousness.
Cantaber, -rī *m* Cantabrian.
Cantabria, -riae *f district of N Spain.*
Cantabricus *adj see n.*
cantāmen, -inis *nt* charm.
cantharis, -idis *f* beetle; Spanish fly.
cantharus, -ī *m* tankard.
canthērīnus *adj* of a horse.
canthērius, -ī *and* **iī** *m* gelding.
canticum, -ī *nt* aria in Latin comedy; song.
cantilēna, -ae *f* old song, gossip; ~**am eandem canere** keep harping on the same theme.
cantiō, -ōnis *f* song; charm.
cantitō, -āre, -āvī, -atum *vt* to sing *or* play often.
Cantium, -ī *and* **iī** *nt* Kent.
cantiunculae, -ārum *fpl* fascinating strains.
cantō, -āre, -āvī, -ātum *vt, vi* to sing; to play; to sing about, recite, celebrate; to proclaim, harp on; to use magic spells; to sound; to drawl.
cantor, -ōris *m*, **-rīx, -rīcis** *f* singer, musician, poet; actor.
cantus, -ūs *m* singing, playing, music; prophecy; magic spell.
cānus *adj* white, grey, hoary; old ♦ *mpl* grey hairs.
Canusīnus *adj see n.*
Canusium, -ī *nt* town in Apulia (*famous for wool*).
capācitās, -ātis *f* spaciousness.
capāx, -ācis *adj* capable of holding, spacious, roomy; capable, able, fit.
capēdō, -inis *f* sacrificial dish.
capēduncula *f* small dish.
capella, -ae *f* she-goat; (*ASTRO*) bright star in Auriga.
Capēna, -ae *f* old Etruscan town.
Capēnās, -us *adj*: **Porta** ~**a** Roman gate leading to the Via Appia.
caper, -rī *m* goat; odour of the armpits.
caperrō, -āre *vi* to wrinkle.
capessō, -ere, -īvī, -ītum *vt* to seize, take hold of, try to reach, make for; to take in hand, engage in; **rem pūblicam** ~ go in for politics.
capillātus *adj* long-haired; ancient.
capillus, -ī *m* hair (*of head or* beard); a hair.
capiō, -ere, cēpī, captum *vt* to take, seize; to catch, capture; (*MIL*) to make prisoner; (*NAUT*) to make, reach (*a goal*); (*fig*) to captivate, charm, cheat; (*pass*) to be maimed, lose the use of; to choose; (*appearance*) to assume; (*habit*) to cultivate; (*duty*) to undertake; (*ideas*) to conceive, form; (*feeling*) to experience; (*harm*) to suffer; to receive, get, inherit; to contain, hold; (*fig*) to bear; (*mind*) to grasp; **cōnsilium**

Noun declensions and verb conjugations are shown on pp xiii to xxv. The present infinitive ending of a verb shows to which conjugation it belongs: **-āre** = 1st; **-ēre** = 2nd; **-ere** = 3rd and **-īre** = 4th. Irregular verbs are shown on p xxvi

~ come to a decision; **impetum** ~ gather momentum; **initium** ~ start; **oculō capī** lose an eye; **mente captus** insane; **cupīdō eum cēpit** he felt a desire.

capis, -dis *f* sacrificial bowl with one handle.

capistrātus *adj* haltered.

capistrum, -ī *nt* halter, muzzle.

capital, -ālis *nt* capital crime.

capitālis *adj* mortal, deadly, dangerous; (*law*) capital; important, excellent.

capitō, -ōnis *m* bighead.

Capitōlīnus *adj* of the Capitol; of Jupiter.

Capitōlium, -ī *nt* Roman hill with temple of Jupiter.

capitulātim *adv* summarily.

capitulum, -ī *nt* small head; person, creature.

Cappadocia, -ae *f* country of Asia Minor.

capra, -ae *f* she-goat; odour of armpits; (*ASTRO*) Capella.

caprea, -ae *f* roe.

Capreae, -ārum *fpl* island of Capri.

capreolus, -ī *m* roebuck; (*pl*) crossbeams.

Capricornus, -ī *m* (*constellation*) Capricorn (*associated with midwinter*).

caprificus, -ī *f* wild fig tree.

caprigenus *adj* of goats.

caprimulgus, -ī *m* goatherd, rustic.

caprīnus *adj* of goats.

capripēs, -edis *adj* goat-footed.

capsa, -ae *f* box (*esp for papyrus rolls*).

capsō *archaic fut of* **capiō**.

capsula, -ae *f* small box; **dē ~ā tōtus** ≈ out of a bandbox.

Capta, -ae *f* Minerva.

captātiō, -ōnis *f* catching at.

captātor, -ōris *m* one who courts; legacy hunter.

captiō, -ōnis *f* fraud; disadvantage; (*argument*) fallacy, sophism.

captiōsē *adv see* **captiōsus**.

captiōsus *adj* deceptive; dangerous; captious.

captiuncula, -ae *f* quibble.

captīvitās, -ātis *f* captivity; capture.

captīvus *adj* captive, captured; of captives ♦ *m/f* prisoner of war.

captō, -āre, -āvī, -ātum *vt* to try to catch, chase; to try to win, court, watch for; to deceive, trap.

captus *ppp of* **capiō** ♦ *m* prisoner.

captus, -ūs *m* grasp, notion.

Capua, -ae *f* chief town of Campania.

capulāris *adj* due for a coffin.

capulus, -ī *m* coffin; handle, hilt.

caput, -itis *nt* head; top, extremity; (*rivers*) source; (*more rarely*) mouth; person, individual; life; civil rights; (*person*) chief, leader; (*towns*) capital; (*money*) principal; (*writing*) substance, chapter; principle, main point, the great thing; ~ **cēnae** main dish; ~**itis accūsāre** charge with a capital offence; ~**itis damnāre** condemn to death; ~**itis dēminūtiō** loss of political rights; ~**itis poena** capital punishment; ~**ita cōnferre** confer in

secret; **in ~ita** per head; **suprā ~ut esse** be imminent.

Cār, -is *m* Carian.

carbaseus *adj* linen, canvas.

carbasus, -ī *f* (*pl* -**a**, -**ōrum** *nt*) Spanish flax, fine linen; garment, sail, curtain.

carbō, -ōnis *m* charcoal, embers.

carbōnārius, -ī *and* **iī** *m* charcoal burner.

carbunculus, -ī *m* small coal; precious stone.

carcer, -is *m* prison; jailbird; barrier, starting place (*for races*); **ad ~ēs ā calce revocārī** have to begin all over again.

carcerārius *adj* of a prison.

carchēsium, -ī *and* **iī** *nt* drinking cup; (*NAUT*) masthead.

cardiacus, -ī *m* dyspeptic.

cardō, -inis *m* hinge; (*ASTRO*) pole, axis, cardinal point; (*fig*) juncture, critical moment.

carduus, -ī *m* thistle.

cārē *adv see* **cārus**.

cārectum, -ī *nt* sedge.

cāreō, -ēre, -uī *vi* (*with abl*) to be free from, not have, be without; to abstain from, be absent from; to want, miss.

cārex, -icis *f* sedge.

Cāria, -ae *f* district of S.W. Asia Minor.

Cāricus *adj* Carian ♦ *f* dried fig.

cariēs (*acc* -**em**, *abl* -**ē**) *f* dry rot.

carīna, -ae *f* keel; ship.

Carīnae, -ārum *fpl* district of Rome.

carīnārius, -ī *and* **iī** *m* dyer of yellow.

cariōsus *adj* crumbling; (*fig*) withered.

cāris, -idis *f* kind of crab.

cāritās, -ātis *f* dearness, high price; esteem, affection.

carmen, -inis *nt* song, tune; poem, poetry, verse; prophecy; (*in law, religion*) formula; moral text.

Carmentālis *adj see n.*

Carmentis, -is, *and* **a, -ae** *f* prophetess, mother of Evander.

carnārium, -ī *and* **iī** *nt* fleshhook; larder.

Carneadēs, -is *m* Greek philosopher (*founder of the New Academy*).

Carneadēus *adj see n.*

carnifex, -icis *m* executioner, hangman; scoundrel; murderer.

carnificīna, -ae *f* execution; torture; ~**am facere** be an executioner.

carnificō, -āre *vt* to behead, mutilate.

carnuf- *etc see* **carnif-**.

carō, -nis *f* flesh.

cārō, -ere *vt* to card.

Carpathius *adj see n.*

Carpathus, -ī *f* island between Crete and Rhodes.

carpatina, -ae *f* leather shoe.

carpentum, -ī *nt* two-wheeled coach.

carpō, -ere, -sī, -tum *vt* to pick, pluck, gather; to tear off; to browse, graze on; (*wool*) to card; (*fig*) to enjoy, snatch; to carp at, slander; to weaken, wear down; to divide up; (*journey*) to go, travel.

carptim *adv* in parts; at different points; at different times.

carptor, -ōris *m* carver.

carptus *ppp of* **carpō.**

carrus, -ī *m* waggon.

Carthāginiēnsis *adj see n.*

Carthāgō, -inis *f* Carthage (*near Tunis*); ~ **Nova** town in Spain (*now* Cartagena).

caruncula, -ae *f* piece of flesh.

cārus *adj* dear, costly; dear, beloved.

Carystēus *adj see n.*

Carystos, -ī *f* town in Euboea (*famous for marble*).

casa, -ae *f* cottage, hut.

cascus *adj* old.

cāseolus, -ī *m* small cheese.

cāseus, -ī *m* cheese.

casia, -ae *f* cinnamon; spurge laurel.

Caspius *adj* Caspian.

Cassandra, -ae *f* Trojan princess and prophetess, doomed never to be believed.

cassēs, -ium *mpl* net, snare; spider's web.

Cassiānus *adj see n.*

cassida, -ae *f* helmet.

Cassiepēa, -ae, Cassiopē, -ēs *f* mother of Andromeda; a constellation.

cassis, -idis *f* helmet.

Cassius, -ī *m* Roman family name.

cassō, -āre *vi* to shake.

cassus *adj* empty; devoid of, without (*abl*); vain, useless; ~ **lūmine** dead; **in ~um** in vain.

Castalia, -ae *f* spring on Parnassus, (*sacred to Apollo and the Muses*).

Castalides, -dum *fpl* Muses.

Castalius, -s *adj see n.*

castanea, -ae *f* chestnut tree; chestnut.

castē *adv see* **castus.**

castellānus *adj* of a fortress ♦ *mpl* garrison.

castellātim *adv* in different fortresses.

castellum, -ī *nt* fortress, castle; (*fig*) defence, refuge.

castēria, -ae *f* rowers' quarters.

castīgābilis *adj* punishable.

castīgātiō, -ōnis *f* correction, reproof.

castīgātor, -ōris *m* reprover.

castīgātus *adj* small, slender.

castīgō, -āre, -āvī, -ātum *vt* to correct, punish; to reprove; to restrain.

castimōnia, -ae *f* purity, morality; chastity, abstinence.

castitās, -ātis *f* chastity.

castor, -oris *m* beaver.

Castor, -oris *m* twin brother of Pollux (*patron of sailors*); star in Gemini.

castoreum, -ī *nt* odorous secretion of the beaver.

castra, -ōrum *ntpl* camp; day's march; army life; (*fig*) party, sect; ~ **movēre** strike camp; ~ **mūnīre** construct a camp; ~ **pōnere** pitch camp; **bīna ~** two camps.

castrēnsis *adj* of the camp, military.

castrō, -āre *vt* to castrate; (*fig*) to weaken.

castrum, -ī *nt* fort.

castus *adj* clean, pure, chaste, innocent; holy, pious.

cāsū *adv* by chance.

casula, -ae *f* little cottage.

cāsus, -ūs *m* fall, downfall; event, chance, accident; misfortune, death; opportunity; (*time*) end; (*GRAM*) case.

Catadūpa, -ōrum *ntpl* Nile cataract near Syene.

catagraphus *adj* painted.

Catamītus, -ī *m* Ganymede.

cataphractēs, -ae *m* coat of mail.

cataphractus *adj* wearing mail.

cataplus, -ī *m* ship arriving.

catapulta, -ae *f* (*MIL*) catapult; (*fig*) missile.

catapultārius *adj* thrown by catapult.

cataracta, -ae *f* waterfall; sluice; drawbridge.

catasta, -ae *f* stage, scaffold.

catē *adv see* **catus.**

catēia, -ae *f* javelin.

catella, -ae *f* small chain.

catellus, -ī *m* puppy.

catēna, -ae *f* chain; fetter; (*fig*) bond, restraint; series.

catēnātus *adj* chained, fettered.

caterva, -ae *f* crowd, band; flock; (*MIL*) troop, body; (*THEAT*) company.

catervātim *adv* in companies.

cathedra, -ae *f* armchair, sedan chair; teacher's chair.

catholicus *adj* (*ECCL*) orthodox, universal.

Catilīna, -ae *m* Catiline (*conspirator suppressed by Cicero*).

Catilīnārius *adj see n.*

catillō, -āre *vt* to lick a plate.

catillus, -ī *m* small dish.

catīnus, -ī *m* dish, pot.

Catō, -ōnis *m* famous censor and author, idealised as the pattern of an ancient Roman; famous Stoic and republican leader against Caesar.

Catoniānus *adj see n.*

Catōnīnī *mpl* Cato's supporters.

catōnium, -ī *and* **iī** *nt* the lower world.

Catulliānus *adj see n.*

Catullus, -ī *m* Latin lyric poet.

catulus, -ī *m* puppy; cub, young of other animals.

catus *adj* clever, wise; sly, cunning.

Caucaseus *adj see n.*

Caucasus, -ī *m* Caucasus mountains.

cauda, -ae *f* tail; ~ **am iactāre** fawn; ~ **am trahere** be made a fool of.

caudeus *adj* wooden.

caudex, -icis *m* trunk; block of wood; book, ledger; (*fig*) blockhead.

caudicālis *adj* of woodcutting.

Caudīnus *adj see n.*

Caudium, -ī *nt Samnite town.*
caulae, -ārum *fpl* opening; sheepfold.
caulis, -is *m* stalk; cabbage.
Cauneus *adj* Caunian.
Caunus, -ī *f town in Caria* ♦ *fpl* dried figs.
caupō, -ōnis *m* shopkeeper, innkeeper.
caupōna, -ae *f* shop, inn.
caupōnius *adj see n.*
caupōnor, -ārī *vt* to trade in.
caupōnula, -ae *f* tavern.
Caurus, -ī *m* north-west wind.
causa, -ae *f* cause, reason; purpose, sake;
    excuse, pretext; opportunity; connection,
    case, position; (*law*) case, suit; (*POL*) cause,
    party; (*RHET*) subject matter; ~**am agere,**
    ōrāre plead a case; ~**am dēfendere** speak for
    the defence; ~**am dīcere** defend oneself; ~**ā**
    for the sake of; **cum ~ā** with good reason;
    quā dē ~ā for this reason; **in ~ā esse** be
    responsible; **per ~am** under the pretext.
causārius *adj* (*MIL*) unfit for service.
causia, -ae *f* Macedonian hat.
causidicus, -ī *m* advocate.
causificor, -ārī *vi* to make a pretext.
causor, -ārī, -ātus *vt, vi* to pretend, make an
    excuse of.
caussa *etc see* **causa.**
causula, -ae *f* petty lawsuit; slight cause.
cautē *adv* carefully, cautiously; with security.
cautēla, -ae *f* caution.
cautēs, -is *f* rock, crag.
cautim *adv* warily.
cautiō, -ōnis *f* caution, wariness; (*law*)
    security, bond, bail; **mihi ~ est** I must take
    care; **mea ~ est** I must see to it.
cautor, -ōris *m* wary person; surety.
cautus *ppp of* **caveō** ♦ *adj* wary, provident;
    safe, secure.
cavaedium, -ī *and* **iī** *nt* inner court of a house.
cavea, -ae *f* cage, stall, coop, hive; (*THEAT*)
    auditorium; theatre; **prīma ~** upper class
    seats; **ultima ~** lower class seats.
caveō, -ēre, cāvī, cautum *vt* to beware of,
    guard against ♦ *vi* (*with* **ab** *or abl*) to be on
    one's guard against; (*with dat*) to look after;
    (*with* **nē**) to take care that . . . not; (*with* **ut**) to
    take good care that; (*with subj or inf*) to take
    care not to, do not; (*law*) to stipulate, decree;
    (*COMM*) to get a guarantee, give a guarantee,
    stand security; **cavē!** look out!
caverna, -ae *f* hollow, cave, vault; (*NAUT*) hold.
cavilla, -ae *f* jeering.
cavillātiō, -ōnis *f* jeering, banter; sophistry.
cavillātor, -ōris *m* scoffer.
cavillor, -ārī, -ātus *vt* to scoff at ♦ *vi* to jeer,
    scoff; to quibble.
cavō, -āre, -āvī, -ātum *vt* to hollow, excavate.
cavus *adj* hollow, concave, vaulted; (*river*)
    deep-channelled ♦ *nt* cavity, hole.
Caystros, -us, -ī *m* river in Lydia (*famous for
    swans*).
-ce *demonstrative particle appended to pronouns
    and adverbs.*

Cēa, -ae *f* Aegean island (*birthplace of
    Simonides*).
cecidī *perf of* **cadō.**
cecīdī *perf of* **caedō.**
cecinī *perf of* **canō.**
Cecropidēs, -idae *m* Theseus; Athenian.
Cecropis, -idis *f* Aglauros; Procne; Philomela;
    Athenian, Attic.
Cecropius *adj* Athenian ♦ *f* Athens.
Cecrops, -is *m* ancient king of Athens.
cēdō, -ere, cessī, cessum *vi* to go, walk; to
    depart, withdraw, retreat; to pass away, die;
    (*events*) to turn out; to be changed (into); to
    accrue (to); to yield, be inferior (to) ♦ *vt* to
    give up, concede, allow; ~ **bonīs, possessiōne**
    make over property (to); ~ **forō** go bankrupt;
    ~ **locō** leave one's post; ~ **memoriā** be
    forgotten.
cedo (*pl* **cette**) *impv* give me, bring here; tell
    me; let me; look at!
cedrus, -ī *f* cedar, perfumed juniper; cedar
    oil.
Celaenō, -ūs *f* a Harpy; a Pleiad.
cēlāta *ntpl* secrets.
celeber, -ris *adj* crowded, populous;
    honoured, famous; repeated.
celebrātiō, -ōnis *f* throng; celebration.
celebrātus *adj* full, much used; festive;
    famous.
celebritās, -ātis *f* crowd; celebration; fame.
celebrō, -āre, -āvī, -ātum *vt* to crowd,
    frequent; to repeat, practise; to celebrate,
    keep (*a festival*); to advertise, glorify.
celer, -is *adj* quick, swift, fast; hasty.
Celerēs, -um *mpl* royal bodyguard.
celeripēs, -edis *adj* swift-footed.
celeritās, -ātis *f* speed, quickness.
celeriter *adv see* **celer.**
celerō, -āre *vt* to quicken ♦ *vi* to make haste.
cella, -ae *f* granary, stall, cell; garret, hut,
    small room; sanctuary of a temple.
cellārius *adj* of the storeroom ♦ *m* steward.
cellula, -ae *f* little room.
cēlō, -āre, -āvī, -ātum *vt* to hide, conceal,
    keep secret; **id mē ~at** he keeps me in the
    dark about it.
celōx, -ōcis *adj* swift ♦ *f* fast ship, yacht.
celsus *adj* high, lofty; (*fig*) great, eminent;
    haughty.
Celtae, -ārum *mpl* Celts (*esp of central Gaul*)
    ♦ *nt* the Celtic nation.
Celtibērī, -ōrum *mpl* people of central Spain.
Celtibēria, -iae *f* Central Spain.
Celtibēricus *adj see n.*
Celticus *adj* Celtic.
cēna, -ae *f* dinner (*the principal Roman meal*);
    inter ~am at table.
cēnāculum, -ī *nt* dining-room; upper room,
    garret.
cēnāticus *adj* of dinner.
cēnātiō, -ōnis *f* dining-room.
cēnātus *ppa* having dined, after dinner ♦ *ppp*
    spent in feasting.

Cenchreae, -ārum *fpl harbour of Corinth.*
cēnitō, -āre *vi* to be accustomed to dine.
cēnō, -āre, -āvī, -ātum *vi* to dine ♦ *vt* to eat, dine on.
cēnseō, -ēre, -uī, -um *vt* (*census*) to assess, rate, take a census, make a property return; (*fig*) to estimate, appreciate, celebrate; (*senate or other body*) to decree, resolve; (*member*) to express an opinion, move, vote; to advise; to judge, think, suppose, consider; **cēnsuī ~endō** for census purposes.
cēnsiō, -ōnis *f* punishment; expression of opinion.
cēnsor, -ōris *m* censor; (*fig*) severe judge, critic.
cēnsōrius *adj* of the censors, to be dealt with by the censors; (*fig*) severe; **homō ~** an ex-censor.
cēnsūra, -ae *f* censorship; criticism.
cēnsus *ppp of* **cēnseō**; **capite ~ī** *the poorest class of Roman citizens.*
cēnsus, -ūs *m register of Roman citizens and their property,* census; registered property; wealth; **~um agere, habēre** hold a census; **sine ~ū** poor.
centaurēum, -ī *nt* centaury.
Centaurēus *adj see n.*
Centaurus, -ī *m* Centaur, half man half horse.
centēnī, -um *num* a hundred each, a hundred.
centēsimus *adj* hundredth ♦ *f* hundredth part; (*interest*) 1 per cent monthly (*12 per cent per annum*).
centiceps *adj* hundred-headed.
centiēns, -ēs *adv* a hundred times.
centimanus *adj* hundred-handed.
centō, -ōnis *m* patchwork; **~ōnēs sarcīre** ≈ *tell tall stories.*
centum *num* a hundred.
centumgeminus *adj* hundred-fold.
centumplex *adj* hundred-fold.
centumpondium, -ī *and* **iī** *nt* a hundred pounds.
centumvirālis *adj* of the centumviri.
centumvirī, -ōrum *mpl a bench of judges who heard special civil cases in Rome.*
centunculus, -ī *m* piece of patchwork, saddlecloth.
centuria, -ae *f* (*MIL*) company; (*POL*) century (*a division of the Roman people according to property*).
centuriātim *adv* by companies, by centuries.
centuriātus *adj* divided by centuries; **comitia ~a** *assembly which voted by centuries.*
centuriātus, -ūs *m* division into centuries; rank of centurion.
centuriō, -āre, -āvī, -ātum *vt* (*MIL*) to assign to companies; (*POL*) to divide by centuries.
centuriō, -ōnis *m* (*MIL*) captain, centurion.
centussis, -is *m* a hundred asses.
cēnula, -ae *f* little dinner.

Ceōs, *acc* **-ō** *see* **Cea.**
Cēphēis *f* Andromeda.
Cēphēius *adj* of Cepheus.
Cēphēus *adj* Ethiopian.
Cepheus, -eī (*acc* **-ea**) *m* king of Ethiopia (*father of Andromeda*).
Cēphīsis *adj see n.*
Cēphīsius *m* Narcissus.
Cēphīsus, -ī *m river in central Greece.*
cēpī *perf of* **capiō.**
cēra, -ae *f* wax; honey cells; writing tablet, notebook; seal; portrait of an ancestor; **prīma ~** first page.
Ceramīcus, -ī *m Athenian cemetery.*
cērārium, -ī *and* **iī** *nt* seal-duty.
cerastēs, -ae *m* a horned serpent.
cerasus, -ī *f* cherry tree; cherry.
cērātus *adj* waxed.
Ceraunia, -ōrum *nt,* **Ceraunii** *m mountains in Epirus.*
Cerbereus *adj see n.*
Cerberus, -ī *m three-headed watchdog of Hades.*
cercopithēcus, -ī *m* monkey.
cercūrus, -ī *m Cyprian type of ship.*
cerdō, -ōnis *m* tradesman.
Cereālia, -ium *ntpl festival of Ceres.*
Cereālis *adj* of Ceres; of corn, of meal.
cerebrōsus *adj* hot-headed.
cerebrum, -ī *nt* brain; understanding; quick temper.
Cerēs, -eris *f goddess of agriculture;* (*fig*) grain, bread.
cēreus *adj* waxen; wax-coloured; (*fig*) supple, easily led ♦ *m* taper.
cēriāria, -ae *f* taper maker.
cērina, -ōrum *ntpl* wax-coloured clothes.
cērintha, -ae *f* honeywort.
cernō, -ere, -crēvī, crētum *vt* to see, discern; to understand, perceive; to decide, determine; (*law*) to decide to take up (an inheritance).
cernuus *adj* face downwards.
cērōma, -atis *nt* wrestlers' ointment.
cērōmaticus *adj* smeared with wax ointment.
cerrītus *adj* crazy.
certāmen, -inis *nt* contest, match; battle, combat; (*fig*) struggle, rivalry.
certātim *adv* emulously.
certātiō, -ōnis *f* contest; debate; rivalry.
certē *adv* assuredly, of course; at least.
certō *adv* certainly, really.
certō, -āre, -āvī, -ātum *vi* to contend, compete; (*MIL*) to fight it out; (*law*) to dispute; (*with inf*) to try hard.
certus *adj* determined, fixed, definite; reliable, unerring; sure, certain; **mihi ~um est** I have made up my mind; **~um scīre, prō ~ō habēre** know for certain, be sure; **~iōrem facere** inform.
cērula, -ae *f* piece of wax; **~ miniāta** red

Noun declensions and verb conjugations are shown on pp xiii to xxv. The present infinitive ending of a verb shows to which conjugation it belongs: **-āre** = 1st; **-ēre** = 2nd; **-ere** = 3rd and **-īre** = 4th. Irregular verbs are shown on p xxvi

pencil.

cērussa, -ae *f* white lead.

cērussātus *adj* painted with white lead.

cerva, -ae *f* hind, deer.

cervīcal, -ālis *nt* pillow.

cervīcula, -ae *f* slender neck.

cervīnus *adj* deer's.

cervīx, -īcis *f* neck; **in ~īcibus esse** be a burden (to), threaten.

cervus, -ī *m* stag, deer; (*MIL*) palisade.

cessātiō, -ōnis *f* delaying; inactivity, idleness.

cessātor, -ōris *m* idler.

cessī *perf of* **cēdō**.

cessiō, -ōnis *f* giving up.

cessō, -āre, -āvī, -ātum *vi* to be remiss, stop; to loiter, delay; to be idle, rest, do nothing; (*land*) to lie fallow; to err.

cestrosphendonē, -ēs *f* (*MIL*) engine for shooting stones.

cestus, -ī *m* girdle (*esp of Venus*).

cētārium, -ī *and* **iī** *nt* fishpond.

cētārius, -ī *and* **iī** *m* fishmonger.

cētera *adv* in other respects.

cēterī, -ōrum *adj* the rest, the others; (*sg*) the rest of.

cēterōquī, -n *adv* otherwise.

cēterum *adv* for the rest, otherwise; but for all that; besides.

Cethēgus, -ī *m* a conspirator with Catiline.

cētr- *etc see* **caetr-**.

cette *etc see* **cedo**.

cētus, -ī *m* (-ē *ntpl*) sea monster, whale.

ceu *adv* just as, as if.

Cēus *adj see* **Cēa**.

Cēyx, -ȳcis *m husband of Alcyone, changed to a kingfisher.*

Chalcidēnsis, (-discus) *adj see n.*

Chalcis, -dis *f chief town of Euboea.*

Chaldaeī, -aeōrum *mpl* Chaldeans; astrologers.

Chaldāicus *adj see n.*

chalybēius *adj* of steel.

Chalybes, -um *mpl a people of Pontus (famous as ironworkers).*

chalybs, -is *m* steel.

Chāones, -um *mpl a people of Epirus.*

Chāonia, -iae *f* Epirus.

Chāonius, -is *adj see n.*

Chaos (*abl* -ō) *nt* empty space, the lower world, chaos.

chara, -ae *f* an unidentified vegetable.

charistia, -ōrum *ntpl a Roman family festival.*

Charites, -um *fpl* the Graces.

Charōn, -ontis *m Charon (ferryman of Hades).*

charta, -ae *f* sheet of papyrus, paper; writing.

chartula, -ae *f* piece of paper.

Charybdis, -is *f monster personifying a whirlpool in the Straits of Messina; (fig) peril.*

Chatti, -ōrum *mpl a people of central Germany.*

Chēlae, -ārum *fpl* (*ASTRO*) the Claws (of Scorpio), Libra.

chelydrus, -ī *m* watersnake.

chelys (*acc* -yn) *f* tortoise; lyre.

cheragra, -ae *f* gout in the hands.

Cherronēsus, Chersonēsus, -ī *f* Gallipoli peninsula; Crimea.

chīliarchus, -ī *m officer in charge of 1000 men;* chancellor of Persia.

Chimaera, -ae *f fire-breathing monster formed of lion, goat and serpent.*

Chimaeriferus *adj birthplace of Chimaera.*

Chios, -ī *f Aegean island (famous for wine).*

Chīus *adj* Chian ♦ *nt* Chian wine; Chian cloth.

chīrographum, -ī *nt* handwriting; document.

Chīrōn, -ōnis *m a learned Centaur (tutor of heroes).*

chīronomos, -ī *m/f,* **chīronomōn, -untis** *m* mime actor.

chiūrūrgia, -ae *f* surgery; (*fig*) violent measures.

chlamydātus *adj* wearing a military cloak.

chlamys, -dis *f* Greek military cloak.

Choerilus, -ī *m inferior Greek poet.*

chorāgium, -i *and* **iī** *nt* producing of a chorus.

chorāgus, -ī *m* one who finances a chorus.

choraulēs, -ae *m* flute-player (accompanying a chorus).

chorda, -ae *f* string (of an instrument); rope.

chorēa, -ae *f* dance.

chorēus, -ī *m* trochee.

chorus, -ī *m* choral dance; chorus, choir of singers *or* dancers; band, troop.

Christiānismus, -ī *m* Christianity.

Christiānus *adj* Christian.

Christus, -ī *m* Christ.

Chrȳsēis, -ēidis *f daughter of Chrȳsēs.*

Chrȳsēs, -ae *m priest of Apollo in the Iliad.*

Chrȳsippēus *adj see n.*

Chrȳsippus, -ī *m Stoic philosopher.*

chrȳsolithos, -ī *m/f* topaz.

chrȳsos, -ī *m* gold.

cibārius *adj* food (*in cpds*); common ♦ *ntpl* rations.

cibātus, -ūs *m* food.

cibōrium, -ī *and* **iī** *nt* kind of drinking cup.

cibus, -ī *m* food, fodder, nourishment.

cicāda, -ae *f* cicada, cricket.

cicātrīcōsus *adj* scarred.

cicātrīx, -īcis *f* scar; (*plants*) mark of an incision.

ciccus, -ī *m* pomegranate pip.

cicer, -is *nt* chickpea.

Cicerō, -ōnis *m great Roman orator and author.*

Cicerōniānus *adj see n.*

cichorēum, -ī *nt* chicory.

Cicōnes, -um *mpl people of Thrace.*

cicōnia, -ae *f* stork.

cicur, -is *adj* tame.

cicūta, -ae *f* hemlock; pipe.

cieō, ciēre, cīvī, citum *vt* to move, stir, rouse; to call, invoke; (*fig*) to give rise to, produce; **calcem ~** make a move (in chess).

Cilicia, -ae *f* country in S. Asia Minor (*famous for piracy*).

Ciliciēnsis, (-us) *adj see n.*

Cilix, -cis, -ssa *adj* Cilician ♦ *nt* goats' hair garment.
Cimbrī, -ōrum *mpl people of N. Germany.*
Cimbricus *adj see n.*
cīmex, -icis *m* bug.
Cimmeriī, -ōrum *mpl people of the Crimea;* mythical race in caves near Cumae.
Cimmerius *adj see n.*
cinaedius *adj* lewd.
cinaedus, -ī *m* sodomite; lewd dancer.
cincinnātus *adj* with curled hair.
Cincinnātus, -ī *m ancient Roman dictator.*
cincinnus, -ī *m* curled hair; (*fig*) rhetorical ornament.
Cincius, -ī *m Roman tribune; Roman historian.*
cincticulus, -ī *m* small girdle.
cinctus *ppp of* **cingō.**
cinctus, -ūs *m* girding; ~ **Gabīnus** *a ceremonial style of wearing the toga.*
cinctūtus *adj* girded.
cinefactus *adj* reduced to ashes.
cinerārius, -ī *and* **iī** *m* hair curler.
cingō, -gere, -xī, -ctum *vt* to surround, enclose; to gird, crown; (*MIL*) to besiege, fortify; to cover, escort; **ferrum ~or** I put on my sword.
cingula, -ae *f* girth (*of animals*).
cingulum, -ī *nt* belt.
cingulus, -ī *m* zone.
ciniflō, -ōnis *m* hair curler.
cinis, -eris *m* ashes; (*fig*) ruin.
Cinna, -ae *m colleague of Marius; poet friend of Catullus.*
cinnamōmum, cinnamum, -ī *nt* cinnamon.
cinxī *perf of* **cingō.**
Cīnyphius *adj of the Cinyps, river of N. Africa; African.*
Cinyrās, -ae *m father of Adonis.*
Cinyrēius *adj see n.*
cippus, -ī *m* tombstone; (*pl*) palisade.
circā *adv* around, round about ♦ *prep* (*with acc*) (*place*) round, in the vicinity of, in; (*time, number*) about; with regard to.
Circaeus *adj see* **Circē.**
circamoerium, -ī *and* **iī** *nt* space on both sides of a wall.
Circē, -ēs *and* **ae** *f goddess with magic powers living in Aeaea.*
circēnsēs, -ium *mpl* the games.
circēnsis *adj* of the Circus.
circinō, -āre *vt* to circle through.
circinus, -ī *m* pair of compasses.
circiter *adv* (*time, number*) about ♦ *prep* (*with acc*) about, near.
circueō, circumeō, -ire, -īvī *and* **iī, -itum** *vt, vi* to go round, surround; (*MIL*) to encircle; to visit, go round canvassing; to deceive.
circuitiō, -ōnis *f* (*MIL*) rounds; (*speech*) evasiveness.
circuitus *ppp of* **circueō.**

circuitus, -ūs *m* revolution; way round, circuit; (*RHET*) period, periphrasis.
circulātor, -ōris *m* pedlar.
circulor, -ārī *vi* to collect in crowds.
circulus, -ī *m* circle; orbit; ring; social group.
circum *adv* round about ♦ *prep* (*with acc*) round, about; near; ~ **insulās mittere** send to the islands round about.
circumagō, -agere, -ēgī, -āctum *vt* to turn, move in a circle, wheel; (*pass: time*) to pass; (: *mind*) to be swayed.
circumarō, -āre *vt* to plough round.
circumcaesūra, -ae *f* outline.
circumcīdō, -dere, -dī, -sum *vt* to cut round, trim; to cut down, abridge.
circumcircā *adv* all round.
circumcīsus *ppp of* **circumcīdō** ♦ *adj* precipitous.
circumclūdō, -dere, -sī, -sum *vt* to shut in, hem in.
circumcolō, -ere *vt* to live round about.
circumcursō, -āre *vi* to run about.
circumdō, -are, -edī, -atum *vt* to put round; to surround, enclose.
circumdūcō, -ūcere, -ūxī, -uctum *vt* to lead round, draw round; to cheat; (*speech*) to prolong, drawl.
circumductus *ppp of* **circumdūcō.**
circumeō *etc see* **circueō.**
circumequitō, -āre *vt* to ride round.
circumferō, -ferre, -tulī, -lātum *vt* to carry round, pass round; to spread, broadcast; to purify; (*pass*) to revolve.
circumflectō, -ctere, -xī, -xum *vt* to wheel round.
circumflō, -āre *vt* (*fig*) to buffet.
circumfluō, -ere, -xī *vt, vi* to flow round; (*fig*) to overflow, abound.
circumfluus *adj* flowing round; surrounded (by water).
circumforāneus *adj* itinerant; (*money*) borrowed.
circumfundō, -undere, -ūdī, -ūsum *vt* to pour round, surround; (*fig*) to crowd round, overwhelm; (*pass*) to flow round.
circumgemō, -ere *vt* to growl round.
circumgestō, -āre *vt* to carry about.
circumgredior, -dī, -ssus *vt, vi* to make an encircling move, surround.
circumiaceō, -ēre *vi* to be adjacent.
circumiciō, -icere, -iēcī, -iectum *vt* to throw round, put round; to surround.
circumiecta *ntpl* neighbourhood.
circumiectus *adj* surrounding.
circumiectus, -ūs *m* enclosure; embrace.
circumit- *etc see* **circuit-.**
circumitiō, -ōnis *f see* **circuitiō.**
circumitus, -ūs *m see* **circuitus.**
circumlātus *ppp of* **circumferō.**
circumligō, -āre, -āvī, -ātum *vt* to tie to, bind

round.

circumlinō, -ere, -tum _vt_ to smear all over, bedaub.

circumluō, -ere _vt_ to wash.

circumluviō, -ōnis _f_ alluvial land.

circummittō, -ittere, -īsī, -issum _vt_ to send round.

circummoeniō (circummūniō), -īre, -īvī, -ītum _vt_ to fortify.

circummūnītiō, -ōnis _f_ investing.

circumpadānus _adj_ of the Po valley.

circumpendeō, -ēre _vi_ to hang round.

circumplaudō, -ere _vt_ to applaud on all sides.

circumplector, -ctī, -xus _vt_ to embrace, surround.

circumplicō, -āre, -āvī, -ātum _vt_ to wind round.

circumpōnō, -pōnere, -posuī, -positum _vt_ to put round.

circumpōtātiō, -ōnis _f_ passing drinks round.

circumrētiō, -īre, -īvī, -ītum _vt_ to ensnare.

circumrōdō, -rosī, -rodere _vt_ to nibble round about; (_fig_) to slander.

circumsaepiō, -īre, -sī, -tum _vt_ to fence round.

circumscindō, -ere _vt_ to strip.

circumscrībō, -bere, -psī, -ptum _vt_ to draw a line round; to mark the limits of; to restrict, circumscribe; to set aside; to defraud.

circumscrīptē _adv_ in periods.

circumscrīptiō, -ōnis _f_ circle, contour; fraud; (_RHET_) period.

circumscrīptor, -ōris _m_ defrauder.

circumscrīptus _ppp of_ **circumscrībō** ♦ _adj_ restricted; (_RHET_) periodic.

circumsecō, -āre _vt_ to cut round.

circumsedeō, -edēre, -ēdī, -essum _vt_ to blockade, beset.

circumsēpiō _etc see_ **circumsaepiō**.

circumsessiō, -ōnis _f_ siege.

circumsessus _ppp of_ **circumsedeō**.

circumsīdō, -ere _vt_ to besiege.

circumsiliō, -īre _vi_ to hop about; (_fig_) to be rampant.

circumsistō, -sistere, -stetī surround.

circumsonō, -āre _vi_ to resound on all sides ♦ _vt_ to fill with sound.

circumsonus _adj_ noisy.

circumspectātrīx, -īcis _f_ spy.

circumspectiō, -ōnis _f_ caution.

circumspectō, -āre _vt, vi_ to look all round, search anxiously, be on the lookout.

circumspectus _ppp of_ **circumspiciō** ♦ _adj_ carefully considered, cautious.

circumspectus, -ūs _m_ consideration; view.

circumspiciō, -icere, -exī, -ectum _vi_ to look all round; to be careful ♦ _vt_ to survey; (_fig_) to consider, search for.

circumstantēs, -antium _mpl_ bystanders.

circumstetī _perf of_ **circumsistō**; _perf of_ **circumstō**.

circumstō, -āre, -etī _vt, vi_ to stand round; to

besiege; (_fig_) to encompass.

circumstrepō, -ere _vt_ to make a clamour round.

circumsurgēns, -entis _pres p_ rising on all sides.

circumtentus _adj_ covered tightly.

circumterō, -ere _vt_ to crowd round.

circumtextus _adj_ embroidered round the edge.

circumtonō, -āre, -uī _vt_ to thunder about.

circumvādō, -dere, -sī _vt_ to assail on all sides.

circumvagus _adj_ encircling.

circumvallō, -āre, -āvī, -ātum _vt_ to blockade, beset.

circumvectiō, -ōnis _f_ carrying about; (_sun_) revolution.

circumvector, -ārī _vi_ to travel round, cruise round; (_fig_) describe.

circumvehor, -hī, -ctus _vt, vi_ to ride round, sail round; (_fig_) to describe.

circumvēlō, -āre _vt_ to envelop.

circumveniō, -enīre, -ēnī, -entum _vt_ to surround, beset; to oppress; to cheat.

circumvertō, circumvortō, -ere _vt_ to turn round.

circumvestiō, -īre _vt_ to envelop.

circumvinciō, -īre _vt_ to lash about.

circumvīsō, -ere _vt_ to look at all round.

circumvolitō, -āre, -āvī, -ātum _vt, vi_ to fly round; to hover around.

circumvolō, -āre _vt_ to fly round.

circumvolvō, -vere _vt_ to roll round.

circus, -ī _m_ circle; the Circus Maximus (_famous Roman racecourse_); a racecourse.

Cirrha, -ae _f_ town near Delphi (_sacred to Apollo_).

Cirrhaeus _adj see n._

cirrus, -ī _m_ curl of hair; fringe.

cis _prep_ (_with acc_) on this side of; (_time_) within.

Cisalpīnus _adj_ on the Italian side of the Alps, Cisalpine.

cisium, -ī _and_ **iī** _nt_ two-wheeled carriage.

Cissēis, -dis _f_ Hecuba.

cista, -ae _f_ box, casket; ballot box.

cistella, -ae _f_ small box.

cistellātrīx, -īcis _f_ keeper of the moneybox.

cistellula, -ae _f_ little box.

cisterna, -ae _f_ reservoir.

cistophorus, -ī _m_ an Asiatic coin.

cistula, -ae _f_ little box.

citātus _adj_ quick, impetuous.

citerior (_sup_ **-imus**) _adj_ on this side, nearer.

Cithaerōn, -ōnis _m_ mountain range between Attica and Boeotia.

cithara, -ae _f_ lute.

citharista, -ae _m_, **citharistria, -ae** _f_ lute player.

citharizō, -āre _vi_ to play the lute.

citharoedus, -ī _m_ a singer who accompanies himself on the lute.

citimus _adj_ nearest.

cito (_com_ **-ius**, _sup_ **-issimē**) _adv_ quickly, soon;

nōn ~ not easily.

citō, -āre, -āvī, -ātum *vt* to set in motion, rouse; to call (by name), appeal to, cite, mention.

citrā *adv* on this side, this way, not so far ♦ *prep* (*with acc*) on this side of, short of; (*time*) before, since; apart from; ~ **quam** before.

citreus *adj* of citrus wood.

citrō *adv* hither, this way; **ultrō** ~**que** to and fro.

citrus, -ī *f* citrus tree; citron tree.

citus *ppp of* **cieō** ♦ *adj* quick.

cīvicus *adj* civic, civil; **corōna** ~**a** civic crown for saving a citizen's life in war.

cīvīlis *adj* of citizens, civil; political, civilian; courteous, democratic; **iūs** ~**e** civil rights; Civil Law; code of legal procedure.

cīvīlitās, -ātis *f* politics; politeness.

cīvīliter *adv* like citizens; courteously.

cīvis, -is *m/f* citizen, fellow citizen.

cīvitās, -ātis *f* citizenship; community state; city; ~**āte dōnāre** naturalize.

clādēs, -is *f* damage, disaster, ruin; defeat; (*fig*) scourge; **dare** ~**em** make havoc.

clam *adv* secretly; unknown ♦ *prep* (*with acc*) unknown to; ~ **mē habēre** keep from me.

clāmātor, -ōris *m* bawler.

clāmitātiō, -ōnis *f* bawling.

clāmitō, -āre, -āvī, -ātum *vt, vi* to bawl, screech, cry out.

clāmō, -āre, -āvī, -ātum *vt, vi* to shout, cry out; to call upon, proclaim.

clāmor, -ōris *m* shout, cry; acclamation.

clāmōsus *adj* noisy.

clanculum *adv* secretly ♦ *prep* (*with acc*) unknown to.

clandestīnō *adv see* **clandestīnus**.

clandestīnus *adj* secret.

clangor, -ōris *m* clang, noise.

clārē *adv* brightly, loudly, clearly, with distinction.

clāreō, -ēre *vi* to be bright, be clear; to be evident; to be renowned.

clārēscō, -ere, clāruī *vi* to brighten, sound clear; to become obvious; to become famous.

clārigātiō, -ōnis *f* formal ultimatum to an enemy; fine for trespass.

clārigō, -āre *vi* to deliver a formal ultimatum.

clārisonus *adj* loud and clear.

clāritās, -ātis *f* distinctness; (*RHET*) lucidity; celebrity.

clāritūdō, -inis *f* brightness; (*fig*) distinction.

Clārius *adj* of Claros ♦ *m* Apollo.

clārō, -āre *vt* to illuminate; to explain; to make famous.

Claros, -ī *f* town in Ionia (*famous for worship of Apollo*).

clārus *adj* (*sight*) bright; (*sound*) loud; (*mind*) clear; (*person*) distinguished; ~ **intonāre**

thunder from a clear sky; **vir** ~**issimus** a courtesy title for eminent men.

classiārius *adj* naval ♦ *mpl* marines.

classicula, -ae *f* flotilla.

classicum, -ī *nt* battle-signal; trumpet.

classicus *adj* of the first class; naval ♦ *mpl* marines.

classis, -is *f* a political class; army; fleet.

clāthrī, -ōrum *mpl* cage.

clāthrātus *adj* barred.

clātrī, -ōrum *mpl see* **clāthrī**.

claudeō, -ēre *vi* to limp; (*fig*) to be defective.

claudicātiō, -ōnis *f* limping.

claudicō, -āre *vi* to be lame; to waver, be defective.

Claudius, -ī *m* patrician family name (*esp Appius Claudius Caecus, famous censor*); the Emperor Claudius.

Claudius, -iānus, -iālis *adj see n*.

claudō, -dere, -sī, -sum *vt* to shut, close; to cut off, block; to conclude; to imprison, confine, blockade; **agmen** ~ bring up the rear.

claudō, -ere *etc see* **claudeō**.

claudus *adj* lame, crippled; (*verse*) elegiac; (*fig*) wavering.

clausī *perf of* **claudō**.

claustra, -ōrum *ntpl* bar, bolt, lock; barrier, barricade, dam.

clausula, -ae *f* conclusion; (*RHET*) ending of a period.

clausum, -ī *nt* enclosure.

clausus *ppp of* **claudō**.

clāva, -ae *f* club, knotty branch; (*MIL*) foil.

clāvārium, -ī *and* **iī** *nt* money for buying shoe nails.

clāvātor, -ōris *m* cudgel-bearer.

clāvicula, -ae *f* vine tendril.

clāviger, -ī *m* (*Hercules*) club bearer; (*Janus*) key-bearer.

clāvis, -is *f* key.

clāvus, -ī *m* nail; tiller, rudder; purple stripe on the tunic (*broad for senators, narrow for equites*); ~**um annī movēre** reckon the beginning of the year.

Cleanthēs, -is *m* Stoic philosopher.

clēmēns, -entis *adj* mild, gentle, merciful; (*weather, water*) mild, calm.

clēmenter *adv* gently, indulgently; gradually.

clēmentia, -ae *f* mildness, forbearance, mercy.

Cleopatra, -ae *f* queen of Egypt.

clepō, -ere, -sī, -tum *vt* to steal.

clepsydra, -ae *f* waterclock (*used for timing speakers*); ~**am dare** give leave to speak; ~**am petere** ask leave to speak.

clepta, -ae *m* thief.

cliēns, -entis *m* client, dependant; follower; vassal-state.

clienta, -ae *f* client.

Noun declensions and verb conjugations are shown on pp xiii to xxv. The present infinitive ending of a verb shows to which conjugation it belongs: -**āre** = 1st; -**ēre** = 2nd; -**ere** = 3rd and -**īre** = 4th. Irregular verbs are shown on p xxvi

clientēla, -ae *f* clientship, protection; clients.

clientulus, -ī *m* insignificant client.

clīnāmen, -inis *nt* swerve.

clīnātus *adj* inclined.

Clīō, -ūs *f* Muse of history.

clipeātus *adj* armed with a shield.

clipeus, -ī *m*, **-um, -ī** *nt* round bronze shield; disc; medallion on a metal base.

clitellae, -ārum *fpl* packsaddle, attribute of an ass.

clitellārius *adj* carrying packsaddles.

Clitumnus, -ī *m* river in Umbria.

clīvōsus *adj* hilly.

clīvus, -ī *m* slope, hill; ~ **sacer** part of the Via Sacra.

cloāca, -ae *f* sewer, drain.

Cloācīna, -ae *f* Venus.

Clōdius, -ī *m* Roman plebeian name (*esp the tribune, enemy of Cicero*).

Cloelia, -ae *f* Roman girl hostage (*who escaped by swimming the Tiber*).

Clōthō (*acc* **-ō**) *f* one of the Fates.

clueō, -ēre, -eor, -ērī *vi* to be called, be famed.

clūnis, -is *m/f* buttock.

clūrīnus *adj* of apes.

Clūsīnus *adj see n.*

Clūsium, -ī *nt* old Etruscan town (*now Chiusi*).

Clūsius, -ī *m* Janus.

Clytaemnēstra, -ae *f* wife of Agamemnon (*whom she murdered*).

Cnidius *adj see n.*

Cnidus, -ī *f* town in Caria (*famous for worship of Venus*).

coacervātiō, -ōnis *f* accumulation.

coacervō, -āre *vt* to heap, accumulate.

coacēscō, -ēscere, -uī *vi* to become sour.

coāctō, -āre *vt* to force.

coāctor, -ōris *m* collector (of money).

coāctōrēs agminis rearguard.

coāctum, -ī *nt* thick coverlet.

coāctus *adj* forced.

coāctus *ppp of* **cōgō**.

coāctus, -ūs *m* compulsion.

coaedificō, -āre, -ātum *vt* to build on.

coaequō, -āre, -āvī, -ātum *vt* to make equal, bring down to the same level.

coagmentātiō, -ōnis *f* combination.

coagmentō, -āre, -āvī, -ātum *vt* to glue, join together.

coagmentum, -ī *nt* joining, joint.

coāgulum, -ī *nt* rennet.

coalēscō, -ēscere, -uī, -itum *vi* to grow together; (*fig*) to agree together; to flourish.

coangustō, -āre *vt* to restrict.

coarct- *etc see* **coart-**.

coarguō, -ere, -ī *vt* to convict, prove conclusively.

coartātiō, -ōnis *f* crowding together.

coartō, -āre, -āvī, -ātum *vt* to compress, abridge.

coccineus, coccinus *adj* scarlet.

coccum, -ī *nt* scarlet.

cochlea, coclea, -ae *f* snail.

cocleāre, -is *nt* spoon.

cocles, -itis *m* man blind in one eye; *surname of Horatius who defended the bridge.*

coctilis *adj* baked; of bricks.

coctus *ppp of* **coquō** ♦ *adj* (*fig*) well considered.

cocus *etc see* **coquus**.

Cōcȳtius *adj see n.*

Cōcȳtos, -us, -ī *m* river in the lower world.

cōda *etc see* **cauda**.

cōdex *etc see* **caudex**.

cōdicillī, -ōrum *mpl* letter, note, petition; codicil.

Codrus, -ī *m* last king of Athens.

coēgī *perf of* **cōgō**.

coel- *etc see* **cael-**.

coemō, -emere, -ēmī, -emptum *vt* to buy up.

coemptiō, -ōnis *f* a form of Roman marriage; mock sale of an estate.

coemptiōnālis *adj* used in a mock sale; worthless.

coen- *etc see* **caen-** *or* **cēn-**.

coeō, -īre, -īvī *and* **iī, -itum** *vi* to meet, assemble; to encounter; to combine, mate; (*wounds*) to close; to agree, conspire ♦ *vt*: ~ **societātem** make a compact.

coepiō, -ere, -ī, -tum *vt, vi* begin (*esp in perf tenses*); **rēs agī ~tae sunt** things began to be done; **coepisse** to have begun.

coeptō, -āre, -āvī, -ātum *vt, vi* to begin, attempt.

coeptum, -ī *nt* beginning, undertaking.

coeptus *ppp of* **coepiō**.

coeptus, -ūs *m* beginning.

coepulōnus, -ī *m* fellow-banqueter.

coerātor *etc see* **cūrātor**.

coerceō, -ēre, -uī, -itum *vt* to enclose; to confine, repress; (*fig*) to control, check, correct.

coercitiō, -ōnis *f* coercion, punishment.

coetus, coitus, -ūs *m* meeting, joining together; assembly, crowd.

cōgitātē *adv* deliberately.

cōgitātiō, -ōnis *f* thought, reflection; idea, plan; faculty of thought, imagination.

cōgitātus *adj* deliberate ♦ *ntpl* ideas.

cōgitō, -āre, -āvī, -ātum *vt, vi* to think, ponder, imagine; to feel disposed; to plan, intend.

cognātiō, -ōnis *f* relationship (by blood); kin, family; (*fig*) affinity, resemblance.

cognātus, -ī *m*, **-a, -ae** *f* relation ♦ *adj* related; (*fig*) connected, similar.

cognitiō, -ōnis *f* acquiring of knowledge, knowledge; idea, notion; (*law*) judicial inquiry; (*comedy*) recognition.

cognitor, -ōris *m* (*law*) attorney; witness of a person's identity; (*fig*) defender.

cognitus *adj* acknowledged.

cognitus *ppp of* **cognōscō**.

cognōmen, -inis *nt* surname; name.

cognōmentum, -ī *nt* surname, name.

cognōminis *adj* with the same name.
cognōminō, -āre, -āvī, -ātum *vt* to give a surname to; **verba ~āta** synonyms.
cognōscō, -ōscere, -ōvī, -itum *vt* to get to know, learn, understand; to know, recognize, identify; (*law*) to investigate; (*MIL*) to reconnoitre.
cōgō, -ere, coēgī, coāctum *vt* to collect, gather together; (*liquids*) to thicken, curdle; to contract, confine; to compel, force; to infer; **agmen ~** bring up the rear; **senātum ~** call a meeting of the senate.
cohaerentia, -ae *f* coherence.
cohaereō, -rēre, -sī, -sum *vi* to stick together, cohere; to cling to; (*fig*) to be consistent, harmonize; to agree, be consistent with.
cohaerēscō, -ere *vi* to stick together.
cohaesus *ppp of* **cohaereō**.
cohērēs, -ēdis *m/f* co-heir.
cohibeō, -ēre, -uī, -itum *vt* to hold together, encircle; to hinder, stop; (*fig*) to restrain, repress.
cohonestō, -āre *vt* to do honour to.
cohorrēscō, -ēscere, -uī *vi* to shudder all over.
cohors, -tis *f* courtyard; (*MIL*) cohort (*about 600 men*); retinue (*esp of the praetor in a province*); (*fig*) company.
cohortātiō, -ōnis *f* encouragement.
cohorticula, -ae *f* small cohort.
cohortor, -ārī, -ātus *vt* to encourage, urge.
coitiō, -ōnis *f* encounter; conspiracy.
coitus *etc see* **coetus**.
colaphus, -ī *m* blow with the fist, box.
Colchis, -idis *f* Medea's country (*at the E. end of the Black Sea*).
Colchis, -us, -icus *adj* Colchian.
cōleus *etc see* **culleus**.
cōlis *etc see* **caulis**.
collabāscō, -ere *vi* to waver also.
collabefactō, -āre *vt* to shake violently.
collabefīō, -fierī, -factus *vi* to be destroyed.
collābor, -bī, -psus *vi* to fall in ruin, collapse.
collacerātus *adj* torn to pieces.
collacrimātiō, -ōnis *f* weeping.
collactea, -ae *f* foster-sister.
collāpsus *ppa of* **collābor**.
collāre, -is *nt* neckband.
Collātia, -iae *f* ancient town near Rome ♦ *m* husband of Lucretia.
Collātīnus *adj* of Collatia.
collātiō, -ōnis *f* bringing together, combination; (*money*) contribution; (*RHET*) comparison; (*PHILOS*) analogy.
collātor, -ōris *m* contributor.
collātus *ppp of* **cōnferō**.
collaudātiō, -ōnis *f* praise.
collaudō, -āre, -āvī, -ātum *vt* to praise highly.

collaxō, -āre *vt* to make porous.
collēcta, -ae *f* money contribution.
collēctīcius *adj* hastily gathered.
collēctiō, -ōnis *f* gathering up; (*RHET*) recapitulation.
collēctus *ppp of* **colligō**.
collēctus, -ūs *m* accumulation.
collēga, -ae *m* colleague; associate.
collēgī *perf of* **colligō**.
collēgium, -ī *and* **iī** *nt* association in office; college, guild (*of magistrates, etc*).
collībertus, -ī *m* fellow freedman.
collibet, collubet, -uit *and* **itum est** *vi* it pleases.
collīdō, -dere, -sī, -sum *vt* to beat together, strike, bruise; (*fig*) to bring into conflict.
colligātiō, -ōnis *f* connection.
colligō, -āre, -āvī, -ātum *vt* to fasten, tie up; (*fig*) to combine; to restrain, check.
colligō, -igere, -ēgī, -ēctum *vt* to gather, collect; to compress, draw together; to check; (*fig*) to acquire; to think about; to infer, conclude; **animum, mentem ~** recover, rally; **sē ~** crouch; recover one's courage; **vāsa ~** (*MIL*) pack up.
Collīna Porta gate in N.E. of Rome.
collīneō, -āre *vt, vi* to aim straight.
collinō, -inere, -ēvī, -itum *vt* to besmear; (*fig*) to deface.
colliquefactus *adj* dissolved.
collis, -is *m* hill, slope.
collīsi *perf of* **collīdō**.
collīsus *ppp of* **collīdō**.
collitus *ppp of* **collinō**.
collocātiō, -ōnis *f* arrangement; giving in marriage.
collocō, -āre, -āvī, -ātum *vt* to place, station, arrange; to give in marriage; (*money*) to invest; (*fig*) to establish; to occupy, employ.
collocuplētō, -āre, -āvī *vt* to enrich.
collocūtiō, -ōnis *f* conversation.
colloquium, -ī *and* **iī** *nt* conversation, conference.
colloquor, -quī, -cūtus *vi* to converse, hold a conference ♦ *vt* to talk to.
collubet *etc see* **collibet**.
collūceō, -ēre *vi* to shine brightly; (*fig*) to be resplendent.
collūdō, -dere, -sī, -sum *vi* to play together *or* with; to practise collusion.
collum, -ī *nt* neck; **~ torquēre, obtorquēre, obstringere** arrest.
colluō, -uere, -uī, -ūtum *vt* to rinse, moisten.
collus *etc see* **collum**.
collūsiō, -ōnis *f* secret understanding.
collūsor, -ōris *m* playmate, fellow gambler.
collūstrō, -āre, -āvī, -ātum *vt* to light up; to survey.
colluviō, -ōnis, -ēs, -em, -ē *f* sweepings, filth; (*fig*) dregs, rabble.

Noun declensions and verb conjugations are shown on pp xiii to xxv. The present infinitive ending of a verb shows to which conjugation it belongs: **-āre** = 1st; **-ēre** = 2nd; **-ere** = 3rd and **-īre** = 4th. Irregular verbs are shown on p xxvi

collybus, -ī *m* money exchange, rate of exchange.

collȳra, -ae *f* vermicelli.

collȳricus *adj see n.*

collȳrium, -ī *and* **iī** *nt* eye lotion.

colō, -ere, -uī, cultum *vt* (*AGR*) to cultivate, work; (*place*) to live in; (*human affairs*) to cherish, protect, adorn; (*qualities, pursuits*) to cultivate, practise; (*gods*) to worship; (*men*) to honour, court; **vītam ~** live.

colocāsia, -ae *f*, **-a, -ōrum** *ntpl* Egyptian bean, caladium.

colōna, -ae *f* country-woman.

colōnia, -ae *f* settlement, colony; settlers.

colōnicus *adj* colonial.

colōnus, -ī *m* crofter, farmer; settler, colonist.

color (colōs), -ōris *m* colour; complexion; beauty, lustre; (*fig*) outward show; (*RHET*) style, tone; colourful excuse; **~ōrem mūtāre** blush, go pale; **homō nullīus ~ōris** an unknown person.

colōrātus *adj* healthily tanned.

colōrō, -āre, -āvī, -ātum *vt* to colour, tan; (*fig*) to give a colour to.

colossus, -ī *m* gigantic statue (*esp that of Apollo at Rhodes*).

colostra, colustra, -ae *f* beestings.

coluber, -rī *m* snake.

colubra, -ae *f* snake.

colubrifer, -ī *adj* snaky.

colubrīnus *adj* wily.

coluī *perf of* **colō.**

cōlum, -ī *nt* strainer.

columba, -ae *f* dove, pigeon.

columbar, -āris *nt* kind of collar.

columbārium, -ī *and* **iī** *nt* dovecote.

columbīnus *adj* pigeon's ♦ *m* little pigeon.

columbus, -ī *m* dove, cock-pigeon.

columella, -ae *f* small pillar.

columen, -inis *nt* height, summit; pillar; (*fig*) chief; prop.

columna, -ae *f* column, pillar; *a pillory in the Forum Romanum*; waterspout.

columnārium, -ī *and* **iī** *nt* pillar tax.

columnārius, -ī *m* criminal.

columnātus *adj* pillared.

colurnus *adj* made of hazel.

colus, -ī *and* **ūs** *f* (*occ m*) distaff.

cōlȳphia, -ōrum *ntpl* food of athletes.

coma, -ae *f* hair (*of the head*); foliage.

comāns, -antis *adj* hairy, plumed; leafy.

cōmarchus, -ī *m* burgomaster.

comātus *adj* long-haired; leafy; **Gallia ~** Transalpine Gaul.

combibō, -ere, -ī *vt* to drink to the full, absorb.

combibō, -ōnis *m* fellow-drinker.

combūrō, -rere, -ssī, -stum *vt* to burn up; (*fig*) to ruin.

combūstus *ppp of* **combūrō.**

comedō, -ēsse, -ēdī, -ēsum *and* **-ēstum** *vt* to eat up, devour; (*fig*) to waste, squander; **sē ~**

pine away.

Cōmēnsis *adj see* **Cōmum.**

comes, -itis *m/f* companion, partner; attendant, follower; one of a magistrate's *or* emperor's retinue; (*medieval title*) count.

comēs, comēst *pres tense of* **comedō.**

comēstus, comēsus *ppp of* **comedō.**

comētēs, -ae *m* comet.

cōmicē *adv* in the manner of comedy.

cōmicus, -ī *m* comedy actor, comedy writer ♦ *adj* of comedy, comic.

cōmis *adj* courteous, friendly.

cōmissābundus *adj* carousing.

cōmissātiō, -ōnis *f* Bacchanalian revel.

cōmissātor, -ōris *m* reveller.

cōmissor, -ārī, -ātus *vi* to carouse, make merry.

cōmitās, -ātis *f* kindness, affability.

comitātus, -ūs *m* escort, retinue; company.

cōmiter *adv see* **cōmis.**

comitia, -iōrum *ntpl* assembly for the election of magistrates and other business (*esp the ~* **centuriāta**); elections.

comitiālis *adj* of the elections; **~ morbus** epilepsy.

comitiātus, -ūs *m* assembly at the elections.

comitium, -ī *and* **iī** *nt* place of assembly.

comitō, -āre, -āvī, -ātum *vt* to accompany.

comitor, -ārī, -ātus *vt, vi* to attend, follow.

commaculō, -āre, -āvī, -ātum *vt* to stain, defile.

commanipulāris, -is *m* soldier in the same company.

commeātus, -ūs *m* passage; leave, furlough; convoy (of troops *or* goods); (*MIL*) lines of communication, provisions, supplies.

commeditor, -ārī *vt* to practise.

commeminī, -isse *vt, vi* to remember perfectly.

commemorābilis *adj* memorable.

commemorātiō, -ōnis *f* recollection, recounting.

commemorō, -āre, -āvī, -ātum *vt* to recall, remind; to mention, relate.

commendābilis *adj* praiseworthy.

commendātīcius *adj* of recommendation *or* introduction.

commendātiō, -ōnis *f* recommendation; worth, excellence.

commendātor, -ōris *m* commender (*male*).

commendātrīx, -rīcis *f* commender (*female*).

commendātus *adj* approved, valued.

commendō, -āre, -āvī, -ātum *vt* to entrust, commit, commend (to one's care *or* charge); to recommend, set off to advantage.

commēnsus *ppa of* **commētior.**

commentāriolum, -ī *nt* short treatise.

commentārius, -ī *and* **iī** *m*, **-ium, -ī** *and* **iī** *nt* notebook; commentary, memoir; (*law*) brief.

commentātiō, -ōnis *f* studying, meditation.

commentīcius *adj* fictitious, imaginary; false.

commentor, -ārī, -ātus *vt, vi* to study, think

over, prepare carefully; to invent, compose, write.

commentor, -ōris *m* inventor.

commentum, -ī *nt* invention, fiction; contrivance.

commentus *ppa of* **comminīscor ♦** *adj* feigned, fictitious.

commeō, -āre *vi* to pass to and fro; to go *or* come often.

commercium, -ī *and* **iī** *nt* trade, commerce; right to trade; dealings, communication.

commercor, -ārī, -ātus *vt* to buy up.

commereō, -ēre, -uī, -itum; -eor, -ērī, -itus *vt* to deserve; to be guilty of.

commētior, -tīrī, -nsus *vt* to measure.

commētō, -āre *vi* to go often.

commictus *ppp of* **commingō**.

commigrō, -āre, -āvī, -ātum *vi* to remove, migrate.

commīlitium, -ī *and* **iī** *nt* service together.

commīlitō, -ōnis *m* fellow soldier.

comminātiō, -ōnis *f* threat.

commingō, -ingere, -īnxī, -īctum *vt* to pollute.

comminīscor, -ī, commentus *vt* to devise, contrive.

comminor, -ārī, -ātus *vt* to threaten.

comminuō, -uere, -uī, -ūtum *vt* to break up, smash; to diminish; to impair.

comminus *adv* hand to hand; near at hand.

commīsceō, -scēre, -scuī, -xtum *vt* to mix together, join together.

commiserātiō, -ōnis *f* (*RHET*) *passage intended to arouse pity.*

commiserēscō, -ere *vt* to pity.

commiseror, -ārī *vt* to bewail **♦** *vi* (*RHET*) to try to excite pity.

commissiō, -ōnis *f* start (*of a contest*).

commissum, -ī *nt* enterprise; offence, crime; secret.

commissūra, -ae *f* joint, connection.

commissus *ppp of* **committō**.

committō, -ittere, -īsī, -issum *vt* to join, connect, bring together; to begin, undertake; (*battle*) to join, engage in; (*offence*) to commit, be guilty of; (*punishment*) to incur, forfeit; to entrust, trust; **sē urbī ~** venture into the city.

commīxtus *ppp of* **commisceō**.

commodē *adv* properly, well; aptly, opportunely; pleasantly.

commoditās, -ātis *f* convenience, ease, fitness; advantage; (*person*) kindliness; (*RHET*) apt expression.

commodō, -āre, -āvī, -ātum *vt* to adjust, adapt; to give, lend, oblige with; (*with dat*) to oblige.

commodulē, -um *adv* conveniently.

commodum, -ī *nt* convenience; advantage, interest; pay, salary; loan; **~ō tuō** at your

leisure; **~a vītae** the good things of life.

commodum *adv* opportunely; just.

commodus *adj* proper, fit, full; suitable, easy, opportune; (*person*) pleasant, obliging.

commōlior, -īrī *vt* to set in motion.

commonefaciō, -facere, -fēcī, -factum *vt* to remind, recall.

commoneō, -ēre, -uī, -itum *vt* to remind, impress upon.

commōnstrō, -āre *vt* to point out.

commorātiō, -ōnis *f* delay, residence; (*RHET*) dwelling (on a topic).

commoror, -ārī, -ātus *vi* to sojourn, wait; (*RHET*) to dwell **♦** *vt* to detain.

commōtiō, -ōnis *f* excitement.

commōtiuncula *f* slight indisposition.

commōtus *ppp of* **commoveō ♦** *adj* excited, emotional.

commoveō, -ovēre, -ōvī, -ōtum *vt* to set in motion, move, dislodge, agitate; (*mind*) to unsettle, shake, excite, move, affect; (*emotions*) to stir up, provoke.

commūne, -is *nt* common property; state; **in ~e** for a common end; equally; in general.

commūnicātiō, -ōnis *f* imparting; (*RHET*) *making the audience appear to take part in the discussion.*

commūnicō, -āre, -āvī, -ātum *vt* to share (by giving *or* receiving); to impart, communicate; **cōnsilia ~ cum** make common cause with.

commūniō, -īre, -īvī *and* **iī, -ītum** *vt* to build (a fortification); to fortify, strengthen.

commūniō, -ōnis *f* sharing in common, communion.

commūnis *adj* common, general, universal; (*person*) affable, democratic; **~ia loca** public places; **~ēs locī** general topics; **~is sēnsus** popular sentiment; **aliquid ~e habēre** have something in common.

commūnitās, -ātis *f* fellowship; sense of fellowship; affability.

commūniter *adv* in common, jointly.

commūnītiō, -ōnis *f* preparing the way.

commurmuror, -ārī, -ātus *vi* to mutter to oneself.

commūtābilis *adj* changeable.

commūtātiō, -iōnis *f* change.

commūtātus, -ūs *m* change.

commūtō, -āre, -āvī, -ātum *vt* to change, exchange, interchange.

cōmō, -ere, -psī, -ptum *vt* to arrange, dress, adorn.

cōmoedia, -ae *f* comedy.

cōmoedicē *adv* as in comedy.

cōmoedus, -ī *m* comic actor.

comōsus *adj* shaggy.

compāctiō, -ōnis *f* joining together.

compāctus *ppp of* **compingō**.

compāgēs, -is, -ō, -inis *f* joint, structure,

framework.

compār, -aris *m/f* comrade, husband, wife ♦ *adj* equal.

comparābilis *adj* comparable.

comparātē *adv* by bringing in a comparison.

comparātiō, -ōnis *f* comparison; (*ASTRO*) relative positions; agreement; preparation, procuring.

comparātīvus *adj* based on comparison.

compāreō, -ēre *vi* to be visible; to be present, be realised.

comparō, -āre, -āvī, -ātum *vt* to couple together, match; to compare; (*POL*) to agree (about respective duties); to prepare, provide; (*custom*) to establish; to procure, purchase, get.

compāscō, -ere *vt* to put (cattle) to graze in common.

compāscuus *adj* for common pasture.

compecīscor, -īscī, -tus *vi* to come to an agreement.

compectum, -tī *nt* agreement.

compediō, -īre, -ītum *vt* to fetter.

compēgī *perf of* **compingō**.

compellātiō, -ōnis *f* reprimand.

compellō, -āre, -āvī, -ātum *vt* to call, address; to reproach; (*law*) to arraign.

compellō, -ellere, -ulī, -ulsum *vt* to drive, bring together, concentrate; to impel, compel.

compendiārius *adj* short.

compendium, -ī *and* **iī** *nt* saving; abbreviating; short cut; **~ī facere** save; abridge; **~ī fierī** be brief.

compēnsātiō, -ōnis *f* (*fig*) compromise.

compēnsō, -āre, -āvī, -ātum *vt* to balance (against), make up for.

compercō, -cere, -sī *vt, vi* to save; to refrain.

comperendinātiō, -iōnis *f* adjournment for two days.

comperendinātus, -ūs *m* adjournment for two days.

comperendinō, -āre *vt* to adjourn for two days.

comperiō, -īre, -ī, -tum (*occ* **-ior**) *vt* to find out, learn; **~tus** detected; found guilty; **~tum habēre** know for certain.

compēs, -edis *f* fetter, bond.

compēscō, -ere, -uī *vt* to check, suppress.

competītor, -ōris *m*, **-rīx, -rīcis** *f* rival candidate.

competō, -ere, -īvī *and* **iī, -ītum** *vi* to coincide, agree; to be capable.

compīlātiō, -ōnis *f* plundering; compilation.

compīlō, -āre, -āvī, -ātum *vt* to pillage.

compingō, -ingere, -ēgī, -āctum *vt* to put together, compose; to lock up, hide away.

compitālia, -ium *and* **iōrum** *ntpl festival in honour of the Lares Compitales.*

compitālicius *adj* of the Compitalia.

compitālis *adj* of crossroads.

compitum, -ī *nt* crossroads.

complaceō, -ēre, -uī *and* **itus sum** *vi* to

please (someone else) as well, please very much.

complānō, -āre *vt* to level, raze to the ground.

complector, -ctī, -xus *vt* to embrace, clasp; to enclose; (*speech, writing*) to deal with, comprise; (*mind*) to grasp, comprehend; to honour, be fond of.

complēmentum, -ī *nt* complement.

compleō, -ēre, -ēvī, -ētum *vt* to fill, fill up; (*MIL*) to man, make up the complement of; (*time, promise, duty*) to complete, fulfil, finish.

complētus *adj* perfect.

complexiō, -ōnis *f* combination; (*RHET*) period; (*logic*) conclusion of an argument; dilemma.

complexus, -ūs *m* embrace; (*fig*) affection, close combat; (*speech*) connection.

complicō, -āre *vt* to fold up.

complōrātiō, -iōnis *f*, **-us, -ūs** *m* loud lamentation.

complōrō, -āre, -āvī, -ātum *vt* to mourn for.

complūrēs, -ium *adj* several, very many.

complūriēns *adv* several times.

complūsculī, -ōrum *adj* quite a few.

compluvium, -ī *and* **iī** *nt roof opening in a Roman house.*

compōnō, -ōnere, -osuī, -ositum *vt* to put together, join; to compose, construct; to compare, contrast; to match, oppose; to put away, store up, stow; (*dead*) to lay out, inter; to allay, quieten, reconcile; to adjust, settle, arrange; to devise, prepare ♦ *vi* to make peace.

comportō, -āre *vt* to collect, bring in.

compos, -tis *adj* in control, in possession; sharing; **vōtī ~** having got one's wish.

compositē *adv* properly, in a polished manner.

compositiō, -ōnis *f* compounding, system; (*words*) arrangement; reconciliation; matching (of fighters).

compositor, -ōris *m* arranger.

compositūra, -ae *f* connection.

compositus *ppp of* **compōnō** ♦ *adj* orderly, regular; adapted, assumed, ready; calm, sedate; (*words*) compound; **compositō, ex compositō** as agreed.

compōtātiō, -ōnis *f* drinking party.

compotiō, -īre *vt* to put in possession (of).

compōtor, -ōris *m*, **-rīx, -rīcis** *f* fellow drinker.

comprānsor, -ōris *m* fellow guest.

comprecātiō, -ōnis *f* public supplication.

comprecor, -ārī, -ātus *vt, vi* to pray to; to pray for.

comprehendō (comprendō), -endere, -endī, -ēnsum *vt* to grasp, catch; to seize, arrest, catch in the act; (*words*) to comprise, recount; (*thought*) to grasp, comprehend; to hold in affection; **numerō ~** count.

comprehēnsibilis *adj* conceivable.

comprehēnsiō, -ōnis *f* grasping, seizing;

perception, idea; (*RHET*) period.
comprehēnsus, comprēnsus *ppp of*
comprehendō.
comprendō *etc see* **comprehendō**.
compressī *perf of* **comprimō**.
compressiō, -ōnis *f* embrace; (*RHET*)
compression.
compressus *ppp of* **comprimō**.
compressus, -ūs *m* compression, embrace.
comprimō, -imere, -essī, -essum *vt* to
squeeze, compress; to check, restrain; to
suppress, withhold; **animam** ~ hold one's
breath; **~essīs manibus** with hands folded,
idle.
comprobātiō, -ōnis *f* approval.
comprobātor, -ōris *m* supporter.
comprobō, -āre, -āvī, -ātum *vt* to prove,
make good; to approve.
comprōmissum, -ī *nt* mutual agreement to
abide by an arbitrator's decision.
comprōmittō, -ittere, -īsī, -issum *vt* to
undertake to abide by an arbitrator's
decision.
cōmpsī *perf of* **cōmō**.
cōmptus *ppp of* **cōmō** ♦ *adj* elegant.
cōmptus, -ūs *m* coiffure; union.
compulī *perf of* **compellō**.
compulsus *ppp of* **compellō**.
compungō, -ungere, -ūnxī, -ūnctum *vt* to
prick, sting, tattoo.
computō, -āre, -āvī, -ātum *vt* to reckon,
number.
Cōmum, -ī *nt* (*also* **Novum Cōmum**) town in N.
Italy (*now* Como).
cōnāmen, -inis *nt* effort; support.
cōnāta, -ōrum *ntpl* undertaking, venture.
cōnātus, -ūs *m* effort; endeavour; inclination,
impulse.
concaedēs, -ium *fpl* barricade of felled trees.
concalefaciō, -facere, -fēcī, -factum *vt* to
warm well.
concaleō, -ēre *vi* to be hot.
concalēscō, -ēscere, -uī *vi* to become hot,
glow.
concallēscō, -ēscere, -uī *vi* to become
shrewd; to become unfeeling.
concastīgō, -āre *vt* to punish severely.
concavō, -āre *vt* to curve.
concavus *adj* hollow; vaulted, bent.
concēdō, -ēdere, -essī, -essum *vi* to
withdraw, depart; to disappear, pass away,
pass; to yield, submit, give precedence,
comply ♦ *vt* to give up, cede; to grant, allow;
to pardon, overlook.
concelebrō, -āre, -āvī, -ātum *vt* to frequent,
fill, enliven; (*study*) to pursue eagerly; to
celebrate; to make known.
concēnātiō, -ōnis *f* dining together.
concentiō, -ōnis *f* chorus.
concenturiō, -āre *vt* to marshal.

concentus, -ūs *m* chorus, concert; (*fig*)
concord, harmony.
conceptiō, -ōnis *f* conception; drawing up
legal formulae.
conceptīvus *adj* (*holidays*) movable.
conceptus *ppp of* **concipiō**.
conceptus, -ūs *m* conception.
concerpō, -ere, -sī, -tum *vt* to tear up; (*fig*) to
abuse.
concertātiō, -ōnis *f* controversy.
concertātor, -ōris *m* rival.
concertātōrius *adj* controversial.
concertō, -āre, -āvī, -ātum *vi* to fight; to
dispute.
concessiō, -ōnis *f* grant, permission; (*law*)
pleading guilty and asking indulgence.
concessō, -āre *vi* to stop, loiter.
concessus *ppp of* **concēdō**.
concessus, -ūs *m* permission.
concha, -ae *f* mussel, oyster, murex; mussel
shell, oyster shell, pearl; purple dye;
trumpet, perfume dish.
conchis, -is *f* kind of bean.
conchīta, -ae *m* catcher of shellfish.
conchȳliātus *adj* purple.
conchȳlium, -ī *and* **iī** *nt* shellfish, oyster,
murex; purple.
concidō, -ere, -ī *vi* to fall, collapse; to subside,
fail, perish.
concīdō, -dere, -dī, -sum *vt* to cut up, cut to
pieces, kill; (*fig*) to ruin, strike down; (*RHET*)
to dismember, enfeeble.
**concieō, -iēre, -īvī, -itum; conciō, -īre,
-ītum** *vt* to rouse, assemble; to stir up,
shake; (*fig*) to rouse, provoke.
conciliābulum, -ī *nt* place for public
gatherings.
conciliātiō, -ōnis *f* union; winning over
(*friends, hearers*); (*PHILOS*) inclination.
conciliātor, -ōris *m* promoter.
conciliātrix, -īcis *m*, **-īcula, -ae** *f* promoter,
matchmaker.
conciliātus, -ūs *m* combination.
conciliātus *adj* beloved; favourable.
conciliō, -āre, -āvī, -ātum *vt* to unite; to win
over, reconcile; to procure, purchase, bring
about, promote.
concilium, -ī *and* **iī** *nt* gathering, meeting;
council; (*things*) union.
concinnē *adv see* **concinnus**.
concinnitās, -ātis, -ūdō, -ūdinis *f* (*RHET*)
rhythmical style.
concinnō, -āre, -āvī, -ātum *vt* to arrange; to
bring about, produce; (*with adj*) to make.
concinnus *adj* symmetrical, beautiful; (*style*)
polished, rhythmical; (*person*) elegant,
courteous; (*things*) suited, pleasing.
concinō, -ere, -uī *vi* to sing, play, sound
together; (*fig*) to agree, harmonize ♦ *vt* to
sing about, celebrate, prophesy.

Noun declensions and verb conjugations are shown on pp xiii to xxv. The present infinitive ending of a verb shows
to which conjugation it belongs: **-āre** = 1st; **-ēre** = 2nd; **-ere** = 3rd and **-īre** = 4th. Irregular verbs are shown on p xxvi

concio *etc see* **concieō.**
concio- *etc see* **contio-.**
concipiō, -ipere, -ēpī, -eptum *vt* to take to oneself, absorb; (*women*) to conceive; (*senses*) to perceive; (*mind*) to conceive, imagine, understand; (*feelings, acts*) to harbour, foster, commit; (*words*) to draw up, intimate formally.
concīsiō, -ōnis *f* breaking up into short clauses.
concīsus *ppp of* **concīdō ♦** *adj* broken up, concise.
concitātē *adv see* **concitātus.**
concitātiō, -ōnis *f* acceleration; (*mind*) excitement, passion; riot.
concitātor, -ōris *m* agitator.
concitātus *ppp of* **concitō ♦** *adj* fast; excited.
concitō, -āre, -āvī, -ātum *vt* to move rapidly, bestir, hurl; to urge, rouse, impel; to stir up, occasion.
concitor, -ōris *m* instigator.
concitus, concītus *ppp of* **concieō;** *ppp of* **conciō.**
conclāmātiō, -ōnis *f* great shout.
conclāmitō, -āre *vi* to keep on shouting.
conclāmō, -āre, -āvī, -ātum *vt, vi* to shout, cry out; to call to help; (*MIL*) to give the signal; (*dead*) to call by name in mourning; **vāsa ~** give the order to pack up; **~ātum est** it's all over.
conclāve, -is *nt* room.
conclūdō, -dere, -sī, -sum *vt* to shut up, enclose; to include, comprise; to end, conclude, round off (*esp with a rhythmical cadence*); (*PHILOS*) to infer, demonstrate.
conclūsē *adv* with rhythmical cadences.
conclūsiō, -ōnis *f* (*MIL*) blockade; end, conclusion; (*RHET*) period, peroration; (*logic*) conclusion.
conclūsiuncula, -ae *f* quibble.
conclūsum, -ī *nt* logical conclusion.
conclūsus *ppp of* **conclūdō.**
concoctus *ppp of* **concoquō.**
concolor, -ōris *adj* of the same colour.
concomitātus *adj* escorted.
concoquō, -quere, -xī, -ctum *vt* to boil down; to digest; (*fig*) to put up with, stomach; (*thought*) to consider well, concoct.
concordia, -ae *f* friendship, concord, union; *goddess of Concord.*
concorditer *adv* amicably.
concordō, -āre *vi* to agree, be in harmony.
concors, -dis *adj* concordant, united, harmonious.
concrēbrēscō, -ēscere, -uī *vi* to gather strength.
concrēdō, -ere, -idī, -itum *vt* to entrust.
concremō, -āre, -āvī, -ātum *vt* to burn.
concrepō, -āre, -uī, -ātum *vi* to rattle, creak, clash, snap (fingers) **♦** *vt* to beat.
concrēscō, -scere, -vī, -tum *vi* to harden, curdle, congeal, clot; to grow, take shape.
concrētiō, -ōnis *f* condensing; matter.

concrētum, -ī *nt* solid matter, hard frost.
concrētus *ppa of* **concrēscō ♦** *adj* hard, thick, stiff, congealed; compounded.
concrīminor, -ārī, -ātus *vi* to bring a complaint.
concruciō, -āre *vt* to torture.
concubīna, -ae *f* (female) concubine.
concubīnātus, -ūs *m* concubinage.
concubīnus, -ī *m* (male) concubine.
concubitus, -ūs *m* reclining together (at table); sexual union.
concubius *adj:* **~iā nocte** during the first sleep **♦** *nt* the time of the first sleep.
conculcō, -āre *vt* to trample under foot, treat with contempt.
concumbō, -mbere, -buī, -bitum *vi* to lie together, lie with.
concupīscō, -īscere, -īvī, -ītum *vt* to covet, long for, aspire to.
concūrō, -āre *vt* to take care of.
concurrō, -rere, -rī, -sum *vi* to flock together, rush in; (*things*) to clash, meet; (*MIL*) to join battle, charge; (*events*) to happen at the same time, concur.
concursātiō, -ōnis *f* running together, rushing about; (*MIL*) skirmishing; (*dreams*) coherent design.
concursātor, -ōris *m* skirmisher.
concursiō, -ōnis *f* meeting, concourse; (*RHET*) repetition for emphasis.
concursō, -āre *vi* to collide; to rush about, travel about; (*MIL*) to skirmish **♦** *vt* to visit, go from place to place.
concursus, -ūs *m* concourse, gathering, collision; uproar; (*fig*) combination; (*MIL*) assault, charge.
concussī *perf of* **concutiō.**
concussus *ppp of* **concutiō.**
concussus, -ūs *m* shaking.
concutiō, -tere, -ssī, -ssum *vt* to strike, shake, shatter; (*weapons*) to hurl; (*power*) to disturb, impair; (*person*) to agitate, alarm; (*self*) to search, examine; to rouse.
condalium, -ī *and* **iī** *nt* slave's ring.
condecet, -ēre *vt impers* it becomes.
condecorō, -āre *vt* to enhance.
condemnātor, -ōris *m* accuser.
condemnō, -āre, -āvī, -ātum *vt* to condemn, sentence; to urge the conviction of; to blame, censure; **ambitūs ~** convict of bribery; **capitis ~** condemn to death; **vōtī ~ātus** obliged to fulfil a vow.
condēnsō, -āre, -eō, -ēre *vt* to compress, move close together.
condēnsus *adj* very dense, close, thick.
condiciō, -ōnis *f* arrangement, condition, terms; marriage contract, match; situation, position, circumstances; manner, mode; **eā ~ōne ut** on condition that; **sub ~ōne** conditionally; **hīs ~ōnibus** on these terms; **vītae ~** way of life.
condīcō, -īcere, -īxī, -ictum *vt, vi* to talk over, agree upon, promise; **ad cēnam ~** have a

dinner engagement.
condidī *perf of* **condō.**
condignē *adv see* **condignus.**
condignus *adj* very worthy.
condīmentum, -ī *nt* spice, seasoning.
condiō, -īre, -īvī, -ītum *vt* to pickle, preserve, embalm; to season; (*fig*) to give zest to, temper.
condiscipulus, -ī *m* school-fellow.
condiscō, -scere, -dicī *vt* to learn thoroughly, learn by heart.
conditiō *etc see* **condiciō.**
condītiō, -ōnis *f* preserving, seasoning.
conditor, -ōris *m* founder, author, composer.
conditōrium, -ī *and* **iī** *nt* coffin, urn, tomb.
condītus *adj* savoury; (*fig*) polished.
conditus *ppp of* **condō.**
condītus *ppp of* **condiō.**
condō, -ere, -idī, -itum *vt* **1.** (*build, found: arts*) to make, compose, write; (: *institutions*) to establish **2.** (*put away for keeping, store up: fruit*) to preserve; (: *person*) to imprison; (: *dead*) to bury; (: *memory*) to lay up; (: *time*) to pass, bring to a close **3.** (*put out of sight, conceal: eyes*) to close; (: *sword*) to sheathe, plunge; (: *troops*) to place in ambush.
condocefaciō, -ere *vt* to train.
condoceō, -ēre, -uī, -tum *vt* to train.
condolēscō, -ēscere, -uī *vi* to begin to ache, feel very sore.
condōnātiō, -ōnis *f* giving away.
condōnō, -āre, -āvī, -ātum *vt* to give, present, deliver up; (*debt*) to remit; (*offence*) to pardon, let off.
condormīscō, -īscere, -īvī *vi* to fall fast asleep.
condūcibilis *adj* expedient.
condūcō, -ūcere, -ūxī, -uctum *vt* to bring together, assemble, connect; to hire, rent, borrow; (*public work*) to undertake, get the contract for; (*taxes*) to farm ♦ *vi* to be of use, profit.
conductī, -ōrum *mpl* hirelings, mercenaries.
conductīcius *adj* hired.
conductiō, -ōnis *f* hiring, farming.
conductor, -ōris *m* hirer, tenant; contractor.
conductum, -ī *nt* anything hired *or* rented.
conductus *ppp of* **condūcō.**
condūplicō, -āre *vt* to double.
condūrō, -āre *vt* to make very hard.
condus, -ī *m* steward.
cōnectō, -ctere, -xuī, -xum *vt* to tie, fasten, link, join; (*logic*) to state a conclusion.
cōnexum, -ī *nt* logical inference.
cōnexus *ppp of* **cōnectō** ♦ *adj* connected; (*time*) following.
cōnexus, -ūs *m* combination.
cōnfābulor, -ārī, -ātus *vi* to talk (to), discuss.
cōnfarreātiō, -ōnis *f the most solemn of Roman marriage ceremonies.*

cōnfarreō, -āre, -ātum *vt* to marry by confarreatio.
cōnfātālis *adj* bound by the same destiny.
cōnfēcī *perf of* **cōnficiō.**
cōnfectiō, -ōnis *f* making, completion; (*food*) chewing.
cōnfector, -ōris *m* maker, finisher; destroyer.
cōnfectus *ppp of* **cōnficiō.**
cōnferciō, -cīre, -tum *vt* to stuff, cram, pack closely.
cōnferō, -ferre, -tulī, -lātum *vt* to gather together, collect; to contribute; to confer, talk over; (*MIL*) to oppose, engage in battle; to compare; (*words*) to condense; to direct, transfer; to transform (into), turn (to); to devote, bestow; to ascribe, assign, impute; (*time*) to postpone; **capita ~** put heads together, confer; **gradum ~ cum** walk beside; **sē ~** go, turn (to); **sermōnēs ~** converse; **signa ~** join battle.
cōnfertim *adv* in close order.
cōnfertus *ppp of* **cōnferciō** ♦ *adj* crowded, full; (*MIL*) in close order.
cōnfervēscō, -vēscere, -buī *vi* to boil up, grow hot.
cōnfessiō, -ōnis *f* acknowledgement, confession.
cōnfessus *ppa of* **cōnfiteor** ♦ *adj* acknowledged, certain; **in ~ō esse/in ~um venīre** be generally admitted.
cōnfestim *adv* immediately.
cōnficiō, -icere, -ēcī, -ectum *vt* to make, effect, complete, accomplish; to get together, procure; to wear out, exhaust, consume, destroy; (*COMM*) to settle; (*space*) to travel; (*time*) to pass, complete; (*PHILOS*) to be an active cause; (*logic*) to deduce; (*pass*) it follows.
cōnfictiō, -ōnis *f* fabrication.
cōnfictus *ppp of* **cōnfingō.**
cōnfīdēns, -entis *pres p of* **cōnfīdō** ♦ *adj* self-confident, bold, presumptuous.
cōnfīdenter *adv* fearlessly, insolently.
cōnfīdentia, -ae *f* confidence, self-confidence; impudence.
cōnfīdentiloquus *adj* outspoken.
cōnfīdō, -dere, -sus sum *vi* to trust, rely, be sure; **sibi ~** be confident.
cōnfīgō, -gere, -xī, -xum *vt* to fasten together; to pierce, shoot; (*fig*) to paralyse.
cōnfingō, -ingere, -inxī, -ictum *vt* to make, invent, pretend.
cōnfīnis *adj* adjoining; (*fig*) akin.
cōnfīnium, -ī *nt* common boundary; (*pl*) neighbours; (*fig*) close connection, borderland between.
cōnfīō, -fierī *occ pass of* **cōnficiō.**
cōnfirmātiō, -ōnis *f* establishing; (*person*) encouragement; (*fact*) verifying; (*RHET*) adducing of proofs.

Noun declensions and verb conjugations are shown on pp xiii to xxv. The present infinitive ending of a verb shows to which conjugation it belongs: **-āre** = 1st; **-ēre** = 2nd; **-ere** = 3rd and **-īre** = 4th. Irregular verbs are shown on p xxvi

cōnfirmātor, -ōris *m* guarantor (*of money*).
cōnfirmātus *adj* resolute; proved, certain.
cōnfirmō, -āre, -āvī, -ātum *vt* to strengthen, reinforce; (*decree*) to confirm, ratify; (*mind*) to encourage; (*fact*) to corroborate, prove, assert; **sē ~** recover; take courage.
cōnfiscō, -āre *vt* to keep in a chest; to confiscate.
cōnfīsiō, -ōnis *f* assurance.
cōnfīsus *ppa of* **cōnfīdō**.
cōnfiteor, -itērī, -essus *vt, vi* to confess, acknowledge; to reveal.
cōnfixus *ppp of* **cōnfīgō**.
cōnflagrō, -āre, -āvī, -ātum *vi* to burn, be ablaze.
cōnflīctiō, -ōnis *f* conflict.
cōnflīctō, -āre, -āvī, -ātum *vt* to strike down, contend (with); (*pass*) to fight, be harassed, be afflicted.
cōnflīctus, -ūs *m* striking together.
cōnflīgō, -gere, -xī, -ctum *vt* to dash together; (*fig*) to contrast ♦ *vi* to fight, come into conflict.
cōnflō, -āre, -āvī, -ātum *vt* to ignite; (*passion*) to inflame; to melt down; (*fig*) to produce, procure, occasion.
cōnfluēns, -entis, -entēs, -entium *m* confluence of two rivers.
cōnfluō, -ere, -xī *vi* to flow together; (*fig*) to flock together, pour in.
cōnfodiō, -odere, -ōdī, -ossum *vt* to dig; to stab.
cōnfore *fut infin of* **cōnsum**.
cōnfōrmātiō, -ōnis *f* shape, form; (*words*) arrangement; (*voice*) expression; (*mind*) idea; (*RHET*) figure.
cōnfōrmō, -āre, -āvī, -ātum *vt* to shape, fashion.
cōnfossus *ppp of* **cōnfodiō** ♦ *adj* full of holes.
cōnfrāctus *ppp of* **cōnfringō**.
cōnfragōsus *adj* broken, rough; (*fig*) hard.
cōnfrēgī *pvrf of* **cōnfringō**.
cōnfremō, -ere, -uī *vi* to murmur aloud.
cōnfricō, -āre *vt* to rub well.
cōnfringō, -ingere, -ēgī, -āctum *vt* to break in pieces, wreck; (*fig*) to ruin.
cōnfugiō, -ugere, -ūgī *vi* to flee for help (to), take refuge (with); (*fig*) to have recourse (to).
cōnfugium, -ī and iī *nt* refuge.
cōnfundō, -undere, -ūdī, -ūsum *vt* to mix, mingle, join; to mix up, confuse, throw into disorder; (*mind*) to perplex, bewilder; to diffuse, spread over.
cōnfūsē *adv* confusedly.
cōnfūsiō, -ōnis *f* combination; confusion, disorder; **ōris ~** going red in the face.
cōnfūsus *ppp of* **cōnfundō** ♦ *adj* confused, disorderly, troubled.
cōnfūtō, -āre, -āvī, -ātum *vt* to keep from boiling over; to repress; to silence, confute.
congelō, -āre, -āvī, -ātum *vt* to freeze, harden ♦ *vi* to freeze over, grow numb.

congeminō, -āre, -āvī, -ātum *vt* to double.
congemō, -ere, -uī *vi* to groan, sigh ♦ *vt* to lament.
conger, -rī *m* sea eel.
congeriēs, -ēī *f* heap, mass, accumulation.
congerō, -rere, -ssī, -stum *vt* to collect, accumulate, build; (*missiles*) to shower; (*speech*) to comprise; (*fig*) to heap (upon), ascribe.
congerō, -ōnis *m* thief.
congerrō, -ōnis *m* companion in revelry.
congestīcius *adj* piled up.
congestus *ppp of* **congerō**.
congestus, -ūs *m* accumulating; heap, mass.
congiālis *adj* holding a congius.
congiārium, -ī and iī *nt* gift of food to the people, gratuity to the army.
congius, -ī and iī *m* Roman liquid measure (*about 6 pints*).
conglaciō, -āre *vi* to freeze up.
conglīscō, -ere *vi* to blaze up.
conglobātiō, -ōnis *f* mustering.
conglobō, -āre, -āvī, -ātum *vt* to make round; to mass together.
conglomerō, -āre *vt* to roll up.
conglūtinātiō, -ōnis *f* gluing, cementing; (*fig*) combination.
conglūtinō, -āre, -āvī, -ātum *vt* to glue, cement; (*fig*) to join, weld together; to contrive.
congraecō, -āre *vt* to squander on luxury.
congrātulor, -ārī, -ātus *vi* to congratulate.
congredior, -dī, -ssus *vt, vi* to meet, accost; to contend, fight.
congregābilis *adj* gregarious.
congregātiō, -ōnis *f* union, society.
congregō, -āre, -āvī, -ātum *vt* to collect, assemble, unite.
congressiō, -ōnis *f* meeting, conference.
congressus *ppa of* **congredior**.
congressus, -ūs *m* meeting, association, union; encounter, fight.
congruēns, -entis *adj* suitable, consistent, proper; harmonious.
congruenter *adv* in conformity.
congruō, -ere, -ī *vi* to coincide; to correspond, suit; to agree, sympathize.
congruus *adj* agreeable.
coniciō, -icere, -iēcī, -iectum *vt* to throw together; to throw, hurl; to put, fling, drive, direct; to infer, conjecture; (*augury*) to interpret; **sē ~** rush, fly; devote oneself.
coniectiō, -ōnis *f* throwing; conjecture, interpretation.
coniectō, -āre *vt* to infer, conjecture, guess.
coniector, -ōris *m* (*male*) interpreter, diviner.
coniectrīx, -rīcis *f* (*female*) interpreter, diviner.
coniectūra, -ae *f* inference, conjecture, guess; interpretation.
coniectūrālis *adj* (*RHET*) involving a question of fact.

coniectus *ppp of* **coniciō.**
coniectus, -ūs *m* heap, mass, concourse; throwing, throw, range; (*eyes, mind*) turning, directing.
cōnifer, cōniger, -ī *adj* cone-bearing.
cōnītor, -tī, -sus *and* **-xus** *vi* to lean on; to strive, struggle on; to labour.
coniugālis *adj* of marriage, conjugal.
coniugātiō, -ōnis *f* etymological relationship.
coniugātor, -ōris *m* uniter.
coniugiālis *adj* marriage- (*in cpds*).
coniugium, -ī *and* **iī** *nt* union, marriage; husband, wife.
coniugō, -āre *vt* to form (*a friendship*); **~āta verba** words related etymologically.
coniūnctē *adv* jointly; on familiar terms; (*logic*) hypothetically.
coniūnctim *adv* together, jointly.
coniūnctiō, -ōnis *f* union, connection, association; (*minds*) sympathy, affinity; (*GRAM*) conjunction.
coniūnctum, -ī *nt* (*RHET*) connection; (*PHILOS*) inherent property (*of a body*).
coniūnctus *ppp of* **coniungō ♦** *adj* near; connected, agreeing, conforming; related, friendly, intimate.
coniungō, -ūngere, -ūnxī, -ūnctum *vt* to yoke, join together, connect; (*war*) to join forces in; to unite in love, marriage, friendship; to continue without a break.
coniūnx, -ugis *m/f* consort, wife, husband, bride.
coniūrātī, -ōrum *mpl* conspirators.
coniūrātiō, -ōnis *f* conspiracy, plot; alliance.
coniūrātus *adj* (*MIL*) after taking the oath.
coniūrō, -āre, -āvī, -ātum *vi* to take an oath; to conspire, plot.
coniux *etc see* **coniūnx.**
cōnīveō, -vēre, -vī *and* **xī** *vi* to shut the eyes, blink; (*fig*) to be asleep; to connive at.
conj- *etc see* **coni-.**
conl- *etc see* **coll-.**
conm- *etc see* **comm-.**
conn- *etc see* **cōn-.**
Conōn, -is *m* Athenian commander; Greek astronomer.
cōnōpēum (-eum), -ēī *nt* mosquito net.
cōnor, -ārī, -ātus *vt* to try, attempt, venture.
conp- *etc see* **comp-.**
conquassātiō, -ōnis *f* severe shaking.
conquassō, -āre, -ātum *vt* to shake, upset, shatter.
conqueror, -rī, -stus *vt, vi* to complain bitterly of, bewail.
conquestiō, -ōnis *f* complaining; (*RHET*) appeal to pity.
conquestus *ppa of* **conqueror.**
conquestus, -ūs *m* outcry.
conquiēscō, -scere, -vī, -tum *vi* to rest, take

a respite; (*fig*) to be at peace, find recreation; (*things*) to stop, be quiet.
conquinīscō, -ere *vi* to cower, squat, stoop down.
conquīrō, -rere, -sīvī, -sītum *vt* to search for, collect.
conquīsītē *adv* carefully.
conquīsītiō, -ōnis *f* search; (*MIL*) levy.
conquīsītor, -ōris *m* recruiting officer; (*THEATRE*) claqueur.
conquīsītus *ppp of* **conquīrō ♦** *adj* select, costly.
conr- *etc see* **corr-.**
cōnsaepiō, -īre, -sī, -tum *vt* to enclose, fence round.
cōnsaeptum, -tī *nt* enclosure.
cōnsalūtātiō, -ōnis *f* mutual greeting.
cōnsalūtō, -āre, -āvī, -ātum *vt* to greet, hail.
cōnsānēscō, -ēscere, -uī *vi* to heal up.
cōnsanguineus *adj* brother, sister, kindred ♦ *mpl* relations.
cōnsanguinitās, -ātis *f* relationship.
cōnscelerātus *adj* wicked.
cōnscelerō, -āre, -āvī, -ātum *vt* to disgrace.
cōnscendō, -endere, -endī, -ēnsum *vt, vi* to climb, mount, embark.
cōnscēnsiō, -ōnis *f* embarkation.
cōnscēnsus *ppp of* **cōnscendō.**
cōnscientia, -ae *f* joint knowledge, being in the know; (*sense of*) consciousness; moral sense, conscience, guilty conscience.
cōnscindō, -ndere, -dī, -ssum *vt* to tear to pieces; (*fig*) to abuse.
cōnsciō, -īre *vt* to be conscious of guilt.
cōnscīscō, -scere, -vī *and* **iī, -ītum** *vt* to decide on publicly; to inflict on oneself; **mortem (sibi) ~** commit suicide.
cōnscīssus *ppp of* **cōnscindō.**
cōnscītus *ppp of* **cōnscīscō.**
cōnscius *adj* sharing knowledge, privy, in the know; aware, conscious (of); conscious of guilt ♦ *m/f* confederate, confidant.
cōnscreor, -ārī *vi* to clear the throat.
cōnscrībō, -bere, -psī, -ptum *vt* to enlist, enrol; to write, compose, draw up, prescribe.
cōnscrīptiō, -ōnis *f* document, draft.
cōnscrīptus *ppp of* **cōnscrībō; patrēs ~ī** patrician and elected plebeian members; senators.
cōnsecō, -āre, -uī, -tum *vt* to cut up.
cōnsecrātiō, -ōnis *f* consecration, deification.
cōnsecrō, -āre, -āvī, -ātum *vt* to dedicate, consecrate, deify; (*fig*) to devote; to immortalise; **caput ~** doom to death.
cōnsectārius *adj* logical, consequent ♦ *ntpl* inferences.
cōnsectātiō, -ōnis *f* pursuit.
cōnsectātrīx, -īcis *f* (*fig*) follower.

Noun declensions and verb conjugations are shown on pp xiii to xxv. The present infinitive ending of a verb shows to which conjugation it belongs: **-āre** = 1st; **-ēre** = 2nd; **-ere** = 3rd and **-īre** = 4th. Irregular verbs are shown on p xxvi

cōnsectiō, -ōnis *f* cutting up.
cōnsector, -ārī, -ātus *vt* to follow, go after, try to gain; to emulate, imitate; to pursue, chase.
cōnsecūtiō, -ōnis *f* (*PHILOS*) consequences, effect; (*RHET*) sequence.
cōnsēdī *perf of* **cōnsīdō.**
cōnsenēscō, -ēscere, -uī *vi* to grow old, grow old together; (*fig*) to fade, pine, decay, become obsolete.
cōnsēnsiō, -ōnis *f* agreement, accord; conspiracy, plot.
cōnsēnsū *adv* unanimously.
cōnsēnsus *ppp of* **cōnsentiō.**
cōnsēnsus, -ūs *m* agreement, concord; conspiracy; (*PHILOS*) common sensation; (*fig*) harmony.
cōnsentāneus *adj* agreeing, in keeping with; **~um est** it is reasonable.
cōnsentiō, -entīre, -ēnsī, -ēnsum *vi* to agree, determine together; to plot, conspire; (*PHILOS*) to have common sensations; (*fig*) to harmonize, suit, be consistent (with); **bellum ~** vote for war.
cōnsequēns, -entis *pres p of* **cōnsequor** ♦ *adj* coherent, reasonable; logical, consequent ♦ *nt* consequence.
cōnsequor, -quī, -cūtus *vt* to follow, pursue; to overtake, reach; (*time*) to come after; (*example*) to follow, copy; (*effect*) to result, be the consequence of; (*aim*) to attain, get; (*mind*) to grasp, learn; (*events*) to happen to, come to; (*standard*) to equal, come up to; (*speech*) to do justice to.
cōnserō, -erere, -ēvī, -itum *vt* to sow, plant; (*ground*) to sow with, plant with; (*fig*) to cover, fill.
cōnserō, -ere, -uī, -tum *vt* to join, string together, twine; (*MIL*) to join battle; **manum/manūs ~** engage in close combat; **ex iūre manum ~** lay claim to (*in an action for possession*).
cōnsertē *adv* connectedly.
cōnsertus *ppp of* **cōnserō.**
cōnserva, -ae *f* fellow slave.
cōnservātiō, -ōnis *f* preserving.
cōnservātor, -ōris *m* preserver.
cōnservitium, -ī *and* **iī** *nt* being fellow slaves.
cōnservō, -āre, -āvī, -ātum *vt* to preserve, save, keep.
cōnservus, -ī *m* fellow slave.
cōnsessor, -ōris *m* companion at table, fellow spectator; (*law*) assessor.
cōnsessus, -ūs *m* assembly; (*law*) court.
cōnsēvī *perf of* **cōnserō.**
cōnsīderātē *adv* cautiously, deliberately.
cōnsīderātiō, -ōnis *f* contemplation.
cōnsīderātus *adj* (*person*) circumspect; (*things*) well-considered.
cōnsīderō, -āre, -āvī, -ātum *vt* to look at, inspect; to consider, contemplate.
cōnsīdō, -īdere, -ēdī, -essum *vi* to sit down, take seats; (*courts*) to be in session; (*MIL*) to

take up a position; (*residence*) to settle; (*places*) to subside, sink; (*fig*) to sink, settle down, subside.
cōnsignō, -āre, -āvī, -ātum *vt* to seal, sign; to attest, vouch for; to record, register.
cōnsilēscō, -ere *vi* to calm down.
cōnsiliārius, -ī *and* **iī** *m* adviser, counsellor; spokesman ♦ *adj* counselling.
cōnsiliātor, -ōris *m* counsellor.
cōnsilior, -ārī, -ātus *vi* to consult; (*with dat*) to advise.
cōnsilium, -ī *and* **iī** *nt* deliberation, consultation; deliberating body, council; decision, purpose; plan, measure, stratagem; advice, counsel; judgement, insight, wisdom; **~ium capere, inīre** come to a decision, resolve; **~ī esse** be an open question; **~iō** intentionally; **eō ~iō ut** with the intention of; **prīvātō ~iō** for one's own purposes.
cōnsimilis *adj* just like.
cōnsipiō, -ere *vi* to be in one's senses.
cōnsistō, -istere, -titī *vi* to stand, rest, take up a position; to consist (of), depend (on); to exist, be; (*fig*) to stand firm, endure; (*liquid*) to solidify, freeze; to stop, pause, halt, come to rest; (*fig*) to come to a standstill, come to an end.
cōnsitiō, -ōnis *f* sowing, planting.
cōnsitor, -ōris *m* sower, planter.
cōnsitus *ppp of* **cōnserō.**
cōnsōbrīnus, -ī *m*, **-a, -ae** *f* cousin.
cōnsociātiō, -ōnis *f* society.
cōnsociō, -āre, -āvī, -ātum *vt* to share, associate, unite.
cōnsōlābilis *adj* consolable.
cōnsōlātiō, -ōnis *f* comfort, encouragement, consolation.
cōnsōlātor, -ōris *m* comforter.
cōnsōlātōrius *adj* of consolation.
cōnsōlor, -ārī, -ātus *vt* to console, comfort, reassure; (*things*) to relieve, mitigate.
cōnsomniō, -āre *vt* to dream about.
cōnsonō, -āre, -uī *vi* to resound; (*fig*) to accord.
cōnsonus *adj* concordant; (*fig*) suitable.
cōnsōpiō, -īre, -ītum *vt* to put to sleep.
cōnsors, -tis *adj* sharing in common; (*things*) shared in common ♦ *m/f* partner, colleague.
cōnsortiō, -ōnis *f* partnership, fellowship.
cōnsortium, -ī *and* **iī** *nt* society, participation.
cōnspectus *ppp of* **cōnspiciō** ♦ *adj* visible; conspicuous.
cōnspectus, -ūs *m* look, view, sight; appearing on the scene; (*fig*) mental picture, survey; **in ~um venīre** come in sight, come near.
cōnspergō, -gere, -sī, -sum *vt* to besprinkle; (*fig*) to spangle.
cōnspiciendus *adj* noteworthy, distinguished.
cōnspiciō, -icere, -exī, -ectum *vt* to observe, catch sight of; to look at (*esp with admiration*),

contemplate; (*pass*) to attract attention, be conspicuous, be notorious; (*mind*) to see, perceive.

cōnspicor, -ārī, -ātus *vt* to observe, see, catch sight of.

cōnspicuus *adj* visible; conspicuous, distinguished.

cōnspīrātiō, -ōnis *f* concord, unanimity; plotting, conspiracy.

cōnspīrō, -āre, -āvī, -ātum *vi* to agree, unite; to plot, conspire; (*music*) to sound together.

cōnspōnsor, -ōris *m* co-guarantor.

cōnspuō, -ere *vt* to spit upon.

cōnspurcō, -āre *vt* to pollute.

cōnspūtō, -āre *vt* to spit upon (*with contempt*).

cōnstabiliō, -īre, -īvī, -itum *vt* to establish.

cōnstāns, -antis *pres p of* **cōnstō** ♦ *adj* steady, stable, constant; consistent; faithful, steadfast.

cōnstanter *adv* steadily, firmly, calmly; consistently.

cōnstantia, -ae *f* steadiness, firmness; consistency, harmony; self-possession, constancy.

cōnsternātiō, -ōnis *f* disorder, tumult; (*horses*) stampede; (*mind*) dismay, alarm.

cōnsternō, -ernere, -rāvī, -rātum *vt* to spread, cover, thatch, pave; **~rāta nāvis** decked ship.

cōnsternō, -āre, -āvī, -ātum *vt* to startle, stampede; to alarm, throw into confusion.

cōnstīpō, -āre *vt* to crowd together.

cōnstitī *perf of* **cōnsistō**.

cōnstituō, -uere, -uī, -ūtum *vt* to put, place, set down; (*MIL*) to station, post, halt; to establish, build, create; to settle, arrange, organize; to appoint, determine, fix; to resolve, decide; **bene ~ūtum corpus** a good constitution.

cōnstitūtiō, -ōnis *f* state, condition; regulation, decree; definition, point at issue.

cōnstitūtum, -ūtī *nt* agreement.

cōnstō, -āre, -itī, -ātum *vi* to stand together; to agree, correspond, tally; to stand firm, remain constant; to exist, be; to consist (of), be composed (of); (*facts*) to be established, be well-known; (*comm*) to cost; **sibi ~** be consistent; **inter omnēs ~at** it is common knowledge; **mihi ~at** I am determined; **ratiō ~at** the account is correct.

cōnstrātum, -ī *nt* flooring, deck.

cōnstrātus *ppp of* **cōnsternō**.

cōnstringō, -ingere, -īnxī, -ictum *vt* to tie up, bind, fetter; (*fig*) to restrain, restrict; (*speech*) to compress, condense.

cōnstructiō, -ōnis *f* building up; (*words*) arrangement, sequence.

cōnstruō, -ere, -xī, -ctum *vt* to heap up; to build, construct.

cōnstuprātor, -ōris *m* debaucher.

cōnstuprō, -āre *vt* to debauch, rape.

cōnsuādeō, -ēre *vi* to advise strongly.

Cōnsuālia, -ium *ntpl* festival of Consus.

cōnsuāsor, -ōris *m* earnest adviser.

cōnsūdō, -āre *vi* to sweat profusely.

cōnsuēfaciō, -facere, -fēcī, -factum *vt* to accustom.

cōnsuēscō, -scere, -vī, -tum *vt* to accustom, inure ♦ *vi* to get accustomed; to cohabit (with); (*perf tenses*) to be accustomed, be in the habit of.

cōnsuētūdō, -inis *f* custom, habit; familiarity, social intercourse; love affair; (*language*) usage, idiom; **~ine/ex ~ine** as usual; **epistulārum ~** correspondence.

cōnsuētus *ppp of* **cōnsuēscō** ♦ *adj* customary, usual.

cōnsuēvī *perf of* **cōnsuēscō**.

cōnsul, -is *m* consul; **~ dēsignātus** consul elect; **~ ōrdinārius** regular consul; **~ suffectus** successor to a consul who has died *during his term of office*; **~ iterum/tertium** consul for the second/third time; **~em creāre, dīcere, facere** elect to the consulship; **L. Domitiō App. Claudiō ~ibus** in the year 54 B.C.

cōnsulāris *adj* consular, consul's; of consular rank ♦ *m* ex-consul.

cōnsulāriter *adv* in a manner worthy of a consul.

cōnsulātus, -ūs *m* consulship; **~um petere** stand for the consulship.

cōnsulō, -ere, -uī, -tum *vi* to deliberate, take thought; (*with dat*) to look after, consult the interests of; (*with dē or in*) to take measures against, pass sentence on ♦ *vt* to consult, ask advice of; to consider; to advise (something); to decide; **bonī/optimī ~** take in good part, be satisfied with.

cōnsultātiō, -ōnis *f* deliberation; inquiry; case.

cōnsultē *adv* deliberately.

cōnsultō *adv* deliberately.

cōnsultō, -āre, -āvī, -ātum *vt, vi* to deliberate, reflect; to consult; (*with dat*) to consult the interests of.

cōnsultor, -ōris *m* counsellor; consulter, client.

cōnsultrīx, -īcis *f* protectress.

cōnsultum, -ī *nt* decree (*esp of the Senate*); consultation; response (*from an oracle*).

cōnsultus *ppp of* **cōnsulō** ♦ *adj* considered; experienced, skilled ♦ *m* lawyer; **iūris ~us** lawyer.

cōnsuluī *perf of* **cōnsulō**.

(cōnsum), futūrum, fore *vi* to be all right.

cōnsummātus *adj* perfect.

cōnsummō, -āre *vt* to sum up; to complete, perfect.

cōnsūmō, -ere, -psī, -ptum *vt* to consume,

use up, eat up; to waste, squander; to
exhaust, destroy, kill; to spend, devote.

cōnsūmptiō, -ōnis *f* wasting.

cōnsūmptor, -ōris *m* destroyer.

cōnsūmptus *ppp of* **cōnsūmō**.

cōnsuō, -uere, -uī, -ūtum *vt* to sew up; (*fig*)
to contrive.

cōnsurgō, -gere, -rēxī, -rēctum *vi* to rise,
stand up; to be roused (to); to spring up,
start.

cōnsurrēctiō, -ōnis *f* standing up.

Cōnsus, -ī *m* ancient Roman god (*connected
with harvest*).

cōnsusurrō, -āre *vi* to whisper together.

cōnsūtus *ppp of* **cōnsuō**.

contābefaciō, -ere *vt* to wear out.

contābēscō, -ēscere, -uī *vi* to waste away.

contabulātiō, -ōnis *f* flooring, storey.

contabulō, -āre, -āvī, -ātum *vt* to board
over, build in storeys.

contāctus *ppp of* **contingō**.

contāctus, -ūs *m* touch, contact; contagion,
infection.

contāgēs, -is *f* contact, touch.

contāgiō, -ōnis *f*, **contāgium, -ī** *and* **iī** *nt*
contact; contagion, infection; (*fig*)
contamination, bad example.

contāminātus *adj* impure, vicious.

contāminō, -āre, -āvī, -ātum *vt* to defile; (*fig*)
to mar, spoil.

contechnor, -ārī, -ātus *vi* to think out plots.

contegō, -egere, -ēxī, -ēctum *vt* to cover up,
cover over; to protect; to hide.

contemerō, -āre *vt* to defile.

contemnō, -nere, -psī, -ptum *vt* to think
light of, have no fear of, despise, defy; to
disparage.

contemplātiō, -ōnis *f* contemplation,
surveying.

contemplātor, -ōris *m* observer.

contemplātus, -ūs *m* contemplation.

**contemplō, -āre, -āvī, -ātum, -or, -ārī,
-ātus** *vt* to look at, observe, contemplate.

contempsī *perf of* **contemnō**.

contemptim *adv* contemptuously,
slightingly.

contemptiō, -ōnis *f* disregard, scorn,
despising.

contemptor, -ōris *m* (male) despiser, defiler.

contemptrīx, -rīcis *f* (female) despiser,
defiler.

contemptus *ppp of* **contemnō** ♦ *adj*
contemptible.

contemptus, -ūs *m* despising, scorn; being
slighted; **~uī esse** be despised.

contendō, -dere, -dī, -tum *vt* to stretch,
draw, tighten; (*instrument*) to tune; (*effort*) to
strain, exert; (*argument*) to assert, maintain;
(*comparison*) to compare, contrast; (*course*)
to direct ♦ *vi* to exert oneself, strive; to
hurry; to journey, march; to contend,
compete, fight; to entreat, solicit.

contentē *adv* (*from* **contendō**) earnestly,

intensely.

contentē *adv* (*from* **contineō**) closely.

contentiō, -ōnis *f* straining, effort; striving
(after); struggle, competition, dispute;
comparison, contrast, antithesis.

contentus *ppp of* **contendō** ♦ *adj* strained,
tense; (*fig*) intent.

contentus *ppp of* **contineō** ♦ *adj* content,
satisfied.

conterminus *adj* bordering, neighbouring.

conterō, -erere, -rīvī, -rītum *vt* to grind,
crumble; to wear out, waste; (*time*) to spend,
pass; (*fig*) to obliterate.

conterreō, -ēre, -uī, -itum *vt* to terrify.

contestātus *adj* proved.

contestor, -ārī, -ātus *vt* to call to witness;
lītem ~ open a lawsuit by calling witnesses.

contexō, -ere, -uī, -tum *vt* to weave,
interweave; to devise, construct; (*recital*) to
continue.

contextē *adv* in a connected fashion.

contextus *adj* connected.

contextus, -ūs *m* connection, coherence.

conticēscō (-iscō), -ēscere, -uī *vi* to become
quiet, fall silent; (*fig*) to cease, abate.

contigī *perf of* **contingō**.

contignātiō, -ōnis *f* floor, storey.

contignō, -āre *vt* to floor.

contiguus *adj* adjoining, near; within reach.

continēns, -entis *pres p of* **contineō** ♦ *adj*
bordering, adjacent; unbroken, continuous;
(*time*) successive, continual, uninterrupted;
(*person*) temperate, continent ♦ *nt* mainland,
continent; essential point (*in an argument*).

continenter *adv* (*place*) in a row; (*time*)
continuously; (*person*) temperately.

continentia, -ae *f* moderation, self-control.

contineō, -inēre, -inuī, -entum *vt* to hold,
keep together; to confine, enclose; to
contain, include, comprise; (*pass*) to consist
of, rest on; to control, check, repress.

contingō, -ingere, -igī, -āctum *vt* to touch,
take hold of, partake of; to be near, border
on; to reach, come to; to contaminate; (*mind*)
to touch, affect, concern ♦ *vi* to happen,
succeed.

contingō, -ere *vt* to moisten, smear.

continuātiō, -ōnis *f* unbroken, succession,
series; (*RHET*) period.

continuī *perf of* **contineō**.

continuō *adv* immediately, without delay;
(*argument*) necessarily.

continuō, -āre, -āvī, -ātum *vt* to join
together, make continuous; to continue
without a break; **verba ~** form a sentence.

continuus *adj* joined (to); continuous,
successive, uninterrupted; **~ā nocte** the
following night; **triduum ~um** three days
running.

cōntiō, -ōnis *f* public meeting; speech,
address; rostrum; **~ōnem habēre** hold a
meeting; deliver an address; **prō ~ōne** in
public.

cōntiōnābundus *adj* delivering a harangue, playing the demagogue.

cōntiōnālis *adj* suitable for a public meeting, demagogic.

cōntiōnārius *adj* fond of public meetings.

cōntiōnātor, -ōris *m* demagogue.

cōntiōnor, -ārī, -ātus *vi* to address a public meeting, harangue; to declare in public; to come to a meeting.

cōntiuncula, -ae *f* short speech.

contorqueō, -quēre, -sī, -tum *vt* to twist, turn; (*weapons*) to throw, brandish; (*words*) to deliver forcibly.

contortē *adv* intricately.

contortiō, -ōnis *f* intricacy.

contortor, -ōris *m* perverter.

contortulus *adj* somewhat complicated.

contortuplicātus *adj* very complicated.

contortus *ppp of* **contorqueō** ♦ *adj* vehement; intricate.

contrā *adv* (place) opposite, face to face; (*speech*) in reply; (*action*) to fight, in opposition, against someone; (*result, with* **esse**) adverse, unsuccessful; (*comparison*) the contrary, conversely, differently; (*argument*) on the contrary, on the other hand; ~ **atque, quam** contrary to what, otherwise than ♦ *prep* (*with acc*) facing, opposite to; against; contrary to, in violation of.

contractiō, -ōnis *f* contracting; shortening; despondency.

contractiuncula, -ae *f* slight despondency.

contractus *ppp of* **contrahō** ♦ *adj* contracted, narrow; short; in seclusion.

contrādīcō, -dīcere, -dīxī, -dictum (*usu two words*) *vt, vi* to oppose, object; (*law*) to be counsel for the other side.

contrādictiō, -ōnis *f* objection.

contrahō, -here, -xī, -ctum *vt* to draw together, assemble; to bring about, achieve; (*COMM*) to contract, make a bargain; to shorten, narrow; to limit, depress; (*blame*) to incur; (*brow*) to wrinkle; (*sail*) to shorten; (*sky*) to overcast.

contrāriē *adv* differently.

contrārius *adj* opposite, from opposite; contrary; hostile, harmful ♦ *nt* opposite, reverse; **ex ~ō** on the contrary.

contrectābiliter *adv* so as to be felt.

contrectātiō, -ōnis *f* touching.

contrectō, -āre, -āvī, -ātum *vt* to touch, handle; (*fig*) to consider.

contremīscō, -īscere, -uī *vi* to tremble all over; (*fig*) to waver ♦ *vt* to be afraid of.

contremō, -ere *vi* to quake.

contribuō, -uere, -uī, -ūtum *vt* to bring together, join, incorporate.

contristō, -āre, -āvī, -ātum *vt* to sadden, darken, cloud.

contrītus *ppp of* **conterō** ♦ *adj* trite, well-worn.

contrōversia, -ae *f* dispute, argument, debate, controversy.

contrōversiōsus *adj* much disputed.

contrōversus *adj* disputed, questionable.

contrucīdō, -āre, -āvī, -ātum *vt* to massacre.

contrūdō, -dere, -sī, -sum *vt* to crowd together.

contruncō, -āre *vt* to hack to pieces.

contrūsus *ppp of* **contrūdō**.

contubernālis, -is *m/f* tent companion; junior officer serving with a general; (*fig*) companion, mate.

contubernium, -ī and iī *nt* service in the same tent, mess; service as junior officer with a general; common tent; slaves' home.

contueor, -ērī, -itus *vt* to look at, consider, observe.

contuitus, -ūs *m* observing, view.

contulī *perf of* **cōnferō**.

contumācia, -ae *f* obstinacy, defiance.

contumāciter *adv see* **contumāx**.

contumāx, -ācis *adj* stubborn, insolent, pig-headed.

contumēlia, -ae *f* (*verbal*) insult, libel, invective; (*physical*) assault, ill-treatment.

contumēliōsē *adv* insolently.

contumēliōsus *adj* insulting, outrageous.

contumulō, -āre *vt* to bury.

contundō, -undere, -udī, -ūsum *vt* to pound, beat, bruise; (*fig*) to suppress, destroy.

contuor *etc see* **contueor**.

conturbātiō, -ōnis *f* confusion, mental disorder.

conturbātus *adj* distracted, diseased.

conturbō, -āre, -āvī, -ātum *vt* to throw into confusion; (*mind*) to derange, disquiet; (*money*) to embarrass.

contus, -ī *m* pole.

contūsus *ppp of* **contundō**.

contūtus *see* **contuitus**.

cōnūbiālis *adj* conjugal.

cōnūbium, -ī and iī *nt* marriage; **iūs ~ī** right of intermarriage.

cōnus, -ī *m* cone; (*helmet*) apex.

convador, -ārī, -ātus *vt* (*law*) to bind over.

convalēscō, -ēscere, -uī *vi* to recover, get better; (*fig*) to grow stronger, improve.

convallis, -is *f* valley with hills on all sides.

convāsō, -āre *vt* to pack up.

convectō, -āre *vt* to bring home.

convector, -ōris *m* fellow passenger.

convehō, -here, -xī, -ctum *vt* to bring in, carry.

convellō, -ellere, -ellī, -ulsum and olsum *vt* to wrench, tear away; to break up; (*fig*) to destroy, overthrow; **signa ~** decamp.

convena, -ae *adj* meeting.

convenae, -ārum *m/f* crowd of strangers, refugees.

Noun declensions and verb conjugations are shown on pp xiii to xxv. The present infinitive ending of a verb shows to which conjugation it belongs: **-āre** = 1st; **-ēre** = 2nd; **-ere** = 3rd and **-īre** = 4th. Irregular verbs are shown on p xxvi

conveniēns, -entis *pres p of* **conveniō ♦** *adj* harmonious, consistent; fit, appropriate.
convenienter *adv* in conformity (with), consistently; aptly.
convenientia, -ae *f* conformity, harmony.
conveniō, -enīre, -ēnī, -entum *vi* to meet, assemble; (*events*) to combine, coincide; (*person*) to agree, harmonize; (*things*) to fit, suit; (*impers*) to be suitable, be proper **♦** *vt* to speak to, interview.
conventīcium, -ī *and* **iī** *nt* payment for attendance at assemblies.
conventīcius *adj* visiting regularly.
conventiculum, -ī *nt* gathering; meeting place.
conventiō, -ōnis *f* agreement.
conventum, -ī *nt* agreement.
conventus *ppp of* **conveniō**.
conventus, -ūs *m* meeting; (*law*) local assizes; (*comm*) corporation; agreement; ~ūs **agere** hold the assizes.
converrō, -rere, -rī, -sum *vt* to sweep up, brush together; (*comedy*) to give a good beating to.
conversātiō, -ōnis *f* associating (with).
conversiō, -ōnis *f* revolution, cycle; change over; (*rhet*) well-rounded period; verbal repetition at end of clauses.
conversō, -āre *vt* to turn round.
conversus *ppp of* **converrō**; *ppp of* **convertō**.
convertō, -tere, -tī, -sum *vt* to turn round, turn back; (*mil*) to wheel; to turn, direct; to change, transform; (*writings*) to translate **♦** *vi* to return, turn, change.
convestiō, -īre, -īvī, -ītum *vt* to clothe, encompass.
convexus *adj* vaulted, rounded; hollow; sloping **♦** *nt* vault, hollow.
convīciātor, -ōris *m* slanderer.
convīcior, -ārī, -ātus *vt* to revile.
convīcium, -ī *and* **iī** *nt* loud noise, outcry; invective, abuse; reproof, protest.
convīctiō, -ōnis *f* companionship.
convīctor, -ōris *m* familiar friend.
convīctus *ppp of* **convīncō**.
convīctus, -ūs *m* community life, intercourse; entertainment.
convincō, -incere, -īcī, -ictum *vt* to refute, convict, prove wrong; to prove, demonstrate.
convīsō, -ere *vt* to search, examine; to pervade.
convītium *see* **convīcium**.
convīva, -ae *m/f* guest.
convīvālis *adj* festive, convivial.
convīvātor, -ōris *m* host.
convīvium, -ī *and* **iī** *nt* banquet, entertainment; guests.
convīvor, -ārī, -ātus *vi* to feast together, carouse.
convocātiō, -ōnis *f* assembling.
convocō, -āre, -āvī, -ātum *vt* to call a meeting of, muster.

convolnerō *see* **convulnerō**.
convolō, -āre, -āvī, -ātum *vi* to flock together.
convolsus *see* **convulsus**.
convolvō, -vere, -vī, -ūtum *vt* to roll up, coil up; to intertwine.
convomō, -ere *vt* to vomit over.
convorrō *see* **converrō**.
convortō *see* **convertō**.
convulnerō, -āre *vt* to wound seriously.
convulsus *ppp of* **convellō**.
cooperiō, -īre, -uī, -tum *vt* to cover over, overwhelm.
cooptātiō, -ōnis *f* electing, nominating (of new members).
cooptō, -āre, -āvī, -ātum *vt* to elect (as a colleague).
coorior, -īrī, -tus *vi* to rise, appear; to break out, begin.
coortus, -ūs *m* originating.
cōpa, -ae *f* barmaid.
cophinus, -ī *m* basket.
cōpia, -ae *f* abundance, plenty, number; resources, wealth, prosperity; (*mil, usu pl*) troops, force; (*words, thought*) richness, fulness, store; (*action*) opportunity, facility, means, access; **prō ~ā** according to one's resources, as good as possible considering.
cōpiolae, -ārum *fpl* small force.
cōpiōsē *adv* abundantly, fully, at great length.
cōpiōsus *adj* abounding, rich, plentiful; (*speech*) eloquent, fluent.
cōpis *adj* rich.
cōpula, -ae *f* rope, leash, grapnel; (*fig*) bond.
cōpulātiō, -ōnis *f* coupling, union.
cōpulātus *adj* connected, binding.
cōpulō, -āre, -āvī, -ātum *vt* to couple, join; (*fig*) to unite, associate.
coqua, -ae *f* cook.
coquīnō, -āre *vi* to be a cook.
coquīnus *adj* of cooking.
coquō, -quere, -xī, -ctum *vt* to cook, boil, bake; to parch, burn; (*fruit*) to ripen; (*stomach*) to digest; (*thought*) to plan, concoct; (*care*) to disquiet, disturb.
coquus (cocus), -ī *m* cook.
cor, cordis *nt* heart; (*feeling*) heart, soul; (*thought*) mind, judgement; **cordī esse** please, be agreeable.
cōram *adv* in one's presence; in person **♦** *prep* (*with abl*) in the presence of, before.
corbis, -is *m/f* basket.
corbīta, -ae *f* slow boat.
corbula, -ae *f* little basket.
corculum, -ī *nt* dear heart.
Corcȳra, -ae *f* island off W. coast of Greece (*now* Corfu).
Corcȳraeus *adj* see n.
cordātē *adv see* **cordātus**.
cordātus *adj* wise.
cordolium, -ī *and* **iī** *nt* sorrow.
Corfiniēnsis *adj see n.*
Corfinium, -ī *nt* town in central Italy.

coriandrum, -ī *nt* coriander.
Corinthiacus, -iēnsis, -ius *adj*: **~ium aes** Corinthian brass (*an alloy of gold, silver and copper*).
Corinthus, -ī *f* Corinth.
corium (corius *m*) **-ī** *and* **iī** *nt* hide, skin; leather, strap.
Cornēlia, -iae *f* mother of the Gracchi.
Cornēliānus, -ius *adj*: **lēgēs ~iae** Sulla's laws.
Cornēlius, -ī *m* famous Roman family name (*esp Scipios, Gracchi, Sulla*).
corneolus *adj* horny.
corneus *adj* of horn.
corneus *adj* of the cornel tree, of cornel wood.
cornicen, -cinis *m* horn-blower.
cornīcula, -ae *f* little crow.
corniculārius, -ī *and* **iī** *m* adjutant.
corniculum, -ī *nt* a horn-shaped decoration.
corniger, -ī *adj* horned.
cornipēs, -edis *adj* horn-footed.
cornix, -īcis *f* crow.
cornū, -ūs, -um, -ī *nt* horn; anything horn-shaped; (*army*) wing; (*bay*) arm; (*book*) roller-end; (*bow*) tip; (*helmet*) crest-socket; (*land*) tongue, spit; (*lyre*) arm; (*moon*) horn; (*place*) side; (*river*) branch; (*yardarm*) point; anything made of horn: bow, funnel, lantern; (*music*) horn; (*oil*) cruet; anything like horn: beak, hoof, wart; (*fig*) strength, courage; **~ cōpiae** *Amalthea's horn, symbol of plenty*.
cornum, -ī *nt* cornelian cherry.
cornum *see* **cornū**.
cornus, -ī *f* cornelian cherry tree; javelin.
corōlla, -ae *f* small garland.
corōllārium, -ī *and* **iī** *nt* garland for actors; present, gratuity.
corōna, -ae *f* garland, crown; (ASTRO) Corona Borealis; (*people*) gathering, bystanders; (MIL) cordon of besiegers *or* defenders; **sub ~ā vēndere, vēnīre** sell, be sold as slaves.
Corōnaeus, -ēus, -ēnsis *adj see* **Corōnēa**.
corōnārium aurum *gold collected in the provinces for a victorious general*.
Corōnēa, -ēae *f* town in central Greece.
corōnō, -āre, -āvī, -ātum *vt* to put a garland on; crown; to encircle.
corporeus *adj* corporeal; of flesh.
corpulentus *adj* corpulent.
corpus, -oris *nt* body; substance, flesh; corpse; trunk, torso; person, individual; (*fig*) structure, corporation, body politic.
corpusculum, -ī *nt* particle; term of endearment.
corrādō, -dere, -sī, -sum *vt* to scrape together, procure.
correctiō, -ōnis *f* amending, improving.
corrēctor, -ōris *m* reformer, critic.
corrēctus *ppp of* **corrigō**.
correpō, -ere, -sī *vi* to creep, slink, cower.

correptē *adv* briefly.
correptus *ppp of* **corripiō**.
corrīdeō, -ēre *vi* to laugh aloud.
corrigia, -ae *f* shoelace.
corrigō, -igere, -ēxī, -ēctum *vt* to make straight; to put right, improve, correct.
corripiō, -ipere, -ipuī, -eptum *vt* to seize, carry off, get along quickly; (*speech*) to reprove, reproach, accuse; (*passion*) to seize upon, attack; (*time, words*) to cut short; **sē gradum, viam ~** hasten, rush.
corrōborō, -āre, -āvī, -ātum *vt* to make strong, invigorate.
corrōdō, -dere, -sī, -sum *vt* to nibble away.
corrogō, -āre *vt* to gather by requesting.
corrūgō, -āre *vt* to wrinkle.
corrumpō, -umpere, -ūpī, -uptum *vt* to break up, ruin, waste; to mar, adulterate, falsify; (*person*) to corrupt, seduce, bribe.
corruō, -ere, -ī *vi* to fall, collapse ♦ *vt* to overthrow, heap up.
corruptē *adv* perversely; in a lax manner.
corruptēla, -ae *f* corruption, bribery; seducer.
corruptiō, -ōnis *f* bribing, seducing; corrupt state.
corruptor, -ōris *m*, **-rīx, -rīcis** *f* corrupter, seducer.
corruptus *ppp of* **corrumpō** ♦ *adj* spoiled, corrupt, bad.
Corsus *adj* Corsican.
cortex, -icis *m/f* bark, rind; cork.
cortīna, -ae *f* kettle, cauldron; tripod of Apollo; (*fig*) vault, circle.
corulus, -ī *f* hazel.
Cōrus *see* **Caurus**.
coruscō, -āre *vt* to butt; to shake, brandish ♦ *vi* to flutter, flash, quiver.
coruscus *adj* tremulous, oscillating; shimmering, glittering.
corvus, -ī *m* raven; (MIL) grapnel.
Corybantēs, -ium *mpl* priests of Cybele.
Corybantius *adj see n*.
cōrycus, -ī *m* punchball.
corylētum, -ī *nt* hazel copse.
corylus, -ī *f* hazel.
corymbifer *m* Bacchus.
corymbus, -ī *m* cluster (*esp of ivy berries*).
coryphaeus, -ī *m* leader.
cōrytos, -us, -ī *m* quiver.
cōs *f* hard rock, flint; grindstone.
Cōs, Coī *f* Aegean island (*famous for wine and weaving*) ♦ *nt* Coan wine ♦ *ntpl* Coan clothes.
cosmēta, -ae *m* master of the wardrobe.
costa, -ae *f* rib; side, wall.
costum, -ī *nt* an aromatic plant, perfume.
cothurnātus *adj* buskined, tragic.
cothurnus, -ī *m* buskin, hunting boot; tragedy, elevated style.
cotīd *see* **cottīd-**.

Noun declensions and verb conjugations are shown on pp xiii to xxv. The present infinitive ending of a verb shows to which conjugation it belongs: **-āre** = 1st; **-ēre** = 2nd; **-ere** = 3rd and **-īre** = 4th. Irregular verbs are shown on p xxvi

cōtis *f see* **cōs**.

cottabus, -ī *m* game of throwing drops of wine.

cottana, -ōrum *ntpl* Syrian figs.

cottīdiānō *adv* daily.

cottīdiānus *adj* daily; everyday, ordinary.

cottīdiē *adv* every day, daily.

coturnīx, -īcis *f* quail.

Cotyttia, -ōrum *ntpl festival of Thracian goddess Cotytto.*

Cōus *adj* Coan.

covinnārius, -ī *and* **iī** *m* chariot fighter.

covinnus, -ī *m* war chariot; coach.

coxa, -ae, coxendīx, -īcis *f* hip.

coxī *perf of* **coquō**.

crābrō, -ōnis *m* hornet.

crambē-, -ēs *f* cabbage; **~ repetīta** stale repetitions.

Crantor, -oris *m Greek Academic philosopher.*

crāpula, -ae *f* intoxication, hangover.

crāpulārius *adj* for intoxication.

crās *adv* tomorrow.

crassē *adv* grossly, dimly.

Crassiānus *adj see* **Crassus**.

crassitūdō, -inis *f* thickness, density.

crassus *adj* thick, gross, dense; *(fig)* dull, stupid.

Crassus, -ī *m famous orator; wealthy politician, triumvir with Caesar and Pompey.*

crāstinum, -ī *nt* the morrow.

crāstinus *adj* of tomorrow; **diē ~ī** tomorrow.

crātēr, -is *m*, **-a, -ae** *f* bowl *(esp for mixing wine and water)*; crater; a constellation.

crātis, -is *f* wickerwork, hurdle; (*AGR*) harrow; (*MIL*) faggots for lining trenches; (*shield*) ribs; *(fig)* frame, joints.

creātiō, -ōnis *f* election.

creātor, -ōris *m*, **-rīx, -rīcis** *f* creator, father, mother.

creātus *m (with abl)* son of.

crēber, -rī *adj* dense, thick, crowded; numerous, frequent; *(fig)* prolific, abundant.

crēbrēscō, -ēscere, -uī *vi* to increase, become frequent.

crēbritās, -ātis *f* frequency.

crēbrō *adv* repeatedly.

crēdibilis *adj* credible.

crēdibiliter *adv see* **crēdibilis**.

crēditor, -ōris *m* creditor.

crēditum, -itī *nt* loan.

crēdō, -ere, -idī, -itum *vt, vi* to entrust, lend; to trust, have confidence in; to believe; to think, suppose; **~erēs** one would have thought.

crēdulitās, -ātis *f* credulity.

crēdulus *adj* credulous, trusting.

cremō, -āre, -āvī, -ātum *vt* to burn, cremate.

Cremōna, -ae *f* town in N. Italy.

Cremōnēnsis *adj see n.*

cremor, -ōris *m* juice, broth.

creō, -āre, -āvī, -ātum *vt* to create, produce, beget; to elect (to an office); to cause, occasion.

creper, -ī *adj* dark; doubtful.

crepida, -ae *f* sandal; **nē sūtor suprā ~am** ≈ *let the cobbler stick to his last.*

crepidātus *adj* wearing sandals.

crepīdō, -inis *f* pedestal, base; bank, pier, dam.

crepidula, -ae *f* small sandal.

crepitācillum, -ī *nt* rattle.

crepitō, -āre *vi* to rattle, chatter, rustle, creak.

crepitus, -ūs *m* rattling, chattering, rustling, creaking.

crepō, -āre, -uī, -itum *vi* to rattle, creak, snap (fingers) ♦ *vt* to make rattle, clap; to chatter about.

crepundia, -ōrum *ntpl* rattle, babies' toys.

crepusculum, -ī *nt* twilight, dusk; darkness.

Crēs, -ētis *m* Cretan.

crēscō, -scere, -vī, -tum *vi* to arise, appear, be born; to grow up, thrive, increase, multiply; to prosper, be promoted, rise in the world.

Crēsius *adj* Cretan.

Crēssa, -ae *f* Cretan.

Crēta, -ae *f* Crete.

crēta, -ae *f* chalk; good mark.

Crētaeus *and* **-icus** *and* **-is, -idis** *adj see n.*

crētātus *adj* chalked; dressed in white.

Crētē *see* **Crēta**.

crēteus *adj* of chalk, of clay.

crētiō, -ōnis *f* declaration of accepting an inheritance.

crētōsus *adj* chalky, clayey.

crētula, -ae *f* white clay for sealing.

crētus *ppp of* **cernō** ♦ *ppa of* **crēscō** ♦ *adj* descended, born.

Creūsa, -ae *f* wife of Jason; wife of Aeneas.

crēvī *perf of* **cernō**; *perf of* **crēscō**.

crībrum, -ī *nt* sieve.

crīmen, -inis *nt* accusation, charge, reproach; guilt, crime; cause of offence; **esse in ~ine** stand accused.

crīminātiō, -ōnis *f* complaint, slander.

crīminātor, -ōris *m* accuser.

crīminō, -āre *vt* to accuse.

crīminor, -ārī, -ātus *dep* to accuse, impeach; *(things)* to complain of, charge with.

crīminōsē *adv* accusingly, slanderously.

crīminōsus *adj* reproachful, slanderous.

crīnālis *adj* for the hair, hair- *(in cpds)* ♦ *nt* hairpin.

crīnis, -is *m* hair; *(comet)* tail.

crīnītus *adj* long-haired; crested; **stēlla ~a** comet.

crispāns, -antis *adj* wrinkled.

crispō, -āre *vt* to curl, swing, wave.

crispus *adj* curled; curly-headed; wrinkled; tremulous.

crista, -ae *f* cockscomb, crest; plume.

cristātus *adj* crested, plumed.

criticus, -ī *m* critic.

croceus *adj* of saffron, yellow.

crocinus *adj* yellow ♦ *nt* saffron oil.

crōciō, -īre *vi* to croak.
crocodīlus, -ī *m* crocodile.
crocōtārius *adj* of saffron clothes.
crocōtula, -ae *f* saffron dress.
crocus, -ī *m*, **-um, -ī** *nt* saffron; yellow.
Croesus, -ī *m* king of Lydia (*famed for wealth*).
crotalistria, -ae *f* castanet dancer.
crotalum, -ī *nt* rattle, castanet.
cruciābilitās, -ātis *f* torment.
cruciāmentum, -ī *nt* torture.
cruciātus, -ūs *m* torture; instrument of torture; (*fig*) ruin, misfortune.
cruciō, -āre, -āvī, -ātum *vt* to torture; to torment.
crūdēlis *adj* hard-hearted, cruel.
crūdēlitās, -ātis *f* cruelty, severity.
crūdēliter *adv see* **crūdēlis**.
crūdēscō, -ēscere, -uī *vi* to grow violent, grow worse.
crūditās, -ātis *f* indigestion.
crūdus *adj* bleeding; (*food*) raw, undigested; (*person*) dyspeptic; (*leather*) rawhide; (*fruit*) unripe; (*age*) immature, fresh; (*voice*) hoarse; (*fig*) unfeeling, cruel, merciless.
cruentō, -āre *vt* to stain with blood, wound.
cruentus *adj* bloody, gory; bloodthirsty, cruel; blood-red.
crumēna, -ae *f* purse; money.
crumilla, -ae *f* purse.
cruor, -ōris *m* blood; bloodshed.
cruppellāriī, -ōrum *mpl* mail-clad fighters.
crūrifragius, -ī *and* **iī** *m* one whose legs have been broken.
crūs, -ūris *nt* leg, shin.
crūsta, -ae *f* hard surface, crust; stucco, embossed *or* inlaid work.
crūstulum, -ī *nt* small pastry.
crūstum, -ī *nt* pastry.
crux, -ucis *f* gallows, cross; (*fig*) torment; **abī in malam ~cem** ≈ *go and be hanged!*
crypta, -ae *f* underground passage, grotto.
cryptoporticus, -ūs *f* covered walk.
crystallinus *adj* of crystal ♦ *ntpl* crystal vases.
crystallum, -ī *nt*, **-us, -ī** *m* crystal.
cubiculāris, cubiculārius *adj* of the bedroom ♦ *m* valet de chambre.
cubiculum, -ī *nt* bedroom.
cubīle, -is *nt* bed, couch; (*animals*) lair, nest; (*fig*) den.
cubital, -ālis *nt* cushion.
cubitālis *adj* a cubit long.
cubitō, -āre *vi* to lie (in bed).
cubitum, -ī *nt* elbow; cubit.
cubitus, -ūs *m* lying in bed.
cubō, -āre, -uī, -itum *vi* to lie in bed; to recline at table; (*places*) to lie on a slope.
cucullus, -ī *m* hood, cowl.
cucūlus, -ī *m* cuckoo.
cucumis, -eris *m* cucumber.
cucurbita, -ae *f* gourd; cupping glass.

cucurrī *perf of* **currō**.
cūdō, -ere *vt* to beat, thresh; (*metal*) to forge; (*money*) to coin.
cūiās, -tis *pron* of what country?, of what town?
cuicuimodī (*gen of* **quisquis** *and* **mōdus**) of whatever kind, whatever like.
cūius *pron* (*interrog*) whose?; (*rel*) whose.
culcita, -ae *f* mattress, pillow; eyepatch.
cūleus *see* **culleus**.
culex, -icis *m/f* gnat.
culīna, -ae *f* kitchen; food.
culleus, cūleus, -ī *m* leather bag for holding liquids; *a fluid measure.*
culmen, -inis *nt* stalk; top, roof, summit; (*fig*) height, acme.
culmus, -ī *m* stalk, straw.
culpa, -ae *f* blame, fault; mischief; **in ~ā sum, mea ~a est** I am at fault *or* to blame.
culpātus *adj* blameworthy.
culpitō, -āre *vt* to find fault with.
culpō, -āre, -āvī, -ātum *vt* to blame, reproach.
cultē *adv* in a refined manner.
cultellus, -ī *m* small knife.
culter, -rī *m* knife, razor.
cultiō, -ōnis *f* cultivation.
cultor, -ōris *m* cultivator, planter, farmer; inhabitant; supporter, upholder; worshipper.
cultrīx, -īcis *f* inhabitant; (*fig*) nurse, fosterer.
cultūra, -ae *f* cultivation, agriculture; (*mind*) care, culture; (*person*) courting.
cultus *ppp of* **colō** ♦ *adj* cultivated; (*dress*) well-dressed; (*mind*) polished, cultured ♦ *ntpl* cultivated land.
cultus, -ūs *m* cultivation, care; (*mind*) training, culture; (*dress*) style, attire; (*way of life*) refinement, civilization; (*gods*) worship; (*men*) honouring.
culullus, -ī *m* goblet.
cūlus, -ī *m* buttocks.
cum *prep* (*with abl*) with; (*denoting accompaniment, resulting circumstances, means, dealings, comparison, possession*); **~ decimō** tenfold; **~ eō quod, ut** with the proviso that; **~ prīmīs** especially; **~ māgnā calamitāte cīvitātis** to the great misfortune of the community; **~ perīculō suō** at one's own peril.
cum *conj* (*time*) when, whenever, while, as, after, since; (*cause*) since, as, seeing that; (*concession*) although; (*condition*) if; (*contrast*) while, whereas; **multī annī sunt ~ in aere meō est** for many years now he has been in my debt; **aliquot sunt annī ~ vōs dēlēgī** it is now some years since I chose you; **~ māximē** just when; just then, just now; **~ prīmum** as soon as; **~ … tum** not only … but also; both … and.

Noun declensions and verb conjugations are shown on pp xiii to xxv. The present infinitive ending of a verb shows to which conjugation it belongs: **-āre** = 1st; **-ēre** = 2nd; **-ere** = 3rd and **-īre** = 4th. Irregular verbs are shown on p xxvi

Cūmae, -ārum *fpl* town near Naples (*famous for its Sibyl*).
Cūmaeānum, -āni *nt* Cicero's Cumaean residence.
Cūmaeus, -ānus *adj see n.*
cumba, cymba, -ae *f* boat, skiff.
cumera, -ae *f* grain chest.
cumīnum, -ī *nt* cumin.
cumque (quomque) *adv* -ever, -soever; at any time.
cumulātē *adv* fully, abundantly.
cumulātus *adj* increased; complete.
cumulō, -āre, -āvī, -ātum *vt* to heap up; to amass, increase; to fill up, overload; (*fig*) to fill, overwhelm, crown, complete.
cumulus, -ī *m* heap, mass; crowning addition, summit.
cūnābula, -ōrum *ntpl* cradle.
cūnae, -ārum *fpl* cradle.
cunctābundus *adj* hesitant, dilatory.
cunctāns, -antis *adj* dilatory, reluctant; sluggish, tough.
cunctanter *adv* slowly.
cunctātiō, -ōnis *f* delaying, hesitation.
cunctātor, -ōris *m* loiterer; one given to cautious tactics (*esp Q Fabius Maximus*).
cunctor, -ārī, -ātus *vi* to linger, delay, hesitate; to move slowly.
cūnctus *adj* the whole of; (*pl*) all together, all.
cuneātim *adv* in the form of a wedge.
cuneātus *adj* wedge-shaped.
cuneus, -ī *m* wedge; (*MIL*) wedge-shaped formation of troops; (*THEATRE*) block of seats.
cunīculus, -ī *m* rabbit; underground passage; (*MIL*) mine.
cunque *see* cumque.
cūpa, -ae *f* vat, tun.
cupidē *adv* eagerly, passionately.
Cupīdineus *adj see* Cupīdō.
cupiditās, -ātis *f* desire, eagerness, enthusiasm; passion, lust; avarice, greed; ambition; partisanship.
cupīdō, -inis *f* desire, eagerness; passion, lust; greed.
Cupīdō, -inis *m* Cupid (*son of Venus*).
cupidus *adj* desirous, eager; fond, loving; passionate, lustful; greedy, ambitious; partial.
cupiēns, -entis *pres p of* cupiō ♦ *adj* eager, desirous.
cupienter *adv see* cupiēns.
cupiō, -ere, -īvī *and* **iī, -ītum** *vt* to wish, desire, long for; (*with dat*) to wish well.
cupītor, -ōris *m* desirer.
cupītus *ppp of* cupiō.
cuppēdia, -ae *f* fondness for delicacies.
cuppēdia, -ōrum *ntpl* delicacies.
cuppēdinārius, -ī *m* confectioner.
cuppēdō, -inis *f* longing, passion.
cuppes, -dis *adj* fond of delicacies.
cupressētum, -ī *nt* cypress grove.
cupresseus *adj* of cypress wood.
cupressifer, -ī *adj* cypress-bearing.

cupressus, -ī *f* cypress.
cūr *adv* why?; (*indirect*) why, the reason for.
cūra, -ae *f* care, trouble, pains (bestowed); anxiety, concern, sorrow (felt); attention (to), charge (of), concern (for); (*MED*) treatment, cure; (*writing*) work; (*law*) trusteeship; (*poet*) love; (*person*) mistress, guardian; ~ **est** I am anxious; **~ae esse** be attended to, looked after.
cūrābilis *adj* troublesome.
cūralium, -ī *and* **iī** *nt* red coral.
cūrātē *adv* carefully.
cūrātiō, -ōnis *f* charge, management; office; treatment, healing.
cūrātor, -ōris *m* manager, overseer; (*law*) guardian.
cūrātūra, -ae *f* dieting.
cūrātus *adj* cared for; earnest, anxious.
curculiō, -ōnis *m* weevil.
curculiunculus, -ī *m* little weevil.
Curēnsis *adj see n.*
Curēs, -ium *mpl* ancient Sabine town.
Cūrētēs, -um *mpl* attendants of Jupiter in Crete.
Cūrētis, -idis *adj* Cretan.
cūria, -ae *f* earliest division of the Roman people; meeting-place of a curia; senate house; senate.
cūriālis, -is *m* member of a curia.
cūriātim *adv* by curiae.
cūriātus *adj* of the curiae; **comitia ~a** earliest Roman assembly.
cūriō, -ōnis *m* president of a curia; ~ **māximus** head of all the curiae.
cūriō, -ōnis *adj* emaciated.
cūriōsē *adv* carefully; inquisitively.
cūriōsitās, -ātis *f* curiosity.
cūriōsus *adj* careful, thoughtful, painstaking; inquiring, inquisitive, officious; careworn.
curis, -ītis *f* spear.
cūrō, -āre, -āvī, -ātum *vt* to take care of, attend to; to bother about; (*with gerundive*) to get something done; (*with inf*) to take the trouble; (*with ut*) to see to it that; (*public life*) to be in charge of, administer; (*MED*) to treat, cure; (*money*) to pay, settle up; **aliud ~ā** never mind; **corpus/cutem ~** take it easy; **prōdigia ~** avert portents.
curriculum, -ī *nt* running, race; course, lap; (*fig*) career; **~ō** at full speed.
currō, -ere, cucurrī, cursum *vi* to run; to hasten, fly ♦ *vt* to run through, traverse; **~entem incitāre** ≈ spur a willing horse.
currus, -ūs *m* car, chariot; triumph; team of horses; ploughwheels.
cursim *adv* quickly, at the double.
cursitō, -āre *vi* to run about, fly hither and thither.
cursō, -āre *vi* to run about.
cursor, -ōris *m* runner, racer; courier.
cursūra, -ae *f* running.
cursus, -ūs *m* running, speed; passage, journey; course, direction; (*things*) movement, flow; (*fig*) rapidity, flow, progress; ~ **honōrum** succession of

magistracies; ~ **rērum** course of events; **~um tenēre** keep on one's course; **~ū** at a run; **māgnō ~ū** at full speed.

curtō, -āre _vt_ to shorten.

curtus _adj_ short, broken off; incomplete.

curūlis _adj_ official, curule; **aedīlis ~** patrician, aediile; **sella ~** magistrates' chair; **equī ~** horses provided for the games by the state.

curvāmen, -inis _nt_ bend.

curvātūra, -ae _f_ curve.

curvō, -āre, -āvī, -ātum _vt_ to curve, bend, arch; (_fig_) to move.

curvus _adj_ bent, curved, crooked; (_person_) aged; (_fig_) wrong.

cuspis, -dis _f_ point; spear, javelin, trident, sting.

custōdēla, -ae _f_ care, guard.

custōdia, -ae _f_ watch, guard, care; (_person_) sentry, guard; (_place_) sentry's post, guardhouse; custody, confinement, prison; **lībera ~** confinement in one's own house.

custōdiō, -īre, -īvī _and_ **iī, -ītum** _vt_ to guard, defend; to hold in custody, keep watch on; to keep, preserve, observe.

custōs, -ōdis _m/f_ guard, bodyguard, protector, protectress; jailer, warder; (_MIL_) sentry, spy; container.

cutīcula, -ae _f_ skin.

cutis, -is _f_ skin; **~em cūrāre** ≈ take it easy.

cyathissō, -āre _vi_ to serve wine.

cyathus, -ī _m_ wine ladle; (_measure_) one-twelfth of a pint.

cybaea, -ae _f_ kind of merchant ship.

Cybēbē, Cybelē, -ēs _f_ Phrygian mother-goddess, Magna Mater.

Cybelēius _adj_ see n.

Cyclades, -um _fpl_ group of Aegean islands.

cyclas, -adis _f_ formal dress with a border.

cyclicus _adj_ of the traditional epic stories.

Cyclōpius _adj_ see n.

Cyclōps, -is _m_ one-eyed giant (_esp_ Polyphemus).

cycnēus _adj_ of a swan, swan's.

cycnus, -ī _m_ swan.

Cydōnius _adj_ Cretan ♦ _ntpl_ quinces.

cygnus see **cycnus.**

cylindrus, -ī _m_ cylinder; roller.

Cyllēnē, -ēs _and_ **ae** _f_ mountain in Arcadia.

Cyllēnēus, -is, -ius _adj_ see n.

Cyllēnius, -ī _m_ Mercury.

cymba see **cumba.**

cymbalum, -ī _nt_ cymbal.

cymbium, -ī _and_ **iī** _nt_ cup.

Cynicē _adv_ like the Cynics.

Cynicus, -ī _m_ a Cynic philosopher (_esp_ Diogenes) ♦ _adj_ Cynic.

cynocephalus, -ī _m_ dog-headed ape.

Cynosūra, -ae _f_ constellation of Ursa Minor.

Cynosūris, -idis _adj_ see n.

Cynthia, -iae _f_ Diana.

Cynthius, -ī _m_ Apollo.

Cynthus, -ī _m_ hill in Delos (_birthplace of Apollo and Diana_).

cyparissus, -ī _f_ cypress.

Cypris, -idis _f_ Venus.

Cyprius _adj_ Cyprian; copper.

Cyprus, -ī _f_ island of Cyprus (_famed for its copper and the worship of Venus_).

Cyrēnaeī, -aicī _mpl_ followers of Aristippus.

Cyrēnaeus, -aicus, -ēnsis _adj_ see n.

Cyrēnē, -ēs _f_, **-ae, -ārum** _fpl_ town and province of N. Africa.

Cyrnēus _adj_ Corsican.

Cyrus, -ī _m_ Persian king.

Cytaeis, -idis _f_ Medea.

Cythēra, -ae _f_ island S. of Greece (_famed for its worship of Venus_).

Cytherēa, -ēae _and_ **-ēia, -ēiae** _and_ **-ēis, -ēidis** _f_ Venus.

Cytherēus, Cythēriacus _adj_ Cytherean; of Venus.

cytisus, -ī _m/f_ cytisus (_a kind of clover_).

Cyzicēnus _adj_ see **Cyzicum.**

Cyzicum, -ī _nt_, **-us, -os, -ī** _f_ town on Sea of Marmora.

_D, d_

Dācī, -ōrum _mpl_ Dacians, a people on the lower Danube.

Dācia, -iae _f_ the country of the Dācī (_now Romania_).

Dācicus, -icī _m_ gold coin of Domitian's reign.

dactylicus _adj_ dactylic.

dactylus, -ī _m_ dactyl.

Daedalēus _adj_ see n.

daedalus _adj_ artistic, skilful in creating; skilfully made, variegated.

Daedalus, -ī _m_ mythical Athenian craftsman and inventor.

Dalmatae, -ārum _mpl_ Dalmatians (_a people on the East coast of the Adriatic_).

Dalmatia, -iae _f_ Dalmatia.

Dalmaticus _adj_ see n.

dāma, -ae _f_ deer; venison.

Damascēnus _adj_ see n.

Damascus, -ī _f_ Damascus.

damma _f_ see **dama.**

damnātiō, -ōnis _f_ condemnation.

damnātōrius _adj_ condemnatory.

damnātus _adj_ criminal; miserable.

damnificus _adj_ pernicious.

Noun declensions and verb conjugations are shown on pp xiii to xxv. The present infinitive ending of a verb shows to which conjugation it belongs: **-āre** = 1st; **-ēre** = 2nd; **-ere** = 3rd and **-īre** = 4th. Irregular verbs are shown on p xxvi

damnō, -āre, -āvī, -ātum *vt* to condemn, sentence; to procure the conviction of; (*heirs*) to oblige; to censure; **capitis/capite ~** condemn to death; **māiestātis, dē māiestāte ~** condemn for treason; **vōtī ~** oblige to fulfil a vow.

damnōsē *adv* ruinously.

damnōsus *adj* harmful, ruinous; spendthrift; wronged.

damnum, -ī *nt* loss, harm, damage; (*law*) fine, damages; **~ facere** suffer loss.

Danaē, -ēs *f* mother of Perseus.

Danaēius *adj see n.*

Danaī, -ōrum *and* **um** *mpl* the Greeks.

Danaides, -idum *fpl* daughters of Danaus.

Danaus, -ī *m* king of Argos and father of 50 daughters.

Danaus *adj* Greek.

danīsta, -ae *m* moneylender.

danīsticus *adj* moneylending.

danō *see* **dō.**

Dānuvius, -ī *m* upper Danube.

Daphnē, -ēs *f* nymph changed into a laurel tree.

Daphnis, -idis (*acc* **-im** *and* **-in**) *m* mythical Sicilian shepherd.

dapinō, -āre *vt* to serve (food).

daps, dapis *f* religious feast; meal, banquet.

dapsilis *adj* sumptuous, abundant.

Dardania, -iae *f* Troy.

Dardanidēs, -idae *m* Trojan (*esp Aeneas*).

Dardanus, -ī *m* son of Jupiter and ancestor of Trojan kings.

Dardanus, -ius, -is, -idis *adj* Trojan.

Darēus, -ī *m* Persian king.

datārius *adj* to give away.

datātim *adv* passing from one to the other.

datiō, -ōnis *f* right to give away; (*laws*) making.

datō, -āre *vt* to be in the habit of giving.

dator, -ōris *m* giver; (*sport*) bowler.

Daulias, -adis *adj see n.*

Daulis, -dis *f* town in central Greece (*noted for the story of Procne and Philomela*).

Daunias, -iadis *f* Apulia.

Daunius *adj* Rutulian; Italian.

Daunus, -ī *m* legendary king of Apulia (*ancestor of Turnus*).

dē *prep* (*with abl: movement*) down from, from; (*origin*) from, of, out of; (*time*) immediately after, in; (*thought, talk, action*) about, concerning; (*reason*) for, because of; (*imitation*) after, in accordance with; **~ industriā** on purpose; **~ integrō** afresh; **~ nocte** during the night; **diem ~ diē** from day to day.

dea, -ae *f* goddess.

dealbō, -āre *vt* to whitewash, plaster.

deambulātiō, -ōnis *f* walk.

deambulō, -āre, -āvī, -ātum *vi* to go for a walk.

deamō, -āre, -āvī, -ātum *vt* to be in love with; to be much obliged to.

dearmātus *adj* disarmed.

deartuō, -āre, -āvī, -ātum *vt* to dismember, ruin.

deasciō, -āre *vt* to smooth with an axe; (*fig*) to cheat.

dēbacchor, -ārī, -ātus *vi* to rage furiously.

dēbellātor, -ōris *m* conqueror.

dēbellō, -āre, -āvī, -ātum *vi* to bring a war to an end ♦ *vt* to subdue; to fight out.

dēbeō, -ēre, -uī, -itum *vt* to owe; (*with inf*) to be bound, ought, should, must; to have to thank for, be indebted for; (*pass*) to be destined.

dēbilis *adj* frail, weak, crippled.

dēbilitās, -ātis *f* weakness, infirmity.

dēbilitātiō, -ōnis *f* weakening.

dēbilitō, -āre, -āvī, -ātum *vt* to cripple, disable; (*fig*) to paralyse, unnerve.

dēbitiō, -ōnis *f* owing.

dēbitor, -ōris *m* debtor.

dēbitum, -ī *nt* debt.

dēblaterō, -āre *vt* to blab.

dēcantō, -āre, -āvī, -ātum *vt* to keep on repeating ♦ *vi* to stop singing.

dēcēdō, -ēdere, -essī, -essum *vi* to withdraw, depart; to retire from a province (*after term of office*); to abate, cease, die; (*rights*) to give up, forgo; (*fig*) to go wrong, swerve (from duty); **dē viā ~** get out of the way.

decem *num* ten.

December, -ris *adj* of December ♦ *m* December.

decempeda, -ae *f* ten-foot rule.

decempedātor, -ōris *m* surveyor.

decemplex, -icis *adj* tenfold.

decemprīmī, -ōrum *mpl* civic chiefs of Italian towns.

decemscalmus *adj* ten-oared.

decemvirālis *adj* of the decemviri.

decemvirātus, -ūs *m* office of decemvir.

decemvirī, -ōrum *and* **um** *mpl* commission of ten men (*for public or religious duties*).

decennis *adj* ten years'.

decēns, -entis *adj* seemly, proper; comely, handsome.

decenter *adv* with propriety.

decentia, -ae *f* comeliness.

dēceptus *ppp of* **dēcipiō.**

dēcernō, -ernere, -rēvī, -rētum *vt* to decide, determine; to decree; to fight it out, decide the issue.

dēcerpō, -ere, -sī, -tum *vt* to pluck off, gather; (*fig*) to derive, enjoy.

dēcertātiō, -ōnis *f* deciding the issue.

dēcertō, -āre, -āvī, -ātum *vi* to fight it out, decide the issue.

dēcessiō, -ōnis *f* departure; retirement (from a province); deduction, disappearance.

dēcessor, -ōris *m* retiring magistrate.

dēcessus, -ūs *m* retirement (from a province); death; (*tide*) ebbing.

decet, -ēre, -uit *vt, vi* it becomes, suits; it is

right, proper.

dēcidō, -ere, -ī *vi* to fall down, fall off; to die; (*fig*) to fail, come down.

dēcidō, -dere, -dī, -sum *vt* to cut off; to settle, put an end to.

deciēns, deciēs *adv* ten times.

decimus, decumus *adj* tenth; **cum ~ō** tenfold; **~um** for the tenth time.

dēcipiō, -ipere, -ēpī, -eptum *vt* to ensnare; to deceive, beguile, disappoint.

dēcīsiō, -ōnis *f* settlement.

dēcīsus *ppp of* **dēcīdō**.

Decius, -ī *m* Roman plebeian name (*esp P Decius Mus, father and son, who devoted their lives in battle*).

Decius, -iānus *adj see* n.

dēclāmātiō, -ōnis *f* loud talking; rhetorical exercise on a given theme.

dēclāmātor, -ōris *m* apprentice in public speaking.

dēclāmātōrius *adj* rhetorical.

dēclāmitō, -āre *vi* to practise rhetoric; to bluster ♦ *vt* to practise pleading.

dēclāmō, -āre, -āvī, -ātum *vi* to practise public speaking, declaim; to bluster.

dēclārātiō, -ōnis *f* expression, making known.

dēclārō, -āre, -āvī, -ātum *vt* to make known; to proclaim, announce, reveal, express, demonstrate.

dēclīnātiō, -ōnis *f* swerving; avoidance; (*RHET*) digression; (*GRAM*) inflection.

dēclīnō, -āre, -āvī, -ātum *vt* to turn aside, deflect; (*eyes*) to close; to evade, shun ♦ *vi* to turn aside, swerve; to digress.

declive *nt* slope, decline.

dēclīvis *adj* sloping, steep, downhill.

dēclīvitās, -ātis *f* sloping ground.

dēcocta, -ae *f* a cold drink.

dēcoctor, -ōris *m* bankrupt.

dēcoctus *ppp of* **dēcoquō** ♦ *adj* (*style*) ripe, elaborated.

dēcōlō, -āre *vi* to run out; (*fig*) to fail.

dēcolor, -ōris *adj* discoloured, faded; **~ aetās** a degenerate age.

dēcolōrātiō, -ōnis *f* discolouring.

dēcolōrō, -āre, -āvī, -ātum *vt* to discolour, deface.

dēcoquō, -quere, -xī, -ctum *vt* to boil down; to cook ♦ *vi* to go bankrupt.

decor, -ōris *m* comeliness, ornament, beauty.

decorē *adv* becomingly, beautifully.

decorō, -āre, -āvī, -ātum *vt* to adorn, embellish; (*fig*) to distinguish, honour.

decōrum, -ī *nt* propriety.

decōrus *adj* becoming, proper; beautiful, noble; adorned.

dēcrepitus *adj* decrepit.

dēcrēscō, -scere, -vī, -tum *vi* to decrease, wane, wear away; to disappear.

dēcrētum, -ī *nt* decree, resolution; (*PHILOS*) doctrine.

dēcrētus *ppp of* **dēcernō**.

dēcrēvī *perf of* **dēcernō**; *perf of* **dēcrēscō**.

decuma, -ae *f* tithe; provincial land tax; largess.

decumāna, -ae *f* wife of a tithe-collector.

decumānus *adj* paying tithes; (*MIL*) of the 10th cohort *or* legion ♦ *m* collector of tithes; **~ī, ~ōrum** *mpl* men of the 10th legion; **porta ~a** main gate of a Roman camp.

decumātēs, -ium *adj pl* subject to tithes.

dēcumbō, -mbere, -buī *vi* to lie down; to recline at table; to fall (in fight).

decumus *see* **decimus**.

decuria, -ae *f* group of ten; panel of judges; social club.

decuriātiō, -ōnis *f*, **decuriātus, -ūs** *m* dividing into decuriae.

decuriō, -āre, -āvī, -ātum *vt* to divide into decuriae *or* groups.

decuriō, -ōnis *m* head of a decuria; (*MIL*) cavalry officer; senator of a provincial town *or* colony.

dēcurrō, -rrere, -currī *and* **rrī, -rsum** *vt, vi* to run down, hurry, flow, sail down; to traverse; (*MIL*) to parade, charge; (*time*) to pass through; (*fig*) to have recourse to.

dēcursiō, -ōnis *f* military manoeuvre.

dēcursus *ppp of* **dēcurrō**.

dēcursus, -ūs *m* descent, downrush; (*MIL*) manoeuvre, attack; (*time*) career.

dēcurtātus *adj* mutilated.

decus, -oris *nt* ornament, glory, beauty; honour, virtue; (*pl*) heroic deeds.

dēcussō, -āre *vt* to divide crosswise.

dēcutiō, -tere, -ssī, -ssum *vt* to strike down, shake off.

dēdecet, -ēre, -uit *vt* it is unbecoming to, is a disgrace to.

dēdecorō, -āre *vt* to disgrace.

dēdecōrus *adj* dishonourable.

dēdecus, -oris *nt* disgrace, shame; vice, crime.

dedī *perf of* **dō**.

dēdicātiō, -ōnis *f* consecration.

dēdicō, -āre, -āvī, -ātum *vt* to consecrate, dedicate; to declare (property in a census return).

dēdidī *perf of* **dēdō**.

dēdignor, -ārī, -ātus *vt* to scorn, reject.

dēdiscō, -scere, -dicī *vt* to unlearn, forget.

dēditīcius, -ī *and* **iī** *m* one who has capitulated.

dēditiō, -ōnis *f* surrender, capitulation.

dēditus *ppp of* **dēdō** ♦ *adj* addicted, devoted; **~ā operā** intentionally.

dēdō, -ere, -idī, -itum *vt* to give up, yield, surrender; to devote.

dēdoceō, -ēre *vt* to teach not to.

dēdoleō, -ēre, -uī *vi* to cease grieving.

dēdūcō, -ūcere, -ūxī, -uctum *vt* to bring down, lead away, deflect; (*MIL*) to lead, withdraw; (*bride*) to bring home; (*colony*) to settle; (*hair*) to comb out; (*important person*) to escort; (*law*) to evict, bring to trial; (*money*) to subtract; (*sail*) to unfurl; (*ship*) to launch; (*thread*) to spin out; (*writing*) to compose; (*fig*) to bring, reduce, divert, derive.

dēductiō, -ōnis *f* leading off; settling a colony; reduction; eviction; inference.

dēductor, -ōris *m* escort.

dēductus *ppp of* **dēdūcō** ♦ *adj* finely spun.

deerrō, -āre, -āvī, -ātum *vi* to go astray.

deesse *infin of* **dēsum**.

dēfaecō, -āre, -āvī, -ātum *vt* to clean; (*fig*) to make clear, set at ease.

dēfatīgātiō, -ōnis *f* tiring out; weariness.

dēfatīgō, -āre, -āvī, -ātum *vt* to tire out, exhaust.

dēfatīscor *etc see* **dēfetīscor**.

dēfectiō, -ōnis *f* desertion; failure, faintness; (*ASTRO*) eclipse.

dēfector, -ōris *m* deserter, rebel.

dēfectus *ppp of* **dēficiō** ♦ *adj* weak, failing.

dēfectus, -ūs *m* failure; eclipse.

dēfendō, -dere, -dī, -sum *vt* to avert, repel; to defend, protect; (*law*) to speak in defence, urge, maintain; (*THEATRE*) to play (a part); **crīmen ~** answer an accusation.

dēfēnsiō, -ōnis *f* defence, speech in defence.

dēfēnsitō, -āre *vt* to defend often.

dēfēnsō, -āre *vt* to defend.

dēfēnsor, -ōris *m* averter; defender, protector, guard.

dēferō, -ferre, -tulī, -lātum *vt* to bring down, bring, carry; to bear away; (*power, honour*) to offer, confer; (*information*) to report; (*law*) to inform against, indict; to recommend (for public services); **ad cōnsilium ~** take into consideration.

dēfervēscō, -vēscere, -vī *and* **buī** *vi* to cool down, calm down.

dēfessus *adj* tired, exhausted.

dēfetīgō *etc see* **dēfatīgō**.

dēfetīscor, -tīscī, -ssus *vi* to grow weary.

dēficiō, -icere, -ēcī, -ectum *vt, vi* to desert, forsake, fail; to be lacking, run short, cease; (*ASTRO*) to be eclipsed; **animō ~** lose heart.

dēfīgō, -gere, -xī, -xum *vt* to fix firmly; to drive in, thrust; (*eyes, mind*) to concentrate; (*fig*) to stupefy, astound; (*magic*) to bewitch.

dēfingō, -ere *vt* to make, portray.

dēfīniō, -īre, -īvī, -ītum *vt* to mark the limit of, limit; to define, prescribe; to restrict; to terminate.

dēfīnītē *adv* precisely.

dēfīnītiō, -ōnis *f* limiting, prescribing, definition.

dēfīnītivus *adj* explanatory.

dēfīnītus *adj* precise.

dēfīō, -ierī *vi* to fail.

dēflagrātiō, -ōnis *f* conflagration.

dēflagrō, -āre, -āvī, -ātum *vi* to be burned down, perish; to cool down, abate ♦ *vt* to burn down.

dēflectō, -ctere, -xī, -xum *vt* to bend down, turn aside; (*fig*) to pervert ♦ *vi* to turn aside, deviate.

dēfleō, -ēre, -ēvī, -ētum *vt* to lament bitterly, bewail ♦ *vi* to weep bitterly.

dēflexus *ppp of* **dēflectō**.

dēflōrēscō, -ēscere, -uī *vi* to shed blooms; (*fig*) to fade.

dēfluō, -ere, -xī, -xum *vi* to flow down, float down; to fall, drop, droop; (*fig*) to come from, be derived; to flow past; (*fig*) to pass away, fail.

dēfodiō, -ōdere, -ōdī, -ossum *vt* to dig, dig out; to bury; (*fig*) to hide away.

dēfore *fut infin of* **dēsum**.

dēfōrmis *adj* misshapen, disfigured, ugly; shapeless; (*fig*) disgraceful, disgusting.

dēfōrmitās, -ātis *f* deformity, hideousness; baseness.

dēfōrmō, -āre, -āvī, -ātum *vt* to form, sketch; to deform, disfigure; to describe; to mar, disgrace.

dēfossus *ppp of* **dēfodiō**.

dēfraudō, -āre *vt* to cheat, defraud; **genium ~** deny oneself.

dēfrēnātus *adj* unbridled.

dēfricō, -āre, -uī, -ātum *and* **tum** *vt* to rub down; (*fig*) to satirize.

dēfringō, -ingere, -ēgī, -āctum *vt* to break off, break down.

dēfrūdō *etc see* **dēfraudō**.

dēfrutum, -ī *nt* new wine boiled down.

dēfugiō, -ugere, -ūgī *vt* to run away from, shirk ♦ *vi* to flee.

dēfuī *perf of* **dēsum**.

dēfūnctus *ppa of* **dēfungor** ♦ *adj* discharged; dead.

dēfundō, -undere, -ūdī, -ūsum *vt* to pour out.

dēfungor, -ungī, -ūnctus *vi* (*with abl*) to discharge, have done with; to die.

dēfutūrus *fut p of* **dēsum**.

dēgener, -is *adj* degenerate, unworthy, base.

dēgenerātum, -ātī *nt* degenerate character.

dēgenerō, -āre, -āvī, -ātum *vi* to degenerate, deteriorate ♦ *vt* to disgrace.

dēgerō, -ere *vt* to carry off.

dēgō, -ere, -ī *vt* (*time*) to pass, spend; (*war*) wage ♦ *vi* to live.

dēgrandinat it is hailing heavily.

dēgravō, -āre *vt* to weigh down, overpower.

dēgredior, -dī, -ssus *vi* to march down, descend, dismount.

dēgrunniō, -īre *vi* to grunt hard.

dēgustō, -āre *vt* to taste, touch; (*fig*) to try, experience.

dehinc *adv* from here; from now, henceforth; then, next.

dehīscō, -ere *vi* to gape, yawn.

dehonestāmentum, -ī *nt* disfigurement.

dehonestō, -āre *vt* to disgrace.

dehortor, -ārī, -ātus *vt* to dissuade, discourage.

Dēianīra, -ae *f wife of Hercules.*

dēiciō, -icere, -iēcī, -iectum *vt* to throw down, hurl, fell; to overthrow, kill; (*eyes*) to lower, avert; (*law*) to evict; (*MIL*) to dislodge; (*ship*) to drive off its course; (*hopes, honours*) to foil, disappoint.

dēiectiō, -ōnis *f* eviction.

dēiectus *ppp of* **dēiciō** ♦ *adj* low-lying; disheartened.

dēiectus, -ūs *m* felling; steep slope.

dēierō, -āre, -āvī, -ātum *vi* to swear solemnly.

dein *etc see* **deinde.**

deinceps *adv* successively, in order.

deinde, dein *adv* from there, next; then, thereafter; next in order.

Dēiotarus, -ī *m* king of Galatia (*defended by Cicero*).

Dēiphobus, -ī *m* son of Priam (*second husband of Helen*).

dēiungō, -ere *vt* to sever.

dēiuvō, -āre *vt* to fail to help.

dej- *etc see* **dei-.**

dēlābor, -bī, -psus *vi* to fall down, fly down, sink; (*fig*) to come down, fall into.

dēlacerō, -āre *vt* to tear to pieces.

dēlāmentor, -ārī *vt* to mourn bitterly for.

dēlāpsus *ppa of* **dēlābor.**

dēlassō, -āre *vt* to tire out.

dēlātiō, -ōnis *f* accusing, informing.

dēlātor, -ōris *m* informer, denouncer.

dēlectābilis *adj* enjoyable.

dēlectāmentum, -ī *nt* amusement.

dēlectātiō, -ōnis *f* delight.

dēlectō, -āre *vt* to charm, delight, amuse.

dēlectus *ppp of* **dēligō.**

dēlectus, -ūs *m* choice; *see also* **dīlēctus.**

dēlēgātiō, -ōnis *f* assignment.

dēlēgī *perf of* **dēligō.**

dēlēgō, -āre, -āvī, -ātum *vt* to assign, transfer, make over; to ascribe.

dēlēnificus *adj* charming.

dēlēnimentum, -ī *nt* solace, allurement.

dēlēniō, -īre, -īvī, -ītum *vt* to soothe, solace; to seduce, win over.

dēlēnītor, -ōris *m* cajoler.

dēleō, -ēre, -ēvī, -ētum *vt* to destroy, annihilate; to efface, blot out.

Dēlia, -ae *f* Diana.

Dēliacus *adj* of Delos.

dēlīberābundus *adj* deliberating.

dēlīberātiō, -ōnis *f* deliberating, consideration.

dēlīberātīvus *adj* deliberative.

dēlīberātor, -ōris *m* consulter.

dēlīberātus *adj* determined.

dēlīberō, -āre, -āvī, -ātum *vt, vi* to consider, deliberate, consult; to resolve, determine; ~**ārī potest** it is in doubt.

dēlībō, -āre, -āvī, -ātum *vt* to taste, sip; to pick, gather; to detract from, mar.

dēlibrō, -āre *vt* to strip the bark off.

dēlibuō, -uere, -uī, -ūtum *vt* to smear, steep.

dēlicātē *adv* luxuriously.

dēlicātus *adj* delightful; tender, soft; voluptuous, spoiled, effeminate; fastidious.

dēliciae, -ārum *fpl* delight, pleasure; whimsicalities, sport; (*person*) sweetheart, darling.

dēliciolae, -ārum *fpl* darling.

dēlicium, -ī *and* **iī** *nt* favourite.

dēlicō, -āre *vt* to explain.

dēlictum, -ī *nt* offence, wrong.

dēlicuus *adj* lacking.

dēligō, -igere, -ēgī, -ēctum *vt* to select, gather; to set aside.

deligō, -āre, -āvī, -ātum *vt* to tie up, make fast.

dēlingō, -ere *vt* to have a lick of.

dēlīni- *etc see* **dēlēni-.**

dēlinquō, -inquere, -īquī, -ictum *vi* to fail, offend, do wrong.

dēliquēscō, -quēscere, -cuī *vi* to melt away; (*fig*) to pine away.

dēliquiō, -ōnis *f* lack.

dēlīrāmentum, -ī *nt* nonsense.

dēlīrātiō, -ōnis *f* dotage.

dēlīrō, -āre *vi* to be crazy, drivel.

dēlīrus *adj* crazy.

dēlitēscō, -ēscere, -uī *vi* to hide away, lurk; (*fig*) to skulk, take shelter under.

dēlītigō, -āre *vi* to scold.

Dēlius, -iacus *adj see n.*

Delmatae *see* **Dalmatae.**

Dēlos, -ī *f* sacred Aegean island (*birthplace of Apollo and Diana*).

Delphī, -ōrum *mpl* town in central Greece (*famous for its oracle of Apollo*); the Delphians.

Delphicus *adj see n.*

delphīnus, -ī *and* **delphīn, -is** *m* dolphin.

Deltōton, -ī *nt* (*constellation*) Triangulum.

dēlubrum, -ī *nt* sanctuary, temple.

dēluctō, -āre, -or, -ārī *vi* to wrestle.

dēlūdificō, -āre *vt* to make fun of.

dēlūdō, -dere, -sī, -sum *vt* to dupe, delude.

dēlumbis *adj* feeble.

dēlumbō, -āre *vt* to enervate.

dēmadēscō, -ēscere, -uī *vi* to be drenched.

dēmandō, -āre *vt* to entrust, commit.

dēmarchus, -ī *m* demarch (*chief of a village in Attica*).

dēmēns, -entis *adj* mad, foolish.

dēmēnsum, -ī *nt* ration.

dēmēnsus *ppa of* **dēmētior.**

dēmenter *adv see* **dēmēns.**

dēmentia, -ae *f* madness, folly.

dēmentiō, -īre *vi* to rave.

Noun declensions and verb conjugations are shown on pp xiii to xxv. The present infinitive ending of a verb shows to which conjugation it belongs: -**āre** = 1st; -**ēre** = 2nd; -**ere** = 3rd and -**īre** = 4th. Irregular verbs are shown on p xxvi

dēmereō, -ēre, -uī, -itum, -eor, -ērī _vt_ to earn, deserve; to do a service to.

dēmergō, -gere, -sī, -sum _vt_ to submerge, plunge, sink; (_fig_) to overwhelm.

dēmessus _ppp of_ **dēmetō.**

dēmētior, -tīrī, -nsus _vt_ to measure out.

dēmetō, -tere, -ssuī, -ssum _vt_ to reap, harvest; to cut off.

dēmigrātiō, -ōnis _f_ emigration.

dēmigrō, -āre _vi_ to move, emigrate.

dēminuō, -uere, -uī, -ūtum _vt_ to make smaller, lessen, detract from; **capite ~** deprive of citizenship.

dēminūtiō, -ōnis _f_ decrease, lessening; (_law_) right to transfer property; **capitis ~** loss of political rights.

dēmīror, -ārī, -ātus _vt_ to marvel at, wonder.

dēmissē _adv_ modestly, meanly.

dēmissīcius _adj_ flowing.

dēmissiō, -ōnis _f_ letting down; (_fig_) dejection.

dēmissus _ppp of_ **dēmittō** ♦ _adj_ low-lying; drooping; humble, unassuming; dejected; (_origin_) descended.

dēmītigō, -āre _vt_ to make milder.

dēmittō, -ittere, -īsī, -issum _vt_ to let down, lower, sink; to send down, plunge; (_beard_) to grow; (_ship_) to bring to land; (_troops_) to move down; (_fig_) to cast down, dishearten, reduce, impress; **sē ~** stoop; descend; be disheartened.

dēmiūrgus, -ī _m_ chief magistrate in a Greek state.

dēmō, -ere, -psī, -ptum _vt_ to take away, subtract.

Dēmocriticus, -ius, -ēus _adj see n._

Dēmocritus, -ī _m_ Greek philosopher (_author of the atomic theory_).

dēmōlior, -īrī _vt_ to pull down, destroy.

dēmōlītiō, -ōnis _f_ pulling down.

dēmōnstrātiō, -ōnis _f_ pointing out, explanation.

dēmōnstrātīvus _adj_ (_RHET_) for display.

dēmōnstrātor, -ōris _m_ indicator.

dēmōnstrō, -āre, -āvī, -ātum _vt_ to point out; to explain, represent, prove.

dēmorior, -ī, -tuus _vi_ to die, pass away ♦ _vt_ to be in love with.

dēmoror, -ārī, -ātus _vi_ to wait ♦ _vt_ to detain, delay.

dēmortuus _ppa of_ **dēmorior.**

Dēmosthenēs, -is _m_ greatest Athenian orator.

dēmoveō, -ovēre, -ōvī, -ōtum _vt_ to remove, turn aside, dislodge.

dēmpsī _perf of_ **dēmō.**

dēmptus _ppp of_ **dēmō.**

dēmūgītus _adj_ filled with lowing.

dēmulceō, -cēre, -sī _vt_ to stroke.

dēmum _adv_ (_time_) at last, not till; (_emphasis_) just, precisely; **ibi ~** just there; **modo ~** only now; **nunc ~** now at last; **post ~** not till after; **tum ~** only then.

dēmurmurō, -āre _vt_ to mumble through.

dēmūtātiō, -ōnis _f_ change.

dēmūtō, -āre _vt_ to change, make worse ♦ _vi_ to change one's mind.

dēnārius, -ī _and_ **iī** _m_ Roman silver coin.

dēnārrō, -āre _vt_ to relate fully.

dēnāsō, -āre _vt_ to take the nose off.

dēnatō, -āre _vi_ to swim down.

dēnegō, -āre, -āvī, ātum _vt_ to deny, refuse, reject ♦ _vi_ to say no.

dēnī, -ōrum _adj_ ten each, in tens; ten; tenth.

dēnicālis _adj_ for purifying after a death.

dēnique _adv_ at last, finally; (_enumerating_) lastly, next; (_summing up_) in short, briefly; (_emphasis_) just, precisely.

dēnōminō, -āre _vt_ to designate.

dēnormō, -āre _vt_ to make irregular.

dēnotō, -āre, -āvī, -ātum _vt_ to point out, specify; to observe.

dēns, dentis _m_ tooth; ivory; prong, fluke.

dēnsē _adv_ repeatedly.

dēnsō, -āre, -āvī, -ātum, dēnseō, -ēre _vt_ to thicken; (_ranks_) to close.

dēnsus _adj_ thick, dense, close; frequent; (_style_) concise.

dentālia, -ium _ntpl_ ploughbeam.

dentātus _adj_ toothed; (_paper_) polished.

dentiō, -īre _vi_ to cut one's teeth; (_teeth_) to grow.

dēnūbō, -bere, -psī, -ptum _vi_ to marry, marry beneath one.

dēnūdō, -āre, -āvī, -ātum _vt_ to bare, strip; (_fig_) to disclose.

dēnūntiātiō, -ōnis _f_ intimation, warning.

dēnūntiō, -āre, -āvī, -ātum _vt_ to intimate, give notice of, declare; to threaten, warn; (_law_) to summon as witness.

dēnuō _adv_ afresh, again, once more.

deonerō, -āre _vt_ to unload.

deorsum, deorsus _adv_ downwards.

deōsculor, -ārī _vt_ to kiss warmly.

dēpacīscor _etc see_ **dēpecīscor.**

dēpāctus _adj_ driven in firmly.

dēpāscō, -scere, -vī, -stum, -scor, -scī _vt_ to feed on, eat up; (_fig_) to devour, destroy, prune away.

dēpecīscor, -īscī, -tus _vt_ to bargain for, agree about.

dēpectō, -ctere, -xum _vt_ to comb; (_comedy_) to flog.

dēpectus _ppa of_ **dēpecīscor.**

dēpecūlātor, -ōris _m_ embezzler.

dēpecūlor, -ārī, -ātus _vt_ to plunder.

dēpellō, -ellere, -ulī, -ulsum _vt_ to expel, remove, cast down; (_MIL_) to dislodge; (_infants_) to wean; (_fig_) to deter, avert.

dēpendeō, -ēre _vi_ to hang down, hang from; to depend on; to be derived.

dēpendō, -endere, -endī, -ēnsum _vt_ to weigh, pay up.

dēperdō, -ere, -idī, -itum _vt_ to lose completely, destroy, ruin.

dēpereō, -īre, -iī _vi_ to perish, be completely destroyed; to be undone ♦ _vt_ to be hopelessly

in love with.
dēpexus *ppp of* **dēpectō**.
dēpingō, -ingere, -inxī, -ictum *vt* to paint;
(*fig*) to portray, describe.
dēplangō, -gere, -xī *vt* to bewail frantically.
dēplexus *adj* grasping.
dēplōrābundus *adj* weeping bitterly.
dēplōrō, -āre, -āvī, -ātum *vi* to weep bitterly
♦ *vt* to bewail bitterly, mourn; to despair of.
dēpluit, -ere *vi* to rain down.
dēpōnō, -ōnere, -osuī, -ositum *vt* to lay
down; to set aside, put away, get rid of; to
wager; to deposit, entrust, commit to the
care of; (*fig*) to give up.
dēpopulātiō, -ōnis *f* ravaging.
dēpopulātor, -ōris *m* marauder.
dēpopulor, -ārī, -ātus; -ō, -āre *vt* to ravage,
devastate; (*fig*) to waste, destroy.
dēportō, -āre, -āvī, -ātum *vt* to carry down,
carry off; to bring home (from a province);
(*law*) to banish for life; (*fig*) to win.
dēposcō, -scere, -poscī *vt* to demand,
require, claim.
dēpositum, -ī *nt* trust, deposit.
dēpositus *ppp of* **dēpōnō** ♦ *adj* dying, dead,
despaired of.
dēprāvātē *adv* perversely.
dēprāvātiō, -ōnis *f* distorting.
dēprāvō, -āre, -āvī, -ātum *vt* to distort; (*fig*)
to pervert, corrupt.
dēprecābundus *adj* imploring.
dēprecātiō, -ōnis *f* averting by prayer;
imprecation, invocation; plea for
indulgence.
dēprecātor, -ōris *m* intercessor.
dēprecor, -ārī, -ātus *vt* to avert (by prayer);
to deprecate, intercede for.
**dēprehendō, dēprendō, -endere, -endī,
-ēnsum** *vt* to catch, intercept; to overtake,
surprise; to catch in the act, detect; (*fig*) to
perceive, discover.
dēprehēnsiō, -ōnis *f* detection.
dēprehēnsus, dēprēnsus *ppp of*
dēprehendō.
dēpressī *perf of* **dēprimō**.
dēpressus *ppp of* **dēprimō** ♦ *adj* low.
dēprimō, -imere, -essī, -essum *vt* to press
down, weigh down; to dig deep; (*ship*) to
sink; (*fig*) to suppress, keep down.
dēproelior, -ārī *vi* to fight it out.
dēprōmō, -ere, psī, -ptum *vt* to fetch, bring
out, produce.
dēproperō, -āre *vi* to hurry up ♦ *vt* to hurry
and make.
dēpsō, -ere *vt* to knead.
dēpudet, -ēre, -uit *v impers* not to be ashamed.
dēpūgis *adj* thin-buttocked.
dēpugnō, -āre, -āvī, -ātum *vi* to fight it out,
fight hard.
dēpulī *perf of* **dēpellō**.

dēpulsiō, -ōnis *f* averting; defence.
dēpulsō, -āre *vt* to push out of the way.
dēpulsor, -ōris *m* repeller.
dēpulsus *ppp of* **dēpellō**.
dēpūrgō, -āre *vt* to clean.
dēputō, -āre *vt* to prune; to consider, reckon.
dēpȳgis *etc see* **dēpūgis**.
dēque *adv* down.
dērēctā, -ē, -ō *adv* straight.
dērēctus *ppp of* **dērigō** ♦ *adj* straight, upright,
at right angles; straightforward.
dērelictiō, -ōnis *f* disregarding.
dērelinquō, -inquere, -īquī, -ictum *vt* to
abandon, forsake.
dērepente *adv* suddenly.
dērēpō, -ere *vi* to creep down.
dēreptus *ppp of* **dēripiō**.
dērīdeō, -dēre, -sī, -sum *vt* to laugh at,
deride.
dērīdiculum, -ī *nt* mockery, absurdity; object
of derision.
dērīdiculus *adj* laughable.
dērigēscō, -ēscere, -uī *vi* to stiffen, curdle.
dērigō, -igere, -ēxī, -ēctum *vt* to turn, aim,
direct; (*fig*) to regulate.
dēripiō, -ipere, -ipuī, -eptum *vt* to tear off,
pull down.
dērīsor, -ōris *m* scoffer.
dērīsus *ppp of* **dērīdeō**.
dērīsus, -ūs *m* scorn, derision.
dērīvātiō, -ōnis *f* diverting.
dērīvō, -āre, -āvī, -ātum *vt* to lead off, draw
off.
dērogō, -āre *vt* (*law*) to propose to amend;
(*fig*) to detract from.
dērōsus *adj* gnawed away.
dēruncinō, -āre *vt* to plane off; (*comedy*) to
cheat.
dēruō, -ere, -ī *vt* to demolish.
dēruptus *adj* steep ♦ *ntpl* precipice.
dēsaeviō, -īre *vi* to rage furiously; to cease
raging.
dēscendō, -endere, -endī, -ēnsum *vi* to
come down, go down, descend, dismount;
(*MIL*) to march down; (*things*) to fall, sink,
penetrate; (*fig*) to stoop (to), lower oneself.
dēscēnsiō, -ōnis *f* going down.
dēscēnsus, -ūs *m* way down.
dēscīscō, -īscere, -īvī *and* **iī, -ītum** *vi* to
desert, revolt; to deviate, part company.
dēscrībō, -bere, -psī, -ptum *vt* to copy out; to
draw, sketch; to describe; *see also* **dīscrībō**.
dēscrīptiō, -ōnis *f* copy; drawing, diagram;
description.
dēscrīptus *ppp of* **dēscrībō**; *see also* **dīscrīptus**.
dēsecō, -āre, -uī, -tum *vt* to cut off.
dēserō, -ere, -uī, -tum *vt* to desert, abandon,
forsake; (*bail*) to forfeit.
dēsertor, -ōris *m* deserter.
dēsertus *ppp of* **dēserō** ♦ *adj* desert,

uninhabited ♦ *ntpl* deserts.

dēserviō, -īre *vi* to be a slave (to), serve.

dēses, -idis *adj* idle, inactive.

dēsiccō, -āre *vt* to dry, drain.

dēsideō, -idēre, -ēdī *vi* to sit idle.

dēsīderābilis *adj* desirable.

dēsīderātiō, -ōnis *f* missing.

dēsīderium, -ī *and* **iī** *nt* longing, sense of loss; want; petition; **mē ~ tenet urbis** I miss Rome.

dēsīderō, -āre, -āvī, -ātum *vt* to feel the want of, miss; to long for, desire; (*casualties*) to lose.

dēsidia, -ae *f* idleness, apathy.

dēsidiōsē *adv* idly.

dēsidiōsus *adj* lazy, idle; relaxing.

dēsīdō, -īdere, -ēdī *vi* to sink, settle down; (*fig*) to deteriorate.

dēsignātiō, -ōnis *f* specifying; election (of magistrates).

dēsignātor *etc see* **dissignātor**.

dēsignātus *adj* elect.

dēsignō, -āre, -āvī, -ātum *vt* to trace out; to indicate, define; (*POL*) to elect; (*art*) to depict.

dēsiī *perf of* **dēsinō**.

dēsiliō, -ilīre, -iluī, -ultum *vi* to jump down, alight.

dēsinō, -nere, -ī *vt* to leave off, abandon ♦ *vi* to stop, desist; to end (in).

dēsipiēns, -ientis *adj* silly.

dēsipientia, -ae *f* folly.

dēsipiō, -ere *vi* to be stupid, play the fool.

dēsistō, -istere, -titī, -titum *vi* to stop, leave off, desist.

dēsitus *ppp of* **dēsinō**.

dēsōlō, -āre, -āvī, -ātum *vt* to leave desolate, abandon.

dēspectō, -āre *vt* to look down on, command a view of; to despise.

dēspectus *ppp of* **dēspiciō** ♦ *adj* contemptible.

dēspectus, -ūs *m* view, prospect.

dēspēranter *adv* despairingly.

dēspērātiō, -ōnis *f* despair.

dēspērātus *adj* despaired of, hopeless; desperate, reckless.

dēspērō, -āre, -āvī, -ātum *vt, vi* to despair, give up hope of.

dēspexī *perf of* **dēspiciō**.

dēspicātiō, -ōnis *f* contempt.

dēspicātus *adj* despised, contemptible.

dēspicātus, -ūs *m* contempt.

dēspicientia, -ae *f* contempt.

dēspiciō, -icere, -exī, -ectum *vt* to look down on; to despise ♦ *vi* to look down.

dēspoliātor, -ōris *m* robber.

dēspoliō, -āre *vt* to rob, plunder.

dēspondeō, -ondēre, -ondī *and* **opondī, -ōnsum** *vt* to pledge, promise; to betroth; to devote; to give up, despair of; **animum ~** despair.

dēspūmō, -āre *vt* to skim off.

dēspuō, -ere *vi* to spit on the ground ♦ *vt* to reject.

dēsquāmō, -āre *vt* to scale, peel.

dēstillō, -āre *vi* to drop down ♦ *vt* to distil.

dēstimulō, -āre *vt* to run through.

dēstinātiō, -ōnis *f* resolution, appointment.

dēstinātus *adj* fixed, decided.

dēstinō, -āre, -āvī, -ātum *vt* to make fast; to appoint, determine, resolve; (*archery*) to aim at; (*fig*) to intend to buy ♦ *nt* mark; intention; **~ātum est mihi** I have decided.

dēstitī *perf of* **dēsistō**.

dēstituō, -uere, -uī, -ūtum *vt* to set apart, place; to forsake, leave in the lurch.

dēstitūtiō, -ōnis *f* defaulting.

dēstitūtus *ppp of* **dēstituō**.

dēstrictus *ppp of* **dēstringō** ♦ *adj* severe.

dēstringō, -ingere, -inxī, -ictum *vt* (*leaves*) to strip; (*body*) to rub down; (*sword*) to draw; to graze, skim; (*fig*) to censure.

dēstruō, -ere, -xī, -ctum *vt* to demolish; to destroy.

dēsubitō *adv* all of a sudden.

dēsūdāscō, -ere *vi* to sweat all over.

dēsūdō, -āre *vi* to exert oneself.

dēsuēfactus *adj* unaccustomed.

dēsuētūdō, -inis *f* disuse.

dēsuētus *adj* unaccustomed, unused.

dēsultor, -ōris *m* circus rider; (*fig*) fickle lover.

dēsultūra, -ae *f* jumping down.

dēsum, deesse, -fuī *vi* to be missing, fail, fail in one's duty.

dēsūmō, -ere, -psī, -ptum *vt* to select.

dēsuper *adv* from above.

dēsurgō, -ere *vi* to rise.

dētegō, -egere, -ēxī, -ēctum *vt* to uncover, disclose; (*fig*) to reveal, detect.

dētendō, -endere, -ēnsum *vt* (*tent*) to strike.

dētentus *ppp of* **dētineō**.

dētergō, -gere, -sī, -sum *vt* to wipe away, clear away; to clean; to break off.

dēterior, -ōris *adj* lower; inferior, worse.

dēterius *adv* worse.

dēterminātiō, -ōnis *f* boundary, end.

dēterminō, -āre, -āvī, -ātum *vt* to bound, limit; to settle.

dēterō, -erere, -rīvī, -rītum *vt* to rub, wear away; (*style*) to polish; (*fig*) to weaken.

dēterreō, -ēre, -uī, -itum *vt* to frighten away; to deter, discourage, prevent.

dētersus *ppp of* **dētergeō**.

dētestābilis *adj* abominable.

dētestātiō, -ōnis *f* execration, curse; averting.

dētestor, -ārī, -ātus *vt* to invoke, invoke against; to curse, execrate; to avert, deprecate.

dētexō, -ere, -uī, -tum *vt* to weave, finish weaving; (*comedy*) to steal; (*fig*) to describe.

dētineō, -inēre, -inuī, -entum *vt* to hold back, detain; to keep occupied.

dētondeō, -ondēre, -ondī, -ōnsum *vt* to shear off, strip.

dētonō, -āre, -uī *vi* to cease thundering.

dētorqueō, -quēre, -sī, -tum *vt* to turn aside,

direct; to distort, misrepresent.
dētractātiō, -ōnis *f* declining.
dētrectātor, -ōris *m* disparager.
dētractiō, -ōnis *f* removal, departure.
dētractō *etc see* **dētrectō**.
dētractus *ppp of* **dētrahō**.
dētrahō, -here, -xī, -ctum *vt* to draw off, take away, pull down; to withdraw, force to leave; to detract, disparage.
dētrectō, -āre, -āvī, -ātum *vt* to decline, shirk; to detract from, disparage.
dētrīmentōsus *adj* harmful.
dētrīmentum, -ī *nt* loss, harm; (*MIL*) defeat; ~ **capere** suffer harm.
dētrītus *ppp of* **dēterō**.
dētrūdō, -dere, -sī, -sum *vt* to push down, thrust away; to dislodge, evict; to postpone; (*fig*) to force.
dētruncō, -āre, -āvī, -ātum *vt* to cut off, behead, mutilate.
dētrūsus *ppp of* **dētrūdō**.
dēturbō, -āre, -āvī, -ātum *vt* to dash down, pull down; (*fig*) to cast down, deprive.
Deucaliōn, -ōnis *m* son of Prometheus (*survivor of the Flood*).
Deucaliōnēus *adj see* **Deucaliōn**.
deūnx, -cis *m* eleven twelfths.
deūrō, -rere, -ssī, -stum *vt* to burn up; to frost.
deus, -ī (*voc* **deus**, *pl* **dī, deos, deum, dis**) *m* god; **dī meliōra!** Heaven forbid!; **dī tē ament!** bless you!
deūstus *ppp of* **deūrō**.
deūtor, -ī *vi* to maltreat.
dēvastō, -āre *vt* to lay waste.
dēvehō, -here, -xī, -ctum *vt* to carry down, convey; (*pass*) to ride down, sail down.
dēvellō, -ellere, -ellī *and* **olsī, -ulsum** *vt* to pluck, pull out.
dēvēlō, -āre *vt* to unveil.
dēveneror, -ārī *vt* to worship; to avert by prayers.
dēveniō, -enīre, -ēnī, -entum *vi* to come, reach, fall into.
dēverberō, -āre, -āvī, -ātum *vt* to thrash soundly.
dēversor, -ārī *vi* to lodge, stay (as guest).
dēversor, -ōris *m* guest.
dēversōriolum, -ī *nt* small lodging.
dēversōrium, -ī *and* **iī** *nt* inn, lodging.
dēversōrius *adj* for lodging.
dēverticulum, -ī *nt* by-road, by-pass; digression; lodging place; (*fig*) refuge.
dēvertō, -tere, -tī, -sum *vi* to turn aside, put up; to have recourse to; to digress.
dēvertor, -tī, versus *vi see* **dēvertō**.
dēvexus *adj* sloping, going down, steep.
dēvinciō, -cīre, -xī, -ctum *vt* to tie up; (*fig*) to bind, lay under an obligation.
dēvincō, -incere, -īcī, -ictum *vt* to defeat

completely, win the day.
dēvītātiō, -ōnis *f* avoiding.
dēvītō, -āre *vt* to avoid.
dēvius *adj* out of the way, devious; (*person*) solitary, wandering off the beaten track; (*fig*) inconstant.
dēvocō, -āre, -āvī, -ātum *vt* to call down, fetch; to entice away.
dēvolō, -āre *vi* to fly down.
dēvolvō, -vere, -vī, -ūtum *vt* to roll down, fall; (*wool*) to spin off.
dēvorō, -āre, -āvī, -ātum *vt* to swallow, gulp down; to engulf, devour; (*money*) to squander; (*tears*) to repress; (*trouble*) to endure patiently.
dēvors-, dēvort- *see* **dēvers-, dēvert-**.
dēvortia, -ōrum *ntpl* byways.
dēvōtiō, -ōnis *f* devoting; (*magic*) spell.
dēvōtō, -āre *vt* to bewitch.
dēvōtus *ppp of* **dēvoveō ♦** *adj* faithful; accursed.
dēvoveō, -ovēre, -ōvī, -ōtum *vt* to devote, vow, dedicate; to give up; to curse; to bewitch.
dēvulsus *ppp of* **dēvellō**.
dextella, -ae *f* little right hand.
dexter, -erī *and* **rī** *adj* right, right-hand; handy, skilful; favourable.
dexteritās, -ātis *f* adroitness.
dextra *f* right hand, right-hand side; hand; pledge of friendship.
dextra *prep* (*with acc*) on the right of.
dextrē (*compar* **-erius**) *adv* adroitly.
dextrōrsum, -rsus, -vorsum *adv* to the right.
dī *pl of* **deus**.
diabathrārius, -ī *and* **iī** *m* slipper maker.
diabolus, -ī *m* devil.
diāconus, -ī *m* (*ECCL*) deacon.
diadēma, -tis *nt* royal headband, diadem.
diaeta, -ae *f* diet; living room.
dialectica, -ae, -ē, -ēs *f* dialectic, logic **♦** *ntpl* logical questions.
dialecticē *adv* dialectically.
dialecticus *adj* dialectical **♦** *m* logician.
Diālis *adj* of Jupiter **♦** *m* high priest of Jupiter.
dialogus, -ī *m* dialogue, conversation.
Diāna, -ae *f* virgin goddess of hunting (*also identified with the moon and Hecate, and patroness of childbirth*).
Diānius *adj* of Diana **♦** *nt* sanctuary of Diana.
diāria, -ōrum *ntpl* daily allowance of food *or* pay.
dibaphus, -ī *f* Roman state robe.
dica, -ae *f* lawsuit.
dicācitās, -ātis *f* raillery, repartee.
dicāculus *adj* pert.
dicātiō, -ōnis *f* declaration of citizenship.
dicāx, -ācis *adj* witty, smart.
dichorēus, -ī *m* double trochee.
diciō, -ōnis *f* power, sway, authority.

Noun declensions and verb conjugations are shown on pp xiii to xxv. The present infinitive ending of a verb shows to which conjugation it belongs: **-āre** = 1st; **-ēre** = 2nd; **-ere** = 3rd and **-īre** = 4th. Irregular verbs are shown on p xxvi

dicis causā for the sake of appearance.
dicō, -āre, -āvī, -ātum vt to dedicate,
consecrate; to deify; to devote, give over.
dīcō, -cere, -xī, dictum vt to say, tell; to
mention, mean, call, name; to pronounce;
(*RHET*) to speak, deliver; (*law*) to plead;
(*poetry*) to describe, celebrate; (*official*) to
appoint; (*time, place*) to settle, fix ♦ vi to
speak (in public); **causam ~** plead; **iūs ~**
deliver judgment; **sententiam ~** vote; **~cō**
namely; **~xī** I have finished; **dictum factum**
no sooner said than done.
dicrotum, -ī nt bireme.
Dictaeus adj Cretan.
dictamnus, -ī f dittany (*a kind of wild
marjoram*).
dictāta, -ōrum ntpl lessons, rules.
dictātor, -ōris m dictator.
dictātōrius adj dictator's.
dictātūra, -ae f dictatorship.
Dictē, -ēs f mountain in Crete (*where Jupiter
was brought up*).
dictiō, -ōnis f speaking, declaring; style,
expression, oratory; (*oracle*) response.
dictitō, -āre vt to keep saying, assert; to plead
often.
dictō, -āre, -āvī, -ātum vt to say repeatedly;
to dictate; to compose.
dictum, -ī nt saying, word; proverb; bon mot,
witticism; command.
dictus ppp of **dīcō**.
Dictynna, -ae f Britomartis; Diana.
Dictynnaeus adj see n.
didicī perf of **discō**.
dīdō, -ere, -idī, -itum vt to distribute,
broadcast.
Dīdō, -ūs and **-ōnis** (*acc* -ō) f Queen of Carthage.
dīdūcō, -ūcere, -ūxī, -uctum vt to separate,
split, open up; (*MIL*) to disperse; (*fig*) to part,
divide.
diēcula, -ae f one little day.
diērēctus adj crucified; **abī ~** go and be
hanged.
diēs, -ēī m/f day; set day (*usu fem*); a day's
journey; (*fig*) time; **~ meus** my birthday; **~em
dīcere** impeach; **~em obīre** die; **~em dē ~ē,
~em ex ~ē** from day to day; **in ~em** to a later
day; for today; **in ~ēs** daily.
Diēspiter, -ris m Jupiter.
diffāmō, -āre, -āvī, -ātum vt to divulge; to
malign.
differentia, -ae f difference, diversity;
species.
differitās, -ātis f difference.
differō, -erre, distulī, dīlātum vt to disperse;
to divulge, publish; (*fig*) to distract, disquiet;
(*time*) to put off, delay ♦ vi to differ, be
distinguished.
differtus adj stuffed, crammed.
difficilis adj difficult; (*person*) awkward, surly.
difficiliter adv with difficulty.
difficultās, -ātis f difficulty, distress,
hardship; surliness.

difficulter adv with difficulty.
diffīdēns, -entis adj nervous.
diffīdenter adv without confidence.
diffīdentia, -ae f mistrust, diffidence.
diffīdō, -dere, -sus vi to distrust, despair.
diffindō, -ndere, -dī, -ssum vt to split, open
up; (*fig*) to break off.
diffingō, -ere vt to remake.
diffissus ppp of **diffindō**.
diffīsus ppa of **diffīdō**.
diffiteor, -ērī vt to disown.
diffluēns, -entis adj (*RHET*) loose.
diffluō, -ere vi to flow away; to melt away; (*fig*)
to wallow.
diffringō, -ere vt to shatter.
diffugiō, -ugere, -ūgī vi to disperse,
disappear.
diffugium, -ī and **iī** nt dispersion.
diffunditō, -āre vt to pour out, waste.
diffundō, -undere, -ūdī, -ūsum vt to pour
off; to spread, diffuse; to cheer, gladden.
diffūsē adv expansively.
diffūsilis adj diffusive.
diffūsus ppp of **diffundō** ♦ adj spreading;
(*writing*) loose.
Dīgentia, -ae f tributary of the Anio (*near
Horace's villa*).
dīgerō, -rere, -ssī, -stum vt to divide,
distribute; to arrange, set out; to interpret.
dīgestiō, -ōnis f (*RHET*) enumeration.
dīgestus ppp of **dīgerō**.
digitulus, -ī m little finger.
digitus, -ī m finger; toe; inch; (*pl*) skill in
counting; **~um porrigere, prōferre** take the
slightest trouble; **~um trānsversum nōn
discēdere** not swerve a finger's breadth;
attingere caelum ~ō reach the height of
happiness; **licērī ~ō** bid at an auction;
mōnstrārī ~ō be a celebrity; **extrēmī, summī
~ī** the fingertips; **concrepāre ~īs** snap the
fingers.
dīgladior, -ārī vi to fight fiercely.
dignātiō, -ōnis f honour, dignity.
dignē adv see **dignus**.
dignitās, -ātis f worth, worthiness; dignity,
rank, position; political office.
dignō, -āre vt to think worthy.
dignor, -ārī vt to think worthy; to deign.
dignōscō, -ere vt to distinguish.
dignus adj worth, worthy; (*things*) fitting,
proper.
dīgredior, -dī, -ssus vi to separate, part; to
deviate, digress.
dīgressiō, -ōnis f parting; deviation,
digression.
dīgressus ppa of **dīgredior**.
dīgressus, -ūs m parting.
dīiūdicātiō, -ōnis f decision.
dīiūdicō, -āre vt to decide; to discriminate.
dīiun- etc see **disiun-**.
dīlābor, -bī, -psus vi to dissolve,
disintegrate; to flow away; (*troops*) to
disperse; (*fig*) to decay, vanish.

dīlacerō, -āre _vt_ to tear to pieces.
dīlāminō, -āre _vt_ to split in two.
dīlaniō, -āre, -āvī, -ātum _vt_ to tear to shreds.
dīlapidō, -āre _vt_ to demolish.
dīlāpsus _ppa of_ **dīlābor.**
dīlargior, -īrī _vt_ to give away liberally.
dīlātiō, -ōnis _f_ putting off, adjournment.
dīlātō, -āre, -āvī, -ātum _vt_ to expand;
  (_pronunciation_) to broaden.
dīlātor, -ōris _m_ procrastinator.
dīlātus _ppp of_ **differō.**
dīlaudō, -āre _vt_ to praise extravagantly.
dīlēctus _ppp of_ **dīligō ♦** _adj_ beloved.
dīlēctus, -ūs _m_ selection, picking; (_MIL_) levy;
  ~um habēre hold a levy, recruit.
dīlēxī _perf of_ **dīligō.**
dīligēns, -entis _adj_ painstaking,
  conscientious, attentive (to); thrifty.
dīligenter _adv see_ **dīligēns.**
dīligentia, -ae _f_ carefulness, attentiveness;
  thrift.
dīligō, -igere, -ēxī, -ēctum _vt_ to prize
  especially, esteem, love.
dīlōrīcō, -āre _vt_ to tear open.
dīlūceō, -ēre _vi_ to be evident.
dīlūcēscit, -cēscere, -xit _vi_ to dawn, begin to
  grow light.
dīlūcidē _adv see_ **dīlūcidus.**
dīlūcidus _adj_ clear, distinct.
dīlūculum, -ī _nt_ dawn.
dīlūdium, -ī _and_ **iī** _nt_ interval.
dīluō, -uere, -uī, -ūtum _vt_ to wash away,
  dissolve, dilute; to explain; (_fig_) to weaken,
  do away with.
dīluviēs, -iēī _f_, **-ium, -ī** _and_ **iī** _nt_ flood, deluge.
dīluviō, -āre _vt_ to inundate.
dīmānō, -āre _vi_ to spread abroad.
dīmēnsiō, -ōnis _f_ measuring.
dīmēnsus _adj_ measured.
dīmētior, -tīrī, -nsus _vt_ to measure out.
dīmētō, -āre, -or, -ārī _vt_ to mark out.
dīmicātiō, -ōnis _f_ fighting, struggle.
dīmicō, -āre, -āvī, -ātum _vi_ to fight, struggle,
  contend.
dīmidiātus _adj_ half, halved.
dīmidius _adj_ half **♦** _nt_ half.
dīmissiō, -ōnis _f_ sending away; discharging.
dīmissus _ppp of_ **dīmittō.**
dīmittō, -ittere, -īsī, -issum _vt_ to send away,
  send round; to let go, lay down; (_meeting_) to
  dismiss; (_MIL_) to disband, detach; (_fig_) to
  abandon, forsake.
dimminuō, -ere _vt_ to dash to pieces.
dīmoveō, -ovēre, -ōvī, -ōtum _vt_ to part,
  separate; to disperse; to entice away.
Dindymēnē, -ēnēs _f_ Cybele.
Dindymus, -ī _m_ mountain in Mysia (_sacred to_
  Cybele).
dīnōscō _see_ **dīgnōscō.**
dīnumerātiō, -ōnis _f_ reckoning up.

dīnumerō, -āre _vt_ to count, reckon up; to pay
  out.
diōbolāris _adj_ costing two obols.
dioecēsis, -is _f_ district; (_ECCL_) diocese.
dioecētēs, -ae _m_ treasurer.
Diogenēs, -is _m_ famous Cynic philosopher; a
  Stoic philosopher.
Diomēdēs, -is _m_ Greek hero at the Trojan War.
Diomēdēus _adj see n._
Diōnaeus _adj_ Boeotian.
Diōnē, -ēs _and_ **-a, -ae** _f_ mother of Venus; Venus.
Dionȳsius, -ī _m_ tyrant of Syracuse.
Dionȳsus, -ī _m_ Bacchus; **-ia, -iōrum** _ntpl_ Greek
  festival of Bacchus.
diōta, -ae _f_ a two-handled wine jar.
diplōma, -tis _nt_ letter of recommendation.
Dipylon, -ī _nt_ Athenian gate.
Dircaeus _adj_ Boeotian.
Dircē, -ēs _f_ famous spring in Boeotia.
dīrēctus _ppp of_ **dīrigō ♦** _adj_ straight;
  straightforward, simple; _see also_ **dērēctus.**
dīrēmī _perf of_ **dirimō.**
diremptus _ppp of_ **dirimō.**
diremptus, -ūs _m_ separation.
dīreptiō, -ōnis _f_ plundering.
dīreptor, -ōris _m_ plunderer.
dīreptus _ppp of_ **dīripiō.**
dīrēxī _perf of_ **dīrigō.**
dīribeō, -ēre _vt_ to sort out (_votes taken from_
  ballot-boxes).
dīribitiō, -ōnis _f_ sorting.
dīribitor, -ōris _m_ ballot-sorter.
dīrigō, -igere, -ēxī, -ēctum _vt_ to put in line,
  arrange; _see also_ **dērigō.**
dirimō, -imere, -ēmī, -emptum _vt_ to part,
  divide; to interrupt, break off; to put an end
  to.
dīripiō, -ipere, -ipuī, -eptum _vt_ to tear in
  pieces; to plunder, ravage; to seize; (_fig_) to
  distract.
dīritās, -ātis _f_ mischief, cruelty.
dīrumpō, disrumpō, -umpere, -ūpī,
  -uptum _vt_ to burst, break in pieces; (_fig_) to
  break off; (_pass_) to burst (with passion).
dīruō, -ere, -ī, -tum _vt_ to demolish; to scatter;
  aere ~tus having one's pay stopped.
dīruptus _ppp of_ **dīrumpō.**
dīrus _adj_ ominous, fearful; (_pers_) dread,
  terrible **♦** _fpl_ bad luck; the Furies **♦** _ntpl_
  terrors.
dīrutus _ppp of_ **dīruō ♦** _adj_ bankrupt.
dīs, dītis _adj_ rich.
Dīs, Dītis _m_ Pluto.
discēdō, -ēdere, -ēssī, -essum _vi_ to go away,
  depart; to part, disperse; (_MIL_) to march
  away; (_result of battle_) to come off; (_POL_) to go
  over (to a different policy); to pass away,
  disappear; to leave out of consideration; **ab**
  signīs ~ break the ranks; **victor** ~ come off
  best.

Noun declensions and verb conjugations are shown on pp xiii to xxv. The present infinitive ending of a verb shows
to which conjugation it belongs: **-āre** = 1st; **-ēre** = 2nd; **-ere** = 3rd and **-īre** = 4th. Irregular verbs are shown on p xxvi

disceptātiō, -ōnis *f* discussion, debate.
disceptātor, -ōris *m*, **-rīx, -rīcis** *f* arbitrator.
disceptō, -āre *vt* to debate, discuss; (*law*) to decide.
discernō, -ernere, -rēvī, -rētum *vt* to divide, separate; to distinguish between.
discerpō, -ere, -sī, -tum *vt* to tear apart, disperse; (*fig*) to revile.
discessiō, -ōnis *f* separation, departure; (*senate*) division.
discessus, -ūs *m* parting; departure; marching away.
discidium, -ī *and* **iī** *nt* disintegration; separation, divorce; discord.
discīdō, -ere *vt* to cut in pieces.
discinctus *ppp of* **discingō** ♦ *adj* ungirt; negligent; dissolute.
discindō, -ndere, -dī, -ssum *vt* to tear up, cut open.
discingō, -gere, -xī, -ctum *vt* to ungird.
disciplīna, -ae *f* teaching, instruction; learning, science, school, system; training, discipline; habits.
discipulus, -ī *m*, **-a, -ae** *f* pupil, apprentice.
discissus *ppp of* **discindō**.
disclūdō, -dere, -sī, -sum *vt* to keep apart, separate out.
discō, -ere, didicī *vt* to learn, be taught, be told.
discolor, -ōris *adj* of a different colour; variegated; different.
discondūcit it is not worthwhile.
disconveniō, -īre *vi* to disagree, be inconsistent.
discordābilis *adj* disagreeing.
discordia, -ae *f* discord, disagreement.
discordiōsus *adj* seditious.
discordō, -āre *vi* to disagree, quarrel; to be unlike.
discors, -dis *adj* discordant, at variance; inconsistent.
discrepantia, -ae *f* disagreement.
discrepātiō, -ōnis *f* dispute.
discrepitō, -āre *vi* to be quite different.
discrepō, -āre, -uī *vi* to be out of tune; to disagree, differ; to be disputed.
discrētus *ppp of* **discernō**.
discrībō, -bere, -psī, -ptum *vt* to distribute, apportion, classify.
discrīmen, -inis *nt* interval, dividing line; distinction, difference; turning point, critical moment; crisis, danger.
discrīminō, -āre *vt* to divide.
discrīptē *adv* in good order.
discrīptiō, -ōnis *f* apportioning, distributing.
discrīptus *ppp of* **discrībō** ♦ *adj* secluded; well-arranged.
discruciō, -āre *vt* to torture; (*fig*) to torment, trouble.
discumbō, -mbere, -buī, -bitum *vi* to recline at table; to go to bed.
discupiō, -ere *vi* to long.
discurrō, -rrere, -currī *and* **rrī, -rsum** *vi* to

run about, run different ways.
discursus, -ūs *m* running hither and thither.
discus, -ī *m* quoit.
discussus *ppp of* **discutiō**.
discutiō, -tere, -ssī, -ssum *vt* to dash to pieces, smash; to scatter; to dispel.
disertē, -im *adv* distinctly; eloquently.
disertus *adj* fluent, eloquent; explicit.
disiciō, -icere, -iēcī, -iectum *vt* to scatter, cast asunder; to break up, destroy; (*MIL*) to rout.
disiectō, -āre *vt* to toss about.
disiectus *ppp of* **disiciō**.
disiectus, -ūs *m* scattering.
disiūnctiō, -ōnis *f* separation, differing; (*logic*) statement of alternatives; (*RHET*) a sequence of short co-ordinate clauses.
disiūnctius *adv* rather in the manner of a dilemma.
disiūnctus *ppp of* **disiungō** ♦ *adj* distinct, distant, removed; (*speech*) disjointed; (*logic*) opposite.
disiungō, -ungere, -ūnxī, -ūnctum *vt* to unyoke; to separate, remove.
dispālēscō, -ere *vi* to be noised abroad.
dispandō, -āndere, -ānsum *and* **-essum** *vt* to spread out.
dispār, -aris *adj* unlike, unequal.
disparilis *adj* dissimilar.
disparō, -āre, -āvī, -ātum *vt* to segregate.
dispart- *etc see* **dispert-**.
dispectus *ppp of* **dispiciō**.
dispellō, -ellere, -ulī, -ulsum *vt* to scatter, dispel.
dispendium, -ī *and* **iī** *nt* expense, loss.
dispennō *etc see* **dispandō**.
dispēnsātiō, -ōnis *f* management, stewardship.
dispēnsātor, -ōris *m* steward, treasurer.
dispēnsō, -āre, -āvī, -ātum *vi* to weigh out, pay out; to manage, distribute; (*fig*) to regulate.
dispercutiō, -ere *vt* to dash out.
disperdō, -ere, -idī, -itum *vt* to ruin, squander.
dispereō, -īre, -iī *vi* to go to ruin, be undone.
dispergō, -gere, -sī, -sum *vt* to disperse, spread over, space out.
dispersē *adv* here and there.
dispersus *ppp of* **dispergō**.
dispertiō, -īre, -īvī, -ītum; -ior, -īrī *vt* to apportion, distribute.
dispertītiō, -ōnis *f* division.
dispessus *ppp of* **dispandō**.
dispiciō, -icere, -exī, -ectum *vt* to see clearly, see through; to distinguish, discern; (*fig*) to consider.
displiceō, -ēre *vi* (*with dat*) to displease; **sibi ~** be in a bad humour.
displōdō, -dere, -sum *vt* to burst with a crash.
dispōnō, -ōnere, -osuī, -ositum *vt* to set out, arrange; (*MIL*) to station.

dispositē *adv* methodically.
dispositiō, -ōnis *f* arrangement.
dispositūra, -ae *f* arrangement.
dispositus *ppp of* **dispōnō** ♦ *adj* orderly.
dispositus, -ūs *m* arranging.
dispudet, -ēre, -uit *v impers* to be very ashamed.
dispulsus *ppp of* **dispellō**.
disputātiō, -ōnis *f* argument.
disputātor, -ōris *m* debater.
disputō, -āre, -āvī, -ātum *vt* to calculate; to examine, discuss.
disquīrō, -ere *vt* to investigate.
disquīsītiō, -ōnis *f* inquiry.
disrumpō *etc see* **dīrumpō**.
dissaepiō, -īre, -sī, -tum *vt* to fence off, separate off.
dissaeptum, -ī *nt* partition.
dissāvior, -ārī *vt* to kiss passionately.
dissēdī *perf of* **dissideō**.
dissēminō, -āre *vt* to sow, broadcast.
dissēnsiō, -ōnis *f* disagreement, conflict.
dissēnsus, -ūs *m* dissension.
dissentāneus *adj* contrary.
dissentiō, -entīre, -ēnsī, -ēnsum *vi* to disagree, differ; to be unlike, be inconsistent.
dissēp- *etc see* **dissaep-**.
disserēnō, -āre *vi* to clear up.
disserō, -erere, -ēvī, -itum *vt* to sow, plant at intervals.
disserō, -ere, -uī, -tum *vt* to set out in order, arrange; to examine, discuss.
disserpō, -ere *vi* to spread imperceptibly.
dissertō, -āre *vt* to discuss, dispute.
dissideō, -idēre, -ēdī, -essum *vi* to be distant; to disagree, quarrel; to differ, be unlike, be uneven.
dissignātiō, -ōnis *f* arrangement.
dissignātor, -ōris *m* master of ceremonies; undertaker.
dissignō, -āre *vt* to arrange, regulate; *see also* **dēsignō**.
dissiliō, -īre, -uī *vi* to fly apart, break up.
dissimilis *adj* unlike, different.
dissimiliter *adv* differently.
dissimilitūdō, -inis *f* unlikeness.
dissimulanter *adv* secretly.
dissimulantia, -ae *f* dissembling.
dissimulātiō, -ōnis *f* disguising, dissembling; Socratic irony.
dissimulātor, -ōris *m* dissembler.
dissimulō, -āre, -āvī, -ātum *vt* to dissemble, conceal, pretend that ... not, ignore.
dissipābilis *adj* diffusible.
dissipātiō, -ōnis *f* scattering, dispersing.
dissipō, dissupō, -āre, -āvī, -ātum *vt* to scatter, disperse; to spread, broadcast; to squander, destroy; (*MIL*) to put to flight.
dissitus *ppp of* **disserō**.

dissociābilis *adj* disuniting; incompatible.
dissociātiō, -ōnis *f* separation.
dissociō, -āre, -āvī, -ātum *vt* to disunite, estrange.
dissolūbilis *adj* dissoluble.
dissolūtē *adv* loosely, negligently.
dissolūtiō, -ōnis *f* breaking up, destruction; looseness; (*law*) refutation; (*person*) weakness.
dissolūtum, -ī *nt* asyndeton.
dissolūtus *ppp of* **dissolvō** ♦ *adj* loose; lax, careless; licentious.
dissolvō, -vere, -vī, -ūtum *vt* to unloose, dissolve; to destroy, abolish; to refute; to pay up, discharge (debt); to free, release.
dissonus *adj* discordant, jarring, disagreeing, different.
dissors, -tis *adj* not shared.
dissuādeō, -dēre, -sī, -sum *vt* to advise against, oppose.
dissuāsiō, -ōnis *f* advising against.
dissuāsor, -ōris *m* opposer.
dissultō, -āre *vi* to fly asunder.
dissuō, -ere *vt* to undo, open up.
dissupō *etc see* **dissipō**.
distaedet, -ēre *v impers* to weary, disgust.
distantia, -ae *f* diversity.
distendō (-nō), -dere, -dī, -tum *vt* to stretch out, swell.
distentus *ppp of* **distendō** ♦ *adj* full ♦ *ppp of* **distineō** ♦ *adj* busy.
disterminō, -āre *vt* to divide, limit.
distichon, -ī *nt* couplet.
distinctē *adv* distinctly, lucidly.
distinctiō, -ōnis *f* differentiating, difference; (*GRAM*) punctuation; (*RHET*) distinction between words.
distinctus *ppp of* **distinguō** ♦ *adj* separate, distinct; ornamented, set off; lucid.
distinctus, -ūs *m* difference.
distineō, -inēre, -inuī, -entum *vt* to keep apart, divide; to distract; to detain, occupy; to prevent.
distinguō, -guere, -xī, -ctum *vt* to divide, distinguish, discriminate; to punctuate; to adorn, set off.
distō, -āre *vi* to be apart, be distant; to be different.
distorqueō, -quēre, -sī, -tum *vt* to twist, distort.
distortiō, -ōnis *f* contortion.
distortus *ppp of* **distorqueō** ♦ *adj* deformed.
distractiō, -ōnis *f* parting, variance.
distractus *ppp of* **distrahō** ♦ *adj* separate.
distrahō, -here, -xī, -ctum *vt* to tear apart, separate, estrange; to sell piecemeal, retail; (*mind*) to distract, perplex; **aciem ~** break up a formation; **contrōversiās ~** end a dispute; **vōcēs ~** leave a hiatus.
distribuō, -uere, -uī, -ūtum *vt* to distribute,

divide.

distribūtē _adv_ methodically.

distribūtiō, -ōnis _f_ distribution, division.

districtus _ppp of_ **distringō ♦** _adj_ busy, occupied; perplexed; severe.

distringō, -ngere, -nxī, -ctum _vt_ to draw apart; to engage, distract; (_MIL_) to create a diversion against.

distruncō, -āre _vt_ to cut in two.

distulī _perf of_ **differō**.

disturbō, -āre, -āvī, -ātum _vt_ to throw into confusion; to demolish; to frustrate, ruin.

dītēscō, -ere _vi_ to grow rich.

dīthyrambicus _adj_ dithyrambic.

dīthyrambus, -ī _m_ dithyramb.

dītiae, -ārum _fpl_ wealth.

dītiō _etc see_ **diciō**.

dītō, -āre _vt_ to enrich.

diū (_comp_ **diūtius**, _sup_ **diūtissimē**) _adv_ long, a long time; long ago; by day.

diurnum, -ī _nt_ day-book; **ācta ~a** Roman daily gazette.

diurnus _adj_ daily, for a day; by day, day- (_in cpds_).

dīus _adj_ divine, noble.

diūtinē _adv_ long.

diūtinus _adj_ long, lasting.

diūturnitās, -ātis _f_ long time, long duration.

diūturnus _adj_ long, lasting.

dīva, -ae _f_ goddess.

dīvāricō, -āre _vt_ to spread.

dīvellō, -ellere, -ellī, -ulsum _vt_ to tear apart, tear in pieces; (_fig_) to tear away, separate, estrange.

dīvēndō, -ere, -itum _vt_ to sell in lots.

dīverberō, -āre _vt_ to divide, cleave.

dīverbium, -ī _and_ **iī** _nt_ (_comedy_) passage in dialogue.

dīversē _adv_ in different directions, variously.

dīversitās, -ātis _f_ contradiction, disagreement, difference.

dīversus, dīvorsus _ppp of_ **dīvertō ♦** _adj_ in different directions, apart; different; remote; opposite, conflicting; hostile ♦ _mpl_ individuals.

dīvertō, -tere, -tī, -sum _vi_ to turn away; differ.

dīves, -itis _adj_ rich.

dīvexō, -āre _vt_ to pillage.

dīvidia, -ae _f_ worry, concern.

dīvidō, -idere, -īsī, -īsum _vt_ to divide, break open; to distribute, apportion; to separate, keep apart; to distinguish; (_jewel_) to set off; **sententiam ~** _take the vote separately on the parts of a motion_.

dīviduus _adj_ divisible; divided.

dīvīnātiō, -ōnis _f_ foreseeing the future, divination; (_law_) inquiry to select the most suitable prosecutor.

dīvīnē _adv_ by divine influence; prophetically; admirably.

dīvīnitās, -ātis _f_ divinity; divination; divine

quality.

dīvīnitus _adv_ from heaven, by divine influence; excellently.

dīvīnō, -āre, -āvī, -ātum _vt_ to foresee, prophesy.

dīvīnus _adj_ divine, of the gods; prophetic; superhuman, excellent ♦ _m_ soothsayer ♦ _nt_ sacrifice; oath; **rēs ~a** religious service, sacrifice; **~a hūmānaque** all things in heaven and earth; **~ī crēdere** believe on oath.

dīvīsī _perf of_ **dīvīdō**.

dīvīsiō, -ōnis _f_ division; distribution.

dīvīsor, -ōris _m_ distributor; bribery agent.

dīvīsus _ppp of_ **dīvīdō ♦** _adj_ separate.

dīvīsus, -ūs _m_ division.

dīvitiae, -ārum _fpl_ wealth; (_fig_) richness.

dīvor- _etc see_ **dīver-**.

dīvortium, -ī _and_ **iī** _nt_ separation; divorce (by consent); road fork, watershed.

dīvulgātus _adj_ widespread.

dīvulgō, -āre, -āvī, -ātum _vt_ to publish, make public.

dīvulsus _ppp of_ **dīvellō**.

dīvum, -ī _nt_ sky; **sub ~ō** in the open air.

dīvus _adj_ divine; deified ♦ _m_ god.

dīxī _perf of_ **dīcō**.

dō, dare, dedī, datum _vt_ to give; to permit, grant; to put, bring, cause, make; to give up, devote; to tell; to impute; **fābulam ~** produce a play; **in fugam ~** put to flight; **litterās ~** post a letter; **manūs ~** surrender; **nōmen ~** enlist; **operam ~** take pains, do one's best; **poenās ~** pay the penalty; **vēla ~** set sail; **verba ~** cheat.

doceō, -ēre, -uī, -tum _vt_ to teach; to inform, tell; **fābulam ~** produce a play.

dochmius, -ī _and_ **iī** _m_ dochmiac foot.

docilis _adj_ easily trained, docile.

docilitās, -ātis _f_ aptness for being taught.

doctē _adv_ skilfully, cleverly.

doctor, -ōris _m_ teacher, instructor.

doctrīna, -ae _f_ instruction, education, learning; science.

doctus _ppp of_ **doceō ♦** _adj_ learned, skilled; cunning, clever.

documentum, -ī _nt_ lesson, example, proof.

Dōdōna, -ae _f_ town in Epirus (_famous for its oracle of Jupiter_).

Dōdōnaeus, -is, -idis _adj see_ **Dōdōna**.

dōdrāns, -antis _m_ three-fourths.

dogma, -tis _nt_ philosophical doctrine.

dolābra, -ae _f_ pickaxe.

dolēns, -entis _pres p of_ **doleō ♦** _adj_ painful.

dolenter _adv_ sorrowfully.

doleō, -ēre, -uī, -itum _vt, vi_ to be in pain, be sore; to grieve, lament, be sorry (for); to pain; **cuī ~et meminit** ≈ _once bitten, twice shy_.

dōliāris _adj_ tubby.

dōliolum, -ī _nt_ small cask.

dōlium, -ī _and_ **iī** _nt_ large wine jar.

dolō, -āre, -āvī, -ātum _vt_ to hew, shape with an axe.

dolō, -ōnis _m_ pike; sting; fore-topsail.

Dolopes, -um *mpl people of Thessaly.*
Dolopia, -iae *f the country of the people of Thessaly.*
dolor, -ōris *m* pain, pang; sorrow, trouble; indignation, resentment; (*RHET*) pathos.
dolōsē *adv see* **dolōsus.**
dolōsus *adj* deceitful, crafty.
dolus, -ī *m* deceit, guile, trick; ~ **malus** wilful fraud.
domābilis *adj* tameable.
domesticus *adj* domestic, household; personal, private; of one's own country, internal ♦ *mpl* members of a household; **bellum** ~ civil war.
domī *adv* at home.
domicilium, -ī *and* **iī** *nt* dwelling.
domina, -ae *f* mistress, lady of the house; wife, mistress; (*fig*) lady.
domināns, -antis *pres p of* **dominor** ♦ *adj* (*words*) literal ♦ *m* tyrant.
dominātiō, -ōnis *f* mastery, tyranny.
dominātor, -ōris *m* lord.
dominātrīx, -rīcis *f* queen.
dominātus, -ūs *m* mastery, sovereignty.
dominicus *adj* (*ECCL*) the Lord's.
dominium, -ī *and* **iī** *nt* absolute ownership; feast.
dominor, -ārī, -ātus *vi* to rule, be master; (*fig*) to lord it.
dominus, -ī *m* master, lord; owner; host; despot; (*ECCL*) the Lord.
Domitiānus *adj m* Roman Emperor.
Domitius, -ī *m* Roman plebeian name (*esp with surname Ahenobarbus*).
domitō, -āre *vt* to break in.
domitor, -ōris *m*, **-rīx, -rīcis** *f* tamer; conqueror.
domitus *ppp of* **domō.**
domitus, -ūs *m* taming.
domō, -āre, -uī, -itum *vt* to tame, break in; to conquer.
domus, -ūs *and* **ī** *f* house (*esp in town*); home, native place; family; (*PHILOS*) sect; **-ī** at home; in peace; **-ī habēre** have of one's own, have plenty of; **~um** home(wards); **-ō** from home.
dōnābilis *adj* deserving a present.
dōnārium, -ī *and* **iī** *nt* offering; altar, temple.
dōnātiō, -ōnis *f* presenting.
dōnātīvum, -ī *nt* largess, gratuity.
dōnec (dōnicum, dōnique) *conj* until; while, as long as.
dōnō, -āre, -āvī, -ātum *vt* to present, bestow; to remit, condone (for another's sake); (*fig*) to sacrifice.
dōnum, -ī *nt* gift; offering.
dorcas, -dis *f* gazelle.
Dōrēs, -um *mpl* Dorians (*mostly the Greeks of the Peloponnese*).
Dōricus *adj* Dorian; Greek.
Dōris, -dis *f* a sea nymph; the sea.

dormiō, -īre, -īvī, -ītum *vi* to sleep, be asleep.
dormītātor, -ōris *m* dreamer.
dormītō, -āre *vi* to be drowsy, nod.
dorsum, -ī *nt* back; mountain ridge.
dōs, dōtis *f* dowry; (*fig*) gift, talent.
Dossēnus, -ī *m* hunchback, clown.
dōtālis *adj* dowry (*in cpds*), dotal.
dōtātus *adj* richly endowed.
dōtō, -āre *vt* to endow.
drachma (drachuma), -ae *f* a Greek silver coin.
dracō, -ōnis *m* serpent, dragon; (*ASTRO*) Draco.
dracōnigena, -ae *adj* sprung from dragon's teeth.
drāpeta, -ae *m* runaway slave.
Drepanum, -ī, -a, -ōrum *nt* town in W. Sicily.
dromas, -dis *m* dromedary.
dromos, -ī *m* racecourse at Sparta.
Druidēs, -um, -ae, -ārum *mpl* Druids.
Drūsiānus *adj see* **Drūsus.**
Drūsus, -ī *m* Roman surname (*esp famous commander in Germany under Augustus*).
Dryades, -um *fpl* woodnymphs, Dryads.
Dryopes, -um *mpl* a people of Epirus.
dubiē *adv* doubtfully.
dubitābilis *adj* doubtful.
dubitanter *adv* doubtingly, hesitatingly.
dubitātiō, -ōnis *f* wavering, uncertainty, doubting; hesitancy, irresolution; (*RHET*) misgiving.
dubitō, -āre, -āvī, -ātum *vt, vi* to waver, be in doubt, wonder, doubt; to hesitate, stop to think.
dubium *nt* doubt.
dubius *adj* wavering, uncertain; doubtful, indecisive; precarious; irresolute ♦ *nt* doubt; **in ~um vocāre** call in question; **in ~um venīre** be called in question; **sine ~ō, haud ~ē** undoubtedly.
ducēnī, -ōrum *adj* 200 each.
ducentēsima, -ae *f* one-half per cent.
ducentī, -ōrum *num* two hundred.
ducentiēs, -iēns *adv* 200 times.
dūcō, -cere, -xī, ductum *vt* to lead, guide, bring, take; to draw, draw out; to reckon, consider; (*MIL*) to lead, march, command; (*breath*) to inhale; (*ceremony*) to conduct; (*changed aspect*) to take on, receive; (*dance*) to perform; (*drink*) to quaff; (*metal*) to shape, beat out; (*mind*) to attract, induce, deceive; (*oars*) to pull; (*origin*) to derive, trace; (*time*) to prolong, put off, pass; (*udders*) to milk; (*wool*) to spin; (*a work*) to construct, compose, make; (*COMM*) to calculate; **īlia ~** become broken-winded; **in numerō hostium ~** regard as an enemy; **ōs ~** make faces; **parvī ~** think little of; **ratiōnem ~** have regard for; **uxōrem ~** marry.
ductim *adv* in streams.
ductitō, -āre *vt* to lead on, deceive; to marry.

Noun declensions and verb conjugations are shown on pp xiii to xxv. The present infinitive ending of a verb shows to which conjugation it belongs: **-āre** = 1st; **-ēre** = 2nd; **-ere** = 3rd and **-īre** = 4th. Irregular verbs are shown on p xxvi

ductō, -āre *vt* to lead, draw; to take home; to cheat.

ductor, -ōris *m* leader, commander; guide, pilot.

ductus *ppp of* **dūcō**.

ductus, -ūs *m* drawing, drawing off; form; command, generalship.

dūdum *adv* a little while ago, just now; for long; **haud** ~ not long ago; **iam** ~ **adsum** I have been here a long time; **quam** ~ how long.

duellum *etc see* **bellum**.

Duillius, -ī *m* consul who defeated the Carthaginians at sea.

duim *pres subj of* **dō**.

dulce, -iter *adv see* **dulcis**.

dulcēdō, -inis *f* sweetness; pleasantness, charm.

dulcēscō, -ere *vi* to become sweet.

dulciculus *adj* rather sweet.

dulcifer, -ī *adj* sweet.

dulcis *adj* sweet; pleasant, lovely; kind, dear.

dulcitūdō, -inis *f* sweetness.

dūlicē *adv* like a slave.

Dūlichium, -ī *nt* island in the Ionian Sea near Ithaca.

Dūlichius *adj* of Dulichium; of Ulysses.

dum *conj* while, as long as; provided that, if only; until ♦ *adv* (*enclitic*) now, a moment; (*with neg*) yet.

dūmētum, -ī *nt* thicket, thornbushes.

dummodo *conj* provided that.

dūmōsus *adj* thorny.

dumtaxat *adv* at least; only, merely.

dūmus, -ī *m* thornbush.

duo, duae, duo *num* two.

duodeciēns, -ēs *adv* twelve times.

duodecim *num* twelve.

duodecimus *adj* twelfth.

duodēnī, -ōrum *adj* twelve each, in dozens.

duodēquadrāgēsimus *adj* thirty-eighth.

duodēquadrāgintā *num* thirty-eight.

duodēquīnquāgēsimus *adj* forty-eighth.

duodētrīciēns *adv* twenty-eight times.

duodētrīgintā *num* twenty-eight.

duodēvīcēnī *adj* eighteen each.

duodēvīgintī *num* eighteen.

duoetvīcēsimānī, -ānōrum *mpl* soldiers of the 22nd legion.

duoetvīcēsimus *adj* twenty-second.

duovirī, duumvirī, -ōrum *mpl* a board of two men; colonial magistrates; ~ **nāvālēs** naval commissioners (for supply and repair); ~ **sacrōrum** keepers of the Sibylline Books.

duplex, -icis *adj* double, twofold; both; (*person*) false.

duplicārius, -ī *and* **iī** *m* soldier receiving double pay.

dupliciter *adv* doubly, on two accounts.

duplicō, -āre, -āvī, -ātum *vt* to double, increase; to bend.

duplus *adj* double, twice as much ♦ *nt* double ♦ *f* double the price.

dupondius, -ī *and* **iī** *m* coin worth two asses.

dūrābilis *adj* lasting.

dūrāmen, -inis *nt* hardness.

dūrateus *adj* wooden.

dūrē, -iter *adv* stiffly; hardily; harshly, roughly.

dūrēscō, -ēscere, -uī *vi* to harden.

dūritās, -ātis *f* harshness.

dūritia, -ae, -ēs, -em *f* hardness; hardiness; severity; want of feeling.

dūrō, -āre, -āvī, -ātum *vt* to harden, stiffen; to make hardy, inure; (*mind*) to dull ♦ *vi* to harden; to be patient, endure; to hold out, last; (*mind*) to be steeled.

dūruī *perf of* **dūrēscō**.

dūrus *adj* hard, harsh, rough; hardy, tough; rude, uncultured; (*character*) severe, unfeeling, impudent, miserly; (*CIRCS*) hard, cruel.

duumvirī *etc see* **duovirī**.

dux, ducis *m* leader, guide; chief, head; (*MIL*) commander, general.

dūxī *perf of* **dūcō**.

Dymantis, -antidis *f* Hecuba.

Dymās, -antis *m* father of Hecuba.

dynamis, -is *f* plenty.

dynastēs, -ae *m* ruler, prince.

Dyrrhachīnus *adj see n*.

Dyrrhachium (Dyrrachium), -ī *nt* Adriatic port (*now* Durazzo).

E, e

ē *prep see* **ex**.

ea *f pron* she, it ♦ *adj see* **is**.

eā *adv* there, that way.

eādem *adv* the same way; at the same time.

eadem *f adj see* **idem**.

eaīdem, eapse *f of* **ipse**.

eapse *f of* **ipse**.

eātenus *adv* so far.

ebenus *etc see* **hebenus**.

ēbibō, -ere, -ī *vt* to drink up, drain; to squander; to absorb.

ēblandior, -īrī *vt* to coax out, obtain by flattery; ~**ītus** obtained by flattery.

Eborācum, -ī *nt* York.

ēbrietās, ātis *f* drunkenness.

ēbriolus *adj* tipsy.

ēbriōsitās, -ātis *f* addiction to drink.

ēbriōsus *adj* drunkard; (*berry*) juicy.

ēbrius *adj* drunk; full; (*fig*) intoxicated.

ēbulliō, -īre *vi* to bubble up ♦ *vt* to brag about.

ebulus, -ī *m*, **-um, -ī** *nt* danewort, dwarf elder.

ebur, -is *nt* ivory; ivory work.

Eburācum, -ī *nt* York.
eburātus *adj* inlaid with ivory.
eburneolus *adj* of ivory.
eburneus, eburnus *adj* of ivory; ivory-white.
ēcastor *interj* by Castor!
ecce *adv* look!, here is!, there is!; lo and
   behold!; **~a, ~am, ~illam, ~istam** here she is!;
   ~um, ~illum here he is!; **~ōs, ~ās** here they
   are!
eccerē *interj* there now!
eccheuma, -tis *nt* pouring out.
ecclēsia, -ae *f a Greek assembly*; (*ECCL*)
   congregation, church.
eccum *etc see* **ecce.**
ecdicus, -ī *m* civic lawyer.
ecf- *see* **eff-.**
echidna, -ae *f* viper; **~ Lernaea** hydra.
echīnus, -ī *m* sea-urchin; hedgehog; a rinsing
   bowl.
Echīōn, -onis *m* Theban hero.
Echīonidēs *m* Pentheus.
Echīonius *adj* Theban.
Ēchō, -us *f* wood nymph; echo.
ecloga, -ae *f* selection; eclogue.
ecquandō *adv* ever.
ecquī, -ae, -od *adj interrog* any.
ecquid, -ī *adv* whether.
ecquis, -id *pron interrog* anyone, anything.
ecquō *adv* anywhere.
eculeus, -ī *m* foal; rack.
edācitās, -ātis *f* gluttony.
edāx, -ācis *adj* gluttonous; (*fig*) devouring,
   carking.
ēdentō, -āre *vt* to knock the teeth out of.
ēdentulus *adj* toothless; old.
edepol *interj* by Pollux, indeed.
ēdī *perf of* **edō.**
ēdīcō, -īcere, -īxī, -ictum *vt* to declare; to
   decree, publish an edict.
ēdictiō, -ōnis *f* decree.
ēdictō, -āre *vt* to proclaim.
ēdictum, -ī *nt* proclamation, edict (*esp a
   praetor's*).
ēdidī *perf of* **ēdō.**
ēdiscō, -ere, ēdidicī *vt* to learn well, learn by
   heart.
ēdisserō, -ere, -uī, -tum *vt* to explain in
   detail.
ēdissertō, -āre *vt* to explain fully.
ēditīcius *adj* chosen by the plaintiff.
ēditiō, -ōnis *f* publishing, edition; statement;
   (*law*) designation of a suit.
ēditus *ppp of* **ēdō** ♦ *adj* high; descended ♦ *nt*
   height; order.
edō, edere *and* **ēsse, ēdī, ēsum** *vt* to eat; (*fig*)
   to devour.
ēdō, -ere, -idī, -itum *vt* to put forth,
   discharge; to emit; to give birth to, produce;
   (*speech*) to declare, relate, utter; (*action*) to
   cause, perform; (*book*) to publish; (*POL*) to

promulgate; **lūdōs ~** put on a show; **tribūs ~**
   nominate tribes of jurors.
ēdoceō, -ere, -uī, -ctum *vt* to instruct
   clearly, teach thoroughly.
ēdomō, -āre, -uī, -itum *vt* to conquer,
   overcome.
Ēdōnus *adj* Thracian.
ēdormiō, -īre *vi* to have a good sleep ♦ *vt* to
   sleep off.
ēdormīscō, -ere *vt* to sleep off.
ēducātiō, -ōnis *f* bringing up, rearing.
ēducātor, -ōris *m* foster father, tutor.
ēducātrīx, -īcis *f* nurse.
ēducō, -āre, -āvī, -ātum *vt* to bring up, rear,
   train; to produce.
ēdūcō, -ūcere, -ūxī, -uctum *vt* to draw out,
   bring away; to raise up, erect; (*law*) to
   summon; (*MIL*) to lead out, march out; (*ship*)
   to put to sea; (*young*) to hatch, rear, train.
edūlis *adj* edible.
ēdūrō, -āre *vi* to last out.
ēdūrus *adj* very hard.
effarciō *etc see* **efferciō.**
effātus *ppa of* **effor** ♦ *adj* solemnly pronounced,
   declared ♦ *nt* axiom; (*pl*) predictions.
effectiō, -ōnis *f* performing; efficient cause.
effector, -ōris *m*, **-rīx, -rīcis** *f* producer,
   author.
effectus *ppp of* **efficiō.**
effectus, -ūs *m* completion, performance;
   effect.
effēminātē *adv see* **effēminātus.**
effēminātus *adj* effeminate.
effēminō, -āre, -āvī, -ātum *vt* to make a
   woman of; to enervate.
efferātus *adj* savage.
efferciō, -cīre, -tum *vt* to cram full.
efferitās, -ātis *f* wildness.
efferō, -āre, -āvī, -ātum *vt* to make wild; (*fig*)
   to exasperate.
efferō (ecferō), -re, extulī, ēlātum *vt* to
   bring out, carry out; to lift up, raise; (*dead*)
   to carry to the grave; (*emotion*) to transport;
   (*honour*) to exalt; (*news*) to spread abroad;
   (*soil*) to produce; (*trouble*) to endure to the
   end; **sē ~** rise; be conceited.
effertus *ppp of* **efferciō** ♦ *adj* full, bulging.
efferus *adj* savage.
effervēscō, -vēscere, -buī *vi* to boil over; (*fig*)
   to rage.
effervō, -ere *vi* to boil up.
effētus *adj* exhausted.
efficācitās, -ātis *f* power.
efficāciter *adv* effectually.
efficāx, -ācis *adj* capable, effective.
efficiēns, -entis *pres p of* **efficiō** ♦ *adj* effective,
   efficient.
efficienter *adv* efficiently.
efficientia, -ae *f* power, efficacy.
efficiō, -icere, -ēcī, -ectum *vt* to make,

accomplish; to cause, bring about; (*numbers*) to amount to; (*soil*) to yield; (*theory*) to make out, try to prove.

effictus *ppp of* **effingō**.

effigiēs, -ēī, -a, -ae *f* likeness, copy; ghost; portrait, statue; (*fig*) image, ideal.

effingō, -ngere, -nxī, -ctum *vt* to form, fashion; to portray, represent; to wipe clean; to fondle.

efflāgitātiō, -ōnis *f* urgent demand.

efflāgitātus, -ūs *m* urgent request.

efflāgitō, -āre *vt* to demand urgently.

efflīctim *adv* desperately.

efflīctō, -āre *vt* to strike dead.

efflīgō, -gere, -xī, -ctum *vt* to exterminate.

efflō, -āre, -āvī, -ātum *vt* to breathe out, blow out ♦ *vi* to billow out; **animam ~** expire.

efflōrēscō, -ēscere, -uī *vi* to blossom forth.

effluō, -ere, -xī *vi* to run out, issue, emanate; (*fig*) to pass away, vanish; (*rumour*) to get known; **ex animō ~** become forgotten.

effluvium, -ī *and* **iī** *nt* outlet.

effodiō, -odere, -ōdī, -ossum *vt* to dig up; (*eyes*) to gouge out; (*house*) to ransack.

effor, -ārī, -ātus *vt* to speak, utter; (*augury*) to ordain; (*logic*) to state a proposition.

effossus *ppp of* **effodiō**.

effrēnātē *adv see* **effrēnātus**.

effrēnātiō, -ōnis *f* impetuousness.

effrēnātus *adj* unbridled, violent, unruly.

effrēnus *adj* unbridled.

effringō, -ingere, -ēgī, -āctum *vt* to break open, smash.

effugiō, -ugere, -ūgī *vi* to run away, escape ♦ *vt* to flee from, escape; to escape the notice of.

effugium, -ī *and* **iī** *nt* flight, escape; means of escape.

effulgeō, -gēre, -sī *vi* to shine out, blaze.

effultus *adj* supported.

effundō, -undere, -ūdī, -ūsum *vt* to pour forth, pour out; (*crops*) to produce in abundance; (*missiles*) to shoot; (*rider*) to throw; (*speech*) to give vent to; (*effort*) to waste; (*money*) to squander; (*reins*) to let go; **sē ~, ~undī** rush out; indulge (in).

effūsē *adv* far and wide; lavishly, extravagantly.

effūsiō, -ōnis *f* pouring out, rushing out; profusion, extravagance; exuberance.

effūsus *ppp of* **effundō** ♦ *adj* vast, extensive; loose, straggling; lavish, extravagant.

effūtiō, -īre *vt* to blab, chatter.

ēgelidus *adj* mild, cool.

egēns, -entis *pres p of* **egeō** ♦ *adj* needy.

egēnus *adj* destitute.

egeō, -ēre, -uī *vi* to be in want; (*with abl or gen*) to need, want.

Ēgeria, -ae *f* nymph who taught Numa.

ēgerō, -rere, -ssī, -stum *vt* to carry out; to discharge, emit.

egestās, -ātis *f* want, poverty.

ēgestus *ppp of* **ēgerō**.

ēgī *perf of* **agō**.

ego *pron* I; **~met** I (*emphatic*).

ēgredior, -dī, -ssus *vi* to go out, come out; to go up, climb; (*MIL*) to march out; (*NAUT*) to disembark, put to sea; (*speech*) to digress ♦ *vt* to go beyond, quit; (*fig*) to overstep, surpass.

ēgregiē *adv* uncommonly well, singularly.

ēgregius *adj* outstanding, surpassing; distinguished, illustrious.

ēgressus *ppa of* **ēgredior**.

ēgressus, -ūs *m* departure; way out; digression; (*NAUT*) landing; (*river*) mouth.

eguī *perf of* **egeō**.

ēgurgitō, -āre *vt* to lavish.

ehem *interj* (*expressing surprise*) ha!, so!

ēheu *interj* (*expressing pain*) alas!

eho *interj* (*expressing rebuke*) look here!

eī *dat of* **is**.

ei *interj* (*expressing alarm*) oh!

eia *interj* (*expressing delight, playful remonstrance, encouragement*) aha!, come now!, come on!

ēiaculor, -ārī *vt* to shoot out.

ēiciō, -icere, -iēcī, -iectum *vt* to throw out, drive out, put out; (*joint*) to dislocate; (*mind*) to banish; (*NAUT*) to bring to land, run aground, wreck; (*rider*) to throw; (*speech*) to utter; (*THEAT*) to hiss off; **sē ~** rush out, break out.

ēiectāmenta, -ōrum *ntpl* refuse.

ēiectiō, -ōnis *f* banishment.

ēiectō, -āre *vt* to throw up.

ēiectus *ppp of* **ēiciō** ♦ *adj* shipwrecked.

ēiectus, -ūs *m* emitting.

ēierō, ēiūrō, -āre *vt* to abjure, reject on oath, forswear; (*office*) to resign; **bonam cōpiam ~** declare oneself bankrupt.

ēiulātiō, -ōnis *f*, **ēiulātus, -ūs** *m* wailing.

ēiulō, -āre *vi* to wail, lament.

ēius *pron* his, her, its; **~modī** such.

ej- *etc see* **ei-**.

ēlābor, -bī, -psus *vi* to glide away, slip off; to escape, get off; to pass away.

ēlabōrātus *adj* studied.

ēlabōrō, -āre, -āvī, -ātum *vi* to exert oneself, take great pains ♦ *vt* to work out, elaborate.

ēlāmentābilis *adj* very mournful.

ēlanguēscō, -ēscere, -ī *vi* to grow faint; to relax.

ēlāpsus *ppa of* **ēlābor**.

ēlātē *adv* proudly.

ēlātiō, -ōnis *f* ecstasy, exaltation.

ēlātrō, -āre *vt* to bark out.

ēlātus *ppp of* **efferō** ♦ *adj* high; exalted.

ēlavō, -avāre, -āvī, -autum *and* **-ōtum** *vt* to wash clean; (*comedy*) to rob.

Elea, -ae *f* town in S. Italy (*birthplace of Parmenides*).

Eleātēs, -āticus *adj see n.*

ēlecebra, -ae *f* snare.

ēlēctē *adv* choicely.

ēlēctilis *adj* choice.

ēlectiō, -ōnis f choice, option.
ēlectō, -āre vt to coax out.
ēlectō, -āre vt to select.
Ēlectra, -ae f a Pleiad (*daughter of Atlas; sister of Orestes*).
ēlectrum, -ī nt amber; an alloy of gold and silver.
ēlēctus ppp of **ēligō** ♦ adj select, choice.
ēlēctus, -ūs m choice.
ēlegāns, -antis adj tasteful, refined, elegant; fastidious; (*things*) fine, choice.
ēleganter adv with good taste.
ēlegantia, -ae f taste, finesse, elegance; fastidiousness.
ēlēgī perf of **ēligō**.
elegī, -ōrum mpl elegiac verses.
elegīa, -ae f elegy.
Eleleides, -eidum fpl Bacchantes.
Eleleus, -eī m Bacchus.
elementum, -ī nt element; (pl) first principles, rudiments; beginnings; letters (of alphabet).
elenchus, -ī m a pear-shaped pearl.
elephantomacha, -ae m fighter mounted on an elephant.
elephantus, -ī, elephās, -antis m elephant; ivory.
Ēlēus, -ius, -ias adj Elean; Olympian.
Eleusīn, -is f Eleusis (*Attic town famous for its mysteries of Demeter*).
Eleusīus adj see **Eleusīn**.
eleutheria, -ae f liberty.
ēlevō, -āre vt to lift, raise; to alleviate; to make light of, lessen, disparage.
ēliciō, -ere, -uī, -itum vt to lure out, draw out; (*god*) to call down; (*spirit*) to conjure up; (*fig*) to elicit, draw.
ēlīdō, -dere, -sī, -sum vt to dash out, squeeze out; to drive out; to crush, destroy.
ēligō, -igere, -ēgī, -ēctum vt to pick, pluck out; to choose.
ēlīminō, -āre vt to carry outside.
ēlīmō, -āre vt to file; (*fig*) to perfect.
ēlinguis adj speechless; not eloquent.
ēlinguō, -āre vt to tear the tongue out of.
Ēlis, -idis f district and town in W. Peloponnese (*famous for Olympia*).
Elissa, -ae f Dido.
ēlīsus ppp of **ēlīdō**.
elixus adj boiled.
elleborōsus adj quite mad.
elleborus, -ī m, **-um, -ī** nt hellebore.
ellum, ellam there he (she) is!
ēlocō, -āre vt to lease, farm out.
ēlocūtiō, -ōnis f delivery, style.
ēlocūtus ppa of **ēloquor**.
ēlogium, -ī and **iī** nt short saying; inscription; (*will*) clause.
ēloquēns, -entis adj eloquent.
ēloquenter adv see adj.

ēloquentia, -ae f eloquence.
ēloquium, -ī and **iī** nt eloquence.
ēloquor, -quī, -cūtus vt, vi to speak out, speak eloquently.
ēlūceō, -cēre, -xī vi to shine out, glitter.
ēluctor, -ārī, -ātus vi to struggle, force a way out ♦ vt to struggle out of, surmount.
ēlūcubrō, -āre, -or, -ārī, -ātus vt to compose by lamplight.
ēlūdificor, -ārī, -ātus vt to cheat, play up.
ēlūdō, -dere, -sī, -sum vt to parry, ward off, foil; to win off at play; to outplay, outmanoeuvre; to cheat, make fun of ♦ vi to finish one's sport.
ēlūgeō, -gēre, -xī vt to mourn for.
ēlumbis adj feeble.
ēluō, -uere, -uī, -ūtum vt to wash clean; (*money*) to squander; (*fig*) to wash away, get rid of.
ēlūsus ppp of **ēlūdō**.
ēlūtus ppp of **ēluō** ♦ adj insipid.
ēluviēs, -em -ē f discharge; overflowing.
ēluviō, -ōnis f deluge.
Ēlysium, -ī nt Elysium.
Ēlysius adj Elysian.
em interj there you are!
ēmancipātiō, -ōnis f giving a son his independence; conveyance of property.
ēmancipō, -āre vt to declare independent; to transfer, give up, sell.
ēmānō, -āre, -āvī, -ātum vi to flow out; to spring (from); (*news*) to leak out, become known.
Ēmathia, -ae f district of Macedonia; Macedonia, Thessaly.
Ēmathius adj Macedonian, Pharsalian; ~des, ~dum fpl Muses.
ēmātūrēscō, -ēscere, -uī vi to soften.
emāx, -ācis adj fond of buying.
emblēma, -tis nt inlaid work, mosaic.
embolium, -ī and **iī** nt interlude.
ēmendābilis adj corrigible.
ēmendātē adv see **ēmendātō**.
ēmendātiō, -ōnis f correction.
ēmendātor, -ōris m, **-rīx, -rīcis** f corrector.
ēmendātus adj faultless.
ēmendō, -āre, -āvī, -ātum vt to correct, improve.
ēmēnsus ppa of **ēmētior** ♦ adj traversed.
ēmentior, -īrī, -ītus vi to tell lies ♦ vt to pretend, fabricate; ~ītus pretended.
ēmercor, -ārī vt to purchase.
ēmereō, -ēre, -uī, -itum, -eor, -ērī vt to earn fully, deserve; to lay under an obligation; to complete one's term of service.
ēmergō, -gere, -sī, -sum vt to raise out; (*fig*) to extricate ♦ vi to rise, come up, emerge; (*fig*) to get clear, extricate oneself; (*impers*) it becomes evident.
ēmeritus ppa of **ēmereor** ♦ adj superannuated,

worn-out ♦ *m* veteran.
ēmersus *ppp of* **ēmergō**.
emetica, -ae *f* emetic.
ēmētior, -tīrī, -nsus *vt* to measure out; to traverse, pass over; (*time*) to live through; (*fig*) to impart.
ēmetō, -ere *vt* to harvest.
ēmī *perf of* **emō**.
ēmicō, -āre, -uī, -ātum *vi* to dart out, dash out, flash out; (*fig*) to shine.
ēmigrō, -āre, -āvī, -ātum *vi* to remove, depart.
ēminēns, -entis *pres p of* **ēmineō** ♦ *adj* high, projecting; (*fig*) distinguished, eminent.
ēminentia, -ae *f* prominence; (*painting*) light.
ēmineō, -ēre, -uī *vi* to stand out, project; to be prominent, be conspicuous, distinguish oneself.
ēminor, -ārī *vi* to threaten.
ēminus *adv* at *or* from a distance.
ēmīror, -ārī *vt* to marvel at.
ēmissārium, -ī *and* **iī** *nt* outlet.
ēmissārius, -ī *and* **iī** *m* scout.
ēmissīcius *adj* prying.
ēmissiō, -ōnis *f* letting go, discharge.
ēmissus *ppp of* **ēmittō**.
ēmissus, -ūs *m* emission.
ēmittō, -ittere, -īsī, -issum *vt* to send out, let out; to let go, let slip; (*missile*) to discharge; (*person*) to release, free; (*sound*) to utter; (*writing*) to publish.
emō, -ere, ēmī, emptum *vt* to buy, procure; to win over; **bene ~** buy cheap; **male ~** buy dear; **in diem ~** buy on credit.
ēmoderor, -ārī *vt* to give expression to.
ēmodulor, -ārī *vt* to sing through.
ēmōlior, -īrī *vt* to accomplish.
ēmollīō, -īre, -iī, -ītum *vt* to soften; to mollify; to enervate.
ēmolumentum, -ī *nt* profit, advantage.
ēmoneō, -ēre *vt* to strongly advise.
ēmorior, -ī, -tuus *vi* to die; (*fig*) to pass away.
ēmortuālis *adj* of death.
ēmoveō, -ovēre, -ōvī, -ōtum *vt* to remove, drive away.
Empedoclēs, -is *m* Sicilian philosopher.
Empedoclēus *adj see n*.
empīricus, -ī *m* empirical doctor.
emporium, -ī *and* **iī** *nt* market, market town.
emptiō, -ōnis *f* buying; a purchase.
emptitō, -āre *vt* to often buy.
emptor, -ōris *m* purchaser.
emptus *ppp of* **emō**.
ēmulgeō, -ēre *vt* to drain.
ēmunctus *ppp of* **ēmungō** ♦ *adj* discriminating.
ēmungō, -gere, -xī, -ctum *vt* to blow the nose of; (*comedy*) to cheat.
ēmūniō, -īre, -īvī, -ītum *vt* to strengthen, secure; to build up; to make roads through.
ēn *interj* (*drawing attention*) look!, see!; (*excited question*) really, indeed!; (*command*) come now!

ēnārrābilis *adj* describable.
ēnārrō, -āre, -āvī, -ātum *vt* to describe in detail.
ēnāscor, -scī, -tus *vi* to sprout, grow.
ēnatō, -āre *vi* to swim ashore; (*fig*) to escape.
ēnātus *ppa of* **ēnāscor**.
ēnāvigō, -āre *vi* to sail clear, clear ♦ *vt* to sail over.
Enceladus, -ī *m* giant under Etna.
endromis, -dis *f* sports wrap.
Endymiōn, -ōnis *m a beautiful youth loved by the Moon, and doomed to lasting sleep.*
ēnecō, -āre, -uī *and* **-āvī, -tum** *and* **ātum** *vt* to kill; to wear out; to torment.
ēnervātus *adj* limp.
ēnervis *adj* enfeebled.
ēnervō, -āre, -āvī, -ātum *vt* to weaken, unman.
ēnicō *etc see* **ēnecō**.
enim *conj* (*affirming*) yes, truly, in fact; (*explaining*) for, for instance, of course; **at ~** but it will be objected; **quid ~** well?; **sed ~** but actually.
enimvērō *conj* certainly, yes indeed.
Enīpeus, -eī *m* river in Thessaly.
ēnīsus *ppa of* **ēnītor**.
ēniteō, -ēre, -uī *vi* to shine, brighten up; (*fig*) to be brilliant, distinguish oneself.
ēnitēscō, -ēscere, -uī *vi* to shine, be brilliant.
ēnītor, -tī, -sus *and* **xus** *vi* to struggle up, climb; to strive, make a great effort ♦ *vt* to give birth to; to climb.
ēnīxē *adv* earnestly.
ēnīxus *ppa of* **ēnītor** ♦ *adj* strenuous.
Enniānus *adj see n*.
Ennius, -ī *m greatest of the early Latin poets.*
Ennosigaeus, -ī *m* Earthshaker, Neptune.
ēnō, -āre, -āvī *vi* to swim out, swim ashore; to fly away.
ēnōdātē *adv* lucidly.
ēnōdātiō, -ōnis *f* unravelling.
ēnōdis *adj* free from knots; plain.
ēnōdō, -āre, -āvī, -ātum *vt* to elucidate.
ēnōrmis *adj* irregular; immense.
ēnōtēscō, -ēscere, -uī *vi* to get known.
ēnotō, -āre *vt* to make a note of.
ēnsiculus, -ī *m* little sword.
ēnsiger, -ī *adj* with his sword.
ēnsis, -is *m* sword.
enthymēma, -tis *nt* argument.
ēnūbō, -bere, -psī *vi* to marry out of one's station; to marry and go away.
ēnucleātē *adv* plainly.
ēnucleātus *adj* (*style*) straightforward; (*votes*) honest.
ēnucleō, -āre *vt* to elucidate.
ēnumerātiō, -ōnis *f* enumeration; (*RHET*) recapitulation.
ēnumerō, -āre *vt* to count up; to pay out; to relate.
ēnūntiātiō, -ōnis *f* proposition.
ēnūntiātum, -ī *nt* proposition.
ēnūntiō, -āre *vt* to disclose, report; to

express; to pronounce.

ēnūptiō, -ōnis *f* marrying out of one's station.

ēnūtriō, -īre *vt* to feed, bring up.

eō, īre, īvī *and* **iī, itum** *vi* to go; (*MIL*) to march; (*time*) to pass; (*event*) to proceed, turn out; in **alia omnia** ~ vote against a bill; **in sententiam** ~ support a motion; **sīc eat** so may he fare!; **ī** (*mocking*) go on!

eō *adv* (*place*) thither, there; (*purpose*) with a view to; (*degree*) so far, to such a pitch; (*time*) so long; (*cause*) on that account, for the reason; (*with compar*) the; **accēdit eō** besides; **rēs erat eō locī** such was the state of affairs; **eō magis** all the more.

eōdem *adv* to the same place, purpose *or* person; ~ **locī** in the same place.

Ēōs *f* dawn ♦ *m* morning star; Oriental.

Ēous *adj* at dawn, eastern.

Epamīnōndās, -ae *m* Theban general.

epāstus *adj* eaten up.

ephēbus, -ī *m* youth (*18 to 20*).

ephēmeris, -idis *f* diary.

Ephesius *adj see n.*

Ephesus, -ī *f* Ionian town in Asia Minor.

ephippiātus *adj* riding a saddled horse.

ephippium, -ī *and* **iī** *nt* saddle.

ephorus, -ī *m* a Spartan magistrate, ephor.

Ephyra, -ae, -ē, -ēs *f* Corinth.

Ephyrēius *adj see* **Ephyra.**

Epicharmus, -ī *m* Greek philosopher and comic poet.

epichysis, -is *f* kind of jug.

epicōpus *adj* rowing.

Epicūrēus, epicus *adj* epic.

Epicūrus, -ī *m* famous Greek philosopher.

Epidaurius *adj see n.*

Epidaurus, -ī *f* town in E. Peloponnese.

epidīcticus *adj* (*RHET*) for display.

epigramma, -tis *nt* inscription; epigram.

epilogus, -ī *m* peroration.

epimēnia, -ōrum *ntpl* a month's rations.

Epimēthis, -dis *f* Pyrrha (*daughter of Epimetheus*).

epirēdium, -ī *and* **iī** *nt* trace.

Ēpīrōtēs, -ōtae *m* native of Epirus.

Ēpīrōticus, -ēnsis *adj see n.*

Ēpīrus, -os, -ī *f* district of N.W. Greece.

episcopus, -ī *m* bishop.

epistolium, -ī *and* **iī** *nt* short note.

epistula, -ae *f* letter; **ab ~īs** secretary.

epitaphium, -ī *and* **iī** *nt* funeral oration.

epithēca, -ae *f* addition.

epitoma, -ae, -ē, -ēs *f* abridgement.

epityrum, -ī *nt* olive salad.

epops, -is *m* hoopoe.

epos (*pl* -ē) *nt* epic.

ēpōtō, -āre, -āvī, -um *vt* to drink up, drain; to waste in drink; to absorb.

epulae, -ārum *fpl* dishes; feast, banquet.

epulāris *adj* at a banquet.

epulō, -ōnis *m* guest at a feast; priest in charge of religious banquets.

epulor, -ārī, -ātus *vi* to be at a feast ♦ *vt* to feast on.

epulum, -ī *nt* banquet.

equa, -ae *f* mare.

eques, -itis *m* horseman, trooper; (*pl*) cavalry; knight, member of the equestrian order.

equester, -ris *adj* equestrian; cavalry- (*in cpds*).

equidem *adv* (*affirming*) indeed, of course, for my part; (*concessive*) to be sure.

equīnus *adj* horse's.

equīria, -ōrum *ntpl* horseraces.

equitātus, -ūs *m* cavalry.

equitō, -āre *vi* to ride.

equuleus *etc see* **eculeus.**

equulus, -ī *m* colt.

equus, -ī *m* horse; (*ASTRO*) Pegasus; ~ **bipēs** seahorse; **~ō merēre** serve in the cavalry; **~īs virīsque** with might and main.

era, -ae *f* mistress (of the house); (*goddess*) Lady.

ērādīcō, -āre *vt* to root out, destroy.

ērādō, -dere, -sī, -sum *vt* to erase, obliterate.

Eratō *f* Muse of lyric poetry.

Eratosthenēs, -is *m* famous Alexandrian geographer.

Erebēus *adj see n.*

Erebus, -ī *m* god of darkness; the lower world.

Erechtheus, -eī *m* legendary king of Athens.

Erechthēus *adj see n.*

Erechthīdae *mpl* Athenians.

Erechthis, -idis *f* Orithyia; Procris.

ērēctus *ppp of* **ērigō** ♦ *adj* upright, lofty; noble, haughty; alert, tense; resolute.

ērēpō, -ere, -sī *vi* to creep out, clamber up ♦ *vt* to crawl over, climb.

ēreptiō, -ōnis *f* seizure, robbery.

ēreptor, -ōris *m* robber.

ēreptus *ppp of* **ēripiō.**

ergā *prep* (*with acc*) towards; against.

ergastulum, -ī *nt* prison (*esp for slaves*); (*pl*) convicts.

ergō *adv* therefore, consequently; (*questions, commands*) then, so; (*resuming*) well then; (*with gen*) for the sake of, because of.

Erichthonius, -ī *m* a king of Troy; a king of Athens ♦ *adj* Trojan; Athenian.

ēricius, -ī *and* **iī** *m* hedgehog; (*MIL*) beam with iron spikes.

Ēridanus, -ī *m* mythical name of river Po.

erifuga, -ae *m* runaway slave.

ērigō, -igere, -ēxī, -ēctum *vt* to make upright, raise up, erect; to excite; to encourage.

Erigonē, -ēs *f* (*constellation*) Virgo.

Erigonēius *adj see n.*

Noun declensions and verb conjugations are shown on pp xiii to xxv. The present infinitive ending of a verb shows to which conjugation it belongs: **-āre** = 1st; **-ēre** = 2nd; **-ere** = 3rd and **-īre** = 4th. Irregular verbs are shown on p xxvi

erīlis *adj* the master's, the mistress's.

Erīnуs, -yos *f* Fury; (*fig*) curse, frenzy.

Eriphуla, -ae *f* mother of Alcmaeon (*who killed her*).

ēripiō, -ipere, -ipuī, -eptum *vt* to tear away, pull away, take by force; to rob; to rescue; **sē ~ escape.**

ērogātiō, -ōnis *f* paying out.

ērogitō, -āre *vt* to enquire.

ērogō, -āre, -āvī, -ātum *vt* to pay out, expend; to bequeath.

errābundus *adj* wandering.

errāticus *adj* roving, shifting.

errātiō, -ōnis *f* wandering, roving.

errātum, -ī *nt* mistake, error.

errātus, -ūs *m* wandering.

errō, -āre, -āvī, -ātum *vi* to wander, stray, lose one's way; to waver; to make a mistake, err ♦ *vt* to traverse; **stēllae ~antēs** planets.

errō, -ōnis *m* vagabond.

error, -ōris *m* wandering; meander, maze; uncertainty; error, mistake, delusion; deception.

ērubēscō, -ēscere, -uī *vi* to blush; to feel ashamed ♦ *vt* to blush for, be ashamed of; to respect.

ērūca, -ae *f* colewort.

ēructō, -āre *vt* to belch, vomit; to talk drunkenly about; to throw up.

ērudiō, -īre, -iī, -ītum *vt* to educate, instruct.

ērudītē *adv* learnedly.

ērudītiō, -ōnis *f* education, instruction; learning, knowledge.

ērudītulus *adj* somewhat skilled.

ērudītus *ppp of* **ērudiō** ♦ *adj* learned, educated, accomplished.

ērumpō, -umpere, -ūpī, -uptum *vt* to break open; to make break out ♦ *vi* to burst out, break through; to end (in).

ēruō, -ere, -ī, -tum *vt* to uproot, tear out; to demolish, destroy; to elicit, draw out; to rescue.

ēruptiō, -ōnis *f* eruption; (*MIL*) sally.

ēruptus *ppp of* **ērumpō.**

erus, -ī *m* master (of the house); owner.

ērutus *ppp of* **ēruō.**

ervum, -ī *nt* vetch.

Erycīnus *adj* of Eryx; of Venus; Sicilian ♦ *f* Venus.

Erymanthius, -is *adj see n.*

Erymanthus *and* **-ī** *m* mountain range in Arcadia, (*where Hercules killed the bear*).

Eryx, -cis *m* town and mountain in the extreme W. of Sicily.

esca, -ae *f* food, tit-bits; bait.

escārius *adj* of food; of bait ♦ *ntpl* dishes.

ēscendō, -endere, -endī, -ēnsum *vi* to climb up, go up ♦ *vt* to mount.

ēscēnsiō, -ōnis *f* raid (from the coast); disembarkation.

esculentus *adj* edible, tasty.

Esquiliae, -iārum *fpl* Esquiline hill in Rome.

Esquilīnus *adj* Esquiline ♦ *f* Esquiline gate.

essedārius, -ī *and* **iī** *m* chariot fighter.

essedum, -ī *nt* war chariot.

essitō, -āre *vt* to usually eat.

ēst *pres of* **edō.**

ēstrīx, -īcis *f* glutton.

ēsuriālis *adj* of hunger.

ēsuriō, -īre, -ītum *vi* to be hungry ♦ *vt* to hunger for.

ēsurītiō, -ōnis *f* hunger.

ēsus *ppp of* **edō.**

et *conj* and; (*repeated*) both … and; (*adding emphasis*) in fact, yes; (*comparing*) as, than ♦ *adv* also, too; even.

etenim *conj* (*adding an explanation*) and as a matter of fact, in fact.

etēsiae, -ārum *fpl* Etesian winds.

etēsius *adj see n.*

ēthologus, -ī *m* mimic.

etiam *adv* also, besides; (*emphatic*) even, actually; (*affirming*) yes, certainly; (*indignant*) really!; (*time*) still, as yet; again; **~ atque ~** again and again; **~ cavēs!** do be careful!; **nihil ~** nothing at all.

etiamdum *adv* still, as yet.

etiamnum, etiamnunc *adv* still, till now, till then; besides.

etiamsī *conj* even if, although.

etiamtum, etiamtunc *adv* till then, still.

Etrūria, -ae *f* district of Italy north of Rome.

Etruscus *adj* Etruscan.

etsī *conj* even if, though; and yet.

etymologia, -ae *f* etymology.

eu *interj* well done!, bravo!

Euan *m* Bacchus.

Euander *and* **rus, -rī** *m* Evander (*ancient king on the site of Rome*).

Euandrius *adj see n.*

euax *interj* hurrah!

Euboea, -oeae *f* Greek island.

Euboicus *adj* Euboean.

euge, eugepae *interj* bravo!, cheers!

Euhan *m* Bacchus.

euhāns, -antis *adj* shouting the Bacchic cry.

Euhias *f* Bacchante.

Euhius, -ī *m* Bacchus.

euhoe *interj* ecstatic cry of Bacchic revellers.

Euius, -ī *m* Bacchus.

Eumenides, -um *fpl* Furies.

eunūchus, -ī *m* eunuch.

Euphrātēs, -is *m* river Euphrates.

Eupolis, -dis *m* Athenian comic poet.

Eurīpidēs, -is *m* Athenian tragic poet.

Eurīpidēus *adj see n.*

Eurīpus, -ī *m* strait between Euboea and mainland; a channel, conduit.

Eurōpa, -ae *and* **ē, -ēs** *f* mythical princess of Tyre (*who was carried by a bull to Crete*); continent of Europe.

Eurōpaeus *adj see n.*

Eurōtās, -ae *m* river of Sparta.

Eurōus *adj* eastern.

Eurus, -ī *m* east wind; south-east wind.

Eurydicē, -ēs *f* wife of Orpheus.

Eurystheus, -eī *m* king of Mycenae (*who imposed the labours on Hercules*).
euschēmē *adv* gracefully.
Euterpē, -ēs *f* Muse of music.
Euxīnus *m* the Black (Sea).
ēvādō, -dere, -sī, -sum *vi* to come out; to climb up; to escape; to turn out, result, come true ♦ *vt* to pass, mount; to escape from.
ēvagor, -ārī, -ātus *vi* (*MIL*) to manoeuvre; (*fig*) to spread ♦ *vt* to stray beyond.
ēvalēscō, -ēscere, -uī *vi* to grow, increase; to be able; to come into vogue.
Ēvander *etc see* **Euander.**
ēvānēscō, -ēscere, -uī *vi* to vanish, die away, lose effect.
ēvangelium, -ī *and* **iī** *nt* (*ECCL*) Gospel.
ēvānidus *adj* vanishing.
ēvāsī *perf of* **ēvādō.**
ēvastō, -āre *vt* to devastate.
ēvehō, -here, -xī, -ctum *vt* to carry out; to raise up, exalt; to spread abroad; (*pass*) to ride, sail, move out.
ēvellō, -ellere, -ellī, -ulsum *vt* to tear out, pull out; to eradicate.
ēveniō, -enīre, -ēnī, -entum *vi* to come out; to turn out, result; to come to pass, happen, befall.
ēventum, -ī *nt* result, issue; occurrence, event; fortune, experience.
ēventus, -ūs *m* result, issue; success; fortune, fate.
ēverberō, -āre *vt* to beat violently.
ēverriculum, -ī *nt* dragnet.
ēverrō, -rere, -rī, -sum *vt* to sweep out, clean out.
ēversiō, -ōnis *f* overthrow, destruction.
ēversor, -ōris *m* destroyer.
ēversus *ppp of* **ēverrō;** *ppp of* **ēvertō.**
ēvertō, -tere, -tī, -sum *vt* to turn out, eject; to turn up, overturn; to overthrow, ruin, destroy.
ēvestīgātus *adj* tracked down.
ēvictus *ppp of* **ēvincō.**
ēvidēns, -entis *adj* visible, plain, evident.
ēvidenter *adv see* **evidēns.**
ēvidentia, -ae *f* distinctness.
ēvigilō, -āre, -āvī, -ātum *vi* to be wide awake ♦ *vt* to compose carefully.
ēvīlēscō, -ere *vi* to become worthless.
ēvinciō, -cīre, -xī, -ctum *vt* to garland, crown.
ēvincō, -incere, -īcī, -ictum *vt* to overcome, conquer; to prevail over; to prove.
ēvirō, -āre *vt* to castrate.
ēviscerō, -āre *vt* to disembowel, tear to pieces.
ēvītābilis *adj* avoidable.
ēvītō, -āre, -āvī, -ātum *vt* to avoid, clear.
ēvocātī, -ōrum *mpl* veteran volunteers.
ēvocātor, -ōris *m* enlister.

ēvocō, -āre, -āvī, -ātum *vt* to call out, summon; to challenge; to call up; to call forth, evoke.
ēvolō, -āre, -āvī, -ātum *vi* to fly out, fly away; to rush out; (*fig*) to rise, soar.
ēvolūtiō, -ōnis *f* unrolling (a book).
ēvolvō, -vere, -vī, -ūtum *vt* to roll out, roll along; to unroll, unfold; (*book*) to open, read; (*fig*) to disclose, unravel, disentangle.
ēvomō, -ere, -uī, -itum *vt* to vomit up, disgorge.
ēvulgō, -āre, -āvī, -ātum *vt* to divulge, make public.
ēvulsiō, -ōnis *f* pulling out.
ēvulsus *ppp of* **ēvellō.**
ex, ē *prep* (*with abl*) (*place*) out of, from, down from; (*person*) from; (*time*) after; immediately after, since; (*change*) from being; (*source, material*) of; (*cause*) by reason of, through; (*conformity*) in accordance with; **ex itinere** on the march; **ex parte** in part; **ex quō** since; **ex rē, ex ūsū** for the good of; **ē rē pūblicā** constitutionally; **ex sententiā** to one's liking; **aliud ex aliō** one thing after another; **ūnus ex** one of.
exacerbō, -āre *vt* to exasperate.
exāctiō, -ōnis *f* expulsion; supervision; tax; (*debts*) calling in.
exāctor, -ōris *m* expeller; superintendent; tax collector.
exāctus *ppp of* **exigō** ♦ *adj* precise, exact.
exacuō, -uere, -uī, -ūtum *vt* to sharpen; (*fig*) to quicken, inflame.
exadversum, -us *adv, prep* (*with acc*) right opposite.
exaedificātiō, -ōnis *f* construction.
exaedificō, -āre *vt* to build up; to finish the building of.
exaequātiō, -ōnis *f* levelling.
exaequō, -āre, -āvī, -ātum *vt* to level out; to compensate; to put on an equal footing; to equal.
exaestuō, -āre *vi* to boil up.
exaggerātiō, -ōnis *f* exaltation.
exaggerō, -āre, -āvī, -ātum *vt* to pile up; (*fig*) to heighten, enhance.
exagitātor, -ōris *m* critic.
exagitō, -āre, -āvī, -ātum *vt* to disturb, harass; to scold, censure; to excite, incite.
exagōga, -ae *f* export.
exalbēscō, -ēscere, -uī *vi* to turn quite pale.
exāmen, -inis *nt* swarm, crowd; tongue of a balance; examining.
examinō, -āre, -āvī, -ātum *vt* to weigh; to consider, test.
examussim *adv* exactly, perfectly.
exanclō, -āre *vt* to drain; to endure to the end.
exanimālis *adj* dead; deadly.
exanimātiō, -ōnis *f* panic.
exanimis *adj* lifeless, breathless; terrified.

Noun declensions and verb conjugations are shown on pp xiii to xxv. The present infinitive ending of a verb shows to which conjugation it belongs: **-āre** = 1st; **-ēre** = 2nd; **-ere** = 3rd and **-īre** = 4th. Irregular verbs are shown on p xxvi

exanimō, -āre, -āvī, -ātum *vt* to wind; to kill; to terrify, agitate; (*pass*) to be out of breath.

exanimus *see* **exanimis**.

exārdēscō, -dēscere, -sī, -sum *vi* to catch fire, blaze up; (*fig*) to be inflamed, break out.

exārēscō, -ēscere, -uī *vi* to dry, dry up.

exarmō, -āre *vt* to disarm.

exarō, -āre, -āvī, -ātum *vt* to plough up; to cultivate, produce; (*brow*) to furrow; (*writing*) to pen.

exārsī *perf of* **exārdēscō**.

exasciātus *adj* hewn out.

exasperō, -āre, -āvī, -ātum *vt* to roughen; (*fig*) to provoke.

exauctōrō, -āre, -āvī, -ātum *vt* (*MIL*) to discharge, release; to cashier.

exaudiō, -īre, -īvī, -ītum *vt* to hear clearly; to listen to; to obey.

exaugeō, -ēre *vt* to increase.

exaugurātiō, -ōnis *f* desecrating.

exaugurō, -āre *vt* to desecrate.

exauspicō, -āre *vi* to take an omen.

exbibō *etc see* **ēbibō**.

excaecō, -āre *vt* to blind; (*river*) to block up.

excandēscentia, -ae *f* growing anger.

excandēscō, -ēscere, -uī *vi* to burn, be inflamed.

excantō, -āre *vt* to charm out, spirit away.

excarnificō, -āre *vt* to tear to pieces.

excavō, -āre *vt* to hollow out.

excēdō, -ēdere, -essī, -essum *vi* to go out, go away; to die, disappear; to advance, proceed (to); to digress ♦ *vt* to leave; to overstep, exceed.

excellēns, -entis *pres p of* **excellō** ♦ *adj* outstanding, excellent.

excellenter *adv see* **excellēns**.

excellentia, -ae *f* superiority, excellence.

excellō, -ere *vi* to be eminent, excel.

excelsē *adv* loftily.

excelsitās, -ātis *f* loftiness.

excelsum, -ī *nt* height.

excelsus *adj* high, elevated; eminent, illustrious.

exceptiō, -ōnis *f* exception, restriction; (*law*) objection.

exceptō, -āre *vt* to catch, take out.

exceptus *ppp of* **excipiō**.

excernō, -ernere, -rēvī, -rētum *vt* to sift out, separate.

excerpō, -ere, -sī, -tum *vt* to take out; to select, copy out extracts; to leave out, omit.

excessus, -ūs *m* departure, death.

excetra, -ae *f* snake.

excidiō, -ōnis *f* destruction.

excidium, -ī *and* **iī** *nt* overthrow, destruction.

excidō, -ere, -ī *vi* to fall out, fall; (*speech*) to slip out, escape; (*memory*) to get forgotten, escape; (*person*) to fail, lose; (*things*) to disappear, be lost.

excīdō, -dere, -dī, -sum *vt* to cut off, hew out, fell; to raze; (*fig*) to banish.

excieō *vt see* **exciō**.

exciō, -īre, -īvī *and* **iī, -ītum** *and* **ītum** *vt* to call out, rouse, summon; to occasion, produce; to excite.

excipiō, -ipere, -ēpī, -eptum *vt* to take out, remove; to exempt, make an exception of, mention specifically; to take up, catch, intercept, overhear; to receive, welcome, entertain; to come next to, follow after, succeed.

excīsiō, -ōnis *f* destroying.

excīsus *ppp of* **excīdō**.

excitātus *adj* loud, strong.

excitō, -āre, -āvī, -ātum *vt* to rouse, wake up, summon; to raise, build; to call on (to stand up); (*fig*) to encourage, revive, excite.

excitus, excītus *ppp of* **exciō**.

exclāmātiō, -ōnis *f* exclamation.

exclāmō, -āre, -āvī, -ātum *vi* to cry out, shout ♦ *vt* to exclaim, call.

exclūdō, -dere, -sī, -sum *vt* to shut out, exclude; to shut off, keep off; (*egg*) to hatch out; (*eye*) to knock out; (*fig*) to prevent, except.

exclūsiō, -ōnis *f* shutting out.

exclūsus *ppp of* **exclūdō**.

excoctus *ppp of* **excoquō**.

excōgitātiō, -ōnis *f* thinking out, devising.

excōgitō, -āre, -āvī, -ātum *vt* to think out, contrive.

excolō, -olere, -oluī, -ultum *vt* to work carefully; to perfect, refine.

excoquō, -quere, -xī, -ctum *vt* to boil away; to remove with heat, make with heat; to dry up.

excors, -dis *adj* senseless, stupid.

excrēmentum, -ī *nt* excretion.

excreō *etc see* **exscreō**.

excrēscō, -scere, -vī, -tum *vi* to grow, rise up.

excrētus *ppp of* **excernō**.

excruciō, -āre, -āvī, -ātum *vt* to torture, torment.

excubiae, -ārum *fpl* keeping guard, watch; sentry.

excubitor, -ōris *m* sentry.

excubō, -āre, -uī, -itum *vi* to sleep out of doors; to keep watch; (*fig*) to be on the alert.

excūdō, -dere, -dī, -sum *vt* to strike out, hammer out; (*egg*) to hatch; (*fig*) to make, compose.

exculcō, -āre *vt* to beat, tramp down.

excultus *ppp of* **excolō**.

excurrō, -rrere, -currī *and* **rrī, -rsum** *vi* to run out, hurry out; to make an excursion; (*MIL*) to make a sortie; (*place*) to extend, project; (*fig*) to expand.

excursiō, -ōnis *f* raid, sortie; (*gesture*) stepping forward; (*fig*) outset.

excursor, -ōris *m* scout.

excursus, -ūs *m* excursion, raid, charge.

excūsābilis *adj* excusable.

excūsātē *adv* excusably.

excūsātiō, -ōnis *f* excuse, plea.

excūsō, -āre, -āvī, -ātum *vt* to excuse; to apologize for; to plead as an excuse.

excussus *ppp of* **excutiō**.

excūsus *ppp of* **excūdō**.

excutiō, -tere, -ssī, -ssum *vt* to shake out, shake off; to knock out, drive out, cast off; (*fig*) to discard, banish; to examine, inspect.

exdorsuō, -āre *vt* to fillet.

exec- *etc see* **exsec-**.

exedō, -ēsse, -ēdī, -ēsum *vt* to eat up; to wear away, destroy; (*feelings*) to prey on.

exedra, -ae *f* hall, lecture room.

exedrium, -ī *and* **iī** *nt* sitting room.

exēmī *perf of* **eximō**.

exemplar, -āris *nt* copy; likeness; model, ideal.

exemplārēs *mpl* copies.

exemplum, -ī *nt* copy; example, sample, precedent, pattern; purport, nature; warning, object lesson; ~ **dare** set an example; ~**ī causā, gratiā** for instance.

exemptus *ppp of* **eximō**.

exenterō, -āre *vt* (*comedy*) to empty, clean out; to torture.

exeō, -īre, -iī, -itum *vi* to go out, leave; to come out, issue; (*MIL*) to march out; (*time*) to expire; to spring up, rise ♦ *vt* to pass beyond; to avoid; ~ **ex potestāte** lose control.

exeq- *etc see* **exseq-**.

exerceō, -ēre, -uī, -itum *vt* to keep busy, supervise; (*ground*) to work, cultivate; (*MIL*) to drill, exercise; (*mind*) to engage, employ; (*occupation*) to practise, follow, carry on; (*trouble*) to worry, harass; **sē** ~ practise, exercise.

exercitātiō, -ōnis *f* practice, exercise, experience.

exercitātus *adj* practised, trained, versed; troubled.

exercitium, -ī *and* **iī** *nt* exercising.

exercitō, -āre *vt* to exercise.

exercitor, -ōris *m* trainer.

exercitus *ppp of* **exerceō** ♦ *adj* disciplined; troubled; troublesome.

exercitus, -ūs *m* army (*esp the infantry*); assembly; troop, flock; exercise.

exerō *etc see* **exserō**.

exēsor, -ōris *m* corroder.

exēsus *ppp of* **exedō**.

exhālātiō, -ōnis *f* vapour.

exhālō, -āre *vt* to exhale, breathe out ♦ *vi* to steam; to expire.

exhauriō, -rīre, -sī, -stum *vt* to drain off; to empty; to take away, remove; (*fig*) to exhaust, finish; (*trouble*) to undergo, endure to the end.

exhērēdō, -āre *vt* to disinherit.

exhērēs, -ēdis *adj* disinherited.

exhibeō, -ere, -uī, -itum *vt* to hold out, produce (in public); to display, show; to

cause, occasion.

exhilarātus *adj* delighted.

exhorrēscō, -ēscere, -uī *vi* to be terrified ♦ *vt* to be terrified at.

exhortātiō, -ōnis *f* encouragement.

exhortor -ārī, -ātus *vt* to encourage.

exigō, -igere, -ēgī, -āctum *vt* to drive out, thrust; (*payment*) to exact, enforce; to demand, claim; (*goods*) to dispose of; (*time*) to pass, complete; (*work*) to finish; (*news*) to ascertain; to test, examine, consider.

exiguē *adv* briefly, slightly, hardly.

exiguitās, -ātis *f* smallness, meagreness.

exiguus *adj* small, short, meagre ♦ *nt* a little bit.

exiliō *etc see* **exsiliō**.

exīlis *adj* thin, small, meagre; poor; (*style*) flat, insipid.

exīlitās, -ātis *f* thinness, meagreness.

exīliter *adv* feebly.

exilium *etc see* **exsilium**.

exim *see* **exinde**.

eximiē *adv* exceptionally.

eximius *adj* exempt; select; distinguished, exceptional.

eximō, -imere, -ēmī, -emptum *vt* to take out, remove; to release, free; to exempt; (*time*) to waste; (*fig*) to banish.

exin *see* **exinde**.

exināniō, -īre, -iī, -ītum *vt* to empty; to pillage.

exinde *adv* (*place*) from there, next; (*time*) then, thereafter, next; (*measure*) accordingly.

exīstimātiō, -ōnis *f* opinion, judgment; reputation, character; (*money*) credit.

exīstimātor, -ōris *m* judge, critic.

exīstimō, -āre, -āvī, -ātum *vt* to value, estimate, judge, think, consider.

existō *etc see* **exsistō**.

exīstumō *vt see* **exīstimō**.

exitiābilis *adj* deadly, fatal.

exitiālis *adj* deadly.

exitiōsus *adj* pernicious, fatal.

exitium, -ī *and* **iī** *nt* destruction, ruin.

exitus, -ūs *m* departure; way out, outlet; conclusion, end; death; outcome, result.

exlēx, -ēgis *adj* above the law, lawless.

exoculō, -āre *vt* to knock the eyes out of.

exodium, -ī *and* **iī** *nt* afterpiece.

exolēscō, -scere, -vī, -tum *vi* to decay, become obsolete.

exolētus *adj* full-grown.

exonerō, -āre, -āvī, -ātum *vt* to unload, discharge; (*fig*) to relieve, exonerate.

exoptātus *adj* welcome.

exoptō, -āre, -āvī, -ātum *vt* to long for, desire.

exōrābilis *adj* sympathetic.

exōrātor, -ōris *m* successful pleader.

exōrdior, -dīrī, -sus *vt* to lay the warp; to begin.

exōrdium, -ī *and* **iī** *nt* beginning; (*RHET*) introductory section.

exorior, -īrī, -tus *vi* to spring up, come out, rise; to arise, appear, start.

exōrnātiō, -ōnis *f* embellishment.

exōrnātor, -ōris *m* embellisher.

exōrnō, -āre, -āvī, -ātum *vt* to equip, fit out; to embellish, adorn.

exōrō, -āre, -āvī, -ātum *vt* to prevail upon, persuade; to obtain, win by entreaty.

exōrsus *ppa of* **exōrdior** ♦ *adj* begun ♦ *ntpl* preamble.

exōrsus, -ūs *m* beginning.

exortus *ppa of* **exorior.**

exortus, -ūs *m* rising; east.

exos, -ossis *adj* boneless.

exōsculor, -ārī, -ātus *vt* to kiss fondly.

exossō, -āre *vt* to bone.

exōstra, -ae *f* stage mechanism; (*fig*) public.

exōsus *adj* detesting.

exōticus *adj* foreign.

expallēscō, -ēscere, -uī *vi* to turn pale, be afraid.

expalpō, -āre *vt* to coax out.

expandō, -ere *vt* to unfold.

expatrō, -āre *vt* to squander.

expavēscō, -ere, expāvī *vi* to be terrified ♦ *vt* to dread.

expect- *etc see* **exspect-.**

expediō, -īre, -īvī *and* **iī, -ītum** *vt* to free, extricate, disentangle; to prepare, clear (for action); to put right, settle; to explain, relate; (*impers*) it is useful, expedient.

expedītē *adv* readily, freely.

expedītiō, -ōnis *f* (*MIL*) expedition, enterprise.

expedītus *ppp of* **expediō** ♦ *adj* light-armed; ready, prompt; at hand ♦ *m* light-armed soldier; **in ~ō esse, habēre** be, have in readiness.

expellō, -ellere, -ulī, -ulsum *vt* to drive away, eject, expel; to remove, repudiate.

expendō, -endere, -endī, -ēnsum *vt* to weigh out; to pay out; (*penalty*) to suffer; (*mind*) to ponder, consider, judge.

expēnsum, -ī *nt* payment, expenditure.

expergēfaciō, -facere, -fēcī, -factum *vt* to rouse, excite.

expergīscor, -gīscī, -rēctus *vi* to wake up; to bestir oneself.

expergō, -ere, -ī, -itum *vt* to awaken.

experiēns, -entis *pres p of* **experior** ♦ *adj* enterprising.

experientia, -ae *f* experiment; endeavour; experience, practice.

experīmentum, -ī *nt* proof, test; experience.

experior, -īrī, -tus *vt* to test, make trial of; to attempt, experience; (*law*) to go to law; (*perf tenses*) to know from experience.

experrēctus *ppa of* **expergīscor.**

expers, -tis *adj* having no part in, not sharing; free from, without.

expertus *ppa of* **experior** ♦ *adj* proved, tried; experienced.

expetessō, -ere *vt* to desire.

expetō, -ere, -īvī *and* **iī, -ītum** *vt* to aim at, tend towards; to desire, covet; to attack; to demand, require ♦ *vi* to befall, happen.

expiātiō, -ōnis *f* atonement.

expictus *ppp of* **expingō.**

expīlātiō, -ōnis *f* pillaging.

expīlātor, -ōris *m* plunderer.

expīlō, -āre, -āvī, -ātum *vt* to rob, plunder.

expingō, -ingere, -inxī, -ictum *vt* to portray.

expiō, -āre, -āvī, -ātum *vt* to purify; to atone for, make amends for; to avert (evil).

expīrō *etc see* **exspīrō.**

expiscor, -ārī, -ātus *vt* to try to find out, ferret out.

explānātē *adv see* **explānātus.**

explānātiō, -ōnis *f* explanation.

explānātor, -ōris *m* interpreter.

explānātus *adj* distinct.

explānō, -āre, -āvī, -ātum *vt* to state clearly, explain; to pronounce clearly.

explaudō *etc see* **explōdō.**

explēmentum, -ī *nt* filling.

expleō, -ēre, -ēvī, -ētum *vt* to fill up; to complete; (*desire*) to satisfy, appease; (*duty*) to perform, discharge; (*loss*) to make good; (*time*) to fulfil, complete.

explētiō, -ōnis *f* satisfying.

explētus *ppp of* **expleō** ♦ *adj* complete.

explicātē *adv* plainly.

explicātiō, -ōnis *f* uncoiling; expounding, analyzing.

explicātor, -ōris *m*, **-rīx, -rīcis** *f* expounder.

explicātus *adj* spread out; plain, clear.

explicātus, -ūs *m* explanation.

explicitus *adj* easy.

explicō, -āre, -āvī *and* **uī, -ātum** *and* **itum** *vt* to unfold, undo, spread out; (*book*) to open; (*MIL*) to deploy, extend; (*difficulty*) to put in order, settle; (*speech*) to develop, explain; to set free.

explōdō, -dere, -sī, -sum *vt* to hiss off, drive away; (*fig*) to reject.

explōrātē *adv* with certainty.

explōrātiō, -ōnis *f* spying.

explōrātor, -ōris *m* spy, scout.

explōrātus *adj* certain, sure.

explōrō, -āre, -āvī, -ātum *vt* to investigate, reconnoitre; to ascertain; to put to the test.

explōsī *perf of* **explōdō.**

explōsiō, -ōnis *f* driving off (the stage).

explōsus *ppp of* **explōdō.**

expoliō, -īre, -īvī, -ītum *vt* to smooth off, polish; (*fig*) to refine, embellish.

expolītiō, -ōnis *f* smoothing off; polish, finish.

expōnō, -ōnere, -osuī, -ositum *vt* to set out, put out; (*child*) to expose; (*NAUT*) to disembark; (*money*) to offer; (*fig*) to set forth, expose, display; (*speech*) to explain, expound.

exporrigō, -igere, -ēxī, -ēctum *vt* to extend, smooth out.

exportātiō, -ōnis *f* exporting.

exportō, -āre, -āvī, -ātum *vt* to carry out, export.

exposcō, -ere, expoposcī *vt* to implore, pray for; to demand.

expositīcius *adj* foundling.

expositiō, -ōnis *f* narration, explanation.

expositus *ppp of* **expōnō ♦** *adj* open, affable; vulgar.

expostulātiō, -ōnis *f* complaint

expostulō, -āre, -āvī, -ātum *vt* to demand urgently; to complain of, expostulate.

expōtus *ppp of* **ēpōtō.**

expressus *ppp of* **exprimō ♦** *adj* distinct, prominent.

exprimō, -imere, -essī, -essum *vt* to squeeze out, force out; to press up; (*fig*) to extort, wrest; (*art*) to mould, model; (*words*) to imitate, portray, translate, pronounce.

exprobrātiō, -ōnis *f* reproach.

exprobrō, -āre, -āvī, -ātum *vt* to reproach, cast up.

exprōmō, -ere, -psī, -ptum *vt* to bring out, fetch out; (*acts*) to exhibit, practise; (*feelings*) to give vent to; (*speech*) to disclose, state.

expugnābilis *adj* capable of being taken by storm.

expugnācior, -ōris *adj* more effective.

expugnātiō, -ōnis *f* storming, assault.

expugnātor, -ōris *m* stormer.

expugnō, -āre, -āvī, -ātum *vt* to storm, reduce; to conquer; (*fig*) to overcome, extort.

expulī *perf of* **expellō.**

expulsiō, -ōnis *f* expulsion.

expulsor, -ōris *m* expeller.

expulsus *ppp of* **expellō.**

expultrīx, -īcis *f* expeller.

expungō, -ungere, -ūnxī, -ūnctum *vt* to prick out, cancel.

expūrgātiō, -ōnis *f* excuse.

expūrgō, -āre *vt* to purify; to justify.

exputō, -āre *vt* to consider, comprehend.

exquīrō, -rere, -sīvī, -sītum *vt* to search out, investigate, to inquire; to devise.

exquīsītē *adv* with particular care.

exquīsītus *ppp of* **exquīrō ♦** *adj* well thought out, choice.

exsaeviō, -īre *vi* to cease raging.

exsanguis *adj* bloodless, pale; feeble.

exsarciō, -cīre, -tum *vt* to repair.

exsatiō, -āre *vt* to satiate, satisfy.

exsaturābilis *adj* appeasable.

exsaturō, -āre *vt* to satiate.

exsce- *etc see* **esce-.**

exscindō, -ndere, -dī, -ssum *vt* to extirpate.

exscreō, -āre *vt* to cough up.

exscrībō, -bere, -psī, -ptum *vt* to copy out; to note down.

exsculpō, -ere, -sī, -tum *vt* to carve out; to erase; (*fig*) to extort.

exsecō, -āre, -uī, -tum *vt* to cut out; to castrate.

exsecrābilis *adj* cursing, deadly.

exsecrātiō, -ōnis *f* curse; solemn oath.

exsecrātus *adj* accursed.

exsecror, -ārī, -ātus *vt* to curse; to take an oath.

exsectiō, -ōnis *f* cutting out.

exsecūtiō, -ōnis *f* management; discussion.

exsecūtus *ppa of* **exsequor.**

exsequiae, -ārum *fpl* funeral, funeral rites.

exsequiālis *adj* funeral.

exsequor, -quī, -cūtus *vt* to follow, pursue; to follow to the grave; (*duty*) to carry out, accomplish; (*speech*) to describe, relate; (*suffering*) to undergo; (*wrong*) to avenge, punish.

exserciō *vt see* **exsarciō.**

exserō, -ere, -uī, -tum *vt* to put out, stretch out; to reveal.

exsertō, -āre *vt* to stretch out repeatedly.

exsertus *ppp of* **exserō ♦** *adj* protruding.

exsibilō, -āre *vt* to hiss off.

exsiccātus *adj* (*style*) uninteresting.

exsiccō, -āre, -āvī, -ātum *vt* to dry up; to drain.

exsicō *etc see* **exsecō.**

exsignō, -āre *vt* to write down in detail.

exsiliō, -īre, -uī *vi* to jump up, spring out; to start.

exsilium, -ī *and* **iī** *nt* banishment, exile; retreat.

exsistō, -istere, -titī, -titum *vi* to emerge, appear; to arise, spring (from); to be, exist.

exsolvō, -vere, -vī, -ūtum *vt* to undo, loosen, open; to release, free; to get rid of, throw off; (*debt, promise*) to discharge, fulfil, pay up; (*words*) to explain.

exsomnis *adj* sleepless, watchful.

exsorbeō, -ēre, -uī *vt* to suck, drain; to devour, endure.

exsors, -tis *adj* chosen, special; free from.

exspargō *etc see* **exspergō.**

exspatior, -ārī, -ātus *vi* to go off the course.

exspectābilis *adj* to be expected.

exspectātiō, -ōnis *f* waiting, expectation.

exspectātus *adj* looked for, welcome.

exspectō, -āre, -āvī, -ātum *vt* to wait for, till; to see; to expect; to hope for, dread; to require.

exspergō, -gere, -sum *vt* to scatter; to diffuse.

exspēs *adj* despairing.

exspīrātiō, -ōnis *f* exhalation.

exspīrō, -āre, -āvī, -ātum *vt* to breathe out, exhale; to emit ♦ *vi* to rush out; to expire,

---

Noun declensions and verb conjugations are shown on pp xiii to xxv. The present infinitive ending of a verb shows to which conjugation it belongs: **-āre** = 1st; **-ēre** = 2nd; **-ere** = 3rd and **-īre** = 4th. Irregular verbs are shown on p xxvi

come to an end.

exsplendēscō, -ere *vi* to shine.

exspoliō, -āre *vt* to pillage.

exspuō, -uere, -uī, -ūtum *vt* to spit out, eject; (*fig*) to banish.

exsternō, -āre *vt* to terrify.

exstillō, -āre *vi* to drip.

exstimulātor, -ōris *m* instigator.

exstimulō, -āre *vt* to goad on; to excite.

exstinctiō, -ōnis *f* annihilation.

exstinctor, -ōris *m* extinguisher; destroyer.

exstinguō, -guere, -xī, -ctum *vt* to put out, extinguish; to kill, destroy, abolish.

exstirpō, -āre *vt* to root out, eradicate.

exstitī *perf of* **exsistō**.

exstō, -āre *vi* to stand out, project; to be conspicuous, be visible; to be extant, exist, be.

exstructiō, -ōnis *f* erection.

exstruō, -ere, -xī, -ctum *vt* to heap up; to build up, construct.

exsūdō, -āre *vi* to come out in sweat ♦ *vt* (*fig*) to toil through.

exsūgō, -gere, -xī, -ctum *vt* to suck out.

exsul, -is *m/f* exile.

exsulō, -āre, -āvī, -ātum *vi* to be an exile.

exsultātiō, -ōnis *f* great rejoicing.

exsultim *adv* friskily.

exsultō, -āre, -āvī, -ātum *vi* to jump up, prance; (*fig*) to exult, run riot, boast; (*speech*) to range at will.

exsuperābilis *adj* superable.

exsuperantia, -ae *f* superiority.

exsuperō, -āre, -āvī, -ātum *vi* to mount up; to gain the upper hand, excel ♦ *vt* to go over; to surpass; to overpower.

exsurdō, -āre *vt* to deafen; (*fig*) to dull.

exsurgō, -gere, -rēxī, -rēctum *vi* to rise, stand up; to recover.

exsuscitō, -āre *vt* to wake up; (*fire*) to fan; (*mind*) to excite.

exta, -ōrum *ntpl* internal organs.

extābēscō, -ēscere, -uī *vi* to waste away; to vanish.

extāris *adj* sacrificial.

extemplō *adv* immediately, on the spur of the moment; **quom ~** as soon as.

extemporālis *adj* extempore.

extempulō *see* **extemplō**.

extendō, -dere, -dī, -tum *and* **extēnsum** *vt* to stretch out, spread, extend; to enlarge, increase; (*time*) to prolong; **sē ~** exert oneself; **īre per ~tum fūnem** walk the tightrope.

extēnsus *ppp of* **extendō**.

extentō, -āre *vt* to strain, exert.

extentus *ppp of* **extendō** ♦ *adj* broad.

extenuātiō, -ōnis *f* (*RHET*) diminution.

extenuō, -āre, -āvī, -ātum *vt* to thin out, rarefy; to diminish, weaken.

exter *adj* from outside; foreign.

exterebrō, -āre *vt* to bore out; to extort.

extergeō, -gēre, -sī, -sum *vt* to wipe off, clean; to plunder.

exterior, -ōris *adj* outer, exterior.

exterius *adv* on the outside.

exterminō, -āre *vt* to drive out, banish; (*fig*) to put aside.

externus *adj* outward, external; foreign, strange.

exterō, -erere, -rīvī, -rītum *vt* to rub out, wear away.

exterreō, -ēre, -uī, -itum *vt* to frighten.

extersus *ppp of* **extergeō**.

exterus *see* **exter**.

extexō, -ere *vt* to unweave; (*fig*) to cheat.

extimēscō, -ēscere, -uī *vi* to be very frightened ♦ *vt* to be very afraid of.

extimus *adj* outermost, farthest.

extin- *etc see* **exstin-**.

extispex, -icis *m* diviner.

extollō, -ere *vt* to lift up, raise; (*fig*) to exalt, beautify; (*time*) to defer.

extorqueō, -quēre, -sī, -tum *vt* to wrench out, wrest; to dislocate; (*fig*) to obtain by force, extort.

extorris *adj* banished, in exile.

extortor, -ōris *m* extorter.

extortus *ppp of* **extorqueō**.

extrā *adv* outside; **~ quam** except that, unless ♦ *prep* (*with acc*) outside, beyond; free from; except.

extrahō, -here, -xī, -ctum *vt* to draw out, pull out; to extricate, rescue; to remove; (*time*) to prolong, waste.

extrāneus, -ī *m* stranger ♦ *adj* external, foreign.

extraōrdinārius *adj* special, unusual.

extrārius *adj* external; unrelated ♦ *m* stranger.

extrēmitās, -ātis *f* extremity, end.

extrēmum, -ī *nt* end; **ad ~** at last.

extrēmum *adv* for the last time.

extrēmus *adj* outermost, extreme; last; utmost, greatest, meanest.

extrīcō, -āre, -āvī, -ātum *vt* to disentangle, extricate; to clear up.

extrīnsecus *adv* from outside, from abroad; on the outside.

extrītus *ppp of* **exterō**.

extrūdō, -dere, -sī, -sum *vt* to drive out; to keep out; (*sale*) to push.

extulī *perf of* **efferō**.

extumeō, -ēre *vi* to swell up.

extundō, -undere, -udī, -ūsum *vt* to beat out, hammer out; (*comedy*) to extort; (*fig*) to form, compose.

exturbō, -āre, -āvī, -ātum *vt* to drive out, throw out, knock out; (*wife*) to put away; (*fig*) to banish, disturb.

exūberō, -āre *vi* to abound.

exul *etc see* **exsul**.

exulcerō, -āre, -āvī, -ātum *vt* to aggravate.

exululō, -āre *vi* to howl wildly ♦ *vt* to invoke with cries.

exūnctus *ppp of* **exungō**.

exundō, -āre *vi* to overflow; to be washed up.
exungō, -ere *vt* to anoint liberally.
exuō, -uere, -uī, -ūtum *vt* to draw out, put off; to lay aside; to strip.
exūrō, -rere, -ssī, -stum *vt* to burn up; to dry up; to burn out; (*fig*) to inflame.
exūstiō, -ōnis *f* conflagration.
exūtus *ppp of* **exuō**.
exuviae, -ārum *fpl* clothing, arms; hide; spoils.

$$F, f$$

faba, -ae *f* bean.
fabālis *adj* bean- (*in cpds*).
fābella, -ae *f* short story, fable; play.
faber, -rī *m* craftsman (*in metal, stone, wood*), tradesman, smith; (*MIL*) artisan; ~ **ferrārius** blacksmith; ~ **tignārius** carpenter ♦ *adj* skilful.
Fabius, -ī *m* Roman family name (*esp Q F Maximus Cunctator, dictator against Hannibal*).
Fabius, -iānus *adj see n.*
fabrē *adv* skilfully.
fabrēfaciō, -facere, -fēcī, -factum *vt* to make, build, forge.
fabrica, -ae *f* art, trade; work of art; workshop; (*comedy*) trick.
fabricātiō, -ōnis *f* structure.
fabricātor, -ōris *m* artificer.
Fabricius, -ī *m* Roman family name (*esp C F Luscinus, incorruptible commander against Pyrrhus*).
Fabricius, -iānus *adj see n.*
fabricō, -āre; -or, -ārī, -ātus *vt* to make, build, forge.
fabrīlis *adj* artificer's ♦ *ntpl* tools.
fābula, -ae *f* story; common talk; play, drama; fable; ~**ae!** nonsense!; **lupus in** ~**ā** ≈ *talk of the devil!*
fābulor, -ārī, -ātus *vi* to talk, converse ♦ *vt* to say, invent.
fābulōsus *adj* legendary.
facessō, -ere, -īvī, -ītum *vt* to perform, carry out; to cause (trouble) ♦ *vi* to go away, retire.
facētē *adv* humorously; brilliantly.
facētiae, -ārum *fpl* wit, clever talk, humour.
facētus *adj* witty, humorous; fine, genteel, elegant.
faciēs, -ēī *f* form, shape; face, looks; appearance, aspect, character.

facile *adv* easily; unquestionably; readily; pleasantly.
facilis *adj* easy; well-suited; ready, quick; (*person*) good-natured, approachable; (*fortune*) prosperous.
facilitās, -ātis *f* ease, readiness; (*speech*) fluency; (*person*) good nature, affability.
facinorōsus *adj* criminal.
facinus, -oris *nt* deed, action; crime.
faciō, -ere, fēcī, factum (*imp* **fac**, *pass* **fīō**) *vt* to make, create, compose, cause; to do, perform; (*profession*) to practise; (*property*) to put under; (*value*) to regard, think of; (*words*) to represent, pretend, suppose ♦ *vi* to do, act; (*religion*) to offer sacrifice; (*with* **ad** *or dat*) to be of use; **cōpiam** ~ afford an opportunity; **damnum** ~ suffer loss; **metum** ~ excite fear; **proelium** ~ join battle; **rem** ~ make money; **verba** ~ talk; **māgnī** ~ think highly of; **quid tibi faciam?** how am I to answer you?; **quid tē faciam?** what am I to do with you?; **fac sciam** let me know; **fac potuisse** suppose one could have.
factiō, -ōnis *f* making, doing; group, party, faction (*esp in politics and chariot racing*).
factiōsus *adj* factious, oligarchical.
factitō, -āre, -āvi, -ātum *vt* to keep making or doing; to practise; to declare (to be).
factor, -ōris *m* (*sport*) batsman.
factum, -ī *nt* deed, exploit.
factus *ppp of* **faciō**.
facula, -ae *f* little torch.
facultās, -ātis *f* means, opportunity; ability; abundance, supply, resources.
fācundē *adv see* **fācundus**.
fācundia, -ae *f* eloquence.
fācundus *adj* fluent, eloquent.
faeceus *adj* impure.
faecula, -ae *f* wine lees.
faenebris *adj* of usury.
faenerātiō, -ōnis *f* usury.
faenerātō *adv* with interest.
faenerātor, -ōris *m* moneylender.
faenerō, -āre; -or, -ārī, -ātus *vt* to lend at interest; to ruin with usury; (*fig*) to trade in.
faenīlia, -um *ntpl* hayloft.
faenum, -ī *nt* hay; ~ **habet in cornū** he is dangerous.
faenus, -oris *nt* interest; capital lent at interest; (*fig*) profit, advantage.
faenusculum, -ī *nt* a little interest.
Faesulae, -ārum *fpl* town in Etruria (*now Fiesole*).
Faesulānus *adj see n.*
faex, faecis *f* sediment, lees; brine (*of pickles*); (*fig*) dregs.
fāgineus, fāginus *adj* of beech.
fāgus, -ī *f* beech.
fala, -ae *f* siege tower, used in assaults; (*Circus*) pillar.

Noun declensions and verb conjugations are shown on pp xiii to xxv. The present infinitive ending of a verb shows to which conjugation it belongs: **-āre** = 1st; **-ēre** = 2nd; **-ere** = 3rd and **-īre** = 4th. Irregular verbs are shown on p xxvi

falārica, -ae f a missile, firebrand.
falcārius, -ī *and* **iī** m sicklemaker.
falcātus adj scythed; sickle-shaped.
falcifer, -ī adj scythe-carrying.
Falernus adj Falernian (*of a district in N. Campania famous for its wine*) ♦ nt Falernian wine.
Faliscī, -ōrum mpl a people of S.E. Etruria (*with chief town Falerii*).
Faliscus adj see n.
fallācia, -ae f trick, deception.
fallāciter adv see **fallāx.**
fallāx, -ācis adj deceitful, deceptive.
fallō, -lere, fefellī, -sum vt to deceive, cheat, beguile; to disappoint, fail, betray; (*promise*) to break; to escape the notice of, be unknown to; (*pass*) to be mistaken; **mē ~lit** I am mistaken; I do not know.
falsē adv wrongly, by mistake; fraudulently.
falsidicus adj lying.
falsificus adj deceiving.
falsiiūrius adj perjurious.
falsiloquus adj lying.
falsiparēns, -entis adj with a pretended father.
falsō adv see **falsē.**
falsus ppp of **fallō** ♦ adj false, mistaken; deceitful; forged, falsified; sham, fictitious ♦ nt falsehood, error.
falx, falcis f sickle, scythe; pruning hook; (*MIL*) siege hook.
fāma, -ae f talk, rumour, tradition; public opinion; reputation, fame; infamy.
famēlicus adj hungry.
famēs, -is f hunger; famine; (*fig*) greed; (*RHET*) poverty of expression.
fāmigerātiō, -ōnis f rumour.
fāmigerātor, -ōris m telltale.
familia, -ae f domestics, slaves of a household; family property, estate; family, house; school, sect; **pater ~ās** master of a household; **~am dūcere** be head of a sect, company *etc.*
familiāris adj domestic, household, family; intimate, friendly; (*entrails*) relating to the sacrificer ♦ m servant; friend.
familiāritās, -ātis f intimacy, friendship.
familiāriter adv on friendly terms.
fāmōsus adj celebrated; infamous; slanderous.
famula, -ae f maidservant, handmaid.
famulāris adj of servants.
famulātus, -ūs m slavery.
famulor, -ārī vi to serve.
famulus, -ī m servant, attendant ♦ adj serviceable.
fānāticus adj inspired; frantic, frenzied.
fandī gerund of **for.**
fandum, -ī nt right.
fānum, -ī nt sanctuary temple.
fār, farris nt spelt; corn; meal.
farciō, -cīre, -sī, -tum vt to stuff, fill full.
farīna, -ae f meal, flour.

farrāgō, -inis f mash, hotch-potch; medley.
farrātus adj of corn; filled with corn.
farsī perf of **farciō.**
fartem, -im f acc filling; mincemeat.
fartor, -ōris m fattener, poulterer.
fartus ppp of **farciō.**
fās nt divine law; right; ~ **est** it is lawful, possible.
fascia, -ae f band, bandage; streak of cloud.
fasciculus, -ī m bundle, packet.
fascinō, -āre vt to bewitch, (*esp with the evil eye*).
fascinum, -ī nt, **-us, -ī** m charm.
fasciola, -ae f small bandage.
fascis, -is m bundle, faggot; soldier's pack, burden; (*pl*) rods and axe carried before the highest magistrates; high office (*esp the consulship*).
fassus ppa of **fateor.**
fāstī, -ōrum mpl register of days for legal and public business; calendar; registers of magistrates and other public records.
fastīdiō, -īre, -iī, -ītum vt to loathe, dislike, despise ♦ vi to feel squeamish, be disgusted; to be disdainful.
fastīdiōsē adv squeamishly; disdainfully.
fastīdiōsus adj squeamish, disgusted; fastidious, nice; disagreeable.
fastīdium, -ī *and* **iī** nt squeamishness, distaste; disgust, aversion; disdain, pride.
fastīgātē adv in a sloping position.
fastīgātus adj sloping up *or* down.
fastīgium, -ī *and* **iī** nt gable, pediment; slope; height, depth; top, summit; (*fig*) highest degree, acme, dignity; (*speech*) main headings.
fāstus adj lawful for public business.
fastus, -ūs m disdain, pride.
Fāta ntpl the Fates.
fātālis adj fateful, destined; fatal, deadly.
fātāliter adv by fate.
fateor, -tērī, -ssus vt to confess, acknowledge; to reveal, bear witness to.
fāticanus, -inus adj prophetic.
fātidicus adj prophetic ♦ m prophet.
fātifer, -ī adj deadly.
fatīgātiō, -ōnis f weariness.
fatīgō, -āre, -āvī, -ātum vt to tire, exhaust; to worry, importune; to wear down, torment.
fātiloqua, -ae f prophetess.
fatīscō, -ere; -or, -ī vi to crack, split; (*fig*) to become exhausted.
fatuitās, -ātis f silliness.
fātum, -ī nt divine word, oracle; fate, destiny; divine will; misfortune, doom, death; ~**ō obīre** die a natural death.
fātur, fātus 3rd pers, ppa of **for.**
fatuus adj silly; unwieldy ♦ m fool.
faucēs, -ium fpl throat; pass, narrow channel, chasm; (*fig*) jaws.
Faunus, -ī m father of Latinus (*god of forests and herdsmen, identified with Pan*); (*pl*) woodland spirits, Fauns.

fauste *adv see* **faustus.**
faustitās, -ātis *f* good fortune, fertility.
faustus *adj* auspicious, lucky.
fautor, -ōris *m* supporter, patron.
fautrīx, -īcis *f* protectress.
favea, -ae *f* pet slave.
faveō, -ēre, fāvī, fautum *vi* (*with dat*) to favour, befriend, support; **~ linguīs** keep silence.
favilla, -ae *f* embers, ashes; (*fig*) spark.
favitor *etc see* **fautor.**
Favōnius, -ī *m* west wind, zephyr.
favor, -ōris *m* favour, support; applause.
favōrābilis *adj* in favour; pleasing.
favus, -ī *m* honeycomb.
fax, facis *f* torch, wedding torch, funeral torch; marriage, death; (ASTRO) meteor; (*fig*) flame, fire, instigator; guide; **facem praeferre** act as guide.
faxim, faxō *old subj and fut of* **faciō.**
febrīcula, -ae *f* slight fever.
febris, -is *f* fever.
Februārius, -ī *m* February ♦ *adj* of February.
februum, -ī *nt* purification; **Februa** *pl festival of purification in February.*
fēcī *perf of* **faciō.**
fēcunditās, -ātis *f* fertility; (*style*) exuberance.
fēcundō, -āre *vt* to fertilise.
fēcundus *adj* fertile, fruitful; fertilising; (*fig*) abundant, rich, prolific.
fefellī *perf of* **fallō.**
fel, fellis *nt* gall bladder, bile; poison; (*fig*) animosity.
fēlēs, -is *f* cat.
fēlicitās, -ātis *f* happiness, good luck.
fēliciter *adv* abundantly; favourably; happily.
fēlīx, -īcis *adj* fruitful; auspicious, favourable; fortunate, successful.
fēmella, -ae *f* girl.
fēmina, -ae *f* female, woman.
fēmineus *adj* woman's, of women; unmanly.
femur, -oris *and* **inis** *nt* thigh.
fēn- *etc see* **faen-.**
fenestra, -ae *f* window; (*fig*) loophole.
fera, -ae *f* wild beast.
ferācius *adv* more fruitfully.
fērālis *adj* funereal; of the Feralia; deadly ♦ *ntpl festival of the dead in February.*
ferāx, -ācis *adj* fruitful, productive.
ferbuī *perf of* **ferveō.**
ferculum, -ī *nt* litter, barrow; dish, course.
ferē *adv* almost, nearly, about; quite, just; usually, generally, as a rule; (*with neg*) hardly; **nihil ~** hardly anything.
ferentārius, -ī *and* **iī** *m* a light-armed soldier.
Feretrius, -ī *m an epithet of Jupiter.*
feretrum, -ī *nt* bier.
fēriae, -ārum *fpl* festival, holidays; (*fig*) peace, rest.

fēriātus *adj* on holiday, idle.
ferīnus *adj* of wild beasts ♦ *f* game.
feriō, -īre *vt* to strike, hit; to kill, sacrifice; (*comedy*) to cheat; **foedus ~** conclude a treaty.
feritās, -ātis *f* wildness, savagery.
fermē *see* **ferē.**
fermentum, -ī *nt* yeast; beer; (*fig*) passion, vexation.
ferō, ferre, tulī, lātum *vt* to carry, bring, bear; to bring forth, produce; to move, stir, raise; to carry off, sweep away, plunder; (*pass*) to rush, hurry, fly, flow, drift; (*road*) to lead; (*trouble*) to endure, suffer, sustain; (*feelings*) to exhibit, show; (*speech*) to talk about, give out, celebrate; (*bookkeeping*) to enter; (*CIRCS*) to allow, require; **sē ~** rush, move; profess to be, boast; **condiciōnem, lēgem ~** propose terms, a law; **iūdicem ~** sue; **sententiam, suffrāgium ~** vote; **signa ~** march; attack; **aegrē, graviter ~** be annoyed at; **laudibus ~** extol; **in oculīs ~** be very fond of; **prae sē ~** show, declare; **fertur, ferunt** it is said, they say; **ut mea fert opīniō** in my opinion.
ferōcia, -ae *f* courage; spirit; pride, presumption.
ferōcitās, -ātis *f* high spirits, aggressiveness; presumption.
ferōciter *adv* bravely; insolently.
Fērōnia, -ae *f* old Italian goddess.
ferōx, -ōcis *adj* warlike, spirited, daring; proud, insolent.
ferrāmentum, -ī *nt* tool, implement.
ferrārius *adj* of iron; **faber ~** blacksmith ♦ *f* iron-mine, iron-works.
ferrātus *adj* ironclad, ironshod ♦ *mpl* men in armour.
ferreus *adj* of iron, iron; (*fig*) hard, cruel; strong, unyielding.
ferrūgineus *adj* rust-coloured, dark.
ferrūgō, -inis *f* rust; dark colour; gloom.
ferrum, -ī *nt* iron; sword; any iron implement; force of arms; **~ et ignis** devastation.
fertilis *adj* fertile, productive; fertilising.
fertilitās, -ātis *f* fertility.
ferula, -ae *f* fennel; staff, rod.
ferus *adj* wild; uncivilised, cruel ♦ *m* beast.
fervēfaciō, -ere, -tum *vt* to boil.
fervēns, -entis *pres p of* **ferveō** ♦ *adj* hot; raging; (*fig*) impetuous, furious.
ferventer *adv* hotly.
ferveō, -vēre, -buī *vi* to boil, burn; (*fig*) to rage, bustle, be agitated.
fervēscō, -ere *vi* to boil up, grow hot.
fervidus *adj* hot, raging; (*fig*) fiery, violent.
fervō, -vere, -vī *vi see* **ferveō.**
fervor, -ōris *m* seething; heat; (*fig*) ardour, passion.
Fescennīnus *adj* Fescennine (*a kind of ribald*

Noun declensions and verb conjugations are shown on pp xiii to xxv. The present infinitive ending of a verb shows to which conjugation it belongs: **-āre** = 1st; **-ēre** = 2nd; **-ere** = 3rd and **-īre** = 4th. Irregular verbs are shown on p xxvi

song, perhaps from Fescennium in Etruria).
fessus *adj* tired, worn out.
festīnanter *adv* hastily.
festīnātiō, -ōnis *f* haste, hurry.
festīnō, -āre *vi* to hurry, be quick ♦ *vt* to hasten, accelerate.
festīnus *adj* hasty, quick.
fēstīvē *adv* gaily; humorously.
fēstīvitās, -ātis *f* gaiety, merriment; humour, fun.
fēstīvus *adj* gay, jolly; delightful; (*speech*) humorous.
festūca, -ae *f* rod (*with which slaves were manumitted*).
fēstus *adj* festal, on holiday ♦ *nt* holiday; feast.
fētiālis, -is *m* priest who carried out the ritual in making war and peace.
fētūra, -ae *f* breeding; brood.
fētus *adj* pregnant; newly delivered; (*fig*) productive, full of.
fētus, -ūs *m* breeding, bearing, producing; brood, young; fruit, produce; (*fig*) production.
fiber, -rī *m* beaver.
fibra, -ae *f* fibre; section of lung *or* liver; entrails.
fībula, -ae *f* clasp, brooch; clamp.
ficedula, -ae *f* fig pecker.
fictē *adv* falsely.
fictilis *adj* clay, earthen ♦ *nt* jar; clay figure.
fictor, -ōris *m* sculptor; maker, inventor.
fictrīx, -īcis *f* maker.
fictūra, -ae *f* shaping, invention.
fictus *ppp of* **fingō** ♦ *adj* false, fictitious ♦ *nt* falsehood.
ficulnus *adj* of the fig tree.
ficus, -ī *and* **ūs** *f* fig tree; fig.
fidēle *adv* faithfully, surely, firmly.
fidēlia, -ae *f* pot, pail; **dē eādem ~ā duōs parietēs dealbāre** ≈ *kill two birds with one stone.*
fidēlis *adj* faithful, loyal; trustworthy, sure.
fidēlitās, -ātis *f* faithfulness, loyalty.
fidēliter *adv* faithfully, surely, firmly.
Fīdēnae, -ārum *fpl* ancient Latin town.
Fīdēnās, -ātis *adj see n.*
fīdēns, -entis *pres p of* **fīdō** ♦ *adj* bold, resolute.
fīdenter *adv see* **fīdens.**
fīdentia, -ae *f* self-confidence.
fidēs, -ēī *f* trust, faith, belief; trustworthiness, honour, loyalty, truth; promise, assurance, word; guarantee, safe-conduct, protection; (*COMM*) credit; (*law*) good faith; **~ mala** dishonesty; **rēs ~que** entire resources; **~em facere** convince; **~em servāre ergā** keep faith with; **dī vostram ~em!** for Heaven's sake!; **ex fidē bonā** in good faith.
fidēs, -is *f* (*usu pl*) stringed instrument, lyre, lute; (*ASTRO*) Lyra.
fīdī *perf of* **findō.**
fidicen, -inis *m* musician; lyric poet.
fidicina, -ae *f* music girl.
fidicula, -ae *f* small lute.

Fidius, -ī *m* an epithet of Jupiter.
fīdō, -dere, -sus *vi* (*with dat or abl*) to trust, rely on.
fīdūcia, -ae *f* confidence, assurance; self-confidence; (*law*) trust, security.
fīdūciārius *adj* to be held in trust.
fīdus *adj* trusty, reliable; sure, safe.
fīgō, -gere, -xī, -xum *vt* to fix, fasten, attach; to drive in, pierce; (*speech*) to taunt.
figulāris *adj* a potter's.
figulus, -ī *m* potter; builder.
figūra, -ae *f* shape, form; nature, kind; phantom; (*RHET*) figure of speech.
figūrō, -āre *vt* to form, shape.
fīlātim *adv* thread by thread.
fīlia, -ae *f* daughter.
fīlicātus *adj* with fern patterns.
fīliola, -ae *f* little daughter.
fīliolus, -ī *m* little son.
fīlius, -ī *and* **iī** *m* son; **terrae ~** a nobody.
filix, -cis *f* fern.
fīlum, -ī *nt* thread; band of wool, fillet; string, shred, wick; contour, shape; (*speech*) texture, quality.
fimbriae, -ārum *fpl* fringe, end.
fimus, -ī *m* dung; dirt.
findō, -ndere, -dī, -ssum *vt* to split, divide; to burst.
fingō, -ere, finxī, fictum *vt* to form, shape, make; to mould, model; to dress, arrange; to train; (*mind, speech*) to imagine, suppose, represent, sketch; to invent, fabricate; **vultum ~** compose the features.
fīniō, -īre, -īvī, -ītum *vt* to bound, limit; to restrain; to prescribe, define, determine; to end, finish, complete ♦ *vi* to finish, die.
fīnis, -is *m* (*occ f*) boundary, border; (*pl*) territory; bound, limit; end; death; highest point, summit; aim, purpose; **~ bonōrum** the chief good; **quem ad ~em?** how long?; **~e genūs** up to the knee.
fīnītē *adv* within limits.
fīnitimus *adj* neighbouring, adjoining; akin, like ♦ *mpl* neighbours.
fīnītor, -ōris *m* surveyor.
fīnitumus *adj see* **fīnitimus.**
fīnītus *ppp of* **fīniō** ♦ *adj* (*RHET*) well-rounded.
finxī *perf of* **fingō.**
fīō, fierī, factus *vi* to become, arise; to be made, be done; to happen; **quī fit ut?** how is it that?; **ut fit** as usually happens; **quid mē fiet?** what will become of me?
firmāmen, -inis *nt* support.
firmāmentum, -ī *nt* support, strengthening; (*fig*) mainstay.
firmātor, -ōris *m* establisher.
firmē *adv* powerfully, steadily.
firmitās, -ātis *f* firmness, strength; steadfastness, stamina.
firmiter *adv see* **firmē.**
firmitūdō, -inis *f* strength, stability.
firmō, -āre, -āvī, -ātum *vt* to strengthen, support, fortify; (*mind*) to encourage,

steady; (*fact*) to confirm, prove, assert.

firmus *adj* strong, stable, firm; (*fig*) powerful, constant, sure, true.

fiscella, -ae *f* wicker basket.

fiscina, -ae *f* wicker basket.

fiscus, -ī *m* purse, moneybox; public exchequer; imperial treasury, the emperor's privy purse.

fissilis *adj* easy to split.

fissiō, -ōnis *f* dividing.

fissum, -ī *nt* slit, fissure.

fissus *ppp of* **findō**.

fistūca, -ae *f* rammer.

fistula, -ae *f* pipe, tube; panpipes; (*MED*) ulcer.

fistulātor, -ōris *m* panpipe player.

fīsus *ppa of* **fīdō**.

fīxī *perf of* **fīgō**.

fīxus *ppp of* **fīgō** ♦ *adj* fixed, fast, permanent.

flābellifera, -ae *f* fanbearer.

flābellum, -ī *nt* fan.

flābilis *adj* airy.

flābra, -ōrum *ntpl* blasts, gusts; wind.

flacceō, -ēre *vi* to flag, lose heart.

flaccēscō, -ere *vi* to flag, droop.

flaccidus *adj* flabby, feeble.

flaccus *adj* flap-eared.

Flaccus, -ī *m surname of Horace.*

flagellō, -āre *vt* to whip, lash.

flagellum, -ī *nt* whip, lash; strap, thong; (*vine*) shoot; (*polyp*) arm; (*feelings*) sting.

flāgitātiō, -ōnis *f* demand.

flāgitātor, -ōris *m* demander, dun.

flāgitiōsē *adv* infamously.

flāgitiōsus *adj* disgraceful, profligate.

flāgitium, -ī *and* **iī** *nt* offence, disgrace, shame; scoundrel.

flāgitō, -āre, -āvī, -ātum *vt* to demand, importune, dun; (*law*) to summon.

flagrāns, -antis *pres p of* **flagrō** ♦ *adj* hot, blazing; brilliant; passionate.

flagranter *adv* passionately.

flagrantia, -ae *f* blazing; (*fig*) shame.

flagrō, -āre *vi* to blaze, burn, be on fire; (*feelings*) to be excited, be inflamed; (*ill-will*) to be the victim of.

flagrum, -ī *nt* whip, lash.

flāmen, -inis *m* priest of a particular deity.

flāmen, -inis *nt* blast, gale, wind.

flāminica, -ae *f* wife of a priest.

Flāminīnus, -ī *m* Roman surname (*esp the conqueror of Philip V of Macedon*).

flāminium, -ī *and* **iī** *nt* priesthood.

Flāminius, -ī *m* Roman family name (*esp the consul defeated by Hannibal*).

Flāminius, -iānus *adj:* **Via ~ia** *road from Rome N.E. to Ariminum.*

flamma, -ae *f* flame, fire; torch, star; fiery colour; (*fig*) passion; danger, disaster.

flammeolum, -ī *nt* bridal veil.

flammēscō, -ere *vi* to become fiery.

flammeus *adj* fiery, blazing; flame-coloured ♦ *nt* bridal veil.

flammifer, -ī *adj* fiery.

flammō, -āre, -āvī, -ātum *vi* to blaze ♦ *vt* to set on fire, burn; (*fig*) to inflame, incense.

flammula, -ae *f* little flame.

flātus, -ūs *m* blowing, breath; breeze; (*fig*) arrogance.

flāvēns, -entis *adj* yellow, golden.

flāvēscō, -ere *vi* to turn yellow.

Flāviānus *adj see* **n**.

Flāvius, -ī *m* Roman family name (*esp the emperors Vespasian, Titus and Domitian*).

flāvus *adj* yellow, golden.

flēbilis *adj* lamentable; tearful, mournful.

flēbiliter *adv see* **flēbilis**.

flectō, -ctere, -xī, -xum *vt* to bend, turn; to turn aside, wheel; (*promontory*) to round; (*mind*) to direct, persuade, dissuade ♦ *vi* to turn, march.

fleō, -ēre, -ēvī, -ētum *vi* to weep, cry ♦ *vt* to lament, mourn for.

flētus, -ūs *m* weeping, tears.

flexanimus *adj* moving.

flexī *perf of* **flectō**.

flexibilis *adj* pliant, flexible; fickle.

flexilis *adj* pliant.

flexiloquus *adj* ambiguous.

flexiō, -ōnis *f* bending, winding, (*voice*) modulation.

flexipēs, -edis *adj* twining.

flexuōsus *adj* tortuous.

flexūra, -ae *f* bending.

flexus *ppp of* **flectō** ♦ *adj* winding.

flexus, -ūs *m* winding, bending; change.

flīctus, -ūs *m* collision.

flō, -āre, -āvī, -ātum *vt, vi* to blow; (*money*) to coin.

floccus, -ī *m* bit of wool; triviality; **~ī nōn faciō** ≈ *I don't care a straw for.*

Flōra, -ae *f* goddess of flowers.

Flōrālis *adj see* **n**.

flōrēns, -entis *pres p of* **floreō** ♦ *adj* in bloom; bright; prosperous, flourishing.

flōreō, -ēre, -uī *vi* to blossom, flower; (*age*) to be in one's prime; (*wine*) to froth; (*fig*) to flourish, prosper; (*places*) to be gay with.

flōrēscō, -ere *vi* to begin to flower; to grow prosperous.

flōreus *adj* of flowers, flowery.

flōridulus *adj* pretty, little.

flōridus *adj* of flowers, flowery; fresh, pretty; (*style*) florid, ornate.

flōrifer, -ī *adj* flowery.

flōrilegus *adj* flower-sipping.

flōrus *adj* beautiful.

flōs, -ōris *m* flower, blossom; (*wine*) bouquet; (*age*) prime, heyday; (*youth*) downy beard, youthful innocence; (*fig*) crown, glory; (*speech*) ornament.

---

flōsculus, -ī *m* little flower; (*fig*) pride, ornament.
flūctifragus *adj* surging.
flūctuātiō, -ōnis *f* wavering.
flūctuō, -āre *vi* to toss, wave; (*fig*) to rage, swell, waver.
flūctuōsus *adj* stormy.
flūctus, -ūs *m* wave; flowing, flood; (*fig*) disturbance; **~ūs** (*pl*) **in simpulō** ≈ *a storm in a teacup.*
fluēns, -entis *pres p of* **fluō** ♦ *adj* lax, loose, enervated; (*speech*) fluent.
fluenta, -ōrum *ntpl* stream, flood.
fluenter *adv* in a flowing manner.
fluentisonus *adj* wave-echoing.
fluidus *adj* flowing, fluid; lax, soft; relaxing.
fluitō, -āre *vi* to flow, float about; to wave, flap, move unsteadily; (*fig*) to waver.
flūmen, -inis *nt* stream, river; (*fig*) flood, flow, fluency; **adversō ~ine** upstream; **secundō ~ine** downstream.
flūmineus *adj* river- (*in cpds*).
fluō, -ere, -xī, -xum *vi* to flow; to overflow, drip; (*fig*) to fall in, fall away, vanish; (*speech*) to run evenly; (*CIRCS*) to proceed, tend.
flūtō *etc see* **fluitō.**
fluviālis *adj* river- (*in cpds*).
fluviātilis *adj* river- (*in cpds*).
flūvidus *etc see* **fluidus.**
fluvius, -ī *and* **iī** *m* river, stream.
fluxi *perf of* **fluō.**
fluxus *adj* flowing, loose, leaky; (*person*) lax, dissolute; (*thing*) frail, fleeting, unreliable.
fōcāle, -is *nt* scarf.
foculus, -ī *m* stove, fire.
focus, -ī *m* hearth, fireplace; pyre, altar; (*fig*) home.
fodicō, -āre *vt* to nudge, jog.
fodiō, -ere, fōdī, fossum *vt* to dig; to prick, stab; (*fig*) to goad.
foedē *adv see* **foedus.**
foederātus *adj* confederated.
foedifragus *adj* perfidious.
foeditās, -ātis *f* foulness, hideousness.
foedō, -āre, -āvī, -ātum *vt* to mar, disfigure; to disgrace, sully.
foedus *adj* foul, hideous, revolting; vile, disgraceful.
foedus, -eris *nt* treaty, league; agreement, compact; law.
foen- *etc see* **faen-.**
foeteō, -ēre *vi* to stink.
foetidus *adj* stinking.
foetor, -ōris *m* stench.
foetu- *etc see* **fētu-.**
foliātum, -ī *nt* nard oil.
folium, -ī *and* **iī** *nt* leaf.
folliculus, -ī *m* small bag; eggshell.
follis, -is *m* bellows; punchball; purse.
fōmentum, -ī *nt* poultice, bandage; (*fig*) alleviation.
fōmes, -itis *m* tinder, kindling.

fōns, fontis *m* spring, source; water; (*fig*) origin, fountainhead.
fontānus *adj* spring- (*in cpds*).
fonticulus, -ī *m* little spring.
for, fārī, fātus *vt, vi* to speak, utter.
forābilis *adj* penetrable.
forāmen, -inis *nt* hole, opening.
forās *adv* out, outside.
forceps, -ipis *m/f* tongs, forceps.
forda, -ae *f* cow in calf.
fore, forem *fut infin, imperf subj of* **sum.**
forēnsis *adj* public, forensic; of the marketplace.
foris, -is *f* (*usu pl*) door; (*fig*) opening, entrance.
forīs *adv* out of doors, outside, abroad; from outside, from abroad; **~ cēnāre** dine out.
fōrma, -ae *f* form, shape, appearance; mould, stamp, last; (*person*) beauty; (*fig*) idea, nature, kind.
fōrmāmentum, -ī *nt* shape.
fōrmātūra, -ae *f* shaping.
Formiae, -ārum *fpl* town in S. Latium.
Formiānus *adj* of Formiae ♦ *nt* villa at Formiae.
formīca, -ae *f* ant.
formīcinus *adj* crawling.
formīdābilis *adj* terrifying.
formīdō, -āre, -āvī, -ātum *vt, vi* to fear, be terrified.
formīdō, -inis *f* terror, awe, horror; scarecrow.
formīdolōsē *adv see* **formīdolōsus.**
formīdolōsus *adj* fearful, terrifying; afraid.
fōrmō, -āre, -āvī, -ātum *vt* to shape, fashion, form.
fōrmōsitās, -ātis *f* beauty.
fōrmōsus *adj* beautiful, handsome.
fōrmula, -ae *f* rule, regulation; (*law*) procedure, formula; (*PHILOS*) principle.
fornācula, -ae *f* small oven.
fornāx, -ācis *f* furnace, oven, kiln.
fornicātus *adj* arched.
fornix, -icis *m* arch, vault; brothel.
forō, -āre *vt* to pierce.
Foroiūliēnsis *adj see* **Forum Iuli.**
fors, fortis *f* chance, luck ♦ *adv* perchance; **~te** by chance, as it happened; perhaps; **nē ~te** in case; **sī ~te** if perhaps; in the hope that.
forsan, forsit, forsitan *adv* perhaps.
fortasse, -is *adv* perhaps, possibly; (*irony*) very likely.
forticulus *adj* quite brave.
fortis *adj* strong, sturdy; brave, manly, resolute.
fortiter *adv* vigorously; bravely.
fortitūdō, -inis *f* courage, resolution; strength.
fortuītō *adv* by chance.
fortuītus *adj* casual, accidental.
fortūna, -ae *f* chance, luck, fortune; good luck, success; misfortune; circumstances, lot; (*pl*) possessions; **~ae fīlius** Fortune's

favourite; **~am habēre** be successful.
fortūnātē *adv see* **fortunātus**.
fortūnātus *adj* happy, lucky; well off, rich, blessed.
fortūnō, -āre *vt* to bless, prosper.
forulī, -ōrum *mpl* bookcase.
forum, -ī *nt* public place, market; market town; *Roman Forum between the Palatine and Capitol*; public affairs, law courts, business; **~ boārium** cattle market; **~ olitōrium** vegetable market; **~ piscātōrium** fish market; **~ agere** hold an assize; **~ attingere** enter public life; **cēdere ~ō** go bankrupt; **utī ~ō** take advantage of a situation.
Forum Iūli colony in S. Gaul (*now* Fréjus).
forus, -ī *m* gangway; block of seats; (*bees*) cell frame.
fossa, -ae *f* ditch, trench.
fossiō, -ōnis *f* digging.
fossor, -ōris *m* digger.
fossus *ppp of* **fodiō**.
fōtus *ppp of* **foveō**.
fovea, -ae *f* pit, pitfall.
foveō, -ēre, fōvī, fōtum *vt* to warm, keep warm; (*MED*) to foment; to fondle, keep; (*fig*) to cherish, love, foster, pamper, encourage; **castra ~** remain in camp.
frāctus *ppp of* **frangō ♦** *adj* weak, faint.
frāga, -ōrum *ntpl* strawberries.
fragilis *adj* brittle, fragile; frail, fleeting.
fragilitās, -ātis *f* frailness.
fragmen, -inis *nt* (*pl*) fragments, ruins, wreck.
fragmentum, -ī *nt* fragment, remnant.
fragor, -ōris *m* crash, din; disintegration.
fragōsus *adj* crashing, roaring, breakable; rough.
frāgrāns, -antis *adj* fragrant.
framea, -ae *f* German spear.
frangō, -angere, -ēgī, -āctum *vt* to break, shatter, wreck; to crush, grind; (*fig*) to break down, weaken, humble; (*emotion*) to touch, move; **cervīcem ~** strangle.
frāter, -ris *m* brother; cousin; (*fig*) friend, ally.
frāterculus, -ī *m* brother.
frāternē *adv* like a brother.
frāternitās, -ātis *f* brotherhood.
frāternus *adj* brotherly, a brother's, fraternal.
frātricīda, -ae *m* fratricide.
fraudātiō, -ōnis *f* deceit, fraud.
fraudātor, -ōris *m* swindler.
fraudō, -āre, -āvī, -ātum *vt* to cheat, defraud; to steal, cancel.
fraudulentus *adj* deceitful, fraudulent.
fraus, -audis *f* deceit, fraud; delusion, error; offence, wrong; injury, damage; **lēgī ~dem facere** evade the law; **in ~dem incidere** be disappointed; **sine ~de** without harm.
fraxineus, fraxinus *adj* of ash.
fraxinus, -ī *f* ash tree; ashen spear.

Fregellae, -ārum *fpl town in S. Latium*.
Fregellānus *adj see n*.
frēgī *perf of* **frangō**.
fremebundus *adj* roaring.
fremitus, -ūs *m* roaring, snorting, noise.
fremō, -ere, -uī, -itum *vi* to roar, snort, grumble ♦ *vt* to shout for, complain.
fremor, -ōris *m* murmuring.
frendō, -ere *vi* to gnash the teeth.
frēnō, -āre, -āvī, -ātum *vt* to bridle; (*fig*) to curb, restrain.
frēnum, -ī *nt* (*pl* **-a**, **-ōrum** *nt*, **-ī**, **-ōrum** *m*) bridle, bit; (*fig*) curb, check; **~ōs dare** give vent to; **~um mordēre** ≈ *take the bit between one's teeth*.
frequēns, -entis *adj* crowded, numerous, populous; regular, repeated, frequent; **~ senatus** a crowded meeting of the senate.
frequentātiō, -ōnis *f* accumulation.
frequenter *adv* in large numbers; repeatedly, often.
frequentia, -ae *f* full attendance, throng, crowd.
frequentō, -āre, -āvī, -ātum *vt* to crowd, populate; to visit repeatedly, frequent; to repeat; (*festival*) to celebrate, keep.
fretēnsis *adj* of the Straits of Messina.
fretum, -ī *nt* strait; sea; (*fig*) violence; **~ Siciliēnse** Straits of Messina.
fretus, -ūs *m* strait.
frētus *adj* relying, confident.
fricō, -āre, -uī, -tum *vt* to rub, rub down.
frictus *ppp of* **frigō**.
frīgefactō, -āre *vt* to cool.
frīgeō, -ēre *vi* to be cold; (*fig*) to be lifeless, flag; to be coldly received, fall flat.
frīgerāns, -antis *adj* cooling.
frīgēscō, -ere *vi* to grow cold; to become inactive.
frīgida, -ae *f* cold water.
frīgidē *adv* feebly.
frīgidulus *adj* rather cold, faint.
frīgidus *adj* cold, cool; chilling; (*fig*) dull, torpid; (*words*) flat, uninteresting.
frīgō, -gere, -xī, -ctum *vt* to roast, fry.
frīgus, -oris *nt* cold; cold weather, winter; death; (*fig*) dullness, inactivity; coldness, indifference.
friguttiō, -īre *vi* to stammer.
friō, -āre *vt* to crumble.
fritillus, -ī *m* dice box.
frīvolus *adj* empty, paltry.
frīxī *perf of* **frīgō**.
frondātor, -ōris *m* vinedresser, pruner.
frondeō, -ēre *vi* to be in leaf.
frondēscō, -ere *vi* to become leafy, shoot.
frondeus *adj* leafy.
frondifer, -ī *adj* leafy.
frondōsus *adj* leafy.
frōns, -ondis *f* leaf, foliage; garland of leaves.

Noun declensions and verb conjugations are shown on pp xiii to xxv. The present infinitive ending of a verb shows to which conjugation it belongs: **-āre** = 1st; **-ēre** = 2nd; **-ere** = 3rd and **-īre** = 4th. Irregular verbs are shown on p xxvi

frōns, -ontis _f_ forehead, brow; front, facade; (_fig_) look, appearance, exterior; **~ontem contrahere** frown; **ā ~onte** in front; **in ~onte** in breadth.

frontālia, -um _ntpl_ frontlet.

frontō, -ōnis _m_ a broad-browed man.

frūctuārius _adj_ productive; paid for out of produce.

fructuōsus _adj_ productive; profitable.

frūctus _ppa of_ **fruor**.

frūctus, -ūs _m_ enjoyment; revenue, income; produce, fruit; (_fig_) consequence, reward; **~uī esse** be an asset (to); **~um percipere** reap the fruits (of).

frūgālis _adj_ thrifty, worthy.

frūgālitās, -ātis _f_ thriftiness, restraint.

frūgāliter _adv_ temperately.

frūgēs _etc see_ **frūx**.

frūgī _adj_ (_indecl_) frugal, temperate, honest; useful.

frūgifer, -ī _adj_ fruitful, fertile.

frūgiferēns, -entis _adj_ fruitful.

frūgilegus _adj_ food-gatherering.

frūgiparus _adj_ fruitful.

frūmentārius _adj_ of corn, corn- (_in cpds_) ♦ _m_ corn dealer; **lēx ~a** law about the distribution of corn; **rēs ~a** commissariat.

frūmentātiō, -ōnis _f_ foraging.

frūmentātor, -ōris _m_ corn merchant, forager.

frūmentor, -ārī, -ātus _vi_ to go foraging.

frūmentum, -ī _nt_ corn, grain, (_pl_) crops.

frūnīscor, -ī _vt_ to enjoy.

fruor, -uī, -ūctus _vt, vi_ (_usu with abl_) to enjoy, enjoy the company of; (_law_) to have the use and enjoyment of.

frūstillātim _adv_ in little bits.

frūstrā _adv_ in vain, for nothing; groundlessly; in error; **~ esse** be deceived; **~ habēre** foil.

frūstrāmen, -inis _nt_ deception.

frūstrātiō, -ōnis _f_ deception, frustration.

frūstrō, -āre; -or, -ārī, -ātus _vt_ to deceive, trick.

frūstulentus _adj_ full of crumbs.

frūstum, -ī _nt_ bit, scrap.

frutex, -icis _m_ bush, shrub; (_comedy_) blockhead.

fruticētum, -ī _nt_ thicket.

fruticor, -ārī _vi_ to sprout.

fruticōsus _adj_ bushy.

frūx, -ūgis _f_, **-ūgēs, -ūgum** fruits of the earth, produce; (_fig_) reward, success; virtue; **sē ad ~ūgem bonam recipere** reform.

fuam _old pres subj of_ **sum**.

fūcātus _adj_ counterfeit, artificial.

fūcō, -āre, -āvī, -ātum _vt_ to paint, dye (_esp red_).

fūcōsus _adj_ spurious.

fūcus, -ī _m_ red dye, rouge; bee glue; (_fig_) deceit, pretence.

fūcus, -ī _m_ drone.

fūdī _perf of_ **fundō**.

fuga, -ae _f_ flight, rout; banishment; speed,

swift passing; refuge; (_fig_) avoidance, escape; **~am facere, in ~am dare** put to flight.

fugācius _adv_ more timidly.

fugāx, -ācis _adj_ timorous, shy, fugitive; swift, transient; (_with gen_) avoiding.

fūgī _perf of_ **fugiō**.

fugiēns, -entis _pres p of_ **fugiō** ♦ _adj_ fleeting, dying; averse (to).

fugiō, -ere, fūgī, -itum _vi_ to flee, run away, escape; to go into exile; (_fig_) to vanish, pass swiftly ♦ _vt_ to flee from, escape from; to shun, avoid; (_fig_) to escape, escape notice of; **~e quaerere** do not ask; **mē ~it** I do not notice _or_ know.

fugitīvus, -ī _m_ runaway slave, truant, deserter ♦ _adj_ fugitive.

fugitō, -āre _vt_ to flee from, shun.

fugō, -āre, -āvī, -ātum _vt_ to put to flight; to banish; to rebuff.

fulcīmen, -inis _nt_ support.

fulciō, -cīre, -sī, -tum _vt_ to prop, support; to strengthen, secure; (_fig_) to sustain, bolster up.

fulcrum, -ī _nt_ bedpost; couch.

fulgeō, -gēre, -sī _vi_ to flash, lighten; to shine; (_fig_) to be illustrious.

fulgidus _adj_ flashing.

fulgō _etc see_ **fulgeō**.

fulgor, -ōris _m_ lightning; flash, brightness; (_fig_) splendour.

fulgur, -is _nt_ lightning; thunderbolt; splendour.

fulgurālis _adj_ on lightning as an omen.

fulgurātor, -ōris _m_ interpreter of lightning.

fulgurītus _adj_ struck by lightning.

fulgurō, -āre _vi_ to lighten.

fulica, -ae _f_ coot.

fūlīgō, -inis _f_ soot; black paint.

fulix, -cis _f see_ **fulica**.

fullō, -ōnis _m_ fuller.

fullōnius _adj_ fuller's.

fulmen, -inis _nt_ thunderbolt; (_fig_) disaster.

fulmenta, -ae _f_ heel of a shoe.

fulmineus _adj_ of lightning; (_fig_) deadly.

fulminō, -āre _vi_ to lighten; (_fig_) to threaten.

fulsī _perf of_ **fulciō**; _perf of_ **fulgeō**.

fultūra, -ae _f_ support.

fultus _ppp of_ **fulciō**.

Fulvia, -iae _f_ wife of M. Antony.

Fulvius, -ī _m Roman family name._

fulvus _adj_ yellow, tawny, dun.

fūmeus _adj_ smoking.

fūmidus _adj_ smoky, smoking.

fūmifer, -ī _adj_ smoking.

fūmificō, -āre _vi_ to burn incense.

fūmificus _adj_ steaming.

fūmō, -āre _vi_ to smoke, steam.

fūmōsus _adj_ smoky, smoked.

fūmus, -ī _m_ smoke, steam.

fūnāle, -is _nt_ cord; wax torch; chandelier.

fūnambulus, -ī _m_ tightrope walker.

fūnctiō, -ōnis _f_ performance.

fūnctus _ppa of_ **fungor**.

fūnda, -ae *f* sling; dragnet.
fundāmen, -inis *nt* foundation.
fundāmentum, -ī *nt* foundation; **~a agere, iacere** lay the foundations.
Fundānus *adj see* **Fundī.**
fundātor, -ōris *m* founder.
Fundī, -ōrum *mpl coast town in Latium.*
funditō, -āre *vt* to sling.
funditor, -ōris *m* slinger.
funditus *adv* utterly, completely; at the bottom.
fundō, -āre, -āvī, -ātum *vt* to found; to secure; (*fig*) to establish, make secure.
fundō, -ere, fūdī, fūsum *vt* to pour, shed, spill; (*metal*) to cast; (*solids*) to hurl, scatter, shower; (*MIL*) to rout; (*crops*) to produce in abundance; (*speech*) to utter; (*fig*) to spread, extend.
fundus, -ī *m* bottom; farm, estate; (*law*) authorizer.
fūnebris *adj* funeral- (*in cpds*); murderous.
fūnerātus *adj* killed.
fūnereus *adj* funeral- (*in cpds*); fatal.
fūnestō, -āre *vt* to pollute with murder, desecrate.
fūnestus *adj* deadly, fatal; sorrowful, in mourning.
fungīnus *adj* of a mushroom.
fungor, -gi, fūnctus *vt, vi* (*usu with abl*) to perform, discharge, do; to be acted on.
fungus, -ī *m* mushroom, fungus; (*candle*) clot on the wick.
fūniculus, -ī *m* cord.
fūnis, -is *m* rope, rigging; **~em dūcere** be the master.
fūnus, -eris *nt* funeral; death; corpse; ruin, destruction.
fūr, fūris *m* thief; slave.
fūrācissimē *adv* most thievishly.
fūrāx, -ācis *adj* thieving.
furca, -ae *f* fork; fork-shaped pole; pillory.
furcifer, -ī *m* gallows rogue.
furcilla, -ae *f* little fork.
furcillō, -āre *vt* to prop up.
furcula, -ae *f* forked prop; **~ae Caudīnae** Pass of Caudium.
furenter *adv* furiously.
furfur, -is *m* bran; scurf.
Furia, -ae *f* Fury, avenging spirit; madness, frenzy, rage.
furiālis *adj* of the Furies; frantic, fearful; infuriating.
furiāliter *adv* madly.
furibundus *adj* mad, frenzied.
furiō, -āre, -āvī, -ātum *vt* to madden.
furiōsē *adv* in a frenzy.
furiōsus *adj* mad, frantic.
furnus, -ī *m* oven.
furō, -ere *vi* to rave, rage, be mad, be crazy.
fūror, -ārī, -ātus *vt* to steal; to pillage; to impersonate.
furor, -ōris *m* madness, frenzy, passion.
fūrtificus *adj* thievish.
fūrtim *adv* by stealth, secretly.
fūrtīvē *adv* secretly.
fūrtīvus *adj* stolen; secret, furtive.
fūrtō *adv* secretly.
fūrtum, -ī *nt* theft, robbery; (*pl*) stolen goods; (*fig*) trick, intrigue.
fūrunculus, -ī *m* pilferer.
furvus *adj* black, dark.
fuscina, -ae *f* trident.
fuscō, -āre *vt* to blacken.
fuscus *adj* dark, swarthy; (*voice*) husky, muffled.
fūsē *adv* diffusely.
fūsilis *adj* molten, softened.
fūsiō, -ōnis *f* outpouring.
fūstis, -is *m* stick, club, cudgel; (*MIL*) beating to death.
fūstuārium, -ī *and* **iī** *nt* beating to death.
fūsus *ppp of* **fundō** ♦ *adj* broad, diffuse; copious.
fūsus, -ī *m* spindle.
futtile *adv* in vain.
futtilis *adj* brittle; worthless.
futtilitās, -ātis *f* futility.
futūrum, -ī *nt* future.
futūrus *fut p of* **sum** ♦ *adj* future, coming.

G, g

Gabiī, -iōrum *mpl ancient town in Latium.*
Gabinius, -ī *m* Roman family name (*esp Aulus, tribune 67 B.C.*).
Gabinius, -iānus *adj:* **lēx ~ia** *law giving Pompey command against the pirates.*
Gabīnus *adj see* **Gabiī.**
Gādēs, -ium *fpl town in Spain (now Cadiz).*
Gāditānus *adj see n.*
gaesum, -ī *nt* Gallic javelin.
Gaetūlī, -ōrum *mpl African people N of Sahara.*
Gaetūlus, -icus *adj* Gaetulian; African.
Gāius, -ī *m* Roman praenomen (*esp emperor Caligula*).
Gāius, -ia *m/f* (*wedding ceremony*) bridegroom, bride.
Galatae, -ārum *mpl Galatians of Asia Minor.*
Galatia, -iae *f* Galatia.
Galba, -ae *m* Roman surname (*esp emperor 68–9*).
galbaneus *adj* of galbanum, a Syrian plant.

galbinus *adj* greenish-yellow ♦ *ntpl* pale green clothes.
galea, -ae *f* helmet.
galeātus *adj* helmeted.
galērītus *adj* rustic.
galērum, -ī *nt*, **-us, -ī** *m* leather hood, cap; wig.
galla, -ae *f* oak apple.
Gallī, -ōrum *mpl* Gauls (*people of what is now France and N. Italy*).
Gallia, -iae *f* Gaul.
Gallicānus *adj* of Italian Gaul.
Gallicus *adj* Gallic ♦ *f* a Gallic shoe.
gallīna, -ae *f* hen; **~ae albae fīlius** fortune's favourite.
gallīnāceus *adj* of poultry.
gallīnārius, -ī *and* **iī** *m* poultry farmer.
Gallograecī, -ōrum *mpl* Galatians.
Gallograecia, -iae *f* Galatia.
gallus, -ī *m* cock.
Gallus, -ī *m* Gaul; Roman surname (*esp the lyric poet; priest of Cybele*).
ganēa, -ae *f* low eating house.
ganeō, -ōnis *m* profligate.
ganeum, -ī *nt* low eating house.
Gangaridae, -ārum *mpl* a people on the Ganges.
Gangēs, -is *m* river Ganges.
Gangēticus *adj see n.*
ganniō, -īre *vi* to yelp; (*fig*) to grumble.
gannītus, -ūs *m* yelping.
Ganymēdēs, -is *m* Ganymede, (*cup bearer in Olympus*).
Garamantes, -um *mpl* N. African tribe.
Garamantis, -idis *adj see n.*
Gargānus, -ī *m* mountain in E. Italy.
garriō, -īre *vi* to chatter.
garrulitās, -ātis *f* chattering.
garrulus *adj* talkative, babbling.
garum, -ī *nt* fish sauce.
Garumna, -ae *f* river Garonne.
gaudeō, -ēre, gāvīsus *vt, vi* to rejoice, be pleased, delight (in); **in sē, in sinū ~** be secretly pleased.
gaudium, -ī *and* **iī** *nt* joy, delight, enjoyment.
gaulus, -ī *m* bucket.
gausape, -is *nt*, **-a, -ōrum** *pl* a woollen cloth, frieze.
gāvīsus *ppa of* **gaudeō.**
gāza, -ae *f* treasure, riches.
gelidē *adv* feebly.
gelidus *adj* cold, frosty; stiff, numb; chilling ♦ *f* cold water.
gelō, -āre *vt* to freeze.
Gelōnī, -ōrum *mpl* Scythian tribe (*now Ukraine*).
gelū, -ūs *nt* frost, cold; chill.
gemebundus *adj* groaning.
gemellipara, -ae *f* mother of twins.
gemellus *adj* twin, double; alike ♦ *m* twin.
geminātiō, -ōnis *f* doubling.
geminō, -āre, -āvī, -ātum *vt* to double, bring together; to repeat ♦ *vi* to be double.

geminus *adj* twin, double, both; similar ♦ *mpl* twins (*esp Castor and Pollux*).
gemitus, -ūs *m* groan, sigh; moaning sound.
gemma, -ae *f* bud, precious stone, jewel; jewelled cup, signet.
gemmātus *adj* bejewelled.
gemmeus *adj* jewelled; sparkling.
gemmifer, -ī *adj* gem-producing.
gemmō, -āre *vi* to bud, sprout; to sparkle.
gemō, -ere, -uī, -itum *vi* to sigh, groan, moan ♦ *vt* to bewail.
Gemōniae, -ārum *fpl* steps in Rome on which bodies of criminals were thrown.
genae, -ārum *fpl* cheeks; eyes, eye sockets.
geneālogus, -ī *m* genealogist.
gener, -ī *m* son-in-law.
generālis *adj* of the species; universal.
generāliter *adv* generally.
generāscō, -ere *vi* to be produced.
generātim *adv* by species, in classes; in general.
generātor, -ōris *m* producer.
generō, -āre, -āvī, -ātum *vt* to breed, procreate.
generōsus *adj* high-born, noble; well-stocked; generous, chivalrous; (*things*) noble, honourable.
genesis, -is *f* birth; horoscope.
genethliacon, -ī *nt* birthday poem.
genetīvus *adj* native, inborn.
genetrīx, -īcis *f* mother.
geniālis *adj* nuptial; joyful, genial.
geniāliter *adv* merrily.
geniculātus *adj* jointed.
genista, -ae *f* broom.
genitābilis *adj* productive.
genitālis *adj* fruitful, generative; of birth.
genitāliter *adv* fruitfully.
genitor, -ōris *m* father, creator.
genitus *ppp of* **gignō.**
genius, -ī *and* **iī** *m* guardian spirit; enjoyment, inclination; talent; **~iō indulgēre** enjoy oneself.
gēns, gentis *f* clan, family, stock, race; tribe, people, nation; descendant; (*pl*) foreign peoples; **minimē gentium** by no means; **ubi gentium** where in the world.
genticus *adj* national.
gentīlicius *adj* family.
gentīlis *adj* family, hereditary; national ♦ *m* kinsman.
gentīlitās, -ātis *f* clan relationship.
genū, -ūs *nt* knee.
genuālia, -um *ntpl* garters.
genuī *perf of* **gignō.**
genuīnus *adj* natural.
genuīnus *adj* of the cheek ♦ *mpl* back teeth.
genus, -eris *nt* birth, descent, noble birth, descendant, race; kind, class, species, respect, way; (*logic*) genus, general term; **id ~ of** that kind; **in omnī ~ere** in all respects.
geōgraphia, -ae *f* geography.
geōmetrēs, -ae *m* geometer.

geōmetria, -ae *f* geometry.
geōmetricus *adj* geometrical ♦ *ntpl* geometry.
germānē *adv* sincerely.
Germānī, -ōrum *mpl* Germans.
Germānia, -iae *f* Germany.
Germānicus *adj, m cognomen of Nero Claudius Drusus and his son.*
germānitās, -ātis *f* brotherhood, sisterhood; relation of sister colonies.
germānus *adj* of the same parents, full (brother, sister); genuine, true ♦ *m* full brother ♦ *f* full sister.
germen, -inis *nt* bud, shoot; embryo; (*fig*) germ.
gerō, -rere, -ssī, -stum *vt* to carry, wear; to bring; (*plants*) to bear, produce; (*feelings*) to entertain, show; (*activity*) to conduct, manage, administer, wage; (*time*) spend; **mōrem ~** comply, humour; **persōnam ~** play a part; **sē ~** behave; **sē medium ~** be neutral; **prae sē ~** exhibit; **rēs ~stae** exploits.
gerō, -ōnis *nt* carrier.
gerrae, -ārum *fpl* trifles, nonsense.
gerrō, -ōnis *m* idler.
gerulus, -ī *m* carrier.
Gēryōn, -onis *m mythical three-bodied king killed by Hercules.*
gessī *perf of* **gerō**.
gestāmen, -inis *nt* arms, ornaments, burden; litter, carriage.
gestiō, -ōnis *f* performance.
gestiō, -īre *vi* to jump for joy, be excited; to be very eager.
gestitō, -āre *vt* to always wear *or* carry.
gestō, -āre *vt* to carry about, usually wear; to fondle; to blab; (*pass*) to go for a ride, drive, sail.
gestor, -ōris *m* telltale.
gestus *ppp of* **gerō**.
gestus, -ūs *m* posture, gesture; gesticulation.
Getae, -ārum *mpl Thracian tribe on the lower Danube.*
Geticus *adj* Getan, Thracian.
gibbus, -ī *m* hump.
Gigantes, -um *mpl Giants, sons of Earth.*
Gigantēus *adj see n.*
gignō, -ere, genuī, genitum *vt* to beget, bear, produce; to cause.
gilvus *adj* pale yellow, dun.
gingīva, -ae *f* gum.
glaber, -rī *adj* smooth, bald ♦ *m* favourite slave.
glaciālis *adj* icy.
glaciēs, -ēī *f* ice.
glaciō, -āre *vt* to freeze.
gladiātor, -ōris *m* gladiator; (*pl*) gladiatorial show.
gladiātōrius *adj* of gladiators ♦ *nt* gladiators' pay.
gladiātūra, -ae *f* gladiator's profession.

gladius, -ī *and* **iī** *m* sword; (*fig*) murder, death; **~ium stringere** draw the sword; **suō sibi ~iō iugulāre** ≈ *beat at his own game.*
glaeba, -ae *f* sod, clod of earth; soil; lump.
glaebula, -ae *f* small lump; small holding.
glaesum *etc see* **glēsum**.
glandifer, -ī *adj* acorn-bearing.
glandium, -ī *and* **iī** *nt* glandule (*in meat*).
glāns, -andis *f* acorn, nut; bullet.
glārea, -ae *f* gravel.
glāreōsus *adj* gravelly.
glaucūma, -ae *f* cataract; **~am ob oculōs obicere** ≈ *throw dust in the eyes of.*
glaucus *adj* bluish grey.
glēba *etc see* **glaeba**.
glēsum, -ī *nt* amber.
glīs, -īris *m* dormouse.
glīscō, -ere *vi* to grow, swell, blaze up.
globōsus *adj* spherical.
globus, -ī *m* ball, sphere; (*MIL*) troop; mass, crowd, cluster.
glōmerāmen, -inis *nt* bell.
glomerō, -āre, -āvī, -ātum *vt* to form into a ball, gather, accumulate.
glomus, -eris *nt* ball of thread, clue.
glōria, -ae *f* glory, fame; ambition, pride, boasting; (*pl*) glorious deeds.
glōriātiō, -ōnis *f* boasting.
glōriola, -ae *f* a little glory.
glōrior, -ārī, -ātus *vt, vi* to boast, pride oneself.
glōriōsē *adv see* **glōriōsus**.
glōriōsus *adj* famous, glorious; boastful.
glūten, -inis *nt* glue.
glūtinātor, -ōris *m* bookbinder.
gluttiō, -īre *vt* to gulp down.
gnāruris, gnārus *adj* knowing, expert; known.
gnātus *see* **nātus**.
gnāvus *see* **nāvus**.
Gnōsius *and* **iacus** *and* **ias** *adj* of Cnossos, Cretan.
Gnōsis, -idis *f* Ariadne.
Gnōsus, -ī *f* Cnossos (*ancient capital of Crete*) ♦ *f* Ariadne.
gōbiō, -ōnis, gōbius, -ī *and* **iī** *m* gudgeon.
Gorgiās, -ae *m Sicilian sophist and teacher of rhetoric.*
Gorgō, -ōnis *f mythical monster capable of turning men to stone, Medusa.*
Gorgoneus *adj:* **equus ~** Pegasus; **lacus ~** Hippocrene.
Gortȳna, -ae *f* Cretan town.
Gortȳnius, -iacus *adj* Gortynian, Cretan.
gōrȳtos, -ī *m* quiver.
grabātus, -ī *m* camp bed, low couch.
Gracchānus *adj see n.*
Gracchus, -ī *m* Roman surname (*esp the famous tribunes Tiberius and Gaius*).
gracilis *adj* slender, slight, meagre, poor;

(*style*) plain.

gracilitās, -ātis *f* slimness, leanness; (*style*) simplicity.

grāculus, -ī *m* jackdaw.

gradātim *adv* step by step, gradually.

gradātiō, -ōnis *f* (*RHET*) climax.

gradior, -adī, -essus *vi* to step, walk.

Grādīvus, -ī *m* Mars.

gradus, -ūs *m* step, pace; stage, step towards; firm stand, position, standing; (*pl*) stair, steps; (*hair*) braid; (*MATH*) degree; (*fig*) degree, rank; **citātō, plēnō ~ū** at the double; **suspēnsō ~ū** on tiptoe; **dē ~ū deicī** be disconcerted.

Graecē *adv* in Greek.

Graecia, -iae *f* Greece; **Māgna ~** S. Italy.

graecissō, -āre *vi* to ape the Greeks.

graecor, -ārī *vi* to live like Greeks.

Graeculus *adj* (*contemptuous*) Greek.

Graecus *adj* Greek.

Grāiugena, -ae *m* Greek.

Grāius *adj* Greek.

grallātor, -ōris *m* stiltwalker.

grāmen, -inis *nt* grass; herb.

grāmineus *adj* grassy; of cane.

grammaticus *adj* literary, grammatical ♦ *m* teacher of literature and language ♦ *f/ntpl* grammar, literature, philology.

grānāria, -ōrum *ntpl* granary.

grandaevus *adj* aged, very old.

grandēscō, -ere *vi* to grow.

grandiculus *adj* quite big.

grandifer, -ī *adj* productive.

grandiloquus, -ī *m* grand speaker; boaster.

grandinat, -āre *vi* it hails.

grandis *adj* large, great, tall; old; strong; (*style*) grand, sublime; **~ nātū** old.

granditās, -ātis *f* grandeur.

grandō, -inis *f* hail.

grānifer, -ī *adj* grain-carrying.

grānum, -ī *nt* seed, grain.

graphicē *adv* nicely.

graphicus *adj* fine, masterly.

graphium, -ī and iī *nt* stilus, pen.

grassātor, -ōris *m* vagabond; robber, footpad.

grassor, -ārī, -ātus *vi* to walk about, prowl, loiter; (*action*) to proceed; (*fig*) to attack, rage against.

grātē *adv* with pleasure; gratefully.

grātēs *fpl* thanks.

grātia, -ae *f* charm, grace; favour, influence, regard, friendship; kindness, service; gratitude, thanks; **~am facere** excuse; **~am referre** return a favour; **in ~am redīre cum** be reconciled to; **~ās agere** thank; **~ās habēre** feel grateful; **~ā** (*with gen*) for the sake of; **eā ~ā** on that account; **~īs** for nothing.

Grātiae, -ārum *fpl* the three Graces.

grātificātiō, -ōnis *f* obligingness.

grātificor, -ārī *vi* to do a favour, oblige ♦ *vt* to make a present of.

grātiīs, grātīs *adv* for nothing.

grātiōsus *adj* in favour, popular; obliging.

grātor, -ārī, -ātus *vi* to rejoice, congratulate.

grātuītō *adv* for nothing.

grātuītus *adj* free, gratuitous.

grātulābundus *adj* congratulating.

grātulātiō, -ōnis *f* rejoicing; congratulation; public thanksgiving.

grātulor, -ārī, -ātus *vt, vi* to congratulate; to give thanks.

grātus *adj* pleasing, welcome, dear; grateful, thankful; (*acts*) deserving thanks; **~um facere** do a favour.

gravātē *adv* reluctantly, grudgingly.

gravātim *adv* unwillingly.

gravēdinōsus *adj* liable to colds.

gravēdō, -inis *f* cold in the head.

graveolēns, -entis *adj* strong-smelling.

gravēscō, -ere *vi* to become heavy; to grow worse.

graviditās, -ātis *f* pregnancy.

gravidō, -āre *vt* to impregnate.

gravidus *adj* pregnant; loaded, full.

gravis *adj* heavy; loaded, pregnant; (*smell*) strong, offensive; (*sound*) deep, bass; (*body*) sick; (*food*) indigestible; (*fig*) oppressive, painful, severe; important, influential, dignified.

gravitās, -ātis *f* weight, severity, sickness; importance, dignity, seriousness; **annōnae ~** high price of corn.

graviter *adv* heavily; strongly, deeply; severely, seriously, violently; gravely, with dignity; **~ ferre** be vexed at.

gravō, -āre *vt* to load, weigh down; to oppress, aggravate.

gravor, -ārī *vt, vi* to feel annoyed, object to, disdain.

gregālis *adj* of the herd, common ♦ *m* comrade.

gregārius *adj* common; (*MIL*) private.

gregātim *adv* in crowds.

gremium, -ī *nt* bosom, lap.

gressus *ppa* of **gradior**.

gressus, -ūs *m* step; course.

grex, -egis *m* flock, herd; company, troop.

grunniō, -īre *vi* to grunt.

grunnītus, -ūs *m* grunting.

grūs, -uis *f* crane.

grȳps, -ȳpis *m* griffin.

gubernāclum (gubernāculum), -ī *nt* rudder, tiller; helm, government.

gubernātiō, -ōnis *f* steering, management.

gubernātor, -ōris *m* steersman, pilot, governor.

gubernātrīx, -īcis *f* directress.

gubernō, -āre, -āvī, -ātum *vt* to steer, pilot; to manage, govern.

gula, -ae *f* gullet, throat; gluttony, palate.

gulōsus *adj* dainty.

gurges, -itis *m* abyss, deep water, flood; (*person*) spendthrift.

gurguliō, -ōnis *f* gullet, windpipe.

gurgustium, -ī and iī *nt* hovel, shack.

gustātus, -ūs *m* sense of taste; flavour.
gustō, -āre, -āvī, -ātum *vt* to taste; to have a
snack; (*fig*) to enjoy, overhear; **prīmīs labrīs**
~ have a superficial knowledge of.
gustus, -ūs *m* tasting; preliminary dish.
gutta, -ae *f* drop; spot, speck.
guttātim *adv* drop by drop.
guttur, -is *nt* throat, gluttony.
gūtus, -ī *m* flask.
Gyās, -ae *m* giant with a hundred arms.
Gȳgaeus *adj see n.*
Gȳgēs, -is *and* **ae** *m* king of Lydia (*famed for
his magic ring*).
gymnasiarchus, -ī *m* master of a
gymnasium.
gymnasium, -ī *and* **iī** *nt* sports ground, school.
gymnasticus *adj* gymnastic.
gymnicus *adj* gymnastic.
gynaecēum, -ēī *and* **īum, -ī̄** *nt* women's
quarters.
gypsātus *adj* coated with plaster.
gypsum, -ī *nt* plaster of Paris; a plaster
figure.
gȳrus, -ī *m* circle, coil, ring; course.

H, h

ha *interj* (*expressing joy or laughter*) hurrah!, ha
ha!
habēna, -ae *f* strap; (*pl*) reins; (*fig*) control;
~ās **dare, immittere** allow to run freely.
habeō, -ēre, -uī, -itum *vt* to have, hold; to
keep, contain, possess; (*fact*) to know; (*with
infin*) to be in a position to; (*person*) to treat,
regard, consider; (*action*) to make, hold,
carry out ♦ *vi* to have possessions;
ōrātiōnem ~ make a speech; **in animō** ~
intend; **prō certō** ~ be sure; **sē** ~ find oneself,
be; **sibi, sēcum** ~ keep to oneself; (*fight*) ~**et a**
hit!; **bene** ~**et** it is well; **sīc** ~**et** so it is; **sīc**
~**ētō** be sure of this.
habilis *adj* manageable, handy; suitable,
nimble, expert.
habilitās, -ātis *f* aptitude.
habitābilis *adj* habitable.
habitātiō, -ōnis *f* dwelling, house.
habitātor, -ōris *m* tenant, inhabitant.
habitō, -āre, -āvī, -ātum *vt* to inhabit ♦ *vi* to
live, dwell; to remain, be always (in).
habitūdō, -inis *f* condition.
habitus *ppp of* **habeō** ♦ *adj* stout; in a humour.
habitus, -ūs *m* condition, appearance; dress;

character, quality; disposition, feeling.
hāc *adv* this way.
hāctenus *adv* thus far, so far; till now.
Hadria, -ae *f* town in N. Italy; Adriatic Sea.
Hadriānus, -ānī *m* emperor Hadrian.
Hadriāticus *and* **acus** *adj of emperor Hadrian.*
haedilia, -ae *f* little kid.
haedinus *adj* kid's.
haedulus, -ī *m* little kid.
haedus, -ī *m* kid; (*ASTRO, usu pl*) the Kids (*a
cluster in Auriga*).
Haemonia, -ae *f* Thessaly.
Haemonius *adj* Thessalian.
Haemus, -ī *m* mountain range in Thrace.
haereō, -rēre, -sī, -sum *vi* to cling, stick, be
attached; (*nearness*) to stay close, hang on;
(*continuance*) to linger, remain (at);
(*stoppage*) to stick fast, come to a standstill,
be at a loss.
haerēscō, -ere *vi* to adhere.
haeresis, -is *f* sect.
haesī *perf of* **haereō.**
haesitantia, -ae *f* stammering.
haesitātiō, -ōnis *f* stammering; indecision.
haesitō, -āre *vi* to get stuck; to stammer; to
hesitate, be uncertain.
hahae, hahahae *see* **ha.**
hālitus, -ūs *m* breath, vapour.
hallex, -icis *m* big toe.
hallūc- *see* **ālūc-.**
hālō, -āre *vi* to be fragrant ♦ *vt* to exhale.
hāluc *etc see* **ālūc.**
halyaeetos, -ī *m* osprey.
hama, -ae *f* water bucket.
Hamādryas, -adis *f* woodnymph.
hāmātilis *adj* with hooks.
hāmātus *adj* hooked.
Hamilcar, -is *m* father of Hannibal.
hāmus, -ī *m* hook; talons.
Hannibal, -is *m* famous Carthaginian general in
2nd Punic War.
hara, -ae *f* stye, pen.
harēna, -ae *f* sand; desert, seashore; arena (*in
the amphitheatre*).
harēnōsus *adj* sandy.
hariola, -ae *f*, **hariolus, -ī** *m* soothsayer.
hariolor, -ārī *vi* to prophesy; to talk nonsense.
harmonia, -ae *f* concord, melody; (*fig*)
harmony.
harpagō, -āre *vt* to steal.
harpagō, -ōnis *m* grappling hook; (*person*)
robber.
harpē, -ēs *f* scimitar.
Harpȳiae, -ārum *fpl* Harpies (*mythical
monsters, half woman, half bird*).
harundifer, -ī *adj* reed-crowned.
harundineus *adj* reedy.
harundinōsus *adj* abounding in reeds.
harundō, -inis *f* reed, cane; fishing rod; shaft,
arrow; (*fowling*) limed twig; (*music*) pipe,

Noun declensions and verb conjugations are shown on pp xiii to xxv. The present infinitive ending of a verb shows
to which conjugation it belongs: **-āre** = 1st; **-ēre** = 2nd; **-ere** = 3rd and **-īre** = 4th. Irregular verbs are shown on p xxvi

flute; (*toy*) hobbyhorse; (*weaving*) comb; (*writing*) pen.

haruspex, -icis *m* diviner (*from entrails*); prophet.

haruspica, -ae *f* soothsayer.

haruspicīnus *adj* of divination by entrails ♦ *f art* of such divination.

haruspicium, -ī *and* **iī** *nt* divination.

Hasdrubal, -is *m* brother of Hannibal.

hasta, -ae *f* spear, pike; sign of an auction sale; **sub ~ā vēndere** put up for auction.

hastātus *adj* armed with a spear ♦ *mpl* first line of Roman army in battle; **prīmus ~** 1st company of hastati.

hastīle, -is *nt* shaft, spear, javelin; vine prop.

hau, haud *adv* not, not at all.

hauddum *adv* not yet.

haudquāquam *adv* not at all, not by any means.

hauriō, -rīre, -sī, -stum *vt* to draw, draw off, derive; to drain, empty, exhaust; to take in, drink, swallow, devour.

haustus *ppp of* **hauriō.**

haustus, -ūs *m* drawing (water); drinking; drink, draught.

haut *etc see* **haud.**

hebdomas, -dis *f* week.

Hēbē, -ēs *f* goddess of youth (*cup bearer to the gods*).

hebenus, -ī *f* ebony.

hebeō, -ēre *vi* to be blunt, dull, sluggish.

hebes, -tis *adj* blunt, dull, sluggish; obtuse, stupid.

hebēscō, -ere *vi* to grow dim *or* dull.

hebetō, -āre *vt* to blunt, dull, dim.

Hebrus, -ī *m* Thracian river (*now* Maritza).

Hecatē, -ēs *f* goddess of magic (*and often identified with Diana*).

Hecatēius, -ēis *adj see n.*

hecatombē, -ēs *f* hecatomb.

Hector, -is *m* son of Priam (*chief warrior of the Trojans against the Greeks*).

Hectoreus *adj* of Hector; Trojan.

Hecuba, -ae *and* **ē, -ēs** *f* wife of Priam.

hedera, -ae *f* ivy.

hederiger, -ī *adj* wearing ivy.

hederōsus *adj* covered with ivy.

hēdychrum, -ī *nt* a cosmetic perfume.

hei, heia *etc see* **ei, eia.**

Helena, -ae *and* **ē, -ēs** *f* Helen (*wife of Menelaus, abducted by Paris*).

Helenus, -ī *m* son of Priam (*with prophetic powers*).

Hēliades, -um *fpl* daughters of the Sun (*changed to poplars or alders, and their tears to amber*).

Helicē, -ēs *f* the Great Bear.

Helicōn, -ōnis *m* mountain in Greece sacred to Apollo and the Muses.

Helicōniades, -um *fpl* the Muses.

Helicōnius *adj see* **Helicōn.**

Hellas, -dis *f* Greece.

Hellē, -ēs *f* mythical Greek princess (*carried by the golden-fleeced ram, and drowned in the Hellespont*).

Hellēspontius, -iacus *adj see n.*

Hellēspontus, -ī *m* Hellespont (*now Dardanelles*).

helluō, -ōnis *m* glutton.

helluor, -ārī *vi* to be a glutton.

helvella, -ae *f* a savoury herb.

Helvētiī, -ōrum *mpl* people of E. Gaul (*now Switzerland*).

Helvētius, -cus *adj see n.*

hem *interj* (*expressing surprise*) eh?, well well!

hēmerodromus, -ī *m* express courier.

hēmicillus, -ī *m* mule.

hēmicyclium, -ī *and* **iī** *nt* semicircle with seats.

hēmīna, -ae *f* half a pint.

hendecasyllabī, -ōrum *mpl* hendecasyllabics, verses of eleven syllables.

heptēris, -is *f* ship with seven banks of oars.

hera *etc see* **era.**

Hēra, -ae *f* Greek goddess identified with Juno.

Hēraclītus, -ī *m* early Greek philosopher.

Hēraea, -aeōrum *ntpl* festival of Hera.

herba, -ae *f* blade, young plant; grass, herb, weed.

herbēscō, -ere *vi* to grow into blades.

herbeus *adj* grass-green.

herbidus *adj* grassy.

herbifer, -ī *adj* grassy.

herbōsus *adj* grassy, made of turf; made of herbs.

herbula, -ae *f* little herb.

hercīscō, -ere *vt* to divide an inheritance.

hercle *interj* by Hercules!

herctum, -ī *nt* inheritance.

Hercule *interj* by Hercules!

Herculēs, -is *and* **ī** *m* mythical Greek hero, later deified.

Herculeus *adj*: **arbor ~** poplar; **urbs ~** Herculaneum.

here *etc see* **herī.**

hērēditārius *adj* inherited; about an inheritance.

hērēditās, -ātis *f* inheritance; **~ sine sacrīs** a gift without awkward obligations.

hērēdium, -ī *and* **iī** *nt* inherited estate.

hērēs, -ēdis *m/f* heir, heiress; (*fig*) master, successor.

herī *adv* yesterday.

herīlis *etc see* **erilis.**

Hermēs, -ae *m* Greek god identified with Mercury; Hermes pillar.

Hernicī, -ōrum *mpl* people of central Italy.

Hernicus *adj see n.*

Hērodotus, -ī *m* first Greek historian.

hērōicus *adj* heroic, epic.

hērōīna, -ae *f* demigoddess.

hērōis, -dis *f* demigoddess.

hērōs, -is *m* demigod, hero.

hērōus *adj* heroic, epic.

herus *etc see* **erus.**

Hēsiodēus, -īus *adj see n.*
Hēsiodus, -ī m Hesiod (*Greek didactic poet*).
Hesperia, -iae *f* Italy; Spain.
Hesperides, -idum *fpl* keepers of a garden in
the far West.
Hesperius, -is *adj* western.
Hesperus, -ī m evening star.
hesternus *adj* of yesterday.
heu *interj* (*expressing dismay or pain*) oh!, alas!
heus *interj* (*calling attention*) ho!, hallo!
hexameter, -rī m hexameter verse.
hexēris, -is *f* ship with six banks of oars.
hiātus, -ūs m opening, abyss; open mouth,
gaping; (*GRAM*) hiatus.
Hibērēs, -um *mpl* Spaniards.
Hibēria, -iae *f* Spain.
hīberna, -ōrum *ntpl* winter quarters.
hībernācula, -ōrum *ntpl* winter tents.
Hibernia, -ae *f* Ireland.
hībernō, -āre *vi* to winter, remain in winter
quarters.
hībernus *adj* winter, wintry.
Hibērus, -icus *adj* Spanish.
Hibērus, -ī m river Ebro.
hibīscum, -ī *nt* marsh mallow.
hibrida, hybrida, -ae *m/f* mongrel, half-
breed.
hīc, haec, hōc *pron, adj* this; he, she, it; my, the
latter, the present; **hīc homō** I; **hōc magis** the
more; **hōc est** that is.
hīc *adv* here; herein; (*time*) at this point.
hīce, haece, hōce *emphatic forms of* **hīc, haec,
hōc.**
hīcine, haecine, hōcine *emphatic forms of* **hīc,
haec, hōc.**
hiemālis *adj* winter, stormy.
hiemō, -āre *vi* to pass the winter; to be
wintry, stormy.
hiems, (hiemps), -is *f* winter; stormy
weather, cold.
Hierōnymus, -ī m Jerome.
Hierosolyma, -ōrum *ntpl* Jerusalem.
Hierosolymārius *adj see n.*
hietō, -āre *vi* to yawn.
hilare *adv see* **hilaris.**
hilaris *adj* cheerful, merry.
hilaritās, -ātis *f* cheerfulness.
hilaritūdō, -inis *f* merriment.
hilarō, -āre *vt* to cheer, gladden.
hilarulus *adj* a gay little thing.
hilarus *etc see* **hilaris.**
hīllae, -ārum *fpl* smoked sausage.
Hīlōtae, -ārum *mpl* Helots (*of Sparta*).
hīlum, -ī *nt* something, a whit.
hinc *adv* from here, hence; on this side; from
this source, for this reason; (*time*)
henceforth.
hinniō, -īre *vi* to neigh.
hinnītus, -ūs m neighing.
hinnuleus, -ī m fawn.

hiō, -āre *vi* to be open, gape, yawn; (*speech*) to
be disconnected, leave a hiatus ♦ *vt* to sing.
hippagōgī, -ōrum *fpl* cavalry transports.
hippocentaurus, -ī m centaur.
hippodromos, -ī m racecourse.
Hippolytus, -ī m son of Theseus (*slandered by
stepmother Phaedra*).
hippomanes, -is *nt* mare's fluid; membrane
on foal's forehead.
Hippōnactēus *adj* of Hipponax ♦ m iambic
verse used by Hipponax.
Hippōnax, -ctis m Greek satirist.
hippotoxotae, -ārum *mpl* mounted
archers.
hīra, -ae *f* the empty gut.
hircīnus *adj* of a goat.
hircōsus *adj* goatish.
hircus, -ī m he-goat; goatish smell.
hirnea, -ae *f* jug.
hirq- *etc see* **hirc-.**
hirsūtus *adj* shaggy, bristly; uncouth.
hirtus *adj* hairy, shaggy; rude.
hirūdō, -inis *f* leech.
hirundinīnus *adj* swallows'.
hirundō, -inis *f* swallow.
hīscō, -ere *vi* to gape; to open the mouth ♦ *vt*
to utter.
Hispānia, -iae *f* Spain.
Hispāniēnsis, -us *adj* Spanish.
hispidus *adj* hairy, rough.
Hister, -rī m lower Danube.
historia, -ae *f* history, inquiry; story.
historicus *adj* historical ♦ m historian.
histricus *adj* of the stage.
histriō, -ōnis m actor.
histriōnālis *adj* of an actor.
histriōnia, -ae *f* acting.
hiulcē *adv* with hiatus.
hiulcō, -āre *vt* to split open.
hiulcus *adj* gaping, open; (*speech*) with hiatus.
hodiē *adv* today; nowadays, now; up to the
present.
hodiernus *adj* today's.
holitor, -ōris m market gardener.
holitōrius *adj* for market gardeners.
holus, -eris *nt* vegetables.
holusculum, -ī *nt* small cabbage.
Homēricus *adj see n.*
Homērus, -ī m Greek epic poet, Homer.
homicīda, -ae m killer, murderer.
homicīdium, -ī *and* **iī** *nt* murder.
homō, -inis *m/f* human being, man; (*pl*)
people, the world; (*derogatory*) fellow,
creature; **inter ~inēs esse** be alive; see the
world.
**homullus, -ī, homunciō, -ōnis,
homunculus, -ī** m little man, poor creature,
mortal.
honestās, -ātis *f* good character, honourable
reputation; sense of honour, integrity;

(*things*) beauty.
honestē *adv* decently, virtuously.
honestō, -āre *vt* to honour, dignify, embellish.
honestus *adj* honoured, respectable; honourable, virtuous; (*appearance*) handsome ♦ *m* gentleman ♦ *nt* virtue, good; beauty.
honor, -ōris *m* honour, esteem; public office, position, preferment; award, tribute, offering; ornament, beauty; ~**ōris causā** out of respect; for the sake of; ~**ōrem praefārī** apologize for a remark.
honōrābilis *adj* a mark of respect.
honōrārius *adj* done out of respect, honorary.
honōrātē *adv* honourably.
honōrātus *adj* esteemed, distinguished; in high office; complimentary.
honōrificē *adv* in complimentary terms.
honōrificus *adj* complimentary.
honōrō, -āre, -āvī, -ātum *vt* to do honour to, embellish.
honōrus *adj* complimentary.
honōs *etc see* **honor.**
hōra, -ae *f* hour; time, season; (*pl*) clock; **in ~ās** hourly; **in ~am vīvere** ≈ live from hand to mouth.
hōraeum, -ī *nt* pickle.
Horātius, -ī *m* Roman family name (*esp the defender of Rome against Porsenna*); the lyric poet Horace.
Horātius *adj see n.*
hordeum, -ī *nt* barley.
horia, -ae *f* fishing smack.
hōrnō *adv* this year.
hōrnōtinus *adj* this year's.
hōrnus *adj* this year's.
hōrologium, -ī *and* **iī** *nt* clock.
horrendus *adj* fearful, terrible; awesome.
horrēns, -entis *pres p of* **horreō** ♦ *adj* bristling, shaggy.
horreō, -ēre, -uī *vi* to stand stiff, bristle; to shiver, shudder, tremble ♦ *vt* to dread; to be afraid, be amazed.
horrēscō, -ere *vi* to stand on end, become rough; to begin to quake; to start, be terrified ♦ *vt* to dread.
horreum, -ī *nt* barn, granary, store.
horribilis *adj* terrifying; amazing.
horridē *adv see* **horridus.**
horridulus *adj* protruding a little; unkempt; (*fig*) uncouth.
horridus *adj* bristling, shaggy, rough, rugged; shivering; (*manners*) rude, uncouth; frightening.
horrifer, -ī *adj* chilling; terrifying.
horrificē *adv* in awesome manner.
horrificō, -āre *vt* to ruffle; to terrify.
horrificus *adj* terrifying.
horrisonus *adj* dread-sounding.
horror, -ōris *m* bristling; shivering, ague; terror, fright, awe, a terror.
hōrsum *adv* this way.

hortāmen, -inis *nt* encouragement.
hortāmentum, -ī *nt* encouragement.
hortātiō, -ōnis *f* harangue, encouragement.
hortātor, -ōris *m* encourager.
hortātus, -ūs *m* encouragement.
Hortēnsius, -ī *m* Roman family name (*esp an orator in Cicero's time*).
hortor, -ārī, -ātus *vt* to urge, encourage, exhort, harangue.
hortulus, -ī *m* little garden.
hortus, -ī *m* garden; (*pl*) park.
hospes, -itis *m*, **hospita, -ae** *f* host, hostess; guest, friend; stranger, foreigner ♦ *adj* strange.
hospitālis *adj* host's, guest's; hospitable.
hospitālitās, -ātis *f* hospitality.
hospitāliter *adv* hospitably.
hospitium, -ī *and* **iī** *nt* hospitality, friendship; lodging, inn.
hostia, -ae *f* victim, sacrifice.
hostiātus *adj* provided with victims.
hosticus *adj* hostile; strange ♦ *nt* enemy territory.
hostīlis *adj* of the enemy, hostile.
hostīliter *adv* in hostile manner.
hostīmentum, -ī *nt* recompense.
hostiō, -īre *vt* to requite.
hostis, -is *m/f* enemy.
hūc *adv* hither, here; to this, to such a pitch; ~ **illūc** hither and thither.
hui *interj* (*expressing surprise*) ho!, my word!
hūiusmodī such.
hūmānē, -iter *adv* humanly; gently, politely.
hūmānitās, -ātis *f* human nature, mankind; humanity, kindness, courtesy; culture, refinement.
hūmānitus *adv* in accordance with human nature; kindly.
hūmānus *adj* human, humane, kind, courteous; cultured, refined, well-educated; ~**ō māior** superhuman.
humātiō, -ōnis *f* burying.
hūme-, hūmi- *see* **ūme-, ūmi-.**
humilis *adj* low, low-lying, shallow; (*condition*) lowly, humble, poor; (*language*) commonplace; (*mind*) mean, base.
humilitās, -ātis *f* low position, smallness, shallowness; lowliness, insignificance; meanness, baseness.
humiliter *adv* meanly, humbly.
humō, -āre, -āvī, -ātum *vt* to bury.
humus, -ī *f* earth, ground; land; ~**ī** on the ground.
hyacinthinus *adj* of the hyacinthus.
hyacinthus, -ī *m* iris, lily.
Hyades, -um *fpl* Hyads (*a group of stars in Taurus*).
hyaena, -ae *f* hyena.
hyalus, -ī *m* glass.
Hybla, -ae *f* mountain in Sicily (*famous for bees*).
Hyblaeus *adj see n.*
hybrida *etc see* **hibrida.**

Hydaspēs, -is *m* tributary of river Indus (*now* Jelum).

Hȳdra, -ae *f* hydra (*a mythical dragon with seven heads*).

hydraulus, -ī *m* water organ.

hydria, -ae *f* ewer.

Hydrochous, -ī *m* Aquarius.

hydrōpicus *adj* suffering from dropsy.

hydrōps, -is *m* dropsy.

hydrus, -ī *m* serpent.

Hylās, -ae *m* a youth loved by Hercules.

Hymēn, -enis, Hymenaeus, -ī *m* god of marriage; wedding song; wedding.

Hymettius *adj see n.*

Hymettus, -ī *m* mountain near Athens (*famous for honey and marble*).

Hypanis, -is *m* river of Sarmatia (*now* Bug).

Hyperboreī, -ōrum *mpl fabulous people in the far North.*

Hyperboreus *adj see n.*

Hyperīōn, -onis *m father of the Sun*; the Sun.

hypodidasculus, -ī *m* assistant teacher.

hypomnēma, -tis *nt* memorandum.

Hyrcānī, -ōrum *mpl people on the Caspian Sea.*

Hyrcānus *adj* Hyrcanian.

I, i

Iacchus, -ī *m* Bacchus; wine.

iaceō, -ēre, -uī *vi* to lie; to be ill, lie dead; (*places*) to be situated, be flat *or* low-lying, be in ruins; (*dress*) to hang loose; (*fig*) to be inactive, be downhearted; (*things*) to be dormant, neglected, despised.

iaciō, -ere, iēcī, iactum *vt* to throw; to lay, build; (*seed*) to sow; (*speech*) to cast, let fall, mention.

iactāns, -antis *pres p of* **iactō** ♦ *adj* boastful.

iactanter *adv* ostentatiously.

iactantia, -ae *f* boasting, ostentation.

iactātiō, -ōnis *f* tossing, gesticulation; boasting, ostentation; ~ **populāris** publicity.

iactātus, -ūs *m* waving.

iactitō, -āre *vt* to mention, bandy.

iactō, -āre, -āvī, -ātum *vt* to throw, scatter; to shake, toss about; (*mind*) to disquiet; (*ideas*) to consider, discuss, mention; (*speech*) to boast of; **sē ~** waver, fluctuate; to behave ostentatiously, be officious.

iactūra, -ae *f* throwing overboard; loss, sacrifice.

iactus *ppp of* **iaciō.**

iactus, -ūs *m* throwing, throw; **intrā tēlī iactum** within spear's range.

iacuī *perf of* **iaceō.**

iaculābilis *adj* missile.

iaculātor, -ōris *m* thrower, shooter; light-armed soldier.

iaculātrīx, -īcis *f* huntress.

iaculor, -ārī, -ātus *vt* to throw, hurl, shoot; to throw the javelin; to shoot at, hit; (*fig*) to aim at, attack.

iaculum, -ī *nt* javelin; fishing net.

iāien- *etc see* **iēn-.**

iam *adv* (*past*) already, by then; (*present*) now, already; (*future*) directly, very soon; (*emphasis*) indeed, precisely; (*inference*) therefore, then surely; (*transition*) moreover, next; **iam dūdum** for a long time, long ago; immediately; **iam iam** right now, any moment now; **non ~** no longer; **iam ... iam** at one time ... at another; **iam nunc** just now; **iam prīdem** long ago, for a long time; **iam tum** even at that time; **sī iam** supposing for the purpose of argument.

iambēus *adj* iambic.

iambus, -ī *m* iambic foot; iambic poetry.

Iānālis *adj see* **Iānus.**

Iāniculum, -ī *nt Roman hill across the Tiber.*

iānitor, -ōris *m* doorkeeper, porter.

iānua, -ae *f* door; entrance; (*fig*) key.

Iānuārius *adj* of January ♦ *m* January.

Iānus, -ī *m god of gateways and beginnings*; archway, arcade.

Iapetīonidēs, -ae *m* Atlas.

Iapetus, -ī *m a Titan (father of Atlas and Prometheus).*

Iāpyx, -gis *adj* Iapygian; Apulian ♦ *m west-north-west wind from Apulia.*

Iāsōn, -onis *m* Jason (*leader of Argonauts, husband of Medea*).

Iāsonius *adj see n.*

iaspis, -dis *f* jasper.

Ibēr- *etc see* **Hībēr-.**

ibi *adv* there; then; in this, at it.

ibīdem *adv* in the same place; at that very moment.

Ibis, -is *and* **idis** *f* ibis.

Īcarium, -ī *nt* Icarian Sea.

Īcarius *adj see n.*

Īcarus, -ī *m* son of Daedalus (*drowned in the Aegean*).

īcō, -ere, -ī, ictum *vt* to strike; **foedus ~** make a treaty.

ictericus *adj* jaundiced.

ictis, -dis *f* weasel.

ictus *ppp of* **īcō.**

ictus, -ūs *m* stroke, blow; wound; (*metre*) beat.

Īda, -ae, -ē, -ēs *f mountain in Crete; mountain near Troy.*

Īdaeus *adj* Cretan; Trojan.

idcircō *adv* for that reason; for the purpose.

Noun declensions and verb conjugations are shown on pp xiii to xxv. The present infinitive ending of a verb shows to which conjugation it belongs: **-āre** = 1st; **-ēre** = 2nd; **-ere** = 3rd and **-īre** = 4th. Irregular verbs are shown on p xxvi

īdem, eadem, idem *pron* the same; also, likewise.

identidem *adv* repeatedly, again and again.

ideō *adv* therefore, for this reason, that is why.

idiōta, -ae *m* ignorant person, layman.

īdōlon, -ī *nt* apparition.

idōneē *adv see* **idōneus**.

idōneus *adj* fit, proper, suitable, sufficient.

īdūs, -uum *fpl* Ides (*the 15th March, May, July, October, the 13th of other months*).

iēcī *perf of* **iaciō**.

iecur, -oris *and* **inoris** *nt* liver; (*fig*) passion.

iecusculum, -ī *nt* small liver.

iēiūniōsus *adj* hungry.

iēiūnitās, -ātis *f* fasting; (*fig*) meagreness.

iēiūnium, -ī *and* **iī** *nt* fast; hunger; leanness.

iēiūnus *adj* fasting, hungry; (*things*) barren, poor, meagre; (*style*) feeble.

ientāculum, -ī *nt* breakfast.

igitur *adv* therefore, then, so.

ignārus *adj* ignorant, unaware; unknown.

ignāvē, -iter *adv* without energy.

ignāvia, -ae *f* idleness, laziness; cowardice.

ignāvus *adj* idle, lazy, listless; cowardly; relaxing.

ignēscō, -ere *vi* to take fire, burn.

igneus *adj* burning, fiery.

igniculus, -ī *m* spark; (*fig*) fire, vehemence.

ignifer, -ī *adj* fiery.

ignigena, -ae *m* the fireborn (Bacchus).

ignipēs, -edis *adj* fiery-footed.

ignipotēns, -entis *adj* fire-working (Vulcan).

ignis, -is *m* fire, a fire; firebrand, lightning; brightness, redness; (*fig*) passion, love.

ignōbilis *adj* unknown, obscure; low-born.

ignōbilitās, -ātis *f* obscurity; low birth.

ignōminia, -ae *f* dishonour, disgrace.

ignōminiōsus *adj* (*person*) degraded, disgraced; (*things*) shameful.

ignōrābilis *adj* unknown.

ignōrantia, -ae *f* ignorance.

ignōrātiō, -ōnis *f* ignorance.

ignōrō, -āre, -āvī, -ātum *vt* to not know, be unacquainted with; to disregard.

ignōscō, -scere, -vī, -tum *vt, vi* to forgive, pardon.

ignōtus *adj* unknown; low-born; ignorant.

īlex, -icis *f* holm oak.

īlia, -um *ntpl* groin; entrails; ~ dūcere become broken-winded.

Īlia, -ae *f* mother of Romulus and Remus.

Īliadēs, -adae *m* son of Ilia; Trojan.

Īlias, -dis *f* the Iliad; a Trojan woman.

īlicet *adv* it's all over, let us go; immediately.

īlicō *adv* on the spot; instantly.

īlignus *adj* of holm oak.

Īlīthyia, -ae *f* Greek goddess of childbirth.

Īlium, -on, -ī *nt*, **-os, -ī** *f* Troy.

Īlius, -acus *adj* Trojan.

illā *adv* that way.

illābefactus *adj* unbroken.

illābor, -bī, -psus *vi* to flow into, fall down.

illabōrō, -āre *vi* to work (at).

illāc *adv* that way.

illacessītus *adj* unprovoked.

illacrimābilis *adj* unwept; inexorable.

illacrimō, -āre; -or, -ārī *vi* to weep over, lament; to weep.

illaesus *adj* unhurt.

illaetābilis *adj* cheerless.

illāpsus *ppa of* **illābor**.

illaqueō, -āre *vt* to ensnare.

illātus *ppp of* **īnferō**.

illaudātus *adj* wicked.

ille, -a, -ud *pron and adj* that, that one; he, she, it; the famous; the former, the other; **ex ~ō** since then.

illecebra, -ae *f* attraction, lure, bait, decoy bird.

illecebrōsus *adj* seductive.

illectus *ppp of* **illiciō**.

illēctus *adj* unread.

illepidē *adv see* **illepidus**.

illepidus *adj* inelegant, churlish.

illex, -icis *m/f* lure.

illēx, -ēgis *adj* lawless.

illexī *perf of* **illiciō**.

illībātus *adj* unimpaired.

illīberālis *adj* ungenerous, mean, disobliging.

illīberālitās, -ātis *f* meanness.

illīberāliter *adv see* **illīberālis**.

illic, -aec, -ūc *pron* he, she, it; that.

illīc *adv* there, yonder; in that matter.

illiciō, -icere, -exī, -ectum *vt* to seduce, decoy, mislead.

illicitātor, -ōris *m* sham bidder (at an auction).

illicitus *adj* unlawful.

illīdō, -dere, -sī, -sum *vt* to strike, dash against.

illigō, -āre, -āvī, -ātum *vt* to fasten on, attach; to connect; to impede, encumber, oblige.

illim *adv* from there.

illīmis *adj* clear.

illinc *adv* from there; on that side.

illinō, -inere, -ēvī, -itum *vt* to smear over, cover, bedaub.

illiquefactus *adj* melted.

illīsī *perf of* **illīdō**.

illīsus *ppp of* **illīdō**.

illitterātus *adj* uneducated, uncultured.

illitus *ppp of* **illinō**.

illō *adv* (to) there; to that end.

illōtus *adj* dirty.

illūc *adv* (to) there; to that; to him/her.

illūceō, -ēre *vi* to blaze.

illūcēscō, -cēscere, -xī *vi* to become light, dawn.

illūdō, -dere, -sī, -sum *vt, vi* to play, amuse oneself; to abuse; to jeer at, ridicule.

illūminātē *adv* luminously.

illūminō, -āre, -āvī, -ātum *vt* to light up; to enlighten; to embellish.

illūsiō, -ōnis *f* irony.

illūstris *adj* bright, clear; distinct, manifest;

distinguished, illustrious.
illūstrō, -āre, -āvī, -ātum *vt* to illuminate; to make clear, explain; to make famous.
illūsus *ppp of* **illūdō.**
illuviēs, -ēī *f* dirt, filth; floods.
Illyria, -ae *f*, **-cum, -cī** *nt* Illyria.
Illyricus, -us *adj see* **Illyricum.**
Illyriī, -ōrum *mpl* people E. of the Adriatic.
Ilva, -ae *f* Italian island (*now* Elba).
imāginārius *adj* fancied.
imāginātiō, -ōnis *f* fancy.
imāginor, -ārī, *vt* to picture to oneself.
imāgō, -inis *f* likeness, picture, statue; portrait of ancestor; apparition, ghost; echo, mental picture, idea; (*fig*) semblance, mere shadow; (*RHET*) comparison.
imbēcillē *adv* faintly.
imbēcillitās, -ātis *f* weakness, helplessness.
imbēcillus *adj* weak, frail; helpless.
imbellis *adj* non-combatant; peaceful; cowardly.
imber, -ris *m* rain, heavy shower; water; (*fig*) stream, shower.
imberbis, imberbus *adj* beardless.
imbibō, -ere, -ī *vt* (*mind*) to conceive; to resolve.
imbrex, -icis *f* tile.
imbricus *adj* rainy.
imbrifer, -ī *adj* rainy.
imbuō, -uere, -uī, -ūtum *vt* to wet, steep, dip; (*fig*) to taint, fill; to inspire, accustom, train; to begin, be the first to explore.
imitābilis *adj* imitable.
imitāmen, -inis *nt* imitation; likeness.
imitāmenta, -ōrum *ntpl* pretence.
imitātiō, -ōnis *f* imitation.
imitātor,-ōris *m*, **-rīx,-rīcis** *f* imitator.
imitātus *adj* copied.
imitor, -ārī, -ātus *vt* to copy, portray; to imitate, act like.
immadēscō, -ēscere, -uī *vi* to become wet.
immāne *adv* savagely.
immānis *adj* enormous, vast; monstrous, savage, frightful.
immānitās, -ātis *f* vastness; savageness, barbarism.
immānsuētus *adj* wild.
immātūritās, -ātis *f* over-eagerness.
immātūrus *adj* untimely.
immedicābilis *adj* incurable.
immemor, -is *adj* unmindful, forgetful, negligent.
immemorābilis *adj* indescribable, not worth mentioning.
immemorātus *adj* hitherto untold.
immēnsitās, -ātis *f* immensity.
immēnsum, -ī *nt* infinity, vast extent ♦ *adv* exceedingly.
immēnsus *adj* immeasurable, vast, unending.
immerēns, -entis *adj* undeserving.

immergō, -gere, -sī, -sum *vt* to plunge, immerse.
immeritō *adv* unjustly.
immeritus *adj* undeserving, innocent; undeserved.
immersābilis *adj* never foundering.
immersus *ppp of* **immergō.**
immētātus *adj* unmeasured.
immigrō, -āre, -āvī, -ātum *vi* to move (into).
immineō, -ēre, -uī *vi* to overhang, project; to be near, adjoin, impend; to threaten, be a menace to; to long for, grasp at.
imminuō, -uere, -uī, -ūtum *vt* to lessen, shorten; to impair; to encroach on, ruin.
imminūtiō, -ōnis *f* mutilation; (*RHET*) understatement.
immisceō, -scēre, -scuī, -xtum *vt* to intermingle, blend; **sē ~** join, meddle with.
immiserābilis *adj* unpitied.
immisericorditer *adv* unmercifully.
immisericors, -dis *adj* pitiless.
immissiō, -ōnis *f* letting grow.
immissus *ppp of* **immittō.**
immītis *adj* unripe; severe, inexorable.
immittō, -ittere, -īsī, -issum *vt* to let in, put in; to graft on; to let go, let loose, let grow; to launch, throw; to incite, set on.
immīxtus *ppp of* **immisceō.**
immo *adv* (*correcting preceding words*) no, yes; on the contrary, or rather; **~ sī** ah, if only.
immōbilis *adj* motionless; immovable.
immoderātē *adv* extravagantly.
immoderātiō, -ōnis *f* excess.
immoderātus *adj* limitless; excessive, unbridled.
immodestē *adv* extravagantly.
immodestia, -ae *f* license.
immodestus *adj* immoderate.
immodicē *adv see* **immodicus.**
immodicus *adj* excessive, extravagant, unruly.
immodulātus *adj* unrhythmical.
immolātiō, -ōnis *f* sacrifice.
immolātor, -ōris *m* sacrificer.
immōlītus *adj* erected.
immolō, -āre, -āvī, -ātum *vt* to sacrifice; to slay.
immorior, -ī, -tuus *vi* to die upon; to waste away.
immorsus *adj* bitten; (*fig*) stimulated.
immortālis *adj* immortal, everlasting.
immortālitās, -ātis *f* immortality; lasting fame.
immortāliter *adv* infinitely.
immōtus *adj* motionless, unmoved, immovable.
immūgiō, -īre, -īī *vi* to roar (in).
immulgeō, -ēre *vt* to milk.
immundus *adj* unclean, dirty.
immūniō, -īre, -īvī *vt* to strengthen.

Noun declensions and verb conjugations are shown on pp xiii to xxv. The present infinitive ending of a verb shows to which conjugation it belongs: **-āre** = 1st; **-ēre** = 2nd; **-ere** = 3rd and **-īre** = 4th. Irregular verbs are shown on p xxvi

immūnis *adj* with no public obligations, untaxed, free from office; exempt, free (from).
immūnitās, -ātis *f* exemption, immunity, privilege.
immūnītus *adj* undefended; (*roads*) unmetalled.
immurmurō, -āre *vi* to murmur (at).
immūtābilis *adj* unalterable.
immūtābilitās, -ātis *f* immutability.
immūtātiō, -ōnis *f* exchange; (*RHET*) metonymy.
immūtātus *adj* unchanged.
immūtō, -āre, -āvī, -ātum *vt* to change; (*words*) to substitute by metonymy.
impācātus *adj* aggressive.
impāctus *ppp of* **impingō**.
impār, -aris *adj* unequal, uneven, unlike; no match for, inferior; (*metre*) elegiac.
imparātus *adj* unprepared, unprovided.
impariter *adv* unequally.
impāstus *adj* hungry.
impatiēns, -entis *adj* unable to endure, impatient.
impatienter *adv* intolerably.
impatientia, -ae *f* want of endurance.
impavidē *adv see* **impavidus**.
impavidus *adj* fearless, undaunted.
impedīmentum, -ī *nt* hindrance, obstacle; (*pl*) baggage, luggage, supply train.
impediō, -īre, -īvī and iī, -ītum *vt* to hinder, entangle; to encircle; (*fig*) to embarrass, obstruct, prevent.
impedītiō, -ōnis *f* obstruction.
impedītus *adj* (*MIL*) hampered with baggage, in difficulties; (*place*) difficult, impassable; (*mind*) busy, obsessed.
impēgī *perf of* **impingō**.
impellō, -ellere, -ulī, -ulsum *vt* to strike, drive; to set in motion, impel, shoot; to incite, urge on; (*fig*) to overthrow, ruin.
impendeō, -ēre *vi* to overhang; to be imminent, threaten.
impendiō *adv* very much.
impendium, -ī and iī *nt* expense, outlay; interest on a loan.
impendō, -endere, -endī, -ēnsum *vt* to weigh out, pay out, spend; (*fig*) to devote.
impenetrābilis *adj* impenetrable.
impēnsa, -ae *f* expense, outlay.
impēnsē *adv* very much; earnestly.
impēnsus *ppp of* **impendō** ♦ *adj* (*cost*) high, dear; (*fig*) great, earnest.
imperātor, -ōris *m* commander-in-chief, general; emperor; chief, master.
imperātōrius *adj* of a general; imperial.
imperātum, -ī *nt* order.
imperceptus *adj* unknown.
impercussus *adj* noiseless.
imperditus *adj* not slain.
imperfectus *adj* unfinished, imperfect.
imperfossus *adj* not stabbed.
imperiōsus *adj* powerful, imperial; tyrannical.
imperītē *adv* awkwardly.
imperītia, -ae *f* inexperience.
imperītō, -āre *vt, vi* to rule, command.
imperītus *adj* inexperienced, ignorant.
imperium, -ī and iī *nt* command, order; mastery, sovereignty, power; military command, supreme authority; empire; (*pl*) those in command, the authorities.
impermissus *adj* unlawful.
imperō, -āre, -āvī, -ātum *vt, vi* to order, command; to requisition, demand; to rule, govern, control; to be emperor.
imperterritus *adj* undaunted.
impertiō, -īre, -īvī and iī, -ītum *vt* to share, communicate, impart.
imperturbātus *adj* unruffled.
impervius *adj* impassable.
impetibilis *adj* intolerable.
impetis (*gen*), **-e** (*abl*) *m* force; extent.
impetrābilis *adj* attainable; successful.
impetrātiō, -ōnis *f* favour.
impetriō, -īre *vt* to succeed with the auspices.
impetrō, -āre, -āvī, -ātum *vt* to achieve; to obtain, secure (*a request*).
impetus, -ūs *m* attack, onset; charge; rapid motion, rush; (*mind*) impulse, passion.
impexus *adj* unkempt.
impiē *adv* wickedly.
impietās, -ātis *f* impiety, disloyalty, unfilial conduct.
impiger, -rī *adj* active, energetic.
impigrē *adv see adj*.
impigritās, -ātis *f* energy.
impingō, -ingere, -ēgī, -āctum *vt* to dash, force against; to force upon; (*fig*) to bring against, drive.
impiō, -āre *vt* to make sinful.
impius *adj* (*to gods*) impious; (*to parents*) undutiful; (*to country*) disloyal; wicked, unscrupulous.
implācābilis *adj* implacable.
implācābiliter *adv see adj*.
implācātus *adj* unappeased.
implacidus *adj* savage.
impleō, -ēre, -ēvī, -ētum *vt* to fill; to satisfy; (*time, number*) to make up, complete; (*duty*) to discharge, fulfil.
implexus *adj* entwined; involved.
implicātiō, -ōnis *f* entanglement.
implicātus *adj* complicated, confused.
implicitē *adv* intricately.
implicō, -āre, -āvī and uī, -ātum and itum *vt* to entwine, enfold, clasp; (*fig*) to entangle, involve; to connect closely, join.
implōrātiō, -ōnis *f* beseeching.
implōrō, -āre, -āvī, -ātum *vt* to invoke, entreat, appeal to.
implūmis *adj* unfledged.
impluō, -ere *vi* to rain upon.
impluvium, -ī and iī *nt* roof-opening of the Roman atrium; rain basin in the atrium.
impolītē *adv* without ornament.

impolītus *adj* unpolished, inelegant.

impollūtus *adj* unstained.

impōnō, -ōnere, -osuī, -ositum *vt* to put in, lay on, place; to embark; (*fig*) to impose, inflict, assign; to put in charge; (*tax*) to impose; (*with dat*) to impose upon, cheat.

importō, -āre, -āvī, -ātum *vt* to bring in, import; (*fig*) to bring upon, introduce.

importūnē *adv see adj.*

importūnitās, -ātis *f* insolence, ill nature.

importūnus *adj* unsuitable; troublesome; ill-natured, uncivil, bullying.

importuōsus *adj* without a harbour.

impos, -tis *adj* not master (of).

impositus, impostus *ppp of* **impōnō.**

impotēns, -entis *adj* powerless, weak; with no control over; headstrong, violent.

impotenter *adv* weakly; violently.

impotentia, -ae *f* poverty; want of self-control, violence.

impraesentiārum *adv* at present.

imprānsus *adj* fasting, without breakfast.

imprecor, -ārī *vt* to invoke.

impressiō, -ōnis *f* (*MIL*) thrust, raid; (*mind*) impression; (*speech*) emphasis; (*rhythm*) beat.

impressus *ppp of* **imprimō.**

imprīmīs *adv* especially.

imprimō, -imere, -essī, -essum *vt* to press upon, impress, imprint, stamp.

improbātiō, -ōnis *f* blame.

improbē *adv* badly, wrongly; persistently.

improbitās, -ātis *f* badness, dishonesty.

improbō, -āre, -āvī, -ātum *vt* to disapprove, condemn, reject.

improbulus *adj* a little presumptuous.

improbus *adj* bad, inferior (in quality); wicked, perverse, cruel; unruly, persistent, rebellious.

imprōcērus *adj* undersized.

imprōdictus *adj* not postponed.

imprōmptus *adj* unready, slow.

improperātus *adj* lingering.

improsper, -ī *adj* unsuccessful.

improsperē *adv* unfortunately.

imprōvidē *adv see adj.*

imprōvidus *adj* unforeseeing, thoughtless.

imprōvīsus *adj* unexpected; ~ō, de ~ō, ex ~ō unexpectedly.

imprūdēns, -entis *adj* unforeseeing, not expecting; ignorant, unaware.

imprūdenter *adv* thoughtlessly, unawares.

imprūdentia, -ae *f* thoughtlessness; ignorance; aimlessness.

impūbēs, -eris *and* **is** *adj* youthful; chaste.

impudēns, -entis *adj* shameless, impudent.

impudenter *adv see adj.*

impudentia, -ae *f* impudence.

impudīcitia, -ae *f* lewdness.

impudīcus *adj* shameless; immodest.

impugnātiō, -ōnis *f* assault.

impugnō, -āre, -āvī, -ātum *vt* to attack; (*fig*) to oppose, impugn.

impulī *perf of* **impellō.**

impulsiō, -ōnis *f* pressure; (*mind*) impulse.

impulsor, -ōris *m* instigator.

impulsus *ppp of* **impellō.**

impulsus, -ūs *m* push, pressure, impulse; (*fig*) instigation.

impūne *adv* safely, with impunity.

impūnitās, -ātis *f* impunity.

impūnītē *adv* with impunity.

impūnītus *adj* unpunished.

impūrātus *adj* vile.

impūrē *adv see adj.*

impūritās, -ātis *f* uncleanness.

impūrus *adj* unclean; infamous, vile.

imputātus *adj* unpruned.

imputō, -āre, -āvī, -ātum *vt* to put to one's account; to ascribe, credit, impute.

īmulus *adj* little tip of.

īmus *adj* lowest, deepest, bottom of; last.

in *prep* (*with abl*) in, on, at; among; in the case of; (*time*) during; (*with acc*) into, on to, to, towards; against; (*time*) for, till; (*purpose*) for; ~ armīs under arms; ~ equō on horseback; ~ eō esse ut be in the position of; be on the point of; ~ hōrās hourly; ~ modum in the manner of; ~ rem of use; ~ universum in general.

inaccessus *adj* unapproachable.

inacēscō, -ere *vi* to turn sour.

Īnachidēs, -idae *m* Perseus; Epaphus.

Īnachis, -idis *f* Io.

Īnachius *adj* of Inachus, Argive, Greek.

Īnachus, -ī *m* first king of Argos.

inadsuētus *adj* unaccustomed.

inadūstus *adj* unsinged.

inaedificō, -āre, -āvī, -ātum *vt* to build on, erect; to wall up, block up.

inaequābilis *adj* uneven.

inaequālis *adj* uneven; unequal; capricious.

inaequāliter *adv see adj.*

inaequātus *adj* unequal.

inaequō, -āre *vt* to level up.

inaestimābilis *adj* incalculable; invaluable; valueless.

inaestuō, -āre *vi* to rage in.

inamābilis *adj* hateful.

inamārēscō, -ere *vi* to become bitter.

inambitiōsus *adj* unambitious.

inambulātiō, -ōnis *f* walking about.

inambulō, -āre *vi* to walk up and down.

inamoenus *adj* disagreeable.

inanimus *adj* lifeless, inanimate.

ināniō, -īre *vt* to make empty.

inānis *adj* empty, void; poor, unsubstantial; useless, worthless, vain, idle ♦ *nt* (*PHILOS*) space; (*fig*) vanity.

inānitās, -ātis *f* empty space; inanity.

Noun declensions and verb conjugations are shown on pp xiii to xxv. The present infinitive ending of a verb shows to which conjugation it belongs: **-āre** = 1st; **-ēre** = 2nd; **-ere** = 3rd and **-īre** = 4th. Irregular verbs are shown on p xxvi

ināniter *adv* idly, vainly.
inarātus *adj* fallow.
inārdēscō, -dēscere, -sī *vi* to be kindled, flare up.
inass- *etc see* **inads-**.
inattenuātus *adj* undiminished.
inaudāx, -ācis *adj* timorous.
inaudiō, -īre *vt* to hear of, learn.
inaudītus *adj* unheard of, unusual; without a hearing.
inaugurātō *adv* after taking the auspices.
inaugurō, -āre *vi* to take auspices ♦ *vt* to consecrate, inaugurate.
inaurēs, -ium *fpl* earrings.
inaurō, -āre, -āvī, -ātum *vt* to gild; (*fig*) to enrich.
inauspicātō *adv* without taking the auspices.
inauspicātus *adj* done without auspices.
inausus *adj* unattempted.
incaeduus *adj* uncut.
incalēscō, -ēscere, -uī *vi* to grow hot; (*fig*) to warm, glow.
incalfaciō, -ere *vt* to heat.
incallidē *adv* unskilfully.
incallidus *adj* stupid, simple.
incandēscō, -ēscere, -uī *vi* to become hot; to turn white.
incānēscō, -ēscere, -uī *vi* to grow grey.
incantātus *adj* enchanted.
incānus *adj* grey.
incassum *adv* in vain.
incastīgātus *adj* unrebuked.
incautē *adv* negligently.
incautus *adj* careless, heedless; unforeseen, unguarded.
incēdō, -ēdere, -ēssī, -ēssum *vi* to walk, parade, march; (MIL) to advance; (*feelings*) to come upon.
incelebrātus *adj* not made known.
incēnātus *adj* supperless.
incendiārius, -ī *and* **iī** *m* incendiary.
incendium, -ī *and* **iī** *nt* fire, conflagration; heat; (*fig*) fire, vehemence, passion.
incendō, -ere, -ī, incēnsum *vt* to set fire to, burn; to light, brighten; (*fig*) to inflame, rouse, incense.
incēnsiō, -ōnis *f* burning.
incēnsus *ppp of* **incendō**.
incēnsus *adj* not registered.
incēpī *perf of* **incipiō**.
inceptiō, -ōnis *f* undertaking.
inceptō, -āre *vt* to begin, attempt.
inceptor, -ōris *m* originator.
inceptum, -ī *nt* beginning, undertaking, attempt.
inceptus *ppp of* **incipiō**.
incērō, -āre *vt* to cover with wax.
incertō *adv* not for certain.
incertus *adj* uncertain, doubtful, unsteady ♦ *nt* uncertainty.
incēssō, -ere, -īvī *vt* to attack; (*fig*) to assail.
incēssus, -ūs *m* gait, pace, tramp; invasion; approach.

incestē *adv see adj*.
incestō, -āre *vt* to pollute, dishonour.
incestus *adj* sinful; unchaste, incestuous ♦ *nt* incest.
incestus, -ūs *m* incest.
incho- *etc see* **incoh-**.
incidō, -idere, -idī, -āsum *vi* to fall upon, fall into; to meet, fall in with, come across; to befall, occur, happen; **in mentem ~** occur to one.
incīdō, -dere, -dī, -sum *vt* to cut open; to cut up; to engrave, inscribe; to interrupt, cut short.
incīle, -is *nt* ditch.
incīlō, -āre *vt* to rebuke.
incingō, -gere, -xī, -ctum *vt* to gird, wreathe; to surround.
incinō, -ere *vt* to sing, play.
incipiō, -ipere, -ēpī, -eptum *vt, vi* to begin.
incipissō, -ere *vt* to begin.
incīsē *adv* in short clauses.
incīsim *adv* in short clauses.
incīsiō, -ōnis *f* clause.
incīsum, -ī *nt* clause.
incīsus *ppp of* **incīdō**.
incitāmentum, -ī *nt* incentive.
incitātē *adv* impetuously.
incitātiō, -ōnis *f* inciting; rapidity.
incitātus *ppp of* **incitō** ♦ *adj* swift, rapid; **equō ~ō** at a gallop.
incitō, -āre, -āvī, -ātum *vt* to urge on, rush; to rouse, encourage, excite; to inspire; to increase; **sē ~** rush; **currentem ~ ≈** *spur a willing horse*.
incitus *adj* swift.
incitus *adj* immovable; **ad ~ās, ~a redigere** bring to a standstill.
inclāmō, -āre *vt, vi* to call out, cry out to; to scold, abuse.
inclārēscō, -ēscere, -uī *vi* to become famous.
inclēmēns, -entis *adj* severe.
inclēmenter *adv* harshly.
inclēmentia, -ae *f* severity.
inclīnātiō, -ōnis *f* leaning, slope; (*fig*) tendency, inclination, bias; (CIRCS) change; (*voice*) modulation.
inclīnātus *adj* inclined, prone; falling; (*voice*) deep.
inclīnō, -āre, -āvī, -ātum *vt* to bend, turn; to turn back; (*fig*) to incline, direct, transfer; to change ♦ *vi* to bend, sink; (MIL) to give way; (*fig*) to change, deteriorate; to incline, tend, turn in favour.
inclitus *etc see* **inclutus**.
inclūdō, -dere, -sī, -sum *vt* to shut in, keep in, enclose; to obstruct, block; (*fig*) to include; (*time*) to close, end.
inclūsiō, -ōnis *f* imprisonment.
inclūsus *ppp of* **inclūdō**.
inclutus *adj* famous, glorious.
incoctus *ppp of* **incoquō**.
incoctus *adj* uncooked, raw.
incōgitābilis *adj* thoughtless.

incōgitāns, -antis *adj* thoughtless.
incōgitantia, -ae *f* thoughtlessness.
incōgitō, -āre *vt* to contrive.
incognitus *adj* unknown, unrecognised; (*law*) untried.
incohātus *adj* unfinished.
incohō, -āre, -āvī, -ātum *vt* to begin, start.
incola, -ae *f* inhabitant, resident.
incolō, -ere, -uī *vt* to live in, inhabit ♦ *vi* to live, reside.
incolumis *adj* safe and sound, unharmed.
incolumitās, -ātis *f* safety.
incomitātus *adj* unaccompanied.
incommendātus *adj* unprotected.
incommodē *adv* inconveniently, unfortunately.
incommoditās, -ātis *f* inconvenience, disadvantage.
incommodō, -āre *vi* to be inconvenient, annoy.
incommodum, -ī *nt* inconvenience, disadvantage, misfortune.
incommodus *adj* inconvenient, troublesome.
incommūtābilis *adj* unchangeable.
incompertus *adj* unknown.
incompositē *adv see adj.*
incompositus *adj* in disorder, irregular.
incōmptus *adj* undressed, inelegant.
inconcessus *adj* forbidden.
inconciliō, -āre *vt* to win over (by guile); to trick, inveigle, embarrass.
inconcinnus *adj* inartistic, awkward.
inconcussus *adj* unshaken, stable.
inconditē *adv* confusedly.
inconditus *adj* undisciplined, not organised; (*language*) artless.
inconsīderātē *adv see adj.*
inconsīderātus *adj* thoughtless, ill-advised.
inconsōlābilis *adj* incurable.
inconstāns, -antis *adj* fickle, inconsistent.
inconstanter *adv* inconsistently.
inconstantia, -ae *f* fickleness, inconsistency.
inconsultē *adv* indiscreetly.
inconsultū without consulting.
inconsultus *adj* indiscreet, ill-advised; unanswered; not consulted.
inconsūmptus *adj* unconsumed.
incontāminātus *adj* untainted.
incontentus *adj* untuned.
incontinēns, -entis *adj* intemperate.
incontinenter *adv* without self-control.
incontinentia, -ae *f* lack of self-control.
inconveniēns, -entis *adj* ill-matched.
incoquō, -quere, -xī, -ctum *vt* to boil; to dye.
incorrēctus *adj* unrevised.
incorruptē *adv* justly.
incorruptus *adj* unspoiled; uncorrupted, genuine.
incrēbrēscō, incrēbēscō, -ēscere, -uī *vi* to increase, grow, spread.

incrēdibilis *adj* incredible, extraordinary.
incrēdibiliter *adv see adj.*
incrēdulus *adj* incredulous.
incrēmentum, -ī *nt* growth, increase; addition; offspring.
increpitō, -āre *vt* to rebuke; to challenge.
increpō, -āre, -uī, -itum *vi* to make a noise, sound; (*news*) to be noised abroad ♦ *vt* to cause to make a noise; to exclaim against, rebuke.
incrēscō, -scere, -vī *vi* to grow in, increase.
incrētus *adj* sifted in.
incruentātus *adj* unstained with blood.
incruentus *adj* bloodless, without bloodshed.
incrūstō, -āre *vt* to encrust.
incubō, -āre, -uī, -itum *vi* to lie in or on; (*fig*) to brood over.
incubuī *perf of* **incubō**; *perf of* **incumbō**.
inculcō, -āre, -āvī, -ātum *vt* to force in; to force upon, impress on.
inculpātus *adj* blameless.
incultē *adv* uncouthly.
incultus *adj* uncultivated; (*fig*) neglected, uneducated, rude.
incultus, -ūs *m* neglect, squalor.
incumbō, -mbere, -buī, -bitum *vi* to lean, recline on; to fall upon, throw oneself upon; to oppress, lie heavily upon; (*fig*) to devote attention to, take pains with; to incline.
incūnābula, -ōrum *ntpl* swaddling clothes; (*fig*) cradle, infancy, birthplace, origin.
incūrātus *adj* neglected.
incūria, -ae *f* negligence.
incūriōsē *adv* carelessly.
incūriōsus *adj* careless, indifferent.
incurrō, -rrere, -rrī *and* **curri, -rsum** *vi* to run into, rush, attack; to invade; to meet with, get involved in; (*events*) to occur, coincide.
incursiō, -ōnis *f* attack; invasion, raid; collision.
incursō, -āre *vt, vi* to run into, assault; to frequently invade; (*fig*) to meet, strike.
incursus, -ūs *m* assault, striking; (*mind*) impulse.
incurvō, -āre *vt* to bend, crook.
incurvus *adj* bent, crooked.
incūs, -ūdis *f* anvil.
incūsātiō, -ōnis *f* blaming.
incūsō, -āre, -āvī, -ātum *vt* to find fault with, accuse.
incussī *perf of* **incutiō**.
incussus *ppp of* **incutiō**.
incussus, -ūs *m* shock.
incustōdītus *adj* unguarded, unconcealed.
incūsus *adj* forged.
incutiō, -tere, -ssī, -ssum *vt* to strike, dash against; to throw; (*fig*) to strike into, inspire with.
indāgātiō, -ōnis *f* search.
indāgātor, -ōris *m* explorer.

indāgātrīx, -rīcis *f* female explorer.
indāgō, -āre *vt* to track down; (*fig*) to trace, investigate.
indāgō, -inis *f* (*hunt*) drive, encirclement.
indaudiō *etc see* **inaudiō**.
inde *adv* from there, from that, from them; on that side; from then, ever since; after that, then.
indēbitus *adj* not due.
indēclīnātus *adj* constant.
indecor, -is *adj* dishonourable, a disgrace.
indecōrē *adv* indecently.
indecorō, -āre *vt* to disgrace.
indecōrus *adj* unbecoming, unsightly.
indēfēnsus *adj* undefended.
indēfessus *adj* unwearied, tireless.
indēflētus *adj* unwept.
indēiectus *adj* undemolished.
indēlēbilis *adj* imperishable.
indēlībātus *adj* unimpaired.
indemnātus *adj* unconvicted.
indēplōrātus *adj* unlamented.
indēprēnsus *adj* undetected.
indeptus *ppa of* **indipīscor**.
indēsertus *adj* unforsaken.
indēstrictus *adj* unscathed.
indētōnsus *adj* unshorn.
indēvītātus *adj* unerring.
index, -icis *m* forefinger; witness, informer; (*book, art*) title, inscription; (*stone*) touchstone; (*fig*) indication, pointer, sign.
India, -iae *f* India.
indicātiō, -ōnis *f* value.
indīcente mē without my telling.
indicium, -ī *and* **iī** *nt* information, evidence; reward for information; indication, sign, proof; ~ **profitērī, offerre** ≈ *turn King's evidence*; ~ **postulāre, dare** ask, grant permission to give evidence.
indicō, -āre, -āvī, -ātum *vt* to point out; to disclose, betray; to give information, give evidence; to put a price on.
indīcō, -īcere, -īxī, -ictum *vt* to declare, proclaim, appoint.
indictus *ppp of* **indīcō**.
indictus *adj* not said, unsung; **causā ~ā** without a hearing.
Indicus *adj see n.*
indidem *adv* from the same place *or* thing.
indidī *perf of* **indō**.
indifferēns, -entis *adj* neither good nor bad.
indigena, -ae *m* native ♦ *adj* native.
indigēns, -entis *adj* needy.
indigentia, -ae *f* need; craving.
indigeō, -ēre, -uī *vi* (*with abl*) to need, want, require; to crave.
indiges, -etis *m* national deity.
indigestus *adj* confused.
indignābundus *adj* enraged.
indignāns, -antis *adj* indignant.
indignātiō, -ōnis *f* indignation.
indignē *adv* unworthily; indignantly.
indignitās, -ātis *f* unworthiness, enormity;

insulting treatment; indignation.
indignor, -ārī, -ātus *vt* to be displeased with, be angry at.
indignus *adj* unworthy, undeserving; shameful, severe; undeserved.
indigus *adj* in want.
indīligēns, -entis *adj* careless.
indīligenter *adv see adj.*
indīligentia, -ae *f* carelessness.
indipīscor, -ī, indeptus *vt* to obtain, get, reach.
indīreptus *adj* unplundered.
indiscrētus *adj* closely connected, indiscriminate, indistinguishable.
indisertē *adv* without eloquence.
indisertus *adj* not eloquent.
indispositus *adj* disorderly.
indissolūbilis *adj* imperishable.
indistinctus *adj* confused, obscure.
inditus *ppp of* **indō**.
indīviduus *adj* indivisible; inseparable ♦ *nt* atom.
indō, -ere, -idī, -itum *vt* to put in *or* on; to introduce; to impart, impose.
indocilis *adj* difficult to teach, hard to learn; untaught.
indoctē *adv* unskilfully.
indoctus *adj* untrained, illiterate, ignorant.
indolentia, -ae *f* freedom from pain.
indolēs, -is *f* nature, character, talents.
indolēscō, -ēscere, -uī *vi* to feel sorry.
indomitus *adj* untamed, wild; ungovernable.
indormiō, -īre *vi* to sleep on; to be careless.
indōtātus *adj* with no dowry; unhonoured; (*fig*) unadorned.
indubitō, -āre *vi* to begin to doubt.
indubius *adj* undoubted.
indūcō, -ūcere, -ūxī, -uctum *vt* to bring in, lead on; to introduce; to overlay, cover over; (*fig*) to move, persuade, seduce; (*bookkeeping*) to enter; (*dress*) to put on; (*public show*) to exhibit; (*writing*) to erase; **animum, in animum ~** determine, imagine.
inductiō, -ōnis *f* leading, bringing on; (*mind*) purpose, intention; (*logic*) induction.
inductus *ppp of* **indūcō**.
indugredior *etc see* **ingredior**.
induī *perf of* **induō**.
indulgēns, -entis *pres p of* **indulgeō** ♦ *adj* indulgent, kind.
indulgenter *adv* indulgently.
indulgentia, -ae *f* indulgence, gentleness.
indulgeō, -gēre, -sī *vi* (*with dat*) to be kind to, indulge, give way to; to indulge in ♦ *vt* to concede; **sibi ~** take liberties.
induō, -uere, -uī, -ūtum *vt* (*dress*) to put on; (*fig*) to assume, entangle.
indup- *etc see* **imp-**.
indūrēscō, -ēscere, -uī *vi* to harden.
indūrō, -āre *vt* to harden.
Indus, -ī *m* Indian; Ethiopian; mahout.
Indus *adj see n.*
industria, -ae *f* diligence; **dē, ex ~ā** on

purpose.
industriē adv see **industrius**.
industrius adj diligent, painstaking.
indūtiae, -ārum fpl truce, armistice.
indūtus ppp of **induō**.
indūtus, -us m wearing.
induviae, -ārum fpl clothes.
indūxī perf of **indūcō**.
inēbriō, -āre vt to intoxicate; (fig) to saturate.
inedia, -ae f starvation.
inēditus adj unpublished.
inēlegāns, -antis adj tasteless.
inēleganter adv without taste.
inēluctābilis adj inescapable.
inēmorior, -ī vi to die in.
inemptus adj unpurchased.
inēnārrābilis adj indescribable.
inēnōdābilis adj inexplicable.
ineō, -īre, -īvī and **iī, -itum** vi to go in, come in;
   to begin ♦ vt to enter; to begin, enter upon,
   form, undertake; **cōnsilium** ~ form a plan;
   grātiam ~ win favour; **numerum** ~
   enumerate; **ratiōnem** ~ calculate, consider,
   contrive; **suffrāgium** ~ vote; **viam** ~ find out a
   way.
ineptē adv see adj.
ineptia, -ae f stupidity; (pl) nonsense.
ineptiō, -īre vi to play the fool.
ineptus adj unsuitable; silly, tactless, absurd.
inermis, inermus adj unarmed, defenceless;
   harmless.
inerrāns, -antis adj fixed.
inerrō, -āre vi to wander about in.
iners, -tis adj unskilful; inactive, indolent,
   timid; insipid.
inertia, -ae f lack of skill; idleness, laziness.
inērudītus adj uneducated.
inēscō, -āre vt to entice, deceive.
inēvectus adj mounted.
inēvītābilis adj inescapable.
inexcītus adj peaceful.
inexcūsābilis adj with no excuse.
inexercitātus adj untrained.
inexhaustus adj unexhausted.
inexōrābilis adj inexorable; (things) severe.
inexperrēctus adj unawakened.
inexpertus adj inexperienced; untried.
inexpiābilis adj inexpiable; implacable.
inexplēbilis adj insatiable.
inexplētus adj incessant.
inexplicābilis adj inexplicable; impracticable,
   unending.
inexplōrātō adv without making a
   reconnaissance.
inexplōrātus adj unreconnoitred.
inexpugnābilis adj impregnable, safe.
inexspectātus adj unexpected.
inexstinctus adj unextinguished; insatiable,
   imperishable.
inexsuperābilis adj insurmountable.

inextrīcābilis adj inextricable.
īnfabrē adv unskilfully.
īnfabricātus adj unfashioned.
īnfacētus adj not witty, crude.
īnfācundus adj ineloquent.
īnfāmia, -ae f disgrace, scandal.
īnfāmis adj infamous, disreputable.
īnfāmō, -āre, -āvī, -ātum vt to disgrace,
   bring into disrepute.
īnfandus adj unspeakable, atrocious.
īnfāns, -antis adj mute, speechless; young,
   infant; tongue-tied; childish ♦ m/f infant,
   child.
īnfantia, -ae f inability to speak; infancy; lack
   of eloquence.
īnfatuō, -āre vt to make a fool of.
īnfaustus adj unlucky.
īnfector, -ōris m dyer.
īnfectus ppp of **īnficiō**.
īnfectus adj undone, unfinished; **rē ~ā** without
   achieving one's purpose.
īnfēcunditās, -ātis f infertility.
īnfēcundus adj unfruitful.
īnfēlīcitās, -ātis f misfortune.
īnfēlīciter adv see adj.
īnfēlīcō, -āre vt to make unhappy.
īnfēlīx, -īcis adj unfruitful; unhappy, unlucky.
īnfēnsē adv aggressively.
īnfēnsō, -āre vt to make dangerous, make
   hostile.
īnfēnsus adj hostile, dangerous.
īnferciō, -īre vt to cram in.
īnferiae, -ārum fpl offerings to the dead.
īnferior, -ōris compar of **īnferus**.
īnferius compar of **īnfrā**.
īnfernē adv below.
īnfernus adj beneath; of the lower world,
   infernal ♦ mpl the shades ♦ ntpl the lower
   world.
īnferō, -re, intulī, illātum vt to carry in,
   bring in, put on; to move forward; (fig) to
   introduce, cause; (book-keeping) to enter;
   (logic) to infer; **bellum** ~ make war (on);
   pedem ~ advance; **sē** ~ repair, rush, strut
   about; **signa** ~ attack, charge.
īnferus (compar ~**ior**, superl **īnfimus**) adj lower,
   below ♦ mpl the dead, the lower world ♦
   compar lower; later; inferior ♦ superl lowest,
   bottom of; meanest, humblest.
īnfervēscō, -vēscere, -buī vi to boil.
īnfestē adv aggressively.
īnfestō, -āre vt to attack.
īnfestus adj unsafe; dangerous, aggressive.
īnficēt- see **īnfacēt-**.
īnficiō, -icere, -ēcī, -ectum vt to dip, dye,
   discolour; to taint, infect; (fig) to instruct,
   corrupt, poison.
īnfidēlis adj faithless.
īnfidēlitās, -ātis f disloyalty.
īnfidēliter adv treacherously.

Noun declensions and verb conjugations are shown on pp xiii to xxv. The present infinitive ending of a verb shows
to which conjugation it belongs: **-āre** = 1st; **-ēre** = 2nd; **-ere** = 3rd and **-īre** = 4th. Irregular verbs are shown on p xxvi

infīdus *adj* unsafe, treacherous.
īnfīgō, -gere, -xī, -xum *vt* to thrust, drive in; (*fig*) to impress, imprint.
īnfimus *superl of* **īnferus.**
īnfindō, -ere *vt* to cut into, plough.
īnfinitās, -ātis *f* boundless extent, infinity.
īnfinītē *adv* without end.
īnfinitiō, -ōnis *f* infinity.
īnfinītus *adj* boundless, endless, infinite; indefinite.
īnfirmātiō, -ōnis *f* invalidating, refuting.
īnfirmē *adv* feebly.
īnfirmitās, -ātis *f* weakness; infirmity, sickness.
īnfirmō, -āre *vt* to weaken; to invalidate, refute.
īnfirmus *adj* weak, indisposed; weak-minded; (*things*) trivial.
īnfit *vi* (*defec*) begins.
īnfitiālis *adj* negative.
īnfitiās eō deny.
īnfitiātiō, -ōnis *f* denial.
īnfitiātor, -ōris *m* denier (of a debt).
īnfitior, -ārī, -ātus *vt* to deny, repudiate.
īnfixus *ppp of* **īnfīgō.**
īnflammātiō, -ōnis *f* (*fig*) exciting.
īnflammō, -āre, -āvī, -ātum *vt* to set on fire, light; (*fig*) to inflame, rouse.
īnflātē *adv* pompously.
īnflātiō, -ōnis *f* flatulence.
īnflātus, -ūs *m* blow; inspiration ♦ *adj* blown up, swollen; (*fig*) puffed up, conceited; (*style*) turgid.
īnflectō, -ctere, -xī, -xum *vt* to bend, curve; to change; (*voice*) to modulate; (*fig*) to affect, move.
īnflētus *adj* unwept.
īnflexiō, -ōnis *f* bending.
īnflexus *ppp of* **īnflectō.**
īnflīgō, -gere, -xī, -ctum *vt* to dash against, strike; to inflict.
īnflō, -āre, -āvī, -ātum *vt* to blow, inflate; (*fig*) to inspire, puff up.
īnfluō, -ere, -xī, -xum *vi* to flow in; (*fig*) to stream, pour in.
īnfodiō, -odere, -ōdī, -ossum *vt* to dig in, bury.
īnfōrmātiō, -ōnis *f* sketch, idea.
īnfōrmis *adj* shapeless; hideous.
īnfōrmō, -āre, -āvī, -ātum *vt* to shape, fashion; to sketch; to educate.
īnfortūnātus *adj* unfortunate.
īnfortūnium, -ī *and* **iī** *nt* misfortune.
īnfossus *ppp of* **īnfodiō.**
īnfrā (*compar* **īnferius**) *adv* underneath, below ♦ *compar* lower down ♦ *prep* (*with acc*) below, beneath, under; later than.
īnfrāctiō, -ōnis *f* weakening.
īnfrāctus *ppp of* **īnfringō.**
īnfragilis *adj* strong.
īnfremō, -ere, -uī *vi* to growl.
īnfrēnātus *ppp of* **īnfrēnō.**
īnfrēnātus *adj* without a bridle.

īnfrendō, -ere *vi* to gnash.
īnfrēnis, -us *adj* unbridled.
īnfrēnō, -āre, -āvī, -ātum *vt* to put a bridle on, harness; (*fig*) to curb.
īnfrequēns, -entis *adj* not crowded, infrequent; badly attended.
īnfrequentia, -ae *f* small number; emptiness.
īnfringō, -ingere, -ēgī, -āctum *vt* to break, bruise; (*fig*) to weaken, break down, exhaust.
īnfrōns, -ondis *adj* leafless.
īnfūcātus *adj* showy.
īnfula, -ae *f* woollen band, fillet, badge of honour.
īnfumus *etc see* **īnfimus.**
īnfundō, -undere, -ūdī, -ūsum *vt* to pour in *or* on; to serve; (*fig*) to spread.
īnfuscō, -āre *vt* to darken; to spoil, tarnish.
īnfūsus *ppp of* **īnfundō.**
ingeminō, -āre *vt* to redouble ♦ *vi* to be redoubled.
ingemīscō, -īscere, -uī *vi* to groan, sigh ♦ *vt* to sigh over.
ingemō, -ere, -uī *vt, vi* to sigh for, mourn.
ingenerō, -āre, -āvī, -ātum *vt* to engender, produce, create.
ingeniātus *adj* with a natural talent.
ingeniōsē *adv* cleverly.
ingeniōsus *adj* talented, clever; (*things*) naturally suited.
ingenitus *ppp of* **ingignō** ♦ *adj* inborn, natural.
ingenium, -ī *and* **iī** *nt* nature; (*disposition*) bent, character; (*intellect*) ability, talent, genius; (*person*) genius.
ingēns, -entis *adj* huge, mighty, great.
ingenuē *adv* liberally, frankly.
ingenuitās, -ātis *f* noble birth, noble character.
ingenuus *adj* native, innate; free-born; noble, frank; delicate.
ingerō, -rere, -ssī, -stum *vt* to carry in; to heap on; to throw, hurl; (*fig*) to press, obtrude.
ingignō, -ignere, -enuī, -enitum *vt* to engender, implant.
inglōrius *adj* inglorious.
ingluviēs, -ēī *f* maw; gluttony.
ingrātē *adv* unwillingly; ungratefully.
ingrātiīs, ingrātīs *adv* against one's will.
ingrātus *adj* disagreeable, unwelcome; ungrateful, thankless.
ingravēscō, -ere *vi* to grow heavy, become worse, increase.
ingravō, -āre *vt* to weigh heavily on; to aggravate.
ingredior, -dī, -ssus *vt, vi* to go in, enter; to walk, march; to enter upon, engage in; to commence, begin to speak.
ingressiō, -ōnis *f* entrance; beginning; pace.
ingressus, -ūs *m* entrance; (*MIL*) inroad; beginning; walking; gait.
ingruō, -ere, -ī *vi* to fall upon, assail.
inguen, -inis *nt* groin.
ingurgitō, -āre *vt* to pour in; **sē ~** gorge

oneself; (*fig*) to be absorbed in.
ingustātus *adj* untasted.
inhabilis *adj* unwieldy, awkward; unfit.
inhabitābilis *adj* uninhabitable.
inhabitō, -āre *vt* to inhabit.
inhaereō, -rēre, -sī, -sum *vi* to stick in, cling
  to; to adhere, be closely connected with; to
  be always in.
inhaerēscō, -ere *vi* to take hold, cling fast.
inhālō, -āre *vt* to breathe on.
inhibeō, -ēre, -uī, -itum *vt* to check, restrain,
  use, practise; ~ **rēmīs/nāvem** back water.
inhibitiō, -ōnis *f* backing water.
inhiō, -āre *vi* to gape ♦ *vt* to gape at, covet.
inhonestē *adv see adj.*
inhonestō, -āre *vt* to dishonour.
inhonestus *adj* dishonourable, inglorious;
  ugly.
inhonōrātus *adj* unhonoured; unrewarded.
inhonōrus *adj* defaced.
inhorreō, -ēre, -uī *vt* to stand erect, bristle.
inhorrēscō, -ēscere, -uī *vi* to bristle up; to
  shiver, shudder, tremble.
inhospitālis *adj* inhospitable.
inhospitālitās, -ātis *f* inhospitality.
inhospitus *adj* inhospitable.
inhūmānē *adv* savagely; uncivilly.
inhūmānitās, -ātis *f* barbarity; discourtesy,
  churlishness, meanness.
inhūmāniter *adv* = **inhūmānē.**
inhūmānus *adj* savage, brutal; ill-bred,
  uncivil, uncultured.
inhumātus *adj* unburied.
inibi *adv* there, therein; about to happen.
īniciō, -icere, -iēcī, -iectum *vt* to throw into,
  put on; (*fig*) to inspire, cause; (*speech*) to
  hint, mention; **manum** ~ take possession.
iniectus, -ūs *m* putting in, throwing over.
inimīcē *adv* hostilely.
inimīcitia, -ae *f* enmity.
inimīcō, -āre *vt* to make enemies.
inimīcus *adj* unfriendly, hostile; injurious ♦
  m/f enemy; **~issimus** greatest enemy.
inīquē *adv* unequally, unjustly.
inīquitās, -ātis *f* unevenness; difficulty;
  injustice, unfair demands.
inīquus *adj* unequal, uneven; adverse,
  unfavourable, injurious; unfair, unjust;
  excessive; impatient, discontented ♦ *m*
  enemy.
initiō, -āre *vt* to initiate.
initium, -ī and iī *nt* beginning; (*pl*) elements,
  first principles; holy rites, mysteries.
initus *ppp of* **ineō.**
initus, -ūs *m* approach; beginning.
iniūcundē *adv see adj.*
iniūcunditās, -ātis *f* unpleasantness.
iniūcundus *adj* unpleasant.
iniungō, -ungere, -ūnxī, -ūnctum *vt* to join,
  attach; (*fig*) to impose, inflict.

iniūrātus *adj* unsworn.
iniūria, -ae *f* wrong, injury, injustice; insult,
  outrage; severity, revenge; unjust
  possession; **~ā** unjustly.
iniūriōsē *adv* wrongfully.
iniūriōsus *adj* unjust, wrongful; harmful.
iniūrius *adj* wrong, unjust.
iniūssū without orders (from).
iniūssus *adj* unbidden.
iniūstē *adv see adj.*
iniūstitia, -ae *f* injustice, severity.
iniūstus *adj* unjust, wrong; excessive, severe.
inl- *etc see* **ill-.**
inm- *etc see* **imm-.**
innābilis *adj* that none may swim.
innāscor, -scī, -tus *vi* to be born in, grow up
  in.
innatō, -āre *vt* to swim in, float on; to swim,
  flow into.
innātus *ppa of* **innāscor** ♦ *adj* innate, natural.
innāvigābilis *adj* unnavigable.
innectō, -ctere, -xuī, -xum *vt* to tie, fasten
  together, entwine; (*fig*) to connect; to
  contrive.
innītor, -tī, -xus and sus *vi* to rest, lean on; to
  depend.
innō, -āre *vi* to swim in, float on, sail on.
innocēns, -entis *adj* harmless; innocent;
  upright, unselfish.
innocenter *adv* blamelessly.
innocentia, -ae *f* innocence; integrity,
  unselfishness.
innocuē *adv* innocently.
innocuus *adj* harmless; innocent; unharmed.
innōtēscō, -ēscere, -uī *vi* to become known.
innovō, -āre *vt* to renew; **sē** ~ return.
innoxius *adj* harmless, safe; innocent;
  unharmed.
innuba, -ae *adj* unmarried.
innūbilus *adj* cloudless.
innūbō, -bere, -psī *vi* to marry into.
innumerābilis *adj* countless.
innumerābilitās, -ātis *f* countless number.
innumerābiliter *adv* innumerably.
innumerālis *adj* numberless.
innumerus *adj* countless.
innuō, -ere, -ī *vi* to give a nod.
innūpta, -ae *adj* unmarried.
Īnō, -ūs *f* daughter of Cadmus.
inoblītus *adj* unforgetful.
inobrutus *adj* not overwhelmed.
inobservābilis *adj* unnoticed.
inobservātus *adj* unobserved.
inoffēnsus *adj* without hindrance,
  uninterrupted.
inofficiōsus *adj* irresponsible; disobliging.
inolēns, -entis *adj* odourless.
inolēscō, -scere, -vī *vi* to grow in.
inōminātus *adj* inauspicious.
inopia, -ae *f* want, scarcity, poverty,

Noun declensions and verb conjugations are shown on pp xiii to xxv. The present infinitive ending of a verb shows
to which conjugation it belongs: **-āre** = 1st; **-ēre** = 2nd; **-ere** = 3rd and **-īre** = 4th. Irregular verbs are shown on p xxvi

helplessness.
inopīnāns, -antis *adj* unaware.
inopīnātō *adv* unexpectedly.
inopīnātus *adj* unexpected; off one's guard.
inopīnus *adj* unexpected.
inopiōsus *adj* in want.
inops, -is *adj* destitute, poor, in need (of); helpless, weak; (*speech*) poor in ideas.
inōrātus *adj* unpleaded.
inōrdinātus *adj* disordered, irregular.
inōrnātus *adj* unadorned, plain; uncelebrated.
Īnōus *adj see* **n**.
inp- *etc see* **imp-**.
inquam *vt* (*defec*) to say; (*emphatic*) I repeat, maintain.
inquiēs, -ētis *adj* restless.
inquiētō, -āre *vt* to unsettle, make difficult.
inquiētus *adj* restless, unsettled.
inquilīnus, -ī *m* inhabitant, tenant.
inquinātē *adv* filthily.
inquinātus *adj* filthy, impure.
inquinō, -āre, -āvī, -ātum *vt* to defile, stain, contaminate.
inquīrō, -rere, -sīvī, -sītum *vt* to search for, inquire into; (*law*) to collect evidence.
inquīsītiō, -ōnis *f* searching, inquiry; (*law*) inquisition.
inquīsītor, -ōris *m* searcher, spy; investigator.
inquīsītus *ppp of* **inquīrō**.
inquīsītus *adj* not investigated.
inr- *etc see* **irr-**.
īnsalūtātus *adj* ungreeted.
īnsānābilis *adj* incurable.
īnsānē *adv* madly.
īnsānia, -ae *f* madness; folly, mania, poetic rapture.
īnsāniō, -īre, -īvī, -ītum *vi* to be mad, rave; to rage; to be inspired.
īnsānitās, -ātis *f* unhealthiness.
īnsānum *adv* (*slang*) frightfully.
īnsānus *adj* mad; frantic, furious; outrageous.
īnsatiābilis *adj* insatiable; never cloying.
īnsatiābiliter *adv see* **adj**.
īnsatietās, -ātis *f* insatiateness.
īnsaturābilis *adj* insatiable.
īnsaturābiliter *adv see* **adj**.
īnscendō, -endere, -endī, -ēnsum *vt, vi* to climb up, mount, embark.
īnscēnsiō, -ōnis *f* going on board.
īnscēnsus *ppp of* **īnscendō**.
īnsciēns, -entis *adj* unaware; stupid.
īnscienter *adv* ignorantly.
īnscientia, -ae *f* ignorance, inexperience; neglect.
īnscītē *adv* clumsily.
īnscītia, -ae *f* ignorance, stupidity, inattention.
īnscītus *adj* ignorant, stupid.
īnscius *adj* unaware, ignorant.
īnscrībō, -bere, -psī, -ptum *vt* to write on, inscribe; to ascribe, assign; (*book*) to entitle; (*for sale*) to advertise.

īnscrīptiō, -ōnis *f* inscribing, title.
īnscrīptus *ppp of* **īnscrībō**.
īnsculpō, -ere, -sī, -tum *vt* to carve in, engrave on.
īnsectātiō, -ōnis *f* hot pursuit; (*words*) abusing, persecution.
īnsectātor, -ōris *m* persecutor.
īnsector, -ārī, -ātus; -ō, -āre *vt* to pursue, attack, criticise.
īnsectus *adj* notched.
īnsēdābiliter *adv* incessantly.
īnsēdī *perf of* **īnsīdō**.
īnsenēscō, -ēscere, -uī *vi* to grow old in.
īnsēnsilis *adj* imperceptible.
īnsepultus *adj* unburied.
īnsequēns, -entis *pres p of* **īnsequor** ♦ *adj* the following.
īnsequor, -quī, -cūtus *vt* to follow, pursue hotly; to proceed; (*time*) to come after, come next; (*fig*) to attack, persecute.
īnserō, -erere, -ēvī, -itum *vt* to graft; (*fig*) to implant.
īnserō, -ere, -uī, -tum *vt* to let in, insert; to introduce, mingle, involve.
īnsertō, -āre *vt* to put in.
īnsertus *ppp of* **īnserō**.
īnserviō, -īre, -iī, -ītum *vt, vi* to be a slave (to); to be devoted, submissive (to).
īnsessus *ppp of* **īnsīdō**.
īnsībilō, -āre *vi* to whistle in.
īnsideō, -ēre *vi* to sit on or in; to remain fixed ♦ *vt* to hold, occupy.
īnsidiae, -ārum *fpl* ambush; (*fig*) trap, trickery.
īnsidiātor, -ōris *nt* soldier in ambush; (*fig*) waylayer, plotter.
īnsidior, -ārī, -ātus *vi* to lie in ambush; (*with dat*) to lie in wait for, plot against.
īnsidiōsē *adv* insidiously.
īnsidiōsus *adj* artful, treacherous.
īnsīdō, -īdere, -ēdī, -essum *vi* to settle on; (*fig*) to become fixed, rooted in ♦ *vt* to occupy.
īnsigne, -is *nt* distinguishing mark, badge, decoration; (*pl*) insignia, honours; (*speech*) purple passages.
īnsigniō, -īre *vt* to distinguish.
īnsignis *adj* distinguished, conspicuous.
īnsignītē *adv* remarkably.
īnsignīter *adv* markedly.
īnsilia, -um *ntpl* treadle (of a loom).
īnsiliō, -īre, -uī *vi* to jump into or onto.
īnsimulātiō, -ōnis *f* accusation.
īnsimulō, -āre, -āvī, -ātum *vt* to charge, accuse, allege (*esp falsely*).
īnsincērus *adj* adulterated.
īnsinuātiō, -ōnis *f* ingratiating.
īnsinuō, -āre, -āvī, -ātum *vt* to bring in, introduce stealthily ♦ *vi* to creep in, worm one's way in, penetrate; **sē ~** ingratiate oneself; to make one's way into.
īnsipiēns, -entis *adj* senseless, foolish.
īnsipienter *adv* foolishly.

īnsipientia, -ae *f* folly.

īnsistō, -istere, -titī *vi* to stand on, step on; to stand firm, halt, pause; to tread on the heels, press on, pursue; to enter upon, apply oneself to, begin; to persist, continue.

īnsitiō, -ōnis *f* grafting; grafting time.

īnsitīvus *adj* grafted; (*fig*) spurious.

īnsitor, -ōris *m* grafter.

īnsitus *ppp of* **īnserō ♦** *adj* innate; incorporated.

īnsociābilis *adj* incompatible.

īnsōlābiliter *adv* unconsolably.

īnsolēns, -entis *adj* unusual, unaccustomed; excessive, extravagant, insolent.

īnsolenter *adv* unusually; immoderately, insolently.

īnsolentia, -ae *f* inexperience, novelty, strangeness; excess, insolence.

īnsolēscō, -ere *vi* to become insolent, elated.

īnsolidus *adj* soft.

īnsolitus *adj* unaccustomed, unusual.

īnsomnia, -ae *f* sleeplessness.

īnsomnis *adj* sleepless.

īnsomnium, -ī *and* **iī** *nt* dream.

īnsonō, -āre, -uī *vi* to resound, sound; to make a noise.

īnsōns, -ontis *adj* innocent; harmless.

īnsōpītus *adj* sleepless.

īnspectō, -āre *vt* to look at.

īnspectus *ppp of* **īnspiciō**.

īnspērāns, -antis *adj* not expecting.

īnspērātus *adj* unexpected; ~ō, ex ~ō unexpectedly.

īnspergō, -gere, -sī, -sum *vt* to sprinkle on.

īnspiciō, -icere, -exī, -ectum *vt* to look into; to examine, inspect; (*MIL*) to review; (*mind*) to consider, get to know.

īnspīcō, -āre *vt* to sharpen.

īnspīrō, -āre, -āvī, -ātum *vt, vi* to blow on, breathe into.

īnspoliātus *adj* unpillaged.

īnspūtō, -āre *vt* to spit on.

īnstābilis *adj* unsteady, not firm; (*fig*) inconstant.

īnstāns, -antis *pres p of* **īnstō ♦** *adj* present; urgent, threatening.

īnstanter *adv* vehemently.

īnstantia, -ae *f* presence; vehemence.

īnstar *nt* (*indecl*) likeness, appearance; as good as, worth.

īnstaurātiō, -ōnis *f* renewal.

īnstaurātīvus *adj* renewed.

īnstaurō, -āre, -āvī, -ātum *vt* to renew, restore; to celebrate; to requite.

īnsternō, -ernere, -rāvī, -rātum *vt* to spread over, cover.

īnstīgātor, -ōris *m* instigator.

īnstīgātrīx, -rīcis *f* female instigator.

īnstīgō, -āre *vt* to goad, incite, instigate.

īnstillō, -āre *vt* to drop on, instil.

īnstimulātor, -ōris *m* instigator.

īnstimulō, -āre *vt* to urge on.

īnstinctor, -ōris *m* instigator.

īnstinctus *adj* incited, inspired.

īnstinctus, -ūs *m* impulse, inspiration.

īnstipulor, -ārī, -ātus *vi* to bargain for.

īnstita, -ae *f* flounce of a lady's tunic.

īnstitī *perf of* **īnsistō**.

īnstitiō, -ōnis *f* stopping.

īnstitor, -ōris *m* pedlar.

īnstituō, -uere, -uī, -ūtum *vt* to set, implant; to set up, establish, build, appoint; to marshal, arrange, organize; to teach, educate; to undertake, resolve on.

īnstitūtiō, -ōnis *f* custom; arrangement; education; (*pl*) principles of education.

īnstitūtum, -ī *nt* way of life, tradition, law; stipulation, agreement; purpose; (*pl*) principles.

īnstō, -āre, -itī *vi* to stand on or in; to be close, be hard on the heels of, pursue; (*events*) to approach, impend; (*fig*) to press on, work hard at; (*speech*) to insist, urge.

īnstrātus *ppp of* **īnsternō**.

īnstrēnuus *adj* languid, slow.

īnstrepō, -ere *vi* to creak.

īnstructiō, -ōnis *f* building; setting out.

īnstructius *adv* in better style.

īnstructor, -ōris *m* preparer.

īnstructus *ppp of* **īnstruō ♦** *adj* provided, equipped; prepared, versed.

īnstructus, -ūs *m* equipment.

īnstrūmentum, -ī *nt* tool, instrument; equipment, furniture, stock; (*fig*) means, provision; dress, embellishment.

īnstruō, -ere, -xī, -ctum *vt* to erect, build up; (*MIL*) to marshal, array; to equip, provide, prepare; (*fig*) to teach, train.

īnsuāsum, -ī *nt* a dark colour.

īnsuāvis *adj* disagreeable.

īnsūdō, -āre *vi* to perspire on.

īnsuēfactus *adj* accustomed.

īnsuēscō, -scere, -vī, -tum *vt* to train, accustom ♦ *vi* to become accustomed.

īnsuētus *ppp of* **īnsuēscō**.

īnsuētus *adj* unaccustomed, unused; unusual.

īnsula, -ae *f* island; block of houses.

īnsulānus, -ī *m* islander.

īnsulsē *adv see adj*.

īnsulsitās, -ātis *f* lack of taste, absurdity.

īnsulsus *adj* tasteless, absurd, dull.

īnsultō, -āre, -vt, vi to jump on, leap in; (*fig*) to exult, taunt, insult.

īnsultūra, -ae *f* jumping on.

īnsum, inesse, īnfuī *vi* to be in *or* on; to belong to.

īnsūmō, -ere, -psī, -ptum *vt* to spend, devote.

īnsuō, -uere, -uī, -ūtum *vt* to sew in, sew up in.

Noun declensions and verb conjugations are shown on pp xiii to xxv. The present infinitive ending of a verb shows to which conjugation it belongs: **-āre** = 1st; **-ēre** = 2nd; **-ere** = 3rd and **-īre** = 4th. Irregular verbs are shown on p xxvi

īnsuper *adv* above, on top; besides, over and above; (*prep with abl*) besides.
īnsuperābilis *adj* unconquerable, impassable.
īnsurgō, -gere, -rēxī, -rēctum *vi* to stand up, rise to; to rise, grow, swell; to rise against.
īnsusurrō, -āre *vt, vi* to whisper.
īnsūtus *ppp of* **īnsuō**.
intābēscō, -ēscere, -uī *vi* to melt away, waste away.
intāctilis *adj* intangible.
intāctus *adj* untouched, intact; untried; undefiled, chaste.
intāminātus *adj* unsullied.
intēctus *ppp of* **integō**.
intēctus *adj* uncovered, unclad; frank.
integellus *adj* fairly whole *or* pure.
integer, -rī *adj* whole, complete, unimpaired, intact; sound, fresh, new; (*mind*) unbiassed, free; (*character*) virtuous, pure, upright; (*decision*) undecided, open; **in ~rum restituere** restore to a former state; **ab, dē, ex ~rō** afresh; **~rum est mihi** I am at liberty (to).
integō, -egere, -ēxī, -ēctum *vt* to cover over; to protect.
integrāscō, -ere *vi* to begin all over again.
integrātiō, -ōnis *f* renewing.
integrē *adv* entirely; honestly; correctly.
integritās, -ātis *f* completeness, soundness; integrity, honesty; (*language*) correctness.
integrō, -āre *vt* to renew, replenish, repair; (*mind*) to refresh.
integumentum, -ī *nt* cover, covering, shelter.
intellēctus *ppp of* **intellegō**.
intellēctus, -ūs *m* understanding; (*word*) meaning.
intellegēns, -entis *pres p of* **intellegō** ♦ *adj* intelligent, a connoisseur.
intellegenter *adv* intelligently.
intellegentia, -ae *f* discernment, understanding; taste.
intellegō, -egere, -ēxī, -ēctum *vt* to understand, perceive, realize; to be a connoisseur.
intemerātus *adj* pure, undefiled.
intemperāns, -antis *adj* immoderate, extravagant; incontinent.
intemperanter *adv* extravagantly.
intemperantia, -ae *f* excess, extravagance; arrogance.
intemperātē *adv* dissolutely.
intemperātus *adj* excessive.
intemperiae, -ārum *fpl* inclemency; madness.
intemperiēs, -ēī *f* inclemency, storm; (*fig*) fury.
intempestīvē *adv* inopportunely.
intempestīvus *adj* unseasonable, untimely.
intempestus *adj* (*night*) the dead of; unhealthy.
intemptātus *adj* untried.
intendō, -dere, -dī, -tum *vt* to stretch out, strain, spread; (*weapon*) to aim; (*tent*) to pitch; (*attention, course*) to direct, turn; (*fact*) to increase, exaggerate; (*speech*) to maintain; (*trouble*) to threaten ♦ *vi* to make for, intend; **animō ~** purpose; **sē ~** exert oneself.
intentē *adv* strictly.
intentiō, -ōnis *f* straining, tension; (*mind*) exertion, attention; (*law*) accusation.
intentō, -āre *vt* to stretch out, aim; (*fig*) to threaten with, attack.
intentus *ppp of* **intendō** ♦ *adj* taut; attentive, intent; strict; (*speech*) vigorous.
intentus, -ūs *m* stretching out.
intepeō, -ēre *vi* to be warm.
intepēscō, -ēscere, -uī *vi* to be warmed.
inter *prep* (*with acc*) between, among, during, in the course of; in spite of; **~ haec** meanwhile; **~ manūs** within reach; **~ nōs** confidentially; **~ sē** mutually, one another; **~ sīcāriōs** in the murder court; **~ viam** on the way.
interāmenta, -ōrum *ntpl* ship's timbers.
interaptus *adj* joined together.
interārēscō, -ere *vi* to wither away.
interbibō, -ere *vi* to drink up.
interbītō, -ere *vi* to fall through.
intercalāris *adj* intercalary.
intercalārius *adj* intercalary.
intercalō, -āre *vt* to intercalate.
intercapēdō, -inis *f* interruption, respite.
intercēdō, -ēdere, -ēssī, -ēssum *vi* to come between, intervene; to occur; to become surety; to interfere, obstruct; (*tribune*) to protest, veto.
interceptiō, -ōnis *f* taking away.
interceptor, -ōris *m* embezzler.
interceptus *ppp of* **intercipiō**.
intercēssiō, -ōnis *f* (*law*) becoming surety; (*tribune*) veto.
intercēssor, -ōris *m* mediator, surety; interposer of the veto; obstructor.
intercīdō, -ere, -ī *vi* to fall short; to happen in the meantime; to get lost, become obsolete, be forgotten.
intercīdō, -dere, -dī, -sum *vt* to cut through, sever.
intercinō, -ere *vt* to sing between.
intercipiō, -ipere, -ēpi, -eptum *vt* to intercept; to embezzle, steal; to cut off, obstruct.
intercīsē *adv* piecemeal.
intercīsus *ppp of* **intercīdō**.
interclūdō, -dere, -sī, -sum *vt* to cut off, block, shut off, prevent; **animam ~** suffocate.
interclūsiō, -ōnis *f* stoppage.
interclūsus *ppp of* **interclūdō**.
intercolumnium, -ī *and* **iī** *nt* space between two pillars.
intercurrō, -ere *vi* to mingle with; to intercede; to hurry in the meantime.
intercursō, -āre *vi* to crisscross; to attack

between the lines.
intercursus, -ūs *m* intervention.
intercus, -tis *adj*: **aqua ~** dropsy.
interdīcō, -īcere, -īxī, -ictum *vt, vi* to forbid, interdict; (*praetor*) to make a provisional order; **aquā et ignī ~** banish.
interdictiō, -ōnis *f* prohibiting, banishment.
interdictum, -ī *nt* prohibition; provisional order (by a praetor).
interdiū *adv* by day.
interdō, -are *vt* to make at intervals; to distribute; **nōn ~uim** I wouldn't care.
interductus, -ūs *m* punctuation.
interdum *adv* now and then, occasionally.
intereā *adv* meanwhile, in the meantime; nevertheless.
interēmī *perf of* **interimō**.
interemptus *ppp of* **interimō**.
intereō, -īre, -iī, -itum *vi* to be lost, perish, die.
interequitō, -āre *vt, vi* to ride between.
interesse *infin of* **intersum**.
interfātiō, -ōnis *f* interruption.
interfātur, -ārī, -ātus *vi* to interrupt.
interfectiō, -ōnis *f* killing.
interfector, -ōris *m* murderer.
interfectrīx, -rīcis *f* murderess.
interfectus *ppp of* **interficiō**.
interficiō, -icere, -ēcī, -ectum *vt* to kill, destroy.
interfīō, -ierī *vi* to pass away.
interfluō, -ere, -xī *vt, vi* to flow between.
interfodiō, -ere *vt* to pierce.
interfugiō, -ere *vi* to flee among.
interfuī *perf of* **intersum**.
interfulgeō, -ēre *vi* to shine amongst.
interfūsus *ppp* lying between; marked here and there.
interiaceō, -ēre *vi* to lie between.
interibi *adv* in the meantime.
intericiō, -icere, -iēcī, -iectum *vt* to put amongst or between, interpose, mingle; **annō ~iectō** after a year.
interiectus, -ūs *m* coming in between; interval.
interiī *perf of* **intereō**.
interim *adv* meanwhile, in the meantime; sometimes; all the same.
interimō, -imere, -ēmī, -emptum *vt* to abolish, destroy, kill.
interior, -ōris *adj* inner, interior; nearer, on the near side; secret, private; more intimate, more profound.
interitiō, -ōnis *f* ruin.
interitus, -ūs *m* destruction, ruin, death.
interiūnctus *adj* joined together.
interius *adv* inwardly; too short.
interlābor, -ī *vi* to glide between.
interlegō, -ere *vt* to pick here and there.
interlinō, -inere, -ēvī, -itum *vt* to smear in

parts; to erase here and there.
interloquor, -quī, -cūtus *vi* to interrupt.
interlūceō, -cēre, -xī *vi* to shine through, be clearly seen.
interlūnia, -ōrum *ntpl* new moon.
interluō, -ere *vt* to wash, flow between.
intermēnstruus *adj* of the new moon ♦ *nt* new moon.
interminātus *ppa of* **interminor** ♦ *adj* forbidden.
interminātus *adj* endless.
interminor, -ārī, -ātus *vi* to threaten; to forbid threateningly.
intermisceō, -scēre, -scuī, -xtum *vt* to mix, intermingle.
intermissiō, -ōnis *f* interruption.
intermittō, -ittere, -īsī, -issum *vt* to break off; to interrupt; to omit, neglect; to allow to elapse ♦ *vi* to cease, pause.
intermixtus *ppp of* **intermisceō**.
intermorior, -ī, -tuus *vi* to die suddenly.
intermortuus *adj* falling unconscious.
intermundia, -ōrum *ntpl* space between worlds.
intermūrālis *adj* between two walls.
internātus *adj* growing among.
internecīnus *adj* murderous, of extermination.
interneciō, -ōnis *f* massacre, extermination.
internecīvus *adj* = **internecīnus**.
internectō, -ere *vt* to enclasp.
internōdia, -ōrum *ntpl* space between joints.
internōscō, -scere, -vī, -tum *vt* to distinguish between.
internūntia, -iae *f* messenger, mediator, go-between.
internūntiō, -āre *vi* to exchange messages.
internūntius, -ī *and* **iī** *m* messenger, mediator, go-between.
internus *adj* internal, civil ♦ *ntpl* domestic affairs.
interō, -erere, -rīvī, -rītum *vt* to rub in; (*fig*) to concoct.
interpellātiō, -ōnis *f* interruption.
interpellātor, -ōris *m* interrupter.
interpellō, -āre, -āvī, -ātum *vt* to interrupt; to disturb, obstruct.
interpolis *adj* made up.
interpolō, -āre *vt* to renovate, do up; (*writing*) to falsify.
interpōnō, -ōnere, -osuī, -ositum *vt* to put between *or* amongst, insert; (*time*) to allow to elapse; (*person*) to introduce, admit; (*pretext etc*) to put forward, interpose; **fidem ~** pledge one's word; **sē ~** interfere, become involved.
interpositiō, -ōnis *f* introduction.
interpositus *ppp of* **interpōnō**.
interpositus, -ūs *m* obstruction.
interpres, -tis *m/f* agent, negotiator;

Noun declensions and verb conjugations are shown on pp xiii to xxv. The present infinitive ending of a verb shows to which conjugation it belongs: **-āre** = 1st; **-ēre** = 2nd; **-ere** = 3rd and **-īre** = 4th. Irregular verbs are shown on p xxvi

interpreter, explainer, translator.
interpretātiō, -ōnis _f_ interpretation, exposition, meaning.
interpretātus _adj_ translated.
interpretor, -ārī, -ātus _vt_ to interpret, explain, translate, understand.
interprimō, -imere, -essī, -essum _vt_ to squeeze.
interpūnctiō, -ōnis _f_ punctuation.
interpūnctus _adj_ well-divided ♦ _ntpl_ punctuation.
interquiēscō, -scere, -vī _vi_ to rest awhile.
interrēgnum, -ī _nt_ regency, interregnum; interval between consuls.
interrēx, -ēgis _m_ regent; deputy consul.
interritus _adj_ undaunted, unafraid.
interrogātiō, -ōnis _f_ question; (_law_) cross-examination; (_logic_) syllogism.
interrogātiuncula, -ae _f_ short argument.
interrogō, -āre, -āvī, -ātum _vt_ to ask, put a question; (_law_) to cross-examine, bring to trial.
interrumpō, -umpere, -ūpī, -uptum _vt_ to break up, sever; (_fig_) to break off, interrupt.
interruptē _adv_ interruptedly.
intersaepiō, -īre, -sī, -tum _vt_ to shut off, close.
interscindō, -ndere, -dī, -ssum _vt_ to cut off, break down.
interserō, -erere, -ēvī, -itum _vt_ to plant at intervals.
interserō, -ere, -uī, -tum _vt_ to interpose.
intersitus _ppp of_ **interserō**.
interspīrātiō, -ōnis _f_ pause for breath.
interstinguō, -guere, -ctum _vt_ to mark, spot; to extinguish.
interstringō, -ere _vt_ to strangle.
intersum, -esse, -fuī _vi_ to be between; to be amongst, be present at; (_time_) to elapse; ~est there is a difference; it is of importance, it concerns, it matters; **meā ~est** it is important for me.
intertextus _adj_ interwoven.
intertrahō, -here, -xī _vt_ to take away.
intertrīmentum, -ī _nt_ wastage; loss, damage.
interturbātiō, -ōnis _f_ confusion.
intervallum, -ī _nt_ space, distance, interval; (_time_) pause, interval, respite; difference.
intervellō, -ere _vt_ to pluck out; to tear apart.
interveniō, -enīre, -ēnī, -entum _vi_ to come on the scene, intervene; to interfere (with), interrupt; to happen, occur.
interventor, -ōris _m_ intruder.
interventus, -ūs _m_ appearance, intervention; occurrence.
intervertō, -tere, -tī, -sum _vt_ to embezzle; to rob, cheat.
intervīsō, -ere, -ī, -um _vt_ to have a look at, look and see; to visit occasionally.
intervolitō, -āre _vi_ to fly about, amongst.
intervomō, -ere _vt_ to throw up (amongst).
intervortō _vt see_ **intervertō**.
intestābilis _adj_ infamous, wicked.

intestātō _adv_ without making a will.
intestātus _adj_ intestate; not convicted by witnesses.
intestīnus _adj_ internal ♦ _nt and ntpl_ intestines, entrails.
intexō, -ere, -uī, -tum _vt_ to inweave, embroider, interlace.
intibum, -ī _nt_ endive.
intimē _adv_ most intimately, cordially.
intimus _adj_ innermost; deepest, secret; intimate ♦ _m_ most intimate friend.
intingō (intinguō), -gere, -xī, -ctum _vt_ to dip in.
intolerābilis _adj_ unbearable; irresistible.
intolerandus _adj_ intolerable.
intolerāns, -antis _adj_ impatient; unbearable.
intoleranter _adv_ excessively.
intolerantia, -ae _f_ insolence.
intonō, -āre, -uī, -ātum _vi_ to thunder, thunder out.
intōnsus _adj_ unshorn, unshaven; long-haired, bearded; uncouth.
intorqueō, -quēre, -sī, -tum _vt_ to twist, wrap round; to hurl at.
intortus _ppp of_ **intorqueō** ♦ _adj_ twisted, curled; confused.
intrā _adv_ inside, within ♦ _prep_ (_with acc_) inside, within; (_time_) within, during; (_amount_) less than, within the limits of.
intrābilis _adj_ navigable.
intractābilis _adj_ formidable.
intractātus _adj_ not broken in; unattempted.
intremīscō, -īscere, -uī _vi_ to begin to shake.
intremō, -ere _vi_ to tremble.
intrepidē _adv see adj_.
intrepidus _adj_ calm, brave; undisturbed.
intrīcō, -āre _vt_ to entangle.
intrīnsecus _adv_ on the inside.
intrītus _adj_ not worn out.
intrīvī _perf of_ **interō**.
intrō _adv_ inside, in.
intrō, -āre, -āvī, -ātum _vt, vi_ to go in, enter; to penetrate.
intrōdūcō, -ūcere, -ūxī, -uctum _vt_ to bring in, introduce, escort in; to institute.
intrōductiō, -ōnis _f_ bringing in.
intrōeō, -īre, -iī, -itum _vi_ to go into, enter.
intrōferō, -ferre, -tulī, -lātum _vt_ to carry inside.
intrōgredior, -dī, -ssus _vi_ to step inside.
intrōitus, -ūs _m_ entrance; beginning.
intrōlātus _ppp of_ **intrōferō**.
intrōmittō, -ittere, -īsī, -issus _vt_ to let in, admit.
intrōrsum, intrōrsus _adv_ inwards, inside.
intrōrumpō, -ere _vi_ to break into.
intrōspectō, -āre _vt_ to look in at.
intrōspiciō, -icere, -exī, -ectum _vt_ to look inside; to look at, examine.
intubum _etc see_ **intibum**.
intueor, -ērī, -itus _vt_ to look at, watch; to contemplate, consider; to admire.
intumēscō, -ēscere, -uī _vi_ to begin to swell,

rise; to increase; to become angry.

intumulātus *adj* unburied.

intuor *etc see* **intueor.**

inturbidus *adj* undisturbed; quiet.

intus *adv* inside, within, in; from within.

intūtus *adj* unsafe; unguarded.

inula, -ae *f* elecampane.

inultus *adj* unavenged; unpunished.

inumbrō, -āre *vt* to shade; to cover.

inundō, -āre, -āvī, -ātum *vt, vi* to overflow, flood.

inunguō, -unguere, -ūnxī, -ūnctum *vt* to anoint.

inurbānē *adv see adj.*

inurbānus *adj* rustic, unmannerly, unpolished.

inurgeō, -ēre *vi* to push, butt.

inūrō, -rere, -ssī, -stum *vt* to brand; (*fig*) to brand, inflict.

inūsitātē *adv* strangely.

inūsitātus *adj* unusual, extraordinary.

inūstus *ppp of* **inūrō.**

inūtilis *adj* useless; harmful.

inūtilitās, -ātis *f* uselessness, harmfulness.

inūtiliter *adv* unprofitably.

invādō, -dere, -sī, -sum *vt, vi* to get in, make one's way in; to enter upon; to fall upon, attack, invade; to seize, take possession of.

invalēscō, -ēscere, -uī *vi* to grow stronger.

invalidus *adj* weak; inadequate.

invāsī *perf of* **invādō.**

invectiō, -ōnis *f* importing; invective.

invectus *ppp of* **invehō.**

invehō, -here, -xī, -ctum *vt* to carry in, bring in; **sē ~** attack.

invehor, -hī, -ctus *vi* to ride, drive, sail in or into, enter; to attack; to inveigh against.

invēndibilis *adj* unsaleable.

inveniō, -enīre, -ēnī, -entum *vt* to find, come upon; to find out, discover; to invent, contrive; to win, get.

inventiō, -ōnis *f* invention; (*RHET*) compiling the subject-matter.

inventor, -ōris *m* inventor, discoverer.

inventrīx, -rīcis *f* inventor, discoverer.

inventus *ppp of* **inveniō** ♦ *nt* invention, discovery.

invenustus *adj* unattractive; unlucky in love.

inverēcundus *adj* immodest, shameless.

invergō, -ere *vt* to pour upon.

inversiō, -ōnis *f* transposition; irony.

inversus *ppp of* **invertō** ♦ *adj* upside down, inside out; perverted.

invertō, -tere, -tī, -sum *vt* to turn over, invert; to change, pervert.

invesperāscit, -ere *vi* it is dusk.

investīgātiō, -ōnis *f* search.

investīgātor, -ōris *m* investigator.

investīgō, -āre, -āvī, -ātum *vt* to follow the trail of; (*fig*) to track down, find out.

inveterāscō, -scere, -vī *vi* to grow old (in); to become established, fixed, inveterate; to grow obsolete.

inveterātiō, -ōnis *f* chronic illness.

inveterātus *adj* of long standing, inveterate.

invexī *perf of* **invehō.**

invicem *adv* in turns, alternately; mutually, each other.

invictus *adj* unbeaten; unconquerable.

invidentia, -ae *f* envy.

invideō, -idēre, -īdī, -īsum *vt, vi* to cast an evil eye on; (*with dat*) to envy, grudge; to begrudge.

invidia, -ae *f* envy, jealousy, ill-will; unpopularity.

invidiōsē *adv* spitefully.

invidiōsus *adj* envious, spiteful; enviable; invidious, hateful.

invidus *adj* envious, jealous, hostile.

invigilō, -āre *vi* to be awake over; to watch over, be intent on.

inviolābilis *adj* invulnerable; inviolable.

inviolātē *adv* inviolately.

inviolātus *adj* unhurt; inviolable.

invīsitātus *adj* unseen, unknown, strange.

invīsō, -ere, -ī, -um *vt* to go and see, visit, have a look at; to inspect.

invīsus *adj* hateful, detested; hostile.

invīsus *adj* unseen.

invītāmentum, -ī *nt* attraction, inducement.

invītātiō, -ōnis *f* invitation; entertainment.

invītātus, -ūs *m* invitation.

invītē *adv* unwillingly.

invītō, -āre, -āvī, -ātum *vt* to invite; to treat, entertain; to summon; to attract, induce.

invītus *adj* against one's will, reluctant.

invius *adj* trackless, impassable; inaccessible.

invocātus *ppp of* **invocō.**

invocātus *adj* unbidden, uninvited.

invocō, -āre, -āvī, -ātum *vt* to call upon, invoke; to appeal to; to call.

involātus, -ūs *m* flight.

involitō, -āre *vi* to play upon.

involō, -āre *vi* to fly at, pounce on, attack.

involūcre, -is *nt* napkin.

involūcrum, -ī *nt* covering, case.

involūtus *ppp of* **involvō** ♦ *adj* complicated.

involvō, -vere, -vī, -ūtum *vt* to roll on; to wrap up, envelop, entangle.

involvolus, -ī *m* caterpillar.

invulnerātus *adj* unwounded.

iō *interj* (*joy*) hurrah!; (*pain*) oh!; (*calling*) ho there!

Iōannēs, -is *m* John.

iocātiō, -ōnis *f* joke.

iocor, -ārī, -ātus *vt, vi* to joke, jest.

iocōsē *adv* jestingly.

iocōsus *adj* humorous, playful.

ioculāris *adj* laughable, funny ♦ *ntpl* jokes.

ioculārius *adj* ludicrous.

Noun declensions and verb conjugations are shown on pp xiii to xxv. The present infinitive ending of a verb shows to which conjugation it belongs: **-āre** = 1st; **-ēre** = 2nd; **-ere** = 3rd and **-īre** = 4th. Irregular verbs are shown on p xxvi

ioculātor, -ōris _m_ jester.
ioculor, -ārī _vi_ to joke.
ioculus, -ī _m_ a bit of fun.
iocus, -ī _m_ (_pl_ **-a, -ōrum** _nt_) joke, jest; **extrā**
~**um** joking apart; **per** ~**um** for fun.
Iōnes, -um _mpl_ Ionians.
Iōnia, -iae _f_ Ionia, coastal district of Asia Minor.
Iōnium, -ī _nt_ Ionian Sea, W. of Greece.
Iōnius, -icus _adj_ Ionian.
iōta _nt_ (_indecl_) Greek letter I.
Iovis _gen of_ **Iuppiter**.
Īphianasse, -ae _f_ Iphigenia.
Īphigenīa, -ae _f_ daughter of Agamemnon
(_who sacrificed her at Aulis to Diana_).
ipse, -a, -um, -īus _prep_ self, himself _etc_; in
person, for one's own part, of one's own
accord, by oneself; just, precisely, very; the
master, the host.
ipsissimus his very own self; **nunc ~um** right
now.
īra, -ae _f_ anger, rage; object of indignation.
īrācundē _adv_ angrily.
īrācundia, -ae _f_ irascibility, quick temper;
rage, resentment.
īrācundus _adj_ irascible, choleric; resentful.
īrāscor, -ī _vi_ to be angry, get furious.
īrātē _adv see adj._
īrātus _adj_ angry, furious.
īre _infin of_ **eō**.
Īris, -dis (_acc_ **-m**) _f_ messenger of the gods; the
rainbow.
īrōnīa, -ae _f_ irony.
irrāsus _adj_ unshaven.
irraucēscō, -cēscere, -sī _vi_ to become hoarse.
irredivīvus _adj_ irreparable.
irreligātus _adj_ not tied.
irreligiōsē _adv see adj._
irreligiōsus _adj_ impious.
irremeābilis _adj_ from which there is no
returning.
irreparābilis _adj_ irretrievable.
irrepertus _adj_ undiscovered.
irrēpō, -ere, -sī _vi_ to steal into, insinuate
oneself into.
irreprehēnsus _adj_ blameless.
irrequiētus _adj_ restless.
irresectus _adj_ not slackened.
irresolūtus _adj_ not slackened.
irrētiō, -īre, -iī, -ītum _vt_ to ensnare, entangle.
irretortus _adj_ not turned back.
irreverentia, -ae _f_ disrespect.
irrevocābilis _adj_ irrevocable; implacable.
irrevocātus _adj_ without an encore.
irrīdeō, -dēre, -sī, -sum _vi_ to laugh, joke ♦ _vt_
to laugh at, ridicule.
irrīdiculē _adv_ unwittily.
irrīdiculum, -ī _nt_ laughing stock.
irrigātiō, -ōnis _f_ irrigation.
irrigō, -āre, -āvī, -ātum _vt_ to water, irrigate;
to inundate; (_fig_) to shed over, flood, refresh.
irriguus _adj_ well-watered, swampy;
refreshing.
irrīsiō, -ōnis _f_ ridicule, mockery.

irrīsor, -ōris _m_ scoffer.
irrīsus _ppp of_ **irrīdeō**.
irrīsus, -ūs _m_ derision.
irrītābilis _adj_ excitable.
irrītāmen, -inis _nt_ excitement, provocation.
irrītātiō, -ōnis _f_ incitement, irritation.
irrītō, -āre, -āvī, -ātum _vt_ to provoke, incite,
enrage.
irritus _adj_ invalid, null and void; useless, vain,
ineffective; (_person_) unsuccessful; **ad ~um**
cadere come to nothing.
irrogātiō, -ōnis _f_ imposing.
irrogō, -āre _vt_ to propose (a measure) against;
to impose.
irrōrō, -āre _vt_ to bedew.
irrumpō, -umpere, -ūpī, -uptum _vt, vi_ to
rush in, break in; to intrude, invade.
irruō, -ere, -ī _vi_ to force a way in, rush in,
attack; (_speech_) to make a blunder.
irruptiō, -ōnis _f_ invasion, raid.
irruptus _ppp of_ **irrumpō**.
irruptus _adj_ unbroken.
is, ea, id _pron_ he, she, it; this, that, the; such;
nōn is sum quī I am not the man to; **id** (_with_
_vi_) for this reason; **id quod** what; **ad id**
hitherto; for the purpose; besides; **in eō est**
it has come to this; one is on the point of; it
depends on this.
Ismara, -ōrum _ntpl_, **-us, -ī** _m_ Mt Ismarus in
Thrace.
Ismarius _adj_ Thracian.
Īsocratēs, -is _m_ Athenian orator and teacher of
rhetoric.
istāc _adv_ that way.
iste, -a, -ud, -īus _pron_ that of yours; (_law_) your
client, the plaintiff, the defendant;
(_contemptuous_) the fellow; that, such.
Isthmius _adj, ntpl_ the Isthmian Games.
Isthmus (-os), -ī _m_ Isthmus of Corinth.
istic, -aec, -uc _and_ **oc** _pron_ that of yours, that.
istīc _adv_ there; in this, on this occasion.
istinc _adv_ from there; of that.
istīusmodī such, of that kind.
istō, istōc _adv_ to you, there, yonder.
istōrsum _adv_ in that direction.
istūc _adv_ (to) there, to that.
ita _adv_ thus, so; as follows; yes; accordingly;
itane? really?; **nōn ita** not so very; **ita ut** just
as; **ita ... ut** so, to such an extent that; on
condition that; only in so far as; **ita ... ut nōn**
without; **ut ... ita** just as ... so; although ...
nevertheless.
Italī, -ōrum _mpl_ Italians.
Italia, -iae _f_ Italy.
Italicus, -is, -us _adj_ Italian.
itaque _conj_ and so, therefore, accordingly.
item _adv_ likewise, also.
iter, -ineris _nt_ way, journey, march; a day's
journey or march; route, road, passage; (_fig_)
way, course; ~ **mihi est** I have to go to; ~ **dare**
grant a right of way; ~ **facere** to journey,
march, travel; **ex, in ~inere** on the way, on
the march; **māgnīs ~ineribus** by forced

marches.
iterātiō, -ōnis *f* repetition.
iterō, -āre, -āvī, -ātum *vt* to repeat, renew; to plough again.
iterum *adv* again, a second time; ~ **atque** ~ repeatedly.
Ithaca, -ae, -ē, -ēs *f* island W. of Greece (*home of Ulysses*).
Ithacēnsis, -us *adj* Ithacan.
Ithacus, -ī *m* Ulysses.
itidem *adv* in the same way, similarly.
itiō, -ōnis *f* going.
itō, -āre *vi* to go.
itus, -ūs *m* going, movement, departure.
iuba, -ae *f* mane; crest.
Iuba, -ae *m* king of Numidia (*supporter of Pompey*).
iubar, -is *nt* brightness, light.
iubātus *adj* crested.
iubeō, -bēre, -ssī, -ssum *vt* to order, command, tell; (*greeting*) to bid; (*MED*) to prescribe; (*POL*) to decree, ratify, appoint.
iūcundē *adv* agreeably.
iūcunditās, -ātis *f* delight, enjoyment.
iūcundus *adj* delightful, pleasing.
Iūdaea, -ae *f* Judaea, Palestine.
Iūdaeus, -ī *m* Jew.
Iūdaeus, iūdaicus *adj* Jewish.
iūdex, -icis *m* judge; (*pl*) panel of jurors; (*fig*) critic.
iūdicātiō, -ōnis *f* judicial inquiry; opinion.
iūdicātum, -ī *nt* judgment, precedent.
iūdicātus, -ūs *m* office of judge.
iūdiciālis *adj* judicial, forensic.
iūdiciārius *adj* judiciary.
iūdicium, -ī *and* **iī** *nt* trial; court of justice; sentence; judgment, opinion; discernment, taste, tact; **in ~ vocāre, ~ō arcessere** sue, summon.
iūdicō, -āre, -āvī, -ātum *vt* to judge, examine, sentence, condemn; to form an opinion of, decide; to declare.
iugālis *adj* yoked together; nuptial.
iugātiō, -ōnis *f* training (*of a vine*).
iūgerum, -ī *nt* a land measure (*240 x 120 feet*).
iūgis *adj* perpetual, never-failing.
iūglāns, -andis *f* walnut tree.
iugō, -āre, -āvī, -ātum *vt* to couple, marry.
iugōsus *adj* hilly.
Iugulae, -ārum *fpl* Orion's Belt.
iugulō, -āre, -āvī, -ātum *vt* to cut the throat of, kill, murder.
iugulus, -ī *m*, **-um, -ī** *nt* throat.
iugum, -ī *nt* (*animals*) yoke, collar; pair, team; (*MIL*) yoke of subjugation; (*mountain*) ridge, height, summit; (*ASTRO*) Libra; (*loom*) crossbeam; (*ship*) thwart; (*fig*) yoke, bond.
Iugurtha, -ae *m* king of Numidia (*rebel against Rome*).
Iugurthīnus *adj see n.*

Iūlēus *adj* of Iulus; of Caesar; of July.
Iūlius, -ī *m* Roman family name (*esp Caesar*); (*month*) July.
Iūlius, -iānus *adj see n.*
Iūlus, -ī *m* son of Aeneas, Ascanius.
iūmentum, -ī *nt* beast of burden, packhorse.
iunceus *adj* of rushes; slender.
iuncōsus *adj* rushy.
iūnctiō, -ōnis *f* union.
iūnctūra, -ae *f* joint; combination; relationship.
iūnctus *ppp of* **iungō** ♦ *adj* connected, attached.
iuncus, -ī *m* rush.
iungō, -gere, iūnxī, iūnctum *vt* to join together, unite; to yoke, harness; to mate; (*river*) to span, bridge; (*fig*) to bring together, connect, associate; (*agreement*) to make; (*words*) to compound.
iūnior, -ōris *adj* younger.
iūniperus, -ī *f* juniper.
Iūnius, -ī *m* Roman family name; (*month*) June.
Iūnius *adj* of June.
Iūnō, -ōnis *f* Roman goddess wife of Jupiter, patroness of women and marriage.
Iūnōnālis *adj see n.*
Iūnōnicola, -ae *m* worshipper of Juno.
Iūnōnigena, -ae *m* Vulcan.
Iūnōnius *adj* = **Iūnōnālis.**
Iuppiter, Iovis *m* Jupiter (*king of the gods, god of sky and weather*); ~ **Stygius** Pluto; **sub Iove** in the open air.
iūrātor, -ōris *m* sworn judge.
iūrecōnsultus *etc see* **iūriscōnsultus.**
iūreiūrō, -āre *vi* to swear.
iūreperītus *etc see* **iūrisperītus.**
iūrgium, -ī *and* **iī** *nt* quarrel, brawl.
iūrgō, -āre *vi* to quarrel, squabble ♦ *vt* to scold.
iūridiciālis *adj* of law, juridical.
iūriscōnsultus, -ī *m* lawyer.
iūrisdictiō, -ōnis *f* administration of justice; authority.
iūrisperītus *adj* versed in the law.
iūrō, -āre, -āvī, -ātum *vi, vt* to swear, take an oath; to conspire; **in nōmen ~** swear allegiance to; **in verba ~** take a prescribed form of oath; **~ātus** having sworn, under oath.
iūs, iūris *nt* broth, soup.
iūs, iūris *nt* law, right, justice; law court; jurisdiction, authority; **~ gentium** international law; **~ pūblicum** constitutional law; **summum ~** the strict letter of the law; **~ dīcere** administer justice; **suī iūris** independent; **iūre** rightly, justly.
iūsiūrandum, iūrisiūrandī *nt* oath.
iussī *perf of* **iubeō.**
iussū *abl m* by order.
iussus *ppp of* **iubeō** ♦ *nt* order, command, prescription.

---

iūstē *adv* duly, rightly.
iūstificus *adj* just dealing.
iūstitia, -ae *f* justice, uprightness, fairness.
iūstitium, -ī *and* **iī** *nt* cessation of legal business.
iūstus *adj* just, fair; lawful, right; regular, proper ♦ *nt* right ♦ *ntpl* rights; formalities, obsequies.
iūtus *ppp of* **iuvō**.
iuvenālis *adj* youthful ♦ *ntpl* youthful games.
Iuvenālis, -is *m* Juvenal (*Roman satirist*).
iuvenāliter *adv* vigorously, impetuously.
iuvenca, -ae *f* heifer; girl.
iuvencus, -ī *m* bullock; young man ♦ *adj* young.
iuvenēscō, -ēscere, -uī *vi* to grow up; to grow young again.
iuvenīlis *adj* youthful.
iuvenīliter *adv see adj.*
iuvenis *adj* young ♦ *m/f* young man *or* woman (*20-45 years*), man, warrior.
iuvenor, -ārī *vi* to behave indiscreetly.
iuventa, -ae *f* youth.
iuventās, -ātis *f* youth.
iuventūs, -ūtis *f* youth, manhood; men, soldiers.
iuvō, -āre, iūvī, iūtum *vt* to help, be of use to; to please, delight; **~at mē** I am glad.
iuxtā *adv* near by, close; alike, just the same ♦ *prep* (*with acc*) close to, hard by; next to; very like, next door to; **~ ac, cum, quam** just the same as.
iuxtim *adv* near; equally.
īvī *perf of* **eō**.
Ixīōn, -onis *m* Lapith king (*bound to a revolving wheel in Tartarus*).
Ixīoneus *adj see n.*
Ixīonidae, -ārum *mpl* Centaurs.
Ixīonidēs, -ae *m* Pirithous.

J, j

J *see* **I**.

K, k

Kalendae, -ārum *fpl* Kalends, first day of each month.
Karthāgō *see* **Carthāgō**.

L, l

labāscō, -ere *vi* to totter, waver.
lābēcula, -ae *f* aspersion.
labefaciō, -facere, -fēcī, -factum (*pass* -fīō, -fierī) *vt* to shake; (*fig*) to weaken, ruin.
labefactō, -āre, -āvī, -ātum *vt* to shake; (*fig*) to weaken, destroy.
labellum, -ī *nt* lip.
lābellum, -ī *nt* small basin.
Laberius, -ī *m* Roman family name (*esp a writer of mimes*).
lābēs, -is *f* sinking, fall; ruin, destruction.
lābēs, -is *f* spot, blemish; disgrace, stigma; (*person*) blot.
labia, -iae *f* lip.
Labiēnus, -ī *m* Roman surname (*esp Caesar's officer who went over to Pompey*).
labiōsus *adj* large-lipped.
labium, -ī *and* **iī** *nt* lip.
labō, -āre *vi* to totter, be unsteady, give way; to waver, hesitate, collapse.
lābor, -bī, -psus *vi* to slide, glide; to sink, fall; to slip away, pass away; (*fig*) to fade, decline, perish; to be disappointed, make a mistake.
labor (-ōs), -ōris *m* effort, exertion, labour, work, task; hardship, suffering, distress; (*ASTRO*) eclipse.
labōrifer, -ī *adj* sore afflicted.
labōriōsē *adv* laboriously, with difficulty.
labōriōsus *adj* troublesome, difficult; industrious.
labōrō, -āre, -āvī, -ātum *vi* to work, toil, take pains; to suffer, be troubled (with), be in distress; to be anxious, worried ♦ *vt* to work out, make, produce.
labōs *etc see* **labor**.
labrum, -ī *nt* lip; edge, rim; **primīs ~īs gustāre** acquire a smattering of.
lābrum, -ī *nt* tub, vat; bath.
lābrusca, -ae *f* wild vine.
lābruscum, -ī *nt* wild grape.

labyrinthēus *adj* labyrinthine.
labyrinthus, -ī *m* labyrinth, maze (*esp that of Cnossos in Crete*).
lac, lactis *nt* milk.
Lacaena, -ae *f* Spartan woman ♦ *adj* Spartan.
Lacedaemōn (-ō), -onis (*acc* -ona) *f* Sparta.
Lacedaemonius *adj* Spartan.
lacer, -ī *adj* torn, mangled, lacerated; tearing.
lacerātiō, -ōnis *f* tearing.
lacerna, -ae *f* cloak (*worn in cold weather*).
lacernātus *adj* cloaked.
lacerō, -āre, -āvī, -ātum *vt* to tear, lacerate, mangle; (*ship*) to wreck; (*speech*) to slander, abuse; (*feeling*) to torture, distress; (*goods, time*) to waste, destroy.
lacerta, -ae *f* lizard; a seafish.
lacertōsus *adj* brawny.
lacertus, -ī *m* upper arm, arm; (*pl*) brawn, muscle.
lacertus, -ī *m* lizard; a sea fish.
lacessō, -ere, -īvī *and* **iī, -ītum** *vt* to strike, provoke, challenge; (*fig*) to incite, exasperate.
Lachesis, -is *f* one of the Fates.
lacinia, -ae *f* flap, corner (*of dress*).
Lacīnium, -ī *nt* promontory in S. Italy, with a temple of Juno.
Lacinius *adj see n.*
Lacō (-ōn), -ōnis *m* Spartan; Spartan dog.
Lacōnicus *adj* Spartan ♦ *nt* sweating bath.
lacrima, -ae *f* tear; (*plant*) gumdrop.
lacrimābilis *adj* mournful.
lacrimābundus *adj* bursting into tears.
lacrimō, -āre, -āvī, -ātum *vt, vi* to weep, weep for.
lacrimōsus *adj* tearful; lamentable.
lacrimula, -ae *f* tear, crocodile tear.
lacrum- *etc see* **lacrim-.**
lactāns, -antis *adj* giving milk; sucking.
lactātiō, -ōnis *f* allurement.
lactēns, -entis *adj* sucking; milky, juicy.
lacteolus *adj* milk-white.
lactēs, -ium *fpl* guts, small intestines.
lactēscō, -ere *vi* to turn to milk.
lacteus *adj* milky, milk-white.
lactō, -āre *vt* to dupe, wheedle.
lactūca, -ae *f* lettuce.
lacūna, -ae *f* hole, pit; pool, pond; (*fig*) deficiency.
lacūnar, -āris *nt* panel ceiling.
lacūnō, -āre *vt* to panel.
lacūnōsus *adj* sunken.
lacus, -ūs *m* vat, tank; lake; reservoir, cistern.
laedō, -dere, -sī, -sum *vt* to hurt, strike, wound; (*fig*) to offend, annoy, break.
Laelius, -ī *m* Roman family name (*esp the friend of Scipio*).
laena, -ae *f* a lined cloak.
Lāērtēs, -ae *m* father of Ulysses.
Lāērtiadēs *m* Ulysses.

Lāērtius *adj see n.*
laesī *perf of* **laedō.**
laesiō, -ōnis *f* attack.
Laestrygonēs, -um *mpl* fabulous cannibals of Campania, founders of Formiae.
Laestrygonius *adj see n.*
laesus *ppp of* **laedō.**
laetābilis *adj* joyful.
laetē *adv* gladly.
laetificō, -āre *vt* to gladden.
laetificus *adj* glad, joyful.
laetitia, -ae *f* joy, delight, exuberance.
laetor, -ārī, -ātus *vi* to rejoice, be glad.
laetus *adj* glad, cheerful; delighting (in); pleasing, welcome; (*growth*) fertile, rich; (*style*) exuberant.
laevē *adv* awkwardly.
laevus *adj* left; stupid; ill-omened, unfortunate; (*augury*) lucky, favourable ♦ *f* left hand.
laganum, -ī *nt* a kind of oilcake.
lagēos, -ī *f* a Greek vine.
lagoena, -ae *f* flagon.
lagōis, -idis *f* a kind of grouse.
lagōna, -ae *f* flagon.
Lāiadēs, -ae *m* Oedipus.
Lāius, -ī *m* father of Oedipus.
lallō, -āre *vi* to sing a lullaby.
lāma, -ae *f* bog.
lamberō, -āre *vt* to tear to pieces.
lambō, -ere, -ī *vt* to lick, touch; (*river*) to wash.
lāmenta, -ōrum *ntpl* lamentation.
lāmentābilis *adj* mournful, sorrowful.
lāmentārius *adj* sorrowful.
lāmentātiō, -ōnis *f* weeping, lamentation.
lāmentor, -ārī, -ātus *vi* to weep, lament ♦ *vt* to weep for, bewail.
lamia, -ae *f* witch.
lāmina (lammina, lāmna), -ae *f* plate, leaf (*of metal, wood*); blade; coin.
lampas, -dis *f* torch; brightness, day.
Lamus, -ī *m* Laestrygonian king.
lāna, -ae *f* wool.
lānārius, -ī *and* **iī** *m* wool-worker.
lānātus *adj* woolly.
lancea, -ae *f* spear, lance.
lancinō, -āre *vt* to tear up; to squander.
lāneus *adj* woollen.
languefaciō, -ere *vt* to make weary.
langueō, -ēre *vi* to be weary, be weak, droop; to be idle, dull.
languēscō, -ēscere, -uī *vi* to grow faint, droop.
languidē *adv see adj.*
languidulus *adj* languid.
languidus *adj* faint, languid, sluggish; listless, feeble.
languor, -ōris *m* faintness, fatigue, weakness; dullness, apathy.
laniātus, -ūs *m* mangling; (*mind*) anguish.

Noun declensions and verb conjugations are shown on pp xiii to xxv. The present infinitive ending of a verb shows to which conjugation it belongs: **-āre** = 1st; **-ēre** = 2nd; **-ere** = 3rd and **-īre** = 4th. Irregular verbs are shown on p xxvi

laniēna, -ae *f* butcher's shop.
lānificium, -ī *and* **iī** *nt* wool-working.
lānificus *adj* wool-working.
lāniger, -ī *adj* fleecy ♦ *m/f* ram, sheep.
laniō, -āre, -āvī, -ātum *vt* to tear to pieces, mangle.
lanista, -ae *m* trainer of gladiators, fencing master; (*fig*) agitator.
lānitium, -ī *and* **iī** *nt* woolgrowing.
lanius, -ī *and* **iī** *m* butcher.
lanterna, -ae *f* lamp.
lanternārius, -ī *and* **iī** *m* guide.
lānūgō, -inis *f* down, woolliness.
Lānuvīnus *adj see n.*
Lānuvium, -ī *nt* Latin town on the Appian Way.
lānx, lancis *f* dish, platter; (*balance*) scale.
Lāomedōn, -ontis *m* king of Troy (*father of Priam*).
Lāomedontēus *adj and* **ontiadēs, -ae** *m* son of Lāomedōn; (*pl*) Trojans.
Lāomedontius *adj* Trojan.
lapathum, -ī *nt*, **-us, -ī** *f* sorrel.
lapicīda, -ae *m* stonecutter.
lapicīdīnae, -ārum *fpl* quarries.
lapidārius *adj* stone- (*in cpds*).
lapidātiō, -ōnis *f* throwing of stones.
lapidātor, -ōris *m* stone thrower.
lapideus *adj* of stones, stone- (*in cpds*).
lapidō, -āre *vt* to stone ♦ *vi* to rain stones.
lapidōsus *adj* stony; hard as stone.
lapillus, -ī *m* stone, pebble; precious stone, mosaic piece.
lapis, -dis *m* stone; milestone, boundary stone, tombstone; precious stone; marble; auctioneer's stand; (*abuse*) blockhead; **bis ad eundem (offendere)** ≈ *make the same mistake twice*; **Juppiter ~** the Jupiter stone.
Lapithae, -ārum *and* **-um** *mpl* Lapiths (*mythical people of Thessaly*).
Lapithaeus, -ēius *adj see n.*
lappa, -ae *f* goosegrass.
lāpsiō, -ōnis *f* tendency.
lāpsō, -āre *vi* to slip, stumble.
lāpsus *ppa of* **lābor**.
lāpsus, -ūs *m* fall, slide, course, flight; error, failure.
laqueāria, -ium *ntpl* panelled ceiling.
laqueātus *adj* panelled, with a panelled ceiling.
laqueus, -ī *m* noose, snare, halter; (*fig*) trap.
Lār, Laris *m* tutelary deity, household god; hearth, home.
lārdum *etc see* **lāridum**.
largē *adv* plentifully, generously, very much.
largificus *adj* bountiful.
largifluus *adj* copious.
largiloquus *adj* talkative.
largior, -īrī, -ītus *vt* to give freely, lavish; to bestow, confer ♦ *vi* to give largesses.
largitās, -ātis *f* liberality, abundance.
largiter *adv* = **large**.
largītiō, -ōnis *f* giving freely, distributing; bribery.

largītor, -ōris *m* liberal giver, dispenser; spendthrift; briber.
largus *adj* copious, ample; liberal, bountiful.
lāridum, -ī *nt* bacon fat.
Lārissa (Lārīsa), -ae *f* town in Thessaly.
Lārissaeus, -ēnsis *adj see n.*
Lārius, -ī *m* lake Como.
larix, -cis *f* larch.
larva, -ae *f* ghost; mask.
larvātus *adj* bewitched.
lasanum, -ī *nt* pot.
lasārpīcifer, -ī *adj* producing asafoetida.
lascīvia, -ae *f* playfulness; impudence, lewdness.
lascīviō, -īre *vi* to frolic, frisk; to run wild, be irresponsible.
lascīvus *adj* playful, frisky; impudent, lustful.
laserpīcium, -ī *and* **iī** *nt* silphium.
lassitūdō, -inis *f* fatigue, heaviness.
lassō, -āre, *vt* to tire, fatigue.
lassulus *adj* rather weary.
lassus *adj* tired, exhausted.
lātē *adv* widely, extensively; **longē ~que** far and wide, everywhere.
latebra, -ae *f* hiding place, retreat; (*fig*) loophole, pretext.
latebricola, -ae *adj* low-living.
latebrōsē *adv* in hiding.
latebrōsus *adj* secret, full of coverts; porous.
latēns, -entis *pres p of* **lateō** ♦ *adj* hidden, secret.
latenter *adv* in secret.
lateō, -ēre, -uī *vi* to lie hid, lurk, skulk; to be in safety, live a retired life; to be unknown, escape notice.
later, -is *m* brick, tile; **~em lavāre** ≈ *waste one's time.*
laterāmen, -inis *nt* earthenware.
laterculus, -ī *m* small brick, tile; kind of cake.
latericius *adj* of bricks ♦ *nt* brickwork.
lāterna *etc see* **lanterna**.
latēscō, -ere *vi* to hide oneself.
latex, -icis *m* water; any other liquid.
Latiar, -iaris *nt* festival of Jupiter Latiaris.
Latiaris *adj* Latin.
latibulum, -ī *nt* hiding place, den, lair.
lāticlāvius *adj* with a broad purple stripe ♦ *m* senator, patrician.
lātifundium, -ī *and* **iī** *nt* large estate.
Latīnē *adv* in Latin, into Latin; **~ loquī** speak Latin, speak plainly, speak correctly; **~ reddere** translate into Latin.
Latīnitās, -ātis *f* good Latin, Latinity; Latin rights.
Latīnus *adj* Latin ♦ *m* legendary king of the Laurentians.
lātiō, -ōnis *f* bringing; proposing.
latitō, -āre *vi* to hide away, lurk, keep out of the way.
lātitūdō, -inis *f* breadth, width; size; broad pronunciation.
Latium, -ī *nt* district of Italy including Rome; Latin rights.

Latius = **Latiaris, Latinus.**
Lātōis, -idis *f* Diana.
Lātōis , -ius *adj see n.*
lātom- *etc see* **lautum-.**
Lātōna, -ae *f* mother of Apollo and Diana.
Lātōnigenae, -ārum *pl* Apollo and Diana.
Lātōnius *adj*, *f* Diana.
lātor, -ōris *m* proposer.
Lātōus *adj* of Latona ♦ *m* Apollo.
lātrātor, -ōris *m* barker.
lātrātus, -ūs *m* barking.
lātrō, -āre *vi* to bark; to rant, roar ♦ *vt* to bark
at; to clamour for.
latrō, -ōnis *m* mercenary soldier; bandit,
brigand; (*chess*) man.
latrōcinium, -ī *and* **iī** *nt* highway robbery,
piracy.
latrōcinor, -ārī, -ātus *vi* to serve as a
mercenary; to be a brigand *or* pirate.
latrunculus, -ī *m* brigand; (*chess*) man.
lātumiae *etc see* **lautumiae.**
lātus *ppp of* **ferō.**
lātus *adj* broad, wide; extensive;
(*pronunciation*) broad; (*style*) diffuse.
latus, -eris *nt* side, flank; lungs; body; ~ **dare**
expose oneself; ~ **tegere** walk beside; **~eris**
dolor pleurisy; **ab ~ere** on the flank.
latusculum, -ī *nt* little side.
laudābilis *adj* praiseworthy.
laudābiliter *adv* laudably.
laudātiō, -ōnis *f* commendation, eulogy;
panegyric, testimonial.
laudātor, -ōris *m*, **-rīx, -rīcis** *f* praiser,
eulogizer; speaker of a funeral oration.
laudātus *adj* excellent.
laudō, -āre, -āvī, -ātum *vt* to praise,
commend, approve; to pronounce a funeral
oration over; to quote, name.
laurea, -ae *f* bay tree; crown of bay; triumph.
laureātus *adj* crowned with bay; (*despatches*)
victorious.
Laurentēs, -um *mpl* Laurentians (*people of
ancient Latium*).
Laurentius *adj see n.*
laureola, -ae *f* triumph.
laureus *adj* of bay.
lauricomus *adj* bay-covered.
lauriger, -ī *adj* crowned with bay.
laurus, -ī *f* bay tree; bay crown; victory,
triumph.
laus, laudis *f* praise, approval; glory, fame;
praiseworthy act, merit, worth.
lautē *adv* elegantly, splendidly; excellently.
lautia, -ōrum *ntpl* State banquet.
lautitia, -ae *f* luxury.
lautumiae, -ārum *fpl* stone quarry; prison.
lautus *ppp of* **lavō** ♦ *adj* neat, elegant,
sumptuous; fine, grand, distinguished.
lavābrum, -ī *nt* bath.
lavātiō, -ōnis *f* washing, bath; bathing gear.

Lāvīnium, -ī *nt* town of ancient Latium.
Lāvīnius *adj see n.*
lavō, -āre, lāvī, lautum (lavātum *and*
lōtum) *vt* to wash, bathe; to wet, soak, wash
away.
laxāmentum, -ī *nt* respite, relaxation.
laxē *adv* loosely, freely.
laxitās, -ātis *f* roominess.
laxō, -āre, -āvī, -ātum *vt* to extend, open out;
to undo; to slacken; (*fig*) to release, relieve;
to relax, abate ♦ *vi* (*price*) to fall off.
laxus *adj* wide, loose, roomy; (*time*) deferred;
(*fig*) free, easy.
lea, -ae *f* lioness.
leaena, -ae *f* lioness.
Lēander, -rī *m* Hero's lover (*who swam the
Hellespont*).
lebēs, -ētis *m* basin, pan, cauldron.
lectīca, -ae *f* litter, sedan chair.
lectīcārius, -ī *and* **iī** *m* litter-bearer.
lectīcula, -ae *f* small litter; bier.
lēctiō, -ōnis *f* selecting; reading, calling the
roll.
lectisterniātor, -ōris *m* arranger of couches.
lectisternium, -ī *and* **iī** *nt* religious feast.
lēctitō, -āre *vt* to read frequently.
lēctiuncula, -ae *f* light reading.
lēctor, -ōris *m* reader.
lectulus, -ī *m* couch, bed.
lectus, -ī *m* couch, bed; bier.
lēctus *ppp of* **legō** ♦ *adj* picked; choice,
excellent.
Lēda, -ae *and* **ē, -ēs** *f* mother of Castor, Pollux,
Helen and Clytemnestra.
Lēdaeus *adj see n.*
lēgātiō, -ōnis *f* mission, embassy; members
of a mission; (*MIL*) staff appointment,
command of a legion; **lībera ~** free
commission (to visit provinces); **vōtīva ~**
free commission for paying a vow in a
province.
lēgātor, -ōris *m* testator.
lēgātum, -ī *nt* legacy, bequest.
lēgātus, -ī *m* delegate, ambassador; deputy;
lieutenant; commander (of a legion).
lēgifer, -ī *adj* law-giving.
legiō, -ōnis *f* legion (*up to 6000 men*); (*pl*)
troops, army.
legiōnārius *adj* legionary.
lēgirupa, -ae; -iō, -iōnis *m* lawbreaker.
lēgitimē *adv* lawfully, properly.
lēgitimus *adj* lawful, legal; right, proper.
legiuncula, -ae *f* small legion.
lēgō, -āre, -āvī, -ātum *vt* to send, charge,
commission; to appoint as deputy or
lieutenant; (*will*) to leave, bequeath.
legō, -ere, lēgī, lēctum *vt* to gather, pick; to
choose, select; (*sail*) to furl; (*places*) to
traverse, pass, coast along; (*view*) to scan;
(*writing*) to read, recite; **senātum ~** call the

Noun declensions and verb conjugations are shown on pp xiii to xxv. The present infinitive ending of a verb shows
to which conjugation it belongs: **-āre** = 1st; **-ēre** = 2nd; **-ere** = 3rd and **-īre** = 4th. Irregular verbs are shown on p xxvi

roll of the senate.

lēgulēius, -ī *and* **iī** *m* pettifogging lawyer.

legūmen, -inis *nt* pulse, bean.

lembus, -ī *m* pinnace, cutter.

Lemnias *f* Lemnian woman.

Lemnicola, -ae *m* Vulcan.

lēmniscātus *adj* beribboned.

lēmniscus, -ī *m* ribbon (*hanging from a victor's crown*).

Lēmnius *adj see n.*

Lēmnos (-us), -ī *f* Aegean island, abode of Vulcan.

Lemurēs, -um *mpl* ghosts.

lēna, -ae *f* procuress; seductress.

Lēnaeus *adj* Bacchic ♦ *m* Bacchus.

lēnīmen, -inis *nt* solace, comfort.

lēnīmentum, -ī *nt* sop.

lēniō, -īre, -īvī *and* **iī, -ītum** *vt* to soften, soothe, heal, calm.

lēnis *adj* soft, smooth, mild, gentle, calm.

lēnitās, -ātis *f* softness, smoothness, mildness, tenderness.

lēniter *adv* softly, gently; moderately, half-heartedly.

lēnitūdō, -inis *f* smoothness, mildness.

lēnō, -ōnis *m* pander, brothel keeper; go-between.

lēnōcinium, -ī *and* **iī** *nt* pandering; allurement; meretricious ornament.

lēnōcinor, -ārī, -ātus *vi* to pay court to; to promote.

lēnōnius *adj* pander's.

lēns, lentis *f* lentil.

lentē *adv* slowly; calmly, coolly.

lentēscō, -ere *vi* to become sticky, soften; to relax.

lentīscifer, -ī *adj* bearing mastic trees.

lentīscus, -ī *f* mastic tree.

lentitūdō, -inis *f* slowness, dullness, apathy.

lentō, -āre *vt* to bend.

lentulus *adj* rather slow.

lentus *adj* sticky, sluggish; pliant; slow, lasting, lingering; (*person*) calm, at ease, indifferent.

lēnunculus, -ī *m* skiff.

leō, -ōnis *m* lion.

Leōnidās, -ae *m* Spartan king who fell at Thermopylae.

leōnīnus *adj* lion's.

Leontīnī, -ōrum *mpl* town in Sicily.

Leontīnus *adj see n.*

lepas, -dis *f* limpet.

lepidē *adv* neatly, charmingly; (*reply*) very well, splendidly.

lepidus *adj* pleasant, charming, neat, witty.

lepōs (lepor), -ōris *m* pleasantness, charm; wit.

lepus, -oris *m* hare.

lepusculus, -ī *m* young hare.

Lerna, -ae *and* **ē, -ēs** *f* marsh near Argos (*where Hercules killed the Hydra*).

Lernaeus *adj* Lernaean.

Lesbias, -iadis *f* Lesbian woman.

Lesbis, Lesbius *adj see n.*

Lesbos (-us), -ī *f* Aegean island (*home of Alcaeus and Sappho*).

Lesbous *f* Lesbian woman.

lētālis *adj* deadly.

Lēthaeus *adj* of Lethe; infernal; soporific.

lēthargicus, -ī *m* lethargic person.

lēthargus, -ī *m* drowsiness.

Lēthē, -ēs *f* river in the lower world, which caused forgetfulness.

lētifer, -ī *adj* fatal.

lētō, -āre *vt* to kill.

lētum, -ī *nt* death; destruction.

Leucadius *adj see n.*

Leucas, -dis *and* **dia, -diae** *f* island off W. Greece.

Leucothea, -ae, -ē, -ēs *f* Ino (*a sea goddess*).

Leuctra, -ōrum *ntpl* battlefield in Boeotia.

Leuctricus *adj see n.*

levāmen, -inis *nt* alleviation, comfort.

levāmentum, -ī *nt* mitigation, consolation.

levātiō, -ōnis *f* relief; diminishing.

lēvī *perf of* **linō**.

leviculus *adj* rather vain.

levidēnsis *adj* slight.

levipēs, -edis *adj* light-footed.

levis *adj* (*weight*) light; (*MIL*) light-armed; (*fig*) easy, gentle; (*importance*) slight, trivial; (*motion*) nimble, fleet; (*character*) fickle, unreliable.

lēvis *adj* smooth; (*youth*) beardless, delicate.

levisomnus *adj* light-sleeping.

levitās, -ātis *f* lightness; nimbleness; fickleness, frivolity.

lēvitās, -ātis *f* smoothness; fluency.

leviter *adv* lightly; slightly; easily.

levō, -āre *vt* to lighten, ease; (*fig*) to alleviate, lessen; to comfort, relieve; to impair; (*danger*) to avert; **sē ~** rise.

lēvō, -āre *vt* to smooth, polish.

lēvor, -ōris *m* smoothness.

lēx, lēgis *f* law, statute; bill; rule, principle; contract, condition; **lēgem ferre** propose a bill; **lēgem perferre** carry a motion; **lēge agere** proceed according to law; **sine lēge** out of control.

lībāmen, -inis *nt* offering, libation.

lībāmentum, -ī *nt* offering, libation.

lībātiō, -ōnis *f* libation.

lībella, -ae *f* small coin, as; level; **ad ~am** exactly; **ex ~ā** sole heir.

libellus, -ī *m* small book; notebook, diary, letter; notice, programme, handbill; petition, complaint; lampoon.

libēns, -entis *adj* willing, glad.

libenter *adv* willingly, with pleasure.

liber, -rī *m* inner bark (of a tree); book; register.

Līber, -ī *m* Italian god of fertility (*identified with Bacchus*).

līber, -ī *adj* free, open, unrestricted, undisturbed; (*with abl*) free from; (*speech*) frank; (*POL*) free, not slave, democratic.

Lībera, -ae f Proserpine; Ariadne.
Līberālia, -ālium ntpl festival of Liber in March.
līberālis adj of freedom, of free citizens, gentlemanly, honourable; generous, liberal; handsome.
līberālitās, -ātis f courtesy, kindness; generosity; bounty.
līberāliter adv courteously, nobly; generously.
līberātiō, -ōnis f delivery, freeing; (law) acquittal.
līberātor, -ōris m liberator, deliverer.
līberē adv freely, frankly, boldly.
līberī, -ōrum mpl children.
līberō, -āre, -āvī, -ātum vt to free, set free, release; to exempt; (law) to acquit; (slave) to give freedom to; **fidem** ~ keep one's promise; **nōmina** ~ cancel debts.
līberta, -ae f freedwoman.
lībertās, -ātis f freedom, liberty; status of a freeman; (POL) independence; freedom of speech, outspokenness.
lībertīnus adj of a freedman, freed ♦ m freedman ♦ f freedwoman.
lībertus, -ī m freedman.
libet (lubet), -ēre, -uit and **itum est** vi (impers) it pleases; **mihi** ~ I like; **ut** ~ as you please.
libīdinōsē adv wilfully.
libīdinōsus adj wilful, arbitrary, extravagant; sensual, lustful.
libīdō (lubīdō), -inis f desire, passion; wilfulness, caprice; lust.
libita, -ōrum ntpl pleasure, fancy.
Libitīna, -ae f goddess of burials.
lībō, -āre, -āvī, -ātum vt to taste, sip, touch; to pour (a libation), offer; to extract, take out; to impair.
lībra, -ae f pound; balance, pair of scales; **ad** ~**am** of equal size.
lībrāmentum, -ī nt level surface, weight (to give balance or movement); (water) fall.
lībrāria, -ae f head spinner.
lībrāriolus, -ī m copyist.
lībrārium, -ī and **iī** nt bookcase.
lībrārius adj of books ♦ m copyist.
lībrātus adj level; powerful.
lībrīlis adj weighing a pound.
lībritor, -ōris m slinger.
lībrō, -āre, -āvī, -ātum vt to poise, hold balanced; to swing, hurl.
lībum, -ī nt cake.
Liburna, -ae f a fast galley, frigate.
Liburnī, -ōrum mpl people of Illyria.
Liburnus adj Liburnian.
Libya, -ae, -ē, -ēs f Africa.
Libycus adj African.
Libyes, -um mpl Libyans, people in N. Africa.
Libyssus, Libystinus, Libystis adj = **Libycus**.
licēns, -entis adj free, bold, unrestricted.
licenter adv freely, lawlessly.

licentia, -ae f freedom, license; lawlessness, licentiousness.
liceō, -ēre, -uī vi to be for sale, value at.
liceor, -ērī, -itus vt, vi to bid (at an auction), bid for.
licet, -ēre, -uit and **itum est** vi (impers) it is permitted, it is lawful; (reply) all right ♦ conj although; **mihi** ~ I may.
Licinius, -ī m Roman family name (esp with surname Crassus).
Licinius adj see n.
licitātiō, -ōnis f bidding (at a sale).
licitor, -ārī, vi to make a bid.
licitus adj lawful.
līcium, -ī and **iī** nt thread.
lictor, -ōris m lictor (an attendant with fasces preceding a magistrate).
licuī perf of **liceō**; perf of **liquēscō**.
liēn, -ēnis m spleen.
ligāmen, -inis nt band, bandage.
ligāmentum, -ī nt bandage.
Liger, -is m river Loire.
lignārius, -ī and **iī** m carpenter.
lignātiō, -ōnis f fetching wood.
lignātor, -ōris m woodcutter.
ligneolus adj wooden.
ligneus adj wooden.
lignor, -ārī vi to fetch wood.
lignum, -ī nt wood, firewood, timber; **in silvam** ~**a ferre** ≈ carry coals to Newcastle.
ligō, -āre, -āvī, -ātum vt to tie up, bandage; (fig) to unite.
ligō, -ōnis m mattock, hoe.
ligula, -ae f shoestrap.
Ligur, -ris m/f Ligurian.
Liguria, -riae f district of N.W. Italy.
ligūriō (ligurriō), -īre vt to lick; to eat daintily; (fig) to feast on, lust after.
ligūrītiō, -ōnis f daintiness.
Ligus, -ris m/f Ligurian.
Ligusticus, -stīnus adj see n.
ligustrum, -ī nt privet.
līlium, -ī and **iī** nt lily; (MIL) spiked pit.
līma, -ae f file; (fig) revision.
līmātius adv more elegantly.
līmātulus adj refined.
līmāx, -ācis f slug, snail.
limbus, -ī m fringe, hem.
līmen, -inis nt threshold, lintel; doorway, entrance; house, home; (fig) beginning.
līmes, -itis m path between fields, boundary; path, track, way; frontier, boundary line.
līmō, -āre, -āvī, -ātum vt to file; (fig) to polish, refine; to file down, investigate carefully; to take away from.
līmōsus adj muddy.
limpidus adj clear, limpid.
līmus adj sidelong, askance.
līmus, -ī m mud, slime, dirt.
līmus, -ī m ceremonial apron.

līnea, -ae _f_ line, string; plumbline; boundary; **ad ~am, rectā ~ā** vertically; **extrēmā ~ā amāre** love at a distance.

līneāmentum, -ī _nt_ line; feature; outline.

līneus _adj_ flaxen, linen.

lingō, -ere _vt_ to lick.

lingua, -ae _f_ tongue; speech, language; tongue of land; **~ Latīna** Latin.

lingula, -ae _f_ tongue of land.

līniger, -ī _adj_ linen-clad.

linō, -ere, lēvī, litum _vt_ to daub, smear; to overlay; (_writing_) to rub out; (_fig_) to befoul.

linquō, -ere, līquī _vt_ to leave, quit; to give up, let alone; (_pass_) to faint, swoon; **~itur ut** it remains to.

linteātus _adj_ canvas.

linteō, -ōnis _m_ linen weaver.

linter, -ris _f_ boat; trough.

linteum, -ī _nt_ linen cloth, canvas; sail.

linteus _adj_ linen.

lintriculus, -ī _m_ small boat.

līnum, -ī _nt_ flax; linen; thread, line, rope; net.

Lipara, -ae, -ē, -ēs _f_ island N. of Sicily (_now_ Lipari).

Liparaeus, -ēnsis _adj see n._

lippiō, -īre _vi_ to have sore eyes.

lippitūdō, -inis _f_ inflammation of the eyes.

lippus _adj_ blear-eyed, with sore eyes; (_fig_) blind.

liquefaciō, -facere, -fēcī, -factum (_pass_ -fīō) _vt_ to melt, dissolve; to decompose; (_fig_) to enervate.

liquēns, -entis _adj_ fluid, clear.

liquēscō, -ere, licuī _vi_ to melt; to clear; (_fig_) to grow soft, waste away.

liquet, -ēre, licuit _vi_ (_impers_) it is clear, it is evident; **nōn ~** not proven.

līquī _perf of_ **linquō**.

liquidō _adv_ clearly.

liquidus _adj_ fluid, liquid, flowing; clear, transparent, pure; (_mind_) calm, serene ♦ _nt_ liquid water.

liquō, -āre _vt_ to melt; to strain.

liquor, -ī _vi_ to flow; (_fig_) to waste away.

liquor, -ōris _m_ fluidity; liquid, the sea.

Līris, -is _m_ river between Latium and Campania.

līs, lītis _f_ quarrel, dispute; lawsuit; matter in dispute; **lītem aestimāre** assess damages.

litātiō, -ōnis _f_ favourable sacrifice.

lītera _etc see_ **littera**.

lītigātor, -ōris _m_ litigant.

lītigiōsus _adj_ quarrelsome, contentious; disputed.

lītigium, -ī _and_ **iī** _nt_ quarrel.

lītigō, -āre _vi_ to quarrel; to go to law.

litō, -āre, -āvī, -ātum _vi_ to offer an acceptable sacrifice, obtain favourable omens; (_with dat_) to propitiate ♦ _vt_ to offer successfully.

lītorālis _adj_ of the shore.

lītoreus _adj_ of the shore.

littera, -ae _f_ letter (of the alphabet).

litterae, -ārum _fpl_ writing; letter, dispatch; document, ordinance; literature; learning, scholarship; **~ās discere** learn to read and write; **homō trium ~ārum** thief (_of fur_); **sine ~īs** uncultured.

litterārius _adj_ of reading and writing.

litterātē _adv_ in clear letters; literally.

litterātor, -ōris _m_ grammarian.

litterātūra, -ae _f_ writing, alphabet.

litterātus _adj_ with letters on it, branded; educated, learned.

litterula, -ae _f_ small letter; short note; (_pl_) studies.

litūra, -ae _f_ correction, erasure, blot.

litus _ppp of_ **linō**.

lītus, -oris _nt_ shore, beach, coast; bank; **~ arāre** labour in vain.

lituus, -ī _m_ augur's staff; trumpet; (_fig_) starter.

līvēns, -entis _pres p of_ **līveō** ♦ _adj_ bluish, black and blue.

līveō, -ēre _vi_ to be black and blue; to envy.

līvēscō, -ere _vi_ to turn black and blue.

Līviānus _adj_ = **Līvius**.

līvidulus _adj_ a little jealous.

līvidus _adj_ bluish, black and blue; envious, malicious.

Līvius, -ī Roman family name (_esp the first Latin poet_); _the famous historian, Livy._

Līvius _adj see n._

līvor, -ōris _m_ bluish colour; envy, malice.

lixa, -ae _m_ sutler, camp-follower.

locātiō, -ōnis _f_ leasing; lease, contract.

locātōrius _adj_ concerned with leases.

locitō, -āre _vt_ to let frequently.

locō, -āre, -āvī, -ātum _vt_ to place, put; to give in marriage; to let, lease, hire out; to contract for; (_money_) to invest.

loculus, -ī _m_ little place; (_pl_) satchel, purse.

locuplēs, -ētis _adj_ rich, opulent; reliable, responsible.

locuplētō, -āre _vt_ to enrich.

locus, -ī _m_ (_pl_ **-ī** _m and_ **-a** _nt_) place, site, locality, region; (_MIL_) post; (_theatre_) seat; (_book_) passage; (_speech_) topic, subject, argument; (_fig_) room, occasion; situation, state; rank, position; **~ī** individual spots; **~a** regions, ground; **~ī commūnēs** general arguments; **~ō** (_with gen_) instead of; **in ~ō** opportunely; **eō ~ī** in the position; **intereā ~ī** meanwhile.

lōcusta, -ae _f_ locust.

locūtiō, -ōnis _f_ speech; pronunciation.

locūtus _ppa of_ **loquor**.

lōdīx, -īcis _f_ blanket.

logica, -ōrum _ntpl_ logic.

logos (-us), -ī _m_ word; idle talk; witticism.

lōlīg- _etc see_ **lollīg-**.

lolium, -ī _and_ **iī** _nt_ darnel.

lollīgō, -inis _f_ cuttlefish.

lōmentum, -ī _nt_ face cream.

Londinium, -ī _nt_ London.

longaevus _adj_ aged.

longē _adv_ far, far off; (_time_) long; (_compar_) by far, very much; **~ esse** be far away, of no

avail; ~ **latēque** everywhere.
longinquitās, -ātis f length; distance; duration.
longinquus adj distant, remote; foreign, strange; lasting, wearisome; (hope) long deferred.
longitūdō, -inis f length; duration; **in ~inem** lengthwise.
longiusculus adj rather long.
longulē adv rather far.
longulus adj rather long.
longurius, -ī and **iī** m long pole.
longus adj long; vast; (time) long, protracted, tedious; (hope) far-reaching; ~a **nāvis** warship; ~um **est** it would be tedious; **nē** ~um **faciam** ≈ to cut a long story short.
loquācitās, -ātis f talkativeness.
loquāciter adv see adj.
loquāculus adj somewhat talkative.
loquāx, -ācis adj talkative, chattering.
loquella, -ae f language, words.
loquor, -quī, cūtus vt, vi to speak, talk, say; to talk about, mention; (fig) to indicate; **rēs** ~quitur **ipsa** the facts speak for themselves.
lōrārius, -ī and **iī** m flogger.
lōrātus adj strapped.
lōreus adj of leather strips.
lōrīca, -ae f breastplate; parapet.
lōrīcātus adj mailed.
lōripēs, -edis adj bandylegged.
lōrum, -ī nt strap; whip, lash; leather charm; (pl) reins.
lōtos (-us), -ī f lotus.
lōtus ppp of **lavō**.
lubēns see **libēns**.
lubentia, -ae f pleasure.
lubet, lubīdō see **libet, libīdō**.
lūbricō, -āre vt to make slippery.
lūbricus adj slippery, slimy; gliding, fleeting; (fig) dangerous, hazardous.
Lūca bōs f elephant.
Lūcania, -iae f district of S. Italy.
Lūcanica f kind of sausage.
Lūcanus adj Lucanian ♦ m the epic poet Lucan.
lūcar, -āris nt forest tax.
lucellum, -ī nt small gain.
lūceō, -cēre, -xī vi to shine, be light; (impers) to dawn, be daylight; (fig) to shine, be clear; **meridiē nōn ~cēre** ≈ (argue) that black is white.
Lūcerēs, -um mpl a Roman patrician tribe.
Lūceria, -iae f town in Apulia.
Lūcerīnus adj see n.
lucerna, -ae f lamp; (fig) ≈ midnight oil.
lūcēscō, -ere vi to begin to shine, get light, dawn.
lūcidē adv clearly.
lūcidus adj bright, clear; (fig) lucid.
lūcifer, -ī adj light-bringing ♦ m morning star, Venus; day.
lūcifugus adj shunning the light.

Lūcīlius, -ī m Roman family name (esp the first Latin satirist).
Lūcīna, -ae f goddess of childbirth.
lūcīscō etc see **lūcēscō**.
Lucmō (Lucumō), -ōnis m Etruscan prince or priest.
Lucrētia, -iae f wife of Collatinus, ravished by Tarquin.
Lucrētius, -ī m Roman family name (esp the philosophic poet).
lucrifuga, -ae m non-profiteer.
Lucrīnēnsis adj see n.
Lucrīnus, -ī m lake near Baiae (famous for oysters).
lucror, -ārī, -ātus vt to gain, win, acquire.
lucrōsus adj profitable.
lucrum, -ī nt profit, gain; greed; wealth; ~ī **facere** gain, get the credit of; ~ō **esse** be of advantage; **in ~īs pōnere** count as gain.
luctāmen, -inis nt struggle, exertion.
luctātiō, -ōnis f wrestling; fight, contest.
luctātor, -ōris m wrestler.
lūctificus adj baleful.
lūctisonus adj mournful.
luctor, -ārī, -ātus vi to wrestle; to struggle, fight.
lūctuōsus adj sorrowful, lamentable.
lūctus, -ūs m mourning, lamentation; mourning (dress).
lūcubrātiō, -ōnis f work by lamplight, nocturnal study.
lūcubrō, -āre, -āvī, -ātum vi to work by night ♦ vt to compose by night.
lūculentē adv splendidly, right.
lūculenter adv very well.
lūculentus adj bright; (fig) brilliant, excellent, rich, fine.
Lūcullus, -ī m Roman surname (esp the conqueror of Mithridates).
lūcus, -ī m grove; wood.
lūdia, -ae f woman gladiator.
lūdibrium, -ī and **iī** nt mockery, derision; laughing stock; sport, play; ~iō **habēre** make fun of.
lūdibundus adj playful; safely, easily.
lūdicer, -rī adj playful; theatrical.
lūdicrum, -ī nt public show, play; sport.
lūdificātiō, -ōnis f ridicule; tricking.
lūdificātor, -ōris m mocker.
lūdificō, -āre; -or, -ārī, -ātus vt to make a fool of, ridicule; to delude, thwart.
lūdiō, -ōnis m actor.
lūdius, -ī and **iī** m actor; gladiator.
lūdō, -dere, -sī, -sum vi to play; to sport, frolic; to dally, make love ♦ vt to play at; to amuse oneself with; to mimic, imitate; to ridicule, mock; to delude.
lūdus, -ī m game, sport, play; (pl) public spectacle, games; school; (fig) child's play; fun, jest; (love) dalliance; ~um **dare** humour;

~ōs facere put on a public show; make fun of.
luella, -ae *f* atonement.
luēs, -is *f* plague, pest; misfortune.
Lugdūnēnsis *adj see n.*
Lugdūnum, -ī *nt* town in E. Gaul (*now* Lyons).
lūgeō, -gēre, -xī *vt, vi* to mourn; to be in mourning.
lūgubris *adj* mourning; disastrous; (*sound*) plaintive ♦ *ntpl* mourning dress.
lumbī, -ōrum *mpl* loins.
lumbrīcus, -ī *m* worm.
lūmen, -inis *m* light; lamp, torch; day; eye; life; (*fig*) ornament, glory; clarity.
lūmināre, -is *nt* window.
lūminōsus *adj* brilliant.
lūna, -ae *f* moon; month; crescent.
lūnāris *adj* of the moon.
lūnātus *adj* crescent-shaped.
lūnō, -āre *vt* to bend into a crescent.
luō, -ere, -ī *vt* to pay; to atone for; to avert by expiation.
lupa, -ae *f* she-wolf; prostitute.
lupānar, -āris *nt* brothel.
lupātus *adj* toothed ♦ *m and ntpl* curb.
Lupercal, -ālis *nt* a grotto sacred to Pan.
Lupercālia, -ālium *ntpl* festival of Pan in February.
Lupercus, -ī *m* Pan; priest of Pan.
lupīnum, -ī *nt* lupin; sham money, counters.
lupīnus *adj* wolf's.
lupīnus, -ī *m* lupin; sham money, counters.
lupus, -ī *m* wolf; (*fish*) pike; toothed bit; grapnel; ~ **in fābulā** ≈ *talk of the devil.*
lūridus *adj* pale yellow, ghastly pallid.
lūror, -ōris *m* yellowness.
lūscinia, -ae *f* nightingale.
luscitiōsus *adj* purblind.
luscus *adj* one-eyed.
lūsiō, -ōnis *f* play.
Lūsitānia, -iae *f* part of W. Spain (*including what is now Portugal*).
Lūsitānus *adj see n.*
lūsitō, -āre *vi* to play.
lūsor, -ōris *m* player; humorous writer.
lūstrālis *adj* lustral, propitiatory; quinquennial.
lūstrātiō, -ōnis *f* purification; roving.
lūstrō, -āre, -āvī, -ātum *vt* to purify; (*motion*) to go round, encircle, traverse; (*MIL*) to review; (*eyes*) to scan, survey; (*mind*) to consider; (*light*) to illuminate.
lustror, -ārī *vi* to frequent brothels.
lustrum, -ī *nt* den, lair; (*pl*) wild country; (*fig*) brothels; debauchery.
lūstrum, -ī *nt* purificatory sacrifice; (*time*) five years.
lūsus *ppp of* **lūdō.**
lūsus, -ūs *m* play, game, sport; dalliance.
lūteolus *adj* yellow.
Lutetia, -ae *f* town in N. Gaul (*now* Paris).
lūteus *adj* yellow, orange.
luteus *adj* of clay; muddy, dirty, (*fig*) vile.
lutitō, -āre *vt* to throw mud at.

lutulentus *adj* muddy, filthy; (*fig*) foul.
lūtum, -ī *nt* dyer's weed; yellow.
lutum, -ī *nt* mud, mire; clay.
lūx, lūcis *f* light; daylight; day; life; (*fig*) public view; glory, encouragement, enlightenment; **lūce** in the daytime; **prīmā lūce** at daybreak; **lūce carentēs** the dead.
lūxī *perf of* **lūceō**; *perf of* **lūgeō.**
luxor, -ārī *vi* to live riotously.
luxuria, -ae, -ēs, -ēī *f* rankness, profusion; extravagance, luxury.
luxuriō, -āre, -or, -ārī *vi* to grow to excess, be luxuriant; (*fig*) to be exuberant, run riot.
luxuriōsē *adv* voluptuously.
luxuriōsus *adj* luxuriant; excessive, extravagant; voluptuous.
luxus, -ūs *m* excess, debauchery, pomp.
Lyaeus, -ī *m* Bacchus; wine.
Lycaeus, -ī *m* mountain in Arcadia (*sacred to Pan*).
Lycāōn, -onis *m* father of Callisto, the Great Bear.
Lycāonius *adj see n.*
Lycēum (Lycīum), -ī *nt* Aristotle's school at Athens.
lychnūchus, -ī *m* lampstand.
lychnus, -ī *m* lamp.
Lycia, -ae *f* country in S.W. Asia Minor.
Lycius *adj* Lycian.
Lyctius *adj* Cretan.
Lycurgus, -ī *m* Thracian king killed by Bacchus; Spartan lawgiver; Athenian orator.
Lȳdia, -iae *f* country of Asia Minor.
Lȳdius *adj* Lydian; Etruscan.
Lȳdus, -ī *m* Lydian.
lympha, -ae *f* water.
lymphāticus *adj* crazy, frantic.
lymphātus *adj* distracted.
Lynceus, -eī *m* keen-sighted Argonaut.
lynx, lyncis *m/f* lynx.
lyra, -ae *f* lyre; lyric poetry.
lyricus *adj* of the lyre, lyrical.
Lysiās, -ae *m* Athenian orator.

M, m

Macedō, -onis *m* Macedonian.
Macedonia *f* Macedonia.
Macedonicus, -onius *adj see n.*
macellum, -ī *nt* market.
maceō, -ēre *vi* to be lean.
macer, -rī *adj* lean, meagre; poor.
māceria, -ae *f* wall.
mācerō, -āre *vt* to soften; (*body*) to enervate; (*mind*) to distress.

macēscō, -ere *vi* to grow thin.
machaera, -ae *f* sword.
machaerophorus, -ī *m* soldier armed with a sword.
Machāōn, -onis *m* legendary Greek surgeon.
Machāonius *adj see n.*
māchina, -ae *f* machine, engine; (*fig*) scheme, trick.
māchināmentum, -ī *nt* engine.
māchinātiō, -ōnis *f* mechanism, machine; (*fig*) contrivance.
māchinātor, -ōris *m* engineer; (*fig*) contriver.
māchinor, -ārī, -ātus *vt* to devise, contrive; (*fig*) to plot, scheme.
maciēs, -ēī *f* leanness, meagreness; poorness.
macilentus *adj* thin.
macrēscō, -ere *vi* to grow thin.
macritūdō, -inis *f* leanness.
macrocollum, -ī *nt* large size of paper.
mactābilis *adj* deadly.
mactātus, -ūs *m* sacrifice.
macte blessed; well done!
mactō, -āre, -āvī, -ātum *vt* to sacrifice; to punish, kill.
mactō, -āre *vt* to glorify.
macula, -ae *f* spot, stain; (*net*) mesh; (*fig*) blemish, fault.
maculō, -āre, -āvī, -ātum *vt* to stain, defile.
maculōsus *adj* dappled, mottled; stained, polluted.
madefaciō, -facere, -fēcī, -factum (*pass* **-fīō, -fierī**) *vt* to wet, soak.
madeō, -ēre *vi* to be wet, be drenched; to be boiled soft; (*comedy*) to be drunk; (*fig*) to be steeped in.
madēscō, -ere *vi* to get wet, become moist.
madidus *adj* wet, soaked; sodden; drunk.
madulsa, -ae *m* drunkard.
Maeander (-ros), -rī *m a winding river of Asia Minor*; winding, wandering.
Maecēnās, -ātis *m friend of Augustus, patron of poets.*
maena, -ae *f* sprat.
Maenala, -ōrum *ntpl mountain range in Arcadia.*
Maenalis, -ius *adj* of Maenalus; Arcadian.
Maenalus (-os), -ī *m* Maenala.
Maenas, -dis *f* Bacchante.
Maeniānum *nt* balcony.
Maenius, -ī *m Roman family name*; **~ia columna** whipping post in the Forum.
Maeonia, -ae *f* Lydia.
Maeonidēs, -dae *m* Homer.
Maeonius, -s *adj* Lydian; Homeric; Etruscan.
Maeōticus, -us *adj* Scythian, Maeotic.
Maeōtis, -dis *f* Sea of Azov.
maereō, -ēre *vi* to mourn, be sad.
maeror, -ōris *m* mourning, sorrow, sadness.
maestiter *adv see adj.*
maestitia, -ae *f* sadness, melancholy.
maestus *adj* sad, sorrowful; gloomy; mourning.

māgālia, -um *ntpl* huts.
mage *etc see* **magis.**
magicus *adj* magical.
magis (mage) *adv* more; **eō ~** the more, all the more.
magister, -rī *m* master, chief, director; (*school*) teacher; (*fig*) instigator; **~ equitum** chief of cavalry, second in command to a dictator; **~ mōrum** censor; **~ sacrōrum** chief priest.
magisterium, -ī *and* **iī** *nt* presidency, tutorship.
magistra, -ae *f* mistress, instructress.
magistrātus, -ūs *m* magistracy, office; magistrate, official.
magnanimitās, -ātis *f* greatness.
māgnanimus *adj* great, brave.
Magnēs, -ētis *m* Magnesian; magnet.
Magnēsia *f district of Thessaly.*
Magnēsius, -ēssus, -ētis *adj see n.*
magnidicus *adj* boastful.
magnificē *adv* grandly; pompously.
magnificentia, -ae *f* greatness, grandeur; pomposity.
magnificō, -āre *vt* to esteem highly.
magnificus (*compar* **-entior** *superl* **-entissimus**) *adj* great, grand, splendid; pompous.
magniloquentia, -ae *f* elevated language; pomposity.
magniloquus *adj* boastful.
magnitūdō, -inis *f* greatness, size, large amount; dignity.
magnopere *adv* greatly, very much.
magnus (*compar* **māior** *superl* **māximus**) *adj* great, large, big, tall; (*voice*) loud; (*age*) advanced; (*value*) high, dear; (*fig*) grand, noble, important; **avunculus ~** great-uncle; **~a loquī** boast; **~ī aestimāre** think highly of; **~ī esse** be highly esteemed; **~ō stāre** cost dear; **~ō opere** very much.
magus, -ī *m* wise man; magician ♦ *adj* magic.
Māia, -ae *f mother of Mercury.*
māiestās, -ātis *f* greatness, dignity, majesty; treason; **~ātem laedere, minuere** offend against the sovereignty of; **lēx ~ātis** law against treason.
māior, -ōris *compar of* **māgnus**; **~ nātū** older, elder.
māiōrēs, -ōrum *mpl* ancestors; **in ~us crēdere/ferre** exaggerate.
Māius, -ī *m* May ♦ *adj* of May.
māiusculus *adj* somewhat greater; a little older.
māla, -ae *f* cheek, jaw.
malacia, -ae *f* dead calm.
malacus *adj* soft.
male (*compar* **pēius, superl pessimē**) *adv* badly, wrongly, unfortunately; not; (*with words having bad sense*) very much; **~ est animō** I

feel ill; ~ **sānus** insane; ~ **dīcere** abuse, curse; ~ **facere** harm.

maledicē _adv_ abusively.

maledictiō, -ōnis _f_ abuse.

maledictum, -ī _nt_ curse.

maledicus _adj_ scurrilous.

malefactum, -ī _nt_ wrong.

maleficē _see adj._

maleficium, -ī _and_ **iī** _nt_ misdeed, wrong, mischief.

maleficus _adj_ wicked ♦ _m_ criminal.

malesuādus _adj_ seductive.

malevolēns, -entis _adj_ spiteful.

malevolentia, -ae _f_ ill-will.

malevolus _adj_ ill-disposed, malicious.

mālifer, -ī _adj_ apple-growing.

malīgnē _adv_ spitefully; grudgingly.

malīgnitās, -ātis _f_ malice; stinginess.

malīgnus _adj_ unkind, ill-natured, spiteful; stingy; (_soil_) unfruitful; (_fig_) small, scanty.

malitia, -ae _f_ badness, malice; roguishness.

malitiōsē _adv see adj._

malitiōsus _adj_ wicked, crafty.

maliv- _etc see_ **malev-**.

mālle _infin of_ **mālō**.

malleolus, -ī _m_ hammer; (_MIL_) fire-brand.

malleus, -ī _m_ hammer, mallet, maul.

mālō, -le, -uī _vt_ to prefer; would rather.

malobathrum, -ī _nt_ an oriental perfume.

māluī _perf of_ **mālō**.

mālum, -ī _nt_ apple, fruit.

malum, -ī _nt_ evil, wrong, harm, misfortune; (_interj_) mischief.

mālus, -ī _f_ apple tree.

mālus, -ī _m_ mast, pole.

malus (_compar_ **pēior** _superl_ **pessimus**) _adj_ bad, evil, harmful; unlucky; ugly; **ī in ~am rem** go to hell!

malva, -ae _f_ mallow.

Māmers, -tis _m_ Mars.

Māmertīnī, -ōrum _mpl_ mercenary troops who occupied Messana.

mamma, -ae _f_ breast; teat.

mammilla, -ae _f_ breast.

mānābilis _adj_ penetrating.

manceps, -ipis _m_ purchaser; contractor.

mancipium, -ī _and_ **iī** _nt_ formal purchase; property; slave.

mancipō, -āre _vt_ to sell, deliver up.

mancup- _etc see_ **mancip-**.

mancus _adj_ crippled.

mandātum, -ī _nt_ commission, command; (_law_) contract.

mandātus, -ūs _m_ command.

mandō, -āre, -āvī, -ātum _vt_ to entrust, commit; to commission, command.

mandō, -ere, -ī, mānsum _vt_ to chew, eat, devour.

mandra, -ae _f_ drove of cattle.

mandūcus, -ī _m_ masked figure of a glutton.

māne _nt_ (_indecl_) morning ♦ _adv_ in the morning, early.

maneō, -ēre, mānsī, mānsum _vi_ to remain;

to stay, stop; to last, abide, continue ♦ _vt_ to wait for, await; **in condiciōne ~** abide by an agreement.

Mānēs, -ium _mpl_ ghosts, shades of the dead; the lower world; bodily remains.

mangō, -ōnis _m_ dealer.

manicae, -ārum _fpl_ sleeves, gloves; handcuffs.

manicātus _adj_ with long sleeves.

manicula, -ae _f_ little hand.

manifestō, -āre _vt_ to disclose.

manifestō _adv_ clearly, evidently.

manifestus _adj_ clear, obvious; convicted, caught.

manipl- _etc see_ **manipul-**.

manipulāris _adj_ of a company ♦ _m_ private (in the ranks); fellow soldier.

manipulātim _adv_ by companies.

manipulus, -ī _m_ bundle (_esp of hay_); (_MIL_) company.

Manlius, -iānus _adj see n._

Manlius, -ī _m_ Roman family name (_esp the saviour of the Capitol from the Gauls_); a severe disciplinarian.

mannus, -ī _m_ Gallic horse.

mānō, -āre, -āvī, -ātum _vi_ to flow, drip, stream; (_fig_) to spread, emanate.

mānsī _perf of_ **maneō**.

mānsiō, -ōnis _f_ remaining, stay.

mānsitō, -āre _vi_ to stay on.

mānsuēfaciō, -facere, -fēcī, -factum (_pass_ **-fīō, -fierī**) _vt_ to tame.

mānsuēscō, -scere, -vī, -tum _vt_ to tame ♦ _vi_ to grow tame, grow mild.

mānsuētē _adv see adj._

mānsuētūdō, -inis _f_ tameness; gentleness.

mānsuētus _ppp of_ **mānsuēscō** ♦ _adj_ tame; mild, gentle.

mānsus _ppp of_ **mandō**; _ppp of_ **maneō**.

mantēle, -is _nt_ napkin, towel.

mantēlum, -ī _nt_ cloak.

mantica, -ae _f_ knapsack.

manticinor, -ārī, -ātus _vi_ to be a prophet.

mantō, -āre _vi_ to remain, wait.

Mantua, -ae _f_ birthplace of Vergil in N. Italy.

manuālis _adj_ for the hand.

manubiae, -ārum _fpl_ money from sale of booty.

manūbrium, -ī _and_ **iī** _nt_ handle, haft.

manuleātus _adj_ with long sleeves.

manūmissiō, -ōnis _f_ emancipation (of a slave).

manūmittō, -ittere, -īsī, -issum _vt_ to emancipate, make free.

manupretium, -ī _and_ **iī** _nt_ pay, wages, reward.

manus, -ūs _f_ hand; corps, band, company; (_elephant_) trunk; (_art_) touch; (_work_) handiwork, handwriting; (_war_) force, valour, hand to hand fighting; (_fig_) power; ~ **extrēma** finishing touch; ~ **ferrea** grappling iron; **~um dare** give up, yield; **~ū** artificially; **~ū mittere** emancipate; **ad ~um** at hand; **in ~ū** obvious; subject; **in ~ūs venīre** come to hand; **in ~ibus** well known; at hand; **in ~ibus habēre** be

engaged on; fondle; **per ~ūs** forcibly; **per ~ūs trādere** hand down.
mapālia, -um *ntpl* huts.
mappa, -ae *f* napkin, cloth.
Marathōn, -ōnis *f* Attic village famous for Persian defeat.
Marathōnius *adj see n.*
Marcellia, -iōrum *ntpl* festival of the Marcelli.
Marcellus, -ī *m* Roman surname (*esp the captor of Syracuse*).
marceō, -ēre *vi* to droop, be faint.
marcēscō, -ere *vi* to waste away, grow feeble.
Marciānus *adj see n.*
marcidus *adj* withered; enervated.
Marcius, -ī *m* Roman family name (*esp Ancus, fourth king*).
Marcius *adj see n.*
mare, -is *nt* sea; **~ nostrum** Mediterranean; **~ inferum** Tyrrhenian Sea; **~ superum** Adriatic.
Mareōticus *adj* Mareotic; Egyptian.
margarīta, -ae *f* pearl.
marginō, -āre *vt* to put a border *or* kerb on.
margō, -inis *m/f* edge, border, boundary; **~ cēnae** side dishes.
Mariānus *adj see n.*
Marīca, -ae *f* nymph of Minturnae.
marīnus *adj* of the sea.
marītālis *adj* marriage- (*in cpds*).
maritimus *adj* of the sea, maritime, coastal ♦ *ntpl* coastal area.
marītō, -āre *vt* to marry.
marītus, -ī *m* husband ♦ *adj* nuptial.
Marius, -ī *m* Roman family name (*esp the victor over Jugurtha and the Teutons*).
Marius *adj see n.*
marmor, -is *nt* marble; statue, tablet; sea.
marmoreus *adj* of marble; like marble.
Marō, -ōnis *m* surname of Vergil.
marra, -ae *f* kind of hoe.
Mars, Martis *m* god of war, father of Romulus; war, conflict; planet Mars; **aequō Marte** on equal terms; **suō Marte** by one's own exertions.
Marsī, -ōrum *mpl* people of central Italy, famous as fighters.
Marsicus, -us *adj* Marsian.
marsuppium, -ī *and* **iī** *nt* purse.
Mārtiālis *adj* of Mars.
Mārticola, -ae *m* worshipper of Mars.
Mārtigena, -ae *m* son of Mars.
Mārtius *adj* of Mars; of March; warlike.
mās, maris *m* male, man ♦ *adj* male; manly.
māsculus *adj* male, masculine; manly.
Masinissa, -ae *m* king of Numidia.
massa, -ae *f* lump, mass.
Massicum, -ī *nt* Massic wine.
Massicus, -ī *m* mountain in Campania, famous for vines.

Massilia, -ae *f* Greek colony in Gaul (*now Marseilles*).
Massiliēnsis *adj see n.*
mastīgia, -ae *nt* scoundrel.
mastrūca, -ae *f* sheepskin.
mastrūcātus *adj* wearing sheepskin.
matara, -ae *and* **is, -is** *f* Celtic javelin.
matelliō, -ōnis *m* pot.
māter, -ris *f* mother; **Māgna ~** Cybele.
mātercula, -ae *f* poor mother.
māteria, -ae; -ēs, -ēi *f* matter, substance; wood, timber; (*fig*) subject matter, theme; occasion, opportunity; (*person*) ability, character.
māteriārius, -ī *and* **iī** *m* timber merchant.
māteriātus *adj* timbered.
māteriēs *etc see* **māteria.**
māterior, -ārī *vi* to fetch wood.
māternus *adj* mother's.
mātertera, -ae *f* aunt (maternal).
mathēmaticus, -ī *m* mathematician; astrologer.
mātricīda, -ae *m* matricide.
mātricīdium, -ī *and* **iī** *nt* a mother's murder.
mātrimōnium, -ī *and* **iī** *nt* marriage.
mātrimus *adj* whose mother is still alive.
mātrōna, -ae *f* married woman, matron, lady.
mātrōnālis *adj* a married woman's.
matula, -ae *f* pot.
mātūrē *adv* at the right time; early, promptly.
mātūrēscō, -ēscere, -uī *vi* to ripen.
mātūritās, -ātis *f* ripeness; (*fig*) maturity, perfection, height.
mātūrō, -āre, -āvī, -ātum *vt* to bring to maturity; to hasten, be too hasty with ♦ *vi* to make haste.
mātūrus *adj* ripe, mature; timely, seasonable; early.
Mātūta, -ae *f* goddess of dawn.
mātūtīnus *adj* morning, early.
Mauritānia, -ae *f* Mauretania (*now* Morocco).
Maurus, -ī *m* Moor ♦ *adj* Moorish, African.
Maurūsius *adj see n.*
Māvors, -tis *m* Mars.
Māvortius *adj see n.*
maxilla, -ae *f* jaw.
maximē *adv* most, very much, especially; precisely, just; certainly, yes; **cum ~** just as; **quam ~** as much as possible.
maximitās, -ātis *f* great size.
maximus *superl of* **magnus.**
māxum- *etc see* **māxim-.**
māzonomus, -ī *m* dish.
meāpte my own.
meātus, -ūs *m* movement, course.
mēcastor *interj* by Castor!
mēcum with me.
meddix tuticus *m* senior Oscan magistrate.
Mēdēa, -ae *f* Colchian wife of Jason, expert in magic.

Noun declensions and verb conjugations are shown on pp xiii to xxv. The present infinitive ending of a verb shows to which conjugation it belongs: **-āre** = 1st; **-ēre** = 2nd; **-ere** = 3rd and **-īre** = 4th. Irregular verbs are shown on p xxvi

Mēdēis *adj* magical.
medentēs, -entum *mpl* doctors.
medeor, -ērī *vi (with dat)* to heal, remedy.
mediastīnus, -ī *m* drudge.
mēdica, -ae *f* lucern (*kind of clover*).
medicābilis *adj* curable.
medicāmen, -inis *nt* drug, medicine;
  cosmetic; (*fig*) remedy.
medicāmentum, -ī *nt* drug, medicine; potion,
  poison; (*fig*) relief; embellishment.
medicātus, -ūs *m* charm.
medicīna, -ae *f* medicine; cure; (*fig*) remedy,
  relief.
medicō, -āre, -āvī, -ātum *vt* to cure; to steep,
  dye.
medicor, -ārī *vt, vi* to cure.
medicus *adj* healing ♦ *m* doctor.
medietās, -ātis *f* mean.
medimnum, -ī *nt*, **-us, -ī** *m* bushel.
mediocris *adj* middling, moderate, average.
mediocritās, -ātis *f* mean, moderation;
  mediocrity.
mediocriter *adv* moderately, not particularly;
  calmly.
Mediolānēnsis *adj see n.*
Mediolānum, -ī *nt* town in N. Italy (*now*
  Milan).
meditāmentum, -ī *nt* preparation, drill.
meditātiō, -ōnis *f* thinking about;
  preparation, practice.
· **meditātus** *adj* studied.
mediterrāneus *adj* inland.
meditor, -ārī, -ātus *vt, vi* to think over,
  contemplate, reflect; to practise, study.
medius *adj* middle, the middle of;
  intermediate; intervening; middling,
  moderate; neutral ♦ *nt* middle; public ♦ *m*
  mediator; **~um complectī** clasp round the
  waist; **~um sē gerere** be neutral; **~ō** midway;
  ~ō temporis meanwhile; **in ~um** for the
  common good; **in ~um prōferre** publish; **dē
  ~ō tollere** do away with; **ē ~ō abīre** die,
  disappear; **in ~ō esse** be public; **in ~ō positus**
  open to all; **in ~ō relinquere** leave undecided.
medius fidius *interj* by Heaven!
medix *etc see* **meddix.**
medulla, -ae *f* marrow, pith.
medullitus *adv* from the heart.
medullula, -ae *f* marrow.
Mēdus, -ī *m* Mede, Persian.
Mēdus *adj see n.*
Medūsa, -ae *f* Gorgon, whose look turned
  everything to stone.
Medūsaeus *adj*: **~ equus** Pegasus.
Megalēnsia (Megalēsia), -um *ntpl festival of
  Cybele in April.*
Megara, -ae *f*, **-ōrum** *ntpl town in Greece near
  the Isthmus.*
Megarēus *and* **icus** *adj* Megarean.
megistānes, -um *mpl* grandees.
mehercle, mehercule, mehercules *interj* by
  Hercules!
mēiō, -ere *vi* to make water.

mel, mellis *nt* honey.
melancholicus *adj* melancholy.
melē *pl* melos.
Meleager (-ros), -rī *m prince of Calydon.*
melicus *adj* musical; lyrical.
melilōtos, -ī *f* kind of clover.
melimēla, -ōrum *ntpl* honey apples.
Mēlīnum, -ī *nt* Melian white.
melior, -ōris *adj* better.
melisphyllum, -ī *nt* balm.
Melita, -ae *f* Malta.
Melitēnsis *adj* Maltese.
melius *nt* melior ♦ *adv* better.
meliusculē *adv* fairly well.
meliusculus *adj* rather better.
mellifer, -ī *adj* honey-making.
mellītus *adj* honeyed; sweet.
melos, -ī *nt* tune, song.
Melpomenē, -ēs *f Muse of tragedy.*
membrāna, -ae *f* skin, membrane, slough;
  parchment.
membrānula, -ae *f* piece of parchment.
membrātim *adv* limb by limb; piecemeal; in
  short sentences.
membrum, -ī *nt* limb, member; part, division;
  clause.
mēmet *emphatic form of* **mē.**
meminī, -isse *vi (with gen)* to remember,
  think of; to mention.
Memnōn, -onis *m Ethiopian king, killed at Troy.*
Memnonius *adj see n.*
memor, -is *adj* mindful, remembering; in
  memory (of).
memorābilis *adj* memorable, remarkable.
memorandus *adj* noteworthy.
memorātus, -ūs *m* mention.
memorātus *adj* famed.
memoria, -ae *f* memory, remembrance; time,
  lifetime; history; **haec ~** our day; **~ae
  prōdere** hand down to posterity; **post
  hominum ~am** since the beginning of
  history.
memoriola, -ae *f* weak memory.
memoriter *adv* from memory; accurately.
memorō, -āre, -āvī, -ātum *vt* to mention,
  say, speak.
Memphis, -is *and* **idos** *f town in middle Egypt.*
Memphītēs *and* **ītis** *and* **īticus** *adj* of
  Memphis; Egyptian.
Menander (-ros), -rī *m Greek writer of comedy.*
Menandrēus *adj see n.*
menda, -ae *f* fault.
mendācium, -ī *and* **iī** *nt* lie.
mendāciunculum, -ī *nt* fib.
mendāx, -ācis *adj* lying; deceptive, unreal ♦
  m liar.
mendīcitās, -ātis *f* beggary.
mendīcō, -āre; -or, -ārī, *vi* to beg, go begging.
mendīcus *adj* beggarly, poor ♦ *m* beggar.
mendōsē *adv see adj.*
mendōsus *adj* faulty; wrong, mistaken.
mendum, -ī *nt* fault, blunder.
Menelāēus *adj see n.*

Menelāus, -ī m brother of Agamemnon, husband of Helen.

Menoetiadēs, -ae m Patroclus.

mēns, mentis f mind, understanding; feelings, heart; idea, plan, purpose; courage; **venit in mentem** it occurs; **mente captus** insane; **eā mente ut** with the intention of.

mēnsa, -ae f table; meal, course; counter, bank; **secunda ~** dessert.

mēnsārius, -ī and **iī** m banker.

mēnsiō, -ōnis f (metre) quantity.

mēnsis, -is m month.

mēnsor, -ōris m measurer, surveyor.

mēnstruālis adj for a month.

mēnstruus adj monthly; for a month ♦ nt a month's provisions.

mēnsula, -ae f little table.

mēnsūra, -ae f measure, measurement; standard, standing; amount, size, capacity.

mēnsus ppa of **mētior.**

menta, -ae f mint.

Menteus adj see n.

mentiēns, -ientis m fallacy.

mentiō, -ōnis f mention, hint.

mentior, -īrī, -ītus vi to lie, deceive ♦ vt to say falsely; to feign, imitate.

mentītus adj lying, false.

Mentor, -is m artist in metalwork; ornamental cup.

mentum, -ī nt chin.

meō, -āre vi to go, pass.

mephītis, -is f noxious vapour, malaria.

merācus adj pure.

mercābilis adj buyable.

mercātor, -ōris m merchant, dealer.

mercātūra, -ae f commerce; purchase; goods.

mercātus, -ūs m trade, traffic; market, fair.

mercēdula, -ae f poor wages, small rent.

mercēnārius adj hired, mercenary ♦ m servant.

mercēs, -ēdis f pay, wages, fee; bribe; rent; (fig) reward, retribution, cost.

mercimōnium, -ī and **iī** nt wares, goods.

mercor, -ārī, -ātus vt to trade in, purchase.

Mercurius, -ī m messenger of the gods, god of trade, thieves, speech and the lyre; **stēlla ~ī** planet Mercury.

Mercuriālis adj see n.

merda, -ae f dung.

merenda, -ae f lunch.

mereō, -ēre, -uī; -eor, -ērī, -itus vt, vi to deserve; to earn, win, acquire; (MIL) to serve; **bene ~ dē** do a service to, serve well; **~ equō** serve in the cavalry.

meretrīcius adj a harlot's.

meretrīcula, -ae f pretty harlot.

meretrīx, -īcis f harlot.

mergae, -ārum fpl pitchfork.

merges, -itis f sheaf.

mergō, -gere, -sī, -sum vt to dip, immerse, sink; (fig) to bury, plunge, drown.

mergus, -ī m (bird) diver.

meridiānus adj midday; southerly.

merīdiātiō, -ōnis f siesta.

merīdiēs, -ēī f midday, noon; south.

**merīdiō, -āre, **vi to take a siesta.

meritō, -āre vt to learn.

meritō adv deservedly.

meritōrius adj money-earning ♦ ntpl lodgings.

meritum, -ī nt service, kindness, merit; blame.

meritus ppp of **mereō** ♦ adj deserved, just.

merops, -is f bee-eater.

mersī perf of **mergō.**

mersō, -āre vt to immerse, plunge; to overwhelm.

mersus ppp of **mergō.**

merula, -ae f blackbird.

merum, -ī nt wine.

merus adj pure, undiluted; bare, mere.

merx, mercis f goods, wares.

Messalla, -ae m Roman surname (esp **~ Corvīnus** Augustan orator, soldier and literary patron).

Messallīna, -īnae f wife of emperor Claudius; wife of Nero.

Messāna, -ae f Sicilian town (now Messina).

messis, -is f harvest.

messor, -ōris m reaper.

messōrius adj a reaper's.

messuī perf of **metō.**

messus ppp of **metō.**

mēta, -ae f pillar at each end of the Circus course; turning point, winning post; (fig) goal, end, limit.

metallum, -ī nt mine, quarry; metal.

mētātor, -ōris m surveyor.

Metaurus, -ī m river in Umbria, famous for the defeat of Hasdrubal.

Metellus, -ī m Roman surname (esp the commander against Jugurtha).

Mēthymna, -ae f town in Lesbos.

Mēthymnaeus adj see n.

mētior, -tīrī, -nsus vt to measure, measure out; to traverse; (fig) to estimate, judge.

metō, -tere, -ssuī, -ssum vt to reap, gather; to mow, cut down.

mētor, -ārī, -ātus vt to measure off, lay out.

metrēta, -ae f liquid measure (about 9 gallons).

metuculōsus adj frightful.

metuō, -uere, -uī, -ūtum vt to fear, be apprehensive.

metus, -ūs m fear, alarm, anxiety.

meus adj my, mine.

mī dat of **ego;** voc and mpl of **meus.**

mīca, -ae f crumb, grain.

micō, -āre, -uī vi to quiver, flicker, beat, flash, sparkle.

Midās, -ae m Phrygian king whose touch turned

Noun declensions and verb conjugations are shown on pp xiii to xxv. The present infinitive ending of a verb shows to which conjugation it belongs: **-āre** = 1st; **-ēre** = 2nd; **-ere** = 3rd and **-īre** = 4th. Irregular verbs are shown on p xxvi

everything to gold.

migrātiō, -ōnis *f* removal, change.

migrō, -āre, -āvī, -ātum *vi* to remove, change, pass away ♦ *vt* to transport, transgress.

mīles, -itis *m* soldier, infantryman; army troops.

Mīlēsius *adj see n.*

Mīlētus, -tī *f* town in Asia Minor.

mīlia, -um *ntpl* thousands; **~ passuum** miles.

mīliārium (milliārium), -ī *and* **iī** *nt* milestone.

mīlitāris *adj* military, a soldier's.

mīlitāriter *adv* in a soldierly fashion.

mīlitia, -ae *f* military service, war; the army; **~ae** on service; **domī ~aeque** at home and abroad.

mīlitō, -āre *vi* to serve, be a soldier.

milium, -ī *and* **iī** *nt* millet.

mīlle, (*pl* **~ia**) *num* a thousand; **~ passūs** a mile.

mīllensimus, -ēsimus *adj* thousandth.

mīllia *etc see* **mīlia.**

mīlliārium *etc see* **mīliārium.**

mīlliēns, -ēs *adv* a thousand times.

Milō, -ōnis *m* tribune who killed Clodius and was defended by Cicero.

Milōniānus *adj see n.*

Miltiadēs, -is *m* Athenian general, victor at Marathon.

mīluīnus *adj* resembling a kite; rapacious.

mīluus (mīlvus), -ī *m* kite; gurnard.

mīma, -ae *f* actress.

Mimallonis, -dis *f* Bacchante.

mīmicē *adv see adj.*

mīmicus *adj* farcical.

Mimnermus, -ī *m* Greek elegiac poet.

mīmula, -ae *f* actress.

mīmus, -ī *m* actor; mime, farce.

mina, -ae *f* Greek silver coin.

mināciter *adv see adj.*

minae, -ārum *fpl* threats; (*wall*) pinnacles.

minanter *adv* threateningly.

minātiō, -ōnis *f* threat.

mināx, -ācis *adj* threatening; projecting.

Minerva, -ae *f* goddess of wisdom and arts, esp weaving; (*fig*) talent, genius; working in wool; **sūs ~am ≈** *"teach your grandmother!"*

miniānus *adj* red-leaded.

miniātulus *adj* painted red.

minimē *adv* least, very little; (*reply*) no, not at all.

minimus *adj* least, smallest, very small; youngest.

miniō, -āre, -āvī, -ātum *vt* to colour red.

minister, -rī *m,* **~ra, ~rae** *f* attendant; servant; helper, agent, tool.

ministerium, -ī *and* **iī** *nt* service, office, duty; retinue.

ministrātor, -ōris *m,* **~rīx, ~rīcis** *f* assistant, handmaid.

ministrō, -āre *vt* to serve, supply; to manage.

minitābundus *adj* threatening.

minitor, -ārī, -ō, -āre *vt, vi* to threaten.

minium, -ī *and* **iī** *nt* vermilion, red lead.

Mīnōis, -idis *f* Ariadne.

Mīnōius, -us *adj see n.*

minor, -ārī, -ātus *vt, vi* to threaten; to project.

minor, -ōris *adj* smaller, less, inferior; younger; (*pl*) descendants.

Mīnōs, -is *m* king of Crete, judge in the lower world.

Mīnōtaurus, -ī *m* monster of the Cretan labyrinth, half bull, half man.

Minturnae, -ārum *fpl* town in S. Latium.

Minturnēnsis *adj see n.*

minum- *etc see* **minim-.**

minuō, -uere, -uī, -ūtum *vt* to make smaller, lessen; to chop up; to reduce, weaken ♦ *vi* (*tide*) to ebb.

minus *nt* minor ♦ *adv* less; not, not at all; **quō ~** (*prevent*) from.

minusculus *adj* smallish.

minūtal, -ālis *nt* mince.

minūtātim *adv* bit by bit.

minūtē *adv* in a petty manner.

minūtus *ppp of* **minuō** ♦ *adj* small; paltry.

mīrābilis *adj* wonderful, extraordinary.

mīrābiliter *adv see adj.*

mīrābundus *adj* astonished.

mīrāculum, -ī *nt* marvel, wonder; amazement.

mīrandus *adj* wonderful.

mīrātiō, -ōnis *f* wonder.

mīrātor, -ōris *m* admirer.

mīrātrīx, -īcis *adj* admiring.

mīrē *adv see adj.*

mīrificē *adv see adj.*

mīrificus *adj* wonderful.

mirmillō *see* **murmillō.**

mīror, -ārī, -ātus *vt* to wonder at, be surprised at, admire ♦ *vi* to wonder, be surprised.

mīrus *adj* wonderful, strange; **~um quam, quantum** extraordinarily.

miscellānea, -ōrum *ntpl* (*food*) hotchpotch.

misceō, -scēre, -scuī, -xtum *vt* to mix, mingle, blend; to join, combine; to confuse, embroil.

misellus *adj* poor little.

Mīsēnēnsis *adj see n.*

Mīsēnum, -ī *nt* promontory and harbour near Naples.

miser, -ī *adj* wretched, poor, pitiful, sorry.

miserābilis *adj* pitiable, sad, plaintive.

miserābiliter *adv see adj.*

miserandus *adj* deplorable.

miserātiō, -ōnis *f* pity, compassion, pathos.

miserē *adv see adj.*

misereō, -ēre, -uī, -eor, -ērī, -itus *vt, vi* (*with gen*) to pity, sympathize with; **~et mē** I pity, I am sorry.

miserēscō, -ere *vi* to feel pity.

miseria, -ae *f* misery, trouble, distress.

misericordia, -ae *f* pity, sympathy, mercy.

misericors, -dis *adj* sympathetic, merciful.

miseriter *adv* sadly.

miseror, -ārī, -ātus *vt* to deplore; to pity.

mīsī *perf of* **mittō.**
missa, -ae *f* (*ECCL*) mass.
missilis *adj* missile.
missiō, -ōnis *f* sending; release; (*MIL*) discharge; (*gladiators*) quarter; (*events*) end; **sine ~ōne** to the death.
missitō, -āre *vt* to send repeatedly.
missus *ppp of* **mittō.**
missus, -ūs *m* sending; throwing; **~ sagittae** bowshot.
mitella, -ae *f* turban.
mītēscō, -ere *vi* to ripen; to grow mild.
Mithridātēs, -is *m king of Pontus, defeated by Pompey.*
Mithridātēus, -icus *adj see n.*
mītigātiō, -ōnis *f* soothing.
mītigō, -āre, -āvī, -ātum *vt* to ripen, soften; to calm, pacify.
mītis *adj* ripe, mellow; soft, mild; gentle.
mitra, -ae *f* turban.
mittō, -ere, mīsī, missum *vt* to send, dispatch; to throw, hurl; to let go, dismiss; to emit, utter; (*news*) to send word; (*gift*) to bestow; (*event*) to end; (*speech*) to omit, stop; **sanguinem ~** bleed ; **ad cēnam ~** invite to dinner; **missum facere** forgo.
mītulus, -ī *m* mussel.
mixtim *adv* promiscuously.
mixtūra, -ae *f* mingling.
Mnēmosynē, -ēs *f mother of the Muses.*
mnēmosynon, -ī *nt* souvenir.
mōbilis *adj* movable; nimble, fleet; excitable, fickle.
mōbilitās, -ātis *f* agility, rapidity; fickleness.
mōbiliter *adv* rapidly.
mōbilitō, -āre *vt* to make rapid.
moderābilis *adj* moderate.
moderāmen, -inis *nt* control; government.
moderanter *adv* with control.
moderātē *adv* with restraint.
moderātim *adv* gradually.
moderātiō, -ōnis *f* control, government; moderation; rules.
moderātor, -ōris *m* controller, governor.
moderātrīx, -īcis *f* mistress, controller.
moderātus *adj* restrained, orderly.
moderor, -ārī, -ātus *vt, vi* (*with dat*) to restrain, check; (*with acc*) to manage, govern, guide.
modestē *adv* with moderation; humbly.
modestia, -ae *f* temperate behaviour, discipline; humility.
modestus *adj* sober, restrained; well-behaved, disciplined; modest, unassuming.
modiālis *adj* holding a peck.
modicē *adv* moderately; slightly.
modicus *adj* moderate; middling, small, mean.
modificātus *adj* measured.
modius, -ī *and* **iī** *m* corn measure, peck.
modo *adv* only; at all, in any way; (*with imp*)

just; (*time*) just now, a moment ago, in a moment ♦ *conj* if only; **nōn ~** not only; **non ~ ... sed** not only ... but also ...; **~ nōn** all but, almost; **~ ... ~** sometimes ... sometimes; **~ ... tum** at first ... then.
modulātē *adv* melodiously.
modulātor, -ōris *m* musician.
modulātus *adj* played, measured.
modulor, -ārī, - ātus *vt* to modulate, play, sing.
modulus, -ī *m* measure.
modus, -ī *m* measure; size; metre, music; way, method; limit, end; **ēius ~ī** such; **~ō, in, ~um** like.
moecha, -ae *f* adulteress.
moechor, -ārī *vi* to commit adultery.
moechus, -ī *m* adulterer.
moenera *etc see* **mūnus.**
moenia, -um *ntpl* defences, walls; town, stronghold.
moeniō *etc see* **mūniō.**
Moesī, -ōrum *mpl people on lower Danube* (*now* Bulgaria).
mola, -ae *f* millstone, mill; grains of spelt.
molāris, -is *m* millstone; (*tooth*) molar.
mōlēs, -is *f* mass, bulk, pile; dam, pier, massive structure; (*fig*) greatness, weight, effort, trouble.
molestē *adv see adj.*
molestia, -ae *f* trouble, annoyance, worry; (*style*) affectation.
molestus *adj* irksome, annoying; (*style*) laboured.
mōlīmen, -inis *nt* exertion, labour; importance.
mōlīmentum, -ī *nt* great effort.
mōlior, -īrī, -ītus *vt* to labour at, work, build; to wield, move, heave; to undertake, devise, occasion ♦ *vi* to exert oneself, struggle.
mōlītiō, -ōnis *f* laborious work.
mōlītor, -ōris *m* builder.
mollēscō, -ere *vi* to soften, become effeminate.
molliculus *adj* tender.
molliō, -īre, -īvī, -ītum *vt* to soften, make supple; to mitigate, make easier; to demoralize.
mollis *adj* soft, supple; tender, gentle; (*character*) sensitive, weak, unmanly; (*poetry*) amatory; (*opinion*) changeable; (*slope*) easy.
molliter *adv* softly, gently; calmly; voluptuously.
mollitia, -ae, -ēs, -ēī *f* softness, suppleness; tenderness, weakness, effeminacy.
mollitūdō, -inis *f* softness; susceptibility.
molō, -ere *vt* to grind.
Molossī, -ōrum *mpl Molossians, people in Epirus.*
Molossicus, -us *adj see n.*
Molossis, -idis *f country of the Molossians.*

Noun declensions and verb conjugations are shown on pp xiii to xxv. The present infinitive ending of a verb shows to which conjugation it belongs: **-āre** = 1st; **-ēre** = 2nd; **-ere** = 3rd and **-īre** = 4th. Irregular verbs are shown on p xxvi

Molossus, -ī *m* Molossian hound.
mōly, -os *nt* a magic herb.
mōmen, -inis *nt* movement, momentum.
mōmentum, -ī *nt* movement; change; (*time*) short space, moment; (*fig*) cause, influence, importance; **nullīus ~ī** unimportant.
momordī *perf of* **mordeō.**
Mona, -ae *f* Isle of Man; Anglesey.
monachus, -ī *m* monk.
monēdula, -ae *f* jackdaw.
moneō, -ēre, -uī, -itum *vt* to remind, advise, warn; to instruct, foretell.
monēris, -is *f* galley with one bank of oars.
monērula *etc see* **monēdula.**
monēta, -ae *f* mint; money; stamp.
monīle, -is *nt* necklace, collar.
monim- *etc see* **monum-.**
monitiō, -ōnis *f* admonishing.
monitor, -ōris *m* admonisher; prompter; teacher.
monitum, -ī *nt* warning; prophecy.
monitus, -ūs *m* admonition; warning.
monogrammus *adj* shadowy.
monopodium, -ī *and* **iī** *nt* table with one leg.
mōns, montis *m* mountain.
mōnstrātor, -ōris *m* shower, inventor.
mōnstrātus *adj* distinguished.
mōnstrē *adv see adj.*
mōnstrō, -āre, -āvī, -ātum *vt* to point out, show; to inform, instruct; to appoint; to denounce.
mōnstrum, -ī *nt* portent, marvel; monster.
mōnstruōsus *adj* unnatural.
montānus *adj* mountainous; mountain- (*in cpds*), highland.
monticola, -ae *m* highlander.
montivagus *adj* mountain-roving.
montuōsus, montōsus *adj* mountainous.
monumentum, -ī *nt* memorial, monument; record.
Mopsopius *adj* Athenian.
mora, -ae *f* delay, pause; hindrance; space of time, sojourn; **~am facere** put off.
mora, -ae *f* division of the Spartan army.
mōrālis *adj* moral.
morātor, -ōris *m* delayer.
morātus *adj* mannered, of a nature; (*writing*) in character.
morbidus *adj* unwholesome.
morbus, -ī *m* illness, disease; distress.
mordāciter *adv see adj.*
mordāx, -ācis *adj* biting, sharp, pungent; (*fig*) snarling, carking.
mordeō, -dēre, momordī, -sum *vt* to bite; to bite into, grip; (*cold*) to nip; (*words*) to sting, hurt, mortify.
mordicus *adv* with a bite; (*fig*) doggedly.
mōres *pl of* **mōs.**
morētum, -ī *nt* salad.
moribundus *adj* dying, mortal; deadly.
mōrigeror, -ārī, -ātus *vi* (*with dat*) to gratify, humour.
mōrigerus *adj* obliging, obedient.

morior, -ī, -tuus *vi* to die; to decay, fade.
moritūrus *fut p of* **morior.**
mōrologus *adj* foolish.
moror, -ārī, -ātus *vi* to delay, stay, loiter ♦ *vt* to detain, retard; to entertain; (*with neg*) to heed, object; **nihil, nīl ~** have no objection to; to not care for; to withdraw a charge against.
mōrōsē *adv see adj.*
mōrōsitās, -ātis *f* peevishness.
mōrōsus *adj* peevish, difficult.
Morpheus, -eos *m* god of dreams.
mors, mortis *f* death; corpse; **mortem sibi cōnscīscere** commit suicide; **mortis poena** capital punishment.
morsiuncula, -ae *f* little kiss.
morsus *ppp of* **mordeō** ♦ *ntpl* little bits.
morsus, -ūs *m* bite; grip; (*fig*) sting, vexation.
mortālis *adj* mortal; transient; man-made ♦ *m* human being.
mortālitās, -ātis *f* mortality, death.
mortārium, -ī *and* **iī** *nt* mortar.
mortifer, -ī *adj* fatal.
mortuus *ppa of* **morior** ♦ *adj* dead ♦ *m* dead man.
mōrum, -ī *nt* blackberry, mulberry.
mōrus, -ī *f* black mulberry tree.
mōrus *adj* foolish ♦ *m* fool.
mōs, mōris *m* nature, manner; humour, mood; custom, practice, law; (*pl*) behaviour, character, morals; **~ māiōrum** national tradition; **mōrem gerere** oblige, humour; **mōre, in mōrem** like.
Mosa, -ae *m* river Meuse.
Mōsēs, -is *m* Moses.
mōtiō, -ōnis *f* motion.
mōtō, -āre *vt* to keep moving.
mōtus *ppp of* **moveō.**
mōtus, -ūs *m* movement; dance, gesture; (*mind*) impulse, emotion; (*POL*) rising, rebellion; **terrae ~** earthquake.
movēns, -entis *pres p of* **moveō** ♦ *adj* movable ♦ *ntpl* motives.
moveō, -ēre, mōvī, mōtum *vt* to move, set in motion; to disturb; to change; to dislodge, expel; to occasion, begin; (*opinion*) to shake; (*mind*) to affect, influence, provoke ♦ *vi* to move; **castra ~** strike camp; **sē ~** budge; to dance.
mox *adv* presently, soon, later on; next.
Mōysēs *see* **Mōsēs.**
mūcidus *adj* snivelling; mouldy.
Mūcius, -ī *m* Roman family name (*esp Scaevola, who burned his right hand before Porsena*).
mūcrō, -ōnis *m* point, edge; sword.
mūcus, -ī *m* mucus.
mūgilis, -is *m* mullet.
muginor, -ārī *vi* to hesitate.
mūgiō, -īre *vi* to bellow, groan.
mūgītus, -ūs *m* lowing, roaring.
mūla, -ae *f* she-mule.
mulceō, -cēre, -sī, -sum *vt* to stroke, caress;

to soothe, alleviate, delight.

Mulciber, -is *and* **ī** *m* Vulcan.

mulcō, -āre, -āvī, -ātum *vt* to beat, ill-treat, damage.

mulctra, -ae *f*, **-ārium, -ārī,** *and* **ārii, -um, -ī** *nt* milkpail.

mulgeō, -ēre, mulsī *vt* to milk.

muliebris *adj* woman's, feminine; effeminate.

muliebriter *adv* like a woman; effeminately.

mulier, -is *f* woman; wife.

mulierārius *adj* woman's.

muliercula, -ae *f* girl.

mulierōsitās, -ātis *f* fondness for women.

mulierōsus *adj* fond of women.

mūlīnus *adj* mulish.

mūliō, -ōnis *m* mule driver.

mūliōnius *adj* mule driver's.

mullus, -ī *m* red mullet.

mulsi *perf of* **mulceō;** *perf of* **mulgeō.**

mulsus *ppp of* **mulceō.**

mulsus *adj* honeyed, sweet ♦ *nt* honey-wine, mead.

multa, -ae *f* penalty, fine; loss.

multangulus *adj* many-angled.

multāticius *adj* fine- (*in cpds*).

multātiō, -ōnis *f* fining.

multēsimus *adj* very small.

multicavus *adj* many-holed.

multīcia, -ōrum *ntpl* transparent garments.

multifāriam *adv* in many places.

multifidus *adj* divided into many parts.

multifōrmis *adj* of many forms.

multiforus *adj* many-holed.

multigeneris, -us *adj* of many kinds.

multiiugis, -us *adj* yoked together; complex.

multiloquium, -ī *and* **ii** *nt* talkativeness.

multiloquus *adj* talkative.

multimodīs *adv* variously.

multiplex, -icis *adj* with many folds, tortuous; many-sided, manifold, various; (*comparison*) far greater; (*character*) fickle, sly.

multiplicō, -āre, -āvī, -ātum *vt* to multiply, enlarge.

multipotēns, -entis *adj* very powerful.

multitūdō, -inis *f* great number, multitude, crowd.

multivolus *adj* longing for much.

multō *adv* much, far, by far; (*time*) long.

multō, -āre, -āvī, -ātum *vt* to punish, fine.

multum *adv* much, very, frequently.

multus (*compar* **plūs** *superl* **plūrimus**) *adj* much, many; (*speech*) lengthy, tedious; (*time*) late; **~ā nocte** late at night; **nē ~a** ≈ *to cut a long story short.*

mūlus, -ī *m* mule.

Mulvius *adj* Mulvian (*a Tiber bridge above Rome*).

mundānus, -ī *m* world citizen.

munditia, -ae, -ēs, -ēī *f* cleanness; neatness, elegance.

mundus *adj* clean, neat, elegant; **in ~ō esse** be in readiness.

mundus, -ī *m* toilet gear; universe, world, heavens; mankind.

mūnerigerulus, -ī *m* bringer of presents.

mūnerō, -āre, -or, -ārī *vt* to present, reward.

mūnia, -ōrum *ntpl* official duties.

mūniceps, -ipis *m/f* citizen (*of a municipium*), fellow-citizen.

mūnicipālis *adj* provincial.

mūnicipium, -ī *and* **i ī** *nt* provincial town, burgh.

mūnificē *adv see adj.*

mūnificentia, -ae *f* liberality.

mūnificō, -āre *vt* to treat generously.

mūnificus *adj* liberal.

mūnīmen, -inis *nt* defence.

mūnīmentum, -ī *nt* defencework, protection.

mūniō, -īre, -iī, -ītum *vt* to fortify, secure, strengthen; (*road*) to build; (*fig*) to protect.

mūnis *adj* ready to oblige.

mūnītiō, -ōnis *f* building; fortification; (*river*) bridging.

mūnītō, -āre *vt* (*road*) to open up.

mūnītor, -ōris *m* sapper, builder.

mūnus, -eris *nt* service, duty; gift; public show; entertainment; tax; (*funeral*) tribute; (*book*) work.

mūnusculum, -ī *nt* small present.

mūraena, -ae *f* a fish.

mūrālis *adj* wall- (*in cpds*), mural, for fighting from *or* attacking walls.

mūrex, -icis *m* purple-fish; purple dye, purple; jagged rock.

muria, -ae *f* brine.

murmillō, -ōnis *m* kind of gladiator.

murmur, -is *nt* murmur, hum, rumbling, roaring.

murmurillum, -ī *nt* low murmur.

murmurō, -āre *vi* to murmur, rumble; to grumble.

murra, -ae *f* myrrh.

murreus *adj* perfumed; made of the stone called murra.

murrina, -ae *f* myrrh wine.

murrina, -ōrum *ntpl* murrine vases.

murt- *etc see* **myrt-**.

mūrus, -ī *m* wall; dam; defence.

mūs, mūris *m/f* mouse, rat.

Mūsa, -ae *f* goddess inspiring an art; poem; (*pl*) studies.

mūsaeus *adj* poetic, musical.

musca, -ae *f* fly.

mūscipula, -ae *f*, **-um, -ī** *nt* mousetrap.

mūscōsus *adj* mossy.

mūsculus, -ī *m* mouse; muscle; (MIL) shed.

mūscus, -ī *m* moss.

mūsicē *adv* very pleasantly.

mūsicus *adj* of music, of poetry ♦ *m* musician ♦ *f* music, culture ♦ *ntpl* music.

Noun declensions and verb conjugations are shown on pp xiii to xxv. The present infinitive ending of a verb shows to which conjugation it belongs: **-āre** = 1st; **-ēre** = 2nd; **-ere** = 3rd and **-īre** = 4th. Irregular verbs are shown on p xxvi

mussitō, -āre *vi* to say nothing; to mutter ♦ *vt* to bear in silence.
mussō, -āre *vt, vi* to say nothing, brood over; to mutter, murmur.
mustāceum, -ī *nt*, **-us, -ī** *m* wedding cake.
mūstēla, -ae *f* weasel.
mustum, -ī *nt* unfermented wine, must; vintage.
mūtābilis *adj* changeable, fickle.
mūtābilitās, -ātis *f* fickleness.
mūtātiō, -ōnis *f* change, alteration; exchange.
mutilō, -āre, -āvī, -ātum *vt* to cut off, maim; to diminish.
mutilus *adj* maimed.
Mutina, -ae *f* town in N. Italy (now Modena).
Mutinēnsis *adj see n.*
mūtiō *etc see* **muttiō.**
mūtō, -āre, -āvī, -ātum *vt* to shift; to change, alter; to exchange, barter ♦ *vi* to change; **~āta verba** figurative language.
muttiō, -īre *vi* to mutter, mumble.
mūtuātiō, -ōnis *f* borrowing.
mūtuē *adv* mutually, in turns.
mūtuitō, -āre *vt* to try to borrow.
mūtuō *adv* = **mūtuē.**
mūtuor, -ārī, -ātus *vt* to borrow.
mūtus *adj* dumb, mute; silent, still.
mūtuum, -ī *nt* loan.
mūtuus *adj* borrowed, lent; mutual, reciprocal; **~um dare** lend; **~um sūmere** borrow; **~um facere** return like for like.
Mycēnae, -ārum *fpl* Agamemnon's capital in S. Greece.
Mycēnaeus, -ēnsis *adj*, **-is, -idis** *f* Iphigenia.
Mygdonius *adj* Phrygian.
myoparō, -ōnis *m* pirate galley.
myrīca, -ae *f* tamarisk.
Myrmidones, -um *mpl* followers of Achilles.
Myrōn, -ōnis *m* famous Greek sculptor.
myropōla, -ae *m* perfumer.
myropōlium, -ī *and* **ī ī** *nt* perfumer's shop.
myrothēcium, -ī *and* **ī ī** *nt* perfume-box.
myrrh- *etc see* **murr-.**
myrtētum, -ī *nt* myrtlegrove.
myrteus *adj* myrtle- (*in cpds*).
Myrtoum mare Sea N.W. of Crete.
myrtum, -ī *nt* myrtle-berry.
myrtus, -ī *and* **ūs** *f* myrtle.
Mȳsia, -iae *f* country of Asia Minor.
Mȳsius, -us *adj see n.*
mysta, -ae *m* priest of mysteries.
mystagōgus, -ī *m* initiator.
mystērium, -ī *and* **ī ī** *nt* secret religion, mystery; secret.
mysticus *adj* mystic.
Mytilēnae, -ārum *fpl*; **-ē, -es** *f* capital of Lesbos.
Mytilēnaeus *adj see n.*
Mytilēnēnsis *adj see n.*

N, n

nablium, -ī *and* **ī ī** *nt* kind of harp.
nactus *ppa of* **nancīscor.**
nae *etc see* **nē.**
naenia *etc see* **nēnia.**
Naeviānus *adj see n.*
Naevius, -ī *m* early Latin poet.
naevus, -ī *m* mole (on the body).
Nāias, -adis *and* **s, -dis** *f* water nymph, Naiad.
Nāicus *adj see n.*
nam *conj* (*explaining*) for; (*illustrating*) for example; (*transitional*) now; (*interrog*) but; (*enclitic*) an emphatic particle.
namque *conj* for, for indeed, for example.
nancīscor, -i, nactus *and* **nanctus** *vt* to obtain, get; to come upon, find.
nānus, -ī *m* dwarf.
Napaeae, -ārum *fpl* dell nymphs.
nāpus, -ī *m* turnip.
Narbō, -ōnis *m* town in S. Gaul.
Narbōnēnsis *adj see n.*
narcissus, -ī *m* narcissus.
nardus, -ī *f*, **-um, -ī** *nt* nard, nard oil.
nāris, -is *f* nostril; (*pl*) nose; (*fig*) sagacity, scorn.
nārrābilis *adj* to be told.
nārrātiō, -ōnis *f* narrative.
nārrātor, -ōris *m* storyteller, historian.
nārrātus, -ūs *m* narrative.
nārrō, -āre, -āvī, -ātum *vt* to tell, relate, say; **male ~** bring bad news.
narthēcium, -ī *and* **ī ī** *nt* medicine chest.
nāscor, -scī, -tus *vi* to be born; to originate, grow, be produced.
Nāsō, -ōnis *m* surname of Ovid.
nassa, -ae *f* wicker basket for catching fish; (*fig*) snare.
nasturtium, -ī *and* **ī ī** *nt* cress.
nāsus, -ī *m* nose.
nāsūtē *adv* sarcastically.
nāsūtus *adj* big-nosed; satirical.
nāta, -ae *f* daughter.
nātālicius *adj* of one's birthday, natal ♦ *f* birthday party.
nātālis *adj* of birth, natal ♦ *m* birthday ♦ *mpl* birth, origin.
nātātiō, -ōnis *f* swimming.
natātor, -ōris *m* swimmer.
nātiō, -ōnis *f* tribe, race; breed, class.
natis, -is *f* (*usu pl*) buttocks.
nātīvus *adj* created; inborn, native, natural.
natō, -āre *vi* to swim, float; to flow, overflow; (*eyes*) to swim, fail; (*fig*) to waver.
nātrīx, -īcis *f* watersnake.
nātū *abl* by birth, in age; **grandis ~, māgnō ~** quite old; **māior ~** older; **māximus ~** oldest.

nātūra, -ae f birth; nature, quality, character; natural order of things; the physical world; (*physics*) element; **rērum** ~ Nature.

nātūrālis *adj* by birth; by nature, natural.

nātūrāliter *adv* by nature.

nātus *ppa of* **nāscor** ♦ *adj* born, made (for); old, of age; **prō, ē rē nātā** under the circumstances, as things are; **annōs vīgintī** ~ 20 years old.

nauarchus, -ī *m* captain.

naucī: nōn esse, facere, habēre to be worthless, consider worthless.

nauclēricus *adj* skipper's.

nauclērus, -ī *m* skipper.

naufragium, -ī *and* **iī** *nt* shipwreck, wreck; ~ **facere** be shipwrecked.

naufragus *adj* shipwrecked, wrecked; (*sea*) dangerous to shipping ♦ *m* shipwrecked man; (*fig*) ruined man.

naulum, -ī *nt* fare.

naumachia, -ae f mock sea fight.

nausea, -ae f seasickness.

nauseō, -āre *vi* to be sick; (*fig*) to disgust.

nauseola, -ae f squeamishness.

nauta, (nāvita), -ae *m* sailor, mariner.

nauticus *adj* nautical, sailors' ♦ *mpl* seamen.

nāvālis *adj* naval, of ships ♦ *nt and ntpl* dockyard; rigging.

nāvicula, -ae f boat.

nāviculāria, -ae f shipping business.

nāviculārius, -ī *and* **iī** *m* ship-owner.

nāvifragus *adj* dangerous.

nāvigābilis *adj* navigable.

nāvigātiō, -ōnis f voyage.

nāviger, -ī *adj* ship-carrying.

nāvigium, -ī *and* **iī** *nt* vessel, ship.

nāvigō, -āre, -āvī, -ātum *vi* to sail, put to sea ♦ *vt* to sail across, navigate.

nāvis, -is f ship; ~ **longa** warship; ~ **mercātōria** merchantman; ~ **onerāria** transport; ~ **praetōria** flagship; ~**em dēdūcere** launch; ~**em solvere** set sail; ~**em statuere** heave to; ~**em subdūcere** beach; ~**ibus atque quadrīgīs** with might and main.

nāvita *etc see* **nauta**.

nāvitās, -ātis f energy.

nāviter *adv* energetically; absolutely.

nāvō, -āre *vt* to perform energetically; **operam** ~ be energetic; to come to the assistance (of).

nāvus *adj* energetic.

Naxos, -ī f Aegean island (*famous for wines and the story of Ariadne*).

nē *interj* truly, indeed.

nē *adv* not ♦ *conj* that not, lest; (*fear*) that; (*purpose*) so that ... not, to avoid, to prevent.

-ne *enclitic* (*introducing a question*).

Neāpolis, -is f Naples.

Neāpolītānus *adj see* **n**.

nebula, -ae f mist, vapour, cloud.

nebulō, -ōnis *m* idler, good-for-nothing.

nebulōsus *adj* misty, cloudy.

nec *etc see* **neque**.

necdum *adv* and not yet.

necessāriē, -ō *adv* of necessity, unavoidably.

necessārius *adj* necessary, inevitable; indispensable; (*kin*) related ♦ *m/f* relative ♦ *ntpl* necessities.

necesse *adj* (*indecl*) necessary, inevitable; needful.

necessitās, -ātis f necessity, compulsion; requirement, want; relationship, connection.

necessitūdō, -inis f necessity, need, want; connection; friendship (*pl*) relatives.

necessum *etc see* **necesse**.

necne *adv* or not.

necnōn *adv* also, besides.

necō, -āre, -āvī, -ātum *vt* to kill, murder.

necopīnāns, -antis *adj* unaware.

necopīnātō *adv see adj*.

necopīnātus *adj* unexpected.

necopīnus *adj* unexpected; unsuspecting.

nectar, -is *nt* nectar (*the drink of the gods*).

nectareus *adj* of nectar.

nectō, -ctere, -xī *and* **xuī, -xum** *vt* to tie, fasten, connect; to weave; (*fig*) to bind, enslave (*esp for debt*); to contrive, frame.

nēcubi *conj* so that nowhere.

nēcunde *conj* so that from nowhere.

nēdum *adv* much less, much more.

nefandus *adj* abominable, impious.

nefāriē *adv see adj*.

nefārius *adj* heinous, criminal.

nefās *nt* (*indecl*) wickedness, sin, wrong ♦ *interj* horror!, shame!

nefāstus *adj* wicked; unlucky; (*days*) closed to public business.

negātiō, -ōnis f denial.

negitō, -āre *vt* to deny, refuse.

neglēctiō, -ōnis f neglect.

neglēctus *ppp of* **neglegō**.

neglēctus, -ūs *m* neglecting.

neglegēns, -entis *pres p of* **neglegō** ♦ *adj* careless, indifferent.

neglegenter *adv* carelessly.

neglegentia, -ae f carelessness, neglect, coldness.

neglegō, -egere, -ēxī, -ēctum *vt* to neglect, not care for; to slight, disregard; to overlook.

negō, -āre, -āvī, -ātum *vt, vi* to say no; to say not, deny; to refuse, decline.

negōtiālis *adj* business- (*in cpds*).

negōtiāns, -antis *m* businessman.

negōtiātiō, -ōnis f banking business.

negōtiātor, -ōris *m* businessman, banker.

negōtiolum, -ī *nt* trivial matter.

negōtior, -ārī, -ātus *vi* to do business, trade.

negōtiōsus *adj* busy.

Noun declensions and verb conjugations are shown on pp xiii to xxv. The present infinitive ending of a verb shows to which conjugation it belongs: **-āre** = 1st; **-ēre** = 2nd; **-ere** = 3rd and **-īre** = 4th. Irregular verbs are shown on p xxvi

negōtium, -ī *and* **iī** *nt* business, work; trouble; matter, thing; **quid est ~ī?** what is the matter?

Nēlēius *adj see* n.

Nēleus, -eī *m* father of Nestor.

Nēlēus *adj see* n.

Nemea, -ae *f* town in S. Greece, where Hercules killed the lion.

Nemea, -ōrum *ntpl* Nemean Games.

Nemeaeus *adj* Nemean.

nēmō, -inis *m/f* no one, nobody ♦ *adj* no; **~ nōn** everybody; **nōn ~** many; **~ ūnus** not a soul.

nemorālis *adj* sylvan.

nemorēnsis *adj* of the grove.

nemoricultrīx, -īcis *f* forest dweller.

nemorivagus *adj* forest-roving.

nemorōsus *adj* well-wooded; leafy.

nempe *adv* (confirming) surely, of course, certainly; (in questions) do you mean?

nemus, -ōris *nt* wood, grove.

nēnia, -ae *f* dirge; incantation; song, nursery rhyme.

neō, nēre, nēvī, nētum *vt* to spin; to weave.

Neoptolemus, -ī *m* Pyrrhus (son of Achilles).

nepa, -ae *f* scorpion.

nepōs, -ōtis *m* grandson; descendant; spendthrift.

nepōtīnus, -ī *m* little grandson.

neptis, -is *f* granddaughter.

Neptūnius *adj:* **~ hērōs** Theseus.

Neptūnus, -ī *m* Neptune (god of the sea); sea.

nēquam *adj* (indecl) worthless, bad.

nēquāquam *adv* not at all, by no means.

neque, nec *adv* not ♦ *conj* and not, but not; neither, nor; **~ ... et** not only not ... but also.

nequeō, -īre, -īvī, -itum *vi* to be unable, cannot.

nēquīquam *adv* fruitlessly, for nothing; without good reason.

nēquior, nēquissimus *compar, superl of* **nēquam.**

nēquiter *adv* worthlessly, wrongly.

nēquitia, -ae, -ēs *f* worthlessness, badness.

Nērēis, -ēidis *f* Nereid, sea nymph.

Nērēius *adj see* n.

Nēreus, -eī *m* a sea god; the sea.

Nēritius *adj* of Neritos; Ithacan.

Nēritos, -ī *m* island near Ithaca.

Nerō, -ōnis *m* Roman surname (esp the emperor).

Nerōniānus *adj see* n.

nervōsē *adv* vigorously.

nervōsus *adj* sinewy, vigorous.

nervulī, -ōrum *mpl* energy.

nervus, -ī *m* sinew; string; fetter, prison; (shield) leather; (pl) strength, vigour, energy.

nesciō, -īre, -īvī *and* **iī, -ītum** *vt* to not know, be ignorant of; to be unable; **~ quis, quid** somebody, something; **~ an** probably.

nescius *adj* ignorant, unaware; unable; unknown.

Nestor, -oris *m* Greek leader at Troy (famous

for his great age and wisdom).

neu *etc see* **nēve.**

neuter, -rī *adj* neither; neuter.

neutiquam *adv* by no means, certainly not.

neutrō *adv* neither way.

nēve, neu *conj* and not; neither, nor.

nēvī *perf of* **neō.**

nex, necis *f* murder, death.

nexilis *adj* tied together.

nexum, -ī *nt* personal enslavement.

nexus *ppp of* **nectō.**

nexus, -ūs *m* entwining, grip; (law) bond, obligation, (esp enslavement for debt).

nī *adv* not ♦ *conj* if not, unless; that not; **quid nī?** why not?

nīcētērium, -ī *and* **iī** *nt* prize.

nictō, -āre *vi* to wink.

nīdāmentum, -ī *nt* nest.

nīdor, -ōris *m* steam, smell.

nīdulus, -ī *m* little nest.

nīdus, -ī *m* nest; (pl) nestlings; (fig) home.

niger, -rī *adj* black, dark; dismal, ill-omened; (character) bad.

nigrāns, -antis *adj* black, dusky.

nigrēscō, -ere *vi* to blacken, grow dark.

nigrō, -āre *vi* to be black.

nigror, -ōris *m* blackness.

nihil, nīl *nt* (indecl) nothing ♦ *adv* not; **~ ad nōs** it has nothing to do with us; **~ est** it's no use; **~ est quod** there is no reason why; **~ nisi** nothing but, only; **~ nōn** everything; **nōn ~** something.

nihilum, -ī *nt* nothing; **~ī esse** be worthless; **~ō minus** none the less.

nīl, nīlum *see* **nihil, nihilum.**

Nīliacus *adj* of the Nile; Egyptian.

Nīlus, -ī *m* Nile; conduit.

nimbifer, -ī *adj* stormy.

nimbōsus *adj* stormy.

nimbus, -ī *m* cloud, rain, storm.

nimiō *adv* much, far.

nīmīrum *adv* certainly, of course.

nimis *adv* too much, very much; **nōn ~** not very.

nimium *adv* too, too much; very, very much.

nimius *adj* too great, excessive; very great ♦ *nt* excess.

ningit, ninguit, -ere *vi* it snows.

ninguēs, -ium *fpl* snow.

Nioba, -ae, -ē, -ēs *f* daughter of Tantalus (changed to a weeping rock).

Niobēus *adj see* n.

Nīreus, -eī *and* **eos** *m* handsomest of the Greeks at Troy.

Nīsaeus, -ēius *adj see* n.

Nīsēis, -edis *f* Scylla.

nisi *conj* if not, unless; except, but.

nīsus *ppa of* **nītor.**

nīsus, -ūs *m* pressure, effort; striving, soaring.

Nīsus, -ī *m* father of Scylla.

nītēdula, -ae *f* dormouse.

nitēns, -entis *pres p of* **niteō** ♦ *adj* bright;

brilliant, beautiful.

niteō, -ēre *vi* to shine, gleam; to be sleek, be greasy; to thrive, look beautiful.

nitēscō, -ere, nituī *vi* to brighten, shine, glow.

nitidiusculē *adv* rather more finely.

nitidiusculus *adj* a little shinier.

nitidē *adv* magnificently.

nitidus *adj* bright, shining; sleek; blooming; smart, spruce; (*speech*) refined.

nitor, -ōris *m* brightness, sheen; sleekness, beauty; neatness, elegance.

nītor, -tī, -sus *and* **xus** *vi* to rest on, lean on; to press, stand firmly; to press forward, climb; to exert oneself, strive, labour; to depend on.

nitrum, -ī *nt* soda.

nivālis *adj* snowy.

niveus *adj* of snow, snowy, snow-white.

nivōsus *adj* snowy.

nix, nivis *f* snow.

nīxor, -ārī *vi* to rest on; to struggle.

nīxus *ppp of* **nītor**.

nīxus, -ūs *m* pressure; labour.

nō, nāre, nāvī *vi* to swim, float; to sail, fly.

nōbilis *adj* known, noted, famous, notorious; noble, high-born; excellent.

nōbilitās, -ātis *f* fame; noble birth; the nobility; excellence.

nōbilitō, -āre, -āvī, -ātum *vt* to make famous *or* notorious.

nocēns, -entis *pres p of* **noceō** ♦ *adj* harmful; criminal, guilty.

noceō, -ēre, -uī, -itum *vi* (*with dat*) to harm, hurt.

nocīvus *adj* injurious.

noctifer, -ī *m* evening star.

noctilūca, -ae *f* moon.

noctivagus *adj* night-wandering.

noctū *adv* by night.

noctua, -ae *f* owl.

noctuābundus *adj* travelling by night.

nocturnus *adj* night- (*in cpds*), nocturnal.

nōdō, -āre, -āvī, -ātum *vt* to knot, tie.

nōdōsus *adj* knotty.

nōdus, -ī *m* knot; knob; girdle; (*fig*) bond, difficulty.

nōlō, -le, -uī *vt, vi* to not wish, be unwilling; refuse; ~ī, ~īte do not.

Nomas, -dis *m/f* nomad; Numidian.

nōmen, -inis *nt* name; title; (*COMM*) demand, debt; (*GRAM*) noun; (*fig*) reputation, fame; account, pretext; ~ dare profitērī enlist; ~ dēferre accuse; ~ina facere enter the items of a debt.

nōmenclātor, -ōris *m slave who told his master the names of people*.

nōminātim *adv* by name, one by one.

nōminātiō, -ōnis *f* nomination.

nōminitō, -āre *vt* to usually name.

nōminō, -āre, -āvī, -ātum *vt* to name, call; to mention; to make famous; to nominate; to accuse, denounce.

nomisma, -tis *nt* coin.

nōn *adv* not; no.

Nōnae, -ārum *fpl* Nones (*7th day of March, May, July, October, 5th of other months*).

nōnāgēsimus *adj* ninetieth.

nōnāgiēns, -ēs *adv* ninety times.

nōnāgintā *num* ninety.

nōnānus *adj* of the ninth legion.

nōndum *adv* not yet.

nōngentī, -ōrum *num* nine hundred.

nonna, -ae *f* nun.

nōnne *adv* do not?, is not? *etc.*; (*indirect*) whether not.

nōnnullus *adj* some.

nōnnunquam *adv* sometimes.

nōnus *adj* ninth ♦ *f* ninth hour.

nōnusdecimus *adj* nineteenth.

Nōricum, -ī *nt country between the Danube and the Alps*.

Nōricus *adj see* **n**.

nōrma, -ae *f* rule.

nōs *pron* we, us; I, me.

nōscitō, -āre *vt* to know, recognise; to observe, examine.

nōscō, -scere, -vī, -tum *vt* to get to know, learn; to examine; to recognise, allow; (*perf*) to know.

nōsmet *pron* (*emphatic*) *see* **nōs**.

noster, -rī *adj* our, ours; for us; my; (*with names*) my dear, good old ♦ *m* our friend ♦ *mpl* our side, our troops; ~rī, ~rum of us.

nostrās, -ātis *adj* of our country, native.

nota, -ae *f* mark, sign, note; (*writing*) note, letter; (*pl*) memoranda, shorthand, secret writing; (*books*) critical mark, punctuation; (*wine, etc*) brand, quality; (*gesture*) sign; (*fig*) sign, token; (*censor's*) black mark; (*fig*) stigma, disgrace.

notābilis *adj* remarkable; notorious.

notābiliter *adv* perceptibly.

notārius, -ī *and* **iī** *m* shorthand writer; secretary.

notātiō, -ōnis *f* marking; choice; observation; (*censor*) stigmatizing; (*words*) etymology.

notēscō, -ere, nōtuī *vi* to become known.

nothus *adj* bastard; counterfeit.

nōtiō, -ōnis *f* (*law*) cognisance, investigation; (*PHILOS*) idea.

nōtitia, -ae, -ēs, -ēī *f* fame; acquaintance; (*PHILOS*) idea, preconception.

notō, -āre, -āvī, -ātum *vt* to mark, write; to denote; to observe; to brand, stigmatize.

nōtuī *perf of* **nōtēscō**.

nōtus *ppp of* **nōscō** ♦ *adj* known, familiar; notorious ♦ *mpl* acquaintances.

Notus (-os), -ī *m* south wind.

novācula, -ae *f* razor.

Noun declensions and verb conjugations are shown on pp xiii to xxv. The present infinitive ending of a verb shows to which conjugation it belongs: **-āre** = 1st; **-ēre** = 2nd; **-ere** = 3rd and **-īre** = 4th. Irregular verbs are shown on p xxvi

novālis, -is *f*, **-e**, **-is** *nt* fallow land; field; crops.
novātrix, -icis *f* renewer.
novē *adv* unusually.
novellus *adj* young, fresh, new.
novem *num* nine.
November, -ris *adj* of November ♦ *m* November.
novendecim *num* nineteen.
novendiālis *adj* nine days'; on the ninth day.
novēnī, -ōrum *adj* in nines; nine.
Novēnsilēs, -ium *mpl* new gods.
noverca, -ae *f* stepmother.
novercālis *adj* stepmother's.
nōvī *perf of* **nōscō**.
novīcius *adj* new.
noviēns, -ēs *adv* nine times.
novissimē *adv* lately; last of all.
novissimus *adj* latest, last, rear.
novitās, -ātis *f* newness, novelty; strangeness.
novō, -āre, -āvī, -ātum *vt* to renew, refresh; to change; (*words*) to coin; **rēs ~** effect a revolution.
novus *adj* new, young, fresh, recent; strange, unusual; inexperienced; **~ homō** upstart, first of his family to hold curule office; **~ae rēs** revolution; **~ae tabulae** cancellation of debts; **quid ~ī** what news?
nox, noctis *f* night; darkness, obscurity; **nocte, noctū** by night; **dē nocte** during the night.
noxa, -ae *f* hurt, harm; offence, guilt; punishment.
noxia, -ae *f* harm, damage; guilt, fault.
noxius *adj* harmful; guilty.
nūbēcula, -ae *f* cloudy look.
nūbēs, -is *f* cloud; (*fig*) gloom; veil.
nūbifer, -ī *adj* cloud-capped; cloudy.
nūbigena, -ae *m* cloudborn, Centaur.
nūbilis *adj* marriageable.
nūbilus *adj* cloudy; gloomy, sad ♦ *ntpl* clouds.
nūbō, -bere, -psī, -ptum *vi* (*women*) to be married.
nucleus, -ī *m* nut, kernel.
nūdius day since, days ago; **~ tertius** the day before yesterday.
nūdō, -āre, -āvī, -ātum *vt* to bare, strip, expose; (*MIL*) to leave exposed; to plunder; (*fig*) to disclose, betray.
nūdus *adj* naked, bare; exposed, defenceless; wearing only a tunic; (*fig*) destitute, poor; mere; unembellished, undisguised; **vestīmenta dētrahere ~ō ≈** draw blood from a stone.
nūgae, -ārum *fpl* nonsense, trifles; (*person*) waster.
nūgātor, -ōris *m* silly creature, liar.
nūgātōrius *adj* futile.
nūgāx, -ācis *adj* frivolous.
nūgor, -ārī, -ātus *vi* to talk nonsense; to cheat.
nullus, -īus (*dat* **-ī**) *adj* no, none; not, not at all; non-existent, of no account ♦ *m/f* nobody.

num *interrog particle* surely not? (*indirect*) whether, if.
Numa, -ae *m* second king of Rome.
nūmen, -inis *nt* nod, will; divine will, power; divinity, god.
numerābilis *adj* easy to count.
numerātus *adj* in cash ♦ *nt* ready money.
numerō, -āre, -āvī, -ātum *vt* to count, number; (*money*) to pay out; (*fig*) to reckon, consider as.
numerō *adv* just now, quickly, too soon.
numerōsē *adv* rhythmically.
numerōsus *adj* populous; rhythmical.
numerus, -ī *m* number; many, numbers; (*MIL*) troop; (*fig*) a cipher; (*pl*) mathematics; rank, category, regard; rhythm, metre, verse; **in ~ō esse, habērī** be reckoned as; **nullō ~ō** of no account.
Numida *adj see n.*
Numidae, -ārum *mpl* Numidians (*people of N. Africa*).
Numidia, -iae *f* the country of the Numidians.
Numidicus *adj see n.*
Numitor, -ōris *m* king of Alba (*grandfather of Romulus*).
nummārius *adj* money- (*in cpds*), financial; mercenary.
nummātus *adj* moneyed.
nummulī, -ōrum *mpl* some money, cash.
nummus, -ī *m* coin, money, cash; (*Roman coin*) sestertius; (*Greek coin*) two-drachma piece.
numnam, numne *see* **num**.
numquam *adv* never; **~ nōn** always; **nōn ~** sometimes.
numquid (*question*) do you? does he? *etc*; (*indirect*) whether.
nunc *adv* now; at present, nowadays; but as it is; **~ ... ~** at one time ... at another.
nuncupātiō, -ōnis *f* pronouncing.
nuncupō, -āre, -āvī, -ātum *vt* to call, name; to pronounce formally.
nūndinae, -ārum *fpl* market day; market; trade.
nūndinātiō, -ōnis *f* trading.
nūndinor, -ārī *vi* to trade, traffic; to flock together ♦ *vt* to buy.
nūndinum, -ī *nt* market time; **trīnum ~** 17 days.
nunq- *etc see* **numq-**.
nūntiātiō, -ōnis *f* announcing.
nūntiō, -āre, -āvī, -ātum *vt* to announce, report, tell.
nūntius *adj* informative, speaking ♦ *m* messenger; message, news; injunction; notice of divorce ♦ *nt* message.
nūper *adv* recently, lately.
nūpsī *perf of* **nūbō**.
nūpta, -ae *f* bride, wife.
nūptiae, -ārum *fpl* wedding, marriage.
nūptiālis *adj* wedding- (*in cpds*), nuptial.
nurus, -ūs *f* daughter-in-law; young woman.
nūsquam *adv* nowhere; in nothing, for nothing.

nūtō, -āre *vi* to nod; to sway, totter, falter.
nūtrīcius, -ī *m* tutor.
nūtrīcō, -āre, -or, -ārī *vt* to nourish, sustain.
nūtrīcula, -ae *f* nurse.
nūtrīmen, -inis *nt* nourishment.
nūtrīmentum, -ī *nt* nourishment, support.
nūtriō, -īre, -īvī, -ītum *vt* to suckle, nourish, rear, nurse.
nūtrīx, -īcis *f* nurse, foster mother.
nūtus, -ūs *m* nod; will, command; (*physics*) gravity.
nux, nucis *f* nut; nut tree, almond tree.
Nyctēis, -idis *f* Antiopa.
nympha, -ae, -ē, -ēs *f* bride; nymph; water.
Nysa, -ae *f* birthplace of Bacchus.
Nysaeus, -ēis, -ius *adj see n.*

O, o

ō *interj* (*expressing joy, surprise, pain, etc*) oh!; (*with voc*) O!
ob *prep* (*with acc*) in front of; for, on account of, for the sake of; **quam ~ rem** accordingly.
obaerātus *adj* in debt ♦ *m* debtor.
obambulō, -āre *vi* to walk past, prowl about.
obarmō, -āre *vt* to arm (against).
obarō, -āre *vt* to plough up.
obc- *etc see* **occ-**.
obdō, -ere, -idī, -itum *vt* to shut; to expose.
obdormīscō, -īscere, -īvī *vi* to fall asleep ♦ *vt* to sleep off.
obdūcō, -ūcere, -ūxī, -uctum *vt* to draw over, cover; to bring up; (*drink*) to swallow; (*time*) to pass.
obductō, -āre *vt* to bring as a rival.
obductus *ppp of* **obdūcō**.
obdūrēscō, -ēscere, -uī *vi* to harden; to become obdurate.
obdūrō, -āre *vi* to persist, stand firm.
obduticō, -ōnis *f* veiling.
obeō, -īre, -īvī, and iī, -itum *vi* to go to, meet; to die; (*ASTRO*) to set ♦ *vt* to visit, travel over; to survey, go over; to envelop; (*duty*) to engage in, perform; (*time*) to meet; **diem ~ die**; (*law*) to appear on the appointed day.
obequitō, -āre *vi* to ride up to.
oberrō, -āre *vi* to ramble about; to make a mistake.
obēsus *adj* fat, plump; coarse.
ōbex, -icis *m/f* bolt, bar, barrier.
obf- *etc see* **off-**.
obg- *etc see* **ogg-**.

obhaerēscō, -rēscere, -sī *vi* to stick fast.
obiaceō, -ēre *vi* to lie over against.
obiciō, -icere, -iēcī, -iectum *vt* to throw to, set before; (*defence*) to put up, throw against; (*fig*) to expose, give up; (*speech*) to taunt, reproach.
obiectātiō, -ōnis *f* reproach.
obiectō, -āre *vt* to throw against; to expose, sacrifice; to reproach; (*hint*) to let on.
obiectus *ppp of* **obiciō** ♦ *adj* opposite, in front of; exposed ♦ *ntpl* accusations.
obiectus, -ūs *m* putting in the way, interposing.
obīrātus *adj* angered.
obiter *adv* on the way; incidentally.
obitus *ppp of* **obeō**.
obitus, -ūs *m* death, ruin; (*ASTRO*) setting; visit.
obiūrgātiō, -ōnis *f* reprimand.
obiūrgātor, -ōris *m* reprover.
obiūrgātōrius *adj* reproachful.
obiūrgitō, -āre *vt* to keep on reproaching.
obiūrgō, -āre, -āvī, -ātum *vt* to scold, rebuke; to deter by reproof.
oblanguēscō, -ēscere, -uī *vi* to become feeble.
oblātrātrīx, -īcis *f* nagging woman.
oblātus *ppp of* **offerō**.
oblectāmentum, -ī *nt* amusement.
oblectātiō, -ōnis *f* delight.
oblectō, -āre, -āvī, -ātum *vt* to delight, amuse, entertain; to detain; (*time*) to spend pleasantly; **sē ~** enjoy oneself.
oblīdō, -dere, -sī, -sum *vt* to crush, strangle.
obligātiō, -ōnis *f* pledge.
obligō, -āre, -āvī, -ātum *vt* to tie up, bandage; to put under an obligation, embarrass; (*law*) to render liable, make guilty; to mortgage.
oblīmō, -āre *vt* to cover with mud.
oblinō, -inere, -ēvī, -itum *vt* to smear over; to defile; (*fig*) to overload.
oblīquē *adv* sideways; indirectly.
oblīquō, -āre *vt* to turn aside, veer.
oblīquus *adj* slanting, downhill; from the side, sideways; (*look*) askance, envious; (*speech*) indirect.
oblīsus *ppp of* **oblīdō**.
oblitēscō, -ere *vi* to hide away.
oblitterō, -āre, -āvī, -ātum *vt* to erase, cancel; (*fig*) to consign to oblivion.
oblitus *ppp of* **oblinō**.
oblītus *ppa of* **oblīvīscor**.
oblīviō, -ōnis *f* oblivion, forgetfulness.
oblīviōsus *adj* forgetful.
oblīvīscor, -vīscī, -tus *vt, vi* to forget.
oblīvium, -ī and iī *nt* forgetfulness, oblivion.
oblocūtor, -ōris *m* contradicter.
oblongus *adj* oblong.
obloquor, -quī, -cūtus *vi* to contradict, interrupt; to abuse; (*music*) to accompany.

Noun declensions and verb conjugations are shown on pp xiii to xxv. The present infinitive ending of a verb shows to which conjugation it belongs: **-āre** = 1st; **-ēre** = 2nd; **-ere** = 3rd and **-īre** = 4th. Irregular verbs are shown on p xxvi

obluctor, -ārī _vi_ to struggle against.
obmōlior, -īrī _vt_ to throw up (_as a defence_).
obmurmurō, -āre _vi_ to roar in answer.
obmūtēscō, -ēscere, -uī _vi_ to become silent;
to cease.
obnātus _adj_ growing on.
obnītor, -tī, -xus _vi_ to push against, struggle;
to stand firm, resist.
obnīxē _adv_ resolutely.
obnīxus _ppa of_ **obnītor** ♦ _adj_ steadfast.
obnoxiē _adv_ slavishly.
obnoxiōsus _adj_ submissive.
obnoxius _adj_ liable, addicted; culpable;
submissive, slavish; under obligation,
indebted; exposed (to danger).
obnūbō, -bere, -psī, -ptum _vt_ to veil, cover.
obnūntiātiō, -ōnis _f_ announcement of an
adverse omen.
obnūntiō, -āre _vt_ to announce an adverse
omen.
oboediēns, -entis _pres p of_ **oboediō** ♦ _adj_
obedient.
oboedienter _adv_ readily.
oboedientia, -ae _f_ obedience.
oboediō, -īre _vi_ to listen; to obey, be subject
to.
oboleō, -ēre, -uī _vt_ to smell of.
oborior, -īrī, -tus _vi_ to arise, spring up.
obp- _etc see_ **opp-**.
obrēpō, -ere, -sī, -tum _vt, vi_ to creep up to,
steal upon, surprise; to cheat.
obrētiō, -īre _vt_ to entangle.
obrigēscō, -ēscere, -uī _vi_ to stiffen.
obrogō, -āre, -āvī, -ātum _vt_ to invalidate (_by
making a new law_).
obruō, -ere, -ī, -tum _vt_ to cover over, bury,
sink; to overwhelm, overpower ♦ _vi_ to fall to
ruin.
obrussa, -ae _f_ test, touchstone.
obrutus _ppp of_ **obruō**.
obsaepiō, -īre, -sī, -tum _vt_ to block, close.
obsaturō, -āre _vt_ to sate, glut.
obscaen- _etc see_ **obscen-**.
obscēnē _adv_ indecently.
obscēnitās, -ātis _f_ indecency.
obscēnus _adj_ filthy; indecent; ominous.
obscūrātiō, -ōnis _f_ darkening,
disappearance.
obscūrē _adv_ secretly.
obscūritās, -ātis _f_ darkness; (_fig_)
uncertainty; (_rank_) lowliness.
obscūrō, -āre, -āvī, -ātum _vt_ to darken; to
conceal, suppress; (_speech_) to obscure;
(_pass_) to become obsolete.
obscūrus _adj_ dark, shady, hidden; (_fig_)
obscure, indistinct; unknown, ignoble;
(_character_) reserved.
obsecrātiō, -ōnis _f_ entreaty; public prayer.
obsecrō, -āre _vt_ to implore, appeal to.
obsecundō, -āre _vi_ to comply with, back up.
obsēdī _perf of_ **obsideō**.
obsēp- _etc see_ **obsaep-**.
obsequēns, -entis _pres p of_ **obsequor** ♦ _adj_

compliant; (_gods_) gracious.
obsequenter _adv_ compliantly.
obsequentia, -ae _f_ complaisance.
obsequiōsus _adj_ complaisant.
obsequium, -ī _and_ **iī** _nt_ compliance,
indulgence; obedience, allegiance.
obsequor, -quī, -cūtus _vi_ to comply with,
yield to, indulge.
obserō, -āre _vt_ to bar, close.
obserō, -erere, -ēvī, -itum _vt_ to sow, plant; to
cover thickly.
observāns, -antis _pres p of_ **observō** ♦ _adj_
attentive, respectful.
observantia, -ae _f_ respect.
observātiō, -ōnis _f_ watching; caution.
observitō, -āre _vt_ to observe carefully.
observō, -āre, -āvī, -ātum _vt_ to watch, watch
for; to guard; (_laws_) to keep, comply with;
(_person_) to pay respect to.
obses, -idis _m/f_ hostage; guarantee.
obsessiō, -ōnis _f_ blockade.
obsessor, -ōris _m_ frequenter; besieger.
obsessus _ppp of_ **obsideō**.
obsideō, -idēre, -ēdī, -essum _vt_ to sit at,
frequent; (_MIL_) to blockade, besiege; to block,
fill, take up; to guard, watch for ♦ _vi_ to sit.
obsidiō, -ōnis _f_ siege, blockade; (_fig_)
imminent danger.
obsidium, -ī _and_ **iī** _nt_ siege, blockade;
hostageship.
obsīdō, -ere _vt_ to besiege, occupy.
obsignātor, -ōris _m_ sealer; witness.
obsignō, -āre, -āvī, -ātum _vt_ to seal up; to
sign and seal; (_fig_) to stamp.
obsistō, -istere, -titī, -titum _vi_ to put oneself
in the way, resist.
obsitus _ppp of_ **obserō**.
obsolefīō, -fierī _vi_ to wear out, become
degraded.
obsolēscō, -scere, -vī, -tum _vi_ to wear out,
become out of date.
obsolētius _adv_ more shabbily.
obsolētus _ppa of_ **obsolēscō** ♦ _adj_ worn out,
shabby; obsolete; (_fig_) ordinary, mean.
obsōnātor, -ōris _m_ caterer.
obsōnātus, -ūs _m_ marketing.
obsōnium, -ī _and_ **iī** _nt_ food eaten with bread,
(_usu fish_).
obsōnō, -āre, -or, -ārī _vi_ to cater, buy
provisions; to provide a meal.
obsonō, -āre _vi_ to interrupt.
obsorbeō, -ēre _vt_ to swallow, bolt.
obstantia, -ium _ntpl_ obstructions.
obstetrīx, -īcis _f_ midwife.
obstinātiō, -ōnis _f_ determination,
stubbornness.
obstinātē _adv_ firmly, obstinately.
obstinātus _adj_ firm, resolute; stubborn.
obstinō, -āre _vi_ to be determined, persist.
obstipēscō _etc see_ **obstupēscō**.
obstīpus _adj_ bent, bowed, drawn back.
obstitī _perf of_ **obsistō**; _perf of_ **obstō**.
obstō, -āre, -itī _vi_ to stand in the way; to

obstruct, prevent.

obstrepō, -ere, -uī, -itum *vi* to make a noise; to shout against, cry down, molest ♦ *vt* to drown (in noise); to fill with noise.

obstrictus *ppp of* **obstringō**.

obstringō, -ingere, -inxī, -ictum *vt* to bind up, tie round; (*fig*) to confine, hamper; to lay under an obligation.

obstructiō, -ōnis *f* barrier.

obstructus *ppp of* **obstruō**.

obstrūdō (obtrūdō), -dere, -sī, -sum *vt* to force on to; to gulp down.

obstruō, -ere, -xī, -ctum *vt* to build up against, block; to shut, hinder.

obstupefaciō, -facere, -fēcī, -factum (*pass* **-fīō, -fierī**) *vt* to astound, paralyse.

obstupēscō, -ēscere, -uī *vi* to be astounded, paralysed.

obstupidus *adj* stupefied.

obsum, -esse, -fuī *vi* to be against, harm.

obsuō, -uere, -uī, -ūtum *vt* to sew on, sew up.

obsurdēscō, -ēscere, -uī *vi* to grow deaf; to turn a deaf ear.

obsūtus *ppp of* **obsuō**.

obtegō, -egere, -ēxī, -ēctum *vt* to cover over; to conceal.

obtemperātiō, -ōnis *f* obedience.

obtemperō, -āre, -āvī, -ātum *vi* (*with dat*) to comply with, obey.

obtendō, -dere, -dī, -tum *vt* to spread over, stretch over against; to conceal; to make a pretext of.

obtentus *ppp of* **obtendō**; *ppp of* **obtineō**.

obtentus, -ūs *m* screen; pretext.

obterō, -erere, -rīvī, -rītum *vt* to trample on, crush; to disparage.

obtestātiō, -ōnis *f* adjuring; supplication.

obtestor, -ārī, -ātus *vt* to call to witness; to entreat.

obtexō, -ere, -uī *vt* to overspread.

obticeō, -ēre *vi* to be silent.

obticēscō, -ēscere, -uī *vi* to be struck dumb.

obtigī *perf of* **obtingō**.

obtigō *see* **obtegō**.

obtineō, -inēre, -inuī, -entum *vt* to hold, possess; to maintain; to gain, obtain ♦ *vi* to prevail, continue.

obtingō, -ngere, -gī *vi* to fall to one's lot; to happen.

obtorpēscō, -ēscere, -uī *vi* to become numb, lose feeling.

obtorqueō, -quēre, -sī, -tum *vt* to twist about, wrench.

obtrectātiō, -ōnis *f* disparagement.

obtrectātor, -ōris *m* disparager.

obtrectō, -āre *vt, vi* to detract, disparage.

obtrītus *ppp of* **obterō**.

obtrūdō *etc see* **obstrūdō**.

obtruncō, -āre *vt* to cut down, slaughter.

obtueor, -ērī, -or, -ī *vt* to gaze at, see clearly.

obtulī *perf of* **offerō**.

obtundō, -undere, -udī, -ūsum *and* **-ūnsum** *vt* to beat, thump; to blunt; (*speech*) to deafen, annoy.

obturbō, -āre *vt* to throw into confusion; to bother, distract.

obturgēscō, -ere *vi* to swell up.

obtūrō, -āre *vt* to stop up, close.

obtūsus, obtūnsus *ppp of* **obtundō** ♦ *adj* blunt; (*fig*) dulled, blurred, unfeeling.

obtūtus, -ūs *m* gaze.

obumbrō, -āre *vt* to shade, darken; (*fig*) to cloak, screen.

obuncus *adj* hooked.

obūstus *adj* burnt, hardened in fire.

obvallātus *adj* fortified.

obveniō, -enīre, -ēnī, -entum *vi* to come up; to fall to; to occur.

obversor, -ārī *vi* to move about before; (*visions*) to hover.

obversus *ppp of* **obvertō** ♦ *adj* turned towards ♦ *mpl* enemy.

obvertō, -tere, -tī, -sum *vt* to direct towards, turn against.

obviam *adv* to meet, against; ~ **ire** to go to meet.

obvius *adj* in the way, to meet; opposite, against; at hand, accessible; exposed.

obvolvō, -vere, -vī, -ūtum *vt* to wrap up, muffle up; (*fig*) to cloak.

occaecō, -āre, -āvī, -ātum *vt* to blind, obscure, conceal; to benumb.

occallēscō, -ēscere, -uī *vi* to grow a thick skin; to become hardened.

occanō, -ere *vi* to sound the attack.

occāsiō, -ōnis *f* opportunity, convenient time; (*MIL*) surprise.

occāsiuncula, -ae *f* opportunity.

occāsus, -ūs *m* setting; west; downfall, ruin.

occātiō, -ōnis *f* harrowing.

occātor, -ōris *m* harrower.

occēdō, -ere *vi* to go up to.

occentō, -āre *vt, vi* to serenade; to sing a lampoon.

occēpī *perf of* **occipiō**.

occepsō *archaic fut of* **occipiō**.

occeptō, -āre *vt* to begin.

occidēns, -entis *pres p of* **occidō** ♦ *m* west.

occīdiō, -ōnis *f* massacre; ~**ōne occīdere** annihilate.

occīdō, -dere, -dī, -sum *vt* to fell; to cut down, kill; to pester.

occidō, -idere, -idī, -āsum *vi* to fall; to set; to die, perish, be ruined.

occiduus *adj* setting; western; failing.

occinō, -ere, -uī *vi* to sing inauspiciously.

occipiō, -ipere, -ēpī, -eptum *vt, vi* to begin.

occipitium, -ī *and* **iī** *nt* back of the head.

occīsiō, -ōnis *f* massacre.

occīsor, -ōris *m* killer.

---

occīsus *ppp of* **occīdō.**
occlāmitō, -āre *vi* to bawl.
occlūdō, -dere, -sī, -sum *vt* to shut up; to stop.
occō, -āre *vt* to harrow.
occubō, -āre *vi* to lie.
occulcō, -āre *vt* to trample down.
occulō, -ere, -uī, -tum *vt* to cover over, hide.
occultātiō, -ōnis *f* concealment.
occultātor, -ōris *m* hider.
occultē *adv* secretly.
occultō, -āre, -āvī, -ātum *vt* to conceal, secrete.
occultus *ppp of* **occulō ♦** *adj* hidden, secret; (*person*) reserved, secretive ♦ *nt* secret, hiding.
occumbō, -mbere, -buī, -bitum *vi* to fall, die.
occupātiō, -ōnis *f* taking possession; business; engagement.
occupātus *adj* occupied, busy.
occupō, -āre, -āvī, -ātum *vt* to take possession of, seize; to occupy, take up; to surprise, anticipate; (*money*) to lend, invest.
occurrō, -rere, -rī, -sum *vi* to run up to, meet; to attack; to fall in with; to hurry to; (*fig*) to obviate, counteract; (*words*) to object; (*thought*) to occur, suggest itself.
occursātiō, -ōnis *f* fussy welcome.
occursō, -āre *vi* to run to meet, meet; to oppose; (*thought*) to occur.
occursus, -ūs *m* meeting.
Ōceanītis, -ītidis *f daughter of Ocean.*
Ōceanus, -ī *m* Ocean, a stream encircling the earth; the Atlantic.
ocellus, -ī *m* eye; darling, gem.
ōcior, -ōris *adj* quicker, swifter.
ōcius *adv* more quickly; sooner, rather; quickly.
ocrea, -ae *f* greave.
ocreātus *adj* greaved.
Octāviānus *adj* of Octavius ♦ *m* Octavian (*a surname of Augustus*).
Octāvius, -ī *m* Roman family name (*esp the emperor Augustus; his father*).
octāvum *adv* for the eighth time.
octāvus *adj* eighth ♦ *f* eighth hour.
octāvusdecimus *adj* eighteenth.
octiēns, -ēs *adv* eight times.
octingentēsimus *adj* eight hundredth.
octingentī, -ōrum *num* eight hundred.
octipēs, -edis *adj* eight-footed.
octō *num* eight.
October, -ris *adj* of October ♦ *m* October.
octōgēnī, -ōrum *adj* eighty each.
octōgēsimus *adj* eightieth.
octōgiēns, -ēs *adv* eighty times.
octōgintā *num* eighty.
octōiugis *adj* eight together.
octōnī, -ōrum *adj* eight at a time, eight each.
octōphoros *adj* (*litter*) carried by eight bearers.
octuplicātus *adj* multiplied by eight.

octuplus *adj* eightfold.
octussis, -is *m* eight asses.
oculātus *adj* with eyes; visible; **~ā diē vendere** sell for cash.
oculus, -ī *m* eye; sight; (*plant*) bud; (*fig*) darling, jewel; **~ōs adicere ad** glance at, covet; **ante ~ōs pōnere** imagine; **ex ~īs** out of sight; **esse in ~īs** be in view; be a favourite.
ōdī, -isse *vt* to hate, dislike.
odiōsē *adv see adj.*
odiōsus *adj* odious, unpleasant.
odium, -ī *and* **iī** *nt* hatred, dislike, displeasure; insolence; **~iō esse** be hateful, be disliked.
odor (-ōs), -ōris *m* smell, perfume, stench; (*fig*) inkling, suggestion.
odōrātiō, -ōnis *f* smelling.
odōrātus *adj* fragrant, perfumed.
odōrātus, -ūs *m* sense of smell; smelling.
odōrifer, -ī *adj* fragrant; perfume-producing.
odōrō, -āre *vt* to perfume.
odōror, -ārī, -ātus *vt* to smell, smell out; (*fig*) to search out; to aspire to; to get a smattering of.
odōrus *adj* fragrant; keen-scented.
odōs *etc see* **odor.**
Odrysius *adj* Thracian.
Odyssēa, -ae *f* Odyssey.
Oeagrius *adj* Thracian.
Oebalia, -iae *f* Tarentum.
Oebalidēs, -idae *m* Castor, Pollux.
Oebalis, -idis *f* Helen.
Oebalius *adj* Spartan.
Oebalus, -ī *m* king of Sparta.
Oedipūs, -odis *and* **ī** *m king of Thebes; solver of riddles.*
oenophorum, -ī *nt* wine basket.
Oenopia, -ae *f* Aegina.
Oenotria, -ae *f* S.E. Italy.
Oenotrius *adj* Italian.
oestrus, -ī *m* gadfly; (*fig*) frenzy.
Oeta, -ae, -ē, -ēs *f mountain range in Thessaly, associated with Hercules.*
Oetaeus *adj see n.*
ofella, -ae *f* morsel.
offa, -ae *f* pellet, lump; swelling.
offectus *ppp of* **officiō.**
offendō, -endere, -endī, -ēnsum *vt* to hit; to hit on, come upon; to offend, blunder; to take offence; to fail, come to grief.
offēnsa, -ae *f* displeasure, enmity; offence, injury.
offēnsiō, -ōnis *f* stumbling; stumbling block; misfortune, indisposition; offence, displeasure.
offēnsiuncula, -ae *f* slight displeasure; slight check.
offēnsō, -āre *vt, vi* to dash against.
offēnsus *ppp of* **offendō ♦** *adj* offensive; displeased ♦ *nt* offence.
offēnsus, -ūs *m* shock; offence.
offerō, -re, obtulī, oblātum *vt* to present, show; to bring forward, offer; to expose; to cause, inflict; **sē ~** encounter.

offerumenta, -ae *f* present.
officīna, -ae *f* workshop factory.
officiō, -icere, -ēcī, -ectum *vt* to obstruct; to interfere with; to hurt, prejudice.
officiōsē *adv* courteously.
officiōsus *adj* obliging; dutiful.
officium, -ī *and* **iī** *nt* service, attention; ceremonial; duty, sense of duty; official duty, function.
offīgō, -ere *vt* to fasten, drive in.
offirmātus *adj* determined.
offirmō, -āre *vt, vi* to persevere in.
offlectō, -ere *vt* to turn about.
offrēnātus *adj* checked.
offūcia, -ae *f* (*cosmetic*) paint; (*fig*) trick.
offulgeō, -gēre, -sī *vi* to shine on.
offundō, -undere, -ūdī, -ūsum *vt* to pour out to; to pour over; to spread; to cover, fill.
offūsus *ppp of* **offundō**.
ogganniō, -īre *vi* to growl at.
oggerō, -ere *vt* to bring, give.
Ogygius *adj* Theban.
oh *interj* (*expressing surprise, joy, grief*) oh!
ohē *interj* (*expressing surfeit*) stop!, enough!
oi *interj* (*expressing complaint, weeping*) oh!, oh dear!
oiei *interj* (*lamenting*) oh dear!
Oīleus, -eī *m* father of the less famous Ajax.
olea, -ae *f* olive; olive tree.
oleāginus *adj* of the olive tree.
oleārius *adj* oil- (*in cpds*) ♦ *m* oil seller.
oleaster, -rī *m* wild olive.
olēns, -entis *pres p of* **oleō** ♦ *adj* fragrant; stinking, musty.
oleō, -ēre, -uī *vt, vi* to smell, smell of; (*fig*) to betray.
oleum, -ī *nt* olive oil, oil; wrestling school; ~ **et operam perdere** waste time and trouble.
olfaciō, -facere, -fēcī, -factum *vt* to smell, scent.
olfactō, -āre *vt* to smell at.
olidus *adj* smelling, rank.
ōlim *adv* once, once upon a time; at the time, at times; for a good while; one day (in the future).
olit- *etc see* **holit-**.
olīva, -ae *f* olive, olive tree; olive branch, olive staff.
olīvētum, -ī *nt* olive grove.
olīvifer, -ī *adj* olive-bearing.
olīvum, -ī *nt* oil; wrestling school; perfume.
olla, -ae *f* pot, jar.
olle, ollus *etc see* **ille**.
olor, -ōris *m* swan.
olōrīnus *adj* swan's.
olus *etc see* **holus**.
Olympia, -ae *f* site of the Greek games in Elis.
Olympia, -ōrum *ntpl* Olympic Games.
Olympiacus *adj* = **Olympicus**.
Olympias, -adis *f* Olympiad, period of four

years.
Olympicus, -us *adj* Olympic.
Olympionīcēs, -ae *m* Olympic winner.
Olympus, -ī *m* mountain in N. Greece, abode of the gods; heaven.
omāsum, -ī *nt* tripe; paunch.
ōmen, -inis *nt* omen, sign; solemnity.
ōmentum, -ī *nt* bowels.
ōminor, -ārī, -ātus *vt* to forebode, prophesy.
ōmissus *ppp of* **ōmittō** ♦ *adj* remiss.
ōmittō, -ittere, -īsī, -issum *vt* to let go; to leave off, give up; to disregard, overlook; (*speech*) to pass over, omit.
omnifer, -ī *adj* all-sustaining.
omnigenus *adj* of all kinds.
omnimodīs *adv* wholly.
omnīnō *adv* entirely, altogether, at all; in general; (*concession*) to be sure, yes; (*number*) in all, just; ~ **nōn** not at all.
omniparēns, -entis *adj* mother of all.
omnipotēns, -entis *adj* almighty.
omnis *adj* all, every, any; every kind of; the whole of ♦ *nt* the universe ♦ *mpl* everybody ♦ *ntpl* everything.
omnituēns, -entis *adj* all-seeing.
omnivagus *adj* roving everywhere.
omnivolus *adj* willing everything.
onager, -rī *m* wild ass.
onerārius *adj* (*beast*) of burden; (*ship*) transport.
onerō, -āre, -āvī, -ātum *vt* to load, burden; (*fig*) to overload, oppress; to aggravate.
onerōsus *adj* heavy, burdensome, irksome.
onus, -eris *nt* load, burden, cargo; (*fig*) charge, difficulty.
onustus *adj* loaded, burdened; (*fig*) filled.
onyx, -chis *m/f* onyx; onyx box.
opācitās, -ātis *f* shade.
opācō, -āre *vt* to shade.
opācus *adj* shady; dark.
ope *abl of* **ops**.
opella, -ae *f* light work, small service.
opera, -ae *f* exertion, work; service; care, attention; leisure, time; (*person*) workman, hired rough; ~**am dare** pay attention; do one's best; ~**ae pretium** worth while; ~**ā meā** thanks to me.
operārius *adj* working ♦ *m* workman.
operculum, -ī *nt* cover, lid.
operīmentum, -ī *nt* covering.
operiō, -īre, -uī, -tum *vt* to cover; to close; (*fig*) to overwhelm, conceal.
operor, -ārī, -ātus *vi* to work, take pains, be occupied.
operōsē *adv* painstakingly.
operōsus *adj* active, industrious; laborious, elaborate.
opertus *ppp of* **operiō** ♦ *adj* covered, hidden ♦ *nt* secret.
opēs *pl of* **ops**.

Noun declensions and verb conjugations are shown on pp xiii to xxv. The present infinitive ending of a verb shows to which conjugation it belongs: **-āre** = 1st; **-ēre** = 2nd; **-ere** = 3rd and **-īre** = 4th. Irregular verbs are shown on p xxvi

opicus *adj* barbarous, boorish.
opifer, -ī *adj* helping.
opifex, -icis *m/f* maker; craftsman, artisan.
ōpiliō, -ōnis *m* shepherd.
opīmitās, -ātis *f* abundance.
opīmus *adj* rich, fruitful, fat; copious,
sumptuous; (*style*) overloaded; **spolia ~a**
spoils of an enemy commander killed by a
Roman general.
opīnābilis *adj* conjectural.
opīnātiō, -ōnis *f* conjecture.
opīnātor, -ōris *m* conjecturer.
opīnātus, -ūs *m* supposition.
opīniō, -ōnis *f* opinion, conjecture, belief;
reputation, esteem; rumour; **contrā, praeter**
~ōnem contrary to expectation.
opīniōsus *adj* dogmatic.
opīnor, -ārī, -ātus *vi* to think, suppose,
imagine ♦ *adj* imagined.
opiparē *adv see adj.*
opiparus *adj* rich, sumptuous.
opitulor, -ārī, -ātus *vi* (*with dat*) to help.
oportet, -ēre, -uit *vt* (*impers*) ought, should.
oppēdō, -ere *vi* to insult.
opperior, -īrī, -tus *vt, vi* to wait, wait for.
oppetō, -ere, -īvī, -ītum *vt* to encounter; to
die.
oppidānus *adj* provincial ♦ *mpl* townsfolk.
oppidō *adv* quite, completely, exactly.
oppidulum, -ī *nt* small town.
oppidum, -ī *nt* town.
oppignerō, -āre *vt* to pledge.
oppilō, -āre *vt* to stop up.
oppleō, -ēre, -ēvī, -ētum *vt* to fill, choke up.
oppōnō, -ōnere, -osuī, -ositum *vt* to put
against, set before; to expose; to present;
(*argument*) to adduce, reply, oppose;
(*property*) to pledge, mortgage.
opportūnitās, -ātis *f* suitableness,
advantage; good opportunity.
opportūnē *adv* opportunely.
opportūnus *adj* suitable, opportune; useful;
exposed.
oppositiō, -ōnis *f* opposing.
oppositus *ppp of* **oppōnō** ♦ *adj* against,
opposite.
oppositus, -ūs *m* opposing.
oppsuī *perf of* **oppōnō**.
oppressiō, -ōnis *f* violence; seizure;
overthrow.
oppressus *ppp of* **opprimō**.
oppressus, -ūs *m* pressure.
opprimō, -imere, -essī, -essum *vt* to press
down, crush; to press together, close; to
suppress, overwhelm, overthrow; to
surprise, seize.
opprobrium, -ī *and* **iī** *nt* reproach, disgrace,
scandal.
opprobrō, -āre *vt* to taunt.
oppugnātiō, -ōnis *f* attack, assault.
oppugnātor, -ōris *m* assailant.
oppugnō, -āre, -āvī, -ātum *vt* to attack,
assault.

ops, -opis *f* power, strength; help.
Ops goddess of plenty.
ops- *etc see* **obs-**.
optābilis *adj* desirable.
optātiō, -ōnis *f* wish.
optātus *adj* longed for ♦ *nt* wish; **~ātō**
according to one's wish.
optimās, -ātis *adj* aristocratic ♦ *mpl* the
nobility.
optimē *adv* best, very well; just in time.
optimus *adj* best, very good; excellent; **~ō iūre**
deservedly.
optiō, -ōnis *f* choice ♦ *m* assistant.
optīvus *adj* chosen.
optō, -āre, -āvī, -ātum *vt* to choose; to wish
for.
optum- *etc see* **optim-**.
opulēns, -entis *adj* rich.
opulentia, -ae *f* wealth; power.
opulentō, -āre *vt* to enrich.
opulentē, -er *adv* sumptuously.
opulentus *adj* rich, sumptuous, powerful.
opum *fpl* resources, wealth.
opus, -eris *nt* work, workmanship; (*art*) work,
building, book; (*MIL*) siege work; (*colloq*)
business; (*with* **esse**) need; **virō ~ est** a man is
needed; **māgnō ~ere** much, greatly.
opusculum, -ī *nt* little work.
ōra, -ae *f* edge, boundary; coast; country,
region; (*NAUT*) hawser.
ōrāculum, -ī *nt* oracle, prophecy.
ōrātē *adv see adj.*
ōrātiō, -ōnis *f* speech, language; a speech,
oration; eloquence; prose; emperor's
message; **~ōnem habēre** deliver a speech.
ōrātiuncula, -ae *f* short speech.
ōrātor, -ōris *m* speaker, spokesman, orator.
ōrātōrius *adj* oratorical.
ōrātrīx, -īcis *f* suppliant.
ōrātus, -ūs *m* request.
orbātor, -ōris *m* bereaver.
orbiculātus *adj* round.
orbis, -is *m* circle, ring, disc, orbit; world;
(*movement*) cycle, rotation; (*style*) rounding
off; **~ lacteus** Milky Way; **~ signifer** Zodiac; **~**
fortūnae wheel of Fortune; **~ terrārum** the
earth, world; **in ~em cōnsistere** form a
circle; **in ~em īre** go the rounds.
orbita, -ae *f* rut, track, path.
orbitās, -ātis *f* childlessness, orphanhood,
widowhood.
orbitōsus *adj* full of ruts.
orbō, -āre, -āvī, -ātum *vt* to bereave, orphan,
make childless.
orbus *adj* bereaved, orphan, childless;
destitute.
orca, -ae *f* vat.
orchas, -dis *f* kind of olive.
orchēstra, -ae *f* senatorial seats (in the
theatre).
Orcus, -ī *m* Pluto; the lower world; death.
ōrdinārius *adj* regular.
ōrdinātim *adv* in order, properly.

ōrdinātiō, -ōnis f orderly arrangement.
ōrdinātus adj appointed.
ōrdinō, -āre, -āvī, -ātum vt to arrange, regulate, set in order.
ōrdior, -dīrī, -sus vt, vi to begin, undertake.
ōrdō, -inis m line, row, series; order, regularity, arrangement; (MIL) rank, line, company, (pl) captains; (building) course, layer; (seats) row; (POL) class, order, station; **ex ~ine** in order, in one's turn; one after the other; **extrā ~inem** irregularly, unusually.
Orēas, -dis f mountain nymph.
Orestēs, -is and **ae** m son of Agamemnon, whom he avenged by killing his mother.
Orestēus adj see n.
orexis, -is f appetite.
organum, -ī nt instrument, organ.
orgia, -ōrum ntpl Bacchic revels; orgies.
orichalcum, -ī nt copper ore, brass.
ōricilla, -ae f lobe.
oriēns, -entis pres p of orior ♦ m morning; east.
orīgō, -inis f beginning, source; ancestry, descent; founder.
Orīōn, -onis and **ōnis** m mythical hunter and constellation.
orior, -īrī, -tus vi to rise; to spring, descend.
oriundus adj descended, sprung.
ōrnāmentum, -ī nt equipment, dress; ornament, decoration; distinction, pride of.
ōrnātē adv elegantly.
ōrnātus ppp of ōrnō ♦ adj equipped, furnished; embellished, excellent.
ōrnātus, -ūs m preparation; dress, equipment; embellishment.
ōrnō, -āre, -āvī, -ātum vt to fit out, equip, dress, prepare; to adorn, embellish, honour.
ornus, -ī f manna ash.
ōrō, -āre, -āvī, -ātum vt to speak, plead; to beg, entreat; to pray.
Orontēs, -is and **ī** m river of Syria.
Orontēus adj Syrian.
Orpheus, -eī and **eos** (acc **-ea**) m legendary Thracian singer, who went down to Hades for Eurydice.
Orphēus, -icus adj see n.
ōrsus ppa of ōrdior ♦ ntpl beginning; utterance.
ōrsus, -ūs m beginning.
ortus ppa of orior ♦ adj born, descended.
ortus, -ūs m rising; east; origin, source.
Ortygia, -ae and **ē, -ēs** f Delos.
Ortygius adj see n.
oryx, -gis m gazelle.
oryza, -ae f rice.
os, ossis nt bone; (fig) very soul.
ōs, -ōris nt mouth; face; entrance, opening; effrontery; **ūnō ōre** unanimously; **in ōre esse** be talked about; **quō ōre redībō** how shall I have the face to go back?
oscen, -inis m bird of omen.

ōscillum, -ī nt little mask.
ōscitāns, -antis pres p of ōscitō ♦ adj listless, drowsy.
ōscitanter adv half-heartedly.
ōscitō, -āre; -or, -ārī vi to yawn, be drowsy.
ōsculātiō, -ōnis f kissing.
ōsculor, -ārī, -ātus vt to kiss; to make a fuss of.
ōsculum, -ī nt sweet mouth; kiss.
Oscus adj Oscan.
Osīris, -is and **idis** m Egyptian god, husband of Isis.
Ossa, -ae f mountain in Thessaly.
osseus adj bony.
ossifraga, -ae f osprey.
ostendō, -dere, -dī, -tum vt to hold out, show, display; to expose; to disclose, reveal; (speech) to say, make known.
ostentātiō, -ōnis f display; showing off, ostentation; pretence.
ostentātor, -ōris m displayer, boaster.
ostentō, -āre vt to hold out, proffer, exhibit; to show off, boast of; to make known, indicate.
ostentum, -ī nt portent.
ostentus ppp of ostendō.
ostentus, -ūs m display, appearance; proof.
Ostia, -ae f, **-ōrum** ntpl port at the Tiber mouth.
ōstiārium, -ī and **iī** nt door tax.
ōstiātim adv from door to door.
Ōstiēnsis adj see n.
ōstium, -ī and **iī** nt door; entrance, mouth.
ostrea, -ae f oyster.
ostreōsus adj rich in oysters.
ostreum, -ī nt oyster.
ostrifer, -ī adj oyster-producing.
ostrīnus adj purple.
ostrum, -ī nt purple; purple dress or coverings.
ōsus, ōsūrus ppa and fut p of ōdī.
Othō, -ōnis m author of a law giving theatre seats to Equites; Roman emperor after Galba.
Othōniānus adj see n.
ōtiolum, -ī nt bit of leisure.
ōtior, -ārī vi to have a holiday, be idle.
ōtiōsē adv leisurely; quietly; fearlessly.
ōtiōsus adj at leisure, free; out of public affairs; neutral, indifferent; quiet, unexcited; (things) free, idle ♦ m private citizen, civilian.
ōtium, -ī and **iī** nt leisure, time (for), idleness, retirement; peace, quiet.
ovātiō, -ōnis f minor triumph.
ovīle, -is nt sheep fold, goat fold.
ovillus adj of sheep.
ovis, -is f sheep.
ovō, -āre vi to rejoice; to celebrate a minor triumph.
ōvum, -ī nt egg.

Noun declensions and verb conjugations are shown on pp xiii to xxv. The present infinitive ending of a verb shows to which conjugation it belongs: **-āre** = 1st; **-ēre** = 2nd; **-ere** = 3rd and **-īre** = 4th. Irregular verbs are shown on p xxvi

P, p

pābulātiō, -ōnis *f* foraging.
pābulātor, -ōris *m* forager.
pābulor, -ārī *vi* to forage.
pābulum, -ī *nt* food, fodder.
pācālis *adj* of peace.
pācātus *adj* peaceful, tranquil ♦ *nt* friendly country.
Pachȳnum, -ī *nt* S.E. point of Sicily (*now* Cape Passaro).
pācifer, -ī *adj* peace-bringing.
pācificātiō, -ōnis *f* peacemaking.
pācificātor, -ōris *m* peacemaker.
pācificātōrius *adj* peacemaking.
pācificō, -āre *vi* to make a peace ♦ *vt* to appease.
pācificus *adj* peacemaking.
pacīscor, -īscī, -tus *vi* to make a bargain, agree ♦ *vt* to stipulate for; to barter.
pācō, -āre, -āvī, -ātum *vt* to pacify, subdue.
pactiō, -ōnis *f* bargain, agreement, contract; collusion; (*words*) formula.
Pactōlus, -ī *m* river of Lydia (*famous for its gold*).
pactor, -ōris *m* negotiator.
pactum, -ī *nt* agreement, contract.
pactus *ppa of* **pacīscor** ♦ *adj* agreed, settled; betrothed.
Pācuvius, -ī *m* Latin tragic poet.
Padus, -ī *m* river Po.
paeān, -ānis *m* healer, epithet of Apollo; hymn of praise, shout of joy; (*metre*) paeon.
paedagōgus, -ī *m* slave who took children to school.
paedor, -ōris *m* filth.
paelex, -icis *f* mistress, concubine.
paelicātus, -ūs *m* concubinage.
Paelignī, -ōrum *mpl* people of central Italy.
Paelignus *adj see* n.
paene *adv* almost, nearly.
paenīnsula, -ae *f* peninsula.
paenitendus *adj* regrettable.
paenitentia, -ae *f* repentance.
paenitet, -ēre, -uit *vt, vi* (*impers*) to repent, regret, be sorry; to be dissatisfied; **an ~et** is it not enough?
paenula, -ae *f* travelling cloak.
paenulātus *adj* wearing a cloak.
paeōn, -ōnis *m* metrical foot of one long and three short syllables.
paeōnius *adj* healing.
Paestānus *adj see* n.
Paestum, -ī *nt* town in S. Italy.
paetulus *adj* with a slight cast in the eye.
paetus *adj* with a cast in the eye.
pāgānus *adj* rural ♦ *m* villager, yokel.

pāgātim *adv* in every village.
pāgella, -ae *f* small page.
pāgina, -ae *f* (*book*) page, leaf.
pāginula, -ae *f* small page.
pāgus, -ī *m* village, country district; canton.
pāla, -ae *f* spade; (*ring*) bezel.
palaestra, -ae *f* wrestling school, gymnasium; exercise, wrestling; (*RHET*) exercise, training.
palaestricē *adv* in gymnastic fashion.
palaestricus *adj* of the wrestling school.
palaestrīta, -ae *m* head of a wrestling school.
palam *adv* openly, publicly, well-known ♦ *prep* (*with abl*) in the presence of.
Palātīnus *adj* Palatine; imperial.
Palātium, -ī *nt* Palatine Hill in Rome; palace.
palātum, -ī *nt* palate; taste, judgment.
palea, -ae *f* chaff.
paleāria, -ium *ntpl* dewlap.
Palēs, -is *f goddess of shepherds.*
Palīlis *adj* of Pales ♦ *ntpl festival of Pales.*
palimpsēstus, -ī *m* palimpsest.
Palinūrus, -ī *m pilot of Aeneas; promontory in S. Italy.*
paliūrus, -ī *m* Christ's thorn.
palla, -ae *f* woman's robe; tragic costume.
Palladium, -dī *nt image of Pallas.*
Palladius *adj* of Pallas.
Pallantēus *adj see* n.
Pallas, -dis *and* **dos** *f* Athene, Minerva; oil; olive tree.
Pallās, -antis *m ancestor or son of Evander.*
pallēns, -entis *pres p of* **palleō** ♦ *adj* pale; greenish.
palleō, -ēre, -uī *vi* to be pale or yellow; to fade; to be anxious.
pallēscō, -escere, -uī *vi* to turn pale, turn yellow.
palliātus *adj* wearing a Greek cloak.
pallidulus *adj* palish.
pallidus *adj* pale, pallid, greenish; in love.
palliolum, -ī *nt* small cloak, cape, hood.
pallium, -ī *and* **iī** *nt* coverlet; Greek cloak.
pallor, -ōris *m* paleness, fading; fear.
palma, -ae *f* (*hand*) palm, hand; (*oar*) blade; (*tree*) palm, date; branch; (*fig*) prize, victory, glory.
palmāris *adj* excellent.
palmārius *adj* prizewinning.
palmātus *adj* palm-embroidered.
palmes, -itis *m* pruned shoot, branch.
palmētum, -ī *nt* palm grove.
palmifer, -ī *adj* palm-bearing.
palmōsus *adj* palm-clad.
palmula, -ae *f* oar blade.
pālor, -ārī, -ātus *vi* to wander about, straggle.
palpātiō, -ōnis *f* flatteries.
palpātor, -ōris *m* flatterer.
palpebra, -ae *f* eyelid.
palpitō, -āre *vi* to throb, writhe.
palpō, -āre; -or, -ārī *vt* to stroke; to coax, flatter.
palpus, -ī *m* coaxing.

paludāmentum, -ī *nt* military cloak.
paludātus *adj* in a general's cloak.
paludōsus *adj* marshy.
palumbēs, -is *m/f* wood pigeon.
pālus, -ī *m* stake, pale.
palūs, -ūdis *f* marsh, pool, lake.
palūster, -ris *adj* marshy.
pampineus *adj* of vineshoots.
pampinus, -ī *m* vineshoot.
Pān, -ānos (*acc* -āna) *m* Greek god of shepherds, hills and woods, esp associated with Arcadia.
panacēa, -ae *f* a herb supposed to cure all diseases.
Panaetius, -ī *m* Stoic philosopher.
Panchāaeus *adj see n.*
Panchāaius *adj see n.*
Panchāia, -iae *f part of Arabia.*
panchrēstus *adj* good for everything.
pancratium, -ī *and* **iī** *nt* all-in boxing and wrestling match.
pandiculor, -āre *vi* to stretch oneself.
Pandīōn, -onis *m* king of Athens, father of Procne and Philomela.
Pandīonius *adj see n.*
pandō, -ere, -ī, pānsum *and* **passum** *vt* to spread out, stretch, extend; to open; (*fig*) to disclose, explain.
pandus *adj* curved, bent.
pangō, -ere, panxī *and* **pepigī, pāctum** *vt* to drive in, fasten; to make, compose; to agree, settle.
pānicula, -ae *f* tuft.
pānicum, -ī *nt* Italian millet.
pānis, -is *m* bread, loaf.
Pāniscus, -ī *m* little Pan.
panniculus, -ī *m* rag.
Pannonia, -ae *f* country on the middle Danube.
Pannonius *adj see n.*
pannōsus *adj* ragged.
pannus, -ī *m* piece of cloth, rag, patch.
Panormus, -ī *f* town in Sicily (*now* Palermo).
pānsa *adj* splayfoot.
pānsus *ppp of* **pandō**.
panthēra, -ae *f* panther.
Panthoidēs, -ae *m* Euphorbus.
Panthūs, -ī *m* priest of Apollo at Troy.
panticēs, -um *mpl* bowels; sausages.
panxī *perf of* **pangō**.
papae *interj* (*expressing wonder*) ooh!
pāpas, -ae *m* tutor.
papāver, -is *nt* poppy.
papāvereus *adj see n.*
Paphius *adj see n.*
Paphos, -ī *f* town in Cyprus, sacred to Venus.
pāpiliō, -ōnis *m* butterfly.
papilla, -ae *f* teat, nipple; breast.
pappus, -ī *m* woolly seed.
papula, -ae *f* pimple.
papȳrifer, -ī *adj* papyrus-bearing.
papȳrum, -ī *nt* papyrus; paper.

papȳrus, -ī *m/f* papyrus; paper.
pār, paris *adj* equal, like; a match for; proper, right ♦ *m* peer, partner, companion ♦ *nt* pair;
pār parī respondēre return like for like;
parēs cum paribus facillimē congregantur ≈ birds of a feather flock together; **lūdere pār impār** play at evens and odds.
parābilis *adj* easy to get.
parasīta, -ae *f* woman parasite.
parasītaster, -rī *m* sorry parasite.
parasīticus *adj* of a parasite.
parasītus, -ī *m* parasite, sponger.
parātē *adv* with preparation; carefully; promptly.
parātiō, -ōnis *f* trying to get.
paratragoedō, -āre *vi* to talk theatrically.
parātus *ppp of* **parō** ♦ *adj* ready; equipped; experienced.
parātus, -ūs *m* preparation, equipment.
Parca, -ae *f* Fate.
parcē *adv* frugally; moderately.
parcō, -cere, pepercī, -sum *vt, vi* (*with dat*) to spare, economize; to refrain from, forgo; (*with inf*) to forbear, stop.
parcus *adj* sparing, thrifty; niggardly, scanty; chary.
pardus, -ī *m* panther.
pārēns, -entis *pres p of* **pāreō** ♦ *adj* obedient ♦ *mpl* subjects.
parēns, -entis *m/f* parent, father, mother; ancestor; founder.
parentālis *adj* parental ♦ *ntpl* festival in honour of dead ancestors and relatives.
parentō, -āre *vi* to sacrifice in honour of dead parents or relatives; to avenge (*with the death of another*).
pāreō, -ēre, -uī, -itum *vi* to be visible, be evident; (*with dat*) to obey, submit to, comply with; ~**et** it is proved.
pariēs, -etis *m* wall.
parietinae, -ārum *fpl* ruins.
Parīlia, -ium *ntpl* festival of Pales.
parīlis *adj* equal.
pariō, -ere, peperī, -tum *vt* to give birth to; to produce, create, cause; to procure.
Paris, -idis *m* son of Priam (*abductor of Helen*).
pariter *adv* equally, alike; at the same time, together.
paritō, -āre *vt* to get ready.
Parius *adj see* **Paros**.
parma, -ae *f* shield, buckler.
parmātus *adj* armed with a buckler.
parmula, -ae *f* little shield.
Parnāsis, -idis *adj* Parnassian.
Parnāsius *adj* = **Parnāsis**.
Parnāsus, -ī *m* mount Parnassus in central Greece, sacred to the Muses.
parō, -āre, -āvī, -ātum *vt* to prepare, get ready, provide; to intend, set about; to procure, get, buy; to arrange.

Noun declensions and verb conjugations are shown on pp xiii to xxv. The present infinitive ending of a verb shows to which conjugation it belongs: **-āre** = 1st; **-ēre** = 2nd; **-ere** = 3rd and **-īre** = 4th. Irregular verbs are shown on p xxvi

parocha, -ae _f_ provision of necessaries (_to officials travelling_).
parochus, -ī _m_ purveyor; host.
paropsis, -dis _f_ dish.
Paros, -ī _f_ Aegean island (_famous for white marble_).
parra, -ae _f_ owl.
Parrhasis, -idis, -ius _adj_ Arcadian.
parricīda, -ae _m_ parricide, assassin; traitor.
parricīdium, -ī _and_ **iī** parricide, murder; high treason.
pars, -tis _f_ part, share, fraction; party, side; direction; respect, degree; (_with pl verb_) some; (_pl_) stage part, role; duty, function; **māgna ~** the majority; **māgnam ~tem** largely; **in eam ~tem** in that direction, on that side, in that sense; **nullā ~te** not at all; **omnī ~te** entirely; **ex ~te** partly; **ex alterā ~te** on the other hand; **ex māgnā ~te** to a large extent; **prō ~te** to the best of one's ability; **~tēs agere** play a part; **duae ~tēs** two-thirds; **trēs ~tēs** three-fourths; **multīs ~ibus** a great deal.
parsimōnia, -ae _f_ thrift, frugality.
parthenicē, -ēs _f_ a plant.
Parthenopē, -ēs _f_ old name of Naples.
Parthenopēius _adj see n._
Parthī, -ōrum _mpl_ Parthians (_Rome's great enemy in the East_).
Parthicus, -us _adj see n._
particeps, -ipis _adj_ sharing, partaking ♦ _m_ partner.
participō, -āre _vt_ to share, impart, inform.
particula, -ae _f_ particle.
partim _adv_ partly, in part; mostly; some ... others.
partiō, -īre, -īvī, -ītum, -ior, -īrī _vt_ to share, distribute, divide.
partītē _adv_ methodically.
partītiō, -ōnis _f_ distribution, division.
parturiō, -īre _vi_ to be in labour; (_fig_) to be anxious ♦ _vt_ to teem with, be ready to produce; (_mind_) to brood over.
partus _ppp of_ **pariō** ♦ _ntpl_ possessions.
partus, -ūs _m_ birth; young.
parum _adv_ too little, not enough; not very, scarcely.
parumper _adv_ for a little while.
parvitās, -ātis _f_ smallness.
parvulus, parvolus _adj_ very small, slight; quite young ♦ _m_ child.
parvus (_comp_ **minor** _superl_ **minimus**) _adj_ small, little, slight; (_time_) short; (_age_) young; **~ī esse** be of little value.
Pascha, -ae _f_ Easter.
pāscō, -scere, -vī, -stum _vt_ to feed, put to graze; to keep, foster; (_fig_) to feast, cherish ♦ _vi_ to graze, browse.
pāscuus _adj_ for pasture ♦ _nt_ pasture.
Pāsiphaē, -ēs _f_ wife of Minos (_mother of the Minotaur_).
passer, -is _m_ sparrow; (_fish_) plaice; **~ marīnus** ostrich.

passerculus, -ī _m_ little sparrow.
passim _adv_ here and there, at random; indiscriminately.
passum, -ī _nt_ raisin wine.
passus _ppp of_ **pandō** ♦ _adj_ spread out, dishevelled; dried.
passus _ppa of_ **patior**.
passus, -ūs _m_ step, pace; footstep; **mille ~ūs** mile; **mīlia ~uum** miles.
pastillus, -ī _m_ lozenge.
pāstor, -ōris _m_ shepherd.
pāstōrālis _adj_ shepherd's, pastoral.
pāstōricius, pāstōrius _adj_ shepherd's.
pāstus _ppp of_ **pāscō**.
pāstus, -ūs _m_ pasture, food.
Patara, -ae _f_ town in Lycia (_with oracle of Apollo_).
Pataraeus _and_ **eus** _adj see n._
Patavīnus _adj see n._
Patavium, -ī _nt_ birthplace of Livy (_now Padua_).
patefaciō, -facere, -fēcī, -factum (_pass_ **-fīō, -fierī**) _vt_ to open, open up; to disclose.
patefactiō, -ōnis _see_ disclosing.
patefīō _etc see_ **patefaciō**.
patella, -ae _f_ small dish, plate.
patēns, -entis _pres p of_ **pateō** ♦ _adj_ open, accessible, exposed; broad; evident.
patenter _adv_ clearly.
pateō, -ēre, -uī _vi_ to be open, accessible, exposed; to extend; to be evident, known.
pater, -ris _m_ father; (_pl_) forefathers; senators.
patera, -ae _f_ dish, saucer, bowl.
paterfamiliās, patrisfamiliās _m_ master of the house.
paternus _adj_ father's, paternal; native.
patēscō, -ere _vi_ to open out; to extend; to become evident.
patibilis _adj_ endurable; sensitive.
patibulātus _adj_ pilloried.
patibulum, -ī _nt_ fork-shaped yoke, pillory.
patiēns, -entis _pres p of_ **patior** ♦ _adj_ able to endure; patient; unyielding.
patienter _adv_ patiently.
patientia, -ae _f_ endurance, stamina; forbearance; submissiveness.
patina, -ae _f_ dish, pan.
patior, -tī, -ssus _vt_ to suffer, experience; to submit to; to allow, put up with; **facile ~** be well pleased with; **aegrē ~** be displeased with.
Patrae, -ārum _fpl_ Greek seaport (_now_ Patras).
patrātor, -ōris _m_ doer.
patrātus _adj:_ **pater ~** officiating priest.
Patrēnsis _adj see n._
patria, -ae _f_ native land, native town, home.
patricius _adj_ patrician ♦ _m_ aristocrat.
patrimōnium, -ī _and_ **iī** _nt_ inheritance, patrimony.
patrimus _adj_ having a father living.
patrissō, -āre _vi_ to take after one's father.
patrītus _adj_ of one's father.
patrius _adj_ father's; hereditary, native.

patrō, -āre, -āvī, -ātum *vt* to achieve, execute, complete.
patrōcinium, -ī *and* **iī** *nt* patronage, advocacy, defence.
patrōcinor, -ārī *vi* (*with dat*) to defend, support.
patrōna, -ae *f* patron goddess; protectress, safeguard.
patrōnus, -ī *m* patron, protector; (*law*) advocate, counsel.
patruēlis *adj* cousin's ♦ *m* cousin.
patruus, -ī *m* (paternal) uncle ♦ *adj* uncle's.
patulus *adj* open; spreading, broad.
paucitās, -ātis *f* small number, scarcity.
pauculus *adj* very few.
paucus *adj* few, little ♦ *mpl* a few, the select few ♦ *ntpl* a few words.
paulātim *adv* little by little, gradually.
paulisper *adv* for a little while.
Paullus, -i *m* = **Paulus**.
paulō *adv* a little, somewhat.
paululus *adj* very little ♦ *nt* a little bit.
paulum *adv* = **paulō**.
paulus *adj* little.
Paulus, -ī *m* Roman surname (*esp victor of Pydna*).
pauper, -is *adj* poor; meagre ♦ *mpl* the poor.
pauperculus *adj* poor.
pauperiēs, -ēī *f* poverty.
pauperō, -āre *vt* to impoverish; to rob.
paupertās, -ātis *f* poverty, moderate means.
pausa, -ae *f* stop, end.
pauxillātim *adv* bit by bit.
pauxillulus *adj* very little.
pauxillus *adj* little.
pavefactus *adj* frightened.
paveō, -ēre, pāvī *vi* to be terrified, quake ♦ *vt* to dread, be scared of.
pavēscō, -ere *vt, vi* to become alarmed (at).
pāvī *perf of* **pāscō**.
pavidē *adv* in a panic.
pavidus *adj* quaking, terrified.
pavīmentātus *adj* paved.
pavīmentum, -ī *nt* pavement, floor.
paviō, -īre *vt* to strike.
pavitō, -āre *vi* to be very frightened; to shiver.
pāvō, -ōnis *m* peacock.
pavor, -ōris *m* terror, panic.
pāx, pācis *f* peace; (*gods*) grace; (*mind*) serenity ♦ *interj* enough!; **pāce tuā** by your leave.
peccātum, -ī *nt* mistake, fault, sin.
peccō, -āre, -āvī, -ātum *vi* to make a mistake, go wrong, offend.
pecorōsus *adj* rich in cattle.
pecten, -inis *m* comb; (*fish*) scallop; (*loom*) reed; (*lyre*) plectrum.
pectō, -ctere, -xī, -xum *vt* to comb.
pectus, -oris *nt* breast; heart, feeling; mind, thought.
pecū *nt* flock of sheep; (*pl*) pastures.
pecuārius *adj* of cattle ♦ *m* cattle breeder ♦ *ntpl* herds.
pecūlātor, -ōris *m* embezzler.
pecūlātus, -ūs *m* embezzlement.
pecūliāris *adj* one's own; special.
pecūliātus *adj* provided with money.
pecūliōsus *adj* with private property.
pecūlium, -ī *and* **iī** *nt* small savings, private property.
pecūnia, -ae *f* property; money.
pecūniārius *adj* of money.
pecūniōsus *adj* moneyed, well-off.
pecus, -oris *nt* cattle, herd, flock; animal.
pecus, -udis *f* sheep, head of cattle, beast.
pedālis *adj* a foot long.
pedārius *adj* (*senator*) without full rights.
pedes, -itis *m* foot soldier, infantry ♦ *adj* on foot.
pedester, -ris *adj* on foot, pedestrian; infantry- (*in cpds*); on land; (*writing*) in prose, prosaic.
pedetemptim *adv* step by step, cautiously.
pedica, -ae *f* fetter, snare.
pedis, -is *m* louse.
pedisequa, -ae *f* handmaid.
pedisequus, -ī *m* attendant, lackey.
peditātus, -ūs *m* infantry.
pedum, -ī *nt* crook.
Pēgaseus *and* **is, -idis** *adj* Pegasean.
Pēgasus, -ī *m* mythical winged horse (*associated with the Muses*).
pēgma, -tis *nt* bookcase; stage elevator.
pēierō, -āre *vi* to perjure oneself.
pēior, -ōris *compar of* **malus**.
pēius *adv* worse.
pelagius *adj* of the sea.
pelagus, -ī (*pl* **-ē**) *nt* sea, open sea.
pelamys, -dis *f* young tunny fish.
Pelasgī, -ōrum *mpl* Greeks.
Pelasgias *and* **is** *and* **us** *adj* Grecian.
Pēleus, -eī *and* **eos** (*acc* **-ea**) *m* king of Thessaly (*father of Achilles*).
Peliās, -ae *m* uncle of Jason.
Pēlias *and* **iacus** *and* **ius** *adj see* **Pēlion**.
Pēlīdēs, -īdae *m* Achilles; Neoptolemus.
Pēlion, -ī *nt* mountain in Thessaly.
Pella, -ae, -ē, -ēs *f* town of Macedonia (*birthplace of Alexander*).
pellācia, -ae *f* attraction.
Pellaeus *adj* of Pella; Alexandrian; Egyptian.
pellāx, -ācis *adj* seductive.
pellēctiō, -ōnis *f* reading through.
pellectus *ppp of* **pelliciō**.
pellegō *etc see* **perlegō**.
polliciō, -icere, -exī, -ectum *vt* to entice, inveigle.
pellicula, -ae *f* skin, fleece.
pelliō, -ōnis *m* furrier.

Noun declensions and verb conjugations are shown on pp xiii to xxv. The present infinitive ending of a verb shows to which conjugation it belongs: **-āre** = 1st; **-ēre** = 2nd; **-ere** = 3rd and **-īre** = 4th. Irregular verbs are shown on p xxvi

pellis, -is *f* skin, hide; leather, felt; tent.
pellītus *adj* wearing skins, with leather coats.
pellō, -ere, pepulī, pulsum *vt* to push, knock, drive; to drive off, rout, expel; (*lyre*) to play; (*mind*) to touch, affect; (*feeling*) to banish.
pellūc- *etc see* **perlūc-**.
Pelopēis *and* **ēius** *and* **ēus** *adj see* n.
Pelopidae, -idārum *mpl* house of Pelops.
Pelopōias *adj see* n.
Peloponnēsiacus, -ius *adj see* n.
Peloponnēsus, -ī *f* Peloponnese, S. Greece.
Pelops, -is *m* son of Tantalus (*grandfather of Agamemnon*).
pelōris, -idis *f* a large mussel.
pelta, -ae *f* light shield.
peltastae, -ārum *mpl* peltasts.
peltātus *adj* armed with the pelta.
Pēlūsiacus *adj see* n.
Pēlūsium, -ī *nt* Eygptian town at the E. mouth of the Nile.
Pēlūsius *adj see* n.
pelvis, -is *f* basin.
penārius *adj* provision- (*in cpds*).
Penātēs, -ium *mpl* spirits of the larder, household gods; home.
penātiger, -ī *adj* carrying his home gods.
pendeō, -ēre, pependī *vi* to hang; to overhang, hover; to hang down, be flabby; (*fig*) to depend; to gaze, listen attentively; (*mind*) to be in suspense, be undecided.
pendō, -ere, pependī, pēnsum *vt* to weigh; to pay; (*fig*) to ponder, value ♦ *vi* to weigh.
pendulus *adj* hanging; in doubt.
Pēnēēis *and* **ēius** *and* **ēus** *adj see* n.
Pēnelopē, ēs *and* **a, -ae** *f* wife of Ulysses (*famed for her constancy*).
Pēnelopēus *adj see* n.
penes *prep* (*with acc*) in the power or possession of; in the house of, with.
penetrābilis *adj* penetrable; piercing.
penetrālis *adj* penetrating; inner, inmost ♦ *ntpl* inner room, interior, sanctuary; remote parts.
penetrō, -āre, -āvī, -ātum *vt, vi* to put into, penetrate, enter.
Pēnēus, -ī *m* chief river of Thessaly.
pēnicillus, -ī *m* painter's brush, pencil.
pēniculus, -ī *m* brush; sponge.
pēnis, -is *m* penis.
penitē *adj* inwardly.
penitus *adv* inside, deep within; deeply, from the depths; utterly, thoroughly.
penna, pinna, -ae *f* feather, wing; flight.
pennātus *adj* winged.
penniger, -ī *adj* feathered.
pennipotēns, -entis *adj* winged.
pennula, -ae *f* little wing.
pēnsilis *adj* hanging, pendent.
pēnsiō, -ōnis *f* payment, instalment.
pēnsitō, -āre *vt* to pay; to consider.
pēnsō, -āre, -āvī, -ātum *vt* to weight out; to compensate, repay; to consider, judge.
pēnsum, -ī *nt* spinner's work; task, duty;

weight, value; **~ī esse** be of importance; **~ī habēre** care at all about.
pēnsus *ppp of* **pendō**.
pentēris, -is *f* quinquereme.
Pentheus, -eī *and* **eos** *m* king of Thebes (*killed by Bacchantes*).
pēnūria, -ae *f* want, need.
penus, -ūs *and* **ī** *m/f*, **-um, -ī, -us, -oris** *nt* provisions, store of food.
pependī *perf of* **pendeō**; *perf of* **pendō**.
peperī *perf of* **parcō**.
peperī *perf of* **pariō**.
pepigī *perf of* **pangō**.
peplum, -ī *nt*, **-us, -ī** *m* state robe of Athena.
pepulī *perf of* **pellō**.
per *prep* (*with acc: space*) through, all over; (: *time*) throughout, during; (: *means*) by, by means of; (: *cause*) by reason of, for the sake of; **~ īram** in anger; **~ manūs** from hand to hand; **~ mē** as far as I am concerned; **~ vim** forcibly; **~ ego tē deōs ōrō** in Heaven's name I beg you.
pēra, -ae *f* bag.
perabsurdus *adj* very absurd.
peraccommodātus *adj* very convenient.
perācer, -ris *adj* very sharp.
peracerbus *adj* very sour.
peracēscō, -ēscere, -uī *vi* to get vexed.
perāctiō, -ōnis *f* last act.
perāctus *ppp of* **peragō**.
peracūtē *adv* very acutely.
peracūtus *adj* very sharp, very clear.
peradulēscēns, -entis *adj* very young.
peraequē *adv* quite equally, uniformly.
peragitātus *adj* harried.
peragō, -agere, -ēgī, -āctum *vt* to carry through, complete; to pass through, pierce; to disturb; (*law*) to prosecute to a conviction; (*words*) to go over, describe.
peragrātiō, -ōnis *f* travelling.
peragrō, -āre, -āvī, -ātum *vt* to travel through, traverse.
peramāns, -antis *adj* very fond.
peramanter *adv* devotedly.
perambulō, -āre *vt* to walk through, traverse.
peramoenus *adj* very pleasant.
peramplus *adj* very large.
perangustē *adv see adj*.
perangustus *adj* very narrow.
perantīquus *adj* very old.
perappositus *adj* very suitable.
perarduus *adj* very difficult.
perargūtus *adj* very witty.
perarō, -āre *vt* to furrow; to write (on wax).
perattentē *adv see adj*.
perattentus *adj* very attentive.
peraudiendus *adj* to be heard to the end.
perbacchor, -ārī *vt* to carouse through.
perbeātus *adj* very happy.
perbellē *adv* very nicely.
perbene *adv* very well.
perbenevolus *adj* very friendly.
perbenignē *adv* very kindly.

perbibō, -ere, -ī *vt* to drink up, imbibe.
perbītō, -ere *vi* to perish.
perblandus *adj* very charming.
perbonus *adj* very good.
perbrevis *adj* very short.
perbreviter *adv* very briefly.
perca, -ae *f* perch.
percalefactus *adj* quite hot.
percalēscō, -ēscere, -uī *vi* to become quite hot.
percallēscō, -ēscere, -uī *vi* to become quite hardened ♦ *vt* to become thoroughly versed in.
percārus *adj* very dear.
percautus *adj* very cautious.
percelebrō, -āre *vt* to talk much of.
perceler, -is *adj* very quick.
perceleriter *adv see adj.*
percellō, -ellere, -ulī, -ulsum *vt* to knock down, upset; to strike; (*fig*) to ruin, overthrow; to discourage, unnerve.
percēnseō, -ēre, -uī *vt* to count over; (*place*) to travel through; (*fig*) to review.
perceptiō, -ōnis *f* harvesting; understanding, idea.
perceptus *ppp of* **percipiō.**
percieō, -iēre, -iō, -īre *vt* to rouse, excite.
percipiō, -ipere, -ēpī, -eptum *vt* to take, get hold of; to gather in; (*senses*) to feel; (*mind*) to learn, grasp, understand.
percitus *ppp of* **percieō** ♦ *adj* roused, excited; excitable.
percoctus *ppp of* **percoquō.**
percolō, -āre *vt* to filter through.
percolō, -olere, -oluī, -ultum *vt* to embellish; to honour.
percōmis *adj* very friendly.
percommodē *adv* very conveniently.
percommodus *adj* very suitable.
percontātiō, -ōnis *f* asking questions.
percontātor, -ōris *m* inquisitive person.
percontor, -ārī, -ātus *vt* to question, inquire.
percontumāx, -ācis *adj* very obstinate.
percoquō, -quere, -xī, -ctum *vt* to cook thoroughly, heat, scorch, ripen.
percrēbēscō, percrēbrēscō, -ēscere, -uī *vi* to be spread abroad.
percrepō, -āre, -uī *vi* to resound.
perculī *perf of* **percellō.**
perculsus *ppp of* **percellō.**
percultus *ppp of* **percolō.**
percunct- *etc see* **percont-.**
percupidus *adj* very fond.
percupiō, -ere *vi* to wish very much.
percūriōsus *adj* very inquisitive.
percūrō, -āre *vt* to heal completely.
percurrō, -rrere, -currī *and* **rrī, -rsum** *vt* to run through, hurry over; (*fig*) to run over, look over ♦ *vi* to run along; to pass.
percursātiō, -ōnis *f* travelling through.

percursiō, -ōnis *f* running over.
percursō, -āre *vi* to rove about.
percursus *ppp of* **percurrō.**
percussiō, -ōnis *f* beating; (*fingers*) snapping; (*music*) time.
percussor, -ōris *m* assassin.
percussus *ppp of* **percutiō.**
percussus, -ūs *m* striking.
percutiō, -tere, -ssī, -ssum *vt* to strike, beat; to strike through, kill; (*feeling*) to shock, impress, move; (*colloq*) to trick.
perdēlīrus *adj* quite crazy.
perdidī *perf of* **perdō.**
perdifficilis *adj* very difficult.
perdifficiliter *adv* with great difficulty.
perdignus *adj* most worthy.
perdīligēns, -entis *adj* very diligent.
perdīligenter *adv see adj.*
perdiscō, -scere, -dicī *vt* to learn by heart.
perdisertē *adv* very eloquently.
perditē *adv* desperately; recklessly.
perditor, -ōris *m* destroyer.
perditus *ppp of* **perdō** ♦ *adj* desperate, ruined; abandoned, profligate.
perdiū *adv* for a very long time.
perdiūturnus *adj* protracted.
perdīves, -itis *adj* very rich.
perdīx, -īcis *m/f* partridge.
perdō, -ere, -idī, -itum *vt* to destroy, ruin; to squander, waste; to lose; **dī tē ~uint** curse you!
perdoceō, -ēre, -uī, -tum *vt* to teach thoroughly.
perdolēscō, -ēscere, -uī *vi* to take it to heart.
perdomō, -āre, -uī, -itum *vt* to subjugate, tame completely.
perdormīscō, -ere *vi* to sleep on.
perdūcō, -ūcere, -ūxī, -uctum *vt* to bring, guide to; to induce, seduce; to spread over; to prolong, continue.
perductō, -āre *vt* to guide.
perductor, -ōris *m* guide; pander.
perductus *ppp of* **perdūcō.**
perduelliō, -ōnis *f* treason.
perduellis, -is *m* enemy.
perduint *archaic subj of* **perdō.**
perdūrō, -āre *vi* to endure, hold out.
peredō, -edere, -ēdī, -ēsum *vt* to consume, devour.
peregrē *adv* away from home, abroad; from abroad.
peregrīnābundus *adj* travelling.
peregrīnātiō, -ōnis *f* living abroad, travel.
peregrīnātor, -ōris *m* traveller.
peregrīnitās, -ātis *f* foreign manners.
peregrīnor, -ārī, -ātus *vi* to be abroad, travel; to be a stranger.
peregrīnus *adj* foreign, strange ♦ *m* foreigner, alien.
perēlegāns, -antis *adj* very polished.

Noun declensions and verb conjugations are shown on pp xiii to xxv. The present infinitive ending of a verb shows to which conjugation it belongs: **-āre** = 1st; **-ēre** = 2nd; **-ere** = 3rd and **-īre** = 4th. Irregular verbs are shown on p xxvi

perēleganter *adv* in a very polished manner.
perēloquēns, -entis *adj* very eloquent.
perēmī *perf of* **perimō.**
peremnia, -ium *ntpl* auspices taken on crossing a river.
peremptus *ppp of* **perimō.**
perendiē *adv* the day after tomorrow.
perendinus *adj* (the day) after tomorrow.
perennis *adj* perpetual, unfailing.
perennitās, -ātis *f* continuance.
perennō, -āre *vi* to last a long time.
pereō, -īre, -iī, -itum *vi* to be lost, pass away, perish, die; (*fig*) to be wasted, be in love, be undone.
perequitō, -āre *vt, vi* to ride up and down.
pererrō, -āre, -āvī, -ātum *vt* to roam over, cover.
perērudītus *adj* very learned.
perēsus *ppp of* **peredō.**
perexcelsus *adj* very high.
perexiguē *adv* very meagrely.
perexiguus *adj* very small, very short.
perfacetē *adv* very wittily.
perfacētus *adj* very witty.
perfacilē *adv* very easily.
perfacilis *adj* very easy; very courteous.
perfamiliāris *adj* very intimate ♦ *m* very close friend.
perfectē *adv* fully.
perfectiō, -ōnis *f* completion, perfection.
perfector, -ōris *m* perfecter.
perfectus *ppp of* **perficiō** ♦ *adj* complete, perfect.
perferō, -ferre, -tulī, -lātum *vt* to carry through, bring, convey; to bear, endure, put up with; (*work*) to finish, bring to completion; (*law*) to get passed; (*message*) to bring news.
perficiō, -icere, -ēcī, -ectum *vt* to carry out, finish, complete; to perfect; to cause, make.
perficus *adj* perfecting.
perfidēlis *adj* very loyal.
perfidia, -ae *f* treachery, dishonesty.
perfidiōsē *adv see adj.*
perfidiōsus *adj* treacherous, dishonest.
perfidus *adj* treacherous, faithless.
perfīgō, -gere, -xī, -xum *vt* to pierce.
perflābilis *adj* that can be blown through.
perflāgitiōsus *adj* very wicked.
perflō, -āre *vt* to blow through, blow over.
perfluctuō, -āre *vt* to flood through.
perfluō, -ere, -xī *vi* to run out, leak.
perfodiō, -odere, -ōdī, -ossum *vt* to dig through, excavate, pierce.
perforō, -āre, -āvī, -ātum *vt* to bore through, pierce.
perfortiter *adv* very bravely.
perfossor, -ōris *m*: ~ parietum burglar.
perfossus *ppp of* **perfodiō.**
perfrāctus *ppp of* **perfringō.**
perfrēgī *perf of* **perfringō.**
perfremō, -ere *vi* to snort along.
perfrequēns, -entis *adj* much frequented.
perfricō, -āre, -uī, -tum *and* **ātum** *vt* to rub all over; **ōs** ~ put on a bold face.
perfrigefaciō, -ere *vt* to make shudder.
perfrīgēscō, -gēscere, -xī *vi* to catch a bad cold.
perfrīgidus *adj* very cold.
perfringō, -ingere, -ēgī, -āctum *vt* to break through, fracture, wreck; (*fig*) to violate; to affect powerfully.
perfrīxī *perf of* **perfrīgēscō.**
perfrūctus *ppa of* **perfruor.**
perfruor, -uī, -ūctus *vi* (*with abl*) to enjoy to the full; to fulfil.
perfuga, -ae *m* deserter.
perfugiō, -ugere, -ūgī *vi* to flee for refuge, desert to.
perfugium, -ī *and* **iī** *nt* refuge, shelter.
perfūnctiō, -ōnis *f* performing.
perfūnctus *ppa of* **perfungor.**
perfundō, -undere, -ūdī, -ūsum *vt* to pour over, drench, besprinkle; to dye; (*fig*) to flood, fill.
perfungor, -gī, perfūnctus *vi* (*with abl*) to perform, discharge; to undergo.
perfurō, -ere *vi* to rage furiously.
perfūsus *ppp of* **perfundō.**
Pergama, -ōrum *ntpl* Troy.
Pergamēnus *adj see n.*
Pergamus *adj* Trojan.
Pergamum, -ī *nt* town in Mysia (*famous for its library*).
pergaudeō, -ēre *vi* to be very glad.
pergō, -gere, -rēxī, -rēctum *vi* to proceed, go on, continue ♦ *vt* to go on with, continue.
pergraecor, -ārī *vi* to have a good time.
pergrandis *adj* very large; very old.
pergraphicus *adj* very artful.
pergrātus *adj* very pleasant.
pergravis *adj* very weighty.
pergraviter *adv* very seriously.
pergula, -ae *f* balcony; school; brothel.
perhibeō, -ēre, -uī, -itum *vt* to assert, call, cite.
perhīlum *adv* very little.
perhonōrificē *adv* very respectfully.
perhonōrificus *adj* very complimentary.
perhorrēscō, -ēscere, -uī *vi* to shiver, tremble violently ♦ *vt* to have a horror of.
perhorridus *adj* quite horrible.
perhūmāniter *adv see adj.*
perhūmānus *adj* very polite.
Periclēs, -is *and* **ī** *m* famous Athenian statesman and orator.
perīclitātiō, -ōnis *f* experiment.
perīclitor, -ārī, -ātus *vt* to test, try; to risk, endanger ♦ *vi* to attempt, venture; to run a risk, be in danger.
perīculōsē *adv see adj.*
perīculōsus *adj* dangerous, hazardous.
perīculum (perīclum), -ī *nt* danger, risk; trial, attempt; (*law*) lawsuit, writ.
peridōneus *adj* very suitable.
periī *perf of* **pereō.**
perillūstris *adj* very notable; highly honoured.

perimbēcillus *adj* very weak.
perimō, -imere, -ēmī, -emptum *vt* to destroy, prevent, kill.
perincommodē *adv see adj.*
perincommodus *adj* very inconvenient.
perinde *adv* just as, exactly as.
perindulgēns, -entis *adj* very tender.
perinfirmus *adj* very feeble.
peringeniōsus *adj* very clever.
perinīquus *adj* very unfair; very discontented.
perinsignis *adj* very conspicuous.
perinvītus *adj* very unwilling.
periodus, -ī *f* sentence, period.
Peripatēticī, -ōrum *mpl* Peripatetics (*followers of Aristotle*).
peripetasmata, -um *ntpl* curtains.
perīrātus *adj* very angry.
periscelis, -dis *f* anklet.
peristrōma, -atis *nt* coverlet.
peristylum, -ī *nt* colonnade, peristyle.
perītē *adv* expertly.
perītia, -ae *f* practical knowledge, skill.
perītus *adj* experienced, skilled, expert.
periūcundē *adv see adj.*
periūcundus *adj* very enjoyable.
periūrium, -ī *and* **iī** *nt* perjury.
periūrō *see* **pēierō**.
periūrus *adj* perjured, lying.
perlābor, -bī, -psus *vi* to glide along *or* through, move on.
perlaetus *adj* very glad.
perlāpsus *ppa of* **perlābor**.
perlātē *adv* very extensively.
perlateō, -ēre *vi* to lie quite hidden.
perlātus *ppp of* **perferō**.
perlegō, -egere, -ēgī, -ēctum *vt* to survey; to read through.
perlevis *adj* very slight.
perleviter *adv see adj.*
perlibēns, -entis *adj* very willing.
perlibenter *adv see adj.*
perlīberālis *adj* very genteel.
perlīberāliter *adv* very liberally.
perlibet, -ēre *vi* (*impers*) (I) should very much like.
perliciō *etc see* **pelliciō**.
perlitō, -āre, -āvī, -ātum *vi* to sacrifice with auspicious results.
perlongē *adv* very far.
perlongus *adj* very long, very tedious.
perlub- *etc see* **perlib-**.
perlūceō, -cēre, -xī *vi* to shine through, be transparent; (*fig*) to be quite intelligible.
perlūcidulus *adj* transparent.
perlūcidus *adj* transparent; very bright.
perlūctuōsus *adj* very mournful.
perluō, -ere *vt* to wash thoroughly; (*pass*) to bathe.
perlūstrō, -āre *vt* to traverse; (*fig*) to survey.

permāgnus *adj* very big, very great.
permānanter *adv* by flowing through.
permānāscō, -ere *vi* to penetrate.
permaneō, -anēre, -ānsī, -ānsum *vi* to last, persist, endure to the end.
permānō, -āre, -āvī, -ātum *vi* to flow *or* ooze through, penetrate.
permānsiō, -ōnis *f* continuing, persisting.
permarīnus *adj* of seafaring.
permātūrēscō, -ēscere, -uī *vi* to ripen fully.
permediocris *adj* very moderate.
permēnsus *ppa of* **permētior**.
permeō, -āre *vt, vi* to pass through, penetrate.
permētior, -tīrī, -nsus *vt* to measure out; to traverse.
permīrus *adj* very wonderful.
permisceō, -scēre, -scuī, -xtum *vt* to mingle, intermingle; to throw into confusion.
permissiō, -ōnis *f* unconditional surrender; permission.
permissus *ppp of* **permittō**.
permissus, -ūs *m* leave, permission.
permitiālis *adj* destructive.
permitiēs, -ēī *f* ruin.
permittō, -ittere, -īsī, -issum *vt* to let go, let pass; to hurl; to give up, entrust, concede; to allow, permit.
permixtē *adv see adj.*
permixtiō, -ōnis *f* mixture; disturbance.
permixtus *ppp of* **permisceō** ♦ *adj* promiscuous, disordered.
permodestus *adj* very moderate.
permolestē *adv* with much annoyance.
permolestus *adj* very troublesome.
permōtiō, -ōnis *f* excitement; emotion.
permōtus *ppp of* **permoveō**.
permoveō, -ovēre, -ōvī, -ōtum *vt* to stir violently; (*fig*) to influence, induce; to excite, move deeply.
permulceō, -cēre, -sī, -sum *vt* to stroke, caress; (*fig*) to charm, flatter; to soothe, appease.
permulsus *ppp of* **permulceō**.
permultus *adj* very much, very many.
permūniō, -īre, -īvī, -ītum *vt* to finish fortifying; to fortify strongly.
permūtātiō, -ōnis *f* change, exchange.
permūtō, -āre, -āvī, -ātum *vt* to change completely; to exchange; (*money*) to remit by bill of exchange.
perna, -ae *f* ham.
pernecessārius *adj* very necessary; very closely related.
pernecesse *adj* indispensable.
pernegō, -āre *vi* to deny flatly.
perniciābilis *adj* ruinous.
perniciēs, -ēī *f* destruction, ruin, death.
perniciōsē *adv see adj.*
perniciōsus *adj* ruinous.

pernīcitās, -ātis *f* agility, swiftness.
pernīciter *adv* nimbly.
pernimius *adj* much too much.
pernīx, -īcis *adj* nimble, agile, swift.
pernōbilis *adj* very famous.
pernoctō, -āre *vi* to stay all night.
pernōscō, -scere, -vī, -tum *vt* to examine thoroughly; to become fully acquainted with, know thoroughly.
pernōtēscō, -ēscere, -uī *vi* to become generally known.
pernōtus *ppp of* **pernōscō**.
pernox, -octis *adj* all night long.
pernumerō, -āre *vt* to count up.
pērō, -ōnis *m* rawhide boot.
perobscūrus *adj* very obscure.
perodiōsus *adj* very troublesome.
perofficiōsē *adv* very attentively.
peroleō, -ēre *vi* to give off a strong smell.
peropportūnē *adv* very opportunely.
peropportūnus *adj* very timely.
peroptātō *adv* very much to one's wish.
peropus est it is most essential.
perōrātiō, -ōnis *f* peroration.
perōrnātus *adj* very ornate.
perōrnō, -āre *vt* to give great distinction to.
perōrō, -āre, -āvī, -ātum *vt* to plead at length; (*speech*) to bring to a close; to conclude.
perōsus *adj* detesting.
perpācō, -āre *vt* to quieten completely.
perparcē *adv* very stingily.
perparvulus *adj* very tiny.
perparvus *adj* very small.
perpāstus *adj* well fed.
perpauculus *adj* very very few.
perpaucus *adj* very little, very few.
perpaulum, -ī *nt* a very little.
perpauper, -is *adj* very poor.
perpauxillum, -ī *nt* a very little.
perpellō, -ellere, -ulī, -ulsum *vt* to urge, force, influence.
perpendiculum, -ī *nt* plumbline; **ad ~** perpendicularly.
perpendō, -endere, -endī, -ēnsum *vt* to weigh carefully, judge.
perperam *adv* wrongly, falsely.
perpes, -etis *adj* continuous.
perpessiō, -ōnis *f* suffering, enduring.
perpessus *ppa of* **perpetior**.
perpetior, -tī, -ssus *vt* to endure patiently, allow.
perpetrō, -āre, -āvī, -ātum *vt* to perform, carry out.
perpetuitās, -ātis *f* continuity, uninterrupted duration.
perpetuō *adv* without interruption, forever, utterly.
perpetuō, -āre *vt* to perpetuate, preserve.
perpetuus *adj* continuous, entire; universal; **in ~um** forever.
perplaceō, -ēre *vi* to please greatly.
perplexē *adv* obscurely.

perplexor, -ārī *vi* to cause confusion.
perplexus *adj* confused, intricate, obscure.
perplicātus *adj* interlaced.
perpluō, -ere *vi* to let the rain through, leak.
perpoliō, -īre, -īvī, -ītum *vt* to polish thoroughly.
perpolītus *adj* finished, refined.
perpopulor, -ārī, -ātus *vt* to ravage completely.
perpōtātiō, -ōnis *f* drinking bout.
perpōtō, -āre *vi* to drink continuously ♦ *vt* to drink off.
perprimō, -ere *vt* to lie on.
perpugnāx, -ācis *adj* very pugnacious.
perpulcher, -rī *adj* very beautiful.
perpulī *perf of* **perpellō**.
perpūrgō, -āre, -āvī, -ātum *vt* to make quite clean; to explain.
perpusillus *adj* very little.
perquam *adv* very, extremely.
perquīrō, -rere, -sīvī, -sītum *vt* to search for, inquire after; to examine carefully.
perquīsītius *adv* more accurately.
perrārō *adv* very seldom.
perrārus *adj* very uncommon.
perreconditus *adj* very abstruse.
perrēpō, -ere *vt* to crawl over.
perrēptō, -āre, -āvī, -ātum *vt, vi* to creep about *or* through.
perrēxī *perf of* **pergō**.
perrīdiculē *adv see adj.*
perrīdiculus *adj* very laughable.
perrogātiō, -ōnis *f* passing (of a law).
perrogō, -āre *vt* to ask one after another.
perrumpō, -umpere, -ūpī, -uptum *vt, vi* to break through, force a way through; (*fig*) to break down.
perruptus *ppp of* **perrumpō**.
Persae, -ārum *mpl* Persians.
persaepe *adv* very often.
persalsē *adv see adj.*
persalsus *adj* very witty.
persalūtātiō, -ōnis *f* greeting everyone in turn.
persalūtō, -āre *vt* to greet in turn.
persānctē *adv* most solemnly.
persapiēns, -entis *adj* very wise.
persapienter *adv see adj.*
perscienter *adv* very discreetly.
perscindō, -ndere, -dī, -ssum *vt* to tear apart.
perscītus *adj* very smart.
perscrībō, -bere, -psī, -ptum *vt* to write in full; to describe, report; (*record*) to enter; (*money*) to make over in writing.
perscrīptiō, -ōnis *f* entry; assignment.
perscrīptor, -ōris *m* writer.
perscrīptus *ppp of* **perscrībō**.
perscrūtor, -ārī, -ātus *vt* to search, examine thoroughly.
persecō, -āre, -uī, -tum *vt* to dissect; to do away with.
persector, -ārī *vt* to investigate.

persecūtiō, -ōnis *f* (*law*) prosecution.
persecūtus *ppa of* **persequor**.
persedeō, -edēre, -ēdī, -essum *vi* to remain sitting.
persegnis *adj* very slow.
Persēius *adj see* **Perseus**.
persentiō, -entīre, -ēnsī *vt* to see clearly; to feel deeply.
persentīscō, -ere *vi* to begin to see; to begin to feel.
Persephonē, -ēs *f* Proserpine.
persequor, -quī, -cūtus *vt* to follow all the way; to pursue, chase, hunt after; to overtake; (*pattern*) to be a follower of, copy; (*enemy*) to proceed against, take revenge on; (*action*) to perform, carry out; (*words*) to write down, describe.
Persēs, -ae *m last king of Macedonia*.
Persēs, -ae *m* Persian.
Perseus, -eī *and* **eos** (*acc* **-ea**) *m son of Danaë* (*killer of Medusa, rescuer of Andromeda*).
Persēus *adj see* n.
persevērāns, -antis *pres p of* **persevērō** ♦ *adj* persistent.
persevēranter *adv see adj.*
persevērantia, -ae *f* persistence.
persevērō, -āre, -āvī, -ātum *vi* to persist ♦ *vt* to persist in.
persevērus *adj* very strict.
Persicus *adj* Persian; of Perses.
Persicum *nt* peach.
persīdō, -īdere, -ēdī, -essum *vi* to sink down into.
persignō, -āre *vt* to record.
persimilis *adj* very like.
persimplex, -icis *adj* very simple.
Persis, -idis *f* Persia.
persistō, -istere, -titī *vi* to persist.
persōlus *adj* one and only.
persolūtus *ppp of* **persolvō**.
persolvō, -vere, -vī, -ūtum *vt* to pay, pay up; to explain.
persōna, -ae *f* mask; character, part; person, personality.
persōnātus *adj* masked; in an assumed character.
personō, -āre, -uī, -itum *vi* to resound, ring (with); to play ♦ *vt* to make resound; to cry aloud.
perspectē *adv* intelligently.
perspectō, -āre *vt* to have a look through.
perspectus *ppp of* **perspiciō** ♦ *adj* well-known.
perspeculor, -ārī *vt* to reconnoitre.
perspergō, -gere, -sī, -sum *vt* to besprinkle.
perspicāx, -ācis *adj* sharp, shrewd.
perspicientia, -ae *f* full understanding.
perspiciō, -icere, -exī, -ectum *vt* to see through; to examine, observe.
perspicuē *adv* clearly.
perspicuitās, -ātis *f* clarity.

perspicuus *adj* transparent; clear, evident.
persternō, -ernere, -rāvī, -rātum *vt* to pave all over.
perstimulō, -āre *vt* to rouse violently.
perstitī *perf of* **persistō**; *perf of* **perstō**.
perstō, -āre, -itī, -ātum *vi* to stand fast; to last; to continue, persist.
perstrātus *ppp of* **persternō**.
perstrepō, -ere *vi* to make a lot of noise.
perstrictus *ppp of* **perstringō**.
perstringō, -ingere, -inxī, -ictum *vt* to graze, touch lightly; (*words*) to touch on, belittle, censure; (*senses*) to dull, deaden.
perstudiōsē *adv* very eagerly.
perstudiōsus *adj* very fond.
persuādeō, -dēre, -sī, -sum *vi* (*with dat*) to convince, persuade; ~**sum habeō, mihi ~sum est** I am convinced.
persuāsiō, -ōnis *f* convincing.
persuāsus, -ūs *m* persuasion.
persubtīlis *adj* very fine.
persultō, -āre *vt, vi* to prance about, frisk over.
pertaedet, -dēre, -sum est *vt* (*impers*) to be weary of, be sick of.
pertegō, -egere, -ēxī, -ēctum *vt* to cover over.
pertemptō, -āre *vt* to test carefully; to consider well; to pervade, seize.
pertendō, -ere, -ī *vi* to push on, persist ♦ *vt* to go on with.
pertenuis *adj* very small, very slight.
perterebrō, -āre *vt* to bore through.
pertergeō, -gēre, -sī, -sum *vt* to wipe over; to touch lightly.
perterrefaciō, -ere *vt* to scare thoroughly.
perterreō, -ēre, -uī, -itum *vt* to frighten thoroughly.
perterricrepus *adj* with a terrifying crash.
perterritus *adj* terrified.
pertexō, -ere, -uī, -tum *vt* to accomplish.
pertica, -ae *f* pole, staff.
pertimefactus *adj* very frightened.
pertimēscō, -ēscere, -uī *vt, vi* to be very alarmed, be very afraid of.
pertinācia, -ae *f* perseverance, stubbornness.
pertināciter *adv see adj.*
pertināx, -ācis *adj* very tenacious; unyielding, stubborn.
pertineō, -ēre, -uī *vi* to extend, reach; to tend, lead to, concern; to apply, pertain, belong; **quod ~et ad** as far as concerns.
pertingō, -ere *vi* to extend.
pertolerō, -āre *vt* to endure to the end.
pertorqueō, -ēre *vt* to distort.
pertractātē *adv* in a hackneyed fashion.
pertractātiō, -ōnis *f* handling.
pertractō, -āre *vt* to handle, feel all over; (*fig*) to treat, study.
pertractus *ppp of* **pertrahō**.

Noun declensions and verb conjugations are shown on pp xiii to xxv. The present infinitive ending of a verb shows to which conjugation it belongs: **-āre** = 1st; **-ēre** = 2nd; **-ere** = 3rd and **-īre** = 4th. Irregular verbs are shown on p xxvi

pertrahō, -here, -xī, -ctum *vt* to drag across, take forcibly; to entice.
pertrect- *etc see* **pertract-**.
pertristis *adj* very sad, very morose.
pertulī *perf of* **perferō**.
pertumultuōsē *adv* very excitedly.
pertundō, -undere, -udī, -ūsum *vt* to perforate.
perturbātē *adv* in confusion.
perturbātiō, -ōnis *f* confusion, disturbance; emotion.
perturbātrīx, -īcis *f* disturber.
perturbātus *ppp of* **perturbō** ♦ *adj* troubled; alarmed.
perturbō, -āre, -āvī, -ātum *vt* to throw into disorder, upset, alarm.
perturpis *adj* scandalous.
pertūsus *ppp of* **pertundō** ♦ *adj* in holes, leaky.
perungō, -ungere, -ūnxī, -ūnctum *vt* to smear all over.
perurbānus *adj* very refined; over-fine.
perūrō, -rere, -ssī, -stum *vt* to burn up, scorch; to inflame, chafe; to freeze, nip.
Perusia, -iae *f* Etruscan town (*now* Perugia).
Perusīnus *adj see n.*
perūstus *ppp of* **perūrō**.
perūtilis *adj* very useful.
pervādō, -dere, -sī, -sum *vt, vi* to pass through, spread through; to penetrate, reach.
pervagātus *adj* widespread, well-known; general.
pervagor, -ārī, -ātus *vi* to range, rove about; to extend, spread ♦ *vt* to pervade.
pervagus *adj* roving.
pervariē *adv* very diversely.
pervastō, -āre, -āvī, -ātum *vt* to devastate.
pervāsus *ppp of* **pervādō**.
pervectus *ppp of* **pervehō**.
pervehō, -here, -xī, -ctum *vt* to carry, convey, bring through; (*pass*) to ride, drive, sail through; to attain.
pervellō, -ere, -ī *vt* to pull, twitch, pinch; to stimulate; to disparage.
perveniō, -enīre, -ēnī, -entum *vi* to come to, arrive, reach; to attain to.
pervēnor, -ārī *vi* to chase through.
perversē *adv* perversely.
perversitās, -ātis *f* perverseness.
perversus (pervorsus) *ppp of* **pervertō** ♦ *adj* awry, squint; wrong, perverse.
pervertō, -tere, -tī, -sum *vt* to overturn, upset; to overthrow, undo; (*speech*) to confute.
pervesperī *adv* very late.
pervestīgātiō, -ōnis *f* thorough search.
pervestīgō, -āre, -āvī, -ātum *vt* to track down; to investigate.
pervetus, -eris *adj* very old.
pervetustus *adj* antiquated.
pervicācia, -ae *f* obstinacy; firmness.
pervicāciter *adv see adj.*
pervicāx, -ācis *adj* obstinate, wilful; dogged.

pervictus *ppp of* **pervincō**.
pervideō, -idēre, -īdī, -īsum *vt* to look over, survey; to consider; to discern.
pervigeō, -ēre, -uī *vi* to continue to flourish.
pervigil, -is *adj* awake, watchful.
pervigilātiō, -ōnis *f* vigil.
pervigilium, -ī *and* **iī** *nt* vigil.
pervigilō, -āre, -āvī, -ātum *vt, vi* to stay awake all night, keep vigil.
pervīlis *adj* very cheap.
pervincō, -incere, -īcī, -ictum *vt, vi* to conquer completely; to outdo, surpass; to prevail upon, effect; (*argument*) to carry a point, maintain, prove.
pervīvō, -ere *vi* to survive.
pervius *adj* passable, accessible.
pervolgō *etc see* **pervulgō**.
pervolitō, -āre *vt, vi* to fly about.
pervolō, -āre, -āvī, -ātum *vt, vi* to fly through *or* over, fly to.
pervolō, -elle, -oluī *vi* to wish very much.
pervolūtō, -āre *vt* (*books*) to read through.
pervolvō, -vere, -vī, -ūtum *vt* to tumble about; (*book*) to read through; (*pass*) to be very busy (with).
pervor- *etc see* **perver-**.
pervulgātus *adj* very common.
pervulgō, -āre, -āvī, -ātum *vt* to make public, impart; to haunt.
pēs, pedis *m* foot; (*length*) foot; (*verse*) foot, metre; (*sailrope*) sheet; **pedem cōnferre** come to close quarters; **pedem referre** go back; **ante pedēs** self-evident; **pedibus** on foot, by land; **pedibus īre in sententiam** take sides; **pedibus aequīs** (*NAUT*) with the wind right aft; **servus ā pedibus** footman.
pessimē *superl of* **male**.
pessimus *superl of* **malus**.
pessulus, -ī *m* bolt.
pessum *adv* to the ground, to the bottom; ~ **dare** put an end to, ruin, destroy; ~ **īre** sink, perish.
pestifer, -ī *adj* pestilential; baleful, destructive.
pestilēns, -entis *adj* unhealthy; destructive.
pestilentia, -ae *f* plague, pest; unhealthiness.
pestilitās, -ātis *f* plague.
pestis, -is *f* plague, pest; ruin, destruction.
petasātus *adj* wearing the petasus.
petasunculus, -ī *m* small leg of pork.
petasus, -ī *m* broadbrimmed hat.
petessō, -ere *vt* to be eager for.
petītiō, -ōnis *f* thrust, attack; request, application; (*office*) candidature, standing for; (*law*) civil suit, right of claim.
petītor, -ōris *m* candidate; plaintiff.
petīturiō, -īre *vt* to long to be a candidate.
petītus *ppp of* **petō**.
petītus, -ūs *m* falling to.
petō, -ere, -īvī *and* **iī, -ītum** *vt* to aim at, attack; (*place*) to make for, go to; to seek, look for, demand, ask; to go and fetch; (*law*) to sue; (*love*) to court; (*office*) to stand for.

petorritum, -ī *nt* carriage.

petrō, -ōnis *m* yokel.

Petrōnius, -ī *m arbiter of fashion under Nero.*

petulāns, -antis *adj* pert, impudent, lascivious.

petulanter *adv see adj.*

petulantia, -ae *f* pertness, impudence.

petulcus *adj* butting.

pexus *ppp of* **pectō.**

Phaeāccius *and* **cus, -x** *adj* Phaeacian.

Phaeāces, -cum *mpl fabulous islanders in the Odyssey.*

Phaedra, -ae *f stepmother of Hippolytus.*

Phaedrus, -ī *m pupil of Socrates; writer of Latin fables.*

Phaethōn, -ontis *m son of the Sun (killed while driving his father's chariot).*

Phaethonteus *adj see n.*

Phaethontiades, -um *fpl sisters of Phaethon.*

phalangae, -ārum *fpl* wooden rollers.

phalangītae, -ārum *mpl* soldiers of a phalanx.

phalanx, -gis *f* phalanx; troops, battle order.

Phalaris, -dis *m tyrant of Agrigentum.*

phalerae, -ārum *fpl* medallions, badges; (*horse*) trappings.

phalerātus *adj* wearing medallions; ornamented.

Phalēreus, -icus *adj see n.*

Phalērum, -ī *nt harbour of Athens.*

pharetra, -ae *f* quiver.

pharetrātus *adj* wearing a quiver.

Pharius *adj see n.*

pharmaceutria, -ae *f* sorceress.

pharmacopōla, -ae *m* quack doctor.

Pharsālicus, -ius *adj see n.*

Pharsālus (-os), -ī *f* town in Thessaly (*where Caesar defeated Pompey*).

Pharus (-os), -ī *f island off Alexandria with a famous lighthouse;* lighthouse.

phasēlus, -ī *m/f* French beans; (*boat*) pinnace.

Phāsiacus *adj* Colchian.

Phāsiānus, -āna *m/f* pheasant.

Phāsis, -dis *and* **dos** *m river of Colchis.*

Phāsis *adj see n.*

phasma, -tis *nt* ghost.

Pherae, -ārum *fpl town in Thessaly (home of Admetus).*

Pheraeus *adj see n.*

phiala, -ae *f* saucer.

Phīdiacus *adj see n.*

Phīdiās, -ae *m famous Athenian sculptor.*

philēma, -tis *nt* kiss.

Philippī, -ōrum *mpl town in Macedonia (where Brutus and Cassius were defeated).*

Philippēus *adj see n.*

Philippicae *fpl Cicero's speeches against Antony.*

Philippicus *adj see n.*

Philippus, -ī *m* king of Macedonia; gold coin.

philitia, (phīditia), -ōrum *ntpl* public meals at Sparta.

Philō (-ōn), -ōnis *m* Academic philosopher (*teacher of Cicero*).

Philoctētēs, -ae *m Greek archer who gave Hercules poisoned arrows.*

philologia, -ae *f* study of literature.

philologus *adj* scholarly, literary.

Philomēla, -ae *f sister of Procne;* nightingale.

philosophē *adv see adj.*

philosophia, -ae *f* philosophy.

philosophor, -ārī, -ātus *vi* to philosophize.

philosophus, -ī *m* philosopher ♦ *adj* philosophical.

philtrum, -ī *nt* love potion.

philyra, -ae *f* inner bark of the lime tree.

phīmus, -ī *m* dice box.

Phlegethōn, -ontis *m a river of Hades.*

Phlegethontis *adj see n.*

Phlīāsius *adj see n.*

Phlīūs, -ūntis *f town in Peloponnese.*

phōca, -ae *f* seal.

Phōcaicus *adj see n.*

Phōcēus *adj see n.*

Phōcis, -idis *f country of central Greece.*

Phōcius *adj see n.*

Phoebas, -adis *f* prophetess.

Phoebē, -ēs *f* Diana, the moon.

Phoebēius, -ēus *adj see n.*

Phoebigena, -ae *m son of Phoebus, Aesculapius.*

Phoebus, -ī *m* Apollo; the sun.

Phoenīcē, -cēs *f* Phoenicia.

Phoenīces, -cum *mpl* Phoenicians.

phoenīcopterus, -ī *m* flamingo.

Phoenīssus *adj* Phoenician ♦ *f* Dido.

Phoenīx, -īcis *m friend of Achilles.*

phoenīx, -īcis *m* phoenix.

Phorcis, -idos = **Phorcȳnis.**

Phorcus, -ī *m son of Neptune (father of Medusa).*

Phorcȳnis, -ȳnidos *f* Medusa.

Phraātēs, -ae *m king of Parthia.*

phrenēsis, -is *f* delirium.

phrenēticus *adj* mad, delirious.

Phrixēus *adj see n.*

Phrixus, -ī *m* Helle's brother (*who took the ram with the golden fleece to Colchis*).

Phryges, -um *mpl* Phrygians; Trojans.

Phrygia, -iae *f* Phrygia (*country of Asia Minor*); Troy.

Phrygius *adj* Phrygian, Trojan.

Phthīa, -ae *f home of Achilles in Thessaly.*

Phthīōta, -ōtēs, -ōtae *m native of Phthia.*

phthisis *f* consumption.

Phthīus *adj see n.*

phy *interj* bah!

phylaca, -ae *f* prison.

phylarchus, -ī *m* chieftain.

physica, -ae *and* **ē, -ēs** *f* physics.

physicē *adv* scientifically.

Noun declensions and verb conjugations are shown on pp xiii to xxv. The present infinitive ending of a verb shows to which conjugation it belongs: **-āre** = 1st; **-ēre** = 2nd; **-ere** = 3rd and **-īre** = 4th. Irregular verbs are shown on p xxvi

physicus *adj* of physics, natural ♦ *m* natural philosopher ♦ *ntpl* physics.
physiognōmōn, -onis *m* physiognomist.
physiologia, -ae *f* natural philosophy, science.
piābilis *adj* expiable.
piāculāris *adj* atoning ♦ *ntpl* sin offerings.
piāculum, -ī *nt* sin offering; victim; atonement, punishment; sin, guilt.
piāmen, -inis *nt* atonement.
pīca, -ae *f* magpie.
picāria, -ae *f* pitch hut.
picea, -ae *f* pine.
Picēns, -entis *adj* = **Picēnus**.
Picēnum, -ēnī *nt* Picenum.
Picēnus *adj* of Picenum in E. Italy.
piceus *adj* pitch black; of pitch.
pictor, -ōris *m* painter.
pictūra, -ae *f* painting; picture.
pictūrātus *adj* painted; embroidered.
pictus *ppp of* **pingō** ♦ *adj* coloured, tattooed; (*style*) ornate; (*fear*) unreal.
pīcus, -ī *m* woodpecker.
piē *adv* religiously, dutifully.
Pīeris, -dis *f* Muse.
Pīerius *adj* of the Muses, poetic.
pietās, -ātis *f* sense of duty (*to gods, family, country*), piety, filial affection, love, patriotism.
piger, -rī *adj* reluctant, slack, slow; numbing, dull.
piget, -ēre, -uit *vt* (*impers*) to be annoyed, dislike; to regret, repent.
pigmentārius, -ī *and* **iī** *m* dealer in paints.
pigmentum, -ī *nt* paint, cosmetic; (*style*) colouring.
pignerātor, -ōris *m* mortgagee.
pignerō, -āre *vt* to pawn, mortgage.
pigneror, -ārī, -ātus *vt* to claim, accept.
pignus, -oris *and* **eris** *nt* pledge, pawn, security; wager, stake; (*fig*) assurance, token; (*pl*) children, dear ones.
pigritia, -ae, -ēs, -ēī *f* sluggishness, indolence.
pigrō, -āre, -or, -ārī *vi* to be slow, be slack.
pīla, -ae *f* mortar.
pīla, -ae *f* pillar; pier.
pila, -ae *f* ball, ball game.
pīlānus, -ī *m* soldier of the third line.
pīlātus *adj* armed with javelins.
pīlentum, -ī *nt* carriage.
pilleātus *adj* wearing the felt cap.
pilleolus, -ī *m* skullcap.
pilleum, -ī *nt*, **pilleus, -ī** *m* felt cap presented to freed slaves; (*fig*) liberty.
pilōsus *adj* hairy.
pīlum, -ī *nt* javelin.
pīlus, -ī *m* division of triarii; **prīmus ~** chief centurion.
pilus, -ī *m* hair; a whit.
Pimplēa, -ae *and* **is, -idis** *f* Muse.
Pimplēus *adj* of the Muses.
Pindaricus *adj see n.*

Pindarus, -ī *m* Pindar (*Greek lyric poet*).
Pindus, -ī *m* mountain range in Thessaly.
pīnētum, -ī *nt* pine wood.
pīneus *adj* pine- (*in cpds*).
pingō, -ere, pinxī, pictum *vt* to paint, embroider; to colour; (*fig*) to embellish, decorate.
pinguēscō, -ere *vi* to grow fat, become fertile.
pinguis *adj* fat, rich, fertile; (*mind*) gross, dull; (*ease*) comfortable, calm; (*weather*) thick ♦ *nt* grease.
pīnifer, -ī, pīniger, -ī *adj* pine-clad.
pinna, -ae *f* feather; wing, arrow; battlement; (*fish*) fin.
pinnātus *adj* feathered, winged.
pinniger, -ī *adj* winged; finny.
pinnipēs, -edis *adj* wing-footed.
pinnirapus, -ī *m* plume-snatcher.
pinnula, -ae *f* little wing.
pīnotērēs, -ae *m* hermit crab.
pīnsō, -ere *vt* to beat, pound.
pīnus, -ūs *and* **ī** *f* stone pine, Scots fir; ship, torch, wreath.
pinxī *perf of* **pingō**.
piō, -āre *vt* to propitiate, worship; to atone for, avert; to avenge.
piper, -is *nt* pepper.
pīpilō, -āre *vi* to chirp.
Pīraea, -ōrum *ntpl* Piraeus (*port of Athens*).
Pīraeeus *and* **us, -ī** *m* main port of Athens.
Pīraeus *adj see n.*
pīrāta, -ae *m* pirate.
pīrāticus *adj* pirate ♦ *f* piracy.
Pīrēnē, -ēs *f* spring in Corinth.
Pīrēnis, -idis *adj see n.*
Pīrithous, -ī *m* king of the Lapiths.
pirum, -ī *nt* pear.
pirus, -ī *f* pear tree.
Pīsa, -ae *f* Greek town near the Olympic Games site.
Pīsae, -ārum *fpl* town in Etruria (*now* Pisa).
Pīsaeus *adj see n.*
Pīsānus *adj see n.*
piscārius *adj* fish- (*in cpds*), fishing- (*in cpds*).
piscātor, -ōris *m* fisherman.
piscātōrius *adj* fishing- (*in cpds*).
piscātus, -ūs *m* fishing; fish; catch, haul.
pisciculus, -ī *m* little fish.
piscīna, -ae *f* fishpond; swimming pool.
piscīnārius, -ī *and* **iī** *m* person keen on fish ponds.
piscis -is *m* fish; (*ASTRO*) Pisces.
piscor, -ārī, -ātus *vi* to fish.
piscōsus *adj* full of fish.
pisculentus *adj* full of fish.
Pīsistratidae, -idārum *mpl* sons of Pisistratus.
Pīsistratus, -ī *m* tyrant of Athens.
pistillum, -ī *nt* pestle.
pistor, -ōris *m* miller; baker.
pistrilla, -ae *f* little mortar.
pistrīnum, -ī *nt* mill, bakery; drudgery.
pistris, -is *and* **īx, -īcis** *f* sea monster, whale;

swift ship.

pithēcium, -ī *and* **iī** *nt* little ape.

pītuīta, -ae *f* phlegm; catarrh, cold in the head.

pītuītōsus *adj* phlegmatic.

pius *adj* dutiful, conscientious; godly, holy; filial, affectionate; patriotic; good, upright ♦ *mpl* the blessed dead.

pix, picis *f* pitch.

plācābilis *adj* easily appeased.

plācābilitās, -ātis *f* readiness to condone.

plācāmen, -inis, plācāmentum, -ī *nt* peace-offering.

plācātē *adv* calmly.

plācātiō, -ōnis *f* propitiating.

plācātus *ppp of* **plācō** ♦ *adj* calm, quiet, reconciled.

placenta, -ae *f* cake.

Placentia, -iae *f* town in N. Italy (*now* Piacenza).

Placentīnus *adj see n.*

placeō, -ēre, -uī, -itum *vi* (*with dat*) to please, satisfy; **~et** it seems good, it is agreed, resolved; **mihi ~eō** I am pleased with myself.

placidē *adv* peacefully, gently.

placidus *adj* calm, quiet, gentle.

placitum, -ī *nt* principle, belief.

placitus *ppa of* **placeō** ♦ *adj* pleasing; agreed on.

plācō, -āre, -āvī, -ātum *vt* to calm, appease, reconcile.

plāga, -ae *f* blow, stroke, wound.

plaga, -ae *f* region, zone.

plaga, -ae *f* hunting net, snare, trap.

plagiārius, -ī *and* **iī** *m* plunderer, kidnapper.

plāgigerulus *adj* much flogged.

plāgōsus *adj* fond of punishing.

plagula, -ae *f* curtain.

planctus, -ūs *m* beating the breast, lamentation.

plānē *adv* plainly, clearly; completely, quite; certainly.

plangō, -gere, -xī, -ctum *vt, vi* to beat noisily; to beat in grief; to lament loudly, bewail.

plangor, -ōris *m* beating; loud lamentation.

plānipēs, -edis *m* ballet dancer.

plānitās, -ātis *f* perspicuity.

plānitiēs, -ēī, (-a, -ae) *f* level ground, plain.

planta, -ae *f* shoot, slip; sole, foot.

plantāria, -ium *ntpl* slips, young trees.

plānus *adj* level, flat; plain, clear ♦ *nt* level ground; **dē ~ō** easily.

planus, -ī *m* impostor.

platalea, -ae *f* spoonbill.

platea, -ae *f* street.

Platō, -ōnis *m* Plato (*founder of the Academic school of philosophy*).

Platōnicus *adj see n.*

plaudō, -dere, -sī, -sum *vt* to clap, beat, stamp ♦ *vi* to clap, applaud; to approve, be

pleased with.

plausibilis *adj* praiseworthy.

plausor, -ōris *m* applauder.

plaustrum, -ī *nt* waggon, cart; (*ASTRO*) Great Bear; **~ percellere** *upset the applecart.*

plausus *ppp of* **plaudō**.

plausus, -ūs *m* flapping; clapping, applause.

Plautīnus *adj see n.*

Plautus, -ī *m* early Latin comic poet.

plēbēcula, -ae *f* rabble.

plēbēius *adj* plebeian; common, low.

plēbicola, -ae *m* friend of the people.

plēbiscītum, -ī *nt* decree of the people.

plēbs (plēbēs), -is *f* common people, plebeians; lower classes, masses.

plēctō, -ere *vt* to punish.

plēctrum, -ī *nt* plectrum; lyre, lyric poetry.

Plēias, -dis *f* Pleiad; (*pl*) the Seven Sisters.

plēnē *adv* fully, entirely.

plēnus *adj* full, filled; (*fig*) sated; (*age*) mature; (*amount*) complete; (*body*) stout, plump; (*female*) pregnant; (*matter*) solid; (*style*) copious; (*voice*) loud; **ad ~um** abundantly.

plērumque *adv* generally, mostly.

plērusque *adj* a large part, most; (*pl*) the majority, the most; very many.

plexus *adj* plaited, interwoven.

Plīas *see* **Plēias**.

plicātrīx, -īcis *f* clothes folder.

plicō, -āre, -āvī *and* **uī, -ātum** *and* **itum** *vt* to fold, coil.

Plīnius, -ī *m* Roman family name (*esp Pliny the Elder, who died in the eruption of Vesuvius*); Pliny the Younger, writer of letters.

plōrātus, -ūs *m* wailing.

plōrō, -āre, -āvī, -ātum *vi* to wail, lament ♦ *vt* to weep for, bewail.

plōstellum, -ī *nt* cart.

ploxenum, -ī *nt* cart box.

pluit, -ere, -it *vi* (*impers*) it is raining.

plūma, -ae *f* soft feather, down.

plumbeus *adj* of lead; (*fig*) heavy, dull, worthless.

plumbum, -ī *nt* lead; bullet, pipe, ruler; **~ album** tin.

plūmeus *adj* down, downy.

plūmipēs, -edis *adj* feather-footed.

plūmōsus *adj* feathered.

plūrimus *superl of* **multus**.

plūs, -ūris *compar of* **multus** ♦ *adv* more.

plūsculus *adj* a little more.

pluteus, -ī *m* shelter, penthouse; parapet; couch; bookcase.

Plūtō, -ōnis *m* king of the lower world.

Plūtōnius *adj see n.*

pluvia, -ae *f* rain.

pluviālis *adj* rainy.

pluvius *adj* rainy, rain- (*in cpds*).

pōcillum, -ī *nt* small cup.

pōculum, -ī *nt* cup; drink, potion.

podagra, -ae *f* gout.
podagrōsus *adj* gouty.
podium, -ī *and* **iī** *nt* balcony.
poēma, -tis *nt* poem.
poena, -ae *f* penalty, punishment; **poenas dare** to be punished.
Poenī, -ōrum *mpl* Carthaginians.
Poenus, Pūnicus *adj* Punic.
poēsis, -is *f* poetry, poem.
poēta, -ae *m* poet.
poēticē *adv* poetically.
poēticus *adj* poetic ♦ *f* poetry.
poētria, -ae *f* poetess.
pol *interj* by Pollux!, truly.
polenta, -ae *f* pearl barley.
poliō, -īre, -īvī, -ītum *vt* to polish; to improve, put in good order.
polītē *adv* elegantly.
polītīa, -ae *f* Plato's Republic.
politicus *adj* political.
polītus *adj* polished, refined, cultured.
pollen, -inis *nt* fine flour, meal.
pollēns, -entis *pres p of* **polleō** ♦ *adj* powerful, strong.
pollentia, -ae *f* power.
polleō, -ēre *vi* to be strong, be powerful.
pollex, -icis *m* thumb.
polliceor, -ērī, -itus *vt* to promise, offer.
pollicitātiō, -ōnis *f* promise.
pollicitor, -ārī, -ātus *vt* to promise.
pollicitum, -ī *nt* promise.
Polliō, -ōnis *m* Roman surname (*esp C. Asinius, soldier, statesman and literary patron under Augustus*).
pollis, -inis *m/f see* **pollen**.
pollūcibiliter *adv* sumptuously.
pollūctus *adj* offered up ♦ *nt* offering.
polluō, -uere, -uī, -ūtum *vt* to defile, pollute, dishonour.
Pollūx, -ūcis *m* twin brother of Castor (*famous as a boxer*).
polus, -ī *m* pole, North pole; sky.
Polyhymnia, -ae *f* a Muse.
Polyphēmus, -ī *m* one-eyed Cyclops.
pōlypus, -ī *m* polypus.
pōmārium, -ī *and* **iī** *nt* orchard.
pōmārius, -ī *and* **iī** *m* fruiterer.
pōmerīdiānus *adj* afternoon.
pōmērium, -ī *and* **iī** *nt* free space round the city boundary.
pōmifer, -ī *adj* fruitful.
pōmoerium *see* **pōmērium**.
pōmōsus *adj* full of fruit.
pompa, -ae *f* procession; retinue, train; ostentation.
Pompeiānus *adj see n.*
Pompeiī, -ōrum *mpl Campanian town buried by an eruption of Vesuvius.*
Pompeius, -ī *m* Roman family name (*esp Pompey the Great*).
Pompeius, -ānus *adj see n.*
Pompilius, -ī *m* Numa (*second king of Rome*).
Pompilius *adj see n.*

Pomptīnus *adj* Pomptine (*name of marshy district in S. Latium*).
pōmum, -ī *nt* fruit; fruit tree.
pōmus, -ī *f* fruit tree.
ponderō, -āre *vt* to weigh; to consider, reflect on.
ponderōsus *adj* heavy, weighty.
pondō *adv* in weight; pounds.
pondus, -eris *nt* weight; mass, burden; (*fig*) importance, authority; (*character*) firmness; (*pl*) balance.
pōne *adv* behind.
pōnō, -ere, posuī, positum *vt* to put, place, lay, set; to lay down, lay aside; (*fig*) to regard, reckon; (*art*) to make, build; (*camp*) to pitch; (*corpse*) to lay out, bury; (*example*) to take; (*food*) to serve; (*hair*) to arrange; (*hope*) to base, stake; (*hypothesis*) to suppose, assume; (*institution*) to lay down, ordain; (*money*) to invest; (*sea*) to calm; (*theme*) to propose; (*time*) to spend, devote; (*tree*) to plant; (*wager*) to put down ♦ *vi* (*wind*) to abate.
pōns, pontis *m* bridge; drawbridge; (*ship*) gangway, deck.
ponticulus, -ī *m* small bridge.
Ponticus *adj see* **Pontus**.
pontifex, -icis *m* high priest, pontiff.
pontificālis *adj* pontifical.
pontificātus, -ūs *m* high priesthood.
pontificius *adj* pontiff's.
pontō, -ōnis *m* ferryboat.
pontus, -ī *m* sea.
Pontus, -ī *m* Black Sea; *kingdom of Mithridates in Asia Minor.*
popa, -ae *m* minor priest.
popanum, -ī *nt* sacrificial cake.
popellus, -ī *m* mob.
popīna, -ae *f* eating house, restaurant.
popīnō, -ōnis *m* glutton.
popl- *etc see* **pūbl-**.
poples, -itis *m* knee.
poposcī *perf of* **poscō**.
poppysma, -tis *nt* clicking of the tongue.
populābilis *adj* destroyable.
populābundus *adj* ravaging.
populāris *adj* of, from, for the people; popular, democratic; native ♦ *m* fellow countryman ♦ *mpl* the people's party, the democrats.
populāritās, -ātis *f* courting popular favour.
populāriter *adv* vulgarly; democratically.
populātiō, -ōnis *f* plundering; plunder.
populātor, -ōris *m* ravager.
pōpuleus *adj* poplar- (*in cpds*).
pōpulifer, -ī *adj* rich in poplars.
populor, -ārī, -ātus; -ō, -āre *vt* to ravage, plunder; to destroy, ruin.
populus, -ī *m* people, nation; populace, the public; large crowds; district.
pōpulus, -ī *f* poplar tree.
porca, -ae *f* sow.
porcella, -ae *f*, **-us, -ī** *m* little pig.

porcīna, -ae f pork.
porcīnārius, -ī and iī m pork seller.
Porcius, -ī m family name of Cato.
Porcius adj see n.
porculus, -ī m porker.
porcus, -ī m pig, hog.
porgō etc see **porrigō**.
Porphyriōn, -ōnis m a Giant.
porrēctiō, -ōnis f extending.
porrēctus ppp of **porrigō** ♦ adj long, protracted; dead.
porrēxī perf of **porrigō**.
porriciō, -ere vt to make an offering of; **inter caesa et porrēcta** ≈ at the eleventh hour.
porrigō, -igere, -ēxī, -ēctum vt to stretch, spread out, extend; to offer, hold out.
porrīgō, -inis f scurf, dandruff.
porrō adv forward, a long way off; (time) in future, long ago; (sequence) next, moreover, in turn.
porrum, -ī nt leek.
Porsena, Porsenna, Porsinna, -ae f king of Clusium in Etruria.
porta, -ae f gate; entrance, outlet.
portātiō, -ōnis f carrying.
portendō, -dere, -dī, -tum vt to denote, predict.
portentificus adj marvellous.
portentōsus adj unnatural.
portentum, -ī nt omen, unnatural happening; monstrosity, monster; (story) marvel.
porthmeus, -eī and eos m ferryman.
porticula, -ae f small gallery.
porticus, -ūs m portico, colonnade; (MIL) gallery; (PHILOS) Stoicism.
portiō, -ōnis f share, instalment; **prō ~ōne** proportionally.
portitor, -ōris m customs officer.
portitor, -ōris m ferryman.
portō, -āre, -āvī, -ātum vt to carry, convey, bring.
portōrium, -ī and iī nt customs duty, tax.
portula, -ae f small gate.
portuōsus adj well-off for harbours.
portus, -ūs m harbour, port; (fig) safety, haven.
pōsca, -ae f a vinegar drink.
poscō, -ere, poposcī vt to ask, require, demand; to call on.
Posīdōnius, -ī m Stoic philosopher (teacher of Cicero).
positiō, -ōnis f position, climate.
positor, -ōris m builder.
positūra, -ae f position; formation.
positus ppp of **pōnō** ♦ adj situated.
posse infin of **possum**.
possēdī perf of **possideō**; perf of **possīdō**.
possessiō, -ōnis f seizing; occupation; possession, property.
possessiuncula, -ae f small estate.

possessor, -ōris m occupier, possessor.
possessus ppp of **possideō** and **possīdō**.
possideō, -idēre, -ēdī, -essum vt to hold, occupy; to have, possess.
possīdō, -īdere, -ēdī, -essum vt to take possession of.
possum, -sse, -tuī vi to be able, can; to have power, avail.
post adv (place) behind; (time) after; (sequence) next ♦ prep (with acc) behind; after, since; **paulō ~** soon after; **~ urbem conditam** since the foundation of the city.
posteā adv afterwards, thereafter; next, then; **~ quam** conj after.
posterior, -ōris adj later, next; inferior, less important.
posteritās, -ātis f posterity, the future.
posterius adv later.
posterus adj next, following ♦ mpl posterity.
postferō, -re vt to put after, sacrifice.
postgenitī, -ōrum mpl later generations.
posthabeō, -ēre, -uī, -itum vt to put after, neglect.
posthāc adv hereafter, in future.
postibi adv then, after that.
postīculum, -ī nt small back building.
postīcus adj back- (in cpds), hind- (in cpds) ♦ nt back door.
postideā adv after that.
postilla adv afterwards.
postis, -is m doorpost, door.
postlīminium, -ī and iī nt right of recovery.
postmerīdiānus adj in the afternoon.
postmodo, postmodum adv shortly, presently.
postpōnō, -ōnere, -osuī, -ositum vt to put after, disregard.
postputō, -āre vt to consider less important.
postquam conj after, when.
postrēmō adv finally.
postrēmus adj last, rear; lowest, worst.
postrīdiē adv next day, the day after.
postscaenium, -ī and iī nt behind the scenes.
postscrībō, -ere vt to write after.
postulātiō, -ōnis f demand, claim; complaint.
postulātum, -ī nt demand, claim.
postulātus, -ūs m claim.
postulō, -āre, -āvī, -ātum vt to demand, claim; (law) to summon, prosecute; to apply for a writ (to prosecute).
postumus adj last, last-born.
postus etc see **positus**.
posuī perf of **pōnō**.
pōtātiō, -ōnis f drinking.
pōtātor, -ōris m toper.
pote etc see **potis**.
potēns, -entis adj able, capable; powerful, strong, potent; master of, ruling over; successful in carrying out.
potentātus, -ūs m political power.

Noun declensions and verb conjugations are shown on pp xiii to xxv. The present infinitive ending of a verb shows to which conjugation it belongs: **-āre** = 1st; **-ēre** = 2nd; **-ere** = 3rd and **-īre** = 4th. Irregular verbs are shown on p xxvi

potenter *adv* powerfully; competently.
potentia, -ae *f* power, force, efficacy; tyranny.
potērium, -ī *and* **iī** *nt* goblet.
potesse *archaic infin of* **possum.**
potestās, -ātis *f* power, ability; control, sovereignty, authority; opportunity, permission; (*person*) magistrate; (*things*) property; **~ātem suī facere** allow access to oneself.
potin can (you)?, is it possible?
pōtiō, -ōnis *f* drink, draught, philtre.
potiō, -īre *vt* to put into the power of.
potior, -īrī, -ītus *vi* (*with gen and abl*) to take possession of, get hold of, acquire; to be master of.
potior, -ōris *adj* better, preferable.
potis *adj* (*indecl*) able; possible.
potissimum *adv* especially.
potissimus *adj* chief, most important.
pōtitō, -āre *vt* to drink much.
potius *adv* rather, more.
pōtō, -āre, -āvī, -ātum *and* **um** *vt* to drink.
pōtor, -ōris *m* drinker.
pōtrīx, -īcis *f* woman tippler.
potuī *perf of* **possum.**
pōtulenta, -ōrum *ntpl* drinks.
pōtus *ppp of* **pōtō** ♦ *adj* drunk.
pōtus, -ūs *m* drink.
prae *adv* in front, before; in comparison ♦ *prep* (*with abl*) in front of; compared with; (*cause*) because of, for; **~ sē** openly; **~ sē ferre** display; **~ manū** to hand.
praeacūtus *adj* pointed.
praealtus *adj* very high, very deep.
praebeō, -ēre, -uī, -itum *vt* to hold out, proffer; to give, supply; to show, represent; **sē ~** behave, prove.
praebibō, -ere, -ī *vt* to toast.
praebitor, -ōris *m* purveyor.
praecalidus *adj* very hot.
praecānus *adj* prematurely grey.
praecautus *ppp of* **praecaveō.**
praecaveō, -avēre, -āvī, -autum *vt* to guard against ♦ *vi* to beware, take precautions.
praecēdō, -dere, -ssī, -ssum *vt* to go before; to surpass ♦ *vi* to lead the way; to excel.
praecellō, -ere *vi* to excel, be distinguished ♦ *vt* to surpass.
praecelsus *adj* very high.
praecentiō, -ōnis *f* prelude.
praecentō, -āre *vi* to sing an incantation for.
praeceps, -ipitis *adj* head first, headlong; going down, precipitous; rapid, violent, hasty; inclined (to); dangerous ♦ *nt* edge of an abyss, precipice; danger ♦ *adv* headlong; into danger.
praeceptiō, -ōnis *f* previous notion; precept.
praeceptor, -ōris *m* teacher.
praeceptrīx, -rīcis *f* teacher.
praeceptum, -ī *nt* maxim, precept; order.
praeceptus *ppp of* **praecipiō.**
praecerpō, -ere, -sī, -tum *vt* to gather prematurely; to forestall.
praecīdō, -dere, -dī, -sum *vt* to cut off, damage; (*fig*) to cut short, put an end to.
praecinctus *ppp of* **praecingō.**
praecingō, -ingere, -inxī, -inctum *vt* to gird in front; to surround.
praecinō, -inere, -inuī, -entum *vt* to play before; to chant a spell ♦ *vt* to predict.
praecipiō, -ipere, -ēpī, -eptum *vt* to take beforehand, get in advance; to anticipate; to teach, admonish, order.
praecipitanter *adv* at full speed.
praecipitem *acc of* **praeceps.**
praecipitō, -āre, -āvī, -ātum *vt* to throw down, throw away, hasten; (*fig*) to remove, carry away, ruin ♦ *vi* to rush headlong, fall; to be hasty.
praecipuē *adv* especially, chiefly.
praecipuus *adj* special; principal, outstanding.
praecīsē *adv* briefly, absolutely.
praecīsus *ppp of* **praecīdō** ♦ *adj* steep.
praeclārē *adv* very clearly; excellently.
praeclārus *adj* very bright; beautiful, splendid; distinguished, noble.
praeclūdō, -dere, -sī, -sum *vt* to close, shut against; to close to, impede.
praecō, -ōnis *m* crier, herald; auctioneer.
praecōgitō, -āre *vt* to premeditate.
praecognitus *adj* foreseen.
praecolō, -olere, -oluī, -ultum *vt* to cultivate early.
praecompositus *adj* studied.
praecōnium, -ī *and* **iī** *nt* office of a crier; advertisement; commendation.
praecōnius *adj* of a public crier.
praecōnsūmō, -ere, -ptum *vt* to use up beforehand.
praecontrectō, -āre *vt* to consider beforehand.
praecordia, -ōrum *ntpl* midriff; stomach; breast, heart; mind.
praecorrumpō, -umpere, -ūpī, -uptum *vt* to bribe beforehand.
praecox, -cis *adj* early, premature.
praecultus *ppp of* **praecolō.**
praecurrentia, -ium *ntpl* antecedents.
praecurrō, -rrere, -currī *and* **rrī, -rsum** *vi* to hurry on before, precede; to excel ♦ *vt* to anticipate; to surpass.
praecursiō, -ōnis *f* previous occurrence; (*RHET*) preparation.
praecursor, -ōris *m* advance guard; scout.
praecutiō, -ere *vt* to brandish before.
praeda, -ae *f* booty, plunder; (*animal*) prey; (*fig*) gain.
praedābundus *adj* plundering.
praedamnō, -āre *vt* to condemn beforehand.
praedātiō, -ōnis *f* plundering.
praedātor, -ōris *m* plunderer.
praedātōrius *adj* marauding.
praedēlassō, -āre *vt* to weaken beforehand.
praedēstinō, -āre *vt* to predetermine.

praediātor, -ōris *m* buyer of landed estates.
praediātōrius *adj* relating to the sale of
estates.
praedicābilis *adj* laudatory.
praedicātiō, -ōnis *f* proclamation;
commendation.
praedicātor, -ōris *m* eulogist.
praedicō, -āre, -āvī, -ātum *vt* to proclaim,
make public; to declare; to praise, boast.
praedīcō, -īcere, -īxī, -ictum *vt* to mention
beforehand, prearrange; to foretell; to
warn, command.
praedictiō, -ōnis *f* foretelling.
praedictum, -ī *nt* prediction; command;
prearrangement.
praedictus *ppp of* **praedīcō.**
praediolum, -ī *nt* small estate.
praediscō, -ere *vt* to learn beforehand.
praedispositus *adj* arranged beforehand.
praeditus *adj* endowed, provided.
praedium, -ī *and* **iī** *nt* estate.
praedīves, -itis *adj* very rich.
praedō, -ōnis *m* robber, pirate.
praedor, -ārī, -ātus *vt, vi* to plunder, rob; (*fig*)
to profit.
praedūcō, -ūcere, -ūxī, -uctum *vt* to draw in
front.
praedulcis *adj* very sweet.
praedūrus *adj* very hard, very tough.
praeēmineō, -ēre *vt* to surpass.
praeeō, -īre, -īvī *and* **iī, -itum** *vi* to lead the
way, go first; (*formula*) to dictate, recite first
♦ *vt* to precede, outstrip.
praeesse *infin of* **praesum.**
praefātiō, -ōnis *f* formula; preface.
praefātus *ppa of* **praefor.**
praefectūra, -ae *f* superintendence;
governorship; *Italian town governed by Roman
edicts,* prefecture; district, province.
praefectus *ppp of* **praeficiō** ♦ *m* overseer,
director, governor, commander; ~ **classis**
admiral; ~ **legiōnis** colonel; ~ **urbis** *or* **urbī**
city prefect (of Rome).
praeferō, -ferre, -tulī, -lātum *vt* to carry in
front, hold out; to prefer; to show, display; to
anticipate; (*pass*) to hurry past, outflank.
praeferōx, -ōcis *adj* very impetuous, very
insolent.
praefervidus *adj* very hot.
praefestīnō, -āre *vi* to be too hasty; to hurry
past.
praefica, -ae *f* hired mourner.
praeficiō, -icere, -ēcī, -ectum *vt* to put in
charge, give command over.
praefidēns, -entis *adj* over-confident.
praefigō, -gere, -xī, -xum *vt* to fasten in
front, set up before; to tip, point; to transfix.
praefiniō, -īre, -īvī *and* **iī, -ītum** *vt* to
determine, prescribe.
praefiscinē, -ī *adv* without offence.

praeflōrō, -āre *vt* to tarnish.
praefluō, -ere *vt, vi* to flow past.
praefocō, -āre *vt* to choke.
praefodiō, -odere, -ōdī *vt* to dig in front of;
to bury beforehand.
praefor, -ārī, -ātus *vt, vi* to say in advance,
preface; to pray beforehand; to predict.
praefrāctē *adv* resolutely.
praefrāctus *ppp of* **praefringō** ♦ *adj* abrupt;
stern.
praefrīgidus *adj* very cold.
praefringō, -ingere, -ēgī, -āctum *vt* to break
off, shiver.
praefuī *perf of* **praesum.**
praefulciō, -cīre, -sī, -tum *vt* to prop up; to
use as a prop.
praefulgeō, -ulgēre, -ulsī *vt* to shine
conspicuously; to outshine.
praegelidus *adj* very cold.
praegestiō, -īre *vi* to be very eager.
praegnāns, -antis *adj* pregnant; full.
praegracilis *adj* very slim.
praegrandis *adj* very large, very great.
praegravis *adj* very heavy; very wearisome.
praegravō, -āre *vt* to weigh down; to eclipse.
praegredior, -dī, -ssus *vt, vi* to go before; to
go past; to surpass.
praegressiō, -ōnis *f* precession, precedence.
praegustātor, -ōris *m* taster.
praegustō, -āre *vt* to taste beforehand.
praehibeō, -ēre *vt* to offer, give.
praeiaceō, -ēre *vt* to lie in front of.
praeiūdicium, -ī *and* **iī** *nt* precedent, example;
prejudgment.
praeiūdicō, -āre, -āvī, -ātum *vt* to prejudge,
decide beforehand.
praeiuvō, -āre *vt* to give previous assistance
to.
praelabor, -bī, -psus *vt, vi* to move past, move
along.
praelambō, -ere *vt* to lick first.
praelātus *ppp of* **praeferō.**
praelegō, -ere *vt* to coast along.
praeligō, -āre *vt* to bind, tie up.
praelongus *adj* very long, very tall.
praeloquor, -quī, -cūtus *vi* to speak first.
praelūceō, -cēre, -xī *vi* to light, shine; to
outshine.
praelūstris *adj* very magnificent.
praemandāta *ntpl* warrant of arrest.
praemandō, -āre, -āvī, -ātum *vt* to bespeak.
praemātūrē *adv* too soon.
praemātūrus *adj* too early, premature.
praemedicātus *adj* protected by charms.
praemeditātiō, -ōnis *f* thinking over the
future.
praemeditātus *adj* premeditated.
praemeditor, -ārī, -ātus *vt* to think over,
practise.
praemetuenter *adv* anxiously.

praemetuō, -ere *vi* to be anxious ♦ *vt* to fear the future.
praemissus *ppp of* **praemittō**.
praemittō, -ittere, -īsī, -issum *vt* to send in advance.
praemium, -ī *and* **iī** *nt* prize, reward.
praemolestia, -ae *f* apprehension.
praemōlior, -īrī *vt* to prepare thoroughly.
praemoneō, -ēre, -uī, -itum *vt* to forewarn, foreshadow.
praemonitus, -ūs *m* premonition.
praemōnstrātor, -ōris *m* guide.
praemōnstrō, -āre *vt* to guide; to predict.
praemordeō, -ēre *vt* to bite off; to pilfer.
praemorior, -ī, -tuus *vi* to die too soon.
praemūniō, -īre, -īvī, -ītum *vt* to fortify, strengthen, secure.
praemūnītiō, -ōnis *f (RHET)* preparation.
praenārrō, -āre *vt* to tell beforehand.
praenatō, -āre *vt* to flow past.
Praeneste, -is *ntlf* Latin town (*now* Palestrina).
Praenestīnus *adj see n.*
praeniteō, -ēre, -uī *vi* to seem more attractive.
praenōmen, -inis *nt* first name.
praenōscō, -ere *vt* to foreknow.
praenōtiō, -ōnis *f* preconceived idea.
praenūbilus *adj* very gloomy.
praenūntia, -iae *f* harbinger.
praenūntiō, -āre *vt* to foretell.
praenūntius, -ī *and* **iī** *m* harbinger.
praeoccupō, -āre, -āvī, -ātum *vt* to take first, anticipate.
praeolit mihi I get a hint of.
praeoptō, -āre, -āvī, -ātum *vt* to choose rather, prefer.
praepandō, -ere *vt* to spread out; to expound.
praeparātiō, -ōnis *f* preparation.
praeparō, -āre, -āvī, -ātum *vt* to prepare, prepare for; **ex ~ātō** by arrangement.
praepediō, -īre, -īvī, -ītum *vt* to shackle, tether; to hamper.
praependeō, -ēre *vi* to hang down in front.
praepes, -etis *adj* swift, winged; of good omen ♦ *f* bird.
praepilātus *adj* tipped with a ball.
praepinguis *adj* very rich.
praepolleō, -ēre *vi* to be very powerful, be superior.
praeponderō, -āre *vt* to outweigh.
praepōnō, -ōnere, -osuī, -ositum *vt* to put first, place in front; to put in charge, appoint commander; to prefer.
praeportō, -āre *vt* to carry before.
praepositiō, -ōnis *f* preference; (*GRAM*) preposition.
praepositus *ppp of* **praepōnō** ♦ *m* overseer, commander.
praepossum, -sse, -tuī *vi* to gain the upper hand.
praeposterē *adv* the wrong way round.
praeposterus *adj* inverted, perverted;

absurd.
praepotēns, -entis *adj* very powerful.
praeproperanter *adv* too hastily.
praeproperē *adv* too hastily.
praeproperus *adj* overhasty, rash.
praepūtium, -ī *and* **iī** *nt* foreskin.
praequam *adv* compared with.
praequestus *adj* complaining beforehand.
praeradiō, -āre *vt* to outshine.
praerapidus *adj* very swift.
praereptus *ppp of* **praeripiō**.
praerigēscō, -ēscere, -uī *vi* to become very stiff.
praeripiō, -ipere, -ipuī, -eptum *vt* to take before, forestall; to carry off prematurely; to frustrate.
praerōdō, -dere, -sum *vt* to bite the end of, nibble off.
praerogātīva, -ae *f* tribe or century with the first vote, the first vote; previous election; omen, sure token.
praerogātīvus *adj* voting first.
praerōsus *ppp of* **praerōdō**.
praerumpō, -umpere, -ūpī, -uptum *vt* to break off.
praeruptus *ppp of* **praerumpō** ♦ *adj* steep, abrupt; headstrong.
praes, -aedis *m* surety; property of a surety.
praesaep- *etc see* **praesēp-**.
praesāgiō, -īre *vt* to have a presentiment of, forebode.
praesāgītiō, -ōnis *f* foreboding.
praesāgium, -ī *and* **iī** *nt* presentiment; prediction.
praesāgus *adj* foreboding, prophetic.
praesciō, -īre, -iī *vt* to know before.
praescīscō, -ere *vt* to find out beforehand.
praescius *adj* foreknowing.
praescrībō, -bere, -psī, -ptum *vt* to write first; to direct, command; to dictate, describe; to put forward as a pretext.
praescrīptiō, -ōnis *f* preface, heading; order, rule; pretext.
praescrīptum, -ī *nt* order, rule.
praescrīptus *ppp of* **praescrībō**.
praesecō, -āre, -uī, -tum *and* **-ātum** *vt* to cut off, pare.
praesēns, -entis *adj* present, in person; (*things*) immediate, ready, prompt; (*mind*) resolute; (*gods*) propitious ♦ *ntpl* present state of affairs; **in ~ēns** for the present; **~in rē ~entī** on the spot.
praesēnsiō, -ōnis *f* foreboding; preconception.
praesēnsus *ppp of* **praesentiō**.
praesentārius *adj* instant, ready.
praesentia, -ae *f* presence; effectiveness.
praesentiō, -entīre, -ēnsī, -ēnsum *vt* to presage, have a foreboding of.
praesēpe, -is *nt*, **-ēs, -is** *f* stable, fold, pen; hovel; hive.
praesēpiō, -īre, -sī, -tum *vt* to barricade.
praesēpis *f* = **praesēpe**.

praesertim *adv* especially.
praeserviō, -īre *vi* to serve as a slave.
praeses, -idis *m* guardian, protector; chief, ruler.
praesideō, -idēre, -ēdī *vi* to guard, defend; to preside over, direct.
praesidiārius *adj* garrison-.
praesidium, -ī *and* **iī** *nt* defence, protection; support, assistance; guard, garrison, convoy; defended position, entrenchment.
praesignificō, -āre *vt* to foreshadow.
praesignis *adj* conspicuous.
praesonō, -āre, -uī *vi* to sound before.
praespargō, -ere *vt* to strew before.
praestābilis *adj* outstanding; preferable.
praestāns, -antis *pres p of* **praestō** ♦ *adj* outstanding, pre-eminent.
praestantia, -ae *f* pre-eminence.
praestes, -itis *adj* presiding, guardian.
praestīgiae, -ārum *fpl* illusion, sleight of hand.
praestīgiātor, -ōris *m*, **-rīx, -rīcis** *f* conjurer, cheat.
praestinō, -āre *vt* to buy.
praestitī *perf of* **praestō.**
praestituō, -uere, -uī, -ūtum *vt* to prearrange, prescribe.
praestitus *ppp of* **praestō.**
praestō *adv* at hand, ready.
praestō, -āre, -itī, -itum *and* **ātum** *vi* to be outstanding, be superior; (*impers*) it is better ♦ *vt* to excel; to be responsible for, answer for; (*duty*) to discharge, perform; (*quality*) to show, prove; (*things*) to give, offer, provide; **sē ~** behave, prove.
praestōlor, -ārī, -ātus *vt, vi* to wait for, expect.
praestrictus *ppp of* **praestringō.**
praestringō, -ingere, -inxī, -ictum *vt* to squeeze; to blunt, dull; (*eyes*) to dazzle.
praestruō, -ere, -xī, -ctum *vt* to block up; to build beforehand.
praesul, -is *m/f* public dancer.
praesultātor, -ōris *m* public dancer.
praesultō, -āre *vi* to dance before.
praesum, -esse, -fuī *vi* (*with dat*) to be at the head of, be in command of; to take the lead; to protect.
praesūmō, -ere, -psī, -ptum *vt* to take first; to anticipate; to take for granted.
praesūtus *adj* sewn over at the point.
praetemptō, -āre *vt* to feel for, grope for; to test in advance.
praetendō, -dere, -dī, -tum *vt* to hold out, put before, spread in front of; to give as an excuse, allege.
praetentō *etc see* **praetemptō.**
praetentus *ppp of* **praetendō** ♦ *adj* lying over against.
praetepeō, -ēre, -uī *vi* to glow before.

praeter *adv* beyond; excepting ♦ *prep* (*with acc*) past, along; except, besides; beyond, more than, in addition to, contrary to.
praeteragō, -ere *vt* to drive past.
praeterbītō, -ere *vt, vi* to pass by.
praeterdūcō, -ere *vt* to lead past.
praetereā *adv* besides; moreover; henceforth.
praetereō, -īre, -iī, -itum *vi* to go past ♦ *vt* to pass, overtake; to escape, escape the notice of; to omit, leave out, forget, neglect; to reject, exclude; to surpass; to transgress.
praeterequitāns, -antis *adj* riding past.
praeterfluō, -ere *vt, vi* to flow past.
praetergredior, -dī, -ssus *vt* to pass, march past; to surpass.
praeterhāc *adv* further, more.
praeteritus *ppp of* **praetereō** ♦ *adj* past, gone by ♦ *ntpl* the past.
praeterlābor, -bī, -psus *vt* to flow past, move past ♦ *vi* to slip away.
praeterlātus *adj* driving, flying past.
praetermeō, -āre *vi* to pass by.
praetermissiō, -ōnis *f* omission, passing over.
praetermittō, -ittere, -īsī, -issum *vt* to let pass; to omit, neglect; to make no mention of; to overlook.
praeterquam *adv* except, besides.
praetervectiō, -ōnis *f* passing by.
praetervehor, -hī, -ctus *vt, vi* to ride past, sail past; to march past; to pass by, pass over.
praetervolō, -āre *vt, vi* to fly past; to escape.
praetexō, -ere, -uī, -tum *vt* to border, fringe; to adorn; to pretend, disguise.
praetextātus *adj* wearing the toga praetexta, under age.
praetextus *ppp of* **praetexō** ♦ *adj* wearing the toga praetexta ♦ *f* toga with a purple border; Roman tragedy ♦ *nt* pretext.
praetextus, -ūs *m* splendour; pretence.
praetimeō, -ēre *vi* to be afraid in advance.
praetinctus *adj* dipped beforehand.
praetor, -ōris *m* chief magistrate, commander; praetor; propraetor, governor.
praetōriānus *adj* of the emperor's bodyguard.
praetōrium, -ī *and* **iī** *nt* general's tent, camp headquarters; governor's residence; council of war; palace, grand building; emperor's bodyguard.
praetōrius *adj* praetor's, praetorian; of a propraetor; of the emperor's bodyguard ♦ *m* ex-praetor; **~ia cohors** bodyguard of general *or* emperor; **porta ~ia** camp gate facing the enemy.
praetorqueō, -ēre *vt* to strangle first.
praetrepidāns, -antis *adj* very impatient.
praetruncō, -āre *vt* to cut off.
praetulī *perf of* **praeferō.**
praetūra, -ae *f* praetorship.

Noun declensions and verb conjugations are shown on pp xiii to xxv. The present infinitive ending of a verb shows to which conjugation it belongs: **-āre** = 1st; **-ēre** = 2nd; **-ere** = 3rd and **-īre** = 4th. Irregular verbs are shown on p xxvi

praeumbrāns, -antis _adj_ obscuring.
praeūstus _adj_ hardened at the point; frostbitten.
praeut _adv_ compared with.
praevaleō, -ēre, -uī _vi_ to be very powerful, have most influence, prevail.
praevalidus _adj_ very strong, very powerful; too strong.
praevāricātiō, -ōnis _f_ collusion.
praevāricātor, -ōris _m_ advocate guilty of collusion.
praevāricor, -ārī, -ātus _vi_ (_with dat_) to favour by collusion.
praevehor, -hī, -ctus _vi_ to ride, fly in front, flow past.
praeveniō, -enīre, -ēnī, -entum _vt, vi_ to come before; to anticipate, prevent.
praeverrō, -ere _vt_ to sweep before.
praevertō, -ere, -ī; -or, -ī _vt_ to put first, prefer; to turn to first, attend first to; to oustrip; to anticipate, frustrate, prepossess.
praevideō, -idēre, -īdī, -īsum _vt_ to foresee.
praevitiō, -āre _vt_ to taint beforehand.
praevius _adj_ leading the way.
praevolō, -āre _vi_ to fly in front.
pragmaticus _adj_ of affairs ♦ _m_ legal expert.
prandeō, -ēre, -ī _vi_ to take lunch ♦ _vt_ to eat.
prandium, -ī and iī _nt_ lunch.
prānsor, -ōris _m_ guest at lunch.
prānsus _adj_ having lunched, fed.
prasinus _adj_ green.
prātēnsis _adj_ meadow.
prātulum, -ī _nt_ small meadow.
prātum, -ī _nt_ meadow; grass.
prāvē _adv_ wrongly, badly.
prāvitās, -ātis _f_ irregularity; perverseness, depravity.
prāvus _adj_ crooked, deformed; perverse, bad, wicked.
Prāxitelēs, -is _m_ famous Greek sculptor.
Prāxitelius _adj_ see n.
precāriō _adv_ by request.
precārius _adj_ obtained by entreaty.
precātiō, -ōnis _f_ prayer.
precātor, -ōris _m_ intercessor.
preces _pl of_ **prex**.
preciae, -ārum _fpl_ kind of vine.
precor, -ārī, -ātus _vt, vi_ to pray, beg, entreat; to wish (well), curse.
prehendō, -endere, -endī, -ēnsum _vt_ to take hold of, catch; to seize, detain; to surprise; (_eye_) to take in; (_mind_) to grasp.
prehēnsō _etc see_ **prēnsō**.
prehēnsus _ppp of_ **prehendō**.
prēlum, -ī _nt_ wine press, oil press.
premō, -mere, -ssī, -ssum _vt_ to press, squeeze; to press together, compress; (_eyes_) to close; (_reins_) to tighten; (_trees_) to prune; to press upon, lie, sit, stand on, cover, conceal, surpass; to press hard on, follow closely; (_coast_) to hug; to press down, lower, burden; (_fig_) to overcome, rule; (_words_) to disparage; to press in, sink, stamp, plant; to press back,

repress, check, stop.
prendō _etc see_ **prehendō**.
prēnsātiō, -ōnis _f_ canvassing.
prēnsō (prehēnsō), -āre, -āvī, -ātum _vt_ to clutch at, take hold of, buttonhole.
prēnsus _ppp of_ **prehendō**.
presbyter, -ī _m_ (_ECCL_) elder.
pressē _adv_ concisely, accurately, simply.
pressī _perf of_ **premō**.
pressiō, -ōnis _f_ fulcrum.
pressō, -āre _vt_ to press.
pressus _ppp of_ **premō** ♦ _adj_ (_style_) concise, compressed; (_pace_) slow; (_voice_) subdued.
pressus, -ūs _m_ pressure.
prēstēr, -ēris _m_ waterspout.
pretiōsē _adv_ expensively.
pretiōsus _adj_ valuable, expensive; extravagant.
pretium, -ī and iī _nt_ price, value; worth; money, fee, reward; **māgnī -ī, in -iō** valuable; **operae ~** worth while.
prex, -ecis _f_ request, entreaty; prayer; good wish; curse.
Priamēis, -ēidis _f_ Cassandra.
Priamēius _adj_ see **Priamus**.
Priamidēs, -idae _m_ son of Priam.
Priamus, -ī _m_ king of Troy.
Priāpus, -ī _m_ god of fertility and of gardens.
prīdem _adv_ long ago, long.
prīdiē _adv_ the day before.
prīmaevus _adj_ youthful.
prīmānī, -ōrum _mpl_ soldiers of the 1st legion.
prīmārius _adj_ principal, first-rate.
prīmigenus _adj_ original.
prīmipīlāris, -is _m_ chief centurion.
prīmipīlus, -ī _m_ chief centurion.
prīmitiae, -ārum _fpl_ first fruits.
prīmitus _adv_ originally.
prīmō _adv_ at first; firstly.
prīmōrdium, -ī and iī _nt_ beginning; **~ia rērum** atoms.
prīmōris _adj_ first, foremost, tip of; principal ♦ _mpl_ nobles; (_MIL_) front line.
prīmulum _adv_ first.
prīmulus _adj_ very first.
prīmum _adv_ first, to begin with, in the first place; for the first time; **cum, ubi, ut ~** as soon as; **quam ~** as soon as possible; **~ dum** in the first place.
prīmus _adj_ first, foremost, tip of; earliest; principal, most eminent; **~ veniō** I am the first to come; **prima lux** dawn, daylight; **~ō mēnse** at the beginning of the month; **~īs digitīs** with the fingertips; **~ās agere** play the leading part; **~ās dare** give first place to; **in ~īs** in the front line; especially.
prīnceps, -ipis _adj_ first, in front, chief, most eminent ♦ _m_ leader, chief; first citizen, emperor; (_MIL_) company, captain, captaincy ♦ _pl_ (_MIL_) the second line.
prīncipālis _adj_ original; chief; the emperor's.
prīncipātus, -ūs _m_ first place; post of commander-in-chief; emperorship.

prīncipiālis *adj* from the beginning.
prīncipium, -ī *and* **iī** *nt* beginning, origin; first to vote ♦ *pl* first principles; (*MIL*) front line; camp headquarters.
prior, -ōris (*nt* -**us**) *adj* former, previous, first; better, preferable ♦ *mpl* forefathers.
prīscē *adv* strictly.
prīscus *adj* former, ancient, old-fashioned.
prīstinus *adj* former, original; of yesterday.
prius *adv* previously, before; in former times; ~ **quam** before, sooner than.
prīvātim *adv* individually, privately; at home.
prīvātiō, -ōnis *f* removal.
prīvātus *adj* individual, private; not in public office ♦ *m* private citizen.
Prīvernās, -ātis *adj see n.*
Prīvernum, -ī *nt* old Latin town.
prīvīgna, -ae *f* stepdaughter.
prīvīgnus, -ī *m* stepson; *pl* stepchildren.
prīvilēgium, -ī *and* **iī** *nt* law in favour of *or* against an individual.
prīvō, -āre, -āvī, -ātum *vt* to deprive, rob; to free.
prīvus *adj* single, one each; own, private.
prō *adv* (*with* **ut** *and* **quam**) in proportion (as) ♦ *prep* (*with abl*) in front of, on the front of; for, on behalf of, instead of, in return for; as, as good as; according to, in proportion to, by virtue of; ~ **eō ac** just as; ~ **eō quod** just because; ~ **eō quantum, ut** in proportion as.
prō *interj* (*expressing wonder or sorrow*) O!, alas!
proāgorus, -ī *m* chief magistrate (*in Sicilian towns*).
proavītus *adj* ancestral.
proavus, -ī *m* great-grandfather, ancestor.
probābilis *adj* laudable; credible, probable.
probābilitās, -ātis *f* credibility.
probābiliter *adv* credibly.
probātiō, -ōnis *f* approval; testing.
probātor, -ōris *m* approver.
probātus *adj* tried, excellent; acceptable.
probē *adv* well, properly; thoroughly, well done!
probitās, -ātis *f* goodness, honesty.
probō, -āre, -āvī, -ātum *vt* to approve, approve of; to appraise; to recommend; to prove, show.
probrōsus *adj* abusive; disgraceful.
probrum, -ī *nt* abuse, reproach; disgrace; infamy, unchastity.
probus *adj* good, excellent; honest, upright.
procācitās, -ātis *f* impudence.
procāciter *adv* insolently.
procāx, -ācis *adj* bold, forward, insolent.
prōcēdō, -ēdere, -essī, -essum *vi* to go forward, advance; to go out, come forth; (*time*) to go on, continue; (*fig*) to make progress, get on; (*events*) to turn out, succeed.
procella, -ae *f* hurricane, storm; (*MIL*) charge.

procellōsus *adj* stormy.
procer, -is *m* chief, noble, prince.
prōcēritās, -ātis *f* height; length.
prōcērus *adj* tall; long.
prōcessiō, -ōnis *f* advance.
prōcessus, -ūs *m* advance, progress.
prōcidō, -ere, -ī *vi* to fall forwards, fall down.
prōcinctus, -ūs *m* readiness (for action).
prōclāmātor, -ōris *m* bawler.
prōclāmō, -āre *vi* to cry out.
prōclīnātus *adj* tottering.
prōclīnō, -āre *vt* to bend.
prōclīvē *adv* downwards; easily.
prōclīvis, -us *adj* downhill, steep; (*mind*) prone, willing; (*act*) easy; **in -ī** easy.
prōclīvitās, -ātis *f* descent; tendency.
prōclīvus *etc see* **proclīvis**.
Procnē, -ēs *f* wife of Tereus (*changed to a swallow*); swallow.
prōcōnsul, -is *m* proconsul, governor.
prōcōnsulāris *adj* proconsular.
prōcōnsulātus, -ūs *m* proconsulship.
prōcrāstinātiō, -ōnis *f* procrastination.
prōcrāstinō, -āre *vt* to put off from day to day.
prōcreātiō, -ōnis *f* begetting.
prōcreātor, -ōris *m* creator, parent.
prōcreātrīx, -īcis *f* mother.
prōcreō, -āre *vt* to beget, produce.
prōcrēscō, -ere *vi* to be produced, grow up.
Procrūstēs, -ae *m* Attic highwayman (*who tortured victims on a bed*).
prōcubō, -āre *vi* to lie on the ground.
prōcūdō, -dere, -dī, -sum *vt* to forge; to produce.
procul *adv* at a distance, far, from afar.
prōculcō, -āre *vt* to trample down.
prōcumbō, -mbere, -buī, -bitum *vi* to fall forwards, bend over; to sink down, be broken down.
prōcūrātiō, -ōnis *f* management; (*religion*) expiation.
prōcūrātor, -ōris *m* administrator, financial agent; (*province*) governor.
prōcūrātrīx, -īcis *f* governess.
prōcūrō, -āre, -āvī, -ātum *vt* to take care of, manage; to expiate ♦ *vi* to be a procurator.
prōcurrō, -rrere, -currī *and* **rrī, -rsum** *vi* to rush forward; to jut out.
prōcursātiō, -ōnis *f* charge.
prōcursātor, -ōris *m* skirmisher.
prōcursō, -āre *vi* to make a sally.
prōcursus, -ūs *m* charge.
prōcurvus *adj* curving forwards.
procus, -ī *m* nobleman.
procus, -ī *m* wooer, suitor.
Procyōn, -ōnis *m* Lesser Dog Star.
prōdeambulō, -āre *vi* to go out for a walk.
prōdeō, -īre, -iī, -itum *vi* to come out, come forward, appear; to go ahead, advance; to

project.

prōdesse *infin of* **prōsum**.

prōdīcō, -īcere, -īxī, -ictum *vt* to appoint, adjourn.

prōdictātor, -ōris *m* vice-dictator.

prōdigē *adv* extravagantly.

prōdigentia, -ae *f* profusion.

prōdigiāliter *adv* unnaturally.

prōdigiōsus *adj* unnatural, marvellous.

prōdigium, -ī *and* **iī** *nt* portent; unnatural deed; monster.

prōdigō, -igere, -ēgī, -āctum *vt* to squander.

prōdigus *adj* wasteful; lavish, generous.

prōditiō, -ōnis *f* betrayal.

prōditor, -ōris *m* traitor.

prōditus *ppp of* **prōdō**.

prōdō, -ere, -idī, -itum *vt* to bring forth, produce; to make known, publish; to betray, give up; (*tradition*) to hand down.

prōdoceō, -ēre *vt* to preach.

prodromus, -ī *m* forerunner.

prōdūcō, -ūcere, -ūxī, -uctum *vt* to bring forward, bring out; to conduct; to drag in front; to draw out, extend; (*acting*) to perform; (*child*) to beget, bring up; (*fact*) to bring to light; (*innovation*) to introduce; (*rank*) to promote; (*slave*) to put up for sale; (*time*) to prolong, protract, put off; (*tree*) to cultivate; (*vowel*) to lengthen.

prōductē *adv* long.

prōductiō, -ōnis *f* lengthening.

prōductō, -āre *vt* to spin out.

prōductus *ppp of* **prōdūcō** ♦ *adj* lengthened, long.

proēgmenon, -ī *nt* a preferred thing.

proeliātor, -ōris *m* fighter.

proelior, -ārī, -ātus *vi* to fight, join battle.

proelium, -ī *and* **iī** *nt* battle, conflict.

profānō, -āre *vt* to desecrate.

profānus *adj* unholy, common; impious; ill-omened.

profātus *ppa of* **profor**.

profectiō, -ōnis *f* departure; source.

profectō *adv* really, certainly.

profectus *ppa of* **proficīscor**.

profectus *ppp of* **prōficiō**.

prōfectus, -ūs *m* growth, progress, profit.

prōferō, -ferre, -tulī, -lātum *vt* to bring forward, forth or out; to extend, enlarge; (*time*) to prolong, defer; (*instance*) to mention, quote; (*knowledge*) to publish, reveal; **pedem ~** proceed; **signa ~** advance.

professiō, -ōnis *f* declaration; public register; profession.

professor, -ōris *m* teacher.

professōrius *adj* authoritative.

professus *ppa of* **profiteor**.

profēstus *adj* not holiday, working.

prōficiō, -icere, -ēcī, -ectum *vi* to make progress, profit; to be of use.

proficīscor, -icīscī, -ectus *vi* to set out, start; to originate, proceed.

profiteor, -itērī, -essus *vt* to declare, profess; to make an official return of; to promise, volunteer.

prōflīgātor, -ōris *m* spendthrift.

prōflīgātus *adj* dissolute.

prōflīgō, -āre, -āvī, -ātum *vt* to dash to the ground; to destroy, overthrow; to bring almost to an end; to degrade.

prōflō, -āre *vt* to breathe out.

prōfluēns, -entis *pres p of* **prōfluō** ♦ *adj* flowing; fluent ♦ *f* running water.

prōfluenter *adv* easily.

prōfluentia, -ae *f* fluency.

prōfluō, -ere, -xī *vi* to flow on, flow out; (*fig*) to proceed.

prōfluvium, -ī *and* **iī** *nt* flowing.

profor, -ārī, -ātus *vi* to speak, give utterance.

profugiō, -ugere, -ūgī *vi* to flee, escape; to take refuge (with) ♦ *vt* to flee from.

profugus *adj* fugitive; exiled; nomadic.

prōfuī *perf of* **prōsum**.

profundō, -undere, -ūdī, -ūsum *vt* to pour out, shed; to bring forth, produce; to prostrate; to squander; **sē ~** burst forth, rush out.

profundus *adj* deep, vast, high; infernal; (*fig*) profound; (*words*) immoderate ♦ *nt* depths, abyss.

profūsē *adv* in disorder, extravagantly.

profūsus *ppp of* **profundō** ♦ *adj* lavish; excessive.

prōgener, -ī *m* grandson-in-law.

prōgenerō, -āre *vt* to beget.

prōgeniēs, -ēī *f* descent; offspring, descendants.

prōgenitor, -ōris *m* ancestor.

prōgignō, -ignere, -enuī, -enitum *vt* to beget, produce.

prōgnātus *adj* born, descended ♦ *m* son, descendant.

Prognē *see* **Procnē**.

prognōstica, -ōrum *ntpl* weather signs.

prōgredior, -dī, -ssus *vi* to go forward, advance; to go out.

prōgressiō, -ōnis *f* advancing, increase; (*RHET*) climax.

prōgressus *ppa of* **prōgredior**.

prōgressus, -ūs *m* advance, progress; (*events*) march.

prōh *see* **prō** *interj*.

prohibeō, -ēre, -uī, -itum *vt* to hinder, prevent; to keep away, protect; to forbid.

prohibitiō, -ōnis *f* forbidding.

prōiciō, -icere, -iēcī, -iectum *vt* to throw down, fling forwards; to banish; (*building*) to make project; (*fig*) to discard, renounce; to forsake; (*words*) to blurt out; (*time*) to defer; **sē ~** rush forward, run into danger; to fall prostrate.

prōiectiō, -ōnis *f* forward stretch.

prōiectus *ppp of* **prōiciō** ♦ *adj* projecting, prominent; abject, useless; downcast; addicted (to).

prōiectus, -ūs *m* jutting out.

proinde, proin *adv* consequently, therefore;

just (as).

prōlābor, -bī, -psus vi to slide, move forward; to fall down; (fig) to go on, come to; to slip out; to fail, fall, sink into ruin.

prōlāpsiō, -ōnis f falling.

prōlāpsus ppa of **prōlābor.**

prōlātiō, -ōnis f extension; postponement; adducing.

prōlātō, -āre vt to extend; to postpone.

prōlātus ppp of **prōferō.**

prōlectō, -āre vt to entice.

prōlēs, -is f offspring child; descendants, race.

prōlētārius, -ī and iī m citizen of the lowest class.

prōliciō, -cere, -xī vt to entice.

prōlixē adv fully, copiously, willingly.

prōlixus adj long, wide, spreading; (person) obliging; (circs) favourable.

prōlogus, -ī m prologue.

prōloquor, -quī, -cūtus vt to speak out.

prōlubium, -ī and iī nt inclination.

prōlūdō, -dere, -sī, -sum vi to practise.

prōluō, -uere, -uī, -ūtum vt to wash out, wash away.

prōlūsiō, -ōnis f prelude.

prōluviēs, -ēī f flood; excrement.

prōmereō, -ēre, -uī; prōmereor, -ērī, -itus vt to deserve, earn.

prōmeritum, -ī nt desert, merit, guilt.

Promētheus, -eī and eos m demigod who stole fire from the gods.

Promētheūs adj see n.

prōminēns, -entis pres p of **prōmineō** ♦ adj projecting ♦ nt headland, spur.

prōmineō, -ēre, -uī vi to jut out, overhang; to extend.

prōmiscam, -ē, -uē adv indiscriminately.

prōmiscuus (prōmiscus) adj indiscriminate, in common; ordinary; open to all.

prōmīsī perf of **prōmittō.**

prōmissiō, -ōnis f promise.

prōmissor, -ōris m promiser.

prōmissum, -ī nt promise.

prōmissus ppp of **prōmittō** ♦ adj long.

prōmittō, -ittere, -īsī, -issum vt to let grow; to promise, give promise of.

prōmō, -ere, -psī, -ptum vt to bring out, produce; to disclose.

prōmont- etc see **prōmunt-.**

prōmōtus ppp of **prōmoveō** ♦ ntpl preferable things.

prōmoveō, -overe, -ōvī, -ōtum vt to move forward, advance; to enlarge; to postpone; to disclose.

prōmpsī perf of **prōmō.**

prōmptē adv readily; easily.

prōmptō, -āre vt to distribute.

prōmptū abl m: **in ~** at hand, in readiness; obvious, in evidence; easy.

prōmptus ppp of **prōmō** ♦ adj at hand, ready; prompt, resolute; easy.

prōmulgātiō, -ōnis f promulgating.

prōmulgō, -āre, -āvī, -ātum vt to make public, publish.

prōmulsis, -idis f hors d'oeuvre.

prōmunturium, -ī and iī nt headland, promontory, ridge.

prōmus, -ī m cellarer, butler.

prōmūtuus adj as a loan in advance.

prōnepōs, -ōtis m great-grandson.

pronoea, -ae f providence.

prōnōmen, -inis nt pronoun.

prōnuba, -ae f matron attending a bride.

prōnūntiātiō, -ōnis f declaration; (RHET) delivery; (logic) proposition.

prōnūntiātor, -ōris m narrator.

prōnūntiātum, -ātī nt proposition.

prōnūntiō, -āre, -āvī, -ātum vt to declare publicly, announce; to recite, deliver; to narrate; to nominate.

prōnurus, -ūs f granddaughter-in-law.

prōnus adj leaning forward; headlong; downwards; sloping, sinking; (fig) inclined, disposed, favourable; easy.

prooemium, -ī and iī nt prelude, preface.

propāgātiō, -ōnis f propagating; extension.

propāgātor, -ōris m enlarger.

propāgō, -āre, -āvī, -ātum vt to propagate; to extend; to prolong.

propāgō, -inis f (plant) layer, slip; (men) offspring, posterity.

prōpalam adv openly, known.

prōpatulum, -ī nt open space.

prōpatulus adj open.

prope adv (comp **propius,** superl **proximē**) near; nearly ♦ prep (with acc) near, not far from.

propediem adv very soon.

prōpellō, -ellere, -ulī, -ulsum vt to drive, push forward, impel; to drive away, keep off.

propemodum, -o adv almost.

prōpendeō, -endēre, -endī, -ēnsum vi to hang down; to preponderate; to be disposed (to).

prōpēnsē adv willingly.

prōpēnsiō, -ōnis f inclination.

prōpēnsus adj inclining; inclined, well-disposed; important.

properanter adv hastily, quickly.

properantia, -ae f haste.

properātiō, -ōnis f haste.

properātō adv quickly.

properātus adj speedy.

properē adv quickly.

properipēs, -edis adj swiftfooted.

properō, -āre, -āvī, -ātum vt to hasten, do with haste ♦ vi to make haste, hurry.

Propertius, -ī m Latin elegiac poet.

properus adj quick, hurrying.

prōpexus *adj* combed forward.
propīnō, -āre *vt* to drink as a toast; to pass on (a cup).
propinquitās, -ātis *f* nearness; relationship, friendship.
propinquō, -āre *vi* to approach ♦ *vt* to hasten.
propinquus *adj* near, neighbouring; related ♦ *m/f* relation ♦ *nt* neighbourhood.
propior, -ōris *adj* nearer; more closely related, more like; (*time*) more recent.
propitiō, -āre *vt* to appease.
propitius *adj* favourable, gracious.
propius *adv* nearer, more closely.
propōla, -ae *f* retailer.
prōpolluō, -ere *vt* to defile further.
prōpōnō, -ōnere, -osuī, -ositum *vt* to set forth, display; to publish, declare; to propose, resolve; to imagine; to expose; (*logic*) to state the first premise; **ante oculōs ~** picture to oneself.
Propontiacus *adj* see *n*.
Propontis, -idis and **idos** *f* Sea of Marmora.
prōporrō *adv* furthermore; utterly.
prōportiō, -ōnis *f* symmetry, analogy.
prōpositiō, -ōnis *f* purpose; theme; (*logic*) first premise.
prōpositum, -ī *nt* plan, purpose; theme; (*logic*) first premise.
prōpositus *ppp of* **prōpōnō**.
prōpraetor, -ōris *m* propraetor, governor; vice-praetor.
propriē *adv* properly, strictly; particularly.
proprietās, -ātis *f* peculiarity, property.
proprītim *adv* properly.
proprius *adj* one's own, peculiar; personal, characteristic; permanent; (*words*) literal, regular.
propter *adv* near by ♦ *prep* (*with acc*) near, beside; on account of; by means of.
proptereā *adv* therefore.
prōpudium, -ī and **iī** *nt* shameful act; villain.
prōpugnāculum, -ī *nt* bulwark, tower; defence.
prōpugnātiō, -ōnis *f* defence.
prōpugnātor, -ōris *m* defender, champion.
prōpugnō, -āre *vi* to make a sortie; to fight in defence.
prōpulsātiō, -ōnis *f* repulse.
prōpulsō, -āre, -āvī, -ātum *vt* to repel, avert.
prōpulsus *ppp of* **prōpellō**.
Propylaea, -ōrum *ntpl* gateway to the Acropolis of Athens.
prō quaestōre *m* proquaestor.
prōquam *conj* according as.
prōra, -ae *f* prow, bows; ship.
prōrēpō, -ere, -sī, -tum *vi* to crawl out.
prōrēta -ae *m* man at the prow.
prōreus, -eī *m* man at the prow.
prōripiō, -ipere, -ipuī, -eptum *vt* to drag out; to hurry away; **sē ~** rush out, run away.
prōrogātiō, -ōnis *f* extension; deferring.
prōrogō, -āre, -āvī, -ātum *vt* to extend, prolong, continue; to defer.

prōrsum *adv* forwards; absolutely.
prōrsus *adv* forwards; absolutely; in short.
prōrumpō, -umpere, -ūpī, -uptum *vt* to fling out; (*pass*) to rush forth ♦ *vi* to break out, burst forth.
prōruō, -ere, -ī, -tum *vt* to throw down, demolish ♦ *vi* to rush forth.
prōruptus *ppp of* **prōrumpō**.
prōsāpia, -ae *f* lineage.
proscaenium, -ī and **iī** *nt* stage.
proscindō, -ndere, -dī, -ssum *vt* to plough up; (*fig*) to revile.
prōscrībō, -bere, -psī, -ptum *vt* to publish in writing; to advertise; to confiscate; to proscribe, outlaw.
prōscrīptiō, -ōnis *f* advertisement; proscription.
prōscrīpturiō, -īre *vi* to want to have a proscription.
prōscrīptus *ppp of* **prōscrībō** ♦ *m* outlaw.
prōsecō, -āre, -uī, -tum *vt* to cut off (for sacrifice).
prōsēminō, -āre *vt* to scatter; to propagate.
prōsentiō, -entīre, -ēnsī *vt* to see beforehand.
prōsequor, -quī, -cūtus *vt* to attend, escort; to pursue, attack; to honour (with); (*words*) to proceed with, continue.
Proserpina, -ae *f* Proserpine (*daughter of Ceres and wife of Pluto*).
proseucha, -ae *f* place of prayer.
prōsiliō, -īre, -uī *vi* to jump up, spring forward; to burst out, spurt.
prōsocer, -ī *m* wife's grandfather.
prōspectō, -āre *vt* to look out at, view; to look forward to, await; (*place*) to look towards.
prōspectus *ppp of* **prōspiciō**.
prōspectus, -ūs *m* sight, view, prospect; gaze.
prōspeculor, -ārī *vi* to look out, reconnoitre ♦ *vt* to watch for.
prosper, prosperus *adj* favourable, successful.
prosperē *adv* see *adj*.
prosperitās, -ātis *f* good fortune.
prosperō, -āre *vt* to make successful, prosper.
prosperus *etc see* **prosper**.
prōspicientia, -ae *f* foresight.
prōspiciō, -icere, -exī, -ectum *vi* to look out, watch; to see to, take precautions ♦ *vt* to descry, watch for; to foresee; to provide; (*place*) to command a view of.
prōsternō, -ernere, -rāvī, -rātum *vt* to throw in front, prostrate; to overthrow, ruin; **sē ~** fall prostrate; to demean oneself.
prōstibulum, -ī *nt* prostitute.
prōstituō, -uere, -uī, -ūtum *vt* to put up for sale, prostitute.
prōstō, -āre, -itī *vi* to project; to be on sale; to prostitute oneself.
prōstrātus *ppp of* **prōsternō**.
prōsubigō, -ere *vt* to dig up.

prōsum, -desse, -fuī *vi* (*with dat*) to be useful to, benefit.

Prōtagorās, -ae *m* Greek sophist (*native of Abdera*).

prōtēctus *ppp of* **prōtegō.**

prōtegō, -egere, -ēxī, -ēctum *vt* to cover over, put a projecting roof on; (*fig*) to shield, protect.

prōtēlō, -āre *vt* to drive off.

prōtēlum, -ī *nt* team of oxen; (*fig*) succession.

prōtendō, -dere, -dī, -tum *vt* to stretch out, extend.

prōtentus *ppp of* **prōtendō.**

prōterō, -erere, -rīvī, -rītum *vt* to trample down, crush; to overthrow.

prōterreō, -ēre, -uī, -itum *vt* to scare away.

protervē *adv* insolently; boldly.

protervitās, -ātis *f* forwardness, insolence.

protervus *adj* forward, insolent, violent.

Prōtesilāēus *adj see n.*

Prōtesilāus, -ī *m* first Greek killed at Troy.

Prōteus, -eī *and* **eos** *m* seagod with power to assume many forms.

prothȳmē *adv* gladly.

prōtinam *adv* immediately.

prōtinus *adv* forward, onward; continuously; right away, forthwith.

prōtollō, -ere *vt* to stretch out; to put off.

prōtractus *ppp of* **prōtrahō.**

prōtrahō, -here, -xī, -ctum *vt* to draw on (to); to drag out; to bring to light, reveal.

prōtrītus *ppp of* **prōterō.**

prōtrūdō, -dere, -sī, -sum *vt* to thrust forward, push out; to postpone.

prōtulī *perf of* **prōferō.**

prōturbō, -āre, -āvī, -ātum *vt* to drive off; to overthrow.

prout *conj* according as.

prōvectus *ppp of* **prōvehō** ♦ *adj* advanced.

prōvehō, -here, -xī, -ctum *vt* to carry along, transport; to promote, advance, bring to; (*speech*) to prolong; (*pass*) to drive, ride, sail on.

prōveniō, -enīre, -ēnī, -entum *vi* to come out, appear; to arise, grow; to go on, prosper, succeed.

prōventus, -ūs *m* increase; result, success.

prōverbium, -ī *and* **iī** *nt* saying, proverb.

prōvidēns, -entis *pres p of* **prōvideō** ♦ *adj* prudent.

prōvidenter *adv* with foresight.

prōvidentia, -ae *f* foresight, forethought.

prōvideō, -idēre, -īdī, -īsum *vi* to see ahead; to take care, make provision ♦ *vt* to foresee; to look after, provide for; to obviate.

prōvidus *adj* foreseeing, cautious, prudent; provident.

prōvincia, -ae *f* sphere of action, duty, province.

prōvinciālis *adj* provincial ♦ *mpl* provincials.

prōvīsiō, -ōnis *f* foresight; precaution.

prōvīsō *adv* with forethought.

prōvīsō, -ere *vi* to go and see.

prōvīsor, -ōris *m* foreseer; provider.

prōvīsus *ppp of* **prōvideō.**

prōvīsus, -ūs *m* looking forward; foreseeing; providing providence.

prōvīvō, -vere, -xī *vi* to live on.

prōvocātiō, -ōnis *f* challenge; appeal.

prōvocātor, -ōris *m* kind of gladiator.

prōvocō, -āre, -āvī, -ātum *vt* to challenge, call out; to provoke; to bring about ♦ *vi* to appeal.

prōvolō, -āre *vi* to fly out, rush out.

prōvolvō, -vere, -vī, -ūtum *vt* to roll forward, tumble over; (*pass*) to fall down, humble oneself, be ruined; **sē ~** wallow.

prōvomō, -ere *vt* to belch forth.

proximē *adv* next, nearest; (*time*) just before *or* after; (*with acc*) next to, very close to, very like.

proximitās, -ātis *f* nearness; near relationship; similarity.

proximus *adj* nearest, next; (*time*) previous, last, following, next; most akin, most like ♦ *m* next of kin ♦ *nt* next door.

proxum *etc see* **proxim-.**

prūdēns, -entis *adj* foreseeing, aware; wise, prudent, circumspect; skilled, versed (in).

prūdenter *adv* prudently; skilfully.

prūdentia, -ae *f* prudence, discretion; knowledge.

pruīna, -ae *f* hoar frost.

pruīnōsus *adj* frosty.

prūna, -ae *f* live coal.

prūnitius *adj* of plum tree wood.

prūnum, -ī *nt* plum.

prūnus, -ī *f* plum tree.

prūriō, -īre *vi* to itch.

prytanēum, -ī *nt* Greek town hall.

prytanis, -is *m* Greek chief magistrate.

psallō, -ere *vi* to play the lyre *or* lute.

psaltērium, -ī *and* **iī** *nt* kind of lute.

psaltria, -ae *f* girl musician.

psecas, -adis *f* slave who perfumed the lady's hair.

psēphisma, -tis *nt* decree of the people.

Pseudocatō, -ōnis *m* sham Cato.

pseudomenos, -ī *m* sophistical argument.

pseudothyrum, -ī *nt* back door.

psithius *adj* psithian (*kind of Greek vine*).

psittacus, -ī *m* parrot.

psychomantēum (-īum), -ī *nt* place of necromancy.

-pte *enclitic* (*to pronouns*) self, own.

ptisanārium, -ī *and* **iī** *nt* gruel.

Ptolemaeēus, -us *adj see n.*

Ptolemaeus, -ī *m* Ptolemy (*name of Egyptian kings*).

pūbēns, -entis *adj* full-grown; (*plant*) juicy.

pūbertās, -ātis *f* manhood; signs of puberty.
pūbēs (pūber), -eris *adj* grown up, adult;
(*plant*) downy.
pūbēs, -is *f* hair at age of puberty; groin;
youth, men, people.
pūbēscō, -ēscere, -uī *vi* to grow to manhood,
become mature; to become clothed.
pūblicānus *adj* of public revenue ♦ *m* tax
farmer.
pūblicātiō, -ōnis *f* confiscation.
pūblicē *adv* by *or* for the State, at the public
expense; all together.
pūblicitus *adv* at the public expense; in
public.
pūblicō, -āre, -āvī, -ātum *vt* to confiscate; to
make public.
Pūblicola, -ae *m* P. Valerius (*an early Roman
consul*).
pūblicum, -ī *nt* State revenue; State territory;
public.
pūblicus *adj* of the State, public, common ♦ *m*
public official; **~a causa** criminal trial; **rēs ~a**
the State; **dē ~ō** at the public expense; **in ~ō**
in public.
Publius, -ī *m* Roman first name.
pudendus *adj* shameful.
pudēns, -entis *adj* bashful, modest.
pudenter *adv* modestly.
pudet, -ēre, -uit *and* **itum est** *vt* (*impers*) to
shame, be ashamed.
pudibundus *adj* modest.
pudīcē *adv see adj.*
pudīcitia, -ae *f* modesty, chastity.
pudīcus *adj* modest, chaste.
pudor, -ōris *m* shame, modesty, sense of
honour; disgrace.
puella, -ae *f* girl; sweetheart, young wife.
puellāris *adj* girlish, youthful.
puellula, -ae *f* little girl.
puellus, -ī *m* little boy.
puer, -ī *m* boy, child; son; slave.
puerīlis *adj* boyish, child's; childish, trivial.
puerīliter *adv* like a child; childishly.
pueritia, -ae *f* childhood, youth.
puerperium, -ī *and* **iī** *nt* childbirth.
puerperus *adj* to help childbirth ♦ *f* woman in
labour.
puertia *etc see* **pueritia.**
puerulus, -ī *m* little boy, slave.
pugil, -is *m* boxer.
pugilātiō, -iōnis *f*, **-us, -ūs** *m* boxing.
pugillāris *adj* that can be held in the hand ♦
mpl, ntpl writing tablets.
pugillātōrius *adj:* **follis ~** punchball.
pugiō, -ōnis *m* dirk, dagger.
pugiunculus, -ī *m* small dagger.
pugna, -ae *f* fight, battle.
pugnācitās, -ātis *f* fondness for a fight.
pugnāciter *adv* aggressively.
pugnāculum, -ī *nt* fortress.
pugnātor, -ōris *m* fighter.
pugnāx, -ācis *adj* fond of a fight, aggressive;
obstinate.

pugneus *adj* with the fist.
pugnō, -āre, -āvī, -ātum *vi* to fight; to
disagree; to struggle; **sēcum ~** be
inconsistent; **~ātum est** the battle was
fought.
pugnus, -ī *m* fist.
pulchellus *adj* pretty little.
pulcher, -rī *adj* beautiful, handsome; fine,
glorious.
pulchrē *adv* excellently; well done!
pulchritūdō, -inis *f* beauty, excellence.
pūlēium, pūlegium, -ī *and* **iī** *nt* pennyroyal.
pūlex, -icis *m* flea.
pullārius, -ī *and* **iī** *m* keeper of the sacred
chickens.
pullātus *adj* dressed in black.
pullulō, -āre *vi* to sprout.
pullus, -ī *m* young (of animals), chicken.
pullus *adj* dark-grey; mournful ♦ *nt* dark grey
clothes.
pulmentārium, -ārī *and* **-āriī, -um, -ī** *nt*
relish; food.
pulmō, -ōnis *m* lung.
pulmōneus *adj* of the lungs.
pulpa, -ae *f* fleshy part.
pulpāmentum, -ī *nt* tit-bits.
pulpitum, -ī *nt* platform, stage.
puls, pultis *f* porridge.
pulsātiō, -ōnis *f* beating.
pulsō, -āre, -āvī, -ātum *vt* to batter, knock,
strike.
pulsus *ppp of* **pellō.**
pulsus, -ūs *m* push, beat, blow; impulse.
pultiphagus, -ī *m* porridge eater.
pultō, -āre *vt* to beat, knock at.
pulvereus *adj* of dust, dusty, fine as dust;
raising dust.
pulverulentus *adj* dusty; laborious.
pulvillus, -ī *m* small cushion.
pulvīnar, -āris *nt* sacred couch; seat of
honour.
pulvīnus, -ī *m* cushion, pillow.
pulvis, -eris *m* dust, powder; arena; effort.
pulvisculus, -ī *m* fine dust.
pūmex, -icis *m* pumice stone; stone, rock.
pūmiceus *adj* of soft stone.
pūmicō, -āre *vt* to smooth with pumice stone.
pūmiliō, -ōnis *mlf* dwarf, pygmy.
pūnctim *adv* with the point.
pūnctum, -ī *nt* point, dot; vote; (*time*) moment;
(*speech*) short section.
pūnctus *ppp of* **pungō.**
pungō, -ere, pupugī, pūnctum *vt* to prick,
sting, pierce; (*fig*) to vex.
Pūnicānus *adj* in the Carthaginian style.
Pūnicē *adv* in Punic.
pūniceus *adj* reddish, purple.
Pūnicum, -ī *nt* pomegranate.
Pūnicus *adj* Punic, Carthaginian; purple-red.
pūniō (poeniō), -īre; -ior, -īrī *vt* to punish; to
avenge.
pūnītor, -ōris *m* avenger.
pūpa, -ae *f* doll.

pūpilla, -ae *f* ward; (*eye*) pupil.
pūpillāris *adj* of a ward, of an orphan.
pūpillus, -ī *m* orphan, ward.
puppis, -is *f* after part of a ship, stern; ship.
pupugī *perf of* **pungō**.
pūpula, -ae *f* (*eye*) pupil.
pūpulus, -ī *m* little boy.
pūrē *adv* cleanly, brightly; plainly, simply,
   purely, chastely.
pūrgāmen, -inis *nt* sweepings, dirt; means of
   expiation.
pūrgāmentum, -ī *nt* refuse, dirt.
pūrgātiō, -ōnis *f* purging; justification.
pūrgō, -āre, -āvī, -ātum *vt* to cleanse, purge,
   clear away; to exculpate, justify; to purify.
pūriter *adv* cleanly, purely.
purpura, -ae *f* purple-fish, purple; purple
   cloth; finery, royalty.
purpurātus *adj* wearing purple ♦ *m* courtier.
purpureus *adj* red, purple, black; wearing
   purple; bright, radiant.
purpurissum, -ī *nt* kind of rouge.
pūrus *adj* clear, unadulterated, free from
   obstruction *or* admixture; pure, clean; plain,
   unadorned; (*moral*) pure, chaste ♦ *nt* clear
   sky.
pūs, pūris *nt* pus; (*fig*) malice.
pusillus *adj* very little; petty, paltry.
pūsiō, -ōnis *m* little boy.
pūstula, -ae *f* pimple, blister.
putāmen, -inis *nt* peeling, shell, husk.
putātiō, -ōnis *f* pruning.
putātor, -ōris *m* pruner.
puteal, -ālis *nt* low wall round a well *or* sacred
   place.
puteālis *adj* well- (*in cpds*).
pūteō, -ēre *vi* to stink.
Puteolānus *adj see n.*
Puteolī, -ōrum *mpl town on the Campanian
   coast.*
puter, putris, -ris *adj* rotten, decaying;
   crumbling, flabby.
putēscō, -ēscere, -uī *vi* to become rotten.
puteus, -ī *m* well; pit.
pūtidē *adv see* **pūtidus**.
pūtidiusculus *adj* somewhat nauseating.
pūtidus *adj* rotten, stinking; (*speech*) affected,
   nauseating.
putō, -āre, -āvī, -ātum *vt* to think, suppose;
   to think over; to reckon, count; (*money*) to
   settle; (*tree*) to prune.
pūtor, -ōris *m* stench.
putrefaciō, -facere, -fēcī, -factum *vt* to
   make rotten; to make crumble.
putrēscō, -ere *vi* to rot, moulder.
putridus *adj* rotten, decayed; withered.
putris *etc see* **puter**.
putus *adj* perfectly pure.
putus, -ī *m* boy.
pycta, -ēs, -ae *m* boxer.

Pydna, -ae *f town in Macedonia.*
Pydnaeus *adj see n.*
pȳga, -ae *f* buttocks.
Pygmaeus *adj* Pygmy.
Pyladēs, -ae and is *m friend of Orestes.*
Pyladēus *adj see n.*
Pylae, -ārum *fpl* Thermopylae.
Pylaicus *adj see n.*
Pylius *adj see n.*
Pylos, -ī *f Pylus (Peloponnesian town, home of
   Nestor).*
pyra, -ae *f* funeral pyre.
Pȳramaeus *adj see* **Pȳramus**.
pȳramis, -idis *f* pyramid.
Pȳramus, -ī *m lover of Thisbe.*
Pȳrēnē, -ēs *f* Pyrenees.
pyrethrum, -ī *nt* Spanish camomile.
Pyrgēnsis *adj see* **Pyrgī**.
Pyrgī, -ōrum *mpl ancient town in Etruria.*
pyrōpus, -ī *m* bronze.
Pyrrha, -ae and ē, -ēs *f wife of Deucalion.*
Pyrrhaeus *adj see n.*
Pyrrhō, -ōnis *m Greek philosopher (founder of
   the Sceptics).*
Pyrrhōnēus *adj see n.*
Pyrrhus, -ī *m son of Achilles; king of Epirus,
   enemy of Rome.*
Pȳthagorās, -ae *m Greek philosopher who
   founded a school in S. Italy.*
Pȳthagorēus, -icus *adj* Pythagorean.
Pȳthius, -icus *adj* Pythian, Delphic ♦ *m* Apollo
   ♦ *f* priestess of Apollo ♦ *ntpl* Pythian Games.
Pȳthō, -ūs *f* Delphi.
Pȳthōn, -ōnis *m serpent killed by Apollo.*
pȳtisma, -tis *nt* what is spit out.
pȳtissō, -āre *vi* to spit out wine.
pyxis, -dis *f* small box, toilet box.

Q, q

quā *adv* where, which way; whereby; as far as;
   partly ... partly.
quācumque *adv* wherever; anyhow.
quādam: ~ tenus *adv* only so far.
quadra, -ae *f* square; morsel; table.
quadrāgēnī, -ōrum *adj* forty each.
quadrāgēsimus *adj* fortieth ♦ *f* 2 ½ per cent
   tax.
quadrāgiēns, -ēs *adv* forty times.
quadrāgintā *num* forty.
quadrāns, -antis *m* quarter; (*coin*) quarter as.
quadrantārius *adj* of a quarter.

Noun declensions and verb conjugations are shown on pp xiii to xxv. The present infinitive ending of a verb shows
to which conjugation it belongs: **-āre** = 1st; **-ēre** = 2nd; **-ere** = 3rd and **-īre** = 4th. Irregular verbs are shown on p xxvi

quadrātum, -ī *nt* square; (*ASTRO*) quadrature.
quadrātus *ppp of* **quadrō** ♦ *adj* square; **~ō agmine** in battle order.
quadriduum, -ī *nt* four days.
quadriennium, -ī *and* **iī** *nt* four years.
quadrifāriam *adv* in four parts.
quadrifidus *adj* split in four.
quadrīgae, -ārum *fpl* team of four; chariot.
quadrīgārius, -ī *and* **iī** *m* chariot racer.
quadrīgātus *adj* stamped with a chariot.
quadrīgulae, -ārum *fpl* little four horse team.
quadriiugī, -ōrum *mpl* team of four.
quadriiugis, -us *adj* of a team of four.
quadrilībris *adj* weighing four pounds.
quadrimulus *adj* four years old.
quadrīmus *adj* four years old.
quadringēnārius *adj* of four hundred each.
quadringēnī, -ōrum *adj* four hundred each.
quadringentēsimus *adj* four-hundredth.
quadringentī, -ōrum *num* four hundred.
quadringentiēns, -ēs *adv* four hundred times.
quadripertītus *adj* fourfold.
quadrirēmis, -is *f* quadrireme.
quadrivium, -ī *and* **iī** *nt* crossroads.
quadrō, -āre *vt* to make square; to complete ♦ *vi* to square, fit, agree.
quadrum, -i *nt* square.
quadrupedāns, -antis *adj* galloping.
quadrupēs, -edis *adj* four-footed, on all fours ♦ *m/f* quadruped.
quadruplātor, -ōris *m* informer, twister.
quadruplex, -icis *adj* four-fold.
quadruplum, -ī *nt* four times as much.
quaeritō, -āre *vt* to search diligently for; to earn (a living); to keep on asking.
quaerō, -rere, -sīvī *and* **siī, -sītum** *vt* to look for, search for; to seek, try to get; to acquire, earn; (*plan*) to think out, work out; (*question*) to ask, make inquiries; (*law*) to investigate; (*with infin*) to try, wish; **quid ~ris?** in short; **sī ~ris/~rimus** to tell the truth.
quaesītiō, -ōnis *f* inquisition.
quaesītor, -ōris *m* investigator, judge.
quaesītus *ppp of* **quaerō** ♦ *adj* special; far-fetched ♦ *nt* question ♦ *ntpl* gains.
quaesīvī *perf of* **quaerō**.
quaesō, -ere *vt* to ask, beg.
quaesticulus, -ī *m* slight profit.
quaestiō, -ōnis *f* seeking, questioning; investigation, research; criminal trial; court; **servum in ~ōnem ferre** take a slave for questioning by torture; **~ōnēs perpetuae** standing courts.
quaestiuncula, -ae *f* trifling question.
quaestor, -ōris *m* quaestor, treasury official.
quaestōrius *adj* of a quaestor ♦ *m* ex-quaestor ♦ *nt* quaestor's tent or residence.
quaestuōsus *adj* lucrative, productive; money-making; wealthy.
quaestūra, -ae *f* quaestorship; public money.
quaestus, -ūs *m* profit, advantage; money-making, occupation; **~uī habēre** make money

out of; **~um facere** make a living.
quālibet *adv* anywhere; anyhow.
quālis *adj* (*interrog*) what kind of?; (*relat*) such as, even as.
quāliscumque *adj* of whatever kind; any, whatever.
qualiscunque *adj* = **qualiscumque**.
quālitās, -ātis *f* quality, nature.
quāliter *adv* just as.
quālubet *adv* anywhere; anyhow.
quālus, -ī *m* wicker basket.
quam *adv* (*interrog, excl*) how?, how much?; (*comparison*) as, than; (*with superl*) as ... as possible; (*emphatic*) very; **dīmidium ~ quod** half of what; **quīntō diē ~** four days after.
quamdiū *adv* how long?; as long as.
quamlibet, quamlubet *adv* as much as you like, however.
quamobrem *adv* (*interrog*) why?; (*relat*) why ♦ *conj* therefore.
quamquam *conj* although; and yet.
quamvīs *adv* however, ever so ♦ *conj* however much, although.
quānam *adv* what way.
quandō *adv* (*interrog*) when?; (*relat*) when; (*with sī, nē, num*) ever ♦ *conj* when; since.
quandōcumque, quandocunque *adv* whenever, as often as; some day.
quandōque *adv* whenever; some day ♦ *conj* seeing that.
quandō quidem *conj* seeing that, since.
quanquam *etc see* **quamquam**.
quantillus *adj* how little, how much.
quantopere *adv* how much; (*after* **tantopere**) as.
quantulus *adj* how little, how small.
quantuluscumque *adj* however small, however trifling.
quantum *adv* how much; as much as; **~cumque** as much as ever; **~libet** however much; **~vīs** as much as you like; although.
quantus *adj* how great; so great as, such as; **~ī** how dear, how highly; **~ō** (*with compar*) how much; the; **in ~um** as far as.
quantuscumque *adj* however great, whatever size.
quantuslibet *adj* as great as you like.
quantus quantus *adj* however great.
quantusvīs *adj* however great.
quāpropter *adv* why; and therefore.
quāquā *adv* whatever way.
quārē *adv* how, why; whereby; and therefore.
quartadecumānī, -ōrum *mpl* men of the fourteenth legion.
quartānus *adj* every four days ♦ *f* quartan fever ♦ *mpl* men of the fourth legion.
quartārius, -ī *and* **iī** *m* quarter pint.
quartus *adj* fourth; **quartum/quartō** for the fourth time.
quartusdecimus *adj* fourteenth.
quasi *adv* as if; as it were; (*numbers*) about.
quasillus, -ī *m*, **-um, -ī** *nt* wool basket.
quassātiō, -ōnis *f* shaking.

quassō, -āre, -āvī, -ātum *vt* to shake, toss; to shatter, damage.
quassus *ppp of* **quatiō ♦** *adj* broken.
quatefaciō, -facere, -fēcī *vt* to shake, give a jolt to.
quātenus *adv* (*interrog*) how far?; how long?; (*relat*) as far as; in so far as, since.
quater *adv* four times; ~ **deciēs** fourteen times.
quaternī, -ōrum *adj* four each, in fours.
quatiō, -tere, -ssum *vt* to shake, disturb, brandish; to strike, shatter; (*fig*) to agitate, harass.
quattuor *num* four.
quattuordecim *num* fourteen.
quattuorvirātus, -ūs *m* membership of quattuorviri.
quattuorvirī, -ōrum *mpl* board of four officials.
-que *conj* and; both . . . and; (*after neg*) but.
quemadmodum *adv* (*interrog*) how?; (*relat*) just as.
queō, -īre, -īvī *and* **iī, -itum** *vi* to be able, can.
quercētum, -ī *nt* oak forest.
querceus *adj* of oak.
quercus, -ūs *f* oak; garland of oak leaves; acorn.
querēla, querella, -ae *f* complaint; plaintive sound.
queribundus *adj* complaining.
querimōnia, -ae *f* complaint; elegy.
queritor, -ārī *vi* to complain much.
quernus *adj* oak- (*in cpds*).
queror, -rī, -stus *vt, vi* to complain, lament; (*birds*) to sing.
querquetulānus *adj* of oakwoods.
querulus *adj* complaining; plaintive, warbling.
questus *ppa of* **queror.**
questus, -ūs *m* complaint, lament.
quī, quae, quod *pron* (*interrog*) what?, which?; (*relat*) who, which, that; what; and this, he, etc.; (*with* **sī, nisi, nē, num**) any.
quī *adv* (*interrog*) how?; (*relat*) with which, whereby; (*indef*) somehow; (*excl*) indeed.
quia *conj* because; ~**nam** why?
quicquam *nt see* **quisquam.**
quicque *nt see* **quisque.**
quicquid *nt see* **quisquis.**
quīcum with whom, with which.
quīcumque, quīcunque *pron* whoever, whatever, all that; every possible.
quid *nt see* **quis ♦** *adv* why?
quīdam, quaedam, quoddam *pron* a certain, a sort of, a . . . .
quiddam *nt* something.
quidem *adv* (*emphatic*) in fact; (*qualifying*) at any rate; (*conceding*) it is true; (*alluding*) for instance; **nē . . . ~** not even.
quidlibet *nt* anything.

quidnam *nt see* **quisnam.**
quidnī *adv* why not?
quidpiam *nt* = **quispiam.**
quidquam *nt* = **quisquam.**
quidquid *nt* = **quisquis.**
quiēs, -ētis *f* rest, peace, quiet; sleep, dream, death; neutrality; lair.
quiēscō, -scere, -vī, -tum *vi* to rest, keep quiet; to be at peace, keep neutral; to sleep; (*with acc and infin*) to stand by and see; (*with infin*) to cease.
quiētē *adv* peacefully, quietly.
quiētus *ppa of* **quiēscō ♦** *adj* at rest; peaceful, neutral; calm, quiet, asleep.
quīlibet, quaelibet, quodlibet *pron* any, anyone at all.
quīn *adv* (*interrog*) why not?; (*correcting*) indeed, rather **♦** *conj* who not; but that, but, without; (*preventing*) from; (*doubting*) that.
quīnam, quaenam, quodnam *pron* which?, what?
Quīnct- *etc see* **Quīnt-.**
quīncūnx, -ūncis *m* five-twelfths; number five on a dice; **in ~ūncem dispositī** arranged in oblique lines.
quīndeciēns, -ēs *adv* fifteen times.
quīndecim *num* fifteen; ~ **prīmī** fifteen chief magistrates.
quīndecimvirālis *adj* of the council of fifteen.
quīndecimvirī, -ōrum *mpl* council of fifteen.
quīngēnī, -ōrum *adj* five hundred each.
quīngentēsimus *adj* five-hundredth.
quīngentī, -ōrum *num* five hundred.
quīngentiēns, -ēs *adv* five hundred times.
quīnī, -ōrum *adj* five each; five; ~ **dēnī** fifteen each; ~ **vīcēnī** twenty-five each.
quīnquāgēnī, -ōrum *adj* fifty each.
quīnquāgēsimus *adj* fiftieth **♦** *f* 2 per cent tax.
quīnquāgintā *num* fifty.
Quīnquātria, -iōrum *and* **ium** *ntpl festival of Minerva.*
Quīnquātrūs, -uum *fpl festival of Minerva.*
quīnque *num* five.
quīnquennālis *adj* quinquennial; lasting five years.
quīnquennis *adj* five years old; quinquennial.
quīnquennium, -ī *and* **iī** *nt* five years.
quīnquepartītus *adj* fivefold.
quīnqueprīmī, -ōrum *mpl* five leading men.
quīnquerēmis *adj* five-banked **♦** *f* quinquereme.
quīnquevirātus, -ūs *m* membership of the board of five.
quīnquevirī, -ōrum *mpl* board of five.
quīnquiēns, -ēs *adv* five times.
quīnquiplicō, -āre *vt* to multiply by five.
quīntadecimānī, -ōrum *mpl* men of the fifteenth legion.
quīntānus *adj* of the fifth **♦** *f street in a camp*

between the 5th and 6th maniples ♦ *mpl* men of
the fifth legion.
Quīntiliānus, -ī *m* Quintilian (*famous teacher
of rhetoric in Rome*).
Quīntīlis *adj* of July.
quīntum, -ō *adv* for the fifth time.
Quīntus, -ī *m* Roman first name.
quīntus *adj* fifth.
quīntusdecimus *adj* fifteenth.
quippe *adv* (*affirming*) certainly, of course ♦
conj (*explaining*) for in fact, because, since; ~
quī since I, he *etc*.
quippiam *etc see* **quispiam**.
quippinī *adv* certainly.
Quirīnālis *adj* of Romulus; Quirinal (hill).
Quirīnus, -ī *m* Romulus ♦ *adj* of Romulus.
Quirīs, -ītis *m* inhabitant of Cures; Roman
citizen; citizen.
quirītātiō, -ōnis *f* shriek.
Quirītēs *pl* inhabitants of Cures; Roman
citizens.
quirītō, -āre *vi* to cry out, wail.
quis, quid *pron* who?, what?; (*indef*) anyone,
anything.
quīs *poetic form of* **quibus**.
quisnam, quaenam, quidnam *pron* who?,
what?
quispiam, quaepiam, quodpiam *and*
quidpiam *pron* some, some one, something.
quisquam, quaequam, quicquam *and*
quidquam *pron* any, anyone, anything; **nec** ~
and no one.
quisque, quaeque, quodque *pron* each,
every, every one; **quidque, quicque**
everything; **decimus** ~ every tenth; **optimus**
~ all the best; **prīmus** ~ the first possible.
quisquiliae, -ārum *fpl* refuse, rubbish.
quisquis, quaequae, quodquod, quidquid
and **quicquid** *pron* whoever, whatever, all.
quīvīs, quaevīs, quodvīs, quidvīs *pron* any
you please, anyone, anything.
quīvīscumque, quaevīscumque,
quodvīscumque *pron* any whatsoever.
quō *adv* (*interrog*) where?; whither?; for what
purpose?, what for?; (*relat*) where, to which
(place), to whom; (*with compar*) the (more);
(*with sī*) anywhere ♦ *conj* (*with subj*) in order
that; **nōn** ~ not that.
quoad *adv* how far?; how long? ♦ *conj* as far as,
as long as; until.
quōcircā *conj* therefore.
quōcumque *adv* whithersoever.
quod *conj* as for, in that, that; because; why; ~
sī but if.
quōdam modo *adv* in a way.
quoi, quōius *old forms of* **cui, cūius**.
quōlibet *adv* anywhere, in any direction.
quom *etc see* **cum** *conj*.
quōminus *conj* that not; (*preventing*) from.
quōmodo *adv* (*interrog*) how?; (*relat*) just as;
~**cumque** howsoever; ~**nam** how?
quōnam *adv* where, where to?
quondam *adv* once, formerly; sometimes;

(*fut*) one day.
quōniam *conj* since, seeing that.
quōpiam *adv* anywhere.
quōquam *adv* anywhere.
quoque *adv* also, too.
quōquō *adv* to whatever place, wherever.
quōquō modo *adv* howsoever.
quōquō versus, -um *adv* in every direction.
quōrsus, quōrsum *adv* where to?, in what
direction?, what for?, to what end?
quot *adj* how many?; as many as, every.
quotannīs *adv* every year.
quotcumque *adj* however many.
quotēnī, -ōrum *adj* how many.
quotīd- *etc see* **cottīd-**.
quotiēns, -ēs *adv* how often?; (*relat*) as often
as.
quotiēnscumque *adv* however often.
quotquot *adj* however many.
quotumus *adj* which number?, what date?.
quotus *adj* what number, how many; ~
quisque how few; **~a hōra** what time.
quotuscumque *adj* whatever number,
however big.
quōūsque *adv* how long, till when; how far.
quōvīs *adv* anywhere.
quum *etc see* **cum** *conj*.

R, r

rabidē *adv* furiously.
rabidus *adj* raving, mad; impetuous.
rabiēs, -em, -ē *f* madness, rage, fury.
rabiō, -ere *vi* to rave.
rabiōsē *adv* wildly.
rabiōsulus *adj* somewhat rabid.
rabiōsus *adj* furious, mad.
rabula, -ae *m* wrangling lawyer.
racēmifer, -ī *adj* clustered.
racēmus, -ī *m* stalk of a cluster; bunch of
grapes; grape.
radiātus *adj* radiant.
rādīcitus *adv* by the roots; utterly.
rādīcula, -ae *f* small root.
radiō, -āre *vt* to irradiate ♦ *vi* to radiate, shine.
radius, -i *and* **ī ī** *m* stick, rod; (*light*) beam, ray;
(*loom*) shuttle; (MATH) rod for drawing
figures, radius of a circle; (*plant*) long olive;
(*wheel*) spoke.
rādīx, -īcis *f* root; radish; (*hill*) foot; (*fig*)
foundation, origin.
rādō, -dere, -sī, -sum *vt* to scrape, shave,
scratch; to erase; to touch in passing, graze,
pass along.
raeda, -ae *f* four-wheeled carriage.

raedārius, -ī *and* **iī** *m* driver.
Raetī, -ōrum *mpl* Alpine people between Italy and Germany.
Raetia, -iae *f* country of the Raetī.
Raeticus *and* **ius** *and* **us** *adj see n.*
rāmālia, -ium *ntpl* twigs, brushwood.
rāmentum, -ī *nt* shavings, chips.
rāmeus *adj* of branches.
rāmex, -icis *m* rupture, blood vessels of the lungs.
Ramnēnsēs, Ramnēs, -ium *mpl* one of the original Roman tribes; a century of equites.
rāmōsus *adj* branching.
rāmulus, -ī *m* twig, sprig.
rāmus, -ī *m* branch, bough.
rāna, -ae *f* frog; frogfish.
rancēns, -entis *adj* putrid.
rancidulus *adj* rancid.
rancidus *adj* rank, rancid; disgusting.
rānunculus, -ī *m* tadpole.
rapācida, -ae *m* son of a thief.
rapācitās, -ātis *f* greed.
rapāx, -ācis *adj* greedy, grasping, ravenous.
raphanus, -ī *m* radish.
rapidē *adv* swiftly, hurriedly.
rapiditās, -ātis *f* rapidity.
rapidus *adj* tearing, devouring; swift, rapid; hasty, impetuous.
rapīna, -ae *f* pillage, robbery; booty, prey.
rapiō, -ere, -uī, -tum *vt* to tear, snatch, carry off; to seize, plunder; to hurry, seize quickly.
raptim *adv* hastily, violently.
raptiō, -ōnis *f* abduction.
raptō, -āre, -āvī, -ātum *vt* to seize and carry off, drag away, move quickly; to plunder, lay waste; (*passion*) to agitate.
raptor, -ōris *m* plunderer, robber, ravisher.
raptus *ppp of* **rapiō** ♦ *nt* plunder.
raptus, -ūs *m* carrying off, abduction; plundering.
rāpulum, -ī *nt* small turnip.
rāpum, -ī *nt* turnip.
rārēfaciō, -facere, -fēcī, -factum (*pass* -fīō, -fierī) *vt* to rarefy.
rārēscō, -ere *vi* to become rarefied, grow thin; to open out.
rāritās, -ātis *f* porousness, open texture; thinness, fewness.
rārō, -ē *adv* seldom.
rārus *adj* porous, open in texture; thin, scanty; scattered, straggling, here and there; (*MIL*) in open order; few, infrequent; uncommon, rare.
rāsī *perf of* **rādō.**
rāsilis *adj* smooth, polished.
rāstrum, -ī *nt* hoe, mattock.
rāsus *ppp of* **rādō.**
ratiō, -ōnis *f* 1. (*reckoning of*) account, calculation; list, register; affair, business.

2. (*relation*) respect, consideration; procedure, method, system, way, kind.
3. (*reason*) reasoning, thought; cause, motive; science, knowledge, philosophy; ~ atque ūsus theory and practice; ~ est it is reasonable; Stōicōrum ~ Stoicism; ~ōnem dūcere, inīre calculate; ~ōnem habēre take account of, have to do with, consider; ~ōnem reddere give an account of; cum ~ōne reasonably; meae ~ōnēs my interests; ā ~ōnibus accountant.
ratiōcinātiō, -ōnis *f* reasoning; syllogism.
ratiōcinātīvus *adj* syllogistic.
ratiōcinātor, -ōris *m* accountant.
ratiōcinor, -ārī, -ātus *vt, vi* to calculate; to consider; to argue, infer.
ratiōnālis *adj* rational; syllogistic.
ratis, -is *f* raft; boat.
ratiuncula, -ae *f* small calculation; slight reason; petty syllogism.
ratus *ppa of* **reor** ♦ *adj* fixed, settled, sure; valid; **prō ~ā (parte)** proportionally; **~um dūcere, facere, habēre** ratify.
raucisonus *adj* hoarse.
raucus *adj* hoarse; harsh, strident.
raudus, -eris *nt* copper coin.
raudusculum, -ī *nt* bit of money.
Ravenna, -ae *f* port in N.E. Italy.
Ravennās, -ātis *adj see n.*
rāvis, -im *f* hoarseness.
rāvus *adj* grey, tawny.
rea, -ae *f* defendant, culprit.
rēapse *adv* in fact, actually.
Reāte, -is *nt* ancient Sabine town.
Reātīnus *adj see n.*
rebellātiō, -ōnis *f* revolt.
rebellātrīx, -īcis *f* rebellious.
rebelliō, -ōnis *f* revolt.
rebellis *adj* rebellious ♦ *mpl* rebels.
rebellium, -ī *and* **iī** *nt* revolt.
rebellō, -āre *vi* to revolt.
rebītō, -ere *vi* to return.
reboō, -āre *vi* to re-echo ♦ *vt* to make resound.
recalcitrō, -āre *vi* to kick back.
recaleō, -ēre *vi* to be warm again.
recalēscō, -ere *vi* to grow warm again.
recalfaciō, -facere, -fēcī *vt* to warm again.
recalvus *adj* bald in front.
recandēscō, -ēscere, -uī *vi* to whiten (*in response to*); to glow.
recantō, -āre, -āvī, -ātum *vt* to recant; to charm away.
reccidī *perf of* **recidō.**
recēdō, -ēdere, -essī, -essum *vi* to move back, withdraw, depart; (*place*) to recede; (*head*) to be severed.
recellō, -ere *vi* to spring back.
recēns, -entis *adj* fresh, young, recent; (*writer*) modern; (*with ab*) immediately after ♦ *adv* newly, just.

Noun declensions and verb conjugations are shown on pp xiii to xxv. The present infinitive ending of a verb shows to which conjugation it belongs: **-āre** = 1st; **-ēre** = 2nd; **-ere** = 3rd and **-īre** = 4th. Irregular verbs are shown on p xxvi

recēnseō, -ēre, -uī, -um _vt_ to count; to review.

recēnsiō, -ōnis _f_ revision.

recēnsus _ppp of_ **recēnseō**.

recēpī _perf of_ **recipiō**.

receptāculum, -ī _nt_ receptacle, reservoir; refuge, shelter.

receptō, -āre _vt_ to take back; to admit, harbour; to tug hard at.

receptor, -ōris _m_ (male) receiver, shelterer.

receptrīx, -īcis _f_ (female) receiver, shelterer.

receptum, -ī _nt_ obligation.

receptus _ppp of_ **recipiō**.

receptus, -ūs _m_ withdrawal; retreat; return; refuge; **~uī canere** sound the retreat.

recessī _perf of_ **recēdō**.

recessim _adv_ backwards.

recessus, -ūs _m_ retreat, departure; recess, secluded spot; (_tide_) ebb.

recidīvus _adj_ resurrected; recurring.

recidō, -idere, -cidī, -āsum _vi_ to fall back; to recoil, relapse; (_fig_) to fall, descend.

recīdō, -dere, -dī, -sum _vt_ to cut back, cut off.

recingō, -gere, -ctum _vt_ to ungird, loose.

recinō, -ere _vt, vi_ to re-echo, repeat; to sound a warning.

reciper- _etc see_ **recuper-**.

recipiō, -ipere, -ēpī, -eptum _vt_ to take back, retake; to get back, regain, rescue; to accept, admit; (_MIL_) to occupy; (_duty_) to undertake; (_promise_) to pledge, guarantee; **sē ~** withdraw, retreat; **nōmen ~** receive notice of a prosecution.

reciprocō, -āre _vt_ to move to and fro; (_ship_) to bring round to another tack; (_proposition_) to reverse ♦ _vi_ (_tide_) to rise and fall.

reciprocus _adj_ ebbing.

recīsus _ppp of_ **recīdō**.

recitātiō, -ōnis _f_ reading aloud, recital.

recitātor, -ōris _m_ reader, reciter.

recitō, -āre, -āvī, -ātum _vt_ to read out, recite.

reclāmātiō, -ōnis _f_ outcry (_of disapproval_).

reclāmitō, -āre _vi_ to cry out against.

reclāmō, -āre _vi_ to cry out, protest; to reverberate.

reclīnis _adj_ leaning back.

reclīnō, -āre, -āvī, -ātum _vt_ to lean back.

reclūdō, -dere, -sī, -sum _vt_ to open up; to disclose.

reclūsus _ppp of_ **reclūdō**.

recoctus _ppp of_ **recoquō**.

recōgitō, -āre _vi_ to think over, reflect.

recognitiō, -ōnis _f_ review.

recognōscō, -ōscere, -ōvī, -itum _vt_ to recollect; to examine, review.

recolligō, -igere, -ēgī, -ēctum _vt_ to gather up; (_fig_) to recover, reconcile.

recolō, -olere, -oluī, -ultum _vt_ to recultivate; to resume; to reflect on, contemplate; to revisit.

recommīnīscor, -ī _vi_ to recollect.

recompositus _adj_ rearranged.

reconciliātiō, -ōnis _f_ restoration, reconciliation.

reconciliō, -āre, -āvī, -ātum _vt_ to win back again, restore, reconcile.

reconcinnō, -āre _vt_ to repair.

reconditus _ppp of_ **recondō** ♦ _adj_ hidden, secluded; abstruse, profound; (_disposition_) reserved.

recondō, -ere, -idī, -itum _vt_ to store away, stow; to hide away, bury.

reconflō, -āre _vt_ to rekindle.

recoquō, -quere, -xī, -ctum _vt_ to cook again, boil again; to forge again, recast; (_fig_) to rejuvenate.

recordātiō, -ōnis _f_ recollection.

recordor, -ārī, -ātus _vt, vi_ to recall, remember; to ponder over.

recreō, -āre, -āvī, -ātum _vt_ to remake, reproduce; to revive, refresh.

recrepō, -āre _vt, vi_ to ring, re-echo.

recrēscō, -scere, -vī _vi_ to grow again.

recrūdēscō, -ēscere, -uī _vi_ (_wound_) to open again; (_war_) to break out again.

rēctā _adv_ straight forward, right on.

rēctē _adv_ straight; correctly, properly, well; quite; (_inf_) good, all right, no thank you.

rēctiō, -ōnis _f_ government.

rēctor, -ōris _m_ guide, driver, helmsman; governor, master.

rēctum, -ī _nt_ right, virtue.

rēctus _ppp of_ **regō** ♦ _adj_ straight; upright, steep; right, correct, proper; (_moral_) good, virtuous.

recubō, -āre _vi_ to lie, recline.

recultus _ppp of_ **recolō**.

recumbō, -mbere, -buī _vi_ to lie down, recline; to fall, sink down.

recuperātiō, -ōnis _f_ recovery.

recuperātor, -ōris _m_ recapturer; (_pl_) board of justices who tried civil cases requiring a quick decision, esp cases involving foreigners.

recuperātōrius _adj_ of the recuperatores.

recuperō, -āre, -āvī, -ātum _vt_ to get back, recover, recapture.

recūrō, -āre _vt_ to restore.

recurrō, -ere, -ī _vi_ to run back; to return, recur; to revert.

recursō, -āre _vi_ to keep coming back, keep recurring.

recursus, -ūs _m_ return, retreat.

recurvō, -āre _vt_ to bend back, curve.

recurvus _adj_ bent, curved.

recūsātiō, -ōnis _f_ refusal, declining; (_law_) objection, counterplea.

recūsō, -āre, -āvī, -ātum _vt_ to refuse, decline, be reluctant; (_law_) to object, plead in defence.

recussus _adj_ reverberating.

redāctus _ppp of_ **redigō**.

redambulō, -āre _vi_ to come back.

redamō, -āre _vt_ to love in return.

redārdēscō, -ere _vi_ to blaze up again.

redarguō, -ere, -ī *vt* to refute, contradict.
redauspicō, -āre *vi* to take auspices for going back.
redditus *ppp of* **reddō**.
reddō, -ere, -idī, -itum *vt* to give back, return, restore; to give in, response, repay; to give up, deliver, pay; (*copy*) to represent, reproduce; (*speech*) to report, repeat, recite, reply; to translate; (*with adj*) to make; **iūdicium** ~ fix the date for a trial; **iūs** ~ administer justice.
redēgī *perf of* **redigō**.
redēmī *perf of* **redimō**.
redemptiō, -ōnis *f* ransoming; bribing; (*revenue*) farming.
redemptō, -āre *vt* to ransom.
redemptor, -ōris *m* contractor.
redemptūra, -ae *f* contracting.
redemptus *ppp of* **redimō**.
redeō, -īre, -iī, -itum *vi* to go back, come back, return; (*speech*) to revert; (*money*) to come in; (*CIRCS*) to be reduced to, come to.
redhālō, -āre *vt* to exhale.
redhibeō, -ēre *vt* to take back.
redigō, -igere, -ēgī, -āctum *vt* to drive back, bring back; (*money*) to collect, raise; (*to a condition*) to reduce, bring; (*number*) to reduce; **ad irritum** ~ make useless.
rediī *perf of* **redeō**.
redimīculum, -ī *nt* band.
redimiō, -īre, -iī, -ītum *vt* to bind, crown, encircle.
redimō, -imere, -ēmī, -emptum *vt* to buy back; to ransom, redeem; to release, rescue; (*good*) to procure; (*evil*) to avert; (*fault*) to make amends for; (*COMM*) to undertake by contract, hire.
redintegrō, -āre, -āvī, -ātum *vt* to restore, renew, refresh.
redipīscor, -ī *vt* to get back.
reditiō, -ōnis *f* returning.
reditus, -ūs *m* return, returning; (*money*) revenue.
redivīvus *adj* renovated.
redoleō, -ēre, -uī *vi* to give out a smell ♦ *vt* to smell of, smack of.
redomitus *adj* broken in again.
redōnō, -āre *vt* to restore; to give up.
redūcō, -ūcere, -ūxī, -uctum *vt* to draw back; to lead back, bring back; to escort home; to marry again; (*troops*) to withdraw; (*fig*) to restore; (*to a condition*) to make into.
reductiō, -ōnis *f* restoration.
reductor, -ōris *m* man who brings back.
reductus *ppp of* **redūcō** ♦ *adj* secluded, aloof.
reduncus *adj* curved back.
redundantia, -ae *f* extravagance.
redundō, -āre, -āvī, -ātum *vi* to overflow; to abound, be in excess; (*fig*) to stream.
reduvia, -ae *f* hangnail.

redux, -cis *adj* (*gods*) who brings back; (*men*) brought back, returned.
refectus *ppp of* **reficiō**.
refellō, -ere, -ī *vt* to disprove, rebut.
referciō, -cīre, -sī, -tum *vt* to stuff, cram, choke full.
referiō, -īre *vt* to hit back; to reflect.
referō, -ferre, -ttulī, -lātum *vt* to bring back, carry back; to give back, pay back, repay; to repeat, renew; (*authority*) to refer to, trace back to; (*blame, credit*) to ascribe; (*likeness*) to reproduce, resemble; (*memory*) to recall; (*news*) to report, mention; (*opinion*) to reckon amongst; (*record*) to enter; (*senate*) to lay before, move; (*speech*) to reply, say in answer; **grātiam** ~ be grateful, requite; **pedem, gradum** ~ return; retreat; **ratiōnēs** ~ present an account; **sē** ~ return.
rēfert, -ferre, -tulit *vi* (*impers*) it is of importance, it matters, it concerns; **meā** ~ it matters to me.
refertus *ppp of* **referciō** ♦ *adj* crammed, full.
referveō, -ēre *vi* to boil over.
refervēscō, -ere *vi* to bubble up.
reficiō, -icere, -ēcī, -ectum *vt* to repair, restore; (*body, mind*) to refresh, revive; (*money*) to get back, get in return; (*POL*) to re-elect.
refīgō, -gere, -xī, -xum *vt* to unfasten, take down; (*fig*) to annul.
refingō, -ere *vt* to remake.
refīxus *ppp of* **refīgō**.
reflāgitō, -āre *vt* to demand back.
reflātus, -ūs *m* contrary wind.
reflectō, -ctere, -xī, -xum *vt* to bend back, turn back; (*fig*) to bring back ♦ *vi* to give way.
reflexus *ppp of* **reflectō**.
reflō, -āre, -āvī, -ātum *vi* to blow contrary ♦ *vt* to breathe out again.
refluō, -ere *vi* to flow back, overflow.
refluus *adj* ebbing.
reformīdō, -āre *vt* to dread; to shun in fear.
refōrmō, -āre *vt* to reshape.
refōtus *ppp of* **refoveō**.
refoveō, -ovēre, -ōvī, -ōtum *vt* to refresh, revive.
refrāctāriolus *adj* rather stubborn.
refrāctus *ppp of* **refringō**.
refrāgor, -ārī, -ātus *vi* (*with dat*) to oppose, thwart.
refrēgī *perf of* **refringō**.
refrēnō, -āre, *vt* to curb, restrain.
refricō, -āre, -uī, -ātum *vt* to scratch open; to reopen, renew ♦ *vi* to break out again.
refrīgerātiō, -ōnis *f* coolness.
refrīgerō, -āre, -āvī, -ātum *vi* to cool, cool off; (*fig*) to flag.
refrīgēscō, -gēscere, -xī *vi* to grow cold; (*fig*) to flag, grow stale.

refringō, -ingere, -ēgī, -āctum *vt* to break open; to break off; (*fig*) to break, check.

refrīxī *perf of* **refrīgēscō**.

refugiō, -ugere, -ūgī *vi* to run back, flee, shrink ♦ *vt* to run away from, shun.

refugium, -ī *and* **iī** *nt* refuge.

refugus *adj* fugitive, receding.

refulgeō, -gēre, -sī *vi* to flash back, reflect light.

refundō, -undere, -ūdī, -ūsum *vt* to pour back, pour out; (*pass*) to overflow.

refūsus *ppp of* **refundō**.

refūtātiō, -ōnis *f* refutation.

refūtātus, -ūs *m* refutation.

refūtō, -āre, -āvī, -ātum *vt* to check, repress; to refute, disprove.

rēgālis *adj* king's, royal, regal.

rēgāliter *adv* magnificently; tyrannically.

regerō, -rere, -ssī, -stum *vt* to carry back, throw back.

rēgia, -ae *f* palace; court; (*camp*) royal tent; (*town*) capital.

rēgiē *adv* regally; imperiously.

rēgificus *adj* magnificent.

regignō, -ere *vt* to reproduce.

Rēgillānus *and* **ēnsis** *adj see* **Rēgillus**.

Rēgillus, -ī *m Sabine town*; lake in Latium (*scene of a Roman victory over the Latins*).

regimen, -inis *nt* guiding, steering; rudder; rule, command, government; ruler.

rēgīna, -ae *f* queen, noblewoman.

Rēgīnus *adj see* **Rēgium**.

regiō, -ōnis *f* direction, line; boundary line; quarter, region; district, ward, territory; (*fig*) sphere, province; **ē ~ōne** in a straight line; (*with gen*) exactly opposite.

regiōnātim *adv* by districts.

Rēgium, -ī *and* **iī** *nt* town in extreme S. of Italy, (*now* Reggio).

rēgius *adj* king's, kingly, royal; princely, magnificent.

reglūtinō, -āre *vt* to unstick.

rēgnātor, -ōris *m* ruler.

rēgnātrīx, -īcis *adj* imperial.

rēgnō, -āre, -āvī, -ātum *vi* to be king, rule, reign; to be supreme, lord it; (*things*) to prevail, predominate ♦ *vt* to rule over.

rēgnum, -ī *nt* kingship, monarchy; sovereignty, supremacy; despotism; kingdom; domain.

regō, -ere, rēxī, rēctum *vt* to keep straight, guide, steer; to manage, direct; to control, rule, govern; **~ fīnēs** (*law*) mark out the limits.

regredior, -dī, -ssus *vi* to go back, come back, return; (*MIL*) to retire.

regressus *ppa of* **regredior**.

regressus, -ūs *m* return; retreat.

rēgula, -ae *f* rule, ruler; stick, board; (*fig*) rule, pattern, standard.

rēgulus, -ī *m* petty king, chieftain; prince.

Rēgulus, -ī *m Roman consul taken prisoner by the Carthaginians.*

regustō, -āre *vt* to taste again.

rēiciō, -icere, -iēcī, -iectum *vt* to throw back, throw over the shoulder, throw off; to drive back, repel; to cast off, reject; to reject with contempt, scorn; (*jurymen*) to challenge, refuse; (*matter for discussion*) to refer; (*time*) to postpone; **sē ~** fling oneself.

rēiectāneus *adj* to be rejected.

rēiectiō, -ōnis *f* rejection; (*law*) challenging.

rēiectō, -āre *vt* to throw back.

rēiectus *ppp of* **rēiciō**.

relābor, -bī, -psus *vi* to glide back, sink back, fall back.

relanguēscō, -ēscere, -ī *vi* to faint; to weaken.

relātiō, -ōnis *f* (*law*) retorting; (*pl*) magistrate's report; (*RHET*) repetition.

relātor, -ōris *m* proposer of a motion.

relātus *ppp of* **referō**.

relātus, -ūs *m* official report; recital.

relaxātiō, -ōnis *f* easing.

relaxō, -āre, -āvī, -ātum *vt* to loosen, open out; (*fig*) to release, ease, relax, cheer.

relēctus *ppp of* **relegō**.

relēgātiō, -ōnis *f* banishment.

relēgō, -āre, -āvī, -ātum *vt* to send away, send out of the way; to banish; (*fig*) to reject; to refer, ascribe.

relegō, -egere, -ēgī, -ēctum *vt* to gather up; (*place*) to traverse, sail over again; (*speech*) to go over again, reread.

relentēscō, -ere *vi* to slacken off.

relēvī *perf of* **relinō**.

relevō, -āre, -āvī, -ātum *vt* to lift up; to lighten; (*fig*) to relieve, ease, comfort.

relictiō, -ōnis *f* abandoning.

relictus *ppp of* **relinquō**.

rēlicuus *etc see* **reliquus**.

religātiō, -ōnis *f* tying up.

religiō, -ōnis *f* religious scruple, reverence, awe; religion; superstition; scruples, conscientiousness; holiness, sanctity (*in anything*); object of veneration, sacred place; religious ceremony, observance.

religiōsē *adv* devoutly; scrupulously, conscientiously.

religiōsus *adj* devout, religious; superstitious; involving religious difficulty; scrupulous, conscientious; (*objects*) holy, sacred.

religō, -āre, -āvī, -ātum *vt* to tie up, fasten behind; (*ship*) to make fast, moor; (*fig*) to bind.

relinō, -inere, -ēvī *vt* to unseal.

relinquō, -inquere, -īquī, -ictum *vt* to leave, leave behind; to bequeath; to abandon, forsake; (*argument*) to allow; (*pass*) to remain.

rēliquiae, -ārum *fpl* leavings, remainder, relics.

reliquus *adj* remaining, left; (*time*) subsequent, future; (*debt*) outstanding ♦ *nt* remainder, rest; arrears ♦ *mpl* the rest; **~um est** it remains, the next point is; **~ī facere**

leave behind, leave over, omit; in **~um** for the future.

rell- *etc see* **rel-**.

relūceō, -cēre, -xī *vi* to blaze.

relūcēscō, -cēscere, -xī *vi* to become bright again.

reluctor, -ārī, -ātus *vi* to struggle against, resist.

remaneō, -anēre, -ānsī *vi* to remain behind; to remain, continue, endure.

remānō, -āre *vi* to flow back.

remānsiō, -ōnis *f* remaining behind.

remedium, -ī *and* **iī** *nt* cure, remedy, medicine.

remēnsus *ppa of* **remētior**.

remeō, -āre *vi* to come back, go back, return.

remētior, -tīrī, -nsus *vt* to measure again; to go back over.

rēmex, -igis *m* rower, oarsman.

Rēmī, -ōrum *mpl* people of Gaul (*in region of what is now* Rheims).

rēmigātiō, -ōnis *f* rowing.

rēmigium, -ī *and* **iī** *nt* rowing; oars; oarsmen.

rēmigō, -āre *vi* to row.

remigrō, -āre *vi* to move back, return (home).

reminīscor, -ī *vt, vi* (*usu with gen*) to remember, call to mind.

remisceō, -scēre, -xtum *vt* to mix up, mingle.

remissē *adv* mildly, gently.

remissiō, -ōnis *f* release; (*tension*) slackening, relaxing; (*payment*) remission; (*mind*) slackness, mildness, relaxation; (*illness*) abating.

remissus *ppp of* **remittō** ♦ *adj* slack; negligent; mild, indulgent, cheerful.

remittō, -ittere, -īsī, -issum *vt* to let go back, send back, release; to slacken, loosen, relax; to emit, produce; (*mind*) to relax, relieve; (*notion*) to discard, give up; (*offence, penalty*) to let off, remit; (*right*) to resign, sacrifice; (*sound*) to give back ♦ *vi* to abate.

remixtus *ppp of* **remisceō**.

remōlior, -īrī, -ītus *vt* to heave back.

remollēscō, -ere *vi* to become soft again, be softened.

remolliō, -īre *vt* to weaken.

remora, -ae *f* hindrance.

remorāmina, -um *ntpl* hindrances.

remordeō, -dēre, -sum *vt* (*fig*) to worry, torment.

remoror, -ārī, -ātus *vi* to linger, stay behind ♦ *vt* to hinder, delay, defer.

remorsus *ppp of* **remordeō**.

remōtē *adv* far.

remōtiō, -ōnis *f* removing.

remōtus *ppp of* **removeō** ♦ *adj* distant, remote; secluded; (*fig*) far removed, free from.

removeō, -ovēre, -ōvī, -ōtum *vt* to move back, withdraw, set aside; to subtract.

remūgiō, -īre *vi* to bellow in answer, re-echo.

remulceō, -cēre, -sī *vt* to stroke; (*tail*) to droop.

remulcum, -ī *nt* towrope.

remūnerātiō, -ōnis *f* recompense, reward.

remūneror, -ārī, -ātus *vt* to repay, reward.

remurmurō, -āre *vi* to murmur in answer.

rēmus, -ī *m* oar.

Remus, -ī *m* brother of Romulus.

renārrō, -āre *vt* to tell over again.

renāscor, -scī, -tus *vi* to be born again; to grow, spring up again.

renātus *ppa of* **renāscor**.

renāvigō, -āre *vi* to sail back.

reneō, -ēre *vt* to unspin, undo.

rēnēs, -um *mpl* kidneys.

renīdeō, -ēre *vi* to shine back, be bright; to be cheerful, smile, laugh.

renīdēscō, -ere *vi* to reflect the gleam of.

renītor, -ī *vi* to struggle, resist.

renō, -āre *vi* to swim back.

rēnō, -ōnis *m* fur.

renōdō, -āre *vt* to tie back in a knot.

renovāmen, -inis *nt* new condition.

renovātiō, -ōnis *f* renewal; compound interest.

renovō, -āre, -āvī, -ātum *vt* to renew, restore; to repair, revive, refresh; (*speech*) to repeat; **faenus ~** take compound interest.

renumerō, -āre *vt* to pay back.

renūntiātiō, -ōnis *f* report, announcement.

renūntiō, -āre, -āvī, -ātum *vt* to report, bring back word; to announce, make an official statement; (*election*) to declare elected, return; (*duty*) to refuse, call off, renounce.

renūntius, -ī *and* **iī** *m* reporter.

renuō, -ere, -ī *vt, vi* to deny, decline, refuse.

renūtō, -āre *vi* to refuse firmly.

reor, rērī, ratus *vi* to think, suppose.

repāgula, -ōrum *ntpl* (*door*) bolts, bars.

repandus *adj* curving back, turned up.

reparābilis *adj* retrievable.

reparcō, -ere *vi* to be sparing with, refrain.

reparō, -āre, -āvī, -ātum *vt* to retrieve, recover; to restore, repair; to purchase; (*mind, body*) to refresh; (*troops*) to recruit.

repastinātiō, -ōnis *f* digging up again.

repellō, -ellere, -pulī, -ulsum *vt* to push back, drive back, repulse; to remove, reject.

rependō, -endere, -endī, -ēnsum *vt* to return by weight; to pay, repay; to requite, compensate.

repēns, -entis *adj* sudden; new.

repēnsus *ppp of* **rependō**.

repentē *adv* suddenly.

repentīnō *adv* suddenly.

repentīnus *adj* sudden, hasty; upstart.

repercō *etc see* **reparcō**.

repercussus *ppp of* **repercutiō**.

repercussus, -ūs *m* reflection, echo.

Noun declensions and verb conjugations are shown on pp xiii to xxv. The present infinitive ending of a verb shows to which conjugation it belongs: **-āre** = 1st; **-ēre** = 2nd; **-ere** = 3rd and **-īre** = 4th. Irregular verbs are shown on p xxvi.

repercutiō, -tere, -ssī, -ssum *vt* to make rebound, reflect, echo.

reperiō, -īre, repperī, -tum *vt* to find, find out; to get, procure; to discover, ascertain; to devise, invent.

repertor, -ōris *m* discoverer, inventor, author.

repertus *ppp of* **reperiō** ♦ *ntpl* discoveries.

repetītiō, -ōnis *f* repetition; (*RHET*) anaphora.

repetītor, -ōris *m* reclaimer.

repetītus *ppp of* **repetō** ♦ *adj:* **altē/longē ~** far-fetched.

repetō, -ere, -īvī *and* **iī, -ītum** *vt* to go back to, revisit; to fetch back, take back; (*MIL*) to attack again; (*action, speech*) to resume, repeat; (*memory*) to recall, think over; (*origin*) to trace, derive; (*right*) to claim, demand back; **rēs ~** demand satisfaction; reclaim one's property; **pecūniae ~undae** extortion.

repetundae, -ārum *fpl* extortion (*by a provincial governor*).

repexus *adj* combed.

repleō, -ēre, -ēvī, -ētum *vt* to fill up, refill; to replenish, make good, complete; to satiate, fill to overflowing.

replētus *adj* full.

replicātiō, -ōnis *f* rolling up.

replicō, -āre *vt* to roll back, unroll, unfold.

rēpō, -ere, -sī, -tum *vi* to creep, crawl.

repōnō, -ōnere, -osuī, -ositum *vt* to put back, replace, restore; to bend back; to put (*in the proper place*); (*performance*) to repeat; (*something received*) to repay; (*store*) to lay up, put away; (*task*) to lay aside, put down; (*hope*) to place, rest; (*with* **prō**) substitute; **in numerō, in numerum ~** count, reckon among.

reportō, -āre, -āvī, -ātum *vt* to bring back, carry back; (*prize*) to win, carry off; (*words*) to report.

reposcō, -ere *vt* to demand back; to claim, require.

repositus *ppp of* **repōnō** ♦ *adj* remote.

repostor, -ōris *m* restorer.

repostus *etc see* **repositus.**

repōtia, -ōrum *ntpl* second drinking.

repperī *perf of* **reperiō.**

reppulī *perf of* **repellō.**

repraesentātiō, -ōnis *f* vivid presentation; (*COMM*) cash payment.

repraesentō, -āre, -āvī, -ātum *vt* to exhibit, reproduce; to do at once, hasten; (*COMM*) to pay cash.

reprehendō, -endere, -endī, -ēnsum *vt* to hold back, catch, restrain; to hold fast, retain; to blame, rebuke, censure; to refute.

reprehēnsiō, -ōnis *f* check; blame, reprimand, refutation.

reprehēnsō, -āre *vt* to keep holding back.

reprehēnsor, -ōris *m* censurer, critic, reviser.

reprehēnsus *ppp of* **reprehendō.**

reprendō *etc see* **reprehendō.**

repressor, -ōris *m* restrainer.

repressus *ppp of* **reprimō.**

reprimō, -imere, -essī, -essum *vt* to keep back, force back; to check, restrain, suppress.

reprōmissiō, -ōnis *f* counterpromise.

reprōmittō, -ittere, -īsī, -issum *vt* to promise in return, engage oneself.

rēptō, -āre *vi* to creep about, crawl along.

repudiātiō, -ōnis *f* rejection.

repudiō, -āre, -āvī, -ātum *vt* to reject, refuse, scorn; (*wife*) to divorce.

repudium, -ī *and* **iī** *nt* divorce; repudiation.

repuerāscō, -ere *vi* to become a child again; to behave like a child.

repugnanter *adv* reluctantly.

repugnantia, -ium *ntpl* contradictions.

repugnō, -āre, -āvī, -ātum *vi* to oppose, resist; to disagree, be inconsistent.

repulsa, -ae *f* refusal, denial, repulse; (*election*) rebuff.

repulsō, -āre *vi* to throb, reverberate.

repulsus *ppp of* **repellō.**

repulsus, -ūs *m* (*light*) reflection; (*sound*) echoing.

repungō, -ere *vt* to prod again.

repūrgō, -āre, -āvī, -ātum *vt* to clear again, cleanse again; to purge away.

reputātiō, -ōnis *f* pondering over.

reputō, -āre, -āvī, -ātum *vt* to count back; to think over, consider.

requiēs, -ētis *f* rest, relaxation, repose.

requiēscō, -scere, -vī, -tum *vi* to rest, find rest; to cease ♦ *vt* to stay.

requiētus *adj* rested, refreshed.

requīritō, -āre *vt* to keep asking after.

requīrō, -rere, -sīvī *and* **siī, -sītum** *vt* to search for, look for; to ask, inquire after; (*with* **ex** *or* **ab**) to question; to need, want, call for; to miss, look in vain for.

requīsītus *ppp of* **requīrō.**

rēs, reī *f* thing, object; circumstance, case, matter, affair; business, transaction; fact, truth, reality; possessions, wealth, money; advantage, interest; (*law*) case; (*MIL*) campaign, operations; (*POL*) politics, power, the State; (*writing*) subject matter, story, history; **~ mihi est tēcum** I have to do with you; **~ dīvīna** sacrifice; **~ mīlitāris** war; **~ pūblica** public affairs, politics, the State, republic; **~ rūstica** agriculture; **rem facere** get rich; **rem gerere** wage war, fight; **ad rem** to the point, to the purpose; **in rem** usefully; **ob rem** to the purpose; **ob eam rem** therefore; **ī in malam rem** go to the devil!; **contrā rem pūblicam** unconstitutional; **ē rē pūblicā** constitutionally; **rē vērā** in fact, actually; **eā rē** for that reason; **tuā rē, ex tuā rē** to your advantage; **ab rē** unhelpfully; **ē rē (nātā)** as things are; **prō rē** according to circumstances; **rēs adversae** failure, adversity; **rēs dubiae** danger; **rēs gestae**

achievements, career; **rēs novae** revolution; **rēs prosperae, secundae** success, prosperity; **rērum māximus** greatest in the world; **rērum scrīptor** historian.

resacrō *etc see* **resecrō**.

resaeviō, -īre *vi* to rage again.

resalūtō, -āre *vt* to greet in return.

resānēscō, -ēscere, -uī *vi* to heal up again.

resarciō, -cīre, -tum *vt* to patch up, repair.

rescindō, -ndere, -dī, -ssum *vt* to cut back, cut open, break down; to open up; (*law, agreement*) to repeal, annul.

rescīscō, -īscere, -īvī *and* **iī, -ītum** *vt* to find out, learn.

rescissus *ppp of* **rescindō**.

rescrībō, -bere, -psī, -ptum *vt* to write back, reply; to rewrite, revise; (*emperors*) to give a decision; (MIL) to transfer, re-enlist; (*money*) to place to one's credit, pay back.

rescrīptus *ppp of* **rescrībō** ♦ *nt* imperial rescript.

resecō, -āre, -uī, -tum *vt* to cut back, cut short; to curtail; **ad vīvum ~** cut to the quick.

resecrō, -āre *vt* to pray again; to free from a curse.

resectus *ppp of* **resecō**.

resecūtus *ppa of* **resequor**.

resēdī *perf of* **resideō**; *perf of* **resīdō**.

resēminō, -āre *vt* to reproduce.

resequor, -quī, -cūtus *vt* to answer.

reserō, -āre, -āvī, -ātum *vt* to unbar, unlock; to disclose.

reservō, -āre, -āvī, -ātum *vt* to keep back, reserve; to preserve, save.

reses, -idis *adj* remaining; inactive; idle; calm.

resideō, -idēre, -ēdī *vi* to remain behind; to be idle, be listless; (*fig*) to remain, rest.

resīdō, -īdere, -ēdī *vi* to sit down, sink down, settle; to subside; (*fig*) to abate, calm down.

residuus *adj* remaining, left over; (*money*) outstanding.

resignō, -āre *vt* to unseal, open; (*fig*) to reveal; (COMM) to cancel, pay back.

resiliō, -īre, -uī *vi* to spring back; to recoil, rebound, shrink.

resīmus *adj* turned up.

rēsīna, -ae *f* resin.

rēsīnātus *adj* smeared with resin.

resipiō, -ere *vt* to savour of, smack of.

resipīscō, -īscere, -iī *and* **uī** *vi* to come to one's senses.

resistō, -istere, -titī *vi* to stand still, stop, halt; to resist, oppose; to rise again.

resolūtus *ppp of* **resolvō**.

resolvō, -vere, -vī, -ūtum *vt* to unfasten, loosen, open, release; to melt, dissolve; to relax; (*debt*) to pay up; (*difficulty*) to banish, dispel; (*tax*) to abolish; (*words*) to explain.

resonābilis *adj* answering.

resonō, -āre *vi* to resound, re-echo ♦ *vt* to echo the sound of; to make resound.

resonus *adj* echoing.

resorbeō, -ēre *vt* to suck back, swallow again.

respectō, -āre *vi* to look back; to gaze about, watch ♦ *vt* to look back at, look for; to have regard for.

respectus *ppp of* **respiciō**.

respectus, -ūs *m* looking back; refuge; respect, regard.

respergō, -gere, -sī, -sum *vt* to besprinkle, splash.

respersiō, -ōnis *f* sprinkling.

respersus *ppp of* **respergō**.

respiciō, -icere, -exī, -ectum *vt* to look back at, see behind; (*help*) to look to; (*care*) to have regard for, consider, respect ♦ *vi* to look back, look.

respīrāmen, -inis *nt* windpipe.

respīrātiō, -ōnis *f* breathing; exhalation; taking breath, pause.

respīrātus, -ūs *m* inhaling.

respīrō, -āre, -āvī, -ātum *vt, vi* to breathe, blow back; to breathe again, revive; (*things*) to abate.

resplendeō, -ēre *vi* to flash back, shine brightly.

respondeō, -ondēre, -ondī, -ōnsum *vt* to answer, reply; (*lawyer, priest, oracle*) to advise, give a response; (*law court*) to appear; (*pledge*) to promise in return; (*things*) to correspond, agree, match; **pār parī ~** return like for like, give tit for tat.

respōnsiō, -ōnis *f* answering; refutation.

respōnsitō, -āre *vi* to give advice.

respōnsō, -āre *vt, vi* to answer back; to defy.

respōnsor, -ōris *m* answerer.

respōnsum, -ī *nt* answer, reply; response, opinion, oracle.

rēspūblica, reīpūblicae *f* public affairs, politics, the State, republic.

respuō, -ere, -ī *vt* to spit out, eject; to reject, refuse.

restagnō, -āre *vi* to overflow; to be flooded.

restaurō, -āre *vt* to repair, rebuild.

resticula, -ae *f* rope, cord.

restinctiō, -ōnis *f* quenching.

restinctus *ppp of* **restinguō**.

restinguō, -guere, -xī, -ctum *vt* to extinguish, quench; (*fig*) to destroy.

restiō, -ōnis *m* rope maker.

restipulātiō, -ōnis *f* counterobligation.

restipulor, -ārī *vt* to stipulate in return.

restis, -is *f* rope.

restitī *perf of* **resistō**; *perf of* **restō**.

restitō, -āre *vi* to stay behind, hesitate.

restituō, -uere, -uī, -ūtum *vt* to replace, restore; to rebuild, renew; to give back, return; (*to a condition*) to reinstate; (*decision*) to quash, reverse; (*character*) to reform.

Noun declensions and verb conjugations are shown on pp xiii to xxv. The present infinitive ending of a verb shows to which conjugation it belongs: **-āre** = 1st; **-ēre** = 2nd; **-ere** = 3rd and **-īre** = 4th. Irregular verbs are shown on p xxvi

restitūtiō, -ōnis *f* restoration; reinstating.
restitūtor, -ōris *m* restorer.
restitūtus *ppp of* **restituō**.
restō, -āre, -itī *vi* to stand firm; to resist; to remain, be left; to be in store (for); **quod ~at** for the future.
restrictē *adv* sparingly; strictly.
restrictus *ppp of* **restringō** ♦ *adj* tight, short; niggardly; severe.
restringō, -ngere, -nxī, -ctum *vt* to draw back tightly, bind fast; (*teeth*) to bare; (*fig*) to check.
resultō, -āre *vi* to rebound; to re-echo.
resūmō, -ere, -psī, -ptum *vt* to take up again, get back, resume.
resupīnō, -āre *vt* to turn back, throw on one's back.
resupīnus *adj* lying back, face upwards.
resurgō, -gere, -rēxī, -rēctum *vi* to rise again, revive.
resuscitō, -āre *vt* to revive.
retardātiō, -ōnis *f* hindering.
retardō, -āre, -āvī, -ātum *vt* to retard, detain, check.
rēte, -is *nt* net; (*fig*) snare.
retēctus *ppp of* **retegō**.
retegō, -egere, -ēxī, -ēctum *vt* to uncover, open; to reveal.
retemptō, -āre *vt* to try again.
retendō, -endere, -endī, -entum *and* **ēnsum** *vt* to slacken, relax.
retēnsus *ppp of* **retendō**.
retentiō, -ōnis *f* holding back.
retentō *etc see* **retemptō**.
retentō, -āre *vt* to keep back, hold fast.
retentus *ppp of* **retendō**; *ppp of* **retineō**.
retēxī *perf of* **retegō**.
retexō, -ere, -uī, -tum *vt* to unravel; (*fig*) to break up, cancel; to renew.
rētiārius, -ī *and* **iī** *m* net-fighter.
reticentia, -ae *f* saying nothing; pause.
reticeō, -ēre, -uī *vi* to be silent, say nothing ♦ *vt* to keep secret.
rēticulum, -ī *nt* small net, hairnet; network bag.
retināculum, -ī *nt* tether, hawser.
retinēns, -entis *pres p of* **retineō** ♦ *adj* tenacious, observant.
retinentia, -ae *f* memory.
retineō, -inēre, -inuī, -entum *vt* to hold back, detain, restrain; to keep, retain, preserve.
retinniō, -īre *vi* to ring.
retonō, -āre *vi* to thunder in answer.
retorqueō, -quēre, -sī, -tum *vt* to turn back, twist.
retorridus *adj* dried up, wizened.
retortus *ppp of* **retorqueō**.
retractātiō, -ōnis *f* hesitation.
retractō, -āre, -āvī, -ātum *vt* to rehandle, take up again; to reconsider, revise; to withdraw ♦ *vi* to draw back, hesitate.
retractus *ppp of* **retrahō** ♦ *adj* remote.

retrahō, -here, -xī, -ctum *vt* to draw back, drag back; to withdraw, remove.
retrectō *etc see* **retractō**.
retribuō, -uere, -uī, -ūtum *vt* to restore, repay.
retrō *adv* back, backwards, behind; (*time*) back, past.
retrōrsum *adv* backwards, behind; in reverse order.
retrūdō, -dere, -sum *vt* to push back; to withdraw.
rettulī *perf of* **referō**.
retundō, -undere, -udī *and* **tudī, -ūsum** *and* **ūnsum** *vt* to blunt; (*fig*) to check, weaken.
retūnsus, retūsus *ppp of* **retundō** ♦ *adj* blunt, dull.
reus, -ī *m* the accused, defendant; guarantor, debtor, one responsible; culprit, criminal; **vōtī ~** one who has had a prayer granted.
revalēscō, -ēscere, -uī *vi* to recover.
revehō, -here, -xī, -ctum *vt* to carry back, bring back; (*pass*) to ride, drive, sail back.
revellō, -ellere, -ellī, -ulsum (**olsum**) *vt* to pull out, tear off; to remove.
revēlō, -āre *vt* to unveil, uncover.
reveniō, -enīre, -ēnī, -entum *vi* to come back, return.
rēvērā *adv* in fact, actually.
reverendus *adj* venerable, awe-inspiring.
reverēns, -entis *pres p of* **revereor** ♦ *adj* respectful, reverent.
reverenter *adv* respectfully.
reverentia, -ae *f* respect, reverence, awe.
revereor, -ērī, -itus *vt* to stand in awe of; to respect, revere.
reversiō (**revorsiō**)**, -ōnis** *f* turning back; recurrence.
reversus *ppa of* **revertor**.
revertō, -ere, -ī; revertor, -tī, -sus *vi* to turn back, return; to revert.
revexī *perf of* **revehō**.
revictus *ppp of* **revincō**.
revinciō, -cīre, -xī, -ctum *vt* to tie back, bind fast.
revincō, -incere, -īcī, -ictum *vt* to conquer, repress; (*words*) to refute, convict.
revinctus *ppp of* **revinciō**.
revirēscō, -ēscere, -uī *vi* to grow green again; to be rejuvenated; to grow strong again, flourish again.
revīsō, -ere *vt*, *vi* to come back to, revisit.
revīvēscō, -vīscō, -vīscere, -xī *vi* to come to life again, revive.
revocābilis *adj* revocable.
revocāmen, -inis *nt* recall.
revocātiō, -ōnis *f* recalling; (*word*) withdrawing.
revocō, -āre, -āvī, -ātum *vt* to call back, recall; (*action*) to revoke; (*former state*) to recover, regain; (*growth*) to check; (*guest*) to invite in return; (*judgment*) to apply, refer; (*law*) to summon again; (*performer*) to encore; (*troops*) to withdraw.

revolō, -āre *vi* to fly back.
revolsus *etc see* **revulsus.**
revolūbilis *adj* that may be rolled back.
revolūtus *ppp of* **revolvō.**
revolvō, -vere, -vī, -ūtum *vt* to roll back, unroll, unwind; (*speech*) to relate, repeat; (*thought*) to think over; (*writing*) to read over; (*pass*) to revolve, return, come round.
revomō, -ere, -uī *vt* to disgorge.
revor- *etc see* **rever-.**
revulsus *ppp of* **revellō.**
rēx, rēgis *m* king; tyrant, despot; leader; patron, rich man.
rēxī *perf of* **regō.**
Rhadamanthus, -ī *m judge in the lower world.*
Rhaeti *etc see* **Raetī.**
Rhamnūs, -ūntis *f town in Attica (famous for its statue of Nemesis).*
Rhamnūsis, -ūsidis *f Nemesis.*
Rhamnūsius *adj see n.*
rhapsōdia, -ae *f a book of Homer.*
Rhea, -ae *f Cybele.*
Rhea Silvia, -ae, -ae *f mother of Romulus and Remus.*
Rhēgium *etc see* **Rēgium.**
Rhēnānus *adj* Rhenish.
rhēnō *etc see* **rēnō.**
Rhēnus, -ī *m* Rhine.
Rhēsus, -ī *m* Thracian king (*killed at Troy*).
rhētor, -oris *m* teacher of rhetoric; orator.
rhētorica, -ae *and* **ē, -ēs** *f* art of oratory, rhetoric.
rhētoricē *adv* rhetorically, in an oratorical manner.
rhētoricī, -ōrum *mpl* teachers of rhetoric.
rhētoricus *adj* rhetorical, on rhetoric.
rhīnocerōs, -ōtis *m* rhinoceros.
rhō *nt (indecl)* Greek letter rho.
Rhodanus, -ī *m* Rhone.
Rhodius *adj see* **Rhodopē.**
Rhodopē, -ēs *f mountain range in Thrace.*
Rhodopēius *adj* Thracian.
Rhodos (Rhodus), -ī *f island of Rhodes.*
Rhoetēum, -ī *nt promontory on the Dardanelles (near Troy).*
Rhoetēus *adj* Trojan.
rhombus, -ī *m* magician's circle; (*fish*) turbot.
rhomphaea, -ae *f long barbarian javelin.*
rhythmicus, -ī *m* teacher of prose rhythm.
rhythmos (-us), -i *m* rhythm, symmetry.
rīca, -ae *f* sacrificial veil.
rīcinium, -ī *and* **iī** *nt small cloak with hood.*
rictum, -ī *nt*, **-us, -ūs** *m* open mouth, gaping jaws.
rīdeō, -dēre, -sī, -sum *vi* to laugh, smile ♦ *vt* to laugh at, smile at; to ridicule
rīdibundus *adj* laughing.
rīdiculāria, -ium *ntpl* jokes.
rīdiculē *adv* jokingly; absurdly.
rīdiculus *adj* amusing, funny; ridiculous, silly

♦ *m* jester ♦ *nt* joke.
rigēns, -entis *pres p of* **rigeō** ♦ *adj* stiff, rigid, frozen.
rigeō, -ēre *vi* to be stiff.
rigēscō, -ēscere, -uī *vi* to stiffen, harden; to bristle.
rigidē *adv* rigorously.
rigidus *adj* stiff, rigid, hard; (*fig*) hardy, strict, inflexible.
rigō, -āre *vt* to water, moisten, bedew; to convey (water).
rigor, -ōris *m* stiffness, hardness; numbness, cold; strictness, severity.
riguī *perf of* **rigēscō.**
riguus *adj* irrigating; watered.
rīma, -ae *f* crack, chink.
rīmor, -ārī, -ātus *vt* to tear open; to search for, probe, examine; to find out.
rīmōsus *adj* cracked, leaky.
ringor, -ī *vi* to snarl.
rīpa, -ae *f* river bank; shore.
Rīphaeī, -ōrum *mpl mountain range in N. Scythia.*
Rīphaeus *adj see* **Rīphaeī.**
rīpula, -ae *f* riverbank.
riscus, -ī *m* trunk, chest.
rīsī *perf of* **rīdeō.**
rīsor, -ōris *m* scoffer.
rīsus, -ūs *m* laughter, laugh; laughing stock.
rīte *adv* with the proper formality *or* ritual; duly, properly, rightly; in the usual manner; fortunately.
rītus, -ūs *m* ritual, ceremony; custom, usage; **~ū** after the manner of.
rīvālis, -is *m* rival in love.
rīvālitās, -ātis *f* rivalry in love.
rīvulus, -ī *m* brook.
rīvus, -ī *m* stream, brook; **ē ~ō flūmina māgna facere** ≈ make a mountain of a molehill.
rixa, -ae *f* quarrel, brawl, fight.
rixor, -ārī, -ātus *vi* to quarrel, brawl, squabble.
rōbiginōsus *adj* rusty.
rōbīgō, -inis *f* rust; blight, mould, mildew.
rōboreus *adj* of oak.
rōborō, -āre *vt* to strengthen, invigorate.
rōbur, -oris *nt* oak; hard wood; prison, dungeon (*at Rome*); (*fig*) strength, hardness, vigour; best part, élite, flower.
rōbustus *adj* of oak; strong, hard; robust, mature.
rōdō, -dere, -sī, -sum *vt* to gnaw; (*rust*) to corrode; (*words*) to slander.
rogālis *adj* of a pyre.
rogātiō, -ōnis *f* proposal, motion, bill; request; (*RHET*) question.
rogātiuncula, -ae *f* unimportant bill; question.
rogātor, -ōris *m* proposer; polling clerk.
rogātus, -ūs *m* request.

Noun declensions and verb conjugations are shown on pp xiii to xxv. The present infinitive ending of a verb shows to which conjugation it belongs: **-āre** = 1st; **-ēre** = 2nd; **-ere** = 3rd and **-īre** = 4th. Irregular verbs are shown on p xxvi

rogitō, -āre *vt* to ask for, inquire eagerly.
rogō, -āre, -āvī, -ātum *vt* to ask, ask for; (*bill*) to propose, move; (*candidate*) to put up for election; **lēgem ~, populum ~** introduce a bill; **magistrātum populum ~** nominate for election to an office; **militēs sacrāmentō ~** administer the oath to the troops; **mālō emere quam rogāre** I'd rather buy it than borrow it.
rogus, -ī *m* funeral pyre.
Rōma, -ae *f* Rome.
Rōmānus *adj* Roman.
Rōmuleus, -us *adj* of Romulus; Roman.
Rōmulidae, -idārum *mpl* the Romans.
Rōmulus, -ī *m* founder and first king of Rome.
rōrāriī, -ōrum *mpl* skirmishers.
rōridus *adj* dewy.
rōrifer, -ī *adj* dew-bringing.
rōrō, -āre *vi* to distil dew; to drip, trickle ♦ *vt* to bedew, wet.
rōs, rōris *m* dew; moisture, water; (*plant*) rosemary; **~ marīnus** rosemary.
rosa, -ae *f* rose; rose bush.
rosāria, -ōrum *ntpl* rose garden.
rōscidus *adj* dewy; wet.
Roscius, -ī *m*: L. ~ Othō *tribune in 67 BC, whose law reserved theatre seats for the equites;* Q. ~ Gallus *famous actor defended by Cicero;* Sex. ~ *of Ameria, defended by Cicero.*
Roscius, -iānus *adj see n.*
rosētum, -ī *nt* rosebed.
roseus *adj* rosy; of roses.
rōsī *perf of* **rōdō.**
rōstrātus *adj* beaked, curved; **columna ~a** *column commemorating a naval victory.*
rōstrum, -ī *nt* (*bird*) beak, bill; (*animal*) snout, muzzle; (*ship*) beak, end of prow; (*pl*) orators' platform in the Forum.
rōsus *ppp of* **rōdō.**
rota, -ae *f* wheel; potter's wheel, torture wheel; car, disc.
rotō, -āre, -āvī, -ātum *vt* to turn, whirl, roll; (*pass*) to revolve.
rotundē *adv* elegantly.
rotundō, -āre *vt* to round off.
rotundus *adj* round, circular, spherical; (*style*) well-turned, smooth.
rubefaciō, -facere, -fēcī, -factum *vt* to redden.
rubēns, -entis *pres p of* **rubeō** ♦ *adj* red; blushing.
rubeō, -ēre *vi* to be red; to blush.
ruber, -rī *adj* red; **mare ~rum** Red Sea; Persian Gulf; **ōceanus ~** Indian Ocean; **Saxa ~ra** *stone quarries between Rome and Veii.*
rubēscō, -ēscere, -uī *vi* to redden, blush.
rubēta, -ae *f* toad.
rubēta, -ōrum *ntpl* bramble bushes.
rubeus *adj* of bramble.
Rubicō, -ōnis *m stream marking the frontier between Italy and Gaul.*
rubicundulus *adj* reddish.
rubicundus *adj* red, ruddy.

rūbīg- *etc see* **rōbīg-.**
rubor, -ōris *m* redness; blush; bashfulness; shame.
rubrīca, -ae *f* red earth, red ochre.
rubuī *perf of* **rubēscō.**
rubus, -ī *m* bramble bush; bramble, blackberry.
ructō, -āre; -or, -ārī *vt, vi* to belch.
ructus, -us *m* belching.
rudēns, -entis *pres p of* **rudō** ♦ *m* rope; (*pl*) rigging.
Rudiae, -iārum *fpl* town in S. Italy (*birthplace of Ennius*).
rudiārius, -ī *and* **iī** *m* retired gladiator.
rudīmentum, -ī *nt* first attempt, beginning.
Rudīnus *adj see* **Rudiae.**
rudis *adj* unwrought, unworked, raw; coarse, rough, badly-made; (*age*) new, young; (*person*) uncultured, unskilled, clumsy; ignorant (of), inexperienced (in).
rudis, -is *f* stick, rod; foil (*for fighting practice*); (*fig*) discharge.
rudō, -ere, -īvī, -ītum *vi* to roar, bellow, bray; to creak.
rūdus, -eris *nt* rubble, rubbish; piece of copper.
rūdus, -eris *nt* copper coin.
Rūfulī, -ōrum *mpl* military tribunes (*chosen by the general*).
rūfulus *adj* red-headed.
rūfus *adj* red, red-haired.
rūga, -ae *f* wrinkle, crease.
rūgō, -āre *vi* to become creased.
rūgōsus *adj* wrinkled, shrivelled, corrugated.
ruī *perf of* **ruō.**
ruīna, -ae *f* fall, downfall; collapse, falling in; debris, ruins; destruction, disaster, ruin (*fig*).
ruīnōsus *adj* collapsing; ruined.
rumex, -icis *f* sorrel.
rūmificō, -āre *vt* to report.
Rūmīna, -ae *f goddess of nursing mothers;* **fīcus ~ālis** the fig tree of Romulus and Remus (*under which the she-wolf suckled them*).
rūminātiō, -ōnis *f* chewing the cud; (*fig*) ruminating.
rūminō, -āre *vt, vi* to chew the cud.
rūmor, -ōris *m* noise, cheering; rumour, hearsay; public opinion; reputation.
rumpia *etc see* **rhomphaea.**
rumpō, -ere, rūpī, ruptum *vt* to break, burst, tear; to break down, burst through; (*activity*) to interrupt; (*agreement*) to violate, annul; (*delay*) to put an end to; (*voice*) to give vent to; (*way*) to force through.
rūmusculī, -ōrum *mpl* gossip.
rūna, -ae *f* dart.
runcō, -āre *vt* to weed.
ruō, -ere, -ī, -tum *vi* to fall down, tumble; to rush, run, hurry; to come to ruin ♦ *vt* to dash down, hurl to the ground; to throw up, turn up.
rūpēs, -is *f* rock, cliff.

rūpī *perf of* **rumpō.**
ruptor, -ōris *m* violator.
ruptus *ppp of* **rumpō.**
rūricola, -ae *adj* rural, country- (*in cpds*).
rūrigena, -ae *m* countryman.
rūrsus, rūrsum (rūsum) *adv* back,
    backwards; on the contrary, in return;
    again.
rūs, rūris *nt* the country, countryside; estate,
    farm; **rūs** to the country; **rūrī** in the country;
    rūre from the country.
ruscum, -ī *nt* butcher's-broom.
russus *adj* red.
rūsticānus *adj* country- (*in cpds*), rustic.
rūsticātiō, -ōnis *f* country life.
rūsticē *adv* in a countrified manner,
    awkwardly.
rūsticitās, -ātis *f* country manners, rusticity.
rūsticor, -ārī *vi* to live in the country.
rūsticulus, -ī *m* yokel.
rūsticus *adj* country- (*in cpds*), rural; simple,
    rough, clownish ♦ *m* countryman.
rūsum *see* **rūrsus.**
rūta, -ae *f* (*herb*) rue; (*fig*) unpleasantness.
ruta caesa *ntpl* minerals and timber on an
    estate.
rutilō, -āre *vt* to colour red ♦ *vi* to glow red.
rutilus *adj* red, auburn.
rutrum, -ī *nt* spade, shovel, trowel.
rūtula, -ae *f* little piece of rue.
Rutulī, -ōrum *mpl* ancient Latin people.
Rutulus *adj* Rutulian.
Rutupiae, -iārum *fpl* seaport in Kent (*now*
    Richborough).
Rutupīnus *adj see n.*
rutus *ppp of* **ruō.**

S, s

Saba, -ae *f* town in Arabia Felix.
Sabaeus *adj see n.*
Sabāzia, -iōrum *ntpl* festival of Bacchus.
Sabāzius, -ī *m* Bacchus.
sabbata, -ōrum *ntpl* Sabbath, Jewish holiday.
Sabellus, -ī *m* Sabine, Samnite.
Sabellus, -icus *adj see n.*
Sabīnī, -ōrum *mpl* Sabines (*a people of central
    Italy*).
Sabīnus *adj* Sabine ♦ *f* Sabine woman ♦ *nt*
    Sabine estate; Sabine wine; **herba ~a** savin (*a
    kind of juniper*).
Sabrīna, -ae *f* river Severn.

saburra, -ae *f* sand, ballast.
Sacae, -ārum *mpl* tribe of Scythians.
saccipērium, -ī *and* **iī** *nt* purse-pocket.
saccō, -āre *vt* to strain, filter.
sacculus, -ī *m* little bag, purse.
saccus, -ī *m* bag, purse, wallet.
sacellum, -ī *nt* chapel.
sacer, -rī *adj* sacred, holy; devoted for
    sacrifice, forfeited; accursed, criminal,
    infamous; **Mōns ~** hill to which the Roman
    plebs seceded; **Via ~ra** street from the Forum to
    the Capitol.
sacerdōs, -ōtis *m/f* priest, priestess.
sacerdōtium, -ī *and* **iī** *nt* priesthood.
sacrāmentum, -ī *nt deposit made by parties to a
    lawsuit*; civil lawsuit, dispute; (*MIL*) oath of
    allegiance, engagement.
sacrārium, -ī *and* **iī** *nt* shrine, chapel.
sacrātus *adj* holy, hallowed; **~āta lēx** a law
    whose violation was punished by devotion to the
    infernal gods.
sacricola, -ae *m/f* sacrificing priest *or*
    priestess.
sacrifer, -ī *adj* carrying holy things.
sacrificālis *adj* sacrificial.
sacrificātiō, -ōnis *f* sacrificing.
sacrificium, -ī *and* **iī** *nt* sacrifice.
sacrificō, -āre *vt, vi* to sacrifice.
sacrificulus, -ī *m* sacrificing priest; **rēx ~** high
    priest.
sacrificus *adj* sacrificial.
sacrilēgium, -ī *and* **iī** *nt* sacrilege.
sacrilegus *adj* sacrilegious; profane, wicked
    ♦ *m* templerobber.
sacrō, -āre, -āvī, -ātum *vt* to consecrate; to
    doom, curse; to devote, dedicate; to make
    inviolable; (*poetry*) to immortalize.
sacrōsanctus *adj* inviolable, sacrosanct.
sacruficō *etc see* **sacrificō.**
sacrum, -rī *nt* holy thing, sacred vessel;
    shrine; offering, victim; rite; (*pl*) sacrifice,
    worship, religion; **~ra facere** sacrifice; **inter
    ~rum saxumque** ≈ with one's back to the wall;
    hērēditās sine ~rīs a gift with no awkward
    obligations.
saeclum *etc see* **saeculum.**
saeculāris *adj* centenary; (*ECCL*) secular,
    pagan.
saeculum, -ī *nt* generation, lifetime, age; the
    age, the times; century; **in ~a** (*ECCL*) for ever.
saepe *adv* often, frequently.
saepe numerō *adv* very often.
saepēs, -is *f* hedge, fence.
saepīmentum, -ī *nt* enclosure.
saepiō, -īre, -sī, -tum *vt* to hedge round,
    fence in, enclose; (*fig*) to shelter, protect.
saeptus *ppp of* **saepiō** ♦ *nt* fence, wall; stake,
    pale; (*sheep*) fold; (*Rome*) voting area in the
    Campus Martius.
saeta, -ae *f* hair, bristle.

Noun declensions and verb conjugations are shown on pp xiii to xxv. The present infinitive ending of a verb shows
to which conjugation it belongs: **-āre** = 1st; **-ēre** = 2nd; **-ere** = 3rd and **-īre** = 4th. Irregular verbs are shown on p xxvi

saetiger, -ī _adj_ bristly.
saetōsus _adj_ bristly, hairy.
saevē, -iter _adv_ fiercely, cruelly.
saevidicus _adj_ furious.
saeviō, -īre, -iī, -ītum _vi_ to rage, rave.
saevitia, -ae _f_ rage; ferocity, cruelty.
saevus _adj_ raging, fierce; cruel, barbarous.
sāga, -ae _f_ fortune teller.
sagācitās, -ātis _f_ (_dogs_) keen scent; (_mind_) shrewdness.
sagāciter _adv_ keenly; shrewdly.
sagātus _adj_ wearing a soldier's cloak.
sagāx, -ācis _adj_ (_senses_) keen, keen-scented; (_mind_) quick, shrewd.
sagīna, -ae _f_ stuffing, fattening; food, rich food; fatted animal.
sagīnō, -are _vt_ to cram, fatten; to feed, feast.
sāgiō, -īre _vi_ to perceive keenly.
sagitta, -ae _f_ arrow.
sagittārius, -ī _and_ **iī** _m_ archer.
sagittifer, -ī _adj_ armed with arrows.
sagmen, -inis _nt_ tuft of sacred herbs (_used as a mark of inviolability_).
sagulum, -ī _nt_ short military cloak.
sagum, -ī _nt_ military cloak; woollen mantle.
Saguntīnus _adj see_ **Saguntum**.
Saguntum, -ī _nt_, **-us (os), -ī** _f_ town in E. Spain.
sāgus _adj_ prophetic.
sāl, salis _m_ salt; brine, sea; (_fig_) shrewdness, wit, humour, witticism; good taste.
salacō, -ōnis _m_ swaggerer.
Salamīnius _adj see_ **Salamīs**.
Salamīs, -īnis _f_ Greek island near Athens; town in Cyprus.
salapūtium, -ī _and_ **iī** _nt_ manikin.
salārius _adj_ salt- (_in cpds_) ♦ _nt_ allowance, salary.
salāx, -ācis _adj_ lustful, salacious.
salebra, -ae _f_ roughness, rut.
Saliāris _adj_ of the Salii; sumptuous.
salictum, -ī _nt_ willow plantation.
salientēs, -ium _fpl_ springs.
salignus _adj_ of willow.
Saliī, -ōrum _mpl_ priests of Mars.
salillum, -ī _nt_ little saltcellar.
salīnae, -ārum _fpl_ saltworks.
salīnum, -ī _nt_ saltcellar.
saliō, -īre, -uī, -tum _vi_ to leap, spring; to throb.
saliunca, -ae _f_ Celtic nard.
salīva, -ae _f_ saliva, spittle; taste.
salix, -icis _f_ willow.
Sallustiānus _adj see_ **Sallustius**.
Sallustius, -ī _m_ Sallust (_Roman historian_); _his wealthy grand-nephew._
Salmōneus, -eos _m_ son of Aeolus (_punished in Tartarus for imitating lightning_).
Salmōnis, -idis _f his daughter Tyro._
salsāmentum, -ī _nt_ brine, pickle; salted fish.
salsē _adv_ wittily.
salsus _adj_ salted; salt, briny; (_fig_) witty.
saltātiō, -ōnis _f_ dancing, dance.
saltātor, -ōris _m_ dancer.

saltātōrius _adj_ dancing- (_in cpds_).
saltātrīx, -īcis _f_ dancer.
saltātus, -ūs _m_ dance.
saltem _adv_ at least, at all events; **nōn ~** not even.
saltō, -āre _vt_, _vi_ to dance.
saltuōsus _adj_ wooded.
saltus, -ūs _m_ leap, bound.
saltus, -ūs _m_ woodland pasture, glade; pass, ravine.
salūber _adj see_ **salūbris**.
salūbris _adj_ health-giving, wholesome; healthy, sound.
salūbritās, -ātis _f_ healthiness; health.
salūbriter _adv_ wholesomely; beneficially.
saluī _perf of_ **saliō**.
salum, -ī _nt_ sea, high sea.
salūs, -ūtis _f_ health; welfare, life; safety; good wish, greeting; **~ūtem dīcere** greet; bid farewell.
salūtāris _adj_ wholesome, healthy; beneficial; **~ littera** letter A (_for_ **absolvō** = _acquittal_).
salūtāriter _adv_ beneficially.
salūtātiō, -ōnis _f_ greeting; formal morning visit, levee.
salūtātor, -ōris _m_ morning caller; male courtier.
salūtātrīx, -rīcis _f_ morning caller; female courtier.
salūtifer, -ī _adj_ health-giving.
salūtigerulus _adj_ carrying greetings.
salūtō, -āre, -āvī, -ātum _vt_ to greet, salute, wish well; to call on, pay respects to.
salvē _adv_ well, in good health; all right.
salvē _impv of_ **salveō**.
salveō, -ēre _vi_ to be well, be in good health; **~ē, ~ētō, ~ēte** hail!, good day!, goodbye!; **~ēre iubeō** I bid good day.
salvus, salvos _adj_ safe, alive, intact, well; without violating; all right; **~ sīs** good day to you!; **~a rēs est** all is well; **~ā lēge** without breaking the law.
Samaous _adj see_ **Samē**.
Samarobrīva, -ae _f_ Belgian town (_now Amiens_).
sambūca, -ae _f_ harp.
sambūcistria, -ae _f_ harpist.
Samē, -ēs _f_ old name of the Greek island Cephallenia.
Samius _adj_ Samian ♦ _ntpl_ Samian pottery.
Samnīs, -ītis _adj_ Samnite.
Samnium, -ī _and_ **iī** _nt_ district of central Italy.
Samos (-us), -ī _f_ Aegean island off Asia Minor (_famous for its pottery and as the birthplace of Pythagoras_).
Samothrāces, -um _mpl_ Samothracians.
Samothrācia, -iae _and_ **a, -ae** _f_ Samothrace (_island in the N. Aegean_).
Samothrācius _adj see n._
sānābilis _adj_ curable.
sānātiō, -ōnis _f_ healing.
sanciō, -cīre, -xī, -ctum _vt_ to make sacred or inviolable; to ordain, ratify; to enact a

punishment against.
sanctimōnia, -ae *f* sanctity; chastity.
sanctiō, -ōnis *f* decree, penalty for violating
a law.
sanctitās, -ātis *f* sacredness; integrity,
chastity.
sanctitūdō, -inis *f* sacredness.
sanctō *adv* solemnly, religiously.
sanctor, -ōris *m* enacter.
sanctus *ppp of* **sanciō** ♦ *adj* sacred, inviolable;
holy, venerable; pious, virtuous, chaste.
sandaligerula, -ae *f* sandalbearer.
sandalium, -ī *and* **iī** *nt* sandal, slipper.
sandapila, -ae *f* common bier.
sandyx, -ycis *f* scarlet.
sānē *adv* sensibly; (*intensive*) very, doubtless;
(*ironical*) to be sure, of course; (*concessive*) of
course, indeed; (*in answer*) certainly, surely;
(*with impv*) then, if you please; ~ **quam** very
much; **haud** ~ not so very, not quite.
sanguen *etc see* **sanguis.**
sanguināns, -antis *adj* bloodthirsty.
sanguinārius *adj* bloodthirsty.
sanguineus *adj* bloody, of blood; blood-red.
sanguinolentus *adj* bloody; blood-red;
sanguinary.
sanguis, -inis *m* blood, bloodshed; descent,
family; offspring; (*fig*) strength, life; **~inem
dare** shed one's blood; **~inem mittere** let
blood.
saniēs, -em, -ē *f* diseased blood, matter;
venom.
sānitās, -ātis *f* (*body*) health, sound condition;
(*mind*) sound sense, sanity; (*style*)
correctness, purity.
sanna, -ae *f* grimace, mocking.
sanniō, -ōnis *m* clown.
sānō, -āre, -āvī, -ātum *vt* to cure, heal; (*fig*) to
remedy, relieve.
Sanquālis avis *f* osprey.
sānus *adj* (*body*) sound, healthy; (*mind*) sane,
sensible; (*style*) correct; **male** ~ mad,
inspired; **sānun es?** are you in your senses?
sanxī *perf of* **sanciō.**
sapa, -ae *f* new wine.
sapiēns, -entis *pres p of* **sapiō** ♦ *adj* wise,
discreet ♦ *m* wise man, philosopher; man of
taste.
sapienter *adv* wisely, sensibly.
sapientia, -ae *f* wisdom, discernment;
philosophy; knowledge.
sapiō, -ere, -īvī *and* **uī** *vi* to have a flavour or
taste; to have sense, be wise ♦ *vt* to taste of,
smell of, smack of; to understand.
sapor, -ōris *m* taste, flavour; (*food*) delicacy;
(*fig*) taste, refinement.
Sapphicus *adj see* **Sapphō.**
Sapphō, -ūs *f famous Greek lyric poetess, native
of Lesbos.*
sarcina, -ae *f* bundle, burden; (*MIL*) pack.

sarcinārius *adj* baggage- (*in cpds*).
sarcinātor, -ōris *m* patcher.
sarcinula, -ae *f* little pack.
sarciō, -cīre, -sī, -tum *vt* to patch, mend,
repair.
sarcophagus, -ī *m* sepulchre.
sarculum, -ī *nt* light hoe.
Sardēs (-is), -ium *fpl* Sardis (*capital of Lydia*).
Sardiānus *adj see* **Sardēs.**
Sardinia, -iniae *f* island of Sardinia.
sardonyx, -chis *f* sardonyx.
Sardus, -ous, -iniēnsis *adj see* **Sardinia.**
sariō, -īre, -īvī *and* **uī** *vt* to hoe, weed.
sarīsa, -ae *f* Macedonian lance.
sarīsophorus, -ī *m* Macedonian lancer.
Sarmatae, -ārum *mpl* Sarmatians (*a people of
S.E. Russia*).
Sarmaticus, -is *adj see* **Sarmatae.**
sarmentum, -ī *nt* twigs, brushwood.
Sarpēdōn, -onis *m king of Lycia.*
Sarra, -ae *f* Tyre.
sarrācum, -ī *nt* cart.
Sarrānus *adj* Tyrian.
sarriō *etc see* **sariō.**
sarsī *perf of* **sarciō.**
sartāgō, -inis *f* frying pan.
sartor, -ōris *m* hoer, weeder.
sartus *ppp of* **sarciō.**
sat *etc see* **satis.**
satagō, -ere *vi* to have one's hands full, be in
trouble; to bustle about, fuss.
satelles, -itis *m/f* attendant, follower;
assistant, accomplice.
satiās, -ātis *f* sufficiency; satiety.
satietās, -ātis *f* sufficiency; satiety.
satin, satine *see* **satisne.**
satiō, -āre, -āvī, -ātum *vt* to satisfy, appease;
to fill, saturate; to glut, cloy, disgust.
satiō, -ōnis *f* sowing, planting; (*pl*) fields.
satis, sat *adj* enough, sufficient ♦ *adv* enough,
sufficiently; tolerably, fairly, quite; ~ **accipiō**
take sufficient bail; ~ **agō, agitō** have one's
hands full, be harassed; ~ **dō** offer sufficient
bail; ~ **faciō** satisfy; give satisfaction, make
amends; (*creditor*) pay.
satisdatiō, -ōnis *f* giving security.
satisdō *see* **satis.**
satisfaciō *see* **satis.**
satisfactiō, -ōnis *f* amends, apology.
satisne *adv* quite, really.
satius *compar of* **satis;** better, preferable.
sator, -ōris *m* sower, planter; father;
promoter.
satrapēs, -is *m* satrap (*Persian governor*).
satur, -ī *adj* filled, sated; (*fig*) rich.
satura, -ae *f* mixed dish; medley; (*poem*)
satire; **per ~am** confusingly.
satureia, -ōrum *ntpl* (*plant*) savory.
saturitās, -ātis *f* repletion; fulness, plenty.
Saturnālia, -ium *and* **iōrum** *ntpl festival of*

Noun declensions and verb conjugations are shown on pp xiii to xxv. The present infinitive ending of a verb shows
to which conjugation it belongs: **-āre** = 1st; **-ēre** = 2nd; **-ere** = 3rd and **-īre** = 4th. Irregular verbs are shown on p xxvi

Saturn in December.
Saturnia, -iae *f* Juno.
Saturnīnus, -ī *m revolutionary tribune in 103 and 100 B.C.*
Saturnius *adj see n.*
Saturnus, -ī *m* Saturn (*god of sowing, ruler of the Golden Age*); *the planet Saturn.*
saturō, -āre, -āvī, -ātum *vt* to fill, glut, satisfy; to disgust.
satus *ppp of* **serō ♦** *m* son ♦ *f* daughter ♦ *ntpl* crops.
satus, -ūs *m* sowing, planting; begetting.
satyriscus, -ī *m* little satyr.
satyrus, -ī *m* satyr.
sauciātiō, -ōnis *f* wounding.
sauciō, -āre *vt* to wound, hurt.
saucius *adj* wounded, hurt; ill, stricken.
Sauromatae *etc see* **Sarmatae.**
sāviātiō, -ōnis *f* kissing.
sāviolum, -ī *nt* sweet kiss.
sāvior, -ārī *vt* to kiss.
sāvium, -ī *and* **iī** *nt* kiss.
saxātilis *adj* rock- (*in cpds*).
saxētum, -ī *nt* rocky place.
saxeus *adj* of rock, rocky.
saxificus *adj* petrifying.
saxōsus *adj* rocky, stony.
saxulum, -ī *nt* small rock.
saxum, -ī *nt* rock, boulder; the Tarpeian Rock.
scaber, -rī *adj* rough, scurfy; mangy, itchy.
scabiēs, -em, -ē *f* roughness, scurf; mange, itch.
scabillum, -ī *nt* stool; a castanet played with the foot.
scabō, -ere, scābī *vt* to scratch.
Scaea porta, -ae, -ae *f the west gate of Troy.*
scaena, -ae *f* stage, stage setting; (*fig*) limelight, public life; outward appearance, pretext.
scaenālis *adj* theatrical.
scaenicus *adj* stage- (*in cpds*), theatrical ♦ *m* actor.
Scaevola, -ae *m early Roman who burned his hand off before Porsenna; famous jurist of Cicero's day.*
scaevus *adj* on the left; perverse ♦ *f* omen.
scālae, -ārum *fpl* steps, ladder, stairs.
scalmus, -ī *m* tholepin.
scalpellum, -ī *nt* scalpel, lancet.
scalpō, -ere, -sī, -tum *vt* to carve, engrave; to scratch.
scalprum, -ī *nt* knife, penknife; chisel.
scalpurriō, -īre *vi* to scratch.
Scamander, -rī *m* river of Troy (*also called Xanthus*).
scammōnea, -ae *f* (*plant*) scammony.
scamnum, -ī *nt* bench, stool; throne.
scandō, -ere *vt, vi* to climb, mount.
scapha, -ae *f* boat, skiff.
scaphium, -ī *and* **iī** *nt* a boat-shaped cup.
scapulae, -ārum *fpl* shoulder blades;

shoulders.
scāpus, -ī *m* shaft; (*loom*) yarnbeam.
scarus, -ī *m* (*fish*) scar.
scatebra, -ae *f* gushing water.
scateō, -ēre; -ō, -ere *vi* to bubble up, gush out; (*fig*) to abound, swarm.
scatūrigines, -um *fpl* springs.
scatūriō, -īre *vi* to gush out; (*fig*) to be full of.
scaurus *adj* large-ankled.
scelerātē *adv* wickedly.
scelerātus *adj* desecrated; wicked, infamous, accursed; pernicious.
scelerō, -āre *vt* to desecrate.
scelerōsus *adj* vicious, accursed.
scelestē *adv* wickedly.
scelestus *adj* wicked, villainous, accursed; unlucky.
scelus, -eris *nt* wickedness, crime, sin; (*person*) scoundrel; (*event*) calamity.
scēn- *etc see* **scaen-.**
scēptrifer, -ī *adj* sceptered.
scēptrum, -ī *nt* staff, sceptre; kingship, power.
scēptūchus, -ī *m* sceptre-bearer.
scheda *etc see* **scida.**
schēma, -ae *f* form, figure, style.
Schoenēis, -ēidis *f* Atalanta.
Schoenēius *adj see* **Schoenēis.**
Schoeneus, -eī *m father of Atalanta.*
schoenobatēs, -ae *m* rope dancer.
schola, -ae *f* learned discussion, dissertation; school; sect, followers.
scholasticus *adj* of a school ♦ *m* rhetorician.
scida, -ae *f* sheet of paper.
sciēns, -entis *pres p of* **sciō ♦** *adj* knowing, purposely; versed in, acquainted with.
scienter *adv* expertly.
scientia, -ae *f* knowledge, skill.
scīlicet *adv* evidently, of course; (*concessive*) no doubt; (*ironical*) I suppose, of course.
scilla *etc see* **squilla.**
scindō, -ndere, -dī, -ssum *vt* to cut open, tear apart, split, break down; to divide, part.
scintilla, -ae *f* spark.
scintillō, -āre *vi* to sparkle.
scintillula, -ae *f* little spark.
sciō, -īre, -īvī, -ītum *vt* to know; to have skill in; (*with infin*) to know how to; **quod ~iam** as far as I know; **~ītō** you may be sure.
Scīpiadēs, -ae *m* Scipio.
scīpiō, -ōnis *m* staff.
Scīpiō, -ōnis *m* famous Roman family name (*esp the conqueror of Hannibal* Africanus); Aemilianus (*destroyer of Carthage and patron of literature*).
scirpeus *adj* rush (*in cpds*) ♦ *f* wickerwork frame.
scirpiculus, -ī *m* rush basket.
scirpus, -ī *m* bulrush.
scīscitor, -ārī, -ātus; -ō, -āre *vt* to inquire; to question.
scīscō, -scere, -vī, -tum *vt* to inquire, learn; (*POL*) to approve, decree, appoint.

scissus *ppp of* **scindō** ♦ *adj* split; (*voice*) harsh.
scītāmenta, -ōrum *ntpl* dainties.
scītē *adv* cleverly, tastefully.
scītor, -ārī, -ātus *vt, vi* to inquire; to consult.
scītulus *adj* neat, smart.
scītum, -ī *nt* decree, statute.
scītus *ppp of* **sciō**; *ppp of* **scīscō** ♦ *adj* clever, shrewd, skilled; (*words*) sensible, witty; (*appearance*) fine, smart.
scītus, -ūs *m* decree.
sciūrus, -ī *m* squirrel.
scīvī *perf of* **sciō**; *perf of* **scīscō**.
scobis, -is *f* sawdust, filings.
scomber, -rī *m* mackerel.
scōpae, -ārum *fpl* broom.
Scopās, -ae *m* famous Greek sculptor.
scopulōsus *adj* rocky.
scopulus, -ī *m* rock, crag, promontory; (*fig*) danger.
scorpiō, -ōnis, -us *and* **os, -ī** *m* scorpion; (*MIL*) a kind of catapult.
scortātor, -ōris *m* fornicator.
scorteus *adj* of leather.
scortor, -ārī *vi* to associate with harlots.
scortum, -ī *nt* harlot, prostitute.
screātor, -ōris *m* one who clears his throat noisily.
screātus, -ūs *m* clearing the throat.
scrība, -ae *m* clerk, writer.
scrībō, -bere, -psī, -ptum *vt* to write, draw; to write down, describe; (*document*) to draw up; (*law*) to designate; (*MIL*) to enlist.
scrīnium, -ī *and* **iī** *nt* book box, lettercase.
scrīptiō, -ōnis *f* writing; composition; text.
scrīptitō, -āre, -āvī, -ātum *vt* to write regularly, compose.
scrīptor, -ōris *m* writer, author; secretary; **rērum ~** historian.
scrīptula, -ōrum *ntpl* lines of a squared board.
scrīptum, -ī *nt* writing, book, work; (*law*) ordinance; **duōdecim ~a** Twelve Lines (*a game played on a squared board*).
scrīptūra, -ae *f* writing; composition; document; (*POL*) tax on public pastures; (*will*) provision.
scrīptus *ppp of* **scrībō**.
scrīptus, -ūs *m* clerkship.
scrīpulum, -ī *nt* small weight, scruple.
scrobis, -is *f* ditch, trench; grave.
scrōfa, -ae *f* breeding sow.
scrōfipāscus, -ī *m* pig breeder.
scrūpeus *adj* stony, rough.
scrūpōsus *adj* rocky, jagged.
scrūpulōsus *adj* stony, rough; (*fig*) precise.
scrūpulum *etc see* **scrīpulum**.
scrūpulus, -ī *m* small sharp stone; (*fig*) uneasiness, doubt, scruple.
scrūpus, -ī *m* sharp stone; (*fig*) uneasiness.
scrūta, -ōrum *ntpl* trash.

scrūtor, -ārī, -ātus *vt* to search, probe into, examine; to find out.
sculpō, -ere, -sī, -tum *vt* to carve, engrave.
sculpōneae, -ārum *fpl* clogs.
sculptilis *adj* carved.
sculptor, -ōris *m* sculptor.
sculptus *ppp of* **sculpō**.
scurra, -ae *m* jester; dandy.
scurrīlis *adj* jeering.
scurrīlitās, -ātis *f* scurrility.
scurror, -ārī *vi* to play the fool.
scūtāle, -is *nt* sling strap.
scūtātus *adj* carrying a shield.
scutella, -ae *f* bowl.
scutica, -ae *f* whip.
scutra, -ae *f* flat dish.
scutula, -ae *f* small dish.
scutula *f* wooden roller; secret letter.
scutulāta, -ae *f* a checked garment.
scūtulum, -ī *nt* small shield.
scūtum, -ī *nt* shield.
Scylla, -ae *f* dangerous rock *or* sea monster (*in the Straits of Messina*).
Scyllaeus *adj see* **Scylla**.
scymnus, -ī *m* cub.
scyphus, -ī *m* wine cup.
Scyrius, -ias *adj see* **Scyros**.
Scyros *and* **us, -ī** *f* Aegean island near Euboea.
scytala *see* **scutula**.
Scytha *and* **ēs, -ae** *m* Scythian.
Scythia, -iae *f* Scythia (*country N.E. of the Black Sea*).
Scythicus *adj* Scythian.
Scythis, -idis *f* Scythian woman.
sē *pron* himself, herself, itself, themselves; one another; **apud ~** at home; in his senses; **inter ~** mutually.
sēbum, -ī *nt* tallow, suet, grease.
sēcēdō, -ēdere, -essī, -essum *vi* to withdraw, retire; to revolt, secede.
sēcernō, -ernere, -rēvī, -rētum *vt* to separate, set apart; to dissociate; to distinguish.
sēcessiō, -ōnis *f* withdrawal; secession.
sēcessus, -ūs *m* retirement, solitude; retreat, recess.
sēclūdō, -dere, -sī, -sum *vt* to shut off, seclude; to separate, remove.
sēclūsus *ppp of* **sēclūdō** ♦ *adj* remote.
secō, -āre, -uī, -tum *vt* to cut; to injure; to divide; (*MED*) to operate on; (*motion*) to pass through; (*dispute*) to decide.
sēcrētiō, -ōnis *f* separation.
sēcrētō *adv* apart, in private, in secret.
sēcrētum, -ī *nt* privacy, secrecy; retreat, remote place; secret, mystery.
sēcrētus *ppp of* **sēcernō** ♦ *adj* separate; solitary, remote; secret, private.
secta, -ae *f* path; method, way of life; (*POL*) party; (*PHILOS*) school.

sectārius *adj* leading.
sectātor, -ōris *m* follower, adherent.
sectilis *adj* cut; for cutting.
sectiō, -ōnis *f* auctioning of confiscated goods.
sector, -ōris *m* cutter; buyer at a public sale.
sector, -ārī, -ātus *vt* to follow regularly, attend; to chase, hunt.
sectūra, -ae *f* digging.
sectus *ppp of* **secō**.
sēcubitus, -ūs *m* lying alone.
sēcubō, -āre, -uī *vi* to sleep by oneself; to live alone.
secuī *perf of* **secō**.
sēcul- *etc see* **saecul-**.
sēcum with himself *etc.*
secundānī, -ōrum *mpl* men of the second legion.
secundārius *adj* second-rate.
secundō *adv* secondly.
secundō, -āre *vt* to favour, make prosper.
secundum *prep (place)* behind, along; *(time)* after; *(rank)* next to; *(agreement)* according to, in favour of ♦ *adv* behind.
secundus *adj* following, next, second; inferior; favourable, propitious, fortunate ♦ *fpl (play)* subsidiary part; *(fig)* second fiddle ♦ *ntpl* success, good fortune; ~**ō flūmine** downstream; **rēs ~ae** prosperity, success.
secūricula, -ae *f* little axe.
secūrifer, -ī *adj* armed with an axe.
secūriger, -ī *adj* armed with an axe.
secūris, -is *f* axe; *(fig)* death blow; *(POL)* authority, supreme power.
sēcūritās, -ātis *f* freedom from anxiety, composure; negligence; safety, feeling of security.
sēcūrus *adj* untroubled, unconcerned; carefree, cheerful; careless.
secus *nt (indecl)* sex.
secus *adv* otherwise, differently; badly; **nōn ~** even so.
secūtor, -ōris *m* pursuer.
sed *conj* but; but also, but in fact.
sēdātē *adv* calmly.
sēdātiō, -ōnis *f* calming.
sēdātus *ppp of* **sēdō** ♦ *adj* calm, quiet, composed.
sēdecim *num* sixteen.
sēdēcula, -ae *f* low stool.
sedentārius *adj* sitting.
sedeō, -ēre, sēdī, sessum *vi* to sit; *(army)* to be encamped, blockade; *(magistrates)* to be in session; *(clothes)* to suit, fit; *(places)* to be low-lying; *(heavy things)* to settle, subside; *(weapons)* to stick fast; *(inactivity)* to be idle; *(thought)* to be firmly resolved.
sēdēs, -is *f* seat, chair; abode, home; site, ground, foundation.
sēdī *perf of* **sedeō**.
sedīle, -is *nt* seat, chair.
sēditiō, -ōnis *f* insurrection, mutiny.
sēditiōsē *adv* seditiously.

sēditiōsus *adj* mutinous, factious; quarrelsome; troubled.
sēdō, -āre, -āvī, -ātum *vt* to calm, allay, lull.
sēdūcō, -ūcere, -ūxī, -uctum *vt* to take away, withdraw; to divide.
sēductiō, -ōnis *f* taking sides.
sēductus *ppp of* **sēdūcō** ♦ *adj* remote.
sēdulitās, -ātis *f* earnestness, assiduity; officiousness.
sēdulō *adv* busily, diligently; purposely.
sēdulus *adj* busy, diligent, assiduous; officious.
seges, -itis *f* cornfield; crop.
Segesta, -ae *f* town in N.W. Sicily.
Segestānus *adj see* **Segesta**.
segmentātus *adj* flounced.
segmentum, -ī *nt* brocade.
segne, -iter *adv* slowly, lazily.
segnipēs, -edis *adj* slow of foot.
segnis *adj* slow, sluggish, lazy.
segnitia, -ae *and* **ēs, -em, -ē** *f* slowness, sluggishness, sloth.
sēgregō, -āre, -āvī, -ātum *vt* to separate, put apart; to dissociate.
sēiugātus *adj* separated.
sēiugis, -is *m* chariot and six.
sēiūnctim *adv* separately.
sēiūnctiō, -ōnis *f* separation.
sēiūnctus *ppp of* **sēiungō**.
sēiungō, -gere, sēiūnxī, sēiūnctum *vt* to separate, part.
sēlēctiō, -ōnis *f* choice.
sēlēctus *ppp of* **sēligō**.
Seleucus, -ī *m* king of Syria.
sēlībra, -ae *f* half pound.
sēligō, -igere, -ēgī, -ēctum *vt* to choose, select.
sella, -ae *f* seat, chair, stool, sedan chair; ~ **cūrūlis** chair of office for higher magistrates.
sellisternia, -ōrum *ntpl* sacred banquets to goddesses.
sellula, -ae *f* stool; sedan chair.
sellulārius, -ī *and* **iī** *m* mechanic.
sēmanimus *etc see* **sēmianimis**.
semel *adv* once; once for all; first; ever; ~ **atque iterum** again and again; ~ **aut iterum** once or twice.
Semelē, -ēs *f* mother of Bacchus.
Semelēius *adj see* **Semelē**.
sēmen, -inis *nt* seed; *(plant)* seedling, slip; *(men)* race, child; *(physics)* particle; *(fig)* origin, instigator.
sēmentifer, -ī *adj* fruitful.
sēmentis, -is *f* sowing, planting; young corn.
sēmentīvus *adj* of seed time.
sēmermis *etc see* **sēmiermis**.
sēmēstris *adj* half-yearly, for six months.
sēmēsus *adj* half-eaten.
sēmet *pron* self, selves.
sēmiadapertus *adj* half-open.
sēmianimis, -us *adj* half-dead.
sēmiapertus *adj* half-open.
sēmibōs, -ovis *adj* half-ox.

sēmicaper, -rī *adj* half-goat.
sēmicremātus, sēmicremus *adj* half-
burned.
sēmicubitālis *adj* half a cubit long.
sēmideus *adj* half-divine ♦ *m* demigod.
sēmidoctus *adj* half-taught.
sēmiermis, -us *adj* half-armed.
sēmiēsus *adj* half-eaten.
sēmifactus *adj* half-finished.
sēmifer, -ī *adj* half-beast; half-savage.
sēmigermānus *adj* half-German.
sēmigravis *adj* half-overcome.
sēmigrō, -āre *vi* to go away.
sēmihiāns, -antis *adj* half-opened.
sēmihomō, -inis *m* half-man, half-human.
sēmihōra, -ae *f* half an hour.
sēmilacer, -ī *adj* half-mangled.
sēmilautus *adj* half-washed.
sēmilīber, -ī *adj* half-free.
sēmilixa, -ae *m* not much better than a camp
follower.
sēmimarīnus *adj* half in the sea.
sēmimās, -āris *m* hermaphrodite ♦ *adj*
castrated.
sēmimortuus *adj* half-dead.
sēminārium, -ī and iī *nt* nursery, seed plot.
sēminātor, -ōris *m* originator.
sēminecis *adj* half-dead.
sēminium, -ī and iī *nt* procreation; breed.
sēminō, -āre *vt* to sow; to produce; to beget.
sēminūdus *adj* half-naked; almost unarmed.
sēmipāgānus *adj* half-rustic.
sēmiplēnus *adj* half-full, half-manned.
sēmiputātus *adj* half-pruned.
Semīramis, -is and idis *f* queen of Assyria.
Semīramius *adj see n.*
sēmirāsus *adj* half-shaven.
sēmireductus *adj* half turned back.
sēmirefectus *adj* half-repaired.
sēmirutus *adj* half-demolished, half in ruins.
sēmis, -issis *m* (*coin*) half an as; (*interest*) ½
per cent per month (*i.e. 6 per cent per annum*);
(*area*) half an acre.
sēmisepultus *adj* half-buried.
sēmisomnus *adj* half-asleep.
sēmisupīnus *adj* half lying back.
sēmita, -ae *f* path, way.
sēmitālis *adj* of byways.
sēmitārius *adj* frequenting byways.
sēmiūst- *etc see* **sēmūst-**.
sēmivir, -ī *adj* half-man; emasculated;
unmanly.
sēmivīvus *adj* half-dead.
sēmodius, -ī and iī *m* half a peck.
sēmōtus *ppp of* **sēmoveō** ♦ *adj* remote;
distinct.
sēmoveō, -ovēre, -ōvī, -ōtum *vt* to put
aside, separate.
semper *adv* always, ever, every time.
sempiternus *adj* everlasting, lifelong.

Semprōnius, -ī *m* Roman family name (*esp
the Gracchi*).
Semprōnius, -iānus *adj see n.*
sēmūncia, -ae *f* half an ounce; a twenty-
fourth.
sēmūnciārius *adj* (*interest*) at the rate of one
twenty-fourth.
sēmūstulātus *adj* half-burned.
sēmūstus *adj* half-burned.
senāculum, -ī *nt* open air meeting place (*of
the Senate*).
sēnāriolus, -ī *m* little trimeter.
sēnārius, -ī and iī *m* (iambic) trimeter.
senātor, -ōris *m* senator.
senātōrius *adj* senatorial, in the Senate.
senātus, -ūs *m* Senate; meeting of the Senate.
senātūscōnsultum, -ī *nt* decree of the
Senate.
Seneca, -ae *m* Stoic philosopher, tutor of Nero.
senecta, -ae *f* old age.
senectus *adj* old, aged.
senectūs, -ūtis *f* old age; old men.
seneō, -ēre *vi* to be old.
senēscō, -ēscere, -uī *vi* to grow old; (*fig*) to
weaken, wane, pine away.
senex, -is (*compar* -ior) *adj* old (*over 45*) ♦ *m/f*
old man, old woman.
sēnī, -ōrum *adj* six each, in sixes; six; ~ dēnī
sixteen each.
senīlis *adj* of an old person, senile.
seniō, -ōnis *m* number six on a dice.
senior *compar of* **senex.**
senium, -ī and iī *nt* weakness of age, decline;
affliction; peevishness.
Senonēs, -um *mpl* tribe of S. Gaul.
sēnsī *perf of* **sentiō.**
sēnsifer, -ī *adj* sensory.
sēnsilis *adj* having sensation.
sēnsim *adv* tentatively, gradually.
sēnsus *ppp of* **sentiō** ♦ *ntpl* thoughts.
sēnsus, -ūs *m* (*body*) feeling, sensation,
sense; (*intellect*) understanding, judgment,
thought; (*emotion*) sentiment, attitude,
frame of mind; (*language*) meaning, purport,
sentence; **commūnis ~** universal human
feelings, human sympathy, social instinct.
sententia, -ae *f* opinion, judgment; purpose,
will; (*law*) verdict, sentence; (*POL*) vote,
decision; (*language*) meaning, sentence,
maxim, epigram; **meā ~ā** in my opinion; **dē
meā ~ā** in accordance with my wishes; **ex
meā ~ā** to my liking; **ex animī meī ~ā** to the
best of my knowledge and belief; **in ~am
pedibus īre** support a motion.
sententiola, -ae *f* phrase.
sententiōsē *adv* pointedly.
sententiōsus *adj* pithy.
senticētum, -ī *nt* thornbrake.
sentīna, -ae *f* bilge water; (*fig*) dregs, scum.
sentiō, -īre, sēnsī, sēnsum *vt* (*senses*) to

Noun declensions and verb conjugations are shown on pp xiii to xxv. The present infinitive ending of a verb shows
to which conjugation it belongs: **-āre** = 1st; **-ēre** = 2nd; **-ere** = 3rd and **-īre** = 4th. Irregular verbs are shown on p xxvi

feel, see, perceive; (*CIRCS*) to experience, undergo; (*mind*) to observe, understand; (*opinion*) to think, judge; (*law*) to vote, decide.

sentis, -is *m* thorn, brier.

sentīscō, -ere *vt* to begin to perceive.

sentus *adj* thorny; untidy.

senuī *perf of* **senēscō**.

seorsum, seorsus *adv* apart, differently.

sēparābilis *adj* separable.

sēparātim *adv* apart, separately.

sēparātiō, -ōnis *f* separation, severing.

sēparātius *adv* less closely.

sēparātus *adj* separate, different.

sēparō, -āre, -āvī, -ātum *vt* to part, separate, divide; to distinguish.

sepeliō, -elīre, -elīvī *and* **eliī, -ultum** *vt* to bury; (*fig*) to overwhelm, overcome.

sēpia, -ae *f* cuttlefish.

Sēplasia, -ae *f street in Capua where perfumes were sold.*

sēpōnō, -ōnere, -osuī, -ositum *vt* to put aside, pick out; to reserve; to banish; to appropriate; to separate.

sēpositus *ppp of* **sēpōnō ♦** *adj* remote; distinct, choice.

sēpse *pron* oneself.

septem *num* seven.

September, -ris *m* September **♦** *adj* of September.

septemdecim *etc see* **septendecim**.

septemfluus *adj* with seven streams.

septemgeminus *adj* sevenfold.

septemplex, -icis *adj* sevenfold.

septemtriō *etc see* **septentriōnēs**.

septemvirālis *adj* of the septemviri **♦** *mpl* the septemviri.

septemvirātus, -ūs *m* office of septemvir.

septemvirī, -ōrum *mpl* board of seven officials.

septēnārius, -ī *and* **iī** *m* verse of seven feet.

septendecim *num* seventeen.

septēnī, -ōrum *adj* seven each, in sevens.

septentriō, -ōnis *m*, **-ōnēs, -ōnum** *mpl* Great Bear, Little Bear; north; north wind.

septentriōnālis *adj* northern **♦** *ntpl* northern regions.

septiēns, -ēs *adv* seven times.

septimānī, -ōrum *mpl* men of the seventh legion.

septimum *adv* for the seventh time; ~ **decimus** seventeenth.

septimus *adj* seventh.

septingentēsimus *adj* seven hundredth.

septingentī, -ōrum *adj* seven hundred.

septuāgēsimus *adj* seventieth.

septuāgintā *adj* seventy.

septuennis *adj* seven years old.

septumus *adj see* **septimus**.

septūnx, -ūncis *m* seven ounces, seven-twelfths.

sepulcrālis *adj* funeral.

sepulcrētum, -ī *nt* cemetery.

sepulcrum, -ī *nt* grave, tomb.

sepultūra, -ae *f* burial, funeral.

sepultus *ppp of* **sepeliō**.

Sequāna, -ae *f* river Seine.

Sequānī, -ōrum *mpl* *people of N. Gaul*.

sequāx, -ācis *adj* pursuing, following.

sequens, -entis *pres p of* **sequor ♦** *adj* following, next.

sequester, -rī *and* **ris** *m* trustee; agent, mediator.

sequestrum, -rī *nt* deposit.

sēquius *compar of* **secus**; otherwise; **nihilō ~** nonetheless.

sequor, -quī, -cūtus *vt*, *vi* to follow; to accompany, go with; (*time*) to come after, come next, ensue; (*enemy*) to pursue; (*objective*) to make for, aim at; (*pulling*) to come away easily; (*share, gift*) to go to, come to; (*words*) to come naturally.

sera, -ae *f* door bolt, bar.

Serāpēum, -ēī *nt temple of Serapis*.

Serāpis, -is *and* **idis** *m chief Egyptian god*.

serēnitās, -ātis *f* fair weather.

serēnō, -āre *vt* to clear up, brighten up.

serēnus *adj* fair, clear; (*wind*) fair-weather; (*fig*) cheerful, happy **♦** *nt* clear sky, fair weather.

Sēres, -um *mpl* Chinese.

serēscō, -ere *vi* to dry off.

sēria, -ae *f* tall jar.

sērica, -ōrum *ntpl* silks.

Sēricus *adj* Chinese; silk.

seriēs, -em, -ē *f* row, sequence, succession.

sēriō *adv* in earnest, seriously.

sēriola, -ae *f* small jar.

Serīphius *adj see* **Serīphus**.

Serīphus (-os), -ī *f* Aegean island.

sērius *adj* earnest, serious.

sērius *compar of* **sērō**.

sermō, -ōnis *m* conversation, talk; learned discussion, discourse; common talk, rumour; language, style; every day language, prose; (*pl*) Satires (of Horace).

sermōcinor, -ārī *vi* to converse.

sermunculus, -ī *m* gossip, rumour.

serō, -ere, sēvī, -satum *vt* to sow, plant; (*fig*) to produce, sow the seeds of.

serō, -ere, -tum *vt* to sew, join, wreathe; (*fig*) to compose, devise, engage in.

sērō (*compar* **-ius**) *adv* late; too late.

serpēns, -entis *m/f* snake, serpent; (*constellation*) Draco.

serpentigena, -ae *m* offspring of a serpent.

serpentipēs, -edis *adj* serpent-footed.

serperastra, -ōrum *ntpl* splints.

serpō, -ere, -sī, -tum *vi* to creep, crawl; (*fig*) to spread slowly.

serpyllum, -ī *nt* wild thyme.

serra, -ae *f* saw.

serrācum *etc see* **sarrācum**.

serrātus *adj* serrated, notched.

serrula, -ae *f* small saw.

Sertōriānus *adj see* **Sertōrius**.

Sertōrius, -ī m commander under Marius, who held out against Sulla in Spain.
sertus ppp of serō ♦ ntpl garlands.
serum, -ī nt whey, serum.
sērum, -ī nt late hour.
sērus adj late; too late; ~ā nocte late at night.
serva, -ae f maidservant, slave.
servābilis adj that cannot be saved.
servātor, -ōris m deliverer; watcher.
servātrīx, -īcis f deliverer.
servīlis adj of slaves, servile.
servīliter adv slavishly.
Servīlius, -ī m Roman family name of many consuls.
Servīlius, -ānus adj see n.
serviō, -īre, -īvī and **iī, -ītum** vi to be a slave; (with dat) to serve, be of use to, be good for; (property) to be mortgaged.
servitium, -ī and **iī** nt slavery, servitude; slaves.
servitūdō, -inis f slavery.
servitūs, -ūtis f slavery, service; slaves; (property) liability.
Servius, -ī m sixth king of Rome; famous jurist of Cicero's day.
servō, -āre, -āvī, -ātum vt to save, rescue; to keep, preserve, retain; to store, reserve; to watch, observe, guard; (place) to remain in.
servolus, -ī m young slave.
servos, -ī m see servus.
servula, -ae f servant girl.
servulus, -ī m young slave.
servus, -ī m slave, servant ♦ adj slavish, serving; (property) liable to a burden.
sescēnāris adj a year and a half old.
sescēnī, -ōrum adj six hundred each.
sescentēsimus adj six hundredth.
sescentī, -ōrum num six hundred; an indefinitely large number.
sescentiēns, -ēs adv six hundred times.
sēsē etc see sē.
seselis, -is f (plant) seseli.
sesqui adv one and a half times.
sesquialter, -ī adj one and a half.
sesquimodius, -ī and **iī** m a peck and a half.
sesquioctāvus adj of nine to eight.
sesquiopus, -eris nt a day and a half's work.
sesquipedālis adj a foot and a half.
sesquipēs, -edis m a foot and a half.
sesquiplāga, -ae f a blow and a half.
sesquiplex, -icis adj one and a half times.
sesquitertius adj of four to three.
sessilis adj for sitting on.
sessiō, -ōnis f sitting; seat; session; loitering.
sessitō, -āre, -āvī vi to sit regularly.
sessiuncula, -ae f small meeting.
sessor, -ōris m spectator; resident.
sēstertium, -ī nt 1000 sesterces; **dēna ~ia** 10,000 sesterces; **centēna mīlia ~ium** 100,000 sesterces; **deciēns ~ium** 1,000,000 sesterces.

sēstertius, -ī and **iī** m sesterce, a silver coin.
Sestius, -ī m tribune defended by Cicero.
Sestius, -iānus adj of a Sestius.
Sestos (-us), -ī f town on Dardanelles (home of Hero).
Sestus adj see Sestos.
sēt- etc see saet-.
Sētia, -iae f town in S. Latium (famous for wine).
Sētiaīnus adj see Sētia.
sētius compar of secus.
seu etc see sīve.
sevērē adv sternly, severely.
sevēritās, -ātis f strictness, austerity.
sevērus adj strict, stern; severe, austere; grim, terrible.
sēvī perf of serō.
sēvocō, -āre vt to call aside; to withdraw, remove.
sēvum etc see sēbum.
sex num six.
sexāgēnārius adj sixty years old.
sexāgēnī, -ōrum adj sixty each.
sexāgēsimus adj sixtieth.
sexāgiēns, -ēs adv sixty times.
sexāgintā num sixty.
sexangulus adj hexagonal.
sexcēn- etc see sescēn-.
sexcēnārius adj of six hundred.
sexennis adj six years old, after six years.
sexennium, -ī and **iī** nt six years.
sexiēns, -ēs adv six times.
sexprīmī, -ōrum mpl a provincial town, council.
sextadecimānī, -ōrum mpl men of the sixteenth legion.
sextāns, -antis m a sixth; (coin, weight) a sixth of an as.
sextārius, -ī and **iī** m pint.
Sextīlis, -is m August ♦ adj of August.
sextula, -ae f a sixth of an ounce.
sextum adv for the sixth time.
sextus adj sixth; ~ decimus sixteenth.
sexus, -ūs m sex.
sī conj if; if only; to see if; **sī forte** in the hope that; **sī iam** assuming for the moment; **sī minus** if not; **sī quandō** whenever; **sī quidem** if indeed; since; **sī quis** if anyone, whoever; **mīrum sī** surprising that; **quod sī** and if, but if.
sībila, -ōrum ntpl whistle, hissing.
sībilō, -āre vi to hiss, whistle ♦ vt to hiss at.
sībilus, -ī m whistle, hissing.
sībilus adj hissing.
Sibulla, Sibylla, -ae f prophetess, Sibyl.
Sibyllīnus adj see Sibylla.
sīc adv so, thus, this way, as follows; as one is, as things are; on this condition; yes.
sīca, -ae f dagger.
Sicānī, -ōrum mpl ancient people of Italy

Noun declensions and verb conjugations are shown on pp xiii to xxv. The present infinitive ending of a verb shows to which conjugation it belongs: **-āre** = 1st; **-ēre** = 2nd; **-ere** = 3rd and **-īre** = 4th. Irregular verbs are shown on p xxvi

(*later of Sicily*).
Sicānia, -iae *f* Sicily.
Sicānus, -ius *adj* Sicanian, Sicilian.
sīcārius, -ī *and* **iī** *m* assassin, murderer.
siccē *adv* (*speech*) firmly.
siccitās, -ātis *f* dryness, drought; (*body*)
  firmness; (*style*) dullness.
siccō, -āre, -āvī, -ātum *vt* to dry; to drain,
  exhaust; (*sore*) to heal up.
siccoculus *adj* dry-eyed.
siccus *adj* dry; thirsty, sober; (*body*) firm,
  healthy; (*argument*) solid, sound; (*style*) flat,
  dull ♦ *nt* dry land.
Sicilia, -ae *f* Sicily.
sicilicula, -ae *f* little sickle.
Siciliēnsis, -s, -dis *adj* Sicilian.
sīcine is this how?
sīcubi *adv* if anywhere, wheresoever.
Siculus *adj* Sicilian.
sīcunde *adv* if from anywhere.
sīcut, sīcutī *adv* just as, as in fact;
  (*comparison*) like, as; (*example*) as for
  instance; (*with subj*) as if.
Sicyōn, -ōnis *f* town in N. Peloponnese.
Sicyōnius *adj see* **Sicyōn**.
sīdereus *adj* starry; (*fig*) radiant.
Sidicīnī, -ōrum *mpl* people of Campania.
Sidicīnus *adj see n.*
sīdō, -ere, -ī *vi* to sit down, settle; to sink,
  subside; to stick fast.
Sīdōn, -ōnis *f* famous Phoenician town.
Sīdōnis, -ōnidis *adj* Phoenician ♦ *f* Europa;
  Dido.
Sīdōnius *adj* Sidonian, Phoenician.
sīdus, -eris *nt* constellation; heavenly body,
  star; season, climate, weather; destiny; (*pl*)
  sky; (*fig*) fame, glory.
siem *archaic subj of* **sum**.
Sigambrī *etc see* **Sugambrī**.
Sigēum, -ī *nt* promontory near Troy.
Sigēus, -ius *adj* Sigean.
sigilla, -ōrum *ntpl* little figures; seal.
sigillātus *adj* decorated with little figures.
signātor, -ōris *m* witness (to a document).
signifer, -ī *adj* with constellations; ~ **orbis**
  Zodiac ♦ *m* (*MIL*) standard-bearer.
significanter *adv* pointedly, tellingly.
significātiō, -ōnis *f* indication, signal, token;
  sign of approval; (*RHET*) emphasis; (*word*)
  meaning.
significō, -āre, -āvī, -ātum *vt* to indicate,
  show; to betoken, portend; (*word*) to mean.
signō, -āre, -āvī, -ātum *vt* to mark, stamp,
  print; (*document*) to seal; (*money*) to coin,
  mint; (*fig*) to impress, designate, note.
signum, -ī *nt* mark, sign, token; (*MIL*) standard;
  signal, password; (*art*) design, statue;
  (*document*) seal; (*ASTRO*) constellation; **~a**
  cōnferre join battle; **~a cōnstituere** halt; **~a**
  convertere wheel about; **~a ferre** move camp;
  attack; **~a inferre** attack; **~a prōferre**
  advance; **~a sequī** march in order; **ab ~īs**
  discēdere leave the ranks; **sub ~īs īre** march

in order.
Sīla, -ae *f* forest in extreme S. Italy
sīlānus, -ī *m* fountain, jet of water.
silēns, -entis *pres p of* **sileō** ♦ *adj* still, silent ♦
  mpl the dead.
silentium, -ī *and* **iī** *nt* stillness, silence; (*fig*)
  standstill, inaction.
Sīlēnus, -ī *m* old and drunken companion of
  Bacchus.
sileō, -ēre, -uī *vi* to be still, be silent; to cease
  ♦ *vt* to say nothing about.
siler, -is *nt* willow.
silēscō, -ere *vi* to calm down, fall silent.
silex, -icis *m* flint, hard stone; rock.
silicernium, -ī *and* **iī** *nt* funeral feast.
silīgō, -inis *f* winter wheat; fine flour.
siliqua, -ae *f* pod, husk; (*pl*) pulse.
sillybus, -ī *m* label bearing a book's title.
Silurēs, -um *mpl* British tribe in S. Wales.
silūrus, -ī *m* sheatfish.
sīlus *adj* snub-nosed.
silva, -ae *f* wood, forest; plantation,
  shrubbery; (*plant*) flowering stem; (*LIT*)
  material.
Silvānus, -ī *m* god of uncultivated land.
silvēscō, -ere *vi* to run to wood.
silvestris *adj* wooded, forest- (*in cpds*); wild;
  pastoral.
silvicola, -ae *m/f* sylvan.
silvicultrīx, -īcis *adj* living in the woods.
silvifragus *adj* tree-breaking.
silvōsus *adj* woody.
sīmia, -ae *f* ape.
simile, -is *nt* comparison, parallel.
similis *adj* like, similar; ~ **atque** like what; **vērī**
  ~ probable.
similiter *adv* similarly.
similitūdō, -inis *f* likeness, resemblance;
  imitation; analogy; monotony; (*RHET*) simile.
sīmiolus, -ī *m* monkey.
simītu *adv* at the same time, together.
sīmius, -ī *and* **iī** *m* ape.
Simoīs, -entis *m* river of Troy.
Simōnidēs, -is *m* Greek lyric poet of Ceos
  (*famous for dirges*).
Simōnidēus *adj see n.*
simplex, -icis *adj* single, simple; natural,
  straightforward; (*character*) frank, sincere.
simplicitās, -ātis *f* singleness; frankness,
  innocence.
simpliciter *adv* simply, naturally; frankly.
simplum, -ī *nt* simple sum.
simpulum, -ī *nt* small ladle; **excitāre fluctūs in**
  ~ō ≈ raise a storm in a teacup.
simpuvium, -ī *and* **iī** *nt* libation bowl.
simul *adv* at the same time, together, at once;
  likewise, also; both ... and; ~ **ac atque, ut** as
  soon as ♦ *conj* as soon as.
simulācrum, -ī *nt* likeness, image, portrait,
  statue; phantom, ghost; (*writing*) symbol;
  (*fig*) semblance, shadow.
simulāmen, -inis *nt* copy.
simulāns, -antis *pres p of* **simulō** ♦ *adj*

imitative.

simulātē *adv* deceitfully.

simulātiō, -ōnis *f* pretence, shamming, hypocrisy.

simulātor, -ōris *m* imitator; pretender, hypocrite.

simulatque *conj* as soon as.

simulō, -āre, -āvī, -ātum *vt* to imitate, represent; to impersonate; to pretend, counterfeit.

simultās, -ātis *f* feud, quarrel.

sīmulus *adj* snub-nosed.

sīmus *adj* snub-nosed.

sīn *conj* but if; ~ **aliter, minus** but if not.

sināpi, -is *nt,* **-is, -is** *f* mustard.

sincērē *adv* honestly.

sincēritās, -ātis *f* integrity.

sincērus *adj* clean, whole, genuine; (*fig*) pure, sound, honest.

sincipitāmentum, -ī *nt* half a head.

sinciput, -itis *nt* half a head; brain.

sine *prep* (*with abl*) without, -less (*in cpds*).

singillātim *adv* singly, one by one.

singulāris *adj* one at a time, single, sole; unique, extraordinary.

singulāriter *adv* separately; extremely.

singulārius *adj* single.

singulī, -ōrum *adj* one each, single, one.

singultim *adv* in sobs.

singultō, -āre *vi* to sob, gasp, gurgle ♦ *vt* to gasp out.

singultus, -ūs *m* sob, gasp, death rattle.

singulus *etc see* **singulī**.

sinister, -rī *adj* left; (*fig*) perverse, unfavourable; (*Roman auspices*) lucky; (*Greek auspices*) unlucky.

sinistra, -rae *f* left hand, left-hand side.

sinistrē *adv* badly.

sinistrōrsus, -um *adv* to the left.

sinō, -ere, sīvī, situm *vt* to let, allow; to let be; **nē dī sīrint** God forbid!

Sinōpē, -ēs *f* Greek colony on the Black Sea.

Sinōpēnsis, -eus *adj see* **Sinōpē**.

Sinuessa, -ae *f* town on the borders of Latium and Campania.

Sinuessānus *adj see* **Sinuessa**.

sīnum *etc see* **sīnus**.

sinuō, -āre, -āvī, -ātum *vt* to wind, curve.

sinuōsus *adj* winding, curved.

sinus, -ūs *m* curve, fold; (*fishing*) net; (GEOG) bay, gulf, valley; (*hair*) curl; (*ship*) sail; (*toga*) fold, pocket, purse; (*person*) bosom; (*fig*) protection, love, heart, hiding place; **in -ū gaudēre** be secretly glad.

sīnus, -ī *m* large cup.

sīparium, -ī and iī *nt* act curtain.

sīphō, -ōnis *m* siphon; fire engine.

sīquandō *adv* if ever.

sīquī, sīquis *pron* if any, if anyone, whoever.

sīquidem *adv* if in fact ♦ *conj* since.

sīrempse *adj* the same.

Sīrēn, -ēnis *f* Siren.

sīris, sīrit *perf subj of* **sinō**.

Sīrius, -ī *m* Dog Star ♦ *adj* of Sirius.

sirpe, -is *nt* silphium.

sīrus, -ī *m* corn pit.

sīs (*for* **sī vīs**) *adv* please.

sistō, -ere, stitī, statum *vt* to place, set, plant; (*law*) to produce in court; (*monument*) to set up; (*movement*) to stop, arrest, check ♦ *vi* to stand, rest; (*law*) to appear in court; (*movement*) to stand still, stop, stand firm; **sē** ~ appear, present oneself; **tūtum** ~ see safe; **vadimōnium** ~ duly appear in court; **~ī nōn potest** the situation is desperate.

sistrum, -ī *nt* Egyptian rattle, cymbal.

sisymbrium, -ī and iī *nt* fragrant herb, perhaps mint.

Sīsyphius *adj,* **-idēs, -idae** *m* Ulysses.

Sīsyphus, -ī *m* criminal condemned in Hades to roll a rock repeatedly up a hill.

sitella, -ae *f* lottery urn.

Sīthonis, -idis *adj* Thracian.

Sīthonius *adj* Thracian.

sitīculōsus *adj* thirsty, dry.

sitiēns, -entis *pres p of* **sitiō** ♦ *adj* thirsty, dry; parching; (*fig*) eager.

sitienter *adv* eagerly.

sitiō, -īre *vi* to be thirsty; to be parched ♦ *vt* to thirst for, covet.

sitis, -is *f* thirst; drought.

sittybus *etc see* **sillybus**.

situla, -ae *f* bucket.

situs *ppp of* **sinō** ♦ *adj* situated, lying; founded; (*fig*) dependent.

situs, -ūs *m* situation, site; structure; neglect, squalor, mould; (*mind*) dullness.

sīve *conj* or if; or; whether ... or.

sīvī *perf of* **sinō**.

smaragdus, -ī *m/f* emerald.

smīlax, -acis *f* bindweed.

Smintheus, -eī *m* Apollo.

Smyrna, -ae *f* Ionian town in Asia Minor.

Smyrnaeus *adj see* **Smyrna**.

sobol- *etc see* **subol-**.

sobriē *adv* temperately: sensibly.

sobrīna, -ae *f* cousin (*on the mother's side*).

sobrīnus, -ī *m* cousin (*on the mother's side*).

sobrius *adj* sober; temperate, moderate; (*mind*) sane, sensible.

soccus, -ī *m* slipper (*esp the sock worn by actors in comedy*); comedy.

socer, -ī *m* father-in-law.

sociābilis *adj* compatible.

sociālis *adj* of allies, confederate; conjugal.

sociāliter *adv* sociably.

sociennus, -ī *m* friend.

societās, -ātis *f* fellowship, association; alliance.

sociō, -āre, -āvī, -ātum *vt* to unite, associate,

Noun declensions and verb conjugations are shown on pp xiii to xxv. The present infinitive ending of a verb shows to which conjugation it belongs: **-āre** = 1st; **-ēre** = 2nd; **-ere** = 3rd and **-īre** = 4th. Irregular verbs are shown on p xxvi

share.

sociofraudus, -ī *m* deceiver of friends.

socius *adj* associated, allied ♦ *m* friend, companion; partner, ally.

sōcordia, -ae *f* indolence, apathy; folly.

sōcordius *adv* more carelessly, lazily.

sōcors, -dis *adj* lazy, apathetic; stupid.

Sōcratēs, -is *m famous Athenian philosopher.*

Sōcraticus *adj* of Socrates, Socratic ♦ *mpl* the followers of Socrates.

socrus, -ūs *f* mother-in-law.

sodālicium, -ī *and* **iī** *nt* fellowship; secret society.

sodālicius *adj* of fellowship.

sodālis, -is *m/f* companion, friend; member of a society, accomplice.

sodālitās, -ātis *f* companionship, friendship; society, club; secret society.

sodālitius *etc see* **sodālicius.**

sodēs *adv* please.

sōl, sōlis *m* sun; sunlight, sun's heat; (*poetry*) day; (*myth*) Sun god; **~ oriēns, ~is ortus** east; **~ occidēns, ~is occāsus** west.

sōlāciolum, -ī *nt* a grain of comfort.

sōlācium, -ī *and* **iī** *nt* comfort, consolation, relief.

sōlāmen, -inis *nt* solace, relief.

sōlāris *adj* of the sun.

sōlārium, -ī *and* **iī** *nt* sundial; clock; balcony, terrace.

sōlātium *etc see* **sōlācium.**

sōlātor, -ōris *m* consoler.

soldūriī, -ōrum *mpl* retainers.

soldus *etc see* **solidus.**

solea, -ae *f* sandal, shoe; fetter; (*fish*) sole.

soleārius, -ī *and* **iī** *m* sandal maker.

soleātus *adj* wearing sandals.

soleō, -ēre, -itus *vi* to be accustomed, be in the habit, usually do; **ut ~ as** usual.

solidē *adv* for certain.

soliditās, -ātis *f* solidity.

solidō, -āre *vt* to make firm, strengthen.

solidus *adj* solid, firm, dense; whole, complete; (*fig*) sound, genuine, substantial ♦ *nt* solid matter, firm ground.

sōliferreum, -ī *nt* an all-iron javelin.

sōlistimus *adj* (*AUG*) most favourable.

sōlitārius *adj* solitary, lonely.

sōlitūdō, -inis *f* solitariness, loneliness; destitution; (*place*) desert.

solitus *ppa of* **soleō** ♦ *adj* usual, customary ♦ *nt* custom; **plūs ~ō** more than usual.

solium, -ī *and* **iī** *nt* seat, throne; tub; (*fig*) rule.

sōlivagus *adj* going by oneself; single.

sollemne, -is *nt* religious rite, festival; usage, practice.

sollemnis *adj* annual, regular; religious, solemn; usual, ordinary.

sollemniter *adv* solemnly.

sollers, -tis *adj* skilled, clever, expert; ingenious.

sollerter *adv* cleverly.

sollertia, -ae *f* skill, ingenuity.

sollicitātiō, -ōnis *f* inciting.

sollicitō, -āre, -āvī, -ātum *vt* to stir up, disturb; to trouble, distress, molest; to rouse, urge, incite, tempt, tamper with.

sollicitūdō, -inis *f* uneasiness, anxiety.

sollicitus *adj* agitated, disturbed; (*mind*) troubled, worried, alarmed; (*things*) anxious, careful; (*cause*) disquieting.

solliferreum *etc see* **sōliferreum.**

sollistimus *etc see* **sōlistimus.**

soloecismus, -ī *m* grammatical mistake.

Solōn, -ōnis *m famous Athenian lawgiver.*

sōlor, -ārī, -ātus *vt* to comfort, console; to relieve, ease.

sōlstitiālis *adj* of the summer solstice; midsummer.

sōlstitium, -ī *and* **iī** *nt* summer solstice; midsummer, summer heat.

solum, -ī *nt* ground, floor, bottom; soil, land, country; (*foot*) sole; (*fig*) basis; **~ō aequāre** raze to the ground.

sōlum *adv* only, merely.

sōlus (*gen* **-īus**, *dat* **-ī**) *see* **vicis;** *adj* only, alone; lonely, forsaken; (*place*) lonely, deserted.

solūtē *adv* loosely, freely, carelessly, weakly, fluently.

solūtiō, -ōnis *f* loosening; payment.

solūtus *ppp of* **solvō** ♦ *adj* loose, free; (*from distraction*) at ease, at leisure, merry; (*from obligation*) exempt; (*from restraint*) free, independent, unprejudiced; (*moral*) lax, weak, insolent; (*language*) prose, unrhythmical; (*speaker*) fluent; **ōrātiō ~a, verba ~a** prose.

solvō, -vere, -vī, -ūtum *vt* to loosen, undo; to free, release, acquit, exempt; to dissolve, break up, separate; to relax, slacken, weaken; to cancel, remove, destroy; to solve, explain; to pay, fulfil; (*argument*) to refute; (*discipline*) to undermine; (*feelings*) to get rid of; (*hair*) to let down; (*letter*) to open; (*sail*) to unfurl; (*siege*) to raise; (*troops*) to dismiss ♦ *vi* to set sail; to pay; **nāvem ~** set sail; **poenās ~** be punished; **praesēns ~** pay cash; **rem ~** pay; **sacrāmentō ~** discharge; **~vendō esse** be solvent.

Solyma, -ōrum *ntpl* Jerusalem.

Solymus *adj* of the Jews.

somniculōsē *adv* sleepily.

somniculōsus *adj* sleepy.

somnifer, -ī *adj* soporific; fatal.

somniō, -āre *vt* to dream, dream about; to talk nonsense.

somnium, -ī *and* **iī** *nt* dream; nonsense, fancy.

somnus, -ī *m* sleep; sloth.

sonābilis *adj* noisy.

sonipēs, -edis *m* steed.

sonitus, -ūs *m* sound, noise.

sonivius *adj* noisy.

sonō, -āre, -uī, -itum *vi* to sound, make a noise ♦ *vt* to utter, speak, celebrate; to sound like.

sonor, -ōris *m* sound, noise.

sonōrus *adj* noisy, loud.
sōns, sontis *adj* guilty.
sonticus *adj* critical; important.
sonus, -ī *m* sound, noise; (*fig*) tone.
sophistēs, -ae *m* sophist.
Sophoclēs, -is *m famous Greek tragic poet.*
Sophoclēus *adj* of Sophocles, Sophoclean.
sophus *adj* wise.
sōpiō, -īre, -īvī, -ītum *vt* to put to sleep; (*fig*)
  to calm, lull.
sopor, -ōris *m* sleep; apathy.
sopōrifer, -ī *adj* soporific, drowsy.
sopōrō, -āre *vt* to lull to sleep; to make
  soporific.
sopōrus *adj* drowsy.
Sōracte, -is *nt mountain in S. Etruria.*
sorbeō, -ēre, -uī *vt* to suck, swallow; (*fig*) to
  endure.
sorbillō, -āre *vt* to sip.
sorbitiō, -ōnis *f* drink, broth.
sorbum, -ī *nt* service berry.
sorbus, -ī *f* service tree.
sordeō, -ēre *vi* to be dirty, be sordid; to seem
  shabby; to be of no account.
sordēs, -is *f* dirt, squalor, shabbiness;
  mourning; meanness; vulgarity; (*people*)
  rabble.
sordēscō, -ere *vi* to become dirty.
sordidātus *adj* shabbily dressed, in
  mourning.
sordidē *adv* meanly, vulgarly.
sordidulus *adj* soiled, shabby.
sordidus *adj* dirty, squalid, shabby; in
  mourning; poor, mean; base, vile.
sōrex, -icis *m* shrewmouse.
sōricinus *adj* of the shrewmouse.
sōrītēs, -ae *m* chain syllogism.
soror, -ōris *f* sister.
sorōricīda, -ae *m* murderer of a sister.
sorōrius *adj* of a sister.
sors, sortis *f* lot; allotted duty; oracle,
  prophecy; fate, fortune; (*money*) capital,
  principal.
sōrsum *etc see* **seōrsum.**
sortilegus *adj* prophetic ♦ *m* soothsayer.
sortior, -īrī, -ītus *vi* to draw *or* cast lots ♦ *vt* to
  draw lots for, allot, obtain by lot; to
  distribute, share; to choose; to receive.
sortītiō, -ōnis *f* drawing lots, choosing by lot.
sortītus *ppa of* **sortior** ♦ *adj* assigned, allotted;
  ~ō by lot.
sortītus, -ūs *m* drawing lots.
Sosius, -ī *m Roman family name (esp two
  brothers Sosii, famous booksellers in Rome).*
sōspes, -itis *adj* safe and sound, unhurt;
  favourable, lucky.
sōspita, -ae *f* saviour.
sōspitālis *adj* beneficial.
sōspitō, -āre *vt* to preserve, prosper.
sōtēr, -ēris *m* saviour.

spādīx, -īcis *adj* chestnut-brown.
spadō, -ōnis *m* eunuch.
spargō, -gere, -sī, -sum *vt* to throw, scatter,
  sprinkle; to strew, spot, moisten; to
  disperse, spread abroad.
sparsus *ppp of* **spargō** ♦ *adj* freckled.
Sparta, -ae, -ē, -ēs *f famous Greek city.*
Spartacus, -ī *m gladiator who led a revolt
  against Rome.*
Spartānus, -icus *adj* Spartan.
Spartiātēs, -iātae *m* Spartan.
spartum, -ī *nt* Spanish broom.
sparulus, -ī *m* bream.
sparus, -ī *m* hunting spear.
spatha, -ae *f* broadsword.
spatior, -ārī, -ātus *vi* to walk; to spread.
spatiōsē *adv* greatly; after a time.
spatiōsus *adj* roomy, ample, large; (*time*)
  prolonged.
spatium, -ī *and* **iī** *nt* space, room, extent;
  (*between points*) distance; (*open space*)
  square, walk, promenade; (*race*) lap, track,
  course; (*time*) period, interval; (*opportunity*)
  time, leisure; (*metre*) quantity.
speciēs, -ēī *f* seeing, sight; appearance, form,
  outline; (*thing seen*) sight; (*mind*) idea; (*in
  sleep*) vision, apparition; (*fair show*) beauty,
  splendour; (*false show*) pretence, pretext;
  (*classification*) species; **in ~em** for the sake of
  appearances; like; **per ~em** under the
  pretence; **sub ~ē** under the cloak.
specillum, -ī *nt* probe.
specimen, -inis *nt* sign, evidence, proof;
  pattern, ideal.
speciōsē *adv* handsomely.
speciōsus *adj* showy, beautiful; specious,
  plausible.
spectābilis *adj* visible; notable, remarkable.
spectāclum, spectāculum, -ī *nt* sight,
  spectacle; public show, play; theatre, seats.
spectāmen, -inis *nt* proof.
spectātiō, -ōnis *f* looking; testing.
spectātor, -ōris *m* onlooker, observer,
  spectator; critic.
spectātrīx, -īcis *f* observer.
spectātus *ppp of* **spectō** ♦ *adj* tried, proved;
  worthy, excellent.
spectiō, -ōnis *f* the right to take auspices.
spectō, -āre, -āvī, -ātum *vt* to look at,
  observe, watch; (*place*) to face; (*aim*) to look
  to, bear in mind, contemplate, tend towards;
  (*judging*) to examine, test.
spectrum, -ī *nt* spectre.
specula, -ae *f* watchtower, lookout; height.
spēcula, -ae *f* slight hope.
speculābundus *adj* on the lookout.
speculāris *adj* transparent ♦ *ntpl* window.
speculātor, -ōris *m* explorer, investigator;
  (*MIL*) spy, scout.
speculātōrius *adj* for spying, scouting ♦ *f* spy

Noun declensions and verb conjugations are shown on pp xiii to xxv. The present infinitive ending of a verb shows
to which conjugation it belongs: **-āre** = 1st; **-ēre** = 2nd; **-ere** = 3rd and **-īre** = 4th. Irregular verbs are shown on p xxvi

boat.

speculātrīx, -īcis *f* watcher.

speculor, -ārī, -ātus *vt* to spy out, watch for, observe.

speculum, -ī *nt* mirror.

specus, -ūs *m*, *nt* cave; hollow, chasm.

spēlaeum, -ī *nt* cave, den.

spēlunca, -ae *f* cave, den.

spērābilis *adj* to be hoped for.

spērāta, -ātae *f* bride.

Spercheīs, -idis *adj see* **Spercheūs.**

Spercheūs (-os), -ī *m* *river in Thessaly.*

spernō, -ere, sprēvī, sprētum *vt* to remove, reject, scorn.

spērō, -āre, -āvī, -ātum *vt* to hope, hope for, expect; to trust; to look forward to.

spēs, speī *f* hope, expectation; **praeter spem** unexpectedly; **spē dēiectus** disappointed.

Speusippus, -ī *m* *successor of Plato in the Academy.*

sphaera, -ae *f* ball, globe, sphere.

Sphinx, -ingis *f* *fabulous monster near Thebes.*

spīca, -ae *f* (*grain*) ear; (*plant*) tuft; (ASTRO) brightest star in Virgo.

spīceus *adj* of ears of corn.

spīculum, -ī *nt* point, sting; dart, arrow.

spīna, -ae *f* thorn; prickle; fish bone; spine, back; (*pl*) difficulties, subtleties.

spīnētum, -ī *nt* thorn hedge.

spīneus *adj* of thorns.

spīnifer, -ī *adj* prickly.

spīnōsus *adj* thorny, prickly; (*style*) difficult.

spintēr, -ēris *nt* elastic bracelet.

spīnus, -ī *f* blackthorn, sloe.

spīra, -ae *f* coil; twisted band.

spīrābilis *adj* breathable, life-giving.

spīrāculum, -ī *nt* vent.

spīrāmentum, -ī *nt* vent, pore; breathing space.

spīritus, -ūs *m* breath, breathing; breeze, air; inspiration; character, spirit, courage, arrogance.

spīrō, -āre, -āvī, -ātum *vi* to breathe, blow; to be alive; to be inspired ♦ *vt* to emit, exhale; (*fig*) to breathe, express.

spissātus *adj* condensed.

spissē *adv* closely; slowly.

spissēscō, -ere *vi* to thicken.

spissus *adj* thick, compact, crowded; slow; (*fig*) difficult.

splendeō, -ēre *vi* to be bright, shine; to be illustrious.

splendēscō, -ere *vi* to become bright.

splendidē *adv* brilliantly, magnificently, nobly.

splendidus *adj* bright, brilliant, glittering; (*sound*) clear; (*dress, house*) magnificent; (*person*) illustrious; (*appearance*) showy.

splendor, -ōris *m* brightness, lustre; magnificence; clearness; nobility.

spoliātiō, -ōnis *f* plundering.

spoliātor, -ōris *m* robber.

spoliātrīx, -īcis *f* robber.

spoliō, -āre, -āvī, -ātum *vt* to strip; to rob, plunder.

spolium, -ī *and* **iī** *nt* (*beast*) skin; (*enemy*) spoils, booty.

sponda, -ae *f* bed frame; bed, couch.

spondālium, -ī *and* **iī** *nt* hymn accompanied by the flute.

spondeō, -ēre, spopondī, spōnsum *vt* to promise, pledge, vow; (*law*) to go bail for; (*marriage*) to betroth.

spondēus, -ī *m* spondee.

spongia, -ae *f* sponge; coat of mail.

spōnsa, -ae *f* fiancée, bride.

spōnsālia, -ium *ntpl* engagement.

spōnsiō, -ōnis *f* promise, guarantee; (*law*) agreement that the loser in a suit pays the winner a sum; bet.

spōnsor, -ōris *m* guarantor, surety.

spōnsus *ppp of* **spondeō** ♦ *m* fiancé, bridegroom ♦ *nt* agreement, covenant.

spōnsus, -ūs *m* contract, surety.

sponte *f* (*abl*) voluntarily, of one's own accord; unaided, by oneself; spontaneously.

spopondī *perf of* **spondeō.**

sportella, -ae *f* fruit basket.

sportula, -ae *f* small basket; gift to clients, dole.

sprētiō, -ōnis *f* contempt.

sprētor, -ōris *m* despiser.

sprētus *ppp of* **spernō.**

sprēvī *perf of* **spernō.**

spūma, -ae *f* foam, froth.

spūmēscō, -ere *vi* to become frothy.

spūmeus *adj* foaming, frothy.

spūmifer, -ī *adj* foaming.

spūmiger, -ī *adj* foaming.

spūmō, -āre *vi* to foam, froth.

spūmōsus *adj* foaming.

spuō, -uere, -uī, -ūtum *vi* to spit ♦ *vt* to spit out.

spurcē *adv* obscenely.

spurcidicus *adj* obscene.

spurcificus *adj* obscene.

spurcitia, -ae *and* **ēs, -ēī** *f* filth, smut.

spurcō, -āre *vt* to befoul.

spurcus *adj* filthy, nasty, foul.

spūtātilicus *adj* despicable.

spūtātor, -ōris *m* spitter.

spūtō, -āre *vt* to spit out.

spūtum, -ī *nt* spit, spittle.

squāleō, -ēre, -uī *vi* to be rough, stiff, clotted; to be parched; to be neglected, squalid, filthy; to be in mourning.

squālidē *adv* rudely.

squālidus *adj* rough, scaly; neglected, squalid, filthy; (*speech*) unpolished.

squālor, -ōris *m* roughness; filth, squalor.

squāma, -ae *f* scale; scale armour.

squāmeus *adj* scaly.

squāmifer, -ī *adj* scaly.

squāmiger, -ī *adj* scaly ♦ *mpl* fishes.

squāmōsus *adj* scaly.

squilla, -ae *f* prawn, shrimp.

st *interj* sh!

stabilīmentum, -ī *nt* support.

stabiliō, -īre *vt* to make stable; to establish.

stabilis *adj* firm, steady; (*fig*) steadfast, unfailing.

stabilitās, -ātis *f* firmness, steadiness, reliability.

stabulō, -āre *vt* to house, stable ♦ *vi* to have a stall.

stabulum, -ī *nt* stall, stable, steading; lodging, cottage; brothel.

stacta, -ae *f* myrrh oil.

stadium, -ī *and* **iī** *nt* stade, furlong; racetrack.

Stagīra, -ōrum *ntpl* town in Macedonia (*birthplace of Aristotle*).

Stagīrītēs, -ītae *m* Aristotle.

stagnō, -āre *vi* to form pools; to be inundated ♦ *vt* to flood.

stagnum, -ī *nt* standing water, pool, swamp; waters.

stāmen, -inis *nt* warp; thread; (*instrument*) string; (*priest*) fillet.

stāmineus *adj* full of threads.

stata *adj*: **Stata māter** Vesta.

statārius *adj* standing, stationary, steady; calm ♦ *f* refined comedy ♦ *mpl* actors in this comedy.

statēra, -ae *f* scales.

statim *adv* steadily; at once, immediately; ~ **ut** as soon as.

statiō, -ōnis *f* standing still; station, post, residence; (*pl*) sentries; (*NAUT*) anchorage.

Statius, -ī *m* Caecilius (*early writer of comedy*); Papinius (*epic and lyric poet of the Silver Age*).

statīvus *adj* stationary ♦ *ntpl* standing camp.

stator, -ōris *m* attendant, orderly.

Stator, -ōris *m* the Stayer (*epithet of Jupiter*).

statua, -ae *f* statue.

statūmen, -inis *nt* (*ship*) rib.

statuō, -uere, -uī, -ūtum *vt* to set up, place; to bring to a stop; to establish, constitute; to determine, appoint; to decide, settle; to decree, prescribe; (*with infin*) to resolve, propose; (*with acc and infin*) to judge, consider, conclude; (*army*) to draw up; (*monument*) to erect; (*price*) to fix; (*sentence*) to pass; (*tent*) to pitch; (*town*) to build; **condiciōnem** ~ dictate (to); **finem** ~ put an end (to); **iūs** ~ lay down a principle; **modum** ~ impose restrictions; **apud animum** ~ make up one's mind; **dē sē** ~ commit suicide; **gravius** ~ **in** deal severely with.

statūra, -ae *f* height, stature.

status *ppp of* **sistō** ♦ *adj* appointed, due.

status, -ūs *m* posture, attitude; position; (*social*) standing, status, circumstances; (*POL*) situation, state, form of government; (*nature*) condition; **reī pūblicae** ~ the political situation; constitution; **dē ~ū movēre** dislodge.

statūtus *ppp of* **statuō**.

stega, -ae *f* deck.

stēliō *see* **stēlliō**.

stēlla, -ae *f* star; ~ **errāns** planet.

stēllāns, -antis *adj* starry.

stēllātus *adj* starred; set in the sky.

stēllifer, -ī *adj* starry.

stēlliger, -ī *adj* starry.

stēlliō, -ōnis *m* newt.

stemma, -tis *nt* pedigree.

stercoreus *adj* filthy.

stercorō, -āre *vt* to manure.

stercus, -oris *nt* dung.

sterilis *adj* barren, sterile; bare, empty; unprofitable, fruitless.

sterilitās, -ātis *f* barrenness.

sternāx, -ācis *adj* bucking.

sternō, -ere, strāvī, strātum *vt* to spread, cover, strew; to smooth, level; to stretch out, extend; to throw to the ground, prostrate; to overthrow; (*bed*) to make; (*horse*) to saddle; (*road*) to pave.

sternūmentum, -ī *nt* sneezing.

sternuō, -ere, -ī *vt, vi* to sneeze.

Steropē, -ēs *f* a Pleiad.

sterquilīnium, -ī *and* **iī, (-um, -ī)** *nt* dung heap.

stertō, -ere, -uī *vi* to snore.

Stēsichorus, -ī *m* Greek lyric poet.

stetī *perf of* **stō**.

Sthenelēius *and* **eis** *and* **ēidis** *adj see n.*

Sthenelus, -ī *m* father of Eurystheus; father of Cycnus.

stigma, -tis *nt* brand.

stigmatiās, -ae *m* branded slave.

stilla, -ae *f* drop.

stillicidium, -ī *and* **iī** *nt* dripping water, rainwater from the eaves.

stillō, -āre, -āvī, -ātum *vi* to drip, trickle ♦ *vt* to let fall in drops, distil.

stilus, -ī *m* stake; pen; (*fig*) writing, composition, style; ~**um vertere** erase.

stimulātiō, -ōnis *f* incentive.

stimulātrīx, -īcis *f* provocative woman.

stimuleus *adj* smarting.

stimulō, -āre, -āvī, -ātum *vt* to goad; to trouble, torment; to rouse, spur on, excite.

stimulus, -ī *m* goad; (*MIL*) stake; (*pain*) sting, pang; (*incentive*) spur, stimulus.

stinguō, -ere *vt* to extinguish.

stīpātiō, -ōnis *f* crowd, retinue.

stīpātor, -ōris *m* attendant; (*pl*) retinue, bodyguard.

stīpendiārius *adj* tributary, liable to a money tax; (*MIL*) receiving pay ♦ *mpl* tributary peoples.

stīpendium, -ī *and* **iī** *nt* tax tribute; soldier's pay; military service, campaign; ~ **merēre, merērī** serve; ~ **ēmerērī** complete one's period of service.

stīpes, -itis *m* log, trunk; tree; (*insult*) blockhead.

stīpō, -āre, -āvī, -ātum *vt* to press, pack together; to cram, stuff full; to crowd round, accompany in a body.

stips, stipis *f* donation, contribution.

stipula, -ae *f* stalk, blade, stubble; reed.

stipulātiō, -ōnis *f* promise, bargain.

stipulātiuncula, -ae *f* slight stipulation.

stipulātus *adj* promised.

stipulor, -ārī *vt, vi* to demand a formal promise, bargain, stipulate.

stīria, -ae *f* icicle.

stirpēs *etc see* **stirps.**

stirpitus *adj* thoroughly.

stirps, -is *f* lower trunk and roots, stock; plant, shoot; family, lineage, progeny; origin; **ab ~e** utterly.

stīva, -ae *f* plough handle.

stlattārius *adj* seaborne.

stō, stāre, stetī, statum *vi* to stand; to remain in position, stand firm; to be conspicuous; (*fig*) to persist, continue; (*battle*) to go on; (*hair*) to stand on end; (*NAUT*) to ride at anchor; (*play*) to be successful; (*price*) to cost; (*with* **ab, cum, prō**) to be on the side of, support; (*with* **in**) to rest, depend on; (*with* **per**) to be the fault of; **stat sententia** one's mind is made up; **per Āfrānium stetit quōminus dīmicārētur** thanks to Afranius there was no battle.

Stōicē *adv* like a Stoic.

Stōicus *adj* Stoic ♦ *m* Stoic philosopher ♦ *ntpl* Stoicism.

stola, -ae *f* long robe (*esp worn by matrons*).

stolidē *adv* stupidly.

stolidus *adj* dull, stupid.

stomachor, -ārī, -ātus *vi* to be vexed, be annoyed.

stomachōsē *adv see adj.*

stomachōsus *adj* angry, irritable.

stomachus, -ī *m* gullet; stomach; taste, liking; dislike, irritation, chagrin.

stōrea (storia), -ae *f* rush mat, rope mat.

strabō, -ōnis *m* squinter.

strāgēs, -is *f* heap, confused mass; havoc, massacre.

strāgulus *adj* covering ♦ *nt* bedspread, rug.

strāmen, -inis *nt* straw, litter.

strāmentum, -ī *nt* straw, thatch; straw bed; covering, rug.

strāmineus *adj* straw-thatched.

strangulō, -āre, -āvī, -ātum *vt* to throttle, choke.

strangūria, -ae *f* difficult discharge of urine.

stratēgēma, -tis *nt* a piece of generalship, stratagem.

stratēgus, -ī *m* commander, president.

stratiōticus *adj* military.

strātum, -ī *nt* coverlet, blanket; bed, couch; horsecloth, saddle; pavement.

strātus *ppp of* **sternō** ♦ *adj* prostrate.

strāvī *perf of* **sternō.**

strēnuē *adv* energetically, quickly.

strēnuitās, -ātis *f* energy, briskness.

strēnuus *adj* brisk, energetic, busy; restless.

strepitō, -āre *vi* to make a noise, rattle, rustle.

strepitus, -ūs *m* din, clatter, crashing, rumbling; sound.

strepō, -ere, -uī *vi* to make a noise, clang, roar, rumble, rustle *etc* ♦ *vt* to bawl out.

strīāta, -ae *f* scallop.

strictim *adv* superficially, cursorily.

strictūra, -ae *f* mass of metal.

strictus *ppp of* **stringō** ♦ *adj* close, tight.

strīdeō, -ēre, -ī; -ō, -ere, -ī *vi* to creak, hiss, shriek, whistle.

strīdor, -ōris *m* creaking, hissing, grating.

strīdulus *adj* creaking, hissing, whistling.

strigilis *f* scraper, strigil.

strigō, -āre *vi* to stop, jib.

strigōsus *adj* thin, scraggy; (*style*) insipid.

stringō, -ngere, -nxī, -ctum *vt* to draw together, draw tight; to touch, graze; to cut off, prune, trim; (*sword*) to draw; (*mind*) to affect, pain.

stringor, -ōris *m* twinge.

strix, -igis *f* screech owl.

stropha, -ae *f* trick.

Strophades, -um *fpl* islands off S Greece.

strophiārius, -ī *and* **iī** *m* maker of breastbands.

strophium, -ī *and* **iī** *nt* breastband; headband.

structor, -ōris *m* mason, carpenter; (*at table*) server, carver.

structūra, -ae *f* construction, structure; works.

structus *ppp of* **struō.**

struēs, -is *f* heap, pile.

struix, -icis *f* heap, pile.

strūma, -ae *f* tumour.

strūmōsus *adj* scrofulous.

struō, -ere, -xī, -ctum *vt* to pile up; to build, erect; to arrange in order; to make, prepare; to cause, contrive, plot.

strūtheus *adj* sparrow- (*in cpds*).

strūthiocamēlus, -ī *m* ostrich.

Strȳmōn, -onis *m* river between Macedonia and Thrace (*now* Struma).

Strȳmonius *adj* Strymonian, Thracian.

studeō, -ēre, -uī *vi* (*usu with dat*) to be keen, be diligent, apply oneself to; to study; (*person*) to be a supporter of.

studiōsē *adv* eagerly, diligently.

studiōsus *adj* (*usu with gen*) keen on, fond of, partial to; studious ♦ *m* student.

studium, -ī *and* **iī** *nt* enthusiasm, application, inclination; fondness, affection; party spirit, partisanship; study, literary work.

stultē *adv* foolishly.

stultiloquentia, -ae *f* foolish talk.

stultiloquium, -ī *and* **iī** *nt* foolish talk.

stultitia, -ae *f* folly, silliness.

stultividus *adj* simple-sighted.

stultus *adj* foolish, silly ♦ *m* fool.

stupefaciō, -facere, -fēcī, -factum (*pass* **-fīō, -fierī**) *vt* to stun, astound.
stupeō, -ēre, -uī *vi* to be stunned, be astonished; to be brought to a standstill ♦ *vt* to marvel at.
stupēscō, -ere *vi* to become amazed.
stūpeus *etc see* **stuppeus.**
stupiditās, -ātis *f* senselessness.
stupidus *adj* senseless, astounded; dull, stupid.
stupor, -ōris *m* numbness, bewilderment; dullness, stupidity.
stuppa, -ae *f* tow.
stuppeus *adj* of tow.
stuprō, -āre, -āvī, -ātum *vt* to defile; to ravish.
stuprum, -ī *nt* debauchery, unchastity.
sturnus, -ī *m* starling.
Stygius *adj* of the lower world, Stygian.
stylus *etc see* **stilus.**
Stymphalicus, (-ius, -is) *adj* Stymphalian.
Stymphalum, -ī *nt*, **Stymphalus, -ī** *m* district of Arcadia (*famous for birds of prey killed by Hercules*).
Styx, -ygis *and* **ygos** *f* river of Hades.
Styxius *adj see* n.
suādēla, -ae *f* persuasion.
suādeō, -dēre, -sī, -sum *vi* (*with dat*) to advise, urge, recommend.
suāsiō, -ōnis *f* speaking in favour (of a proposal); persuasive type of oratory.
suāsor, -ōris *m* adviser; advocate.
suāsus *ppp of* **suādeō.**
suāsus, -ūs *m* advice.
suāveolēns, -entis *adj* fragrant.
suāviātiō *etc see* **sāviātiō.**
suāvidicus *adj* charming.
suāviloquēns, -entis *adj* charming.
suāviloquentia, -ae *f* charm of speech.
suāvior *etc see* **sāvior.**
suāvis *adj* sweet, pleasant, delightful.
suāvitās, -ātis *f* sweetness, pleasantness, charm.
suāviter *adv see* **suāvis.**
suāvium *etc see* **sāvium.**
sub *prep* 1. *with abl* (*place*) under, beneath; (*hills, walls*) at the foot of, close to; (*time*) during, at; (*order*) next to; (*rule*) under, in the reign of. 2. *with acc* (*place*) under, along under; (*hills, walls*) up to, to; (*time*) up to, just before, just after; ~ **ictum venīre** come within range; ~ **manum** to hand.
subabsurdē *adv see adj.*
subabsurdus *adj* somewhat absurd.
subaccūsō, -āre *vt* to find some fault with.
subāctiō, -ōnis *f* working (the soil).
subāctus *ppp of* **subigō.**
subadroganter *adv* a little conceitedly.
subagrestis *adj* rather boorish.
subalāris *adj* carried under the arms.

subamārus *adj* rather bitter.
subaquilus *adj* brownish.
subauscultō, -āre *vt, vi* to listen secretly, eavesdrop.
subbasilicānus, -ī *m* lounger.
subblandior, -īrī *vi* (*with dat*) to flirt with.
subc- *etc see* **succ-.**
subdidī *perf of* **subdō.**
subdifficilis *adj* rather difficult.
subdiffīdō, -ere *vi* to be a little doubtful.
subditīcius *adj* sham.
subditīvus *adj* sham.
subditus *ppp of* **subdō** ♦ *adj* spurious.
subdō, -ere, -idī, -itum *vt* to put under, plunge into; to subdue; to substitute, forge.
subdoceō, -ēre *vt* to teach as an assistant.
subdolē *adv* slily.
subdolus *adj* sly, crafty, underhand.
subdubitō, -āre *vi* to be a little undecided.
subdūcō, -ūcere, -ūxī, -uctum *vt* to pull up, raise; to withdraw, remove; to take away secretly, steal; (*account*) to balance; (*ship*) to haul up, beach; **sē ~** steal away, disappear.
subductiō, -ōnis *f* (*ship*) hauling up; (*thought*) reckoning.
subductus *ppp of* **subdūcō.**
subedō, -ēsse, -ēdī *vt* to wear away underneath.
subēgī *perf of* **subigō.**
subeō, -īre, -iī, -itum *vi* to go under, go in; to come up to, climb, advance; to come immediately after; to come to the assistance; to come as a substitute, succeed; to come secretly, steal in; to come to mind, suggest itself ♦ *vt* to enter, plunge into; to climb; to approach, attack; to take the place of; to steal into; to submit to, undergo, suffer; (*mind*) to occur to.
sūber, -is *nt* cork tree; cork.
subesse *infin of* **subsum.**
subf- *etc see* **suff-.**
subg- *etc see* **sugg-.**
subhorridus *adj* somewhat uncouth.
subiaceō, -ēre, -uī *vi* to lie under, be close (to); to be connected (with).
subiciō, -icere, -iēcī, -iectum *vt* to put under, bring under; to bring up, throw up; to bring near; to submit, subject, expose; to subordinate, deal with under; to append, add on, answer; to adduce, suggest; to substitute; to forge; to suborn; **sē ~** grow up.
subiectē *adv* submissively.
subiectiō, -ōnis *f* laying under; forging.
subiectō, -āre *vt* to lay under, put to; to throw up.
subiector, -ōris *m* forger.
subiectus *ppp of* **subiciō** ♦ *adj* neighbouring, bordering; subject, exposed.
subigitātiō, -ōnis *f* lewdness.
subigitō, -āre *vt* to behave improperly to.

subigō, -igere, -ēgī, -āctum *vt* to bring up to; to impel, compel; to subdue, conquer; (*animal*) to tame, break in; (*blade*) to sharpen; (*boat*) to row, propel; (*cooking*) to knead; (*earth*) to turn up, dig; (*mind*) to train.

subiī *perf of* **subeō**.

subimpudēns, -entis *adj* rather impertinent.

subinānis *adj* rather empty.

subinde *adv* immediately after; repeatedly.

subīnsulsus *adj* rather insipid.

subinvideō, -ēre *vi* to be a little envious of.

subinvīsus *adj* somewhat odious.

subinvītō, -āre *vt* to invite vaguely.

subīrāscor, -scī, -tus *vi* to be rather angry.

subīrātus *adj* rather angry.

subitārius *adj* sudden, emergency (*in cpds*).

subitō *adv* suddenly.

subitus *ppp of* **subeō** ♦ *adj* sudden, unexpected; (*man*) rash; (*troops*) hastily raised ♦ *nt* surprise, emergency.

subiūnctus *ppp of* **subiungō**.

subiungō, -ungere, -ūnxī, -ūnctum *vt* to harness; to add, affix; to subordinate, subdue.

sublābor, -bī, -psus *vi* to sink down; to glide away.

sublāpsus *ppa of* **sublābor**.

sublātē *adv* loftily.

sublātiō, -ōnis *f* elevation.

sublātus *ppp of* **tollō** ♦ *adj* elated.

sublectō, -āre *vt* to coax.

sublēctus *ppp of* **sublegō**.

sublegō, -egere, -ēgī, -ēctum *vt* to gather up; to substitute; (*child*) to kidnap; (*talk*) to overhear.

sublestus *adj* slight.

sublevātiō, -ōnis *f* alleviation.

sublevō, -āre, -āvī, -ātum *vt* to lift up, hold up; to support, encourage; to lighten, alleviate.

sublica, -ae *f* pile, palisade.

sublicius *adj* on piles.

sublīgāculum, -ī, subligar, -āris *nt* loincloth.

sublīgō, -āre *vt* to fasten on.

sublīmē *adv* aloft, in the air.

sublīmis *adj* high, raised high, lifted up; (*character*) eminent, aspiring; (*language*) lofty, elevated.

sublīmitās, -ātis *f* loftiness.

sublīmus *etc see* **sublīmis**.

sublingiō, -ōnis *m* scullion.

sublinō, -inere, -ēvī, -itum *vt*: **ōs ~** to fool, bamboozle.

sublitus *ppp of* **sublinō**.

sublūceō, -ēre *vi* to glimmer.

sublue, -ere *vt* (*river*) to flow past the foot of.

sublūstris *adj* faintly luminous.

sublūtus *ppp of* **subluō**.

subm- *etc see* **summ-**.

subnātus *adj* growing up underneath.

subnectō, -ctere, -xuī, -xum *vt* to tie under, fasten to.

subnegō, -āre *vt* to half refuse.

subnexus *ppp of* **subnectō**.

subniger, -rī *adj* darkish.

subnīxus *and* **sus** *adj* supported, resting (on); relying (on).

subnuba, -ae *f* rival.

subnūbilus *adj* overcast.

subō, -āre *vi* to be in heat.

subobscēnus *adj* rather indecent.

subobscūrus *adj* somewhat obscure.

subodiōsus *adj* rather odious.

suboffendō, -ere *vi* to give some offence.

subolēs, -is *f* offspring, children.

subolēscō, -ere *vi* to grow up.

subolet, -ēre *vi* (*impers*) there is a faint scent; **~ mihi** I detect, have an inkling.

suborior, -īrī *vi* to spring up in succession.

subōrnō, -āre, -āvī, -ātum *vt* to fit out, equip; to instigate secretly, suborn.

subortus, -ūs *m* rising up repeatedly.

subp- *etc see* **supp-**.

subrancidus *adj* slightly tainted.

subraucus *adj* rather hoarse.

subrēctus *ppp of* **subrigō**.

subrēmigō, -āre *vi* to paddle under (water).

subrēpō, -ere, -sī, -tum *vi* to creep along, steal up to.

subreptus *ppp of* **subripiō**.

subrīdeō, -dēre, -sī *vi* to smile.

subrīdiculē *adv* rather funnily.

subrigō, -igere, -ēxī, -ēctum *vt* to lift, raise.

subringor, -ī *vi* to make a wry face, be rather vexed.

subripiō, -ipere, -ipuī *and* **upuī, -eptum** *vt* to take away secretly, steal.

subrogō, -āre *vt* to propose as successor.

subrōstrānī, -ōrum *mpl* idlers.

subrubeō, -ēre *vi* to blush slightly.

subrūfus *adj* ginger-haired.

subruō, -ere, -ī, -tum *vt* to undermine, demolish.

subrūsticus *adj* rather countrified.

subrutus *ppp of* **subruō**.

subscrībō, -bere, -psī, -ptum *vt* to write underneath; (*document*) to sign, subscribe; (*censor*) to set down; (*law*) to add to an indictment, prosecute; (*fig*) to record; (*with dat*) to assent to, approve.

subscrīptiō, -ōnis *f* inscription underneath; signature; (*censor*) noting down; (*law*) subscription (to an indictment); register.

subscrīptor, -ōris *m* subscriber (to an indictment).

subscrīptus *ppp of* **subscrībō**.

subsecīvus *etc see* **subsicīvus**.

subsecō, -āre, -uī, -ctum *vt* to cut off, clip.

subsēdī *perf of* **subsīdō**.

subsellium, -ī *and* **iī** *nt* bench, seat; (*law*) the bench, the court.

subsentiō, -entīre, -ēnsī *vt* to have an inkling of.

subsequor, -quī, -cūtus *vt, vi* to follow closely; to support; to imitate.

subserviō, -īre *vi* to be a slave; (*fig*) to comply

(with).

subsicīvus *adj* left over; (*time*) spare; (*work*) overtime.

subsidiārius *adj* in reserve ♦ *mpl* reserves.

subsidium, -ī *and* **iī** *nt* reserve ranks, reserve troops; relief, aid, assistance.

subsīdō, -īdere, -ēdī, -essum *vi* to sit down, crouch, squat; to sink down, settle, subside; (*ambush*) to lie in wait; (*residence*) to stay, settle ♦ *vt* to lie in wait for.

subsignānus *adj* special reserve (troops).

subsignō, -āre *vt* to register; to guarantee.

subsiliō, -īre, -uī *vi* to leap up.

subsistō, -istere, -titī *vi* to stand still, make a stand; to stop, halt; to remain, continue, hold out; (*with dat*) to resist ♦ *vt* to withstand.

subsortior, -īrī, -ītus *vt* to choose as a substitute by lot.

subsortītiō, -ōnis *f* choosing of substitutes by lot.

substantia, -ae *f* means, wealth.

substernō, -ernere, -rāvī, -rātum *vt* to scatter under, spread under; (*fig*) to put at one's service.

substitī *perf of* **subsistō**.

substituō, -uere, -uī, -ūtum *vt* to put next; to substitute; (*idea*) to present, imagine.

substitūtus *ppp of* **substituō**.

substō, -āre *vi* to hold out.

substrātus *ppp of* **substernō**.

substrictus *ppp of* **substringō** ♦ *adj* narrow, tight.

substringō, -ngere, -nxī, -ctum *vt* to bind up; to draw close; to check.

substructiō, -ōnis *f* foundation.

substruō, -ere, -xī, -ctum *vt* to lay, pave.

subsultō, -āre *vi* to jump up.

subsum, -esse *vi* to be underneath; to be close to, be at hand; (*fig*) to underlie, be latent in.

subsūtus *adj* fringed at the bottom.

subtēmen, -inis *nt* woof; thread.

subter *adv* below, underneath ♦ *prep* (*with acc and abl*) beneath; close up to.

subterdūcō, -cere, -xī *vt* to withdraw secretly.

subterfugiō, -ugere, -ūgī *vt* to escape from, evade.

subterlābor, -ī *vt, vi* to flow past under; to slip away.

subterrāneus *adj* underground.

subtexō, -ere, -uī, -tum *vt* to weave in; to veil, obscure.

subtīlis *adj* slender, fine; (*senses*) delicate, nice; (*judgment*) discriminating, precise; (*style*) plain, direct.

subtīlitās, -ātis *f* fineness; (*judgment*) acuteness, exactness; (*style*) plainness, directness.

subtīliter *adv* finely; accurately; simply.

subtimeō, -ēre *vt* to be a little afraid of.

subtractus *ppp of* **subtrahō**.

subtrahō, -here, -xī, -ctum *vt* to draw away from underneath; to take away secretly; to withdraw, remove.

subtristis *adj* rather sad.

subturpiculus *adj* a little bit mean.

subturpis *adj* rather mean.

subtus *adv* below, underneath.

subtūsus *adj* slightly bruised.

subūcula, -ae *f* shirt, vest.

sūbula, -ae *f* awl.

subulcus, -ī *m* swineherd.

Subūra, -ae *f* a disreputable quarter of Rome.

Subūrānus *adj see* **Subūra**.

suburbānitās, -ātis *f* nearness to Rome.

suburbānus *adj* near Rome ♦ *nt* villa near Rome ♦ *mpl* inhabitants of the towns near Rome.

suburbium, -ī *and* **iī** *nt* suburb.

suburgeō, -ēre *vt* to drive close (to).

subvectiō, -ōnis *f* transport.

subvectō, -āre *vt* to carry up regularly.

subvectus *ppp of* **subvehō**.

subvectus, -ūs *m* transport.

subvehō, -here, -xī, -ctum *vt* to carry up, transport upstream.

subveniō, -enīre, -ēnī, -entum *vi* (*with dat*) to come to the assistance of, relieve, reinforce.

subventō, -āre *vi* (*with dat*) to come quickly to help.

subvereor, -ērī *vi* to be a little afraid.

subversor, -ōris *m* subverter.

subversus *ppp of* **subvertō**.

subvertō, -tere, -tī, -sum *vt* to turn upside down, upset; to overthrow, subvert.

subvexī *perf of* **subvehō**.

subvexus *adj* sloping upwards.

subvolō, -āre *vi* to fly upwards.

subvolvō, -ere *vt* to roll uphill.

subvortō *etc see* **subvertō**.

succavus *adj* hollow underneath.

succēdō, -ēdere, -essī, -essum *vt, vi* (*with dat*) to go under, pass into, take on; (*with dat, acc,* **in**) to go up, climb; (*with dat, acc,* **ad, sub**) to march on, advance to; (*with dat,* **in**) to come to take the place of, relieve; (*with dat,* **in, ad**) to follow after, succeed, succeed to; (*result*) to turn out, be successful.

succendō, -endere, -endī, -ēnsum *vt* to set fire to, kindle; (*fig*) to fire, inflame.

succēnseō *etc see* **suscēnseō**.

succēnsus *ppp of* **succendō**.

succenturiātus *adj* in reserve.

succenturiō, -ōnis *m* under-centurion.

successī *perf of* **succēdō**.

successiō, -ōnis *f* succession.

successor, -ōris *m* successor.

successus *ppp of* **succēdō**.

Noun declensions and verb conjugations are shown on pp xiii to xxv. The present infinitive ending of a verb shows to which conjugation it belongs: **-āre** = 1st; **-ēre** = 2nd; **-ere** = 3rd and **-īre** = 4th. Irregular verbs are shown on p xxvi

successus, -ūs *m* advance uphill; result, success.
succīdia, -ae *f* leg *or* side of meat, flitch.
succīdō, -dere, -dī, -sum *vt* to cut off, mow down.
succīdō, -ere, -ī *vi* to sink, give way.
succiduus *adj* sinking, failing.
succīnctus *ppp of* **succingō**.
succingō, -gere, -xī, -ctum *vt* to gird up, tuck up; to equip, arm.
succingulum, -ī *nt* girdle.
succinō, -ere *vi* to chime in.
succīsus *ppp of* **succīdō**.
succlāmātiō, -ōnis *f* shouting, barracking.
succlāmō, -āre, -āvī, -ātum *vt* to shout after, interrupt with shouting.
succontumēliōsē *adv* somewhat insolently.
succrēscō, -ere *vi* to grow up (from *or* to).
succrispus *adj* rather curly.
succumbō, -mbere, -buī, -bitum *vi* to fall, sink under; to submit, surrender.
succurrō, -rere, -rī, -sum *vi* to come quickly up; to run to the help of, succour; (*idea*) to occur.
succus *etc see* **sūcus**.
succussus, -ūs *m* shaking.
succustōs, -ōdis *m* assistant keeper.
succutiō, -tere, -ssī, -ssum *vt* to toss up.
sūcidus *adj* juicy, fresh, plump.
sūcinum, -ī *nt* amber.
sūctus *ppp of* **sūgō**.
sucula, -ae *f* winch, windlass.
sucula, -ae *f* piglet; (*pl*) the Hyads.
sūcus, -ī *m* juice, sap; medicine, potion; taste, flavour; (*fig*) strength, vigour, life.
sūdārium, -ī *and* **iī** *nt* handkerchief.
sūdātōrius *adj* for sweating ♦ *nt* sweating bath.
sudis, -is *f* stake, pile, pike, spike.
sūdō, -āre, -āvī, -ātum *vi* to sweat, perspire; to be drenched with; to work hard ♦ *vt* to exude.
sūdor, -ōris *m* sweat, perspiration; moisture; hard work, exertion.
sudus *adj* cloudless, clear ♦ *nt* fine weather.
sueō, -ēre *vi* to be accustomed.
suēscō, -scere, -vī, -tum *vi* to be accustomed ♦ *vt* to accustom.
Suessa, -ae *f* town in Latium.
Suessiōnēs, -um *mpl* people of Gaul (*now* Soissons).
suētus *ppp of* **suēscō** ♦ *adj* accustomed; usual.
Suēvī, -ōrum *mpl* people of N.E. Germany.
sūfes, -etis *m* chief magistrate of Carthage.
suffarcinātus *adj* stuffed full.
suffectus *ppp of* **sufficiō** ♦ *adj* (*consul*) appointed to fill a vacancy during the regular term of office.
sufferō, -re *vt* to support, undergo, endure.
suffēs *etc see* **sūfes**.
sufficiō, -icere, -ēcī, -ectum *vt* to dye, tinge; to supply, provide; to appoint in place of (another), substitute ♦ *vi* to be adequate,

suffice.
suffīgō, -gere, -xī, -xum *vt* to fasten underneath, nail on.
suffīmen, -inis, suffīmentum, -ī *nt* incense.
suffiō, -īre *vt* to fumigate, perfume.
suffīxus *ppp of* **suffīgō**.
sufflāmen, -inis *nt* brake.
sufflō, -āre *vt* to blow up; to puff up.
suffōcō, -āre *vt* to choke, stifle.
suffodiō, -odere, -ōdī, -ossum *vt* to stab; to dig under, undermine.
suffossus *ppp of* **suffodiō**.
suffrāgātiō, -ōnis *f* voting for, support.
suffrāgātor, -ōris *m* voter, supporter.
suffrāgātōrius *adj* supporting a candidate.
suffrāgium, -ī *and* **iī** *nt* vote, ballot; right of suffrage; (*fig*) judgment, approval; ~ **ferre** vote.
suffrāgor, -ārī, -ātus *vi* to vote for; to support, favour.
suffringō, -ere *vt* to break.
suffugiō, -ugere, -ūgī *vt* to run for shelter ♦ *vt* to elude.
suffugium, -ī *and* **iī** *nt* shelter, refuge.
suffulciō, -cīre, -sī, -tum *vt* to prop up, support.
suffundō, -undere, -ūdī, -ūsum *vt* to pour in; to suffuse, fill; to tinge, colour, blush; to overspread.
suffūror, -ārī *vi* to filch.
suffuscus *adj* darkish.
suffūsus *ppp of* **suffundō**.
Sugambrī, -ōrum *mpl* people of N.W. Germany.
suggerō, -rere, -ssī, -stum *vt* to bring up to, supply; to add on, put next.
suggestum, -ī *nt* platform.
suggestus *ppp of* **suggerō**.
suggestus, -ūs *m* platform, stage.
suggrandis *adj* rather large.
suggredior, -dī, -ssus *vi* to come up close, approach ♦ *vt* to attack.
sūgillātiō, -ōnis *f* affronting.
sūgillātus *adj* bruised; insulted.
sūgō, -gere, -xī, -ctum *vt* to suck.
suī *gen of* **sē**.
suī *perf of* **suō**.
suillus *adj* of pigs.
sulcō, -āre *vt* to furrow, plough.
sulcus, -ī *m* furrow; trench; track.
sulfur *etc see* **sulpur**.
Sulla, -ae *m* famous Roman dictator.
Sullānus *adj see n.*
sullāturiō, -īre *vi* to hanker after being a Sulla.
Sulmō, -ōnis *m* town in E. Italy (*birthplace of Ovid*).
Sulmōnēnsis *adj see n.*
sultis *adv* please.
sum, esse, fuī *vi* to be, exist; ~ **ab** belong to; ~ **ad** be designed for; ~ **ex** consist of; **est, sunt** there is, are; **est mihi** I have; **mihi tēcum nīl est** I have nothing to do with you; **est quod** something; there is a reason for; **est ubi**

sometimes; **est ut** it is possible that; **est** (_with gen_) to belong to, be the duty of, be characteristic of; (_with infin_) it is possible, it is permissible; **sunt quī** some; **fuit Ilium** Troy is no more.

sūmen, -inis _nt_ udder, teat; sow.

summa, -ae _f_ main part, chief point, main issue; gist, summary; sum, amount, the whole; supreme power; **~ rērum** the general interest, the whole responsibility; **~ summārum** the universe; **ad ~am** in short, in fact; in conclusion; **in ~ā** in all; after all.

Summānus, -ī _m_ god of nocturnal thunderbolts.

summās, -ātis _adj_ high-born, eminent.

summātim _adv_ cursorily, summarily.

summātus, -ūs _m_ sovereignty.

summē _adv_ in the highest degree, extremely.

summergō, -gere, -sī, -sum _vt_ to plunge under, sink.

summersus _ppp of_ **summergō.**

sumministrō, -āre, -āvī, -ātum _vt_ to provide, furnish.

summissē _adv_ softly; humbly, modestly.

summissiō, -ōnis _f_ lowering.

summissus _ppp of_ **summittō** ♦ _adj_ low; (_voice_) low, calm; (_character_) mean, grovelling, submissive, humble.

summittō, -ittere, -īsī, -issum _vt_ (_growth_) to send up, raise, rear; to despatch, supply; to let down, lower, reduce, moderate; to supersede; to send secretly; **animum ~** submit; **sē ~** condescend.

summolestē _adv_ with some annoyance.

summolestus _adj_ a little annoying.

summoneō, -ēre, -uī _vt_ to drop a hint to.

summorōsus _adj_ rather peevish.

summōtor, -ōris _m_ clearer.

summōtus _ppp of_ **summoveō.**

summoveō, -ovēre, -ōvī, -ōtum _vt_ to move away, drive off; to clear away (to make room); to withdraw, remove, banish; (_fig_) to dispel.

summum, -ī _nt_ top, surface.

summum _adv_ at the most.

summus _adj_ highest, the top of, the surface of; last, the end of; (_fig_) utmost, greatest, most important; (_person_) distinguished, excellent ♦ _m_ head of the table.

summūtō, -āre _vt_ to substitute.

sūmō, -ere, -psī, -ptum _vt_ to take, take up; to assume, arrogate; (_action_) to undertake; (_argument_) to assume, take for granted; (_dress_) to put on; (_punishment_) to exact; (_for a purpose_) to use, spend.

sūmptiō, -ōnis _f_ assumption.

sūmptuārius _adj_ sumptuary.

sūmptuōsē _adv see adj._

sūmptuōsus _adj_ expensive, lavish, extravagant.

sūmptus _ppp of_ **sūmō.**

sūmptus, -ūs _m_ expense, cost.

Sūnium, -ī _and_ **iī** _nt_ S.E. promontory of Attica.

suō, suere, suī, sūtum _vt_ to sew, stitch, join together.

suōmet, suōpte _emphatic abl of_ **suus.**

suovetaurīlia, -ium _ntpl_ sacrifice of a pig, sheep and bull.

supellex, -ectilis _f_ furniture, goods, outfit.

super _etc adj see_ **superus.**

super _adv_ above, on the top; besides, moreover; left, remaining ♦ _prep_ (_with abl_) upon, above; concerning; besides; (_time_) at; (_with acc_) over, above, on; beyond; besides, over and above.

superā _etc see_ **suprā.**

superābilis _adj_ surmountable, conquerable.

superaddō, -ere, -itum _vt_ to add over and above.

superāns, -antis _pres p of_ **superō** ♦ _adj_ predominant.

superātor, -ōris _m_ conqueror.

superbē _adv_ arrogantly, despotically.

superbia, -ae _f_ arrogance, insolence, tyranny; pride, lofty spirit.

superbiloquentia, -ae _f_ arrogant speech.

superbiō, -īre _vi_ to be arrogant, take a pride in; to be superb.

superbus _adj_ arrogant, insolent, overbearing; fastidious; superb, magnificent.

supercilium, -ī _and_ **iī** _nt_ eyebrow; (_hill_) brow, ridge; (_fig_) arrogance.

superēmineō, -ēre _vt_ to overtop.

superesse _infin of_ **supersum.**

superficiēs, -ēī _f_ surface; (_law_) a building (_esp on another's land_).

superfiō, -ierī _vi_ to be left over.

superfixus _adj_ fixed on top.

superfluō, -ere _vi_ to overflow.

superfuī _perf of_ **supersum.**

superfundō, -undere, -ūdī, -ūsum _vt, vi_ to pour over, shower; (_pass_) to overflow, spread out.

superfūsus _ppp of_ **superfundō.**

supergredior, -dī, -ssus _vt_ to surpass.

superiaciō, -iacere, -iēcī, -iectum _and_ **iactum** _vt_ to throw over, overspread; to overtop; (_fig_) to exaggerate.

superiectus _ppp of_ **superiaciō.**

superimmineō, -ēre _vi_ to overhang.

superimpendēns, -entis _adj_ overhanging.

superimpōnō, -ōnere, -osuī, -ositum _vt_ to place on top.

superimpositus _ppp of_ **superimpōnō.**

superincidēns, -entis _adj_ falling from above.

superincubāns, -antis _adj_ lying upon.

superincumbō, -ere _vi_ to fling oneself down upon.

superingerō, -ere _vt_ to pour down.

superiniciō, -icere, -iēcī, -iectum _vt_ to throw upon, put on top.

Noun declensions and verb conjugations are shown on pp xiii to xxv. The present infinitive ending of a verb shows to which conjugation it belongs: **-āre** = 1st; **-ēre** = 2nd; **-ere** = 3rd and **-īre** = 4th. Irregular verbs are shown on p xxvi

superiniectus *ppp of* **superinicō.**
superīnsternō, -ere *vt* to lay over.
superior, -ōris *adj* higher, upper; (*time, order*)
preceding, previous, former; (*age*) older;
(*battle*) victorious, stronger; (*quality*)
superior, greater.
superlātiō, -ōnis *f* exaggeration.
superlātus *adj* exaggerated.
supernē *adv* at the top, from above.
supernus *adj* upper; celestial.
superō, -āre, -āvī, -ātum *vi* to rise above,
overtop; to have the upper hand; to be in
excess, be abundant; to be left over, survive
♦ *vt* to pass over, surmount, go beyond; to
surpass, outdo; (*MIL*) to overcome, conquer;
(*NAUT*) to sail past, double.
superobruō, -ere *vt* to overwhelm.
superpendēns, -entis *adj* overhanging.
superpōnō, -ōnere, -osuī, -ositum *vt* to
place upon; to put in charge of.
superpositus *ppp of* **superpōnō.**
superscandō, -ere *vt* to climb over.
supersedeō, -edēre, -ēdī, -essum *vi* to
forbear, desist from.
superstes, -itis *adj* standing over; surviving.
superstitiō, -ōnis *f* awful fear, superstition.
superstitiōsē *adv* superstitiously;
scrupulously.
superstitiōsus *adj* superstitious; prophetic.
superstō, -āre *vt, vi* to stand over, stand on.
superstrātus *adj* spread over.
superstruō, -ere, -xī, -ctum *vt* to build on
top.
supersum, -esse, -fuī *vi* to be left, remain; to
survive; to be in abundance, be sufficient; to
be in excess.
supertegō, -ere *vt* to cover over.
superurgēns, -entis *adj* pressing from
above.
superus (*compar* **-ior,** *superl* **suprēmus,**
summus) *adj* upper, above ♦ *mpl* the gods
above; the living ♦ *ntpl* the heavenly bodies;
higher places; **mare ~um** Adriatic Sea.
supervacāneus *adj* extra, superfluous.
supervacuus *adj* superfluous, pointless.
supervādō, -ere *vt* to climb over, surmount.
supervehor, -hī, -ctus *vt* to ride past, sail
past.
superveniō, -enīre, -ēnī, -entum *vt* to
overtake, come on top of ♦ *vi* to come on the
scene, arrive unexpectedly.
superventus, -ūs *m* arrival.
supervolitō, -āre *vt* to fly over.
supervolō, -āre *vt, vi* to fly over.
supīnō, -āre, -āvī, -ātum *vt* to upturn, lay on
its back.
supīnus *adj* lying back, face up; sloping, on a
slope; backwards; (*mind*) indolent, careless.
suppāctus *ppp of* **suppingō.**
suppaenitet, -ēre *vt impers* to be a little sorry.
suppalpor, -ārī *vi* to coax gently.
suppār, -aris *adj* nearly equal.
supparasītor, -ārī *vi* to flatter gently.

supparus, -ī *m*, **supparum, -ī** *nt* woman's
linen garment; topsail.
suppeditātiō, -ōnis *f* abundance.
suppeditō, -āre, -āvī, -ātum *vi* to be at hand,
be in full supply, be sufficient; to be rich in
♦ *vt* to supply, furnish.
suppēdō, -ere *vi* to break wind quietly.
suppetiae, -ārum *fpl* assistance.
suppetior, -ārī, -ātus *vi* to come to the
assistance of.
suppetō, -ere, -īvī, *and* **iī, -ītum** *vi* to be
available, be in store; to be equal to, suffice
for.
suppīlō, -āre *vt* to steal.
suppingō, -ingere, -āctum *vt* to fasten
underneath.
supplantō, -āre *vt* to trip up.
supplēmentum, -ī *nt* full complement;
reinforcements.
suppleō, -ēre *vt* to fill up, make good, make
up to the full complement.
supplex, -icis *adj* suppliant, in entreaty.
supplicātiō, -ōnis *f* day of prayer, public
thanksgiving.
suppliciter *adv* in supplication.
supplicium, -ī *and* **iī** *nt* prayer, entreaty;
sacrifice; punishment, execution, suffering;
~iō afficere execute.
supplicō, -āre, -āvī, -ātum *vi* (*with dat*) to
entreat, pray to, worship.
supplōdō, -dere, -sī *vt* to stamp.
supplōsiō, -ōnis *f* stamping.
suppōnō, -ōnere, -osuī, -ositum *vt* to put
under, apply; to subject; to add on; to
substitute, falsify.
supportō, -āre *vt* to bring up, transport.
suppositīcius *adj* spurious.
suppositiō, -ōnis *f* substitution.
suppositus *ppp of* **suppōnō.**
supposuī *perf of* **suppōnō.**
suppressiō, -ōnis *f* embezzlement.
suppressus *ppp of* **supprimō** ♦ *adj* (*voice*) low.
supprimō, -imere, -essī, -essum *vt* to sink;
to restrain, detain, put a stop to; to keep
secret, suppress.
supprōmus, -ī *m* underbutler.
suppudet, -ēre *vt* (*impers*) to be a little
ashamed.
suppūrō, -āre *vi* to fester.
suppus *adj* head downwards.
supputō, -āre *vt* to count up.
suprā *adv* above, up on top; (*time*) earlier,
previously; (*amount*) more; **~ quam** beyond
what ♦ *prep* (*with acc*) over, above; beyond;
(*time*) before; (*amount*) more than, over.
suprāscandō, -ere *vt* to surmount.
suprēmum *adv* for the last time.
suprēmus *adj* highest; last, latest; greatest,
supreme ♦ *ntpl* moment of death; funeral
rites; testament.
sūra, -ae *f* calf (of the leg).
sūrculus, -ī *m* twig, shoot; graft, slip.
surdaster, -rī *adj* rather deaf.

surditās, -ātis *f* deafness.
surdus *adj* deaf; silent.
surēna, -ae *m* grand vizier (*of the Parthians*).
surgō, -ere, surrēxī, surrēctum *vi* to rise,
get up, stand up; to arise, spring up, grow.
surpere *etc* = **surripere** *etc*.
surr- *etc see* **subr-**.
surrēxī *perf of* **surgō**.
surruptīcius *adj* stolen.
surrupuī *perf of* **subripiō**.
sūrsum, sūrsus *adv* upwards, up, high up; ~
deōrsum up and down.
sūs, suis *m/f* pig, boar, hog, sow.
Sūsa, -ōrum *ntpl* ancient Persian capital.
suscēnseō, -ēre, -uī *vi* to be angry, be
irritated.
susceptiō, -ōnis *f* undertaking.
susceptus *ppp of* **suscipiō**.
suscipiō, -ipere, -ēpī, -eptum *vt* to take up,
undertake; to receive, catch; (*child*) to
acknowledge; to beget; to take under one's
protection.
suscitō, -āre, -āvī, -ātum *vt* to lift, raise; to
stir, rouse, awaken; to encourage, excite.
suspectō, -āre *vt, vi* to look up at, watch; to
suspect, mistrust.
suspectus *ppp of* **suspiciō** ♦ *adj* suspected,
suspicious.
suspectus, -ūs *m* looking up; esteem.
suspendium, -ī *and* **iī** *nt* hanging.
suspendō, -endere, -endī, -ēnsum *vt* to
hang, hang up; (*death*) to hang; (*building*) to
support; (*mind*) to keep in suspense;
(*movement*) to check, interrupt; (*pass*) to
depend.
suspēnsus *ppp of* **suspendō** ♦ *adj* raised,
hanging, poised; with a light touch; (*fig*) in
suspense, uncertain, anxious; dependent; **~ō
gradū** on tiptoe.
suspicāx, -ācis *adj* suspicious.
suspiciō, -icere, -exī, -ectum *vt* to look up at,
look up to; to admire, respect; to mistrust.
suspiciō, -ōnis *f* mistrust, suspicion.
suspīciōsē *adv* suspiciously.
suspīciōsus *adj* suspicious.
suspicor, -ārī, -ātus *vt* to suspect; to surmise,
suppose.
suspīrātus, -ūs *m* sigh.
suspīritus, -ūs *m* deep breath, difficult
breathing; sigh.
suspīrium, -ī *and* **iī** *nt* deep breath, sigh.
suspīrō, -āre, -āvī, -ātum *vi* to sigh ♦ *vt* to
sigh for; to exclaim with a sigh.
susque dēque *adv* up and down.
sustentāculum, -ī *nt* prop.
sustentātiō, -ōnis *f* forbearance.
sustentō, -āre, -āvī, -ātum *vt* to hold up,
support; (*fig*) to uphold, uplift; (*food, means*)
to sustain, support; (*enemy*) to check, hold;
(*trouble*) to suffer; (*event*) to hold back,
postpone.

sustineō, -inēre, -inuī, -entum *vt* to hold up,
support; to check, control; (*fig*) to uphold,
maintain; (*food, means*) to sustain, support;
(*trouble*) to bear, suffer, withstand; (*event*) to
put off.
sustollō, -ere *vt* to lift up, raise; to destroy.
sustulī *perf of* **tollō**.
susurrātor, -ōris *m* whisperer.
susurrō, -āre *vt, vi* to murmur, buzz, whisper.
susurrus, -ūs *m* murmuring, whispering.
susurrus *adj* whispering.
sūtēla, -ae *f* trick.
sūtilis *adj* sewn.
sūtor, -ōris *m* shoemaker; ~ **nē suprā
crepidam** ≈ *let the cobbler stick to his last*.
sūtōrius *adj* shoemaker's; ex-cobbler.
sūtrīnus *adj* shoemaker's.
sūtūra, -ae *f* seam.
sūtus *ppp of* **suō**.
suus *adj* his, her, its, their; one's own, proper,
due, right ♦ *mpl* one's own troops, friends,
followers *etc* ♦ *nt* one's own property.
Sybaris, -is *f* town in S. Italy (*noted for its
debauchery*).
Sybarīta, -ītae *m* Sybarite.
Sȳchaeus, -ī *m* husband of Dido.
sȳcophanta, -ae *m* slanderer, cheat,
sycophant.
sȳcophantia, -ae *f* deceit.
sȳcophantiōsē *adv* deceitfully.
sȳcophantor, -ārī, *vi* to cheat.
Syēnē, -ēs *f* town in S. Egypt (*now* Assuan).
syllaba, -ae *f* syllable.
syllabātim *adv* syllable by syllable.
symbola, -ae *f* contribution.
symbolus, -ī *m* token, symbol.
symphōnia, -ae *f* concord, harmony.
symphōniacus *adj* choir (*in cpds*).
Symplēgades, -um *fpl* clashing rocks in the
Black Sea.
synedrus, -ī *m* senator (*in Macedonia*).
Synephēbī, -ōrum *mpl* Youths Together
(*comedy by Caecilius*).
syngrapha, -ae *f* promissory note.
syngraphus, -ī *m* written contract; passport,
pass.
Synnada, -ōrum *ntpl* town in Phrygia (*famous
for marble*).
Synnadēnsis *adj see n*.
synodūs, -ontis *m* bream.
synthesis, -is *f* dinner service; suit of clothes;
dressinggown.
Syphāx, -ācis *m* king of Numidia.
Syrācūsae, -ārum *fpl* Syracuse.
Syrācūsānus, Syrācūsānius, Syrācosius
adj Syracusan.
Syria, -iae *f* country at the E. end of the
Mediterranean.
Syrius, -us *and* **iacus, -iscus** *adj* Syrian.

Noun declensions and verb conjugations are shown on pp xiii to xxv. The present infinitive ending of a verb shows
to which conjugation it belongs: **-āre** = 1st; **-ēre** = 2nd; **-ere** = 3rd and **-īre** = 4th. Irregular verbs are shown on p xxvi

syrma, -ae f robe with a train; (*fig*) tragedy.
Syrtis, -is f Gulf of Sidra in N. Africa; sandbank.

T, t

tabella, -ae f small board, sill; writing tablet, voting tablet, votive tablet; picture; (*pl*) writing, records, dispatches.
tabellārius adj about voting ♦ m courier.
tābeō, -ēre vi to waste away; to be wet.
taberna, -ae f cottage; shop; inn; (*circus*) stalls.
tabernāculum, -ī nt tent; ~ **capere** choose a site (for auspices).
tabernāriī, -ōrum mpl shopkeepers.
tābēs, -is f wasting away, decaying, melting; putrefaction; plague, disease.
tābēscō, -ēscere, -uī vi to waste away, melt, decay; (*fig*) to pine, languish.
tābidulus adj consuming.
tābidus adj melting, decaying; pining; corrupting, infectious.
tābificus adj melting, wasting.
tabula, -ae f board, plank; writing tablet; votive tablet; map; picture; auction; (*pl*) account books, records, lists, will; ~ **Sullae** Sulla's proscriptions; **XII ~ae** Twelve Tables of Roman laws; **~ae novae** cancellation of debts.
tabulārium, -ī and **ii** nt archives.
tabulātiō, -ōnis f flooring, storey.
tabulātum, -ī nt flooring, storey; (*trees*) layer, row.
tābum, -ī nt decaying matter; disease, plague.
taceō, -ēre, -uī, -itum vi to be silent, say nothing; to be still, be hushed ♦ vt to say nothing about, not speak of.
tacitē adv silently; secretly.
taciturnitās, -ātis f silence, taciturnity.
taciturnus adj silent, quiet.
tacitus ppp of **taceō** ♦ adj silent, mute, quiet; secret, unmentioned; tacit, implied; **per ~um** quietly.
Tacitus, -ī m famous Roman historian.
tāctilis adj tangible.
tāctiō, -ōnis f touching; sense of touch.
tāctus ppp of **tangō**.
tāctus, -ūs m touch, handling, sense of touch; influence.
taeda, -ae f pitch pine, pinewood; torch; plank; (*fig*) wedding.
taedet, -ēre, -uit and **taesum est** vt (*impers*) to be weary (of), loathe.
taedifer, -ī adj torch-bearing.
taedium, -ī and **ii** nt weariness, loathing.

Taenaridēs, -idae m Spartan (*esp Hyacinthus*).
Taenarius, -is adj of Taenarus; Spartan.
Taenarum (-on), -ī nt, **Taenarus (-os), -ī** m/f town and promontory in S. Greece (*now* Matapan); the lower world.
taenia, -ae f hairband, ribbon.
taesum est perf of **taedet**.
taeter, -rī adj foul, hideous, repulsive.
taetrē adv hideously.
taetricus see **tetricus**.
tagāx, -ācis adj light-fingered.
Tagus, -ī m river of Lusitania (*now* Tagus).
tālāris adj reaching to the ankles ♦ ntpl winged sandals; a garment reaching to the ankles.
tālārius adj of dice.
Talāsius, -ī and **ii** m god of weddings; wedding cry.
tālea, -ae f rod, stake.
talentum, -ī nt talent, *a Greek weight about 25.4kg*; a large sum of money (*esp the Attic talent of 60 minae*).
tāliō, -ōnis f retaliation in kind.
tālis adj such; the following.
talpa, -ae f mole.
tālus, -ī m ankle; heel; (*pl*) knuckle bones, oblong dice.
tam adv so, so much, so very.
tamdiū adv so long, as long.
tamen adv however, nevertheless, all the same.
Tāmesis, -is and **a, -ae** m Thames.
tametsī conj although.
tamquam adv as, just as, just like ♦ conj as if.
Tanagra, -ae f town in Boeotia.
Tanais, -is m river in Sarmatia (*now* Don).
Tanaquil, -ilis f wife of the elder Tarquin.
tandem adv at last, at length, finally; (*question*) just.
tangō, -ere, tetigī, tāctum vt to touch, handle; (*food*) to taste; (*with force*) to hit, strike; (*with liquid*) to sprinkle; (*mind*) to affect, move; (*place*) to reach; to border on; (*task*) to take in hand; (*by trick*) to take in, fool; (*in words*) to touch on, mention; **dē caelō tāctus** struck by lightning.
tanquam see **tamquam**.
Tantaleus adj, **-idēs, -idae** m Pelops, Atreus, Thyestes or Agamemnon.
Tantalis, -idis f Niobe or Hermione.
Tantalus, -ī m father of Pelops (*condemned to hunger and thirst in Tartarus, or to the threat of an overhanging rock*).
tantillus adj so little, so small.
tantisper adv so long, just for a moment.
tantopere adv so much.
tantulus adj so little, so small.
tantum adv so much, so, as; only, merely; ~ **modo** only; ~ **nōn** all but, almost; ~ **quod** only just.
tantummodo adv only.
tantundem adv just as much, just so much.
tantus adj so great; so little ♦ nt so much; so little; **~ī esse** be worth so much, be so dear,

be so important; ~**ō** so much, so far; (*with compar*) so much the; ~**ō opere** so much; **in** ~**um** to such an extent; **tria** ~**a** three times as much.

tantusdem *adj* just so great.

tapēta, -ae *m*, **-ia, -ium** *ntpl* carpet, tapestry, hangings.

Taprobanē, -ēs *f* Ceylon.

tardē *adv* slowly, tardily.

tardēscō, -ere *vi* to become slow, falter.

tardipēs, -edis *adj* limping.

tarditās, -ātis *f* slowness, tardiness; (*mind*) dullness.

tardiusculus *adj* rather slow.

tardō, -āre, -āvī, -ātum *vt* to retard, impede ♦ *vi* to delay, go slow.

tardus *adj* slow, tardy, late; (*mind*) dull; (*speech*) deliberate.

Tarentīnus *adj* Tarentine.

Tarentum, -ī *nt* town in S. Italy (*now* Taranto).

tarmes, -itis *m* woodworm.

Tarpēius *adj* Tarpeian; **mōns** ~ *the Tarpeian Rock on the Capitoline Hill from which criminals were thrown.*

tarpezīta, -ae *m* banker.

Tarquiniēnsis *adj* of Tarquinii.

Tarquiniī, -iōrum *mpl* ancient town in Etruria.

Tarquinius *adj* of Tarquin.

Tarquinius, -ī *m* Tarquin (*esp Priscus, the fifth king of Rome, and Superbus, the last king*).

Tarracīna, -ae *f*, **-ae, -ārum** *fpl* town in Latium.

Tarracō, -ōnis *f* town in Spain (*now* Tarragona).

Tarracōnēnsis *adj see n.*

Tarsēnsis *adj see n.*

Tarsus, -ī *f* capital of Cilicia.

Tartareus *adj* infernal.

Tartarus (-os), -ī *m*, **-a, -ōrum** *ntpl* Tartarus, the lower world (*esp the part reserved for criminals*).

tat *interj* hallo there!

Tatius, -ī *m* Sabine king (*who ruled jointly with Romulus*).

Tatius *adj see n.*

Taum, -ī *nt* Firth of Tay.

taureus *adj* bull's ♦ *f* whip of bull's hide.

Taurī, -ōrum *mpl* Thracians of the Crimea.

Tauricus *adj see n.*

tauriformis *adj* bull-shaped.

Taurīnī, -ōrum *mpl* people of N. Italy (*now* Turin).

taurīnus *adj* bull's.

Tauromenītānus *adj see n.*

Tauromenium, -ī *and* **iī** *nt town in E. Sicily.*

taurus, -ī *m* bull.

Taurus, -ī *m* mountain range in S.E. Asia Minor.

taxātiō, -ōnis *f* valuing.

taxeus *adj* of yews.

taxillus, -ī *m* small dice.

taxō, -āre *vt* to value, estimate.

taxus, -ī *f* yew.

Tāygeta, -ōrum *ntpl*, **Tāygetus, -ī** *m* mountain range in S. Greece.

Tāygetē, -ēs *f* a Pleiad.

tē *acc and abl of* **tū**.

-te *suffix for* **tū**.

Teānēnsis *adj see n.*

Teānum, -ī *nt* town in Apulia; town in Campania.

techina, -ae *f* trick.

Tecmessa, -ae *f* wife of Ajax.

tēctor, -ōris *m* plasterer.

tēctōriolum, -ī *nt* a little plaster.

tēctōrium, -ī *and* **iī** *nt* plaster, stucco.

tēctōrius *adj* of a plasterer.

tēctum, -ī *nt* roof, ceiling, canopy; house, dwelling, shelter.

tēctus *ppp of* **tegō** ♦ *adj* hidden; secret, reserved, close.

tēcum with you.

Tegea, -ae *f* town in Arcadia.

Tegeaeus *adj* Arcadian ♦ *m the god Pan* ♦ *f* Atalanta.

Tegeātae, -ātārum *mpl* Tegeans.

teges, -etis *f* mat.

tegillum, -ī *nt* hood, cowl.

tegimen, -inis *nt* covering.

tegimentum, -ī *nt* covering.

tegm- *etc see* **tegim-**.

tegō, -ere, tēxī, -tēctum *vt* to cover; to hide, conceal; to protect, defend; to bury; **latus** ~ walk by the side of.

tēgula, -ae *f* tile; (*pl*) tiled roof.

tegum- *etc see* **tegim**.

Tēius *adj* of Teos.

tēla, -ae *f* web; warp; yarnbeam, loom; (*fig*) plan.

Telamōn, -ōnis *m* father of Ajax.

Tēlegonus, -ī *m* son of Ulysses and Circe.

Tēlemachus, -ī *m* son of Ulysses and Penelope.

Tēlephus, -ī *m* king of Mysia (*wounded by Achilles' spear*).

tellūs, -ūris *f* the earth; earth, ground; land, country.

tēlum, -ī *nt* weapon, missile; javelin, sword; (*fig*) shaft, dart.

temerārius *adj* accidental; rash, thoughtless.

temerē *adv* by chance, at random; rashly, thoughtlessly; **nōn** ~ not for nothing; not easily; hardly ever.

temeritās, -ātis *f* chance; rashness, thoughtlessness.

temerō, -āre, -āvī, -ātum *vt* to desecrate, disgrace.

tēmētum, -ī *nt* wine, alcohol.

temnō, -ere *vt* to slight, despise.

tēmō, -ōnis *m* beam (of plough *or* carriage); cart; (*ASTRO*) the Plough.

Tempē *ntpl* famous valley in Thessaly.

temperāmentum, -ī *nt* moderation,

Noun declensions and verb conjugations are shown on pp xiii to xxv. The present infinitive ending of a verb shows to which conjugation it belongs: **-āre** = 1st; **-ēre** = 2nd; **-ere** = 3rd and **-īre** = 4th. Irregular verbs are shown on p xxvi

compromise.

temperāns, -antis *pres p of* **temperō ♦** *adj* moderate, temperate.

temperanter *adv* with moderation.

temperantia, -ae *f* moderation, self-control.

temperātē *adv* with moderation.

temperātiō, -ōnis *f* proper mixture, composition, constitution; organizing power.

temperātor, -ōris *m* organizer.

temperātus *ppp of* **temperō ♦** *adj* moderate, sober.

temperī *adv* in time, at the right time.

temperiēs, -ēī *f* due proportion; temperature, mildness.

temperō, -āre, -āvī, -ātum *vt* to mix in due proportion, blend, temper; to regulate, moderate, tune; to govern, rule ♦ *vi* to be moderate, forbear, abstain; (*with dat*) to spare, be lenient to.

tempestās, -ātis *f* time, season, period; weather; storm; (*fig*) storm, shower.

tempestīvē *adv* at the right time, appropriately.

tempestīvitās , -ātis *f* seasonableness.

tempestīvus *adj* timely, seasonable, appropriate; ripe, mature; early.

templum, -ī *nt* space marked off for taking auspices; open space, region, quarter; sanctuary; temple.

temporārius *adj* for the time, temporary.

temptābundus *adj* making repeated attempts.

temptāmentum, -ī *nt* trial, attempt, proof.

temptāmina, -um *ntpl* attempts, essays.

temptātiō, -ōnis *f* trial, proof; attack.

temptātor, -ōris *m* assailant.

temptō, -āre, -āvī, -ātum *vt* to feel, test by touching; to make an attempt on, attack; to try, essay, attempt; to try to influence, tamper with, tempt, incite; **vēnās ~** feel the pulse.

tempus, -oris *nt* time; right time, opportunity; danger, emergency, circumstance; (*head*) temple; (*verse*) unit of metre; (*verb*) tense; **~ore** at the right time, in time; **ad ~us** at the right time; for the moment; **ante ~us** too soon; **ex ~ore** on the spur of the moment; to suit the circumstances; **in ~ore** in time; **in ~us** temporarily; **per ~us** just in time; **prō ~ore** to suit the occasion.

tēmulentus *adj* intoxicated.

tenācitās, -ātis *f* firm grip; stinginess.

tenāciter *adv* tightly, firmly.

tenāx, -ācis *adj* gripping, tenacious; sticky; (*fig*) firm, persistent; stubborn; stingy.

tendicula, -ae *f* little snare.

tendō, -ere, tetendī, tentum *and* **tēnsum** *vt* to stretch, spread; to strain; (*arrow*) to aim, shoot; (*bow*) to bend; (*course*) to direct; (*lyre*) to tune; (*tent*) to pitch; (*time*) to prolong; (*trap*) to lay ♦ *vi* to encamp; to go, proceed; to

aim, tend; (*with infin*) to endeavour, exert oneself.

tenebrae, -ārum *fpl* darkness, night; unconsciousness, death, blindness; (*place*) dungeon, haunt, the lower world; (*fig*) ignorance, obscurity.

tenebricōsus *adj* gloomy.

tenebrōsus *adj* dark, gloomy.

Tenedius *adj see n.*

Tenedos (-us), -ī *f Aegean island near Troy.*

tenellulus *adj* dainty little.

teneō, -ēre, -uī *vt* to hold, keep; to possess, occupy, be master of; to attain, acquire; (*argument*) to maintain, insist; (*category*) to comprise; (*goal*) to make for; (*interest*) to fascinate; (*law*) to bind, be binding on; (*mind*) to grasp, understand, remember; (*movement*) to hold back, restrain ♦ *vi* to hold on, last, persist; (*rumour*) to prevail; **cursum ~** keep on one's course; **sē ~** remain; to refrain.

tener, -ī *adj* tender, delicate; young, weak; effeminate; (*poet*) erotic.

tenerāscō, -ere *vi* to grow weak.

tenerē *adv* softly.

teneritās, -ātis *f* weakness.

tenor, -ōris *m* steady course; **ūnō ~ōre** without a break, uniformly.

tēnsa, -ae *f carriage bearing the images of the gods in procession.*

tēnsus *ppp of* **tendō ♦** *adj* strained.

tentā- *etc see* **temptā-**.

tentīgō, -inis *f* lust.

tentō *etc see* **temptō**.

tentōrium, -ī *and* **iī** *nt* tent.

tentus *ppp of* **tendō**.

tenuiculus *adj* paltry.

tenuis *adj* thin, fine; small, shallow; (*air*) rarefied; (*water*) clear; (*condition*) poor, mean, insignificant; (*style*) refined, direct, precise.

tenuitās, -ātis *f* thinness, fineness; poverty, insignificance; (*style*) precision.

tenuiter *adv* thinly; poorly; with precision; superficially.

tenuō, -āre, -āvī, -ātum *vt* to make thin, attenuate, rarefy; to lessen, reduce.

tenus *prep* (*with gen or abl*) as far as, up to, down to; **verbō ~** in name, nominally.

Teos, -ī *f town on coast of Asia Minor* (*birthplace of Anacreon*).

tepefaciō, -facere, -fēcī, -factum *vt* to warm.

tepeō, -ēre *vi* to be warm, be lukewarm; (*fig*) to be in love.

tepēscō, -ēscere, -uī *vi* to grow warm; to become lukewarm, cool off.

tepidus *adj* warm, lukewarm.

tepor, -ōris *m* warmth; coolness.

ter *adv* three times, thrice.

terdeciēns *and* **ēs** *adv* thirteen times.

terebinthus, -ī *f* turpentine tree.

terebra, -ae *f* gimlet.

terebrō, -āre *vt* to bore.

terēdō, -inis *f* grub.

Terentia, -iae *f* Cicero's wife.

Terentius, -ī *m* Roman family name (*esp the comic poet Terence*).

Terentius, -iānus *adj see* n.

teres, -etis *adj* rounded (*esp cylindrical*), smooth, shapely; (*fig*) polished, elegant.

Tēreus, -eī *and* **eos** *m* king of Thrace (*husband of Procne, father of Itys*).

tergeminus *adj* threefold, triple.

tergeō, -gēre, -sī, -sum *vt* to wipe off, scour, clean; to rub up, burnish.

terginum, -ī *nt* rawhide.

tergiversātiō, -ōnis *f* refusal, subterfuge.

tergiversor, -ārī, -ātus *vi* to hedge, boggle, be evasive.

tergō *etc see* **tergeō**.

tergum, -ī *nt* back; rear; (*land*) ridge; (*water*) surface; (*meat*) chine; (*skin*) hide, leather, anything made of leather; **~a vertere** take to flight; **ā ~ō** behind, in the rear.

tergus, -oris *see* **tergum**.

termes, -itis *m* branch.

Terminālia, -ium *ntpl* Festival of the god of Boundaries.

terminātiō, -ōnis *f* decision; (*words*) clausula.

terminō, -āre, -āvī, -ātum *vt* to set bounds to, limit; to define, determine; to end.

terminus, -ī *m* boundary line, limit, bound; god of boundaries.

ternī, -ōrum *adj* three each; three.

terō, -ere, -trīvī, trītum *vt* to rub, crush, grind; to smooth, sharpen; to wear away, use up; (*road*) to frequent; (*time*) to waste; (*word*) to make commonplace.

Terpsichorē, -ēs *f* Muse of dancing.

terra, -ae *f* dry land, earth, ground, soil; land, country; **orbis ~ārum** the world; **ubi ~ārum** where in the world.

terrēnus *adj* of earth; terrestrial, land- (*in cpds*) ♦ *nt* land.

terreō, -ēre, -uī, -itum *vt* to frighten, terrify; to scare away; to deter.

terrestris *adj* earthly, on earth, land- (*in cpds*).

terribilis *adj* terrifying, dreadful.

terricula, -ōrum *ntpl* scare, bogy.

terrificō, -āre *vt* to terrify.

terrificus *adj* alarming, formidable.

terrigena, -ae *m* earth-born.

terriloquus *adj* alarming.

territō, -āre *vt* to frighten, intimidate.

territōrium, -ī *and* **iī** *nt* territory.

territus *adj* terrified.

terror, -ōris *m* fright, alarm, terror; a terror.

tersī *perf of* **tergeō**.

tersus *ppp of* **tergeō** ♦ *adj* clean; neat, terse.

tertiadecimānī, -ōrum *mpl* men of the thirteenth legion.

tertiānus *adj* recurring every second day ♦ *f* a

fever ♦ *mpl* men of the third legion.

tertiō *adv* for the third time; thirdly.

tertium *adv* for the third time.

tertius *adj* third; **~ decimus (decumus)** thirteenth.

terūncius, -ī *and* **iī** *m* quarter-as; a fourth; (*fig*) farthing.

tesqua (tesca), -ōrum *ntpl* waste ground, desert.

tessella, -ae *f* cube of mosaic stone.

tessera, -ae *f* cube, dice; (*MIL*) password; token (*for mutual recognition of friends*); ticket (*for doles*).

tesserārius, -ī *and* **iī** *m* officer of the watch.

testa, -ae *f* brick, tile; (*earthenware*) pot, jug, sherd; (*fish*) shell, shellfish.

testāmentārius *adj* testamentary ♦ *m* forger of wills.

testāmentum, -ī *nt* will, testament.

testātiō, -ōnis *f* calling to witness.

testātus *ppa of* **testor** ♦ *adj* public.

testiculus, -ī *m* testicle.

testificātiō, -ōnis *f* giving evidence, evidence.

testificor, -ārī, -ātus *vt* to give evidence, vouch for; to make public, bring to light; to call to witness.

testimōnium, -ī *and* **iī** *nt* evidence, testimony; proof.

testis, -is *m/f* witness; eyewitness.

testis, -is *m* testicle.

testor, -ārī, -ātus *vt* to give evidence, testify; to prove, vouch for; to call to witness, appeal to ♦ *vi* to make a will.

testū (*abl* **-ū**) *nt* earthenware lid, pot.

testūdineus *adj* of tortoiseshell, tortoise- (*in cpds*).

testūdō, -inis *f* tortoise; tortoiseshell; lyre, lute; (*MIL*) shelter for besiegers, covering of shields; (*building*) vault.

testum, -ī *nt* earthenware lid, pot.

tēte *emphatic acc of* **tū**.

tetendī *perf of* **tendō**.

tēter *etc see* **taeter**.

Tēthys, -os *f* sea goddess; the sea.

tetigī *perf of* **tangō**.

tetrachmum, tetradrachmum, -ī *nt* four drachmas.

tetraō, -ōnis *m* blackcock, grouse *or* capercailzie.

tetrarchēs, -ae *m* tetrarch, ruler.

tetrarchia, -ae *f* tetrarchy.

tetricus *adj* gloomy, sour.

tetulī *archaic perf of* **ferō**.

Teucer, -rī *m* son of Telamon of Salamis; son-in-law of Dardanus.

Teucrī, -rōrum *mpl* Trojans.

Teucria, -riae *f* Troy.

Teutonī, -ōrum *and* **es, -um** *mpl* Teutons (*a German people*).

Noun declensions and verb conjugations are shown on pp xiii to xxv. The present infinitive ending of a verb shows to which conjugation it belongs: **-āre** = 1st; **-ēre** = 2nd; **-ere** = 3rd and **-īre** = 4th. Irregular verbs are shown on p xxvi

Teutonicus *adj* Teutonic, German.
tēxī *perf of* **tegō**.
texō, -ere, -uī, -tum *vt* to weave; to plait; to build, make; (*fig*) to compose, contrive.
textilis *adj* woven ♦ *nt* fabric.
textor, -ōris *m* weaver.
textrīnum, -ī *nt* weaving; shipyard.
textūra, -ae *f* web, fabric.
textus *ppp of* **texō** ♦ *nt* web, fabric.
textus, -ūs *m* texture.
texuī *perf of* **texō**.
Thāis, -idis *f an Athenian courtesan.*
thalamus, -ī *m* room, bedroom; marriage bed; marriage.
thalassicus *adj* sea-green.
thalassinus *adj* sea-green.
Thalēs, -is *and* **ētis** *m* early Greek philosopher (*one of the seven wise men*).
Thalia, -ae *f Muse of comedy.*
thallus, -ī *m* green bough.
Thamyrās, -ae *m blinded Thracian poet.*
Thapsitānus *adj see* **Thapsus**.
Thapsus (-os), -ī *f town in N. Africa (scene of Caesar's victory).*
Thasius *adj see* **Thasus**.
Thasus (-os), -ī *f Greek island in N. Aegean.*
Thaumantias, -dis *f Iris.*
theātrālis *adj* of the theatre, in the theatre.
theātrum, -ī *nt* theatre; audience; (*fig*) theatre, stage.
Thēbae, -ārum *fpl Thebes (capital of Boeotia); town in Upper Egypt.*
Thēbais, -aidis *f Theban woman; epic poem by Statius.*
Thēbānus *adj* Theban.
thēca, -ae *f case, envelope.*
Themis, -dis *f goddess of justice.*
Themistoclēs, -ī *and* **is** *m famous Athenian statesman.*
Themistoclēus *adj see* **Themistoclēs**.
thēnsaurārius *adj* of treasure.
thēnsaurus *see* **thēsaurus**.
theologus, -ī *m* theologian.
Theophrastus, -ī *m* Greek philosopher (*successor to Aristotle*).
Theopompēus, -īnus *adj see n.*
Theopompus, -ī *m Greek historian.*
thermae, -ārum *fpl* warm baths.
Thermōdōn, -ontis *m river of Pontus (where the Amazons lived).*
Thermōdontēus, -ontiacus *adj* Amazonian.
thermopōlium *nt* restaurant serving warm drinks.
thermopōtō, -āre *vt* to refresh with warm drinks.
Thermopylae, -ārum *fpl famous Greek pass defended by Leonidas.*
thēsaurus, -ī *m* treasure, store; storehouse, treasury.
Thēseus, -eī *and* **eos** *m Greek hero (king of Athens).*
Thēsēus, -ēius *adj*, **-īdēs, -īdae** *m* Hippolytus; (*pl*) Athenians.

Thespiae, -ārum *fpl Boeotian town near Helicon.*
Thespiēnsis *and* **as, -adis** *adj* Thespian.
Thespis, -is *m traditional founder of Greek tragedy.*
Thessalia, -iae *f Thessaly (district of N. Greece).*
Thessalicus, -us *and* **is, -idis** *adj* Thessalian.
Thetis, -idis *and* **idos** *f sea nymph (mother of Achilles);* the sea.
thiasus, -ī *m* Bacchic dance.
Thoantēus *adj see n.*
Thoās, -antis *m king of Crimea (killed by Orestes);* king of Lemnos *(father of Hypsipyle).*
tholus, -ī *m* rotunda.
thōrāx, -ācis *m* breastplate.
Thrāca, -ae, (-ē, -ēs), (-ia, -iae) *f Thrace.*
Thracius, (Thrēicius) *adj* Thracian.
Thrasea, -ae *m Stoic philosopher under Nero.*
Thrasymachus, -ī *m Greek sophist.*
Thrāx, -ācis *m* Thracian; *kind of gladiator.*
Thrēssa, -ae, (Thrēissa, -ae) *f Thracian woman.*
Thrēx, -ēcis *m kind of gladiator.*
Thūcydidēs, -is *m famous Greek historian.*
Thūcydidius *adj* Thucydidean.
Thūlē, -ēs *f island in the extreme N. (perhaps Shetland).*
thunnus *see* **thynnus**.
thūr, -is *nt* = **tūs, tūris**.
Thūriī, -iōrum *mpl town in S. Italy.*
Thūrīnus *adj see n.*
thūs *see* **tūs**.
thȳa (thȳia), -ae *f citrus tree.*
Thybris, -is *and* **idis** *m* river Tiber.
Thyestēs, -ae *m brother of Atreus (whose son's flesh he served up to him to eat).*
Thyestēus *adj*, **-iadēs, -iadae** *m* Aegisthus.
Thyias (Thȳas), -adis *f Bacchante.*
Thȳlē *see* **Thūlē**.
thymbra, -ae *f savory.*
thymum, -ī *nt* garden thyme.
Thȳnia, -iae *f Bithynia.*
thynnus, -ī *m* tunnyfish.
Thȳnus, (-iacus), (-ias) *adj* Bithynian.
Thyōneus, -eī *m* Bacchus.
thyrsus, -ī *m* Bacchic wand.
tiāra, -ae *f*, **-ās, -ae** *m* turban.
Tiberiānus *adj see n.*
Tiberīnus, -īnis *adj*, **-īnus, -īnī** *m* Tiber.
Tiberis (Tibris), -is *m* river Tiber.
Tiberius, -ī *m* Roman praenomen (*esp the second emperor*).
tibi *dat of* **tū**.
tībia, -ae *f* shinbone; pipe, flute.
tībīcen, -inis *m* flute player; pillar.
tībīcina, -ae *f* flute player.
tībīcinium, -ī *and* **iī** *nt* flute playing.
Tibullus, -ī *m Latin elegiac poet.*
Tībur, -is *nt town on the river Anio (now Tivoli).*
Tīburs, -tis, (-tīnus), (-nus) *adj* Tiburtine.
Tīcīnus, -ī *m tributary of the river Po.*

Tigellīnus, -ī *m favourite of Nero.*

tigillum, -ī *nt small log, small beam.*

tignārius *adj working in wood;* **faber ~** carpenter.

tignum, -ī *nt timber, trunk, log.*

Tigrānēs, -is *m king of Armenia.*

tigris, -is *and* **idis** *f tiger.*

tīlia, -ae *f lime tree.*

Tīmaeus, -ī *m Sicilian historian; Pythagorean philosopher; a dialogue of Plato.*

timefactus *adj frightened.*

timeō, -ēre, -uī *vt, vi to fear, be afraid.*

timidē *adv timidly.*

timiditās, -ātis *f timidity, cowardice.*

timidus *adj timid, cowardly.*

timor, -ōris *m fear, alarm; a terror.*

tinctilis *adj dipped in.*

tinctus *ppp of* **tingō.**

tinea, -ae *f moth, bookworm.*

tingō, -gere, -xī, -ctum *vt to dip, soak; to dye, colour; (fig) to imbue.*

tinnīmentum, -ī *nt ringing noise.*

tinniō, -īre *vt, vi to ring, tinkle.*

tinnītus, -ūs *m ringing, jingle.*

tinnulus *adj ringing, jingling.*

tintinnābulum, -ī *nt bell.*

tintinō, -āre *vi to ring.*

tīnus, -ī *m a shrub, laurustinus.*

tinxī *perf of* **tingō.**

Tīphys, -os *m helmsman of the Argo.*

tippula, -ae *f water spider.*

Tīresiās, -ae *m blind soothsayer of Thebes.*

Tīridātēs, -ae *m king of Armenia.*

tīrō, -ōnis *m recruit, beginner.*

Tīrō, -ōnis *m Cicero's freedman secretary.*

tīrōcinium, -ī *and* **iī** *nt first campaign; recruits; (fig) first attempt, inexperience.*

Tīrōniānus *adj see* **Tīrō.**

tīrunculus, -ī *m young beginner.*

Tīryns, -this *f ancient town in S.E. Greece (home of Hercules).*

Tīrynthius *adj of Tiryns, of Hercules* ♦ *m Hercules.*

tis *archaic gen of* **tū.**

Tīsiphonē, -ēs *f a Fury.*

Tīsiphonēus *adj guilty.*

Tītān, -ānis, (-ānus, -ānī) *m Titan (an ancient race of gods); the sun.*

Tītānius, (-āniacus), (-ānis) *adj see n.*

Tīthōnius *adj see n.*

Tīthōnus, -ī *m consort of Aurora (granted immortality without youth).*

tītillātiō, -ōnis *f tickling.*

tītillō, -āre *vt to tickle.*

titubanter *adv falteringly.*

titubātiō, -ōnis *f staggering.*

titubō, -āre *vi to stagger, totter; to stammer; to waver, falter.*

titulus, -ī *m inscription, label, notice; title of honour; fame; pretext.*

Tityos, -ī *m giant punished in Tartarus.*

Tmōlus, -ī *m mountain in Lydia.*

toculiō, -ōnis *m usurer.*

tōfus, -ī *m tufa.*

toga, -ae *f toga (dress of the Roman citizen); (fig) peace; ~* **candida** *dress of election candidates; ~* **picta** *ceremonial dress of a victor in triumph; ~* **praetexta** *purple-edged toga of magistrates and children; ~* **pūra, virīlis** *plain toga of manhood.*

togātus *adj wearing the toga* ♦ *m Roman citizen; client* ♦ *f drama on a Roman theme.*

togula, -ae *f small toga.*

tolerābilis *adj bearable, tolerable; patient.*

tolerābiliter *adv patiently.*

tolerāns, -antis *pres p of* **tolerō** ♦ *adj patient.*

toleranter *adv patiently.*

tolerantia, -ae *f endurance.*

tolerātiō, -ōnis *f enduring.*

tolerātus *adj tolerable.*

tolerō, -āre, -āvī, -ātum *vt to bear, endure; to support, sustain.*

tollēnō, -ōnis *m crane, derrick, lift.*

tollō, -ere, sustulī, sublātum *vt to lift, raise; to take away, remove; to do away with, abolish, destroy; (anchor) to weigh; (child) to acknowledge, bring up; (mind) to elevate, excite, cheer; (passenger) to take on board;* **signa ~** *decamp.*

Tolōsa, -ae *f Toulouse.*

Tolōsānus *adj see* **Tolōsa.**

tolūtim *adv at a trot.*

tomāculum, -ī *nt sausage.*

tōmentum, -ī *nt stuffing, padding.*

Tomis, -is *f town on the Black Sea (to which Ovid was exiled).*

Tomītānus *adj see* **Tomis.**

Tonāns, -antis *m Thunderer (epithet of Jupiter).*

tondeō, -ēre, totondī, tōnsum *vt to shear, clip, shave; to crop, reap, mow; to graze, browse on; (fig) to fleece, rob.*

tonitrālis *adj thunderous.*

tonitrus, -ūs *m, -ua, -uōrum* *ntpl thunder.*

tonō, -āre, -uī *vi to thunder* ♦ *vt to thunder out.*

tōnsa, -ae *f oar.*

tōnsillae, -ārum *fpl tonsils.*

tōnsor, -ōris *m barber.*

tōnsōrius *adj for shaving.*

tōnstrīcula, -ae *f barber girl.*

tōnstrīna, -ae *f barber's shop.*

tōnstrīx, -īcis *f woman barber.*

tōnsūra, -ae *f shearing, clipping.*

tōnsus *ppp of* **tondeō.**

tōnsus, -ūs *m coiffure.*

tōphus *see* **tōfus.**

topiārius *adj of ornamental gardening* ♦ *m topiarist* ♦ *f topiary.*

topicē, -ēs *f the art of finding topics.*

Noun declensions and verb conjugations are shown on pp xiii to xxv. The present infinitive ending of a verb shows to which conjugation it belongs: **-āre** = 1st; **-ēre** = 2nd; **-ere** = 3rd and **-īre** = 4th. Irregular verbs are shown on p xxvi

toral, -ālis *nt* valance.
torcular, -āris *and* **um, -ī** *nt* press.
toreuma, -tis *nt* embossed work, relief.
tormentum, -ī *nt* windlass, torsion catapult, artillery; shot; rack, torture; (*fig*) torment, anguish.
tormina, -um *ntpl* colic.
torminōsus *adj* subject to colic.
tornō, -āre, -āvī, -ātum *vt* to turn (in a lathe), round off.
tornus, -ī *m* lathe.
torōsus *adj* muscular.
torpēdō, -inis *f* numbness, lethargy; (*fish*) electric ray.
torpeō, -ēre *vi* to be stiff, be numb; to be stupefied.
torpēscō, -ēscere, -uī *vi* to grow stiff, numb, listless.
torpidus *adj* benumbed.
torpor, -ōris *m* numbness, torpor, listlessness.
torquātus *adj* wearing a neckchain.
Torquātus, -ī *m surname of Manlius.*
torqueō, -quēre, -sī, -tum *vt* to turn, twist, bend, wind; (*missile*) to whirl, hurl, brandish; (*body*) to rack, torture; (*mind*) to torment.
torquēs *and* **is, -is** *m/f* neckchain, necklace, collar.
torrēns, -entis *pres p of* **torreō** ♦ *adj* scorching, hot; rushing, rapid ♦ *m* torment.
torreō, -ēre, -uī, tostum *vt* to parch, scorch, roast.
torrēscō, -ere *vi* to become parched.
torridus *adj* parched, dried up; frostbitten.
torris, -is *m* brand, firebrand.
torsī *perf of* **torqueō.**
tortē *adv* awry.
tortilis *adj* twisted, winding.
tortor, -ārī *vi* to writhe.
tortor, -ōris *m* torturer, executioner.
tortuōsus *adj* winding; (*fig*) complicated.
tortus *ppp of* **torqueō** ♦ *adj* crooked; complicated.
tortus, -ūs *m* twisting, writhing.
torulus, -ī *m* tuft (of hair).
torus, -ī *m* knot, bulge; muscle, brawn; couch, bed; (*earth*) bank, mound; (*language*) ornament.
torvitās, -ātis *f* wildness, grimness.
torvus *adj* wild, grim, fierce.
tostus *ppp of* **torreō.**
tot *adj* (*indecl*) so many, as many.
totidem *adj* (*indecl*) just as many, the same number of.
totiēns, totiēs *adv* so often, as often.
totondī *perf of* **tondeō.**
tōtus (*gen* **-īus,** *dat* **-ī**) *adj* entire, the whole, all; entirely, completely taken up with; **ex ~ō** totally; **in ~ō** on the whole.
toxicum, -ī *nt* poison.
trabālis *adj* for beams; **clāvus ~** large nail.
trabea, -ae *f* ceremonial robe.
trabeātus *adj* wearing a ceremonial robe.

trabs, -abis *f* beam, timber; tree; ship; roof.
Trāchīn, -īnis *f* town in Thessaly (*where Hercules cremated himself*).
Trāchīnius *adj see* **Trāchīn.**
tractābilis *adj* manageable, tractable.
tractātiō, -ōnis *f* handling, treatment.
tractātus, -ūs *m* handling.
tractim *adv* slowly, little by little.
tractō, -āre, -āvī, -ātum *vt* to maul; to handle, deal with, manage; (*activity*) to conduct, perform; (*person*) to treat; (*subject*) to discuss, consider.
tractus *ppp of* **trahō** ♦ *adj* fluent.
tractus, -ūs *m* dragging, pulling, drawing, train, track; (*place*) extent, region, district; (*movement*) course; (*time*) lapse; (*word*) drawling.
trādidī *perf of* **trādō.**
trāditiō, -ōnis *f* surrender; handing down.
trāditor, -ōris *m* traitor.
trāditus *ppp of* **trādō.**
trādō, -ere, -idī, -itum *vt* to hand over, deliver, surrender; to commit, entrust; to betray; to bequeath, hand down; (*narrative*) to relate, record; (*teaching*) to propound; **sē ~** surrender, devote oneself.
trādūcō (trānsdūcō), -ūcere, -ūxī, -uctum *vt* to bring across, lead over, transport across; to transfer; to parade, make an exhibition of (in public); (*time*) to pass, spend.
trāductiō, -ōnis *f* transference; (*time*) passage; (*word*) metonymy.
trāductor, -ōris *m* transferrer.
trāductus *ppp of* **trādūcō.**
trādux, -ucis *m* vine layer.
tragicē *adv* dramatically.
tragicocōmoedia, -ae *f* tragicomedy.
tragicus *adj* of tragedy, tragic; in the tragic manner, lofty; terrible, tragic ♦ *m* writer of tragedy.
tragoedia, -ae *f* tragedy; (*fig*) bombast.
tragoedus, -ī *m* tragic actor.
trāgula, -ae *f* kind of javelin.
trahea, -ae *f* sledge.
trahō, -here, -xī, -ctum *vt* to draw, drag, pull, take with one; to pull out, lengthen; to draw together, contract; to carry off, plunder; (*liquid*) to drink, draw; (*money*) to squander; (*wool*) to spin; (*fig*) to attract; (*appearance*) to take on; (*consequence*) to derive, get; (*praise, blame*) to ascribe, refer; (*thought*) to ponder; (*time*) to spin out.
trāiciō, -icere, -iēcī, -iectum *vt* to throw across, shoot across; (*troops*) to get across, transport; (*with weapon*) to pierce, stab; (*river, etc*) to cross; (*fig*) to transfer ♦ *vi* to cross.
trāiectiō, -ōnis *f* crossing, passage; (*fig*) transferring; (*RHET*) exaggeration; (*words*) transposition.
trāiectus *ppp of* **trāiciō.**
trāiectus, -ūs *m* crossing, passage.

trālāt- *etc see* **trānslāt-**.
Trallēs, -ium *fpl town in Lydia.*
Tralliānus *adj see n.*
trālūceō *etc see* **trānslūceō**.
trāma, -ae *f* woof, web.
trāmes, -itis *m* footpath, path.
trāmittō *etc see* **trānsmittō**.
trānatō *etc see* **trānsnatō**.
trānō, -āre, -āvī, -ātum *vt, vi* to swim across; (*air*) to fly through.
tranquillē *adv* quietly.
tranquillitās, -ātis *f* quietness, calm; (*fig*) peace, quiet.
tranquillō, -āre *vt* to calm.
tranquillus *adj* quiet, calm ♦ *nt* calm sea.
trāns *prep* (*with acc*) across, over, beyond.
trānsabeō, -īre, -iī *vt* to pierce.
trānsāctor, -ōris *m* manager.
trānsāctus *ppp of* **trānsigō**.
trānsadigō, -ere *vt* to drive through, pierce.
Trānsalpīnus *adj* Transalpine.
trānscendō (trānsscendō), -endere, -endī, -ēnsum *vt, vi* to pass over, surmount; to overstep, surpass, transgress.
trānscrībō (trānsscrībō), -bere, -psī, -ptum *vt* to copy out; (*fig*) to make over, transfer.
trānscurrō, -rere, -rī, -sum *vt, vi* to run across, run past, traverse.
trānscursus, -ūs *m* running through; (*speech*) cursory remark.
trānsd- *etc see* **trād-**.
trānsēgī *perf of* **trānsigō**.
trānsenna, -ae *f* net, snare; trellis, latticework.
trānseō, -īre, -iī, -itum *vt, vi* to pass over, cross over; to pass along *or* through; to pass by; to outstrip, surpass, overstep; (*change*) to turn into; (*speech*) to mention briefly, leave out, pass on; (*time*) to pass, pass away.
trānsferō, -ferre, -tulī, -lātum *vt* to bring across, transport, transfer; (*change*) to transform; (*language*) to translate; (*RHET*) to use figuratively; (*time*) to postpone; (*writing*) to copy.
trānsfīgō, -gere, -xī, -xum *vt* to pierce; to thrust through.
trānsfīxus *ppp of* **trānsfīgō**.
trānsfodiō, -odere, -ōdī, -ossum *vt* to run through, stab.
trānsfōrmis *adj* changed in shape.
trānsfōrmō, -āre *vt* to change in shape.
trānsfossus *ppp of* **trānsfodiō**.
trānsfuga, -ae *m/f* deserter.
trānsfugiō, -ugere, -ūgī *vi* to desert, come over.
trānsfugium, -ī *and* **iī** *nt* desertion.
trānsfundō, -undere, -ūdī, -ūsum *vt* to decant, transfuse.
trānsfūsiō, -ōnis *f* transmigration.

trānsfūsus *ppp of* **trānsfundō**.
trānsgredior, -dī, -ssus *vt, vi* to step across, cross over, cross; to pass on; to exceed.
trānsgressiō, -ōnis *f* passage; (*words*) transposition.
trānsgressus *ppa of* **trānsgredior**.
trānsgressus, -ūs *m* crossing.
trānsiciō *etc see* **trāiciō**.
trānsigō, -igere, -ēgī, -āctum *vt* to carry through, complete, finish; (*difference*) to settle; (*time*) to pass, spend; (*with* **cum**) to put an end to; (*with weapon*) to stab.
trānsiī *perf of* **trānseō**.
trānsiliō, trānssiliō, -īre, -uī *vi* to jump across ♦ *vt* to leap over; (*fig*) to skip, disregard; to exceed.
trānsitiō, -ōnis *f* passage; desertion; (*disease*) infection.
trānsitō, -āre *vi* to pass through.
trānsitus *ppp of* **trānseō**.
trānsitus, -ūs *m* passing over, passage; desertion; passing by; transition.
trānslātīcius, trālātīcius *adj* traditional, customary, common.
trānslātiō, trālātiō, -ōnis *f* transporting, transferring; (*language*) metaphor.
trānslātīvus *adj* transferable.
trānslātor, -ōris *m* transferrer.
trānslātus *ppp of* **trānsferō**.
trānslegō, -ere *vt* to read through.
trānslūceō, -ēre *vi* to be reflected; to shine through.
trānsmarīnus *adj* overseas.
trānsmeō, -āre *vi* to cross.
trānsmigrō, -āre *vi* to emigrate.
trānsmissiō, -ōnis *f* crossing.
trānsmissus *ppp of* **trānsmittō**.
trānsmissus, -ūs *m* crossing.
trānsmittō, -ittere, -īsī, -issum *vt* to send across, put across; to let pass through; to transfer, entrust, devote; to give up, pass over; (*place*) to cross over, go through, pass ♦ *vi* to cross.
trānsmontānus *adj* beyond the mountains.
trānsmoveō, -ovēre, -ōvī, -ōtum *vt* to move, transfer.
trānsmūtō, -āre *vt* to shift.
trānsnatō, trānatō, -āre *vi* to swim across ♦ *vt* to swim.
trānsnō *etc see* **trānō**.
Trānspadānus *adj* north of the Po.
trānspectus, -ūs *m* view.
trānspiciō, -ere *vt* to look through.
trānspōnō, -ōnere, -osuī, -ositum *vt* to transfer.
trānsportō, -āre *vt* to carry across, transport, remove.
trānspositus *ppp of* **trānspōnō**.
Trānsrhēnānus *adj* east of the Rhine.
trānss- *etc see* **trāns-**.

Noun declensions and verb conjugations are shown on pp xiii to xxv. The present infinitive ending of a verb shows to which conjugation it belongs: **-āre** = 1st; **-ēre** = 2nd; **-ere** = 3rd and **-īre** = 4th. Irregular verbs are shown on p xxvi

Trānstiberīnus *adj* across the Tiber.
trānstineō, -ēre *vi* to get through.
trānstrum, -ī *nt* thwart.
trānstulī *perf of* **trānsferō**.
trānsultō, -āre *vi* to jump across.
trānsūtus *adj* pierced.
trānsvectiō, -ōnis *f* crossing.
trānsvectus *ppp of* **trānsvehō**.
trānsvehō, -here, -xī, -ctum *vt* to carry across, transport.
trānsvehor, -hī, -ctus *vi* to cross, pass over; (*parade*) to ride past; (*time*) to elapse.
trānsverberō, -āre *vt* to pierce through, wound.
trānsversus (trāversus) *adj* lying across, crosswise, transverse; **digitum ~um** a finger's breadth; **dē ~ō** unexpectedly; **ex ~ō** sideways.
trānsvolitō, -āre *vt* to fly through.
trānsvolō, -āre *vt, vi* to fly across, fly through; to move rapidly across; to fly past, disregard.
trānsvorsus *etc see* **trānsversus**.
trapētus, -ī *m* olive mill, oil mill.
trapezīta *etc see* **tarpezīta**.
Trapezūs, -ūntis *f* Black Sea town (*now* Trebizond).
Trasumennus (Trasimēnus), -ī *m* lake in Etruria (*where Hannibal defeated the Romans*).
trāv- *see* **trānsv-**.
trāvectiō *etc see* **trānsvectiō**.
traxī *perf of* **trahō**.
trecēnī, -ōrum *adj* three hundred each.
trecentēsimus *adj* three-hundredth.
trecentī, -ōrum *num* three hundred.
trecentiēns, -ēs *adv* three hundred times.
trechedīpna, -ōrum *ntpl* dinner shoes (of parasites).
tredecim *num* thirteen.
tremebundus *adj* trembling.
tremefaciō, -facere, -fēcī, -factum *vt* to shake.
tremendus *adj* formidable, terrible.
tremēscō (tremīscō), -ere *vi* to begin to shake ♦ *vt* to be afraid of.
tremō, -ere, -uī *vi* to tremble, quake, quiver ♦ *vt* to tremble at, dread.
tremor, -ōris *m* shaking, quiver, tremor; earthquake.
tremulus *adj* trembling, shivering.
trepidanter *adv* with agitation.
trepidātiō, -ōnis *f* agitation, alarm, consternation.
trepidē *adv* hastily, in confusion.
trepidō, -āre, -āvī, -ātum *vi* to be agitated, bustle about, hurry; to be alarmed; to flicker, quiver ♦ *vt* to start at.
trepidus *adj* restless, anxious, alarmed; alarming, perilous.
trēs, trium *num* three.
trēssis, -is *m* three asses.
trēsvirī, triumvirōrum *mpl* three commissioners, triumvirs.

Trēverī, -ōrum *mpl* people of E. Gaul (*about what is now* Trèves).
Trēvericus *adj see* n.
triangulum, -ī *nt* triangle.
triangulus *adj* triangular.
triāriī, -ōrum *mpl* the third line (*in Roman battle order*), the reserves.
tribuārius *adj* of the tribes.
tribūlis, -is *m* fellow tribesman.
tribulum, -ī *nt* threshing sledge.
tribulus, -ī *m* star thistle.
tribūnal, -ālis *nt* platform; judgment seat; camp platform, cenotaph.
tribūnātus, -ūs *m* tribuneship, rank of tribune.
tribūnicius *adj* of a tribune ♦ *m* ex-tribune.
tribūnus, -ī *m* tribune; ~ **plēbis** tribune of the people, a magistrate who defended the rights of the plebeians; ~ **mīlitum** *or* **mīlitāris** military tribune, an officer under the legatus; ~ī **aerāriī** paymasters.
tribuō, -uere, -uī, -ūtum *vt* to assign, allot; to give, bestow, pay; to concede, allow; to ascribe, attribute; (*subject*) to divide; (*time*) to devote.
tribus, -ūs *m* tribe.
tribūtārius *adj*: **-ae tabellae** letters of credit.
tribūtim *adv* by tribes.
tribūtiō, -ōnis *f* distribution.
tribūtum, -ī *nt* contribution, tribute, tax.
tribūtus *ppp of* **tribuō**.
tribūtus *adj* arranged by tribes.
trīcae, -ārum *fpl* nonsense; tricks, vexations.
trīcēnī, -ōrum *adj* thirty each, in thirties.
triceps, -ipitis *adj* three-headed.
trīcēsimus *adj* thirtieth.
trichila, -ae *f* arbour, summerhouse.
trīciēns, -ēs *adv* thirty times.
trīclīnium, -ī *and* **iī** *nt* dining couch; dining room.
trīcō, -ōnis *m* mischief-maker.
trīcor, -ārī *vi* to make mischief, play tricks.
tricorpor, -is *adj* three-bodied.
tricuspis, -idis *adj* three-pointed.
tridēns, -entis *adj* three-pronged ♦ *m* trident.
tridentifer, -ī *adj* trident-wielding.
tridentiger, -ī *adj* trident-wielding.
trīduum, -ī *nt* three days.
triennia, -ium *ntpl* a triennial festival.
triennium, -ī *and* **iī** *nt* three years.
triēns, -entis *m* a third; (*coin*) a third of an as; (*measure*) a third of a pint.
trientābulum, -ī *nt* land given by the State as a third of a debt.
trientius *adj* sold for a third.
triērarchus, -ī *m* captain of a trireme.
triēris, -is *f* trireme.
trietēricus *adj* triennial ♦ *ntpl* festival of Bacchus.
trietēris, -idis *f* three years; a triennial festival.
trifāriam *adv* in three parts, in three places.
trifaux, -aucis *adj* three-throated.

trifidus *adj* three-forked.
trifōrmis *adj* triple.
trifūr, -ūris *m* archthief.
trifurcifer, -ī *m* hardened criminal.
trigeminus *adj* threefold, triple ♦ *mpl* triplets.
trigintā *num* thirty.
trigōn, -ōnis *m* a ball game.
trilībris *adj* three-pound.
trilinguis *adj* three-tongued.
trilīx, -icis *adj* three-ply, three-stranded.
trimēstris *adj* of three months.
trimetrus, -ī *m* trimeter.
trīmus *adj* three years old.
Trīnacria, -iae *f* Sicily.
Trīnacrius, -is, -idis *adj* Sicilian.
trīnī, -ōrum *adj* three each, in threes; triple.
Trinobantēs, -um *mpl* British tribe in East Anglia.
trinōdis *adj* three-knotted.
triōbolus, -ī *m* half-a-drachma.
Triōnēs, -um *mpl* the Plough; the Little Bear.
tripartītō *adv* in *or* into three parts.
tripartītus, tripertītus *adj* divided into three parts.
tripectorus *adj* three-bodied.
tripedālis *adj* three-foot.
tripert- *etc see* **tripart-**.
tripēs, -edis *adj* three-legged.
triplex, -icis *adj* triple, threefold ♦ *nt* three times as much ♦ *mpl* three-leaved writing tablet.
triplus *adj* triple.
Triptolemus, -ī *m* inventor of agriculture, judge in Hades.
tripudiō, -āre *vi* to dance.
tripudium, -ī *and* **iī** *nt* ceremonial dance, dance; a favourable omen (*when the sacred chickens ate greedily*).
tripūs, -odis *f* tripod; the Delphic oracle.
triquetrus *adj* triangular; Sicilian.
trirēmis *adj* with three banks of oars ♦ *f* trireme.
trīs *etc see* **trēs**.
triscurria, -ōrum *ntpl* sheer fooling.
tristē *adv* sadly; severely.
trīstī = **trīvistī**.
tristiculus *adj* rather sad.
tristificus *adj* ominous.
tristimōnia, -ae *f* sadness.
tristis *adj* sad, glum, melancholy; gloomy, sombre, dismal; (*taste*) bitter; (*smell*) offensive; (*temper*) severe, sullen, ill-humoured.
tristitia, -ae *f* sadness, sorrow, melancholy; moroseness, severity.
tristitiēs, -ēī *f* sorrow.
trisulcus *adj* three-forked.
tritavus, -ī *m* great-great-great-grandfather.
trīticeus *adj* of wheat, wheaten.
trīticum, -ī *nt* wheat.

Trītōn, -ōnis *m* sea god (*son of Neptune*); African lake (*where Minerva was born*).
Trītōnius, -ōniacus, -ōnis *adj* of Lake Triton, of Minerva ♦ *f* Minerva.
trītūra, -ae *f* threshing.
trītus *ppp of* **terō** ♦ *adj* well-worn; (*judgment*) expert; (*language*) commonplace, trite.
trītus, -ūs *m* rubbing, friction.
triumphālis *adj* triumphal ♦ *ntpl* insignia of a triumph.
triumphō, -āre, -āvī, -ātum *vi* to celebrate a triumph; to triumph, exult ♦ *vt* to triumph over, win by conquest.
triumphus, -ī *m* triumphal procession, victory parade; triumph, victory.
triumvir, -ī *m* commissioner, triumvir; mayor (*of a provincial town*).
triumvirālis *adj* triumviral.
triumvirātus, -ūs *m* office of triumvir, triumvirate.
triumvirī, -ōrum *mpl* three commissioners, triumvirs.
trivenēfica, -ae *f* old witch.
trivī *perf of* **terō**.
Trivia, -ae *f* Diana.
triviālis *adj* common, popular.
trivium, -ī *and* **iī** *nt* crossroads; public street.
trivius *adj* of the crossroads.
Trōas, -adis *f* the district of Troy, Troad; Trojan woman ♦ *adj* Trojan.
trochaeus, -ī *m* trochee; tribrach.
trochlea, -ae *f* block and tackle.
trochus, -ī *m* hoop.
Trōglodytae, -ārum *mpl* cave dwellers of Ethiopia.
Trōia, -ae *f* Troy.
Trōilus, -ī *m* son of Priam.
Trōiugena, -ae *m/f* Trojan; Roman.
Trōius *and* **ānus** *and* **cus** *adj* Trojan.
tropaeum, -ī *nt* victory memorial, trophy; victory; memorial, token.
Trōs, -ōis *m* king of Phrygia; Trojan.
trucīdātiō, -ōnis *f* butchery.
trucīdō, -āre, -āvī, -ātum *vt* to slaughter, massacre.
truculentē *adv see* **truculentus**.
truculentia, -ae *f* ferocity, inclemency.
truculentus *adj* ferocious, grim, wild.
trudis, -is *f* pike.
trūdō, -dere, -sī, -sum *vt* to push, thrust, drive; (*buds*) to put forth.
trulla, -ae *f* ladle, scoop; washbasin.
truncō, -āre, -āvī, -ātum *vt* to lop off, maim, mutilate.
truncus, -ī *m* (*tree*) trunk, bole; (*human*) trunk, body; (*abuse*) blockhead ♦ *adj* maimed, broken, stripped (of); defective.
trūsī *perf of* **trūdō**.
trūsitō, -āre *vt* to keep pushing.
trūsus *ppp of* **trūdō**.

Noun declensions and verb conjugations are shown on pp xiii to xxv. The present infinitive ending of a verb shows to which conjugation it belongs: **-āre** = 1st; **-ēre** = 2nd; **-ere** = 3rd and **-īre** = 4th. Irregular verbs are shown on p xxvi

trutina, -ae *f* balance, scales.
trux, -ucis *adj* savage, grim, wild.
trȳgōnus, -ī *m* stingray.
tū *pron* you, thou.
tuātim *adv* in your usual fashion.
tuba, -ae *f* trumpet, war trumpet.
tūber, -is *nt* swelling, lump; (*food*) truffle.
tuber, -is *f* kind of apple tree.
tubicen, -inis *m* trumpeter.
tubilūstria, -ōrum *ntpl* festival of trumpets.
tuburcinor, -ārī *vi* to gobble up, guzzle.
tubus, -ī *m* pipe.
tuditō, -āre *vt* to strike repeatedly.
tueor, -ērī, -itus *and* **tūtus** *vt* to see, watch, look; to guard, protect, keep.
tugurium, -ī *and* **iī** *nt* hut, cottage.
tuitiō, -ōnis *f* defence.
tuitus *ppa of* **tueor.**
tulī *perf of* **ferō.**
Tulliānum, -ī *nt* State dungeon of Rome.
Tulliānus *adj see* **Tullius.**
Tulliola, -ae *f* little Tullia (*Cicero's daughter*).
Tullius, -ī *and* **iī** *m* Roman family name (*esp the sixth king*); *the orator Cicero.*
Tullus, -ī *m* third king of Rome.
tum *adv* (*time*) then, at that time; (*sequence*) then, next ♦ *conj* moreover, besides; ~ ... ~ at one time ... at another; ~ ... **cum** at the time when, whenever; **cum** ... ~ not only ... but; ~ **dēmum** only then; ~ **ipsum** even then; ~ **māximē** just then; ~ **vērō** then more than ever.
tumefaciō, -facere, -fēcī, -factum *vt* to make swell; (*fig*) to puff up.
tumeō, -ēre *vi* to swell, be swollen; (*emotion*) to be excited; (*pride*) to be puffed up; (*language*) to be turgid.
tumēscō, -ēscere, -uī *vi* to begin to swell, swell up.
tumidus *adj* swollen, swelling; (*emotion*) excited, enraged; (*pride*) puffed up; (*language*) bombastic.
tumor, -ōris *m* swelling, bulge; hillock; (*fig*) commotion, excitement.
tumulō, -āre *vt* to bury.
tumulōsus *adj* hilly.
tumultuārius *adj* hasty; (*troops*) emergency.
tumultuātiō, -ōnis *f* commotion.
tumultuō, -āre; -or, -ārī *vi* to make a commotion, be in an uproar.
tumultuōsē *adv see* **tumultuōsus.**
tumultuōsus *adj* uproarious, excited, turbulent.
tumultus, -ūs *m* commotion, uproar, disturbance; (*MIL*) rising, revolt, civil war; (*weather*) storm; (*mind*) disorder.
tumulus, -ī *m* mound, hill; burial mound, barrow.
tunc *adv* (*time*) then, at that time; (*sequence*) then, next; ~ **dēmum** only then; ~ **quoque** then too; even so.
tundō, -ere, tutudī, tūnsum *and* **tūsum** *vt* to beat, thump, hammer; (*grain*) to pound;

(*speech*) to din, importune.
Tūnēs, -ētis *m* Tunis.
tunica, -ae *f* tunic; (*fig*) skin, husk.
tunicātus *adj* wearing a tunic.
tunicula, -ae *f* little tunic.
tūnsus *ppp of* **tundō.**
tuor *etc see* **tueor.**
turba, -ae *f* disorder, riot, disturbance; brawl, quarrel; crowd, mob, troop, number.
turbāmenta, -ōrum *ntpl* propaganda.
turbātē *adv* in confusion.
turbātiō, -ōnis *f* confusion.
turbātor, -ōris *m* agitator.
turbātus *ppp of* **turbō** ♦ *adj* troubled, disorderly.
turbellae, -ārum *fpl* stir, row.
turben *etc see* **turbō.**
turbidē *adv* in disorder.
turbidus *adj* confused, wild, boisterous; (*water*) troubled, muddy; (*fig*) disorderly, troubled, alarmed, dangerous.
turbineus *adj* conical.
turbō, -āre, -āvī, -ātum *vt* to disturb, throw into confusion; (*water*) to trouble, make muddy.
turbō, -inis *m* whirl, spiral, rotation; reel, whorl, spindle; (*toy*) top; (*wind*) tornado, whirlwind; (*fig*) storm.
turbulentē *and* **er** *adv* wildly.
turbulentus *adj* agitated, confused, boisterous, stormy; troublemaking, seditious.
turdus, -ī *m* thrush.
tūreus *adj* of incense.
turgeō, -gēre, -sī *vi* to swell, be swollen; (*speech*) to be bombastic.
turgēscō, -ere *vi* to swell up, begin to swell; (*fig*) to become enraged.
turgidulus *adj* poor swollen.
turgidus *adj* swollen, distended; bombastic.
tūribulum, -ī *nt* censer.
tūricremus *adj* incense-burning.
tūrifer, -ī *adj* incense-producing.
tūrilegus *adj* incense-gathering.
turma, -ae *f* troop, squadron (*of cavalry*); crowd.
turmālis *adj* of a troop; equestrian.
turmātim *adv* troop by troop.
Turnus, -ī *m* Rutulian king (*chief opponent of Aeneas*).
turpiculus *adj* ugly little; slightly indecent.
turpificātus *adj* debased.
turpilucricupidus *adj* fond of filthy lucre.
turpis *adj* ugly, deformed, unsightly; base, disgraceful ♦ *nt* disgrace.
turpiter *adv* repulsively; shamefully.
turpitūdō, -inis *f* deformity; disgrace, infamy.
turpō, -āre *vt* to disfigure, soil.
turriger, -ī *adj* turreted.
turris, -is *f* tower, turret; siege tower; (*elephant*) howdah; (*fig*) mansion.
turrītus *adj* turreted; castellated; towering.

tursī *perf of* **turgeō**.
turtur, -is *m* turtledove.
tūs, tūris *nt* incense, frankincense.
Tusculānēnsis *adj* at Tusculum.
Tusculānum, -ānī *nt* villa at Tusculum (*esp Cicero's*).
Tusculānus *adj* Tusculan.
tūsculum, -ī *nt* a little incense.
Tusculum, -ī *nt* Latin town near Rome.
Tusculus *adj* Tusculan.
Tuscus *adj* Etruscan.
tussiō, -īre *vi* to cough, have a cough.
tussis, -is *f* cough.
tūsus *ppp of* **tundō**.
tūtāmen, -inis *nt* defence.
tūtāmentum, -ī *nt* protection.
tūte *emphatic form of* **tū**.
tūtē *adv* safely, in safety.
tūtēla, -ae *f* keeping, charge, protection; (*of minors*) guardianship, wardship; (*person*) watcher, guardian; ward, charge.
tūtemet *emphatic form of* **tū**.
tūtor, -ārī, -ātus, -ō, -āre *vt* to watch, guard, protect; to guard against.
tūtor, -ōris *m* protector; (*law*) guardian.
tutudī *perf of* **tundō**.
tūtus *ppp of* **tueō** ♦ *adj* safe, secure; cautious ♦ *nt* safety.
tuus *adj* your, yours, thy, thine; your own, your proper; of you.
Tȳdeus, -eī *and* **eos** *m* father of Diomede.
Tȳdīdēs, -īdae *m* Diomede.
tympanotrība, -ae *m* timbrel player.
tympanum (typanum), -ī *nt* drum, timbrel (*esp of the priests of Cybele*); (*mechanism*) wheel.
Tyndareus, -eī *m* king of Sparta (*husband of Leda*).
Tyndaridae, -idārum *mpl* Castor and Pollux.
Tyndaris, -idis *f* Helen; Clytemnestra.
Typhōeus, -eos *m* giant under Etna.
Typhōius, -is *adj see n*.
typus, -ī *m* figure.
tyrannicē *adv see* **tyrannicus**.
tyrannicīda, -ae *m* tyrannicide.
tyrannicus *adj* tyrannical.
tyrannis, -idis *f* despotism, tyranny.
tyrannoctonus, -ī *m* tyrannicide.
tyrannus, -ī *m* ruler, king; despot, tyrant.
Tyrās, -ae *m* river Dniester.
Tyrius *adj* Tyrian, Phoenician, Carthaginian; purple.
tyrotarīchos, -ī *m* dish of salt fish and cheese.
Tyrrhēnia, -iae *f* Etruria.
Tyrrhēnus *adj* Etruscan, Tyrrhenian.
Tyrtaeus, -ī *m* Spartan war poet.
Tyrus (-os), -ī *f* Tyre (*famous Phoenician seaport*).

U, u

ūber, -is *nt* breast, teat; (*fig*) richness.
ūber, -is *adj* fertile, plentiful, rich (in); (*language*) full, copious.
ūberius (*superl* **-rime**) *compar adj* more fully, more copiously.
ūbertās, -ātis *f* richness, plenty, fertility.
ūbertim *adv* copiously.
ubī *adv* (*interrog*) where?; (*relat*) where?, in which?, with whom?; when?
ubīcumque *adv* wherever; everywhere.
Ubiī, -ōrum *mpl* German tribe on the lower Rhine.
ubīnam *adv* where (in fact)?
ubīquāque *adv* everywhere.
ubīque *adv* everywhere, anywhere.
ubiubī *adv* wherever.
ubīvīs *adv* anywhere.
ūdus *adj* wet, damp.
ulcerō, -āre *vt* to make sore, wound.
ulcerōsus *adj* full of sores; wounded.
ulcīscor, -ī, ultus *vt* to take vengeance on, punish; to take vengeance for, avenge.
ulcus, -eris *nt* sore, ulcer; ~ **tangere** touch on a delicate subject.
ūlīgō, -inis *f* moisture, marshiness.
Ulixēs, -is *m* Ulysses, Odysseus (*king of Ithaca, hero of Homer's Odyssey*).
ullus (*gen* **-īus**, *dat* **-ī**) *adj* any.
ulmeus *adj* of elm.
ulmus, -ī *f* elm; (*pl*) elm rods.
ulna, -ae *f* elbow; arm; (*measure*) ell.
ulterior, -ōris *compar adj* farther, beyond, more remote.
ulterius *compar of* **ultrā**.
ultimus *superl adj* farthest, most remote, the end of; (*time*) earliest, latest, last; (*degree*) extreme, greatest, lowest ♦ *ntpl* the end; **~um** for the last time; **ad ~um** finally.
ultiō, -ōnis *f* vengeance, revenge.
ultor, -ōris *m* avenger, punisher.
ultrō *adv* beyond, farther, besides ♦ *prep* (*with acc*) beyond, on the far side of; (*time*) past; (*degree*) over and above.
ultrīx, -īcis *adj* avenging.
ultrō *adv* on the other side, away; besides; of one's own accord, unasked, voluntarily.
ultrō tribūta *ntpl* State expenditure for public works.
ultus *ppa of* **ulcīscor**.
ulula, -ae *f* screech owl.
ululātus, -ūs *m* wailing, shrieking, yells, whoops.

Noun declensions and verb conjugations are shown on pp xiii to xxv. The present infinitive ending of a verb shows to which conjugation it belongs: **-āre** = 1st; **-ēre** = 2nd; **-ere** = 3rd and **-īre** = 4th. Irregular verbs are shown on p xxvi

ululō, -āre, -āvī, -ātum *vi* to shriek, yell, howl ♦ *vt* to cry out to.
ulva, -ae *f* sedge.
umbella, -ae *f* parasol.
Umber, -rī *adj* Umbrian ♦ *m* Umbrian dog.
umbilīcus, -ī *m* navel; (*fig*) centre; (*book*) roller end; (*sea*) cockle *or* pebble.
umbō, -ōnis *m* boss (*of a shield*); shield; elbow.
umbra, -ae *f* shadow, shade; (*dead*) ghost; (*diner*) uninvited guest; (*fish*) grayling; (*painting*) shade; (*place*) shelter, school, study; (*unreality*) semblance, mere shadow.
umbrāculum, -ī *nt* arbour; school; parasol.
umbrāticola, -ae *m* lounger.
umbrāticus *adj* fond of idling; in retirement.
umbrātilis *adj* in retirement, private, academic.
Umbria, -riae *f* Umbria (*district of central Italy*).
umbrifer, -ī *adj* shady.
umbrō, -āre *vt* to shade.
umbrōsus *adj* shady.
ūmectō, -āre *vt* to wet, water.
ūmectus *adj* damp, wet.
ūmeō, -ēre *vi* to be damp, be wet.
umerus, -ī *m* upper arm, shoulder.
ūmēscō, -ere *vi* to become damp, get wet.
ūmidē *adv* with damp.
ūmidulus *adj* dampish.
ūmidus *adj* wet, damp, dank, moist.
ūmor, -ōris *m* liquid, fluid, moisture.
umquam, unquam *adv* ever, at any time.
ūnā *adv* together.
ūnanimāns, -antis *adj* in full agreement.
ūnanimitās, -ātis *f* concord.
ūnanimus *adj* of one accord, harmonious.
ūncia, -ae *f* a twelfth; (*weight*) ounce; (*length*) inch.
ūnciārius *adj* of a twelfth; (*interest*) 8⅓ per cent.
ūnciātim *adv* little by little.
uncīnātus *adj* barbed.
ūnciola, -ae *f* a mere twelfth.
ūnctiō, -ōnis *f* anointing.
ūnctitō, -āre *vt* to anoint regularly.
ūnctiusculus *adj* rather too unctuous.
ūnctor, -ōris *m* anointer.
ūnctūra, -ae *f* anointing (*of the dead*).
ūnctus *ppp of* **ungō** ♦ *adj* oiled; greasy, resinous; (*fig*) rich, sumptuous ♦ *nt* sumptuous dinner.
uncus, -ī *m* hook, grappling-iron.
uncus *adj* hooked, crooked, barbed.
unda, -ae *f* wave, water; (*fig*) stream, surge.
unde *adv* from where, whence; from whom, from which; ~ **petitur** the defendant; ~ **unde** from wherever; somehow or other.
ūndeciēns *and* **ēs** *adv* eleven times.
ūndecim *num* eleven.
ūndecimus *adj* eleventh.
undecumque *adv* from wherever.
ūndēnī, -ōrum *adj* eleven each, eleven.
ūndēnōnāgintā *num* eighty-nine.
ūndeoctōgintā *num* seventy-nine.

ūndēquadrāgintā *num* thirty-nine.
ūndēquīnquāgēsimus *adj* forty-ninth.
ūndēquīnquāgintā *num* forty-nine.
ūndēsexāgintā *num* fifty-nine.
ūndētrīcēsimus *adj* twenty-ninth.
ūndēvīcēsimānī, -ōrum *mpl* men of the nineteenth legion.
ūndēvīcēsimus *adj* nineteenth.
ūndēvīgintī *num* nineteen.
undique *adv* from every side, on all sides, everywhere; completely.
undisonus *adj* sea-roaring.
undō, -āre *vi* to surge; (*fig*) to roll, undulate.
undōsus *adj* billowy.
ūnetvīcēsimānī, -ōrum *mpl* men of the twenty-first legion.
ūnetvīcēsimus *adj* twenty-first.
ungō (unguō), -gere, ūnxī, ūnctum *vt* to anoint, smear, grease.
unguen, -inis *nt* fat, grease, ointment.
unguentārius, -ī *and* **iī** *m* perfumer.
unguentātus *adj* perfumed.
unguentum, -ī *nt* ointment, perfume.
unguiculus, -ī *m* fingernail.
unguis, -is *m* nail (*of finger or toe*); claw, talon, hoof; **ad ~em** with perfect finish; **trānsversum ~em** a hair's breadth; **dē tenerō ~ī** from earliest childhood.
ungula, -ae *f* hoof, talon, claw.
unguō *etc see* **ungō**.
ūnicē *adv* solely, extraordinarily.
ūnicolor, -ōris *adj* all one colour.
ūnicus *adj* one and only, sole; unparalleled, unique.
ūnifōrmis *adj* simple.
ūnigena, -ae *adj* only-begotten; of the same parentage.
ūnimanus *adj* with only one hand.
ūniō, -ōnis *m* a single large pearl.
ūniter *adv* together in one.
ūniversālis *adj* general.
ūniversē *adv* in general.
ūniversitās, -ātis *f* the whole; the universe.
ūniversus *adj* all taken together, entire, general ♦ *mpl* the community as a whole ♦ *nt* the universe; **in ~um** in general.
unquam *etc see* **umquam**.
ūnus *num* one ♦ *adj* sole, single, only; one and the same; the outstanding one; an individual; ~ **et alter** one or two; ~ **quisque** every single one; **nēmō ~** not a single one; **ad ~um** to a man.
ūnxī *perf of* **ungō**.
ūpiliō, -ōnis *m* shepherd.
upupa, -ae *f* hoopoe; crowbar.
Urania, -ae *and* **ē, -ēs** *f* Muse of astronomy.
urbānē *adv* politely; wittily, elegantly.
urbānitās, -ātis *f* city life; refinement, politeness; wit.
urbānus *adj* town (*in cpds*), city (*in cpds*); refined, polite; witty, humorous; impertinent ♦ *m* townsman.
urbicapus, -ī *m* taker of cities.

urbs, urbis *f* city; Rome.
urceolus, -ī *m* jug.
urceus, -ī *m* pitcher, ewer.
ūrēdō, -inis *f* blight.
urgeō, -gēre, -sī *vt, vi* to force on, push
forward; to press hard on, pursue closely; to
crowd, hem in; to burden, oppress;
(*argument*) to press, urge; (*work, etc*) to urge
on, ply hard, follow up.
ūrīna, -ae *f* urine.
ūrīnātor, -ōris *m* diver.
urna, -ae *f* water jar, urn; voting urn, lottery
urn, cinerary urn, money jar.
urnula, -ae *f* small urn.
ūrō, -ere, ūssī, ūstum *vt* to burn; to scorch,
parch; (*cold*) to nip; (*MED*) to cauterize;
(*rubbing*) to chafe, hurt; (*passion*) to fire,
inflame; (*vexation*) to annoy, oppress.
ursa, -ae *f* she-bear, bear; (*ASTRO*) Great Bear,
Lesser Bear.
ursī *perf of* **urgeō**.
ursīnus *adj* bear's.
ursus, -ī *m* bear.
urtīca, -ae *f* nettle.
ūrus, -ī *m* wild ox.
Usipetēs, -etum, (-iī, -iōrum) *mpl* German
tribe on the Rhine.
ūsitātē *adv* in the usual manner.
ūsitātus *adj* usual, familiar.
uspiam *adv* anywhere, somewhere.
usquam *adv* anywhere; in any way, at all.
usque *adv* all the way (to, from), right on,
right up to; (*time*) all the time, as long as,
continuously; (*degree*) even, as much as; ~
quāque everywhere; every moment, on
every occasion.
ūssī *perf of* **ūrō**.
ūstor, -ōris *m* cremator.
ūstulō, -āre *vt* to burn.
ūstus *ppp of* **ūrō**.
ūsūcapiō, -apere, -ēpī, -aptum *vt* to acquire
ownership of, take over.
ūsūcapiō, -ōnis *f* ownership by use *or*
possession.
ūsūra, -ae *f* use, enjoyment; interest, usury.
ūsūrārius *adj* for use and enjoyment; paying
interest.
ūsurpātiō, -ōnis *f* making use (of).
ūsurpō, -āre, -āvī, -ātum *vt* to make use of,
employ, exercise; (*law*) to take possession
of, enter upon; (*senses*) to perceive, make
contact with; (*word*) to call by, speak of.
ūsus *ppa of* **ūtor**.
ūsus, -ūs *m* use, enjoyment, practice;
experience, skill; usage, custom;
intercourse, familiarity; usefulness, benefit,
advantage; need, necessity; ~ **est, venit**
there is need (of); ~**uī esse, ex** ~**ū esse** be of
use, be of service; ~**ū venīre** happen; ~ **et**
frūctus use and enjoyment, usufruct.

ut, utī *adv* how; (*relat*) as; (*explaining*)
considering how, according as; (*place*)
where; ~ **in ōrātōre** for an orator ♦ *conj* **1.** *with*
indic: (*manner*) as; (*concessive*) while, though;
(*time*) when, as soon as. **2.** *with subj*:
(*expressing the idea of a verb*) that, to;
(*purpose*) so that, to; (*causal*) seeing that;
(*concessive*) granted that, although; (*result*)
that, so that; (*fear*) that not; ~ ... **ita** while ...
nevertheless; ~ **nōn** without; ~ **quī** seeing
that I, he, *etc*; ~ **quisque māximē** the more.
utcumque (utcunque) *adv* however;
whenever; one way or another.
ūtēnsilis *adj* of use ♦ *ntpl* necessaries.
ūter, -ris *m* bag, skin, bottle.
uter (*gen* -**rīus**, *dat* -**rī**), **-ra, -rum** *pron* which (of
two), the one that; one or the other.
utercumque, utracumque, utrumcumque
pron whichever (of two).
uterlibet, utralibet, utrumlibet *pron*
whichever (of the two) you please, either
one.
uterque, utraque, utrumque *pron* each (of
two), either, both.
uterum, -ī *nt*, **uterus, -ī** *m* womb; child; belly.
utervīs, utravīs, utrumvīs *pron* whichever
(of two) you please; either.
ūtī *infin of* **ūtor**.
utī *etc see* **ut**.
ūtibilis *adj* useful, serviceable.
Utica, -ae *f* town near Carthage (*where Cato*
committed suicide).
Uticēnsis *adj see n*.
ūtilis *adj* useful, expedient, profitable; fit (for).
ūtilitās, -ātis *f* usefulness, expediency,
advantage.
ūtiliter *adv* usefully, advantageously.
utinam *adv* I wish!, would that!, if only!
utique *adv* at least, by all means, especially.
ūtor, ūtī, ūsus *vi* (*with abl*) to use, employ; to
possess, enjoy; to practise, experience;
(*person*) to be on intimate terms with, find;
ūtendum rogāre borrow.
utpote *adv* inasmuch as, as being.
ūtrārius, -ī *and* **iī** *m* watercarrier.
ūtriculārius, -ī *and* **iī** *m* bagpiper.
utrimque (utrinque) *adv* on both sides, on
either side.
utrō *adv* in which direction.
utrobīque *see* **utrubīque**.
utrōque *adv* in both directions, both ways.
utrubī *adv* on which side.
utrubīque *adv* on both sides, on either side.
utrum *adv* whether.
utut *adv* however.
ūva, -ae *f* grape, bunch of grapes; vine;
cluster.
ūvēscō, -ere *vi* to become wet.
ūvidulus *adj* moist.
ūvidus *adj* wet, damp; drunken.

Noun declensions and verb conjugations are shown on pp xiii to xxv. The present infinitive ending of a verb shows
to which conjugation it belongs: **-āre** = 1st; **-ēre** = 2nd; **-ere** = 3rd and **-īre** = 4th. Irregular verbs are shown on p xxvi

uxor, -ōris *f* wife.
uxorcula, -ae *f* little wife.
uxōrius *adj* of a wife; fond of his wife.

V, v

vacāns, -antis *pres p of* **vacō** ♦ *adj* unoccupied; (*woman*) single.
vacātiō, -ōnis *f* freedom, exemption; exemption from military service; payment for exemption from service.
vacca, -ae *f* cow.
vaccīnium, -ī *and* **iī** *nt* hyacinth.
vaccula, -ae *f* heifer.
vacēfīō, -ierī *vi* to become empty.
vacillō, -āre *vi* to stagger, totter; to waver, be unreliable.
vacīvē *adv* at leisure.
vacīvitās, -ātis *f* want.
vacīvus *adj* empty, free.
vacō, -āre, -āvī, -ātum *vi* to be empty, vacant, unoccupied; to be free, aloof (from); to have time for, devote one's time to; **~at** there is time.
vacuātus *adj* empty.
vacuēfaciō, -facere, -fēcī, -factum *vt* to empty, clear.
vacuitās, -ātis *f* freedom, exemption; vacancy.
vacuus *adj* empty, void, wanting; vacant; free (from), clear; disengaged, at leisure; (*value*) worthless; (*woman*) single ♦ *nt* void, space.
vadimōnium, -ī *and* **iī** *nt* bail, security; **~ sistere** appear in court; **~ dēserere** default.
vādō, -ere *vi* to go, go on, make one's way.
vador, -ārī, -ātus *vt* to bind over by bail.
vadōsus *adj* shallow.
vadum, -ī *nt* shoal, shallow, ford; water, sea; bottom.
vae *interj* woe!, alas!
vafer, -rī *adj* crafty, subtle.
vafrē *adv* artfully.
vagē *adv* far afield.
vāgīna, -ae *f* sheath, scabbard; (*grain*) husk.
vāgiō, -īre *vi* to cry.
vāgītus, -ūs *m* crying, bleating.
vagor, -ārī, -ātus *vi* to wander, rove, go far afield; (*fig*) to spread.
vāgor, -ōris *m* cry.
vagus *adj* wandering, unsettled; (*fig*) fickle, wavering, vague.
vah *interj* (*expressing surprise, joy, anger*) oh!, ah!
valdē *adv* greatly, intensely; very.
valē, valēte *interj* goodbye, farewell.

valēns, -entis *pres p of* **valeō** ♦ *adj* strong, powerful, vigorous; well, healthy.
valenter *adv* strongly.
valentulus *adj* strong.
valeō, -ēre, -uī, -itum *vi* to be strong; to be able, have the power (to); to be well, fit, healthy; (*fig*) to be powerful, effective, valid; (*force*) to prevail; (*money*) to be worth; (*word*) to mean; **~ apud** have influence over, carry weight with; **~ēre iubeō** say goodbye to; **~ē dīcō** say goodbye; **~eās** away with you!
valēscō, -ere *vi* to grow strong, thrive.
valētūdinārium, -ī *and* **iī** *nt* hospital.
valētūdō, -inis *f* state of health, health; illness.
valgus *adj* bow-legged.
validē *adv* powerfully, very.
validus *adj* strong, powerful, able; sound, healthy; effective.
vallāris *adj* (*decoration*) for scaling a rampart.
vallēs, vallis, -is *f* valley.
vallō, -āre, -āvī, -ātum *vt* to palisade, entrench, fortify.
vallum, -ī *nt* rampart, palisade, entrenchment.
vallus, -ī *m* stake; palisade, rampart; (*comb*) tooth.
valvae, -ārum *fpl* folding door.
vānēscō, -ere *vi* to disappear, pass away.
vānidicus, -ī *m* liar.
vāniloquentia, -ae *f* idle talk.
vāniloquus *adj* untruthful; boastful.
vānitās, -ātis *f* emptiness; falsehood, worthlessness, fickleness; vanity.
vānitūdō, -inis *f* falsehood.
vannus, -ī *f* winnowing fan.
vānus *adj* empty; idle, useless, groundless; false, untruthful, unreliable; conceited.
vapidus *adj* spoilt, corrupt.
vapor, -ōris *m* steam, vapour; heat.
vapōrārium, -ī *and* **iī** *nt* steam pipe.
vapōrō, -āre *vt* to steam, fumigate, heat ♦ *vi* to burn.
vappa, -ae *f* wine that has gone flat; (*person*) good-for-nothing.
vāpulō, -āre *vi* to be flogged, beaten; to be defeated.
variantia, -ae *f* diversity.
variātiō, -ōnis *f* difference.
vāricō, -āre *vi* to straddle.
vāricōsus *adj* varicose.
vāricus *adj* with feet wide apart.
variē *adv* diversely, with varying success.
varietās, -ātis *f* difference, diversity.
variō, -āre, -āvī, -ātum *vt* to diversify, variegate; to make different, change, vary ♦ *vi* to change colour; to differ, vary.
varius *adj* coloured, spotted, variegated; diverse, changeable, various; (*ability*) versatile; (*character*) fickle.
Varius, -ī *m* epic poet (*friend of Vergil and Horace*).
varix, -icis *f* varicose vein.

Varrō, -ōnis *m consul defeated at Cannae; antiquarian writer of Cicero's day.*

Varrōniānus *adj see* **Varrō.**

vārus *adj* knock-kneed; crooked; contrary.

vas, vadis *m* surety, bail.

vās, vāsis (*pl* **vāsa, -ōrum**) *nt* vessel, dish; utensil, implement; (*MIL*) baggage.

vāsārium, -ī *and* **iī** *nt* furnishing allowance (of a governor).

vāsculārius, -ī *and* **iī** *m* metalworker.

vāsculum, -ī *nt* small dish.

vastātiō, -ōnis *f* ravaging.

vastātor, -ōris *m* ravager.

vastē *adv* (*size*) enormously; (*speech*) coarsely.

vastificus *adj* ravaging.

vastitās, -ātis *f* desolation, desert; devastation, destruction.

vastitiēs, -ēī *f* ruin.

vastō, -āre, -āvī, -ātum *vt* to make desolate, denude; to lay waste, ravage.

vastus *adj* empty, desolate, uncultivated; ravaged, devastated; (*appearance*) uncouth, rude; (*size*) enormous, vast.

vāsum *etc see* **vās.**

vātēs, -is *m/f* prophet, prophetess; poet, bard.

Vāticānus *adj* Vatican (*hill on right bank of Tiber*).

vāticinātiō, -ōnis *f* prophesying, prediction.

vāticinātor, -ōris *m* prophet.

vāticinor, -ārī, -ātus *vi* to prophesy; to celebrate in verse; to rave, rant.

vāticinus *adj* prophetic.

-ve *conj* or; either ... or.

vēcordia, -ae *f* senselessness; insanity.

vēcors, -dis *adj* senseless, foolish, mad.

vectīgal, -ālis *nt* tax; honorarium (to a magistrate); income.

vectiō, -ōnis *f* transport.

vectis, -is *m* lever, crowbar; (*door*) bolt, bar.

Vectis, -is *f* Isle of Wight.

vectō, -āre *vt* to carry; (*pass*) to ride.

vector, -ōris *m* carrier; passenger, rider.

vectōrius *adj* transport (*in cpds*).

vectūra, -ae *f* transport; (*payment*) carriage, fare.

vectus *ppp of* **vehō.**

Vediovis, -is = **Vēiovis.**

vegetus *adj* lively, sprightly.

vēgrandis *adj* small.

vehemēns, -entis *adj* impetuous, violent; powerful, strong.

vehementer *adv* violently, eagerly; powerfully, very much.

vehementia, -ae *f* vehemence.

vehiculum, -ī *nt* carriage, cart; (*sea*) vessel.

vehō, -here, -xī, -ctum *vt* to carry, convey; (*pass*) to ride, sail, drive.

Vēiēns, -entis, (-entānus), (-us) *adj see* **Vēiī.**

Vēiī, -ōrum *mpl* ancient town in S. Etruria.

Vēiovis, -is *m* ancient Roman god (*anti-Jupiter*).

vel *conj* or, or perhaps; or rather; or else; either ... or ♦ *adv* even, if you like; perhaps; for instance; ~ **māximus** the very greatest.

Vēlābrum, -ī *nt* low ground between Capitol and Palatine hills.

vēlāmen, -inis *nt* covering, garment.

vēlāmentum, -ī *nt* curtain; (*pl*) draped olive branches carried by suppliants.

vēlārium, -ī *and* **iī** *nt* awning.

vēlātī, -ōrum *mpl* supernumerary troops.

vēlēs, -itis *m* light-armed soldier, skirmisher.

vēlifer, -ī *adj* carrying sail.

vēlificātiō, -ōnis *f* sailing.

vēlificō, -āre *vi* to sail ♦ *vt* to sail through.

vēlificor, -ārī *vi* to sail; (*with dat*) to make an effort to obtain.

Velīnus, -ī *m* a Sabine lake.

vēlitāris *adj* of the light-armed troops.

vēlitātiō, -ōnis *f* skirmishing.

vēlitēs *pl of* **vēles.**

vēlitor, -ārī *vi* to skirmish.

vēlivolus *adj* sail-winged.

velle *infin of* **volō.**

vellicō, -āre *vt* to pinch, pluck, twitch; (*speech*) to taunt, disparage.

vellō, -ere, vellī *and* **vulsī, vulsum** *vt* to pluck, pull, pick; to pluck out, tear up.

vellus, -eris *nt* fleece, pelt; wool; fleecy clouds.

vēlō, -āre, -āvī, -ātum *vt* to cover up, clothe, veil; (*fig*) to conceal.

vēlōcitās, -ātis *f* speed, rapidity.

vēlōciter *adv* rapidly.

vēlōx, -ōcis *adj* fast, quick, rapid.

vēlum, -ī *nt* sail; curtain, awning; **rēmis ~īsque** with might and main; ~**a dare** set sail.

velut, velutī *adv* as, just as; for instance; just as if.

vēmēns *etc see* **vehemēns.**

vēna, -ae *f* vein, artery; vein of metal; water course; (*fig*) innermost nature of feelings, talent, strength; ~**ās temptāre** feel the pulse; ~**ās tenēre** have one's finger on the pulse (of).

vēnābulum, -ī *nt* hunting spear.

Venāfrānus *adj see n.*

Venāfrum, -ī *nt* Samnite town famous for olive oil.

vēnālicius *adj* for sale ♦ *m* slave dealer.

vēnālis *adj* for sale; bribable ♦ *m* slave offered for sale.

vēnāticus *adj* hunting (*in cpds*).

vēnātiō, -ōnis *f* hunting; a hunt; public show of fighting wild beasts; game.

vēnātor, -ōris *m* hunter.

vēnātōrius *adj* hunter's.

vēnātrīx, -īcis *f* huntress.

vēnātūra, -ae *f* hunting.

vēnātus, -ūs *m* hunting.

vēndibilis *adj* saleable; (*fig*) popular.

Noun declensions and verb conjugations are shown on pp xiii to xxv. The present infinitive ending of a verb shows to which conjugation it belongs: **-āre** = 1st; **-ēre** = 2nd; **-ere** = 3rd and **-īre** = 4th. Irregular verbs are shown on p xxvi

vēnditātiō, -ōnis *f* showing off, advertising.
vēnditātor, -ōris *m* braggart.
vēnditiō, -ōnis *f* sale.
vēnditō, -āre *vt* to try to sell; to praise up, advertise; **sē ~** ingratiate oneself (with).
vēnditor, -ōris *m* seller.
vēndō (*pass* **vēneō**), **-ere, -idī, -itum** *vt* to sell; to betray; to praise up.
venēficium, -ī *and* **iī** *nt* poisoning; sorcery.
venēficus *adj* poisonous; magic ♦ *m* sorcerer ♦ *f* sorceress.
venēnātus *adj* poisonous; magic.
venēnifer, -ī *adj* poisonous.
venēnō, -āre *vt* to poison.
venēnum, -ī *nt* drug, potion; dye; poison; magic charm; (*fig*) mischief; charm.
vēneō, -īre, -iī, -itum *vi* to be sold.
venerābilis *adj* honoured, venerable.
venerābundus *adj* reverent.
venerātiō, -ōnis *f* respect, reverence.
venerātor, -ōris *m* reverencer.
Venereus, Venerius *adj* of Venus ♦ *m* highest throw at dice.
veneror, -ārī, -ātus *vt* to worship, revere, pray to; to honour, respect; to ask for, entreat.
Venetia, -iae *f* district of the Veneti.
Veneticus *adj see n.*
Venetus *adj* Venetian; (*colour*) blue.
vēnī *perf of* **veniō**.
venia, -ae *f* indulgence, favour, kindness; permission, leave; pardon, forgiveness; **bonā tuā ~ā** by your leave; **bonā ~ā audīre** give a fair hearing.
vēnī *ī perf of* **vēneō**.
veniō, -īre, vēnī, ventum *vi* to come; (*fig*) to fall into, incur, go as far as; **in amīcitiam ~** make friends (with); **in spem ~** entertain hopes.
vēnor, -ārī, -ātus *vt, vi* to hunt, chase.
venter, -ris *m* stomach, belly; womb, unborn child.
ventilātor, -ōris *m* juggler.
ventilō, -āre *vt* to fan, wave, agitate.
ventiō, -ōnis *f* coming.
ventitō, -āre *vi* to keep coming, come regularly.
ventōsus *adj* windy; like the wind; fickle; conceited.
ventriculus, -ī *m* belly; (*heart*) ventricle.
ventriōsus *adj* pot-bellied.
ventulus, -ī *m* breeze.
ventus, -ī *m* wind.
vēnūcula, -ae *f* kind of grape.
vēnum, vēnō for sale.
vēnumdō (vēnundō), -āre, -edī, -atum *vt* to sell, put up for sale.
venus, -eris *f* charm, beauty; love, mating.
Venus, -eris *f* goddess of love; planet Venus; highest throw at dice.
Venusia, -iae *f* town in Apulia (*birthplace of Horace*).
Venusīnus *adj see* **Venusia**.

venustās, -ātis *f* charm, beauty.
venustē *adv* charmingly.
venustulus *adj* charming little.
venustus *adj* charming, attractive, beautiful.
vēpallidus *adj* very pale.
veprēcula, -ae *f* little brier bush.
veprēs, -is *m* thornbush, bramblebush.
vēr, vēris *nt* spring; **~ sacrum** offerings of firstlings.
vērātrum, -ī *nt* hellebore.
vērāx, -ācis *adj* truthful.
verbēna, -ae *f* vervain; (*pl*) sacred boughs carried by heralds or priests.
verber, -is *nt* lash, scourge; (*missile*) strap; (*pl*) flogging, strokes.
verberābilis *adj* deserving a flogging.
verberātiō, -ōnis *f* punishment.
verbereus *adj* deserving a flogging.
verberō, -āre, -āvī, -ātum *vt* to flog, beat, lash.
verberō, -ōnis *m* scoundrel.
verbōsē *adv* verbosely.
verbōsus *adj* wordy.
verbum, -ī *nt* word; saying, expression; (*GRAM*) verb; (*pl*) language, talk; **~ ē (dē, prō) ~ō** literally; **ad ~um** word for word; **~ō** orally; briefly; **~a dare** cheat, fool; **~a facere** talk; **meīs ~īs** in my name.
vērē *adv* really, truly, correctly.
verēcundē *adv see adj.*
verēcundia, -ae *f* modesty, shyness; reverence, dread; shame.
verēcundor, -ārī *vi* to be bashful, feel shy.
verēcundus *adj* modest, shy, bashful.
verendus *adj* venerable.
vereor, -ērī, -itus *vt, vi* to fear, be afraid; to revere, respect.
verētrum, -ī *nt* the private parts.
Vergiliae, -ārum *fpl* the Pleiads.
Vergilius, -ī *m* Vergil, Virgil (*famous epic poet*).
vergō, -ere *vt* to turn, incline ♦ *vi* to turn, incline, decline; (*place*) to face.
vēridicus *adj* truthful.
vērī similis *adj* probable.
vērī similitūdō, -inis *f* probability.
vēritās, -ātis *f* truth, truthfulness; reality, real life; (*character*) integrity; (*language*) etymology.
veritus *ppa of* **vereor**.
vermiculātus *adj* inlaid with wavy lines, mosaic.
vermiculus, -ī *m* grub.
vermina, -um *ntpl* stomach pains.
vermis, -is *m* worm.
verna, -ae *f* slave born in his master's home.
vernāculus *adj* of home-born slaves; native.
vernīlis *adj* slavish; (*remark*) smart.
vernīliter *adv* slavishly.
vernō, -āre *vi* to bloom, be spring-like; to be young.
vernula, -ae *f* young home-born slave; native.

vernus–vetustās

vernus *adj* of spring.

vērō *adv* in fact, assuredly; (*confirming*) certainly, yes; (*climax*) indeed; (*adversative*) but in fact; **minimē ~** certainly not.

Vērōna, -ae *f* town in N. Italy (*birthplace of Catullus*).

Vērōnēnsis *adj see* **Vērōna.**

verpus, -ī *m* circumcised man.

verrēs, -is *m* boar.

Verrēs, -is *m praetor prosecuted by Cicero.*

verrīnus *adj* boar's, pork (*in cpds*).

Verrius *and* **īnus** *adj see n.*

verrō, -rere, -rī, -sum *vt* to sweep, scour; to sweep away, carry off.

verrūca, -ae *f* wart; (*fig*) slight blemish.

verrūcōsus *adj* warty.

verruncō, -āre *vi* to turn out successfully.

versābundus *adj* rotating.

versātilis *adj* revolving; versatile.

versicolor, -ōris *adj* of changing *or* various colours.

versiculus, -ī *m* short line; (*pl*) unpretentious verses.

versificātor, -ōris *m* versifier.

versipellis *adj* of changed appearance; crafty ♦ *m* werewolf.

versō, -āre, -āvī, -ātum *vt* to keep turning, wind, twist; (*fig*) to upset, disturb, ruin; (*mind*) to ponder, consider.

versor, -ārī, -ātus *vi* to live, be, be situated; to be engaged (in), be busy (with).

versum *adv* turned, in the direction.

versūra, -ae *f* borrowing to pay a debt; loan.

versus *ppp of* **vertō** ♦ *adv* turned, in the direction.

versus, -ūs *m* line, row; verse; (*dance*) step.

versūtē *adv* craftily.

versūtiae, -ārum *fpl* tricks.

versūtiloquus *adj* sly.

versūtus *adj* clever; crafty, deceitful.

vertex, -icis *m* whirlpool, eddy; whirlwind; crown of the head, head; top, summit; (*sky*) pole.

verticōsus *adj* eddying, swirling.

vertīgō, -inis *f* turning round; dizziness.

vertō, -tere, -tī, -sum *vt* to turn; to turn over, invert; to turn round; to turn into, change, exchange; (*cause*) to ascribe, impute; (*language*) to translate; (*war*) to overthrow, destroy; (*pass*) to be (in), be engaged (in) ♦ *vi* to turn; to change; to turn out; **in fugam ~** put to flight; **terga ~** flee; **solum ~** emigrate; **vitiō ~ blame; annō ~tente** in the course of a year.

Vertumnus, -ī *m* god of seasons.

verū, -ūs *nt* spit; javelin.

vērum *adv* truly, yes; but actually; but, yet; **~ tamen** nevertheless.

vērum, -ī *nt* truth, reality; right; **~ī similis** probable.

vērus *adj* true, real, actual; truthful; right,

reasonable.

verūtum, -ī *nt* javelin.

verūtus *adj* armed with the javelin.

vervēx, -ēcis *m* wether.

vēsānia, -ae *f* madness.

vēsāniēns, -entis *adj* raging.

vēsānus *adj* mad, insane; furious, raging.

vescor, -ī *vi* (*with abl*) to feed, eat; to enjoy.

vescus *adj* little, feeble; corroding.

vēsīca, -ae *f* bladder; purse; football.

vēsīcula, -ae *f* small bladder, blister.

vespa, -ae *f* wasp.

Vespasiānus, -ī *m* Roman emperor.

vesper, -is *and* **ī** *m* evening; supper; evening star; west; **~e, ~ī** in the evening.

vespera, -ae *f* evening.

vesperāscō, -ere *vi* to become evening, get late.

vespertīliō, -ōnis *m* bat.

vespertīnus *adj* evening (*in cpds*), in the evening; western.

vesperūgō, -inis *f* evening star.

Vesta, -ae *f* Roman goddess of the hearth.

Vestālis *adj* Vestal ♦ *f* virgin priestess of Vesta.

vester, -rī *adj* your, yours.

vestibulum, -ī *nt* forecourt, entrance.

vestīgium, -ī *and* **ī ī** *nt* footstep, footprint, track; (*fig*) trace, sign, vestige; (*time*) moment, instant; **ē ~iō** instantly.

vestīgō, -āre, -āvī, -ātum *vt* to track, trace, search for, discover.

vestīmentum, -ī *nt* clothes.

vestiō, -īre, -iī, -ītum *vt* to clothe, dress; to cover, adorn.

vestipica, -ae *f* wardrobe woman.

vestis, -is *f* clothes, dress; coverlet, tapestry, blanket; (*snake*) slough; **~em mūtāre** change one's clothes; go into mourning.

vestispica *etc see* **vestipica.**

vestītus, -ūs *m* clothes, dress; covering; **mūtāre ~um** go into mourning; **redīre ad suum ~um** come out of mourning.

Vesuvius, -ī *m* the volcano Vesuvius.

veterānus *adj* veteran.

veterāscō, -scere, -vī *vi* to grow old.

veterātor, -ōris *m* expert, old hand; sly fox.

veterātōriē *adv see* **veterātōrius.**

veterātōrius *adj* crafty.

veterīnus *adj* of burden ♦ *f and ntpl* beasts of burden.

veternōsus *adj* lethargic, drowsy.

veternus, -ī *m* lethargy, drowsiness.

vetitus *ppp of* **vetō** ♦ *nt* prohibition.

vetō, -āre, -uī, -itum *vt* to forbid, prohibit, oppose; (*tribune*) to protest.

vetulus *adj* little old, poor old.

vetus, -eris *adj* old, former ♦ *mpl* the ancients ♦ *fpl* the old shops (*in the Forum*) ♦ *ntpl* antiquity, tradition.

vetustās, -ātis *f* age, long standing; antiquity;

Noun declensions and verb conjugations are shown on pp xiii to xxv. The present infinitive ending of a verb shows to which conjugation it belongs: **-āre** = 1st; **-ēre** = 2nd; **-ere** = 3rd and **-īre** = 4th. Irregular verbs are shown on p xxvi

great age, future age.

vetustus *adj* old, ancient; old-fashioned.

vexāmen, -inis *nt* shaking.

vexātiō, -ōnis *f* shaking; trouble, distress.

vexātor, -ōris *m* troubler, opponent.

vexī *perf of* **vehō**.

vexillārius, -ī *and* **iī** *m* standard-bearer, ensign; (*pl*) special reserve of veterans.

vexillum, -ī *nt* standard, flag; company, troop; ~ **prōpōnere** hoist the signal for battle.

vexō, -āre, -āvī, -ātum *vt* to shake, toss, trouble, distress, injure, attack.

via, -ae *f* road, street, way; journey, march; passage; (*fig*) way, method, fashion; the right way; ~**ā** properly; **inter ~ās** on the way.

viālis *adj* of the highways.

viārius *adj* for the upkeep of roads.

viāticātus *adj* provided with travelling money.

viāticus *adj* for a journey ♦ *nt* travelling allowance; (*MIL*) prizemoney, savings.

viātor, -ōris *m* traveller; (*law*) summoner.

vībīx, -īcis *f* weal.

vibrō, -āre, -āvī, -ātum *vt* to wave, shake, brandish, hurl, launch ♦ *vi* to shake, quiver, vibrate; to shimmer, sparkle.

vīburnum, -ī *nt* wayfaring-tree *or* guelder rose.

vīcānus *adj* village (*in cpds*) ♦ *mpl* villagers.

Vica Pota, -ae, -ae *f* goddess of victory.

vicārius *adj* substituted ♦ *m* substitute, proxy; underslave.

vīcātim *adv* from street to street; in villages.

vice (*with gen*) on account of; like.

vicem in turn; (*with gen*) instead of; on account of; like; **tuam** ~ on your account.

vīcēnārius *adj* of twenty.

vīcēnī, -ōrum *adj* twenty each, in twenties.

vicēs *pl of* **vicis**.

vīcēsimānī, -ōrum *mpl* men of the twentieth legion.

vīcēsimārius *adj* derived from the 5 per cent tax.

vīcēsimus *adj* twentieth ♦ *f* a 5 per cent tax.

vīcī *perf of* **vincō**.

vicia, -ae *f* vetch.

vīciēns *and* **ēs** *adv* twenty times.

vīcīnālis *adj* neighbouring.

vīcīnia, -ae *f* neighbourhood, nearness.

vīcīnitās, -ātis *f* neighbourhood, nearness.

vīcīnus *adj* neighbouring, nearby; similar, kindred ♦ *m/f* neighbour ♦ *nt* neighbourhood.

vicis *gen* (*acc* -**em**, *abl* -**e**) *f* interchange, alternation, succession; recompense, retaliation; fortune, changing conditions; duty, function, place; **in ~em** in turn, mutually.

vicissim *adv* in turn, again.

vicissitūdō, -inis *f* interchange, alternation.

victima, -ae *f* victim, sacrifice.

victimārius, -ī *and* **iī** *m* assistant at sacrifices.

victitō, -āre *vi* to live, subsist.

victor, -ōris *m* conqueror, victor, winner ♦ *adj* victorious.

victōria, -ae *f* victory.

victōriātus, -ūs *m* silver coin stamped with Victory.

Victōriola, -ae *f* little statue of Victory.

victrīx, -īcis *f* conqueror ♦ *adj* victorious.

victus *ppp of* **vincō**.

vīctus, -ūs *m* sustenance, livelihood; way of life.

vīculus, -ī *m* hamlet.

vīcus, -ī *m* (*city*) quarter, street; (*country*) village, estate.

vidēlicet *adv* clearly, evidently; (*ironical*) of course; (*explaining*) namely.

videō, -ēre, vīdī, vīsum *vt* to see, look at; (*mind*) to observe, be aware, know; to consider, think over; to see to, look out for; to live to see; (*pass*) to seem, appear; to seem right, be thought proper; **mē ~ē** rely on me; **vīderit** let him see to it; **mihi ~eor esse** I think I am; **sī (tibi) vidētur** if you like.

viduāta *adj* widowed.

viduitās, -ātis *f* bereavement, want; widowhood.

vīdulus, -ī *m* trunk, box.

viduō, -āre *vt* to bereave.

viduus *adj* bereft, bereaved; unmarried; (*with abl*) without ♦ *f* widow; spinster.

Vienna, -ae *f* town in Gaul on the Rhone.

viētus *adj* shrivelled.

vigeō, -ēre, -uī *vi* to thrive, flourish.

vigēscō, -ere *vi* to begin to flourish, become lively.

vigēsimus *etc see* **vīcēsimus**.

vigil, -is *adj* awake, watching, alert ♦ *m* watchman, sentinel; (*pl*) the watch, police.

vigilāns, -antis *pres p of* **vigilō** ♦ *adj* watchful.

vigilanter *adv* vigilantly.

vigilantia, -ae *f* wakefulness; vigilance.

vigilāx, -ācis *adj* watchful.

vigilia, -ae *f* lying awake, sleeplessness; keeping watch, guard; a watch; the watch, sentries; vigil; vigilance.

vigilō, -āre, -āvī, -ātum *vi* to remain awake; to keep watch; to be vigilant ♦ *vt* to spend awake, make while awake at night.

vīgintī *num* twenty.

vīgintīvirātus, -ūs *m* membership of a board of twenty.

vīgintīvirī, -ōrum *mpl* a board *or* commission of twenty men.

vigor, -ōris *m* energy, vigour.

vīlica, -ae *f* wife of a steward.

vīlicō, -āre *vi* to be an overseer.

vīlicus, -ī *m* overseer, manager of an estate, steward.

vīlis *adj* cheap; worthless, poor, mean, common.

vīlitās, -ātis *f* cheapness, low price; worthlessness.

vīliter *adv* cheaply.

vīlla, -ae *f* country house, villa.

vīllic- *etc see* **vīlic-**.

villōsus–vīs

villōsus *adj* hairy, shaggy.
vīllula, -ae *f* small villa.
vīllum, -ī *nt* a drop of wine.
villus, -ī *m* hair, fleece; (*cloth*) nap.
vīmen, -inis *nt* osier; basket.
vīmentum, -ī *nt* osier.
Vīminālis *adj* Viminal (*hill of Rome*).
vīmineus *adj* of osiers, wicker.
vīnāceus *adj* grape (*in cpds*).
Vīnālia, -ium *ntpl* Wine festival.
vīnārius *adj* of wine, wine (*in cpds*) ♦ *m* vintner
♦ *nt* wine flask.
vincibilis *adj* easily won.
vinciō, -cīre, -xī, -ctum *vt* to bind, fetter; to
encircle; (*fig*) to confine, restrain, envelop,
attach.
vinclum *nt see* **vinculum.**
vincō, -ere, vīcī, victum *vt* to conquer,
defeat, subdue; to win, prevail, be
successful; (*fig*) to surpass, excel; (*argument*)
to convince, refute, prove conclusively;
(*life*) to outlive.
vinctus *ppp of* **vinciō.**
vinculum, -ī *nt* bond, fetter, chain; (*pl*) prison.
vīndēmia, -ae *f* vintage grape harvest.
vīndēmiātor, -ōris *m* vintager.
vīndēmiola, -ae *f* small vintage.
Vīndēmitor, -ōris *m* the Vintager (*a star in
Virgo*).
vindex, -icis *m* champion, protector;
liberator; avenger ♦ *adj* avenging.
vindicātiō, -ōnis *f* punishment of offences.
vindiciae, -ārum *fpl* legal claim; ~**ās ab
lībertāte in servitūtem dare** condemn a free
person to slavery.
vindicō, -āre, -āvī, -ātum *vt* to lay claim to;
to claim, appropriate; to liberate, protect,
champion; to avenge, punish; **in lībertātem ~**
emancipate.
vindicta, -ae *f* rod used in manumitting a
slave; defence, deliverance; revenge,
punishment.
vīnea, -ae *f* vineyard; vine; (*MIL*) penthouse
(for besiegers).
vīnētum, -ī *nt* vineyard.
vīnitor, -ōris *m* vine-dresser.
vinnulus *adj* delightful.
vīnolentia, -ae *f* wine drinking.
vīnolentus *adj* drunk.
vīnōsus *adj* fond of wine, drunken.
vīnum, -ī *nt* wine.
vinxī *perf of* **vinciō.**
viola, -ae *f* violet; stock.
violābilis *adj* vulnerable.
violāceus *adj* violet.
violārium, -ī *nt* violet bed.
violārius, -ī and iī *m* dyer of violet.
violātiō, -ōnis *f* desecration.
violātor, -ōris *m* violator, desecrator.
violēns, -entis *adj* raging, vehement.

violenter *adv* violently, furiously.
violentia, -ae *f* violence, impetuosity.
violentus *adj* violent, impetuous, boisterous.
violō, -āre, -āvī, -ātum *vt* to do violence to,
outrage, violate; (*agreement*) to break.
vīpera, -ae *f* viper, adder, snake.
vīpereus *adj* snake's, serpent's.
vīperīnus *adj* snake's, serpent's.
vir, virī *m* man; grown man; brave man, hero;
husband; (*MIL*) footsoldier.
virāgō, -inis *f* heroine, warrior maid.
virecta, -ōrum *ntpl* grassy sward.
vireō, -ēre, -uī *vi* to be green; (*fig*) to be fresh,
flourish.
vīrēs *pl of* **vīs.**
virēscō, -ere *vi* to grow green.
virga, -ae *f* twig; graft; rod, staff, walking
stick, wand; (*colour*) stripe.
virgātor, -ōris *m* flogger.
virgātus *adj* made of osiers; striped.
virgētum, -ī *nt* thicket of osiers.
virgeus *adj* of brushwood.
virgidēmia, -ae *f* crop of flogging.
virginālis *adj* maidenly, of maids.
virginārius *adj* of maids.
virgineus *adj* maidenly, virgin, of virgins.
virginitās, -ātis *f* maidenhood.
virgō, -inis *f* maid, virgin; young woman, girl;
constellation Virgo; a Roman aqueduct.
virgula, -ae *f* wand.
virgulta, -ōrum *ntpl* thicket, shrubbery;
cuttings, slips.
virguncula, -ae *f* little girl.
viridāns, -antis *adj* green.
viridārium, -ī and iī *nt* plantation, garden.
viridis *adj* green; fresh, young, youthful ♦ *ntpl*
greenery.
viriditās, -ātis *f* verdure, greenness;
freshness.
viridor, -ārī *vi* to become green.
virīlis *adj* male, masculine; man's, adult;
manly, brave, bold; ~ **pars** one's individual
part *or* duty; **prō ~ī parte, portiōne** to the best
of one's ability.
virīlitās, -ātis *f* manhood.
virīliter *adv* manfully.
virītim *adv* individually, separately.
virōsus *adj* slimy; rank.
virtūs, -ūtis *f* manhood, full powers; strength,
courage, ability, worth; (*MIL*) valour,
prowess, heroism; (*moral*) virtue; (*things*)
excellence, worth.
vīrus, -ī *nt* slime; poison; offensive smell; salt
taste.
vīs (*acc* **vim**, *abl* **vī**, *pl* **vīrēs**) *f* power, force,
strength; violence, assault; quantity,
amount; (*mind*) energy, vigour; (*word*)
meaning, import; (*pl*) strength; (*MIL*) troops;
per vim forcibly; **dē vī damnārī** be convicted

Noun declensions and verb conjugations are shown on pp xiii to xxv. The present infinitive ending of a verb shows
to which conjugation it belongs: **-āre** = 1st; **-ēre** = 2nd; **-ere** = 3rd and **-īre** = 4th. Irregular verbs are shown on p xxvi

of assault; **prō vīribus** with all one's might.

vīs *2nd pers of* **volō**.

viscātus *adj* limed.

viscerātiō, -ōnis *f* public distribution of meat.

viscō, -āre *vt* to make sticky.

viscum, -ī *nt* mistletoe; bird lime.

viscus, -eris (*usu pl* **-era, -erum**) *nt* internal organs; flesh; womb, child; (*fig*) heart, bowels.

vīsendus *adj* worth seeing.

vīsiō, -ōnis *f* apparition; idea.

vīsitō, -āre *vt* to see often; to visit.

vīsō, -ere, -ī, -um *vt* to look at, survey; to see to; to go and see, visit.

Visurgis, -is *m* river Weser.

vīsus *ppp of* **videō** ♦ *nt* vision.

vīsus, -ūs *m* sight, the faculty of seeing; a sight, vision.

vīta, -ae *f* life, livelihood; way of life; career; biography.

vītābilis *adj* undesirable.

vītābundus *adj* avoiding, taking evasive action.

vītālis *adj* of life, vital ♦ *nt* subsistence ♦ *ntpl* vitals.

vītāliter *adv* with life.

vītātiō, -ōnis *f* avoidance.

Vitellius, -ī *m* Roman emperor in AD 69.

Vitellius, -iānus *adj see n.*

vitellus, -ī *m* little calf; (*egg*) yolk.

vīteus *adj* of the vine.

vīticula, -ae *f* little vine.

vītigenus *adj* produced from the vine.

vitilēna, -ae *f* procuress.

vitiō, -āre, -āvī, -ātum *vt* to spoil, corrupt, violate; to falsify.

vitiōsē *adv* badly, defectively.

vitiōsitās, -ātis *f* vice.

vitiōsus *adj* faulty, corrupt; wicked, depraved; ~ **cōnsul** *a consul whose election had a religious flaw in it.*

vītis, -is *f* vine; vine branch; centurion's staff, centurionship.

vītisator, -ōris *m* vine planter.

vitium, -ī *and* **iī** *nt* fault, flaw, defect; (*moral*) failing, offence, vice; (*religion*) flaw in the auspices.

vītō, -āre, -āvī, -ātum *vt* to avoid, evade, shun.

vītor, -ōris *m* basket maker, cooper.

vitreus *adj* of glass; glassy ♦ *ntpl* glassware.

vītricus, -ī *m* stepfather.

vitrum, -ī *nt* glass; woad.

vitta, -ae *f* headband, sacrificial fillet.

vittātus *adj* wearing a fillet.

vitula, -ae *f* (*of cow*) calf.

vitulīnus *adj* of veal ♦ *f* veal.

vītulor, -ārī *vi* to hold a celebration.

vitulus, -ī *m* calf; foal; ~ **marīnus** seal.

vituperābilis *adj* blameworthy.

vituperātiō, -ōnis *f* blame, censure;

scandalous conduct.

vituperātor, -ōris *m* critic.

vituperō, -āre *vt* to find fault with, disparage; (*omen*) to spoil.

vīvārium, -ī *and* **iī** *nt* fishpond, game preserve.

vīvātus *adj* animated.

vīvāx, -ācis *adj* long-lived; lasting; (*sulphur*) inflammable.

vīvēscō, -ere *vi* to grow, become active.

vīvidus *adj* full of life; (*art*) true to life, vivid; (*mind*) lively.

vīvirādīx, -īcis *f* a rooted cutting, layer.

vīvīscō *etc see* **vīvēscō**.

vīvō, -vere, -xī, -ctum *vi* to live, be alive; to enjoy life; (*fame*) to last, be remembered; (*with abl*) to live on; **~ve** farewell!; **~xērunt** they are dead.

vīvus *adj* alive, living; (*light*) burning; (*rock*) natural; (*water*) running; **~ō videntīque** before his very eyes; **mē ~ō** as long as I live, in my lifetime; **ad ~um resecāre** cut to the quick; **dē ~ō dētrahere** take out of capital.

vix *adv* with difficulty, hardly, scarcely.

vixdum *adv* hardly, as yet.

vīxī *perf of* **vīvō**.

vocābulum, -ī *nt* name, designation; (*GRAM*) noun.

vōcālis *adj* speaking, singing, tuneful ♦ *f* vowel.

vocāmen, -inis *nt* name.

vocātiō, -ōnis *f* invitation; (*law*) summons.

vocātus, -ūs *m* summons, call.

vōciferātiō, -ōnis *f* loud cry, outcry.

vōciferor, -ārī *vt* to cry out loud, shout.

vocitō, -āre, -āvī, -ātum *vt* to usually call; to shout.

vōcīvus *etc see* **vacīvus**.

vocō, -āre, -āvī, -ātum *vt* to call, summon; to call, name; (*gods*) to call upon; (*guest*) to invite; (*MIL*) to challenge; (*fig*) to bring (*into some condition or plight*); ~ **dē** name after; **~in dubium** ~ call in question; **in iūdicium** ~ call to account.

vōcula, -ae *f* weak voice; soft tone; gossip.

volaema *ntpl* kind of large pear.

Volaterrae, -ārum *fpl* old Etruscan town (*now* Volterra).

Volaterrānus *adj see n.*

volāticus *adj* winged; fleeting, inconstant.

volātilis *adj* winged; swift; fleeting.

volātus, -ūs *m* flight.

Volcānius *adj see n.*

Volcānus, -ī *m* Vulcan (*god of fire*); fire.

volēns, -entis *pres p of* **volō** ♦ *adj* willing, glad, favourable; **mihi ~entī est** it is acceptable to me.

volg- *etc see* **vulg-**.

volitō, -āre *vi* to fly about, flutter; to hurry, move quickly; (*fig*) to hover, soar; to get excited.

voln- *etc see* **vuln-**.

volō, -āre, -āvī, -ātum *vi* to fly; to speed.

volō, velle, voluī *vt* to wish, want; to be

willing; to will, purpose, determine;
(*opinion*) to hold, maintain; (*word, action*) to
mean; ~ **dīcere** I mean; **bene** ~ like; **male** ~
dislike; **ōrātum tē** ~ I beg you; **paucīs tē** ~ a
word with you!; **numquid vīs?** (*before leaving*)
is there anything else?; **quid sibi vult?** what
does he mean?; what is he driving at?; **velim
faciās** please do it; **vellem fēcissēs** I wish you
had done it.
volōnēs, -um *mpl* volunteers.
volpēs *etc see* **vulpēs.**
Volscī, -ōrum *mpl people in S. Latium.*
Volscus *adj* Volscian.
volsella, -ae *f* tweezers.
volsus *ppp of* **vellō.**
volt, voltis *older forms of* **vult, vultis.**
Voltumna, -ae *f patron goddess of Etruria.*
voltus *etc see* **vultus.**
volūbilis *adj* spinning, revolving; (*fortune*)
fickle; (*speech*) fluent.
volubilitās, -ātis *f* whirling motion;
roundness; fluency; inconstancy.
volūbiliter *adv* fluently.
volucer, -ris *adj* winged; flying, swift; fleeting.
volucris, -is *f* bird; insect.
volūmen, -inis *nt* roll, book; coil, eddy, fold.
voluntārius *adj* voluntary ♦ *mpl* volunteers.
voluntās, -ātis *f* will, wish, inclination;
attitude, goodwill; last will, testament; **suā**
~**āte** of one's own accord; **ad** ~**ātem** with the
consent (of).
volup *adv* agreeably, to one's satisfaction.
voluptābilis *adj* agreeable.
voluptās, -ātis *f* pleasure, enjoyment; (*pl*)
entertainments, sports.
voluptuārius *adj* pleasureable, agreeable;
voluptuous.
volūtābrum, -ī *nt* wallowing place.
volūtātiō, -ōnis *f* wallowing.
volūtō, -āre *vt* to roll about, turn over; (*mind*)
to occupy, engross; (*thought*) to ponder,
think over; (*pass*) to wallow, flounder.
volūtus *ppp of* **volvō.**
volva, -ae *f* womb; (*dish*) sow's womb.
volvō, -vere, -vī, -ūtum *vt* to roll, turn round;
to roll along; (*air*) to breathe; (*book*) to open;
(*circle*) to form; (*thought*) to ponder, reflect
on; (*time*) to roll on; (*trouble*) to undergo;
(*pass*) to roll, revolve ♦ *vi* to revolve, elapse.
vōmer, -eris *m* ploughshare.
vomica, -ae *f* sore, ulcer, abscess, boil.
vōmis *etc see* **vōmer.**
vomitiō, -ōnis *f* vomiting.
vomitus, -ūs *m* vomiting, vomit.
vomō, -ere, -uī, -itum *vt* to vomit, throw up;

to emit, discharge.
vorāgō, -inis *f* abyss, chasm, depth.
vorāx, -ācis *adj* greedy, ravenous; consuming.
vorō, -āre, -āvī, -ātum *vt* to swallow, devour;
(*sea*) to swallow up; (*reading*) to devour.
vors-, vort- *etc see* **vers-, vert-** *etc.*
vōs *pron* you.
Vosegus, -ī *m* Vosges mountains.
voster *etc see* **vester.**
vōtīvus *adj* votive, promised in a vow.
votō *etc see* **vetō.**
vōtum, -ī *nt* vow, prayer; votive offering;
wish, longing; ~**ī damnārī** have one's prayer
granted.
vōtus *ppp of* **voveō.**
voveō, -ēre, vōvī, vōtum *vt* to vow, promise
solemnly; to dedicate; to wish.
vōx, vōcis *f* voice; sound, cry, call; word,
saying, expression; accent; **unā vōce**
unanimously.
Vulcānus *see* **Volcānus.**
vulgāris *adj* common, general.
vulgāriter *adv* in the common fashion.
vulgātor, -ōris *m* betrayer.
vulgātus *adj* common; generally known,
notorious.
vulgivagus *adj* roving; inconstant.
vulgō *adv* publicly, commonly, usually,
everywhere.
vulgō, -āre, -āvī, -ātum *vt* to make common,
spread; to publish, divulge, broadcast; to
prostitute; to level down.
vulgus, -ī *nt* (*occ m*) the mass of the people,
the public; crowd, herd; rabble; populace.
vulnerātiō, -ōnis *f* wounding, injury.
vulnerō, -āre, -āvī, -ātum *vt* to wound, hurt;
to damage.
vulnificus *adj* wounding, dangerous.
vulnus, -eris *nt* wound, injury; (*things*)
damage, hole; (*fig*) blow, misfortune, pain.
vulpēcula, -ae *f* little fox.
vulpēs, -is *f* fox; (*fig*) cunning.
vulsī *perf of* **vellō.**
vulsus *ppp of* **vellō.**
vulticulus, -ī *m* a mere look (from).
vultum *etc see* **vultus.**
vultuōsus *adj* affected.
vultur, -is *m* vulture.
vulturius, -ī *and* **iī** *m* vulture, bird of prey;
(*dice*) an unlucky throw.
Vulturnus, -ī *m* river in Campania.
vultus, -ūs *m* look, expression (*esp* in the
eyes); face; (*things*) appearance.
vulva *etc see* **volva.**

Noun declensions and verb conjugations are shown on pp xiii to xxv. The present infinitive ending of a verb shows
to which conjugation it belongs: **-āre** = 1st; **-ēre** = 2nd; **-ere** = 3rd and **-īre** = 4th. Irregular verbs are shown on p xxvi

X, x

Xanthippē, -ēs *f wife of Socrates.*
Xanthus, -ī *m river of Troy (identified with Scamander); river of Lycia.*
xenium, -ī *and* **iī** *nt present.*

Xenocratēs, -is *m disciple of Plato.*
Xenophanēs, -is *m early Greek philosopher.*
Xenophōn, -ontis *m famous Greek historian.*
Xenophontēus *adj see n.*
xērampelinae, -ārum *fpl* dark-coloured clothes.
Xerxēs, -is *m Persian king defeated at Salamis.*
xiphiās, -ae *m* swordfish.
xystum, -ī *nt,* **xystus, -ī** *m* open colonnade, walk, avenue.

Z, z

Zacynthius *adj see n.*
Zacynthus (-os), -ī *f* island off W. Greece (*now* Zante).
Zama, -ae *f* town in Numidia (*where Scipio defeated Hannibal*).
Zamēnsis *adj see n.*
zāmia, -ae *f* harm.
Zanclaeus *and* **ēius** *adj see n.*
Zanclē, -ēs *f old name of Messana.*
zēlotypus *adj* jealous.

Zēnō *and* **ōn, -ōnis** *m founder of Stoicism; a philosopher of Elea; an Epicurean teacher of Cicero.*
Zephyrītis, -idis *f* Arsinoe (*queen of Egypt*).
Zephyrus, -ī *m* west wind, zephyr; wind.
Zēthus, -ī *m brother of Amphion.*
Zeuxis, -is *and* **idis** *m famous Greek painter.*
zmaragdus *etc see* **smaragdus.**
Zmyrna *etc see* **Smyrna.**
zōdiacus, -ī *m* zodiac.
zōna, -ae *f* belt, girdle; (GEOG) zone; (ASTRO) Orion's Belt.
zōnārius *adj* of belts; **sector ~** cutpurse ♦ *m* belt maker.
zōnula, -ae *f* little belt.
zōthēca, -ae *f* private room.
zōthēcula, -ae *f* cubicle.

ROMAN LIFE AND CULTURE

KEY EVENTS IN ROMAN HISTORY

B.C.

753	Foundation of Rome. Romulus became first king.
600-510	Rome ruled by Etruscan kings.
510	Expulsion of Tarquin and republic established.
507	Consecration of Temple of Jupiter on Capitol.
451	Code of Twelve Tables laid basis of Roman law.
390	Gauls sacked Rome.
367	Lex Liciniae Sextiae; plebeians allowed to be consul.
354	Treaty with Samnites.
343-341	First Samnite war; Romans occupied northern Campania.
340-338	Latin War; separate treaties made with Latins.
327-304	Second Samnite war; Rome increased influence in southern Italy.
321	Samnites defeated Romans at Caudine Forks; truce.
312	Appian Way, first Roman road, built.
298-290	Third Samnite war; Rome now all-powerful in southern Italy.
287	Hortensian Law; People's Assembly became a law-making body.
282-272	Wars with Tarentum and King Pyrrhus of Epirus.
270	Whole peninsula under Roman power.
264-241	First Punic war; Rome defended Greek cities in Sicily.
260	Fleet built; first naval victory at Mylae against Carthaginians.
241	Roman victory over Carthage secured Sicily, source of corn supply.
226	River Ebro treaty; Carthage should not cross into northern Spain.
218-201	Second Punic war against Hannibal.
216	Rome defeated at Battle of Cannae.
214-205	First Macedonian war with Philip V.
202	Scipio defeated Hannibal at Zama.
201	Peace concluded with Carthage; Rome now controlled the western Mediterranean.
200-196	Second Macedonian war; freedom of Greece proclaimed.
172-168	Third Macedonian war; Perseus crushed at Pydna.
148	Macedonia became a Roman province.
146	Carthage destroyed; Corinth destroyed.
133	Tiberius Gracchus became tribune; his assassination caused class conflict.
123-122	Gaius Gracchus carried out political/economic reforms.
121	Gaius was killed.
111-105	Marius and Sulla conducted war against Jugurtha of Numidia.
91-89	Social war between Rome and allies.
89-85	War with Mithridates VI of Pontus.
83-82	Civil war between Sulla and Marius; Sulla captured Rome.
81-79	Sulla, dictator, restored constitution, introduced reforms.
78	Death of Sulla.

77-72	Pompey fought Sertorius in Spain.
73-71	Spartacus' slave revolt.
70	Pompey and Crassus joint consuls; tribunes restored.
67	End of war against Mithridates; pirates controlled by Pompey.
63	Cicero suppressed Catiline's conspiracy.
60	First Triumvirate (Caesar, Pompey, Crassus) was formed.
58-51	Caesar conquered Gaul.
53	Battle of Carrhae; Rome defeated by Parthians; Crassus killed.
49	Caesar crossed Rubicon; civil war with Pompey began.
48	Pompey defeated by Caesar at Pharsalus; Caesar became dictator.
44	Caesar assassinated; Antony sought revenge against conspirators.
43	Second Triumvirate (Antony, Octavian, Lepidus).
42	Battle of Philippi; Triumvirate defeated Brutus and Cassius.
41-40	Antony and Octavian divided territory.
33-32	Rupture between Antony and Octavian.
31	Battle of Actium; Octavian defeated Antony and Cleopatra at sea.
27	Octavian returned powers to Senate; received name Augustus.
18	Julian laws promoted morality, condemned adultery, regulated divorce.
12	Augustus became Pontifex Maximus, head of state religion.
2	Augustus became 'pater patriae', father of his country; apex of his power.

A.D.

4	Tiberius adopted as Augustus' heir.
6	Annexation of Judaea.
9	Varus' three legions destroyed in Germany.
14	Death of Augustus.
14-37	Tiberius emperor; efficient administrator but unpopular.
14-16	Germanicus' successful campaign in Germany.
19	Germanicus died mysteriously; funeral at Antioch.
21-22	Sefanus organized Praetorian Guard.
26-31	Sefanus powerful in Rome; executed in 31.
37-41	Caligula emperor; cruel and tyrannical, was murdered by a tribune.
41-54	Claudius emperor; conquered Britain; showed political judgement.
57-68	Nero emperor; great fire (64); Christians persecuted.
68-69	Year of four emperors - Galba, Otho, Vitellius, Vespasian.
69-79	Vespasian began Flavian dynasty. Colosseum built.
70	Titus, Vespasian's son, captured Jerusalem, destroyed the Temple.
79-81	Titus emperor. Vesuvius erupted (79), Pompeii destroyed.
81-96	Domitian emperor. Border built in Germany; period ended in terror.
96-98	Nerva emperor after Domitian's assassination.
98-117	Trajan emperor - conqueror of Dacia and Parthian empire.
117-138	Hadrian, cultured traveller, soldier and administrator of empire.
122	Hadrian's Wall built between Solway and Tyne.
138-161	Antoninus Pius emperor; orderly, peaceful rule.
141-143	Antonine's Wall built between Forth and Clyde.
161-180	Marcus Aurelius emperor; Commodus, his son, shared power (177-180).

162	War with Parthia.
175-180	War against Germans on the Danube.
180-192	Commodus emperor.
193-211	Septimius Severus became emperor after crisis; died in Britain. Authorized special benefits for army.
211-217	Deterioration under criminal rule of Caracalla.
212	All free men of the empire became citizens.
284-305	Diocletian and Maximian co-emperors, empire divided into 12 dioceses. Prices imposed throughout empire.
303	Christians persecuted by Diocletian.
312	Constantine's victory at Milvian Bridge gave him Rome.
313	Edict of Milan ended persecution of Christians.
324	Constantine became sole emperor.
325	Council of Nicaea made Christianity religion of the empire.
330	Constantine made Byzantium seat of government; renamed it Constantinople.
337	Constantine died a Christian, trying to reorganize the empire.
379-395	Emperor Theodosius kept empire formally intact.
410	Alaric and Goths captured and destroyed Rome.

GOVERNMENT AND ADMINISTRATION

Republic

There was no written constitution. The Republic evolved from the struggle between the Senate and the People - Senatus Populusque Romanus - SPQR.

The Senate (Senatus)
This was the governing body, largely in the hands of the nobles (nobiles) or patricians (patricii).

- it prepared proposals to bring before the people
- it passed decrees (senatus consulta)
- it dealt with emergencies
- it controlled finances and building contracts
- it appointed magistrates to provinces
- it directed foreign relations
- it supervised state religion

The People (Populus)
The resolutions of the people, plebiscita, could have the force of law, but the Senate was allowed greater control. There were four assemblies:

- comitia curiata — formal duties
- comitia centuriata — elected magistrates
- comitia tributa — elected lesser magistrates
- concilium plebis — passed plebiscita

The Knights (Equites)
A third element, or class, emerged (originally from Rome's cavalry) to engage in trade and finance. These businessmen acquired more political influence and became wealthy. By the time of Cicero, they could enter the Senate. Cicero tried to reconcile the three classes, **senatores**, **equites** and **plebs** by his **concordia ordinum** (harmony of the classes).

Magistrates (Magistratus)
A magistrate was an official elected annually by the people. Offices were held in a strict order - **cursus honorum**. After ten years' military service, a young man could begin on the lowest rung of the ladder as follows:

Age	Office	Number	Duties
28	**Quaestor**	(8)	• administered finance maintained public records
30	**Aedile**	(4)	• maintained roads, water supply organized games and festivals
33(39)	**Praetor**	(6)	• civil judge could introduce laws
39(43)	**Consul**	(2)	• commanded army conducted elections presided over Senate carried out its decrees

Other magistrates:

Tribune (10) (tribunus plebis)	• defended plebs' rights had right of veto
Censor (2)	• conducted census (every 5 years) conducted purification revised roll of senators
Dictator (1)	• ruled in crisis (maximum of 6 months) conducted military and domestic matters

Imperium (supreme power) was held by consuls and praetors and dictators.
Potestas (power to enforce laws) was held by all magistrates.
Lictores (lictors *or* officials) carried **fasces** (bundles of rods) in front of consuls, praetors and dictators as a sign of their authority.

ORGANIZATION OF THE ARMY

Empire

At the time of Augustus there were 28 **legions** (later 25), each legion consisting of approximately 5000 infantrymen, trained for close combat. It was organized as follows:

Legio	Legion	5000 men
10 Cohortes	Cohorts	500 men
6 Centuriae	Centuries	80/100 men

Officers	
Legatus	legionary commander
6 **Tribuni Militum**	tribunes
60 **Centuriones**	centurions (from ranks), in charge of centuries

Recruitment	Citizens
Length of service	20/25 years
Duties	Offensive in important battles, repelling invasion *etc*
Pay	250/300 denarii per day
On retirement	Land or cash bounty

Additional **auxiliary forces** were recruited to help the legions. Particularly necessary were cavalry, drawn from all parts of the Empire, slingers, bowmen, etc. Infantrymen were often recruited locally and formed cohorts of about 500 men.

Auxilia	Auxiliaries	
Ala	Cavalry unit	500 men approx.
16 Turmae	turmae	32 men
Cohors	Infantry unit	500 men

Officers	
Decurio	Decurion (cavalry officer)

Recruitment	Non-citizens
Length of service	25 years
Duties	Frontier skirmishes, occupation, assisting legions

Pay	100 denarii per day
On retirement	Citizenship for self/family

The **Praetorian Guard** was the Emperor's special bodyguard. Three cohorts were based in Rome, six more in nearby towns.

Praetorium	Praetorian Guard	4500 men
9 Cohortes	cohorts	500 men

Officers	
2 **Praefecti Praetorio**	praetorian prefects
Recruitment	Citizens (Italy)
Length of service	16 years
Duties	Preserving emperor's power and safety
Pay	1000 denarii per day
On retirement	5000 denarii

FAMILY TREE

tritavus *m* **tritavia**
(great-great-great-great-grandfather) | (great-great-great-great-grandmother)

atavus *m* **atavia**
(great-great-great-grandfather) | (great-great-great-grandmother)

abavus *m* **abavia**
(great-great-grandfather) | (great-great-grandmother)

proavus *m* **proavia**
(great-grandfather) | (great-grandmother)

avus *m* **avia**
(grandfather) | (grandmother)

noverca *m* **pater** *m* **māter** *m* **vitricus**
(step-mother) | (father) | (mother) | (step-father)

Paternal line
- **patruus maximus** (great-great-granduncle)
- **amita maxima** (great-great-grandaunt)
- **patruus māior** (great-granduncle)
- **amita māior** (great-grandaunt)
- **patruus magnus** (grand-uncle)
- **amita magna** (grand-aunt)
- **patruus** (uncle)
- **amita** (aunt)

Maternal line
- **matertera maxima** (great-great-grandaunt)
- **avunculus maximus** (great-great-granduncle)
- **matertera māior** (great-grandaunt)
- **avunculus māior** (great-granduncle)
- **matertera magna** (grand-aunt)
- **avunculus magnus** (grand-uncle)
- **matertera** (aunt)
- **avunculus** (uncle)

In-laws
prosocer *m* **prosocrus**
(grandfather-in-law) | (grandmother-in-law)

socer *m* **socrus**
(father-in-law) | (mother-in-law)

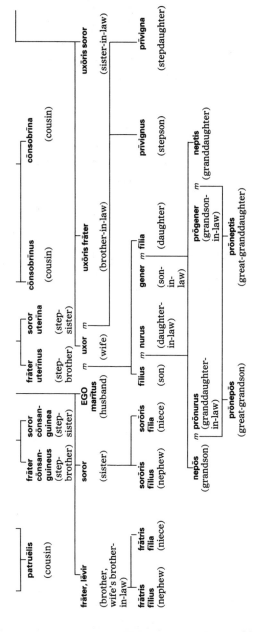

*Note: This is the Family Tree of the man designated **EGO** in the fourth generation from the end.*

MAJOR WRITERS

ENNIUS (Quintus Ennius: b 239 B.C.) **Annales**.

PLAUTUS (Titus Maccus *or* Maccius Plautus: b 254 B.C.) **Amphitruo**; the **Aulularia;** the **Menaechmi** and **Miles Gloriosus**.

TERENCE (Publius Terentius Afer) **Andria; Mother-in-law; Pharmio**.

LUCRETIUS (Titus Lucretius Carus: 94 - 55 B.C.) **De Rerum Natura**.

CATULLUS (Gaius Valerius Catullus: c.84 - c.54 B.C.) Lyric poetry; **Ave atque vale**.

CICERO (Marcus Tullius Cicero: b 106 B.C.) **Pro Caelio; De Legibus;** the **Tusculan Disputations; De Officiis; Philippics**.

JULIUS CAESAR (Gaius Iulius Caesar: b c.102 B.C. and assassinated in 44 B.C.) **Bellum Gallicum; Bellum Civile**.

SALLUST (Gaius Sallustius Crispus: 86 - 35 B.C.) **Bellum Catilinae; Bellum Iugurthinium**.

VIRGIL (Publius Vergilius Maro: 70 - 19 B.C.) **Eclogues; Georgics;** the **Aeneid**.

HORACE (Quintus Horatius Flaccus: b 65 A.D.). **Satires; Odes; Epistles**.

LIVY (Titus Livius: 59 B.C. - 17 A.D.) **Ab Urbe Condita**.

OVID (Publius Ovidius Naso: 43 B.C. - 17 A.D.) the **Heroides, Ars Amatoria;** the **Metamorphoses; Tristia.**

SENECA (Lucius Annaeus Seneca: 4 B.C. - 65 A.D.) **Dialogi; Epistolae; Morales**.

QUINTILIAN (Marcus Fabius Quintilianus: c.35 - c.95 A.D.) **Institutio Oratorio**.

MARTIAL (Marcus Valerius Martialis: 40 - 104 A.D.) the **Epigrams**.

JUVENAL (Decimus Iunius Iuvenalis) **Satires.**

TACITUS (Cornelius Tacitus) **Agricola; Germania; Histories;** the **Annals**.

PLINY (Gnaeus Plinius Secundus: b 61 *or* 62 A.D.) **Letters**.

GEOGRAPHICAL NAMES

The following list of geographical names and their adjectives includes both ancient and medieval Latin forms. The former are printed in Roman type, the latter in Italics. Medieval place names tend to have a variety of Latin forms, but only one has been selected in each case; occasionally both the ancient and the medieval forms have been given. Modern names which have a ready-made Latin form (_e.g._ America) have been omitted, and many names not included in this selection can be easily Latinized on the analogy of those which do appear.

Aachen	_Aquīsgrānum nt_	adj _Aquīsgrānēnsis_
Aberdeen	_Aberdōnia f_	adj _Aberdōnēnsis_
Abergavenny	Gobannium nt	
Aberystwith	_Aberistyvium nt_	
Adige, River	Athesis m	
Adriatic	Mare superum nt	adj Hadriāticus
Aegean	Mare Aegaeum nt	adj Aegaeus
Afghanistan	Ariāna f	adj Ariānus
Africa	Libya f,	adj Libycus,
	Africa f	Africānus
Agrigento	Agrigentum nt	adj Agrigentīnus
Aisne, River	Axona m	
Aix-en-Provence	Aquae Sextiae fpl	adj _Aquēnsis_
Aix-la-Chapelle	_Aquīsgrānum nt_	adj _Aquisgrānēnsis_
Aix-Les-Bains	Aquae Grātiānae fpl	
Ajaccio	_Adiacium nt_	adj _Adiacēnsis_
Aldborough	Isurium (nt)	
	Brigantum	
Alexandria	Alexandrēa,	
	Alexandrīa f	adj Alexandrīnus
Algiers	_Algerium nt_	adj _Algerīnus_
Alps	Alpēs fpl	adj Alpīnus
Alsace	_Alsatia f_	
Amalfi	Amalphis f	adj Amalphītānus
Ambleside	Galava f	
Amiens	_Ambiānum nt_	adj _Ambiānēnsis_
Amsterdam	_Amstelodamum nt_	adj _Amstelodamēnsis_
Ancaster	Causennae fpl	
Angers	_Andegāvum nt_	adj Andegāvēnsis
Anglesey	Mona f	
Aniene, River	Aniō m	adj Aniēnus
Anjou	Andegāvēnsis ager m	
Ankara	Ancyra f	adj Ancyrānus
Antibes	Antipolis f	adj Antipolītānus
Antioch	Antiochīa f	adj Antiochēnus
Antwerp	_Antwerpium nt_	adj _Antwerpiēnsis_
Anzio	Antium nt	adj Antiās, Antiānus
Aosta	Augusta Praetōria f	
Apennines	Mōns Apennīnus m	

Aragon	*Aragōnia f*	
Archangel	*Archangelopolis f*	
Ardennes	Arduenna *f*	
Arezzo	Ārētium *nt*	*adj* Ārētīnus
Argenteuil	*Argentōlium nt*	
Argyll	*Argadia f*	
Arles	Arelās *f*	*adj* Arelātēnsis
Armagh	Armācha *f*	*adj* Armāchānus
Arno, *River*	Arnus *m*	*adj* Arniēnsis
Arras	Atrebatēs *mpl*	*adj* Atrebatēnsis
Artois	Atrebatēs *mpl*	
Assisi	Assīsium *nt*	*adj* Assīsiēnsis
Athens	Athēnae *fpl*	*adj* Athēniēnsis
Atlantic	Mare Atlanticum *nt*	
Augsburg	Augusta (*f*) Vindelicōrum	*adj* Augustānus
Autun	Augustodūnum *nt*	*adj* Augustodūnēnsis
Auvergne	Arvernī *mpl*	*adj* Arvernus
Aventine	Aventīnus *m*	
Avignon	Aveniō *f*	*adj* Aveniōnēnsis
Avon, *River*	Auvona *m*	
Babylon	Babylōn *f*	*adj* Babylōnius
Baden-Baden	Aquae Aurēliae *fpl*	
Balearic Islands	Baliārēs Insulae *fpl*	*adj* Baliāricus
Balkh	Bactra *ntpl*	*adj* Bactriānus
Baltic	*Balticum Mare nt*	
Bangor	*Bangertium nt*	*adj Bangertiēnsis*
Barcelona	Barcinō *f*	*adj* Barcinōnēnsis
Bari	Bārium *nt*	*adj Bārēnsis*
Basle	Basilēa *f*	*adj* Basilēēnsis
Basques	Vasconēs *mpl*	*adj* Vasconicus
Bath	Aquae (*fpl*) Sulis	
Bayeux	*Augustodūrum nt*	
Bayreuth	*Barūthum nt*	
Beauvais	Bellovacī *mpl*	*adj Bellovacēnsis*
Beirut	Bērȳtus *f*	*adj* Bērȳtius
Belgium	Belgae *mpl*	*adj* Belgicus
Bergen	*Bergae fpl*	
Berlin	*Berolīnum nt*	*adj Berolīnēnsis*
Berne	Vērona *f*	
Berwick	*Barvīcum nt*	
Besançon	Vesontiō *m*	*adj Bisuntīnus*
Black Sea	Pontus (Euxīnus) *m*	*adj* Ponticus
Bobbio	*Bobbium nt*	*adj Bobbiēnsis*
Bohemia	Boiohaemī *mpl*	
Bologna	Bonōnia *f*	*adj* Bonōniēnsis
Bonn	*Bonna f*	
Bordeaux	*Burdigala f*	*adj Burdigalēnsis*
Boulogne	Bonōnia *f*	*adj* Bononiēnsis
Bourges	Avāricum *nt*	*adj* Avāricēnsis
Brabant	*Brabantia f*	
Braganza	Brigantia *f*	*adj* Brigantiēnsis

Brancaster	Branodūnum *nt*	
Brandenburg	*Brandenburgia f*	*adj Brandenburgēnsis*
Bremen	*Brēma f*	*adj Brēmēnsis*
Breslau	*Bratislavia f*	*adj Bratislaviēnsis*
Brindisi	Brundisium *nt*	*adj* Brundisīnus
Bristol	*Bristolium nt*	*adj Bristoliēnsis*
Britain	Britannia *f*	*adj* Britannicus
Brittany	Armoricae *fpl*	
Bruges	*Brugae fpl*	*adj Brugēnsis*
Brunswick	*Brunsvīcum nt*	*adj Brunsvīcēnsis*
Brussels	*Bruxellae fpl*	*adj Bruxellēnsis*
Bucharest	*Bucarestum nt*	*adj Bucarestiēnsis*
Burgos	*Burgī mpl*	*adj Burgitānus*
Burgundy	Burgundiōnēs *mpl*	
Cadiz	Gādēs *fpl*	*adj* Gāditānus
Caen	*Cadomum nt*	*adj Cadomēnsis*
Caerleon	Isca *f*	
Caermarthen	Maridūnum *nt*	
Caernarvon	Segontium *nt*	
Caerwent	Venta (*f*) Silurum	
Cagliari	Caralis *f*	*adj* Caralītānus
Cairo	*Cairus f*	
Calais	*Calētum nt*	*adj* Calētanus
Cambrai	*Camerācum nt*	*adj Camerācēnsis*
Cambridge	*Cantabrigia f*	*adj Cantabrigiēnsis*
Campagna	Campānia *f*	*adj* Campānus
Cannes	*Canoē f*	
Canterbury	Durovernum *nt*,	*adj Cantuāriēnsis*
	Cantuāria f	
Capri	Capreae *fpl*	*adj* Capreēnsis
Cardigan	Ceretica *f*	
Carlisle	Luguvallium *nt*	
Cartagena	Carthāgō Nova *f*	
Carthage	Carthāgō *f*	*adj* Carthāginiēnsis
Caspian Sea	Mare Caspium *nt*	
Cevennes	Gebenna *f*	*adj* Gebennicus
Ceylon	Tāprobanē *f*	
Champagne	*Campānia f*	*adj Campānicus*
Chartres	Carnūtēs *mpl*	*adj* Carnōtēnus
Chelmsford	Caesaromagus *m*	
Cherbourg	*Caesaris burgus m*	
Chester	Deva *f*	
Chichester	Rēgnum *nt*	
China	Sēres *mpl*	*adj* Sēricus
Cirencester	Corinium (*nt*)	
	Dobunōrum	
Clairvaux	*Clāra Vallis f*	*adj Clāravallēnsis*
Clermont	Nemossus *f*	
Cluny	*Clīniacum nt*	*adj Clīniacēnsis*
Clyde, *River*	Clōta *f*	
Colchester	Camulodūnum *nt*	
Cologne	Colōnia Agrippīna *f*	*adj Colōniēnsis*

Como, *Lake*	Lārius *m*	*adj* Lārius
Constance, *Lake*	Lacus Brigantīnus *m*	
Copenhagen	*Hafnia f*	
Corbridge	Corstopitum *nt*	
Cordoba	Corduba *f*	*adj* Cordubēnsis
Corfu	Corcȳra *f*	*adj* Corcȳraeus
Corinth	Corinthus *f*	*adj* Corinthius
Cork	*Corcagia f*	*adj Corcagiēnsis*
Cornwall	*Cornubia f*	
Cracow	*Cracovia f*	*adj Cracoviēnsis*
Crete	Crēta *f*	*adj* Crētēnsis, Crēticus
Cumberland	*Cumbria f*	
Cyprus	Cyprus *f*	*adj* Cyprius
Cyrene	Cȳrēnae *fpl*	*adj* Cȳrēnaicus
Damascus	Damascus *f*	*adj* Damascēnus
Danube, *River*	*(lower)* Ister *m*,	
	(upper) Dānuvius *m*	
Dardanelles	Hellēspontus *m*	*adj* Hellēspontius
Dee, *River*	Deva *f*	
Denmark	Dānia *f*	*adj* Dānicus
Derby	*Derventiō m*	
Devon	*Devōnia f*	
Dijon	*Diviō f*	*adj Diviōnēnsis*
Dneiper, *River*	Borysthenēs *m*	
Dneister, *River*	Danaster *m*	
Don, *River* (Russian)	Tanais *m*	
Doncaster	Dānum *nt*	
Dorchester	Durnovāria *f*	
Douro, *River*	Durius *m*	
Dover	Dubrī *mpl*	
Dover, *Straits of*	Fretum Gallicum *nt*	
Dresden	*Dresda f*	*adj Dresdēnsis*
Dublin	*Dublīnum nt*	*adj Dublīnēnsis*
Dumbarton	*Britannodūnum nt*	
Dundee	*Taodūnum nt*	
Dunstable	Durocobrīvae *fpl*	
Durham	*Dunelmum nt*	*adj Dunelmēnsis*
Ebro, *River*	Hibērus *m*	
Eden, *River*	Itūna *f*	
Edinburgh	*Edinburgum nt*	*adj Edinburgēnsis*
Egypt	Aegyptus *f*	*adj* Aegyptius
Elba	Ilva *f*	
Elbe, *River*	Albis *m*	
England	Anglia *f*	*adj* Anglicus
Etna	Aetna *f*	*adj* Aetnaeus
Europe	Eurōpa	*adj* Eurōpaeus
Exeter	Isca (*f*) Dumnoniōrum	
Fiesole	Faesulae *fpl*	*adj* Faesulānus
Flanders	Menapiī *mpl*	
Florence	Flōrentia *f*	*adj Flōrentīnus*
Fontainebleau	*Bellofontānum nt*	
Forth, *River*	Bodotria *f*	

France	Gallia f	adj Gallicus
Frankfurt	Francofurtum nt	
Frejus	Forum (nt) Iūliī	adj Foroiūliēnsis
Friesland	Frīsiī mpl	adj Frīsius
Gallipoli	Callipolis f	adj Callipolitānus
Galloway	Gallovidia f	
Ganges	Gangēs m	adj Gangēticus
Garda, Lake	Bēnācus m	
Garonne, River	Garumna f	
Gaul	Gallia f	adj Gallicus
Gdansk	Gedānum m	
Geneva	Genāva f	adj Genāvēnsis
Geneva, Lake	Lemannus lacus m	
Genoa	Genua f	adj Genuēnsis
Germany	Germānia f	adj Germānicus
Ghent	Gandavum nt	adj Gandavēnsis
Gibraltar	Calpē f	adj Calpētānus
Gibraltar, Straits of	Fretum Gāditānum nt	
Glasgow	Glasgua f	adj Glasguēnsis
Gloucester	Glēvum nt	
Gothenburg	Gothoburgum nt	
Graz	Graecium nt	
Greece	Graecia f	adj Graecus
Greenwich	Grenovīcum nt	
Grenoble	Grātiānopolis f	
Groningen	Groninga f	
Guadalquivir, River	Baetis m	
Guadiana, River	Anas m	
Guernsey	Sarnia f	
Hague, The	Haga (f) Comitis	
Halle	Halla f	adj Hallēnsis
Hamadān	Ecbatana ntpl	
Hamburg	Hamburgum nt	adj Hamburgēnsis
Hanover	Hannovera f	
Harwich	Harvīcum nt	
Havre	Grātiae Portus m	
Hebrides	Ebūdae Insulae fpl	
Hexham	Axelodūnum nt	
Holland	Batāvī mpl	adj Batāvus
Ibiza	Ebusus f	adj Ebusitānus
Ilkley	Olicāna f	
Inn, River	Aenus m	
Ipswich	Gippevīcum nt	
Ireland	Hibernia f	adj Hibernicus
Isar, River	Isara f	
Istanbul	Bȳzantium nt	adj Bȳzantīnus
Italy	Italia f	adj Italicus
Jersey	Caesarea f	
Jerusalem	Hierosolyma ntpl	adj Hierosolymītānus
Jutland	Chersonnēsus Cimbrica f	
Karlsbad	Aquae Carolīnae fpl	

Kent	Cantium *nt*	
Kiel	*Chilonium nt*	
Koblenz	Cōnfluentēs *mpl*	
Lancaster	*Lancastria f*	
Lanchester	Longovicium *nt*	
Land's End	Bolerium Prōmunturium *nt*	
Lausanne	Lausōnium *nt*	*adj* Lausōniēnsis
Lebanon	Libanus *m*	
Leeds	*Ledesia f*	
Leicester	Ratae (*fpl*) Coritānōrum	
Leiden	Lugdūnum (*nt*) Batāvōrum	
Leipsig	*Lipsia f*	*adj* Lipsiēnsis
Lērida	Ilerda *f*	*adj* Ilerdēnsis
Lichfield	*Etocētum nt*	
Limoges	Augustorītum *nt*	
Lincoln	Lindum *nt*	
Lisbon	Olisīpō *m*	*adj* Olisīpōnēnsis
Lizard Point	Damnonium Prōmunturium *nt*	
Loire, *River*	Liger *m*	*adj* Ligericus
Lombardy	*Langobardia f*	
London	Londinium *nt*	*adj* Londiniēnsis
Lorraine	*Lōthāringia f*	
Lucerne	*Lūceria f*	*adj* Lūcernēnsis
Lund	Londinium (*nt*) Gothōrum	
Lyons	Lugdūnum *nt*	*adj* Lugdūnēnsis
Madrid	Matrītum *nt*	*adj* Matrītēnsis
Maggiore, *Lake*	Verbannus *m*	
Main, *River*	Moenus *m*	
Mainz	Mogontiacum *nt*	
Majorca	Baliāris Māior *f*	
Malta	Melita *f*	
Man, *Isle of*	Monapia *f*	
Manchester	*Mancunium nt*	
Marmara, *Sea of*	Propontis *f*	
Marne, *River*	*Māterna f*	
Marseilles	Massilia *f*	*adj* Massiliēnsis
Matapan	Taenarum *nt*	*adj* Taenarius
Mediterranean	Mare internum *nt*	
Melun	Melodūnum *nt*	
Mērida	Ēmerita *f*	*adj* Ēmeritēnsis
Messina	Messāna *f*	*adj* Messānius
Metz	Dīvodūrum *nt*	
Meuse, *River*	Mosa *f*	
Milan	Mediōlānum *nt*	*adj* Mediōlānēnsis
Minorca	Baliāris Minor *f*	
Modena	Mutina *f*	*adj* Mutinēnsis
Mons	Montēs *mpl*	
Monte Cassino	Casīnum *nt*	*adj* Casīnās
Moray	*Moravia f*	

Morocco	Maurētānia *f*	*adj* Maurus
Moscow	*Moscovia f*	
Moselle, *River*	Mosella *f*	
Munich	*Monacum nt*	*adj Monacēnsis*
Nantes	Namnētēs *mpl*	
Naples	Neāpolis *f*	*adj* Neāpolītānus
Neckar, *River*	Nīcer *m*	
Newcastle	Pōns (*m*) Aeliī,	*adj Novocastrēnsis*
	Novum Castrum nt	
Nice	Nīcaea *f*	*adj* Nicaeēnsis
Nile, *River*	Nīlus *m*	*adj* Nīlōticus
Nîmes	Nemausus *f*	*adj* Nemausēnsis
Norway	*Norvēgia f*	*adj Norvēgiānus*
Norwich	*Nordovīcum nt*	
Oder, *River*	Viadrus *m*	
Oporto	Portus Calēnsis *m*	
Orange	Arausiō *f*	
Orkneys	Orcades *fpl*	
Orléans	*Aurēliānum nt*	*adj Aurēliānēnsis*
Oudenarde	*Aldenarda f*	
Oxford	*Oxonia f*	*adj Oxoniēnsis*
Padua	Patavium *nt*	*adj* Patavīnus
Palermo	Panormus *m*	*adj* Panormitānus
Paris	Lutetia *f*, Parīsiī *mpl*	*adj Parīsiēnsis*
Patras	Patrae *fpl*	*adj* Patrēnsis
Persian Gulf	Mare Rubrum *nt*	
Piacenza	Placentia *f*	*adj* Placentīnus
Po, *River*	Padus	*adj* Padānus
Poitiers	Limōnum *nt*	
Poland	*Polōnia f*	
Portsmouth	Māgnus Portus *m*	
Portugal	Lūsitānia *f*	
Pozzuoli	Puteolī *mpl*	*adj* Puteolānus
Prague	*Prāga f*	*adj Prāgēnsis*
Provence	Prōvincia *f*	
Pyrenees	Pȳrēnaeī montēs *mpl*	
Red Sea	Sinus Arābicus *m*	
Rheims	Dūrocortorum *nt*	
Rhine, *River*	Rhēnus *m*	*adj* Rhēnānus
Rhodes	Rhodos *f*	*adj* Rhodius
Rhône, *River*	Rhodanus *m*	
Richborough	Rutupiae *fpl*	*adj* Rutupīnus
Rimini	Arīminum	*adj* Arīminēnsis
Rochester	Dūrobrīvae *fpl*	
Rome	Rōma *f*	*adj* Rōmānus
Rotterdam	*Roterodamum nt*	*adj Roterodamēnsis*
Rouen	*Rothomagus f*	*adj Rothomagēnsis*
Saar, *River*	*Sangona f*	
Salisbury	Sarisberia *f*	
Salzburg	*Iuvāvum nt*	*adj Salisburgēnsis*
Saône, *River*	Arar *m*	

Savoy	*Sabaudia f*	
Scheldt, *River*	Scaldis *m*	
Schleswig	*Slesvīcum nt*	
Scilly Isles	Cassiterides *fpl*	
Scotland	Calēdonia *f*	*adj* Calēdonius
Seine, *River*	Sēquana *f*	
Severn, *River*	Sabrīna *f*	
Seville	Hīspalis *f*	*adj* Hispalēnsis
Shrewsbury	*Salōpia f*	
Sicily	Sicilia *f*	*adj* Siculus
Sidra, *Gulf of*	Syrtis (māior) *f*	
Silchester	Callēva (*f*) Atrebatum	
Soissons	Augusta (*f*) Suessiōnum	
Solway Firth	Itūna (*f*) aestuārium	
Somme, *River*	Samara *f*	
Spain	Hispānia *f*	*adj* Hispānus
St. Albans	Verulamium *nt*	
St. Andrews	*Andreopolis f*	
St. Bernard	(*Great*) Mōns Pennīnus *m*, (*Little*) Alpis Grāia *f*	
St. Gallen	*Sangallēnse coenobium nt*	*adj Sangallēnsis*
St. Gotthard	Alpēs summae *fpl*	
St. Moritz	*Agaunum nt*	*adj* Agaunēnsis
Strasbourg	Argentorātus *f*	*adj* Argentorātēnsis
Swabia	Suēvia *f*	*adj* Suēvicus
Sweden	*Suēcia f*	*adj Suēcicus*
Switzerland	Helvētia *f*	*adj* Helvēticus
Syracuse	Syrācūsae *fpl*	*adj* Syrācūsānus
Tangier	Tingī *f*	*adj* Tingitānus
Taranto	Tarentum *nt*	*adj* Tarentīnus
Tarragona	Tarracō *f*	*adj* Tarracōnēnsis
Tay, *River*	*Taus m*	
Thames, *River*	Tamesis *m*	
Thebes	Thēbae *fpl*	*adj* Thēbānus
Tiber, *River*	Tiberis *m*	*adj* Tiberīnus
Tivoli	Tībur *nt*	*adj* Tīburtīnus
Toledo	Tolētum *nt*	*adj* Tolētānus
Toulon	*Tolōna f*	*adj Tolōnēnsis*
Toulouse	Tolōsa *f*	*adj* Tolōsānus
Tours	Caesarodūnum *nt*	
Trèves, Trier	Augusta (*f*) Treverōrum	
Trieste	Tergeste *nt*	*adj* Tergestīnus
Tripoli	Tripolis *f*	*adj* Tripolitānus
Tunis	Tūnēs *f*	*adj* Tūnētānus
Turin	Augusta (*f*) Taurīnōrum	*adj* Taurīnus
Tuscany	Etrūria *f*	*adj* Etrūscus
Tyrrhenian Sea	Mare īnferum *nt*	
Utrecht	*Ultrāiectum nt*	*adj Ultrāiectēnsis*
Vardar, *River*	Axius *m*	
Venice	Venetī *mpl*, *Venetiae fpl*	*adj* Venetus
Verdun	*Virodūnum nt*	*adj Virodūnēnsis*

Versailles	*Versāliae fpl*	*adj* *Versāliēnsis*
Vichy	Aquae (*fpl*) Sōlis	
Vienna	*Vindobona f*	*adj* *Vindobenēnsis*
Vosges	Vosegus *m*	
Wales	*Cambria f*	
Wallsend	Segedūnum *nt*	
Warsaw	*Varsavia f*	*adj* *Varsaviēnsis*
Wash, *The*	Metaris (*m*) aestuārium	
Wear, *River*	Vedra *f*	
Weser, *River*	Visurgis *m*	
Westminster	*Westmonastērium nt*	*adj* *Westmonastēriēnsis*
Wiesbaden	Mattiacum *nt*	*adj* Mattiacus
Wight, *Isle of*	Vectis *f*	
Winchester	Venta (*f*) Belgārum	
Worcester	Vigornia *f*	
Worms	*Vormatia f*	
Wroxeter	Viroconium *nt*	
York	Eburācum *nt*	*adj* Eburācēnsis
Zuider Zee	Flēvō *m*	
Zurich	*Turicum nt*	*adj* Tigurīnus

NUMERALS

	Cardinal		Ordinal	
1	ūnus	I	prīmus	1st
2	duo	II	secundus, alter	2nd
3	trēs	III	tertius	3rd
4	quattuor	IV	quārtus	4th
5	quīnque	V	quīntus	5th
6	sex	VI	sextus	6th
7	septem	VII	septimus	7th
8	octō	VIII	octāvus	8th
9	novem	IX	nōnus	9th
10	decem	X	decimus	10th
11	undecim	XI	undecimus	11th
12	duodecim	XII	duodecimus	12th
13	tredecim	XIII	tertius decimus	13th
14	quattuordecim	XIV	quārtus decimus	14th
15	quīndecim	XV	quīntus decimus	15th
16	sēdecim	XVI	sextus decimus	16th
17	septendecim	XVII	septimus decimus	17th
18	duodēvīgintī	XVIII	duodēvīcēsimus	18th
19	ūndēvīgintī	XIX	ūndēvīcēsimus	19th
20	vīgintī	XX	vīcēsimus	20th
21	vīgintī ūnus	XXI	vīcēsimus prīmus	21st
28	duodētrīgintā	XXVIII	duodētrīcēsimus	28th
29	ūndētrīgintā	XXIX	ūndētrīcēsimus	29th
30	trīgintā	XXX	trīcēsimus	30th
40	quadrāgintā	XL	quadrāgēsimus	40th
50	quīnquāgintā	L	quīnquāgēsimus	50th
60	sexāgintā	LX	sexāgēsimus	60th
70	septuāgintā	LXX	septuāgēsimus	70th
80	octōgintā	LXXX	octōgēsimus	80th
90	nōnāgintā	XC	nōnāgēsimus	90th
100	centum	C	centēsimus	100th
101	centum et ūnus	CI	centēsimus prīmus	101st
122	centum vīgintī duo	CXXII	centēsimus vīcēsimus alter	122nd
200	ducentī	CC	ducentēsimus	200th
300	trecentī	CCC	trecentēsimus	300th
400	quadringentī	CCCC	quadringentēsimus	400th
500	quīngentī	D	quīngentēsimus	500th
600	sēscentī	DC	sēscentēsimus	600th
700	septingentī	DCC	septingentēsimus	700th
800	octingentī	DCCC	octingentēsimus	800th
900	nōngentī	DCCCC	nōngentēsimus	900th
1000	mīlle	M	mīllēsimus	1000th
1001	mīlle et ūnus	MI	mīllēsimus prīmus	1001st
1102	mīlle centum duo	MCII	mīllēsimus centēsimus alter	1102nd
3000	tria mīlia	MMM	ter mīllēsimus	3000th
5000	quīnque mīlia	IↃↃ	quīnquiēs mīllēsimus	5000th
10,000	decem mīlia	CCIↃↃ	deciēs mīllēsimus	10,000th
100,000	centum mīlia	CCCIↃↃↃ	centiēs mīllēsimus	100,000th
1,000,000	deciēs centēna mīlia	CCCCIↃↃↃↃ	deciēs centiēs mīllēsimus	1,000,000th

NUMERALS

	Distributive		Adverb	
1	singulī	I	semel	1st
2	bīnī	II	bis	2nd
3	ternī (trīnī)	III	ter	3rd
4	quaternī	IV	quater	4th
5	quīnī	V	quīnquiēs	5th
6	sēnī	VI	sexiēs	6th
7	septēnī	VII	septiēs	7th
8	octōnī	VIII	octiēs	8th
9	novēnī	IX	noviēs	9th
10	dēnī	X	deciēs	10th
11	undēnī	XI	undeciēs	11th
12	duodēnī	XII	duodeciēs	12th
13	ternī dēnī	XIII	ter deciēs	13th
14	quaternī dēnī	XIV	quattuordeciēs	14th
15	quīnī dēnī	XV	quīndeciēs	15th
16	sēnī dēnī	XVI	sēdeciēs	16th
17	septēnī dēnī	XVII	septiēs deciēs	17th
18	duodēvīcēnī	XVIII	duodēvīciēs	18th
19	ūndēvīcēnī	XIX	ūndēvīciēs	19th
20	vīcēnī	XX	vīciēs	20th
21	vīcēnī singulī	XXI	semel et vīciēs	21st
28	duodētrīcēnī	XXVIII	duodētrīciēs	28th
29	ūndētrīcēnī	XXIX	ūndētrīciēs	29th
30	trīcēnī	XXX	trīciēs	30th
40	quadrāgēnī	XL	quadrāgiēs	40th
50	quīnquāgēnī	L	quīnquāgiēs	50th
60	sexāgēnī	LX	sexāgiēs	60th
70	septuāgēnī	LXX	septuāgiēs	70th
80	octōgēnī	LXXX	octōgiēs	80th
90	nōnagēnī	XC	nōnāgiēs	90th
100	centēnī	C	centiēs	100th
101	centēnī singulī	CI	semel et centiēs	101st
122	centēnī vīcēnī bīnī	CXXII	centiēs vīciēs bis	122nd
200	ducēnī	CC	ducentiēs	200th
300	trecēnī	CCC	trecentiēs	300th
400	quadringēnī	CCCC	quadringentiēs	400th
500	quīngēnī	D	quīngentiēs	500th
600	sexcēnī	DC	sexcentiēs	600th
700	septingēnī	DCC	septingentiēs	700th
800	octingēnī	DCCC	octingentiēs	800th
900	nōngēnī	DCCCC	nōngentiēs	900th
1000	singula mīlia	M	mīlliēs	1000th
1001	singula mīlia singulī	MI	semel et mīlliēs	1001st
1102	singula mīlia centēnī bīnī	MCII	mīlliēs centiēs bis	1102nd
3000	trīna mīlia	MMM	ter mīlliēs	3000th
5000	quīna mīlia	IↃↃ	quīnquiēs mīlliēs	5000th
10,000	dēna mīlia	CCIↃↃ	deciēs mīlliēs	10,000th
100,000	centēna mīlia	CCCIↃↃↃ	centiēs mīlliēs	100,000th
1,000,000	deciēs centēna mīlia	CCCCIↃↃↃↃ	mīlliēs mīlliēs	1,000,000th

DATES

MONTHS

Three days of the month have special names:

Kalendae the 1st.

Nōnae the 5th of most months, but the 7th of March, May, July and October.

> "In March, July, October, May,
> The Nones are on the 7th day."

Idūs the 13th of most months, but the 15th of March, May, July and October.

If the date is one of these three days, it is expressed in the ablative, with the adjective of the month in agreement, _e.g._

1st January, **Kalendīs Iānuāriīs**, usually abbreviated **Kal. Ian.**

The day immediately before any of these three is expressed by **prīdiē** with the accusative, _e.g._

4th February, **prīdiē Nōnās Februāriās**, usually abbreviated **prid. Non. Feb.**

All other dates are expressed as so many days before the next named day, and in reckoning the interval both the date and the named day are counted, _e.g._ the 11th is the 5th day before the 15th.

The formula is all in the accusative, begining with the words **ante diem**, _e.g._ 11th March, **ante diem quīntum Idūs Martiās**, usually abbreviated **a.d. V Id. Mar.**

The following selection of dates for April and May should be a sufficient guide to the dates of any month in the year:—

APRIL		MAY
Kal. Apr.	1	Kal. Mai.
a.d IV Non. Apr.	2	a.d. VI Non. Mai.
a.d. III Non. Apr.	3	a.d. V Non. Mai.
prid. Non. Apr.	4	a.d. IV Non. Mai.
Non. Apr.	5	a.d. III Non. Mai.
a.d. VIII Id. Apr.	6	prid. Non. Mai.
a.d. VII Id. Apr.	7	Non. Mai.
a.d. VI Id. Apr.	8	a.d. VIII Id. Mai.
a.d. V Id. Apr.	9	a.d. VII Id. Mai.
a.d. IV Id. Apr.	10	a.d. VI Id. Mai.
a.d. III Id. Apr.	11	a.d. V Id. Mai.
prid. Id. Apr.	12	a.d. IV Id. Mai.
Id. Apr.	13	a.d. III Id. Mai.
a.d. XVIII Kal. Mai.	14	prid. Id. Mai.
a.d. XVII Kal. Mai.	15	Id. Mai.
a.d. XVI Kal. Mai.	16	a.d. XVII Kal. Iun.

a.d. XV Kal. Mai.	**17**	a.d. XVI Kal. Iun.
a.d. XII Kal. Mai.	**20**	a.d. XIII Kal. Iun.
a.d. VII Kal. Mai.	**25**	a.d. VIII Kal. Iun.
prid. Kal. Mai.	**30**	a.d. III Kal. Iun.
—	**31**	prid. Kal. Iun.

YEARS

A year is denoted either by giving the names of the consuls or by reckoning the number of years from the traditional date of the foundation of Rome, 753 B.C. (A date B.C. should be subtracted from 754, a date A.D. should be added to 753.)

E.g. "In the year 218 B.C.," *either* P. Cornelio Scipione Ti. Sempronio Longo coss. *or* a. u. c. DXXXVI.

MEASURES

Length

12 ūnciae = 1 pēs
5 pedēs = 1 passus
125 passūs = 1 stadium
8 stadia = mīlle passūs

The Roman mile was about 1.48 km.

Area

100 pedēs quadrātī = 1 scrīpulum
144 scrīpula = 1 āctus quadrātus
2 āctūs quadrātī = 1 iugerum
2 iugera = 1 hērēdium
100 hērēdia = 1 centuria

The **iugerum** was about 2529.28 square metres.

Capacity

	4 cochleāria	= 1 cyathus
	12 cyathī	= 1 sextārius
(_liquid_)	6 sextāriī	= 1 congius
	8 congiī	= 1 amphora
	20 amphorae	= 1 culleus
(_dry_)	8 sextāriī	= 1 sēmodius
	2 sēmodiī	= 1 modius

The **sextārius** was about half a litre, the **modius** about 9 litres.

Weight

4 scrīpula = 1 sextula
6 sextulae = 1 ūncia
12 ūnciae = 1 lībra

The Roman lb. was about 326 gr, and the **ūncia** was therefore about 27 gr. The twelfths of the **lībra** have the following names, which are also used to denote fractions generally, _e.g._ **hērēs ex triente**, heir to a third of an estate.

$\frac{1}{12}$ ūncia	$\frac{5}{12}$ quīncūnx	$\frac{3}{4}$ dōdrāns
$\frac{1}{6}$ sextāns	$\frac{1}{2}$ sēmis	$\frac{5}{6}$ dextāns
$\frac{1}{4}$ quadrāns	$\frac{7}{12}$ septūnx	$\frac{11}{12}$ deūnx
$\frac{1}{3}$ triēns	$\frac{2}{3}$ bēs	

MONEY

Roman

2½ assēs	=	1 sēstertius (*or* nummus)
4 sēstertii	=	1 dēnārius
25 dēnārii	=	1 aureus

The sesterce is represented by a symbol for 2½, properly **II S(ēmis)**, usually standardized in the form HS. The *ntpl* **sēstertia** with the distributive numeral denotes thousands of sesterces, and the numeral adverb with the *gen pl* **sēstertium** (understanding **centena milia**) means hundred thousands, *e.g.*

10,000 sesterces	=	dēna sēstertia	= HS X̄
1,000,000 "	=	deciēs sēstertium	= HS IX̄I

Greek

100 drachumae	= 1 mina
60 minae	= 1 talentum

LATIN VERSE

QUANTITY

Both vowels and syllables in Latin may be described as long or short. A long vowel or syllable is one on which the voice dwells for a longer time than on a short one, in much the same way as a minim is long compared with a crotchet in musical notation.

A syllable is long if the vowel in it is either long in itself or followed by two or more consonants. The letter **x** counts as a double consonant, the letter **h** not at all, and the following pairs of consonants occurring in the same word after a short vowel do not necessarily make the syllable long:

br, cr, dr, fr, gr, pr, tr; fl, gl, pl.

A syllable is short if its vowel is a short one and not followed by two or more consonants (except for the groups noted in the preceding paragraph).

Examples: In **dūcō** both the vowels are long ("by nature") and therefore the two syllables are long.

In **deus** both the vowels are short, neither is followed by more than one consonant, and therefore the two syllables are short; but if a word beginning with a consonant follows, then the syllable **-us** will become long.

In **adsunt** both the vowels are short, but they are both followed by two consonants, and the two syllables are therefore "long by position".

This long or short characteristic of Latin vowels and syllables is called "quantity." To determine the quantities of vowels no general rules can be given, and some of them are now not known for certain. The vowel quantities of words will have to be learned when the words are learned, or else looked up when the need arises. In final syllables, however, there is a certain regularity to be found, and the following table shows the commonest of these:

ENDING

	Long	Short
-a	*1st decl abl sing* *1st conj impv sing* *numerals and most adverbs*	*1st decl nom and voc sing* *all nom and acc ntpl* **ita, quia**
-e	*5th decl abl sing* *2nd conj impv sing* *most adverbs* *Greek nouns*	*all other noun and verb endings* **bene, male** *enclitics*

-i	*all endings, except*	**quasi, nisi:** *and sometimes* **mihi, tibi, sibi, ibi, ubi**
-o	*all endings, except*	*sometimes iambic words, esp* **cito, duo, ego, homo, modo, puto, rogo, scio**
-u	*all endings*	
-as	*all endings, except*	*Greek nouns*
-es	*all endings, except*	*3rd decl nom sing with short* **-e-** *in stem* **es** (be) *and compounds* **penes**
-is	*1st and 2nd decl dat and abl pl* *3rd decl acc pl* *4th conj 2nd pers sing* **vīs, sīs, velīs**	*all others*
-os	*all endings, except*	*2nd decl nom sing* **os** (bone) **compos, impos**
-us	*3rd decl nom sing with long* **-u-** *in stem* *4th decl gen sing and nom and acc pl*	*all others*

METRES

Latin Verse is a pattern of long and short syllables, grouped together in "feet" or in lyric lines.

FEET

The commonest Feet employed in Latin metres are:

Anapaest	(short—short—long)	⏑ ⏑ –
Dactyl	(long—short—short)	– ⏑ ⏑
Iambus	(short—long)	⏑ –
Proceleusmatic	(short—short—short—short)	⏑ ⏑ ⏑ ⏑
Spondee	(long—long)	– –
Tribrach	(short—short—short)	⏑ ⏑ ⏑
Trochee	(long—short)	– ⏑

CAESURA AND DIAERESIS

The longer lines usually have a regular break near the middle, occurring either in the middle of a foot (**Caesura**) or at the end of a foot (**Diaeresis**). This break need not imply a pause in the sense of the words, but merely the end of a word, provided that it does not go too closely with the word following, as in the case of a preposition before a noun. See examples on pages 4–9 where the caesura is marked †, and the diaeresis //.

ELISION

A vowel or a vowel followed by **m** at the end of a word ("open vowel") is regularly elided before a vowel at the beginning of the next word in the same line. In reciting, the elided syllable should not be dropped entirely, but slurred into the following vowel. An open vowel at the end of a line does not elide before a vowel at the beginning of the next line.

FINAL SYLLABLES

Where the metre requires the final syllable in a line to be long, this syllable may in fact be a short one. This position in the line is commonly called a **syllaba anceps**, and marked down as being either long or short. It is perhaps better to regard this syllable, when the vowel is short, as long by position, since metrical length is a matter of duration, and the end of a line calls naturally for a slight pause in reading, even if the sense runs on to the next line. In the metrical schemes which follow, a long final syllable should be understood in this sense: it may in itself be a short one.

Latin metres fall into three fairly distinct categories, associated with three different genres of verse: 1. *Dactylic*
2. *Iambic and Trochaic*
3. *Lyric*

DACTYLIC VERSE

The Dactylic metres are the **Hexameter** and the **Pentameter**. The Hexameter is the medium of epic, didactic and pastoral poetry, of satires and epistles, and other examples of occasional verse. In conjunction with the Pentameter it forms the **Elegiac Couplet**, the metre most commonly used for love poetry, occasional pieces, and the epigram.

Dactylic Hexameter

The first four feet may be either **dactyls** or **spondees**, the 5th is regularly a dactyl, the 6th always a spondee. In Virgil and later poets the last word is either disyllabic or trisyllabic. A **Caesura** normally occurs in either the 3rd or the 4th foot, and pastoral poetry often has the "**Bucolic Diaeresis**" at the end of the 4th foot. In Virgilian and later usage there is a tendency for words and feet to overlap in the first four feet and to coincide in the last two. Similarly in the first part of the line the metrical ictus and the normal accent of the spoken word tend to fall on different syllables, whereas they regularly coincide in the last two feet.

Example:

Clāss(em) āp|teñt tăcĭ|tī⁺ sŏcĭ|ōsqu(e) ād | lītŏră| tōrquēnt

(Virgil, Aen. 4, 289)

Occasional lines will be found in the poets, which deliberately violate the above rules for the sake of obtaining some special effect,

pēr cō|nūbĭă| nōstrā,⁺ pĕr|īncēp|tōs hȳmĕ|nāeōs

(Aen. 4, 316)

The above echoes Greek hexameter, where the final word is Greek and has four syllables, and the caesura comes between the two short syllables of the dactyl in the 3rd foot:

cūm sŏcĭ|īs nā|tōquĕ⁺ pĕ|nātĭ būs| ēt māg|nīs dīs

(Aen. 3, 12)

Note the solemn, archaic touch, suggesting a line of Ennius, where the 5th foot is a spondee, and the last word is monosyllabic.

pār̆tŭrĭ|ent mōn|tēs,[†] nā|scētūr| rĭdĭcŭ|lūs mūs

(Hor, A. P. 139)

The monosyllabic ending, above, creates a comic effect.

Dactylic Pentameter

This line has two equal parts of 2½ feet each. The two feet in the first part may be either **dactyls** or **spondees**, those in the second part are always dactylic. The two half-feet are long (though the final syllable may be a short one), and there is always a diaeresis between the two parts of the line. In Ovid and later poets the last word in the line is regularly disyllabic.

Example:

Aēnē|ān ănĭ|mō // nōxqŭe dĭ|ēsqŭe rĕ|fērt

(Ovid, Her. 7, 26)

SCANSION

The following procedure may assist beginners to scan a normal hexameter or pentameter correctly:—

1. Mark off elisions.
2. Mark the first syllable long, and (Hexameter) the last five dactyl and spondee, or (Pentameter) the last seven syllables, two dactyls and a long syllable.
3. Mark all diphthongs long.
4. Mark all syllables that are long by position, omitting any doubtful cases.
5. Mark any other syllables known to be long.
6. Mark any syllables known to be short.
7. Fill in the few (if any) remaining syllables, and identify the principal caesura.
8. Read the line aloud.

IAMBIC AND TROCHAIC VERSE

The Iambic and Trochaic metres occur mainly in dramatic verse, but some are found elsewhere, as in the lyrics of Catullus and Horace. The principal Iambic metres are the **Senarius**, the **Septenarius**, and the **Octonarius**; the principal Trochaic metres are the Septenarius and Octonarius.

Iambic Senarius

Basically this line consists of six iambic feet, but in practice such a line is very rare.

Example:

Phăsēl|lŭs ĭl|lĕ quēm| vĭ dē|tĭs, hōs|pĭ tēs

(Cat. 4, 1)

In drama the last foot is always iambic, and the 5th regularly a spondee. The **spondee** is also very common in the first four feet, the **dactyl** and the **tribrach** are frequent, occasionally the **anapaest** is found, and, more rarely, the **proceleusmatic**. There is usually a **caesura** in either the third or the fourth foot.

Example:

Ĭn hāc| hăbĭtās|sĕ plătĕ|ā dĭc|tūmst Chrȳ|sĭdēm

(Ter, And. 796)

Iambic Septenarius

This line consists of seven and a half feet, basically iambic, but allowing the same variations as in the Senarius. The 4th foot is regularly an Iambus, and is usually followed by a diaeresis: this is an aid to identifying the line.

Example:

N(am) ĭdcĭr|c(o) āccēr|sōr nūp|tĭ ās| quōd m(i) ād|părā|rĭ sēn|sĭt

(Ter, And. 690)

Iambic Octonarius

This line has eight iambic feet, with the same variations as in the other iambic lines. The 4th and 8th feet are regularly iambic, and a diaeresis follows the 4th foot.

Example:

Cūrā|bĭtūr.| sēd pătĕr| ădēst.| căvĕt(e) ēs|sĕ trĭs|tēm sēn|tĭ āt

(Ter, And. 403)

Trochaic Septenarius

Apart from drama, this line is common in popular verses, and comes into its own in later Latin poetry. It consists of seven and a half **trochees**, but in practice only the seventh foot is regularly trochaic, while the others may be **spondee, dactyl, tribrach**, or (more rarely) **anapaest**. There is usually a **diaeresis** after the 4th foot.

Example:

Crās ă|mēt quī| nūnqu(am) ă|māvĭt,| quīqu(e) ă| māvĭt| crās ă|mēt

(Pervigilium Veneris)

Trochaic Octonarius

This is a line of eight trochees, allowing the same variations as above. There is a diaeresis after the 4th foot.

Example:

Prōin tū| sōllĭcĭ|tūdĭn|(em) īstām| fālsām| quāe t(e) ēx|crŭcĭăt| mīttās

(Ter, Heaut. 177)

LYRIC VERSE

In most lyric metres the line is not to be subdivided into feet, but is itself the unit of scansion, and has a fixed number of syllables. The commonest, which are those used by Catullus and Horace, are the **Hendecasyllabic**, the **Asclepiads**, the **Glyconic** and the **Pherecratic**, which occur either singly or in combinations to form either couplets or stanzas of four lines. Beside these groupings there are the **Alcaic** and **Sapphic** stanzas. Elisions occur much more rarely than in the other metres.

Hendecasyllabic

This is Catullus's favourite line. It consists of eleven syllables in the following pattern:

$$- - - \; \breve{} \breve{} \_ \; \breve{} \_ \; \breve{} - -$$

Either the first or the second syllable may occasionally be short, and there is usually a caesura after the 5th syllable.

Example:

Vīvāmūs, mĕă Lēsbĭ(a), ātqu(e) ămēmūs

(Cat. 5, 1)

Asclepiads

There are two Asclepiad lines, of which the **Lesser** is by far the commoner. It has twelve syllables, in the following pattern with a caesura after the 6th syllable:

$$- - - \smile \smile - - \smile \smile - \smile -$$

Māecēnās, ătăvīs† ēdĭtĕ rēgĭbŭs

(_Hor, Od. I_, 1, 1)

The **Greater Asclepiad** is formed by adding a **choriambus** $- \smile \smile -$ after the 6th syllable with a **diaeresis** both before and after it.

Example:

Nūllām, Vārĕ, săcrā vītĕ prĭus sēvĕrĭs ārbŏrēm

(_Hor, Od. I_, 18, 1)

Glyconic

The **Glyconic** occurs by itself in Catullus, but more usually it is found in combination with the **Lesser Asclepiad** or the **Pherecratic**. It consists of eight syllables ($- - - \smile \smile - \smile -$), so that it is like a Lesser Asclepiad minus the **choriambus**. It has no regular caesura.

Example:

Dōnēc grātŭs ĕrăm tĭbī

(_Hor. Od. III_, 9, 1)

Pherecratic

The **Pherecratic** is a Glyconic minus the second last (short) syllable. It is found only in combination with other lines.

Example:

Sūspēndīssĕ pŏtēntī

(_Hor, Od. I_, 5, 11)

Alcaic Stanza

The **Alcaic stanza** has four lines, of which the first two have the same pattern
⏤⏤⏑⏤⏤⏑⏑⏤⏑⏤. In these there is a regular **caesura** after the 5th syllable. The
third line is ⏤⏤⏑⏤⏤⏑⏤⏑⏤ and the 4th ⏤⏑⏑⏤⏑⏑⏤⏑⏤⏤. Neither of the last two
lines has a regular break in it.

Example:

> Nūnc ēst bĭbēndūm,† nūnc pĕdĕ lībĕrō
> pūlsāndă tēllūs,† nūnc Sălĭārĭbūs
> ōrnārĕ pūlvīnār dĕōrūm
> tēmpŭs ĕrāt dăpĭbūs, sŏdālēs.

> (_Hor, Od. I._ 37, 1-4)

Sapphic Stanza

The **Sapphic stanza** also has four lines, of which the first three are the same:
⏤⏑⏤⏤⏤⏑⏑⏤⏑⏤⏤. As in the Alcaic there is a **caesura** after the 5th syllable. The
last line is a short **Adonic** ⏤⏑⏑⏤⏤

Example:

> Īntĕgēr vītāe† scĕlĕrīsquĕ pūrūs
> nōn ĕgēt Māurīs† iăcŭlīs nĕqu(e) ārcū
> nēc vĕnēnātīs† grăvĭdā săgīttīs,
> Fūscĕ, phărētrā.

> (_Hor, Od. I._ 22, 1-4)

English-Latin

A, a

a, an *art* not translated; (*a certain*) quīdam; **twice a day** bis in diē; **four acres a man** quaterna in singulōs iūgera.
aback *adv*: **taken ~** dēprehēnsus.
abaft *adv* in puppī ♦ *prep* post, pōne.
abandon *vt* relinquere; (*wilfully*) dērelinquere, dēserere; (*to danger*) ōbicere; (*to pleasure*) dēdere; (*plan*) abicere; **~ hope** spem abicere.
abandoned *adj* perditus.
abase *vt* dēprimere; **~ oneself** sē prōsternere.
abash *vt* perturbāre; rubōrem incutere (*dat*).
abate *vt* minuere, imminuere; (*a portion*) remittere ♦ *vi* (*fever*) dēcēdere; (*passion*) dēfervēscere; (*price*) laxāre; (*storm*) cadere.
abatement *n* remissiō *f*, dēminūtiō *f*.
abbess *n* abbātissa *f*.
abbey *n* abbātia *f*.
abbot *n* abbās *m*.
abbreviate *vt* imminuere.
abbreviation *n* (*writing*) nota *f*.
abdicate *vt* sē abdicāre (*abl*).
abdication *n* abdicātiō *f*.
abduct *vt* abripere.
abduction *n* raptus *m*.
aberration *n* error *m*.
abet *vt* adiuvāre, adesse (*dat*), favēre (*dat*).
abettor *n* adiūtor *m*, minister *m*, fautor *m*, socius *m*.
abeyance *n*: **in ~** intermissus; **be in ~** iacēre.
abhor *vt* ōdisse, invīsum habēre.
abhorrence *n* odium *nt*.
abhorrent *adj*: **~ to** aliēnus ab.
abide *vi* (*dwell*) habitāre; (*tarry*) commorārī; (*last*) dūrāre; **~ by** *vt fus* stāre (*abl*), perstāre in (*abl*).
abiding *adj* perpetuus, diūturnus.
ability *n* (*to do*) facultās *f*, potestās *f*; (*physical*) vīrēs *fpl*; (*mental*) ingenium *nt*; **to the best of my ~** prō meā parte, prō virīlī parte.
abject *adj* abiectus, contemptus; (*downcast*) dēmissus.
abjectly *adv* humiliter, dēmissē.
abjure *vt* ēiūrāre.
ablative *n* ablātīvus *m*.
ablaze *adj* flāgrāns, ardēns.
able *adj* perītus, doctus; **be ~** posse, valēre.
able-bodied *adj* rōbustus.
ablution *n* lavātiō *f*.
ably *adv* perītē, doctē.
abnegation *n* abstinentia *f*.

abnormal *adj* inūsitātus; (*excess*) immodicus.
abnormally *adv* inūsitātē, praeter mōrem.
aboard *adv* in nāvī; **go ~** nāvem cōnscendere; **put ~** impōnere.
abode *n* domicilium *nt*, sēdēs *f*.
abolish *vt* tollere, ē mediō tollere, abolēre; (*law*) abrogāre.
abolition *n* dissolūtiō *f*; (*law*) abrogātiō *f*.
abominable *adj* dētestābilis, nefārius.
abominably *adv* nefāriē, foedē.
abominate *vt* dētestārī.
abomination *n* odium *nt*; (*thing*) nefas *nt*.
aboriginal *adj* prīscus.
aborigines *n* aborīginēs *mpl*.
abortion *n* abortus *m*.
abortive *adj* abortīvus; (*fig*) inritus; **be ~** ad inritum redigī.
abound *vi* abundāre, superesse; **~ in** abundāre (*abl*), adfluere (*abl*).
abounding *adj* abundāns, adfluēns; cōpiōsus ab.
about *adv* (*place*) usu expressed by cpd verbs; (*number*) circiter, ferē, fermē ♦ *prep* (*place*) circā, circum (*acc*); (*number*) circā, ad (*acc*); (*time*) sub (*acc*); (*concerning*) dē (*abl*); **~ to die** moritūrus; **I am ~ to go** in eō est ut eam.
above *adv* suprā; **from ~** dēsuper; **over and ~** īnsuper ♦ *prep* suprā (*acc*); (*motion*) super (*acc*); (*rest*) super (*abl*); **be ~** (*conduct*) indignārī.
abreast *adv* (*ships*) aequātīs prōrīs; **walk ~ of** latus tegere (*dat*).
abridge *vt* contrahere, compendī facere.
abridgement *n* epitomē *f*.
abroad *adv* peregrē; (*out of doors*) forīs; **be ~** peregrīnārī; **from ~** peregrē.
abrogate *vt* dissolvere; (*law*) abrogāre.
abrupt *adj* subitus, repentīnus; (*speech*) concīsus.
abscess *n* vomica *f*.
abscond *vi* aufugere.
absence *n* absentia *f*; **in my ~** mē absente; **leave of ~** commeātus *m*.
absent *adj* absēns; **be ~** abesse; **~ oneself** *vi* deesse, nōn adesse.
absent-minded *adj* immemor, parum attentus.
absolute *adj* absolūtus, perfectus; (*not limited*) īnfīnītus; (*not relative*) simplex; **~ power** rēgnum *nt*, dominātus *m*; **~ ruler** rēx.
absolutely *adv* absolūtē, omnīnō.
absolution *n* venia *f*.

absolve *vt* absolvere, exsolvere; (*from punishment*) condōnāre.
absorb *vt* bibere, absorbēre; (*fig*) distringere; **I am ~ed in** tōtus sum in (*abl*).
absorbent *adj* bibulus.
abstain *vi* abstinēre, sē abstinēre; (*from violence*) temperāre.
abstemious *adj* sobrius.
abstinence *n* abstinentia *f*, continentia *f*.
abstinent *adj* abstinēns, sobrius.
abstract *adj* mente perceptus, cōgitātiōne comprehēnsus ♦ *n* epitomē *f* ♦ *vt* abstrahere, dēmere.
abstraction *n* (*idea*) nōtiō *f*; (*inattention*) animus parum attentus.
abstruse *adj* reconditus, obscūrus, abstrūsus.
absurd *adj* ineptus, absurdus.
absurdity *n* ineptiae *fpl*, insulsitās *f*.
absurdly *adv* ineptē, absurdē.
abundance *n* cōpia *f*, abundantia *f*; **there is ~ of** abundē est (*gen*).
abundant *adj* cōpiōsus, abundāns, largus; **be ~** abundāre.
abundantly *adv* abundē, abundanter, adfātim.
abuse *vt* abūtī (*abl*); (*words*) maledīcere (*dat*) ♦ *n* probra *ntpl*, maledicta *ntpl*, convīcium *nt*, contumēlia *f*.
abusive *adj* maledicus, contumēliōsus.
abut *vi* adiacēre; **~ting on** cōnfīnis (*dat*), fīnitimus (*dat*).
abysmal *adj* profundus.
abyss *n* profundum *nt*, vorāgō *f*; (*water*) gurges *m*; (*fig*) barathrum *nt*.
academic *adj* scholasticus; (*style*) umbrātilis; (*sect*) Acadēmicus.
academy *n* schola *f*; (*Plato's*) Acadēmīa *f*.
accede *vi* adsentīrī; **~ to** accipere.
accelerate *vt, vi* adcelerāre, festīnāre; (*process*) mātūrāre.
accent *n* vōx *f*; (*intonation*) sonus *m*; (*mark*) apex *m* ♦ *vt* (*syllable*) acuere; (*word*) sonum admovēre (*dat*).
accentuate *vt* exprimere.
accept *vt* accipere.
acceptable *adj* acceptus, grātus, probābilis; **be ~** placēre.
acceptation *n* significātiō *f*.
access *n* aditus *m*; (*addition*) accessiō *f*; (*illness*) impetus *m*.
accessary *n* socius *m*, particeps *m*.
accessible *adj* (*person*) adfābilis, facilis; **be ~** (*place*) patēre; (*person*) facilem sē praebēre.
accession *n* (*addition*) accessiō *f*; (*king's*) initium rēgnī.
accident *n* cāsus *m*, calamitās *f*.
accidental *adj* fortuītus.
accidentally *adv* cāsū, fortuītō.
acclaim *vt* adclāmāre.
acclamation *n* clāmor *m*, studium *nt*.
acclimatize *vt* aliēnō caelō adsuēfacere.
accommodate *vt* accommodāre, aptāre; (*lodging*) hospitium parāre (*dat*); **~ oneself to** mōrigerārī (*dat*).

accommodating *adj* facilis.
accommodation *n* hospitium *nt*.
accompany *vt* comitārī; (*courtesy*) prōsequī; (*to Forum*) dēdūcere; (*music*) concinere (*dat*).
accomplice *n* socius *m*, particeps *m*, cōnscius *m*.
accomplish *vt* efficere, perficere, patrāre.
accomplished *adj* doctus, perītus.
accomplishment *n* effectus *m*, perfectiō *f*, fīnis *m*; **~s** *pl* artēs *fpl*.
accord *vi* inter sē congruere, cōnsentīre ♦ *vt* dare, praebēre, praestāre ♦ *n* cōnsēnsus *m*, concordia *f*; (*music*) concentus *m*; **of one's own ~** suā sponte, ultrō; **with one ~** unā vōce.
accordance *n*: **in ~ with** ex, ē (*abl*), secundum (*acc*).
according *adv*: **~ to** ex, ē (*abl*), secundum (*acc*); (*proportion*) prō (*abl*); **~ as** prōut.
accordingly *adv* itaque, igitur, ergō.
accost *vt* appellāre, adloquī, compellāre.
account *n* ratiō *f*; (*story*) nārrātiō *f*, expositiō *f*; **on ~ of** ob (*acc*); propter (*acc*), causā (*gen*); **be of no ~** (*person*) nihilī aestimārī, nēquam esse; **on that ~** idcircō ideō; **on your ~** tuā grātiā, tuō nōmine; **give an ~** ratiōnem reddere; **present an ~** ratiōnem referre; **take ~ of** ratiōnem habēre (*gen*); **put down to my ~** mihī expēnsum ferre; **the ~s balance** ratiō cōnstat/convenit.
account *vi*: **~ for** ratiōnēs reddere, adferre (cūr); **that ~s for it** haec causa est; (*PROV*) hinc illae lacrimae.
accountant *n* ā ratiōnibus, ratiōcinātor *m*.
accountable *adj* reus; **I am ~ for** mihi ratiō reddenda est (*gen*).
account book *n* tabulae *fpl*; cōdex acceptī et expēnsī.
accoutred *adj* īnstructus, ōrnātus.
accoutrements *n* ōrnāmenta *ntpl*, arma *ntpl*.
accredited *adj* pūblicā auctōritate missus.
accretion *n* accessiō *f*.
accrue *vi* (*addition*) cēdere; (*advantage*) redundāre.
accumulate *vt* cumulāre, congerere, coacervāre ♦ *vi* crēscere, cumulārī.
accumulation *n* cumulus *m*, acervus *m*.
accuracy *n* cūra *f*; (*writing*) subtīlitās *f*.
accurate *adj* (*work*) exāctus, subtīlis; (*worker*) dīligēns.
accurately *adv* subtīliter, ad amussim, dīligenter.
accursed *adj* sacer; (*fig*) exsecrātus, scelestus.
accusation *n* (*act*) accūsātiō *f*; (*charge*) crīmen *nt*; (*unfair*) īnsimulātiō *f*; (*false*) calumnia *f*; **bring an ~ against** accūsāre; (*to a magistrate*) nōmen dēferre (*gen*).
accusative *n* (*case*) accūsātīvus *m*.
accuse *vt* accūsāre, crīminārī, reum facere; (*falsely*) īnsimulāre; **the ~d** reus; (*said by prosecutor*) iste.
accuser *n* accūsātor *m*; (*civil suit*) petītor *m*; (*informer*) dēlātor *m*.

accustom vt adsuēfacere; ~ **oneself** adsuēscere, consuēscere.

accustomed adj adsuētus; **be** ~ solēre; **become** ~ adsuēscere, consuēscere.

ace n ūniō f; **I was within an** ~ **of going** minimum āfuit quin īrem.

acerbity n acerbitās f.

ache n dolor m ♦ vi dolēre.

achieve vt cōnficere, patrāre; (win) cōnsequī, adsequī.

achievement n factum nt, rēs gesta.

acid adj acidus.

acknowledge vt (fact) agnōscere; (fault) fatērī, cōnfitērī; (child) tollere; (service) grātiās agere prō (abl); **I have to** ~ **your letter of 1st March** accēpī litterās tuās Kal. Mart. datās.

acknowledgement n cōnfessiō f; grātia f.

acme n fastīgium nt, flōs m.

aconite n aconītum nt.

acorn n glāns f.

acoustics n rēs audītōria f.

acquaint vt certiōrem facere, docēre; ~ **oneself with** cognōscere; ~ed **with** gnārus (gen), perītus (gen).

acquaintance n (with fact) cognitiō f, scientia f; (with person) familiāritās f, ūsus m; (person) nōtus m, familiāris m.

acquiesce vi (assent) adquiēscere; (submit) aequō animō patī.

acquiescence n: **with your** ~ tē nōn adversante, pāce tuā.

acquire vt adquīrere, adipīscī, cōnsequī; nanciscī.

acquirements n artēs fpl.

acquisition n (act) comparātiō f, quaestus m; (thing) quaesītum nt.

acquisitive adj quaestuōsus.

acquit vt absolvere; ~ **oneself** sē praestāre, officiō fungī.

acquittal n absolūtiō f.

acre n iūgerum nt.

acrid adj asper, ācer.

acrimonious adj acerbus, truculentus.

acrimony n acerbitās f.

acrobat n fūnambulus m.

acropolis n arx f.

across adv trānsversus ♦ prep trāns (acc).

act n factum nt, facinus nt; (play) āctus m; (POL) āctum nt, senātus cōnsultum nt, dēcrētum nt; **I was in the** ~ **of saying** in eō erat ut dīcerem; **caught in the** ~ dēprehēnsus ♦ vi facere, agere; (conduct) sē gerere; (stage) histriōnem esse, partēs agere; (pretence) simulāre ♦ vt: ~ **a part** partēs agere, persōnam sustinēre; ~ **the part of** agere; ~ **as** esse, munere fungī (gen); ~ **upon** (instructions) exsequī.

action n (doing) āctiō f; (deed) factum nt, facinus nt; (legal) āctiō f, līs f; (MIL) proelium nt; (of play) āctiō f; (of speaker) gestus m; **bring an** ~ **against** lītem intendere, āctiōnem īnstituere (dat); **be in** ~ agere, rem gerere;

(MIL) pugnāre, in aciē dīmicāre; **man of** ~ vir strēnuus.

active adj impiger, strēnuus, sēdulus, nāvus.

actively adv impigrē, strēnuē, nāviter.

activity n (motion) mōtus m; (energy) industria f, sēdulitās f.

actor n histriō m; (in comedy) cōmoedus m; (in tragedy) tragoedus m.

actress n mīma f.

actual adj vērus, ipse.

actually adv rē vērā.

actuate vt movēre, incitāre.

acumen n acūmen nt, ingenī aciēs, argūtiae fpl.

acute adj acūtus, ācer; (pain) ācer; (speech) argūtus, subtīlis.

acutely adv acūtē, ācriter, argūtē.

acuteness n (mind) acūmen nt, aciēs f, subtīlitas f.

adage n prōverbium nt.

adamant n adamās m ♦ adj obstinātus.

adamantine adj adamantinus.

adapt vt accommodāre.

adaptable adj flexibilis, facile accommodandus.

adaptation n accommodātiō f.

add vt addere, adicere, adiungere; **be** ~ed accēdere.

adder n vīpera f.

addicted adj dēditus.

addition n adiūnctiō f, accessiō f; additāmentum nt, incrēmentum nt; **in** ~ īnsuper, praetereā; **in** ~ **to** praeter (acc).

additional adj novus, adiūnctus.

addled adj (egg) inritus; (brain) inānis.

address vt compellāre, alloquī; (crowd) cōntiōnem habēre apud (acc); (letter) īnscrībere; ~ **oneself** (to action) accingī ♦ n adloquium nt; (public) cōntiō f, ōratiō f; (letter) īnscrīptiō f.

adduce vt (argument) adferre; (witness) prōdūcere.

adept adj perītus.

adequate adj idōneus, dignus, pār; **be** ~ sufficere.

adequately adv satis, ut pār est.

adhere vi haerēre, adhaerēre; ~ **to** inhaerēre (dat), inhaerēscere in (abl); (agreement) manēre, stāre in (abl).

adherent n adsectātor m; (of party) fautor m; (of person) cliēns m.

adhesive adj tenax.

adieu interj valē, valēte; **bid** ~ **to** valēre iubēre.

adjacent adj fīnitimus, vīcīnus; **be** ~ **to** adiacēre (dat).

adjoin vi adiacēre (dat).

adjoining adj fīnitimus, adiūnctus; proximus.

adjourn vt (short time) differre; (longer time) prōferre; (case) ampliāre ♦ vi rem differre, prōferre.

adjournment n dīlātiō f, prōlātiō f.

adjudge vt addīcere, adiūdicāre.

adjudicate vi dēcernere.

adjudicator *n* arbiter *m*.
adjunct *n* appendix *f*, accessiō *f*.
adjure *vt* obtestārī, obsecrāre.
adjust *vt* (*adapt*) accommodāre; (*put in order*) compōnere.
adjutant *n* (*MIL*) optiō *m*; (*civil*) adiūtor *m*.
administer *vt* administrāre, gerere; (*justice*) reddere; (*oath to*) iūreiūrandō adigere; (*medicine*) dare, adhibēre.
administration *n* administrātiō *f*.
administrator *n* administrātor *m*, prōcūrātor *m*.
admirable *adj* admīrābilis, ēgregius.
admirably *adv* ēgregiē.
admiral *n* praefectus classis; ~'s ship nāvis praetōria.
admiralty *n* praefectī classium.
admiration *n* admīrātiō *f*, laus *f*.
admire *vt* admīrārī; mīrārī.
admirer *n* laudātor *m*; amātor *m*.
admissible *adj* aequus.
admission *n* (*entrance*) aditus *m*; (*of guilt etc*) cōnfessiō *f*.
admit *vt* (*let in*) admittere, recipere, accipere; (*to membership*) adscīscere; (*argument*) concēdere; (*fault*) fatērī; ~ of patī, recipere.
admittedly *adv* sānē.
admonish *vt* admonēre, commonēre, hortārī.
admonition *n* admonitiō *f*.
ado *n* negōtium *nt*; **make much ~ about nothing** fluctūs in simpulō excitāre; **without more ~** prōtinus, sine morā.
adolescence *n* prīma adulēscentia *f*.
adolescent *adj* adulēscēns ♦ *n* adulēscentulus *m*.
adopt *vt* (*person*) adoptāre; (*custom*) adscīscere; ~ **a plan** consilium capere.
adoption *n* (*person*) adoptiō *f*; (*custom*) adsūmptiō *f*; **by ~** adoptīvus.
adoptive *adj* adoptīvus.
adorable *adj* amābilis, venustus.
adorably *adv* venustē.
adoration *n* (*of gods*) cultus *m*; (*of kings*) venerātiō *f*; (*love*) amor *m*.
adore *vt* (*worship*) venerārī; (*love*) adamāre.
adorn *vt* ōrnāre, exōrnāre, decorāre.
adornment *n* ōrnāmentum *nt*, decus *nt*; ōrnātus *m*.
adrift *adj* fluctuāns; **be ~** fluctuāre.
adroit *adj* sollers, callidus.
adroitly *adv* callidē, scītē.
adroitness *n* sollertia *f*, calliditās *f*.
adulation *n* adūlātiō *f*, adsentātiō *f*.
adulatory *adj* blandus.
adult *adj* adultus.
adulterate *vt* corrumpere, adulterāre.
adulterer *n* adulter *m*.
adulteress *n* adultera *f*.
adulterous *adj* incestus.
adultery *n* adulterium *nt*; **commit ~** adulterāre.
adults *npl* pūberēs *mpl*.
adumbrate *vt* adumbrāre.
advance *vt* prōmovēre; (*a cause*) fovēre;

(*money*) crēdere; (*opinion*) dīcere; (*to honours*) prōvehere; (*time*) mātūrāre ♦ *vi* prōcēdere, prōgredī, adventāre; (*MIL*) signa prōferre, pedem īnferre; (*progress*) prōficere; (*walk*) incēdere; ~ **to the attack** signa īnferre ♦ *n* prōgressus *m*, prōcessus *m*; (*attack*) impetus *m*; (*money*) mūtuae pecūniae; **in ~** mātūrius; **fix in ~** praefīnīre; **get in ~** praecipere.
advanced *adj* prōvectus; **well ~** (*task*) adfectus.
advancement *n* (*POL*) honōs *m*.
advantage *n* (*benefit*) commodum *nt*, bonum *nt*, ūsus *m*; (*of place or time*) opportūnitās *f*; (*profit*) fructus *m*; (*superiority*) praestantia *f*; **it is an ~** bono est; **be of ~ to** prōdesse (*dat*), ūsuī esse (*dat*); **to your ~** in rem tuam; **it is to your ~** tibi expedit, tuā interest; **take ~ of** (*CIRCS*) ūtī; (*person*) dēcipere, fallere; **have an ~ over** praestāre (*dat*); **be seen to ~** māximē placēre.
advantageous *adj* ūtilis, opportūnus.
advantageously *adv* ūtiliter, opportūnē.
advent *n* adventus *m*.
adventitious *adj* fortuītus.
adventure *n* (*exploit*) facinus memorābile *nt*; (*hazard*) perīculum *nt*.
adventurer *n* vir audāx *m*; (*social*) parasītus *m*.
adventurous *adj* audāx.
adversary *n* adversārius *m*, hostis *m*.
adverse *adj* adversus, contrārius, inimīcus.
adversely *adv* contrāriē, inimīcē, male.
adversity *n* rēs adversae *fpl*, calamitās *f*.
advert *vi*: ~ **to** attingere.
advertise *vt* prōscrībere; vēnditāre.
advertisement *n* prōscrīptiō *f*, libellus *m*.
advice *n* cōnsilium *nt*; (*POL*) auctōritās *f*; (*legal*) respōnsum *nt*; **ask ~ of** cōnsulere; **on the ~ of Sulla** auctōre Sullā.
advisable *adj* ūtilis, operae pretium.
advise *vt* monēre, suādēre (*dat*), cēnsēre (*dat*); ~ **against** dissuādēre.
advisedly *adv* cōnsultō.
adviser *n* auctor *m*, suāsor *m*.
advocacy *n* patrōcinium *nt*.
advocate *n* patrōnus *m*, causidicus *m*; (*supporter*) auctor *m*; **be an ~** causam dīcere ♦ *vt* suādēre, cēnsēre.
adze *n* ascia *f*.
aedile *n* aedīlis *m*.
aedile's *adj* aedīlicius.
aedileship *n* aedīlitās *f*.
aegis *n* aegis *f*, (*fig*) praesidium *nt*.
Aeneid *n* Aenēis *f*.
aerial *adj* āerius.
aesthetic *adj* pulchritūdinis amāns, artificiōsus.
afar *adv* procul; **from ~** procul.
affability *n* cōmitās *f*, facilitās *f*, bonitās *f*.
affable *adj* cōmis, facilis, commodus.
affably *adv* cōmiter.
affair *n* negōtium *nt*, rēs *f*.
affect *vt* afficere, movēre, commovēre;

(*concern*) attingere; (*pretence*) simulāre.
affectation n simulātiō f; (*RHET*) adfectātiō f; (*in diction*) īnsolentia f; quaesīta ntpl.
affected adj (*style*) molestus, pūtidus.
affectedly adv pūtidē.
affecting adj miserābilis.
affection n amor m, cāritās f, studium nt; (*family*) pietās f.
affectionate adj amāns, pius.
affectionately adv amanter, piē.
affiance vt spondēre.
affidavit n testimōnium nt.
affinity n affīnitās f, cognātiō f.
affirm vt adfirmāre, adsevērāre.
affirmation n adfirmātiō f.
affirmative adj: **I reply in the** ~ āiō.
affix vt adfīgere, adiungere.
afflict vt adflīctāre, angere, vexāre; affligere.
affliction n miseria f, dolor m, rēs adversae fpl.
affluence n cōpia f, opēs fpl.
affluent adj dīves, opulentus, locuplēs.
afford vt praebēre, dare; **I cannot** ~ rēs mihi nōn suppetit ad.
affray n rixa f, pugna f.
affright vt terrēre ♦ n terror m, pavor m.
affront vt offendere, contumēliam dīcere (*dat*) ♦ n iniūria f, contumēlia f.
afield adv forīs; **far** ~ peregrē.
afloat adj natāns; **be** ~ natāre.
afoot adv pedibus; **be** ~ gerī.
aforesaid adj suprā dictus.
afraid adj timidus; **be** ~ **of** timēre, metuere; verērī.
afresh adv dēnuō, dē integrō.
Africa n Africa f.
aft adv in puppī, puppim versus.
after adj posterior ♦ adv post (*acc*), posteā; **the day** ~ postrīdiē ♦ conj postquam; **the day** ~ postrīdiē quam ♦ prep post (*acc*); (*in rank*) secundum (*acc*); (*in imitation*) ad (*acc*), dē (*abl*); ~ **all** tamen, dēnique; ~ **reading the book** librō lēctō; **one thing** ~ **another** aliud ex aliō; **immediately** ~ statim ab.
aftermath n ēventus m.
afternoon n: **in the** ~ post merīdiem ♦ adj postmerīdiānus.
afterthought n posterior cōgitātiō f.
afterwards adv post, posteā, deinde.
again adv rūrsus, iterum; ~ **and** ~ etiam atque etiam, identidem; **once** ~ dēnuō; (*new point in a speech*) quid?
against prep contrā (*acc*), adversus (*acc*), in (*acc*); ~ **the stream** adversō flūmine; ~ **one's will** invitus.
agape adj hiāns.
age n (*life*) aetās f; (*epoch*) aetās f, saeculum nt; **old** ~ senectūs f; **he is of** ~ suī iūris est; **he is eight years of** ~ octō annōs nātus est, nōnum annum agit; **of the same** ~ aequālis.
aged adj senex, aetāte prōvectus; (*things*) antīquus.
agency n opera f; **through the** ~ **of** per (*acc*).
agent n āctor m, prōcūrātor m; (*in crime*)

minister m.
aggrandize vt augēre, amplificāre.
aggrandizement n amplificātiō f.
aggravate vt (*wound*) exulcerāre; (*distress*) augēre; **become** ~**d** ingravēscere.
aggravating adj molestus.
aggregate n summa f.
aggression n incursiō f, iniūria f.
aggressive adj ferōx.
aggressiveness n ferōcitās f.
aggressor n oppugnātor m.
aggrieved adj īrātus; **be** ~ indignārī.
aghast adj attonitus, stupefactus; **stand** ~ obstupēscere.
agile adj pernix, vēlōx.
agility n pernīcitās f.
agitate vt agitāre; (*mind*) commovēre, perturbāre.
agitation n commōtiō f, perturbātiō f, trepidātiō f; (*POL*) tumultus m.
agitator n turbātor m, concitātor m.
aglow adj fervidus ♦ adv: **be** ~ fervēre.
ago adv abhinc (*acc*); **three days** ~ abhinc trēs diēs; **long** ~ antīquitus, iamprīdem, iamdūdum; **a short time** ~ dūdum.
agog adj sollicitus, ērēctus.
agonize vt cruciāre, torquēre.
agonizing adj horribilis.
agony n cruciātus m, dolor m.
agrarian adj agrārius; ~ **party** agrāriī mpl.
agree vi (*together*) cōnsentīre, congruere; (*with*) adsentīrī (*dat*), sentīre cum; (*bargain*) pacīscī; (*facts*) cōnstāre, convenīre; (*food*) facilem esse ad concoquendum; ~ **upon** cōnstituere, compōnere; **it is agreed** constat (inter omnes).
agreeable adj grātus, commodus, acceptus.
agreeableness n dulcēdō f, iūcunditās f.
agreeably adv iūcundē.
agreement n (*together*) cōnsēnsus m, concordia f; (*with*) adsēnsus m; (*pact*) pactiō f, conventum nt, foedus nt; **according to** ~ compāctō, ex compositō; **be in** ~ cōnsentīre, congruere.
agricultural adj rūsticus, agrestis.
agriculture n rēs rūstica f, agrī cultūra f.
aground adv: **be** ~ sīdere; **run** ~ in lītus ēicī, offendere.
ague n horror m, febris f.
ahead adv ante; **go** ~ anteīre, praeīre; **go-**~ adj impiger; **ships in line** ~ agmen nāvium.
aid vt adiuvāre, succurrere (*dat*), subvenīre (*dat*) ♦ n auxilium nt, subsidium nt.
aide-de-camp n optiō m.
ail vt dolēre ♦ vi aegrōtāre, labōrāre, languēre.
ailing adj aeger, īnfirmus.
ailment n morbus m, valētūdō f.
aim vt intendere; ~ **at** petere; (*fig*) adfectāre, spectāre, sequī; (*with verb*) id agere ut ♦ n fīnis m, prōpositum nt.
aimless adj inānis, vānus.
aimlessly adv sine ratiōne.
aimlessness n vānitās f.

air n āēr m; (*breeze*) aura f; (*look*) vultus m, speciēs f; (*tune*) modus m; **in the open** ~ sub dīvō; ~**s** fastus m; **give oneself** ~**s** sē iactāre.

airily adv hilarē.

airy adj (*of air*) āerius; (*light*) tenuis; (*place*) apertus; (*manner*) hilaris.

aisle n āla f.

ajar adj sēmiapertus.

akin adj cōnsanguineus, cognātus.

alacrity n alacritās f.

alarm n terror m, formīdō f, trepidātiō f; (*sound*) clāmor m; **sound an** ~ ad arma conclāmāre; **give the** ~ increpāre; **be in a state of** ~ trepidāre ♦ vt terrēre, perterrēre, perturbāre.

alarming adj formīdolōsus.

alas interj heu.

albeit conj etsī, etiamsī.

alcove n zōthēca f.

alder n alnus f.

alderman n decuriō m.

ale n cervīsia f.

alehouse n caupōna f, taberna f.

alert adj prōmptus, alacer, vegetus.

alertness n alacritās f.

alien adj externus; ~ **to** abhorrēns ab ♦ n peregrīnus m.

alienate vt aliēnāre, abaliēnāre, āvertere, āvocāre.

alienation n aliēnātiō f.

alight vi (*from horse*) dēscendere, dēsilīre; (*bird*) īnsīdere.

alight adj: **be** ~ ārdēre; **set** ~ accendere.

alike adj pār, similis ♦ adv aequē, pariter.

alive adj vīvus; **be** ~ vīvere.

all adj omnis; (*together*) ūniversus, cūnctus; (*whole*) tōtus; ~ **but** paene; ~ **for** studiōsus (*gen*); ~ **in** cōnfectus; ~ **of** tōtus; ~ **over with** āctum dē (*abl*); ~ **the best men** optimus quisque; ~ **the more** eō plūs, tantō plūs; **at** ~ ullō modō, quid; **it is** ~ **up with** actum est dē (*abl*); **not at** ~ haudquāquam ♦ n fortūnae fpl.

allay vt sēdāre, mītigāre, lēnīre.

allegation n adfirmātiō f; (*charge*) īnsimulātiō f.

allege vt adfirmāre, praetendere; (*in excuse*) excūsāre.

allegiance n fidēs f; **owe** ~ **to** in fidē esse (*gen*); **swear** ~ **to** in verba iūrāre (*gen*).

allegory n allēgoria f, immūtāta ōrātiō f.

alleviate vt mītigāre, adlevāre, sublevāre.

alleviation n levātiō f, levāmentum nt.

alley n (*garden*) xystus m; (*town*) angiportus m.

alliance n societās f, foedus nt.

allied adj foederātus, socius; (*friends*) coniūnctus.

alligator n crocodīlus m.

allocate vt adsignāre, impertīre.

allot vt adsignāre, distribuere; **be** ~**ted** obtingere.

allotment n (*land*) adsignātiō f.

allow vt sinere, permittere (*dat*), concēdere (*dat*), patī; (*admit*) fatērī, concēdere;

(*approve*) comprobāre; **it is** ~**ed** licet (*dat* + *infin*); ~ **for** vt fus ratiōnem habēre (*gen*).

allowance n venia f, indulgentia f; (*pay*) stīpendium nt; (*food*) cibāria ntpl; (*for travel*) viāticum nt; **make** ~ **for** indulgēre (*dat*), ignōscere (*dat*), excūsāre.

alloy n admixtum nt.

all right adj rēctē; **it is** ~ bene est.

allude vi: ~ **to** dēsignāre, attingere, significāre.

allure vt adlicere, pellicere.

allurement n blanditia f, blandīmentum nt, illecebra f.

alluring adj blandus.

alluringly adv blandē.

allusion n mentiō f, indicium nt.

alluvial adj: ~ **land** adluviō f.

ally n socius m ♦ vt sociāre, coniungere.

almanac n fāstī mpl.

almighty adj omnipotēns.

almond n (*nut*) amygdalum nt; (*tree*) amygdala f.

almost adv paene, ferē, fermē, propemodum.

alms n stipem (*no nom*) f.

aloe n aloē f.

aloft adj sublīmis ♦ adv sublīmē.

alone adj sōlus, sōlitārius, ūnus ♦ adv sōlum.

along prep secundum (*acc*), praeter (*acc*) ♦ adv porrō; **all** ~ iamdūdum, ab initiō; ~ **with** unā cum (*abl*).

alongside adv: **bring** ~ adpellere; **come** ~ ad crepīdinem accēdere.

aloof adv procul; **stand** ~ sē removēre ♦ adj sēmōtus.

aloofness n sōlitūdō f, sēcessus m.

aloud adv clārē, māgnā vōce.

alphabet n elementa ntpl.

Alps n Alpēs fpl.

already adv iam.

also adv etiam, et, quoque; īdem.

altar n āra f.

alter vt mūtāre, commūtāre; (*order*) invertere.

alteration n mūtātiō f, commūtātiō f.

altercation n altercātiō f, iūrgium nt.

alternate adj alternus ♦ vt variāre.

alternately adv invicem.

alternation n vicem (*no nom*) f, vicissitūdō f.

alternative adj alter, alius ♦ n optiō f.

although conj quamquam (*indic*), etsī/etiamsī (+ *cond clause*); quamvīs (+ *subj*).

altitude n altitūdō f.

altogether adv omnīnō; (*emphasis*) plānē, prōrsus.

altruism n beneficentia f.

alum n alūmen nt.

always adv semper.

amalgamate vt miscēre, coniungere.

amalgamation n coniūnctiō f, temperātiō f.

amanuensis n librārius m.

amass vt cumulāre, coacervāre.

amateur n idiōta m.

amatory adj amātōrius.

amaze vt obstupefacere; attonāre; **be** ~**d**

obstupēscere.

amazement *n* stupor *m*; **in ~** attonitus, stupefactus.

ambassador *n* lēgātus *m*.

amber *n* sūcinum *nt*.

ambidextrous *adj* utrīusque manūs compos.

ambiguity *n* ambiguitās *f*; (*RHET*) amphibolia *f*.

ambiguous *adj* ambiguus, anceps, dubius.

ambiguously *adv* ambiguē.

ambition *n* glōria *f*, laudis studium.

ambitious *adj* glōriae cupidus, laudis avidus.

amble *vi* ambulāre.

ambrosia *n* ambrosia *f*.

ambrosial *adj* ambrosius.

ambuscade *n* īnsidiae *fpl*.

ambush *n* īnsidiae *fpl* ♦ *vt* īnsidiārī (*dat*).

ameliorate *vt* corrigere, meliōrem reddere.

amelioration *n* prōfectus *m*.

amenable *adj* facilis, docilis.

amend *vt* corrigere, ēmendāre.

amendment *n* ēmendātiō *f*.

amends *n* (*apology*) satisfactiō *f*; **make ~ for** expiāre; **make ~ to** satisfacere (*dat*).

amenity *n* (*scenery*) amoenitās *f*; (*comfort*) commodum *nt*.

amethyst *n* amethystus *f*.

amiability *n* benignitās *f*, suāvitās *f*.

amiable *adj* benignus, suāvis.

amiably *adv* benignē, suāviter.

amicable *adj* amīcus, cōmis.

amicably *adv* amīcē, cōmiter.

amid, amidst *prep* inter (*acc*).

amiss *adv* perperam, secus, incommodē; **take ~** aegrē ferre.

amity *n* amīcitia *f*.

ammunition *n* tēla *ntpl*.

amnesty *n* venia *f*.

among, amongst *prep* inter (*acc*), apud (*acc*).

amorous *adj* amātōrius, amāns.

amorously *adv* cum amōre.

amount *vi*: **~ to** efficere; (*fig*) esse ♦ *n* summa *f*.

amours *n* amōrēs *mpl*.

amphibious *adj* anceps.

amphitheatre *n* amphitheātrum *nt*.

ample *adj* amplus, satis.

amplification *n* amplificātiō *f*.

amplify *vt* amplificāre.

amplitude *n* amplitūdō *f*, cōpia *f*.

amputate *vt* secāre, amputāre.

amuck *adv*: **run ~** bacchārī.

amulet *n* amulētum *nt*.

amuse *vt* dēlectāre, oblectāre.

amusement *n* oblectāmentum *nt*, dēlectātiō *f*; **for ~** animī causā.

amusing *adj* rīdiculus, facētus.

an *indef art see* **a.**

anaemic *adj* exsanguis.

analogous *adj* similis.

analogy *n* prōportiō *f*, comparātiō *f*.

analyse *vt* excutere, perscrūtārī.

analysis *n* explicātiō *f*.

anapaest *n* anapaestus *m*.

anarchical *adj* sēditiōsus.

anarchy *n* reī pūblicae perturbātiō, lēgēs nullae *fpl*, licentia *f*.

anathema *n* exsecrātiō *f*; (*object*) pestis *f*.

ancestor *n* proavus *m*; **~s** *pl* māiōrēs *mpl*.

ancestral *adj* patrius.

ancestry *n* genus *nt*, orīgō *f*.

anchor *n* ancora *f*; **lie at ~** in ancorīs stāre; **weigh ~** ancoram tollere ♦ *vi* ancoram iacere.

anchorage *n* statiō *f*.

ancient *adj* antīquus, prīscus, vetustus; **~ history, ~ world** antīquitās *f*; **from/in ~ times** antīquitus; **the ~s** veterēs.

and *conj* et, atque, ac, -que; **~ . . . not** nec, neque; **~ so** itaque.

anecdote *n* fābella *f*.

anent *prep* dē (*abl*).

anew *adv* dēnuō, ab integrō.

angel *n* angelus *m*.

angelic *adj* angelicus; (*fig*) dīvīnus, eximius.

anger *n* īra *f* ♦ *vt* inrītāre.

angle *n* angulus *m* ♦ *vi* hāmō piscārī.

angler *n* piscātor *m*.

Anglesey *n* Mona *f*.

angrily *adv* īrātē.

angry *adj* īrātus; **be ~** īrāscī (*dat*).

anguish *n* cruciātus *m*, dolor *m*; (*mind*) angor *m*.

angular *adj* angulātus.

animal *n* animal *nt*; (*domestic*) pecus *f*; (*wild*) fera *f*.

animate *vt* animāre.

animated *adj* excitātus, vegetus.

animation *n* ārdor *m*, alacritās *f*.

animosity *n* invidia *f*, inimīcitia *f*.

ankle *n* tālus *m*.

annalist *n* annālium scrīptor.

annals *n* annālēs *mpl*.

annex *vt* addere.

annexation *n* adiectiō *f*.

annihilate *vt* dēlēre, exstinguere, perimere.

annihilation *n* exstinctiō *f*, interneciō *f*.

anniversary *n* diēs anniversārius; (*public*) sollemne *nt*.

annotate *vt* adnotāre.

annotation *n* adnotātiō *f*.

announce *vt* nūntiāre; (*officially*) dēnūntiāre, prōnūntiāre; (*election result*) renūntiāre.

announcement *n* (*official*) dēnūntiātiō *f*; (*news*) nūntius *m*.

announcer *n* nūntius *m*.

annoy *vt* inrītāre, vexāre; **be ~ed with** aegrē ferre.

annoyance *n* molestia *f*, vexātiō *f*; (*felt*) dolor *m*.

annoying *adj* molestus.

annual *adj* annuus, anniversārius.

annually *adv* quotannīs.

annuity *n* annua *ntpl*.

annul *vt* abrogāre, dissolvere, tollere.

annulment *n* abrogātiō *f*.

anoint *vt* ungere, illinere.

anomalous *adj* novus.
anomaly *n* novitās *f.*
anon *adv* mox.
anonymous *adj* incertī auctōris.
anonymously *adv* sine nōmine.
another *adj* alius; (*second*) alter; **of** ~ aliēnus; **one after** ~ alius ex aliō; **one** ~ inter sē, alius alium; **in** ~ **place** alibī; **to** ~ **place** aliō; **in** ~ **way** aliter; **at** ~ **time** aliās.
answer *vt* respondēre (*dat*); (*by letter*) rescrībere (*dat*); (*agree*) respondēre, congruere; ~ **a charge** crīmen dēfendere; ~ **for** *vt fus* (*surety*) praestāre; (*account*) ratiōnem referre; (*substitute*) īnstar esse (*gen*) ♦ *n* respōnsum *nt*; (*to a charge*) dēfēnsiō *f*; ~ **to the name of** vocārī; **give an** ~ respondēre.
answerable *adj* reus; **I am** ~ **for** . . . ratiō mihī reddenda est . . . (*gen*).
ant *n* formīca *f.*
antagonism *n* simultās *f*, inimīcitia *f.*
antagonist *n* adversārius *m*, hostis *m.*
antarctic *adj* antarcticus.
antecedent *adj* antecēdēns, prior.
antediluvian *adj* prīscus, horridus, Deucaliōnēus.
antelope *n* dorcas *f.*
anterior *adj* prior.
anteroom *n* vestibulum *nt.*
anthology *n* excerpta *ntpl*; **make an** ~ excerpere.
anthropology *n* rēs hūmānae *fpl.*
anticipate *vt* (*expect*) exspectāre; (*forestall*) antevenīre, occupāre, (*in thought*) animō praecipere.
anticipation *n* exspectātiō *f*, spēs *f*; praesūmptiō *f.*
antics *n* gestus *m*, ineptiae *fpl.*
anticyclone *n* serēnitās *f.*
antidote *n* remedium *nt*, medicāmen *nt.*
antipathy *n* fastīdium *nt*, odium *nt*; (*things*) repugnantia *f.*
antiphonal *adj* alternus.
antiphony *n* alterna *ntpl.*
antipodes *n* contrāria pars terrae.
antiquarian *adj* historicus.
antiquary *n* antīquārius *m.*
antiquated *adj* prīscus, obsolētus.
antique *adj* antīquus, prīscus.
antiquity *n* antīquitās *f*, vetustas *f*, veterēs *mpl.*
antithesis *n* contentiō *f*, contrārium *nt.*
antlers *n* cornua *ntpl.*
anvil *n* incūs *f.*
anxiety *n* sollicitūdō *f*, metus *m*, cūra *f*; anxietās *f.*
anxious *adj* sollicitus, anxius; avidus; cupidus.
any *adj* ullus; (*interrog*) ecquī; (*after* sī, nisī, num, nē) quī; (*indef*) quīvīs, quīlibet; **hardly** ~ nullus ferē; ~ **further** longius; ~ **longer** (*of time*) diutius.
anybody *pron* aliquis; (*indef*) quīvīs, quīlibet;

(*after* sī, nisī, num, nē) quis; (*interrog*) ecquis, numquis; (*after neg*) quisquam; **hardly** ~ nēmō ferē.
anyhow *adv* ullō modō, quōquō modō.
anyone *pron see* **anybody.**
anything *pron* aliquid; quidvīs, quidlibet; (*interrog*) ecquid, numquid; (*after neg*) quicquam; (*after* sī, nisī, num, nē) quid; **hardly** ~ nihil ferē.
anywhere *adv* usquam, ubīvīs.
apace *adv* citō, celeriter.
apart *adv* seōrsum, sēparātim ♦ *adj* dīversus; **be six feet** ~ sex pedēs distāre; **set** ~ sēpōnere; **stand** ~ distāre; **joking** ~ remōtō iocō; ~ **from** praeter (*acc*).
apartment *n* cubiculum *nt*, conclāve *nt.*
apathetic *adj* lentus, languidus, ignāvus.
apathy *n* lentitūdō *f*, languor *m*, ignāvia *f.*
ape *n* sīmia *f* ♦ *vt* imitārī.
aperture *n* hiātus *m*, forāmen *nt*, rīma *f.*
apex *n* fastīgium *nt.*
aphorism *n* sententia *f.*
apiary *n* alveārium *nt.*
apiece *adv* in singulōs; **two** ~ bīnī.
aplomb *n* cōnfīdentia *f.*
apocryphal *adj* commentīcius.
apologetic *adj* cōnfitēns, veniam petēns.
apologize *vi* veniam petere, sē excūsāre.
apology *n* excūsātiō *f.*
apoplectic *adj* apoplēcticus.
apoplexy *n* apoplēxis *f.*
apostle *n* apostolus *m.*
apothecary *n* medicāmentārius *m.*
appal *vt* perterrēre, cōnsternere.
appalling *adj* dīrus.
apparatus *n* īnstrūmenta *ntpl*, ōrnāmenta *ntpl.*
apparel *n* vestis *f*, vestīmenta *ntpl.*
apparent *adj* manifestus, apertus, ēvidēns.
apparently *adv* speciē, ut vidētur.
apparition *n* vīsum *nt*, speciēs *f.*
appeal *vi* (*to magistrate*) appellāre; (*to people*) prōvocāre ad; (*to gods*) invocāre, testārī; (*to senses*) placēre (*dat*) ♦ *n* appellātiō *f*, prōvocātiō *f*, testātiō *f.*
appear *vi* (*in sight*) appārēre; (*in court*) sistī; (*in public*) prōdīre; (*at a place*) adesse, advenīre; (*seem*) vidērī.
appearance *n* (*coming*) adventus *m*; (*look*) aspectus *m*, faciēs *f*; (*semblance*) speciēs *f*; (*thing*) vīsum *nt*; **for the sake of** ~**s** in speciem; (*formula*) dicis causā; **make one's** ~ prōcēdere, prōdīre.
appeasable *adj* plācābilis.
appease *vt* plācāre, lēnīre, mītigāre, sēdāre.
appeasement *n* plācātiō *f*; (*of enemy*) pācificātiō *f.*
appellant *n* appellātor *m.*
appellation *n* nōmen *nt.*
append *vt* adiungere, subicere.
appendage *n* appendix *f*, adiūnctum *nt.*
appertain *vi* pertinēre.
appetite *n* adpetītus *m*; (*for food*) fāmēs *f.*
applaud *vt* plaudere; (*fig*) laudāre.

applause n plausus m; (fig) adsēnsiō f, adprobātiō f.

apple n pōmum nt; mālum nt; ~ **tree** mālus f; ~ **of my eye** ocellus meus; **upset the ~ cart** plaustrum percellere.

appliance n māchina f, īnstrūmentum nt.

applicable adj aptus, commodus; **be ~** pertinēre.

applicant n petītor m.

application n (work) industria f; (mental) intentiō f; (asking) petītiō f; (MED) fōmentum nt.

apply vt adhibēre, admovēre; (use) ūtī (abl); ~ **oneself to** sē adplicāre, incumbere in (acc) ♦ vi pertinēre; (to a person) adīre (acc); (for office) petere.

appoint vt (magistrate) creāre, facere, cōnstituere; (commander) praeficere; (guardian, heir) īnstituere; (time) dīcere, statuere; (for a purpose) dēstināre; (to office) creāre.

appointment n cōnstitūtum nt; (duty) mandātum nt; (office) magistrātus m; **have an ~ with** cōnstitūtum habēre cum; **keep an ~** ad cōnstitūtum venīre.

apportion vt dispertīre, dīvīdere; (land) adsignāre.

apposite adj aptus, appositus.

appraisal n aestimātiō f.

appraise vt aestimāre.

appreciable adj haud exiguus.

appreciate vt aestimāre.

appreciation n aestimātiō f.

apprehend vt (person) comprehendere; (idea) intellegere, mente comprehendere; (fear) metuere, timēre.

apprehension n comprehēnsiō f; metus m, formīdō f.

apprehensive adj anxius, sollicitus; **be ~ of** metuere.

apprentice n discipulus m, tīrō m.

apprenticeship n tīrōcinium nt.

apprise vt docēre, certiōrem facere.

approach vt appropinquāre ad (acc), accēdere ad; (person) adīre ♦ vi (time) adpropinquāre; (season) appetere ♦ n (act) accessus m, aditus m; (time) adpropinquātiō f; (way) aditus m; **make ~es to** adīre ad, ambīre, petere.

approachable adj (place) patēns; (person) facilis.

approbation n adprobātiō f, adsēnsiō f.

appropriate adj aptus, idōneus, proprius ♦ vt adscīscere, adsūmere.

appropriately adv aptē, commodē.

approval n adprobātiō f, adsēnsus m, favor m.

approve vt, vi adprobāre, comprobāre, adsentīrī (dat); (law) scīscere.

approved adj probātus, spectātus.

approximate adj propinquus ♦ vi: ~ **to** accēdere ad.

approximately adv prope, propemodum; (number) ad (acc).

appurtenances n īnstrūmenta ntpl, apparātus m.

apricot n armēniacum nt; ~ **tree** n armēniaca f.

April n mēnsis Aprīlis m; **of ~** Aprīlis.

apron n operīmentum nt.

apropos of prep quod attinet ad.

apse n apsis f.

apt adj aptus, idōneus; (pupil) docilis, prōmptus; ~ **to** prōnus, prōclīvis ad; **be ~ to** solēre.

aptitude n ingenium nt, facultās f.

aptly adv aptē.

aquarium n piscīna f.

aquatic adj aquātilis.

aqueduct n aquae ductus m.

aquiline adj (nose) aduncus.

arable land n arvum nt.

arbiter n arbiter m.

arbitrarily adv ad libīdinem, licenter.

arbitrary adj libīdinōsus (act); (ruler) superbus.

arbitrate vi dīiūdicāre, disceptāre.

arbitration n arbitrium nt, dīiūdicātiō f.

arbitrator n arbiter m, disceptātor m.

arbour n umbrāculum nt.

arbutus n arbutus f.

arc n arcus m.

arcade n porticus f.

arch n fornix m, arcus m ♦ vt arcuāre ♦ adj lascīvus, vafer.

archaeologist n antīquitātis investīgātor m.

archaeology n antīquitātis investīgātiō f.

archaic adj prīscus.

archaism n verbum obsolētum nt.

archbishop n archiepiscopus m.

arched adj fornicātus.

archer n sagittārius m.

archery n sagittāriōrum ars f.

architect n architectus m.

architecture n architectūra f.

architrave n epistylium nt.

archives n tabulae (pūblicae) fpl.

arctic adj arcticus, septentriōnālis ♦ n septentriōnēs mpl.

ardent adj ārdēns, fervidus, vehemēns.

ardently adv ārdenter, ācriter, vehementer.

ardour n ārdor m, fervor m.

arduous adj difficilis, arduus.

area n regiō f; (MATH) superficiēs f.

arena n harēna f.

argonaut n argonauta m.

argosy n onerāria f.

argue vi (discuss) disserere, disceptāre; (dispute) ambigere; disputāre; (reason) argūmentārī ♦ vt (prove) arguere.

argument n (discussion) contrōversia f, disputātiō f; (reason) ratiō f; (proof, theme) argūmentum nt.

argumentation n argūmentātiō f.

argumentative adj lītigiōsus.

aria n canticum nt.

arid adj āridus, siccus.

aright adv rectē, vērē.

arise vi orīrī, coorīrī, exsistere; ~ **from** nāscī ex, proficīscī ab.

aristocracy *n* optimātēs *mpl*, nōbilēs *mpl*; (*govt*) optimātium dominātus *m*.
aristocrat *n* optimās *m*.
aristocratic *adj* patricius, generōsus.
arithmetic *n* numerī *mpl*, arithmētica *ntpl*.
ark *n* arca *f*.
arm *n* bracchium *nt*; (*upper*) lacertus *m*; (*sea*) sinus *m*; (*weapon*) tēlum *nt* ♦ *vt* armāre ♦ *vi* arma capere.
armament *n* bellī apparātus *m*; cōpiae *fpl*.
armed *adj* (*men*) armātus; **light-~ troops** levis armātūra *f*, vēlitēs *mpl*.
armistice *n* indutiae *fpl*.
armlet *n* armilla *f*.
armour *n* arma *ntpl*; (*kind of*) armātūra *f*.
armourer *n* (armōrum) faber *m*.
armoury *n* armāmentārium *nt*.
armpit *n* āla *f*.
arms *npl* (*MIL*) arma *ntpl*; **by force of ~** vī et armīs; **under ~** in armīs.
army *n* exercitus *m*; (*in battle*) aciēs *f*; (*on march*) agmen *nt*.
aroma *n* odor *m*.
aromatic *adj* frāgrāns.
around *adv* circum (*acc*), circā (*acc*) ♦ *prep* circum (*acc*).
arouse *vt* suscitāre, ērigere, excitāre.
arraign *vt* accūsāre.
arrange *vt* (*in order*) compōnere, ōrdināre, dīgerere, dispōnere; (*agree*) pacīscī; **~ a truce** indūtias compōnere.
arrangement *n* ōrdō *m*, collocātiō *f*, dispositiō *f*; pactum *nt*, cōnstitūtum *nt*.
arrant *adj* summus.
array *n* vestis *f*, habitus *m*; (*MIL*) aciēs *f* ♦ *vt* vestīre, exōrnāre; (*MIL*) īnstruere.
arrears *n* residuae pecūniae *fpl*, reliqua *ntpl*.
arrest *vt* comprehendere, adripere; (*attention*) in sē convertere; (*movement*) morārī, tardāre ♦ *n* comprehēnsiō *f*.
arrival *n* adventus *m*.
arrive *vi* advenīre (ad + *acc*), pervenīre (ad + *acc*).
arrogance *n* superbia *f*, adrogantia *f*, fastus *m*.
arrogant *adj* superbus, adrogāns.
arrogantly *adv* superbē, adroganter.
arrogate *vt* adrogāre.
arrow *n* sagitta *f*.
arsenal *n* armāmentārium *nt*.
arson *n* incēnsiōnis crīmen *nt*.
art *n* ars *f*, artificium *nt*; **fine ~s** ingenuae artēs.
artery *n* artēria *f*.
artful *adj* callidus, vafer, astūtus.
artfully *adv* callidē, astūtē.
artfulness *n* astūtia *f*, dolus *m*.
artichoke *n* cinara *f*.
article *n* rēs *f*, merx *f*; (*clause*) caput *nt*; (*term*) condiciō *f*.
articulate *adj* explānātus, distinctus ♦ *vi* explānāre, exprimere.
articulately *adv* explānātē, clārē.
articulation *n* prōnūntiātiō *f*.
artifice *n* ars *f*, artificium *nt*, dolus *m*.

artificer *n* artifex *m*, opifex *m*, faber *m*.
artificial *adj* (*work*) artificiōsus; (*appearance*) fūcātus.
artificially *adv* arte, manū.
artillery *n* tormenta *ntpl*.
artisan *n* faber *m*, opifex *m*.
artist *n* artifex *m*; pictor *m*.
artistic *adj* artificiōsus, ēlegāns.
artistically *adv* artificiōsē, ēleganter.
artless *adj* (*work*) inconditus; (*person*) simplex.
artlessly *adv* incondītē; simpliciter, sine dolō.
artlessness *n* simplicitās *f*.
as *adv* (*before adj, adv*) tam; (*after* **aequus, īdem, similis**) ac, atque; (*correlative*) quam, quālis, quantus ♦ *conj* (*compar*) ut (+ *indic*), sīcut, velut, quemadmodum; (*cause*) cum (+ *indic*), quōniam, quippe quī; (*time*) dum, ut ♦ *relat pron* quī, quae, quod (+ *subj*); **~ being** utpote; **~ follows** ita; **~ for** quod attinet ad; **~ if** quasī, tamquam si, velut; (= *while*) *usu expressed by pres part*; **~ it were** ut ita dīcam; **~ yet** adhūc; **~ soon ~** simul ac/atque (+ *perf indic*); **~ ... as possible** quam (+ *superl*).
as *n* (*coin*) as *m*.
ascend *vt, vi* ascendere.
ascendancy *n* praestantia *f*, auctōritās *f*.
ascendant *adj* surgēns, potēns; **be in the ~** praestāre.
ascent *n* ascēnsus *m*; (*slope*) clīvus *m*.
ascertain *vt* comperīre, cognōscere.
ascetic *adj* nimis abstinēns, austērus.
asceticism *n* dūritia *f*.
ascribe *vt* adscrībere, attribuere, adsignāre.
ash *n* (*tree*) fraxinus *f* ♦ *adj* fraxineus.
ashamed *adj*: **I am ~** pudet mē; **~ of** pudet (+ *acc of person, + gen of thing*).
ashen *adj* pallidus.
ashes *n* cinis *m*.
ashore *adv* (*motion*) in lītus; (*rest*) in lītore; **go ~** ēgredī.
Asia *n* Asia *f*.
aside *adv* sēparatim, sē- (*in cpd*).
ask *vt* (*question*) rogāre, quaerere; (*request*) petere, poscere; (*beg, entreat*) ōrāre; **~ for** *vt* petere; rogāre; scīscitārī; percontārī.
askance *adv* oblīquē; **look ~ at** līmīs oculīs aspicere, invidēre (*dat*).
askew *adv* prāvē.
aslant *adv* oblīquē.
asleep *adj* sōpītus; **be ~** dormīre; **fall ~** obdormīre, somnum inīre.
asp *n* aspis *f*.
asparagus *n* asparagus *m*.
aspect *n* (*place*) aspectus *m*; (*person*) vultus *m*; (*CIRCS*) status *m*; **have a southern ~** ad merīdiem spectāre; **there is another ~ to the matter** aliter sē rēs habet.
aspen *n* pōpulus *f*.
asperity *n* acerbitās *f*.
asperse *vt* maledīcere (*dat*), calumniārī.
aspersion *n* calumnia *f*; **cast ~s on** calumniārī, īnfamiā aspergere.
asphalt *n* bitūmen *nt*.

asphyxia n strangulātiō f.
asphyxiate vt strangulāre.
aspirant n petītor m.
aspirate n (GRAM) aspīrātiō f.
aspiration n spēs f; (POL) ambitiō f.
aspire vi: ~ **to** adfectāre, petere, spērāre.
ass n asinus m, asellus m; (fig) stultus.
assail vt oppugnāre, adorīrī, aggredī.
assailable adj expugnābilis.
assailant n oppugnātor m.
assassin n sīcārius m, percussor m.
assassinate vt interficere, occīdere, iugulāre.
assassination n caedēs f, parricidium nt.
assault vt oppugnāre, adorīrī, aggredī;
   (speech) invehī in (acc) ♦ n impetus m,
   oppugnātiō f; (personal) vīs f.
assay vt (metal) spectāre; temptāre, cōnārī.
assemble vt convocāre, congregāre, cōgere ♦
   vi convenīre, congregārī.
assembly n coetus m, conventus m; (plebs)
   concilium nt; (Roman people) comitia ntpl;
   (troops) cōntiō f; (things) congeriēs f.
assent vi adsentīrī, adnuere ♦ n adsēnsus m.
assert vt adfirmāre, adsevērāre, dīcere.
assertion n adfirmātiō f, adsevērātiō f, dictum
   nt, sententia f.
assess vt cēnsēre, aestimāre; ~ **damages**
   lītem aestimāre.
assessment n cēnsus m, aestimātiō f.
assessor n cēnsor m; (assistant) cōnsessor m.
assets n bona ntpl.
assiduity n dīligentia f, sēdulitās f, industria f.
assiduous adj dīligēns, sēdulus, industrius.
assign vt tribuere, attribuere; (land)
   adsignāre; (in writing) perscrībere; (task)
   dēlēgāre; (reason) adferre.
assignation n cōnstitūtum nt.
assignment n adsignātiō f, perscrīptiō f; (task)
   mūnus nt, pēnsum nt.
assimilate vt aequāre; (food) concoquere;
   (knowledge) concipere.
assist vt adiuvāre, succurrere (dat), adesse
   (dat).
assistance n auxilium nt, opem (no nom) f;
   come to the ~ of subvenīre (dat); **be of ~ to**
   auxiliō esse (dat).
assistant n adiūtor m, minister m.
assize n conventus m; **hold ~s** conventūs
   agere.
associate vt cōnsociāre, coniungere ♦ vi rem
   inter sē cōnsociāre; ~ **with** familiāriter ūtī
   (abl) ♦ n socius m, sodālis m.
association n societās f; (club) sodālitās f.
assort vt dīgerere, dispōnere ♦ vi congruere.
assortment n (of goods) variae mercēs fpl.
assuage vt lēnīre, mītigāre, sēdāre.
assume vt (for oneself) adsūmere, adrogāre;
   (hypothesis) pōnere; (office) inīre.
assumption n (hypothesis) sūmptiō f, positum
   nt.
assurance n (given) fidēs f, pignus nt; (felt)
   fīdūcia f; (boldness) cōnfīdentia f.
assure vt cōnfirmāre, prōmittere (dat).

assured adj (person) fīdēns; (fact) explōrātus,
   certus.
assuredly adv certō, certē, profectō, sānē.
astern adv ā puppī; (movement) retrō; ~ **of**
   post.
asthma n anhēlitus m.
astonish vt obstupefacere; attonāre.
astonished adj attonitus, stupefactus; **be ~ed**
   at admīrārī.
astonishing adj mīrificus, mīrus.
astonishment n stupor m, admīrātiō f.
astound vt obstupefacere.
astray adj vagus; **go ~** errāre, aberrāre,
   deerrāre.
astride adj vāricus.
astrologer n Chaldaeus m, mathēmaticus m.
astrology n Chaldaeōrum dīvīnātiō f.
astronomer n astrologus m.
astronomy n astrologia f.
astute adj callidus, vafer.
astuteness n calliditās f.
asunder adv sēparātim, dis- (in cpd).
asylum n asȳlum nt.
at prep in (abl), ad (acc); (time) usu expressed by
   abl; (towns, small islands) loc; ~ **the house of**
   apud (acc); ~ **all events** saltem; see also **dawn,**
   hand, house etc.
atheism n deōs esse negāre.
atheist n atheos m; **be an ~** deōs esse negāre.
Athenian adj Atheniensis.
Athens n Athenae fpl; **at/from ~** Athenis; **to ~**
   Athenas.
athirst adj sitiens; (fig) avidus.
athlete n athlēta m.
athletic adj rōbustus, lacertōsus.
athletics n athlētica ntpl.
athwart prep trāns (acc).
atlas n orbis terrārum dēscrīptiō f.
atmosphere n āēr m.
atom n atomus f, corpus indīviduum nt.
atone vi: ~ **for** expiāre.
atonement n expiātiō f, piāculum nt.
atrocious adj immānis, nefārius, scelestus.
atrociously adv nefāriē, scelestē.
atrociousness n immānitās f.
atrocity n nefas nt, scelus nt, flāgitium nt.
atrophy vi marcēscere.
attach vt adiungere, adfīgere, illigāre; (word)
   subicere; ~**ed to** amāns (gen).
attachment n vinculum nt; amor m, studium
   nt.
attack vt oppugnāre, adorīrī, aggredī;
   impetum facere in (acc); (speech) īnsequī,
   invehī in (acc); (disease) ingruere in (acc) ♦ n
   impetus m, oppugnātiō f, incursus m.
attacker n oppugnātor m.
attain vt adsequī, adipīscī, cōnsequī; ~ **to**
   pervenīre ad.
attainable adj impetrābilis, in prōmptū.
attainder n: **bill of ~** prīvilēgium nt.
attainment n adeptiō f.
attainments npl doctrīna f, ērudītiō f.
attaint vt māiestātis condemnāre.

attempt *vt* cōnārī, temptāre; (*with effort*)
mōlīrī ♦ *n* cōnātus *m*, inceptum *nt*; (*risk*)
perīculum *nt*; **first ~s** rudīmenta *ntpl.*

attend *vt* (*meeting*) adesse (*dat*), interesse
(*dat*); (*person*) prōsequī, comitārī; (*master*)
appārēre (*dat*); (*invalid*) cūrāre ♦ *vi* animum
advertere, animum attendere; **~ to** (*task*)
adcūrāre; **~ upon** prōsequī, adsectārī; **~ the
lectures of** audīre; **not ~** aliud agere; **~ first to**
praevertere (*dat*); **well ~ed** frequēns; **thinly
~ed** īnfrequēns.

attendance *n* (*courtesy*) adsectātiō *f*; (*MED*)
cūrātiō *f*; (*service*) apparitiō *f*; **constant ~**
adsiduitās *f*; **full ~** frequentia *f*; **poor ~**
īnfrequentia *f*; **dance ~ on** haerēre (*dat*).

attendant *n* famulus *m*, minister *m*; (*on
candidate*) sectātor *m*; (*on nobleman*)
adsectātor *m*; (*on magistrate*) apparitor *m*.

attention *n* animadversiō *f*, animī attentiō *f*;
(*to work*) cūra *f*; (*respect*) observantia *f*;
attract ~ digitō mōnstrarī; **call ~ to** indicāre;
pay ~ to animadvertere, observāre;
ratiōnem habēre (*gen*); **~ !** hōc age!

attentive *adj* intentus; (*to work*) dīligēns.

attentively *adv* intentē, dīligenter.

attenuate *vt* attenuāre.

attest *vt* cōnfirmāre, testārī.

attestation *n* testificātiō *f*.

attestor *n* testis *m*.

attic *n* cēnāculum *nt*.

attire *vt* vestīre ♦ *n* vestis *f*, habitus *m*.

attitude *n* (*body*) gestus *m*, status *m*, habitus
m; (*mind*) ratiō *f*.

attorney *n* āctor *m*; advocātus *m*.

attract *vt* trahere, attrahere, adlicere.

attraction *n* vīs attrahendī; illecebra *f*,
invītāmentum *nt*.

attractive *adj* suāvis, venustus, lepidus.

attractively *adv* suāviter, vēnustē, lepidē.

attractiveness *n* venustās *f*, lepōs *m*.

attribute *vt* tribuere, attribuere, adsignāre ♦
n proprium *nt*.

attrition *n* attrītus *m*.

attune *vt* modulārī.

auburn *adj* flāvus.

auction *n* auctiō *f*; (*public*) hasta *f*; **hold an ~**
auctiōnem facere; **sell by ~** sub hastā
vēndere.

auctioneer *n* praecō *m*.

audacious *adj* audāx; protervus.

audaciously *adv* audācter, protervē.

audacity *n* audācia *f*, temeritās *f*.

audible *adj*: **be ~** exaudīrī posse.

audibly *adv* clārā vōce.

audience *n* audītōrēs *mpl*; (*interview*) aditus *m*;
give an ~ to admittere.

audit *vt* īnspicere ♦ *n* ratiōnum īnspectiō *f*.

auditorium *n* cavea *f*.

auditory *adj* audītōrius.

auger *n* terebra *f*.

augment *vt* augēre, adaugēre, ♦ *vi* crēscere,
augērī.

augmentation *n* incrēmentum *nt*.

augur *n* augur *m*; **~'s staff** lituus *m* ♦ *vi*
augurārī; (*fig*) portendere.

augural *adj* augurālis.

augurship *n* augurātus *m*.

augury *n* augurium *nt*, auspicium *nt*; ōmen *nt*;
take ~ies augurārī; **after taking ~ies**
augurātō.

august *adj* augustus.

August *n* mēnsis Augustus, Sextīlis; **of ~**
Sextīlis.

aunt *n* (*paternal*) amita *f*; (*maternal*) mātertera
f.

auspices *n* auspicium *nt*; **take ~** auspicārī;
after taking ~ auspicātō; **without taking ~**
inauspicātō.

auspicious *adj* faustus, fēlīx.

auspiciously *adv* fēlīciter, prosperē.

austere *adj* austērus, sevērus, dūrus.

austerely *adv* sevērē.

austerity *n* sevēritās *f*, dūritia *f*.

authentic *adj* vērus, certus.

authenticate *vt* recognōscere.

authenticity *n* auctōritās *f*, fidēs *f*.

author *n* auctor *m*, inventor *m*; scrīptor *m*.

authoress *n* auctor *f*.

authoritative *adj* fīdus; imperiōsus.

authority *n* auctōritās *f*, potestās *f*, iūs *nt*; (*MIL*)
imperium *nt*; (*LIT*) auctor *m*, scrīptor *m*;
enforce ~ iūs suum exsequī; **have great ~**
multum pollēre; **on Caesar's ~** auctōre
Caesare; **an ~ on** perītus (*gen*).

authorize *vt* potestātem facere (*dat*),
mandāre; (*law*) sancīre.

autobiography *n* dē vītā suā scrīptus liber *m*.

autocracy *n* imperium singulāre *nt*, tyrannis *f*.

autocrat *n* tyrannus *m*, dominus *m*.

autocratic *adj* imperiōsus.

autograph *n* manus *f*, chīrographum *nt*.

automatic *adj* necessārius.

automatically *adv* necessāriō.

autonomous *adj* līber.

autonomy *n* lībertās *f*.

Autumn *n* auctumnus *m*.

autumnal *adj* auctumnālis.

auxiliaries *npl* auxilia *ntpl*, auxiliāriī *mpl*.

auxiliary *adj* auxiliāris ♦ *n* adiūtor *m*; **~ forces**
auxilia *ntpl*; novae copiae *fpl*.

avail *vi* valēre ♦ *n* prōdesse (*dat*); **~ oneself of**
ūtī (*abl*) ♦ *n* ūsus *m*; **of no ~** frustrā.

available *adj* ad manum, in prōmptū.

avalanche *n* montis ruīna *f*.

avarice *n* avāritia *f*, cupīditās *f*.

avaricious *adj* avārus, cupidus.

avariciously *adv* avārē.

avenge *vt* ulcīscī (+ *abl*), vindicāre.

avenger *n* ultor *m*, vindex *m*.

avenue *n* xystus *m*; (*fig*) aditus *m*, iānua *f*.

aver *vt* adfirmāre, adsevērāre.

average *n* medium *nt*; **on the ~** ferē.

averse *adj* āversus (ab); **be ~ to** abhorrēre ab.

aversion *n* odium *nt*, fastīdium *nt*.

avert *vt* arcēre, dēpellere; (*by prayer*)
dēprecārī.

aviary n aviārium nt.
avid adj avidus.
avidity n aviditās f.
avidly adv avidē.
avoid vt vītāre, fugere, dēclīnāre; (battle) dētrectāre.
avoidance n fuga f, dēclīnātiō f.
avow vt fatērī, cōnfitērī.
avowal n cōnfessiō f.
avowed adj apertus.
avowedly adv apertē, palam.
await vt exspectāre; (future) manēre.
awake vt suscitāre, exsuscitare ♦ vi expergīscī ♦ adj vigil.
awaken vt exsuscitāre.
award vt tribuere; (law) adiūdicāre ♦ n (decision) arbitrium nt, iūdicium nt; (thing) praemium nt.
aware adj gnārus ♦ adj conscius (gen); be ~ scīre; become ~ of percipere.
away adv ā-, ab- (in cpd); be ~ abesse ab (abl); far ~ procul, longē; make ~ with dē mediō tollere.
awe n formīdō f, reverentia f, rēligiō f; stand in ~ of verērī; (gods) venerārī.
awe-struck adj stupidus.
awful adj terribilis, formīdolōsus, dīrus.
awfully adv formīdolōsē.
awhile adv aliquamdiū, aliquantisper, parumper.
awkward adj incallidus, inconcinnus; (to handle) inhabilis; (fig) molestus.
awkwardly adv incallidē, imperītē.
awkwardness n imperītia f, īnscītia f.
awl n sūbula f.
awning n vēlum nt.
awry adj prāvus, dissidēns.
axe n secūris f.
axiom n prōnūntiātum nt, sententia f.
axiomatic adj ēvidēns, manifestus.
axis n axis m.
axle n axis m.
aye adv semper; for ~ in aeternum.
azure adj caeruleus.

B, b

baa vi bālāre ♦ n bālātus m.
babble vi garrīre, blaterāre.
babbler n garrulus m.
babbling adj garrulus.
babe n īnfāns m/f.
babel n dissonae vōcēs fpl.
baboon n sīmia f.
baby n īnfāns m/f.
Bacchanalian adj Bacchicus.
Bacchante n Baccha f.

bachelor n caelebs m; (degree) baccalaureus m.
back n tergum nt; (animal) dorsum nt; (head) occipitium nt; at one's ~ ā tergō; behind one's ~ (fig) clam (acc); put one's ~ up stomachum movēre (dat); turn one's ~ on sē āvertere ab ♦ adj āversus, postīcus ♦ adv retrō, retrōrsum, re- (in cpds) ♦ vt obsecundāre (dat), adesse (dat); ~ water inhibēre rēmīs, inhibēre nāvem ♦ vi: ~ out of dētrectāre, dēfugere.
backbite vt obtrectāre (dat), maledīcere (dat).
backbone n spīna f.
backdoor n postīcum nt.
backer n fautor m.
background n recessus m, umbra f.
backing n fidēs f, favor m.
backslide vi dēscīscere.
backward adj āversus; (slow) tardus; (late) sērus.
backwardness n tardītās f, pigritia f.
backwards adv retrō, retrōrsum.
bacon n lārdum nt.
bad adj malus, prāvus, improbus, turpis; go ~ corrumpī; be ~ for obesse (dat), nocēre (dat).
badge n īnsigne nt, īnfula f.
badger n mēles f ♦ vt sollicitāre
badly adv male, prāvē, improbē, turpiter.
badness n prāvitās f, nēquitia f, improbitās f.
baffle vt ēlūdere, fallere, frustrārī.
bag n saccus m, folliculus m; hand~ mantica f.
bagatelle n nūgae fpl, floccus m.
baggage n impedīmenta ntpl, vāsa ntpl, sarcinae fpl; ~ train impedīmenta ntpl; without ~ expedītus.
bail n vadimōnium nt; (person) vas m; become ~ for spondēre prō (abl); accept ~ for vadārī; keep one's ~ vadimōnium obīre ♦ vt spondēre prō (abl).
bailiff n (POL) apparitor m; (private) vīlicus m.
bait n esca f, illecebra f ♦ vt lacessere.
bake vt coquere, torrēre.
bakehouse n pistrīna f.
baker n pistor m.
bakery n pistrīna f.
balance n (scales) lībra f, trutina f; (equilibrium) lībrāmentum nt; (money) reliqua ntpl ♦ vt lībrāre; (fig) compēnsāre; the account ~s ratiō cōnstat.
balance sheet n ratiō acceptī et expēnsī.
balcony n podium nt, Maeniānum nt.
bald adj calvus; (style) āridus, iēiūnus.
baldness n calvitium nt; (style) iēiūnitās f.
bale n fascis m; ~ out vt exhaurīre.
baleful adj fūnestus, perniciōsus, tristis.
balk n tignum nt ♦ vt frustrārī, dēcipere.
ball n globus m; (play) pila f; (wool) glomus nt; (dance) saltātiō f.
ballad n carmen nt.
ballast n saburra f.
ballet n saltātiō f.
ballot n suffrāgium nt.
ballot box n urna f.
balm n unguentum nt; (fig) sōlātium nt.
balmy adj lēnis, suāvis.

balsam *n* balsamum *nt*.
balustrade *n* cancellī *mpl*.
bamboozle *vt* cōnfundere.
ban *vt* interdīcere (*dat*), vetāre ♦ *n*
   interdictum *nt*.
banal *adj* trītus.
banana *n* ariēna *f*; (*tree*) pāla *f*.
band *n* vinculum *nt*, redimīculum *nt*; (*head*)
   īnfula *f*; (*men*) caterva *f*, manus *f*, grex *f* ♦ *vi*:
   ~ **together** cōnsociārī.
bandage *n* fascia *f*, īnfula *f* ♦ *vt* obligāre,
   adligāre.
bandbox *n*: **out of a** ~ (*fig*) dē capsulā.
bandeau *n* redimīculum *nt*.
bandit *n* latrō *m*.
bandy *vt* iactāre; ~ **words** altercārī ♦ *adj* vārus.
bane *n* venēnum *nt*, pestis *f*, perniciēs *f*.
baneful *adj* perniciōsus, pestifer.
bang *vt* pulsāre ♦ *n* fragor *m*.
bangle *n* armilla *f*.
banish *vt* pellere, expellere, ēicere; (*law*) aquā
   et ignī interdīcere (*dat*); (*temporarily*)
   relēgāre; (*feeling*) abstergēre.
banishment *n* (*act*) aquae et ignis interdictiō
   f; relēgātiō *f*; (*state*) exsilium *nt*, fuga *f*.
bank *n* (*earth*) agger *m*; (*river*) rīpa *f*; (*money*)
   argentāria *f*.
banker *n* argentārius *m*; (*public*) mēnsārius *m*.
bankrupt *adj*: **be** ~ solvendō nōn esse; **declare**
   oneself ~ bonam cōpiam ēiūrāre; **go** ~
   dēcoquere ♦ *n* dēcoctor *m*.
banner *n* vexillum *nt*.
banquet *n* cēna *f*, epulae *fpl*; convīvium *nt*;
   (*religious*) daps *f* ♦ *vi* epulārī.
banter *n* cavillātiō *f* ♦ *vi* cavillārī.
baptism *n* baptisma *nt*.
baptize *vt* baptizāre.
bar *n* (*door*) sera *f*; (*gate*) claustrum *nt*; (*metal*)
   later *m*; (*wood*) asser *m*; (*lever*) vectis *m*;
   (*obstacle*) impedīmentum *nt*; (*law-court*)
   cancellī *mpl*; (*barristers*) advocātī *mpl*;
   (*profession*) forum *nt*; **of the** ~ forēnsis;
   practise at the ~ causās agere.
bar *vt* (*door*) obserāre; (*way*) obstāre (*dat*),
   interclūdere, prohibēre; (*exception*)
   excipere, exclūdere.
barb *n* acūleus *m*, dēns *m*, hāmus *m*.
barbarian *n* barbarus *m* ♦ *adj* barbarus.
barbarism *n* barbaria *f*.
barbarity *n* saevitia *f*, ferōcia *f*, immānitās *f*,
   inhūmānitās *f*.
barbarous *adj* barbarus, saevus, immānis,
   inhūmānus.
barbarously *adv* barbarē, inhūmānē.
barbed *adj* hāmātus.
barber *n* tōnsor *m*; ~'**s shop** tōnstrīna *f*.
bard *n* vātēs *m/f*; (*Gallic*) bardus *m*.
bare *adj* nūdus; (*mere*) merus; **lay** ~ nūdāre,
   aperīre, dētegere ♦ *vt* nūdāre.
barefaced *adj* impudēns.
barefoot *adj* nūdis pedibus.
bare-headed *adj* capite aperto.
barely *adv* vix.

bargain *n* pactum *nt*, foedus *nt*; **make a** ~
   pacīscī; **make a bad** ~ male emere; **into the** ~
   grātiīs ♦ *vi* pacīscī.
barge *n* linter *f*.
bark *n* cortex *m*; (*dog*) lātrātus *m*; (*ship*) nāvis *f*,
   ratis *f* ♦ *vi* lātrāre.
barking *n* latrātus *m*.
barley *n* hordeum *nt*; **of** ~ hordeāceus.
barn *n* horreum *nt*.
barrack *vt* obstrepere (*dat*).
barracks *n* castra *ntpl*.
barrel *n* cūpa *f*; ligneum vās *nt*.
barren *adj* sterilis.
barrenness *n* sterilitās *f*.
barricade *n* claustrum *nt*, mūnīmentum *nt* ♦ *vt*
   obsaepīre, obstruere; ~ **off** intersaepīre.
barrier *n* impedīmentum *nt*; (*racecourse*)
   carcer *nt*.
barrister *n* advocātus *m*, patrōnus *m*,
   causidicus *m*.
barrow *n* ferculum *nt*; (*mound*) tumulus *m*.
barter *vt* mūtāre ♦ *vi* mercēs mūtāre ♦ *n*
   mūtātiō *f*, commercium *nt*.
base *adj* turpis, vīlis; (*birth*) humilis, ignōbilis;
   (*coin*) adulterīnus.
base *n* fundāmentum *nt*; (*statue*) basis *f*; (*hill*)
   rādīcēs *fpl*; (*MIL*) castra *ntpl*.
baseless *adj* falsus, inānis.
basely *adv* turpiter.
basement *n* basis *f*; (*storey*) īmum tabulātum
   nt.
baseness *n* turpitūdō *f*.
bashful *adj* pudīcus, verēcundus.
bashfulness *n* pudor *m*, verēcundia *f*.
basic *adj* prīmus.
basin *n* alveolus *m*, pelvis *f*; **wash**~ aquālis *m*.
basis *n* fundāmentum *nt*.
bask *vi* aprīcārī.
basket *n* corbis *f*, fiscus *m*; (*for bread*)
   canistrum *nt*; (*for wool*) quasillum *nt*.
basking *n* aprīcātiō *f*.
bas-relief *n* toreuma *nt*.
bass *adj* (*voice*) gravis.
bastard *adj* nothus.
bastion *n* prōpugnāculum *nt*.
bat *n* vespertīliō *m*; (*games*) clāva *f*.
batch *n* numerus *m*.
Bath *n* Aquae Sulis *fpl*.
bath *n* balneum *nt*; (*utensil*) lābrum *nt*, lavātiō *f*
   Turkish ~ Lacōnicum *nt*; **cold** ~ frīgidārium
   nt; **hot** ~ calidārium *nt*; ~ **superintendent**
   balneātor *m* ♦ *vt* lavāre.
bathe *vt* lavāre ♦ *vi* lavārī, perluī.
bathroom *n* balneāria *ntpl*.
baths *n* (*public* ~) balneae *fpl*.
batman *n* cālō *m*.
baton *n* virga *f*, scīpiō *m*.
battalion *n* cohors *f*.
batter *vt* quassāre, pulsāre, verberāre.
battering ram *n* ariēs *m*.
battery *n* (*assault*) vīs *f*.
battle *n* pugna *f*, proelium *nt*, certāmen *nt*; **a** ~
   was fought pugnatum est; **pitched** ~ iūstum

proelium; **line of** ~ aciēs *f*; **drawn** ~ anceps
proelium ♦ *vi* pugnāre, contendere; ~ **order**
aciēs *f*.
battle-axe *n* bipennis *f*.
battlefield, battle-line *n* aciēs *f*.
battlement *n* pinna *f*.
bawl *vt* vōciferārī, clāmitāre.
bay *n* (*sea*) sinus *m*; (*tree*) laurus *f*, laurea *f*; **of** ~
laureus; **at** ~ interclūsus ♦ *adj* (*colour*) spādīx
♦ *vi* (*dog*) lātrāre.
be *vi* esse; (*CIRCS*) versārī; (*condition*) sē habēre;
~ **at** adesse (*dat*); ~ **amongst** interesse (*dat*); ~
in inesse (*dat*); **consul-to-~** cōnsul
dēsignātus; **how are you?** quid agis?; **so ~ it**
estō; *see also* **absent, here** *etc.*
beach *n* lītus *nt*, acta *f* ♦ *vt* (*ship*) subdūcere.
beacon *n* ignis *m*.
bead *n* pilula *f*.
beadle *n* apparitor *m*.
beak *n* rōstrum *nt*.
beaked *adj* rōstrātus.
beaker *n* cantharus *m*, scyphus *m*.
beam *n* (*wood*) trabs *f*, tignum *nt*; (*balance*)
iugum *nt*; (*light*) radius *m*; (*ship*) latus *nt*; **on
the** ~ ā latere ♦ *vi* fulgēre; (*person*) adrīdēre.
beaming *adj* hilaris.
bean *n* faba *f*.
bear *n* ursus *m*, ursa *f*; **Great B~** septentriōnēs
mpl, Arctos *f*; **Little B~** septentriō minor *m*,
Cynosūra *f*; ~'**s** ursīnus ♦ *vt* (*carry*) ferre,
portāre; (*endure*) ferre, tolerāre, patī;
(*produce*) ferre, fundere; (*child*) parere; ~
down upon appropinquāre; ~ **off** ferre; ~ **out**
vt arguere; ~ **up** *vi*: ~ **up under** obsistere (*dat*),
sustinēre; ~ **upon** innītī (*dat*); (*refer*)
pertinēre ad; ~ **with** *vt fus* indulgēre (*dat*); ~
oneself sē gerere; **I cannot** ~ **to** addūcī nōn
possum ut.
bearable *adj* tolerābilis.
beard *n* barba *f* ♦ *vt* ultrō lacessere.
bearded *adj* barbātus.
beardless *adj* imberbis.
bearer *n* bāiulus *m*; (*letter*) tabellārius *m*; (*litter*)
lectīcārius *m*; (*news*) nūntius *m*.
bearing *n* (*person*) gestus *m*, vultus *m*;
(*direction*) regiō *f*; **have no** ~ **on** nihil
pertinēre ad; **I have lost my ~s** ubi sim
nesciō.
beast *n* bestia *f*; (*large*) bēlua *f*; (*wild*) fera *f*;
(*domestic*) pecus *f*.
beastliness *n* foeditās *f*, stuprum *nt*.
beastly *adj* foedus.
beast of burden *n* iūmentum *nt*.
beat *n* ictus *m*; (*heart*) palpitātiō *f*; (*music*)
percussiō *f*; (*oars, pulse*) pulsus *m*.
beat *vt* ferīre, percutere, pulsāre; (*the body in
grief*) plangere; (*punish*) caedere; (*whip*)
verberāre; (*conquer*) vincere, superāre ♦ *vi*
palpitāre, micāre; ~ **back** repellere; ~ **in**
perfringere; ~ **out** excutere; (*metal*)
extundere; ~ **a retreat** receptui canere; ~
about the bush circuitiōne ūtī; **be ~en**
vāpulāre; **dead** ~ cōnfectus.

beating *n* verbera *ntpl*; (*defeat*) clādes *f*;
(*time*) percussiō *f*; **get a** ~ vāpulāre.
beatitude *n* beātitūdō *f*, fēlīcitās *f*.
beau *n* nitidus homō *m*; (*lover*) amāns *m*.
beauteous *adj* pulcher, fōrmōsus.
beautiful *adj* pulcher, formōsus; (*looks*)
decōrus; (*scenery*) amoenus.
beautifully *adv* pulchrē.
beautify *vt* exōrnāre, decorāre.
beauty *n* fōrma *f*, pulchritūdō *f*, amoenitās *f*.
beaver *n* castor *m*, fiber *m*; (*helmet*) buccula *f*.
becalmed *adj* ventō dēstitūtus.
because *conj* quod, quia, quōniam (+ *indic*),
quippe quī; ~ **of** propter (*acc*).
beck *n* nūtus *m*.
beckon *vt* innuere, vocāre.
become *vi* fierī; **what will** ~ **of me?** quid me
fīet? ♦ *vt* decēre, convenīre in (*acc*).
becoming *adj* decēns, decōrus.
becomingly *adv* decōrē, convenienter.
bed *n* cubīle *nt*, lectus *m*, lectulus *m*; **go to** ~
cubitum īre; **make a** ~ lectum sternere; **be
~ridden** lectō tenērī; **camp** ~ grabātus *m*;
flower~ pulvīnus *m*; **marriage** ~ lectus
geniālis *m*; **river~** alveus *m*.
bedaub *vt* illinere, oblinere.
bedclothes *n* strāgula *ntpl*.
bedding *n* strāgula *ntpl*.
bedeck *vt* ōrnāre, exōrnāre.
bedew *vt* inrōrāre.
bedim *vt* obscūrāre.
bedpost *n* fulcrum *nt*.
bedraggled *adj* sordidus, madidus.
bedroom *n* cubiculum *nt*.
bedstead *n* sponda *f*.
bee *n* apis *f*; **queen** ~ rēx *m*.
beech *n* fāgus *f* ♦ *adj* fāginus.
beef *n* būbula *f*.
beehive *n* alvus *f*.
beekeeper *n* apiārius *m*.
beer *n* cervīsia *f*, fermentum *nt*.
beet *n* bēta *f*.
beetle *n* (*insect*) scarabaeus *m*; (*implement*)
fistūca *f*.
beetling *adj* imminēns, mināx.
befall *vi, vt* accidere, ēvenīre (*dat*); (*good*)
contingere (*dat*).
befit *vt* decēre, convenīre in (*acc*).
before *adv* ante, anteā, antehāc ♦ *prep* ante
(*acc*); (*place*) prō (*abl*); (*presence*) apud (*acc*),
cōram (*abl*) ♦ *conj* antequam, priusquam.
beforehand *adv* ante, anteā; prae (*in cpd*).
befoul *vt* inquināre, foedāre.
befriend *vt* favēre (*dat*), adiuvāre; (*in trouble*)
adesse (*dat*).
beg *vt* ōrāre, obsecrāre, precārī, poscere ab,
petere ab; ~ **for** petere ♦ *vi* mendīcāre.
beget *vt* gignere, prōcreāre, generāre.
begetter *n* generātor *m*, creātor *m*.
beggar *m* mendīcus *m*.
beggarly *adj* mendīcus, indigēns.
beggary *n* mendīcitās *f*, indigentia *f*.
begin *vi, vt* incipere, coepisse; (*speech*)

exōrdīrī; (*plan*) īnstituere, incohāre; (*time*)
inīre; ~ **with** incipere ab.
beginning n initium nt, prīncipium nt,
exōrdium nt, inceptiō f; (*learning*) rudīmenta
ntpl, elementa ntpl; (*origin*) orīgō f, fōns m; **at
the ~ of** spring ineunte vēre.
begone interj apage, tē āmovē.
begotten adj genitus, nātus.
begrudge vt invidēre (*dat*).
beguile vt dēcipere, fallere.
behalf n: **on ~ of** prō (*abl*); **on my ~** meō
nōmine.
behave vi sē gerere, sē praebēre (*with adj*);
well ~d bene mōrātus.
behaviour n mōrēs mpl.
behead vt dētruncāre, secūrī percutere.
behest n iūssum nt.
behind adv pōne, post, ā tergō ♦ prep post (*acc*),
pōne (*acc*).
behindhand adv sērō; **be ~** parum prōficere.
behold vt aspicere, cōnspicere, intuērī ♦ interj
ecce, ēn.
beholden adj obnoxius, obstrictus, obligātus.
behoof n ūsus m.
behove vt oportēre.
being n (*life*) animātiō f; (*nature*) nātūra f;
(*person*) homō m/f.
bejewelled adj gemmeus, gemmātus.
belabour vt verberāre, caedere.
belated adj sērus.
belch vi ructāre, ēructāre.
beldam n anus f.
beleaguer vt obsidēre, circumsedēre.
belie vt abhorrēre ab, repugnāre.
belief n fidēs f, opīniō f; (*opinion*) sententia f; **to
the best of my ~** ex animī meī sententiā; **past
~** incrēdibilis.
believe vt, vi (*thing*) crēdere; (*person*) crēdere
(*dat*); (*suppose*) crēdere, putāre, arbitrārī,
opīnārī; **~ in gods** deōs esse crēdere; **make ~**
simulāre.
believer n deōrum cultor m; Christiānus m.
belike adv fortasse.
belittle vt obtrectāre.
bell n tintinnābulum nt; (*public*) campāna f.
belle n fōrmōsa f, pulchra f.
belles-lettres n litterae fpl.
bellicose adj ferōx.
belligerent adj bellī particeps.
bellow vi rūdere, mūgīre ♦ n mūgītus m.
bellows n follis m.
belly n abdōmen nt, venter m; (*sail*) sinus m ♦ vi
tumēre.
belong vi esse (*gen*), proprium esse (*gen*),
inesse (*dat*); (*concern*) attinēre, pertinēre.
belongings n bona ntpl.
beloved adj cārus, dīlectus, grātus.
below adv īnfrā, subter ♦ adj īnferus ♦ prep
īnfrā (*acc*), sub (*abl, acc*).
belt n zōna f; (*sword*) balteus m.
bemoan vt dēplōrāre, lāmentārī.
bemused adj stupefactus, stupidus.
bench n subsellium nt; (*rowing*) trānstrum nt;

(*law*) iūdicēs mpl; **seat on the ~** iūdicātus m.
bend vt flectere, curvāre, inclīnāre; (*bow*)
intendere; (*course*) tendere, flectere; (*mind*)
intendere ♦ vi sē īnflectere; (*person*) sē
dēmittere; **~ back** reflectere; **~ down** vi
dēflectere; sē dēmittere ♦ n flexus m,
ānfrāctus m.
beneath adv subter ♦ prep sub (*acc or abl*).
benediction n bonae precēs fpl.
benedictory adj faustus.
benefaction n beneficium nt, dōnum nt.
benefactor n patrōnus m; **be a ~** bene merērī
(*dē*).
beneficence n beneficentia f, līberālitās f.
beneficent adj beneficus.
beneficial adj ūtilis, salūbris.
benefit n beneficium nt; (*derived*) fructus m;
have the ~ of fruī (*abl*) ♦ vt prōdesse (*dat*),
usuī esse (*dat*).
benevolence n benevolentia f, benignitās f.
benevolent adj benevolus, benignus.
benevolently adv benevolē, benignē.
benighted adj nocte oppressus; (*fig*) ignārus,
indoctus.
benign adj benignus, cōmis.
bent n (*mind*) inclīnātiō f, ingenium nt ♦ adj
curvus, flexus; (*mind*) attentus; **be ~ on**
studēre (*dat*).
benumb vt stupefacere.
benumbed adj stupefactus, torpidus; **be ~**
torpēre.
bequeath vt lēgāre.
bequest n lēgātum nt.
bereave vt orbāre, prīvāre.
bereavement n damnum nt.
bereft adj orbus, orbātus, prīvātus.
berry n bāca f.
berth n statiō f; **give a wide ~ to** dēvītāre.
beryl n bēryllus m.
beseech vt implōrāre, ōrāre, obsecrāre.
beset vt obsidēre, circumsedēre.
beside prep ad (*acc*), apud (*acc*); (*close*) iuxtā
(*acc*); **~ the point** nihil ad rem; **be ~ oneself**
nōn esse apud sē.
besides adv praetereā, accēdit quod; (*in
addition*) īnsuper ♦ prep praeter (*acc*).
besiege vt obsidēre, circumsedēre.
besieger n obsessor m.
besmear vt illinere.
besmirch vt maculāre.
besom n scōpae fpl.
besotted adj stupidus.
bespatter vt aspergere.
bespeak vt (*order*) imperāre; (*denote*)
significāre.
besprinkle vt aspergere.
best adj optimus; **the ~ part** māior pars ♦ n flōs
m, rōbur nt; **do one's ~** prō virīlī parte agere;
do one's ~ to operam dare ut; **have the ~ of it**
vincere; **make the ~ of (a situation)** aequō
animō accipere; **to the ~ of one's ability** prō
virīlī parte; **to the ~ of my knowledge** quod
sciam ♦ adv optimē.

bestial *adj* foedus.
bestir *vt* movēre; ~ **oneself** expergīscī.
bestow *vt* dōnāre, tribuere, dare, cōnferre.
bestride *vt* (*horse*) sedēre in (*abl*).
bet *n* pignus *nt* ♦ *vt* oppōnere ♦ *vi* pignore contendere.
betake *vt* cōnferre, recipere; ~ **o.s. sē** cōnferre.
bethink *vt*: ~ **oneself sē** colligere; ~ **oneself of** respicere.
betide *vi* accidere, ēvenīre.
betoken *vt* significāre; (*foretell*) portendere.
betray *vt* prōdere, trādere; (*feelings*) arguere; **without ~ing one's trust** salvā fidē.
betrayal *n* prōditiō *f*.
betrayer *n* prōditor *m*; (*informer*) index *m*.
betroth *vt* spondēre, dēspondēre.
betrothal *n* spōnsālia *ntpl*.
better *adj* melior; **it is ~ to** praestat (*infin*); **get the ~ of** vincere, superāre; **I am ~** (*in health*) melius est mihī; **I had ~ go** praestat īre; **get ~** convalēscere; **think ~ of** sententiam mūtāre dē ♦ *adv* melius ♦ *vt* corrigere; ~ **oneself** prōficere.
betterment *n* prōfectus *m*.
between *prep* inter (*acc*).
beverage *n* pōtiō *f*.
bevy *n* manus *f*, grex *f*.
bewail *vt* dēflēre, lāmentārī, dēplōrāre.
beware *vt* cavēre.
bewilder *vt* cōnfundere, perturbāre.
bewildered *adj* attonitus.
bewilderment *n* perturbātiō *f*, admīrātiō *f*.
bewitch *vt* fascināre; (*fig*) dēlēnīre.
beyond *adv* ultrā, suprā ♦ *prep* ultrā (*acc*), extrā (*acc*); (*motion*) trāns (*acc*); (*amount*) ultrā, suprā (*acc*); **go/pass ~** excēdere, ēgredī.
bezel *n* pāla *f*.
bias *n* inclīnātiō *f*; (*party*) favor *m* ♦ *vt* inclīnāre.
biassed *adj* prōpēnsior.
bibber *n* pōtor *m*, pōtātor *m*.
Bible *n* litterae sacrae *fpl*.
bibulous *adj* bibulus.
bicephalous *adj* biceps.
bicker *vi* altercārī, iūrgāre.
bid *vt* iubēre; (*guest*) vocāre, invītāre ♦ *vi* (*at auction*) licērī; ~ **for** licērī; ~ **good day** salvēre iubēre; **he ~s fair to make progress** spēs est eum prōfectūrum esse.
biddable *adj* docilis.
bidding *n* iussum *nt*; (*auction*) licitātiō *f*.
bide *vt* manēre, opperīrī.
biennial *adj* biennālis.
bier *n* ferculum *nt*.
bifurcate *vi* sē scindere.
bifurcation *n* (*road*) trivium *nt*.
big *adj* māgnus, grandis, amplus; (*with child*) gravida; **very ~** permāgnus; **talk ~** glōriārī.
bight *n* sinus *m*.
bigness *n* māgnitūdō *f*, amplitūdō *f*.
bigot *n* nimis obstinātus fautor *m*.

bigoted *adj* contumāx.
bigotry *n* contumācia *f*, nimia obstinātiō *f*.
bile *n* bīlis *f*, fel *nt*.
bilgewater *n* sentīna *f*.
bilk *vt* fraudāre.
bill *n* (*bird*) rōstrum *nt*; (*implement*) falx *f*; (*law*) rogātiō *f*, lēx *f*; (*money*) syngrapha *f*; (*notice*) libellus *m*, titulus *m*; **introduce a ~** populum rogāre, lēgem ferre; **carry a ~** lēgem perferre.
billet *n* hospitium *nt* ♦ *vt* in hospitia dīvidere.
billhook *n* falx *f*.
billow *n* fluctus *m*.
billowy *adj* undōsus.
billy goat *n* caper *m*.
bin *n* lacus *m*.
bind *vt* adligāre, dēligāre, vincīre; (*by oath*) adigere; (*by obligation*) obligāre, obstringere; (*wound*) obligāre; ~ **fast** dēvincīre; ~ **together** conligāre; ~ **over** *vt* vadārī.
binding *n* compāgēs *f* ♦ *adj* (*law*) ratus; **it is ~ on** oportet.
bindweed *n* convolvulus *m*.
biographer *n* vītae nārrātor *m*.
biography *n* vīta *f*.
bipartite *adj* bipartītus.
biped *n* bipēs *m*.
birch *n* bētula *f*; (*flogging*) virgae ulmeae *fpl*.
bird *n* avis *f*; ~**s of a feather** parēs cum paribus facillimē congregantur; **kill two ~s with one stone** ūnō saltū duōs aprōs capere, dē eādem fidēliā duōs parietēs dealbāre; ~**'s-eye view of** dēspectus in (*acc*).
birdcatcher *n* auceps *m*.
birdlime *n* viscum *nt*.
birth *n* (*act*) partus *m*; (*origin*) genus *nt*; **low ~** ignōbilitās *f*; **high ~** nōbilitās *f*; **by ~** nātū, ortū.
birthday *n* nātālis *m*.
birthday party *n* nātālicia *ntpl*.
birthplace *n* locus nātālis *m*; (*fig*) incūnābula *ntpl*.
birthright *n* patrimōnium *nt*.
bisect *vt* dīvidere.
bishop *n* epīscopus *m*.
bison *n* ūrus *m*.
bit *n* pars *f*; (*food*) frustum *nt*; (*broken off*) fragmentum *nt*; (*horse*) frēnum *nt*; ~ **by ~** minūtātim; **a ~** *adv* aliquantulum; **a ~ sad** tristior.
bitch *n* canis *f*.
bite *vt* mordēre; (*frost*) ūrere ♦ *n* morsus *m*; **with a ~** mordicus.
biting *adj* mordāx.
bitter *adj* (*taste*) acerbus, amārus; (*words*) asper.
bitterly *adv* acerbē, asperē.
bittern *n* būtiō *m*, ardea *f*.
bitterness *n* acerbitās *f*.
bitumen *n* bitūmen *nt*.
bivouac *n* excubiae *fpl* ♦ *vi* excubāre.
bizarre *adj* īnsolēns.

blab *vt, vi* garrīre, effūtīre.
black *adj* (*dull*) āter; (*glossy*) niger; (*dirt*) sordidus; (*eye*) līvidus; (*looks*) trux; ~ **and blue** līvidus; ♦ *n* ātrum *nt*, nigrum *nt*; **dressed in** ~ ātrātus; (*in mourning*) sordidātus.
blackberry *n* mōrum *nt*.
blackbird *n* merula *f*.
blacken *vt* nigrāre, nigrum reddere; (*character*) īnfāmāre, obtrectāre (*dat*).
blackguard *n* scelestus, scelerātus *m*.
blacking *n* ātrāmentum *nt*.
blacklist *n* prōscrīptiō *f*.
black magic *n* magicae artēs *fpl*.
blackmail *n* minae *fpl* ♦ *vt* minīs cōgere.
black mark *n* nota *f*.
blacksmith *n* faber *m*.
bladder *n* vēsīca *f*.
blade *n* (*grass*) herba *f*; (*oar*) palma *f*; (*sword*) lāmina *f*.
blame *vt* reprehendere, culpāre; **I am to ~** reus sum ♦ *n* reprehēnsiō *f*, culpa *f*.
blameless *adj* innocēns.
blamelessly *adv* innocenter.
blamelessness *n* innocentia *f*, integritās *f*.
blameworthy *adj* accūsābilis, nocēns.
blanch *vi* exalbēscere, pallēscere.
bland *adj* mītis, lēnis.
blandishment *n* blanditiae *fpl*.
blank *adj* vacuus, pūrus; (*look*) stolidus.
blanket *n* lōdīx *f*; **wet** ~ nimium sevērus.
blare *vi* canere, strīdere ♦ *n* clangor *m*, strīdor *m*.
blarney *n* lēnōcinium *nt*.
blaspheme *vi* maledīcere.
blasphemous *adj* maledicus, impius.
blasphemy *n* maledicta *ntpl*, impietās *f*.
blast *n* flātus *m*, īnflātus *m* ♦ *vt* disicere, discutere; (*crops*) rōbīgine adficere.
blatant *adj* raucus.
blaze *n* flamma *f*, ignis *m*, fulgor *m* ♦ *vi* flāgrāre, ārdēre, fulgēre; ~ **up** exārdēscere ♦ *vt*: ~ **abroad** pervulgāre.
blazon *vt* promulgāre.
bleach *vt* candidum reddere.
bleak *adj* dēsertus, tristis, inamoenus.
bleary-eyed *adj* lippus.
bleat *vi* bālāre ♦ *n* bālātus *m*.
bleed *vi* sanguinem fundere ♦ *vt* sanguinem mittere (*dat*); **my heart ~s** animus mihī dolet.
bleeding *adj* crūdus, sanguineus ♦ *n* sanguinis missiō *f*.
blemish *n* macula *f*, vitium *nt* ♦ *vt* maculāre, foedāre.
blend *vt* miscēre, immiscēre, admiscēre ♦ *n* coniūnctiō *f*.
bless *vt* beāre; laudāre; (ECCL) benedīcere; ~ **with** augēre (*abl*); ~ **my soul!** ita mē dī ament!
blessed *adj* beātus, fortūnātus; (*emperors*) dīvus.
blessing *n* (*thing*) commodum *nt*, bonum *nt*; (ECCL) benedictiō *f*.
blight *n* rōbīgō *f*, ūrēdō *f* ♦ *vt* rōbīgine adficere; (*fig*) nocēre (*dat*).

blind *adj* caecus; (*in one eye*) luscus; (*fig*) ignārus, stultus; (*alley*) nōn pervius; (*forces*) necessārius; **turn a ~ eye to** cōnīvēre in (*abl*) ♦ *vt* excaecāre, caecāre; (*fig*) occaecāre; (*with light*) praestringere.
blindfold *adj* capite obvolūtō.
blindly *adv* temerē.
blindness *n* caecitās *f*; (*fig*) temeritās *f*, īnsipientia *f*.
blink *vi* nictāre.
bliss *n* fēlīcitās *f*, laetitia *f*.
blissful *adj* fēlīx, beātus, laetus.
blissfully *adv* fēlīciter, beātē.
blister *n* pustula *f*.
blithe *adj* hilaris, laetus.
blithely *adv* hilare, laetē.
blizzard *n* hiems *f*.
bloated *adj* tumidus, turgidus.
blob *n* gutta *f*, particula *f*.
block *n* (*wood*) stīpes *m*, caudex *m*; (*stone*) massa *f*; (*houses*) īnsula *f*; ~ **letter** quadrāta littera; **stumbling** ~ offēnsiō *f*.
block *vt* claudere, obstruere, interclūdere; ~ **the way** obstāre.
blockade *n* obsidiō *f*; **raise a** ~ obsidiōnem solvere ♦ *vt* obsidēre, interclūdere.
blockhead *n* caudex *m*, bārō *m*, truncus *m*.
blockhouse *n* castellum *nt*.
blond *adj* flāvus.
blood *n* sanguis *m*; (*shed*) cruor *m*; (*murder*) caedēs *f*; (*kin*) genus *nt*; **let** ~ sanguinem mittere; **staunch** ~ sanguinem supprimere; **bad** ~ simultās *f*; **in cold** ~ cōnsultō; **own flesh and** ~ cōnsanguineus.
bloodless *adj* exsanguis; (*victory*) incruentus.
bloodshed *n* caedēs *f*.
bloodshot *adj* sanguineus.
bloodstained *adj* cruentus.
bloodsucker *n* hirūdō *f*.
bloodthirsty *adj* sanguinārius.
blood vessel *n* vēna *f*.
bloody *adj* cruentus.
bloom *n* flōs *m*; **in** ~ flōrēns ♦ *vi* flōrēre, flōrēscere, vigēre.
blossom *n* flōs *m* ♦ *vi* efflōrēscere, flōrēre.
blot *n* macula *f*; (*erasure*) litūra *f* ♦ *vt* maculāre; ~ **out** dēlēre, oblitterāre.
blotch *n* macula *f*.
blotched *adj* maculōsus.
blow *vt, vi* (*wind*) flāre; (*breath*) adflāre, anhēlāre; (*instrument*) canere; (*flower*) efflōrēscere; (*nose*) ēmungere; ~ **out** *vi* exstinguere; ~ **over** *vi* (*storm*) cadere; (*fig*) abīre; ~ **up** *vt* īnflāre; (*destroy*) discutere, disturbāre ♦ *n* ictus *m*; (*on the cheek*) alapa *f*; (*fig*) plāga *f*; (*misfortune*) calamitās *f*; **aim a ~ at** petere; **come to ~s** ad manūs venīre.
blowy *adj* ventōsus.
bludgeon *n* fustis *m*.
blue *adj* caeruleus; **black and** ~ līvidus; **true** ~ fīdissimus; ~ **blood** nōbilitās *f*.
bluff *n* rūpēs *f*, prōmunturium *nt* ♦ *adj*

inurbānus ♦ *vt* fallere, dēcipere, verba dare (*dat*), impōnere (*dat*).

blunder *vi* errāre, offendere ♦ *n* error *m*, errātum *nt*; (*in writing*) mendum *nt*.

blunt *adj* hebes; (*manners*) horridus, rūsticus, inurbānus; **be ~** hebēre ♦ *vt* hebetāre, obtundere, retundere.

bluntly *adv* līberius, plānē et apertē.

blur *n* macula *f* ♦ *vt* obscūrāre.

blurt *vt*: **~ out** ēmittere.

blush *vi* rubēre, ērubēscere ♦ *n* rubor *m*.

bluster *vi* dēclāmitāre, lātrāre.

boa *n* boa *f*.

Boadicea *n* Boudicca *f*.

boar *n* verrēs *m*; (*wild*) aper *m*.

board *n* tabula *f*; (*table*) mēnsa *f*; (*food*) vīctus *m*; (*committee*) concilium *nt*; (*judicial*) quaestiō *f*; (*of ten men*) decemvirī *mpl*; (*gaming*) abacus *m*, alveus *m*; **on ~** in nāvī; **go on ~** in nāvem cōnscendere; **go by the ~** intercidere, perīre; **above ~** sine fraude ♦ *vt* (*building*) contabulāre; (*ship*) cōnscendere; (*person*) vīctum praebēre (*dat*) ♦ *vi*: **~ with** dēvertere ad.

boarder *n* hospes *m*.

boast *vi* glōriārī, sē iactāre; **~ of** glōriārī dē (*abl*) ♦ *n* glōria *f*, glōriātiō *f*, iactātiō *f*.

boastful *adj* glōriōsus.

boastfully *adv* glōriōsē.

boasting *n* glōriātiō *f* ♦ *adj* glōriōsus.

boat *n* linter *f*, scapha *f*, cymba *f*; (*ship*) nāvis *f*; **be in the same ~** (*fig*) in eādem nāvī esse.

boatman *n* nauta *m*.

boatswain *n* hortātor *m*.

bobbin *n* fūsus *m*.

bode *vt* portendere, praesāgīre.

bodiless *adj* sine corpore.

bodily *adj* corporeus.

bodkin *n* acus *f*.

body *n* corpus *nt*; (*dead*) cadāver *nt*; (*small*) corpusculum *nt*; (*person*) homō *m/f*; (*of people*) globus *m*, numerus *m*; (*of troops*) manus *f*, caterva *f*; (*of cavalry*) turma *f*; (*of officials*) collēgium *nt*; (*heavenly*) astrum *nt*; **in a ~** ūniversī, frequentēs.

bodyguard *n* custōs *m*, stīpātōrēs *mpl*; (*emperor's*) praetōriānī *mpl*.

bog *n* palūs *f*.

bogey *n* mōnstrum *nt*.

boggle *vi* tergiversārī, haesitāre.

boggy *adj* palūster.

bogus *adj* falsus, fictus.

Bohemian *adj* līberior, solūtior, libīdinōsus.

boil *vt* coquere; (*liquid*) fervefacere; **~ down** dēcoquere ♦ *vi* fervēre, effervēscere; (*sea*) exaestuāre; (*passion*) exārdēscere, aestuāre; **~ over** effervēscere ♦ *n* (*MED*) fūrunculus *m*.

boiler *n* cortīna *f*.

boiling *adj* (*hot*) fervēns.

boisterous *adj* (*person*) turbulentus, vehemēns; (*sea*) turbidus, agitātus; (*weather*) procellōsus, violentus.

boisterously *adv* turbidē, turbulentē.

boisterousness *n* tumultus *m*, violentia *f*.

bold *adj* audāx, fortis, intrepidus; (*impudent*) impudēns, protervus; (*language*) līber; (*headland*) prōminēns; **make ~** audēre.

boldly *adv* audācter, fortiter, intrepidē; impudenter.

boldness *n* audācia *f*, cōnfīdentia *f*; impudentia *f*, petulantia *f*; (*speech*) lībertās *f*.

bolster *n* pulvīnus *m* ♦ *vt*: **~ up** sustinēre, cōnfirmāre.

bolt *n* (*door*) claustrum *nt*, pessulus *m*, sera *f*; (*missile*) tēlum *nt*, sagitta *f*; (*lightning*) fulmen *nt*; **make a ~ for it** sē prōripere, aufugere; **a ~ from the blue** rēs subita, rēs inopīnāta ♦ *vi* (*door*) obserāre, obdere.

bombard *vt* tormentīs verberāre; (*fig*) lacessere.

bombast *n* ampullae *fpl*.

bombastic *adj* tumidus, īnflātus; **be ~** ampullārī.

bond *n* vinculum *nt*, catēna *f*, compes *f*; (*of union*) cōpula *f*, iugum *nt*, nōdus *m*; (*document*) syngrapha *f*; (*agreement*) foedus *nt* ♦ *adj* servus, addictus.

bondage *n* servitūs *f*, famulātus *m*.

bone *n* os *nt*; (*fish*) spīna *f* ♦ *vt* exossāre.

boneless *adj* exos.

bonfire *n* ignis festus *m*.

bonhomie *n* festīvitās *f*.

bon mot *n* dictum *nt*, sententia *f*.

bonny *adj* pulcher, bellus.

bony *adj* osseus.

boo *vt* explōdere.

book *n* liber *m*; (*small*) libellus *m*; (*scroll*) volūmen *nt*; (*modern form*) cōdex *m*; **~s** (*COMM*) rationēs *fpl*, tabulae *fpl*; **bring to ~** in iūdicium vocāre.

bookbinder *n* glūtinātor *m*.

bookcase *n* librārium *nt*, pēgma *nt*.

bookish *adj* litterārum studiōsus.

book-keeper *n* āctuārius *m*.

bookseller *n* librārius *m*, bibliopōla *m*.

bookshop *n* bibliothēca *f*, librāria taberna *f*.

bookworm *n* tinea *f*.

boom *n* (*spar*) longurius *m*; (*harbour*) ōbex *m/f* ♦ *vi* resonāre.

boon *n* bonum *nt*, beneficium *nt*, dōnum *nt* ♦ *adj* festīvus; **~ companion** sodālis *m*, compōtor *m*.

boor *n* agrestis *m*, rūsticus *m*.

boorish *adj* agrestis, rūsticus, inurbānus.

boorishly *adv* rūsticē.

boost *vt* efferre; (*wares*) vēnditāre.

boot *n* calceus *m*; (*MIL*) caliga *f*; (*rustic*) pērō *m*; (*tragic*) cothurnus *m* ♦ *vi* prōdesse; **to ~** īnsuper, praetereā.

booted *adj* calceātus, caligātus.

booth *n* taberna *f*.

bootless *adj* inūtilis, vānus.

bootlessly *adv* frustrā.

booty *n* praeda *f*, spolia *ntpl*.

border *n* ōra *f*, margō *f*; (*country*) fīnis *m*; (*dress*) limbus *m* ♦ *vt* praetexere, margināre;

fīnīre ♦ *vi*: ~ **on** adiacēre (*dat*), imminēre (*dat*), attingere; (*fig*) fīnitimum esse (*dat*).
bordering *adj* fīnitimus.
bore *vt* perforāre, perterebrāre; (*person*) obtundere, fatīgāre; ~ **out** exterebrāre ♦ *n* terebra *f*; (*hole*) forāmen *nt*; (*person*) homō importūnus *m*, ineptus *m*.
boredom *n* lassitūdō *f*.
borer *n* terebra *f*.
born *adj* nātus; **be** ~ nāscī.
borough *n* mūnicipium *nt*.
borrow *vt* mūtuārī.
borrowed *adj* mūtuus; (*fig*) aliēnus.
borrowing *n* mūtuātiō *f*; (*to pay a debt*) versūra *f*.
bosky *adj* nemorōsus.
bosom *n* sinus *m*; (*fig*) gremium *nt*; ~ **friend** familiāris *m/f*, sodālis *m*; **be a** ~ **friend of** ab latere esse (*gen*).
boss *n* bulla *f*; (*shield*) umbō *m*.
botanist *n* herbārius *m*.
botany *n* herbāria *f*.
botch *vt* male sarcīre, male gerere.
both *pron* ambō, uterque (*gen* **utriusque**, *each of two*) ♦ *adv*: ~ ... **and** et ... et, cum ... tum.
bother *n* negōtium *nt* ♦ *vt* vexāre, molestus esse (*dat*) ♦ *vi* operam dare.
bothersome *adj* molestus.
bottle *n* lagoena *f*, amphora *f* ♦ *vt* (*wine*) diffundere.
bottom *n* fundus *m*; (*ground*) solum *nt*; (*ship*) carīna *f*; **the** ~ **of** īmus; **be at the** ~ **of** (*cause*) auctōrem esse; **go to the** ~ pessum īre, perīre; **send to the** ~ pessum dare; **from the** ~ funditus, ab īnfimō.
bottomless *adj* profundus, fundō carēns.
bottommost *adj* īnfimus.
bough *n* rāmus *m*.
boulder *n* saxum *nt*.
boulevard *n* platea *f*.
bounce *vi* salīre, resultāre.
bound *n* fīnis *m*, modus *m*, terminus *m*; (*leap*) saltus *m*; **set ~s to** modum facere (*dat*) ♦ *vt* fīnīre, dēfīnīre, termināre ♦ *vi* salīre, saltāre ♦ *adj* adligātus, obligātus, obstrictus; **be ~ to** (*duty*) dēbēre; **it is ~ to happen** necesse est ēveniat; **be ~ for** tendere in (*acc*); **be storm~** tempestāte tenērī.
boundaries *npl* fīnes *mpl*.
boundary *n* fīnis *m*; (*of fields*) terminus *m*; (*fortified*) līmes *m*; ~ **stone** terminus *m*.
boundless *adj* immēnsus, īnfīnītus.
boundlessness *n* īnfīnitās *f*, immēnsum *nt*.
bounteous *adj see* **bountiful**.
bounteously *adv* largē, līberāliter, cōpiōsē.
bountiful *adj* largus, līberālis, benignus.
bounty *n* largitās *f*, līberālitās *f*; (*store*) cōpia *f*.
bouquet *n* corollārium *nt*; (*of wine*) flōs *m*.
bourn *n* fīnis *m*.
bout *n* certāmen *nt*; (*drinking*) cōmissātiō *f*.
bovine *adj* būbulus; (*fig*) stolidus.
bow *n* arcus *m*; (*ship*) prōra *f*; (*courtesy*) salūtātiō *f*; **have two strings to one's** ~

duplicī spē ūtī; **rain~** arcus *m* ♦ *vi* flectere, inclīnāre ♦ *vi* caput dēmittere.
bowels *n* alvus *f*; (*fig*) viscera *ntpl*.
bower *n* umbrāculum *nt*, trichila *f*.
bowl *n* (*cooking*) catīnus *m*; (*drinking*) calix *m*; (*mixing wine*) crātēra *f*; (*ball*) pila *f* ♦ *vt* volvere; ~ **over** prōruere.
bow-legged *adj* valgus.
bowler *n* (*game*) dator *m*.
bowstring *n* nervus *m*.
box *n* arca *f*, capsa *f*; (*for clothes*) cista *f*; (*for medicine*) pyxis *f*; (*for perfume*) alabaster *m*; (*tree*) buxus *f*; (*wood*) buxum *nt*; (*blow on ears*) alapa *f* ♦ *vt* inclūdere; ~ **the ears of** alapam dūcere (*dat*), colaphōs īnfringere (*dat*) ♦ *vi* (*fight*) pugnīs certāre.
boxer *n* pugil *m*.
boxing *n* pugilātiō *f*.
boxing glove *n* caestus *m*.
boy *n* puer *m*; **become a** ~ **again** repuerāscere.
boycott *vt* repudiāre.
boyhood *n* pueritia *f*; **from** ~ ā puerō.
boyish *adj* puerīlis.
boyishly *adv* puerīliter.
brace *n* (*building*) fībula *f*; (*strap*) fascia *f*; (*pair*) pār *nt* ♦ *vt* adligāre; (*strengthen*) firmāre.
bracelet *n* armilla *f*.
bracing *adj* (*air*) salūbris.
bracken *n* filix *f*.
bracket *n* uncus *m*.
brackish *adj* amārus.
bradawl *n* terebra *f*.
brag *vi* glōriārī, sē iactāre.
braggart *n* glōriōsus *m*.
braid *vt* nectere.
brain *n* cerebrum *nt*; ingenium *nt*.
brainless *adj* sōcors, stultus.
brainy *adj* ingeniōsus.
brake *n* (*wood*) dūmētum *nt*; (*on wheel*) sufflāmen *nt*.
bramble *n* rubus *m*.
bran *n* furfur *nt*.
branch *n* rāmus *m*; (*kind*) genus *nt* ♦ *vi*: ~ **out** rāmōs porrigere.
branching *adj* rāmōsus.
brand *n* (*fire*) torris *m*, fax *f*; (*mark*) nota *f*; (*sword*) ēnsis *m*; (*variety*) genus *nt* ♦ *vt* (*mark*) inūrere; (*stigma*) notāre; ~ **new** recēns.
brandish *vt* vibrāre.
brass *n* orichalcum *nt*.
bravado *n* ferōcitās *f*; **out of** ~ per speciem ferōcitātis.
brave *adj* fortis, ācer ♦ *vt* adīre, patī.
bravely *adv* fortiter, ācriter.
bravery *n* fortitūdō *f*, virtūs *f*.
bravo *interj* bene, euge, macte.
brawl *n* rixa *f*, iūrgium *nt* ♦ *vi* rixārī.
brawn *n* lacertī *mpl*.
brawny *adj* lacertōsus, rōbūstus.
bray *vi* rūdere.
brazen *adj* aēneus; (*fig*) impudēns.
brazier *n* foculus *m*.
breach *n* (*in wall*) ruīna *f*; (*of friendship*)

dissēnsiō *f* ♦ *vt* perfringere; ~ **of trust** mala fidēs; **commit a** ~ **of promise** prōmissīs nōn stāre.
breach of the peace *n* iūrgium *nt*, tumultus *m*.
bread *n* pānis *m*.
breadth *n* lātitūdō *f*; **in** ~ **in** lātitūdinem (*acc*).
break *vt* frangere, perfringere; ~ **down** *vt* īnfringere, dīruere; ~ **in** *vt* (*animal*) domāre; ~ **into pieces** dīrumpere; ~ **off** *vt* abrumpere, dēfringere; (*action*) dīrimere; ~ **open** effringere, solvere; ~ **through** *vt fus* interrumpere; ~ **up** *vt* dissolvere, interrumpere; ~ **one's word** fidem fallere, violāre; **without** ~**ing the law** salvīs lēgibus ♦ *vi* rumpī, frangī; (*day*) illūcēscere; (*strength*) dēficere; ~ **off** *vi* dēsinere; ~ **into** intrāre; ~ **out** *vi* ērumpere; (*sore*) recrūdēscere; (*trouble*) exārdēscere; ~ **up** *vi* dīlābī, dissolvī; (*meeting*) dīmittī; ~ **through** *vi* inrumpere; ~ **with** dissidēre ab ♦ *n* intermissiō *f*, intervallum *nt*.
breakable *adj* fragilis.
breakage *n* frāctum *nt*.
breakdown *n* (*activity*) mora *f*; (*health*) dēbilitās *f*.
breaker *n* fluctus *m*.
breakfast *n* iēntāculum *nt*, prandium *nt* ♦ *vi* ientāre, prandēre.
breakwater *n* mōlēs *f*.
bream *n* sparulus *m*.
breast *n* pectus *nt*; (*woman's*) mamma *f*; **make a clean** ~ **of** cōnfitērī.
breastplate *n* lōrīca *f*.
breastwork *n* lōrīca *f*, pluteus *m*.
breath *n* spīritus *m*, anima *f*; (*bad*) hālitus *m*; (*quick*) anhēlitus *m*; (*of wind*) aura *f*, adflātus *m*; **below one's** ~ mussitāns; **catch one's** ~ obstipēscere; **hold one's** ~ animam comprimere, continēre; **take a** ~ spīritum dūcere; **take one's** ~ **away** exanimāre; **waste one's** ~ operam perdere; **out of** ~ exanimātus.
breathable *adj* spīrābilis.
breathe *vt, vi* spīrāre, respīrāre; (*quickly*) anhēlāre; ~ **again** respīrāre; ~ **in** *vt, vi* spīritum dūcere; ~ **out** *vt, vi* exspīrāre, exhālāre; ~ **upon** īnspīrāre (*dat*), adflāre (*dat*); ~ **one's last** animam agere, efflāre.
breathing *n* hālitus *m*, respīrātiō *f*.
breathing space *n* respīrātiō *f*.
breathless *adj* exanimātus.
breeches *n* brācae *fpl*.
breed *n* genus *nt* ♦ *vt* generāre, prōcreāre; (*raise*) ēducāre, alere; (*fig*) adferre, efficere; **well-bred** generōsus.
breeder *n* (*animal*) mātrix *f*; (*man*) generātor *m*; (*fig*) nūtrix *f*.
breeding *n* (*act*) fētūra *f*; (*manners*) mōrēs *mpl*; **good** ~ hūmānitās *f*.
breeze *n* aura *f*, flātus *m*.
breezy *adj* ventōsus; (*manner*) hilaris.
brevity *n* brevitās *f*.
brew *vt* coquere ♦ *vi* (*fig*) parārī, imminēre.

bribe *vt* corrumpere ♦ *vi* largīrī ♦ *n* pecūnia *f*, mercēs *f*.
briber *n* corruptor *m*, largītor *m*.
bribery *n* ambitus *m*, largītiō *f*.
brick *n* later *m* ♦ *adj* latericius.
brickwork *n* latericium *nt*.
bridal *adj* nūptiālis; (*bed*) geniālis ♦ *n* nūptiae *fpl*.
bride *n* nūpta *f*.
bridegroom *m* marītus *m*.
bridge *n* pōns *m* ♦ *vt* pontem impōnere (*dat*).
bridle *n* frēnum *nt* ♦ *vt* frēnāre, īnfrēnāre.
brief *adj* brevis; **to be** ~ nē longum sit, nē multa.
briefly *adv* breviter, paucīs verbīs.
briefness *n* brevitās *f*.
brier *n* veprēs *m*, sentis *m*.
brig *n* liburna *f*.
brigade *n* legiō *f*; (*cavalry*) turma *f*.
brigadier *n* lēgātus *m*.
brigand *n* latrō *m*, praedō *m*.
brigandage *n* latrōcinium *nt*.
bright *adj* clārus, lūculentus; (*sky*) serēnus; (*intellect*) ingeniōsus; (*manner*) hilaris, laetus; **be** ~ lūcēre, splendēre.
brighten *vt* illūstrāre; laetificāre ♦ *vi* lūcēscere; (*person*) hilarem fierī.
brightly *adv* clārē.
brightness *n* fulgor *m*, candor *m*; (*sky*) serēnitās *f*.
brilliance *n* splendor *m*, fulgor *m*; (*style*) nitor *m*, lūmen *nt*, īnsignia *ntpl*.
brilliant *adj* clārus, illūstris, splendidus; (*fig*) īnsignis, praeclārus, lūculentus.
brilliantly *adv* splendidē, praeclārē, lūculentē.
brim *n* lābrum *nt*, margō *f*; **fill to the** ~ explēre.
brimstone *n* sulfur *nt*.
brindled *adj* varius.
brine *n* salsāmentum *nt*.
bring *vt* ferre; (*person*) dūcere; (*charge*) intendere; (*to a place*) adferre, addūcere, advehere, dēferre; (*to a destination*) perdūcere; (*to a worse state*) redigere; ~ **about** *vt* efficere; ~ **before** dēferre ad, referre ad; ~ **back** *vt* (*thing*) referre; (*person*) redūcere; ~ **down** *vt* dēdūcere, dēferre; ~ **forth** (*from store*) dēprōmere; (*child*) parere; (*crops*) ferre, ēdere; ~ **forward** *vt* (*for discussion*) iactāre, iacere; (*reason*) adferre; ~ **home** (*bride*) dēdūcere; (*in triumph*) dēportāre; ~ **home to** pervincere; ~ **in** *vt* invehere, indūcere, intrōdūcere; (*import*) importāre; (*revenue*) reddere; ~ **off** *vt* (*success*) reportāre; ~ **on** īnferre, importāre; (*stage*) indūcere; ~ **out** *vt* efferre; (*book*) ēdere; (*play*) dare; (*talent*) ēlicere; ~ **over** perdūcere, trādūcere; ~ **to bear** adferre; ~ **to light** nūdāre, dētegere; ~ **to pass** perficere, peragere; ~ **to shore** ad litus appellere; ~ **together** contrahere, cōgere; (*enemies*) conciliāre; ~ **up** *vt* (*child*) ēducāre, tollere; (*troops*) admovēre; (*topic*) prōferre; ~ **upon oneself** sibī cōnscīscere, sibī contrahere.

brink n ōra f, margō f.
briny adj salsus.
brisk adj alacer, vegetus, ācer.
briskly adv ācriter.
briskness n alacritās f.
bristle n sēta f ♦ vi horrēre, horrēscere.
bristly adj horridus, hirsūtus.
Britain n Brittania f.
Britons n Brittani mpl.
brittle adj fragilis.
broach vt (topic) in medium prōferre.
broad adj lātus; (accent) lātus; (joke)
  inurbānus; (daylight) multus.
broadcast vt dissēmināre.
broaden vt dīlātāre.
broadly adv lātē.
broadsword n gladius m.
brocade n Attalica ntpl.
brochure n libellus m.
brogue n pērō m.
broil n rixa f, iūrgium nt ♦ vt torrēre.
broiling adj torridus.
broken adj frāctus; (fig) cōnfectus; (speech)
  īnfrāctus.
broken-hearted adj dolōre cōnfectus.
broker n īnstitor m.
bronze n aes nt ♦ adj aēneus, aerātus.
brooch n fībula f.
brood n fētus m; (fig) gēns f ♦ vi incubāre (dat);
  (fig) incubāre (dat), fovēre; ~ over meditārī.
brook n rīvus m ♦ vt ferre, patī.
brooklet n rīvulus m.
broom n (plant) genista f; (brush) scōpae fpl.
broth n iūs nt.
brother n frāter m; (full) germānus m; ~ and
  sister marītus mpl.
brotherhood n frāternitās f.
brother-in-law n lēvir m, uxōris frāter m,
  sorōris marītus m.
brotherly adj frāternus.
brow n frōns f; (eye) supercilium nt; (hill)
  dorsum nt.
browbeat vt obiūrgāre, exagitāre.
brown adj fulvus, spādīx; (skin) adūstus.
browse vi pāscī, dēpāscī.
bruise vt atterere, frangere, contundere ♦ n
  vulnus nt.
bruit vt pervulgāre.
brunt n vīs f; bear the ~ of exhaurīre.
brush n pēniculus m; (artist's) pēnicillus m;
  (quarrel) rixa f ♦ vt verrere, dētergēre; (teeth)
  dēfricāre; ~ aside vt aspernārī, neglegere; ~
  up vt (fig) excolere.
brushwood n virgulta ntpl; (for cutting)
  sarmenta ntpl.
brusque adj parum cōmis.
brutal adj atrōx, saevus, inhūmānus.
brutality n atrōcitās f, saevitia f.
brutally adv atrōciter, inhūmānē.
brute n bēlua f, bestia f.
brutish adj stolidus.
bubble n bulla f ♦ vi bullāre; ~ over
  effervēscere; ~ up scatēre.

buccaneer n praedō m, pīrāta m.
buck n cervus m ♦ vi exsultāre.
bucket n situla f, fidēlia f.
buckle n fībula f ♦ vt fībulā nectere; ~ to
  accingī.
buckler n parma f.
buckram n carbasus m.
bucolic adj agrestis.
bucolics n būcolica ntpl.
bud n gemma f, flōsculus m ♦ vi gemmāre.
budge vi movērī, cēdere.
budget n pūblicae pecūniae ratiō f ♦ vi: ~ for
  prōvidēre (dat).
buff adj lūteus.
buffalo n ūrus m.
buffet n (blow) alapa f; (fig) plāga f; (sideboard)
  abacus m ♦ vt iactāre, tundere.
buffoon n scurra m, balatrō m.
buffoonery n scurrilitās f.
bug n cīmex m.
bugbear n terricula ntpl, terror m.
bugle n būcina f.
bugler n būcinātor m.
build vt aedificāre, struere; (bridge) facere;
  (road) mūnīre; ~ on vt (add) adstruere;
  (hopes) pōnere; ~ on sand in aquā
  fundāmenta pōnere; ~ up vt exstruere; (to
  block) inaedificāre; (knowledge) īnstruere; ~
  castles in the air spem inānem pāscere ♦ n
  statūra f.
builder n aedificātor m, structor m.
building n (act) aedificātiō f; (structure)
  aedificium nt.
bulb n bulbus m.
bulge vi tumēre, tumēscere, prōminēre ♦ vi
  tuberculum nt; (of land) locus prōminēns m.
bulk n māgnitūdō f, amplitūdō f; (mass) mōlēs
  f; (most) plērīque, māior pars.
bulky adj amplus, grandis.
bull n taurus m; ~'s taurīnus; take the ~ by the
  horns rem fortiter adgredī.
bulldog n Molossus m.
bullet n glāns f.
bulletin n libellus m.
bullion n aurum īnfectum nt, argentum
  īnfectum nt.
bullock n iuvencus m.
bully n obiūrgātor m, patruus m ♦ vt obiūrgāre,
  exagitāre.
bulrush n scirpus m.
bulwark n prōpugnāculum nt; (fig) arx f.
bump n (swelling) tuber nt, tuberculum nt;
  (knock) ictus m ♦ vi: ~ against offendere.
bumper n plēnum pōculum nt ♦ adj plēnus,
  māximus.
bumpkin n rūsticus m.
bumptious adj adrogāns.
bunch n fasciculus m; (of berries) racēmus m.
bundle n fascis m; (of hay) manipulus m ♦ vt
  obligāre.
bung n obtūrāmentum nt ♦ vt obtūrāre.
bungle vt male gerere.
bunk n lectus m, lectulus m.

buoy n cortex m ♦ vt sublevāre.
buoyancy n levitās f.
buoyant adj levis; (fig) hilaris.
bur n lappa f.
burden n onus nt; **beast of** ~ iūmentum nt ♦ vt
onerāre; **be a** ~ oneri esse.
burdensome adj gravis, molestus.
bureau n scrīnium nt.
burgeon vi gemmāre.
burgess n mūniceps m.
burgh n mūnicipium nt.
burgher n mūniceps m.
burglar n fūr m.
burglary n fūrtum nt.
burial n fūnes nt, humātiō f, sepultūra f.
burin n caelum nt.
burlesque n imitātiō f ♦ vt per iocum imitārī.
burly adj crassus.
burn vt incendere, ūrere; (to ashes) cremāre ♦
vi ārdēre, flāgrāre; ~ **up** ambūrere,
combūrere, exūrere; **be ~ed down**
dēflāgrāre; ~ **out** vi exstinguī; ~ **the midnight
oil** lūcubrāre ♦ n (MED) ambūstum nt.
burning adj igneus.
burnish vt polīre.
burrow n cuniculus m ♦ vi dēfodere.
burst vt rumpere, dīrumpere ♦ vi rumpī,
dīrumpī; ~ **in** inrumpere; ~ **into tears** in
lacrimās effundī; ~ **open** refringere; ~ **out**
ērumpere, prōrumpere; ~ **out laughing**
cachinnum tollere; ~ **through** perrumpere
per (acc); ~ **upon** offerrī (dat), invādere ♦ n
ēruptiō f; (noise) fragor m; ~ **of applause**
clāmōrēs mpl; **with a** ~ **of speed** citātō gradū,
citātō equō.
bury vt sepelīre, humare; (ceremony) efferre;
(hiding) condere; (things) dēfodere; (fig)
obruere; ~ **the hatchet** amīcitiam
reconciliāre.
bush n frutex m; dūmus m; **beat about the** ~
circuitiōne ūtī.
bushel n medimnus m.
bushy adj fruticōsus; (thick) dēnsus; (hair)
hirsūtus.
busily adv strēnuē, impigrē.
business n negōtium nt; (occupation) ars f,
quaestus m; (public life) forum nt; (matter) rēs
f; **it is your** ~ tuum est; **make it one's** ~ **to** id
agere ut; **you have no** ~ **to** nōn tē decet
(infin); **mind one's own** ~ suum negōtium
agere; ~ **days** diēs fāstī mpl.
businessman negōtiātor m.
buskin n cothurnus m.
bust n imāgō f.
bustle vi trepidāre, festīnāre; ~ **about**
discurrere.
busy adj negōtiōsus, occupātus; (active)
operōsus, impiger, strēnuus; ~ **in** occupātus
(abl); ~ **on** intentus (dat); **keep** ~ vt exercēre;
~ **oneself with** pertractāre, studēre (dat).
busybody n: **be a** ~ aliēnīs negōtīs sē
immiscēre.
but conj sed, at; (2nd place) autem, tamen ♦ adv

modo ♦ prep praeter (acc); **nothing** ~ nihil
nisī; ~ **that,** ~ **what** quīn; **not** ~ **what**
nihilōminus.
butcher n lanius m ♦ vt trucīdāre.
butcher's shop n laniēna f.
butchery n strāgēs f, occīdiō f.
butler n prōmus m.
butt n (cask) cadus m; (of ridicule) lūdibrium nt
♦ vi arietāre; ~ **in** interpellāre.
butter n būtyrum nt.
butterfly n pāpiliō m.
buttock n clūnis m/f.
button n bulla f.
buttonhole vt (fig) dētinēre, prēnsāre.
buttress n antērides fpl ♦ vt fulcīre.
buxom adj nitidus.
buy vt emere; ~ **provisions** obsōnāre; ~ **back** vt
redimere; ~ **off** vt redimere; ~ **up** vt coemere.
buyer n emptor m; (at auctions) manceps m.
buzz n strīdor m, susurrus m ♦ vi strīdere,
susurrāre.
buzzard n būteō m.
by prep (near) ad (acc), apud (acc); prope (acc);
(along) secundum (acc); (past) praeter (acc);
(agent) a, ab (abl); (instrument) abl; (time) ante
(acc); (oath) per (acc) ♦ adv prope, iuxtā; ~
and ~ mox; **be** ~ adesse, adstāre; ~ **force of
arms** vī et armīs; ~ **land and sea** terrī
marique.
bygone adj praeteritus.
bystander n arbiter m; pl circumstantēs mpl.
byway n dēverticulum nt, trāmes m, sēmita f.
byword n prōverbium nt.

C, c

cabal n factiō f.
cabbage n brassica f, caulis m.
cabin n casa f; (ship) cubiculum nt.
cabinet n armārium nt.
cable n fūnis m; (anchor) ancorāle nt.
cache n thēsaurus m.
cachet n nota f.
cackle vi strepere n ♦ strepitus m, clangor m.
cacophonous adj dissonus.
cacophony n vōcēs dissonae fpl.
cadaverous adj cadāverōsus.
cadence n clausula numerōsa f, numerus m.
cadet n (son) nātū minor; (MIL) contubernālis
m.
cage n cavea f ♦ vt inclūdere.
caitiff n ignāvus m.
cajole vt blandīrī, dēlēnīre.
cake n placenta f.
calamitous adj exitiōsus, calamitōsus.

calamity n calamitās f, malum nt; (*MIL*) clādēs f.
calculate vt ratiōnem dūcere, inīre.
calculation n ratiō f.
calculator n ratiōcinātor m.
calendar n fāstī mpl.
calends n Kalendae fpl.
calf n (*animal*) vitulus m, vitula f; (*leg*) sūra f.
calibre n (*fig*) ingenium nt, auctōritās f.
call vt vocāre; (*name*) appellāre, nōmināre; (*aloud*) clāmāre; (*to a place*) advocāre, convocāre; ~ **aside** sēvocāre; ~ **down** (*curse*) dētestārī; ~ **for** vt fus postulāre, requīrere; ~ **forth** ēvocāre, excīre, ēlicere; ~ **in** vt advocāre; ~ **together** convocāre; ~ **on** vt fus (*for help*) implōrāre; (*visit*) salūtāre; ~ **off** vt āvocāre, revocāre; ~ **out** vi exclāmāre; ~ **up** vt (*dead*) excitāre, ēlicere; (*MIL*) ēvocāre ♦ n vōx f, clāmor m; (*summons*) invītātiō f; (*visit*) salūtātiō f.
caller n salūtātor m.
calling n ars f, quaestus m.
callous adj dūrus; **become** ~ obdūrēscere.
callow adj rudis.
calm adj tranquillus, placidus; (*mind*) aequus ♦ vi: ~ **down** (*fig*) dēfervēscere ♦ vt sēdāre, tranquillāre ♦ n tranquillitās f; **dead** ~ (*at sea*) malacia f.
calmly adv tranquillē, placidē; aequō animō.
calumniate vt obtrectāre, crīminārī; (*falsely*) calumniārī.
calumniator n obtrectātor m.
calumny n opprobria ntpl, obtrectātiō f.
calve vi parere.
cambric n linteum nt.
camel n camēlus m.
camouflage n dissimulātiō f ♦ vt dissimulāre.
camp n castra ntpl; **summer** ~ aestīva ntpl; **winter** ~ hīberna ntpl; **in** ~ sub pellibus; **pitch** ~ castra pōnere; **strike** ~ castra movēre ♦ adj castrēnsis ♦ vi tendere.
campaign n stīpendium nt, bellum nt; (*rapid*) expedītiō f ♦ vi bellum gerere, stīpendium merēre.
campaigner n mīles m; **old** ~ veterānus m; (*fig*) veterātor m.
campbed n grabātus m.
camp followers n lixae mpl.
can n hirnea f.
can vi posse (+ infin); (*know how*) scīre.
canaille n vulgus nt, plebs f.
canal n fossa nāvigābilis f, eurīpus m.
cancel vt indūcere, abrogāre.
cancellation n (*writing*) litūra f; (*law*) abrogātiō f.
cancer n cancer m; (*fig*) carcinōma nt, ulcus nt.
cancerous adj (*fig*) ulcerōsus.
candelabrum n candēlābrum nt.
candid adj ingenuus, apertus, līber, simplex.
candidate n petītor m; **be a** ~ **for** petere.
candidature n petītiō f.
candidly adv ingenuē.
candle n candēla f.
candlestick n candēlābrum nt.

candour n ingenuitās f, simplicitās f, lībertās f.
cane n (*reed*) harundō f; (*for walking, punishing*) virga f ♦ vt verberāre.
canine adj canīnus.
canister n capsula f.
canker n (*plants*) rōbigō f; (*fig*) aerūgō f, carcinōma nt ♦ vt corrumpere.
Cannae n Cannae fpl.
cannibal n anthrōpophagus m.
cannon n tormentum nt.
cannot nōn posse, nequīre; **I** ~ **help but** ... facere nōn possum quīn ... (*subj*), nōn possum nōn ... (*infin*).
canny adj prūdens, prōvidus, cautus, circumspectus.
canoe n linter f.
canon n nōrma f, rēgula f; (*ECCL*) canonicus m.
canopy n aulaeum nt.
cant n fūcus m, fūcāta verba ntpl ♦ vt oblīquāre.
cantankerous adj importūnus.
cantankerousness n importūnitās f.
canter n lēnis cursus m ♦ vi lēniter currere.
canticle n canticum nt.
canto n carmen nt.
canton n pāgus m.
canvas n carbasus m, linteum nt ♦ adj carbaseus; **under** ~ sub pellibus.
canvass vi ambīre ♦ vt prēnsāre, circumīre.
canvassing n ambitus m, ambitiō f.
cap n pilleus m; (*priest's*) galērus m, apex m.
capability n facultās f, potestās f.
capable adj capāx, doctus, perītus.
capably adv bene, doctē.
capacious adj capāx, amplus.
capacity n capācitās f, amplitūdō f; (*mind*) ingenium nt.
caparison n ephippium nt.
cape n (*GEOG*) prōmunturium nt; (*dress*) chlamys f.
caper vi saltāre; (*animal*) lascīvīre ♦ n saltus m.
capering n lascivia f.
capital adj (*chief*) praecipuus, prīnceps; (*excellent*) ēgregius; (*law*) capitālis; **convict of a** ~ **offence** capitis damnāre ♦ n (*town*) caput nt; (*money*) sors f; (*class*) negōtiātōrēs mpl; **make** ~ **out of** ūtī (*abl*).
capitalist n faenerātor m.
capital punishment n capitis supplicum nt.
capitation tax n capitum exāctiō f.
Capitol n Capitolium nt.
capitulate vi sē dēdere; **troops who have** ~**d** dēditīciī mpl.
capitulation n dēditiō f.
capon n capō m.
caprice n libīdō f, incōnstantia f.
capricious adj incōnstāns, levis.
capriciously adv incōnstanter, leviter.
capriciousness n incōnstantia f, libīdō f.
capsize vt ēvertere ♦ vi ēvertī.
captain m dux m, praefectus m, prīnceps;

(*MIL*) centuriō *m*; (*naval*) nāvarchus *m*; (*of merchant ship*) magister *m* ♦ *vt* praeesse (*dat*), dūcere.
captaincy *n* centuriātus *m*.
caption *n* caput *nt*.
captious *adj* mōrōsus; (*question*) captiōsus.
captiously *adv* mōrōsē.
captiousness *n* mōrōsitās *f*.
captivate *vt* capere, dēlēnīre, adlicere.
captive *n* captīvus *m*.
captivity *n* captīvitās *f*, vincula *ntpl*.
captor *n* (*by storm*) expugnātor *m*; victor *m*.
capture *n* (*by storm*) expugnātiō *f* ♦ *vt* capere.
car *n* currus *m*.
caravan *n* commeātus *m*.
carbuncle *n* (*MED*) fūrunculus *m*; (*stone*) acaustus *m*.
carcass *n* cadāver *nt*.
card *n* charta *f*; (*ticket*) tessera *f*; (*wool*) pecten *nt* ♦ *vt* pectere.
cardamom *n* amōmum *nt*.
cardinal *adj* praecipuus; ~ **point** cardō *m* ♦ *n* (*ECCL*) cardinālis.
care *n* cūra *f*; (*anxiety*) sollicitūdō *f*; (*attention*) dīligentia *f*; (*charge*) custōdia *f*; **take** ~ cavēre; **take** ~ **of** cūrāre ♦ *vi* cūrāre; (*like*) amāre; **I don't** ~ **nīl moror; I couldn't care less about** . . . floccī nōn faciō . . . , pendō; **I don't** ~ **about** mittō, nihil moror; **for all I** ~ **per mē.**
career *n* curriculum *nt*; (*POL*) cursus honōrum; (*completed*) rēs gestae *fpl* ♦ *vi* ruere, volāre.
carefree *adj* sēcūrus.
careful *adj* (*cautious*) cautus; (*attentive*) dīligēns, attentus; (*work*) accūrātus.
carefully *adv* cautē; dīligenter, attentē; accūrātē.
careless *adj* incautus, neglegēns.
carelessly *adv* incautē, neglegenter.
carelessness *n* incūria *f*, neglegentia *f*.
caress *vt* fovēre, blandīrī ♦ *n* blandīmentum *nt*, amplexus *m*.
cargo *n* onus *nt*.
caricature *n* (*picture*) gryllus *m*; (*fig*) imāgō dētorta *f* ♦ *vt* dētorquēre.
carmine *n* coccum *m* ♦ *adj* coccineus.
carnage *n* strāgēs *f*, caedēs *f*.
carnal *adj* corporeus; (*pleasure*) libīdinōsus.
carnival *n* fēriae *fpl*.
carol *n* carmen *nt* ♦ *vi* cantāre.
carouse *vi* perpōtāre, cōmissārī ♦ *n* cōmissātiō *f*.
carp *vi* obtrectāre; ~ **at** carpere, rōdere.
carpenter *n* faber *m*, lignārius *m*.
carpet *n* tapēte *nt*.
carriage *n* (*conveying*) vectūra *f*; (*vehicle*) vehiculum *nt*; (*for journeys*) raeda *f*, petorritum *nt*; (*for town*) carpentum *nt*, pīlentum *nt*; (*deportment*) gestus *m*, incessus *m*; ~ **and pair** bīgae *fpl*; ~ **and four** quadrīgae *fpl*.
carrier *n* vector *m*; (*porter*) bāiulus *m*; **letter** ~ tabellārius *m*.

carrion *n* cadāver *nt*.
carrot *n* carōta *f*.
carry *vt* portāre, vehere, ferre, gerere; (*law*) perferre; (*by assault*) expugnāre; ~ **away** auferre, āvehere; (*by force*) rapere; (*with emotion*) efferre; ~ **all before one** ēvincere; ~ **along** (*building*) dūcere; ~ **back** reportāre; revehere, referre; ~ **down** dēportāre, dēvehere; ~ **in** invehere, intrōferre; ~ **off** auferre, asportāre, āvehere; (*by force*) abripere, ēripere; (*prize*) ferre, reportāre; (*success*) bene gerere; ~ **on** *vt* gerere; (*profession*) exercēre; ~ **out** *vi* efferre, ēgerere, ēvehere; (*task*) exsequī; ~ **out an undertaking** rem suscipere; ~ **over** trānsportāre, trānsferre; ~ **the day** vincere; ~ **one's point** pervincere; ~ **through** perferre; ~ **to** adferre, advehere; ~ **up** pergere; (*flirt*) lascīvīre.
Carthage *n* Carthāgō, Carthāginis *f*.
Carthaginian *adj* Carthāginiēnsis; Pūnicus; **the** ~**s** Poenī *mpl*.
carthorse *n* iūmentum *nt*.
carve *vt* sculpere; (*on surface*) caelāre; (*meat*) secāre; ~ **out** exsculpere.
carver *n* caelātor *m*.
carving *n* caelātūra *f*.
cascade *n* cataracta *m*.
case *n* (*instance*) exemplum *nt*, rēs *f*; (*legal*) āctiō *f*, līs *f*, causa *f*; (*plight*) tempus *nt*; (*GRAM*) cāsus *m*; (*receptacle*) thēca *f*, involucrum *nt*; **in** ~ **sī**; (*to prevent*) nē; **in any** ~ utut est rēs; **in that** ~ **ergō; such is the** ~ **sic sē rēs habet; civil** ~ **causa prīvāta; criminal** ~ **causa pūblica; win a** ~ **causam, lītem obtinēre; lose a** ~ **causam, lītem āmittere.**
casement *n* fenestra *f*.
cash *n* nummī *mpl*; (*ready*) numerātum *nt*, praesēns pecūnia *f*; **pay** ~ **ex arcā absolvere, repraesentāre.**
cash box *n* arca *f*.
cashier *n* dispēnsātor *m* ♦ *vt* (*MIL*) exauctōrāre.
cash payment *n* repraesentātiō *f*.
cask *n* cūpa *f*.
casket *n* arcula *f*, pyxis *f*.
casque *n* galea *f*, cassis *f*.
cast *vt* iacere; (*account*) inīre; (*eyes*) conicere; (*lots*) conicere; (*covering*) exuere; (*metal*) fundere; ~ **ashore** ēicere; ~ **away** prōicere; ~ **down** dēicere; (*humble*) abicere; ~ **in one's teeth** exprobrāre; ~ **lots** sortīrī; ~ **off** *vi* abicere, exuere; ~ **out** prōicere, ēicere, pellere ♦ *n* iactus *m*; (*moulding*) typus *m*, fōrma *f*; **with a** ~ **in the eye** paetus *m*.
castanet *n* crotalum *nt*.
castaway *n* ēiectus *m*.
caste *n* ōrdō *m*.
castigate *vt* animadvertere, castīgāre.
castigation *n* animadversiō *f*, castīgātiō *f*.

castle *n* arx *f*, castellum *nt*.
castrate *vt* castrāre.
casual *adj* fortuītus; (*person*) neglegēns.
casually *adv* temerē.
casualty *n* īnfortūnium *nt*; *pl*: **casualties** occīsī *mpl*.
casuist *n* sophistēs *m*.
cat *n* fēlēs *f*.
cataclysm *n* dīluvium *nt*, ruīna *f*.
catalogue *n* index *m*.
catapult *n* catapulta *f*, ballista *f*.
cataract *n* cataracta *f*.
catarrh *n* gravēdō *f*; **liable to ~** gravēdinōsus.
catastrophe *n* calamitās *f*, ruīna *f*.
catastrophic *adj* calamitōsus, exitiōsus.
catch *vt* capere, dēprehendere, excipere; (*disease*) contrahere, nancīscī; (*fire*) concipere, comprehendere; (*meaning*) intellegere; **~ at** captāre; **~ out** *vi* dēprehendere; **~ up with** adsequī; **~ birds** aucupārī; **~ fish** piscārī ♦ *n* bolus *m*.
categorical *adj* (*statement*) plānus.
categorically *adv* sine exceptiōne.
category *n* numerus *m*, genus *nt*.
cater *vi* obsōnāre.
cateran *n* praedātor *m*.
caterer *n* obsōnātor *m*.
caterpillar *n* ērūca *f*.
caterwaul *vi* ululāre.
catgut *n* chorda *f*.
catharsis *n* pūrgātiō *f*.
cathedral *n* aedēs *f*.
catholic *adj* generālis.
catkin *n* iūlus *m*.
cattle *n* (*collectively*) pecus *nt*; (*singly*) pecus *f*; (*for plough*) armenta *ntpl*.
cattle breeder *n* pecuārius *m*.
cattle market *n* forum boārium *nt*.
cattle thief *n* abāctor *m*.
cauldron *n* cortīna *f*.
cause *n* causa *f*; (*person*) auctor *m*; (*law*) causa *f*; (*party*) partēs *fpl*; **give ~ for** māteriam dare (*gen*); **make common ~ with** facere cum, stāre ab; **plead a ~** causam dīcere; **in the ~ of** prō (*abl*); **without ~** iniūriā ♦ *vt* efficere ut (+ *subj*), facere, facessere (*with* ut); cūrāre (*with gerundive*); (*feelings*) movēre, inicere, ciēre.
causeless *adj* vānus, sine causā.
causeway *n* agger *m*.
caustic *adj* (*fig*) mordāx.
cauterize *vt* adūrere.
caution *n* (*wariness*) cautiō *f*, prūdentia *f*; (*warning*) monitum *nt* ♦ *vt* monēre, admonēre.
cautious *adj* cautus, prōvidus, prūdens.
cautiously *adv* cautē, prūdenter.
cavalcade *n* pompa *f*.
cavalier *n* eques *m* ♦ *adj* adrogāns.
cavalierly *adv* adroganter.
cavalry *n* equitēs *mpl*, equitātus *m* ♦ *adj* equester; **troop of ~** turma *f*.
cavalryman *n* eques *m*.

cave *n* spēlunca *f*, caverna *f*; antrum *nt*; **~ in** *vi* concidere, conlābī.
cavern *n* spēlunca *f*, caverna *f*.
cavil *vi* cavillārī; **~ at** carpere, cavillārī ♦ *n* captiō *f*, cavillātiō *f*.
cavity *n* caverna *f*, cavum *nt*.
cavort *vi* saltāre.
caw *vi* cornīcārī.
cease *vi* dēsinere, dēsistere.
ceaseless *adj* adsiduus, perpetuus.
ceaselessly *adv* adsiduē, perpetuō.
cedar *n* cedrus *f* ♦ *adj* cedrinus.
cede *vt* cēdere, concēdere.
ceiling *n* tēctum *nt*; (*panelled*) lacūnar *nt*, laqueārium *nt*.
celebrate *vt* (*rite*) celebrāre, agitāre; (*in crowds*) frequentāre; (*person, theme*) laudāre, celebrāre, dīcere.
celebrated *adj* praeclārus, illūstris, nōtus; **the ~** ille.
celebration *n* celebrātiō *f*; (*rite*) sollemne *nt*.
celebrity *n* celebritās *f*, fāma *f*; (*person*) vir illūstris.
celerity *n* celeritās *f*, vēlōcitās *f*.
celery *n* apium *nt*.
celestial *adj* caelestis; dīvīnus.
celibacy *n* caelibātus *m*.
celibate *n* caelebs *m*.
cell *n* cella *f*.
cellar *n* cella *f*.
cement *n* ferrūmen *nt* ♦ *vt* coagmentāre.
cemetery *n* sepulchrētum *nt*.
cenotaph *n* tumulus honōrārius, tumulus inānis *m*.
censer *n* tūribulum *nt*, acerra *f*.
censor *n* cēnsor *m* ♦ *vt* cēnsēre.
censorious *adj* cēnsōrius, obtrectātor.
censorship *n* cēnsūra *f*.
censure *n* reprehēnsiō *f*, animadversiō *f*; (*censor's*) nota *f* ♦ *vt* reprehendere, animadvertere, increpāre; notāre.
census *n* cēnsus *m*.
cent *n*: **one per ~** centēsima *f*; **12 per ~ per annum** centēsima *f* (*ie monthly*).
centaur *n* centaurus *m*.
centaury *n* (*plant*) centaurēum *nt*.
centenarian *n* centum annōs nātus *m*, nāta *f*.
centenary *n* centēsimus annus *m*.
centesimal *adj* centēsimus.
central *adj* medius.
centralize *vt* in ūnum locum cōnferre; (*power*) ad ūnum dēferre.
centre *n* centrum *nt*, media pars *f*; **the ~ of** medius.
centuple *adj* centuplex.
centurion *n* centuriō *m*.
century *n* (*MIL*) centuria *f*; (*time*) saeculum *nt*.
ceramic *adj* fictilis.
cereal *n* frūmentum *nt*.
ceremonial *adj* sollemnis ♦ *n* rītus *m*.
ceremonious *adj* (*rite*) sollemnis; (*person*) officiōsus.
ceremoniously *adv* sollemniter; officiōsē.

ceremony n caerimōnia f, rītus m; (politeness) officium nt; (pomp) apparātus m; **master of ceremonies** dēsignātor m.

cerise n coccum nt ♦ adj coccineus.

certain adj (sure) certus; (future) explōrātus; **a ~** quīdam, quaedam, quoddam; **be ~** (know) prō certō scīre/habēre.

certainly adv certē, certō, sine dubiō; (yes) ita, māximē; (concessive) quidem.

certainty n (thing) certum nt; (belief) fidēs f; **for a ~** prō certō, explōrātē; **regard as a ~** prō explōrātō habēre.

certificate n testimōnium nt.

certify vt (writing) recognōscere; (fact) adfirmāre, testificārī.

cessation n fīnis m; (from labour) quiēs f; (temporary) intermissiō f; (of hostilities) indutiae fpl.

chafe vt ūrere; (fig) inrītāre ♦ vi stomachārī.

chaff n palea f ♦ vt lūdere.

chaffinch n fringilla f.

chagrin n dolor m, stomachus m ♦ vt stomachum facere (dat), sollicitāre.

chain n catēna f; (for neck) torquis m; (sequence) seriēs f; **~s** pl vincula ntpl ♦ vt vincīre.

chair n sella f; (of office) sella curūlis f; (sedan) sella gestātōria f, lectīca f; (teacher's) cathedra f.

chairman n (at meeting) magister m; (of debate) disceptātor m.

chalet n casa f.

chalice n calix m.

chalk n crēta f.

chalky adj crētōsus.

challenge n prōvocātiō f ♦ vt prōvocāre, lacessere; (statement) in dubium vocāre; (fig) invītāre, dēposcere.

challenger n prōvocātor m.

chamber n conclāve nt; (bed) cubiculum nt; (bridal) thalamus m; (parliament) cūria f.

chamberlain n cubiculārius m.

chambermaid n serva f, ancilla f.

chameleon n chamaeleōn f.

chamois n rūpicapra f.

champ vt mandere.

champion n prōpugnātor m, patrōnus m; (winner) victor m ♦ vt favēre (dat), adesse (dat).

chance n fors f, fortūna f, cāsus m; (opportunity) occāsiō f; potestās f, facultās f; (prospect) spēs f; **game of ~** ālea f; **by ~** cāsū, fortuītō; **have an eye to the main ~** forō ūtī; **on the ~ of** sī forte ♦ adj fortuītus ♦ vi accidere, ēvenīre; **it chanced that ...** accidit ut ... (+ subj); **~ upon** vt fus incidere in, invenīre ♦ vt periclitārī.

chancel n absis f.

chancellor n cancellārius m.

chancy adj dubius, perīculōsus.

chandelier n candēlābrum nt.

chandler n candēlārum propōla m.

change n mūtātiō f, commūtātiō f, permūtātiō f; (POL) rēs novae fpl; (alternation) vicēs fpl, vicissitūdō f; (money) nummī minōrēs mpl ♦ vt mūtāre, commūtāre, permūtāre ♦ vi mūtārī; **~ hands** abaliēnārī; **~ places** ōrdinem permūtāre, inter sē loca permūtāre.

changeable adj incōnstāns, mūtābilis.

changeableness n incōnstantia f, mūtābilitās f.

changeful adj varius.

changeless adj cōnstāns, immūtābilis.

changeling n subditus m.

channel n canālis m; (sea) fretum nt; (irrigation) rīvus m; (groove) sulcus m.

chant vt cantāre, canere ♦ n cantus m.

chaos n chaos nt; (fig) perturbātiō f.

chaotic adj perturbātus.

chap n rīma f; (man) homō m.

chapel n sacellum nt, aedicula f.

chaplain n diāconus m.

chaplet n corōna f, sertum nt.

chaps n (animal) mālae fpl.

chapter n caput nt.

char vt ambūrere.

character n (inborn) indolēs f, ingenium nt, nātūra f; (moral) mōrēs mpl; (reputation) existimātiō f; (kind) genus nt; (mark) signum nt, littera f; (THEAT) persōna f, partēs fpl; **sustain a ~** persōnam gerere; **I know his ~** sciō quālis sit.

characteristic adj proprius ♦ n proprium nt.

characteristically adv suō mōre.

characterize vt dēscrībere; proprium esse (gen).

charcoal n carbō m.

charge n (law) accūsātiō f, crīmen nt; (MIL) impetus m, dēcursus m; (cost) impēnsa f; (task) mandātum nt, onus nt; (trust) cūra f, tūtēla f; **bring a ~ against** lītem intendere (dat); **entertain a ~ against** nōmen recipere (gen); **give in ~** in custōdiam trādere; **put in ~ of** praeficere (acc, dat); **be in ~ of** praeesse (dat) ♦ vt (law) accūsāre; (falsely) īnsimulāre; (MIL) incurrere in (acc), signa īnferre in (acc), impetum facere in (acc); (duty) mandāre; (cost) ferre, īnferre; (empty space) complēre; (trust) committere; (speech) hortārī; **~ to the account of** expēnsum ferre (dat).

chargeable adj obnoxius.

charger n (dish) lānx f; (horse) equus m.

charily adv cautē, parcē.

chariot n currus m; (races) quadrīgae fpl; (war) essedum nt.

charioteer n aurīga m; (war) essedārius m.

charitable adj benevolus, benignus.

charitably adv benevolē, benignē.

charity n amor m, benignitās f; līberālitās f.

charlatan n planus m.

charm n (spell) carmen nt; (amulet) bulla f; (fig) blanditiae fpl, dulcēdō f, illecebra f; (beauty) venus f, lepōs m ♦ vt (magic) fascināre; (delight) dēlectāre, dēlēnīre.

charming adj venustus, lepidus; (speech) blandus; (scenery) amoenus.

charmingly *adv* venustē, blandē.
chart *n* tabula *f*.
charter *n* diplōma *nt* ♦ *vt* condūcere.
chary *adj* (*cautious*) cautus; (*sparing*) parcus.
chase *vt* fugāre; (*hunt*) vēnārī; (*pursue*) persequī, īnsequī; (*engrave*) caelāre; ~ **away** pellere, abigere ♦ *n* vēnātus *m*, vēnātiō *f*; (*pursuit*) īnsectātiō *f*.
chaser *n* (*in metal*) caelātor *m*.
chasm *n* hiātus *m*.
chaste *adj* castus, pudīcus; (*style*) pūrus.
chasten *vt* castīgāre, corrigere.
chastener *n* castīgātor *m*, corrēctor *m*.
chastise *vt* castīgāre, animadvertere.
chastisement *n* castīgātiō *f*, poena *f*.
chastity *n* castitās *f*, pudīcitia *f*.
chat *vi* colloquī, sermōcinārī ♦ *n* sermō *m*, colloquium *nt*.
chatelaine *n* domina *f*.
chattels *n* bona *ntpl*, rēs mancipī.
chatter *vi* garrīre; (*teeth*) crepitāre ♦ *n* garrulitās *f*, loquācitās *f*.
chatterbox *n* lingulāca *m/f*.
chatterer *n* garrulus *m*, loquāx *m*.
chattering *adj* garrulus, loquāx ♦ *n* garrulitās *f*, loquācitās *f*; (*teeth*) crepitus *m*.
cheap *adj* vīlis; **hold** ~ parvī aestimāre; **buy** ~ bene emere.
cheapen *vt* pretium minuere (*gen*).
cheaply *adv* vīliter, parvō pretiō.
cheapness *n* vīlitās *f*.
cheat *vt* dēcipere, fraudāre, dēfraudāre, frustrārī ♦ *n* fraudātor *m*.
check *vt* cohibēre, coercēre; (*movement*) impedīre, inhibēre; (*rebuke*) reprehendere; (*test*) probāre ♦ *n* impedīmentum *nt*, mora *f*; (*MIL*) offēnsiō *f*; (*rebuke*) reprehēnsiō *f*; (*test*) probātiō *f*; (*ticket*) tessera *f*.
checkmate *n* incitae calcēs *fpl* ♦ *vt* ad incitās redigere.
cheek *n* gena *f*; (*impudence*) ōs *nt*; ~ **s** *pl* mālae *fpl*; **how have you the ~ to say?** quō ōre dīcis?
cheekbone *n* maxilla *f*.
cheeky *adj* impudēns.
cheep *vi* pīpilāre.
cheer *vt* hilarāre, exhilarāre; hortārī; (*in sorrow*) cōnsōlārī ♦ *vi* clāmāre, adclāmāre; ~ **up!** bonō animō es! ♦ *n* (*shout*) clāmor *m*, plausus *m*; (*food*) hospitium *nt*; (*mind*) animus *m*.
cheerful *adj* alacer, hilaris, laetus.
cheerfully *adv* hilare, laetē.
cheerfulness *n* hilaritās *f*.
cheerily *adv* hilare.
cheerless *adj* tristis, maestus.
cheerlessly *adv* triste.
cheery *adj* hilaris.
cheese *n* cāseus *m*.
chef *n* coquus *m*.
cheque *n* perscrīptiō *f*, syngrapha *f*.
chequer *vt* variāre.
chequered *adj* varius; (*mosaic*) tessellātus.
cherish *vt* fovēre, colere.

cherry *n* (*fruit*) cerasum *nt*; (*tree*) cerasus *f*.
chess *n* latrunculī *mpl*.
chessboard *n* abacus *m*.
chest *n* (*box*) arca *f*, arcula *f*; (*body*) pectus *nt*; ~ **of drawers** armārium *nt*.
chestnut *n* castanea *f* ♦ *adj* (*colour*) spādīx.
chevalier *n* eques *m*.
chevaux-de-frise *n* ēricius *m*.
chew *vt* mandere.
chic *adj* expolītus, concinnus.
chicanery *n* (*law*) calumnia *f*; (*fig*) dolus *m*.
chick *n* pullus *m*.
chicken *n* pullus *m*; **don't count your ~s before they're hatched** adhūc tua messis in herbā est.
chicken-hearted *adj* timidus, ignāvus.
chick-pea *n* cicer *nt*.
chide *vt* reprehendere, increpāre, obiūrgāre.
chief *n* prīnceps *m*, dux *m* ♦ *adj* praecipuus, prīmus; ~ **point** caput *nt*.
chief command *n* summa imperiī.
chiefly *adv* in prīmīs, praesertim, potissimum.
chieftain *n* prīnceps *m*, rēgulus *m*.
chilblain *n* perniō *m*.
child *n* īnfāns *m/f*; puer *m*, puerulus *m*, puella *f*; fīlius *m*, fīlia *f*; ~ **'s play** lūdus *m*.
childbed *n* puerperium *nt*.
childbirth *n* partus *m*.
childhood *n* pueritia *f*; **from** ~ ā puerō.
childish *adj* puerīlis.
childishly *adv* puerīliter.
childless *adj* orbus.
childlessness *n* orbitās *f*.
childlike *adj* puerīlis.
children *npl* līberī *mpl*.
chill *n* frīgus *nt* ♦ *adj* frīgidus ♦ *vt* refrīgerāre.
chilly *adj* frīgidus, frīgidior.
chime *vi* sonāre, canere; ~ **in** interpellāre; (*fig*) cōnsonāre ♦ *n* sonus *m*.
chimera *n* chimaera *f*; (*fig*) somnium *nt*.
chimerical *adj* commentīcius.
chimney *n* camīnus *m*.
chin *n* mentum *nt*.
china *n* fictilia *ntpl*.
chink *n* rīma *f*; (*sound*) tinnītus *m* ♦ *vi* crepāre, tinnīre.
chip *n* assula *f*, fragmentum *nt* ♦ *vt* dolāre.
chirp *vi* pīpilāre.
chirpy *adj* hilaris.
chisel *n* scalprum *nt*, scalpellum *nt* ♦ *vt* sculpere.
chit *n* (*child*) pūsiō *m*, puerulus *m*.
chitchat *n* sermunculī *mpl*.
chitterlings *n* hillae *fpl*.
chivalrous *adj* generōsus.
chivalry *n* virtūs *f*; (*men*) iuventūs *f*; (*class*) equitēs *mpl*.
chive *n* caepe *nt*.
chock *n* cuneus *m*.
chock-full *adj* refertus.
choice *n* dēlēctus *m*, ēlēctiō *f*; (*of alternatives*) optiō *f* ♦ *adj* lēctus, eximius, exquīsītus.
choiceness *n* ēlegantia *f*, praestantia *f*.

choir n chorus m.
choke vt suffocāre; (emotion) reprimere; (passage) obstruere.
choler n bīlis f; (anger) īra f, stomachus m.
choleric adj īrācundus.
choose vt legere, ēligere, dēligere; (alternative) optāre; (for office) dēsignāre; (with infin) velle, mālle.
chop vt concīdere; ~ **off** praecīdere ♦ n (meat) offa f.
chopper n secūris f.
choppy adj (sea) asper.
choral adj symphōniacus.
chord n (string) nervus m, chorda f.
chortle vi cachinnāre.
chorus n (singers) chorus m; (song) concentus m, symphōnia f; **in ~** unā vōce.
christen vt baptizāre.
Christian adj Christiānus.
Christianity n Christiānismus m.
chronic adj inveterātus; **become ~** inveterāscere.
chronicle n annālēs mpl, ācta pūblica ntpl ♦ vt in annālēs referre.
chronicler n annālium scrīptor m.
chronological adj: **in ~ order** servātō temporum ōrdine; **make a ~ error** temporibus errāre.
chronology n temporum ratiō f, temporum ōrdō m.
chronometer n hōrologium nt.
chubby adj pinguis.
chuck vt conicere; **~ out** extrūdere.
chuckle vi rīdēre ♦ n rīsus m.
chum n sodālis m.
church n ecclēsia f.
churl n rūsticus m.
churlish adj difficilis, importūnus; avārus.
churlishly adv rūsticē, avārē.
churlishness n mōrōsitās f, avāritia f.
chute n (motion) lāpsus m; (place) dēclīve nt.
cicada n cicāda f.
cincture n cingulum nt.
cinder n cinis m.
cipher n numerus m, nihil nt; (code) notae fpl; **in ~** per notās.
circle n orbis m, circulus m, gȳrus m; **form a ~** in orbem cōnsistere ♦ vi sē circumagere, circumīre.
circlet n īnfula f.
circuit n ambitus m, circuitus m; (assizes) conventus m.
circuitous adj longus; **a ~ route** circuitus m; (speech) ambāgēs fpl.
circular adj rotundus.
circulate vt (news) pervulgāre ♦ vi circumagī; (news) circumferrī, percrēbrēscere.
circulation n ambitus m; **be in ~** in manibus esse; **go out of ~** obsolēscere.
circumcise vt circumcīdere.
circumference n ambitus m.
circumlocution n ambāgēs fpl, circuitiō f.
circumnavigate vt circumvehī.

circumscribe vt circumscrībere; (restrict) coercēre, fīnīre.
circumspect adj cautus, prūdēns.
circumspection n cautiō f, prūdentia f, circumspectiō f.
circumspectly adv cautē, prūdenter.
circumstance n rēs f; **~s** rērum status m; (wealth) rēs f; **as ~s arise** ē rē nātā; **under the ~s** cum haec ita sint, essent; **under no ~s** nēquāquam.
circumstantial adj adventīcius; (detailed) accūrātus; **~ evidence** coniectūra f.
circumstantially adv accūrātē, subtīliter.
circumvallation n circummūnītiō f.
circumvent vt circumvenīre, fallere.
circus n circus m.
cistern n lacus m, cisterna f.
citadel n arx f.
citation n (law) vocātiō f; (mention) commemorātiō f.
cite vt in iūs vocāre; (quote) commemorāre, prōferre.
citizen n cīvis m/f; (of provincial town) mūniceps m; **fellow ~** cīvis m/f; **Roman ~s** Quirītēs mpl ♦ adj cīvīlis, cīvicus.
citizenship n cīvitās f; **deprived of ~** capite dēminūtus; **loss of ~** capitis dēminūtiō f.
citron n (fruit) citrum nt; (tree) citrus f.
city n urbs f, oppidum nt.
civic adj cīvīlis, cīvicus.
civil adj (of citizens) cīvīlis; (war) cīvilis, intestīnus, domesticus; (manners) urbānus, cōmis, officiōsus; (lawsuit) prīvātus.
civilian n togātus m.
civility n urbānitās f, cōmitās f; (act) officium nt.
civilization n exculta hominum vīta f, cultus atque hūmānitās.
civilize vt excolere, expolīre, ad hūmānum cultum dēdūcere.
civil war n bellum cīvīle, bellum domesticum, bellum intestīnum.
clad adj vestītus.
claim vt (for oneself) adrogāre, adserere; (something due) poscere, postulāre, vindicāre; (at law) petere; (statement) adfirmāre ♦ n postulātiō f, postulātum nt; (at law) petītiō f, vindiciae fpl.
claimant n petītor m.
clam n chāma f.
clamber vi scandere.
clammy adj ūmidus, lentus.
clamorous adj vōciferāns.
clamour n strepitus m, clāmōrēs mpl ♦ vi: **~ against** obstrepere (dat).
clamp n cōnfībula f.
clan n gēns f.
clandestine adj fūrtīvus.
clandestinely adv clam, fūrtim.
clang n clangor m, crepitus m ♦ vi increpāre.
clangour n clangor m.
clank n crepitus m ♦ vi crepitāre.
clansman n gentīlis m.

clap *vi* plaudere, applaudere; ~ **eyes on** cōnspicere; ~ **in prison** in vincula conicere ♦ *n* plausus *m*; (*thunder*) fragor *m*.

clapper *n* plausor *m*.

claptrap *n* iactātiō *f*.

claque *n* plausōrēs *mpl*, operae *fpl*.

clarify *vt* pūrgāre; (*knowledge*) illūstrāre ♦ *vi* liquēre.

clarinet *n* tībia *f*.

clarion *n* lituus *m*, cornū *nt*.

clarity *n* perspicuitās *f*.

clash *n* concursus *m*; (*sound*) strepitus *m*, crepitus *m*; (*fig*) discrepantia *f* ♦ *vi* concurrere; (*sound*) increpāre; (*fig*) discrepāre ♦ *vt* conflīgere.

clasp *n* fībula *f*; (*embrace*) amplexus *m* ♦ *vt* implicāre; amplectī, complectī; ~ **together** interiungere.

class *n* (*POL*) ōrdō *m*, classis *f*; (*kind*) genus *nt*; (*school*) classis *f* ♦ *vt* dēscrībere; ~ **as in** numerō (*gen pl*) referre, repōnere, habēre.

classic *n* scrīptor classicus *m*.

classical *adj* classicus; ~ **literature** litterae Graecae et Rōmānae.

classics *npl* scrīptōrēs Graecī et Rōmānī.

classify *vt* dēscrībere, in ōrdinem redigere.

class-mate *n* condiscipulus *m*.

clatter *n* crepitus *m* ♦ *vi* increpāre.

clause *n* (*GRAM*) incīsum *nt*, membrum *nt*; (*law*) caput *nt*; (*will*) ēlogium *nt*; **in short ~s** incīsim.

claw *n* unguis *m*, ungula *f* ♦ *vt* (*unguibus*) lacerāre.

clay *n* argilla *f*; **made of ~** fictilis.

clayey *adj* argillāceus.

claymore *n* gladius *m*.

clean *adj* mundus; (*fig*) pūrus, castus; ~ **slate** novae tabulae *fpl*; **make a ~ sweep of** omnia tollere; **show a ~ pair of heels** sē in pedēs conicere; **my hands are ~** innocēns sum ♦ *adv* prōrsus, tōtus ♦ *vt* pūrgāre.

cleanliness *n* munditia *f*.

cleanly *adj* mundus, nitidus ♦ *adv* mundē, pūrē.

cleanse *vt* pūrgāre, abluere, dētergēre.

clear *adj* clārus; (*liquid*) limpidus; (*space*) apertus, pūrus; (*sound*) clārus; (*weather*) serēnus; (*fact*) manifestus, perspicuus; (*language*) illūstris, dīlūcidus; (*conscience*) rēctus, innocēns; **it is ~** liquet; ~ **of** līber (*abl*), expers (*gen*); **be ~ about** rēctē intellegere; **keep ~ of** ēvītāre; **the coast is ~** arbitrī absunt ♦ *vt* (*of obstacles*) expedīre, pūrgāre; (*of a charge*) absolvere; (*self*) pūrgāre; (*profit*) lucrārī; ~ **away** āmovēre, tollere; ~ **off** *vt* (*debt*) solvere, exsolvere ♦ *vi* facessere; ~ **out** ēluere, dētergēre; ~ **up** *vt* (*difficulty*) illūstrāre, ēnōdāre, explicāre ♦ *vi* (*weather*) disserēnāscere.

clearance *n* pūrgātiō *f*; (*space*) intervallum *nt*.

clearing *n* (*in forest*) lūcus *m*.

clearly *adv* clārē; manifestē, apertē, perspicuē; (*with clause*) vidēlicet.

clearness *n* clāritās *f*; (*weather*) serēnitās *f*;

(*mind*) acūmen *nt*; (*style*) perspicuitās *f*.

clear-sighted *adj* sagāx, perspicāx.

cleavage *n* discidium *nt*.

cleave *vt* (*out*) findere, discindere ♦ *vi* (*cling*): ~ **to** haerēre (*dat*), adhaerēre (*dat*).

cleaver *n* dolabra *f*.

cleft *n* rīma *f*, hiātus *m* ♦ *adj* fissus, discissus.

clemency *n* clēmentia *f*, indulgentia *f*; **with ~** clēmenter.

clement *adj* clēmēns, misericors.

clench *vt* (*nail*) retundere; (*hand*) comprimere.

clerk *n* scrība *m*; (*of court*) lēctor *m*.

clever *adj* callidus, ingeniōsus, doctus, astūtus.

cleverly *adv* doctē, callidē, ingeniōsē.

cleverness *n* calliditās *f*, sollertia *f*.

clew *n* glomus *nt*.

cliché *n* verbum trītum *nt*.

client *n* cliēns *m/f*; (*lawyer's*) cōnsultor *m*; **body of ~s** clientēla *f*.

clientele *n* clientēla *f*.

cliff *n* rūpēs *f*, scopulus *m*.

climate *n* caelum *nt*.

climax *n* (*RHET*) gradātiō *f*; (*fig*) culmen *nt*.

climb *vt*, *vi* scandere, ascendere; ~ **down** dēscendere ♦ *n* ascēnsus *m*.

climber *n* scandēns *m*.

clime *n* caelum *nt*, plāga *f*.

clinch *vt* cōnfirmāre.

cling *vi* adhaerēre; ~ **together** cohaerere.

clink *vi* tinnīre ♦ *n* tinnītus *m*.

clip *vt* tondēre; praecīdere.

clippers *n* forfex *f*.

clique *n* factiō *f*.

cloak *n* (*rain*) lacerna *f*; (*travel*) paenula *f*; (*MIL*) sagum *nt*; palūdāmentum *nt*; (*Greek*) pallium *nt*; (*fig*) involūcrum *nt*; (*pretext*) speciēs *f* ♦ *vt* tegere, dissimulāre.

clock *n* hōrologium *nt*; (*sun*) sōlārium *nt*; (*water*) clepsydra *f*; **ten o'~** quarta hōra.

clockwise *adv* dextrōvorsum, dextrōrsum.

clod *n* glaeba *f*.

clog *n* (*shoe*) sculpōnea *f*; (*fig*) impedīmentum *nt* ♦ *vt* impedīre.

cloister *n* porticus *f*.

cloistered *adj* (*fig*) umbrātilis.

close *adj* (*shut*) clausus; (*tight*) artus; (*narrow*) angustus; (*near*) propinquus; (*compact*) refertus, dēnsus; (*stingy*) parcus; (*secret*) obscūrus; (*weather*) crassus; ~ **at ~ quarters** comminus; **be ~ at hand** īnstāre; **keep ~ to** adhaerēre; ~ **to** prope (*acc*), iuxtā (*acc*) ♦ *adv* prope, iuxtā ♦ *n* angiportus *m*.

close *vt* claudere, operīre; (*finish*) perficere, fīnīre, conclūdere, termināre; (*ranks*) dēnsāre ♦ *vi* claudī; conclūdī, terminārī; (*time*) exīre; (*wound*) coīre; (*speech*) perōrāre; ~ **with** (*fight*) manum cōnserere, signa cōnferre; (*deal*) pacīscī; (*offer*) accipere ♦ *n* fīnis *m*, terminus *m*; (*action*) exitus *m*; (*sentence*) conclūsiō *f*; **at the ~ of summer** aestāte exeunte.

closely *adv* prope; (*attending*) attentē;

(*associating*) coniūnctē; **follow ~** īnstāre (*dat*).
closeness *n* propinquitās *f*; (*weather*) gravitās *f*, crassitūdō *f*; (*with money*) parsimōnia *f*; (*friends*) coniūnctiō *f*; (*manner*) cautiō *f*.
closet *n* cubiculum *nt*, cella *f* ♦ *vt* inclūdere.
clot *n* (*blood*) concrētus sanguis *m* ♦ *vi* concrēscere.
cloth *n* textile *nt*; (*piece*) pannus *m*; (*linen*) linteum *nt*; (*covering*) strāgulum *nt*.
clothe *vt* vestīre.
clothes *n* vestis *f*, vestītus *m*, vestīmenta *ntpl*.
clothier *n* vestiārius *m*.
clothing *n* vestis *f*, vestītus *m*, vestīmenta *ntpl*.
clotted *adj* concrētus.
cloud *n* nūbēs *f*; (*storm*) nimbus *m*; (*dust*) globus *m*; (*disfavour*) invidia *f* ♦ *vt* nūbibus obdūcere; (*fig*) obscūrāre.
clouded *adj* obnūbilus.
cloudiness *n* nūbilum *nt*.
cloudless *adj* pūrus, serēnus.
cloudy *adj* obnūbilus.
clout *n* pannus *m*.
clover *n* trifolium *nt*.
cloven *adj* (*hoof*) bifidus.
clown *n* (*boor*) rūsticus *m*; (*comic*) scurra *m*.
clownish *adj* rūsticus, inurbānus.
clownishness *n* rūsticitās *f*.
cloy *vt* satiāre.
cloying *adj* pūtidus.
club *n* (*stick*) fustis *m*, clāva *f*; (*society*) sodālitās *f*; **~ together** *vi* in commūne cōnsulere, pecūniās cōnferre.
club-footed *adj* scaurus.
cluck *vi* singultīre ♦ *n* singultus *m*.
clue *n* indicium *nt*, vestīgium *nt*.
clump *n* massa *f*; (*earth*) glaeba *f*; (*trees*) arbustum *nt*; (*willows*) salictum *nt*.
clumsily *adv* ineptē, inēleganter; inconditē, īnfabrē.
clumsiness *n* īnscītia *f*.
clumsy *adj* (*person*) inconcinnus, ineptus; (*thing*) inhabilis; (*work*) inconditus.
cluster *n* cumulus *m*; (*grapes*) racēmus *m*; (*people*) corōna *f* ♦ *vi* congregārī.
clutch *vt* prehendere, adripere; ~ **at** captāre *nt*, comprehēnsiō *f*; **from one's ~es** ē manibus; **in one's ~es** in potestāte.
clutter *n* turba *f* ♦ *vt* impedīre, obstruere.
coach *n* currus *m*, raeda *f*, pīlentum *nt*; (*trainer*) magister *m* ♦ *vt* ēdocēre, praecipere (*dat*).
coachman *n* aurīga *m*, raedārius *m*.
coagulate *vt* cōgere ♦ *vi* concrēscere.
coagulation *n* concrētiō *f*.
coal *n* carbō *m*; **carry ~s to Newcastle** in silvam ligna ferre.
coalesce *vi* coīre, coalēscere.
coalition *n* coitiō *f*, cōnspīrātiō *f*.
coarse *adj* (*quality*) crassus; (*manners*) rūsticus, inurbānus; (*speech*) īnfacētus.
coarsely *adv* inurbānē, inēleganter.
coarseness *n* crassitūdō *f*; rūsticitās *f*.
coast *n* lītus *nt*, ōra maritima *f* ♦ *vi*: ~ **along** legere, praetervehī.

coastal *adj* lītorālis, maritimus.
coastline *n* lītus *nt*.
coat *n* pallium *nt*; (*animals*) pellis *f* ♦ *vt* indūcere, inlinere.
coating *n* corium *nt*.
coax *vt* blandīrī, dēlēnīre.
coaxing *adj* blandus ♦ *n* blanditiae *fpl*.
cob *n* (*horse*) mannus *m*; (*swan*) cygnus *m*.
cobble *n* lapis *m* ♦ *vt* sarcīre.
cobbler *n* sūtor *m*.
cobweb *n* arāneum *nt*.
cock *n* gallus *m*, gallus gallīnāceus *m*; (*other birds*) mās *m*; (*tap*) epitonium *nt*; (*hay*) acervus *m*.
cockatrice *n* basiliscus *m*.
cockchafer *n* scarabaeus *m*.
cockcrow *n* gallī cantus *m* ♦ *vt* ērigere.
cockerel *n* pullus *m*.
cockroach *n* blatta *f*.
cocksure *adj* cōnfīdēns.
cod *n* callarias *m*.
coddle *vt* indulgēre (*dat*), permulcēre.
code *n* fōrmula *f*; (*secret*) notae *fpl*.
codicil *n* cōdicillī *mpl*.
codify *vt* in ōrdinem redigere.
coequal *adj* aequālis.
coerce *vt* cōgere.
coercion *n* vīs *f*.
coffer *n* arca *f*, cista *f*; (*public*) fiscus *m*.
coffin *n* arca *f*.
cog *n* dēns *m*.
cogency *n* vīs *f*, pondus *nt*.
cogent *adj* gravis, validus.
cogitate *vi* cōgitāre, meditārī.
cogitation *n* cōgitātiō *f*; meditātiō *f*.
cognate *adj* cognātus.
cognition *n* cognitiō *f*.
cognizance *n* cognitiō *f*; **take ~ of** cognōscere.
cognizant *adj* gnārus.
cohabit *vi* cōnsuēscere.
cohabitation *n* cōnsuētūdō *f*.
coheir *n* cohērēs *m/f*.
cohere *vi* cohaerēre; (*statement*) congruere.
coherence *n* coniūnctiō *f*; (*fig*) convenientia *f*.
coherent *adj* congruēns.
cohesion *n* coagmentātiō *f*.
cohesive *adj* tenāx.
cohort *n* cohors *f*.
coil *n* spīra *f* ♦ *vt* glomerāre.
coin *n* nummus *m* ♦ *vt* cūdere; (*fig*) fingere.
coinage *n* monēta *f*; (*fig*) fictum *nt*.
coincide *vi* concurrere; (*opinion*) cōnsentīre.
coincidence *n* concursus *m*; cōnsēnsus *m*; **by a ~** cāsū.
coincidental *adj* fortuītus.
coiner *n* (*of money*) signātor *m*.
col *n* iugum *nt*.
colander *n* cōlum *nt*.
cold *adj* frīgidus; (*icy*) gelidus; **very ~** perfrīgidus; **be, feel ~** algēre, frīgēre; **get ~** algēscere, frīgēscere ♦ *n* frīgus *nt*; (*felt*) algor *m*; (*malady*) gravēdō *f*; **catch ~** algēscere, frīgus colligere; **catch a ~**

gravēdinem contrahere; **have a ~** gravēdine
labōrāre.
coldish adj frīgidulus, frīgidior.
coldly adv (manner) sine studiō.
coldness n frīgus nt, algor m.
cold water n frīgida f.
colic n tormina ntpl.
collar n collāre nt.
collarbone n iugulum nt.
collate vt cōnferre, comparāre.
collateral adj adiūnctus; (evidence)
cōnsentāneus.
collation n collātiō f; (meal) prandium nt,
merenda f.
colleague n collēga m.
collect vt colligere, cōgere, congerere;
(persons) congregāre, convocāre; (taxes)
exigere; (something due) recipere; **~ oneself**
animum colligere; **cool and ~ed** aequō animō
♦ vi convenīre, congregārī.
collection n (persons) coetus m, conventus m;
(things) congeriēs f; (money) exāctiō f.
collective adj commūnis.
collectively adv commūniter.
collector n (of taxes) exāctor m.
college n collēgium nt.
collide vi concurrere, cōnflīctārī.
collier n carbōnārius m.
collision n concursus m.
collocation n collocātiō f.
collop n offa f.
colloquial adj cottīdiānus.
colloquy n sermō m, colloquium nt.
collude vi praevāricārī.
collusion n praevāricātiō f.
collusive adj praevāricātor.
colonel n lēgātus m.
colonial adj colōnicus ♦ n colōnus m.
colonist n colōnus m.
colonization n dēductiō f.
colonize vt colōniam dēdūcere, cōnstituere in
(acc).
colonnade n porticus f.
colony n colōnia f.
colossal adj ingēns, vastus.
colossus n colossus m.
colour n color m; (paint) pigmentum nt;
(artificial) fūcus m; (complexion) color m;
(pretext) speciēs f; **take on a ~** colōrem
dūcere; **under ~ of** per speciem (gen); **local ~**
māteria dē regiōne sūmpta ♦ vt colōrāre;
(dye) īnficere, fūcāre; (fig) praetendere (dat)
♦ vi rubēre, ērubēscere.
colourable adj speciōsus.
coloured adj (naturally) colōrātus; (artificially)
fūcātus.
colourful adj fūcōsus, varius.
colouring n pigmentum nt; (dye) fūcus m.
colourless adj perlūcidus; (person) pallidus;
(fig) īnsulsus.
colours n (MIL) signum nt, vexillum nt; (POL)
partēs fpl; **sail under false ~** aliēnō nōmine
ūtī; **with flying ~** māximā cum gloriā.
colour sergeant n signifer m.

colt n equuleus m, equulus m.
coltsfoot n farfarus m.
column n columna f; (MIL) agmen nt.
coma n sopor m.
comb n pecten m; (bird) crista f; (loom) pecten
m; (honey) favus m ♦ vt pectere.
combat n pugna f, proelium nt, certāmen nt ♦
vi pugnāre, dīmicāre, certāre ♦ vt pugnāre
cum (abl), obsistere (dat).
combatant n pugnātor m ♦ adj pugnāns; **non ~**
imbellis.
combative adj ferōx, pugnāx.
combination n coniūnctiō f, cōnfūsiō f;
(persons) cōnspīrātiō f; (illegal) coniūrātiō f.
combine vt coniungere, iungere ♦ vi coīre,
coniungī ♦ n societās f.
combustible adj ignī obnoxius.
combustion n dēflāgrātiō f, incendium nt.
come vi venīre, advenīre; (after a journey)
dēvenīre; (interj) age!; **how ~s it that ...?**; quī
fit ut ...?; **~ across** vi invenīre, offendere; **~**
after sequī, excipere, succēdere (dat); **~**
again revenīre, redīre; **~ away** vi abscēdere;
(when pulled) sequī; **~ back** vi revenīre,
redīre; regredī; **~ between** intervenīre,
intercēdere; **~ down** vi dēvenīre,
dēscendere; (from the past) trādī, prōdī; **~**
forward vi prōcēdere, prōdīre; **~ from** vi
(origin) dēfluere; **~ in** vi inīre, introīre;
ingredī; (revenue) redīre; **~ near** accēdere ad
(acc), appropinquāre (dat); **~ nearer and**
nearer adventāre; **~ of** vi (family) ortum esse
ab, ex (abl); **~ off** vi ēvādere, discēdere; **~ on**
vi prōcēdere; (progress) prōficere; (interj)
age, agite; **~ on the scene** intervenīre,
supervenīre, adesse; **~ out** vi exīre, ēgredī;
(hair, teeth) cadere; (flower) flōrēscere; (book)
ēdī; **~ over** vi trānsīre; (feeling) subīre,
occupāre; **~ to** vi advenīre ad, in (acc);
(person) adīre; (amount) efficere; **~ to the**
help of subvenīre (dat); succurrere (dat); **~ to**
nought ad nihilum recidere; **~ to pass**
ēvenīre, fierī; **~ together** convenīre, coīre; **~**
up vi subīre, succēdere; (growth) prōvenīre;
~ upon vt fus invenīre; **he is coming to** animus
eī redit.
comedian n (actor) cōmoedus m; (writer)
cōmicus m.
comedienne n mīma f.
comedy n cōmoedia f.
comeliness n decor m, decōrum nt.
comely adj decōrus, pulcher.
comestibles n vīctus m.
comet n comētēs m.
comfort vt sōlārī, cōnsōlārī, adlevāre ♦ n
sōlācium nt, cōnsōlātiō f.
comfortable adj commodus; **make oneself ~**
corpus cūrāre.
comfortably adv commodē.
comforter n cōnsōlātor m.
comfortless adj incommodus; **be ~** sōlātiō
carēre.
comforts npl commoda ntpl.
comic adj cōmicus; facētus ♦ n scurra m.

comical *adj* facētus, rīdiculus.
coming *adj* futūrus ♦ *n* adventus *m*.
comity *n* cōmitās *f*.
command *vt* iubēre (*+ acc and infin*), imperāre (*dat and* **ut** *+subj*); dūcere; (*feelings*) regere; (*resources*) fruī (*abl*); (*view*) prōspectāre ♦ *n* (*MIL*) imperium *nt*; (*sphere*) prōvincia *f*; (*order*) imperium *nt*, iussum *nt*, mandātum *nt*; **be in ~ (of)** praeesse (*dat*); **put in ~ of** praeficere (*dat*); **~ of language** fācundia *f*.
commandant *n* praefectus *m*.
commandeer *vt* pūblicāre.
commander *n* dux *m*, praefectus *m*.
commander in chief *n* imperātor *m*.
commandment *n* mandātum *nt*.
commemorate *vt* celebrāre, memoriae trādere.
commemoration *n* celebrātiō *f*.
commence *vt* incipere, exōrdīrī, initium facere (*gen*).
commencement *n* initium *nt*, exōrdium *nt*, prīncipium *nt*.
commend *vt* laudāre; (*recommend*) commendāre; (*entrust*) mandāre; **~ oneself** sē probāre.
commendable *adj* laudābilis, probābilis.
commendation *n* laus *f*, commendātiō *f*.
commendatory *adj* commendātīcius.
commensurable *adj* pār.
commensurate *adj* congruēns, conveniēns.
comment *vi* dīcere, scrībere; **~ on** interpretārī; (*with notes*) adnotāre ♦ *n* dictum *nt*, sententia *f*.
commentary *n* commentāriī *mpl*.
commentator *n* interpres *m*.
commerce *n* mercātūra *f*, commercium *nt*; **engage in ~** mercātūrās facere, negōtiārī.
commercial dealings *n* commercium *nt*.
commercial traveller *n* īnstitor *m*.
commination *n* minae *fpl*.
comminatory *adj* mināx.
commingle *vt* intermiscēre.
commiserate *vt* miserērī (*gen*).
commiseration *n* misericordia *f*; (*RHET*) commiserātiō *f*.
commissariat *n* rēs frūmentāria *f*, commeātus *m*; (*staff*) frūmentāriī *mpl*.
commissary *n* lēgātus *m*; reī frūmentāriae praefectus *m*.
commission *n* (*charge*) mandātum *nt*; (*persons*) triumvirī *mpl*, decemvirī *mpl*, etc; (*abroad*) lēgātiō *f*; **get a ~** (*MIL*) tribūnum fierī; **standing ~** (*law*) quaestiō perpetua *f* ♦ *vt* mandāre, adlēgāre.
commissioner *n* lēgātus *m*; **three ~s** triumvirī *mpl*; **ten ~s** decemvirī *mpl*.
commit *vt* (*charge*) committere, mandāre; (*crime*) admittere; (*to prison*) conicere; (*to an undertaking*) obligāre, obstringere; **~ to memory** memoriae trādere; **~ to writing** litterīs mandāre; **~ an error** errāre; **~ a theft** fūrtum facere; *see also* **suicide**.
commitment *n* mūnus *nt*, officium *nt*.

committee *n* dēlēctī *mpl*.
commodious *adj* capāx.
commodity *n* merx *f*, rēs *f*.
commodore *n* praefectus classis *m*.
common *adj* (*for all*) commūnis; (*ordinary*) vulgāris, cottīdiānus; (*repeated*) frequēns, crēber; (*inferior*) nēquam ♦ *n* compāscuus ager *m*, prātum *nt*; **~ man** homō plēbēius *m*; **~ soldier** gregārius mīles *m*.
commonalty *n* plēbs *f*.
commoner *n* homō plēbēius *m*.
common law *n* mōs māiōrum *m*.
commonly *adv* ferē, vulgō.
common people *n* plēbs *f*, vulgus *nt*.
commonplace *n* trītum prōverbium *nt*; (*RHET*) locus commūnis *m* ♦ *adj* vulgāris, trītus.
commons *n* plēbs *f*; (*food*) diāria *ntpl*.
common sense *n* prūdentia *f*.
commonwealth *n* cīvitās *f*, rēs pūblica *f*.
commotion *n* perturbātiō *f*, tumultus *m*; **cause a ~** tumultuārī.
communal *adj* commūnis.
commune *n* pāgus *m* ♦ *vi* colloquī, sermōnēs cōnferre.
communicate *vt* commūnicāre; (*information*) nūntiāre, patefacere ♦ *vi*: **~ with** commūnicāre (*dat*), commercium habēre (*gen*), agere cum (*abl*).
communication *n* (*dealings*) commercium *nt*; (*information*) litterae *fpl*, nūntius *m*; (*passage*) commeātus *m*; **cut off the ~s of** interclūdere.
communicative *adj* loquāx.
communion *n* societās *f*.
communiqué *n* litterae *fpl*, praedicātiō *f*.
communism *n* bonōrum aequātiō *f*.
community *n* cīvitās *f*, commūne *nt*; (*participation*) commūniō *f*.
commutation *n* mūtātiō *f*.
commute *vt* mūtāre, commūtāre.
compact *n* foedus *nt*, conventum *nt* ♦ *adj* dēnsus ♦ *vt* dēnsāre.
companion *n* socius *m*, comes *m/f*; (*intimate*) sodālis *m*; (*at school*) condiscipulus *m*; (*in army*) commīlitō *m*, contubernālis *m*.
companionable *adj* facilis, commodus.
companionship *n* sodālitās *f*, cōnsuētūdō *f*; (*MIL*) contubernium *nt*.
company *n* societās *f*, cōnsuētūdō *f*; (*gathering*) coetus *m*, conventus *m*; (*guests*) cēnantēs *mpl*; (*commercial*) societās *f*; (*magistrates*) collēgium *nt*; (*MIL*) manipulus *m*; (*THEAT*) grex *m*, caterva *f*; **~ of ten** decuria *f*.
comparable *adj* comparābilis, similis.
comparative *adj* māgnus, sī cum aliīs cōnfertur.
comparatively *adv* ut in tālī tempore, ut in eā regiōne, ut est captus hominum; **~ few** perpaucī, nullus ferē.
compare *vt* comparāre, cōnferre; **~d with** ad (*acc*).
comparison *n* comparātiō *f*, collātiō *f*; (*RHET*) similitūdō *f*; **in ~ with** prō (*abl*).
compartment *n* cella *f*, pars *f*.

compass n ambitus m, spatium nt, modus m;
pair of ~es circinus m ♦ vt circumdare,
cingere; (*attain*) cōnsequī.
compassion n misericordia f.
compassionate adj misericors, clēmēns.
compassionately adv clēmenter.
compatibility n convenientia f.
compatible adj congruēns, conveniēns; **be ~**
congruere.
compatibly adv congruenter, convenienter.
compatriot n cīvis m, populāris m.
compeer n pār m; aequālis m.
compel vt cōgere.
compendious adj brevis.
compendiously adv summātim.
compendium n epitomē f.
compensate vt compēnsāre, satisfacere
(*dat*).
compensation n compēnsātiō f; pretium nt,
poena f.
compete vi certāre, contendere.
competence n facultās f; (*law*) iūs nt; (*money*)
quod sufficit.
competent adj perītus, satis doctus, capāx;
(*witness*) locuplēs; **it is ~** licet.
competition n certāmen m, contentiō f.
competitor n competītor m, aemulus m.
compilation n collectānea ntpl, liber m.
compile vt compōnere.
compiler n scrīptor m.
complacency n amor suī m.
complacent adj suī contentus.
complain vi querī, conquerī; **~ of** (*person*)
nōmen dēferre (*gen*).
complainant n accūsātor m, petītor m.
complaint n questus m, querimōnia f; (*law*)
crīmen nt; (*MED*) morbus m, valētūdō f.
complaisance n cōmitās f, obsequium nt,
indulgentia f.
complaisant adj cōmis, officiōsus, facilis.
complement n complēmentum nt; numerus
suus m; **make up the ~ of** complēre.
complete vt (*amount, time*) complēre, explēre;
(*work*) cōnficere, perficere, absolvere,
peragere ♦ adj perfectus, absolūtus, integer;
(*victory*) iūstus; (*amount*) explētus.
completely adv funditus, omnīnō, absolūtē,
plānē; penitus.
completeness n integritās f; (*perfection*)
perfectiō f.
completion n (*process*) absolūtiō f, cōnfectiō f;
(*end*) fīnis m; **bring to ~** absolvere.
complex adj implicātus, multiplex.
complexion n color m.
complexity n implicātiō f.
compliance n accommodātiō f, obsequium nt,
obtemperātiō f.
compliant adj obsequēns, facilis.
complicate vt implicāre, impedīre.
complicated adj implicātus, involūtus,
impedītus.
complication n implicātiō f.
complicity n cōnscientia f.

compliment n blandīmentum nt, honōs m ♦ vt
blandīrī, laudāre; **~ on** grātulārī (*dat*) dē
(*abl*).
complimentary adj honōrificus, blandus.
compliments npl (*as greeting*) salūs f.
comply vi obsequī (*dat*), obtemperāre (*dat*);
mōrem gerere (*dat*), mōrigerārī (*dat*).
component n elementum nt, pars f.
comport vt gerere.
compose vt (*art*) compōnere, condere,
pangere; (*whole*) efficere, cōnflāre; (*quarrel*)
compōnere, dīrimere; (*disturbance*) sēdāre;
be ~d of cōnsistere ex (*abl*), cōnstāre ex
(*abl*).
composed adj tranquillus, placidus.
composer n auctor m, scrīptor m.
composite adj multiplex.
composition n (*process*) compositiō f,
scrīptūra f; (*product*) opus nt, poēma nt,
carmen nt; (*quality*) structūra f.
composure n sēcūritās f, aequus animus m;
(*face*) tranquillitās f.
compound vt miscēre; (*words*) duplicāre,
iungere ♦ vi (*agree*) pacīscī ♦ adj compositus
♦ n (*word*) iūnctum verbum nt; (*area*)
saeptum nt.
compound interest n anatocismus m.
comprehend vt intellegere, comprehendere;
(*include*) continēre, complectī.
comprehensible adj perspicuus.
comprehension n intellegentia f,
comprehēnsiō f.
comprehensive adj capāx; **be ~** lātē patēre,
multa complectī.
compress vt comprimere, coartāre ♦ n
fōmentum nt.
compression n compressus m.
comprise vt continēre, complectī,
comprehendere.
compromise n (*by one side*) accommodātiō f;
(*by both sides*) comprōmissum nt ♦ vi
comprōmittere ♦ vt implicāre, in
suspiciōnem vocāre; **be ~d** in suspiciōnem
venīre.
comptroller n moderātor m.
compulsion n necessitās f, vīs f; **under ~**
coāctus.
compulsory adj necesse, lēge imperātus; **use**
~ measures vim adhibēre.
compunction n paenitentia f.
computation n ratiō f.
compute vt computāre, ratiōnem dūcere.
comrade n socius m, contubernālis m.
comradeship n contubernium nt.
concatenation n seriēs f.
concave adj concavus.
conceal vt cēlāre, abdere, abscondere; (*fact*)
dissimulāre.
concealment n occultātiō f; (*place*) latebrae
fpl; (*of facts*) dissimulātiō f; **in ~** abditus,
occultus; **be in ~** latēre, latitāre; **go into ~**
dēlitēscere.
concede vt concēdere.
conceit n (*idea*) nōtiō f; (*wit*) facētiae fpl; (*pride*)

superbia *f*, adrogantia *f*, vānitās *f*.
conceited *adj* glōriōsus, adrogāns.
conceitedness *n* adrogantia *f*, vānitās *f*.
conceive *vt* concipere, comprehendere,
intellegere.
concentrate *vt* (*in one place*) cōgere,
congregāre; (*attention*) intendere, dēfīgere.
concentrated *adj* dēnsus.
concentration *n* animī intentiō *f*.
concept *n* nōtiō *f*.
conception *n* conceptus *m*; (*mind*)
intellegentia *f*, īnfōrmātiō *f*; (*idea*) nōtiō *f*,
cōgitātiō *f*, cōnsilium *nt*.
concern *vt* (*refer*) attinēre ad (*acc*), interesse
(*gen*); (*worry*) sollicitāre; **it ~s me** meā rēfert,
meā interest; **as far as I am ~ed** per mē ♦ *n*
rēs *f*, negōtium *nt*; (*importance*) mōmentum
nt; (*worry*) sollicitūdō *f*, cūra *f*; (*regret*) dolor
m.
concerned *adj* sollicitus, anxius; **be ~** dolēre;
be ~ about molestē ferre.
concerning *prep* dē (*abl*).
concernment *n* sollicitūdō *f*.
concert *n* (*music*) concentus *m*; (*agreement*)
cōnsēnsus *m*; **in ~** ex compositō, ūnō animō ♦
vt compōnere; (*plan*) inīre.
concession *n* concessiō *f*; **by the ~ of** concessū
(*gen*); **make a ~** concēdere, tribuere.
conciliate *vt* conciliāre.
conciliation *n* conciliātiō *f*.
conciliator *n* arbiter *m*.
conciliatory *adj* pācificus.
concise *adj* brevis; (*style*) dēnsus.
concisely *adv* breviter.
conciseness *n* brevitās *f*.
conclave *n* sēcrētus cōnsessus *m*.
conclude *vt* (*end*) termināre, fīnīre, cōnficere;
(*settle*) facere, compōnere, pangere; (*infer*)
īnferre, colligere.
conclusion *n* (*end*) fīnis *m*; (*of action*) exitus *m*;
(*of speech*) perōrātiō *f*; (*inference*) coniectūra
f; (*decision*) placitum *nt*, sententia *f*; **in ~**
dēnique; **try ~s with** contendere cum.
conclusive *adj* certus, manifestus, gravis.
conclusively *adv* sine dubiō.
concoct *vt* coquere; (*fig*) cōnflāre.
concoction *n* (*fig*) māchinātiō *f*.
concomitant *adj* adiūnctus.
concord *n* concordia *f*; (*music*) harmonia *f*.
concordant *adj* concors.
concordat *n* pactum *nt*, foedus *nt*.
concourse *n* frequentia *f*, celebrātiō *f*;
(*moving*) concursus *m*.
concrete *adj* concrētus; **in the ~** rē.
concretion *n* concrētiō *f*.
concubine *n* concubīna *f*.
concupiscence *n* libīdō *f*.
concur *vi* (*time*) concurrere; (*opinion*)
cōnsentīre, adsentīre.
concurrence *n* (*time*) concursus *m*; (*opinion*)
cōnsēnsus *m*.
concurrent *adj* (*time*) aequālis; (*opinion*)
cōnsentāneus; **be ~** concurrere, cōnsentīre.

concurrently *adv* simul, ūnā.
concussion *n* ictus *m*.
condemn *vt* damnāre, condemnāre;
(*disapprove*) improbāre; **~ to death** capitis
damnāre; **~ for treason** dē māiestāte
damnāre.
condemnation *n* damnātiō *f*; condemnātiō *f*.
condemnatory *adj* damnātōrius.
condense *vt* dēnsāre; (*words*) premere.
condescend *vi* dēscendere, sē submittere.
condescending *adj* cōmis.
condescension *n* cōmitās *f*.
condiment *n* condīmentum *nt*.
condition *n* (*of body*) habitus *m*; (*external*)
status *m*, condiciō *f*, rēs *f*; (*in society*) locus *m*,
fortūna *f*; (*of agreement*) condiciō *f*, lēx *f*; **~s of
sale** mancipī lēx *f*; **on ~ that** eā condicione ut
(*subj*); **in ~** (*animals*) nitidus ♦ *vt* fōrmāre,
regere.
conditional *adj*: **the assistance is ~ on** eā
condiciōne succurritur ut (*subj*).
conditionally *adv* sub condiciōne.
conditioned *adj* (*character*) mōrātus.
condole *vi*: **~ with** cōnsōlārī.
condolence *n* cōnsōlātiō *f*.
condonation *n* venia *f*.
condone *vt* condōnāre, ignōscere (*dat*).
conduce *vi* condūcere (ad), prōficere (ad).
conducive *adj* ūtilis, accommodātus.
conduct *vt* dūcere; (*escort*) dēdūcere; (*to a
place*) addūcere, perdūcere; (*business*)
gerere, administrāre; (*self*) gerere ♦ *n*
mōrēs *mpl*; (*past*) vīta *f*, facta *ntpl*; (*business*)
administrātiō *f*; **safe ~** praesidium *nt*.
conductor *m* dux *m*, ductor *m*.
conduit *n* canālis *m*, aquae ductus *m*.
cone *n* cōnus *m*.
coney *n* cunīculus *m*.
confabulate *vi* colloquī.
confection *n* cuppēdō *f*.
confectioner *n* cuppēdinārius *m*.
confectionery *n* dulcia *ntpl*.
confederacy *n* foederātae cīvitātēs *fpl*,
societās *f*.
confederate *adj* foederātus ♦ *n* socius *m* ♦ *vi*
coniūrāre, foedus facere.
confederation *n* societās *f*.
confer *vt* cōnferre, tribuere ♦ *vi* colloquī,
sermōnem cōnferre; **~ about** agere dē (*abl*).
conference *n* colloquium *nt*, congressus *m*.
conferment *n* dōnātiō *f*.
confess *vt* fatērī, cōnfitērī.
confessedly *adv* manifestō.
confession *n* cōnfessiō *f*.
confidant *n* cōnscius *m*.
confide *vi* fīdere (*dat*), cōnfīdere (*dat*) ♦ *vt*
crēdere, committere.
confidence *n* fidēs *f*, fīdūcia *f*; **have ~ in** fīdere
(*dat*), cōnfīdere (*dat*); **inspire ~ in** fidem
facere (*dat*); **tell in ~** tūtīs auribus dēpōnere.
confident *adj* fīdēns; **~ in** frētus (*abl*); **be ~ that**
certō scīre, prō certō habēre.
confidential *adj* arcānus, intimus.

confidentially *adv* inter nōs.
confidently *adv* fīdenter.
confiding *adj* crēdulus.
configuration *n* figūra *f*, fōrma *f*.
confine *vt* (*prison*) inclūdere, in vincula conicere; (*limit*) termināre, circumscrībere; (*restrain*) coercēre, cohibēre; (*to bed*) dētinēre; **be ~d** (*women*) parturīre.
confinement *n* custōdia *f*, vincula *ntpl*, inclūsiō *f*; (*women*) puerperium *nt*.
confines *n* fīnēs *mpl*.
confirm *vt* (*strength*) corrōborāre, firmāre; (*decision*) sancīre, ratum facere; (*fact*) adfirmāre, comprobāre.
confirmation *n* cōnfirmātiō *f*, adfirmātiō *f*.
confirmed *adj* ratus.
confiscate *vt* pūblicāre.
confiscation *n* pūblicātiō *f*.
conflagration *n* incendium *nt*, dēflāgrātiō *f*.
conflict *n* (*physical*) concursus *m*; (*hostile*) certāmen *nt*, proelium *nt*; (*verbal*) contentiō *f*, contrōversia *f*; (*contradiction*) repugnantia *f*, discrepantia *f* ♦ *vi* inter sē repugnāre.
conflicting *adj* contrārius.
confluence *n* cōnfluēns *m*.
confluent *adj* cōnfluēns.
conform *vt* accommodāre ♦ *vi* sē cōnfōrmāre (ad), obsequī (*dat*), mōrem gerere (*dat*).
conformable *adj* accommodātus, conveniēns.
conformably *adv* convenienter.
conformation *n* structūra *f*, cōnfōrmātiō *f*.
conformity *n* convenientia *f*, cōnsēnsus *m*.
confound *vt* (*mix*) cōnfundere, permiscēre; (*amaze*) obstupefacere; (*thwart*) frustrārī; (*suppress*) opprimere, obruere; **~ you!** dī tē perduint.
confounded *adj* miser, sacer, nefandus.
confoundedly *adv* mīrum quantum nefāriē.
confraternity *n* frāternitās *f*.
confront *vt* sē oppōnere (*dat*), obviam īre (*dat*), sē cōram offerre.
confuse *vt* permiscēre, perturbāre.
confused *adj* perturbātus.
confusedly *adv* perturbātē, prōmiscuē.
confusion *n* perturbātiō *f*; (*shame*) rubor *m*.
confutation *n* refūtātiō *f*.
confute *vt* refūtāre, redarguere, convincere.
congé *n* commeātus *m*.
congeal *vt* congelāre, dūrāre ♦ *vi* concrēscere.
congealed *adj* concrētus.
congenial *adj* concors, congruēns, iūcundus.
congeniality *n* concordia *f*, mōrum similitūdō *f*.
congenital *adj* nātīvus.
conger *n* conger *m*.
congested *adj* refertus, dēnsus; (*with people*) frequentissimus.
congestion *n* congeriēs *f*; frequentia *f*.
conglomerate *vt* glomerāre.
conglomeration *n* congeriēs *f*, cumulus *m*.
congratulate *vt* grātulārī (*dat*).
congratulation *n* grātulātiō *f*.

congratulatory *adj* grātulābundus.
congregate *vt* congregāre, cōgere ♦ *vi* convenīre, congregārī.
congregation *n* conventus *m*, coetus *m*.
congress *n* conventus *m*, cōnsessus *m*, concilium *nt*; senātus *m*.
congruence *n* convenientia *f*.
congruent *adj* conveniēns, congruēns.
congruently *adv* convenienter, congruenter.
congruous *adj see* **congruent.**
conical *adj* turbinātus.
coniferous *adj* cōnifer.
conjectural *adj* opīnābilis.
conjecturally *adv* coniectūrā.
conjecture *n* coniectūra *f* ♦ *vt* conicere, augurārī.
conjoin *vt* coniungere.
conjoint *adj* coniūnctus.
conjointly *adv* coniūnctē, ūnā.
conjugal *adj* coniugālis.
conjugate *vt* dēclīnāre.
conjugation *n* (*GRAM*) dēclīnātiō *f*.
conjunct *adj* coniūnctus.
conjunction *n* coniūnctiō *f*, concursus *m*.
conjure *vt* (*entreat*) obtestārī, obsecrāre; (*spirits*) ēlicere, ciēre ♦ *vi* praestigiīs ūtī.
conjurer *n* praestigiātor *m*.
conjuring *n* praestigiae *fpl*.
connate *adj* innātus, nātūrā īnsitus.
connect *vt* iungere, coniungere, cōpulāre, connectere.
connected *adj* coniūnctus; (*unbroken*) continēns; (*by marriage*) adfīnis; **be ~ed with** contingere; **be closely ~ed with** inhaerēre (*dat*), cohaerēre cum (*abl*).
connectedly *adv* coniūnctē, continenter.
connection *n* coniūnctiō *f*, contextus *m*, seriēs *f*; (*kin*) necessitūdō *f*; (*by marriage*) adfīnitās *f*; **~ between . . . and . . .** ratiō (*gen*) . . . cum . . . (*abl*); **I have no ~ with you** nīl mihī tēcum est.
connivance *n* venia *f*, dissimulātiō *f*.
connive *vi* conīvēre in (*abl*), dissimulāre.
connoisseur *n* intellegēns *m*.
connotation *n* vīs *f*, significātiō *f*.
connote *vt* significāre.
connubial *adj* coniugālis.
conquer *vt* vincere, superāre.
conquerable *adj* superābilis, expugnābilis.
conqueror *n* victor *m*.
conquest *n* victōria *f*; (*town*) expugnātiō *f*; (*prize*) praemium *nt*, praeda *f*; **the ~ of Greece** Graecia capta.
conscience *n* cōnscientia *f*; **guilty ~** mala cōnscientia; **have a clear ~** nullīus culpae sibi cōnscium esse; **have no ~** nullam rēligiōnem habēre.
conscientious *adj* probus, rēligiōsus.
conscientiously *adv* bonā fidē, rēligiōsē.
conscientiousness *n* fidēs *f*, rēligiō *f*.
conscious *adj* sibī cōnscius; (*aware*) gnārus; (*physically*) mentis compos; **be ~** sentīre.
consciously *adv* sciēns.
consciousness *n* animus *m*; (*of action*)

cōnscientia *f*; **he lost ~** animus eum relīquit.
conscript *n* tīrō *m* ♦ *vt* cōnscrībere.
conscription *n* dēlēctus *m*; (*of wealth*)
   pūblicātiō *f*.
consecrate *vt* dēdicāre, cōnsecrāre; (*self*)
   dēvovēre.
consecrated *adj* sacer.
consecration *n* dēdicātiō *f*, cōnsecrātiō *f*;
   (*self*) dēvōtiō *f*.
consecutive *adj* dēinceps, continuus.
consecutively *adv* dēinceps, ōrdine.
consensus *n* cōnsēnsus *m*.
consent *vi* adsentīre (*dat*), adnuere (*infin*);
   (*together*) cōnsentīre ♦ *n* (*one side*) adsēnsus
   m; (*all*) cōnsēnsus *m*; **by common ~** omnium
   cōnsēnsū.
consequence *n* ēventus *m*, exitus *m*; (*logic*)
   conclūsiō *f*; (*importance*) mōmentum *nt*,
   auctōritās *f*; **it is of ~** interest; **what will be
   the ~ of?** quō ēvādet?
consequent *adj* cōnsequēns.
consequential *adj* cōnsentāneus; (*person*)
   adrogāns.
consequently *adv* itaque, igitur, properteā.
conservation *n* cōnservātiō *f*.
conservative *adj* reī pūblicae cōnservandae
   studiōsus; (*estimate*) mediōcris; **~ party**
   optimātēs *mpl*.
conservator *n* custōs *m*, cōnservātor *m*.
conserve *vt* cōnservāre, servāre.
consider *vt* cōnsīderāre, contemplārī; (*reflect*)
   sēcum volūtāre, meditari, dēlīberāre,
   cōgitāre; (*deem*) habēre, dūcere; (*respect*)
   respicere, observāre.
considerable *adj* aliquantus, nōnnullus;
   (*person*) illūstris.
considerably *adv* aliquantum; (*with compar*)
   aliquantō, multō.
considerate *adj* hūmānus, benignus.
considerately *adv* hūmānē, benignē.
consideration *n* cōnsīderātiō *f*, contemplātiō
   f, dēlīberātiō *f*; (*respect*) respectus *m*, ratiō *f*;
   (*importance*) mōmentum *nt*; (*reason*) ratiō *f*;
   (*pay*) pretium *nt*; **for a ~** mercēde, datā
   mercēde; **in ~ of** propter (*acc*), prō (*abl*); **on
   no ~** nēquāquam; **with ~** cōnsultō; **without ~**
   temerē; **take into ~** ad cōnsilium dēferre;
   show ~ for respectum habēre (*gen*).
considered *adj* (*reasons*) exquīsītus.
considering *prep* prō (*abl*), propter (*acc*) ♦ *conj*
   ut, quōniam.
consign *vt* mandāre, committere.
consist *vi* cōnstāre; **~ in** cōnstāre ex (*abl*),
   continērī (*abl*), positum esse in (*abl*); **~ with**
   congruere (*dat*), convenīre (*dat*).
consistence *n* firmitās *f*.
consistency *n* cōnstantia *f*.
consistent *adj* cōnstāns; (*with*) cōnsentāneus,
   cōngruens; (*of movement*) aequābilis; **be ~**
   cohaerēre.
consistently *adv* constanter.
consolable *adj* cōnsōlābilis.
consolation *n* cōnsōlātiō *f*; (*thing*) sōlācium *nt*.

consolatory *adj* cōnsōlātōrius.
console *vt* cōnsōlārī.
consoler *n* cōnsōlātor *m*.
consolidate *vt* (*liquid*) cōgere; (*strength*)
   corrōborāre; (*gains*) obtinēre ♦ *vi*
   concrēscere.
consolidation *n* concrētiō *f*; cōnfirmātiō *f*.
consonance *n* concentus *m*.
consonant *adj* cōnsonus, haud absonus ♦ *n*
   cōnsonāns *f*.
consort *n* cōnsors *m/f*, socius *m*; (*married*)
   coniunx *m/f* ♦ *vi*: **~ with** familiāriter ūtī (*abl*),
   coniūnctissimē vīvere cum (*abl*).
conspectus *n* summārium *nt*.
conspicuous *adj* ēminēns, īnsignis,
   manifestus; **be ~** ēminēre.
conspicuously *adv* manifestō, palam, ante
   oculōs.
conspiracy *n* coniūrātiō *f*.
conspirator *n* coniūrātus *m*.
conspire *vi* coniūrāre; (*for good*) cōnspīrāre.
constable *n* lictor *m*.
constancy *n* cōnstantia *f*, firmitās *f*; **with ~**
   cōnstanter.
constant *adj* cōnstāns; (*faithful*) fīdus, fidēlis;
   (*continuous*) adsiduus.
constantly *adv* adsiduē, saepe, crēbrō.
constellation *n* sīdus *nt*.
consternation *n* trepidātiō *f*, pavor *m*; **throw
   into ~** perterrēre, cōnsternere.
constituency *n* suffrāgātōrēs *mpl*.
constituent *adj*: **~ part** elementum *nt* ♦ *n*
   (*voter*) suffrāgātor *m*.
constitute *vt* creāre, cōnstituere; esse.
constitution *n* nātūra *f*, status *m*; (*body*)
   habitus *m*; (*POL*) cīvitātis fōrma *f*, reī pūblicae
   status *m*, lēgēs *fpl*.
constitutional *adj* lēgitimus, iūstus.
constitutionally *adv* ē rē pūblicā.
constrain *vt* cōgere.
constraint *n* vīs *f*; **under ~** coāctus; **without ~**
   suā sponte.
constrict *vt* comprimere, cōnstringere.
constriction *n* contractiō *f*.
construct *vt* aedificāre, exstruere.
construction *n* aedificātiō *f*; (*method*)
   structūra *f*; (*meaning*) interpretātiō *f*; **put a
   wrong ~ on** in malam partem interpretārī.
construe *vt* interpretārī.
consul *n* cōnsul *m*; **~ elect** cōnsul dēsignātus;
   ex ~ cōnsulāris *m*.
consular *adj* cōnsulāris.
consulship *n* cōnsulātus *m*; **stand for the ~**
   cōnsulātum petere; **hold the ~** cōnsulātum
   gerere; **in my ~** mē cōnsule.
consult *vt* cōnsulere; **~ the interests of**
   cōnsulere (*dat*) ♦ *vi* dēlīberāre, cōnsiliārī.
consultation *n* (*asking*) cōnsultātiō *f*;
   (*discussion*) dēlīberātiō *f*.
consume *vt* cōnsūmere, absūmere; (*food*)
   edere.
consumer *n* cōnsūmptor *m*.
consummate *adj* summus, perfectus ♦ *vt*

perficere, absolvere.
consummation *n* absolūtiō *f*; fīnis *m*, ēventus *m*.
consumption *n* cōnsūmptiō *f*; (*disease*) tābēs *f*, phthisis *f*.
consumptive *adj* pulmōnārius.
contact *n* tāctus *m*, contāgiō *f*; **come in ~ with** contingere.
contagion *n* contāgiō *f*.
contagious *adj* tābificus; **be ~** contāgiīs vulgārī.
contain *vt* capere, continēre; (*self*) cohibēre.
container *n* vās *nt*.
contaminate *vt* contāmināre, īnficere.
contamination *n* contāgiō *f*, lābēs *f*.
contemplate *vt* contemplārī, intuērī; (*action*) in animō habēre; (*prospect*) spectāre.
contemplation *n* contemplātiō *f*; (*thought*) cōgitātiō *f*.
contemplative *adj* cōgitāns, meditāns; **in a ~ mood** cōgitātiōnī dēditus.
contemporaneous *adj* aequālis.
contemporaneously *adv* simul.
contemporary *adj* aequālis.
contempt *n* contemptiō *f*; **be an object of ~** contemptuī esse; **treat with ~** contemptum habēre, conculcāre.
contemptible *adj* contemnendus, abiectus, vīlis.
contemptuous *adj* fastīdiōsus.
contemptuously *adv* contemptim, fastīdiōsē.
contend *vi* certāre, contendere; (*in battle*) dīmicāre, pugnāre; (*in words*) adfirmāre, adsevērāre.
contending *adj* contrārius.
content *adj* contentus ♦ *n* aequus animus *m* ♦ *vt* placēre (*dat*), satisfacere (*dat*); **be ~ed** satis habēre.
contentedly *adv* aequō animō.
contention *n* certāmen *nt*; contrōversia *f*; (*opinion*) sententia *f*.
contentious *adj* pugnāx, lītigiōsus.
contentiously *adv* pugnāciter.
contentiousness *n* contrōversiae studium *nt*.
contentment *n* aequus animus *m*.
contents *n* quod inest, quae insunt; (*of speech*) argūmentum *nt*.
conterminous *adj* adfīnis.
contest *n* certāmen *nt*, contentiō *f* ♦ *vt* (*law*) lēge agere dē (*abl*); (*office*) petere; (*dispute*) repugnāre (*dat*), resistere (*dat*).
contestable *adj* contrōversus.
contestant *n* petītor *m*, aemulus *m*.
context *n* contextus *m*.
contiguity *n* vīcīnia *f*, propinquitās *f*.
contiguous *adj* vīcīnus, adiacēns; **be ~ to** adiacēre (*dat*), contingere.
continence *n* continentia *f*, abstinentia *f*.
continent *adj* continēns, abstinēns ♦ *n* continēns *f*.
continently *adv* continenter, abstinenter.
contingency *n* cāsus *m*, rēs *f*.
contingent *adj* fortuītus ♦ *n* (*MIL*) numerus *m*.

continual *adj* adsiduus, perpetuus.
continually *adv* adsiduē, semper.
continuance *n* perpetuitās *f*, adsiduitās *f*.
continuation *n* continuātiō *f*; (*of a command*) prōrogātiō *f*; (*of a story*) reliqua pars *f*.
continue *vt* continuāre; (*time*) prōdūcere; (*command*) prōrogāre ♦ *vi* (*action*) pergere; (*time*) manēre; (*endurance*) perstāre, dūrāre; **~ to** *imperf indic*.
continuity *n* continuātiō *f*; (*of speech*) perpetuitās *f*.
continuous *adj* continuus, continēns, perpetuus.
continuously *adv* perpetuō, continenter.
contort *vt* contorquēre, dētorquēre.
contortion *n* distortiō *f*.
contour *n* fōrma *f*.
contraband *adj* interdictus, vetitus.
contract *n* pactum *nt*, mandātum *nt*, conventum *nt*; (*POL*) foedus *nt*; **trial for a breach of ~** mandātī iūdicium *nt* ♦ *vt* (*narrow*) contrahere, addūcere; (*short*) dēminuere; (*illness*) contrahere; (*agreement*) pacīscī; (*for work*) locāre; (*to do work*) condūcere ♦ *vi* pacīscī.
contraction *n* contractiō *f*; (*word*) compendium *nt*.
contractor *n* redemptor *m*, conductor *m*.
contradict *vt* (*person*) contrādīcere (*dat*), refrāgārī (*dat*); (*statement*) īnfitiās īre (*dat*); (*self*) repugnāre (*dat*).
contradiction *n* repugnantia *f*, īnfitiae *fpl*.
contradictory *adj* repugnāns, contrārius; **be ~** inter sē repugnāre.
contradistinction *n* oppositiō *f*.
contraption *n* māchina *f*.
contrariety *n* repugnantia *f*.
contrariwise *adv* ē contrāriō.
contrary *adj* contrārius, adversus; (*person*) difficilis, mōrōsus; **~ to** contrā (*acc*), praeter (*acc*); **~ to expectations** praeter opiniōnem ♦ *n* contrārium *nt*; **on the ~** ē contrāriō, contrā; (*retort*) immo.
contrast *n* discrepantia *f* ♦ *vt* comparāre, oppōnere ♦ *vi* discrepāre.
contravene *vt* (*law*) violāre; (*statement*) contrādīcere (*dat*).
contravention *n* violātiō *f*.
contribute *vt* cōnferre, adferre, contribuere. ♦ *vi*: **~ towards** cōnferre ad (*acc*), adiuvāre; **~ to the cost** impēnsās cōnferre.
contribution *n* conlātiō *f*; (*money*) stipem (*no nom*) *f*.
contributor *n* quī cōnfert.
contributory *adj* adiūnctus.
contrite *adj* paenitēns.
contrition *n* paenitentia *f*.
contrivance *n* māchinātiō *f*, excōgitātiō *f*; (*thing*) māchina *f*; (*idea*) cōnsilium *nt*; (*deceit*) dolus *m*.
contrive *vt* māchinārī, excōgitāre, struere; (*to do*) efficere ut.
contriver *n* māchinātor *m*, artifex *m*, auctor *m*.

control n (*restraint*) frēnum nt; (*power*) moderātiō f, potestās f, imperium nt; **have ~ of** praeesse (*dat*); **out of ~** impotēns ♦ vt moderārī (*dat*), imperāre (*dat*).
controller n moderātor m.
controversial adj concertātōrius.
controversy n contrōversia f, disceptātiō f.
controvert vt redarguere, impugnāre, in dubium vocāre.
contumacious adj contumāx, pervicāx.
contumaciously adv contumāciter, pervicāciter.
contumacy n contumācia f, pervicācia f.
contusion n sūgillātiō f.
conundrum n aenigma nt.
convalesce vi convalēscere.
convalescence n melior valētūdō f.
convalescent adj convalēscēns.
convene vt convocāre.
convenience n opportūnitās f, commoditās f; (*thing*) commodum nt; **at your ~** commodō tuō.
convenient adj idōneus, commodus, opportūnus; **be ~** convenīre; **very ~** percommodus.
conveniently adv opportūnē, commodē.
convention n (*meeting*) conventus m; (*agreement*) conventum nt; (*custom*) mōs m, iūsta ntpl.
conventional adj iūstus, solitus.
conventionality n mōs m, cōnsuētūdō f.
converge vi in medium vergere, in eundem locum tendere.
conversant adj perītus, doctus, exercitātus; **be ~ with** versārī in (*abl*).
conversation n sermō m, colloquium nt.
converse n sermō m, colloquium nt; (*opposite*) contrārium nt ♦ vi colloquī, sermōnem cōnferre ♦ adj contrārius.
conversely adv ē contrāriō, contrā.
conversion n mūtātiō f; (*moral*) mōrum ēmendātiō f.
convert vt mūtāre, convertere; (*to an opinion*) dēdūcere ♦ n discipulus m.
convertible adj commūtābilis.
convex adj convexus.
convexity n convexum nt.
convey vt vehere, portāre, convehere; (*property*) abaliēnāre; (*knowledge*) commūnicāre; (*meaning*) significāre; **~ across** trānsmittere, trādūcere, trānsvehere; **~ away** auferre, āvehere; **~ down** dēvehere, dēportāre; **~ into** importāre, invehere; **~ to** advehere, adferre; **~ up** subvehere.
conveyance n vehiculum nt; (*property*) abaliēnātiō f.
convict vt (*prove guilty*) convincere; (*sentence*) damnāre ♦ n reus m.
conviction n (*law*) damnātiō f; (*argument*) persuāsiō f; (*belief*) fidēs f; **carry ~** fidem facere; **have a ~** persuāsum habēre.
convince vt persuādēre (*dat*); **I am firmly ~d**

mihi persuāsum habeō.
convincing adj (*argument*) gravis; (*evidence*) manifestus.
convincingly adv manifestō.
convivial adj convīvalis, festīvus.
conviviality n festīvitās f.
convocation n conventus m.
convoke vt convocāre.
convolution n spīra f.
convoy n praesidium nt ♦ vt prōsequī.
convulse vt agitāre; **be ~d with laughter** sē in cachinnōs effundere.
convulsion n (*MED*) convulsiō f; (*POL*) tumultus m.
convulsive adj spasticus.
coo vi gemere.
cook vt coquere ♦ n coquus m.
cookery n ars coquīnāria f.
cool adj frīgidus; (*conduct*) impudens; (*mind*) impavidus, lentus ♦ n frīgus nt ♦ vt refrīgerāre; (*passion*) restinguere, sēdāre ♦ vi refrīgēscere, refrīgerārī, dēfervēscere.
coolly adv aequō animō; impudenter.
coolness n frīgus nt; (*mind*) aequus animus m; impudentia f.
coop n hara f; (*barrel*) cūpa f ♦ vt inclūdere.
co-operate vi operam cōnferre; **~ with** adiuvāre, socius esse (*gen*).
co-operation n cōnsociātiō f; auxilium nt, opera f.
co-operative adj (*person*) officiōsus.
co-operator n socius m.
co-opt vt cooptāre.
coot n fulica f.
copartner n socius m.
copartnership n societās f.
cope vi: **~ with** contendere cum (*abl*); **able to ~ with** pār (*dat*); **unable to ~ with** impār (*dat*).
copier n librārius m.
coping n fastīgium nt.
copious adj cōpiōsus, largus, plēnus, abundāns.
copiously adv cōpiōsē, abundanter.
copiousness n cōpia f, ūbertās f.
copper n aes nt ♦ adj aēneus.
coppersmith n faber aerārius m.
coppice, copse n dūmētum nt, virgultum nt.
copy n exemplar nt ♦ vt imitārī; (*writing*) exscrībere, trānscrībere.
copyist n librārius m.
coracle n linter f.
coral n cūrālium nt.
cord n fūniculus m.
cordage n fūnēs mpl.
cordial adj cōmis, festīvus, amīcus; (*greetings*) multus.
cordiality n cōmitās f, studium nt.
cordially adv cōmiter, libenter, ex animō.
cordon n corōna f.
core n (*fig*) nucleus m.
cork n sūber nt; (*bark*) cortex m.
corn n frūmentum nt ♦ adj frūmentārius; (*on

the foot) clāvus *m*; **price of ~** annōna *f*.
corndealer *n* frūmentārius *m*.
cornfield *n* seges *f*.
cornel *n* (*tree*) cornus *f*.
corner *n* angulus *m*.
cornet *n* cornū *nt*.
cornice *n* corōna *f*.
coronet *n* diadēma *nt*.
corporal *adj* corporeus.
corporal punishment *n* verbera *ntpl*.
corporation *n* collēgium *nt*; (*civic*)
  magistrātūs *mpl*.
corporeal *adj* corporeus.
corps *n* manus *f*.
corpse *n* cadāver *nt*.
corpulence *n* obēsum corpus *nt*.
corpulent *adj* obēsus, pinguis.
corpuscle *n* corpusculum *nt*.
corral *n* praesēpe *nt*.
correct *vt* corrigere, ēmendāre; (*person*)
  castīgāre ♦ *adj* vērus; (*language*) integer;
  (*style*) ēmendātus.
correction *n* ēmendātiō *f*; (*moral*) corrēctiō *f*;
  (*punishment*) castīgātiō *f*.
correctly *adv* bene, vērē.
correctness *n* (*fact*) vēritās *f*; (*language*)
  integritās *f*; (*moral*) probitās *f*.
corrector *n* ēmendātor *m*, corrēctor *m*.
correspond *vi* (*agree*) respondēre (*dat*),
  congruere (*dat*); (*by letter*) inter sē scrībere.
correspondence *n* similitūdō *f*; epistulae *fpl*.
correspondent *n* epistulārum scrīptor *m*.
corresponding *adj* pār.
correspondingly *adv* pariter.
corridor *n* porticus *f*.
corrigible *adj* ēmendābilis.
corroborate *vt* cōnfirmāre.
corroboration *n* cōnfirmātiō *f*.
corrode *vt* ērōdere, edere.
corrosive *adj* edāx.
corrugate *vt* rūgāre.
corrugated *adj* rūgōsus.
corrupt *vt* corrumpere, dēprāvāre; (*text*)
  vitiāre ♦ *adj* corruptus, vitiātus; (*person*)
  prāvus, vēnālis; (*text*) vitiātus.
corrupter *n* corruptor *m*.
corruptible *adj* (*matter*) dissolūbilis; (*person*)
  vēnālis.
corruption *n* (*of matter*) corruptiō *f*; (*moral*)
  corruptēla *f*, dēprāvātiō *f*; (*bribery*) ambitus
  m.
corsair *n* pīrāta *m*.
cortège *n* pompa *f*.
coruscate *vi* fulgēre.
coruscation *n* fulgor *m*.
Corybant *n* Corybas *m*.
Corybantic *adj* Corybantius.
cosmetic *n* medicāmen *nt*.
cosmic *adj* mundānus.
cosmopolitan *adj* mundānus.
cosmos *n* mundus *m*.
cost *vt* emī, stāre (*dat*); **it ~ me dear** māgnō
  mihi stetit, male ēmī; **it ~ me a talent** talentō

mihi stetit, talentō ēmī; **it ~ me my freedom**
  lībertātem perdidī ♦ *n* pretium *nt*, impēnsa *f*;
  ~ of living annōna *f*; **to your ~** incommodō tuō,
  dētrīmentō tuō; **at the ~ of one's reputation**
  violātā fāmā, nōn salvā existimātiōne; **I sell**
  at ~ price quantī ēmī vēndō.
costliness *n* sūmptus *m*; cāritās *f*.
costly *adj* cārus; (*furnishings*) lautus,
  sūmptuōsus.
costume *n* habitus *m*.
cosy *adj* commodus.
cot *n* lectulus *m*.
cote *n* columbārium *nt*.
cottage *n* casa *f*, tugurium *nt*.
cottager *n* rūsticus *m*.
cotton *n* (*tree*) gossympinus *f*; (*cloth*) xylinum
  nt.
couch *n* lectus *m* ♦ *vi* recumbere ♦ *vt* (*lance*)
  intendere; (*words*) exprimere, reddere.
cough *n* tussis *f* ♦ *vi* tussīre.
council *n* concilium *nt*; (*small*) cōnsilium *nt*.
councillor *n* (*town*) dēcuriō *m*.
counsel *n* (*debate*) cōnsultātiō *f*; (*advice*)
  cōnsilium *nt*; (*law*) advocātus *m*, patrōnus *m*;
  take ~ cōnsiliārī, dēlīberāre; **take ~ of**
  cōnsulere ♦ *vt* suādēre (*dat*), monēre.
counsellor *n* cōnsiliārius *m*.
count *vt* numerāre, computāre; **~ as** dūcere,
  habēre; **~ amongst** pōnere in (*abl*); **~ up** *vt*
  ēnumerāre; **~ upon** cōnfīdere (*dat*); **be ~ed**
  among in numerō esse (*gen*) ♦ *vi* aestimārī,
  habērī ♦ *n* ratiō *f*; (*in indictment*) caput *nt*;
  (*title*) comes *m*.
countenance *n* faciēs *f*, vultus *m*, ōs *nt*; (*fig*)
  favor *m*; **put out of ~** conturbāre ♦ *vt* favēre
  (*dat*), indulgēre (*dat*).
counter *n* (*for counting*) calculus *m*; (*for play*)
  tessera *f*; (*shop*) mēnsa *f* ♦ *adj* contrārius ♦
  adv contrā, obviam ♦ *vt* obsistere (*dat*),
  respondēre (*dat*).
counteract *vt* obsistere (*dat*), adversārī (*dat*);
  (*malady*) medērī (*dat*).
counterattack *vt* in vicem oppugnāre,
  adgredī.
counterattraction *n* altera illecebra *f*.
counterbalance *vt* compēnsāre, exaequāre.
counterclockwise *adv* sinistrōrsus.
counterfeit *adj* falsus, fūcātus, adsimulātus,
  fictus ♦ *vt* fingere, simulāre, imitārī.
countermand *vt* renūntiāre.
counterpane *n* lōdīx *f*, strāgulum *nt*.
counterpart *n* pār *m/f/nt*.
counterpoise *n* aequum pondus *nt* ♦ *vt*
  compēnsāre, exaequāre.
countersign *n* (MIL) tessera *f*.
counting table *n* abacus *m*.
countless *adj* innumerābilis.
countrified *adj* agrestis, rūsticus.
country *n* (*region*) regiō *f*, terra *f*; (*territory*)
  fīnēs *mpl*; (*native*) patria *f*; (*not town*) rūs *nt*;
  (*open*) agrī *mpl*; **of our ~** nostrās; **live in the ~**
  rūsticārī; **living in the ~** rūsticātiō *f*.

country house n vīlla f.
countryman n agricola m; **fellow ~** populāris m, cīvis m.
countryside n agrī mpl, rus nt.
couple n pār nt; **a ~ of** duo ♦ vt cōpulare, coniungere.
couplet n distichon nt.
courage n fortitūdō f, animus m; (MIL) virtūs f; **have the ~ to** audēre; **lose ~** animōs dēmittere; **take ~** bonō animō esse.
courageous adj fortis, ācer; audāx.
courageously adv fortiter, ācriter.
courier n tabellārius m.
course n (movement) cursus m; (route) iter nt; (sequence) seriēs f; (career) dēcursus; (for races) stadium nt, circus m; (of dinner) ferculum nt; (of stones) ōrdō m; (of water) lāpsus m; **of ~** certē, sānē, scīlicet; **as a matter of ~** continuō; **in due ~** mox; **in the ~ of** inter (acc), in (abl); **keep on one's ~** cursum tenēre; **be driven off one's ~**dēicī; **second ~** secunda mēnsa.
court n (space) ārea f; (of house) ātrium nt; (of king) aula f; (suite) cohors f, comitēs mpl; (law) iūdicium nt, iūdicēs mpl; **pay ~ to** ambīre, īnservīre (dat); **hold a ~** forum agere; **bring into ~** in iūs vocāre ♦ vt colere, ambīre; (danger) sē offerre (dat); (woman) petere.
courteous adj cōmis, urbānus, hūmānus.
courteously adv cōmiter, urbānē.
courtesan n meretrīx f.
courtesy n (quality) cōmitās f, hūmānitās f; (act) officium nt.
courtier n aulicus m; **~s** pl aula f.
courtly adj officiōsus.
cousin n cōnsobrīnus m, cōnsobrīna f.
cove n sinus m.
covenant n foedus nt, pactum nt ♦ vi pacīscī.
cover vt tegere, operīre; (hide) vēlāre; (march) claudere; **~ over** obdūcere; **~ up** vi obtegere ♦ n integumentum nt, operculum nt; (shelter) latebrae fpl, suffugium nt; (pretence) speciēs f; **under ~ of** sub (abl), sub speciē (gen); **take ~** dēlitēscere.
covering n integumentum nt, involucrum nt, operculum nt; (of couch) strāgulum nt.
coverlet n lōdīx f.
covert adj occultus; (language) oblīquus ♦ n latebra f, perfugium nt; (thicket) dūmētum nt.
covertly adv occultē, sēcrētō.
covet vt concupīscere, expetere.
covetous adj avidus, cupidus.
covetously adv avidē, cupidē.
covetousness n aviditās f, cupiditās f.
covey n grex f.
cow n vacca f ♦ vt terrēre.
coward n ignāvus m.
cowardice n ignāvia f.
cowardly adj ignāvus.
cower vi subsīdere.
cowherd m bubulcus m.
cowl n cucullus m.
coxswain n rēctor m.

coy adj pudens, verēcundus.
coyly adv pudenter, modestē.
coyness n pudor m, verēcundia f.
cozen vt fallere, dēcipere.
crab n cancer m.
crabbed adj mōrōsus, difficilis.
crack n (chink) rīma f; (sound) crepitus m ♦ vt findere, frangere; (whip) crepitāre (abl) ♦ vi (open) fatīscere; (sound) crepāre, crepitāre.
crackle vi crepitāre.
crackling n crepitus m.
cradle n cūnae fpl; (fig) incūnābula ntpl.
craft n ars f; (deceit) dolus m; (boat) nāvigium nt.
craftily adv callidē, sollerter; dolōsē.
craftsman n artifex m, faber m.
craftsmanship n ars f, artificium nt.
crafty adj callidus, sollers; dolōsus.
crag n rūpēs f, scopulus m.
cram vt farcīre, refercīre; (with food) sagīnāre.
cramp n convulsiō f; (tool) cōnfībula f ♦ vt coercēre, coartāre.
crane n (bird) grus f; (machine) māchina f, trochlea f.
crank n uncus m; (person) ineptus m.
crannied adj rīmōsus.
cranny n rīma f.
crash n (fall) ruīna f; (noise) fragor m ♦ vi ruere; strepere.
crass adj crassus; **~ stupidity** mera stultitia.
crate n crātēs fpl.
crater n crātēr m.
cravat n fōcāle nt.
crave vt (desire) concupīscere, adpetere, exoptāre; (request) ōrāre, obsecrāre.
craven adj ignāvus.
craving n cupīdō f, dēsīderium nt, adpetītiō f.
crawl vi (animal) serpere; (person) rēpere.
crayfish n commarus m.
craze n libīdō f ♦ vt mentem aliēnāre.
craziness n dēmentia f.
crazy adj dēmēns, fatuus.
creak vi crepāre.
creaking n crepitus m.
cream n spūma lactis f; (fig) flōs m.
crease n rūga f ♦ vt rūgāre.
create vt creāre, facere, gignere.
creation n (process) fabricātiō f; (result) opus nt; (human) hominēs mpl.
creative adj (nature) creātrīx; (mind) inventor, inventrīx.
creator n creātor m, auctor m, opifex m.
creature n animal nt; (person) homō m/f.
credence n fidēs f.
credentials n litterae commendātīciae fpl; (fig) auctōritās f.
credibility n fidēs f; (source) auctōritās f.
credible adj crēdibilis; (witness) locuplēs.
credit n (belief) fidēs f; (repute) existimātiō f; (character) auctōritās f, grātia f; (COMM) fidēs f; **be a ~ to** decus esse (gen); **it is to your ~** tibī laudī est; **give ~ for** laudem tribuere (gen);

have ~ fidē stāre ♦ *vt* crēdere (*dat*); (*with money*) acceptum referre (*dat*).
creditable *adj* honestus, laudābilis.
creditably *adv* honestē, cum laude.
creditor *n* crēditor *m.*
credulity *n* crēdulitās *f.*
credulous *adj* crēdulus.
creed *n* dogma *nt.*
creek *n* sinus *m.*
creel *n* vīdulus *m.*
creep *vi* (*animal*) serpere; (*person*) rēpere; (*flesh*) horrēre.
cremate *vt* cremāre.
crescent *n* lūna *f.*
crescent-shaped *adj* lūnātus.
cress *n* nasturtium *nt.*
crest *n* crista *f.*
crested *adj* cristātus.
crestfallen *adj* dēmissus.
crevasse *n* hiātus *m.*
crevice *n* rīma *f.*
crew *n* nautae *mpl*, rēmigēs *mpl*, grex *f*, turba *f.*
crib *n* (*cot*) lectulus *m*; (*manger*) praesēpe *nt.*
cricket *n* gryllus *m.*
crier *n* praecō *m.*
crime *n* scelus *nt*, facinus *nt*, flāgitium *nt.*
criminal *adj* scelestus, facinorōsus, flāgitiōsus ♦ *n* reus *m.*
criminality *n* scelus *nt.*
criminally *adv* scelestē, flāgitiōsē.
crimson *n* coccum *nt* ♦ *adj* coccineus.
cringe *vi* adūlārī, adsentārī.
crinkle *n* rūga *f.*
cripple *vt* dēbilitāre, mūtilāre; (*fig*) frangere ♦ *adj* claudus.
crisis *n* discrīmen *nt.*
crisp *adj* fragilis; (*manner*) alacer; (*hair*) crispus.
crisscross *adj* in quīncūncem dispositus.
criterion *n* index *m*, indicium *nt*; **take as a ~** referre ad (*acc*).
critic *n* iūdex *m*; (*literary*) criticus, grammaticus *m*; (*adverse*) castīgātor *m.*
critical *adj* (*mind*) accūrātus, ēlegāns; (*blame*) cēnsōrius, sevērus; (*danger*) perīculōsus, dubius; **~ moment** discrīmen *nt.*
critically *adv* accūrātē, ēleganter; sevērē; cum perīculō.
criticism *n* iūdicium *nt*; (*adverse*) reprehēnsiō *f.*
criticize *vt* iūdicāre; reprehendere, castīgāre.
croak *vi* (*raven*) crōcīre; (*frog*) coaxāre.
croaking *n* cantus *m* ♦ *adj* raucus.
crock *n* olla *f.*
crockery *n* fictilia *ntpl.*
crocodile *n* crocodīlus *m*; **weep ~ tears** lacrimās cōnfingere.
crocus *n* crocus *m.*
croft *n* agellus *m.*
crone *n* anus *f.*
crony *n* sodālis *m.*
crook *n* pedum *nt* ♦ *vt* incurvāre.
crooked *adj* incurvus, aduncus; (*deformed*)

prāvus; (*winding*) flexuōsus; (*morally*) perversus.
crookedly *adv* perversē, prāvē.
crookedness *n* prāvitās *f.*
croon *vt, vi* cantāre.
crop *n* (*grain*) seges *f*, messis *f*; (*tree*) fructus *m*; (*bird*) ingluviēs *f* ♦ *vt* (*reap*) metere; (*graze*) carpere, tondēre; **~ up** *vi* intervenīre.
cross *n* (*mark*) decussis *m*; (*torture*) crux *f* ♦ *adj* trānsversus, oblīquus; (*person*) acerbus, īrātus ♦ *vt* trānsīre; (*water*) trāicere; (*mountain*) trānscendere; superāre; (*enemy*) obstāre (*dat*), frustrārī; **~ out** *vt* (*writing*) expungere ♦ *vi* trānsīre; **~ over** (*on foot*) trānsgredī; (*by sea*) trānsmittere.
crossbar *n* iugum *nt.*
crossbow *n* scorpiō *m.*
cross-examination *n* interrogātiō *f.*
cross-examine *vt* interrogāre, percontārī.
cross-grained *adj* (*fig*) mōrōsus.
crossing *n* trānsitus *m*; (*on water*) trāiectus *m.*
cross purpose *n*: **be at ~s** dīversa spectāre.
cross-question *vt* interrogāre.
crossroads *n* quadrivium *nt.*
crosswise *adv* ex trānsversō; **divide ~** decussāre.
crotchety *adj* mōrōsus, difficilis.
crouch *vi* subsīdere, sē submittere.
crow *n* cornīx *f*; **as the ~ flies** rēctā regiōne ♦ *vi* cantāre; (*fig*) exsultāre, gestīre.
crowbar *n* vectis *m.*
crowd *n* turba *f*, concursus *m*, frequentia *f*; (*small*) grex *m*; multitūdō *f*; **in ~s** gregātim ♦ *vi* frequentāre, celebrāre ♦ *vt* (*place*) complēre; (*person*) stīpāre.
crowded *adj* frequēns.
crown *n* corōna *f*; (*royal*) diadēma *nt*; (*of head*) vertex *m*; (*fig*) apex *m*, flōs *m*; **the ~ of** summus ♦ *vt* corōnāre; (*fig*) cumulāre, fastīgium impōnere (*dat*).
crucial *adj* gravissimus, māximī mōmentī; **~ moment** discrīmen *nt.*
crucifixion *n* crucis supplicium *nt.*
crucify *vt* crucī suffīgere.
crude *adj* crūdus; (*style*) dūrus, inconcinnus.
crudely *adv* dūrē, asperē.
crudity *n* asperitās *f.*
cruel *adj* crūdēlis, saevus, atrōx.
cruelly *adv* crūdēliter, atrōciter.
cruelty *n* crūdēlitās *f*, saevitia *f*, atrōcitās *f.*
cruise *n* nāvigātiō *f* ♦ *vi* nāvigāre.
cruiser *n* speculātōria nāvis *f.*
crumb *n* mīca *f.*
crumble *vi* corruere, putrem fierī ♦ *vt* putrefacere, friāre.
crumbling *adj* putris.
crumple *vt* rūgāre.
crunch *vt* dentibus frangere.
crupper *n* postilēna *f.*
crush *vt* frangere, contundere, obterere; (*fig*) adflīgere, opprimere, obruere ♦ *n* turba *f*, frequentia *f.*
crust *n* crusta *f*; (*bread*) frustum *nt.*

crusty *adj* (*fig*) stomachōsus.
crutch *n* baculum *nt.*
cry *vt, vi* clāmāre, clāmitāre; (*weep*) flēre;
(*infant*) vāgīre; ~ **down** dētrectāre; ~ **out**
exclāmāre, vōciferārī; ~ **out against**
adclāmāre, reclāmāre; ~ **up** laudāre,
vēnditāre ♦ *n* clāmor *m*, vōx *f*; (*child's*)
vāgītus *m*; (*of grief*) plōrātus *m.*
cryptic *adj* arcānus.
crystal *n* crystallum *nt* ♦ *adj* crystallinus.
cub *n* catulus *m.*
cube *n* cubus *m.*
cubit *n* cubitum *nt.*
cuckoo *n* coccyx *m.*
cucumber *n* cucumis *m.*
cud *n*: **chew the ~** rūminārī.
cudgel *n* fustis *m* ♦ *vt* verberāre.
cue *n* signum *nt*, indicium *nt.*
cuff *n* (*blow*) alapa *f.*
cuirass *n* lōrīca *f.*
culinary *adj* coquīnārius.
cull *vt* legere, carpere, dēlībāre.
culminate *vi* ad summum fastīgium venīre.
culmination *n* fastīgium *nt.*
culpability *n* culpa *f*, noxa *f.*
culpable *adj* nocēns.
culprit *n* reus *m.*
cultivate *vt* (*land*) colere, subigere; (*mind*)
excolere; (*interest*) fovēre, studēre (*dat*).
cultivation *n* cultus *m*, cultūra *f.*
cultivator *n* cultor *m*, agricola *m.*
cultural *adj* hūmānior.
culture *n* hūmānitās *f*, bonae artēs *fpl.*
cultured *adj* doctus, litterātus.
culvert *n* cloāca *f.*
cumber *vt* impedīre, obesse (*dat*); (*load*)
onerāre.
cumbersome *adj* molestus, gravis.
cumulative *adj* alius ex aliō; **be ~** cumulārī.
cuneiform *adj* cuneātus.
cunning *adj* callidus, astūtus ♦ *n* ars *f*, astūtia
f, calliditās *f.*
cunningly *adv* callidē, astūtē.
cup *n* pōculum *nt*; **drink the ~ of** (*fig*) exanclāre,
exhaurīre; **in one's ~s** ēbrius, pōtus.
cupboard *n* armārium *nt.*
Cupid *n* Cupīdō *m*, Amor *m.*
cupidity *n* avāritia *f.*
cupola *n* tholus *m.*
cupping glass *n* cucurbita *f.*
cur *n* canis *m.*
curable *adj* sānābilis.
curative *adj* salūbris.
curator *n* custōs *m.*
curb *vt* frēnāre, īnfrēnāre; (*fig*) coercēre,
cohibēre ♦ *n* frēnum *nt.*
curdle *vt* cōgere ♦ *vi* concrēscere.
curds *n* concrētum lac *nt.*
cure *vt* sānāre, medērī (*dat*) ♦ *n* remedium *nt*;
(*process*) sānātiō *f.*
curio *n* dēliciae *fpl.*
curiosity *n* studium *nt*; (*thing*) mīrāculum *nt.*
curious *adj* (*inquisitive*) cūriōsus, cupidus;

(*artistic*) ēlabōrātus; (*strange*) mīrus, novus.
curiously *adv* cūriōsē; summā arte; mīrum in
modum.
curl *n* (*natural*) cirrus *m*; (*artificial*) cincinnus *m*
♦ *vt* (*hair*) crispāre ♦ *vi* (*smoke*) volvī.
curling irons *n* calamistrī *mpl.*
curly *adj* crispus.
currency *n* (*coin*) monēta *f*; (*use*) ūsus *m*; **gain ~**
(*rumour*) percrēbrēscere.
current *adj* vulgātus, ūsitātus; (*time*) hīc ♦ *n*
flūmen *nt*; **with the ~** secundō flūmine;
against the ~ adversō flūmine.
currently *adv* vulgō.
curriculum *n* īnstitūtiō *f.*
curry *vt* (*favour*) aucupārī.
curse *n* exsecrātiō *f*, maledictum *nt*; (*formula*)
exsecrābile carmen *nt*; (*fig*) pestis *f*; **~s**
(*interj*) malum! ♦ *vt* exsecrārī, maledīcere
(*dat*).
cursed *adj* exsecrātus, sacer; scelestus.
cursorily *adv* breviter, strictim.
cursory *adj* brevis.
curt *adj* brevis.
curtail *vt* minuere, contrahere.
curtailment *n* dēminūtiō *f*, contractiō *f.*
curtain *n* aulaeum *nt* ♦ *vt* vēlāre.
curule *adj* curūlis.
curve *n* flexus *m*, arcus *m* ♦ *vt* flectere,
incurvāre, arcuāre.
cushion *n* pulvīnus *m.*
custodian *n* custōs *m.*
custody *n* custōdia *f*, tūtēla *f*; (*prison*) carcer
m; **hold in ~** custōdīre.
custom *n* mōs *m*, cōnsuētūdō *f*; (*national*)
īnstitūtum *nt*; **~s** *pl* portōria *ntpl.*
customarily *adv* plērumque, dē mōre, vulgō.
customary *adj* solitus, ūsitātus; (*rite*)
sollemnis; **it is ~** mōs est.
customer *n* emptor *m.*
customs officer *n* portitor *m.*
cut *vt* secāre, caedere, scindere; (*corn*)
metere; (*branch*) amputāre; (*acquaintance*)
āversārī; (*hair*) dētondēre; ~ **away**
abscindere, resecāre; ~ **down** rescindere,
caedere, succīdere; ~ **into** incīdere; ~ **off** *vt*
abscīdere, praecīdere; (*exclude*) exclūdere;
(*intercept*) interclūdere, intercipere; (*head*)
abscindere; ~ **out** *vt* excīdere, exsecāre;
(*omit*) ōmittere; ~ **out for** aptus ad, nātus ad
(*acc*); ~ **round** circumcīdere; ~ **short**
praecīdere; (*speech*) incīdere, interrumpere;
~ **through** intercīdere; ~ **up** *vt* concīdere ♦ *n*
vulnus *nt.*
cutlass *n* gladius *m.*
cutlery *n* cultrī *mpl.*
cutter *n* sector *m*; (*boat*) lembus *m.*
cutthroat *n* sīcārius *m.*
cutting *n* (*plant*) propāgō *f* ♦ *adj* acūtus; (*fig*)
acerbus, mordāx.
cuttlefish *n* sēpia *f.*
cyclamen *n* baccar *nt.*
cycle *n* orbis *m.*
cyclone *n* turbō *f.*

cylinder n cylindrus m.
cymbal n cymbalum nt.
cynic n (PHILOS) cynicus m.
cynical adj mordāx, acerbus.
cynically adv mordāciter, acerbē.
cynicism n acerbitās f.
cynosure n cynosūra f.
cypress n cypressus f.

D, d

dabble vi: ~ **in** gustāre, leviter attingere.
dactyl n dactylus m.
dactylic adj dactylicus.
dagger n sīca f, pugiō f.
daily adj diūrnus, cottīdiānus ♦ adv cottīdiē, in diēs.
daintily adv molliter, concinnē; fastīdiōsē.
daintiness n munditia f, concinnitās f; (squeamish) fastīdium nt.
dainty adj mundus, concinnus, mollis; fastīdiōsus ♦ npl: **dainties** cuppēdia ntpl.
dais n suggestus m.
daisy n bellis f.
dale n vallis f.
dalliance n lascīvia f.
dally vi lūdere; morārī.
dam n mōlēs f, agger m; (animal) māter f ♦ vt obstruere, exaggerāre.
damage n damnum nt, dētrīmentum nt, malum nt; (inflicted) iniūria f; (law) damnum nt; **assess ~s** lītem aestimāre ♦ vt laedere, nocēre (dat); (by evidence) laedere; (reputation) violāre.
damageable adj fragilis.
dame n mātrōna f, domina f.
damn vt damnāre, exsecrārī.
damnable adj dētestābilis, improbus.
damnably adv improbē.
damnation n malum nt.
damp adj ūmidus ♦ n ūmor m ♦ vt madefacere; (enthusiasm) restinguere, dēmittere.
damsel n puella f, virgō f.
damson n Damascēnum nt.
dance vi saltāre ♦ n saltātiō f; (religious) tripudium nt.
dancer n saltātor m, saltātrīx f.
dandruff n porrīgō f.
dandy n dēlicātus m.
danger n perīculum nt, discrīmen nt.
dangerous adj perīculōsus, dubius; (in attack) īnfestus.
dangerously adv perīculōsē.
dangle vt suspendere ♦ vi pendēre.

dank adj ūmidus.
dapper adj concinnus, nitidus.
dapple vt variāre, distinguere.
dappled adj maculōsus, distinctus.
dare vt audēre; (challenge) prōvocāre; **I ~ say** haud sciō an.
daring n audācia f ♦ adj audāx.
daringly adv audācter.
dark adj obscūrus, opācus; (colour) fuscus, āter; (fig) obscūrus; **it is getting ~** advesperāscit; **to ~ silēre** ♦ n tenebrae fpl; (mist) cālīgō f; **keep in the ~** cēlāre.
darken vt obscūrāre, occaecāre.
darkish adj subobscūrus.
darkling adj obscūrus.
darkness n tenebrae fpl; (mist) cālīgō f.
darksome adj obscūrus.
darling adj cārus, dīlēctus ♦ n dēliciae fpl, voluptās f.
darn vt resarcīre.
darnel n lolium nt.
dart n tēlum nt; iaculum nt ♦ vi ēmicāre, sē conicere ♦ vt iaculārī, iacere.
dash vt adflīgere; (hope) frangere; ~ **against** illīdere, incutere; ~ **down** dēturbāre; ~ **out** ēlīdere; ~ **to pieces** discutere; ~ **to the ground** prōsternere ♦ vi currere, sē incitāre, ruere ♦ n impetus m; (quality) ferōcia f.
dashing adj ferōx, animōsus.
dastardly adj ignāvus.
date n (fruit) palmula f; (time) tempus nt, diēs m; **out of ~** obsolētus; **become out of ~** exolēscere; **to ~** adhūc; **be up to ~** praesentī mōre ūtī ♦ vt (letter) diem adscrībere; (past event) repetere ♦ vi initium capere.
dative n datīvus m.
daub vt inlinere.
daughter n fīlia f; (little) fīliola f.
daughter-in-law n nurus f.
daunt vt terrēre, perterrēre.
dauntless adj impavidus, intrepidus.
dauntlessly adv impavidē, intrepidē.
dawdle vi cessāre, cunctārī.
dawdler n cunctātor m.
dawn n aurōra f, dīlūculum nt; (fig) orīgō f; prima lux f; **at ~** prīmā lūce ♦ vi dīlūcēscere; **day ~s** diēs illūcēscit; **it ~s upon me** mente concipiō.
day n diēs m/f; (period) aetās f; ~ **about** alternīs diēbus; ~ **by** ~ in diēs; cotīdiē; **by** ~ adj diūrnus ♦ adv interdiū; **during the** ~ interdiū; **every** ~ cotīdiē; **from** ~ **to** ~ in diēs, diem dē diē; **late in the** ~ multō diē; **next** ~ postrīdiē; **one ~/some** ~ ōlim; **the** ~ **after** adv postrīdiē ♦ conj postrīdiē quam; **the** ~ **after tomorrow** perendiē; **the** ~ **before** adv prīdiē ♦ conj prīdiē quam; **the** ~ **before yesterday** nūdius tertius; **the present** ~ haec aetās; **time of** ~ hōra; **twice a** ~ bis (in) diē; ~s **of old** praeteritum tempus; ~s **to come** posteritās; **better** ~s rēs prosperae; **evil** ~s rēs adversae; **three** ~s trīduum nt; **two** ~s biduum nt; **win**

the ~ vincere.
daybook n adversāria *ntpl*.
daybreak n aurōra *f*, prīma lūx *f*.
daylight n diēs *m*; **(become)** ~ illūcēscere.
daystar n lūcifer *m*.
daytime n diēs *m*; **in the** ~ interdiū.
daze *vt* obstupefacere ♦ n stupor *m*.
dazzle *vt* praestringere.
dazzling *adj* splendidus, nitēns.
deacon n diāconus *m*.
deaconess n diāconissa *f*.
dead *adj* mortuus; (*in battle*) occīsus; (*LIT*)
frīgidus; (*place*) iners, sōlitarius; (*senses*)
hebes; ~ **of night** nox intempesta *f*; **be** ~ **to**
nōn sentīre; **in** ~ **earnest** sēriō ac vērō; **rise
from the** ~ revīvīscere ♦ *adv* prōrsus,
omnīnō.
dead beat *adj* cōnfectus.
dead body n cadāver *m*.
dead calm n malacia *f*.
dead certainty n rēs certissima.
deaden *vt* (*senses*) hebetāre, obtundere; (*pain*)
restinguere.
deadlock n incitae *fpl*; **reach a** ~ ad incitās
redigī.
dead loss n mera iactūra.
deadly *adj* fūnestus, exitiōsus, exitiābilis;
(*enmity*) implācābilis; (*pain*) acerbissimus.
dead weight n mōlēs *f*.
deaf *adj* surdus; **become** ~ obsurdēscere; **be** ~
to nōn audīre, obdūrēscere contrā.
deafen *vt* (*with noise*) obtundere.
deafness n surditās *f*.
deal n (*amount*) cōpia *f*; **a good** ~ aliquantum *nt*,
bona pars *f*; (*wood*) abiēs *f* ♦ *adj* abiēgnus ♦ *vt*
(*blow*) dare, īnflīgere; (*share*) dīvidere,
partīrī ♦ *vi* agere, negōtiārī; ~ **with** *vt fus*
(*person*) agere cum (*abl*); (*matter*) tractāre.
dealer n (*wholesale*) negōtiātor *m*, mercātor *m*;
(*retail*) caupō *m*.
dealings n commercium *nt*, negōtium *nt*, rēs *f*.
dean n decānus *m*.
dear *adj* (*love*) cārus, grātus; (*cost*) cārus,
pretiōsus; **my** ~ **Quintus** mī Quīnte;
(*beginning of letter from Marcus*) Marcus
Quintō salūtem; ~ **me!** (*sorrow*) hei!;
(*surprise*) ehem!; **buy** ~ male emere; **sell** ~
bene vēndere.
dearly *adv* (*love*) valdē, ārdenter; (*value*)
magnī.
dearness n cāritās *f*.
dearth n inopia *f*, pēnūria *f*.
death n mors *f*; (*natural*) obitus *m*; (*violent*) nex
f, interitus *m*; **condemn to** ~ capitis damnāre;
put to ~ interficere; **give the** ~ **blow to**
interimere.
deathbed n: **on one's** ~ moriēns, moribundus.
deathless *adj* immortālis.
deathly *adj* pallidus.
debar *vt* prohibēre, exclūdere.
debase *vt* dēprāvāre, corrumpere; (*coin*)
adulterāre; (*self*) prōsternere, dēmittere.
debasement n dēdecus *nt*; (*coin*) adulterium

nt.
debatable *adj* ambiguus, dubius.
debate *vt* disputāre, disceptāre ♦ n
contrōversia *f*, disceptātiō *f*, altercātiō *f*.
debater n disputātor *m*.
debauch *vt* corrumpere, pellicere ♦ n
cōmissātiō *f*.
debauched *adj* perditus, prāvus.
debauchee n cōmissātor *m*.
debaucher n corruptor *m*.
debauchery n luxuria *f*, stuprum *nt*.
debilitate *vt* dēbilitāre.
debility n īnfirmitās *f*.
debit n expēnsum *nt* ♦ *vt* in expēnsum referre.
debonair *adj* urbānus, cōmis.
debouch *vi* exīre.
debris n rūdus *nt*.
debt n aes aliēnum *nt*; (*booked*) nōmen *nt*; (*fig*)
dēbitum *nt*; **be in** ~ in aere aliēnō esse; **pay off**
~ aes aliēnum persolvere; **run up** ~ aes
aliēnum contrahere; **collect** ~s nōmina
exigere; **abolition of** ~s novae tabulae *fpl*.
debtor n dēbitor *m*.
decade n decem annī *mpl*.
decadence n occāsus *m*.
decadent *adj* dēgener, dēterior.
decamp *vi* (*MIL*) castra movēre; (*fig*)
discēdere, aufugere.
decant *vt* dēfundere, diffundere.
decanter n lagoena *f*.
decapitate *vt* dētruncāre.
decay *vi* dīlābī, perīre, putrēscere; (*fig*)
tābēscere, senēscere ♦ n ruīna *f*, lāpsus *m*;
(*fig*) occāsus *m*, dēfectiō *f*.
deceased *adj* mortuus.
deceit n fraus *f*, fallācia *f*, dolus *m*.
deceitful *adj* fallāx, fraudulentus, dolōsus.
deceitfully *adv* fallāciter, dolōsē.
deceive *vt* dēcipere, fallere, circumvenīre,
fraudāre.
deceiver n fraudātor *m*.
December n mēnsis December *m*; **of** ~
December.
decemvir n decemvir *m*; **of the** ~s
decemvirālis.
decemvirate n decemvirātus *m*.
decency n honestum *nt*, decōrum *nt*, pudor *m*.
decent *adj* honestus, pudēns.
decently *adv* honestē, pudenter.
deception n fraus *f*, fallācia *f*.
deceptive *adj* fallāx, fraudulentus.
decide *vt*, *vi* (*dispute*) diiūdicāre, dēcernere,
dīrimere; ~ **to do** statuere, cōnstituere
(*infin*); **I have** ~**d** mihī certum est; ~ **the issue**
dēcernere.
decided *adj* certus, firmus.
decidedly *adv* certē, plānē.
deciduous *adj* cadūcus.
decimate *vt* decimum quemque occīdere.
decipher *vt* expedīre, ēnōdāre.
decision n (*of judge*) iūdicium *nt*; (*of council*)
dēcrētum *nt*; (*of senate*) auctōritās *f*; (*of
referee*) arbitrium *nt*; (*personal*) sententia *f*;

(quality) cōnstantia *f.*
decisive *adj* certus; ~ **moment** discrīmen *nt.*
decisively *adv* sine dubiō.
deck *vt* ōrnāre, exōrnāre ♦ *n*
(ship) pōns *m*; **with a** ~ cōnstrātus.
decked *adj* ōrnātus; *(ship)* cōnstrātus.
declaim *vt, vi* dēclāmāre, prōnūntiāre.
declamation *n* dēclāmātiō *f.*
declamatory *adj* dēclāmātōrius.
declaration *n* adfirmātiō *f*, adsevērātiō *f*;
(formal) prōfessiō *f*; *(of war)* dēnūntiātiō *f.*
declare *vt* affirmāre, adsevērāre; *(secret)*
aperīre, expōnere; *(proclamation)*
dēnūntiāre, ēdīcere; *(property in census)*
dēdicāre; *(war)* indīcere.
declension *n* dēclīnātiō *f.*
declination *n* dēclīnātiō *f.*
decline *n* *(slope)* dēclīve *nt*, dēiectus *m*; *(of age)*
senium *nt*; *(of power)* dēfectiō *f*; *(of nation)*
occāsus *m* ♦ *vi* inclīnāre, occidere; *(fig)*
ruere, dēlābī, dēgenerāre ♦ *vt* dētrectāre,
recūsare; *(GRAM)* dēclīnāre.
decode *vt* expedīre, ēnōdāre.
decompose *vt* dissolvere ♦ *vi* putrēscere.
decomposed *adj* putridus.
decomposition *n* dissolūtiō *f.*
decorate *vt* ōrnāre, decorāre.
decoration *n* ōrnāmentum *nt*; *(medal)* īnsigne
nt.
decorous *adj* pudēns, modestus, decōrus.
decorously *adv* pudenter, modestē.
decorum *n* pudor *m*, honestum *nt.*
decoy *n* illecebra *f* ♦ *vt* adlicere, inescāre.
decrease *n* dēminūtiō *f*, dēcessiō *f* ♦ *vt*
dēminuere, extenuāre ♦ *vi* dēcrēscere.
decree *n* *(of magistrate)* dēcrētum *nt*, ēdictum
nt; *(of senate)* cōnsultum *nt*, auctōritās *f*; *(of*
people) scītum *nt* ♦ *vt* ēdīcere, dēcernere;
(people) scīscere, iubēre; **the senate ~s**
placet senātuī.
decrepit *adj* īnfirmus, dēbilis, dēcrepitus.
decrepitude *n* īnfirmitās *f*, dēbilitās *f.*
decry *vt* obtrectāre, reprehendere.
decurion *n* decuriō *m.*
dedicate *vt* dēdicāre, cōnsecrāre; *(life)*
dēvovēre.
dedication *n* dēdicātiō *f*; dēvōtiō *f.*
dedicatory *adj* commendātīcius.
deduce *vt* colligere, conclūdere.
deduct *vt* dēmere, dētrahere.
deduction *n* *(inference)* conclūsiō *f*,
cōnsequēns *nt*; *(subtraction)* dēductiō *f*,
dēminūtiō *f.*
deed *n*, factum *nt*, facinus *nt*; gestum *nt*; *(legal)*
tabulae *fpl*; **~s** *pl* rēs gestae *fpl.*
deem *vt* dūcere, cēnsēre, habēre.
deep *adj* altus, profundus; *(discussion)*
abstrūsus; *(sleep)* artus; *(sound)* gravis;
(width) lātus; **three ~** *(MIL)* ternī in
lātitūdinem ♦ *n* altum *nt.*
deepen *vt* dēfodere, altiōrem reddere; *(fig)*
augēre ♦ *vi* altiōrem fierī; *(fig)* crēscere.
deepest *adj* īmus.

deeply *adv* altē, graviter; *(inside)* penitus; **very**
~ valdē, vehementer.
deep-seated *adj* *(fig)* inveterātus.
deer *n* cervus *m*, cerva *f*; *(fallow)* dāma *f.*
deface *vt* dēfōrmāre, foedāre.
defaced *adj* dēfōrmis.
defacement *n* dēfōrmitās *f.*
defalcation *n* peculātus *m.*
defamation *n* calumnia *f*, opprobrium *nt.*
defamatory *adj* contumēliōsus, probrōsus.
defame *vt* īnfāmāre, obtrectāre, calumniārī.
default *vi* dēesse; *(money)* nōn solvere ♦ *n*
dēfectiō *f*, culpa *f*; **let judgment go by** ~
vadimōnium dēserere, nōn respondēre.
defaulter *n* reus *m.*
defeat *vt* vincere, superāre; *(completely)*
dēvincere; *(plan)* frustrārī, disicere ♦ *n*
clādēs *f*; *(at election)* repulsa *f*, offēnsiō *f*; *(of*
plan) frustrātiō *f.*
defeatism *n* patientia *f.*
defeatist *n* imbellis *m.*
defect *n* vitium *nt.*
defection *n* dēfectiō *f*, sēditiō *f.*
defective *adj* mancus, vitiōsus.
defence *n* praesidium *nt*, tūtēla *f*; patrōcinium
nt; *(speech)* dēfēnsiō *f*; **speak in** ~ dēfendere.
defenceless *adj* inermis, indēfēnsus; **leave** ~
nūdāre.
defences *npl* mūnīmenta *ntpl*, mūnītiōnēs *fpl.*
defend *vt* dēfendere, tuērī, custōdīre.
defendant *n* reus *m.*
defender *n* dēfēnsor *m*, prōpugnātor *m*; *(law)*
patrōnus *m.*
defensible *adj* iūstus.
defensive *adj* dēfēnsiōnis causā; **be on the** ~
sē dēfendere.
defensively *adv* dēfendendō.
defer *vt* differre, prōlātāre ♦ *vi* mōrem gerere
(dat); **I** ~ **to you in this** hōc tibī tribuō.
deference *n* obsequium *nt*, observantia *f*;
show ~ **to** observāre, īnservīre *(dat).*
deferential *adj* observāns, officiōsus.
deferment *n* dīlātiō *f*, prōlātiō *f.*
defiance *n* ferōcia *f*, minae *fpl.*
defiant *adj* ferōx, mināx.
defiantly *adv* ferōciter, mināciter.
deficiency *n* vitium *nt*; *(lack)* pēnūria *f*, inopia
f.
deficient *adj* vitiōsus, inops; **be** ~ dēesse,
dēficere.
deficit *n* lacūna *f.*
defile *n* faucēs *fpl*, angustiae *fpl* ♦ *vt* inquināre,
contāmināre.
defilement *n* sordēs *f*, foeditās *f.*
define *vt* *(limits)* fīnīre, dēfīnīre, termināre;
(meaning) explicāre.
definite *adj* certus, dēfīnītus.
definitely *adv* dēfīnītē; prōrsus.
definition *n* dēfīnītiō *f*, explicātiō *f.*
definitive *adj* dēfīnītīvus.
deflate *vt* laxāre.
deflect *vt* dēdūcere, dēclīnāre ♦ *vi* dēflectere,
dēgredī.

deflection *n* dēclīnātiō *f*, flexus *m*.
deform *vt* dēfōrmāre.
deformed *adj* dēfōrmis, distortus.
deformity *n* dēfōrmitās *f*, prāvitās *f*.
defraud *vt* fraudāre, dēfraudāre.
defrauder *n* fraudātor *m*.
defray *vt* solvere, suppeditāre.
deft *adj* habilis.
deftly *adv* habiliter.
defunct *adj* mortuus.
defy *vt* contemnere, spernere, adversārī (*dat*);
(*challenge*) prōvocāre, lacessere.
degeneracy *n* dēprāvātiō *f*.
degenerate *adj* dēgener ♦ *vi* dēgenerāre,
dēscīscere.
degradation *n* īnfāmia *f*, ignōminia *f*, nota *f*.
degrade *vt* notāre, abicere; (*from office*)
movēre.
degrading *adj* turpis, indignus.
degree *n* gradus; (*social*) locus *m*; **in some ~**
aliquā ex parte; **by ~s** gradātim, sēnsim.
deification *n* apotheōsis *f*.
deified *adj* (*emperor*) dīvus.
deify *vt* cōnsecrāre, inter deōs referre.
deign *vi* dignārī.
deity *n* deus *m*.
dejected *adj* adflīctus, dēmissus.
dejectedly *adv* animō dēmissō.
dejection *n* maestitia *f*.
delay *vt* dēmorārī, dētinēre, retardāre ♦ *vi*
cunctārī, cessāre ♦ *n* mora *f*, cunctātiō *f*.
delayer *n* morātor *m*, cunctātor *m*.
delectable *adj* iūcundus, amoenus.
delegate *vt* lēgāre, mandāre, committere ♦ *n*
lēgātus *m*.
delegation *n* lēgātiō *f*, lēgātī *mpl*.
delete *vt* dēlēre.
deleterious *adj* perniciōsus, noxius.
deletion *n* (*writing*) litūra *f*.
deliberate *vi* dēlīberāre, cōnsulere ♦ *adj* (*act*)
cōnsīderātus; (*intention*) certus; (*manner*)
cōnsīderātus; (*speech*) lentus.
deliberately *adv* dē industriā.
deliberation *n* dēlīberātiō *f*.
deliberative *adj* dēlīberātīvus.
delicacy *n* (*judgment*) subtīlitās *f*, ēlegantia *f*;
(*manners*) mollitia *f*, luxus *m*; (*health*)
valētūdō *f*; (*food*) cuppēdia *ntpl*.
delicate *adj* mollis; (*health*) īnfirmus; (*shape*)
gracilis; (*feelings*) hūmānus.
delicately *adv* molliter; hūmānē.
delicious *adj* suāvis, lautus.
delight *n* voluptās *f*, gaudium *nt*, dēlectātiō *f* ♦
vt dēlectāre, oblectāre, iuvāre ♦ *vi* gaudēre,
dēlectārī.
delightful *adj* iūcundus, dulcis, festīvus;
(*scenery*) amoenus.
delightfully *adv* iūcundē, suāviter.
delimitation *n* dēfīnītiō *f*.
delineate *vt* dēscrībere, dēpingere.
delineation *n* dēscrīptiō *f*.
delinquency *n* culpa *f*, dēlictum *nt*, noxa *f*.
delinquent *n* nocēns *m/f*, reus *m*.

delirious *adj* dēlīrus, āmēns, furiōsus; **be ~**
furere, dēlīrāre.
delirium *n* furor *m*, āmentia *f*.
deliver *vt* (*from*) līberāre, exsolvere, ēripere;
(*blow*) intendere; (*message*) referre; (*speech*)
habēre; **~ to** dēferre, trādere, dare; **~ up**
dēdere, trādere; **be ~ed of** parere.
deliverance *n* līberātiō *f*.
deliverer *n* līberātor *m*.
delivery *n* (*of things due*) trāditiō *f*; (*of speech*)
āctiō *f*, prōnūntiātiō *f*; (*of child*) partus *m*.
dell *n* convallis *f*.
Delphi *n* Delphī *mpl*.
delude *vt* dēcipere, frustrārī, dēlūdere.
deluge *n* ēluviō *f* ♦ *vt* inundāre.
delusion *n* error *m*, fraus *f*.
delusive *adj* fallāx, inānis.
delve *vt* fodere.
demagogue *n* plēbicola *m*.
demand *vt* poscere, postulāre, imperāre;
(*urgently*) flāgitāre, poscere; (*thing due*)
exigere; (*answer*) quaerere; **~ back** repetere
♦ *n* postulātiō *f*, postulātum *nt*.
demarcation *n* līmes *m*.
demean *vt* (*self*) dēmittere.
demeanour *n* gestus *m*, mōs *m*, habitus *m*.
demented *adj* dēmēns, furiōsus.
demerit *n* culpa *f*, vitium *nt*.
demesne *n* fundus *m*.
demigod *n* hērōs *m*.
demise *n* obitus *m* ♦ *vt* lēgāre.
democracy *n* cīvitās populāris *f*.
democrat *n* homō populāris *m/f*.
democratic *adj* populāris.
demolish *vt* dēmōlīrī, dīruere, dēstruere;
(*argument*) discutere.
demolition *n* ruīna *f*, ēversiō *f*.
demon *n* daemōn *m*.
demonstrate *vt* (*show*) mōnstrāre, ostendere,
indicāre; (*prove*) dēmōnstrāre.
demonstration *n* exemplum *nt*; (*proof*)
dēmōnstrātiō *f*.
demonstrative *adj* (*manner*) vehemēns; (*RHET*)
dēmōnstrātīvus.
demoralization *n* corruptiō *f*, dēprāvātiō *f*.
demoralize *vt* corrumpere, dēprāvāre,
labefactāre.
demote *vt* locō movēre.
demur *vi* gravārī, recūsāre ♦ *n* mora *f*,
dubitātiō *f*.
demure *adj* modestus, verēcundus.
demurely *adv* modestē, verēcundē.
demureness *n* modestia *f*, verēcundia *f*,
pudor *m*.
demurrer *n* (*law*) exceptiō *f*.
den *n* latibulum *nt*, latebra *f*; (*of vice*) lustrum
nt.
denarius *n* dēnārius *m*.
denial *n* īnfitiātiō *f*, negātiō *f*.
denigrate *vt* obtrectāre, calumniārī.
denizen *n* incola *m/f*.
denominate *vt* nōmināre, appellāre.
denomination *n* nōmen *nt*; (*religious*) secta *f*.

denote _vt_ notāre, significāre.
denouement _n_ exitus _m_.
denounce _vt_ dēferre, incūsāre.
denouncer _n_ dēlātor _m_.
dense _adj_ dēnsus; (_crowd_) frequēns; (_person_) stolidus.
density _n_ crassitūdō _f_; (_crowd_) frequentia _f_.
dent _n_ nota _f_.
dentate _adj_ dentātus.
denture _n_ dentēs _mpl_.
denudation _n_ spoliātiō _f_.
denude _vt_ spoliāre, nūdāre.
denunciation _n_ (_report_) indicium _nt_, dēlātiō _f_; (_threat_) minae _fpl_.
deny _vt_ īnfitiārī, īnfitiās īre, negāre, abnuere; (_on oath_) abiūrāre; ~ **oneself** genium dēfraudāre.
depart _vi_ discēdere (_abl_), abīre, exīre, ēgredī.
department _n_ (_district_) regiō _f_, pars _f_; (_duty_) prōvincia _f_, mūnus _nt_.
departure _n_ discessus _m_, abitus _m_, dīgressus _m_, exitus _m_; (_change_) mūtātiō _f_; (_death_) obitus _m_.
depend _vi_ pendēre; (_be dependent_) pendēre ex (_abl_), nītī (_abl_); (_rely_) fīdere, cōnfīdere; ~**ing on** frētus (_abl_).
dependable _adj_ fīdus.
dependant _n_ cliēns _m/f_.
dependence _n_ clientēla _f_; (_reliance_) fīdūcia _f_.
dependency _n_ prōvincia _f_.
dependent _adj_ subiectus, obnoxius.
depict _vt_ dēscrībere, dēpingere; (_to the life_) expingere.
deplete _vt_ dēminuere.
depletion _n_ dēminūtiō _f_.
deplorable _adj_ turpis, nefandus, pessimus.
deplorably _adv_ turpiter, pessimē, miserē.
deplore _vt_ dēplōrāre, dēfiēre, conquerī.
deploy _vt_ explicāre; instruere, dispōnere.
depopulate _vt_ vastāre, nūdāre.
depopulation _n_ vastātiō _f_, sōlitūdō _f_.
deport _vt_ (_banish_) dēportāre; (_self_) gerere.
deportation _n_ exsilium _nt_.
deportment _n_ gestus _m_, habitus _m_.
depose _vt_ dēmovēre, dēpellere; (_evidence_) testārī.
deposit _n_ fīdūcia _f_, dēpositum _nt_ ♦ _vt_ dēpōnere, mandāre.
depositary _n_ sequester _m_.
deposition _n_ (_law_) testimōnium _nt_, indicium _nt_.
depository _n_ apothēca _f_.
depot _n_ (_for arms_) armāmentārium _nt_; (_for trade_) emporium _nt_.
deprave _vt_ dēprāvāre, corrumpere.
depraved _adj_ prāvus.
depravity _n_ dēprāvātiō _f_, turpitūdō _f_.
deprecate _vt_ abōminārī, dēprecārī.
deprecation _n_ dēprecātiō _f_.
depreciate _vt_ obtrectāre, dētrectāre.
depreciation _n_ obtrectātiō _f_; (_price_) vīlitās _f_.
depredation _n_ praedātiō _f_, dīreptiō _f_.
depress _vt_ dēprimere; (_mind_) adflīgere,

frangere; **be ~ed** iacēre, animum dēspondēre.
depressing _adj_ maestus, tristis.
depression _n_ (_place_) cavum _nt_; (_mind_) tristitia _f_, sollicitūdō _f_.
deprivation _n_ prīvātiō _f_, spoliātiō _f_.
deprive _vt_ prīvāre, spoliāre.
depth _n_ altitūdō _f_; (_place_) profundum _nt_, gurges _m_.
deputation _n_ lēgātiō _f_, lēgātī _mpl_.
depute _vt_ lēgāre, mandāre.
deputy _n_ lēgātus _m_; (_substitute_) vicārius _m_.
derange _vt_ conturbāre.
deranged _adj_ īnsānus, mente captus.
derangement _n_ perturbātiō _f_; (_mind_) īnsānia _f_, dēmentia _f_.
derelict _adj_ dēsertus.
dereliction _n_ (_of duty_) neglegentia _f_.
deride _vt_ dērīdēre, inlūdere.
derision _n_ rīsus _m_, irrīsiō _f_.
derisive _adj_ mordāx.
derivation _n_ orīgō _f_.
derive _vt_ dūcere, trahere; (_advantage_) capere, parāre; (_pleasure_) dēcerpere, percipere; **be ~d** dēfluere.
derogate _vi_ dērogāre, dētrahere; ~ **from** imminuere, obtrectāre.
derogation _n_ imminūtiō _f_, obtrectātiō _f_.
derogatory _adj_ indignus; ~ **remarks** obtrectātiō _f_.
derrick _n_ trochlea _f_.
descant _vt_ disserere ♦ _n_ cantus _m_.
descend _vi_ dēscendere; (_water_) dēlābī; (_from heaven_) dēlābī; (_by inheritance_) pervenīre, prōdī; (_morally_) dēlābī, sē dēmittere; **be ~ed from** orīrī ex (_abl_).
descendant _n_ prōgeniēs _f_; ~**s** _pl_ minōrēs _mpl_, posterī _mpl_.
descent _n_ dēscensus _m_; (_slope_) clīvus _m_, dēiectus _m_; (_birth_) genus _nt_; (_hostile_) dēcursus _m_, incursiō _f_; **make a ~ upon** inrumpere in (_acc_), incursāre in (_acc_).
describe _vt_ dēscrībere; (_tell_) nārrāre; (_portray_) dēpingere, exprimere.
description _n_ dēscrīptiō _f_; (_tale_) nārrātiō _f_; (_kind_) genus _nt_.
descry _vt_ cernere, cōnspicere, prōspectāre.
desecrate _vt_ prōfānāre, exaugurāre.
desecration _n_ exaugurātiō _f_, violātiō _f_.
desert _vt_ dēserere, dērelinquere, dēstituere ♦ _vi_ dēscīscere, dēficere ♦ _adj_ dēsertus, sōlitārius ♦ _n_ (_place_) sōlitūdō _f_, loca dēserta _ntpl_; (_merit_) meritum _nt_.
deserted _adj_ dēsertus.
deserter _n_ dēsertor _m_; (_MIL_) trānsfuga _m_.
desertion _n_ dēfectiō _f_, trānsfugium _nt_.
deserve _vt_ merērī; dignus esse quī (+ _subj_); ~ **well of** bene merērī dē (_abl_).
deserved _adj_ meritus.
deservedly _adv_ meritō.
deserving _adj_ dignus.
desiccate _vt_ siccāre.
design _n_ (_drawing_) adumbrātiō _f_; (_plan_)

cōnsilium *nt*, prōpositum *nt*; **by ~** cōnsultō ♦
vt adumbrāre; **in animō** habēre.
designate *vt* dēsignāre, mōnstrāre; (*as heir*)
scrībere; (*as official*) dēsignāre ♦ *adj*
dēsignātus.
designation *n* nōmen *nt*, titulus *m*.
designedly *adv* dē industriā, cōnsultō.
designer *n* auctor *m*, inventor *m*.
designing *adj* vafer, dolōsus.
desirable *adj* optābilis, expetendus, grātus.
desire *n* cupīditās *f*; studium *nt*; (*uncontrolled*)
libīdō *f*; (*natural*) adpetītiō *f* ♦ *vt* cupere;
(*much*) exoptāre, expetere; (*command*)
iubēre.
desirous *adj* cupidus, avidus, studiōsus.
desist *vi* dēsistere.
desk *n* scrīnium *nt*.
desolate *adj* dēsertus, sōlitārius; (*place*)
vastus ♦ *vt* vastāre.
desolation *n* sōlitūdō *f*, vastitās *f*; (*process*)
vastātiō *f*.
despair *vi* dēspērāre dē (*abl*), animum
dēspondēre ♦ *n* dēspērātiō *f*.
despairingly *adv* dēspēranter.
despatch *see* **dispatch.**
desperado *n* homō dēspērātus *m*.
desperate *adj* (*hopeless*) dēspērātus; (*wicked*)
perditus; (*dangerous*) perīculōsus.
desperately *adv* dēspēranter.
desperation *n* dēspērātiō *f*.
despicable *adj* dēspectus, abiectus, turpis.
despicably *adv* turpiter.
despise *vt* contemnere, dēspicere, spernere.
despiser *n* contemptor *m*.
despite *n* malevolentia *f*, odium *nt*.
despoil *vt* spoliāre, nūdāre.
despoiler *n* spoliātor *m*, praedātor *m*.
despond *vi* animum dēspondēre, dēspērāre.
despondency *n* dēspērātiō *f*.
despondent *adj* abiectus, adflīctus, dēmissus;
be ~ animum dēspondēre.
despondently *adv* animō dēmissō.
despot *n* dominus *m*, rēx *m*.
despotic *adj* imperiōsus, superbus.
despotically *adv* superbē.
despotism *n* dominātiō *f*, superbia *f*, rēgnum
nt.
dessert *n* secunda mēnsa *f*.
destination *n* fīnis *m*.
destine *vt* dēstināre, dēsignāre; **~d to be**
futūrus.
destiny *n* fātum *nt*; **of ~** fātālis.
destitute *adj* inops, pauper, prīvātus; **~ of**
expers (*gen*).
destitution *n* inopia *f*, egestās *f*.
destroy *vt* dēlēre, ēvertere, dīrimere,
perdere.
destroyer *n* ēversor *m*.
destructible *adj* fragilis.
destruction *n* exitium *nt*, ēversiō *f*, excidium
nt.
destructive *adj* exitiābilis, perniciōsus.
destructively *adv* perniciōsē.

desuetude *n* dēsuētūdō *f*.
desultorily *adv* carptim.
desultory *adj* varius, incōnstāns.
detach *vt* abiungere, sēiungere, āmovēre,
sēparāre.
detachment *n* (*MIL*) manus *f*, cohors *f*; (*mind*)
integer animus *m*, līber animus.
detail *n*: **~s** *pl* singula *ntpl*; **in ~** singillātim ♦ *vt*
exsequī.
detain *vt* dēmorārī, dētinēre, distinēre,
morārī.
detect *vt* dēprehendere, patefacere.
detection *n* dēprehēnsiō *f*.
detective *n* inquīsītor *m*.
detention *n* retentiō *f*; (*prison*) vincula *ntpl*.
deter *vt* dēterrēre, absterrēre, impedīre.
deteriorate *vi* dēgenerāre.
deterioration *n* dēprāvātiō *f*, lāpsus *m*.
determinate *adj* certus, fīnītus.
determination *n* obstinātiō *f*, cōnstantia *f*;
(*intention*) prōpositum *nt*, sententia *f*.
determine *vt* (*fix*) fīnīre; (*decide*) statuere,
cōnstituere.
determined *adj* obstinātus; (*thing*) certus; **I**
am ~ to mihī certum est (*infin*).
determinedly *adv* cōnstanter.
deterrent *n*: **act as a ~ to** dēterrēre.
detest *vt* ōdisse, dētestārī.
detestable *adj* dētestābilis, odiōsus.
detestation *n* odium *nt*, invidia *f*.
dethrone *vt* rēgnō dēpellere.
detour *n* circuitus *m*; **make a ~** iter flectere;
(*MIL*) agmen circumdūcere.
detract *vi*: **~ from** dērogāre, dētrahere.
detraction *n* obtrectātiō *f*.
detractor *n* obtrectātor *m*, invidus *m*.
detriment *n* damnum *nt*, dētrīmentum *nt*.
detrimental *adj* damnōsus; **be ~ to** dētrīmentō
esse (*dat*).
devastate *vt* vastāre, populārī.
devastation *n* vastātiō *f*, populātiō *f*; (*state*)
vastitās *f*.
develop *vt* ēvolvere, explicāre; (*person*)
ēducāre, alere ♦ *vi* crēscere; **~ into** ēvādere
in (*acc*).
development *n* explicātiō *f*; (*of men*) ēducātiō
f; (*of resources*) cultus *m*; (*of events*) exitus *m*.
deviate *vi* dēcēdere dē viā, aberrāre,
dēclīnāre; (*speech*) dēgredī.
deviation *n* dēclīnātiō *f*; (*from truth*) error *m*;
(*in speech*) dīgressus *m*.
device *n* (*plan*) cōnsilium *nt*; (*machine*)
māchina *f*; (*emblem*) īnsigne *nt*.
devil *n* diabolus *m*; **go to the ~** abī in malam
crucem!; **talk of the ~** lupus in fābulā!
devilish *adj* scelestus, impius.
devil-may-care *adj* praeceps, lascīvus.
devilment *n* malitia *f*.
devilry *n* magicae artēs *fpl*.
devious *adj* dēvius, errābundus.
devise *vt* excōgitāre, commentārī, fingere.
devoid *adj* vacuus, expers; **be ~ of** carēre (*abl*).
devolve *vi* obtingere, obvenīre ♦ *vt* dēferre,

committere.
devote *vt* dēdicāre; (*attention*) dēdere, trādere; (*life*) dēvovēre.
devoted *adj* dēditus, studiōsus; (*victim*) dēvōtus, sacer; **be ~ to** studēre (*dat*), incumbere (*dat*).
devotee *n* cultor *m*.
devotion *n* amor *m*, studium *nt*; rēligiō *f*.
devour *vt* dēvorāre, cōnsūmere; (*fig*) haurīre.
devout *adj* pius, rēligiōsus.
devoutly *adv* piē, rēligiōsē.
dew *n* rōs *m*.
dewy *adj* rōscidus.
dexterity *n* ars *f*, sollertia *f*.
dexterous *adj* sollers, habilis.
dexterously *adv* sollerter, habiliter.
diabolical *adj* scelestus, nefārius.
diadem *n* diadēma *nt*.
diagnose *vt* discernere, diiūdicāre.
diagnosis *n* iūdicium *nt*.
diagonal *adj* oblīquus.
diagram *n* fōrma *f*.
dial *n* sōlārium *nt*.
dialect *n* dialectus *f*, sermō *m*.
dialectic *n* ars disserendī *f*, dialecticē *f* ♦ *adj* dialecticus.
dialectician *n* dialecticus *m*.
dialogue *n* dialogus *m*, colloquium *nt*.
diameter *n* diametros *f*.
diamond *n* adamās *m*.
diaphanous *adj* perlūcidus.
diaphragm *n* praecordia *ntpl*.
diary *n* ephēmeris *f*.
diatribe *n* convīcium *nt*.
dice *n* tālus *m*, tessera *f*; **game of ~** ālea *f*.
dictate *vt* dictāre ♦ *n* praeceptum *nt*; **~s of nature** nātūrae iūdicia *ntpl*.
dictation *n* dictāta *ntpl*; (*fig*) arbitrium *nt*.
dictator *n* dictātor *m*; **~'s** dictātōrius.
dictatorial *adj* imperiōsus, superbus.
dictatorship *n* dictātūra *f*.
diction *n* (*enunciation*) ēlocūtiō *f*; (*words*) ōrātiō *f*.
dictionary *n* verbōrum thēsaurus *m*.
die *n* signum *nt*; **the ~ is cast** iacta ālea est ♦ *vi* morī, perīre, obīre; (*in battle*) cadere, occumbere; **~ off** dēmorī; **~ out** ēmorī; **be dying to** exoptāre.
diet *n* (*food*) diaeta *f*; (*meeting*) conventus *m*.
differ *vi* differre, discrepāre, dissentīre.
difference *n* discrepantia *f*, dissimilitūdō *f*; (*of opinion*) dissēnsiō *f*; **there is a ~** interest.
different *adj* dīversus, varius, dissimilis; **~ from** alius . . . ac; **in ~ directions** dīversī; **they say ~ things** alius aliud dīcit.
differentiate *vt* discernere.
differently *adv* dīversē, variē, alius aliter; **~ from** aliter . . . ac.
difficult *adj* difficilis, arduus; **very ~** perdifficilis, perarduus.
difficulty *n* difficultās *f*, labor *m*, negōtium *nt*; **with ~** difficulter, aegrē, vix; **be in ~** labōrāre.

diffidence *n* diffīdentia *f*; (*shyness*) pudor *m*; **with ~** modestē.
diffident *adj* diffīdēns; (*shy*) modestus, verēcundus.
diffidently *adv* modestē.
diffuse *vt* diffundere, dispergere; **be ~d** diffluere ♦ *adj* fūsus, diffūsus, cōpiōsus.
diffusely *adv* diffūsē, cōpiōsē.
diffuseness *n* cōpia *f*.
dig *vt* fodere; dūcere; (*nudge*) fodicāre; **~ up** *vt* effodere, ēruere.
digest *vt* coquere, concoquere ♦ *n* summārium *nt*.
digestion *n* concoctiō *f*; **with a bad ~** crūdus.
digger *n* fossor *m*.
dignified *adj* gravis, augustus.
dignify *vt* honōrāre, honestāre.
dignity *n* gravitās *f*, māiestās *f*, amplitūdō *f*.
digress *vi* dēvertere, dīgredī, dēclīnāre.
digression *n* dēclīnātiō *f*, dīgressus *m*.
dike *n* (*ditch*) fossa *f*; (*mound*) agger *m*.
dilapidated *adj* ruīnōsus.
dilapidation *n* ruīna *f*.
dilate *vt* dīlātāre; (*speech*) plūra dīcere.
dilatorily *adv* tardē, cunctanter.
dilatoriness *n* mora *f*, cunctātiō *f*.
dilatory *adj* tardus, lentus, segnis.
dilemma *n* nōdus *m*, angustiae *fpl*; **be in a ~** haerēre; **be on the horns of a ~** auribus tenēre lupum.
diligence *n* dīligentia *f*, industria *f*, cūra *f*.
diligent *adj* dīligēns, industrius, sēdulus.
diligently *adv* dīligenter, sēdulō.
dill *n* anēthum *nt*.
dilly-dally *vi* cessāre.
dilute *vt* dīluere, temperāre.
dim *adj* obscūrus; (*fig*) hebes ♦ *vt* obscūrāre; hebetāre.
dimension *n* modus *m*; **~s** *pl* amplitūdō *f*, māgnitūdō *f*.
diminish *vt* minuere, imminuere, extenuāre, īnfringere ♦ *vi* dēcrēscere.
diminution *n* imminūtiō *f*, dēminūtiō *f*.
diminutive *adj* parvulus, exiguus ♦ *n* (*word*) dēminūtum *nt*.
diminutiveness *n* exiguitās *f*.
dimly *adv* obscūrē.
dimness *n* tenebrae *fpl*, cālīgō *f*.
dimple *n* gelasīnus *m*.
din *n* fragor *m*, strepitus *m*; **make a ~** strepere ♦ *vt* obtundere.
dine *vi* cēnāre.
diner *n* convīva *m*.
dinghy *n* scapha *f*.
dingy *adj* sordidus; (*colour*) fuscus.
dining room *n* cēnātiō *f*.
dinner *n* cēna *f*.
dinner party convīvium *nt*.
dint *n* ictus *m*; **by ~ of** per (*acc*).
dip *vt* imbuere, mergere ♦ *vi* mergī; **~ into** (*study*) perstringere.
diploma *n* diplōma *nt*.
diplomacy *n* (*embassy*) lēgātiō *f*; (*tact*)

iūdicium *nt*, sagācitās *f.*
diplomat *n* lēgātus *m.*
diplomatic *adj* sagāx, circumspectus.
diptych *n* tabellae *fpl.*
dire *adj* dīrus, horridus.
direct *vt* regere, dīrigere; (*attention*) attendere, admovēre, advertere; (*course*) tendere; (*business*) administrāre, moderārī; (*letter*) īnscrībere; (*order*) imperāre (*dat*), iubēre; (*to a place*) viam mōnstrāre (*dat*); (*weapon*) intendere ♦ *adj* rēctus, dīrēctus; (*person*) simplex; (*language*) apertus ♦ *adv* rēctā.
direction *n* (*of going*) cursus *m*, iter *nt*; (*of looking*) pars *f*, regiō *f*; (*control*) administrātiō *f*, regimen *nt*; (*order*) praeceptum *nt*, iussum *nt*; **in the ~ of Rome** Rōmam versus; **in all ~s** passim, undique; **in both ~s** utrōque.
directly *adv* (*place*) rēctā; (*time*) prōtinus, continuō, statim; (*language*) apertē ♦ *conj* simulac.
directness *n* (*fig*) simplicitās *f.*
director *n* dux *m*, gubernātor *m*, moderātor *m.*
dirge *n* nēnia *f.*
dirk *n* pūgiō *m.*
dirt *n* sordēs *f*; (*mud*) lūtum *nt.*
dirty *adj* sordidus, foedus; (*speech*) inquinātus ♦ *vt* foedāre, inquināre.
disability *n* vitium *nt.*
disable *vt* dēbilitāre, imminuere.
disabled *adj* mutilus, dēbilis.
disabuse *vt* errōrem dēmere (*dat*).
disaccustom *vt* dēsuēfacere.
disadvantage *n* incommodum *nt*, dētrīmentum *nt*; **it is a ~** dētrīmentō est.
disadvantageous *adj* incommodus, inīquus.
disadvantageously *adv* incommodē.
disaffected *adj* aliēnātus, sēditiōsus.
disaffection *n* aliēnātiō *f*, sēditiō *f.*
disagree *vi* discrepāre, dissentīre, dissidēre.
disagreeable *adj* molestus, incommodus, iniūcundus.
disagreeably *adv* molestē, incommodē.
disagreement *n* discordia *f*, dissēnsiō *f*, discrepantia *f.*
disallow *vt* improbāre, abnuere, vetāre.
disappear *vi* dēperīre, perīre, abīre, diffugere, ēvānēscere.
disappearance *n* dēcessiō *f*, fuga *f.*
disappoint *vt* dēcipere, spē dēicere, frustrārī; **be ~ed in a hope** ā spē dēcidere, dē spē dēicī.
disappointment *n* frustrātiō *f*, malum *nt.*
disapprobation *n* reprehēnsiō *f*, improbātiō *f.*
disapproval *n* improbātiō *f.*
disapprove *vt, vi* improbāre, reprehendere.
disarm *vt* exarmāre, dearmāre; (*fig*) mītigāre.
disarrange *vt* turbāre, cōnfundere.
disarranged *adj* incompositus.
disarrangement *n* turbātiō *f.*
disarray *n* perturbātiō *f* ♦ *vt* perturbāre.
disaster *n* calamitās *f*, cāsus *m*; (*MIL*) clādēs *f.*
disastrous *adj* īnfēlīx, exitiōsus, calamitōsus.
disavow *vt* diffitērī, īnfitiārī.

disavowal *n* īnfitiātiō *f.*
disband *vt* dīmittere.
disbelief *n* diffīdentia *f*, suspiciō *f.*
disbelieve *vt* diffīdere (*dat*).
disburden *vt* exonerāre.
disburse *vt* ērogāre, expendere.
disbursement *n* impēnsa *f.*
disc *n* orbis *m.*
discard *vt* mittere, pōnere, prōicere.
discern *vt* cōnspicere, dīspicere, cernere; (*fig*) intellegere.
discernment *n* iūdicium *nt*, intellegentia *f*, sagācitās *f.*
discharge *vt* (*load*) exonerāre; (*debt*) exsolvere; (*duty*) fungī (*abl*), exsequī; (*officer*) exauctōrāre; (*troops*) missōs facere, dīmittere; (*weapon*) iacere, iaculārī; (*prisoner*) absolvere; (*from body*) ēdere, reddere ♦ *vi* (*river*) effundī, īnfluere ♦ *n* (*bodily*) dēfluxiō *f*; (*MIL*) missiō *f*, dīmissiō *f*; (*of a duty*) perfūnctiō *f.*
disciple *n* discipulus *m.*
discipline *n* (*MIL*) modestia *f*; (*punishment*) castīgātiō *f*; (*study*) disciplīna *f* ♦ *vt* coercēre, castīgāre.
disciplined *adj* modestus.
disclaim *vt* renūntiāre, repudiāre, rēicere.
disclaimer *n* repudiātiō *f.*
disclose *vt* aperīre, patefacere, indicāre.
disclosure *n* indicium *nt.*
discoloration *n* dēcolōrātiō *f.*
discolour *vt* dēcolōrāre.
discoloured *adj* dēcolor.
discomfit *vt* vincere, conturbāre, dēprehendere.
discomfiture *n* clādēs *f*; (*POL*) repulsa *f.*
discomfort *n* molestia *f*, incommodum *nt.*
disconcert *vt* conturbāre, percellere.
disconcerting *adj* molestus.
disconnect *vt* abiungere, sēiungere.
disconnected *adj* dissolūtus, abruptus.
disconnectedly *adv* dissolūtē.
disconsolate *adj* maestus, dēmissus.
disconsolately *adv* animō dēmissō.
discontent *n* offēnsiō *f*, fastīdium *nt*, taedium *nt.*
discontented *adj* invidus, fastīdiōsus, parum contentus.
discontentedly *adv* invītus, inīquō animō.
discontinuance *n* intermissiō *f.*
discontinue *vt* intermittere ♦ *vi* dēsistere, dēsinere.
discord *n* discordia *f*; (*music*) dissonum *nt.*
discordance *n* discrepantia *f*, dissēnsiō *f.*
discordant *adj* discors, discrepāns; (*music*) dissonus, absonus.
discount *vt* dētrahere; (*fig*) praetermittere ♦ *n* dēcessiō *f*; **be at a ~** iacēre.
discountenance *vt* improbāre.
discourage *vt* dēhortārī, dēterrēre; **be ~d** animum dēmittere, animō dēficere.
discouragement *n* animī abiectiō *f*; (*cause*) incommodum *nt.*

discourse n sermō m; (_lecture_) ōrātiō f ♦ vi conloquī, disserere, disputāre.
discourteous adj inurbānus, asper, inhūmānus.
discourteously adv inhūmānē, rūsticē.
discourtesy n inhūmānitās f, acerbitās f.
discover vt (_find_) invenīre, reperīre; (_detect_) dēprehendere; (_reveal_) aperīre, patefacere; (_learn_) cognōscere.
discoverer n inventor m.
discovery n inventum nt.
discredit vt notāre, fidem imminuere (_gen_) ♦ n invidia f, lābēs f; **be in ~** iacēre.
discreditable adj inhonestus, turpis.
discreditably adv inhonestē, turpiter.
discreet adj prūdēns, sagāx, cautus.
discreetly adv prūdenter, sagāciter, cautē.
discrepancy n discrepantia f, dissēnsiō f.
discretion n prūdentia f; (_tact_) iūdicium nt; (_power_) arbitrium nt, arbitrātus m; **at your ~** arbitrātū tuō; **surrender at ~** in dēditiōnem venīre, sine ullā pactiōne sē tradere; **years of ~** adulta aetās f.
discretionary adj līber.
discriminate vt, vi discernere, internōscere, distinguere.
discriminating adj perspicāx, sagāx.
discrimination n discrīmen nt, iūdicium nt.
discursive adj vagus, loquāx; **be ~** excurrere.
discuss vt agere, disputāre, disceptāre dē (_abl_); **~ terms of peace** dē pāce agere.
discussion n disceptātiō f, disputātiō f.
disdain vt contemnere, aspernārī, fastīdīre ♦ n contemptiō f, fastīdium nt.
disdainful adj fastīdiōsus, superbus.
disdainfully adv fastīdiōsē, superbē.
disease n morbus m; pestilentia f.
diseased adj aeger, aegrōtus.
disembark vi ē nave ēgredī ♦ vt mīlitēs ē nāve expōnere.
disembarkation n ēgressus m.
disembodied adj sine corpore.
disembowel vt exenterāre.
disencumber vt exonerāre.
disengage vt expedīre, līberāre; (_mind_) abstrahere, abdūcere.
disengaged adj vacuus, ōtiōsus.
disentangle vt expedīre, explicāre, exsolvere.
disfavour n invidia f.
disfigure vt dēfōrmāre, foedāre.
disfigured adj dēfōrmis.
disfigurement n dēfōrmātiō f.
disfranchise vt cīvitātem adimere (_dat_).
disfranchised adj capite dēminūtus.
disfranchisement n capitis dēminūtiō f.
disgorge vt ēvomere.
disgrace n dēdecus nt, ignōminia f, īnfāmia f ♦ vt dēdecorāre, dēdecorī esse (_dat_).
disgraceful adj ignōminiōsus, flāgitiōsus, turpis; **~ thing** flāgitium nt.
disgracefully adv turpiter, flāgitiōsē.
disgruntled adj mōrōsus, invidus.

disguise n integumentum nt; (_fig_) speciēs f, simulātiō f; **in ~** mūtātā veste ♦ vt obtegere, involvere; (_fact_) dissimulāre; **~ oneself** vestem mūtāre.
disgust vt displicēre (_dat_), fastīdium movēre (_dat_); **be ~ed** stomachārī; **I am ~ed** mē taedet, mē piget ♦ n fastīdium nt, taedium nt.
disgusting adj taeter, foedus, dēfōrmis.
disgustingly adv foedē.
dish n lanx f; (_course_) ferculum nt.
dishearten vt percellere; **be ~ed** animō dēficere, animum dēmittere.
dishevelled adj solūtus, passus.
dishonest adj perfidus, inīquus, improbus.
dishonestly adv improbē, dolō malō.
dishonesty n mala fidēs f, perfidia f, fraus f.
dishonour n dēdecus nt, ignōminia f, turpitūdō f ♦ vt dēdecorāre.
dishonourable adj ignōminiōsus, indecōrus, turpis.
dishonourably adv turpiter, inhonestē.
disillusion vt errōrem adimere (_dat_).
disinclination n odium nt.
disinclined adj invītus, āversus.
disinfect vt pūrgāre.
disingenuous adj dolōsus, fallāx.
disingenuously adv dolōsē.
disinherit vt abdicāre, exhērēdāre.
disinherited adj exhērēs.
disintegrate vt dissolvere ♦ vi dīlābī, dissolvī.
disinter vt effodere, ēruere.
disinterested adj grātuītus, favōris expers.
disinterestedly adv sine favōre.
disinterestedness n innocentia f, integritās f.
disjoin vt sēiungere.
disjointed adj parum cohaerēns.
disk n orbis m.
dislike n odium nt, offēnsiō f, invidia f ♦ vt ōdisse; **I ~** mihī displicet, mē piget (_gen_).
dislocate vt extorquēre.
dislocated adj luxus.
dislodge vt dēmovēre, dēicere, dēpellere, dētrūdere.
disloyal adj īnfīdus, īnfidēlis; (_to gods, kin, country_) impius.
disloyally adv īnfidēliter.
disloyalty n perfidia f, īnfidēlitās f, impietās f.
dismal adj fūnestus, maestus.
dismally adv miserē.
dismantle vt nūdāre; (_building_) dīruere.
dismay n pavor m, formīdō f ♦ vt terrēre, perturbāre.
dismember vt discerpere.
dismiss vt dīmittere; (_troops_) missōs facere; (_from service_) exauctōrāre; (_fear_) mittere, pōnere.
dismissal n missiō f, dīmissiō f.
dismount vi dēgredī, (ex equō) dēscendere.
disobedience n contumācia f.
disobedient adj contumāx.
disobediently adv contrā iūssa.
disobey vt nōn pārēre (_dat_), aspernārī.

disoblige vt displicēre (dat), offendere.
disobliging adj inofficiōsus, difficilis.
disobligingly adv contrā officium.
disorder n turba f, cōnfūsiō f; (MED) morbus m; (POL) mōtus m, tumultus m ♦ vt turbāre, miscēre, sollicitāre.
disorderly adj immodestus, inōrdinātus, incompositus; (POL) turbulentus, sēditiōsus; **in a ~ manner** nullō ōrdine, temerē.
disorganize vt dissolvere, perturbāre.
disown vt (statement) īnfitiārī; (thing) abnuere, repudiāre; (heir) abdicāre.
disparage vt obtrectāre, dētrectāre.
disparagement n obtrectātiō f, probrum nt.
disparager n obtrectātor m, dētrectātor m.
disparate adj dispār.
disparity n discrepantia f, dissimilitūdō f.
dispassionate adj studiī expers.
dispassionately adv sine īrā et studiō.
dispatch vt mittere, dīmittere; (finish) absolvere, perficere; (kill) interficere ♦ n (letter) litterae fpl; (speed) celeritās f.
dispel vt dispellere, discutere.
dispensation n (distribution) partītiō f; (exemption) venia f; (of heaven) sors f; **by divine ~** dīvīnitus.
dispense vt dispertīrī, dīvidere ♦ vi: **~ with** ōmittere, praetermittere, repudiāre.
dispersal n dīmissiō f, diffugium nt.
disperse vt dispergere, dissipāre, dīsicere ♦ vi diffugere, dīlābī.
dispirited adj dēmissō animō; **be ~** animō dēficere, animum dēmittere.
displace vt locō movēre.
display n ostentātiō f, iactātiō f; **for ~** per speciem ♦ vt exhibēre, ostendere, praestāre, sē ferre.
displease vt displicēre (dat), offendere; **be ~d** aegrē ferre, stomachārī, indignārī.
displeasing adj ingrātus, odiōsus.
displeasure n invidia f, offēnsiō f, odium nt.
disport vt: **~ oneself** lūdere.
disposal n (sale) vēnditiō f; (power) arbitrium nt.
dispose vt (troops) dispōnere; (mind) inclīnāre, addūcere ♦ vi: **~ of** abaliēnāre, vēndere; (get rid) tollere; (argument) refellere.
disposed adj adfectus, inclīnātus, prōnus; **well ~** benevolus, bonō animō.
disposition n animus m, adfectiō f, ingenium nt, nātūra f; (of troops) dispositiō f.
dispossess vt dētrūdere, spoliāre.
disproportion n inconcinnitās f.
disproportionate adj impār, inconcinnus.
disproportionately adv inaequāliter.
disprove vt refūtāre, redarguere, refellere.
disputable adj dubius, ambiguus.
disputation n disputātiō f.
dispute n altercātiō f, contrōversia f; (violent) iūrgium nt; **beyond ~** certissimus ♦ vi altercārī, certāre, rixārī ♦ vt negāre, in

dubium vocāre.
disqualification n impedīmentum nt.
disqualify vt impedīre.
disquiet n sollicitūdō f ♦ vt sollicitāre.
disquisition n disputātiō f.
disregard n neglegentia f, contemptiō f ♦ vt neglegere, contemnere, ōmittere.
disrepair n vitium nt; **in ~** male sartus.
disreputable adj inhonestus, īnfāmis.
disrepute n īnfāmia f.
disrespect n neglegentia f, contumācia f.
disrespectful adj contumāx, īnsolēns.
disrespectfully adv īnsolenter.
disrobe vt nūdāre, vestem exuere (dat) ♦ vi vestem exuere.
disrupt vt dīrumpere, dīvellere.
disruption n discidium nt.
dissatisfaction n molestia f, aegritūdō f, dolor m.
dissatisfied adj parum contentus; **I am ~ with ... mē taedet (gen) ....
dissect vt incīdere; (fig) investīgāre.
dissemble vt, vi dissimulāre; mentīrī.
dissembler n simulātor m.
disseminate vt dīvulgāre, dissēmināre.
dissension n discordia f, dissēnsiō f; (violent) iūrgium nt.
dissent vi dissentīre, dissidēre ♦ n dissēnsiō f.
dissertation n disputātiō f.
disservice n iniūria f, incommodum nt.
dissimilar adj dispār, dissimilis.
dissimilarity n discrepantia f, dissimilitūdō f.
dissident adj discors.
dissimulation n dissimulātiō f.
dissipate vt dissipāre, diffundere, disperdere.
dissipated adj dissolūtus, lascīvus, luxuriōsus.
dissipation n dissipātiō f; (vice) luxuria f, licentia f.
dissociate vt dissociāre, sēiungere.
dissociation n sēparātiō f, discidium nt.
dissoluble adj dissolūbilis.
dissolute adj dissolūtus, perditus, libīdinōsus.
dissolutely adv libīdinōsē, luxuriōsē.
dissoluteness n luxuria f.
dissolution n dissolūtiō f, discidium nt.
dissolve vt dissolvere; (ice) liquefacere; (meeting) dīmittere; (contract) dīrimere ♦ vi liquēscere; (fig) solvī.
dissonance n dissonum nt.
dissonant adj dissonus.
dissuade vt dissuādēre (dat), dēhortārī.
dissuasion n dissuāsiō f.
distaff n colus f.
distance n intervallum nt, spatium nt; (long way) longinquitās f; **at a ~** (far) longē; (within sight) procul; (fight) ēminus; **at a ~ of ...** spatiō (gen) ...; **within striking ~** intrā iactum tēlī.
distant adj longinquus; (measure) distāns; (person) parum familiāris; **be ~** abesse (abl).

distaste n fastīdium nt.
distasteful adj molestus, iniūcundus.
distemper n morbus m.
distend vt distendere.
distil vt, vi stillāre.
distinct adj (*different*) dīversus; (*separate*)
distinctus; (*clear*) clārus, argūtus; (*marked*)
distinctus; (*sure*) certus; (*well-drawn*)
expressus.
distinction n discrīmen nt; (*dissimilarity*)
discrepantia f; (*public status*) amplitūdō f;
(*honour*) honōs m, decus nt; (*mark*) īnsigne nt;
there is a ~ interest; **without ~** prōmiscuē.
distinctive adj proprius, īnsignītus.
distinctively adv propriē, īnsignītē.
distinctly adv clārē, distinctē, certē,
expressē.
distinguish vt distinguere, internōscere,
dīiūdicāre, discernere; (*honour*) decorāre,
ōrnāre; **~ oneself** ēminēre.
distinguished adj īnsignis, praeclārus,
ēgregius, amplissimus.
distort vt dētorquēre; (*fig*) dēprāvāre.
distorted adj distortus.
distortion n distortiō f; dēprāvātiō f.
distract vt distrahere, distinēre, āvocāre;
(*mind*) aliēnāre.
distracted adj āmēns, īnsānus.
distraction n (*state*) indīligentia f; (*cause*)
invītāmentum nt; (*madness*) furor m,
dēmentia f; **to ~** cfflīctim.
distraught adj āmēns, dēmēns.
distress n labor m, dolor m, aegrimōnia f,
aerumna f; **be in ~** labōrāre ♦ vt adflīgere,
sollicitāre.
distressed adj adflīctus, sollicitus; **be ~ at** rem
aegrē ferre.
distressing adj tristis, miser, acerbus.
distribute vt distribuere, dīvidere, dispertīre.
distribution n partītiō f, distribūtiō f.
district n regiō f, pars f.
distrust n diffīdentia f ♦ vt diffīdere (*dat*), nōn
crēdere (*dat*).
distrustful adj diffīdēns.
distrustfully adv diffīdenter.
disturb vt perturbāre, conturbāre;
commovēre; (*mind*) sollicitāre.
disturbance n turba f, perturbātiō f; (*POL*)
mōtus m, tumultus m.
disturber n turbātor m.
disunion n discordia f, discidium nt.
disunite vt dissociāre, sēiungere.
disuse n dēsuētūdō f; **fall into ~** obsolēscere.
disused adj dēsuētus, obsolētus.
disyllabic adj disyllabus.
ditch n fossa f, scrobis m.
dithyrambic adj dithyrambicus.
dittany n dictamnum nt.
ditty n carmen nt, cantilēna f.
diurnal adj diūrnus.
divan n lectus m, lectulus m.
dive vi dēmergī.
diver n ūrīnātor m.

diverge vi dēvertere, dīgredī; (*road*) sē
scindere; (*opinions*) discrepāre.
divergence n dīgressiō f; discrepantia f.
divers adj complūrēs.
diverse adj varius, dīversus.
diversify vt variāre.
diversion n (*of water*) dērīvātiō f; (*of thought*)
āvocātiō f; (*to amuse*) oblectāmentum nt;
create a ~ (*MIL*) hostēs dīstringere; **for a ~**
animī causā.
diversity n varietās f, discrepantia f.
divert vt dēflectere, āvertere; (*attention*)
āvocāre, abstrahere; (*water*) dērīvāre; (*to
amuse*) oblectāre, placēre (*dat*).
diverting adj iūcundus; (*remark*) facētus.
divest vt exuere, nūdāre; **~ oneself of** (*fig*)
pōnere, mittere.
divide vt dīvidere; (*troops*) dīdūcere; **~ among**
partīrī, distribuere; **~ from** sēparāre ab,
sēiungere ab; **~ out** dispertīrī, dīvidere ♦ vi
discēdere, sē scindere; (*senate*) in
sententiam īre; **be ~d** (*opinions*) discrepāre.
divination n dīvīnātiō f; (*from birds*) augurium
nt; (*from entrails*) haruspicium nt.
divine adj dīvīnus ♦ vt dīvīnāre, augurārī,
hariolārī; **by ~ intervention** dīvīnitus.
divinely adv dīvīnē.
diviner n dīvīnus m, augur m, haruspex m.
divinity n (*status*) dīvīnitās f; (*god*) deus m, dea
f.
divisible adj dīviduus.
division n (*process*) dīvīsiō f, partītiō f;
(*variance*) discordia f, dissēnsiō f; (*section*)
pars f; (*grade*) classis f; (*of army*) legiō f; (*of
time*) discrīmen nt; (*in senate*) discessiō f.
divorce n dīvortium nt, repudium nt ♦ vt (*wife*)
nūntium mittere (*dat*); (*things*) dīvellere,
sēparāre.
divulge vt aperīre, patefacere, ēvulgāre,
ēdere.
dizziness n vertīgō f.
dizzy adj vertīginōsus; (*fig*) attonitus.
do vt facere, agere; (*duty*) fungī (*abl*); (*wrong*)
admittere; **~ away with** vt fus tollere; (*kill*)
interimere; **~ one's best to** id agere ut (*subj*)
~ without repudiāre; **~ not . . .** nolī/nolīte (+
infin); **how ~ you ~?** quid agis?; **I have nothing
to ~ with you** mihī tēcum nihil est
commercī; **it has nothing to ~ with me** nihil
est ad mē; **that will ~** iam satis est; **be done**
fierī; **have done with** dēfungī (*abl*).
docile adj docilis.
docility n docilitās f.
dock n (*ships*) nāvāle nt; (*law*) cancellī mpl ♦ vt
praecīdere.
dockyard n nāvālia ntpl.
doctor n medicus m; (*UNIV*) doctor m ♦ vt
cūrāre.
doctrine n dogma nt, dēcrētum nt; (*system*)
ratiō f.
document n litterae fpl, tabula f.
dodge vt dēclīnāre, ēvādere ♦ n dolus m.
doe n cerva f.

doer n āctor m, auctor m.
doff vt exuere.
dog n canis m/f; ~ **star** Canīcula f; ~'s canīnus ♦ vt īnsequī, īnstāre (dat).
dogged adj pertināx.
doggedly adv pertināciter.
dogma n dogma nt, praeceptum nt.
dogmatic adj adrogāns.
dogmatically adv adroganter.
doing n factum nt.
dole n sportula f ♦ vt: ~ **out** dispertīrī, dīvidere.
doleful adj lūgubris, flēbilis, maestus.
dolefully adv flēbiliter.
dolefulness n maestitia f, miseria f.
doll n pūpa f.
dolorous adj lūgubris, maestus.
dolour n maestitia f, dolor m.
dolphin n delphīnus m.
dolt n stīpes m, caudex m.
domain n ager m; (king's) rēgnum nt.
dome n tholus m, testūdō f.
domestic adj domesticus, familiāris; (animal) mānsuētus ♦ n famulus m, servus m, famula f, ancilla f; ~s pl familia f.
domesticate vt mānsuēfacere.
domesticated adj mānsuētus.
domesticity n larēs suī mpl.
domicile n domicilium nt, domus f.
dominant adj superior, praepotēns.
dominate vt dominārī in (acc), imperāre (dat); (view) dēspectāre.
domination n dominātiō f, dominātus m.
domineer vi dominārī, rēgnāre.
dominion n imperium nt, rēgnum nt.
don vt induere ♦ n scholasticus m.
donate vt dōnāre.
donation n dōnum nt.
donkey n asellus m.
donor n dōnātor m.
doom n fātum nt ♦ vt damnāre.
door n (front) iānua f; (back) postīcum nt; (double) forēs fpl; **folding ~s** valvae fpl; **out of ~s** forīs; (to) forās; **next ~ to** iuxtā (acc).
doorkeeper n iānitor m.
doorpost n postis m.
doorway n ōstium nt.
dormant adj sōpītus; **lie ~** iacēre.
dormitory n cubiculum nt.
dormouse n glīs m.
dose n pōculum nt.
dot n pūnctum nt.
dotage n senium nt.
dotard n senex dēlīrus m.
dote vi dēsipere; ~ **upon** dēamāre.
doting adj dēsipiēns, peramāns.
dotingly adv perditē.
double adj duplex; (amount) duplus; (meaning) ambiguus ♦ n duplum nt ♦ vt duplicāre; (promontory) superāre; (fold) complicāre ♦ vi duplicārī; (MIL) currere.
double-dealer n fraudātor m.
double-dealing adj fallāx, dolōsus ♦ n fraus

f, dolus m.
doublet n tunica f.
doubly adv bis, dupliciter.
doubt n dubium nt; (hesitancy) dubitātiō f; (distrust) suspiciō f; **give one the benefit of the ~** innocentem habēre; **no ~** sānē; **I do not ~ that** ... non dubito quīn ... (+ subj); **there is no ~ that** nōn dubium est quīn (subj) ♦ vt dubitāre; (distrust) diffīdere (dat), suspicārī.
doubtful adj dubius, incertus; (result) anceps; (word) ambiguus.
doubtfully adv dubiē; (hesitation) dubitanter.
doubtless adv scīlicet, nīmīrum.
doughty adj fortis, strēnuus.
dove n columba f.
dovecote n columbārium nt.
dowdy adj inconcinnus.
dower n dōs f ♦ vt dōtāre.
dowerless adj indōtātus.
down n plūmae fpl, lānūgō f; (thistle) pappus m.
down adv deōrsum; **be ~** iacēre; ~ **with!** perea(n)t; **up and ~** sūrsum deōrsum ♦ prep dē (abl); ~ **from** dē (abl).
downcast adj dēmissus, maestus.
downfall n ruīna f; (fig) occāsus m.
downhearted adj dēmissus, frāctus animī.
downhill adj dēclīvis; (fig) prōclīvis ♦ adv in praeceps.
downpour n imber m.
downright adj dīrēctus; (intensive) merus.
downstream adv secundō flūmine.
downtrodden adj subiectus, oppressus.
downward adj dēclīvis, prōclīvis.
downwards adv deōrsum.
downy adj plūmeus.
dowry n dōs f.
doyen n pater m.
doze vi dormītāre.
dozen n duodecim.
drab adj sordidior.
drachma n drachma f.
draft n (writing) exemplum nt; (MIL) dīlēctus m; (money) syngrapha f; (literary) silva f ♦ vt scrībere; (MIL) mittere.
drag vt trahere ♦ vi (time) trahī; ~ **on** vi (war) prōdūcere ♦ n harpagō m; (fig) impedīmentum nt.
dragnet n ēverriculum nt.
dragon n drācō m.
dragoon n eques m.
drain n cloāca f ♦ vt (water) dērīvāre; (land) siccāre; (drink) exhaurīre; (resources) exhaurīre.
drainage n dērīvātiō f.
drake n anas m.
drama n fābula f; **the ~** scaena f.
dramatic adj scaenicus.
dramatist n fābulārum scrīptor m.
dramatize vt ad scaenam compōnere.
drape vt vēlāre.
drapery n vestīmenta ntpl.
drastic adj vehemēns, efficāx.
draught n (air) aura f; (drink) haustus m; (net)

bolus *m.*
draughts *n* latrunculī *mpl.*
draw *vt* dūcere, trahere; (*bow*) addūcere;
(*inference*) colligere; (*picture*) scrībere,
pingere; (*sword*) stringere, dēstringere;
(*tooth*) eximere; (*water*) haurīre; ~ **aside**
sēdūcere; ~ **away** āvocāre; ~ **back** *vt*
retrahere ♦ *vi* recēdere; ~ **near**
adpropinquāre; ~ **off** dētrahere; (*water*)
dērīvāre; ~ **out** *vi* ēdūcere; (*lengthen*)
prōdūcere; ~ **over** obdūcere; ~ **taut**
addūcere; ~ **together** contrahere; ~ **up** *vt* (*MIL*)
īnstruere; (*document*) scrībere.
drawback *n* scrūpulus *m;* **this was the only** ~
hōc ūnum dēfuit.
drawing *n* dēscrīptiō *f;* (*art*) graphicē *f.*
drawing room *n* sellāria *f.*
drawings *npl* līneāmenta *ntpl.*
drawl *vi* lentē dīcere.
drawling *adj* lentus in dīcendō.
dray *n* plaustrum *nt.*
dread *n* formīdō *f,* pavor *m,* horror *m* ♦ *adj*
dīrus ♦ *vt* expavēscere, extimēscere,
formīdāre.
dreadful *adj* terribilis, horribilis,
formīdolōsus, dīrus.
dreadfully *adv* vehementer, atrōciter.
dream *n* somnium *nt* ♦ *vt, vi* somniāre.
dreamy *adj* somniculōsus.
dreariness *n* (*place*) vastitās *f;* (*mind*) tristitia
f.
dreary *adj* (*place*) vastus; (*person*) tristis.
dregs *n* faex *f;* (*of oil*) amurca *f;* **drain to the** ~
exhaurīre.
drench *vt* perfundere.
dress *n* vestis *f,* vestītus *m,* vestīmenta *ntpl;*
(*style*) habitus *m* ♦ *vt* vestīre; (*wound*) cūrāre;
(*tree*) amputāre ♦ *vi* induī; ~ **up** *vi* vestum
induere.
dressing *n* (*MED*) fōmentum *nt.*
drift *n* (*motion*) mōtus *m;* (*snow*) agger *m;*
(*language*) vīs *f;* **I see the** ~ **of your speech**
videō quōrsum ōrātiō tua tendat ♦ *vi* fluitāre;
(*fig*) lābī, ferrī.
drill *n* terebra *f;* (*MIL*) exercitātiō *f* ♦ *vt* (*hole*)
terebrāre; (*MIL*) exercēre; (*pupil*) īnstruere.
drink *vt, vi* bibere, pōtāre; ~ **a health**
propīnāre, Graecō mōre bibere; ~ **deep of**
exhaurīre; ~ **in** haurīre; ~ **up** ēpōtāre ♦ *n*
pōtiō *f.*
drinkable *adj* pōtulentus.
drinker *n* pōtor *m.*
drinking bout *n* pōtātiō *f.*
drip *vi* stillāre, dēstillāre.
drive *vt* agere; (*force*) cōgere; ~ **away** abigere;
(*fig*) pellere, prōpulsāre; ~ **back** repellere; ~
home dēfīgere; ~ **in/into** īnfīgere in (*acc*);
(*flock*) cōgere in (*acc*); ~ **off** dēpellere; ~ **out**
exigere, expellere, exturbāre; ~ **through**
trānsfīgere ♦ *vi* vehī; ~ **away** āvehī; ~ **back**
revehī; ~ **in** invehī; ~ **on** *vt* impellere; ~ **round**
circumvehī; ~ **past** praetervehī; **what are**
you driving at? quōrsum tua spectat ōrātiō?

♦ *n* gestātiō *f.*
drivel *vi* dēlīrāre.
drivelling *adj* dēlīrus, ineptus ♦ *n* ineptiae *fpl.*
driver *n* aurīga *m;* rēctor *m.*
drizzle *vi* rōrāre.
droll *adj* facētus, ioculāris.
drollery *n* facētiae *fpl.*
dromedary *n* dromas *m.*
drone *n* (*bee*) fūcus *m;* (*sound*) bombus *m* ♦ *vi*
fremere.
droop *vi* dēmittī; (*flower*) languēscere; (*mind*)
animum dēmittere.
drooping *adj* languidus.
drop *n* gutta *f* ♦ *vi* cadere; (*liquid*) stillāre ♦ *vt*
mittere; (*anchor*) iacere; (*hint*) ēmittere;
(*liquid*) īnstillāre; (*work*) dēsistere ab (*abl*) ♦
vi: ~ **behind** cessāre; ~ **in** *vi* vīsere,
supervenīre; ~ **out** excidere.
dross *n* scōria *f;* (*fig*) faex *f.*
drought *n* siccitās *f.*
drouth *n* sitis *f.*
drove *n* grex *f.*
drover *n* bubulcus *m.*
drown *vt* mergere, obruere; (*noise*) obscūrāre
♦ *vi* aquā perīre.
drowse *vi* dormītāre.
drowsily *adv* somniculōsē.
drowsiness *n* sopor *m.*
drowsy *adj* sēmisomnus, somniculōsus.
drub *vt* pulsāre, verberāre.
drudge *n* mediastīnus *m* ♦ *vi* labōrāre.
drudgery *n* labor *m.*
drug *n* medicāmentum *nt* ♦ *vt* medicāre.
Druids *n* Druidae, Druidēs *mpl.*
drum *n* tympanum *nt;* (*container*) urna *f.*
drummer *n* tympanista *m.*
drunk *adj* pōtus, ēbrius, tēmulentus.
drunkard *n* ēbriōsus *m.*
drunken *adj* ēbriōsus, tēmulentus.
drunkenness *n* ēbrietās *f.*
dry *adj* siccus, āridus; (*thirst*) sitiēns; (*speech*)
āridus, frīgidus; (*joke*) facētus; **be** ~ ārēre ♦
vt siccāre ♦ *vi* ārēscere; ~ **up** exārēscere.
dryad *n* dryas *f.*
dry rot *n* rōbīgō *f.*
dual *adj* duplex.
duality *n* duplex nātūra *f.*
dubiety *n* dubium *nt.*
dubious *adj* dubius, incertus; (*meaning*)
ambiguus.
dubiously *adv* dubiē; ambiguē.
duck *n* anas *f* ♦ *vt* dēmergere ♦ *vi* dēmergī, sē
dēmittere.
duckling *n* anaticula *f.*
duct *n* ductus *m.*
dudgeon *n* dolor *m,* stomachus *m.*
due *adj* dēbitus, meritus, iūstus; **be** ~ dēbērī; **it**
is ~ **to me that … not** per mē stat quōminus
(+ *subj*); **be** ~ **to** orīrī ex, fierī (*abl*) ♦ *n* iūs *nt,*
dēbitum *nt;* (*tax*) vectīgal *nt;* (*harbour*)
portōrium *nt;* **give every man his** ~ suum
cuīque tribuere ♦ *adv* rēctā; ~ **to** ob (+ *acc*);
propter (+ *acc*).

duel n certāmen nt.

dug n über nt.

duke n dux m.

dulcet adj dulcis.

dull adj hebes; (weather) subnūbilus; (language) frīgidus; (mind) tardus; **be ~** hebēre; **become ~** hebēscere ♦ vt hebetāre, obtundere, retundere.

dullard n stolidus m.

dulness n (mind) tarditās f, stultitia f.

duly adv rītē, ut pār est.

dumb adj mūtus; **be struck ~** obmūtēscere.

dun n flāgitātor m ♦ vt flāgitāre ♦ adj fuscus.

dunce n bārō m.

dune n tumulus m.

dung n fimus m.

dungeon n carcer m, rōbur nt.

dupe vt dēlūdere, fallere ♦ n crēdulus m.

duplicate n exemplar nt ♦ vt duplicāre.

duplicity n fraus f, perfidia f.

durability n firmitās f, firmitūdō f.

durable adj firmus, perpetuus.

durably adv firmē.

duration n spatium nt; (long) diūturnitās f.

duresse n vīs f.

during prep inter (acc), per (acc).

dusk n crepusculum nt, vesper m; **at ~** prīmā nocte, prīmīs tenebrīs.

dusky adj fuscus.

dust n pulvis m; **throw ~ in the eyes of** tenebrās offundere (dat) ♦ vt dētergēre.

dusty adj pulverulentus.

dutiful adj pius, officiōsus.

dutifully adv piē, officiōsē.

dutifulness n pietās f.

duty n (moral) officium nt; (task) mūnus nt; (tax) vectīgal nt; **be on ~** (MIL) statiōnem agere, excubāre; **do one's ~** officiō fungī; **do ~ for** (pers) in locum sufficī (gen); (thing) adhibērī prō (abl); **it is my ~** dēbeō, mē oportet, meum est; **it is the ~ of a commander** ducis est; **sense of ~** pietās f.

duty call n salūtātiō f.

duty-free adj immūnis.

dwarf n nānus m.

dwell vi habitāre; **~ in** incolere; **~ upon** (theme) commorārī in (abl).

dweller n incola m.

dwelling n domus f, domicilium nt; (place) sēdēs f.

dwindle vi dēcrēscere, extenuārī.

dye n fūcus m, color m ♦ vt īnficere, fūcāre.

dyer n īnfector m.

dying adj moribundus, moriēns.

dynasty n domus (rēgia) f.

dyspepsia n crūditās f.

E, e

each adj & pron quisque; (of two) uterque; **~ other** inter sē; **one ~** singulī; **~ year** quotannīs.

eager adj avidus, cupidus, alācer; **~ for** avidus (+ gen).

eagerly adv avidē, cupidē, ācriter.

eagerness n cupīdō f, ārdor m, studium nt; alacritās f.

eagle n aquila f.

ear n auris f; (of corn) spīca f; **give ~** aurem praebēre, auscultāre; **go in at one ~ and out at the other** surdīs auribus nārrārī; **prick up one's ~s** aurēs ērigere; **with long ~s** aurītus.

earl n comes m.

earlier adv ante; anteā.

early adj (in season) mātūrus; (in day) mātūtīnus; (at beginning) prīmus; (in history) antīquus ♦ adv (in day) māne; (before time) mātūrē, temperī; **~ in life** ab ineunte aetāte.

earn vt merērī, cōnsequī; **~ a living** vīctum quaerere, quaestum facere.

earnest adj (serious) sērius; (eager) ācer, sēdulus ♦ n pignus nt; (money) arrabō m; **in ~** sēdulō, ēnīxē.

earnestly adv sēriō, graviter, sēdulō.

earnestness n gravitās f, studium nt.

earnings n quaestus m.

earring n elenchus m.

earth n (planet) tellūs f; (inhabited) orbis terrārum m; (land) terra f; (soil) solum nt, humus f; (fox's) latibulum nt; **where on ~?** ubī gentium?; **of the ~** terrestris.

earthen adj (ware) fictilis; (mound) terrēnus.

earthenware n fictilia ntpl ♦ adj fictilis.

earthly adj terrestris.

earthquake n terrae mōtus m.

earthwork n agger m.

earthy adj terrēnus.

ease n facilitās f; (leisure) ōtium nt; **at ~** ōtiōsus; (in mind) sēcūrus; **ill at ~** sollicitus ♦ vt laxāre, relevāre; (pain) mītigāre.

easily adv facile; (gladly) libenter; (at leisure) ōtiōsē; **not ~** nōn temerē.

easiness n facilitās f.

east n Oriēns m, sōlis ortus m; **~ wind** eurus m.

Easter n Pascha f.

easterly, eastern adj orientālis.

eastward adv ad orientem.

easy adj facilis; (manner) adfābilis, facilis; (mind) sēcūrus; (speech) expedītus; (discipline) remissus; **~ circumstances** dīvitiae fpl, abundantia f.

eat vt edere; cōnsūmere; vescī (abl); **~ away** rōdere; **~ up** exedere.

eatable adj esculentus.

eating n cibus m.

eaves *n* suggrunda *f*.
eavesdropper *n* sermōnis auceps *m*.
ebb *n* dēcessus *m*, recessus *m*; **at ~tide**
minuente aestū; **be at a low ~** (*fig*) iacēre ♦ *vi*
recēdere.
ebony *n* ebenus *f*.
ebullient *adj* fervēns.
ebullition *n* fervor *m*.
eccentric *adj* īnsolēns.
eccentricity *n* īnsolentia *f*.
echo *n* imāgō *f* ♦ *vt*, *vi* resonāre.
eclipse *n* dēfectus *m*, dēfectiō *f* ♦ *vt* obscūrāre;
be ~d dēficere, labōrāre.
eclogue *n* ecloga *f*.
economic *adj* quaestuōsus, sine iactūrā.
economical *adj* (*person*) frūgī, parcus.
economically *adv* nullā iactūrā factā.
economics *n* reī familiāris dispēnsātiō *f*.
economize *vi* parcere.
economy *n* frūgālitās *f*.
ecstasy *n* alacritās *f*, furor *m*.
ecstatic *adj* gaudiō ēlātus.
eddy *n* vertex *m* ♦ *vi* volūtārī.
edge *n* ōra *f*, margō *f*; (*of dish*) labrum *nt*; (*of
blade*) aciēs *f*; **take the ~ off** obtundere; **on ~**
(*fig*) suspēnsō animō ♦ *vt* (*garment*)
praetexere; (*blade*) acuere ♦ *vi*: **~ in sē**
īnsinuāre.
edging *n* limbus *m*.
edible *adj* esculentus.
edict *n* ēdictum *nt*, dēcrētum *nt*.
edification *n* ērudītiō *f*.
edifice *n* aedificium *nt*.
edify *vt* ērudīre.
edit *vt* recognōscere, recēnsēre.
edition *n* ēditiō *f*.
educate *vt* ērudīre, īnfōrmāre; **~ in** īnstituere
ad (*acc*).
education *n* doctrīna *f*; (*process*) īnstitūtiō *f*.
eel *n* anguilla *f*.
eerie *adj* mōnstruōsus.
efface *vt* dēlēre, tollere.
effect *n* (*result*) ēventus *m*; (*impression*) vīs *f*,
effectus *m*; (*show*) iactātiō *f*; **~s** *pl* bona *ntpl*;
for ~ iactātiōnis causā; **in ~** rē vērā; **to this ~**
in hanc sententiam; **without ~** inritus ♦ *vt*
efficere, facere, patrāre.
effective *adj* valēns, validus; (*RHET*) gravis,
ōrnātus.
effectively *adv* validē, graviter, ōrnātē.
effectiveness *n* vīs *f*.
effectual *adj* efficāx, idōneus.
effectually *adv* efficāciter.
effectuate *vt* efficere, cōnsequī.
effeminacy *n* mollitiēs *f*.
effeminate *adj* mollis, effēminātus.
effeminately *adv* molliter, effēminātē.
effervesce *vi* effervēscere.
effete *adj* effētus.
efficacious *adj* efficāx.
efficaciously *adv* efficāciter.
efficacy *n* vīs *f*.
efficiency *n* virtūs *f*, perītia *f*.

efficient *adj* capāx, perītus; (*logic*) efficiēns.
efficiently *adv* perītē, bene.
effigy *n* simulācrum *nt*, effigiēs *f*.
effloresce *vi* flōrēscere.
efflorescence *n* (*fig*) flōs *m*.
effluvium *n* hālitus *m*.
effort *n* opera *f*, cōnātus *m*; (*of mind*) intentiō *f*;
make an ~ ēnītī.
effrontery *n* audācia *f*, impudentia *f*.
effusive *adj* officiōsus.
egg *n* ōvum *nt*; **lay an ~** ōvum parere ♦ *vt*
impellere, īnstīgāre.
egoism *n* amor suī *m*.
egoist *n* suī amāns *m*.
egotism *n* iactātiō *f*.
egotist *n* glōriōsus *m*.
egregious *adj* singulāris.
egress *n* exitus *m*.
eight *num* octō; **~ each** octōnī; **~ times** octiēns.
eighteen *num* duodēvīgintī.
eighteenth *adj* duodēvīcēsimus.
eighth *adj* octāvus.
eight hundred *num* octingentī.
eight hundredth *adj* octingentēsimus.
eightieth *adj* octōgēsimus.
eighty *num* octōgintā; **~ each** octōgēnī; **~ times**
octōgiēns.
either *pron* alteruter, uterlibet, utervīs ♦ *conj*
aut, vel; **~ ... ~** aut ... aut; vel ... vel.
ejaculation *n* clāmor *m*.
eject *vt* ēicere, expellere.
ejection *n* expulsiō *f*.
eke *vt*: **eke out** parcendō prōdūcere.
elaborate *vt* ēlabōrāre ♦ *adj* ēlabōrātus,
exquīsītus.
elaborately *adv* summō labōre, exquīsītē.
elan *n* ferōcia *f*.
elapse *vi* abīre, intercēdere; **allow to ~**
intermittere; **a year has ~d since** annus est
cum (*indic*).
elated *adj* ēlātus; **be ~** efferrī.
elation *n* laetitia *f*.
elbow *n* cubitum *nt*.
elder *adj* nātū māior, senior ♦ *n* (*tree*)
sambūcus *f*.
elderly *adj* aetāte prōvectus.
elders *npl* patrēs *mpl*.
eldest *adj* nātū māximus.
elecampane *n* inula *f*.
elect *vt* ēligere, dēligere; (*magistrate*) creāre;
(*colleague*) co-optāre ♦ *adj* dēsignātus;
(*special*) lēctus.
election *n* (*POL*) comitia *ntpl*.
electioneering *n* ambitiō *f*.
elector *n* suffrāgātor *m*.
elegance *n* ēlegantia *f*, lepōs *m*, munditia *f*,
concinnitās *f*.
elegant *adj* ēlegāns, concinnus, nitidus.
elegantly *adv* ēleganter, concinnē.
elegiac *adj*: **~ verse** elegī *mpl*, versūs alternī
mpl.
elegy *n* elegīa *f*.
element *n* elementum *nt*; **~s** *pl* initia *ntpl*,

prīncipia *ntpl*; **out of one's** ~ peregrīnus.
elementary *adj* prīmus.
elephant *n* elephantus *m*, elephas *m*.
elevate *vt* efferre, ērigere.
elevated *adj* ēditus, altus.
elevation *n* altitūdō *f*; (*style*) ēlātiō *f*.
eleven *num* ūndecim; ~ **each** ūndēnī; ~ **times** ūndeciēns.
eleventh *adj* ūndecimus.
elf *n* deus *m*.
elicit *vt* ēlicere; (*with effort*) ēruere.
elide *vt* ēlīdere.
eligible *adj* idōneus, aptus.
eliminate *vt* tollere, āmovēre.
elite *n* flōs *m*, rōbur *nt*.
elk *n* alcēs *f*.
ell *n* ulna *f*.
ellipse *n* (*RHET*) dētractiō *f*; (*oval*) ōvum *nt*.
elm *n* ulmus *f* ♦ *adj* ulmeus.
elocution *n* prōnūntiātiō *f*.
elongate *vt* prōdūcere.
elope *vi* aufugere.
eloquence *n* ēloquentia *f*; (*natural*) fācundia *f*, dīcendī vīs *f*.
eloquent *adj* ēloquēns; (*natural*) fācundus; (*fluent*) disertus.
eloquently *adv* fācundē, disertē.
else *adv* aliōquī, aliter ♦ *adj* alius; **or** ~ aliōquī; **who** ~ quis alius.
elsewhere *adv* alibī; ~ **to** aliō.
elucidate *vt* ēnōdāre, illūstrāre.
elucidation *n* ēnōdātiō *f*, explicātiō *f*.
elude *vt* ēvītāre, frustrārī, fallere.
elusive *adj* fallāx.
emaciated *adj* macer.
emaciation *n* maciēs *f*.
emanate *vi* mānāre; (*fig*) ēmānāre, orīrī.
emanation *n* exhālātiō *f*.
emancipate *vt* ēmancipāre, manū mittere, līberāre.
emancipation *n* lībertās *f*.
emasculate *vt* ēnervāre, dēlumbāre.
embalm *vt* condīre.
embankment *n* agger *m*, mōlēs *f*.
embargo *n* interdictum *nt*.
embark *vi* cōnscendere, nāvem cōnscendere; ~ **upon** (*fig*) ingredī ♦ *vt* impōnere.
embarkation *n* cōnscēnsiō *f*.
embarrass *vt* (*by confusing*) perturbāre; (*by obstructing*) impedīre; (*by revealing*) dēprehendere; **be ~ed** haerēre.
embarrassing *adj* incommodus, intempestīvus.
embarrassment *n* (*in speech*) haesitātiō *f*; (*in mind*) sollicitūdō *f*; (*in business*) angustiae *fpl*, difficultās *f*; (*cause*) molestia *f*, impedīmentum *nt*.
embassy *n* lēgātiō *f*.
embedded *adj* dēfixus.
embellish *vt* adōrnāre, exōrnāre, decorāre.
embellishment *n* decus *nt*, exōrnātiō *f*, ōrnāmentum *nt*.
embers *n* cinis *m*, favilla *f*.

embezzle *vt* pecūlārī, dēpecūlārī.
embezzlement *n* pecūlātus *m*.
embezzler *n* pecūlātor *m*.
embitter *vt* exacerbāre.
emblazon *vt* īnsignīre.
emblem *n* īnsigne *nt*.
embodiment *n* exemplar *nt*.
embody *vt* repraesentāre; (*MIL*) cōnscrībere.
embolden *vt* cōnfirmāre; ~ **the hearts of** animōs cōnfirmāre.
emboss *vt* imprimere, caelāre.
embrace *vt* amplectī, complectī; (*items*) continēre, comprehendere; (*party*) sequī; (*opportunity*) adripere ♦ *nt* amplexus *m*, complexus *m*.
embroider *vt* acū pingere.
embroidery *n* vestis picta *f*.
embroil *vt* miscēre, implicāre.
emend *vt* ēmendāre, corrigere.
emendation *n* ēmendātiō *f*, corrēctiō *f*.
emerald *n* smaragdus *m*.
emerge *vi* ēmergere, exsistere; ēgredī.
emergency *n* tempus *nt*, discrīmen *nt* ♦ *adj* subitārius.
emigrate *vi* migrāre, ēmigrāre.
emigration *n* migrātiō *f*.
eminence *n* (*ground*) tumulus *m*, locus ēditus *m*; (*rank*) praestantia *f*, amplitūdō *f*.
eminent *adj* ēgregius, ēminēns, īnsignis, amplus.
eminently *adv* ēgregiē, prae cēterīs, in prīmīs.
emissary *n* lēgātus *m*.
emit *vt* ēmittere.
emolument *n* lucrum *nt*, ēmolumentum *nt*.
emotion *n* animī mōtus *m*, commōtiō *f*, adfectus *m*.
emotional *adj* (*person*) mōbilis; (*speech*) flexanimus.
emperor *n* prīnceps *m*, imperātor *m*.
emphasis *n* pondus *nt*; (*words*) impressiō *f*.
emphasize *vt* exprimere.
emphatic *adj* gravis.
emphatically *adv* adsevēranter, vehementer.
empire *n* imperium *nt*.
employ *vt* ūtī (*abl*); (*for purpose*) adhibēre; (*person*) exercēre.
employed *adj* occupātus.
employees *npl* operae *fpl*.
employer *n* redemptor *m*.
employment *n* (*act*) ūsus *m*; (*work*) quaestus *m*.
empower *vt* permittere (*dat*), potestātem facere (*dat*).
emptiness *n* inānitās *f*.
empty *adj* inānis, vacuus; (*fig*) vānus, inritus ♦ *vt* exhaurīre, exinānīre ♦ *vi* (*river*) īnfluere.
emulate *vt* aemulārī.
emulation *n* aemulātiō *f*.
emulous *adj* aemulus.
emulously *adv* certātim.
enable *vt* potestātem facere (*dat*); efficere ut(*subj*).

enact *vt* dēcernere, ēdīcere, scīscere; (*part*) agere.

enactment *n* dēcrētum *nt*, lēx *f*.

enamoured *adj* amāns; **be ~ of** dēamāre.

encamp *vi* castra pōnere, tendere.

encampment *n* castra *ntpl*.

encase *vt* inclūdere.

enchant *vt* fascināre; (*fig*) dēlectāre.

enchantment *n* fascinātiō *f*; blandīmentum *nt*.

enchantress *n* sāga *f*.

encircle *vt* cingere, circumdare, amplectī.

enclose *vt* inclūdere, saepīre.

enclosure *n* saeptum *nt*, māceria *f*.

encompass *vt* cingere, circumdare, amplectī.

encounter *vt* obviam īre (*dat*), occurrere (*dat*); (*in battle*) concurrere cum (*abl*), congredī cum ♦ *n* occursus *m*, concursus *m*.

encourage *vt* cōnfirmāre, (co)hortārī, sublevāre, favēre (*dat*).

encouragement *n* hortātiō *f*, favor *m*, auxilium *nt*.

encroach *vi* invādere; **~ upon** occupāre; (*fig*) imminuere.

encrust *vt* incrustāre.

encumber *vt* impedīre, onerāre.

encumbrance *n* impedīmentum *nt*, onus *nt*.

end *n* fīnis *m*; (*aim*) prōpositum *nt*; (*of action*) ēventus *m*, exitus *m*; (*of speech*) perōrātiō *f*; **~ to ~** continuī; **at a loose ~** vacuus, ōtiōsus; **for two days on ~** biduum continenter; **in the ~** dēnique; **the ~ of** extrēmus; (*time*) exāctus; **put an ~ to** fīnem facere (*dat*), fīnem impōnere (*dat*); **to the ~ that** eō cōnsiliō ut (*subj*); **to what ~?** quō?, quōrsum? ♦ *vt* fīnīre, cōnficere; (*mutual dealings*) dīrimere ♦ *vi* dēsinere; (*event*) ēvādere; (*sentence*) cadere; (*speech*) perōrāre; (*time*) exīre; **~ up as** ēvādere; **~ with** dēsinere in (*acc*).

endanger *vt* perīclitārī, in discrīmen addūcere.

endear *vt* dēvincīre.

endearing *adj* blandus.

endearment *n* blanditiae *fpl*.

endeavour *vt* cōnārī, ēnītī ♦ *n* cōnātus *m*.

ending *n* fīnis *m*, exitus *m*.

endive *n* intubum *nt*.

endless *adj* īnfīnītus; (*time*) aeternus, perpetuus.

endlessly *adv* sine fīne, īnfīnītē.

endorse *vt* ratum facere.

endow *vt* dōnāre, īnstruere.

endowed *adj* praeditus (+ *abl*).

endowment *n* dōnum *nt*.

endurance *n* patientia *f*.

endure *vi* dūrāre, permanēre ♦ *vt* ferre, tolerāre, patī.

enemy *n* (*public*) hostis *m*, hostēs *mpl*; (*private*) inimīcus *m*; **greatest ~** inimīcissimus *m*; **~ territory** hosticum *nt*.

energetic *adj* impiger, nāvus, strēnuus; (*style*) nervōsus.

energetically *adv* impigrē, nāviter, strēnuē.

energy *n* impigritās *f*, vigor *m*, incitātiō *f*; (*mind*) contentiō *f*; (*style*) nervī *mpl*.

enervate *vt* ēnervāre, ēmollīre.

enervation *n* languor *m*.

enfeeble *vt* īnfīrmāre, dēbilitāre.

enfold *vt* involvere, complectī.

enforce *vt* (*law*) exsequī; (*argument*) cōnfirmāre.

enfranchise *vt* cīvitāte dōnāre; (*slave*) manū mittere.

engage *vt* (*affection*) dēvincīre; (*attention*) distinēre, occupāre; (*enemy*) manum cōnserere cum (*abl*); (*hire*) condūcere; (*promise*) spondēre, recipere; **~ the enemy** proelium cum hostibus committere; **be ~d in** versārī in (*abl*) ♦ *vi*: **~ in** ingredī, suscipere.

engagement *n* (*COMM*) occupātiō *f*; (*MIL*) pugna *f*, certāmen *nt*; (*agreement*) spōnsiō *f*; **keep an ~** fidem praestāre; **break an ~** fidem fallere; **I have an ~ at your house** prōmīsī ad tē.

engaging *adj* blandus.

engender *vt* ingenerāre, ingignere.

engine *n* māchina *f*.

engineer *n* māchinātor *m* ♦ *vt* mōlīrī.

engraft *vt* īnserere.

engrave *vt* īnsculpere, incīdere, caelāre.

engraver *n* sculptor *m*, caelātor *m*.

engraving *n* sculptūra *f*, caelātūra *f*.

engross *vt* dīstringere, occupāre; **~ed in** tōtus in (*abl*).

engulf *vt* dēvorāre, obruere.

enhance *vt* amplificāre, augēre, exaggerāre.

enigma *n* aenigma *nt*, ambāgēs *fpl*.

enigmatic *adj* ambiguus, obscūrus.

enigmatically *adv* per ambāgēs, ambiguē.

enjoin *vt* imperāre (*dat*), iniungere (*dat*).

enjoy *vt* fruī (*abl*); (*advantage*) ūtī (*abl*); (*pleasure*) percipere, dēcerpere; **~ oneself** dēlectārī, geniō indulgēre.

enjoyable *adj* iūcundus.

enjoyment *n* fructus *m*; dēlectātiō *f*, voluptās *f*.

enlarge *vt* augēre, amplificāre, dīlātāre; (*territory*) prōpāgāre; **~ upon** amplificāre.

enlargement *n* amplificātiō *f*, prōlātiō *f*.

enlighten *vt* inlūstrāre; docēre, ērudīre.

enlightenment *n* ērudītiō *f*, hūmānitās *f*.

enlist *vt* scrībere, cōnscrībere; (*sympathy*) conciliāre ♦ *vi* nōmen dare.

enliven *vt* excitāre.

enmesh *vt* impedīre, implicāre.

enmity *n* inimīcitia *f*, simultās *f*.

ennoble *vt* honestāre, excolere.

ennui *n* taedium *nt*.

enormity *n* immānitās *f*; (*deed*) scelus *nt*, nefās *nt*.

enormous *adj* immānis, ingēns.

enormously *adv* immēnsum.

enough *adj* satis (*indecl gen*) ♦ *adv* satis; **more than ~** satis superque; **I have had ~ of ...** mē taedet (*gen*) ....

enquire *vi* quaerere, percontārī; **~ into**

cognōscere, inquīrere in (*acc*).
enquiry *n* percontātiō *f*; (*legal*) quaestiō *f*.
enrage *vt* inrītāre, incendere.
enrapture *vt* dēlectāre.
enrich *vt* dītāre, locuplētāre; ~ **with** augēre (*abl*).
enrol *vt* adscrībere, conscrībere ♦ *vi* nōmen dare.
enshrine *vt* dēdicāre; (*fig*) sacrāre.
enshroud *vt* involvere.
ensign *n* signum *nt*, īnsigne *nt*; (*officer*) signifer *m*.
enslave *vt* in servitūtem redigere.
enslavement *n* servitūs *f*.
ensnare *vt* dēcipere, inlaqueāre, inrētīre.
ensue *vi* īnsequī.
ensure *vt* praestāre; ~ **that** efficere ut (*subj*).
entail *vt* adferre.
entangle *vt* impedīre, implicāre, inrētīre.
entanglement *n* implicātiō *f*.
enter *vi* inīre, ingredī, intrāre; (*riding*) invehī; ~ **into** introīre in (*acc*); ~ **upon** inīre, ingredī ♦ *vt* (*place*) intrare; (*account*) ferre, indūcere; (*mind*) subīre.
enterprise *n* inceptum *nt*; (*character*) prōmptus animus *m*.
enterprising *adj* prōmptus, strēnuus.
entertain *vt* (*guest*) invītāre, excipere; (*state of mind*) habēre, concipere; (*to amuse*) oblectāre.
entertainer *n* acroāma *nt*.
entertainment *n* hospitium *nt*; oblectāmentum *nt*; acroāma *nt*.
enthral *vt* capere.
enthusiasm *n* studium *nt*, fervor *m*; ~ **for** studium *nt* (+ *gen*).
enthusiastic *adj* studiōsus, fervidus.
enthusiastically *adv* summō studiō.
entice *vt* inlicere, ēlicere, invītāre.
enticement *n* illecebra *f*, lēnōcinium *nt*.
entire *adj* integer, tōtus, ūniversus.
entirely *adv* omnīnō, funditus, penitus.
entitle *vt* (*book*) īnscrībere; **be ~d to** merērī, dignum esse quī (*subj*), iūs habēre (*gen*).
entity *n* rēs *f*.
entomb *vt* humāre, sepelīre.
entrails *n* intestīna *ntpl*, exta *ntpl*.
entrance *n* aditus *m*, introitus *m*; (*act*) ingressiō *f*; (*of house*) vestibulum *nt*; (*of harbour*) ōstium *nt*.
entrance *vt* fascināre, cōnsōpīre, capere.
entreat *vt* implōrāre, obsecrāre; (*successfully*) exōrāre.
entreaty *n* precēs *fpl*.
entrenchment *n* mūnītiō *f*.
entrust *vt* committere, crēdere, mandāre; (*for keeping*) dēpōnere.
entry *n* introitus *m*, aditus *m*; **make an ~** (*book*) in tabulās referre.
entwine *vt* implicāre, involvere.
enumerate *vt* numerāre, dīnumerāre.
enunciate *vt* ēdīcere; (*word*) exprimere.
envelop *vt* implicāre, involvere.

envelope *n* involucrum *nt*.
enviable *adj* beātus.
envious *adj* invidus, invidiōsus.
enviously *adv* invidiōsē.
environment *n* vīcīnia *f*; **our ~** ea in quibus versāmur.
envoy *n* lēgātus *m*.
envy *n* invidia *f* ♦ *vt* invidēre (*dat*).
enwrap *vt* involvere.
ephemeral *adj* brevis.
ephor *n* ephorus *m*.
epic *adj* epicus ♦ *n* epos *nt*.
epicure *n* dēlicātus *m*.
epigram *n* sententia *f*; (*poem*) epigramma *nt*.
epilepsy *n* morbus comitiālis *m*.
epilogue *n* epilogus *m*.
episode *n* ēventum *nt*.
epistle *n* epistula *f*, litterae *fpl*.
epitaph *n* epigramma *nt*, titulus *m*.
epithet *n* adsūmptum *nt*.
epitome *n* epitomē *f*.
epoch *n* saeculum *nt*.
equable *adj* aequālis; (*temper*) aequus.
equal *adj* aequus, pār; **be ~ to** aequāre; (*task*) sufficere (*dat*) ♦ *n* pār *m/f* ♦ *vt* aequāre, adaequāre.
equality *n* aequālitās *f*.
equalize *vt* adaequāre, exaequāre.
equally *adv* aequē, pariter.
equanimity *n* aequus animus *m*.
equate *vt* aequāre.
equator *n* aequinoctiālis circulus *m*.
equestrian *adj* equester.
equidistant *adj*: **be ~** aequō spatiō abesse, idem distāre.
equilibrium *n* lībrāmentum *nt*.
equine *adj* equīnus.
equinoctial *adj* aequinoctiālis.
equinox *n* aequinoctium *nt*.
equip *vt* armāre, īnstruere, ōrnāre.
equipment *n* arma *ntpl*, īnstrūmenta *ntpl*, adparātus *m*.
equipoise *n* lībrāmentum *nt*.
equitable *adj* aequus, iūstus.
equitably *adv* iūstē, aequē.
equity *n* aequum *nt*, aequitās *f*.
equivalent *adj* pār, īdem īnstar (*gen*).
equivocal *adj* anceps, ambiguus.
equivocally *adv* ambiguē.
equivocate *vi* tergiversārī.
era *n* saeculum *nt*.
eradicate *vt* ēvellere, exstirpāre.
erase *vt* dēlēre, indūcere.
erasure *n* litūra *f*.
ere *conj* priusquam.
erect *vt* ērigere; (*building*) exstruere; (*statute*) pōnere ♦ *adj* ērēctus.
erection *n* (*process*) exstructiō *f*; (*product*) aedificium *nt*.
erode *vt* rōdere.
erotic *adj* amātōrius.
err *vi* errāre, peccāre.
errand *n* mandātum *nt*.

errant *adj* vagus.
erratic *adj* incōnstāns.
erroneous *adj* falsus.
erroneously *adv* falsō, perperam.
error *n* error *m*; (*moral*) peccātum *nt*; (*writing*) mendum *nt*.
erudite *adj* doctus.
erudition *n* doctrīna *f*, ērudītiō *f*.
erupt *vi* ērumpere.
eruption *n* ēruptiō *f*.
escapade *n* ausum *nt*.
escape *vi* effugere, ēvādere ♦ *vt* fugere, ēvītāre; (*memory*) excidere ex (*abl*); ~ **the notice of** fallere, praeterīre ♦ *n* effugium *nt*, fuga *f*; **way of ~** effugium *nt*.
eschew *vt* vītāre.
escort *n* praesidium *nt*; (*private*) dēductor *m* ♦ *vt* comitārī, prōsequī; (*out of respect*) dēdūcere.
especial *adj* praecipuus.
especially *adv* praecipuē, praesertim, māximē, in prīmīs.
espionage *n* inquīsītiō *f*.
espouse *vt* (*wife*) dūcere; (*cause*) fovēre.
espy *vt* cōnspicere, cōnspicārī.
essay *n* cōnātus *m*; (*test*) perīculum *nt*; (*literary*) libellus *m* ♦ *vt* cōnārī, incipere.
essence *n* vīs *f*, nātūra *f*.
essential *adj* necesse, necessārius.
essentially *adv* necessāriō.
establish *vt* īnstituere, condere; (*firmly*) stabilīre.
established *adj* firmus, certus; **be ~** cōnstāre; **become ~** (*custom*) inveterāscere.
establishment *n* (*act*) cōnstitūtiō *f*; (*domestic*) familia *f*.
estate *n* fundus *m*, rūs *nt*; (*in money*) rēs *f*; (*rank*) ōrdō *m*.
esteem *vt* aestimāre, respicere ♦ *n* grātia *f*, opīniō *f*.
estimable *adj* optimus.
estimate *vt* aestimāre, ratiōnem inīre (*gen*) ♦ *n* aestimātiō *f*, iūdicium *nt*.
estimation *n* opīniō *f*, sententia *f*.
estrange *vt* aliēnāre, abaliēnāre.
estrangement *n* aliēnātiō *f*, discidium *nt*.
estuary *n* aestuārium *nt*.
eternal *adj* aeternus, perennis.
eternally *adv* semper, aeternum.
eternity *n* aeternitās *f*.
etesian winds *n* etēsiae *fpl*.
ether *n* (*sky*) aethēr *m*.
ethereal *adj* aetherius, caelestis.
ethic, ethical *adj* mōrālis.
ethics *n* mōrēs *mpl*, officia *ntpl*.
Etruscan *n* Etruscus *m* ♦ *adj like* **bonus.**
etymology *n* verbōrum notātiō *f*.
eulogist *n* laudātor *m*.
eulogize *vt* laudāre, conlaudāre.
eulogy *n* laudātiō *f*.
eunuch *n* eunūchus *m*.
euphony *n* sonus *m*.
evacuate *vt* (*place*) exinānīre; (*people*) dēdūcere.

evacuation *n* discessiō *f*.
evade *vt* dēclīnāre, dēvītāre, ēlūdere.
evaporate *vt* exhālāre ♦ *vi* exhālārī.
evaporation *n* exhālātiō *f*.
evasion *n* tergiversātiō *f*.
evasive *adj* ambiguus.
eve *n* vesper *m*; (*before festival*) pervigilium *nt*; **on the ~ of** prīdiē (*gen*).
even *adj* aequus, aequālis; (*number*) pār ♦ *adv* et, etiam; (*tentative*) vel; ~ **if** etsī, etiamsī; tametsī; ~ **more** etiam magis; ~ **so** nihilōminus; ~ **yet** etiamnum; **not ~** ... nē quidem ♦ *vt* aequāre.
evening *n* vesper *m* ♦ *adj* vespertīnus; ~ **is drawing on** invesperāscit; **in the ~** vesperī.
evening star *n* Vesper *m*, Hesperus *m*.
evenly *adv* aequāliter, aequābiliter.
evenness *n* aequālitās *f*, aequābilitās *f*.
event *n* ēventum *nt*; (*outcome*) ēventus *m*.
eventide *n* vespertīnum tempus *nt*.
eventuality *n* cāsus *m*.
eventually *adv* mox, aliquandō, tandem.
ever *adv* unquam; (*after* **sī, nisī, num, nē**) quandō; (*always*) semper; (*after interrog*) -nam, tandem; ~ **so** nimium, nimium quantum; **best ~** omnium optimus; **for ~** in aeternum.
everlasting *adj* aeternus, perpetuus, immortālis.
evermore *adv* semper, in aeternum.
every *adj* quisque, omnis; ~ **four years** quintō quōque annō; ~ **now and then** interdum; **in ~ direction** passim; undique; ~ **other day** alternīs diebus; ~ **day** cottīdiē ♦ *adj* cottīdiānus.
everybody *pron* quisque, omnēs *mpl*; ~ **agrees** inter omnēs constat; ~ **knows** nēmō est quīn sciat.
everyday *adj* cottīdiānus.
everyone *pron see* **everybody.**
everything omnia *ntpl*; **your health is ~ to me** meā māximē interest tē valēre.
everywhere *adv* ubīque, passim.
evict *vt* dēicere, dētrūdere.
eviction *n* dēiectiō *f*.
evidence *n* testimōnium *nt*, indicium *nt*; (*person*) testis *m/f*; (*proof*) argūmentum *nt*; **on the ~ of** fidē (*gen*); **collect ~ against** inquīrere in (*acc*); **turn King's ~** indicium profitērī.
evident *adj* manifestus, ēvidēns, clārus; **it is ~** appāret.
evidently *adv* manifestō, clārē.
evil *adj* malus, improbus, scelerātus.
evildoer *n* scelerātus *m*, maleficus *m*.
evil eye *n* fascinum *nt*, malum *nt*, improbitās *f*.
evil-minded *adj* malevolus.
evince *vt* praestāre.
evoke *vt* ēvocāre, ēlicere.
evolution *n* seriēs *f*, prōgressus *m*; (*MIL*) dēcursus *m*, dēcursiō *f*.
evolve *vt* explicāre, ēvolvere ♦ *vi* crēscere.
ewe *n* ovis *f*.
ewer *n* hydria *f*.
exacerbate *vt* exacerbāre, exasperāre.

exact vt exigere ♦ adj accūrātus; (person) dīligēns; (number) exāctus.

exaction n exāctiō f.

exactly adv accūrātē; (reply) ita prōrsus; ~ **as** perinde que.

exactness n cūra f, dīligentia f.

exaggerate vt augēre, in māius extollere.

exalt vt efferre, extollere; laudāre.

exaltation n ēlātiō f.

examination n inquīsītiō f, scrūtātiō f; (of witness) interrogātiō f; (test) probātiō f.

examine vt investīgāre, scrūtārī; īnspicere; (witness) interrogāre; (case) quaerere dē (abl); (candidate) probāre.

examiner n scrūtātor m.

example n exemplum nt, documentum nt; **for** ~ exemplī grātiā; **make an** ~ **of** animadvertere in (acc); **I am an** ~ exemplō sum.

exasperate vt exacerbāre, inrītāre.

exasperation n inrītātiō f.

excavate vt fodere.

excavation n fossiō f.

excavator n fossor m.

exceed vt excēdere, superāre.

exceedingly adv nimis, valdē, nimium quantum.

excel vt praestāre (dat), exsuperāre ♦ vi excellere.

excellence n praestantia f, virtūs f.

excellent adj ēgregius, praestāns, optimus.

excellently adv ēgregiē, praeclārē.

except vt excipere ♦ prep praeter (acc) ♦ adv nisī ♦ conj praeterquam, nisī quod.

exception n exceptiō f; **make an** ~ **of** excipere; **take** ~ **to** gravārī quod; **with the** ~ **of** praeter (acc).

exceptional adj ēgregius, eximius.

exceptionally adv ēgregiē, eximiē.

excerpt vt excerpere ♦ n excerptum nt.

excess n immoderātiō f, intemperantia f ♦ adj supervacāneus; **be in** ~ superesse.

excessive adj immoderātus, immodestus, nimius.

excessively adv immodicē, nimis.

exchange vt mūtāre, permūtāre ♦ n permūtātiō f; (of currencies) collybus m.

exchequer n aerārium nt; (emperor's) fiscus m.

excise n vectīgālia ntpl ♦ vt excīdere.

excision n excīsiō f.

excitable adj mōbilis.

excite vt excitāre, concitāre; (to action) incitāre, incendere; (to hope) ērigere, exacuere; (emotion) movēre, commovēre.

excitement n commōtiō f.

exclaim vt exclāmāre; ~ **against** adclāmāre (dat).

exclamation n clāmor m, exclāmātiō f.

exclude vt exclūdere.

exclusion n exclūsiō f.

exclusive adj proprius.

exclusively adv sōlum.

excogitate vt excōgitāre.

excrescence n tūber nt.

excruciating adj acerbissimus.

exculpate vt pūrgāre, absolvere.

excursion n iter nt; (MIL) excursiō f.

excuse n excūsātiō f; (false) speciēs f ♦ vt excūsāre, ignōscere (dat); (something due) remittere; **plead in** ~ excūsāre; **put forward as an** ~ praetendere.

execrable adj dētestābilis, sacer, nefārius.

execrate vt dētestārī, exsecrārī.

execration n dētestātiō f, exsecrātiō f.

execute vt efficere, patrāre, exsequī; suppliciō afficere; (behead) secūrī percutere.

execution n effectus m; (penalty) supplicium nt, mors f.

executioner n carnifex m.

exemplar n exemplum nt.

exempt adj immūnis, līber ♦ vt līberāre.

exemption n (from tax) immūnitās f; (from service) vacātiō f.

exercise n exercitātiō f, ūsus m; (school) dictāta ntpl ♦ vt exercēre, ūtī (abl); (mind) acuere.

exert vt extendere, intendere, ūtī (abl); ~ **oneself** mōlīrī, ēnītī, sē intendere.

exertion n mōlīmentum nt; (mind) intentiō f.

exhalation n exhālātiō f, vapor m.

exhale vt exhālāre, exspīrāre.

exhaust vt exhaurīre; (tire) dēfatīgāre, cōnficere.

exhaustion n dēfatīgātiō f.

exhaustive adj plēnus.

exhibit vt exhibēre, ostendere, expōnere; (on stage) ēdere.

exhibition n expositiō f, ostentātiō f.

exhilarate vt exhilarāre.

exhort vt hortārī, cohortārī.

exhortation n hortātiō f, hortāmen nt.

exhume vt ēruere.

exigency n necessitās f.

exile n exsilium nt, fuga f; (temporary) relēgātiō f; (person) exsul m; **live in** ~ exsulāre ♦ vt in exsilium pellere, dēportāre; (temporarily) relēgāre.

exist vi esse.

existence n vīta f.

exit n exitus m, ēgressus m.

exodus n discessus m.

exonerate vt absolvere.

exorbitant adj nimius, immoderātus.

exotic adj peregrīnus.

expand vt extendere, dīlātāre.

expanse n spatium nt, lātitūdō f.

expatiate vi: ~ **upon** amplificāre.

expatriate vt extermināre ♦ n extorris m.

expect vt exspectāre, spērāre.

expectancy, expectation n spēs f, exspectātiō f; opīniō f.

expediency n ūtile nt, ūtilitās f.

expedient adj ūtilis, commodus; **it is** ~ expedit ♦ n modus m, ratiō f.

expediently adv commodē.

expedite vt mātūrāre.

expedition n (*MIL*) expedītiō f.
expeditious adj prōmptus, celer.
expeditiously adv celeriter.
expel vt pellere, expellere, ēicere.
expend vt impendere, expendere.
expenditure n impēnsae fpl, sūmptus m.
expense n impēnsae fpl, impendia ntpl; **at my ~**
meō sūmptū; **at the public ~** dē pūblicō.
expensive adj cārus, pretiōsus; (*furnishings*)
lautus.
expensively adv sūmptuōsē, māgnō pretiō.
experience n ūsus m, experientia f ◆ vt
experīrī, patī.
experienced adj perītus, expertus (+ gen).
experiment n experīmentum nt ◆ vi: **~ with**
experīrī.
expert adj perītus, sciēns.
expertly adv perītē, scienter.
expertness n perītia f.
expiate vt expiāre, lūere.
expiatio n (*act*) expiātiō f; (*penalty*) piāculum
nt.
expiatory adj piāculāris.
expiration n (*breath*) exspīrātiō f; (*time*) exitus
m.
expire vi exspīrāre; (*die*) animam agere,
animam efflāre; (*time*) exīre.
expiry n exitus m, fīnis m.
explain vt explicāre, expōnere, explānāre,
interpretārī; (*lucidly*) ēnōdāre; (*in detail*)
ēdisserere.
explanation n explicātiō f, ēnōdātiō f,
interpretātiō f.
explicit adj expressus, apertus.
explicitly adv apertē.
explode vt discutere ◆ vi dīrumpī.
exploit n factum nt, ausum nt; **~s** pl rēs gestae
fpl ◆ vt ūtī (*abl*), fruī (*abl*).
explore vt, vi explōrāre, scrūtārī.
explorer n explōrātor m.
explosion n fragor m.
exponent n interpres m, auctor m.
export vt exportāre ◆ n exportātiō f.
exportation n exportātiō f.
expose vt dētegere, dēnūdāre, patefacere;
(*child*) expōnere; (*to danger*) obicere; (*MIL*)
nūdāre; (*for sale*) prōpōnere; **~ o.s.** se
obicere.
exposed adj apertus, obnoxius.
exposition n explicātiō f, interpretātiō f.
expostulate vi expostulāre, conquerī.
expostulation n expostulātiō f.
exposure n (*of child*) expositiō f; (*of guilt*)
dēprehēnsiō f; (*to hardship*) patientia f.
expound vt expōnere, interpretārī.
expounder n interpres m.
express vt (*in words*) exprimere, dēclārāre,
ēloquī; (*in art*) effingere ◆ adj expressus;
(*speed*) celerrimus.
expression n significātiō f; (*word*) vōx f,
verbum nt; (*face*) vultus m.
expressive adj significāns; **~ of** index (*gen*); **be**
very ~ māximam vim habēre.

expressively adv significanter.
expressiveness n vīs f.
expressly adv plānē.
expulsion n expulsiō f, ēiectiō f.
expurgate vt pūrgāre.
exquisite adj ēlegāns, exquīsītus, eximius;
(*judgment*) subtīlis.
exquisitely adv ēleganter, exquīsītē.
ex-service adj ēmeritus.
extant adj superstes; **be ~** exstāre.
extempore adv ex tempore, subitō ◆ adj
extemporālis.
extemporize vi subita dīcere.
extend vt extendere, dīlātāre; (*hand*)
porrigere; (*line*) dūcere; (*office*) prōrogāre;
(*territory*) propāgāre ◆ vi patēre, porrigī; **~**
into incurrere in (*acc*).
extension n prōductiō f, prōlātiō f; (*of office*)
prōrogātiō f; (*of territory*) propāgātiō f; (*extra*)
incrēmentum nt.
extensive adj effūsus, amplus, lātus.
extensively adv lātē.
extent n spatium nt, amplitūdō f; **to a large ~**
māgnā ex parte; **to some ~** aliquā ex parte;
to this ~ hāctenus; **to such an ~** adeō.
extenuate vt levāre, mītigāre.
exterior adj externus, exterior ◆ n speciēs f.
exterminate vt occīdiōne occīdere,
interimere.
extermination n occīdiō f, interneciō f.
external adj externus.
externally adv extrīnsecus.
extinct adj mortuus; (*custom*) obsolētus.
extinction n exstinctiō f, interitus m.
extinguish vt exstinguere, restinguere.
extinguisher n exstinctor m.
extirpate vt exstirpāre, excīdere.
extol vt laudāre, laudibus efferre.
extort vt extorquēre, exprimere.
extortion n (*offence*) rēs repetundae fpl.
extortionate adj inīquus, rapāx.
extra adv īnsuper, praetereā ◆ adj additus.
extract vt excerpere, extrahere ◆ n: **make ~s**
excerpere.
extraction n ēvulsiō f; (*descent*) genus nt.
extraneous adj adventīcius, aliēnus.
extraordinarily adv mīrificē, eximiē.
extraordinary adj extraōrdinārius; (*strange*)
mīrus, novus; (*outstanding*) eximius,
īnsignis.
extravagance n intemperantia f; (*language*)
immoderātiō f, luxuria f; (*spending*) sūmptus
m.
extravagant adj immoderātus, immodestus;
(*spending*) sūmptuōsus, prōdigus.
extreme adj extrēmus, ultimus.
extremely adv valdē, vehementer.
extremity n extrēmum nt, fīnis m; (*distress*)
angustiae fpl; **the ~ of** extrēmus.
extricate vt expedīre, absolvere; **~ oneself**
ēmergere.
exuberance n ūbertās f, luxuria f.
exuberant adj ūber, laetus, luxuriōsus.

exuberantly *adv* ūbertim.
exude *vt* exsūdāre. ♦ *vi* mānāre.
exult *vi* exsultārī, laetārī, gestīre.
exultant *adj* laetus.
exultantly *adv* laetē.
exultation *n* laetitia *f*.

eye *n* oculus *m*; (*needle*) forāmen *nt*; **cast ~s on**
oculōs conicere in (*acc*); **have an ~ to**
spectāre; **in your ~s** iūdice tē; **keep one's ~s**
on oculōs dēfigere in (*abl*); **lose an ~** alterō
oculō capī; **see ~ to ~** cōnsentīre; **set ~s on**
cōnspicere; **shut one's ~s to** cōnīvēre in
(*abl*); **take one's ~s off** oculōs dēicere ab
(*abl*); **up to the ~s in** tōtus in (*abl*); **with a cast**
in the ~ paetus; **with sore ~s** lippus; **sore ~s**
lippitūdō *f*; **with one's own ~s** cōram; **with**
one's ~s open sciēns ♦ *vt* intuērī, aspicere.
eyeball *n* pūpula *f*.
eyebrow *n* supercilium *nt*.
eyelash *n* palpebrae pilus *m*.
eyelid *n* palpebra *f*.
eyeshot *n* oculōrum coniectus *m*.
eyesight *n* aciēs *f*, oculī *mpl*.
eyesore *n* turpe *nt*; **it is an ~ to me** oculī meī
dolent.
eye tooth *n* dēns canīnus *m*.
eyewash *n* sycophantia *f*.
eyewitness *n* arbiter *m*; **be an ~ of** interesse
(*dat*).

F, f

fable *n* fābula *f*, apologus *m*.
fabled *adj* fābulōsus.
fabric *n* (*built*) structūra *f*; (*woven*) textile *nt*.
fabricate *vt* fabricārī; (*fig*) comminīscī,
fingere.
fabricated *adj* commentīcius.
fabrication *n* (*process*) fabricātiō *f*; (*thing*)
commentum *nt*.
fabricator *n* auctor *m*.
fabulous *adj* commentīcius, fictus.
fabulously *adv* incrēdibiliter.
facade *n* frōns *f*.
face *n* faciēs *f*, ōs *nt*; (*aspect*) aspectus *m*;
(*impudence*) ōs *nt*; **~ to ~** cōram; **how shall**
I have the ~ to go back? quō ōre redībō?; **on**
the ~ of it ad speciem, prīmō aspectū; **put**
a bold ~ on fortēm sē praebēre; **save ~**
factum pūrgāre; **set one's ~ against**
adversārī (*dat*) ♦ *vt* spectāre ad (*acc*);
(*danger*) obviam īre (*dat*), sē oppōnere
(*dat*) ♦ *vi* (*place*) spectāre, vergere; **~**
about (*MIL*) signa convertere.
facetious *adj* facētus, salsus.

facetiously *adv* facētē, salsē.
facetiousness *n* facētiae *fpl*, salēs *mpl*.
facile *adj* facilis.
facilitate *vt* expedīre.
facilities *npl* opportūnitās *f*.
facility *n* facilitās *f*.
facing *adj* adversus ♦ *prep* exadversus (*acc*).
facsimile *n* exemplār *nt*.
fact *n* rēs *f*, vērum *nt*; **as a matter of ~**
enimvērō; **the ~ that** quod; **in ~** rē vērā ♦ *conj*
etenim; (*climax*) dēnique.
faction *n* factiō *f*.
factious *adj* factiōsus, sēditiōsus.
factiously *adv* sēditiōsē.
factor *n* prōcūrātor *m*.
factory *n* officīna *f*.
faculty *n* facultās *f*, vīs *f*.
fad *n* libīdō *f*.
fade *vi* dēflōrēscere, marcēscere.
faded *adj* marcidus.
faggot *n* sarmentum *nt*.
fail *vi* dēficere, dēesse; (*fig*) cadere, dēcidere;
(*in business*) forō cēdere; **~ to** nōn posse; **~ to**
come nōn venīre ♦ *vt* dēficere, dēstituere.
failing *n* culpa *f*, vitium *nt*.
failure *n* (*of supply*) dēfectiō *f*; (*in action*)
offēnsiō *f*; (*at election*) repulsa *f*.
fain *adv* libenter.
faint *adj* (*body*) languidus, dēfessus;
(*impression*) hebes, levis; (*courage*) timidus;
(*colour*) pallidus; **be ~** languēre; hebēre ♦ *vi*
intermorī, animō linquī; **I feel ~** animō male
est.
faint-hearted *adj* animo dēmissus; timidus.
faintly *adv* languidē; leviter.
faintness *n* dēfectiō *f*, languor *m*; levitās *f*.
fair *adj* (*appearance*) pulcher, fōrmōsus; (*hair*)
flāvus; (*skin*) candidus; (*weather*) serēnus;
(*wind*) secundus; (*copy*) pūrus; (*dealings*)
aequus; (*speech*) speciōsus, blandus; (*ability*)
mediocris; (*reputation*) bonus ♦ *n* nūndinae
fpl; **~ and square** sine fūcō ac fallāciīs.
fairly *adv* iūre, iūstē; mediocriter.
fairness *n* aequitās *f*.
fair play *n* aequum et bonum *nt*.
fairy *n* nympha *f*.
faith *n* fidēs *f*; **in good ~** bonā fidē.
faithful *adj* fidēlis, fīdus.
faithfully *adv* fidēliter.
faithfulness *n* fidēlitās *f*.
faithless *adj* īnfidēlis, īnfīdus, perfidus.
faithlessly *adv* īnfidēliter.
faithlessness *n* īnfidēlitās *f*.
fake *vt* simulāre.
falchion *n* falx *f*.
falcon *n* falcō *m*.
fall *vi* cadere; (*gently*) lābī; (*morally*) prōlābī;
(*dead*) concidere, occidere; (*fortress*)
expugnārī, capī; **~ at** accidere; **~ away**
dēficere, dēscīscere; **~ back** recidere; (*MIL*)
pedem referre; **~ between** intercidere; **~**
behind cessāre; **~ by the way** intercidere; **~**
down dēcidere, dēlābī; (*building*) ruere,

corruere; ~ **due** cadere; ~ **flat** sē
prōsternere; (*speech*) frīgēre; ~ **forward**
prōlābī; ~ **foul of** incurrere in (*acc*); ~
headlong sē praecipitāre; ~ **in, into** incidere;
~ **in with** occurrere (*dat*); ~ **off** dēcidere; (*fig*)
dēscīscere; ~ **on** incumbere in (*acc*), incidere
in (*acc*); ~ **out** excidere; (*event*) ēvenīre;
(*hair*) dēfluere; ~ **short of** deesse ad; ~ **to** (*by
lot*) obtingere, obvenīre (*dat*); ~ **to the
ground** (*case*) iacēre; ~ **upon** invādere,
ingruere in (*acc*); (*one's neck*) in collum
invādere ♦ *n* cāsus *m*; (*building*) ruīna *f*;
(*moral*) lāpsus *m*; (*season*) autumnus *m*; **the ~
of Capua** Capua capta.
fallacious *adj* captiōsus, fallāx.
fallaciously *adv* fallāciter.
fallacy *n* captiō *f*.
fallible *adj*: **be ~** errāre solēre.
fallow *adj* (*land*) novālis ♦ *n* novāle *nt*; **lie ~**
cessāre.
false *adj* falsus, fictus.
falsehood *n* falsum *nt*, mendācium *nt*; **tell a ~**
mentīrī.
falsely *adv* falsō.
falsify *vt* vitiāre, interlinere.
falter *vi* (*speech*) haesitāre; (*gait*) titubāre.
faltering *adj* (*speech*) īnfrāctus; (*gait*) titubāns
♦ *n* haesitātiō *f*.
fame *n* fāma *f*, glōria *f*, nōmen *nt*.
famed *adj* illūstris, praeclārus.
familiar *adj* (*friend*) intimus; (*fact*) nōtus;
(*manner*) cōmis; ~ **spirit** genius *m*; **be ~ with**
nōvisse; **be on ~ terms with** familiāriter ūtī
(*abl*).
familiarity *n* ūsus *m*, cōnsuētūdō *f*.
familiarize *vt* adsuēfacere.
familiarly *adv* familiāriter.
family *n* domus *f*, gēns *f* ♦ *adj* domesticus,
familiāris; ~ **property** rēs familiāris *f*.
famine *n* famēs *f*.
famished *adj* famēlicus.
famous *adj* illūstris, praeclārus, nōbilis; **make
~** nōbilitāre; **the ~** ille.
fan *n* flābellum *nt*; (*winnowing*) vannus *f* ♦ *vt*
ventilāre; ~ **the flames of** (*fig*) īnflammāre.
fanatic *n* (*religious*) fānāticus *m*.
fanciful *adj* (*person*) incōnstāns; (*idea*)
commentīcius.
fancy *n* (*faculty*) mēns *f*; (*idea*) opīnātiō *f*;
(*caprice*) libīdō *f*; **take a ~ to** amāre incipere;
~ **oneself** se amāre ♦ *vt* animō fingere,
imāginārī, sibi prōpōnere; ~ **you thinking ...!**
tē crēdere ...! ♦ *adj* dēlicātus.
fancy-free *adj* sēcūrus, vacuus.
fang *n* dēns *m*.
fantastic *adj* commentīcius, mōnstruōsus.
fantasy *n* imāginātiō *f*; (*contemptuous*)
somnium *nt*.
far *adj* longinquus ♦ *adv* longē, procul; (*with
compar*) multō; **be ~ from** longē abesse ab; **be
not ~ from doing** haud multum abest quin
(+*subj*); **by ~** longē; **how ~?** quātenus?,
quoūsque?; **so ~** hāctenus, eātenus; (*limited*)

quādam tenus; **thus ~** hāctenus; ~ **and wide**
lātē; ~ **be it from me to say** equidem dīcere
nōlim; ~ **from thinking** ... **I** adeō nōn crēdō ...
ut; **as ~ as** *prep* tenus (*abl*) ♦ *adv* ūsque ♦ *conj*
quātenus; (*know*) quod.
farce *n* mīmus *m*.
farcical *adj* rīdiculus.
fare *vi* sē habēre, agere ♦ *n* vectūra *f*; (*boat*)
naulum *nt*; (*food*) cibus *m*.
farewell *interj* valē, valēte; **say ~ to** valēre
iubēre.
far-fetched *adj* quaesītus, arcessītus, altē
repetītus.
farm *n* fundus *m*, praedium *nt* ♦ *vt* (*soil*) colere;
(*taxes*) redimere; ~ **out** locāre.
farmer *n* agricola *m*; (*of taxes*) pūblicānus *m*.
farming *n* agrīcultūra *f*.
farrow *vt* parere ♦ *n* fētus *m*.
far-sighted *adj* prōvidus, prūdēns.
farther *adv* longius, ultrā ♦ *adj* ulterior.
farthest *adj* ultimus, extrēmus ♦ *adv*
longissimē.
fasces *n* fascēs *mpl*.
fascinate *vt* dēlēnīre, capere.
fascination *n* dulcēdō *f*, dēlēnīmenta *ntpl*,
lēnōcinia *ntpl*.
fashion *n* mōs *m*, ūsus *m*; (*manner*) modus *m*,
ratiō *f*; (*shape*) fōrma *f* ♦ *vt* fingere, fōrmāre;
after the ~ of rītū (*gen*); **come into ~** in
mōrem venīre; **go out of ~** obsolēscere.
fashionable *adj* ēlegāns; **it is ~** mōris est.
fashionably *adv* ēleganter.
fast *adj* (*firm*) firmus; (*quick*) celer; **make ~**
dēligāre ♦ *adv* firmē; celeriter; **be ~ asleep**
artē dormīre ♦ *vi* iēiūnus esse, cibō
abstinēre ♦ *n* iēiūnium *nt*.
fasten *vt* fīgere, ligāre; ~ **down** dēfīgere; ~ **on**
inligāre; ~ **to** adligāre; ~ **together** conligāre,
cōnfīgere.
fastening *n* iūnctūra *f*.
fastidious *adj* dēlicātus, ēlegāns.
fastidiously *adv* fastīdiōsē.
fastidiousness *n* fastīdium *nt*.
fasting *n* iēiūnium *nt*, inedia *f* ♦ *adj* iēiūnus.
fastness *n* arx *f*, castellum *nt*.
fat *adj* pinguis, opīmus, obēsus; **grow ~**
pinguēscere ♦ *n* adeps *m/f*.
fatal *adj* (*deadly*) fūnestus, exitiābilis; (*fated*)
fātālis.
fatality *n* fātum *nt*, cāsus *m*.
fatally *adv*: **be ~ wounded** vulnere perīre.
fate *n* fātum *nt*, fortūna *f*, sors *f*.
fated *adj* fātālis.
fateful *adj* fātālis; fūnestus.
Fates *npl* (*goddesses*) Parcae *fpl*.
father *n* pater *m*; (*fig*) auctor *m* ♦ *vt* gignere; ~
upon addīcere, tribuere.
father-in-law *n* socer *m*.
fatherland *n* patria *f*.
fatherless *adj* orbus.
fatherly *adj* paternus.
fathom *n* sex pedēs *mpl* ♦ *vt* (*fig*) exputāre.
fathomless *adj* profundus.

fatigue n fatīgātio f, dēfatīgātiō f ♦ vt fatīgāre, dēfatīgāre.
fatness n pinguitūdō f.
fatten vt sagīnāre.
fatty adj pinguis.
fatuity n īnsulsitās f, ineptiae fpl.
fatuous adj fatuus, īnsulsus, ineptus.
fault n culpa f, vitium nt; (written) mendum nt; **count as a ~** vitiō vertere; **find ~ with** incūsāre; **it is not your ~ that** ... nōn per tē stat quōminus (subj).
faultily adv vitiōsē, mendōsē.
faultiness n vitium nt.
faultless adj ēmendātus, integer.
faultlessly adv ēmendātē.
faulty adj vitiōsus, mendōsus.
faun n faunus m.
fauna n animālia ntpl.
favour n grātia f, favor m; (done) beneficium nt; **win ~ with** grātiam inīre apud; **by your ~** bonā veniā tuā ♦ vt favēre (dat), indulgēre (dat).
favourable adj faustus, prosperus, secundus.
favourably adv faustē, fēlīciter, benignē.
favourite adj dīlectus, grātissimus ♦ n dēliciae fpl.
favouritism n indulgentia f, studium nt.
fawn n hinnuleus m ♦ adj (colour) gilvus ♦ vi: ~ **upon** adūlārī.
fawning adj blandus ♦ n adūlātiō f.
fear n timor m, metus m, formīdō f ♦ vt timēre, metuere, formīdāre, verērī; **fearing that** veritus nē (+ imperf subj).
fearful adj timidus; horrendus, terribilis, formīdolōsus.
fearfully adv timidē; formīdolōsē.
fearless adj impavidus, intrepidus.
fearlessly adv impavidē, intrepidē.
fearlessness n fīdentia f, audācia f.
fearsome adj formīdolōsus.
feasible adj: **it is ~** fierī potest.
feast n epulae fpl; (private) convīvium nt; (public) epulum nt; (religious) daps f; (festival) festus diēs m ♦ vi epulārī, convīvārī; (fig) pāscī ♦ vt: ~ **one's eyes on** oculōs pāscere (abl).
feat n factum nt, facinus nt.
feather n penna f; (downy) plūma f; **birds of a ~ flock together** parēs cum paribus facillimē congregantur.
feathered adj pennātus.
feathery adj plūmeus.
feature n līneāmentum nt; (fig) proprium nt.
February n mēnsis Februārius m; **of ~** Februārius.
federal adj sociālis, foederātus.
federate vi societātem facere.
federated adj foederātus.
federation n societās f, foederātae cīvitātēs fpl.
fee n honōs m, mercēs f.
feeble adj imbēcillus, īnfirmus, dēbilis.
feebleness n imbēcillitās f, īnfirmitās f.
feebly adv īnfirmē.

feed vt alere, pāscere ♦ vi pāscī; ~ **on** vescī (abl) ♦ n pābulum nt.
feel vt sentīre; (with hand) tractāre, tangere; (emotion) capere, adficī (abl); (opinion) cēnsēre, sentīre; ~ **one's way** pedetemptim prōgredī ♦ vi sentīre; **I ~ glad** gaudeō; ~ **sure** prō certō habēre.
feeling n sēnsus m, tāctus m; (mind) animus m, adfectus m; (pity) misericordia f; **good ~** voluntās f; **bad ~** invidia f.
feign vt simulāre, fingere.
feignedly adv simulātē, fictē.
feint n simulātiō f.
felicitate vt grātulārī (dat).
felicitation n grātulātiō f.
felicitous adj fēlīx, aptus.
felicity n fēlīcitās f.
feline adj fēlīnus.
fell vt (tree) succīdere; (enemy) sternere, caedere ♦ adj dīrus, crūdēlis, atrōx ♦ n mōns m; (skin) pellis f.
fellow n socius m, aequālis m; (contemptuous) homō m.
fellow citizen n cīvis m/f.
fellow countryman n cīvis m/f, populāris m/f.
fellow feeling n misericordia f.
fellowship n societās f, sodālitās f.
fellow slave n cōnservus m.
fellow soldier n commīlitō m.
fellow student n condiscipulus m.
felon n nocēns m.
felonious adj scelestus, scelerātus.
felony n scelus nt, noxa f.
felt n coāctum nt.
female adj muliebris ♦ n fēmina f.
feminine adj muliebris.
fen n palūs f.
fence n saepēs f; **sit on the ~** quiēscere, medium sē gerere ♦ vt saepīre; ~ **off** intersaepīre ♦ vi bātuere, rudibus lūdere.
fencing n rudium lūdus m; ~ **master** lānista m.
fend vt arcēre ♦ vi prōvidēre.
fennel n ferula f.
fenny adj palūster.
ferment n fermentum nt; (fig) aestus m ♦ vt fermentāre; (fig) excitāre, accendere ♦ vi fervēre.
fermentation n fervor m.
fern n filix f.
ferocious adj ferōx, saevus, truculentus.
ferociously adv truculentē.
ferocity n ferōcitās f, saevitia f.
ferret n viverra m ♦ vt: ~ **out** rīmārī, ēruere.
ferry n trāiectus m; (boat) cymba f, pontō m ♦ vt trānsvehere.
ferryman n portitor m.
fertile adj fertīlis, fēcundus.
fertility n fertīlitās f, fēcunditās f.
fertilize vt fēcundāre, laetificāre.
fervent adj fervidus, ārdēns.
fervently adv ārdenter.
fervid adj fervidus.
fervour n ārdor m, fervor m.

festal *adj* festus.
fester *vi* exulcerārī.
festival *n* diēs festus *m*, sollemne *nt*.
festive *adj* (*time*) festus; (*person*) festīvus.
festivity *n* hilaritās *f*; (*event*) sollemne *nt*.
festoon *n* sertum *nt* ♦ *vt* corōnāre.
fetch *vt* arcessere, addūcere; (*price*) vēnīre
  (*gen*); ~ **out** dēprōmere; ~ **water** aquārī.
fetching *adj* lepidus, blandus.
fetid *adj* foetidus, pūtidus.
fetter *n* compēs *f*, vinculum *nt* ♦ *vt* compedēs
  inicere (*dat*), vincīre; (*fig*) impedīre.
fettle *n* habitus *m*, animus *m*.
feud *n* simultās *f*, inimīcitia *f*.
fever *n* febris *f*.
feverish *adj* febrīculōsus; (*fig*) sollicitus.
few *adj* paucī; **very** ~ perpaucī; **how** ~**?** quotus
  quisque?
fewness *n* paucitās *f*.
fiancé *n* spōnsus *m*.
fiasco *n* calamitās *f*; **be a** ~ frīgēre.
fiat *n* ēdictum *nt*.
fibre *n* fibra *f*.
fickle *adj* incōnstāns, levis, mōbilis.
fickleness *n* incōnstantia *f*, levitās *f*, mōbilitās
  f.
fiction *n* fābula *f*, commentum *nt*.
fictitious *adj* fictus, falsus, commentīcius;
  (*character*) persōnātus.
fictitiously *adv* fictē.
fidelity *n* fidēlitās *f*, fidēs *f*.
fidget *vi* sollicitārī.
field *n* ager *m*; (*ploughed*) arvum *nt*; (*of grain*)
  segēs *f*; (*MIL*) campus *m*, aciēs *f*; (*scope*)
  campus *m*, locus *m*; **in the** ~ (*MIL*) mīlitiae;
  hold the ~ vincere, praevalēre; ~ **of vision**
  cōnspectus *m*.
fiend *n* diabolus *m*.
fiendish *adj* nefārius, improbus.
fierce *adj* saevus, ācer, atrōx; (*look*) torvus.
fiercely *adv* ācriter, atrōciter, saevē.
fierceness *n* saevitia *f*, atrōcitās *f*.
fieriness *n* ārdor *m*, fervor *m*.
fiery *adj* igneus, flammeus; (*fig*) ārdēns,
  fervidus.
fife *n* tībia *f*.
fifteen *num* quīndecim; ~ **each** quīndēnī; ~
  times quīndeciēns.
fifteenth *adj* quīntus decimus.
fifth *adj* quīntus ♦ *n* quīnta pars *f*.
fiftieth *adj* quīnquāgēsimus.
fifty *num* quīnquāgintā.
fig *n* fīcus *f*; (*tree*) fīcus *f*; **of** ~ fīculnus; **not care
  a** ~ **for** floccī nōn facere.
fight *n* pugna *f*, proelium *nt* ♦ *vi* pugnāre,
  dīmicāre; ~ **it out** dēcernere, dēcertāre; ~ **to
  the end** dēpugnāre ♦ *vt* (*battle*) committere;
  (*enemy*) pugnāre cum (*abl*).
fighter *n* pugnātor *m*.
fighting *n* dīmicātiō *f*.
figment *n* commentum *nt*.
figurative *adj* trānslātus; **in** ~ **language**
  trānslātīs per similitūdinem verbīs; **use** ~**ly**
  trānsferre.

figure *n* figūra *f*, fōrma *f*; (*in art*) signum *nt*; (*of
  speech*) figūra *f*, trānslātiō *f*; (*pl, on pottery*)
  sigilla *ntpl* ♦ *vt* figūrāre, fōrmāre; (*art*)
  fingere, effingere; ~ **to oneself** sibi
  prōpōnere.
figured *adj* sigillātus.
figurehead *n* (*of ship*) īnsigne *nt*.
filament *n* fibra *f*.
filch *vt* fūrārī, surripere.
file *n* (*tool*) līma *f*; (*line*) ōrdō *m*, agmen *nt*; (*of
  papers*) fasciculus *m*; ~**s** *pl* tabulae *fpl*; **in
  single** ~ simplicī ōrdine; **the rank and** ~
  gregāriī mīlitēs ♦ *vt* līmāre.
filial *adj* pius.
filigree *n* diatrēta *ntpl*.
fill *vt* implēre, explēre, complēre; (*office*) fungī
  (*abl*); ~ **up** supplēre.
fillet *n* īnfula *f*, vitta *f* ♦ *vt* (*fish*) exossāre.
fillip *n* stimulus *m*.
filly *n* equula *f*.
film *n* membrāna *f*.
filter *n* cōlum *nt* ♦ *vt* dēliquāre ♦ *vi* percōlārī.
filth *n* sordēs *f*, caenum *nt*.
filthily *adv* foedē, inquinātē.
filthiness *n* foeditās *f*, impūritās *f*.
filthy *adj* foedus, impūrus; (*speech*)
  inquinātus.
fin *n* pinna *f*.
final *adj* ultimus, postrēmus, extrēmus.
finally *adv* dēnique, tandem, postrēmō.
finance *n* rēs nummāria *f*; (*state*) vectīgālia
  ntpl.
financial *adj* aerārius.
financier *n* faenerātor *m*.
finch *n* fringilla *f*.
find *vt* invenīre, reperīre; (*supplies*) parāre;
  (*verdict*) iūdicāre; (*pleasure*) capere; ~ **fault
  with** incūsāre; ~ **guilty** damnāre; ~ **out**
  comperīre, cognōscere.
finder *n* inventor *m*.
finding *n* iūdicium *nt*, sententia *f*.
fine *n* (*law*) multa *f*, damnum *nt*; **in** ~ dēnique ♦
  vt multāre ♦ *adj* (*thin*) tenuis, subtīlis;
  (*refined*) ēlegāns, mundus, decōrus;
  (*beautiful*) pulcher, venustus; (*showy*)
  speciōsus; (*of weather*) serēnus.
finely *adv* pulchrē, ēleganter, subtīliter.
fineness *n* tenuitās *f*; ēlegantia *f*; pulchritūdō *f*;
  speciēs *f*; serēnitās *f*.
finery *n* ōrnātus *m*, munditiae *fpl*.
finesse *n* astūtia *f*, ars *f*, argūtiae *fpl*.
finger *n* digitus *m*; **a** ~**'s breadth** trānsversus
  digitus; **not lift a** ~ (*in effort*) nē manum
  quidem vertere ♦ *vt* pertractāre.
fingertips *npl* extrēmī digitī.
finish *n* fīnis *m*; (*art*) perfectiō *f* ♦ *vt* fīnīre,
  perficere; cōnficere; (*with art*) perficere,
  expolīre ♦ *vi* dēsinere; ~ **off** transigere,
  peragere, absolvere.
finishing post *n* mēta *f*.
finishing touch *n* manus extrēma.
finite *adj* circumscrīptus.

fir n abiēs f; **of ~** abiēgnus.

fire n ignis m; (conflagration) incendium nt; (in hearth) focus m; (fig) ārdor m, calor m, impetus m; **be on ~** ārdēre, flagrāre; **catch ~** flammam concipere, ignem comprehendere; **set on ~** accendere, incendere ♦ vt incendere; (fig) īnflammāre; (missile) iaculārī.

firebrand n fax f.

fire brigade n vigilēs mpl.

fireplace n focus m.

fireside n focus m.

firewood n lignum nt.

firm n societās f ♦ adj firmus, stabilis; (mind) cōnstāns; **stand ~** perstāre.

firmament n caelum nt.

firmly adv firmē, cōnstanter.

firmness n firmitās f, firmitūdō f; cōnstantia f.

first adj prīmus, prīnceps; (of two) prior ♦ adv prīmum; **at ~** prīmō, prīncipiō; **at ~ hand** ipse, ab ipsō; **come in ~** vincere; **give ~ aid to** ad tempus medērī (dat); **I was the ~ to see** prīmus vīdī.

first-class adj classicus.

first fruits npl prīmitiae fpl.

firstly adv prīmum.

first-rate adj eximius, lūculentus.

firth n aestuārium nt, fretum nt.

fiscal adj vectīgālis, aerārius.

fish n piscis m ♦ vi piscārī; (fig) expiscārī.

fisher, fisherman n piscātor m.

fishing n piscātus m ♦ adj piscātōrius.

fishing-rod n harundō f.

fish market n forum piscārium nt.

fishmonger n piscārius m.

fish pond n piscīna f.

fissile adj fissilis.

fissure n rīma f.

fist n pugnus m.

fit n (MED) convulsiō f; (of anger, illness) impetus m; **by ~s and starts** temerē, carptim ♦ vt aptāre, accommodāre; (dress) sedēre (dat); **~ out** armāre, īnstruere ♦ adj aptus, idōneus, dignus; **I see ~ to** mihi vidētur; **~ for** aptus ad (+ acc).

fitful adj dubius, incōnstāns.

fitfully adv incōnstanter.

fitly adv dignē, aptē.

fitness n convenientia f.

fitting n adparātus m, īnstrūmentum nt ♦ adj idōneus, dignus; **it is ~** convenit, decet.

fittingly adv dignē, convenienter.

five num quīnque; **~ each** quīnī; **~ times** quīnquiēns; **~ years** quīnquennium nt, lūstrum nt; **~ sixths** quīnque partēs.

five hundred num quīngentī; **~ each** quīngēnī; **~ times** quīngentiēns.

five hundredth adj quīngentēsimus.

fix vt fīgere; (time) dīcere, cōnstituere; (decision) statuere ♦ n angustiae fpl; **put in a ~** dēprehendere.

fixed adj fīxus; (attention) intentus; (decision) certus; (star) inerrāns; **be firmly ~ in** īnsidēre (dat).

fixedly adv intentē.

fixity n stabilitās f; (of purpose) cōnstantia f.

fixtures npl adfīxa ntpl.

flabbergast vt obstupefacere.

flabbiness n mollitia f.

flabby adj flaccidus, mollis.

flag n vexillum nt; **~ officer** praefectus classis m ♦ vi flaccēre, flaccēscere, languēscere.

flagellate vt verberāre.

flagon n lagoena f.

flagrant adj manifestus; flāgitiōsus.

flagrantly adv flāgitiōsē.

flagship n nāvis imperātōria f.

flail n fūstis m.

flair n iūdicium nt.

flake n squāma f; **~s** pl (snow) nix f.

flame n flamma f ♦ vi flagrāre, exārdēscere.

flaming adj flammeus.

flamingo n phoenīcopterus m.

flank n latus nt; cornū m; **on the ~** ab latere, ad latus ♦ vt latus tegere (gen).

flap n flābellum nt; (dress) lacinia f ♦ vt plaudere (abl).

flare n flamma f, fulgor m ♦ vi exārdēscere, flagrāre.

flash n fulgor m; (lightning) fulgur nt; (time) mōmentum nt ♦ vi fulgēre; (motion) micāre.

flashy adj speciōsus.

flask n ampulla f.

flat adj plānus; (ground) aequus; (on back) supīnus; (on face) prōnus; (music) gravis; (style) āridus, frīgidus; **fall ~** (fig) frīgēre ♦ n (land) plānitiēs f; (sea) vadum nt; (house) tabulātum nt.

flatly adv prōrsus.

flatness n plānitiēs f.

flatten vt aequāre, complānāre.

flatter vt adūlārī (dat), adsentārī (dat), blandīrī (dat).

flatterer n adsentātor m.

flattering adj blandus.

flatteringly adv blandē.

flattery n adūlātiō f, adsentātiō f, blanditiae fpl.

flatulence n īnflātiō f.

flatulent adj īnflātus.

flaunt vt iactāre ♦ vi iactāre, glōriārī.

flaunting n iactātiō f ♦ adj glōriōsus.

flauntingly adv glōriōsē.

flautist n tībīcen m.

flavour n gustātus m, sapor m ♦ vt imbuere, condīre.

flavouring n condītiō f.

flavourless adj īnsulsus.

flaw n vitium nt.

flawless adj ēmendātus.

flax n līnum nt.

flaxen adj flāvus.

flay vt dēglūbere.

flea n pūlex m.

fleck n macula f ♦ vt variāre.

fledged adj pennātus.

flee vi fugere, effugere; (for refuge) cōnfugere.

fleece n vellus nt ♦ vt tondēre; (*fig*) spoliāre.
fleecy adj lāneus.
fleet n classis f ♦ adj vēlōx, celer.
fleeting adj fugāx.
fleetness n vēlōcitās f, celeritās f.
flesh n cārō f; (*fig*) corpus nt; **in the ~** vīvus;
  one's own ~ and blood cōnsanguineus; **put
  on ~** pinguēscere.
fleshiness n corpus nt.
fleshliness n libīdō f.
fleshly adj libīdinōsus.
fleshy adj pinguis.
flexibility n lentitia f.
flexible adj flexibilis, lentus.
flicker vi coruscāre.
flickering adj tremulus.
flight n (*flying*) volātus m; (*fleeing*) fuga f;
  (*steps*) scāla f; **put to ~** fugāre, in fugam
  conicere; **take to ~** sē in fugam dare, terga
  vertere.
flightiness n mōbilitās f.
flighty adj mōbilis, incōnstāns.
flimsy adj tenuis, pertenuis.
flinch vi recēdere.
fling vt iacere, conicere; (*missile*) intorquēre; **~
  away** abicere, prōicere; **~ open** patefacere; **~
  in one's teeth** obicere (*dat*); **~ to the ground**
  prōsternere ♦ vi sē incitāre ♦ n iactus m.
flint n silex m.
flinty adj siliceus.
flippancy n lascīvia f.
flippant adj lascīvus, protervus.
flippantly adv petulanter.
flirt vi lūdere, lascīvīre ♦ n lascīvus m, lascīva
  f.
flit vi volitāre.
flitch n succīdia f.
float vi innāre, fluitāre; (*in air*) volitāre; **~
  down** dēfluere.
flock n grex m; (*wool*) floccus m ♦ vi
  concurrere, congregārī, cōnfluere; **~ in**
  adfluere.
flog vt verberāre, virgīs caedere.
flogging n verbera ntpl.
flood n (*deluge*) ēluviō f; (*river*) torrēns m; (*tide*)
  accessus m; (*fig*) flūmen nt ♦ vt inundāre.
floodgate n cataracta f.
floor n solum nt; (*paved*) pavīmentum nt;
  (*storey*) tabulātum nt; (*threshing*) ārea f ♦ vt
  contabulāre; **be ~ed** (*in argument*) iacēre.
flora n herbae fpl.
floral adj flōreus.
florid adj flōridus.
flotilla n classicula f.
flounce vi sē conicere ♦ n īnstita f.
flounder vi volutāre; (*in speech*) haesitāre.
flour n fārīna f.
flourish vi flōrēre, vigēre ♦ vt vibrāre,
  iactāre ♦ n (*RHET*) calamistrī mpl; (*music*)
  clangor m.
flout vt aspernārī, inlūdere (*dat*).
flow vi fluere, mānāre; (*tide*) accēdere; **~ back**
  recēdere; **~ between** interfluere; **~ down**

dēfluere; **~ into** īnfluere in (*acc*); **~ out**
  prōfluere, ēmānāre; **~ past** praeterfluere; **~
  through** permānāre; **~ together** cōnfluere; **~
  towards** adfluere ♦ n flūmen nt, cursus m;
  (*tide*) accessus m; (*words*) flūmen nt.
flower n flōs m, flōsculus m ♦ vi flōrēre,
  flōrēscere.
floweret n flōsculus m.
flowery adj flōridus.
flowing adj prōfluēns; **~ with** abundāns (*abl*).
flowingly adv prōfluenter.
flown adj īnflātus.
fluctuate vi aestuāre, fluctuāre.
fluctuating adj incōnstāns, incertus.
fluctuation n aestus m, dubitātiō f.
fluency n fācundia f, verbōrum cōpia f.
fluent adj disertus, prōfluēns.
fluently adv disertē, prōfluenter.
fluid adj liquidus ♦ n liquor m.
fluidity n liquor m.
fluke n (*anchor*) dēns m; (*luck*) fortuītum nt.
flurry n trepidātiō f ♦ vt sollicitāre, turbāre.
flush n rubor m; **in the first ~ of victory** victōriā
  ēlātus ♦ vi ērubēscere ♦ adj (*full*) abundāns;
  (*level*) aequus.
fluster n trepidātiō f ♦ vt turbāre, sollicitāre.
flute n tībia f; **play the ~** tībiā canere.
fluted adj striātus.
flutter n tremor m; (*fig*) trepidātiō f ♦ vi (*heart*)
  palpitāre; (*mind*) trepidāre; (*bird*) volitāre.
fluvial adj fluviātilis.
flux n fluxus m; **be in a state of ~** fluere.
fly n musca f ♦ vi volāre; (*flee*) fugere; **~ apart**
  dissilīre; **~ at** involāre in (*acc*); **~ away**
  āvolāre; **~ from** fugere; **~ in the face of**
  obviam īre (*dat*); **~ out** ēvolāre; **~ to** advolāre
  ad (*acc*); **~ up** ēvolāre, subvolāre; **let ~ at**
  immittere in (*acc*).
flying adj volucer, volātilis; (*time*) fugāx.
foal n equuleus m, equullus m ♦ vt parere.
foam n spūma f ♦ vi spūmāre; (*with rage*)
  saevīre.
foaming adj spūmeus.
focus vt (*mind*) intendere.
fodder n pābulum nt.
foe n hostis m; (*private*) inimīcus m.
fog n cālīgō f, nebula f.
foggy adj cālīginōsus, nebulōsus.
foible n vitium nt.
foil n (*metal*) lāmina f; (*sword*) rudis f ♦ vt
  ēlūdere, ad inritum redigere.
foist vt inculcāre, interpōnere.
fold n sinus m; (*sheep*) ovīle nt ♦ vt plicāre,
  complicāre; (*hands*) comprimere; (*sheep*)
  inclūdere; **~ back** replicāre; **~ over** plicāre; **~
  together** complicāre; **~ up in** involvere in
  (*abl*).
folding doors npl valvae fpl.
foliage n frondēs fpl.
folk n hominēs mpl ♦ adj patrius.
follow vt sequī; (*calling*) facere; (*candidate*)
  adsectārī; (*enemy*) īnsequī; (*example*)
  imitārī; (*instructions*) pārēre (*dat*);

(*predecessor*) succēdere (*dat*); (*road*)
pergere; (*speaker*) intellegere; ~ **closely**
īnsequī; ~ **hard on the heels of** īnsequī,
īnsistere (*dat*), īnstāre (*dat*); ~ **out** exsequī; ~
to the grave exsequī; ~ **up** subsequī,
īnsistere (*dat*) ♦ *vi* (*time*) īnsequī; (*inference*)
sequī; **as ~s** ita, in hunc modum.

follower *n* comes *m*; (*of candidate*) adsectātor
m; (*of model*) imitātor *m*; (*of teacher*) audītor
m.

following *adj* tālis; īnsequēns, proximus,
posterus; **on the ~ day** postrīdiē, postero diē,
proximo diē ♦ *n* adsectātōrēs *mpl*.

folly *n* stultitia *f*, dēmentia *f*, īnsipientia *f*.

foment *vt* fovēre; (*fig*) augēre.

fond *adj* amāns, studiōsus; ineptus; **be ~ of**
amāre.

fondle *vt* fovēre, mulcēre.

fondly *adv* amanter; ineptē.

food *n* cibus *m*; (*fig*) pābulum *nt*.

fool *n* stultus *m*, ineptus *m*; (*jester*) scurra *m*;
make a ~ of ludibriō habēre; **play the ~**
dēsipere ♦ *vt* dēcipere, lūdere; ~ **away**
disperdere ♦ *vi* dēsipere.

foolery *n* ineptiae *fpl*, nūgae *fpl*.

foolhardy *adj* temerārius.

foolish *adj* stultus, ineptus, īnsipiēns.

foolishly *adv* stultē, ineptē.

foolishness *n* stultitia *f*, īnsipientia *f*.

foot *n* pēs *m*; (*MIL*) peditātus *m*; **a ~ long** pedālis;
on ~ pedes; **set ~ on** īnsistere (*dat*); **set on ~**
īnstituere; **the ~ of** īmus ♦ *vt* (*bill*) solvere.

football *n* follis *m*.

footing *n* locus *m*, status *m*; **keep one's ~**
īnsistere; **on an equal ~** ex aequō.

footman *n* pedisequus *m*.

footpad *n* grassātor *m*.

footpath *n* sēmita *f*, trāmes *m*.

footprint *n* vestīgium *nt*.

foot soldier *n* pedes *m*.

footstep *n* vestīgium *nt*; **follow in the ~s of**
vestīgiīs ingredī (*gen*).

foppish *adj* dēlicātus.

for *prep* (*advantage*) *dat*; (*duration*) *acc*; (*after
noun*) *gen*; (*price*) *abl*; (*behalf*) prō (*abl*); (*cause*)
propter (*acc*), causā (*gen*); (*after neg*) prae
(*abl*); (*feelings*) erga (*acc*); (*lieu*) prō (*abl*);
(*purpose*) ad, in (*acc*); (*time fixed*) in (*acc*) ♦
conj namque; nam (*1st word*), enim (*2nd
word*); (*with pron*) quippe quī; ~ **a long time**
diū; ~ **some time** aliquamdiū.

forage *n* pābulum *nt* ♦ *vi* pābulārī, frūmentārī.

forager *n* pābulātor *m*, frūmentātor *m*.

foraging *n* pābulātiō *f*, frūmentātiō *f*.

forasmuch as *conj* quōniam.

foray *n* incursiō *f*.

forbear *vi* parcere (*dat*), supersedēre (*infin*).

forbearance *n* venia *f*, indulgentia *f*.

forbears *n* māiōrēs *mpl*.

forbid *vt* vetāre (+ *acc and infin*), interdīcere
(*dat and quominus and subj*); **Heaven ~!** dī
meliōra!

forbidding *adj* tristis.

force *n* vīs *f*; (*band of men*) manus *m*; **by ~ of
arms** vī et armis ♦ *vt* cōgere, impellere;
(*way*) rumpere, mōlīrī; (*growth*) festīnāre; ~
an engagement hostes proeliārī cogere; ~
down dētrūdere; ~ **out** extrūdere, expellere,
exturbāre; ~ **upon** inculcāre; ~ **a way in**
intrōrumpere, inrumpere.

forced *adj* (*march*) māgnus; (*style*) quaesītus; ~
march māgnum iter.

forceful *adj* validus.

forceps *n* forceps *m/f*.

forces *npl* (*MIL*) cōpiae *fpl*.

forcible *adj* validus; (*fig*) gravis.

forcibly *adv* vī, violenter; (*fig*) graviter.

ford *n* vadum *nt* ♦ *vt* vadō trānsīre.

fore *adj* prior; **to the ~** praestō ♦ *adv*: ~ **and aft**
in longitūdinem.

forearm *n* bracchium *nt* ♦ *vt*: **be ~ed**
praecavēre.

forebode *vt* ōminārī, portendere; prasentīre.

foreboding *n* praesēnsiō *f*; ōmen *nt*.

forecast *n* praedictiō *f* ♦ *vt* praedīcere,
prōvidēre.

forecourt *n* vestibulum *nt*.

forefathers *n* māiōrēs *mpl*.

forefinger *n* index *m*.

foreground *n* ēminentia *ntpl*.

forehead *n* frōns *f*.

foreign *adj* peregrīnus, externus; (*goods*)
adventīcius; ~ **to** aliēnus ab; ~ **ways**
peregrīnitās *f*.

foreigner *n* peregrīnus *m*, advena *m*.

foreknow *vt* praenōscere.

foreknowledge *n* prōvidentia *f*.

foreland *n* prōmunturium *nt*.

foremost *adj* prīmus, prīnceps.

forenoon *n* antemerīdiānum tempus *nt*.

forensic *adj* forēnsis.

forerunner *n* praenūntius *m*.

foresee *vt* praevidēre.

foreshadow *vt* praemonēre.

foresight *n* prōvidentia *f*.

forest *n* silva *f*.

forestall *vt* occupāre, antevenīre.

forester *n* silvicola *m*.

foretaste *vt* praegustāre.

foretell *vt* praedīcere, vāticinārī.

forethought *n* prōvidentia *f*.

forewarn *vt* praemonēre.

foreword *n* praefātiō *f*.

forfeit *n* multa *f*, damnum *nt* ♦ *vt* āmittere,
perdere, multārī (*abl*); (*bail*) dēserere.

forfeiture *n* damnum *nt*.

forgather *vi* congregārī, convenīre.

forge *n* fornāx *f* ♦ *vt* fabricārī, excūdere;
(*document*) subicere; (*will*) suppōnere;
(*signature*) imitārī; (*money*) adulterīnōs
nummōs percutere.

forged *adj* falsus, adulterīnus, commentīcius.

forger *n* (*of will*) subiector *m*.

forgery *n* falsum *nt*, commentum *nt*.

forget *vt* oblīvīscī (*gen*); (*thing learnt*)
dēdiscere; **be forgotten** memoriā cadere, ex

animō effluere.
forgetful *adj* immemor; (*by habit*) oblīviōsus.
forgetfulness *n* oblīviō *f*.
forgive *vt* ignōscere (*dat*), veniam dare (*dat*).
forgiveness *n* venia *f*.
forgo *vt* dīmittere, renūntiāre; (*rights*) dēcēdere dē iūre.
fork *n* furca *f*; (*small*) furcula *f*; (*road*) trivium *nt*.
forlorn *adj* inops, dēstitūtus, exspēs.
form *n* fōrma *f*, figūra *f*; (*of procedure*) fōrmula *f*; (*condition*) vigor *m*; (*etiquette*) mōs *m*; (*seat*) scamnum *nt*; (*school*) schola *f*; (*hare's*) latibulum *nt* ♦ *vt* fōrmāre, fingere, efficere; (*MIL*) īnstruere; (*plan*) inīre, capere.
formal *adj* iūstus; (*rite*) sollemnis.
formality *n* iūsta *ntpl*, rītus *m*; **as a ~** dicis causā; **with due ~** rītē.
formally *adv* rītē.
formation *n* fōrma *f*, figūra *f*; (*process*) cōnfōrmātiō *f*; **in ~** (*MIL*) īnstructus.
former *adj* prior, prīstinus, vetus; **the ~** ille.
formerly *adv* anteā, ōlim, quondam.
formidable *adj* formīdolōsus.
formidably *adv* formīdolōsē.
formula *n* fōrmula *f*; (*dictated*) praefātiō *f*.
formulate *vt* compōnere.
forsake *vt* dērelinquere, dēstituere, dēserere.
forswear *vt* pēierāre, abiūrāre.
fort *n* castellum *nt*.
forth *adv* forās; (*time*) posthāc.
forthwith *adv* extemplō, statim, prōtinus.
fortieth *adj* quadragēsimus.
fortification *n* (*process*) mūnītiō *f*; (*place*) mūnīmentum *nt*, arx *f*.
fortify *vt* mūnīre, ēmūnīre, commūnīre; (*fig*) cōnfirmāre.
fortitude *n* fortitūdō *f*.
fortnight *n* quīndecim diēs *mpl*.
fortnightly *adv* quīntō decimō quōque diē.
fortress *n* arx *f*, castellum *nt*.
fortuitous *adj* fortuītus.
fortuitously *adv* fortuītō, cāsū.
fortunate *adj* fēlīx, fortūnātus.
fortunately *adv* fēlīciter, bene.
fortune *n* fortūna *f*, fors *f*; (*wealth*) rēs *f*, dīvitiae *fpl*; **good ~** fēlīcitās *f*, secundae rēs *fpl*; **bad ~** adversae rēs *fpl*; **make one's ~** rem facere, rem quaerere; **tell ~s** hariolārī.
fortune-hunter *n* captātor *m*.
fortune-teller *n* hariolus *m*, sāga *f*.
forty *num* quadrāgintā; **~ each** quadrāgēnī; **~ times** quadrāgiēns.
forum *n* forum *nt*.
forward *adj* (*person*) protervus, audāx; (*fruit*) praecox ♦ *adv* porrō, ante; **bring ~** prōferre; **come ~** prōdīre ♦ *vt* (*letter*) perferre; (*cause*) adiuvāre, favēre (*dat*).
forwardness *n* audācia *f*, alacritās *f*.
forwards *adv* porrō, prōrsus; **backwards and ~** rursum prōrsum, hūc illūc.
fosse *n* fossa *f*.
foster *vt* alere, nūtrīre; (*fig*) fovēre.

foster child *n* alumnus *m*, alumna *f*.
foster father *n* altor *m*, ēducātor *m*.
foster mother *n* altrīx *f*, nūtrīx *f*.
foul *adj* foedus; (*speech*) inquinātus; **fall ~ of** inruere in (*acc*).
foully *adv* foedē, inquinātē.
foul-mouthed *adj* maledicus.
foulness *n* foedītās *f*.
found *vt* condere, fundāre, īnstituere; (*metal*) fundere.
foundation *n* fundāmenta *ntpl*.
founder *n* fundātor *m*, conditor *m* ♦ *vi* submergī, naufragium facere.
foundling *n* expositīcia *f*.
fount *n* fōns *m*.
fountain *n* fōns *m*.
fountainhead *n* fōns *m*, orīgō *f*.
four *num* quattuor (*indecl*); **~ each** quaternī; **~ times** quater; **~ days** quadriduum *nt*; **~ years** quadriennium *nt*.
fourfold *adj* quadruplex ♦ *adv* quadrifāriam.
four hundred *num* quadringentī; **~ each** quadringēnī; **~ times** quadringentiēns.
four hundredth *adj* quadringentēsimus.
fourteen *num* quattuordecim; **~ each** quaternī dēnī; **~ times** quater deciēns.
fourteenth *adj* quartus decimus.
fourth *adj* quartus ♦ *n* quadrāns *m*; **three ~s** dōdrāns *m*, trēs partēs *fpl*.
fowl *n* avis *f*; gallīna *f*.
fowler *n* auceps *m*.
fox *n* vulpes *f*; **~'s** vulpīnus.
foxy *adj* astūtus, vafer.
fracas *n* rīxa *f*.
fraction *n* pars *f*.
fractious *adj* difficilis.
fracture *n* frāctum os *nt* ♦ *vt* frangere.
fragile *adj* fragilis.
fragility *n* fragilitās *f*.
fragment *n* fragmentum *nt*.
fragrance *n* odor *m*.
fragrant *adj* suāvis.
fragrantly *adv* suāviter.
frail *adj* fragilis, īnfirmus, dēbilis.
frailty *n* dēbilitās *f*; (*moral*) error *m*.
frame *vt* fabricārī, fingere, effingere; (*document*) compōnere ♦ *n* fōrma *f*; (*of mind*) affectiō *f*, habitus *m*; **in a ~ of mind** animātus.
framer *n* fabricātor *m*, opifex *m*; (*of law*) lātor *m*.
framework *n* compāgēs *f*.
franchise *n* suffrāgium *nt*, cīvitās *f*.
frank *adj* ingenuus, apertus; (*speech*) līber.
frankincense *n* tūs *nt*.
frankly *adv* ingenuē, apertē; līberē.
frankness *n* ingenuitās *f*; (*speech*) lībertās *f*.
frantic *adj* furēns, furiōsus, dēlīrus.
frantically *adv* furenter.
fraternal *adj* frāternus.
fraternally *adv* frāternē.
fraternity *n* frāternitās *f*; (*society*) sodālitās *f*; (*guild*) collēgium *nt*.
fraternize *vi* amīcitiam iungere.
fratricide *n* frātricīda *m*; (*act*) frātris

parricīdium nt.

fraud n fraus f, dolus m, falsum nt; (*criminal*) dolus malus m.

fraudulence n fraus f.

fraudulent adj fraudulentus, dolōsus.

fraudulently adv dolōsē, dolō malō.

fraught adj plēnus.

fray n pugna f, rīxa f ♦ vt terere.

freak n mōnstrum nt; (*caprice*) libīdō f.

freckle n lentīgō f.

freckly adj lentīginōsus.

free adj līber; (*disengaged*) vacuus; (*generous*) līberālis; (*from cost*) grātuītus; (*from duty*) immūnis; (*from encumbrance*) expedītus; **be ~ from** vacāre (*abl*); **I am still ~ to** integrum est mihī (*infin*); **set ~** absolvere, līberāre; (*slave*) manū mittere ♦ adv grātīs, grātuītō ♦ vt līberāre, expedīre, exsolvere.

freebooter n praedō m.

freeborn adj ingenuus.

freedman n lībertus m.

freedom n lībertās f; (*from duty*) immūnitās f.

freehold n praedium līberum nt ♦ adj immūnis.

freely adv līberē; (*lavishly*) cōpiōsē, largē; (*frankly*) apertē; (*voluntarily*) ultrō, suā sponte.

freeman n cīvis m.

free will n voluntās f; **of one's own ~** suā sponte.

freeze vt gelāre, glaciāre ♦ vi concrēscere.

freezing adj gelidus; **it is ~** gelat.

freight n vectūra f; (*cargo*) onus nt ♦ vt onerāre.

freighter n nāvis onerāria f.

frenzied adj furēns, furiōsus, fānāticus.

frenzy n furor m, īnsania f.

frequency n adsiduitās f.

frequent adj frequēns, crēber ♦ vt frequentāre, commeāre in (*acc*).

frequently adv saepe, saepenumerō, frequenter.

fresh adj (*new*) recēns, novus; (*vigorous*) integer; (*water*) dulcis; (*wind*) ācer.

freshen vt renovāre ♦ vi (*wind*) incrēbrēscere.

freshly adv recenter.

freshman n tīrō m.

freshness n novitās f, viriditās f.

fret vi maerēre, angī ♦ vt sollicitāre.

fretful adj mōrōsus, querulus.

fretfulness n mōrōsitās f.

fretted adj laqueātus.

friable adj puter.

friction n trītus m.

friend n amīcus m, familiāris m/f, hospes m, sodālis m; **make ~s with** sē cōnferre ad amīcitiam (*gen*).

friendless adj sine amīcīs.

friendliness n cōmitās f, officium nt.

friendly adj cōmis, facilis, benīgnus; **on ~ terms** familiāriter.

friendship n amīcitia f, familiāritās f.

frigate n liburna f.

fright n horror m, pavor m, terror m; **take ~** extimēscere, expavēscere.

frighten vt terrēre, exterrēre, perterrēre; **~ away** absterrēre; **~ off** dēterrēre; **~ the life out of** exanimāre.

frightful adj horribilis, immānis; (*look*) taeter.

frightfully adv foedē.

frigid adj frīgidus.

frigidity n frīgus nt.

frill n fimbriae fpl; (*RHET*) calamistrī mpl.

fringe n fimbriae fpl.

frisk vi lascīvīre, exsultāre.

frisky adj lascīvus.

fritter vt: **~ away** dissipāre; (*time*) extrahere.

frivolity n levitās f.

frivolous adj levis, inānis.

frivolously adv ināniter.

fro adv: **to and ~** hūc illūc.

frock n stola f.

frog n rāna f.

frolic n lūdus m ♦ vi lūdere, lascīvīre.

frolicsome adj lascīvus, hilaris.

from prep ab (*abl*), ā (*before consonants*); (*out*) ē, ex (*abl*); (*cause*) propter (*acc*); (*prevention*) quōminus, quīn; **~ all directions** undique.

front n frōns f; **in ~** ā fronte, adversus; **in ~ of** prō (+ *abl*).

frontier n līmes m, cōnfīnia ntpl; **~s** fīnēs mpl.

front line n prima aciēs.

frost n gelū nt.

frostbitten adj: **be ~** vī frīgoris ambūrī.

frosty adj gelidus, glaciālis.

froth n spūma f ♦ vi spūmās agere.

frothy adj spūmeus.

froward adj contumāx.

frown n frontis contractiō f ♦ vi frontem contrahere.

frozen adj glaciālis.

fructify vt fēcundāre.

frugal adj parcus, frūgī.

frugality n frūgālitās f, parsimōnia f.

frugally adv parcē, frūgāliter.

fruit n frūctus m; (*tree*) māla ntpl; (*berry*) bāca f; (*fig*) frūctus m; **~s** pl (*of earth*) frūgēs fpl.

fruiterer n pōmārius m.

fruitful adj fēcundus, frūctuōsus.

fruitfully adv ferāciter.

fruitfulness n fēcunditās f, ūbertās f.

fruition n frūctus m.

fruitless adj inūtilis, vānus.

fruitlessly adv nēquīquam, frustrā.

fruit tree n pōmum nt.

frustrate vt frustrārī, ad inritum redigere.

frustration n frustrātiō f.

fry vt frīgere.

frying pan n sartāgō f; **out of the ~ into the fire** incidit in Scyllam quī vult vītāre Charybdim.

fuel n fōmes m.

fugitive adj fugitīvus ♦ n fugitīvus m, trānsfuga m; (*from abroad*) extorris m.

fulfil vt (*duty*) explēre, implēre; (*promise*)

praestāre; (*order*) exsequī, perficere.
fulfilment *n* absolūtiō *f*.
full *adj* plēnus (+ *abl*), refertus, explētus;
(*entire*) integer; (*amount*) solidus; (*brother*)
germānus; (*measure*) iūstus; (*meeting*)
frequēns; (*style*) cōpiōsus; **at ~ length**
porrēctus; **at ~ speed** citātō gradū, citātō
equō.
fuller *n* fullō *m*.
full-grown *adj* adultus.
full moon *n* lūna plēna.
fullness *n* (*style*) cōpia *f*; (*time*) mātūritās *f*.
fully *adv* plēnē, penitus, funditus.
fulminate *vi* intonāre.
fulsome *adj* fastīdiōsus, pūtidus.
fumble *vi* haesitāre.
fume *n* fūmus *m*, hālitus *m* ♦ *vi* stomachārī.
fumigate *vt* suffīre.
fun *n* iocus *m*, lūdus *m*; **for ~** animī causā; **make
~ of** inlūdere, dēlūdere, lūdibriō habēre.
function *n* officium *nt*, mūnus *nt*.
fund *n* cōpia *f*.
fundamental *adj* prīmus ♦ *n* prīncipium *nt*,
elementum *nt*.
funds *npl* sors *f*, pecūniae *fpl*.
funeral *n* fūnus *nt*, exsequiae *fpl* ♦ *adj* fūnebris.
funeral pile *n* rogus *m*.
funeral pyre *n* rogus *m*.
funeral rites *npl* exsequiae *fpl*, īnferiae *fpl*.
funereal *adj* fūnebria, lūgubris.
funnel *n* īnfundibulum *nt*.
funny *adj* ioculāris, rīdiculus.
fur *n* pellis *m*.
furbelow *n* īnstita *f*.
furbish *vt* expolīre; **~ up** interpolāre.
Furies *npl* Furiae *fpl*.
furious *adj* saevus, vehemēns, perīrātus.
furiously *adv* furenter, saevē, vehementer.
furl *vt* (*sail*) legere.
furlong *n* stadium *nt*.
furlough *n* commeātus *m*.
furnace *n* fornāx *f*.
furnish *vt* praebēre, suppeditāre; (*equip*)
īnstruere, ōrnāre.
furniture *n* supellex *f*.
furrow *n* sulcus *m* ♦ *vt* sulcāre.
furry *adj* villōsus.
further *adj* ulterior ♦ *adv* ultrā, porrō; amplius
♦ *vt* adiuvāre, cōnsulere (*dat*).
furtherance *n* prōgressus *m*; (*means*)
īnstrūmentum *nt*.
furthermore *adv* praetereā, porrō.
furthest *adj* ultimus ♦ *adv* longissimē.
furtive *adj* fūrtīvus, clandestīnus.
furtively *adv* clam, fūrtim.
fury *n* furor *m*, saevitia *f*; īra *f*.
fuse *vt* fundere; (*together*) coniungere.
fusion *n* coniūnctiō *f*.
fuss *n* importūnitās *f*, querimōnia *f* ♦ *vi*
conquerī, sollicitārī.
fussy *adj* importūnus, incommodus.
fusty *adj* mūcidus.
futile *adj* inānis, inūtilis, futtilis.

futility *n* vānitās *f*, futtilitās *f*.
future *adj* futūrus, posterus ♦ *n* posterum *nt*,
reliquum *nt*; **in ~** posthāc; **for the ~** in
posterum.
futurity *n* posterum tempus *nt*, posteritās *f*.

G, g

gabble *vi* garrīre.
gable *n* fastīgium *nt*.
gadfly *n* tabānus *m*.
gag *vt* ōs praeligāre (*dat*), ōs obvolvere (*dat*).
gage *n* pignus *nt*.
gaiety *n* laetitia *f*, hilaritās *f*, festīvitās *f*.
gaily *adv* hilare, festīve.
gain *n* lucrum *nt*, quaestus *m* ♦ *vt* comparāre;
adipīscī; (*profit*) lucrārī; (*thing*) parāre,
cōnsequī, capere; (*case*) vincere; (*place*)
pervenīre ad; (*possession of*) potīrī (*gen*);
(*victory*) reportāre; **~ over** conciliāre; **~
ground** incrēbrēscere; **~ possession of**
potior (+ *abl*); **~ the upper hand** rem obtinēre.
gainful *adj* quaestuōsus.
gainsay *vt* contrādīcere (*dat*).
gait *n* incessus *m*, ingressiō *f*.
gaiters *n* ocreae *fpl*.
gala *n* diēs festus *m*.
galaxy *n* circulus lacteus *m*.
gale *n* ventus *m*.
gall *n* fel *nt*, bīlis *m* ♦ *vt* ūrere.
gallant *adj* fortis, audāx; (*courteous*)
officiōsus.
gallantly *adv* fortiter; officiōsē.
gallantry *n* virtūs *f*; urbānitās *f*.
gall bladder *n* fel *nt*.
gallery *n* porticus *f*.
galley *n* nāvis āctuāria *f*; (*cook's*) culīna *f*.
galling *adj* amārus, mordāx.
gallon *n* congius *m*.
gallop *n* cursus *m*; **at the ~** citātō equō,
admissō equō ♦ *vi* admissō equō currere.
gallows *n* īnfēlīx arbor *m*, furca *f*.
gallows bird *n* furcifer *m*.
galore *adv* adfatim.
gamble *n* ālea *f* ♦ *vi* āleā lūdere.
gambler *n* āleātor *m*.
gambling *n* ālea *f*.
gambol *n* lūsus *m* ♦ *vi* lūdere, lascīvīre,
exsultāre.
game *n* lūdus *m*; (*with dice*) ālea *f*; (*hunt*)
praeda *f*; **play the ~** rēctē facere; **public ~s**
lūdī *mpl*; **Olympic ~s** Olympia *npl*; **the ~'s up**
āctum est ♦ *adj* animōsus.
gamester *n* āleātor *m*.
gammon *n* perna *f*.
gander *n* ānser *m*.

gang n grex m, caterva f.
gangster n grassātor m.
gangway n forus m.
gaol n carcer m.
gaoler n custōs m.
gap n hiātus m, lacūna f.
gape vi hiāre, inhiāre; (opening) dēhiscere.
garb n habitus m, amictus m ♦ vt amicīre.
garbage n quisquiliae fpl.
garden n hortus m; (public) hortī mpl.
gardener n hortulānus m; (ornamental)
   topiārius m.
gardening n hortī cultūra f; (ornamental)
   topiāria f.
gargle vi gargarissāre.
garish adj speciōsus, fūcātus.
garland n sertum nt, corōna f ♦ vt corōnāre.
garlic n ālium nt.
garment n vestis f, vestīmentum nt.
garnish vt ōrnāre, decorāre.
garret n cēnāculum nt.
garrison n praesidium nt, dēfēnsōrēs mpl ♦ vt
   praesidiō mūnīre, praesidium collocāre in
   (abl).
garrotte vt laqueō gulam frangere (dat).
garrulity n garrulitās f.
garrulous adj garrulus, loquāx.
gas n vapor m.
gash n vulnus nt ♦ vt caedere, lacerāre.
gasp n anhēlitus m, singultus m ♦ vi anhēlāre.
gastronomy n gula f.
gate n porta f.
gather vt colligere, cōgere; (fruit) legere;
   (inference) colligere, conicere ♦ vi
   congregārī.
gathering n conventus m, coetus m.
gauche adj inconcinnus, illepidus.
gaudily adv splendidē, speciōsē.
gaudy adj speciōsus, fūcātus, lautus.
gauge n modulus m ♦ vt mētīrī.
Gaul n Gallia f; (person) Gallus m.
gaunt adj macer.
gauntlet n manica f.
gauze n Coa ntpl.
gay adj hilaris, festīvus, laetus.
gaze vi intuērī; ~ at intuērī, adspectāre,
   contemplārī.
gazelle n oryx m.
gazette n ācta diūrna ntpl, ācta pūblica ntpl.
gear n īnstrūmenta ntpl; (ship's) armāmenta
   ntpl.
gelding n cantērius m.
gelid adj gelidus.
gem n gemma f.
gender n genus nt.
genealogical adj dē stirpe.
genealogical table n stemma nt.
genealogist n geneālogus m.
genealogy n geneālogia f.
general adj generālis, ūniversus; (usual)
   vulgāris, commūnis; **in ~** omnīnō ♦ n dux m,
   imperātor m; **~'s tent** praetorium nt.
generalissimo n imperātor m.

generality n vulgus nt, plērīque mpl.
generalize vi ūnīversē loquī.
generally adv ferē, plērumque; (discuss)
   īnfīnītē.
generalship n ductus m.
generate vt gignere, generāre.
generation n aetās f, saeculum nt.
generic adj generālis.
generically adv genere.
generosity n līberālitās f, largitās f.
generous adj līberālis, largus, benīgnus.
generously adv līberāliter, largē, benīgnē.
genesis n orīgō f, prīncipium nt.
genial adj cōmis, hilaris.
geniality n cōmitās f, hilaritās f.
genially adv cōmiter, hilare.
genitive n genitīvus m.
genius n (deity) genius m; (talent) ingenium nt,
   indolēs f; **of ~** ingeniōsus.
genre n genus nt.
genteel adj urbānus, polītus.
gentility n urbānitās f, ēlegantia f.
gentle adj (birth) ingenuus; (manner) hūmānus,
   indulgēns, mītis; (slope) lēnis, mollis; (thing)
   placidus, lēnis.
gentleman n vir m, ingenuus m, vir honestus
   m.
gentlemanly adj ingenuus, līberālis,
   honestus.
gentleness n hūmānitās f, indulgentia f,
   lēnitās f.
gentlewoman n ingenua f, mulier honesta f.
gently adv lēniter, molliter, placidē.
gentry n ingenuī mpl, optimātēs mpl;
   (contempt) hominēs mpl.
genuine adj vērus, germānus, sincērus.
genuinely adv germānē, sincērē.
genuineness n fidēs f.
geographical adj geōgraphicus; **~ position**
   situs m.
geography n geōgraphia f.
geometrical adj geōmetricus.
geometry n geōmetria f.
Georgics n Geōrgica ntpl.
germ n germen nt, sēmen nt.
germane adj adfīnis.
germinate vi gemmāre.
gesticulate vi sē iactāre, gestū ūtī.
gesticulation n gestus m.
gesture n gestus m, mōtus m.
get vt adipīscī, nancīscī, parāre; (malady)
   contrahere; (request) impetrāre; (return)
   capere; (reward) ferre; **~ sth done** cūrāre
   (with gerundive); **~ sb to do** persuādēre (dat),
   addūcere; **~ by heart** ēdiscere; **~ in** repōnere;
   ~ the better of superāre; **go and ~** arcessere
   ♦ vi fierī; **~ about** (rumour) palam fierī,
   percrēbrēscere; **~ away** effugere; **~ at**
   (intent) spectāre; **~ behind** cessāre; **~ off**
   absolvī; **~ on** prōficere; **~ out** effugere,
   ēvādere; **~ out of hand** lascīvīre; **~ out of the
   way** dē viā dēcēdere; **~ ready** parāre; **~ rid of**
   abicere, tollere; **~ to** pervenīre ad;

~ **to know** cognōscere; ~ **together** congregārī; ~ **up** exsurgere.
get-up *n* ōrnātus *m*.
ghastliness *n* pallor *m*.
ghastly *adj* pallidus; (*sight*) taeter.
ghost *n* larva *f*, īdōlon *nt*; ~**s** *pl* mānēs *mpl*; **give up the** ~ animam agere, efflāre.
giant *n* Gigas *m*.
gibberish *n* barbaricus sermō *m*.
gibbet *n* furca *f*.
gibe *vi* inrīdēre.
giddiness *n* vertīgō *f*.
giddy *adj* vertīginōsus; (*fig*) levis.
gift *n* dōnum *nt*; (*small*) mūnusculum *nt*; ~**s** *pl* (*mind*) ingenium *nt*.
gifted *adj* ingeniōsus.
gig *n* cisium *nt*.
gigantic *adj* ingēns, immānis.
gild *vt* inaurāre.
gill *n* (*measure*) quartārius *m*; (*fish*) branchia *f*.
gilt *adj* aurātus.
gimlet *n* terebra *f*.
gin *n* pedica *f*, laqueus *m*.
ginger *n* zingiberī *nt*.
gingerly *adv* pedetemptim.
giraffe *n* camēlopardālis *f*.
gird *vt* circumdāre; ~ **on** accingere; ~ **oneself** cingī; ~ **up** succingere.
girder *n* tignum *nt*.
girdle *n* cingulus *m* ♦ *vt* cingere.
girl *n* puella *f*, virgō *f*.
girlhood *n* aetās puellāris *f*.
girlish *adj* puellāris.
girth *n* ambitus *m*, amplitūdō *f*.
gist *n* firmāmentum *nt*.
give *vt* dare, dōnāre, tribuere; (*thing due*) reddere; ~ **away** largīrī; (*bride*) in matrimōnium collocāre; (*secret*) prōdere; ~ **back** reddere, restituere; ~ **birth (to)** pārēre; ~ **in** (*name*) profitērī; ~ **off** ēmittere; ~ **out** (*orders*) ēdere; (*sound*) ēmittere; ~ **thanks** gratias agere; ~ **up** dēdere, trādere; (*hope of*) dēspērāre; (*rights*) dēcēdere dē, renūntiāre; ~ **way** cēdere; (*MIL*) inclīnāre ♦ *vi* labāre; ~ **in** sē victum fatērī; (*MIL*) manūs dare; ~ **out** (*fail*) dēficere; (*pretend*) ferre; ~ **up** dēsistere; ~ **way** cēdere.
giver *n* dator *m*.
glacial *adj* glaciālis.
glad *adj* laetus, alacer, hilaris; **be** ~ gaudēre.
gladden *vt* exhilarāre, oblectāre.
glade *n* saltus *m*.
gladiator *n* gladiātor *m*.
gladiatorial *adj* gladiātōrius; **present a** ~ **show** gladiātōrēs dare.
gladly *adv* laetē, libenter.
gladness *n* laetitia *f*, alacritās *f*, gaudium *nt*.
glamorous *adj* venustus.
glamour *n* venustās *f*.
glance *n* aspectus *m* ♦ *vi* oculōs conicere; ~ **at** aspicere; (*fig*) attingere, perstringere; ~ **off** stringere.

glare *n* fulgor *m* ♦ *vi* fulgēre; ~ **at** torvīs oculīs intuērī.
glaring *adj* (*look*) torvus; (*fault*) manifestus; **be** ~ ante pedēs positum esse.
glass *n* vitrum *nt*; (*mirror*) speculum *nt*.
glassy *adj* vitreus.
glaze *vt* vitrō obdūcere.
gleam *n* fulgor *m*, lūx *f* ♦ *vi* fulgēre, lūcēre.
gleaming *adj* splendidus, nitidus.
glean *vi* spīcās legere.
gleaning *n* spīcilegium *nt*.
glebe *n* fundus *m*.
glee *n* hilaritās *f*, gaudium *nt*.
gleeful *adj* hilaris, festīvus, laetus.
gleefully *adv* hilare, laetē.
glen *n* vallis *f*.
glib *adj* prōfluēns, fācundus.
glibly *adv* prōfluenter.
glide *n* lāpsus *m* ♦ *vi* lābī; ~ **away** ēlābī.
glimmer *vi* sublūcēre ♦ *n*: **a** ~ **of hope** spēcula *f*.
glimpse *n* aspectus *m* ♦ *vt* cōnspicārī.
glint *vi* renīdēre.
glisten *vi* fulgēre, nitēre.
glitter *vi* micāre.
gloaming *n* crepusculum *nt*.
gloat *vi*: ~ **over** inhiāre, animō haurīre, oculōs pāscere (*abl*).
globe *n* globus *m*, sphaera *f*; (*inhabited*) orbis terrārum *m*.
globular *adj* globōsus.
globule *n* globulus *m*, pilula *f*.
gloom *n* tenebrae *fpl*; tristitia *f*.
gloomy *adj* tenebricōsus; tristis, dēmissus.
glorify *vt* illūstrāre, extollere, laudāre.
glorious *adj* illūstris, praeclārus, splendidus.
gloriously *adv* praeclārē, splendidē.
glory *n* laus *f*, glōria *f*, decus *nt* ♦ *vi* glōriārī, sē iactāre.
gloss *n* nitor *m* ♦ *vt*: ~ **over** (*fig*) dissimulāre.
glossy *adj* nitidus.
glove *n* manica *f*.
glow *n* (*light*) lūmen *nt*; (*heat*) ārdor *m*; (*passion*) calor *m* ♦ *vi* lūcēre, ārdēre, calēre, candēre.
glowing *adj* candēns, ārdēns, calidus.
glue *n* glūten *nt* ♦ *vt* glūtināre.
glum *adj* tristis, maestus.
glut *vt* explēre, saturāre ♦ *n* satietās *f*, abundantia *f*.
glutton *n* gāneō *m*, helluō *m*.
gluttonous *adj* edāx, vorāx, avidus.
gluttony *n* gula *f*, edācitās *f*.
gnarled *adj* nōdōsus.
gnash *vt*, *vi* frendere; ~ **one's teeth** dentibus frendere.
gnat *n* culex *m*.
gnaw *vt* rōdere; ~ **away** ērōdere.
gnawing *adj* mordāx.
go *vi* īre, vādere; (*depart*) abīre, discēdere; (*event*) ēvādere; (*mechanism*) movērī; ~ **about** incipere, adgredī; ~ **after** īnsequī; ~ **away** abīre, discēdere; ~ **back** redīre,

regredī; ~ **before** anteīre, praeīre; ~ **by**
praeterīre; (*rule*) sequī, ūtī (*abl*); ~ **down**
dēscendere; (*storm*) cadere; (*star*) occidere;
~ **for** petere; ~ **forward** prōgredī; ~ **in** intrāre,
ingredī; ~ **in for** (*profession*) facere,
exercēre; ~ **off** abīre; ~ **on** pergere; (*event*)
agī; ~ **out** exīre, ēgredī; (*fire*) extinguī; ~ **over**
trānsīre; (*to enemy*) dēscīscere; (*preparation*)
meditarī; (*reading*) legere; (*work done*)
retractāre; ~ **round** circumīre, ambīre; ~
through percurrere; penetrāre; (*suffer*)
perferre; ~ **to** adīre, petere; ~ **up** ascendere;
~ **to the help of** subvenīre (+ *dat*); ~ **to meet**
obviam īre; ~ **with** comitārī; ~ **without**
carēre (*abl*), sē abstinēre (*abl*) ♦ *n* vīs *f*,
ācrimōnia *f*.
goad *n* stimulus *m* ♦ *vt* irrītāre; pungere; (*fig*)
stimulāre.
go-ahead *adj* impiger.
goal *n* fīnis *m*, mēta *f*.
goat *n* caper *m*, capra *f*.
gobble *vt* dēvorāre.
go-between *n* internūntius *m*, internūntia *f*;
(*bribery*) sequester *m*.
goblet *n* pōculum *nt*, scyphus *m*.
god *n* deus *m*.
goddess *n* dea *f*.
godhead *n* dīvīnitās *f*, nūmen *nt*.
godless *adj* impius.
godlike *adj* dīvīnus.
godliness *n* pietās *f*, rēligiō *f*.
godly *adj* pius.
godsend *n* quasi caelō dēmissus.
going *n* itiō *f*; (*way*) iter *nt*; (*departure*)
profectiō *f*, discessus *m*.
goitre *n* strūma *nt*.
gold *n* aurum *nt* ♦ *adj* aureus.
golden *adj* aureus; (*hair*) flāvus.
gold leaf *n* bractea *f*.
goldmine *n* aurāria *f*.
goldsmith *n* aurārius *m*, aurifex *m*.
good *adj* bonus, probus; (*fit*) idōneus, aptus;
(*considerable*) magnus; ~ **day!** salvē, salvēte!;
~ **looks** fōrma *f*, pulchritūdō *f*; ~ **nature**
facilitās *f*, cōmitās *f* ♦ *n* bonum *nt*,
commodum *nt*; **do** ~ **to** prōdesse (*dat*); **make** ~
supplēre, praestāre; **seem** ~ vidērī; ♦ *interj*
bene.
goodbye *interj* valē, valēte; **say** ~ **to** valēre
iubēre.
good-for-nothing *adj* nēquam.
good-humoured *adj* cōmis.
good-looking *adj* pulcher.
goodly *adj* pulcher; (*size*) amplus.
good nature *n* facilitās *f*, cōmitās *f*.
good-natured *adj* facilis, benīgnus,
benevolus.
goodness *n* bonitās *f*; (*character*) virtūs *f*,
probitās *f*, pietās *f*.
goods *npl* bona *ntpl*, rēs *f*; (*for sale*) merx *f*.
good-tempered *adj* mītis, lēnis.
goodwill *n* benevolentia *f*, favor *m*, grātia *f*.
goose *n* ānser *m/f*.

goose flesh *n* horror *m*.
gore *n* cruor *m* ♦ *vt* cornibus cōnfodere.
gorge *n* faucēs *fpl*, gula *f*; (*GEOG*) angustiae *fpl* ♦
vt: ~ **oneself** sē ingurgitāre.
gorgeous *adj* lautus, splendidus.
gorgeously *adv* lautē, splendidē.
gorgeousness *n* lautitia *f*.
gormandize *vi* helluārī.
gory *adj* cruentus.
gospel *n* ēvangelium *nt*.
gossip *n* (*talk*) sermunculus *m*, rūmusculus *m*,
fāma *f*; (*person*) lingulāca *f* ♦ *vi* garrīre.
gouge *vt* ēruere.
gourd *n* cucurbita *f*.
gourmand *n* helluō *m*, gāneō *m*.
gout *n* podagra *f*, articulāris morbus *m*.
gouty *adj* arthrīticus.
govern *vt* (*subjects*) regere; (*state*)
administrāre, gubernāre; (*emotion*)
moderārī (*dat*), cohibēre.
governess *n* ēducātrīx *f*.
government *n* gubernātiō *f*, administrātiō *f*;
(*men*) magistrātūs *mpl*.
governor *n* gubernātor *m*, moderātor *m*;
(*province*) prōcōnsul *m*, prōcūrātor *m*.
gown *n* (*men*) toga *f*; (*women*) stola *f*.
grab *vt* adripere, corripere.
grace *n* grātia *f*, lepōs *m*, decor *m*; (*favour*)
grātia *f*, venia *f*; (*of gods*) pāx *f*; **be in the good**
~**s of** in grātiā esse apud (*acc*); **with a bad** ~
invītus ♦ *vt* decorāre, ōrnāre.
graceful *adj* decōrus, venustus, lepidus.
gracefully *adv* venustē, lepidē.
graceless *adj* illepidus, impudēns.
gracious *adj* benīgnus, prōpitius, misericors.
graciously *adv* benīgnē, līberāliter.
graciousness *n* benīgnitās *f*, līberālitās *f*.
gradation *n* gradus *m*.
grade *n* gradus *m*.
gradient *n* clīvus *m*.
gradual *adj* lēnis.
gradually *adv* gradātim, sēnsim, paulātim.
graft *n* surculus *m*; (*POL*) ambitus *m* ♦ *vt*
īnserere.
grafting *n* īnsitiō *f*.
grain *n* frūmentum *nt*; (*seed*) grānum *nt*;
against the ~ invītā Minervā.
grammar *n* grammatica *f*.
grammarian *n* grammaticus *m*.
granary *n* horreum *nt*.
grand *adj* (*person*) amplus, illūstris, ēgregius;
(*way of life*) lautus, māgnificus; (*language*)
grandis, sublīmis.
granddaughter *n* neptis *f*; **great** ~ prōneptis *f*.
grandeur *n* māiestās *f*, māgnificentia *f*; (*style*)
granditās *f*.
grandfather *n* avus *m*; **great** ~ proavus *m*;
great-great-~ abavus *m*; **of a** ~ avītus.
grandiloquence *n* māgniloquentia *f*.
grandiloquent *adj* grandiloquus, tumidus.
grandiose *adj* māgnificus.
grandmother *n* avia *f*; **great** ~ proavia *f*.
grandson *n* nepōs *m*; **great** ~ prōnepōs *m*.

grant *vt* dare, concēdere, tribuere; (*admit*) fatērī ♦ *n* concessiō *f*.
grape *n* ūva *f*.
graphic *adj* expressus; **give a ~ account of** ante oculōs ponere, oculīs subicere.
grapnel *n* manus ferrea *f*, harpagō *f*.
grapple *vi* luctārī.
grappling iron *n* manus ferrea *f*.
grasp *vt* prēnsāre, comprehendere; (*with mind*) complectī, adsequī, percipere, intellegere; **~ at** captāre, adpetere ♦ *n* manus *f*, comprehēnsiō *f*; (*mind*) captus *m*.
grasping *adj* avārus, rapāx.
grass *n* herba *f*.
grasshopper *n* gryllus *m*.
grassy *adj* herbōsus; herbidus.
grate *n* focus *m* ♦ *vt* atterere; **~ upon** offendere.
grateful *adj* grātus; **feel ~** grātiam habēre.
gratefully *adv* grātē.
gratification *n* voluptās *f*.
gratify *vt* mōrem gerere (*dat*), mōrigerārī (*dat*), grātificārī (*dat*).
gratifying *adj* iūcundus.
gratis *adv* grātuītō, grātīs.
gratitude *n* grātia *f*; **show ~** grātiam referre.
gratuitous *adj* grātuītus.
gratuitously *adv* grātuītō.
gratuity *n* stips *f*; (*MIL*) dōnātīvum *nt*.
grave *n* sepulchrum *nt* ♦ *adj* gravis, austērus ♦ *vt* scalpere.
gravel *n* glārea *f*.
gravely *adv* graviter, sevērē.
gravitate *vi* vergere.
gravity *n* (*person*) sevēritās *f*, tristitia *f*; (*CIRCS*) gravitās *f*, mōmentum *nt*; (*physics*) nūtus *m*; **by force of ~** nūtū suō.
gray *adj* rāvus; (*hair*) cānus.
graze *vi* pāscī ♦ *vt* (*cattle*) pāscere; (*by touch*) stringere.
grazing *n* pāstus *m*.
grease *n* arvīna *f* ♦ *vt* ungere.
greasy *adj* pinguis, ūnctus.
great *adj* māgnus, grandis, ingēns, amplus; (*fame*) īnsignis, praeclārus; **as ~ as** ... tantus ... quantus; **~ deal** plūrimum; **~ many** plūrimī; **how ~** quantus; **very ~** permāgnus.
greatcoat *n* lacerna *f*.
greatest *adj* māximus.
greatly *adv* multum, māgnopere.
greave *n* ocrea *f*.
greed *n* avāritia *f*.
greedily *adv* avārē, cupidē.
greedy *adj* avārus, cupidus; avidus.
Greek *adj* Graecus.
green *adj* viridis; (*unripe*) crūdus; **be ~** virēre.
greenness *n* viriditās *f*.
greens *n* olus *nt*.
greet *vt* salūtāre.
greeting *n* salūs *f*, salūtātiō *f*.
grey *adj* rāvus; (*hair*) cānus.
greyhound *n* vertagus *m*.
grief *n* dolor *m*, maeror *m*, lūctus *m*; **come to ~**

perīre.
grievance *n* querimōnia *f*; iniūria *f*.
grieve *vi* dolēre, maerēre, lūgēre.
grievous *adj* tristis, lūctuōsus; molestus, gravis, acerbus.
grievously *adv* graviter, valdē.
grim *adj* trux, truculentus; atrōx.
grimace *n* ōris dēprāvātiō *f*; **make a ~ ōs** dūcere.
grime *n* sordēs *f*, lutum *nt*.
grimy *adj* sordidus, lutulentus.
grin *n* rīsus *m* ♦ *vi* adrīdēre.
grind *vt* contundere; (*corn*) molere; (*blade*) acuere; **~ down** (*fig*) opprimere.
grindstone *n* cōs *f*.
grip *vt* comprehendere, arripere ♦ *n* comprehēnsiō *f*; **come to ~s with** in complexum venīre (*gen*).
gripe *n* tormina *ntpl*.
grisly *adj* horridus, dīrus.
grist *n* (*fig*) ēmolumentum *nt*.
grit *n* harēna *f*.
groan *n* gemitus *m* ♦ *vi* gemere, ingemere.
groin *n* inguen *nt*.
groom *n* agāsō *m*.
groove *n* canālis *m*, stria *f*.
grope *vi* praetentāre.
gross *adj* crassus, pinguis; (*morally*) turpis, foedus.
grossly *adv* foedē, turpiter; (*very*) valdē.
grossness *n* crassitūdō *f*; turpitūdō *f*.
grotto *n* spēlunca *f*, antrum *nt*.
ground *n* (*bottom*) solum *nt*; (*earth*) terra *f*, humus *f*; (*cause*) ratiō *f*, causa *f*; (*sediment*) faex *f*; **on the ~** humī; **on the ~s that** quod (+ *subj*); **to the ~** humum; **gain ~** prōficere; (*rumour*) incrēbrēscere; **lose ~** cēdere; (*MIL*) inclīnāre ♦ *vt* īnstituere ♦ *vi* (*ship*) sīdere.
grounding *n* īnstitūtiō *f*.
groundless *adj* vānus, inānis.
groundlessly *adv* frustrā, temerē.
grounds *n* faex *f*; (*property*) praedium *nt*; (*reason*) causa *f*; **I have good ~ for doing** nōn sine causā faciō, iūstīs dē causīs faciō.
groundwork *n* fundāmentum *nt*.
group *n* globus *m*, circulus *m* ♦ *vt* dispōnere.
grouse *n* (*bird*) tetraō *m*; (*complaint*) querēla *f* ♦ *vi* querī.
grove *n* nemus *nt*, lūcus *m*.
grovel *vi* serpere, sē prōsternere, sē advolvere.
grovelling *adj* humilis, abiectus.
grow *vi* crēscere, glīscere; (*spread*) percrēbrēscere; (*become*) fierī; **~ old** (con)senēscere; **~ up** adolēscere, pūbēscere; **let ~** (*hair*) prōmittere ♦ *vt* (*crops*) colere; (*beard*) dēmittere.
growl *n* fremitus *m* ♦ *vi* fremere.
grown-up *adj* adultus, grandis.
growth *n* incrēmentum *nt*, auctus *m*.
grub *n* vermiculus *m*.
grudge *n* invidia *f* ♦ *vt* invidēre (*dat*); (*thing*) gravārī.
grudgingly *adv* invītus, gravātē.

gruesome *adj* taeter.
gruff *adj* acerbus, asper.
grumble *vi* querī, mussāre ♦ *n* querēla *f*.
grumpy *adj* mōrōsus, querulus.
grunt *n* grunnītus *m* ♦ *vi* grunnīre.
guarantee *n* (*money*) spōnsiō *f*; (*promise*) fidēs
f; (*person*) praes *m* ♦ *vt* spondēre, praestāre.
guarantor *n* spōnsor *m*.
guard *n* custōdia *f*, praesidium *nt*; (*person*)
custōs *m*; **on ~** in statiōne; **be on one's ~**
cavēre; **keep ~** statiōnem agere; **off one's ~**
imprūdēns, inopīnāns; **be taken off one's ~**
dē gradū dēicī ♦ *vt* custōdīre, dēfendere;
(*keep*) cōnservāre; **~ against** cavēre.
guarded *adj* cautus.
guardedly *adv* cautē.
guardhouse *n* custōdia *f*.
guardian *n* custōs *m*; (*of minors*) tūtor *m*.
guardianship *n* custōdia *f*, tūtēla *f*.
guardian spirit *n* genius *m*.
gudgeon *n* gōbius *m*.
guerdon *n* praemium *nt*, mercēs *f*.
guess *n* coniectūra *f* ♦ *vt* dīvīnāre, conicere.
guest *n* hospes *m*, hospita *f*; (*at dinner*) convīva
m; **uninvited ~** umbra *f*; **~'s** hospitālis.
guffaw *n* cachinnus *m* ♦ *vi* cachinnāre.
guidance *n* moderātiō *f*; **under the ~ of God**
dūcente deō.
guide *n* dux *m*, ductor *m*; (*in policy*) auctor *m* ♦
vt dūcere; (*steer*) regere; (*control*) moderārī.
guild *n* collēgium *nt*.
guile *n* dolus *m*, fraus *f*.
guileful *adj* dolōsus, fraudulentus.
guilefully *adv* dolōsē.
guileless *adj* simplex, innocēns.
guilelessly *adv* sine fraude.
guilt *n* culpa *f*, scelus *nt*.
guiltless *adj* innocēns, īnsōns.
guiltlessly *adv* integrē.
guilty *adj* nocēns, sōns; **find ~** damnāre.
guise *n* speciēs *f*.
guitar *n* fidēs *fpl*; **play the ~** fidibus canere.
gulf *n* sinus *m*; (*chasm*) hiātus *m*.
gull *n* mergus *m* ♦ *vt* dēcipere.
gullet *n* gula *f*, guttur *nt*.
gullible *adj* crēdulus.
gulp *vt* dēvorāre, haurīre.
gum *n* gummī *nt*; (*mouth*) gingīva *f*.
gumption *n* prūdentia *f*.
gurgle *vi* singultāre.
gush *vi* sē prōfundere, ēmicāre ♦ *n*
scatūrīginēs *fpl*.
gust *n* flāmen *nt*, impetus *m*.
gusto *n* studium *nt*.
gusty *adj* ventōsus.
gut *n* intestīnum *nt* ♦ *vt* exenterāre; (*fig*)
extergēre.
gutter *n* canālis *m*.
guzzle *vi* sē ingurgitāre.
gymnasium *n* gymnasium *nt*, palaestra *f*;
head of a ~ gymnasiarchus *m*.
gymnastic *adj* gymnicus; **~s** *pl* palaestra *f*.
gyrate *vi* volvī.

H, h

habit *n* mōs *m*, cōnsuētūdō *f*; (*dress*) habitus *m*,
vestītus *m*; **be in the ~ of** solēre.
habitable *adj* habitābilis.
habitation *n* domus *f*, domicilium *nt*; (*place*)
sēdēs *f*.
habitual *adj* ūsitātus.
habitually *adv* ex mōre, persaepe.
habituate *vt* adsuēfacere, īnsuēscere.
hack *vt* caedere, concīdere ♦ *n* (*horse*)
caballus *m*.
hackneyed *adj* trītus.
Hades *n* īnferī *mpl*.
haft *n* manubrium *nt*.
hag *n* anus *f*.
haggard *adj* ferus.
haggle *vi* altercārī.
hail *n* grandō *f* ♦ *vi*: **it ~s** grandinat ♦ *vt*
salūtāre, adclāmāre ♦ *interj* avē, avēte; salvē,
salvēte; **I ~ from Rome** Rōma mihi patria est.
hair *n* capillus *m*; crīnis *m*; (*single*) pīlus *m*;
(*animals*) sēta *f*, villus *m*; **deviate a ~'s
breadth from** trānsversum digitum
discēdere ab; **split ~s** cavillārī.
hairdresser *n* tōnsor *m*.
hairless *adj* (*head*) calvus; (*body*) glaber.
hairpin *n* crīnāle *nt*.
hairsplitting *adj* captiōsus ♦ *n* cavillātiō *f*.
hairy *adj* pīlōsus.
halberd *n* bipennis *f*.
halcyon *n* alcēdō *f*; **~ days** alcēdōnia *ntpl*.
hale *adj* validus, rōbustus ♦ *vt* trahere, rapere.
half *n* dīmidium *nt*, dīmidia pars *f* ♦ *adj*
dīmidius, dīmidiātus; **~ as much again**
sesquī; **well begun is ~ done** dīmidium factī
quī coepit habet.
half-asleep *adj* sēmisomnus.
half-baked *adj* (*fig*) rudis.
half-dead *adj* sēmianimis, sēmivīvus.
half-full *adj* sēmiplēnus.
half-hearted *adj* incūriōsus, sōcors.
half-heartedly *adv* sine studiō.
half-hour *n* sēmihōra *f*.
half-moon *n* lūna dīmidiāta *f*.
half-open *adj* sēmiapertus.
half pound *n* sēlībra *f*.
half-way *adj* medius; **~ up the hill** in mediō
colle.
half-yearly *adj* sēmestris.
hall *n* ātrium *nt*; (*public*) exedra *f*.
hallo *interj* heus.

hallow *vt* sacrāre.
hallucination *n* error *m*, somnium *nt*.
halo *n* corōna *f*.
halt *vi* īnsistere, cōnsistere ♦ *vt* sistere ♦ *n*:
come to a ~ cōnsistere, agmen cōnstituere ♦
adj claudus.
halter *n* capistrum *nt*; (*fig*) laqueus *m*.
halve *vt* bipartīre.
ham *n* perna *f*.
hamlet *n* vīcus *m*.
hammer *n* malleus *m* ♦ *vt* tundere; ~ out
excūdere.
hamper *n* corbis *f* ♦ *vt* impedīre; (*with debt*)
obstringere.
hamstring *vt* poplitem succīdere (*dat*).
hand *n* manus *f*; **left** ~ laeva *f*, sinistra *f*; **right** ~
dextra *f*; **an old** ~ veterātor *m*; **at** ~ praestō,
ad manum; **be at** ~ adesse; **at first** ~ ipse; **at
second** ~ ab aliō; **on the one** ~ . . . **on the other**
et . . . et, quidem . . . at; **near at** ~ in expedītō,
inibī; **the matter in** ~ quod nunc īnstat, quae
in manibus sunt; **get out of** ~ lascīvīre; **have
a** ~ **in** interesse (*dat*); **have one's ~s full** satis
agere; **lay ~s on** manum adferre, inicere
(*dat*); **live from** ~ **to mouth** ad hōram vīvere;
pass from ~ **to** ~ per manūs trādere; **take in** ~
suscipere; **~s** *pl* (*workmen*) operae *fpl* ♦ *vt*
trādere, porrigere; ~ **down** trādere, ~
prōdere; ~ **over** dēferre, reddere.
handbill *n* libellus *m*.
handbook *n* ars *f*.
handcuffs *n* manicae *fpl*.
handful *n* manipulus *m*.
handicap *n* impedīmentum *nt*.
handicraft *n* artificium *nt*, ars operōsa *f*.
handily *adv* habiliter.
handiness *n* habilitās *f*; commoditās *f*.
handiwork *n* opus *nt*, manus *f*.
handkerchief *n* sūdārium *nt*.
handle *n* (*cup*) ānsa *f*; (*knife*) manubrium *nt*;
(*fig*) ānsa *f*, occāsiō *f* ♦ *vt* tractāre.
handling *n* tractātiō *f*.
handmaid *n* famula *f*.
handsome *adj* fōrmōsus, pulcher; (*gift*)
līberālis.
handsomely *adv* pulchrē; līberāliter.
handsomeness *n* pulchritūdō *f*, fōrma *f*.
hand-to-hand *adv*: **fight** ~ manum cōnserere,
comminus pugnāre.
handwriting *n* manus *f*.
handy *adj* (*to use*) habilis; (*near*) praestō.
hang *vt* suspendere; (*head*) dēmittere; (*wall*)
vestīre ♦ *vi* pendēre; ~ **back** gravārī,
dubitāre; ~ **down** dēpendēre; ~ **on to** haerēre
(*dat*); ~ **over** imminēre (*dat*), impendēre (*dat*);
go and be ~ed in malam crucem!
hanger-on *n* cliēns *m/f*, assecla *m/f*.
hanging *n* (*death*) suspendium *nt*; **~s** *pl* aulaea
ntpl ♦ *adj* pendulus.
hangman *n* carnifex *m*.
hanker *vi*: ~ **after** appetere, exoptāre.
hap *n* fors *f*.
haphazard *adj* fortuītus.

hapless *adj* miser, īnfēlīx.
haply *adv* fortasse.
happen *vi* accidere, ēvenīre, contingere;
(*become*) fierī; **as usually ~s** ut fit; ~ **upon**
incidere in (*acc*); **it ~s that** accidit ut
(*+subj*).
happily *adv* fēlīciter, beātē, bene.
happiness *n* fēlīcitās *f*.
happy *adj* fēlīx, beātus; laetus; (*in some
respect*) fortūnātus.
harangue *n* cōntiō *f* ♦ *vt* cōntiōnārī apud (+
acc), hortārī.
harass *vt* vexāre, lacessere, exagitāre,
sollicitāre.
harassing *adj* molestus.
harbinger *n* praenūntius *m*.
harbour *n* portus *m* ♦ *vt* recipere.
harbour dues *n* portōria *ntpl*.
hard *adj* dūrus; (*CIRCS*) asper, inīquus; (*task*)
difficilis, arduus; ~ **of hearing** surdaster;
grow ~ dūrēscere ♦ *adv* sēdulō, valdē; ~ **by**
prope, iuxtā; **I am** ~ **put to it to do** aegerrimē
faciō.
hard cash *n* praesēns pecūnia *f*.
harden *vt* dūrāre ♦ *vi* dūrēscere; (*fig*)
obdūrēscere; **become ~ed** obdūrēscere.
hard-fought *adj* atrōx.
hard-hearted *adj* crūdēlis, dūrus, inhūmānus.
hardihood *n* audācia *f*.
hardily *adv* sevērē.
hardiness *n* rōbur *nt*; dūritia *f*.
hardly *adv* vix, aegrē; (*severely*) dūriter,
acerbē; ~ **any** nullus ferē.
hardness *n* dūritia *f*; (*fig*) asperitās *f*, inīquitās
f; (*difficulty*) difficultās *f*; ~ **of hearing** surditās
f.
hard-pressed *adj*: **be** ~ labōrāre.
hardship *n* labor *m*, malum *nt*, iniūria *f*.
hard-working *adj* industrius, nāvus, sēdulus.
hardy *adj* dūrus, rōbustus, sevērus.
hare *n* lepus *m*.
hark *interj* auscultā, auscultāte ♦ *vi*: ~ **back to**
repetere.
harm *n* iniūria *f*, damnum *nt*, malum *nt*,
dētrīmentum *nt*; **come to** ~ dētrīmentum
capere, accipere ♦ *vt* laedere, nocēre (*dat*).
harmful *adj* damnōsus, noxius.
harmfully *adv* male.
harmless *adj* innocēns.
harmlessly *adv* innocenter; (*escape*) salvus,
incolumis, inviolātus.
harmonious *adj* cōnsonus, canōrus; (*fig*)
concors; (*things*) congruēns.
harmoniously *adv* modulātē; concorditer;
convenienter.
harmonize *vi* concinere, cōnsentīre,
congruere.
harmony *n* concentus *m*; (*fig*) concordia *f*,
cōnsēnsus *m*.
harness *n* arma *ntpl* ♦ *vt* īnfrēnāre, iungere.
harp *n* fidēs *fpl*; **play the** ~ fidibus canere ♦ *vi*: ~
on (*fig*) cantāre, dictitāre; **be always ~ing on
the same thing** cantilēnam eandem canere.

harpist n fidicen m, fidicina f.
harpoon n iaculum nt.
harpy n Harpyia f.
harrow n rāstrum nt ♦ vt occāre.
harrower n occātor m.
harrowing adj horrendus.
harry vt vexāre, dīripere.
harsh adj dūrus, acerbus, asper; (person) inclēmēns, sevērus.
harshly adv acerbē, asperē; sevērē.
harshness n acerbitās f, asperitās f; crūdēlitās f.
hart n cervus m.
harvest n messis f ♦ vt metere, dēmetere.
harvester n messor m.
hash n farrāgō f ♦ vt comminuere.
haste n festīnātiō f, properātiō f; **in ~** festīnanter; **in hot ~** incitātus; **make ~** festīnāre.
hasten vt mātūrāre, adcelerāre ♦ vi festīnāre, properāre, mātūrāre.
hastily adv properē, raptim; temerē, incōnsultē; īrācundē.
hastiness n temeritās f; (temper) īrācundia f.
hasty adj properus, celer; (action) incōnsultus, temerārius; (temper) īrācundus, ācer; **over ~** praeproperus.
hat n petasus m.
hatch vt exclūdere, parere.
hatchet n dolābra f.
hate n odium nt, invidia f ♦ vt ōdisse.
hated adj: **to be ~ (by sb)** odiō esse (+ dat).
hateful adj odiōsus, invīsus.
hatefully adv odiōsē.
hatred n odium nt.
haughtily adv adroganter, superbē, insolenter.
haughtiness n fastus m, adrogantia f, superbia f.
haughty adj adrogāns, superbus, īnsolēns.
haul vt trahere ♦ n bolus m.
haulage n vectūra f.
haulm n culmus m.
haunch n femur nt.
haunt vt frequentāre ♦ n locus m; (animals) lustrum nt.
have vt habēre, tenēre; (get done) cūrāre (gerundive); **I ~ a house** est mihī domus; **I ~ to go** mihī abeundum est; **~ it out with** rem dēcernere cum; **~ on** gerere, gestāre, indui; **I had better go** melius est īre, praestat īre; **I had rather** mālim, māllem.
haven n portus m; (fig) perfugium nt.
havoc n exitium nt, vastātiō f, ruīna f.
hawk n accipiter m ♦ vt (wares) circumferre.
hawker n īnstitor m.
hay n faenum nt; **make ~ while the sun shines** forō ūtī.
hazard n perīculum nt, discrīmen nt, ālea f ♦ vt perīclitārī, in āleam dare.
hazardous adj perīculōsus.
haze n nebula f.
hazel n corylus f.
hazy adj nebulōsus; (fig) incertus.

he pron hic, ille, is.
head n caput nt; (person) dux m, prīnceps m; (composition) caput nt; (mind) animus m, ingenium nt; **~ over heels** cernuus; **off one's ~** dēmēns; **be at the ~ of** dūcere, praeesse (dat); **come to a ~** caput facere; (fig) in discrīmen addūcī; **give one his ~** indulgēre (dat), habēnās immittere (dat); **keep one's ~** praesentī animō ūtī; **lose one's ~** suī compotem nōn esse; **shake one's ~** abnuere ♦ vt dūcere, praeesse (dat); **~ off** intercipere ♦ vi (in a direction) tendere.
headache n capitis dolor m.
headfirst adj praeceps.
heading n caput nt.
headland n prōmunturium nt.
headlong adj praeceps ♦ adv in praeceps; **rush ~** sē praecipitāre.
headquarters n (MIL) praetōrium nt.
headship n prīncipātus m.
headsman n carnifex m.
headstrong adj impotēns, pervicāx.
headway n prōfectus m.
heady adj incōnsultus; (wine) vehemēns.
heal vt sānāre, medērī (dat) ♦ vi sānēscere; **~ over** obdūcī.
healer n medicus m.
healing adj salūbris.
health n valētūdō f, salūs f; **state of ~** valētūdō f; **ill ~** valētūdō f; **be in good ~** valēre; **drink the ~ of** propīnāre (dat).
healthful adj salūbris.
healthiness n sānitās f.
healthy adj sānus, integer; (conditions) salūber.
heap n acervus m, cumulus m; **in ~s** acervātim ♦ vt acervāre; **~ together** congerere; **~ up** adcumulāre, coacervāre, congerere.
hear vt audīre; (case) cognōscere; **~ clearly** exaudīre; **~ in secret** inaudīre.
hearer n audītor m.
hearing n (sense) audītus m; (act) audītiō f; (of case) cognitiō f; **get a ~** sibī audientiam facere; **hard of ~** surdaster; **without a ~** indictā causā.
hearken vi auscultāre.
hearsay n fāma f, rūmor m.
heart n cor nt; (emotion) animus m, pectus nt; (courage) animus m; (interior) viscera ntpl; **by ~** memoriā, memoriter; **learn by ~** ēdiscere; **the ~ of the matter** rēs ipsa; **lose ~** animum dēspondēre; **take to ~** graviter ferre.
heartache n dolor m, angor m.
heartbroken adj animī frāctus, aeger; **be ~** animō labōrāre.
heartburning n invidia f.
heartfelt adj sincērus.
hearth n focus m; **~ and home** ārae et focī.
heartily adv vehementer, valdē.
heartiness n studium nt, vigor m.
heartless adj dūrus, inhūmānus, crūdēlis.
heartlessly adv inhūmānē.
heartlessness n inhūmānitās f, crūdēlitās f.
hearty adj studiōsus, vehemēns; (health)

rōbustus; (*feeling*) sincērus.
heat *n* ārdor *m*, calor *m*; (*emotion*) ārdor *m*, aestus *m*; (*race*) missus *m* ♦ *vt* calefacere, fervefacere; (*fig*) accendere; **become ~ed** incalēscere.
heatedly *adv* ferventer, ārdenter.
heath *n* inculta loca *ntpl*.
heathcock *n* attagēn *m*.
heathen *n* pāgānus *m*.
heather *n* erīcē *f*.
heave *vt* tollere; (*missile*) conicere; (*sigh*) dūcere ♦ *vi* tumēre, fluctuāre.
heaven *n* caelum *nt*, dī *mpl*; **~ forbid!** dī meliōra; **from ~** dīvīnitus; **in ~'s name** prō deum fidem!; **be in seventh ~** digitō caelum attingere.
heavenly *adj* caelestis, dīvīnus.
heavily *adv* graviter.
heaviness *n* gravitās *f*, pondus *nt*; (*of spirit*) maestitia *f*.
heavy *adj* gravis; (*air*) crassus; (*spirit*) maestus; (*shower*) māgnus, dēnsus.
heckle *vt* interpellāre.
heckler *n* interpellātor *m*.
hectic *adj* violēns, ācer, fervidus.
hector *vt* obstrepere (*dat*).
hedge *n* saepēs *f* ♦ *vt* saepīre; **~ off** intersaepīre ♦ *vi* tergiversārī.
hedgehog *n* echīnus *m*, ēricius *m*.
heed *vt* cūrāre, respicere ♦ *n* cūra *f*, opera *f*; **pay ~** animum attendere; **take ~** cavēre.
heedful *adj* attentus, cautus, dīligēns.
heedfully *adv* attentē, cautē.
heedfulness *n* cūra *f*, dīligentia *f*.
heedless *adj* incautus, immemor, neglegēns.
heedlessly *adv* incautē, neglegenter, temerē.
heedlessness *n* neglegentia *f*.
heel *n* calx *f*; **take to one's ~s** sē in pedēs conicere ♦ *vi* sē inclīnāre.
hegemony *n* prīncipātus *m*.
heifer *n* būcula *f*.
height *n* altitūdō *f*; (*person*) prōcēritās *f*; (*hill*) collis *m*, iugum *nt*; (*fig*) fastīgium *nt*; **the ~ of** summus.
heighten *vt* augēre, exaggerāre.
heinous *adj* atrōx, nefārius.
heinously *adv* atrōciter, nefāriē.
heinousness *n* atrōcitās *f*.
heir *n* hērēs *m*; **sole ~** hērēs ex asse.
heiress *n* hērēs *f*.
heirship *n* hērēditās *f*.
hell *n* Tartarus *m*, īnfernī *mpl*.
hellish *adj* īnfernus, scelestus.
helm *n* gubernāculum *nt*, clāvus *m*.
helmet *n* galea *f*.
helmsman *n* gubernātor *m*.
helots *n* Hīlōtae *mpl*.
help *n* auxilium *nt*, subsidium *nt*; **I am a ~** auxiliō sum ♦ *vt* iuvāre (+ *acc*), auxiliārī, subvenīre (*dat*), succurrere (*dat*) ♦ *vi* prōdesse; **I cannot ~ facere** nōn possum quīn (*subj*); **it can't be ~ed** fierī nōn potest aliter; **so ~ me God** ita me dī ament.

helper *n* adiūtor *m*, adiūtrix *f*.
helpful *adj* ūtilis; **be ~ to** auxiliō esse (*dat*).
helpless *adj* inops.
helplessness *n* inopia *f*.
hem *n* ōra *f*, limbus *m* ♦ *vt*: **~ in** interclūdere, circumsedēre.
hemlock *n* cicūta *f*.
hemp *n* cannabis *f*.
hen *n* gallīna *f*.
hence *adv* hinc; (*consequence*) igitur, ideō.
henceforth, henceforward *adv* dehinc, posthāc, ex hōc tempore.
her *adj* suus, ēius.
herald *n* praecō *m*; (*POL*) fētiālis *m* ♦ *vt* praenūntiāre.
herb *n* herba *f*, olus *nt*.
herbage *n* herbae *fpl*.
herd *n* pecus *nt*; grex *f*, armentum *nt* ♦ *vi* congregārī.
herdsman *n* pāstor *m*.
here *adv* hīc; **be ~** adesse; **~ and there** passim; **here ... there** alibī ... alibī; **from ~** hinc; **~ is ... ecce** (*acc*) ....
hereabouts *adv* hīc ferē.
hereafter *adv* posthāc, posteā.
hereat *adv* hīc.
hereby *adv* ex hōc, hinc.
hereditary *adj* hērēditārius, patrius.
heredity *n* genus *nt*.
herein *adv* hīc.
hereinafter *adv* īnfrā.
hereof *adv* ēius reī.
hereupon *adv* hīc, quō factō.
herewith *adv* cum hōc, ūnā.
heritable *adj* hērēditārius.
heritage *n* hērēditās *f*.
hermaphrodite *n* andrōgynus *m*.
hermit *n* homō sōlitārius *m*.
hero *n* vir fortissimus *m*; (*demigod*) hērōs *m*.
heroic *adj* fortissimus, māgnanimus; (*epic*) hērōicus; (*verse*) hērōus.
heroically *adv* fortissimē, audācissimē.
heroism *n* virtūs *f*, fortitūdō *f*.
heron *n* ardea *f*.
hers *pron* suus, ēius.
herself *pron* ipsa *f*; (*reflexive*) sē.
hesitancy *n* dubitātiō *f*.
hesitant *adj* incertus, dubius.
hesitate *vi* dubitāre, haesitāre.
hesitating *adj* dubius.
hesitatingly *adv* cunctanter.
hesitation *n* dubitātiō *f*; **with ~** dubitanter.
heterogeneous *adj* dīversus, aliēnigenus.
hew *vt* dolāre, caedere; **~ down** excīdere, interscindere.
hexameter *n* hexameter *m*.
heyday *n* flōs *m*.
hiatus *n* hiātus *m*.
hiccup *n* singultus *m* ♦ *vi* singultīre.
hide *vt* cēlāre, abdere, abscondere, occultāre; **~ away** abstrūdere; **~ from** cēlāre (*acc*) ♦ *vi* sē abdere, latēre; **~ away** dēlitēscere ♦ *n* pellis *f*, corium *nt*.

hideous *adj* foedus, dēfōrmis, turpis.
hideously *adv* foedē.
hideousness *n* foeditās *f*, dēfōrmitās *f*.
hiding *n* (*place*) latebra *f*.
hierarchy *n* ōrdinēs *mpl*.
high *adj* altus, excelsus; (*ground*) ēditus; (*pitch*)
    acūtus; (*rank*) amplus; (*price*) cārus; (*tide*)
    māximus; (*wind*) māgnus; ~ **living** luxuria *f*; ~
    treason māiestās *f*; ~ **and mighty** superbus;
    on ~ sublīmis ♦ *adv* altē.
highborn *adj* nōbilis, generōsus.
high-class *adj* (*goods*) lautus.
high-flown *adj* īnflātus, tumidus.
high-handed *adj* superbus, īnsolēns.
high-handedly *adv* superbē, licenter.
high-handedness *n* licentia *f*, superbia *f*.
highland *adj* montānus.
highlander *n* montānus *m*.
highlands *npl* montāna *ntpl*.
highly *adv* (*value*) māgnī; (*intensity*) valdē.
highly-strung *adj* trepidus.
high-minded *adj* generōsus.
high-spirited *adj* ferōx, animōsus.
highway *n* via *f*.
highwayman *n* grassātor *m*, latrō *m*.
hilarious *adj* festīvus, hilaris.
hilariously *adv* festīvē, hilare.
hilarity *n* festīvitās *f*, hilaritās *f*.
hill *n* collis *m*, mōns *m*; (*slope*) clīvus *m*.
hillock *n* tumulus *m*.
hilly *adj* montuōsus, clīvōsus.
hilt *n* manubrium *nt*, capulus *m*.
himself *pron* ipse; (*reflexive*) sē.
hind *n* cerva *f*.
hinder *vt* impedīre, obstāre (*dat*), morārī.
hindmost *adj* postrēmus; (*in column*)
    novissimus.
hindrance *n* impedīmentum *nt*, mora *f*.
hinge *n* cardō *f*.
hint *n* indicium *nt*, suspiciō *f*; **throw out a** ~
    inicere ♦ *vt* subicere, significāre.
hip *n* coxendīx *f*.
hippodrome *n* spatium *nt*.
hire *vt* condūcere; ~ **out** locāre ♦ *n* conductiō *f*,
    locātiō *f*; (*wages*) mercēs *f*.
hired *adj* mercennārius, conductus.
hireling *n* mercennārius *m*.
hirsute *adj* hirsūtus.
his *adj* suus, ēius.
hiss *vi* sībilāre ♦ *vt*: ~ **off stage** explōdere,
    exsībilāre ♦ *n* sībilus *m*.
historian *n* historicus *m*, rērum scrīptor *m*.
historical *adj* historicus.
history *n* historia *f*; **the ~ of Rome** rēs
    Rōmānae *fpl*; **since the beginning of** ~ post
    hominum memoriam; **ancient** ~ antīquitās *f*.
histrionic *adj* scaenicus.
hit *n* ictus *m*, plāga *f*; **a** ~ ! (*in duel*) habet! ♦ *vt*
    ferīre, icere, percutere; ~ **against** offendere;
    ~ **upon** invenīre.
hitch *n* mora *f* ♦ *vt* implicāre; ~ **up** succingere.
hither *adv* hūc; ~ **and thither** hūc illūc ♦ *adj*
    citerior.

hitherto *adv* adhūc, hāctenus, hūcusque.
hive *n* alveārium *nt*.
hoar *adj* cānus ♦ *n* pruīna *f*.
hoard *n* thēsaurus *m*, acervus *m* ♦ *vt* condere,
    recondere.
hoarfrost *n* pruīna *f*.
hoarse *adj* raucus, fuscus.
hoarsely *adv* raucā vōce.
hoary *adj* cānus.
hoax *n* fraus *f*, fallācia *f*, lūdus *m* ♦ *vt* dēcipere,
    fallere.
hobble *vi* claudicāre.
hobby *n* studium *nt*.
hob-nob *vi* familiāriter ūtī (*abl*).
hocus-pocus *n* trīcae *fpl*.
hoe *n* sarculum *nt* ♦ *vt* sarrīre.
hog *n* sūs *m*, porcus *m*; ~**'s** porcīnus.
hogshead *n* dōlium *nt*.
hoist *vt* tollere; (*sail*) vēla dare.
hold *n* (*grasp*) comprehēnsiō *f*; (*power*)
    potestās *f*; (*ship*) alveus *m*; **gain a ~ over**
    obstringere, sibi dēvincīre; **get ~ of** potīrī
    (*abl*); **keep ~ of** retinēre; **lose ~ of** ōmittere;
    take ~ of prehendere, comprehendere ♦ *vt*
    tenēre, habēre; (*possession*) obtinēre,
    possidēre; (*office*) gerere, fungī (*abl*);
    (*capacity*) capere; (*meeting*) habēre; ~ **a**
    meeting concilium habēre; ~ **one's own with**
    parem esse (*dat*); ~ **over** differre, prōlātāre;
    ~ **water** (*fig*) stāre ♦ *vi* manēre, dūrāre;
    (*opinion*) dūcere, existimāre, adfirmāre; ~
    back *vt* retinēre, inhibēre ♦ *vi* gravārī,
    dubitāre; ~ **cheap** parvī facere; ~ **fast** *vt*
    retinēre, amplectī ♦ *vi* haerēre; ~ **good**
    valēre; ~ **out** *vt* porrigere, extendere; (*hope*)
    ostendere ♦ *vi* dūrāre, perstāre; ~ **together**
    cohaerēre; ~ **up** tollere; (*falling*) sustinēre;
    (*movement*) obstāre (*dat*), morārī; ~ **with**
    adsentīre (*dat*).
holdfast *n* fībula *f*.
holding *n* (*land*) agellus *m*.
hole *n* forāmen *nt*, cavum *nt*; **make a ~ in**
    pertundere, perforāre.
holiday *n* ōtium *nt*; **festus diēs** *m*; **on** ~
    fēriātus; ~**s** *pl* fēriae *fpl*.
holily *adv* sanctē.
holiness *n* sanctitās *f*.
hollow *adj* cavus, concavus; (*fig*) inānis, vānus
    ♦ *n* cavum *nt*, caverna *f* ♦ *vt* excavāre.
hollowness *n* (*fig*) vānitās *f*.
holly *n* aquifolium *nt*.
holy *adj* sanctus.
homage *n* observantia *f*, venerātiō *f*; **pay ~ to**
    venerārī, colere.
home *n* domus *f*; (*town, country*) patria *f*; **at** ~
    domī; **from** ~ domō ♦ *adj* domesticus ♦ *adv*
    domum.
homeless *adj* profugus.
homely *adj* simplex, rūsticus; (*speech*)
    plēbēius.
homestead *n* fundus *m*.
homewards *adv* domum.
homicide *n* (*act*) homicīdium *nt*, caedēs *f*;

(*person*) homicīda *m*.
homily *n* sermō *m*.
homogeneous *adj* aequābilis.
homologous *adj* cōnsimilis.
hone *n* cōs *f* ♦ *vt* acuere.
honest *adj* probus, frūgī, integer.
honestly *adv* probē, integrē.
honesty *n* probitās *f*, fidēs *f*.
honey *n* mel *nt*.
honeycomb *n* favus *m*.
honeyed *adj* mellītus, mulsus.
honorarium *n* stips *f*.
honorary *adj* honōrārius.
honour *n* honōs *m*; (*repute*) honestās *f*;
existimātiō *f*; (*chastity*) pudor *m*; (*trust*) fidēs *f*;
(*rank*) dignitās *f*; (*award*) decus *nt*, īnsigne *nt*;
(*respect*) observantia *f* ♦ *vt* honōrāre,
decorāre; (*respect*) observāre, colere; **do ~ to**
honestāre.
honourable *adj* honestus, probus; (*rank*)
illūstris, praeclārus.
honourably *adv* honestē.
hood *n* cucullus *m*.
hoodwink *vt* verba dare (*dat*).
hoof *n* ungula *f*.
hook *n* uncus *m*, hāmus *m* ♦ *vt* hāmō capere.
hooked *adj* aduncus, hāmātus.
hoop *n* circulus *m*; (*toy*) trochus *m*.
hoot *vi* obstrepere; **~ off** (*stage*) explōdere.
hop *n* saltus *m*; **catch on the ~** in ipsō articulō
opprimere ♦ *vi* salīre.
hope *n* spēs *f*; **in the ~ that** sī forte; **give up ~**
spem dēpōnere, dēspērāre; **past ~**
dēspērātus; **entertain ~s** spem habēre ♦ *vt*
spērāre.
hopeful *adj* bonae speī; **be ~** aliquam spem
habēre.
hopefully *adv* nōn sine spē.
hopeless *adj* dēspērātus.
hopelessly *adv* dēspēranter.
hopelessness *n* dēspērātiō *f*.
horde *n* multitūdō *f*.
horizon *n* fīniēns *m*.
horizontal *adj* aequus, lībrātus.
horizontally *adv* ad lībram.
horn *n* cornū *nt*; (*shepherd's*) būcina *f*.
horned *adj* corniger.
hornet *n* crabrō *m*; **stir up a ~'s nest** crabrōnēs
inrītāre.
horny *adj* corneus.
horoscope *n* sīdus nātālicium *nt*.
horrible *adj* horrendus, horribilis, dīrus,
foedus.
horribly *adv* foedē.
horrid *adj* horribilis.
horrify *vt* terrēre, perterrēre.
horror *n* horror *m*, terror *m*; odium *nt*.
horse *n* equus *m*; (*cavalry*) equitēs *mpl*; **flog a
dead ~** asellum currere docēre; **spur a
willing ~** currentem incitāre; **~'s** equīnus.
horseback *n*: **ride on ~back** in equō vehī; **fight
on ~back** ex equō pugnāre.
horseman *n* eques *m*.

horseradish *n* armoracia *f*.
horse soldier *n* eques *m*.
horticulture *n* hortōrum cultus *m*.
hospitable *adj* hospitālis.
hospitably *adv* hospitāliter.
hospital *n* valētūdinārium *nt*.
hospitality *n* hospitālitās *f*, hospitium *nt*.
host *n* hospes *m*; (*inn*) caupō *m*; (*number*)
multitūdō *f*; (*MIL*) exercitus *m*.
hostage *n* obses *m/f*.
hostelry *n* taberna *f*, dēversōrium *nt*.
hostile *adj* hostīlis, īnfēnsus, inimīcus;
īnfestus; **in a ~ manner** īnfēnsē, hostīliter,
inimīcē.
hostility *n* inimīcitia *f*; **hostilities** *pl* bellum *nt*.
hot *adj* calidus, fervidus, aestuōsus; (*boiling*)
fervēns; (*fig*) ārdēns; **be ~** calēre, fervēre,
ārdēre; **get ~** calēscere.
hotch-potch *n* farrāgō *f*.
hotel *n* dēversōrium *nt*.
hot-headed *adj* ārdēns, temerārius, praeceps.
hotly *adv* ārdenter, ācriter.
hot-tempered *adj* īrācundus.
hot water *n* calida *f*.
hound *n* canis *m* ♦ *vt* īnstāre (*dat*).
hour *n* hōra *f*.
hourly *adv* in hōrās.
house *n* domus *f*, aedēs *fpl*; (*country*) vīlla *f*;
(*family*) domus *f*, gēns *f*; **at the ~ of** apud (*acc*);
full ~ frequēns senātus, frequēns theātrum
♦ *vt* hospitiō accipere, recipere; (*things*)
condere.
household *n* familia *f*, domus *f* ♦ *adj*
familiāris, domesticus.
householder *n* paterfamiliās *m*, dominus *m*.
housekeeping *n* reī familiāris cūra *f*.
housemaid *n* ancilla *f*.
housetop *n* fastīgium *nt*.
housewife *n* māterfamiliās *f*, domina *f*.
housing *n* hospitium *nt*; (*horse*) ōrnāmenta
ntpl.
hovel *n* gurgustium *nt*.
hover *vi* pendēre; (*fig*) impendēre.
how *adv* (*interrog*) quemadmodum; quōmodo,
quō pactō; (*excl*) quam; **~ great/big/large**
quantus; **~ long** (*time*) quamdiū; **~ many** quot;
~ much quantum; **~ often** quotiēns.
howbeit *adv* tamen.
however *adv* tamen; autem, nihilōminus;
utcumque, quōquō modō; **~ much** quamvīs,
quantumvīs; **~ great** quantuscumque.
howl *n* ululātus *m* ♦ *vi* ululāre; (*wind*) fremere.
howsoever *adv* utcumque.
hub *n* axis *m*.
hubbub *n* tumūltus *m*.
huckster *n* īnstitor *m*, propōla *m*.
huddle *n* turba *f* ♦ *vi* congregārī.
hue *n* color *m*; **~ and cry** clāmor *m*.
huff *n* offēnsiō *f* ♦ *vt* offendere.
hug *n* complexus *m* ♦ *vt* complectī.
huge *adj* ingēns, immānis, immēnsus, vastus.
hugely *adv* vehementer.
hugeness *n* immānitās *f*.

hulk n alveus m.
hull n alveus m.
hum n murmur nt, fremitus m ♦ vi
  murmurāre, fremere.
human adj hūmānus.
human being n homō m/f.
humane adj hūmānus, misericors.
humanely adv hūmānē, hūmāniter.
humanism n litterae fpl.
humanist n homō litterātus m.
humanity n hūmānitās f; misericordia f.
humanize vt excolere.
humanly adv hūmānitus.
human nature n hūmānitās f.
humble adj humilis, modestus ♦ vt dēprimere;
  (oneself) summittere.
humbleness n humilitās f.
humbly adv summissē, modestē.
humbug n trīcae fpl.
humdrum adj vulgāris; (style) pedester.
humid adj ūmidus, madidus; **be ~** madēre.
humidity n ūmor m.
humiliate vt dēprimere, dēdecorāre.
humiliation n dēdecus nt.
humility n modestia f, animus summissus m.
humorist n homō facētus m.
humorous adj facētus, ioculāris, rīdiculus.
humorously adv facētē.
humour n facētiae fpl; (disposition) ingenium
  nt; (mood) libīdō f; **be in a bad ~** sibī
  displicēre ♦ vt indulgēre (dat), mōrem
  gerere (dat), mōrigerārī (dat).
hump n gibbus m.
hunchback n gibber m.
hundred num centum; **~ each** centēnī; **~ times**
  centiēns.
hundredth adj centēsimus.
hundredweight n centumpondium nt.
hunger n famēs f ♦ vi ēsurīre.
hungrily adv avidē.
hungry adj ēsuriēns, iēiūnus, avidus; **be ~**
  ēsurīre.
hunt n vēnātiō f, vēnātus m ♦ vt vēnārī,
  indāgāre, exagitāre.
hunter n vēnātor m.
hunting n vēnātiō f; (fig) aucupium nt.
hunting spear n vēnābulum nt.
huntress n vēnātrix f.
huntsman n vēnātor m.
hurdle n crātēs f; (obstacle) obex m/f.
hurl vt conicere, ingerere, iaculārī, iācere.
hurly-burly n turba f, tumultus m.
hurrah interj euax, iō.
hurricane n procella f.
hurried adj praeproperus, praeceps, trepidus.
hurriedly adv properātō, cursim, festīnanter.
hurry vt adcelerāre, mātūrāre ♦ vi festīnāre,
  properāre; **~ along** vt rapere; **~ away** vi
  discēdere, properāre; **~ about** vi discurrere;
  ~ on vt mātūrāre; **~ up** vi properāre ♦ n
  festīnātiō f; **in a ~** festīnanter, raptim.
hurt n iniūria f, damnum nt; vulnus nt ♦ vt
  laedere, nocēre (dat); **it ~s** dolet.

hurtful adj nocēns, damnōsus.
hurtfully adv nocenter, damnōsē.
hurtle vi volāre; sē praecipitāre.
husband n vir m, marītus m ♦ vt parcere (dat).
husbandry n agrī cultūra f; (economy)
  parsimōnia f.
hush n silentium nt ♦ vt silentium facere (dat),
  lēnīre ♦ vi tacēre, silēre; **~ up** comprimere,
  cēlāre ♦ interj st!
hushed adj tacitus.
husk n folliculus m, siliqua f ♦ vt dēglūbāre.
husky adj fuscus, raucus.
hustle vt trūdere, īnstāre (dat).
hut n casa f, tugurium nt.
hutch n cavea f.
hyacinth n hyacinthus m.
hybrid n hibrida m/f.
hydra n hydra f.
hyena n hyaena f.
hygiene n salūbritās f.
hygienic adj salūbris.
hymeneal adj nūptiālis.
hymn n carmen nt ♦ vt canere.
hyperbole n superlātiō f.
hypercritical adj Aristarchus m.
hypocaust n hypocaustum nt.
hypocrisy n simulātiō f, dissimulātiō f.
hypocrite n simulātor m, dissimulātor m.
hypocritical adj simulātus, fictus.
hypothesis n positum nt, sūmptiō f,
  coniectūra f.
hypothetical adj sūmptus.

I, i

I pron ego.
iambic adj iambēus.
iambus n iambus m.
ice n glaciēs f.
icicle n stīria f.
icon n simulacrum nt.
icy adj glaciālis, gelidus.
idea n nōtiō f, nōtitia f, imāgō f; (Platonic) fōrma
  f; (expressed) sententia f; **conceive the ~ of**
  īnfōrmāre; **with the ~ that** eō cōnsiliō ut (+
  subj).
ideal adj animō comprehēnsus; (perfect)
  perfectus, optimus ♦ n specimen nt, speciēs
  f, exemplar nt.
identical adj īdem, cōnsimilis.
identify vt agnōscere.
identity n: **establish the ~ of** cognōscere quis
  sit.
Ides n Īdūs fpl.
idiocy n animī imbēcillitās f.

idiom *n* proprium *nt*, sermō *m*.
idiomatic *adj* proprius.
idiomatically *adv* sermōne suō, sermōne
  propriō.
idiosyncrasy *n* proprium *nt*, libīdō *f*.
idiot *n* excors *m*.
idiotic *adj* fatuus, stultus.
idiotically *adv* stultē, ineptē.
idle *adj* ignāvus, dēses, iners; (*unoccupied*)
  ōtiōsus, vacuus; (*useless*) inānis, vānus; **be ~**
  cessāre, dēsidēre; **lie ~** (*money*) iacēre ♦ *vi*
  cessāre.
idleness *n* ignāvia *f*, dēsidia *f*, inertia *f*; ōtium
  nt.
idler *n* cessātor *m*.
idly *adv* ignāvē; ōtiōsē; frustrā, nēquīquam.
idol *n* simulacrum *nt*; (*person*) dēliciae *fpl*.
idolater *n* falsōrum deōrum cultor *m*.
idolatry *n* falsōrum deōrum cultus *m*.
idolize *vt* venerārī.
idyll *n* carmen Theocrītēum *nt*.
if *conj* sī; (*interrog*) num, utrum; **~ anyone** sī
  quis; **~ ever** sī quandō; **~ not** nisī; **~ only** dum,
  dummodo; **~ ... or** sīve ... sīve; **as ~** quasi,
  velut; **but ~** sīn, quodsī; **even ~** etiamsī.
igneous *adj* igneus.
ignite *vt* accendere, incendere ♦ *vi* ignem
  concipere.
ignoble *adj* (*birth*) ignōbilis; (*repute*)
  illīberālis, turpis.
ignominious *adj* ignōminiōsus, īnfāmis,
  turpis.
ignominiously *adv* turpiter.
ignominy *n* ignōminia *f*, īnfāmia *f*, dēdecus *nt*.
ignoramus *n* idiōta *m*, indoctus *m*.
ignorance *n* īnscītia *f*, ignōrātiō *f*.
ignorant *adj* ignārus, indoctus; (*of something*)
  īnscītus, rudis; (*unaware*) īnscius; **be ~ of**
  nescīre, ignōrāre.
ingorantly *adv* īnscienter, īnscītē, indoctē.
ignore *vt* praetermittere.
ilex *n* īlex *f*.
Iliad *n* Ilias *f*.
ill *adj* aeger, aegrōtus, invalidus; (*evil*) malus;
  be ~ aegrōtāre; **fall ~** in morbum incidere; **~
  at ease** sollicitus ♦ *adv* male, improbē ♦ *n*
  malum *nt*, incommodum *nt*, aerumna *f*,
  damnum *nt*.
ill-advised *adj* incōnsultus.
ill-bred *adj* agrestis, inurbānus.
ill-disposed *adj* malevolus, invidus.
illegal *adj* illicitus, vetitus.
illegally *adv* contrā lēgēs.
ill-fated *adj* īnfēlīx.
ill-favoured *adj* turpis.
ill-gotten *adj* male partus.
ill-health *n* valētūdō *f*.
illicit *adj* vetitus.
illimitable *adj* īnfīnītus.
illiteracy *n* litterārum īnscītia *f*.
illiterate *adj* illitterātus, inērudītus.
ill-natured *adj* malevolus, malignus.
illness *n* morbus *m*, valētūdō *f*.

illogical *adj* absurdus.
ill-omened *adj* dīrus, īnfaustus.
ill-starred *adj* īnfēlīx.
ill-tempered *adj* īrācundus, amārus,
  stomachōsus.
ill-timed *adj* immātūrus, intempestīvus.
ill-treat *vt* malefacere (*dat*).
illuminate *vt* illūmināre, illūstrāre.
illumination *n* lūmina *ntpl*.
illusion *n* error *m*, somnium *nt*.
illusive, illusory *adj* fallāx.
illustrate *vt* illūstrāre; (*with instances*)
  exemplō cōnfirmāre.
illustration *n* exemplum *nt*.
illustrious *adj* illūstris, īnsignis, praeclārus.
illustriously *adv* praeclārē.
ill will *n* invidia *f*.
image *n* imāgō *f*, effigiēs *f*; (*idol*) simulacrum
  nt; (*verbal*) figūra *f*, similitūdō *f*.
imagery *n* figūrae *fpl*.
imaginary *adj* commentīcius, fictus.
imagination *n* cōgitātiō *f*, opīnātiō *f*.
imaginative *adj* ingeniōsus.
imagine *vt* animō fingere, animum indūcere,
  ante oculōs pōnere; (*think*) opīnārī, arbitrārī.
imbecile *adj* animō imbēcillus, fatuus, mente
  captus.
imbecility *n* animī imbēcillitās *f*.
imbibe *vt* adbibere; (*fig*) imbuī (*abl*).
imbrue *vt* īnficere.
imbue *vt* imbuere, īnficere, tingere.
imitable *adj* imitābilis.
imitate *vt* imitārī.
imitation *n* imitātiō *f*; (*copy*) imāgō *f*.
imitator *n* imitātor *m*, imitātrix *f*, aemulātor
  m.
immaculate *adj* integer, ēmendātus.
immaculately *adv* integrē, sine vitiō.
immaterial *adj* indifferēns.
immature *adj* immātūrus.
immeasurable *adj* immēnsus, īnfīnītus.
immediate *adj* īnstāns, praesēns; (*neighbour*)
  proximus.
immediately *adv* statim, extemplō,
  cōnfestim.
immemorial *adj* antīquissimus; **from time ~**
  post hominum memoriam.
immense *adj* immēnsus, immānis, ingēns,
  vastus.
immensely *adv* vehementer.
immensity *n* immēnsum *nt*, māgnitūdō *f*.
immerse *vt* immergere, mergere.
immigrant *n* advena *m*.
immigrate *vi* migrāre.
imminent *adj* īnstāns, praesēns; **be ~**
  imminēre, impendēre.
immobile *adj* fīxus, immōbilis.
immoderate *adj* immoderātus, immodestus.
immoderately *adv* immoderātē, immodestē.
immodest *adj* impudīcus, inverēcundus.
immolate *vt* immolāre.
immoral *adj* prāvus, corruptus, turpis.
immorality *n* corruptī mōrēs *mpl*, turpitūdō *f*.

immorally *adv* prāvē, turpiter.
immortal *adj* immortālis, aeternus.
immortality *n* immortālitās *f*.
immortalize *vt* in astra tollere.
immortally *adv* aeternum.
immovable *adj* fīxus, immōbilis.
immune *adj* immūnis, vacuus.
immunity *n* immūnitās *f*, vacātiō *f*.
immure *vt* inclūdere.
immutability *n* immūtābilitās *f*.
immutable *adj* immūtābilis.
imp *n* puer improbus *m*.
impact *n* ictus *m*, incussus *m*.
impair *vt* imminuere, corrumpere.
impale *vt* induere, īnfīgere.
impalpable *adj* tenuissimus.
impart *vt* impertīre, commūnicāre; (*courage*) addere.
impartial *adj* aequus, medius.
impartiality *n* aequābilitās *f*.
impartially *adv* sine favōre.
impassable *adj* invius; (*mountains*) inexsuperābilis; (*fig*) inexplicābilis.
impasse *n* mora *f*, incitae *fpl*.
impassioned *adj* ārdēns, fervidus.
impassive *adj* rigidus, sēnsū carēns.
impatience *n* aviditās *f*; (*of anything*) impatientia *f*.
impatient *adj* trepidus, avidus; impatiēns.
impatiently *adv* aegrē.
impeach *vt* diem dīcere (*dat*), accūsāre.
impeachment *n* accūsātiō *f*, crīmen *nt*.
impeccable *adj* ēmendātus.
impecunious *adj* pauper.
impede *vt* impedīre, obstāre (*dat*).
impediment *n* impedīmentum *nt*.
impel *vt* impellere, incitāre.
impend *vi* impendēre, imminēre, īnstāre.
impenetrable *adj* impenetrābilis; (*country*) invius, impervius.
impenitent *adj*: **I am ~** nīl mē paenitet.
imperative *adj* necessārius.
imperceptible *adj* tenuissimus, obscurus.
imperceptibly *adv* sēnsim.
imperfect *adj* imperfectus, vitiōsus.
imperfection *n* vitium *nt*.
imperfectly *adv* vitiōsē.
imperial *adj* imperātōrius, rēgius.
imperil *vt* in discrīmen addūcere, labefactāre.
imperious *adj* imperiōsus, superbus.
imperiously *adv* superbē.
imperishable *adj* immortālis, aeternus.
impersonate *vt* partēs agere (*gen*).
impertinence *n* importūnitās *f*, protervitās *f*.
impertinent *adj* importūnus, protervus, ineptus.
impertinently *adv* importūnē, ineptē, protervē.
imperturbable *adj* immōtus, gravis.
impervious *adj* impervius, impenetrābilis.
impetuosity *n* ārdor *m*, violentia *f*, vīs *f*.
impetuous *adj* violēns, fervidus, effrēnātus.
impetuously *adv* effrēnātē.

impetus *n* impetus *m*.
impiety *n* impietās *f*.
impinge *vi* incidere.
impious *adj* impius, profānus; **it is ~** nefas est.
impiously *adv* impiē.
impish *adj* improbus.
implacable *adj* implācābilis, inexōrābilis, dūrus.
implacably *adv* dūrē.
implant *vt* īnserere, ingignere.
implement *n* īnstrūmentum *nt* ♦ *vt* implēre, exsequī.
implicate *vt* implicāre, impedīre.
implication *n* indicium *nt*.
implicit *adj* tacitus; absolūtus.
implicitly *adv* absconditē; (*trust*) omnīnō, summā fidē.
implore *vt* implōrāre, obsecrāre.
imply *vt* significāre, continēre; **be ~ied** inesse.
impolite *adj* inurbānus, illepidus.
impolitely *adv* inurbānē.
impolitic *adj* incōnsultus, imprūdēns.
imponderable *adj* levissimus.
import *vt* importāre, invehere; (*mean*) velle ♦ *n* significātiō *f*.
importance *n* gravitās *f*, mōmentum *nt*; (*rank*) dignitās *f*, amplitūdō *f*, auctōritās *f*; **it is of great ~ to me** meā māgnī rēfert.
important *adj* gravis, magnī mōmentī; **it is ~ interest** (+ *gen*) rēfert; **more ~, most ~** antīquior, antīquissimus.
importation *n* invectiō *f*.
imports *npl* importātīcia *ntpl*.
importunate *adj* molestus.
importune *vt* flāgitāre, īnstāre (*dat*).
impose *vt* impōnere; (*by order*) indīcere, iniungere; **~ upon** illūdere, fraudāre, abūtī (*abl*).
imposing *adj* māgnificus, lautus.
imposition *n* fraus *f*; (*tax*) tribūtum *nt*.
impossible *adj*: **it is ~** fierī nōn potest.
impost *n* tribūtum *nt*, vectīgal *nt*.
impostor *n* planus *m*, fraudātor *m*.
imposture *n* fraus *f*, fallācia *f*.
impotence *n* īnfirmitās *f*.
impotent *adj* īnfirmus, dēbilis; (*with rage*) impotēns.
impotently *adv* frustrā; (*rage*) impotenter.
impound *vt* inclūdere; (*confiscate*) pūblicāre.
impoverish *vt* in inopiam redigere.
impracticable *adj*: **be ~** fierī nōn posse.
imprecate *vt* exsecrārī.
imprecation *n* exsecrātiō *f*.
impregnable *adj* inexpugnābilis.
impregnate *vt* imbuere, īnficere.
impress *vt* imprimere; (*on mind*) īnfīgere; (*person*) permovēre; (*MIL*) invītum scrībere.
impression *n* (*copy*) exemplar *nt*; (*mark*) signum *nt*; (*feeling*) impulsiō *f*; (*belief*) opīnātiō *f*; **make an ~ of** exprimere; **make an ~ on** commovēre; **have the ~** opīnārī.
impressionable *adj* crēdulus.
impressive *adj* gravis.

impressively *adv* graviter.
impressiveness *n* gravitās *f.*
imprint *n* impressiō *f*, signum *nt* ♦ *vt* imprimere; (*on mind*) īnfīgere, inūrere.
imprison *vt* inclūdere, in vincula conicere.
imprisonment *n* custōdia *f*, vincula *ntpl.*
improbable *adj* incrēdibilis, haud vērīsimilis.
impromptu *adv* ex tempore.
improper *adj* indecōrus, ineptus.
improperly *adv* prāvē, perperam.
impropriety *n* culpa *f*, offēnsa *f.*
improve *vt* ēmendāre, corrigere; (*mind*) excolere ♦ *vi* prōficere, meliōrem fierī.
improvement *n* ēmendātiō *f*, prōfectus *m.*
improvident *adj* imprōvidus; (*with money*) prōdigus.
improvidently *adv* imprōvidē; prōdigē.
improvise *vt* ex tempore compōnere, excōgitāre.
imprudence *n* imprūdentia *f.*
imprudent *adj* imprūdēns.
imprudently *adv* imprūdenter.
impudence *n* impudentia *f*, audācia *f.*
impudent *adj* impudēns, audāx.
impudently *adv* impudenter, protervē.
impugn *vt* impugnāre, in dubium vocāre.
impulse *n* impetus *m*, impulsus *m.*
impulsive *adj* praeceps, violentus.
impulsively *adv* impetū quōdam animī.
impulsiveness *n* impetus *m*, violentia *f.*
impunity *n* impūnitās *f*; **with ~** impūne.
impure *adj* impūrus, incestus, inquinātus.
impurely *adv* impūrē, incestē, inquinātē.
impurity *n* impūritās *f*, sordēs *fpl.*
imputation *n* crīmen *nt.*
impute *vt* attribuere, adsignāre; **~ as a fault** vitiō vertere.
in *prep* in (*abl*); (*with motion*) in (*acc*); (*authors*) apud (*acc*); (*time*) *abl*; **~ doing this** dum hoc faciō; **~ my youth** adulēscēns; **~ that** quod ♦ *adv* (*rest*) intrā; (*motion*) intrō.
inaccessible *adj* inaccessus.
inaccuracy *n* neglegentia *f*, incūria *f*; (*error*) mendum *nt.*
inaccurate *adj* parum dīligēns, neglegēns.
inaccurately *adv* neglegenter.
inaction *n* inertia *f.*
inactive *adj* iners, quiētus; **be ~** cessāre.
inactivity *n* inertia *f*, ōtium *nt.*
inadequate *adj* impār, parum idōneus.
inadequately *adv* parum.
inadvertency *n* imprūdentia *f.*
inadvertent *adj* imprūdēns.
inadvertently *adv* imprūdenter.
inane *adj* inānis, vānus; ineptus, stultus.
inanely *adv* ineptē.
inanimate *adj* inanimus.
inanity *n* ineptiae *fpl*, stultitia *f.*
inapplicable *adj*: **be ~** nōn valēre.
inappropriate *adj* aliēnus, parum aptus.
inarticulate *adj* īnfāns.
inartistic *adj* sine arte, dūrus, inēlegāns.
inasmuch as *conj* quōniam, cum (*subj*).

inattention *n* incūria *f*, neglegentia *f.*
inattentive *adj* neglegēns.
inattentively *adv* neglegenter.
inaudible *adj*: **be ~** audīrī nōn posse.
inaugurate *vt* inaugurāre, cōnsecrāre.
inauguration *n* cōnsecrātiō *f.*
inauspicious *adj* īnfaustus, īnfēlix.
inauspiciously *adv* malīs ōminibus.
inborn *adj* innātus.
incalculable *adj* inaestimābilis.
incantation *n* carmen *nt.*
incapable *adj* inhabilis, indocilis; **be ~** nōn posse.
incapacitate *vt* dēbilitāre.
incapacity *n* inertia *f*, īnscītia *f.*
incarcerate *vt* inclūdere, in vincula conicere.
incarnate *adj* hūmānā speciē indūtus.
incautious *adj* incautus, temerārius.
incautiously *adv* incautē.
incendiary *adj* incendiārius.
incense *n* tūs *nt* ♦ *vt* inrītāre, stomachum movēre (*dat*); **be ~d** stomachārī.
incentive *n* incitāmentum *nt*, stimulus *m.*
inception *n* initium *nt*, exōrdium *nt.*
incessant *adj* adsiduus.
incessantly *adv* adsiduē.
incest *n* incestus *m.*
inch *n* digitus *m*, ūncia *f.*
incident *n* ēventum *nt*, cāsus *m*, rēs *f.*
incidental *adj* fortuītus.
incidentally *adv* cāsū.
incipient *adj* prīmus.
incisive *adj* ācer.
incite *vt* īnstīgāre, impellere, hortārī, incitāre.
incitement *n* invītāmentum *nt*, stimulus *m.*
inciter *n* īnstimulātor *m.*
incivility *n* importūnitās *f*, inhūmānitās *f.*
inclemency *n* (*weather*) intemperiēs *f.*
inclement *adj* asper, tristis.
inclination *n* inclīnātiō *f*, animus *m*, libīdō *f*; (*slope*) clīvus *m.*
incline *vt* inclīnāre; (*person*) indūcere ♦ *vi* inclīnāre, incumbere; **~ towards** sē adclīnāre ♦ *n* adclīvitās *f*, clīvus *m.*
inclined *adj* inclīnātus, prōpēnsus; **I am ~ to think** haud sciō an.
include *vt* inclūdere, continēre, complectī.
incognito *adv* clam.
incoherent *adj* interruptus; **be ~** nōn cohaerēre.
income *n* fructus *m*, mercēs *f.*
incommensurate *adj* dispār.
incommode *vt* molestiam adferre (*dat*).
incomparable *adj* singulāris, eximius.
incompatibility *n* discrepantia *f*, repugnantia *f.*
incompatible *adj* īnsociābilis, repugnāns; **be ~ with** dissidēre ab, repugnāre (*dat*).
incompetence *n* inertia *f*, īnscītia *f.*
incompetent *adj* iners, īnscītus.
incomplete *adj* imperfectus.
incomprehensible *adj* incrēdibilis.

inconceivable adj incrēdibilis.
inconclusive adj inānis.
incongruous adj absonus, aliēnus.
inconsiderable adj exiguus.
inconsiderate adj imprōvidus, incōnsultus.
inconsistency n discrepantia f, incōnstantia f.
inconsistent adj incōnstāns; **be ~** discrepāre;
be ~ with abhorrēre ab, repugnāre (dat).
inconsistently adv incōnstanter.
inconsolable adj nōn cōnsōlābilis.
inconspicuous adj obscūrus; **be ~** latēre.
inconstancy n incōnstantia f, levitās f.
inconstant adj incōnstāns, levis, mōbilis.
inconstantly adv incōnstanter.
incontestable adj certus.
incontinence n incontinentia f.
incontinent adj intemperāns.
inconvenience n incommodum nt ♦ vt
    incommodāre.
inconvenient adj incommodus.
inconveniently adv incommodē.
incorporate vt īnserere, adiungere.
incorrect adj falsus; **be ~** nōn cōnstāre.
incorrectly adv falsō, perperam.
incorrigible adj improbus, perditus.
incorruptibility n integritās f.
incorruptible adj incorruptus.
increase n incrēmentum nt, additāmentum nt,
    auctus m ♦ vt augēre, amplificāre ♦ vi
    crēscere, incrēscere.
increasingly adv magis magisque.
incredible adj incrēdibilis.
incredibly adv incrēdibiliter.
incredulous adj incrēdulus.
increment n incrēmentum nt.
incriminate vt crīminārī.
inculcate vt inculcāre, īnfīgere.
incumbent adj: **it is ~ on** oportet.
incur vt subīre; (guilt) admittere.
incurable adj īnsānābilis.
incursion n incursiō f.
indebted adj obnoxius; **be ~** dēbēre.
indecency n obscēnitās f.
indecent adj obscēnus, impudīcus.
indecently adv obscēnē.
indecision n dubitātiō f.
indecisive adj anceps, dubius; **the battle is ~**
    ancipitī Marte pugnātur.
indecisively adv incertō ēventū.
indecorous adj indecōrus.
indeed adv profectō, sānē; (concessive)
    quidem; (interrog) itane vērō?; (reply) certē,
    vērō; (with pron) dēmum; (with adj, adv, conj)
    adeō.
indefatigable adj impiger.
indefensible adj: **be ~** dēfendī nōn posse;
    (belief) tenērī nōn posse; (offence) excūsārī
    nōn posse.
indefinite adj incertus, ambiguus, īnfīnītus.
indefinitely adv ambiguē; (time) in incertum.
indelicate adj pūtidus, indecōrus.
independence n lībertās f.
independent adj līber, suī iūris.

indescribable adj inēnārrābilis.
indestructible adj perennis.
indeterminate adj incertus.
index n index m.
indicate vt indicāre, significāre.
indication n indicium nt, signum nt.
indict vt diem dīcere (dat), accūsāre, nōmen
    dēferre (gen).
indictment n accūsātiō f.
indifference n neglegentia f, languor m.
indifferent adj (manner) neglegēns, frīgidus,
    sēcūrus; (quality) mediocris.
indifferently adv neglegenter; mediocriter;
    (without distinction) promiscuē, sine
    discrīmine.
indigence n indigentia f, egestās f.
indigenous adj indigena.
indigent adj indigēns, egēnus.
indigestible adj crūdus.
indigestion n crūditās f.
indignant adj indignābundus, īrātus; **be ~**
    indignārī.
indignantly adv īrātē.
indignation n indignātiō f, dolor m.
indignity n contumēlia f, indignitās f.
indigo n Indicum nt.
indirect adj oblīquus.
indirectly adv oblīquē, per ambāgēs.
indirectness n ambāgēs fpl.
indiscipline n lascīvia f, licentia f.
indiscreet adj incōnsultus, imprūdēns.
indiscreetly adv incōnsultē, imprūdenter.
indiscretion n imprūdentia f; (act) culpa f.
indiscriminate adj prōmiscuus.
indiscriminately adv prōmiscuē, sine
    discrīmine.
indispensable adj necesse, necessārius.
indisposed adj īnfirmus, aegrōtus, (will)
    āversus, aliēnātus; **be ~** aegrōtāre;
    abhorrēre, aliēnārī.
indisposition n īnfirmitās f, valētūdō f.
indisputable adj certus, manifestus.
indisputably adv certē, sine dubiō.
indissoluble adj indissolūbilis.
indistinct adj obscūrus, obtūsus; (speaker)
    balbus.
indistinctly adv obscūrē; **pronounce ~**
    opprimere; **speak ~** balbutīre.
individual adj proprius ♦ n homō m/f, prīvātus
    m; **~s** pl singulī mpl.
individuality n proprium nt.
individually adv singulātim, prīvātim.
indivisible adj indīviduus.
indolence n dēsidia f, ignāvia f, inertia f.
indolent adj dēses, ignāvus, iners.
indolently adv ignāvē.
indomitable adj indomitus.
indoor adj umbrātilis.
indoors adv intus; (motion) intrā.
indubitable adj certus.
indubitably adv sine dubiō.
induce vt indūcere, addūcere, persuādēre
    (dat).

inducement _n_ illecebra _f_, praemium _nt_.
induction _n_ (_logic_) inductiō _f_.
indulge _vt_ indulgēre (_dat_).
indulgence _n_ indulgentia _f_, venia _f_; (_favour_)
   grātia _f_.
indulgent _adj_ indulgēns, lēnis.
indulgently _adv_ indulgenter.
industrious _adj_ industrius, impiger, dīligēns.
industriously _adv_ industriē.
industry _n_ industria _f_, dīligentia _f_, labor _m_.
inebriated _adj_ ēbrius.
inebriation _n_ ēbrietās _f_.
ineffable _adj_ eximius.
ineffective _adj_ inūtilis, invalidus.
ineffectively _adv_ ināniter.
ineffectual _adj_ inritus.
inefficient _adj_ īnscītus, parum strēnuus.
inelegant _adj_ inēlegāns, inconcinnus.
inelegantly _adv_ inēleganter.
inept _adj_ ineptus.
ineptly _adv_ ineptē.
inequality _n_ dissimilitūdō _f_, inīquitās _f_.
inert _adj_ iners, sōcors, immōbilis.
inertia _n_ inertia _f_.
inertly _adv_ tardē, lentē.
inestimable _adj_ inaestimābilis.
inevitable _adj_ necessārius.
inevitably _adv_ necessāriō.
inexact _adj_ parum subtīlis.
inexhaustible _adj_ perennis.
inexorable _adj_ inexōrābilis.
inexpediency _n_ inūtilitās _f_, incommodum _nt_.
inexpedient _adj_ inūtilis; **it is ~** nōn expedit.
inexpensive _adj_ vīlis.
inexperience _n_ imperītia _f_, īnscītia _f_.
inexperienced _adj_ imperītus, rudis, īnscītus.
inexpert _adj_ imperītus.
inexpiable _adj_ inexpiābilis.
inexplicable _adj_ inexplicābilis, inēnōdābilis.
inexpressible _adj_ inēnārrābilis.
inextricable _adj_ inexplicābilis.
infallible _adj_ certus, errōris expers.
infamous _adj_ īnfāmis, flāgitiōsus.
infamously _adv_ flāgitiōsē.
infamy _n_ īnfāmia _f_, flāgitium _nt_, dēdecus _nt_.
infancy _n_ īnfantia _f_; (_fig_) incūnābula _ntpl_.
infant _n_ īnfāns _m/f_.
infantile _adj_ puerīlis.
infantry _n_ peditēs _mpl_, peditātus _m_.
infantryman _n_ pedes _m_.
infatuate _vt_ īnfatuāre.
infatuated _adj_ dēmēns.
infatuation _n_ dēmentia _f_.
infect _vt_ īnficere.
infection _n_ contāgiō _f_.
infer _vt_ īnferre, colligere.
inference _n_ conclūsiō _f_.
inferior _adj_ (_position_) īnferior; (_quality_)
   dēterior.
infernal _adj_ īnfernus.
infest _vt_ frequentāre.
infidel _adj_ impius.
infidelity _n_ perfidia _f_, īnfidēlitās _f_.

infiltrate _vi_ sē īnsinuāre.
infinite _adj_ īnfīnītus, immēnsus.
infinitely _adv_ longē, immēnsum.
infinitesimal _adj_ minimus.
infinity _n_ īnfīnitās _f_.
infirm _adj_ īnfirmus, invalidus.
infirmary _n_ valētūdinārium _nt_.
infirmity _n_ morbus _m_.
inflame _vt_ accendere, incendere, īnflammāre.
   be ~d exārdēscere.
inflammation _n_ (_MED_) īnflātiō _f_.
inflate _vt_ īnflāre.
inflated _adj_ (_fig_) īnflātus, tumidus.
inflexible _adj_ rigidus.
inflexion _n_ (_GRAM_) flexūra _f_; (_voice_) flexiō _f_.
inflict _vt_ īnflīgere, incutere; (_burden_)
   impōnere; (_penalty_) sūmere; **be ~ed with**
   labōrāre ex.
infliction _n_ poena _f_; malum _nt_.
influence _n_ (_physical_) impulsiō _f_, mōmentum
   _nt_; (_moral_) auctōritās _f_; (_partial_) grātia _f_; **have**
   ~ ~ valēre; **have great ~ with** plūrimum posse
   apud; **under the ~ of** īnstinctus (_abl_) ♦ _vt_
   impellere, movēre, addūcere.
influential _adj_ gravis, potēns; grātiōsus.
influenza _n_ gravēdō _f_.
inform _vt_ docēre, certiōrem facere; **~ against**
   nōmen dēferre (_gen_).
informant _n_ index _m_, auctor _m_.
information _n_ indicium _nt_, nūntius _m_.
informer _n_ index _m_, dēlātor _m_; **turn ~** indicium
   profitērī.
infrequent _adj_ rārus.
infrequently _adv_ rārō.
infringe _vt_ violāre, imminuere.
infringement _n_ violātiō _f_.
infuriate _vt_ efferāre.
infuriated _adj_ furibundus.
infuse _vt_ īnfundere; (_fig_) inicere.
ingenious _adj_ ingeniōsus, callidus; (_thing_)
   artificiōsus.
ingeniously _adv_ callidē, summā arte.
ingenuity _n_ ars _f_, artificium _nt_, acūmen _nt_.
ingenuous _adj_ ingenuus, simplex.
ingenuously _adv_ ingenuē, simpliciter.
ingenuousness _n_ ingenuitās _f_.
ingle _n_ focus _m_.
inglorious _adj_ inglōrius, ignōbilis, inhonestus.
ingloriously _adv_ sine glōriā, inhonestē.
ingot _n_ later _m_.
ingrained _adj_ īnsitus.
ingratiate _vt_: **~ oneself with** grātiam inīre ab,
   sē īnsinuāre in familiāritātem (_gen_); **~**
   oneself into sē īnsinuāre in (_acc_).
ingratitude _n_ ingrātus animus _m_.
ingredient _n_ pars _f_.
inhabit _vt_ incolere, habitāre in (_abl_).
inhabitable _adj_ habitābilis.
inhabitant _n_ incola _m/f_.
inhale _vt_ haurīre.
inharmonious _adj_ dissonus.
inherent _adj_ īnsitus; **be ~ in** inhaerēre (_dat_),
   inesse (_dat_).

inherently *adv* nātūrā.
inherit *vt* excipere.
inheritance *n* hērēditās *f*, patrimōnium *nt*;
divide an ~ herctum ciēre; **come into an ~**
hērēditātem adīre.
inheritor *n* hērēs *m/f*.
inhibit *vt* prohibēre, inhibēre.
inhospitable *adj* inhospitālis.
inhuman *adj* inhūmānus, immānis, crūdēlis.
inhumanity *n* inhūmānitās *f*, crūdēlitās *f*.
inhumanly *adv* inhūmānē, crūdēliter.
inimical *adj* inimīcus.
inimitable *adj* singulāris, eximius.
iniquitous *adj* inīquus, improbus, nefārius.
iniquity *n* scelus *nt*, flāgitium *nt*.
initial *adj* prīmus.
initiate *vt* initiāre; (*with knowledge*) imbuere.
initiative *n* initium *nt*; **take the ~** initium
capere, facere; occupāre (*inf*).
inject *vt* inicere.
injudicious *adj* incōnsultus, imprūdēns.
injunction *n* iussum *nt*, praeceptum *nt*.
injure *vt* laedere, nocēre (*dat*).
injurious *adj* damnōsus, nocēns.
injury *n* iniūria *f*, damnum *nt*; (*bodily*) vulnus
nt.
injustice *n* iniūria *f*, inīquitās *f*.
ink *n* ātrāmentum *nt*.
inkling *n* audītiō *f*, suspiciō *f*.
inland *adj* mediterrāneus; **further ~** interior.
inlay *vt* īnserere.
inlet *n* sinus *m*, aestuārium *nt*.
inly *adv* penitus.
inmate *n* inquilīnus *m*.
inmost *adj* intimus.
inn *n* dēversōrium *nt*; caupōna *f*, taberna *f*.
innate *adj* innātus, īnsitus.
inner *adj* interior.
innermost *adj* intimus.
innkeeper *n* caupō *m*.
innocence *n* innocentia *f*.
innocent *adj* innocēns, īnsōns; (*character*)
integer, castus.
innocently *adv* innocenter, integrē, castē.
innocuous *adj* innoxius.
innovate *vt* novāre.
innovation *n* novum *nt*, nova rēs *f*.
innovator *n* novārum rērum auctor *m*.
innuendo *n* verbum inversum *nt*.
innumerable *adj* innumerābilis.
inoffensive *adj* innocēns.
inoffensively *adv* innocenter.
inopportune *adj* intempestīvus.
inopportunely *adv* intempestīvē.
inordinate *adj* immodicus, immoderātus.
inordinately *adv* immoderātē.
inquest *n* quaestiō *f*; **hold an ~ on** quaerere dē.
inquire *vi* exquīrere, rogāre; **~ into** inquīrere
in (*acc*), investigāre.
inquiry *n* quaestiō *f*, investigātiō *f*; (*asking*)
interrogātiō *f*; **make ~** exquīrere; **make ~ies**
about inquīrere in (*acc*); **hold an ~ on**
quaerere dē, quaestiōnem īnstituere dē.

inquisition *n* inquīsītiō *f*.
inquisitive *adj* cūriōsus.
inquisitiveness *n* cūriōsitās *f*.
inquisitor *n* inquīsītor *m*.
inroad *n* incursiō *f*, impressiō *f*; **make an ~**
incursāre.
insane *adj* īnsānus, mente captus; **be ~**
īnsānīre.
insanity *n* īnsānia *f*, dēmentia *f*.
insatiable *adj* īnsatiābilis, inexplēbilis,
īnsaturābilis.
insatiably *adv* īnsaturābiliter.
inscribe *vt* īnscrībere.
inscription *n* epigramma *nt*; (*written*)
īnscrīptiō *f*.
inscrutable *adj* obscūrus.
insect *n* bestiola *f*.
insecure *adj* īnstabilis, intūtus.
insecurity *n* perīcula *ntpl*.
insensate *adj* ineptus, stultus.
insensible *adj* torpidus; (*fig*) dūrus.
insensitive *adj* dūrus.
inseparable *adj* coniūnctus; **be the ~**
companion of ab latere esse (*gen*).
inseparably *adv* coniūnctē.
insert *vt* īnserere, immittere, interpōnere.
insertion *n* interpositiō *f*.
inshore *adv* prope lītus.
inside *adv* intus; (*motion*) intrō ♦ *adj* interior ♦
n pars *f* interior ♦ *prep* intrā (*acc*); **get right ~**
sē īnsinuāre in (*acc*); **turn ~ out** excutere; **on**
the ~ interior.
insidious *adj* īnsidiōsus, subdolus.
insidiously *adv* īnsidiōsē.
insight *n* intellegentia *f*, cognitiō *f*.
insignia *n* īnsignia *ntpl*.
insignificance *n* levitās *f*.
insignificant *adj* levis, exiguus, nullīus
mōmentī; (*position*) humilis.
insincere *adj* simulātus, fūcōsus.
insincerely *adv* simulātē.
insincerity *n* simulātiō *f*, fraus *f*.
insinuate *vt* īnsinuāre; (*hint*) significāre ♦ *vi*
sē īnsinuāre.
insinuating *adj* blandus.
insinuation *n* ambigua verba *ntpl*.
insipid *adj* īnsulsus, frīgidus.
insipidity *n* īnsulsitās *f*.
insist *vi* īnstāre; **~ on** postulāre.
insistence *n* pertinācia *f*.
insistent *adj* pertināx.
insolence *n* īnsolentia *f*, contumācia *f*,
superbia *f*.
insolent *adj* īnsolēns, contumāx, superbus.
insolently *adv* īnsolenter.
insoluble *adj* inexplicābilis.
insolvency *n* reī familiāris naufragium *nt*.
insolvent *adj*: **be ~** solvendō nōn esse.
inspect *vt* īnspicere; (*MIL*) recēnsēre.
inspection *n* cognitiō *f*; (*MIL*) recēnsiō *f*.
inspector *n* cūrātor *m*.
inspiration *n* adflātus *m*, īnstinctus *m*.
inspire *vt* īnstinguere, incendere.

instability n mōbilitās f.
install vt inaugurāre.
instalment n pēnsiō f.
instance n exemplum nt; **for ~** exemplī causā, grātiā; **at the ~** admonitū; **at my ~** mē auctōre ♦ vt memorāre.
instant adj īnstāns, praesēns ♦ n temporis pūnctum nt, mōmentum nt.
instantaneous adj praesēns.
instantaneously adv continuō, īlicō.
instantly adv īlicō, extemplō.
instead of prep prō (abl), locō (gen); (with verb) nōn . . . sed.
instigate vt īnstīgāre, impellere.
instigation n impulsus m, stimulus m; auctōritās f; **at my ~** mē auctōre.
instigator n īnstimulātor m, auctor m.
instil vt imbuere, adspīrāre, inicere.
instinct n nātūra f, ingenium nt, sēnsus m.
instinctive adj nātūrālis.
instinctively adv nātūrā, ingeniō suō.
institute vt īnstituere, inaugurāre.
institution n īnstitūtum nt; societās f.
instruct vt docēre, īnstituere, īnstruere; ērudīre; (order) praecipere (dat).
instruction n doctrīna f, disciplīna f; praeceptum nt; **give ~s** dēnūntiāre, praecipere.
instructor n doctor m, praeceptor m.
instructress n magistra f.
instrument n īnstrūmentum nt; (music) fidēs fpl; (legal) tabulae fpl.
instrumental adj ūtilis.
instrumentalist n fidicen m, fidicina f.
instrumentality n opera f.
insubordinate adj turbulentus, sēditiōsus.
insubordination n intemperantia f, licentia f.
insufferable adj intolerandus, intolerābilis.
insufficiency n inopia f.
insufficient adj minor; **be ~** nōn sufficere.
insufficiently adv parum.
insulate vt sēgregāre.
insult n iniūria f, contumēlia f, probrum nt ♦ vt maledīcere (dat), contumēliam impōnere (dat).
insulting adj contumēliōsus.
insultingly adv contumēliōsē.
insuperable adj inexsuperābilis.
insupportable adj intolerandus, intolerābilis.
insurance n cautiō f.
insure vi cavēre.
insurgent n rebellis m.
insurmountable adj inexsuperābilis.
insurrection n mōtus m, sēditiō f.
intact adj integer, intāctus, incolumis.
integrity n integritās f, innocentia f, fidēs f.
intellect n ingenium nt, mēns f, animus m.
intellectual adj ingeniōsus.
intelligence n intellegentia f, acūmen nt; (MIL) nūntius m.
intelligent adj ingeniōsus, sapiēns, argūtus.
intelligently adv ingeniōsē, sapienter, satis acūtē.

intelligible adj perspicuus, apertus.
intemperance n intemperantia f, licentia f.
intemperate adj intemperāns, intemperātus.
intemperately adv intemperanter.
intend vt (with inf) in animō habēre, velle; (with object) dēstināre.
intense adj ācer, nimius.
intensely adv valdē, nimium.
intensify vt augēre, amplificāre; **be ~ied** ingravēscere.
intensity n vīs f.
intensive adj ācer, multus, adsiduus.
intensively adv summō studiō.
intent adj ērēctus, intentus; **be ~ on** animum intendere in (acc) ♦ n cōnsilium nt; **with ~** cōnsultō.
intention n cōnsilium nt, prōpositum nt; **it is my ~** mihī in animō est; **with the ~ of** eā mente, eō cōnsiliō ut (subj).
intentionally adv cōnsultō, dē industriā.
inter vt humāre.
intercalary adj intercalāris.
intercalate vt intercalāre.
intercede vi intercēdere, dēprecārī.
intercept vt excipere, intercipere; (cut off) interclūdere.
intercession n dēprecātiō f; (tribune's) intercessiō f.
intercessor n dēprecātor m.
interchange vt permūtāre ♦ n permūtātiō f, vicissitūdō f.
intercourse n commercium nt, ūsus m, cōnsuētūdō f.
interdict n interdictum nt ♦ vt interdīcere (dat), vetāre.
interest n (advantage) commodum nt; (study) studium nt; (money) faenus nt, ūsūra f; **compound ~** anatocismus m; **rate of ~** faenus nt; **~ at 12 per cent (per annum)** centēsimae fpl; **it is of ~** interest; **it is in my ~s** meā interest; **consult the ~s of** cōnsulere (dat); **take an ~ in** animum intendere (dat) ♦ vt dēlectāre, capere; (audience) tenēre; **~ oneself in** studēre (dat).
interested adj attentus; (for gain) ambitiōsus.
interesting adj iūcundus, novus.
interfere vi intervenīre: (with) sē interpōnere (dat), sē admiscēre ad; (hinder) officere (dat).
interference n interventus m, intercessiō f.
interim n: **in the ~** interim, intereā.
interior adj interior ♦ n pars interior f; (country) interiōra ntpl.
interject vt exclāmāre.
interjection n interiectiō f.
interlace vt intexere.
interlard vt variāre.
interlock vt implicāre.
interloper n interpellātor m.
interlude n embolium nt.
intermarriage n cōnūbium nt.
intermediary adj medius ♦ n internūntius m.
intermediate adj medius.
interment n humātiō f.

interminable *adj* sempiternus, longus.
intermingle *vt* intermiscēre ♦ *vi* sē immiscēre.
intermission *n* intercapēdō *f*, intermissiō *f*.
intermittent *adj* interruptus.
intermittently *adv* interdum.
intern *vt* inclūdere.
internal *adj* internus; (*POL*) domesticus.
internally *adv* intus, domī.
international *adj*: ~ **law** iūs gentium.
internecine *adj* internecīvus.
interplay *n* vicēs *fpl*.
interpolate *vt* interpolāre.
interpose *vt* interpōnere ♦ *vi* intercēdere.
interposition *n* intercessiō *f*.
interpret *vt* interpretārī.
interpretation *n* interpretātiō *f*.
interpreter *n* interpres *m/f*.
interrogate *vt* interrogāre, percontārī.
interrogation *n* interrogātiō *f*, percontātiō *f*.
interrupt *vt* (*action*) intercipere; (*speaker*) interpellāre; (*talk*) dirimere; (*continuity*) intermittere.
interrupter *n* interpellātor *m*.
interruption *n* interpellātiō *f*; intermissiō *f*.
intersect *vt* dīvidere, secāre.
intersperse *vt* distinguere.
interstice *n* rīma *f*.
intertwine *vt* intexere, implicāre.
interval *n* intervallum *nt*, spatium *nt*; **after an ~** spatiō interpositō; **after an ~ of a year** annō interiectō; **at ~s** interdum; **at frequent ~s** identidem; **leave an ~** intermittere.
intervene *vt* intercēdere, intervenīre.
intervention *n* intercessiō *f*, interventus *m*; **by the ~ of** intercursū (*gen*).
interview *n* colloquium *nt*, aditus *m* ♦ *vt* convenīre.
interweave *vt* implicāre, intexere.
intestate *adj* intestātus ♦ *adv* intestātō.
intestine *adj* intestīnus; (*POL*) domesticus ♦ *npl* intestīna *ntpl*; (*victim's*) exta *ntpl*.
intimacy *n* familiāritās *f*.
intimate *adj* familiāris; **be an ~ friend of** ab latere esse (*gen*); **a very ~ friend** perfamiliāris *m/f* ♦ *vt* dēnūntiāre.
intimately *adv* familiāriter.
intimation *n* dēnūntiātiō *f*; (*hint*) indicium *nt*.
intimidate *vt* minārī (*dat*), terrōrem inicere (*dat*).
intimidation *n* metus *m*, minae *fpl*.
into *prep* in (*acc*), intrā (*acc*).
intolerable *adj* intolerandus, intolerābilis.
intolerably *adv* intoleranter.
intolerance *n* impatientia *f*.
intolerant *adj* impatiēns, intolerāns.
intonation *n* sonus *m*, flexiō *f*.
intone *vt* cantāre.
intoxicate *vt* ēbrium reddere.
intoxicated *adj* ēbrius.
intoxication *n* ēbrietās *f*.
intractable *adj* indocilis, difficilis.
intransigent *adj* obstinātus.

intrepid *adj* intrepidus, impavidus.
intrepidity *n* audācia *f*, fortitūdō *f*.
intricacy *n* implicātiō *f*.
intricate *adj* implicātus, involūtus.
intricately *adv* implicitē.
intrigue *n* factiō *f*, artēs *fpl*, fallācia *f* ♦ *vi* māchinārī, fallāciīs ūtī.
intriguing *adj* factiōsus; blandus.
intrinsic *adj* vērus, innātus.
intrinsically *adv* per sē.
introduce *vt* indūcere, īnferre, importāre; (*acquaintance*) commendāre; (*custom*) īnstituere.
introduction *n* exōrdium *nt*, prooemium *nt*; (*of person*) commendātiō *f*; **letter of ~** litterae commendātīciae *fpl*.
intrude *vi* sē interpōnere, intervenīre.
intruder *n* interpellātor *m*, advena *m*; (*fig*) aliēnus *m*.
intrusion *n* interpellātiō *f*.
intuition *n* sēnsus *m*, cognitiō *f*.
inundate *vt* inundāre.
inundation *n* ēluviō *f*.
inure *vt* dūrāre, adsuēfacere.
invade *vt* invādere.
invalid *adj* aeger, dēbilis; (*null*) inritus.
invalidate *vt* īnfirmāre.
invaluable *adj* inaestimābilis.
invariable *adj* cōnstāns, immūtābilis.
invariably *adv* semper.
invasion *n* incursiō *f*.
invective *n* convīcium *nt*.
inveigh *vi*: ~ **against** invehī in (*acc*), īnsectārī.
inveigle *vt* illicere, pellicere.
invent *vt* fingere, comminīscī, invenīre.
invention *n* inventum *nt*; (*faculty*) inventiō *f*.
inventor *n* inventor *m*, auctor *m*.
inverse *adj* inversus.
inversely *adv* inversō ōrdine.
invert *vt* invertere.
invest *vt* (*in office*) inaugurāre; (*MIL*) obsidēre, circumsedēre; (*money*) locāre.
investigate *vt* investīgāre, indāgāre; (*case*) cognōscere.
investigation *n* investīgātiō *f*, indāgātiō *f*; (*case*) cognitiō *f*.
investment *n* (*MIL*) obsessiō *f*; (*money*) locāta pecūnia *f*.
inveterate *adj* inveterātus, vetus; **become ~** inveterāscere.
invidious *adj* invidiōsus.
invidiously *adv* invidiōsē.
invigorate *vt* recreāre, reficere.
invincible *adj* invictus.
inviolable *adj* inviolātus; (*person*) sacrōsanctus.
inviolably *adv* inviolātē.
inviolate *adj* integer.
invisible *adj* caecus; **be ~** vidērī nōn posse.
invitation *n* invītātiō *f*; **at the ~ of** invītātū (*gen*).
invite *vt* invītāre, vocāre.
inviting *adj* suāvis, blandus.

invitingly *adv* blandē, suāviter.
invocation *n* testātiō *f*.
invoke *vt* invocāre, testārī.
involuntarily *adv* īnscienter, invītus.
involuntary *adj* coāctus.
involve *vt* implicāre, involvere; **be ~d in** inligārī (*abl*).
invulnerable *adj* inviolābilis; **be ~** vulnerārī nōn posse.
inward *adj* interior.
inwardly *adv* intus.
inwards *adv* intrōrsus.
inweave *vt* intexere.
inwrought *adj* intextus.
irascibility *n* īrācundia *f*.
irascible *adj* īrācundus.
irate *adj* īrātus.
ire *n* īra *f*.
iris *n* hyacinthus *m*.
irk *vt* incommodāre; **I am ~ed** mē piget.
irksome *adj* molestus.
irksomeness *n* molestia *f*.
iron *n* ferrum *nt*; **of ~** ferreus ♦ *adj* ferreus.
ironical *adj* inversus.
ironically *adv* inversīs verbīs.
iron mine *n* ferrāria *f*.
ironmonger *n* negōtiātor ferrārius *m*.
ironmongery *n* ferrāmenta *ntpl*.
iron ore *n* ferrum īnfectum *nt*.
iron-tipped *adj* ferrātus.
irony *n* illūsiō *f*, verbōrum inversiō *f*, dissimulātiō *f*.
irradiate *vt* illūstrāre.
irrational *adj* absurdus, ratiōnis expers; (*animal*) brūtus.
irrationally *adv* absurdē, sine ratiōne.
irreconcilable *adj* repugnāns, īnsociābilis.
irrefutable *adj* certus, invictus.
irregular *adj* incompositus; (*ground*) inaequālis; (*meeting*) extraōrdinārius; (*troops*) tumultuārius.
irregularity *n* inaequālitās *f*; (*conduct*) prāvitās *f*, licentia *f*; (*election*) vitium *nt*.
irregularly *adv* nullō ōrdine; (*elected*) vitiō.
irrelevant *adj* aliēnus.
irreligion *n* impietās *f*.
irreligious *adj* impius.
irremediable *adj* īnsānābilis.
irreparable *adj* inrevocābilis.
irreproachable *adj* integer, innocēns.
irresistible *adj* invictus.
irresolute *adj* dubius, anceps.
irresolutely *adv* dubitanter.
irresolution *n* dubitātiō *f*.
irresponsibility *n* licentia *f*.
irresponsible *adj* lascīvus, levis.
irretrievable *adj* inrevocābilis.
irreverence *n* impietās *f*.
irreverent *adj* impius.
irreverently *adv* impiē.
irrevocable *adj* inrevocābilis.
irrigate *vt* inrigāre.
irrigation *n* inrigātiō *f*.

irritability *n* īrācundia *f*.
irritable *adj* īrācundus.
irritate *vt* inrītāre, stomachum movēre (*dat*).
irritation *n* īrācundia *f*, stomachus *m*.
island *n* īnsula *f*.
islander *n* īnsulānus *m*.
isle *n* īnsula *f*.
isolate *vt* sēgregāre, sēparāre.
isolation *n* sōlitūdō *f*.
issue *n* (*result*) ēventus *m*, exitus *m*; (*children*) prōlēs *f*; (*question*) rēs *f*; (*book*) ēditiō *f*; **decide the ~** dēcernere, dēcertāre; **the point at ~** quā dē rē agitur ♦ *vt* distribuere; (*book*) ēdere; (*announcement*) prōmulgāre; (*coin*) ērogāre ♦ *vi* ēgredī, ēmānāre; (*result*) ēvādere, ēvenīre.
isthmus *n* isthmus *m*.
it *pron* hōc, id.
itch *n* (*disease*) scabiēs *f*; (*fig*) cacoēthes *nt* ♦ *vi* prūrīre.
item *n* nōmen *nt*, rēs *f*.
iterate *vt* iterāre.
itinerant *adj* vāgus, circumforāneus.
itinerary *n* iter *nt*.
its *adj* suus, ēius.
itself *pron* ipse, ipsa, ipsum.
ivory *n* ebur *nt* ♦ *adj* eburneus.
ivy *n* hedera *f*.

J, j

jabber *vi* blaterāre.
jackdaw *n* grāculus *m*.
jaded *adj* dēfessus, fatīgātus.
jagged *adj* serrātus.
jail *n* carcer *m*.
jailer *n* custōs *m*, carcerārius *m*.
jam *vt* comprimere; (*way*) obstruere.
jamb *n* postis *m*.
jangle *vi* crepitāre; rixārī.
janitor *n* iānitor *m*.
January *n* mēnsis Iānuārius *m*; **of ~** Iānuārius.
jar *n* urna *f*; (*for wine*) amphora *f*; (*for water*) hydria *f*; (*sound*) offēnsa *f*; (*quarrel*) rixa *f* ♦ *vi* offendere.
jasper *n* iaspis *f*.
jaundice *n* morbus arquātus.
jaundiced *adj* ictericus.
jaunt *n*: **take a ~** excurrere.
jauntily *adv* hilare, festīvē.
jauntiness *n* hilaritās *f*.
jaunty *adj* hilaris, festīvus.
javelin *n* iaculum *nt*, pīlum *nt*; **throw the ~** iaculārī.
jaw *n* māla *f*; **~s** *pl* faucēs *fpl*.

jay n grāculus m.
jealous adj invidus; **be ~ of** invidēre (dat).
jealousy n invidia f.
jeer n irrīsiō f ♦ vi irrīdēre; **~ at** illūdere.
jejune adj iēiūnus, exīlis.
jeopardize vt in perīculum addūcere.
jeopardy n perīculum nt.
jerk n subitus mōtus m.
jest n iocus m.
jester n scurra m.
jet n (mineral) gagātēs m; (of water) saltus m ♦ vi salīre.
jetsam n ēiectāmenta ntpl.
jettison vt ēicere.
jetty n mōlēs f.
Jew n Iūdaeus.
jewel n gemma f.
Jewish adj Iūdaicus.
jig n tripudium nt.
jilt vt repudiāre.
jingle n nēnia f ♦ vi crepitāre, tinnīre.
job n opus nt.
jocose adj see **jocular**.
jocular adj facētus, ioculāris.
jocularity n facētiae fpl.
jocularly adv facētē, per iocum.
jocund adj hilaris, festīvus.
jog vt fodicāre; (fig) stimulāre ♦ vi ambulāre.
join vt iungere, coniungere, cōpulāre ♦ vi coniungī, sē coniungere; **~ in** interesse (dat), sē immiscēre (dat); **~ battle with** proelium committere (+ abl).
joiner n faber m.
joint adj commūnis ♦ n commissūra f; (of body) articulus m, nōdus m; **~ by ~** articulātim.
jointed adj geniculātus.
joint-heir n cohērēs m/f.
jointly adv ūnā, coniūnctē.
joist n tignum nt.
joke n iocus m ♦ vi iocārī, lūdere.
joking n iocus m; **~ apart** remōtō iocō.
jokingly adv per iocum.
jollity n hilaritās f, festīvitās f.
jolly adj hilaris, festīvus.
jolt vt iactāre.
jolting n iactātiō f.
jostle vt agitāre, offendere.
jot n minimum nt; **not a ~** nihil; **not care a ~** nōn floccī facere.
journal n ācta diūrna ntpl.
journey n iter nt.
journeyman n opifex m.
Jove n Iuppiter m.
jovial adj hilaris.
joviality n hilaritās f.
jovially adv hilare.
jowl n māla f; **cheek by ~** iuxtā.
joy n gaudium nt, laetitia f, alacritās f.
joyful adj laetus, hilaris.
joyfully adv laetē, hilare.
joyfulness n gaudium nt, laetitia f.
joyless adj tristis, maestus.

joyous adj see **joyful**.
joyously adv see **joyfully**.
jubilant adj laetus, gaudiō exsultāns.
judge n iūdex m, arbiter m ♦ vt iūdicāre; (think) exīstimāre, cēnsēre; **~ between** dīiūdicāre.
judgeship n iūdicātus m.
judgment n iūdicium nt, arbitrium nt; (opinion) sententia f; (punishment) poena f; (wisdom) iūdicium nt; **in my ~** meō animō, meō arbitrātū; **pass ~ on** statuere dē; **sit in ~** iūdicium exercēre.
judgment seat n tribūnal nt.
judicature n iūrisdictiō f; (men) iūdicēs mpl.
judicial adj iūdiciālis; (law) iūdiciārius.
judiciary n iūdicēs mpl.
judicious adj prūdēns, cōnsīderātus.
judiciously adv prūdenter.
jug n hydria f, urceus m.
juggler n praestīgiātor m.
juggling n praestīgiae fpl.
juice n liquor m, sūcus m.
juicy adj sūcī plēnus.
July n mēnsis Quīnctīlis, Iūlius m; **of ~** Quīnctīlis, Iūlius.
jumble n congeriēs f ♦ vt cōnfundere.
jump n saltus m ♦ vi salīre; **~ across** transilīre; **~ at** (opportunity) captāre, adripere, amplectī; **~ down** dēsilīre; **~ on to** īnsilīre in (acc).
junction n coniūnctiō f.
juncture n tempus nt.
June n mēnsis Iūnius; **of ~** Iūnius.
junior adj iūnior, nātū minor.
juniper n iūniperus f.
Juno n Iūnō, Iūnōnis f.
Jupiter n Iuppiter, Iovis m.
juridical adj iūdiciārius.
jurisconsult n iūriscōnsultus m.
jurisdiction n iūrisdictiō f, diciō f; **exercise ~** iūs dīcere.
jurisprudence n iūrisprūdentia f.
jurist n iūriscōnsultus m.
juror n iūdex m.
jury n iūdicēs mpl.
just adj iūstus, aequus ♦ adv (exactly) prōrsus; (only) modo; (time) commodum, modo; (with adv) dēmum, dēnique; (with pron) adeō dēmum, ipse; **~ as** (comparison) aequē ac, perinde ac, quemadmodum; sīcut; **~ before** (time) cum māximē, sub (acc); **~ now** modo, nunc; **~ so** ita prōrsus, sānē; **only ~** vix.
justice n iūstitia f, aequitās f, iūs nt; (person) praetor m; **administer ~** iūs reddere.
justiciary n praetor m.
justifiable adj iūstus.
justifiably adv iūre.
justification n pūrgātiō f, excūsātiō f.
justify vt excūsāre, pūrgāre.
justly adv iūstē, aequē; iūre, meritō.
jut vi prōminēre, excurrere.
jutting adj prōiectus.
juvenile adj iuvenīlis, puerīlis.

K, k

keel n carīna f.
keen adj ācer; (*mind*) acūtus, argūtus; (*sense*) sagāx; (*pain*) acerbus; **I am ~ on** studeō.
keenly adv ācriter, sagāciter, acūtē, acerbē.
keenness n (*scent*) sagācitās f; (*sight*) aciēs f; (*pain*) acerbitās f; (*eagerness*) studium nt, ārdor m.
keep vt servāre, tenēre, habēre; (*celebrate*) agere, celebrāre; (*guard*) custōdīre; (*obey*) observāre; (*preserve*) cōnservāre; (*rear*) alere, pāscere; (*store*) condere; **~ apart** distinēre; **~ away** arcēre; **~ back** dētinēre, reservāre; **~ down** comprimere; (*exuberance*) dēpāscere; **~ in** cohibēre, claudere; **~ in with** grātiam sequī (*gen*); **~ off** arcēre, dēfendere; **~ one's word** fidem praestāre; **~ one's hands off** manūs abstinēre; **~ house** domī sē retinēre; **~ secret** cēlāre; **~ together** continēre; **~ up** sustinēre, cōnservāre; **~ up with** subsequī; **~ waiting** dēmorārī ♦ vi dūrāre, manēre ♦ n arx f.
keeper n custōs m.
keeping n custōdia f; **in ~ with** prō (*abl*); **be in ~ with** convenīre (*dat*).
keg n cadus m.
ken n cōnspectus m.
kennel n stabulum nt.
kerb n crepīdō f.
kernel n grānum nt, nucleus m.
kettle n lebēs f.
key n clāvis f; (*fig*) claustra ntpl, iānua f; **~ position** cardō m.
kick vi calcitrāre ♦ vt calce ferīre.
kid n haedus m.
kidnap vt surripere.
kidnapper n plagiārius m.
kidney n rēn m.
kidney bean n phasēlus m.
kid's adj haedīnus.
kill vt interficere, interimere; (*in battle*) occīdere; (*murder*) necāre, iugulāre; (*time*) perdere.
killer n interfector m.
kiln n fornāx f.
kin n cognātī mpl, propinqui mpl; **next of ~** proximī mpl.
kind adj bonus, benīgnus, benevolus ♦ n genus nt; **of such a ~** tālis; **what ~ of** quālis ♦ adj cōmis.
kindle vt incendere, succendere, īnflammāre.
kindliness n cōmitās f, hūmānitās f.
kindling n (*fuel*) fōmes m.
kindly adv benīgnē.
kindness n benīgnitās f, benevolentia f; (*act*) beneficium nt, officium nt, grātia f.

kindred n necessitūdō f, cognātiō f; propinquī mpl, cognātī mpl ♦ adj cognātus, adfīnis.
king n rēx m.
kingdom n rēgnum nt.
kingfisher n alcēdō f.
kingly adj rēgius, rēgālis.
kingship n rēgnum nt.
kink n vitium nt.
kinsfolk n cognātī mpl, necessāriī mpl.
kinsman n cognātus m, propinquus m, necessārius m.
kinswoman n cognāta f, propinqua f, necessāria f.
kismet n fātum nt.
kiss n ōsculum nt ♦ vt ōsculārī.
kit n (*MIL*) sarcina f.
kitchen n culīna f.
kitchen garden n hortus m.
kite n mīluus m.
kite's adj mīluīnus.
knack n callid2itās f, artificium nt; **have the ~ of** callēre.
knapsack n sarcina f.
knave n veterātor m.
knavish adj improbus.
knavishly adv improbē.
knead vt depsere, subigere.
knee n genū nt.
kneel vi genibus nītī.
knife n culter m; (*surgeon's*) scalprum nt.
knight n eques m ♦ vt in ōrdinem equestrem recipere.
knighthood n ōrdō equester m.
knightly adj equester.
knit vt texere; (*brow*) contrahere.
knob n bulla f.
knock vt ferīre, percutere; **~ at** pulsāre; **~ against** offendere; **~ down** dēicere, adflīgere; (*at auction*) addīcere; **~ off** dēcutere; (*work*) dēsistere ab; **~ out** ēlīdere, excutere; (*unconscious*) exanimāre; (*fig*) dēvincere; **~ up** suscitāre ♦ n pulsus m, ictus m.
knock-kneed adj vārus.
knoll n tumulus m.
knot n nōdus m ♦ vt nectere.
knotty adj nōdōsus; **~ point** nōdus m.
know vt scīre; (*person*) nōvisse; **~ all about** explōrātum habēre; **~ again** agnōscere; **~ how to** scīre; **not ~** ignōrāre, nescīre; **let me ~** fac sciam, fac mē certiōrem; **get to ~** cognōscere ♦ n **in the ~** cōnscius.
knowing adj prūdēns, callidus.
knowingly adv cōnsultō, sciēns.
knowledge n scientia f, doctrīna f; (*practical*) experientia f; (*of something*) cognitiō f.
knowledgeable adj gnārus, doctus.
known adj nōtus; **make ~** dēclārāre.
knuckle n articulus m.
knuckle bone n tālus m.
kotow vi adulārī.
kudos n glōria f, laus f.

L, l

label n titulus m ♦ vt titulō īnscrībere.
laboratory n officīna f.
laborious adj labōriōsus, operōsus.
laboriously adv operōsē.
laboriousness n labor m.
labour n labor m, opera f; (work done) opus nt; (work allotted) pēnsum nt; (workmen) operae fpl; **be in ~** parturīre ♦ vi labōrāre, ēnītī; **~ at** ēlabōrāre; **~ under a delusion** errōre fallī.
laboured adj adfectātus.
labourer n operārius m; **~s** pl operae fpl.
labyrinth n labyrinthus m.
lace n texta rēticulāta ntpl; (shoe) ligula f ♦ vt nectere.
lacerate vt lacerāre.
laceration n lacerātiō f.
lack n inopia f, dēfectiō f ♦ vt egēre (abl), carēre (abl).
lackey n pedisequus m.
laconic adj brevis.
laconically adv ūnō verbō, paucīs verbīs.
lacuna n lacūna f.
lad n puer m.
ladder n scāla f.
lade vt onerāre.
laden adj onustus, onerātus.
lading n onus nt.
ladle n trulla f.
lady n domina f, mātrōna f, mulier f.
ladylike adj līberālis, honestus.
lag vi cessāre.
lagoon n stagnum nt.
lair n latibulum nt.
lake n lacus m.
lamb n agnus m; (flesh) agnīna f; **ewe ~** agna f.
lame adj claudus; (argument) inānis; **be ~** claudicāre.
lameness n claudicātiō f.
lament n lāmentātiō f, lāmentum nt ♦ vt lūgēre, lāmentārī; (regret) dēplōrāre.
lamentable adj lāmentābilis, miserābilis.
lamentably adv miserābiliter.
lamentation n lāmentātiō f.
lamp n lucerna f, lychnus m.
lampoon n satura f ♦ vt carmine dēstringere.
lance n hasta f, lancea f.
lancer n hastātus m.
lancet n scalpellum nt.
land n terra f; (country) terra f, regiō f; (territory) fīnēs mpl; (native) patria f; (property) praedium nt, ager m; (soil) solum nt ♦ vt expōnere ♦ vi ē nāve ēgredī ♦ adj terrēnus, terrestris.
landfall n adpulsus m.
landing place n ēgressus m.

landlady n caupōna f.
landlord n dominus m; (inn) caupō m.
landmark n lapis m; **be a ~** ēminēre.
landscape n agrōrum prōspectus m.
landslide n terrae lābēs f, lāpsus m.
landwards adv terram versus.
lane n (country) sēmita f; (town) angiportus m.
language n lingua f; (style) ōrātiō f, sermō m; (diction) verba ntpl; **bad ~** maledicta ntpl.
languid adj languidus, remissus.
languidly adv languidē.
languish vi languēre, languēscere; (with disease) tābēscere.
languor n languor m.
lank, lanky adj exīlis, gracilis.
lantern n lanterna f, lucerna f.
lap n gremium nt, sinus m ♦ vt lambere; (cover) involvere.
lapse n (time) lāpsus m; (mistake) errātum nt; **after the ~ of a year** interiectō annō ♦ vi lābī; (agreement) inritum fierī; (property) revertī.
larceny n fūrtum nt.
larch n larix f ♦ adj larignus.
lard n adeps m/f.
larder n cella penāria f.
large adj māgnus, grandis, amplus; **at ~** solūtus; **very ~** permāgnus; **as ~ as ...** tantus ... quantus.
largely adv plērumque.
largesse n largitiō f; (MIL) dōnātivum nt; (civil) congiārium nt; **give ~** largīrī.
lark n alauda f.
lascivious adj libīdinōsus.
lasciviously adv libīdinōsē.
lasciviousness n libīdō f.
lash n flagellum nt, lōrum nt; (eye) cilium nt ♦ vt verberāre; (tie) adligāre; (with words) castīgāre.
lashing n verbera ntpl.
lass n puella f.
lassitude n languor m.
last adj ultimus, postrēmus, suprēmus; (in line) novissimus; (preceding) proximus; **at ~** tandem, dēmum, dēnique; **for the ~ time** postrēmum ♦ n fōrma f; **let the cobbler stick to his ~** nē sūtor suprā crepidam ♦ vi dūrāre, permanēre.
lasting adj diūtinus, diūturnus.
lastly adv postrēmō, dēnique.
latch n pessulus m.
latchet n corrigia f.
late adj sērus; (date) recēns; (dead) dēmortuus; (emperor) dīvus; **~ at night** multā nocte; **till ~ in the day** ad multum diem ♦ adv sērō; **too ~** sērō; **too ~ to** sērius quam quī (subj); **of ~** nūper.
lately adv nūper.
latent adj occultus, latitāns.
later adj posterior ♦ adv posteā, posthāc, mox.
latest adj novissimus.
lath n tigillum nt.
lathe n tornus m.
lather n spūma f.

Latin *adj* Latīnus; **speak** ~ Latīnē loquī;
understand ~ Latīnē scīre; **translate into** ~
Latīnē reddere; **in Latin** latinē.
Latinity *n* Latīnitās *f.*
latitude *n* (*GEOG*) caelum *nt*; (*scope*) lībertās *f.*
latter *adj* posterior; **the** ~ hīc.
latterly *adv* nūper.
lattice *n* trānsenna *f.*
laud *n* laus *f* ♦ *vt* laudāre.
laudable *adj* laudābilis, laude dignus.
laudatory *adj* honōrificus.
laugh *n* rīsus *m*; (*loud*) cachinnus *m* ♦ *vi* rīdēre,
cachinnāre; ~ **at** (*joke*) rīdēre; (*person*)
dērīdēre; ~ **up one's sleeve** in sinū gaudēre.
laughable *adj* rīdiculus.
laughing stock *n* lūdibrium *nt.*
laughter *n* rīsus *m.*
launch *vt* (*missile*) contorquēre; (*ship*)
dēdūcere; ~ **an attack** impetum dare ♦ *vi*: ~
out into ingredī in (*acc*) ♦ *n* celōx *f*, lembus
m.
laureate *adj* laureātus.
laurel *n* laurus *m* ♦ *adj* laureus.
lave *vt* lavāre.
lavish *adj* prōdigus, largus ♦ *vt* largīrī,
profundere.
lavishly *adv* prōdigē, effūsē.
lavishness *n* largitās *f.*
law *n* lēx *f*; (*system*) iūs *nt*; (*divine*) fās *nt*; **civil** ~
iūs cīvīle; **constitutional** ~ iūs pūblicum;
international ~ iūs gentium; **go to** ~ lēge
agere, lītigāre; **break the** ~ lēges violāre;
pass a ~ (*magistrate*) lēgem perferre; (*people*)
lēgem iubēre.
law-abiding *adj* bene mōrātus.
law court *n* iūdicium *nt*; (*building*) basilica *f.*
lawful *adj* lēgitimus; (*morally*) fās.
lawfully *adv* lēgitimē, lēge.
lawgiver *n* lēgum scrīptor *m.*
lawless *adj* exlēx.
lawlessly *adv* licenter.
lawlessness *n* licentia *f.*
lawn *n* prātulum *nt.*
law-suit *n* līs *f*, āctiō *f.*
lawyer *n* iūriscōnsultus *m*, causidicus *m.*
lax *adj* dissolūtus, remissus.
laxity *n* dissolūtiō *f.*
lay *vt* pōnere, locāre; (*ambush*) collocāre,
tendere; (*disorder*) sēdāre; (*egg*) parere;
(*foundation*) iacere; (*hands*) inicere; (*plan*)
capere, inīre; (*trap*) tendere; (*wager*) facere;
~ **aside** pōnere; (*in store*) repōnere; ~ **by**
repōnere; ~ **down** dēpōnere; (*rule*) statuere;
~ **hold of** prehendere, adripere; ~ **in** condere;
~ **a motion before** referre ad; ~ **on** impōnere;
~ **open** patefacere; (*to attack*) nūdāre; ~ **out**
(*money*) impendere, ērogāre; (*camp*) mētārī;
~ **siege to** obsidēre; ~ **to heart** in pectus
dēmittere; ~ **up** recondere; ~ **upon**
iniungere, impōnere; ~ **violent hands on** vim
adferre, adhibēre (*dat*); **whatever they could**
~ **hands on** quod cuīque in manum vēnisset;
~ **waste** vastāre ♦ *n* carmen *nt*, melos *nt.*

lay *adj* (*ECCL*) lāicus.
layer *n* corium *nt*; (*stones*) ōrdō *m*; (*plant*)
propāgō *f.*
layout *n* dēsignātiō *f.*
laze *vi* ōtiārī.
lazily *adv* ignāvē, ōtiōsē.
laziness *n* ignāvia *f*, dēsidia *f*, pigritia *f.*
lazy *adj* ignāvus, dēsidiōsus, piger.
lea *n* prātum *nt.*
lead *vt* dūcere; (*life*) agere; (*wall*) perdūcere;
(*water*) dērīvāre; ~ **across** trādūcere; ~
around circumdūcere; ~ **astray** in errōrem
indūcere; ~ **away** abdūcere; ~ **back**
redūcere; ~ **down** dēdūcere; ~ **in**
intrōdūcere; ~ **on** addūcere; ~ **out** ēdūcere; ~
over trādūcere; ~ **the way** dūcere, praeīre; ~
up to tendere ad, spectare ad; **the road** ~**s** ...
via fert ....
lead *n* plumbum *nt* ♦ *adj* plumbeus.
leaden *adj* (*colour*) līvidus.
leader *n* dux *m*, ductor *m.*
leadership *n* ductus *m.*
leading *adj* prīmus, prīnceps, praecipuus.
leaf, *pl* **leaves** *n* folium *nt*, frōns *f*; (*paper*)
scheda *f*; **put forth leaves** frondēscere.
leaflet *n* libellus *m.*
leafy *adj* frondōsus.
league *n* foedus *nt*, societās *f*; (*distance*) tria
mīlia passuum ♦ *vi* coniūrāre, foedus
facere.
leagued *adj* foederātus.
leak *n* rīma *f* ♦ *vi* mānāre, rimās agere.
leaky *adj* rīmōsus.
lean *adj* macer, exīlis, gracilis ♦ *vi* nītī; ~ **back**
sē reclīnāre; ~ **on** innītī in (*abl*), incumbere
(*dat*); ~ **over** inclīnāre.
leaning *n* prōpēnsiō *f* ♦ *adj* inclīnātus.
leanness *n* gracilitās *f*, maciēs *f.*
leap *n* saltus *m* ♦ *vi* salīre; (*for joy*) exsultāre; ~
down dēsilīre; ~ **on to** īnsilīre in (*acc*).
leap year *n* annus bissextilis *m.*
learn *vt* discere; (*news*) accipere, audīre; (*by
heart*) ēdiscere; (*discover*) cognōscere.
learned *adj* doctus, ērudītus, litterātus.
learnedly *adv* doctē.
learner *n* tīrō *m*, discipulus *m.*
learning *n* doctrīna *f*, ērudītiō *f*, litterae *fpl.*
lease *n* (*taken*) conductiō *f*; (*given*) locātiō *f* ♦ *vt*
condūcere; locāre.
leash *n* cōpula *f.*
least *adj* minimus ♦ *adv* minimē; **at** ~ saltem; **to
say the** ~ ut levissimē dīcam; **not in the** ~
haudquāquam.
leather *n* corium *nt*, alūta *f.*
leathery *adj* lentus.
leave *n* (*of absence*) commeātus *m*; (*permission*)
potestās *f*, venia *f*; **ask** ~ veniam petere; **give**
~ potestātem facere; **obtain** ~ impetrāre; **by
your** ~ pace tuā, bonā tuā veniā ♦ *vt*
relinquere, dēserere; (*legacy*) lēgāre; ~ **alone**
nōn tangere, manum abstinēre ab; ~ **behind**
relinquere; ~ **in the lurch** dēstituere,
dērelinquere; ~ **off** dēsinere, dēsistere ab;

(*temporarily*) intermittere; (*garment*) pōnere; ~ **out** praetermittere, ōmittere ♦ *vi* discēdere ab (+ *abl*), abīre.
leaven *n* fermentum *nt*.
leavings *n* rēliquiae *fpl*.
lecherous *adj* salāx.
lecture *n* acroāsis *f*, audītiō *f* ♦ *vi* docēre, scholam habēre.
lecturer *n* doctor *m*.
lecture room *n* audītōrium *nt*.
ledge *n* līmen *nt*.
ledger *n* cōdex acceptī et expēnsī.
lee *n* pars ā ventō tūta.
leech *n* hirūdō *f*.
leek *n* porrum *nt*.
leer *vi* līmīs oculīs intuērī.
lees *n* faex *f*; (*of oil*) amurca *f*.
left *adj* sinister, laevus ♦ *n* sinistra *f*, laeva *f*; **on the ~** ā laevā, ad laevam, ā sinistrā.
leg *n* crūs *nt*; (*of table*) pēs *m*.
legacy *n* lēgātum *nt*; ~ **hunter** captātor *m*.
legal *adj* lēgitimus.
legalize *vt* sancīre.
legally *adv* secundum lēgēs, lēge.
legate *n* lēgātus *m*.
legation *n* lēgātiō *f*.
legend *n* fābula *f*; (*inscription*) titulus *m*.
legendary *adj* fābulōsus.
legerdemain *n* praestīgiae *fpl*.
legging *n* ocrea *f*.
legible *adj* clārus.
legion *n* legiō *f*; **men of the 10th ~** decumānī *mpl*.
legionary *n* legiōnārius *m*.
legislate *vi* lēgēs scrībere, lēgēs facere.
legislation *n* lēgēs *fpl*, lēgēs scrībendae.
legislator *n* lēgum scrīptor *m*.
legitimate *adj* lēgitimus.
legitimately *adv* lēgitimē.
leisure *n* ōtium *nt*; **at ~** ōtiōsus, vacuus; **have ~ for** vacāre (*dat*).
leisured *adj* ōtiōsus.
leisurely *adj* lentus.
lend *vt* commodāre, mūtuum dare; (*at interest*) faenerārī; (*ear*) aurēs praebēre, admovēre; ~ **a ready ear** aurēs patefacere; ~ **assistance** opem ferre.
length *n* longitūdō *f*; (*time*) diūturnitās *f*; **at ~** tandem, dēmum, dēnique; (*speech*) cōpiōsē.
lengthen *vt* extendere; (*time*) prōtrahere; (*sound*) prōdūcere.
lengthwise *adv* in longitūdinem.
lengthy *adj* longus, prōlixus.
leniency *n* clēmentia *f*.
lenient *adj* clēmēns, mītis.
leniently *adv* clēmenter.
lentil *n* lēns *f*.
leonine *adj* leōnīnus.
leopard *n* pardus *m*.
less *adj* minor ♦ *adv* minus; ~ **than** (*num*) intrā (*acc*); **much ~, still ~** nēdum.
lessee *n* conductor *m*.
lessen *vt* minuere, imminuere, dēminuere ♦

vi dēcrēscere.
lesson *n* documentum *nt*; **be a ~ to** documentō esse (*dat*); ~**s** *pl* dictāta *ntpl*; **give ~s** scholās habēre; **give ~s in** docēre.
lessor *n* locātor *m*.
lest *conj* nē (+ *subj*).
let *vt* (*allow*) sinere; (*lease*) locāre; (*imper*) fac; ~ **alone** ōmittere; (*mention*) nē dīcam; ~ **blood** sanguinem mittere; ~ **down** dēmittere; ~ **fall** ā manibus mittere; (*word*) ēmittere; ~ **fly** ēmittere; ~ **go** mittere, āmittere; (*ship*) solvere; ~ **in** admittere; ~ **loose** solvere; ~ **off** absolvere, ignōscere (*dat*); ~ **oneself go** geniō indulgēre; ~ **out** ēmittere; (*ship*) āmittere, ōmittere; ~ **slip** āmittere, ōmittere.
lethal *adj* mortifer.
lethargic *adj* veternōsus.
lethargy *n* veternus *m*.
letter *n* epistula *f*, litterae *fpl*; (*of alphabet*) littera *f*; **the ~ of the law** scrīptum *nt*; **to the ~** ad praescrīptum; **by ~** per litterās; ~**s** (*learning*) litterae *fpl*; **man of ~s** scrīptor *m*.
lettered *adj* litterātus.
lettuce *n* lactūca *f*.
levee *n* salūtātiō *f*.
level *adj* aequus, plānus ♦ *n* plānitiēs *f*; (*instrument*) lībra *f*; **do one's ~ best** prō virīlī parte agere; **put on a ~ with** exaequāre cum ♦ *vt* aequāre, adaequāre, inaequāre; (*to the ground*) solō aequāre, sternere; (*weapon*) intendere.
level-headed *adj* prūdēns.
levelled *adj* (*weapon*) īnfestus.
lever *n* vectis *m*.
levity *n* levitās *f*; (*fun*) iocī *mpl*, facētiae *fpl*.
levy *vt* (*troops*) scrībere; (*tax*) exigere ♦ *n* dīlectus *m*.
lewd *adj* impudīcus.
lewdness *n* impudīcitia *f*.
liable *adj* obnoxius; **render ~** obligāre.
liaison *n* cōnsuētūdō *f*.
liar *n* mendāx *m*.
libel *n* probrum *nt*, calumnia *f* ♦ *vt* calumniārī.
libellous *adj* probrōsus, fāmōsus.
liberal *adj* līberālis; (*in giving*) largus, benīgnus; ~ **education** bonae artēs *fpl*.
liberality *n* līberālitās *f*, largitiō *f*.
liberally *adv* līberāliter, largē, benīgnē.
liberate *vt* līberāre; (*slave*) manū mittere.
liberation *n* līberātiō *f*.
liberator *n* līberātor *m*.
libertine *n* libīdinōsus *m*.
liberty *n* lībertās *f*; (*excess*) licentia *f*; **I am at ~ to** mihī licet (*inf*); **I am still at ~ to** integrum est mihī (*inf*); **take a ~ with** licentius ūtī (*abl*), familiārius sē gerere in (*acc*).
libidinous *adj* libīdinōsus.
librarian *n* librārius *m*.
library *n* bibliothēca *f*.
licence *n* (*permission*) potestās *f*; (*excess*) licentia *f*.
license *vt* potestātem dare (*dat*).
licentious *adj* dissolūtus.

licentiousness *n* libīdō *f*, licentia *f*.
lick *vt* lambere; mulcēre.
lictor *n* lictor *m*.
lid *n* operculum *nt*.
lie *n* mendācium *nt*; **give the ~ to** redarguere; **tell a ~** mentīrī ♦ *vi* mentīrī; (*lie down*) iacēre; (*place*) situm esse; (*consist*) continērī; **as far as in me ~s** quantum in mē est; **~ at anchor** stāre; **~ between** interiacēre; **~ down** cubāre, discumbere; **~ heavy on** premere; **~ hid** latēre; **~ in wait** īnsidiārī; **~ low** dissimulāre; **~ on** incumbere (*dat*); **~ open** patēre; hiāre.
lien *n* nexus *m*.
lieu *n*: **in ~ of** locō (*gen*).
lieutenant *n* decuriō *m*; legātus *m*.
life *n* vīta *f*; (*in danger*) salūs *f*, caput *nt*; (*biography*) vīta *f*; (*breath*) anima *f*; (*RHET*) sanguis *m*; (*time*) aetās *f*; **come to ~ again** revīvīscere; **draw to the ~** exprimere; **for ~** aetātem; **matter of ~ and death** capitāle *nt*; **prime of ~** flōs aetātis; **way of ~** mōrēs *mpl*.
lifeblood *n* sanguis *m*.
life-giving *adj* almus, vītālis.
lifeguard *n* custōs *m*; (*emperor's*) praetōriānus *m*.
lifeless *adj* exanimis; (*style*) exsanguis.
lifelike *adj* expressus.
lifelong *adj* perpetuus.
lifetime *n* aetās *f*.
lift *vt* tollere, sublevāre; **~ up** efferre, attollere.
light *n* lūx *f*, lūmen *nt*; (*painting*) lūmen *nt*; **bring to ~** in lūcem prōferre; **see in a favourable ~** in meliōrem partem interpretārī; **throw ~ on** lūmen adhibēre (*dat*) ♦ *vt* accendere, incendere; (*illuminate*) illūstrāre, illūmināre; **be lit up** collūcēre ♦ *vi*: **~ upon** invenīre, offendere ♦ *adj* illūstris; (*movement*) agilis; (*weight*) levis; **grow ~** illūcēscere, dīlūcēscere; **make ~ of** parvī pendere.
light-armed *adj* expedītus.
lighten *vi* fulgurāre ♦ *vt* levāre.
lighter *n* linter *f*.
light-fingered *adj* tagāx.
light-footed *adj* celer, pernīx.
light-headed *adj* levis, volāticus.
light-hearted *adj* hilaris, laetus.
lightly *adv* leviter; pernīciter.
lightness *n* levitās *f*.
lightning *n* fulgur *nt*; (*striking*) fulmen *nt*; **be hit by ~** dē caelō percutī; **of ~** fulgurālis.
like *adj* similis, pār; **~ this** ad hunc modum ♦ *adv* similiter, sīcut, rītū (*gen*) ♦ *vt* amāre; **I ~** mihī placet, mē iuvat; **I ~ to** libet (*inf*); **I don't ~** nīl moror, mihī displicet; **look ~** similem esse, referre.
likelihood *n* vērī similitūdō *f*.
likely *adj* vērī similis ♦ *adv* sānē.
liken *vt* comparāre, aequiperāre.
likeness *n* imāgō *f*, īnstar *nt*, similitūdō *f*.
likewise *adv* item; (*also*) etiam.
liking *n* libīdō *f*, grātia *f*; **to one's ~** ex

sententiā.
lily *n* līlium *nt*.
limb *n* membrum *nt*, artus *m*.
lime *n* calx *f*; (*tree*) tilia *f*.
limelight *n* celebritās *f*; **enjoy the ~** mōnstrārī digitō.
limestone *n* calx *f*.
limit *n* fīnis *m*, terminus *m*, modus *m*; **mark the ~s of** dētermināre ♦ *vt* fīnīre, dēfinīre, termināre; (*restrict*) circumscrībere.
limitation *n* modus *m*.
limp *adj* mollis, flaccidus ♦ *vi* claudicāre.
limpid *adj* limpidus.
linden *n* tilia *f*.
line *n* līnea *f*; (*battle*) aciēs *f*; (*limit*) modus *m*; (*outline*) līneāmentum *nt*; (*writing*) versus *m*; **in a straight ~** ē regiōne; **~ of march** agmen *nt*; **read between the ~s** dissimulātā dispicere; **ship of the ~** nāvis longa; **write a ~** pauca scrībere ♦ *vt* (*street*) saepīre.
lineage *n* genus *nt*, stirps *f*.
lineal *adj* (*descent*) gentīlis.
lineaments *n* līneāmenta *ntpl*, ōris ductūs *mpl*.
linen *n* linteum *nt* ♦ *adj* linteus.
liner *n* nāvis *f*.
linger *vi* cunctārī, cessāre, dēmorārī.
lingering *adj* tardus ♦ *n* cunctātiō *f*.
linguist *n*: **be a ~** complūrēs linguās callēre.
link *n* ānulus *m*; (*fig*) nexus *m*, vinculum *nt* ♦ *vt* coniungere.
lintel *n* līmen superum *nt*.
lion *n* leō *m*; **~'s** leōnīnus; **~'s share** māior pars.
lioness *n* leaena *f*.
lip *n* lābrum *nt*; **be on everyone's ~s in** ōre omnium hominum esse, per omnium ōra ferrī.
lip service *n*: **pay ~ to** verbō tenus obsequī (*dat*).
liquefy *vt* liquefacere.
liquid *adj* liquidus ♦ *n* liquor *m*.
liquidate *vt* persolvere.
liquor *n* liquor *m*; vīnum *nt*.
lisp *vi* balbūtīre.
lisping *adj* blaesus.
lissom *adj* agilis.
list *n* index *m*, tabula *f*; (*ship*) inclīnātiō *f* ♦ *vt* scrībere ♦ *vi* (*lean*) sē inclīnāre; (*listen*) auscultāre; (*wish*) cupere.
listen *vi* auscultāre; **~ to** auscultāre, audīre.
listener *n* audītor *m*, auscultātor *m*.
listless *adj* languidus.
listlessness *n* languor *m*.
literally *adv* ad verbum.
literary *adj* (*man*) litterātus; **~ pursuits** litterae *fpl*, studia *ntpl*.
literature *n* litterae *fpl*.
lithe *adj* mollis, agilis.
litigant *n* lītigātor *m*.
litigate *vi* lītigāre.
litigation *n* līs *f*.
litigious *adj* lītigiōsus.
litter *n* (*carriage*) lectīca *f*; (*brood*) fētus *m*; (*straw*) strāmentum *nt*; (*mess*) strāgēs *f* ♦ *vt*

sternere; (*young*) parere.

little *adj* parvus, exiguus; (*time*) brevis; **very ~** perexiguus, minimus; **~ boy** puerulus *m* ♦ *n* paulum *nt*, aliquantulum *nt*; **for a ~** paulisper, parumper; **~ or nothing** vix quicquam ♦ *adv* paulum, nōnnihil; (*with comp*) paulō; **~ by ~** paulātim, sēnsim, gradātim; **think ~ of** parvī aestimāre; **too ~** parum (+ *gen*).

littleness *n* exiguitās *f*.

littoral *n* lītus *nt*.

live *vi* vīvere, vītam agere; (*dwell*) habitāre; **~ down** (*reproach*) ēluere; **~ on** (*food*) vescī (*abl*) ♦ *adj* vīvus.

livelihood *n* vīctus *m*.

liveliness *n* alacritās *f*, hilaritās *f*.

livelong *adj* tōtus.

lively *adj* alacer, hilaris.

liven *vt* exhilarāre.

liver *n* iecur *nt*.

livery *n* vestis famulāris *f*.

livid *adj* līvidus; **be ~** līvēre.

living *adj* vīvus ♦ *n* vīctus *m*; (*earning*) quaestus *m*.

lizard *n* lacerta *f*.

lo *interj* ecce.

load *n* onus *nt* ♦ *vt* onerāre.

loaf *n* pānis *m* ♦ *vi* grassārī.

loafer *n* grassātor *m*.

loam *n* lutum *nt*.

loan *n* mūtuum *nt*, mūtua pecūnia *f*.

loathe *vt* fastīdīre, ōdisse.

loathing *n* fastīdium *nt*.

loathsome *adj* odiōsus, taeter.

lobby *n* vestibulum *nt*.

lobe *n* fibra *f*.

lobster *n* astacus *m*.

local *adj* indigena, locī.

locality *n* locus *m*.

locate *vt* reperīre; **be ~d** situm esse.

location *n* situs *m*.

loch *n* lacus *m*.

lock *n* (*door*) sera *f*; (*hair*) coma *f* ♦ *vt* obserāre.

locomotion *n* mōtus *m*.

locust *n* locusta *f*.

lodge *n* casa *f* ♦ *vi* dēversārī ♦ *vt* īnfīgere; (*complaint*) dēferre.

lodger *n* inquilīnus *m*.

lodging *n* hospitium *nt*, dēversōrium *nt*.

loft *n* cēnāculum *nt*.

loftiness *n* altitūdō *f*, sublīmitās *f*.

lofty *adj* excelsus, sublīmis.

log *n* stīpes *m*; (*fuel*) lignum *nt*.

loggerhead *n*: **be at ~s** rixārī.

logic *n* dialecticē *f*.

logical *adj* dialecticus, ratiōne frētus.

logically *adv* ex ratiōne.

logician *n* dialecticus *m*.

loin *n* lumbus *m*.

loiter *vi* grassārī, cessāre.

loiterer *n* grassātor *m*, cessātor *m*.

loll *vi* recumbere.

lone *adj* sōlus, sōlitārius.

loneliness *n* sōlitūdō *f*.

lonely, lonesome *adj* sōlitārius.

long *adj* longus; (*hair*) prōmissus; (*syllable*) prōductus; (*time*) longus, diūturnus; **in the ~ run** aliquandō; **for a ~ time** diū; **to make a ~ story short** nē longum sit, nē longum faciam ♦ *adv* diū; **~ ago** iamprīdem, iamdūdum; **as ~ as** *conj* dum; **before ~** mox; **for ~** diū; **how ~** quamdiū, quōusque; **I have ~ been wishing** iam prīdem cupiō; **not ~ after** haud multō post; **any ~er** (*time*) diūtius; (*distance*) longius; **no ~er** nōn iam ♦ *vi*: **~ for** dēsīderāre, exoptāre, expetere; **~ to** gestīre.

longevity *n* vīvācitās *f*.

longing *n* dēsīderium *nt*, cupīdō *f* ♦ *adj* avidus.

longingly *adv* avidē.

longitudinally *adv* in longitūdinem.

long-lived *adj* vīvāx.

long-suffering *adj* patiēns.

long-winded *adj* verbōsus, longus.

longwise *adv* in longitūdinem.

look *n* aspectus *m*; (*expression*) vultus *m* ♦ *vi* aspicere; (*seem*) vidērī, speciem praebēre; **~ about** circumspicere; **~ after** prōvidēre (*dat*), cūrāre; **~ at** spectāre ad (+ *acc*), aspicere, intuērī; (*with mind*) contemplārī; **~ back** respicere; **~ down on** dēspectāre; (*fig*) dēspicere; **~ for** quaerere, petere; **~ forward to** exspectāre; **~ here** heus tu, ehodum; **~ into** īnspicere, intrōspicere; **~ out** prōspicere; (*beware*) cavēre; **~ round** circumspicere; **~ through** perspicere; **~ to** ratiōnem habēre (*gen*); (*leader*) spem pōnere in (*abl*); **~ towards** spectāre ad; **~ up** suspicere; **~ up to** suspicere; **~ upon** habēre.

looker-on *n* arbiter *m*.

lookout *n* (*place*) specula *f*; (*man*) vigil *m*, excubiae *fpl*.

looks *npl* speciēs *f*; **good ~** fōrma *f*, pulchritūdō *f*.

loom *n* tēla *f* ♦ *vi* in cōnspectum sē dare.

loop *n* orbis *m*, sinus *m*.

loophole *n* fenestra *f*.

loose *adj* laxus, solūtus, remissus; (*morally*) dissolūtus; **let ~ on** immittere in (*acc*) ♦ *vt* (*undo*) solvere; (*slacken*) laxāre.

loosely *adv* solūtē, remissē.

loosen *vt* (re)solvere; (*structure*) labefacere.

looseness *n* dissolūtiō *f*, dissolūtī mōrēs *mpl*.

loot *n* praeda *f*, rapīna *f*.

lop *vt* amputāre.

lopsided *adj* inaequālis.

loquacious *adj* loquāx.

loquacity *n* loquācitās *f*.

lord *n* dominus *m* ♦ *vi*: **~ it** dominārī.

lordliness *n* superbia *f*.

lordly *adj* superbus; (*rank*) nōbilis.

lordship *n* dominātiō *f*, imperium *nt*.

lore *n* litterae *fpl*, doctrīna *f*.

lose *vt* āmittere, perdere; **~ an eye** alterō oculō capī; **~ heart** animum dēspondēre; **~ one's way** deerrāre ♦ *vi* (*in contest*) vincī.

loss *n* damnum *nt*, dētrīmentum *nt*; **be at a ~** haerēre, haesitāre; **suffer ~** damnum

accipere, facere; **~es** (_in battle_) caesī _mpl._
lost _adj_ āmissus, absēns; **be ~** perīre, interīre;
 give up for ~ dēplōrāre.
lot _n_ sors _f_; **be assigned by ~** sorte obvenīre;
 draw a ~ sortem dūcere; **draw ~s for** sortīrī;
 a ~ of multus, plūrimus.
loth _adj_ invītus.
lottery _n_ sortēs _fpl_; (_fig_) ālea _f._
lotus _n_ lōtos _f._
loud _adj_ clārus, māgnus.
loudly _adv_ māgnā vōce.
loudness _n_ māgna vōx _f._
lounge _vi_ ōtiārī.
louse _n_ pedis _m/f._
lout _n_ agrestis _m._
lovable _adj_ amābilis.
love _n_ amor _m_; **be hopelessly in ~** dēperīre; **fall
 in ~ with** adamāre ♦ _vt_ amāre, dīligere; **I ~ to**
 mē iuvat (_inf_).
love affair _n_ amor _m._
loveless _adj_ amōre carēns.
loveliness _n_ grātia _f_, venustās _f._
lovely _adj_ pulcher, amābilis, venustus.
love poem _n_ carmen amātōrium _nt._
lover _n_ amāns _m_, amātor _m._
lovesick _adj_ amōre aeger.
loving _adj_ amāns.
lovingly _adv_ amanter.
low _adj_ humilis; (_birth_) ignōbilis; (_price_) vīlis;
 (_sound_) gravis; (_spirits_) dēmissus; (_voice_)
 dēmissus; **at ~ water** aestūs dēcessū; **be ~**
 iacēre; **lay ~** interficere ♦ _vi_ mūgīre.
lower _adj_ īnferior; **the ~ world** īnferī _mpl_; **of
 the ~ world** īnfernus ♦ _adv_ īnferius ♦ _vt_
 dēmittere, dēprimere ♦ _vi_ (_cloud_) obscūrārī,
 minārī.
lowering _adj_ mināx.
lowest _adj_ īnfimus, īmus.
lowing _n_ mūgītus _m._
lowland _adj_ campestris.
lowlands _n_ campī _mpl._
lowliness _n_ humilitās _f._
lowly _adj_ humilis, obscūrus.
low-lying _adj_ dēmisssus; **be ~** sedēre.
lowness _n_ humilitās _f_; (_spirit_) tristitia _f._
loyal _adj_ fidēlis, fīdus; (_citizen_) bonus.
loyally _adv_ fidēliter.
loyalty _n_ fidēs _f_, fidēlitās _f._
lubricate _vt_ ungere.
lucid _adj_ clārus, perspicuus.
lucidity _n_ perspicuitās _f._
lucidly _adv_ clārē, perspicuē.
luck _n_ fortūna _f_, fors _f_; **good ~** fēlīcitās _f_; **bad ~**
 īnfortūnium _nt._
luckily _adv_ fēlīciter, faustē, prosperē.
luckless _adj_ īnfēlīx.
lucky _adj_ fēlīx, fortūnātus; (_omen_) faustus.
lucrative _adj_ quaestuōsus.
lucre _n_ lucrum _nt_, quaestus _m._
lucubration _n_ lūcubrātiō _f._
ludicrous _adj_ rīdiculus.
ludicrously _adv_ rīdiculē.
lug _vt_ trahere.

luggage _n_ impedīmenta _ntpl_, sarcina _f._
lugubrious _adj_ lūgubris, maestus.
lukewarm _adj_ tepidus; (_fig_) segnis, neglegēns;
 be ~ tepēre.
lukewarmly _adv_ segniter, neglegenter.
lukewarmness _n_ tepor _m_; (_fig_) neglegentia _f_,
 incūria _f._
lull _vt_ sōpīre; (_storm_) sēdāre ♦ _n_ intermissiō _f._
lumber _n_ scrūta _ntpl._
luminary _n_ lūmen _nt_, astrum _nt._
luminous _adj_ lūcidus, illūstris.
lump _n_ massa _f_; (_on body_) tuber _nt._
lumpish _adj_ hebes, crassus, stolidus.
lunacy _n_ īnsānia _f._
lunar _adj_ lūnāris.
lunatic _n_ īnsānus _m._
lunch _n_ prandium _nt_ ♦ _vi_ prandēre.
lung _n_ pulmō _m_; _pl_ (_RHET_) latera _ntpl._
lunge _n_ ictus _m_ ♦ _vi_ prōsilīre.
lurch _n_: **leave in the ~** dērelinquere, dēstituere
 ♦ _vi_ titubāre.
lure _n_ esca _f_ ♦ _vt_ allicere, illicere, ēlicere.
lurid _adj_ lūridus.
lurk _vi_ latēre, latitāre, dēlitēscere.
luscious _adj_ praedulcis.
lush _adj_ luxuriōsus.
lust _n_ libīdō _f_ ♦ _vi_ libīdine flagrāre,
 concupīscere.
lustful _adj_ libīdinōsus.
lustily _adv_ validē, strēnuē.
lustiness _n_ vigor _m_, nervī _mpl._
lustration _n_ lūstrum _nt._
lustre _n_ fulgor _m_, splendor _m._
lustrous _adj_ illūstris.
lusty _adj_ validus, lacertōsus.
lute _n_ cithara _f_, fidēs _fpl._
lute player _n_ citharista _m_, citharistria _f_,
 fidicen _m_, fidicina _f._
luxuriance _n_ luxuria _f._
luxuriant _adj_ luxuriōsus.
luxuriate _vi_ luxuriārī.
luxuries _pl_ lautitiae _fpl._
luxurious _adj_ luxuriōsus, sūmptuōsus, lautus.
luxuriously _adv_ sūmptuōsē, lautē.
luxury _n_ luxuria _f_, luxus _m._
lynx _n_ lynx _m/f_; **~-eyed** lyncēus.
lyre _n_ lyra _f_, fidēs _fpl_; **play the ~** fidibus canere.
lyric _adj_ lyricus ♦ _n_ carmen _nt._
lyrist _n_ fidicen _m_, fidicina _f._

M, m

mace _n_ scīpiō _m._
machination _n_ dolus _m._
machine _n_ māchina _f._

mackerel n scomber m.
mad adj īnsānus, furiōsus, vēcors, dēmēns; **be**
~ īnsānīre, furere.
madam n domina f.
madden vt furiāre, mentem aliēnāre (dat).
madly adv insānē, furiōsē, dēmenter.
madness n īnsānia f, furor m, dēmentia f;
(animals) rabiēs f.
maelstrom n vertex m.
magazine n horreum nt, apothēca f.
maggot n vermiculus m.
magic adj magicus ♦ n magicae artēs fpl.
magician n magus m, veneficus m.
magistracy n magistrātus m.
magistrate n magistrātus m.
magnanimity n māgnanimitās f, līberalitās f.
magnanimous adj generōsus, līberālis,
māgnanimus.
magnet n magnēs m.
magnificence n māgnificentia f, adparātus m.
magnificent adj māgnificus, amplus,
splendidus.
magnificently adv māgnificē, amplē,
splendidē.
magnify vt amplificāre, exaggerāre.
magnitude n māgnitūdō f.
magpie n pīca f.
maid n virgō f; (servant) ancilla f.
maiden n virgō f.
maidenhood n virginitās f.
maidenly adj virginālis.
mail n (armour) lōrīca f; (letters) epistulae fpl.
maim vt mutilāre.
maimed adj mancus.
main adj prīnceps, prīmus; ~ **point** caput nt
♦ n (sea) altum nt, pelagus nt; **with might and**
~ manibus pedibusque, omnibus nervīs.
mainland n continēns f.
mainly adv praecipuē, plērumque.
maintain vt (keep) tenēre, servāre; (keep up)
sustinēre; (keep alive) alere, sustentāre;
(argue) adfirmāre, dēfendere.
maintenance n (food) alimentum nt.
majestic adj augustus, māgnificus.
majestically adv augustē.
majesty n māiestās f.
major adj māior.
majority n māior pars f, plērīque; **have**
attained one's ~ suī iūris esse.
make vt facere, fingere; (appointment) creāre;
(bed) sternere; (cope) superāre; (compulsion)
cōgere; (consequence) efficere; (craft)
fabricārī; (harbour) capere; (living) quaerere;
(sum) efficere; (with adj) reddere; (with verb)
cōgere; ~ **away with** tollere, interimere; ~
good supplēre, resarcīre; ~ **light of** parvī
facere; ~ **one's way** iter facere; ~ **much of**
māgnī aestimāre, multum tribuere (dat); ~
for petere; ~ **out** arguere; ~ **over** dēlēgāre,
trānsferre; ~ **ready** parāre; ~ **a speech**
ōrātiōnem habēre; ~ **a truce** indutias
compōnere; ~ **war on** bellum inferre; ~ **up**
(loss) supplēre; (total) efficere; (story)

fingere; **be made fierī**.
make-believe n simulātiō f.
maker n fabricātor m, auctor m.
make-up n medicāmina ntpl.
maladministration n (charge) repetundae fpl.
malady n morbus m.
malcontent adj novārum rērum cupidus.
male adj mās, māsculus.
malefactor n nocēns m, reus m.
malevolence n malevolentia f.
malevolent adj malevolus, malignus.
malevolently adv malignē.
malformation n dēprāvātiō f.
malice n invidia f, malevolentia f; **bear** ~
towards invidēre (dat).
malicious adj invidiōsus, malevolus,
malignus.
maliciously adv malignē.
malign adj malignus, invidiōsus ♦ vt
obtrectāre.
malignant adj malevolus.
maligner n obtrectātor m.
malignity n malevolentia f.
malleable adj ductilis.
mallet n malleus m.
mallow n malva f.
malpractices n dēlicta ntpl.
maltreat vt laedere, vexāre.
malversation n pecūlātus m.
man n (human being) homō m/f; (male) vir m;
(MIL) mīles m; (chess) latrunculus m; **to a** ~
omnēs ad ūnum; ~ **who** is qui; **old** ~ senex m;
young ~ adulēscēns m; ~ **of war** nāvis longa f
♦ vt (ship) complēre; (walls) praesidiō
firmāre.
manacle n manicae fpl ♦ vt manicās inicere
(dat).
manage vt efficere, gerere, gubernāre,
administrāre; (horse) moderārī; (with verb)
posse.
manageable adj tractābilis, habilis.
management n administrātiō f, cūra f;
(finance) dispēnsātiō f.
manager n administrātor m, moderātor m;
dispēnsātor m.
mandate n mandātum nt.
mane n iuba f.
manful adj virīlis, fortis.
manfully adv virīliter, fortiter.
manger n praesēpe nt.
mangle vt dīlaniāre, lacerāre.
mangy adj scaber.
manhood n pūbertās f, toga virīlis f.
mania n īnsānia f.
maniac n furiōsus m.
manifest adj manifestus, apertus, clārus ♦ vt
dēclārāre, aperīre.
manifestation n speciēs f.
manifestly adv manifestō, apertē.
manifesto n ēdictum nt.
manifold adj multiplex, varius.
manikin n homunciō m, homunculus m.
manipulate vt tractāre.

manipulation *n* tractātiō *f*.
mankind *n* hominēs *mpl*, genus hūmānum *nt*.
manliness *n* virtūs *f*.
manly *adj* fortis, virīlis.
manner *n* modus *m*, ratiō *f*; (*custom*) mōs *m*,
  ūsus *m*; **~s** *pl* mōrēs *mpl*; **after the ~ of** rītū,
  mōre (*gen*); **good ~s** hūmānitās *f*, modestia *f*.
mannered *adj* mōrātus.
mannerism *n* mōs *m*.
mannerly *adj* bene mōrātus, urbānus.
manoeuvre *n* (*MIL*) dēcursus *m*, dēcursiō *f*; (*fig*)
  dolus *m* ♦ *vi* dēcurrere; (*fig*) māchinārī.
manor *n* praedium *nt*.
mansion *n* domus *f*.
manslaughter *n* homicīdium *nt*.
mantle *n* pallium *nt*; (*women's*) palla *f*.
manual *adj*: **~ labour** opera *f* ♦ *n* libellus *m*, ars
  f.
manufacture *n* fabrica *f* ♦ *vt* fabricārī.
manumission *n* manūmissiō *f*.
manumit *vt* manū mittere, ēmancipāre.
manure *n* fimus *m*, stercus *nt* ♦ *vt* stercorāre.
manuscript *n* liber *m*, cōdex *m*.
many *adj* multī; **as ~ as** tot … quot; **how ~?**
  quot?; **so ~** tot; **in ~ places** multifāriam; **a**
  good ~ complūrēs; **too ~** nimis multī; **the ~**
  vulgus *nt*; **very ~** permultī, plūrimī.
map *n* tabula *f* ♦ *vt*: **~ out** dēscrībere,
  dēsignāre.
maple *n* acer *nt* ♦ *adj* acernus.
mar *vt* corrumpere, dēfōrmāre.
marauder *n* praedātor *m*, dēpopulātor *m*.
marble *n* marmor *nt* ♦ *adj* marmoreus.
March *n* mēnsis Martius *m*; **of ~** Martius.
march *n* iter *nt*; **line of ~** agmen *nt*; **by forced**
  ~es māgnīs itineribus; **on the ~** ex itinere, in
  itinere; **quick ~** plēnō gradū; **a regular day's ~**
  iter iūstum *nt* ♦ *vi* contendere, iter facere,
  incēdere, īre; **~ out** exīre; **~ on** signa
  prōferre, prōgredī ♦ *vt* dūcere; **~ out**
  ēdūcere; **~ in** intrōdūcere.
mare *n* equa *f*.
margin *n* margō *f*; (*fig*) discrīmen *nt*.
marigold *n* caltha *f*.
marine *adj* marīnus *m* ♦ *n* mīles classicus *m*.
mariner *n* nauta *m*.
marital *adj* marītus.
maritime *adj* maritimus.
marjoram *n* amāracus *m*.
mark *n* nota *f*; (*of distinction*) īnsigne *nt*; (*target*)
  scopos *m*; (*trace*) vestīgium *nt*; **beside the ~**
  nihil ad rem; **it is the ~ of a wise man to**
  sapientis est (*inf*); **be wide of the ~** errāre ♦
  vt notāre, dēsignāre; (*observe*)
  animadvertere, animum attendere; **~ out**
  (*site*) mētārī, dēsignāre; (*for purpose*)
  dēnotāre.
marked *adj* īnsignis, manifestus.
markedly *adv* manifestō.
marker *n* index *m*.
market *n* macellum *nt*; **~ day** nūndinae *fpl*; **~**
  town emporium *nt*; **cattle ~** forum boārium
  nt; **fish ~** forum piscārium *nt*.

marketable *adj* vēndibilis.
marketplace *n* forum *nt*.
market prices *npl* annōna *f*.
market town *n* emporium *nt*.
marking *n* macula *f*.
maroon *vt* dērelinquere.
marriage *n* mātrimōnium *nt*, coniugium *nt*;
  (*ceremony*) nūptiae *fpl*; **give in ~** collocāre; **~**
  bed lectus geniālis *m*.
marriageable *adj* nūbilis.
marrow *n* medulla *f*.
marry *vt* (*a wife*) dūcere, in mātrimōnium
  dūcere; (*a husband*) nūbere (*dat*).
marsh *n* pālūs *f*.
marshal *n* imperātor *m* ♦ *vt* īnstruere.
marshy *adj* palūster.
mart *n* forum *nt*.
marten *n* mēlēs *f*.
martial *adj* bellicōsus, ferōx.
martyr *n* dēvōtus *m*; (*ECCL*) martyr *m/f*.
marvel *n* mīrāculum *nt*, portentum *nt* ♦ *vi*
  mīrārī; **~ at** admīrārī.
marvellous *adj* mīrus, mīrificus, mīrābilis.
marvellously *adv* mīrē, mīrum quantum.
masculine *adj* mās, virīlis.
mash *n* farrāgō *f* ♦ *vt* commiscēre,
  contundere.
mask *n* persōna *f* ♦ *vt* persōnam induere (*dat*);
  (*fig*) dissimulāre.
mason *n* structor *m*.
masonry *n* lapidēs *mpl*, caementum *nt*.
masquerade *n* simulātiō *f* ♦ *vi* vestem
  mūtāre; **~ as** speciem sibi induere (*gen*),
  persōnam ferre (*gen*).
mass *n* mōlēs *f*; (*of small things*) congeriēs *f*; (*of*
  people) multitūdō *f*; (*ECCL*) missa *f*; **the ~es**
  vulgus *nt*, plēbs *f* ♦ *vt* congerere, coacervāre.
massacre *n* strāgēs *f*, caedēs *f*, interneciō *f* ♦
  vt trucīdāre.
massive *adj* ingēns, solidus.
massiveness *n* mōlēs *f*, soliditās *f*.
mast *n* mālus *m*.
master *n* dominus *m*; (*school*) magister *m*; **be ~**
  of dominārī in (*abl*); (*skill*) perītum esse
  (*gen*); **become ~ of** potīrī (*abl*); **be one's own**
  ~ suī iūris esse; **not ~ of** impotēns (*gen*); **a**
  past ~ veterātor *m* ♦ *vt* dēvincere; (*skill*)
  ēdiscere; (*passion*) continēre.
masterful *adj* imperiōsus.
masterly *adj* doctus, perītus.
masterpiece *n* praeclārum opus *nt*.
mastery *n* dominātiō *f*, imperium *nt*,
  arbitrium *nt*.
masticate *vt* mandere.
mastiff *n* Molossus *m*.
mat *n* storea *f*.
match *n* (*person*) pār *m/f*; (*marriage*) nūptiae *fpl*;
  (*contest*) certāmen *nt*; **a ~ for** pār (*dat*); **no ~**
  for impār (*dat*) ♦ *vt* exaequāre, adaequāre ♦
  vi congruere.
matchless *adj* singulāris, ūnicus.
mate *n* socius *m*; (*married*) coniunx *m/f* ♦ *vi*
  coniungī.

material adj corporeus; (significant) haud levis ♦ n māteriēs f; (literary) silva f.
materialize vi ēvenīre.
materially adv māgnopere.
maternal adj māternus.
mathematical adj mathēmaticus.
mathematician n mathēmaticus m, geōmetrēs m.
mathematics n ars mathēmatica f, numerī mpl.
matin adj mātūtīnus.
matricide n (act) mātricīdium nt; (person) mātricīda m.
matrimony n mātrimōnium nt.
matrix n fōrma f.
matron n mātrōna f.
matter n māteria f, corpus nt; (affair) rēs f; (MED) pūs nt; **what is the ~ with you?** quid tibī est? vi: **it ~s** interest, rēfert.
matting n storea f.
mattock n dolābra f.
mattress n culcita f.
mature adj mātūrus; (age) adultus ♦ vi mātūrēscere.
maturity n mātūritās f; (age) adulta aetās f.
maul n fistūca f ♦ vt contundere, dīlaniāre.
maw n ingluviēs f.
mawkish adj pūtidus.
mawkishly adv pūtidē.
maxim n dictum nt, praeceptum nt, sententia f.
maximum adj quam māximus, quam plūrimus.
May n mēnsis Māius m; **of ~** Māius.
may vi posse; **I ~** licet mihī.
mayor n praefectus m.
maze n labyrinthus m.
mead n (drink) mulsum nt; (land) prātum nt.
meagre adj exīlis, iēiūnus.
meagrely adv exīliter, iēiūnē.
meagreness n exīlitās f.
meal n (flour) farīna f; (repast) cibus m.
mealy-mouthed adj blandiloquus.
mean adj humilis, abiectus; (birth) ignōbilis; (average) medius, mediocris ♦ n modus m, mediocritās f ♦ vt dīcere, significāre; (word) valēre; (intent) velle, in animō habēre.
meander vi sinuōsō cursū fluere.
meaning n significātiō f, vīs f, sententia f; **what is the ~ of?** quid sibī vult?, quōrsum spectat?.
meanly adv abiectē, humiliter.
meanness n humilitās f; (conduct) illīberālitās f, avāritia f.
means n īnstrūmentum nt; (of doing) facultās f; (wealth) opēs fpl; **by ~ of** per (acc); **by all ~** māximē; **by no ~** nūllō modō, haudquāquam; **of small ~** pauper.
meantime, meanwhile adv intereā, interim.
measles n boa f.
measure n modus m, mēnsūra f; (rhythm) numerī mpl; (plan) cōnsilium nt; (law) rogātiō f, lēx f; **beyond ~** nimium; **in some ~** aliquā ex parte; **take ~s** cōnsulere; **take the ~ of** quālis

sit cognōscere; **without ~** immoderātē ♦ vt mētīrī; **~ out** dīmētīrī; (land) mētārī.
measured adj moderātus.
measureless adj īnfīnītus, immēnsus.
measurement n mēnsūra f.
meat n carō f.
mechanic n opifex m, faber m.
mechanical adj mēchanicus.
mechanical device māchinātiō f.
mechanics n māchinālis scientia f.
mechanism n māchinātiō f.
medal n īnsigne nt.
meddle vi sē interpōnere.
meddlesome adj cūriōsus.
Medes n Mīdi mpl.
mediate vi intercēdere; **~ between** compōnere, conciliāre.
mediator n intercessor m, dēprecātor m.
medical adj medicus.
medicate vt medicāre.
medicinal adj medicus, salūbris.
medicine n (art) medicīna f; (drug) medicāmentum nt.
medicine chest n narthēcium nt.
mediocre adj mediocris.
mediocrity n mediocritās f.
meditate vi meditārī, cōgitāre, sēcum volūtāre.
meditation n cōgitātiō f, meditātiō f.
medium n internūntius m; (means) modus m ♦ adj mediocris.
medley n farrāgō f.
meek adj mītis, placidus.
meekly adv summissō animō.
meet adj idōneus, aptus ♦ n conventus m ♦ vi convenīre ♦ vt obviam īre (dat), occurrere (dat); (fig) obīre; **~ with** invenīre, excipere.
meeting n cōnsilium nt, conventus m.
melancholic adj melancholicus.
melancholy n ātra bīlis f; tristitia f, maestitia f ♦ adj tristis, maestus.
mêlée n turba f, concursus m.
mellow adj mītis; (wine) lēnis; **become ~** mītēscere; **make ~** mītigāre.
mellowness n mātūritās f.
melodious adj canōrus, numerōsus.
melodiously adv numerōsē.
melody n melos nt, modī mpl.
melt vt liquefacere, dissolvere; (fig) movēre ♦ vi liquēscere, dissolvī; (fig) commovērī; **~ away** dēliquēscere.
member n membrum nt; (person) socius m.
membrane n membrāna f.
memento n monumentum nt.
memoir n commentārius m.
memorable adj memorābilis, commemorābilis.
memorandum n hypomnēma nt.
memorial n monumentum nt.
memorize vt ēdiscere.
memory n memoria f; **from ~** memoriter.
menace n minae fpl ♦ vt minārī, minitārī; (things) imminēre (dat).

menacing *adj* mināx.
menacingly *adv* mināciter.
menage *n* familia *f*.
mend *vt* sarcīre, reficere ♦ *vi* meliōrem fierī; (*health*) convalēscere.
mendacious *adj* mendāx.
mendacity *n* mendācium *nt*.
mendicant *n* mendīcus *m*.
mendicity *n* mendīcitās *f*.
menial *adj* servīlis, famulāris ♦ *n* servus *m*, famulus *m*.
menstrual *adj* mēnstruus.
mensuration *n* mētiendī ratiō *f*.
mental *adj* cōgitātiōnis, mentis.
mentality *n* animī adfectus *m*, mēns *f*.
mentally *adv* cōgitātiōne, mente.
mention *n* mentiō *f* ♦ *vt* memorāre, mentiōnem facere (*gen*); (*casually*) inicere; (*briefly*) attingere; **omit to ~** praetermittere.
mentor *n* auctor *m*, praeceptor *m*.
mercantile *adj* mercātōrius.
mercenary *adj* mercennārius, vēnālis ♦ *n* mercennārius mīles *m*.
merchandise *n* mercēs *fpl*.
merchant *n* mercātor *m*.
merchantman *n* nāvis onerāria *f*.
merchant ship *n* nāvis onerāria *f*.
merciful *adj* misericors, clēmens.
mercifully *adv* clēmenter.
merciless *adj* immisericors, inclēmens, inhūmānus.
mercilessly *adv* inhūmānē.
mercurial *adj* hilaris.
mercy *n* misericordia *f*, clēmentia *f*, venia *f*; **at the ~ of** obnoxius (*dat*), in manū (*gen*).
mere *n* lacus *m* ♦ *adj* merus, ipse.
merely *adv* sōlum, tantum, dumtaxat.
meretricious *adj* meretricius; **~ attractions** lēnōcinia *ntpl*.
merge *vt* cōnfundere ♦ *vi* cōnfundī.
meridian *n* merīdiēs *m* ♦ *adj* merīdiānus.
merit *n* meritum *nt*, virtūs *f* ♦ *vt* merērī.
meritorious *adj* laudābilis.
meritoriously *adv* optimē.
mermaid *n* nympha *f*.
merrily *adv* hilare, festīvē.
merriment *n* hilaritās *f*, festīvitās *f*.
merry *adj* hilaris, festīvus; **make ~** lūdere.
merrymaking *n* lūdus *m*, festīvitās *f*.
mesh *n* macula *f*.
mess *n* (*dirt*) sordēs *f*, squālor *m*; (*trouble*) turba *f*; (*food*) cibus *m*; (*MIL*) contubernālēs *mpl*.
message *n* nūntius *m*.
messenger *n* nūntius *m*.
messmate *n* contubernālis *m*.
metal *n* metallum *nt* ♦ *adj* ferreus, aereus.
metamorphose *vt* mūtāre, trānsfōrmāre.
metamorphosis *n* mūtātiō *f*.
metaphor *n* trānslātiō *f*.
metaphorical *adj* trānslātus.
metaphorically *adv* per trānslātiōnem.
metaphysics *n* dialectica *ntpl*.

mete *vt* mētīrī.
meteor *n* fax caelestis *f*.
meteorology *n* prognōstica *ntpl*.
methinks *vi*: **~ I am** mihī videor esse.
method *n* ratiō *f*, modus *m*.
methodical *adj* dispositus; (*person*) dīligēns.
methodically *adv* dispositē.
meticulous *adj* accūrātus.
meticulously *adv* accūrātē.
meticulousness *n* cūra *f*.
metonymy *n* immūtātiō *f*.
metre *n* numerī *mpl*, modī *mpl*.
metropolis *n* urbs *f*.
mettle *n* ferōcitās *f*, virtūs *f*.
mettlesome *adj* ferōx, animōsus.
mew *n* (*bird*) larus *m*; **~s** *pl* stabula *ntpl* ♦ *vi* vāgīre.
miasma *n* hālitus *m*.
mid *adj* medius ♦ *prep* inter (*acc*).
midday *n* merīdiēs *m* ♦ *adj* merīdiānus.
middle *adj* medius ♦ *n* medium *nt*; **in the ~** medius, in mediō; **~ of** medius.
middling *adj* mediocris.
midge *n* culex *m*.
midget *n* pūmiliō *m/f*.
midland *adj* mediterrāneus.
midnight *n* media nox *f*.
midriff *n* praecordia *ntpl*.
midst *n* medium *nt*; **in the ~** medius; **in the ~ of** inter (*acc*); **through the ~ of** per medium.
midsummer *n* sōlstitium *nt* ♦ *adj* sōlstitiālis.
midway *adv* medius.
midwife *n* obstetrix *f*.
midwinter *n* brūma *f* ♦ *adj* brūmālis.
mien *n* aspectus *m*, vultus *m*.
might *n* vīs *f*, potentia *f*; **with ~ and main** omnibus nervīs, manibus pedibusque.
mightily *adv* valdē, magnopere.
mighty *adj* ingēns, validus.
migrate *vi* abīre, migrāre.
migration *n* peregrīnātiō *f*.
migratory *adj* advena.
mild *adj* mītis, lēnis, clēmēns.
mildew *n* rōbīgō *f*.
mildly *adv* lēniter, clēmenter.
mildness *n* clēmentia *f*, mānsuētūdō *f*; (*weather*) caelī indulgentia *f*.
mile *n* mīlle passūs *mpl*; **~s** *pl* mīlia passuum.
milestone *n* lapis *m*, mīliārium *nt*.
militant *adj* ferōx.
military *adj* mīlitāris ♦ *n* mīlitēs *mpl*.
military service *n* mīlitia *f*.
militate *vi*: **~ against** repugnāre (*dat*), facere contrā (*acc*).
militia *n* mīlitēs *mpl*.
milk *n* lac *nt* ♦ *vt* mulgēre.
milk pail *n* mulctra *f*.
milky *adj* lacteus.
mill *n* pistrīnum *nt*.
milled *adj* (*coin*) serrātus.
millennium *n* mīlle annī *mpl*.
miller *n* pistor *m*.
millet *n* mīlium *nt*.

million *num* deciēs centēna mīlia *ntpl.*
millionaire *n* rēx *m.*
millstone *n* mola *f*, molāris *m.*
mime *n* mīmus *m.*
mimic *n* imitātor *m*, imitātrīx *f* ♦ *vt* imitārī.
mimicry *n* imitātiō *f.*
minatory *adj* mināx.
mince *vt* concīdere; **not ~ words** plānē apertēque dīcere ♦ *n* minūtal *nt.*
mind *n* mēns *f*, animus *m*, ingenium *nt*; (*opinion*) sententia *f*; (*memory*) memoria *f*; **be in one's right ~** mentis suae esse; **be of the same ~** eadem sentīre; **be out of one's ~** īnsānīre; **bear in ~** meminisse (*gen*), memorem esse (*gen*); **call to ~** memoriā repetere, recordārī; **have a ~ to** libet; **have in ~** in animō habēre; **put one's ~ to** animum applicāre ad (+ *acc*); **make up one's ~** animum indūcere, animō obstināre, statuere; **put in ~ of** admonēre (*gen*); **speak one's ~** sententiam suam aperīre; **to one's ~** ex sententiā ♦ *vt* cūrāre, attendere; **~ one's own business** suum negōtium agere ♦ *vi* gravārī; **I don't ~** nīl moror; **never ~** mitte.
minded *adj* animātus.
mindful *adj* memor.
mine *n* metallum *nt*; (*MIL*) cuniculus *m*; (*fig*) thēsaurus *m* ♦ *vi* fodere; (*MIL*) cuniculum agere ♦ *pron* meus.
miner *n* fossor *m.*
mineral *n* metallum *nt.*
mingle *vt* miscēre, commiscēre ♦ *vi* sē immiscēre.
miniature *n* minima pictūra *f.*
minimize *vt* dētrectāre.
minimum *n* minimum *nt* ♦ *adj* quam minimum.
minion *n* cliēns *m/f*; dēlicātus *m.*
minister *n* administer *m* ♦ *vi* ministrāre, servīre.
ministry *n* mūnus *nt*, officium *nt.*
minor *adj* minor ♦ *n* pupillus *m*, pupilla *f.*
minority *n* minor pars *f*; **in one's ~** nōndum suī iūris.
Minotaur *n* Mīnōtaurus *m.*
minstrel *n* fidicen *m.*
minstrelsy *n* cantus *m.*
mint *n* (*plant*) menta *f*; (*money*) Monēta *f* ♦ *vt* cūdere.
minute *n* temporis mōmentum *nt.*
minute *adj* minūtus, exiguus, subtīlis.
minutely *adv* subtīliter.
minuteness *n* exiguitās *f*, subtīlitas *f.*
minutiae *n* singula *ntpl.*
minx *n* lascīva *f.*
miracle *n* mīrāculum *nt*, mōnstrum *nt.*
miraculous *adj* mīrus, mīrābilis.
miraculously *adv* dīvīnitus.
mirage *n* falsa speciēs *f.*
mire *n* lutum *nt.*
mirror *n* speculum *nt* ♦ *vt* reddere.
mirth *n* hilaritās *f*, laetitia *f.*
mirthful *adj* hilaris, laetus.
mirthfully *adv* hilare, laetē.

miry *adj* lutulentus.
misadventure *n* īnfortūnium *nt*, cāsus *m.*
misapply *vt* abūtī (*abl*); (*words*) invertere.
misapprehend *vt* male intellegere.
misapprehension *n* error *m.*
misappropriate *vt* intervertere.
misbegotten *adj* nothus.
misbehave *vi* male sē gerere.
miscalculate *vi* errāre, fallī.
miscalculation *n* error *m.*
miscall *vt* maledīcere (*dat*).
miscarriage *n* abortus *m*; (*fig*) error *m.*
miscarry *vi* aborīrī; (*fig*) cadere, inritum esse.
miscellaneous *adj* prōmiscuus, varius.
miscellany *n* farrāgō *f.*
mischance *n* īnfortūnium *nt.*
mischief *n* malum *nt*, facinus *nt*, maleficium *nt*; (*children*) lascīvia *f.*
mischievous *adj* improbus, maleficus; lascīvus.
misconceive *vt* male intellegere.
misconception *n* error *m.*
misconduct *n* dēlictum *nt*, culpa *f.*
misconstruction *n* prāva interpretātiō *f.*
misconstrue *vt* male interpretārī.
miscreant *n* scelerātus *m.*
misdeed *n* maleficium *nt*, dēlictum *nt.*
misdemeanour *n* peccātum *nt*, culpa *f.*
miser *n* avārus *m.*
miserable *adj* miser, infēlīx; **make oneself ~** sē cruciāre.
miserably *adv* miserē.
miserliness *n* avāritia *f.*
miserly *adj* avārus.
misery *n* miseria *f*, aerumna *f.*
misfortune *n* malum *nt*, īnfortūnium *nt*, incommodum *nt*, rēs adversae *fpl.*
misgiving *n* suspiciō *f*, cūra *f*; **have ~s** parum cōnfīdere.
misgovern *vt* male regere.
misgovernment *n* prāva administrātiō *f.*
misguide *vt* fallere, dēcipere.
misguided *adj* dēmēns.
mishap *n* īnfortūnium *nt.*
misinform *vt* falsa docēre.
misinterpret *vt* male interpretārī.
misinterpretation *n* prāva interpretātiō *f.*
misjudge *vt* male iūdicāre.
mislay *vt* āmittere.
mislead *vt* dēcipere, indūcere, auferre.
mismanage *vt* male gerere.
misnomer *n* falsum nōmen *nt.*
misogyny *n* mulierum odium *nt.*
misplace *vt* in aliēnō locō collocāre.
misplaced *adj* (*fig*) vānus.
misprint *n* mendum *nt.*
mispronounce *vt* prāvē appellāre.
misquote *vt* perperam prōferre.
misrepresent *vt* dētorquēre, invertere; (*person*) calumniārī.
misrepresentation *n* calumnia *f.*
misrule *n* prāva administrātiō *f.*
miss *vt* (*aim*) aberrāre (*abl*); (*loss*) requīrere,

dēsīderāre; (*notice*) praetermittere ♦ *n* error *m*; (*girl*) virgō *f*.
misshapen *adj* distortus, dēfōrmis.
missile *n* tēlum *nt*.
missing *adj* absēns; **be ~** dēesse, dēsīderārī.
mission *n* lēgātiō *f*.
missive *n* litterae *fpl*.
misspend *vt* perdere, dissipāre.
misstatement *n* falsum *nt*, mendācium *nt*.
mist *n* nebula *f*, cālīgō *f*.
mistake *n* error *m*; (*writing*) mendum *nt*; **full of ~s** mendōsus ♦ *vt*: **~ for** habēre prō (*abl*); **be ~n** errāre, fallī.
mistletoe *n* viscum *nt*.
mistranslate *vt* prāvē reddere.
mistress *n* domina *f*; (*school*) magistra *f*; (*lover*) amīca *f*.
mistrust *n* diffīdentia *f*, suspiciō *f* ♦ *vt* diffīdere (*dat*).
mistrustful *adj* diffīdēns.
mistrustfully *adv* diffīdenter.
misty *adj* nebulōsus.
misunderstand *vt* male intellegere ♦ *vi* errāre.
misunderstanding *n* error *m*; (*quarrel*) discidium *nt*.
misuse *n* malus ūsus *m* ♦ *vt* abūtī (*abl*).
mite *n* parvulus *m*; (*insect*) vermiculus *m*.
mitigate *vt* mītigāre, lēnīre.
mitigation *n* mītigātiō *f*.
mix *vt* miscēre; **~ in** admiscēre; **~ together** commiscēre; **get ~ed up with** admiscērī cum, sē interpōnere (*dat*).
mixed *adj* prōmiscuus.
mixture *n* (*act*) temperātiō *f*; (*state*) dīversitās *f*.
mnemonic *n* artificium memoriae *nt*.
moan *n* gemitus *m* ♦ *vi* gemere.
moat *n* fossa *f*.
mob *n* vulgus *nt*, turba *f* ♦ *vt* circumfundī in (*acc*).
mobile *adj* mōbilis, agilis.
mobility *n* mōbilitās *f*, agilitās *f*.
mobilize *vt* (*MIL*) ēvocāre.
mock *vt* irrīdēre, lūdibriō habēre, lūdificārī; (*ape*) imitārī; **~ at** inlūdere ♦ *n* lūdibrium *nt* ♦ *adj* simulātus, fictus.
mocker *n* dērīsor *m*.
mockery *n* lūdibrium *nt*, irrīsus *m*.
mode *n* modus *m*, ratiō *f*.
model *n* exemplar *nt*, exemplum *nt* ♦ *vt* fingere.
modeller *n* fictor *m*.
moderate *adj* (*size*) modicus; (*conduct*) moderātus ♦ *vt* temperāre; (*emotion*) temperāre (*dat*) ♦ *vi* mītigārī.
moderately *adv* modicē, moderātē, mediocriter.
moderation *n* moderātiō *f*, modus *m*; (*mean*) mediocritās *f*.
moderator *n* praefectus *m*.
modern *adj* recēns.
modernity *n* haec aetās *f*.

modest *adj* pudīcus, verēcundus.
modestly *adv* verēcundē, pudenter.
modesty *n* pudor *m*, verēcundia *f*.
modicum *n* paullulum *nt*, aliquantulum *nt*.
modification *n* mūtātiō *f*.
modify *vt* immūtāre; (*law*) derogāre aliquid dē.
modulate *vt* (*voice*) īnflectere.
modulation *n* flexiō *f*, inclīnātiō *f*.
moiety *n* dīmidia pars *f*.
moist *adj* ūmidus.
moisten *vt* ūmectāre, rigāre.
moisture *n* ūmor *m*.
molar *n* genuīnus *m*.
mole *n* (*animal*) talpa *f*; (*on skin*) naevus *m*; (*pier*) mōlēs *f*.
molecule *n* corpusculum *nt*.
molehill *n*: **make a mountain out of a ~** ē rīvō flūmina māgna facere, arcem facere ē cloācā.
molest *vt* sollicitāre, vexāre.
molestation *n* vexātiō *f*.
mollify *vt* mollīre, lēnīre.
molten *adj* liquefactus.
moment *n* temporis mōmentum *nt*, temporis pūnctum *nt*; **for a ~** parumper; **in a ~** iam; **without a ~'s delay** nullā interpositā morā; **be of great ~** māgnō mōmentō esse; **it is of ~** interest.
momentary *adj* brevis.
momentous *adj* gravis, māgnī mōmentī.
momentum *n* impetus *m*.
monarch *n* rēx *m*, tyrannus *m*.
monarchical *adj* rēgius.
monarchy *n* rēgnum *nt*.
monastery *n* monastērium *nt*.
monetary *adj* pecūniārius.
money *n* pecūnia *f*; (*cash*) nummī *mpl*; **for ~** mercēde; **ready ~** nummī, praesēns pecūnia; **make ~** rem facere, quaestum facere.
moneybag *n* fiscus *m*.
moneyed *adj* nummātus, pecūniōsus.
moneylender *n* faenerātor *m*.
moneymaking *n* quaestus *m*.
mongoose *n* ichneumōn *m*.
mongrel *n* hibrida *m*.
monitor *n* admonitor *m*.
monk *n* monachus *m*.
monkey *n* sīmia *f*.
monograph *n* libellus *m*.
monologue *n* ōrātiō *f*.
monopolize *vt* absorbēre, sibī vindicāre.
monopoly *n* arbitrium *nt*.
monosyllabic *adj* monosyllabus.
monosyllable *n* monosyllabum *nt*.
monotonous *adj* aequābilis.
monotony *n* taedium *nt*.
monster *n* mōnstrum *nt*, portentum *nt*, bēlua *f*.
monstrosity *n* mōnstrum *nt*.
monstrous *adj* immānis, mōnstruōsus; improbus.
month *n* mēnsis *m*.
monthly *adj* mēnstruus.

monument *n* monumentum *nt.*
monumental *adj* ingēns.
mood *n* adfectiō *f*, adfectus *m*, animus *m*;
(*GRAM*) modus *m*; **I am in the ~ for** libet (*inf*).
moody *adj* mōrōsus, tristis.
moon *n* lūna *f*; **new ~** interlūnium *nt.*
moonlight *n*: **by ~** ad lūnam.
moonshine *n* somnia *ntpl.*
moonstruck *adj* lūnāticus.
moor *vt* religāre ♦ *n* tesqua *ntpl.*
moorings *n* ancorae *fpl.*
moot *n* conventus *m*; **it is a ~ point** discrepat ♦
vt iactāre.
mop *n* pēniculus *m* ♦ *vt* dētergēre.
mope *vi* maerēre.
moral *adj* honestus, probus; (*opposed to
physical*) animī; (*PHILOS*) mōrālis ♦ *n*
documentum *nt.*
morale *n* animus *m*; **~ is low** iacet animus.
morality *n* bonī mōrēs *mpl*, virtūs *f.*
moralize *vi* dē officiīs disserere.
morally *adv* honestē.
morals *npl* mōrēs *mpl.*
morass *n* palūs *f.*
moratorium *n* mora *f.*
morbid *adj* aeger.
mordant *adj* mordāx.
more *adj* plūs, pluris (*in sg + gen, in pl + adj*) ♦
adv plūs, magis, amplius; (*extra*) ultrā; **~ than**
amplius quam; **~ than three feet** amplius trēs
pedēs; **~ and ~** magis magisque; **never ~**
immo; **~ or less** ferē; **no ~** (*time*) nōn diūtius,
nunquam posteā.
moreover *adv* tamen, autem, praetereā.
moribund *adj* moribundus.
morning *n* māne *nt*; **early in the ~** bene māne;
this ~ hodiē māne; **good ~** salvē ♦ *adj*
mātūtīnus.
morning call *n* salūtātiō *f.*
morning watch *n* (*NAUT*) tertia vigilia *f.*
moron *n* sōcors *m.*
morose *adj* acerbus, tristis.
moroseness *n* acerbitās *f*, tristitia *f.*
morrow *n* posterus diēs *m*; **on the ~** posterō
diē, postrīdiē.
morsel *n* offa *f.*
mortal *adj* mortālis, hūmānus; (*wound*)
mortifer ♦ *n* mortālis *m/f*, homō *m/f*; **poor ~**
homunculus *m.*
mortality *n* mortālitās *f*; (*death*) mors *f*; **the ~
was high** plūrimī periērunt.
mortally *adv*: **be ~ wounded** mortiferum
vulnus accipere.
mortar *n* mortārium *nt.*
mortgage *n* pignus *nt*, fīdūcia *f* ♦ *vt* obligāre.
mortification *n* dolor *m*, angor *m.*
mortified *adj*: **be ~ at** aegrē ferre.
mortify *vt* mordēre, vexāre; (*lust*) coercēre ♦
vi putrēscere.
mortise *vt* immittere.
mosaic *n* emblēma *nt*, lapillī *mpl* ♦ *adj*
tessellātus.
mosquito *n* culex *m.*

mosquito net *n* cōnōpēum *nt.*
moss *n* muscus *m.*
mossy *adj* muscōsus.
most *adj* plūrimus, plērusque; **for the ~ part**
māximam partem ♦ *adv* māximē, plūrimum.
mostly *adv* plērumque, ferē.
mote *n* corpusculum *nt.*
moth *n* tinea *f.*
mother *n* māter *f*; **of a ~** māternus.
mother-in-law *n* socrus *f.*
motherless *adj* mātre orbus.
motherly *adj* māternus.
mother tongue *n* patrius sermō *m.*
mother wit *n* Minerva *f.*
motif *n* argūmentum *nt.*
motion *n* mōtus *m*; (*for law*) rogātiō *f*; (*in
debate*) sententia *f*; **propose a ~** ferre; **set in ~**
movēre ♦ *vt* innuere.
motionless *adj* immōbilis.
motive *n* causa *f*, ratiō *f*; **I know your ~ in
asking** sciō cūr rogēs.
motley *adj* versicolor, varius.
mottled *adj* maculōsus.
motto *n* sententia *f.*
mould *n* fōrma *f*; (*soil*) humus *f*; (*fungus*)
mūcor *m* ♦ *vt* fingere, fōrmāre.
moulder *vi* putrēscere ♦ *n* fictor *m.*
mouldering *adj* puter.
mouldiness *n* situs *m.*
mouldy *adj* mūcidus.
moult *vi* pennas exuere.
mound *n* agger *m*, tumulus *m.*
mount *n* mōns *m*; (*horse*) equus *m* ♦ *vt*
scandere, cōnscendere, ascendere ♦ *vi*
ascendere; **~ up** ēscendere.
mountain *n* mōns *m.*
mountaineer *n* montānus *m.*
mountainous *adj* montuōsus.
mourn *vi* maerēre, lūgēre ♦ *vt* dēflēre,
lūgēre.
mourner *n* plōrātor *m*; (*hired*) praefica *f.*
mournful *adj* (*cause*) lūctuōsus, acerbus;
(*sound*) lūgubris, maestus.
mournfully *adv* maestē.
mourning *n* maeror *nt*, lūctus *m*; (*dress*)
sordēs *fpl*; **in ~** fūnestus; **be in ~** lūgere; **put
on ~** vestem mūtāre, sordēs suscipere;
wearing ~ ātrātus.
mouse *n* mūs *m.*
mousetrap *n* mūscipulum *nt.*
mouth *n* ōs *nt*; (*river*) ōstium *nt.*
mouthful *n* bucca *f.*
mouthpiece *n* interpres *m.*
movable *adj* mōbilis ♦ *npl*: **~s** rēs *fpl*, supellex
f.
move *vt* movēre; (*emotion*) commovēre; **~
backwards and forwards** reciprocāre; **~ out
of the way** dēmovēre; **~ up** admovēre ♦ *vi*
movērī; (*residence*) dēmigrāre; (*proposal*)
ferre, cēnsēre; **~ into** immigrāre in (*acc*); **~
on** prōgredī.
movement *n* mōtus *m*; (*process*) cursus *m*;
(*society*) societās *f.*

mover n auctor m.
moving adj flēbilis, flexanimus.
mow vt secāre, dēmetere.
mower n faenisex m.
much adj multus ♦ adv multum; (*with compar*)
multō; **as ~ as** tantum quantum; **so ~** tantum;
(*with verbs*) adeo; **~ less** nēdum; **too ~** nimis ♦
n multum nt.
muck n stercus nt.
mud n lutum nt.
muddle n turba f ♦ vt turbāre.
muffle vt involvere; **~ up** obvolvere.
muffled adj surdus.
mug n pōculum nt.
mulberry n mōrum nt; (*tree*) mōrus f.
mule n mūlus m.
muleteer n mūliō m.
mulish adj obstinātus.
mullet n mullus m.
multifarious adj multiplex, varius.
multiform adj multifōrmis.
multiply vt multiplicāre ♦ vi crēscere.
multitude n multitūdō f.
multitudinous adj crēberrimus.
mumble vt (*words*) opprimere ♦ vi
murmurāre.
munch vt mandūcāre.
mundane adj terrestris.
municipal adj mūnicipālis.
municipality n mūnicipium nt.
munificence n largitās f.
munificent adj largus, mūnificus.
munificently adv mūnificē.
munitions n bellī adparātus m.
mural adj mūrālis.
murder n parricīdium nt, caedēs f; **charge with
~** inter sīcāriōs accūsāre; **trial for ~** quaestiō
inter sīcāriōs ♦ vt interficere, iūgulāre,
necāre.
murderer n sīcārius m, homicīda m, parricīda
m, percussor m.
murderess n interfectrīx f.
murderous adj cruentus.
murky adj tenebrōsus.
murmur n murmur nt; (*angry*) fremitus m ♦ vi
murmurāre; fremere.
murmuring n admurmurātiō f.
muscle n torus m.
muscular adj lacertōsus.
muse vi meditārī ♦ n Mūsa f.
mushroom n fungus m, bōlētus m.
music n (*art*) mūsica f; (*sound*) cantus m, modī
mpl.
musical adj (*person*) mūsicus; (*sound*)
canōrus.
musician n mūsicus m; (*strings*) fidicen m;
(*wind*) tībīcen m.
muslin n sindōn f.
must n (*wine*) mustum nt ♦ vi dēbēre; **I ~ go** mē
oportet īre, mihī eundum est.
mustard n sināpi nt.
muster vt convocāre, cōgere; (*review*)
recēnsēre ♦ vi convenīre, coīre ♦ n
conventus m; (*review*) recēnsiō f.
muster roll n album nt.
mustiness n situs m.
musty adj mūcidus.
mutability n incōnstantia f.
mutable adj incōnstāns, mūtābilis.
mute adj mūtus.
mutilate vt mūtilāre, truncāre.
mutilated adj mūtilus, truncus.
mutilation n lacerātiō f.
mutineer n sēditiōsus m.
mutinous adj sēditiōsus.
mutiny n sēditiō f ♦ vi sēditiōnem facere.
mutter vi mussitāre.
mutton n carō ovilla f.
mutual adj mūtuus.
mutually adv mūtuō, inter sē.
muzzle n ōs nt, rōstrum nt; (*guard*) fiscella f ♦ vt
fiscellā capistrāre.
my adj meus.
myriad n decem mīlia; (*any large no.*) sēscentī.
myrmidon n satelles m.
myrrh n murra f.
myrtle n myrtus f ♦ adj myrteus.
myrtle grove n myrtētum nt.
myself pron ipse, egomet; (*reflexive*) mē.
mysterious adj arcānus, occultus.
mysteriously adv occultē.
mystery n arcānum nt; (*rites*) mystēria ntpl;
(*fig*) latebra f.
mystic adj mysticus.
mystical adj mysticus.
mystification n fraus f, ambāgēs fpl.
mystify vt fraudāre, cōnfundere.
myth n fābula f.
mythical adj fābulōsus.
mythology n fābulae fpl.

N, n

nabob n rēx m.
nadir n fundus m.
nag n caballus m ♦ vt obiūrgitāre.
naiad n nāias f.
nail n clāvus m; (*finger*) unguis m; **hit the ~ on
the head** rem acū tangere ♦ vt clāvīs
adfīgere.
naive adj simplex.
naively adv simpliciter.
naiveté n simplicitās f.
naked adj nūdus.
nakedly adv apertē.
name n nōmen nt; (*repute*) existimātiō f; (*term*)
vocābulum nt; **by ~** nōmine; **have a bad ~**
male audīre; **have a good ~** bene audīre; **in**

the ~ of verbīs (*gen*); (*oath*) per ♦ *vt* appellāre, vocāre, nōmināre; (*appoint*) dīcere.
nameless *adj* nōminis expers, sine nōmine.
namely *adv* nempe, dīcō.
namesake *n* gentīlis *m/f*.
nanny goat *n* capra *f*.
nap *n* brevis somnus *m*; (*cloth*) villus *nt*.
napkin *n* linteum *nt*.
narcissus *n* narcissus *m*.
narcotic *adj* somnifer.
nard *n* nardus *f*.
narrate *vt* nārrāre, ēnārrāre.
narration *n* nārrātiō *f*.
narrative *n* fābula *f*.
narrator *n* nārrātor *m*.
narrow *adj* angustus ♦ *vt* coartāre ♦ *vi* coartārī.
narrowly *adv* aegrē, vix.
narrowness *n* angustiae *fpl*.
narrows *n* angustiae *fpl*.
nasal *adj* nārium.
nascent *adj* nāscēns.
nastily *adv* foedē.
nastiness *n* foeditās *f*.
nasty *adj* foedus, taeter, impūrus.
natal *adj* nātālis.
nation *n* populus *m*; (*foreign*) gēns *f*.
national *adj* pūblicus, cīvīlis; (*affairs*) domesticus.
nationality *n* cīvitās *f*.
native *adj* indigena; (*speech*) patrius ♦ *n* incola *m*, indigena *m/f*.
native land *n* patria *f*.
nativity *n* ortus *m*.
natural *adj* nātūrālis; (*innate*) nātīvus, genuīnus, īnsitus.
naturalization *n* cīvitās *f*.
naturalize *vt* cīvitāte dōnāre.
naturalized *adj* (*person*) cīvitāte dōnātus; (*thing*) īnsitus.
naturally *adv* nātūrāliter, secundum nātūram; (*of course*) scīlicet, certē.
nature *n* nātūra *f*; rērum nātūra *f*; (*character*) indolēs *f*, ingenium *nt*; (*species*) genus *nt*; **course of ~** nātūra *f*; **I know the ~ of** sciō quālis sit.
naught *n* nihil *nt*; **set at ~** parvī facere.
naughty *adj* improbus.
nausea *n* nausea *f*; (*fig*) fastīdium *nt*.
nauseate *vt* fastīdium movēre (*dat*); **be ~d with** fastīdīre.
nauseous *adj* taeter.
nautical *adj* nauticus, maritimus.
naval *adj* nāvālis.
navel *n* umbilīcus *m*.
navigable *adj* nāvigābilis.
navigate *vt, vi* nāvigāre.
navigation *n* rēs nautica *f*; (*sailing*) nāvigātiō *f*.
navigator *n* nauta *m*, gubernātor *m*.
navy *n* classis *f*, cōpiae nāvālēs *fpl*.
nay *adv* nōn; **~ more** immo.
near *adv* prope ♦ *adj* propinquus ♦ *prep* prope

(*acc*), ad (*acc*); **lie ~** adiacēre (*dat*) ♦ *vt* adpropinquāre (*dat*).
nearby *adj* iuxtā.
nearer *adj* propior.
nearest *adj* proximus.
nearly *adv* paene, prope, fermē.
neat *adj* nitidus, mundus, concinnus; (*wine*) pūrus.
neatly *adv* mundē, concinnē.
neatness *n* munditia *f*.
nebulous *adj* nebulōsus; (*fig*) incertus.
necessaries *n* rēs ad vīvendum necessāriae *fpl*.
necessarily *adv* necessāriō, necesse.
necessary *adj* necessārius, necesse; **it is ~** oportet (*+ acc and infin or gerundive of vt*).
necessitate *vt* cōgere (*inf*), efficere ut (*subj*).
necessitous *adj* egēnus, pauper.
necessity *n* necessitās *f*; (*thing*) rēs necessāria *f*; (*want*) paupertās *f*, egestās *f*.
neck *n* collum *nt*.
neckcloth *n* fōcāle *nt*.
necklace *n* monīle *nt*, torquis *m*.
nectar *n* nectar *nt*.
need *n* (*necessity*) necessitās *f*; (*want*) egestās *f*, inopia *f*, indigentia *f*; **there is ~ of** opus est (*abl*); **there is no ~ to** nihil est quod, cūr (*subj*) ♦ *vt* egēre (*abl*), carēre, indigēre (*abl*); **I ~** opus est mihī (*abl*).
needful *adj* necessārius.
needle *n* acus *f*.
needless *adj* vānus, inūtilis.
needlessly *adv* frustrā, sine causā.
needs *adv* necesse ♦ *npl* necessitātēs *fpl*.
needy *adj* egēns, inops, pauper.
nefarious *adj* nefārius, scelestus.
negation *n* negātiō *f*, īnfitiātiō *f*.
negative *adj* negāns ♦ *n* negātiō *f*; **answer in the ~** negāre ♦ *vt* vetāre, contrādīcere (*dat*).
neglect *n* neglegentia *f*, incūria *f*; (*of duty*) dērelictiō *f* ♦ *vt* neglegere, ōmittere.
neglectful *adj* neglegēns, immemor.
negligence *n* neglegentia *f*, incūria *f*.
negligent *adj* neglegēns, indīligēns.
negligently *adv* neglegenter, indīligenter.
negligible *adj* levissimus, minimī mōmentī.
negotiate *vi* agere dē ♦ *vt* (*deal*) peragere; (*difficulty*) superāre.
negotiation *n* āctiō *f*, pactum *nt*.
negotiator *n* lēgātus *m*, conciliātor *m*.
negro *n* Aethiops *m*.
neigh *vi* hinnīre.
neighbour *n* vīcīnus *m*, fīnitimus *m*.
neighbourhood *n* vīcīnia *f*, vīcīnitās *f*.
neighbouring *adj* vīcīnus, fīnitimus, propinquus.
neighbourly *adj* hūmānus, amīcus.
neighing *n* hinnītus *m*.
neither *adv* neque, nec; nēve, neu ♦ *pron* neuter ♦ *adj* neuter, neutra, neutrum (*like alter*); **~ ... nor** nec/neque ... nec/neque.
neophyte *n* tīrō *m*.
nephew *n* frātris fīlius *m*, sorōris fīlius *m*.

Nereid *n* Nērēis *f*.
nerve *n* nervus *m*; (*fig*) audācia *f*; ~s *pl* pavor *m*, trepidātiō *f*; **have the ~ to** audēre ♦ *vt* cōnfirmāre.
nervous *adj* diffīdēns, sollicitus, trepidus.
nervously *adv* trepidē.
nervousness *n* sollicitūdō *f*, diffīdentia *f*.
nest *n* nīdus *m* ♦ *vi* nīdificāre.
nestle *vi* recubāre.
nestling *n* pullus *m*.
net *n* rēte *nt* ♦ *vt* inrētīre.
nether *adj* īnferior.
nethermost *adj* īnfimus, īmus.
netting *n* rēticulum *nt*.
nettle *n* urtīca *f* ♦ *vt* inrītāre, ūrere.
neuter *adj* neuter.
neutral *adj* medius; **be ~** neutrī partī sē adiungere, medium sē gerere.
neutralize *vt* compēnsāre.
never *adv* nunquam.
nevertheless *adv* nihilōminus, at tamen.
new *adj* novus, integer, recēns.
newcomer *n* advena *m/f*.
newfangled *adj* novus, inaudītus.
newly *adv* nūper, modo.
newness *n* novitās *f*.
news *n* nūntius *m*; **what ~?** quid novī?; **~ was brought that** nūntiātum est (+ *acc and infin*).
newspaper *n* ācta diūrna/pūblica *ntpl*.
newt *n* lacerta *f*.
next *adj* proximus; (*time*) īnsequēns ♦ *adv* dēinde, dēinceps; **~ day** postrīdiē; **~ to** iuxtā; **come ~ to** excipere.
nibble *vi* rōdere.
nice *adj* bellus, dulcis; (*exact*) accūrātus; (*particular*) fastīdiōsus.
nicely *adv* bellē, probē.
nicety *n* subtīlitās *f*.
niche *n* aedicula *f*.
nick *n*: **in the ~ of time** in ipsō articulō temporis.
nickname *n* cognōmen *nt*.
niece *n* frātris fīlia *f*, sorōris fīlia *f*.
niggardliness *n* illīberālitās *f*, avāritia *f*.
niggardly *adj* illīberālis, parcus, avārus.
nigh *adv* prope.
night *n* nox *f*; **by ~** noctū; **all ~** pernox; **spend the ~** pernoctāre; **be awake all ~** pervigilāre ♦ *adj* nocturnus.
night bird *n* noctua *f*.
nightfall *n* prīmae tenebrae *fpl*; **at ~** sub noctem.
nightingale *n* luscinia *f*.
nightly *adj* nocturnus ♦ *adv* noctū.
nightmare *n* incubus *m*.
night work *n* lūcubrātiō *f*.
nimble *adj* agilis, pernīx.
nimbleness *n* agilitās *f*, pernīcitās *f*; (*mind*) argūtiae *fpl*.
nimbly *adv* pernīciter.
nine *num* novem; **~ each** novēnī; **~ times** noviēns; **~ days'** novendiālis.
nine hundred *num* nōngentī.
nine hundredth *adj* nōngentēsimus.

nineteen *num* ūndēvigintī; **~ each** ūndēvīcēnī; **~ times** deciēns et noviēns.
nineteenth *adj* ūndēvīcēsimus.
ninetieth *adj* nōnāgēsimus.
ninety *num* nōnāgintā; **~ each** nōnāgēnī; **~ times** nōnāgiēns.
ninth *adj* nōnus.
nip *vt* vellicāre; (*frost*) ūrere.
nippers *n* forceps *m*.
nipple *n* papilla *f*.
no *adv* nōn; (*correcting*) immo; **say ~** negāre ♦ *adj* nullus.
nobility *n* nōbilitās *f*; (*persons*) optimātēs *mpl*, nōbilēs *mpl*.
noble *adj* nōbilis; (*birth*) generōsus; (*appearance*) decōrus.
nobleman *n* prīnceps *m*, optimās *m*.
nobly *adv* nōbiliter, praeclārē.
nobody *n* nēmō *m*.
nocturnal *adj* nocturnus.
nod *n* nūtus *m* ♦ *vi* nūtāre; (*sign*) adnuere; (*sleep*) dormītāre.
noddle *n* caput *nt*.
node *n* nōdus *m*.
noise *n* strepitus *m*, sonitus *m*; (*loud*) fragor *m*; **make a ~** increpāre, strepere ♦ *vt*: **~ abroad** ēvulgāre; **be ~d abroad** percrēbrēscere.
noiseless *adj* tacitus.
noiselessly *adv* tacitē.
noisily *adv* cum strepitū.
noisome *adj* taeter, gravis.
noisy *adj* clāmōsus.
nomadic *adj* vagus.
nomenclature *n* vocābula *ntpl*.
nominally *adv* nōmine, verbō.
nominate *vt* nōmināre, dīcere; (*in writing*) scrībere.
nomination *n* nōminātiō *f*.
nominative *adj* nōminātīvus.
nominee *n* nōminātus *m*.
nonappearance *n* absentia *f*.
nonce *n*: **for the ~** semel.
nonchalance *n* aequus animus *m*.
nonchalantly *adv* aequō animō.
noncombatant *adj* imbellis.
noncommittal *adj* circumspectus.
nondescript *adj* īnsolitus.
none *adj* nullus ♦ *pron* nēmō *m*.
nonentity *n* nihil *nt*, nullus *m*.
nones *n* Nōnae *fpl*.
nonexistent *adj* quī nōn est.
nonplus *vt* ad incitās redigere.
nonresistance *n* patientia *f*.
nonsense *n* nūgae *fpl*, ineptiae *fpl*.
nonsensical *adj* ineptus, absurdus.
nook *n* angulus *m*.
noon *n* merīdiēs *m* ♦ *adj* merīdiānus.
no one *pron* nēmō *m* (*for gen/abl use* nullus).
noose *n* laqueus *m*.
nor *adv* neque, nec; nēve, neu.
norm *n* nōrma *f*.
normal *adj* solitus.
normally *adv* plērumque.

north _n_ septentriōnēs _mpl_ ♦ _adj_
  septentriōnālis.
northeast _adv_ inter septentriōnēs et
  orientem.
northerly _adj_ septentriōnālis.
northern _adj_ septentriōnālis.
North Pole _n_ arctos _f._
northwards _adv_ ad septentriōnēs versus.
northwest _adv_ inter septentriōnēs et
  occidentem ♦ _adj:_ **~ wind** Cōrus _m._
north wind _n_ aquilō _m._
nose _n_ nāsus _m,_ nārēs _fpl;_ **blow the ~**
  ēmungere; **lead by the ~** labiīs ductāre ♦ _vi_
  scrūtārī.
nostril _n_ nāris _f._
not _adv_ nōn, haud; **~ at all** haudquāquam; **~ as if**
  nōn quod, nōn quō; **~ but what** nōn quīn; **~**
  even nē ... quidem; **~ so very** nōn ita; **~ that**
  nōn quō; **and ~** neque; **does ~, did ~** (_interrog_)
  nonne; **if** ... **~** nisi; **that ~** (_purpose_) nē; (_fear_)
  nē nōn; **~ long after** haud multō post; **~ only**
  ... **but also** non modo/solum ... sed etiam; **~**
  yet nōndum.
notability _n_ vir praeclārus _m._
notable _adj_ īnsignis, īnsignītus, memorābilis.
notably _adv_ īnsignītē.
notary _n_ scrība _m._
notation _n_ notae _fpl._
notch _n_ incīsūra _f_ ♦ _vt_ incīdere.
note _n_ (_mark_) nota _f;_ (_comment_) adnotātiō _f;_
  (_letter_) litterulae _fpl;_ (_sound_) vōx _f;_ **make a ~ of**
  in commentāriōs referre ♦ _vt_ notāre;
  (_observe_) animadvertere.
notebook _n_ pugillārēs _mpl._
noted _adj_ īnsignis, praeclārus, nōtus.
noteworthy _adj_ memorābilis.
nothing _n_ nihil, nīl _nt;_ **~ but** merus, nīl nisi;
  come to ~ in inritum cadere; **for ~** frustrā;
  (_gift_) grātīs, grātuītō; **good for ~** nēquam;
  think ~ of nihilī facere.
notice _n_ (_official_) prōscrīptiō _f;_ (_private_) libellus
  _m;_ **attract ~** cōnspicī; **escape ~** latēre; **escape**
  the ~ of fallere; **give ~ of** dēnūntiāre; **take ~**
  of animadvertere ♦ _vt_ animadvertere,
  cōnspicere.
noticeable _adj_ cōnspicuus, īnsignis.
noticeably _adv_ īnsignītē.
notification _n_ dēnūntiātiō _f._
notify _vt_ (_event_) dēnūntiāre, indicāre; (_person_)
  renūntiāre (_dat_), certiōrem facere.
notion _n_ nōtiō _f,_ īnfōrmātiō _f;_ suspiciō _f._
notoriety _n_ īnfāmia _f._
notorious _adj_ fāmōsus, īnfāmis; (_thing_)
  manifestus.
notoriously _adv_ manifestō.
notwithstanding _adv_ nihilōminus, tamen
  ♦ _prep:_ **~ the danger** in tantō discrīmine.
nought _n_ nihil, nīl _nt._
noun _n_ nōmen _nt._
nourish _vt_ alere, nūtrīre.
nourisher _n_ altor _m,_ altrīx _f._
nourishment _n_ cibus _m,_ alimenta _ntpl._
novel _adj_ novus, inaudītus ♦ _n_ fābella _f._
novelty _n_ rēs nova _f;_ novitās _f,_ īnsolentia _f._

November _n_ mēnsis November _m;_ **of ~**
  November.
novice _n_ tīrō _m._
now _adv_ nunc; (_past_) iam; **~ and then**
  interdum; **just ~** nunc; (_lately_) dūdum, modo;
  ~ ... ~ modo ... modo ♦ _conj_ at, autem.
nowadays _adv_ nunc, hodiē.
nowhere _adv_ nusquam.
nowise _adv_ nullō modō, haudquāquam.
noxious _adj_ nocēns, noxius.
nuance _n_ color _m._
nucleus _n_ sēmen _nt._
nude _adj_ nūdus.
nudge _vt_ fodicāre.
nudity _n_ nūdātum corpus _nt._
nugget _n_ massa _f._
nuisance _n_ malum _nt,_ incommodum _nt._
null _adj_ inritus.
nullify _vt_ inritum facere; (_law_) abrogāre.
numb _adj_ torpēns, torpidus; **be ~** torpēre;
  become ~ torpēscere.
number _n_ numerus _m;_ **a ~ of** complūrēs,
  aliquot; **a great ~** multitūdō _f,_ frequentia _f;_ **a**
  small ~ īnfrequentia _f;_ **in large ~s** frequentēs
  ♦ _vt_ numerāre, ēnumerāre.
numberless _adj_ innumerābilis.
numbness _n_ torpor _m._
numerous _adj_ frequēns, crēber, plūrimī.
nun _n_ monacha _f._
nuptial _adj_ nūptiālis.
nuptials _n_ nūptiae _fpl._
nurse _n_ nūtrīx _f_ ♦ _vt_ (_child_) nūtrīre; (_sick_)
  cūrāre; (_fig_) fovēre.
nursery _n_ (_children_) cubiculum _nt;_ (_plants_)
  sēminārium _nt._
nursling _n_ alumnus _m,_ alumna _f._
nurture _n_ ēducātiō _f._
nut _n_ nux _f._
nutrition _n_ alimenta _ntpl._
nutritious _adj_ salūbris.
nutshell _n_ putāmen _nt._
nut tree _n_ nux _f._
nymph _n_ nympha _f._

O, o

O _interj_ ō!
oaf _n_ agrestis _m._
oak _n_ quercus _f;_ (_evergreen_) īlex _f;_ (_timber_)
  rōbur _nt_ ♦ _adj_ quernus, īlignus, rōboreus; **~**
  forest quercētum _nt._
oakum _n_ stuppa _f._
oar _n_ rēmus _m._
oarsman _n_ rēmex _m._
oaten _adj_ avēnāceus.
oath _n_ iūsiūrandum _nt;_ (_MIL_) sacrāmentum _nt;_

(imprecation) exsecrātiō *f*; **false** ~ periūrium *nt*; **take an ~ iūrāre; take an ~ of allegiance to** in verba iūrāre *(gen)*.

oats *n* avēna *f*.

obduracy *n* obstinātus animus *m*.

obdurate *adj* obstinātus, pervicāx.

obdurately *adv* obstinātē.

obedience *n* oboedientia *f*, obsequium *nt*.

obedient *adj* oboediēns, obsequēns; **be ~ to** pārēre *(dat)*, obtemperāre *(dat)*, obsequī *(dat)*.

obediently *adv* oboedienter.

obeisance *n* obsequium *nt*; **make ~ to** adōrāre.

obelisk *n* obeliscus *m*.

obese *adj* obēsus, pinguis.

obesity *n* obēsitās *f*, pinguitūdō *f*.

obey *vt* pārēre *(dat)*, obtemperāre *(dat)*, oboedīre *(dat)*; ~ **orders** dictō pārēre.

obituary *n* mortēs *fpl*.

object *n* rēs *f*; *(aim)* fīnis *m*, prōpositum *nt*; **be an ~ of hate** odiō esse; **with what ~ quō** cōnsiliō ♦ *vi* recūsāre, gravārī; **but, it is ~ed at enim;** ~ **to** improbāre.

objection *n* recūsātiō *f*, mora *f*; **I have no ~ nīl** moror.

objectionable *adj* invīsus, iniūcundus.

objective *adj* externus *nt*, prōpositum *nt*, fīnis *m*.

objurgate *vt* obiūrgāre, culpāre.

oblation *n* dōnum *nt*.

obligation *n* *(legal)* dēbitum *nt*; *(moral)* officium *nt*; **lay under an ~** obligāre, obstringere.

obligatory *adj* dēbitus, necessārius.

oblige *vt* *(force)* cōgere; *(contract)* obligāre, obstringere; *(compliance)* mōrem gerere *(dat)*, mōrigerārī *(dat)*; **I am ~d to** *(action)* dēbeō *(inf)*; *(person)* amāre, grātiam habēre *(dat)*.

obliging *adj* cōmis, officiōsus.

obligingly *adv* cōmiter, officiōsē.

oblique *adj* oblīquus.

obliquely *adv* oblīquē.

obliquity *n* *(moral)* prāvitās *f*.

obliterate *vt* dēlēre, oblitterāre.

obliteration *n* litūra *f*.

oblivion *n* oblīviō *f*.

oblivious *adj* oblīviōsus, immemor.

oblong *adj* oblongus.

obloquy *n* vītuperātiō *f*, opprobrium *nt*.

obnoxious *adj* invīsus.

obscene *adj* obscaenus, impūrus.

obscenity *n* obscaenitās *f*, impūritās *f*.

obscure *adj* obscūrus, caecus ♦ *vt* obscūrāre, officere *(dat)*.

obscurely *adv* obscūrē; *(speech)* per ambāgēs.

obscurity *n* obscūritās *f*; *(speech)* ambāgēs *fpl*.

obsequies *n* exsequiae *fpl*.

obsequious *adj* officiōsus, ambitiōsus.

obsequiously *adv* officiōsē.

obsequiousness *n* adsentātiō *f*.

observance *n* observantia *f*; *(rite)* rītus *m*.

observant *adj* attentus, dīligēns.

observation *n* observātiō *f*, animadversiō *f*; *(remark)* dictum *nt*.

observe *vt* animadvertere, contemplārī; *(see)* cernere, cōnspicere; *(remark)* dīcere; *(adhere to)* cōnservāre, observāre.

observer *n* spectātor *m*, contemplātor *m*.

obsess *vt* occupāre; **I am ~ed by** tōtus sum in *(abl)*.

obsession *n* studium *nt*.

obsolescent *adj*: **be ~** obsolēscere.

obsolete *adj* obsolētus; **become ~** exolēscere.

obstacle *n* impedīmentum *nt*, mora *f*.

obstinacy *n* pertinācia *f*, obstinātus animus *m*.

obstinate *adj* pertināx, obstinātus.

obstinately *adv* obstinātō animō.

obstreperous *adj* clāmōsus, ferus.

obstruct *vt* impedīre, obstruere, obstāre *(dat)*; *(POL)* intercēdere *(dat)*; *(fig)* officere *(dat)*.

obstruction *n* impedīmentum *nt*; *(POL)* intercessiō *f*

obstructionist *n* intercessor *m*.

obtain *vt* adipīscī, nancīscī, cōnsequī; comparāre; *(by request)* impetrāre ♦ *vi* tenēre, obtinēre.

obtrude *vi* sē inculcāre ♦ *vt* ingerere.

obtrusive *adj* importūnus, molestus.

obtuse *adj* hebes, stolidus.

obtusely *adv* stolidē.

obtuseness *n* stupor *m*.

obverse *adj* obversus.

obviate *vt* tollere, praevertere.

obvious *adj* ēvidēns, manifestus, apertus; **it is ~** appāret.

obviously *adv* ēvidenter, apertē, manifestō.

occasion *n* occāsiō *f*, locus *m*; *(reason)* causa *f* ♦ *vt* movēre, facessere, auctōrem esse *(gen)*.

occasional *adj* fortuītus.

occasionally *adv* interdum, nōnnunquam.

occidental *adj* occidentālis.

occult *adj* arcānus.

occupancy *n* possessiō *f*.

occupant *n* habitātor *m*, possessor *m*.

occupation *n* quaestus *m*, occupātiō *f*.

occupier *n* possessor *m*.

occupy *vt* possidēre; *(MIL)* occupāre; *(space)* complēre; *(attention)* distinēre, occupāre.

occur *vi* ēvenīre, accidere; *(to mind)* occurrere, in mentem venīre.

occurrence *n* ēventum *nt*; rēs *f*.

ocean *n* mare *nt*, ōceanus *m*.

October *n* mēnsis Octōber *m*; **of ~** Octōber.

ocular *adj* oculōrum; **give ~ proof of** ante oculōs pōnere, videntī dēmōnstrāre.

odd *adj* *(number)* impār; *(moment)* subsecīvus; *(appearance)* novus, īnsolitus.

oddity *n* novitās *f*; *(person)* homō rīdiculus *m*.

oddly *adv* mīrum in modum.

odds *n* praestantia *f*; **be at ~ with** dissidēre cum; **the ~ are against us** imparēs sumus; **the ~ are in our favour** superiōrēs sumus.

ode *n* carmen *nt*.

odious *adj* invīsus, odiōsus.

odium *n* invidia *f*.

odorous *adj* odōrātus.
odour *n* odor *m.*
of *prep gen*; (*origin*) ex, dē; (*cause*) *abl*; **all ~ us**
nōs omnēs; **the city ~ Rome** urbs Rōma.
off *adv* procul; (*prefix*) ab-; **~ and on** interdum;
~ with you aufer tē; **come ~** ēvādere; **well ~**
beātus; **well ~ for** abundāns (*abl*).
offal *n* quisquiliae *fpl.*
offence *n* offēnsiō *f*; (*legal*) dēlictum *nt*;
commit an ~ dēlinquere.
offend *vt* laedere, offendere; **be ~ed** aegrē
ferre ♦ *vi* dēlinquere; **~ against** peccāre in
(*acc*), violāre.
offender *n* reus *m.*
offensive *adj* odiōsus; (*smell*) gravis;
(*language*) contumēliōsus; **take the ~** bellum
īnferre.
offensively *adv* odiōsē; graviter.
offer *vt* offerre, dare, praebēre; (*hand*)
porrigere; (*violence*) adferre; (*honour*)
dēferre; (*with verb*) profitērī, pollicērī ♦ *n*
condiciō *f*; **~ for sale** venditāre.
offering *n* dōnum *nt*; (*to the dead*) īnferiae *fpl.*
off-hand *adj* neglegēns, incūriōsus.
office *n* (*POL*) magistrātus *m*, mūnus *nt*, honōs
m; (*kindness*) officium *nt*; (*place*) mēnsa *f.*
officer *n* praefectus *m*; lēgātus *m.*
official *adj* pūblicus ♦ *n* adiūtor *m*, minister *m.*
officially *adv* pūblicē.
officiate *vi* operārī, officiō fungī.
officious *adj* molestus.
officiously *adv* molestē.
officiousness *n* occursātiō *f.*
offing *n*: **in the ~** procul.
offset *vt* compēnsāre.
offspring *n* prōgeniēs *f*, līberī *mpl*; (*animal*)
fētus *m.*
often *adv* saepe, saepenumerō; **as ~ as**
quotiēs; totiēs ... quotiēs; **how ~?**
quotiēns?; **so ~** totiēns; **very ~** persaepe.
ogle *vi*: **~ at** līmīs oculīs intuērī.
ogre *n* mōnstrum *nt.*
oh *interj* (*joy, surprise*) ōh!; (*sorrow*) prō!
oil *n* oleum *nt* ♦ *vt* ungere.
oily *adj* oleōsus.
ointment *n* unguentum *nt.*
old *adj* (*person*) senex; (*thing*) vetus; (*ancient*)
antīquus, prīscus; **~ age** senectūs *f*; **be ten
years ~** decem annōs habēre; **ten years ~**
decem annōs nātus; **two years ~** bīmus; **good
~** antīquus; **good ~ days** antīquitās *f*; **grow ~**
senēscere; **of ~** quondam.
olden *adj* prīscus, prīstinus.
older *adj* nātū māior, senior.
oldest *adj* nātū māximus.
old-fashioned *adj* antīquus, obsolētus.
old man *n* senex *m.*
oldness *n* vetustās *f.*
old woman *n* anus *f.*
oligarchy *n* paucōrum dominātiō *f*,
optimātium factiō *f.*
olive *n* olea *f*; **~ orchard** olīvētum *nt.*

Olympiad *n* Olympias *f.*
Olympic *adj* Olympicus; **win an ~ victory**
Olympia vincere.
Olympic Games *n* Olympia *ntpl.*
omen *n* ōmen *nt*, auspicium *nt*; **announce a bad
~** obnūntiāre; **obtain favourable ~s** litāre.
ominous *adj* īnfaustus, mināx.
omission *n* praetermissiō *f*, neglegentia *f.*
omit *vt* ōmittere, praetermittere.
omnipotence *n* īnfīnīta potestās *f.*
omnipotent *adj* omnipotēns.
on *prep* (*place*) in (*abl*), in- (*prefix*); (*time*) *abl*;
(*coast of*) ad (*acc*); (*subject*) dē (*abl*); (*side*) ab
(*abl*) ♦ *adv* porrō, usque; **and so ~** ac
deinceps; **~ hearing the news** nūntiō acceptō;
~ equal terms (*in battle*) aequō Marte; **~ the
following day** posterō/proximō diē;
postrīdiē; **~ this side of** citrā (+ *acc*).
once *adv* semel; (*past*) ōlim, quondam; **at ~**
extemplō, statim; (*together*) simul; **for ~**
aliquandō; **~ and for all** semel; **~ more** dēnuō,
iterum; **~ upon a time** ōlim, quondam.
one *num* ūnus ♦ *pron* quīdam; (*of two*) alter,
altera, alterum; **~ and the same** ūnus; **~
another** inter sē, alius alium; **~ or the other**
alteruter; **~ day** ōlim; **~ each** singulī; **~ would
have thought** crēderēs; **be ~ of** in numerō
esse (*gen*); **be at ~** idem sentīre; **it is all ~**
nihil interest; **the ~** alter, hic; **this is the ~**
hōc illud est.
one-eyed *adj* luscus.
oneness *n* ūnitās *f.*
onerous *adj* gravis.
oneself *pron* ipse; (*reflexive*) sē.
one-sided *adj* inaequālis, inīquus.
onion *n* caepe *nt.*
onlooker *n* spectātor *m.*
only *adj* ūnus, sōlus; (*son*) ūnicus ♦ *adv* sōlum,
tantum, modo; (*with clause*) nōn nisi, nīl nisi,
nihil aliud quam; (*time*) dēmum; **if ~** sī modo;
(*wish*) utinam.
onrush *n* incursus *m.*
onset *n* impetus *m.*
onslaught *n* incursus *m*; **make an ~ on** (*words*)
invehī in (*acc*).
onto *prep* in (+ *acc*).
onus *n* officium *nt.*
onward, onwards *adv* porrō.
onyx *n* onyx *m.*
ooze *vi* mānāre, stillāre.
opaque *adj* haud perlūcidus.
open *adj* apertus; (*wide*) patēns, hiāns;
(*ground*) pūrus, apertus; (*question*) integer;
lie ~ patēre; **stand ~** hiāre; **throw ~**
adaperīre, patefacere; **it is ~ to me** to mihī
integrum est (*inf*); **while the question is still ~**
rē integrā ♦ *vt* aperīre, patefacere; (*book*)
ēvolvere; (*letter*) resolvere; (*speech*)
exōrdīrī; (*with ceremony*) inaugurāre; (*will*)
resignāre ♦ *vi* aperīrī, hiscere; (*sore*)
recrūdēscere; **~ out** extendere, pandere; **~
up** (*country*) aperīre.
open air *n*: **in the ~** sub dīvō.

open-handed *adj* largus, mūnificus.
open-handedness *n* largitās *f*.
open-hearted *adj* ingenuus.
opening *n* forāmen *nt*, hiātus *m*; (*ceremony*)
cōnsecrātiō *f*; (*opportunity*) occāsiō *f*, ānsa *f*
♦ *adj* prīmus.
openly *adv* palam, apertē.
open-mouthed *adj*: **stand ~ at** inhiāre.
operate *vi* rem gerere ♦ *vt* movēre.
operation *n* opus *nt*, āctiō *f*; (*MED*) sectiō *f*.
operative *adj* efficāx.
ophthalmia *n* lippitūdō *f*.
opiate *adj* somnifer.
opine *vi* opīnārī, existimāre.
opinion *n* sententia *f*; (*of person*) existimātiō *f*;
public ~ fāma *f*; **in my ~** meō iūdiciō, meō
animō.
opponent *n* adversārius *m*, hostis *m*.
opportune *adj* opportūnus, tempestīvus.
opportunely *adv* opportūnē.
opportunity *n* occāsiō *f*; (*to act*) facultās *f*;
potestās *f*.
oppose *vt* (*barrier*) obicere; (*contrast*)
oppōnere ♦ *vi* adversārī (*dat*), resistere (*dat*),
obstāre (*dat*); **be ~d to** adversārī (*dat*);
(*opinion*) dīversum esse ab.
opposite *adj* (*facing*) adversus; (*contrary*)
contrārius, dīversus ♦ *prep* contrā (*acc*),
adversus (*acc*); **directly ~** ē regiōne (*gen*)
♦ *adv* ex adversō.
opposition *n* repugnantia *f*; (*party*) factiō
adversa *f*.
oppress *vt* opprimere, adflīgere; (*burden*)
premere, onerāre.
oppression *n* iniūria *f*, servitūs *f*.
oppressive *adj* gravis, inīquus; **become more
~** ingravēscere.
oppressor *n* tyrannus *m*.
opprobrious *adj* turpis.
opprobriously *adv* turpiter.
opprobrium *n* dēdecus *nt*, ignōminia *f*.
optical *adj* oculōrum.
optical illusion *n* oculōrum lūdibrium *nt*.
optimism *n* spēs *f*.
option *n* optiō *f*, arbitrium *nt*; **I have no ~** nōn
est arbitriī meī.
optional *adj*: **it is ~ for you** optiō tua est.
opulence *n* opēs *fpl*, cōpia *f*.
opulent *adj* dīves, cōpiōsus.
or *conj* aut, vel, -ve; (*after* **utrum**) an; **~ else**
aliōquīn; **~ not** (*direct*) annōn; (*indirect*)
necne.
oracle *n* ōrāculum *nt*.
oracular *adj* fātidicus; (*fig*) obscūrus.
oral *adj*: **give an ~ message** vōce nūntiāre.
orally *adv* vōce, verbīs.
oration *n* ōrātiō *f*.
orator *n* ōrātor *m*.
oratorical *adj* ōrātōrius.
oratory *n* ēloquentia *f*, rhētoricē *f*; (*for prayer*)
sacellum *nt*; **of ~** dīcendī, ōrātōrius.
orb *n* orbis *m*.
orbit *n* orbis *m*, ambitus *m*.
orchard *n* pōmārium *nt*.

ordain *vt* ēdīcere, sancīre.
ordeal *n* labor *m*.
order *n* (*arrangement*) ōrdō *m*; (*class*) ōrdō *m*;
(*battle*) aciēs *f*; (*command*) iussum *nt*,
imperium *nt*; (*money*) perscrīptiō *f*; **in ~**
dispositus; (*succession*) deinceps; **in ~ that/to**
ut (*+ subj*); **in ~ that not** nē (*+ subj*); **put in ~**
dispōnere, ōrdināre; **by ~ of** iussū (*gen*); **out
of ~** incompositus; **without ~s from** iniussū
(*gen*) ♦ *vt* (*arrange*) dispōnere, ōrdināre;
(*command*) iubēre (*+ acc and infin*), imperāre
(*dat and ut/nē +subj*).
orderly *adj* ōrdinātus; (*conduct*) modestus ♦ *n*
accēnsus *m*.
ordinance *n* ēdictum *nt*, institūtum *nt*.
ordinarily *adv* plērumque, ferē.
ordinary *adj* ūsitātus, solitus, cottīdiānus.
ordnance *n* tormenta *ntpl*.
ordure *n* stercus *m*.
ore *n* aes *nt*; **iron ~** ferrum īnfectum *nt*.
Oread *n* (*MYTH*) Oreas *f*.
organ *n* (*bodily*) membrum *nt*; (*musical*)
organum *nt*, hydraulus *m*.
organic *adj* nātūrālis.
organically *adv* nātūrā.
organization *n* ōrdinātiō *f*, structūra *f*.
organize *vt* ōrdināre, īnstituere, adparāre.
orgies *n* orgia *ntpl*.
orgy *n* cōmissātiō *f*.
orient *n* oriēns *m*.
oriental *adj* Asiāticus.
orifice *n* ōstium *nt*.
origin *n* orīgō *f*, prīncipium *nt*; (*source*) fōns *m*;
(*birth*) genus *nt*.
original *adj* prīmus, prīstinus; (*LIT*) proprius
♦ *n* exemplar *nt*.
originally *adv* prīncipiō, antīquitus.
originate *vt* īnstituere, auctōrem esse (*gen*)
♦ *vi* exorīrī; **~ in** innāscī in (*abl*), initium
dūcere ab.
originator *n* auctor *m*.
orisons *n* precēs *fpl*.
ornament *n* ōrnāmentum *nt*; (*fig*) decus *nt* ♦ *vt*
ōrnāre, decorāre; **I am ~** ornamentō sum.
ornamental *adj* decōrus; **be ~** decorī esse.
ornamentally *adv* ōrnātē.
ornate *adj* ōrnātus.
ornately *adv* ōrnātē.
orphan *n* orbus *m*, orba *f*.
orphaned *adj* orbātus.
orthodox *adj* antīquus.
orthography *n* orthographia *f*.
oscillate *vi* reciprocāre.
osculate *vt* ōsculārī.
osier *n* vīmen *nt* ♦ *adj* vīmineus.
osprey *n* haliaeetos *m*.
ostensible *adj* speciōsus.
ostensibly *adv* per speciem.
ostentation *n* iactātiō *f*, ostentātiō *f*.
ostentatious *adj* glōriōsus, ambitiōsus.
ostentatiously *adv* glōriōsē.
ostler *n* agāsō *m*.
ostrich *n* strūthiocamēlus *m*.

other *adj* alius; (*of two*) alter; **one or the ~**
alteruter; **every ~ year** tertiō quōque annō;
on the ~ side of ultrā (+ *acc*); **of ~s** aliēnus.
otherwise *adv* aliter; (*if not*) aliōquī.
otter *n* lutra *f*.
ought *vi* dēbēre (+ *infin or gerundive of vt*); **I ~**
mē oportet; **I ~ to have said** dēbuī dīcere.
ounce *n* ūncia *f*; **two ~s** sextāns *m*; **three ~s**
quadrāns *m*; **four ~s** triēns *m*; **five ~s**
quīncūnx *m*; **six ~s** sēmis *m*; **seven ~s** septūnx
m; **eight ~s** bēs *m*; **nine ~s** dōdrāns *m*; **ten ~s**
dextāns *m*; **eleven ~s** deūnx *m*.
our *adj* noster.
ourselves *pron* ipsī; (*reflexive*) nōs.
oust *vt* extrūdere, ēicere.
out *adv* (*rest*) forīs; (*motion*) forās; **~ of** dē, ē/ex
(*abl*); (*cause*) propter (*acc*); (*beyond*) extrā,
ultrā (*acc*); **be ~** (*book*) in manibus esse;
(*calculation*) errāre; (*fire*) exstinctum esse;
(*secret*) palam esse.
outbreak *n* initium *nt*, ēruptiō *f*.
outburst *n* ēruptiō *f*.
outcast *n* profugus *m*.
outcome *n* ēventus *m*, exitus *m*.
outcry *n* clāmor *m*, adclāmātiō *f*; **raise an ~**
against obstrepere (*dat*).
outdistance *vt* praevertere.
outdo *vt* superāre.
outdoor *adj* sub dīvō.
outer *adj* exterior.
outermost *adj* extrēmus.
outfit *n* īnstrūmenta *ntpl*; vestīmenta *ntpl*.
outflank *vt* circumīre.
outgrow *vt* excēdere ex.
outing *n* excursiō *f*.
outlandish *adj* barbarus.
outlaw *n* prōscrīptus *m* ♦ *vt* prōscrībere, aquā
et ignī interdīcere (*dat*).
outlawry *n* aquae et ignis interdictiō *f*.
outlay *n* impēnsa *f*, sūmptus *m*.
outlet *n* ēmissārium *nt*, exitus *m*.
outline *n* ductus *m*, adumbrātiō *f* ♦ *vt*
adumbrāre.
outlive *vt* superesse (*dat*).
outlook *n* prōspectus *m*.
outlying *adj* longinquus, exterior.
outnumber *vt* numerō superiōrēs esse,
multitūdine superāre.
out-of-doors *adv* forīs.
outpost *n* statiō *f*.
outpouring *n* effūsiō *f*.
output *n* fructus *m*.
outrage *n* flāgitium *nt*, iniūria *f* ♦ *vt* laedere,
violāre.
outrageous *adj* flāgitiōsus, indignus.
outrageously *adv* flāgitiōsē.
outrider *n* praecursor *m*.
outright *adv* penitus, prōrsus; semel.
outrun *vt* praevertere.
outset *n* initium *nt*.
outshine *vt* praelūcēre (*dat*).
outside *adj* externus ♦ *adv* extrā, forīs;
(*motion to*) forās; **~ in** inversus; **from ~**

extrīnsecus ♦ *n* exterior pars *f*; (*show*)
speciēs *f*; **at the ~** summum, ad summum; **on
the ~** extrīnsecus ♦ *prep* extrā (*acc*).
outsider *n* aliēnus *m*; (*POL*) novus homō *m*.
outskirts *n* suburbānus ager *m*; **on the ~**
suburbānus.
outspoken *adj* līber.
outspokenness *n* lībertās *f*.
outspread *adj* patulus.
outstanding *adj* ēgregius, īnsignis,
singulāris; (*debt*) residuus.
outstep *vt* excēdere.
outstretched *adj* passus, porrēctus, extentus.
outstrip *vt* praevertere.
outvote *vt* suffrāgiīs superāre.
outward *adj* externus; **~ form** speciēs *f* ♦ *adv*
domō, forās.
outweigh *vt* praeponderāre.
outwit *vt* dēcipere, circumvenīre.
outwork *n* prōpugnāculum *nt*, bracchium *nt*.
outworn *adj* exolētus.
oval *adj* ōvātus ♦ *n* ōvum *nt*.
ovation *n* (*triumph*) ovātiō *f*; **receive an ~** cum
laudibus excipī.
oven *n* furnus *m*, fornāx *f*.
over *prep* (*above*) super (*abl*), suprā (*acc*);
(*across*) super (*acc*); (*extent*) per (*acc*); (*time*)
inter (*acc*); **~ and above** super (*acc*), praeter
(*acc*); **all ~ per**; **~ against** adversus (*acc*) ♦ *adv*
suprā; (*excess*) nimis; (*done*) cōnfectus; **~
again** dēnuō; **~ and above** īnsuper; **~ and ~**
identidem; **be left ~** superesse, restāre; **it is
all ~ with** āctum est dē.
overall *adj* tōtus ♦ *adv* ubīque, passim.
overawe *vt* formīdinem inicere (*dat*).
overbalance *vi* titubāre.
overbearing *adj* superbus.
overboard *adv* ē nāvī, in mare; **throw ~**
excutere, iactāre.
overbold *adj* importūnus.
overburden *vt* praegravāre.
overcast *adj* nūbilus.
overcoat *n* paenula *f*, lacerna *f*.
overcome *vt* superāre, vincere.
overconfidence *n* cōnfīdentia *f*.
overconfident *adj* cōnfīdēns.
overdo *vt* modum excēdere in (*abl*).
overdone *adj* (*style*) pūtidus.
overdraw *vt* (*style*) exaggerāre.
overdue *adj* (*money*) residuus.
overestimate *vt* māiōris aestimāre.
overflow *n* ēluviō *f* ♦ *vi* abundāre, redundāre
♦ *vt* inundāre.
overgrown *adj* obsitus; **be ~** luxuriāre.
overhang *vt, vi* impendēre, imminēre (*dat*).
overhaul *vt* reficere.
overhead *adv* īnsuper.
overhear *vt* excipere, auscultāre.
overjoyed *adj* nimiō gaudiō ēlātus.
overladen *adj* praegravātus.
overland *adv* terrā.
overlap *vt* implicāre.
overlay *vt* indūcere.

overload *vt* (*fig*) obruere.
overlook *vt* (*place*) dēspectāre, imminēre
(*dat*); (*knowledge*) ignōrāre; (*notice*)
neglegere, praetermittere; (*fault*) ignōscere
(*dat*).
overlord *n* dominus *m*.
overmaster *vt* dēvincere.
overmuch *adv* nimis, plūs aequō.
overnight *adj* nocturnus ♦ *adv* noctū.
overpower *vt* superāre, domāre, obruere,
opprimere.
overpraise *vt* in māius extollere.
overrate *vt* māiōris aestimāre.
overreach *vt* circumvenīre.
overriding *adj* praecipuus.
overrule *vt* rescindere.
overrun *vt* pervagārī; (*fig*) obsidēre.
oversea *adj* trānsmarīnus.
oversee *vt* praeesse (*dat*).
overseer *n* cūrātor *m*, custōs *m*.
overset *vt* ēvertere.
overshadow *vt* officere (*dat*).
overshoot *vt* excēdere.
oversight *n* neglegentia *f*.
overspread *vt* offendere (*dat*), obdūcere.
overstep *vt* excēdere.
overt *adj* apertus.
overtake *vt* cōnsequī; (*surprise*) opprimere,
dēprehendere.
overtax *vt* (*fig*) abūtī (*abl*).
overthrow *vt* ēvertere; (*destroy*) prōflīgāre,
dēbellāre ♦ *n* ēversiō *f*, ruīna *f*.
overtly *adv* palam.
overtop *vt* superāre.
overture *n* exōrdium *nt*; **make ~s to** temptāre,
agere cum, lēgātōs mittere ad.
overturn *vt* ēvertere.
overweening *adj* superbus, adrogāns,
īnsolēns.
overwhelm *vt* obruere, dēmergere,
opprimere.
overwhelming *adj* īnsignis,
vehementissimus.
overwhelmingly *adv* mīrum quantum.
overwork *vi* plūs aequō labōrāre ♦ *vt*
cōnficere ♦ *n* immodicus labor *m*.
overwrought *adj* (*emotion*) ēlātus; (*style*)
ēlabōrātus.
owe *vt* dēbēre.
owing *adj*: **be ~** dēbērī; **~ to** (*person*) per;
(*cause*) ob/propter (*acc*).
owl *n* būbō *m*; ulula *f*.
own *adj* proprius; **my ~** meus; **have of one's ~**
domī habēre; **hold one's ~** parem esse ♦ *vt*
possidēre, habēre; (*admit*) fatērī, cōnfitērī.
owner *n* dominus *m*, possessor *m*.
ownership *n* possessiō *f*, mancipium *nt*.
ox *n* bōs *m*.
ox herd *n* bubulcus *m*.
oyster *n* ostrea *f*.

P, p

pace *n* passus *m*; (*speed*) gradus *m*; **keep ~**
gradum cōnferre ♦ *vi* incēdere; **~ up and
down** spatiārī, inambulāre.
pacific *adj* pācificus; (*quiet*) placidus.
pacification *n* pācificātiō *f*.
pacifist *n* imbellis *m*.
pacify *vt* (*anger*) plācāre; (*rising*) sēdāre.
pack *n* (*MIL*) sarcina *f*; (*animals*) grex *m*; (*people*)
turba *f* ♦ *vt* (*kit*) colligere; (*crowd*) stīpāre; **~
together** coartāre; **~ up** colligere,
compōnere ♦ *vi* vāsa colligere; **send ~ing**
missum facere ♦ *adj* (*animal*) clītellārius.
package *n* fasciculus *m*, sarcina *f*.
packet *n* fasciculus *m*; (*ship*) nāvis āctuāria *f*.
packhorse *n* iūmentum *nt*.
packsaddle *n* clītellae *fpl*.
pact *n* foedus *nt*, pactum *nt*.
pad *n* pulvillus *m*.
padding *n* tōmentum *nt*.
paddle *n* rēmus *m* ♦ *vi* rēmigāre.
paddock *n* saeptum *nt*.
paean *n* paeān *m*.
pagan *adj* pāgānus.
page *n* (*book*) pāgina *f*; (*boy*) puer *m*.
pageant *n* pompa *f*, spectāculum *nt*.
pageantry *n* adparātus *m*.
pail *n* situla *f*.
pain *n* dolor *m*; **be in ~** dolēre ♦ *vt* dolōre
adficere.
painful *adj* acerbus; (*work*) labōriōsus.
painfully *adv* acerbē, labōriōsē.
painless *adj* dolōris expers.
painlessly *adv* sine dolōre.
painlessness *n* indolentia *f*.
pains *npl* opera *f*; **take ~** operam dare; **take ~
with** (*art*) ēlabōrāre.
painstaking *adj* dīligēns, operōsus.
painstakingly *adv* dīligenter, summā cūrā.
paint *n* pigmentum *nt*; (*cosmetic*) fūcus *m* ♦ *vt*
pingere; (*red*) fūcāre; (*in words*) dēpingere;
(*portrait*) dēpingere.
paintbrush *n* pēnicillus *m*.
painter *n* pictor *m*.
painting *n* pictūra *f*.
pair *n* pār *nt* ♦ *vt* coniungere, compōnere.
palace *n* rēgia *f*.
palatable *adj* suāvis, iūcundus.
palate *n* palātum *nt*.
palatial *adj* rēgius.
palaver *n* colloquium *nt*, sermunculī *mpl*.
pale *n* pālus *m*, vallus *m*; **beyond the ~**
extrāneus ♦ *adj* pallidus; **look ~** pallēre;
grow ~ pallēscere; **~ brown** subfuscus; **~
green** subviridis ♦ *vi* pallēscere.
paleness *n* pallor *m*.

palimpsest n palimpsēstus m.
paling n saepēs f.
palisade n (MIL) vallum nt.
palish adj pallidulus.
pall n (funeral) pallium nt ♦ vi taedēre.
pallet n grabātus m.
palliasse n strāmentum nt.
palliate vt extenuāre, excūsāre.
palliation n excūsātiō f.
palliative n lēnīmentum nt.
pallid adj pallidus.
pallor n pallor m.
palm n (hand) palma f; (tree) palma f ♦ vt: ~ off impōnere.
palmy adj flōrēns.
palpable adj tractābilis; (fig) manifestus.
palpably adv manifestō, propalam.
palpitate vi palpitāre, micāre.
palpitation n palpitātiō f.
palsied adj membrīs captus.
palsy n paralysis f.
paltry adj vīlis, frīvolus.
pamper vt indulgēre (dat).
pampered adj dēlicātus.
pamphlet n libellus m.
pan n patina f, patella f; (frying) sartāgō f; (of balance) lanx f.
pancake n laganum nt.
pander n lēnō m ♦ vi: ~ to lēnōcinārī (dat).
panegyric n laudātiō f.
panegyrist n laudātor m.
panel n (wall) abacus m; (ceiling) lacūnār nt; (judges) decuria f.
panelled adj laqueātus.
pang n dolor m.
panic n pavor m ♦ vi trepidāre.
panic-stricken adj pavidus.
panniers n clītellae fpl.
panoply n arma ntpl.
panorama n prōspectus m.
panpipe n fistula f.
pant vi anhēlāre.
panther n panthēra f.
panting n anhēlitus m.
pantomime n mīmus m.
pantry n cella penāria f.
pap n mamma f.
paper n charta f.
papyrus n papyrus f.
par n: on a ~ with pār (dat).
parable n parabolē f.
parade n pompa f; (show) adparātus m ♦ vt trādūcere, iactāre ♦ vi pompam dūcere, incēdere.
paradox n verba sēcum repugnantia; ~es pl paradoxa ntpl.
paragon n exemplar nt, specimen nt.
paragraph n caput nt.
parallel adj parallēlus; (fig) cōnsimilis.
paralyse vt dēbilitāre; (with fear) percellere; **be ~d** torpēre.
paralysis n dēbilitās f; (fig) torpēdō f.
paramount adj prīnceps, summus.

paramour n adulter m.
parapet n lōrīca f.
paraphernalia n adparātus m.
paraphrase vt vertere.
parasite n parasītus m.
parasol n umbella f.
parboiled adj subcrūdus.
parcel n fasciculus m ♦ vt: ~ out distribuere, dispertīre.
parch vt torrēre.
parched adj torridus, āridus; **be ~** ārēre.
parchment n membrāna f.
pardon n venia f ♦ vt ignōscere (dat); (offence) condōnāre.
pardonable adj ignōscendus.
pare vt dēglūbere; (nails) resecāre.
parent n parēns m/f, genitor m, genetrīx f.
parentage n stirps f, genus nt.
parental adj patrius.
parenthesis n interclūsiō f.
parings n praesegmina ntpl.
parish n (ECCL) paroecia f.
parity n aequālitās f.
park n hortī mpl.
parlance n sermō m.
parley n colloquium nt ♦ vi colloquī, agere.
parliament n senātus m; **house of ~** cūria f.
parliamentary adj senātōrius.
parlour n exedrium nt.
parlous adj difficilis, perīculōsus.
parochial adj mūnicipālis.
parody n carmen ioculāre nt ♦ vt calumniārī.
parole n fidēs f.
paronomasia n agnōminātiō f.
paroxysm n accessus m.
parricide n (doer) parricīda m; (deed) parricīdium nt.
parrot n psittacus m.
parry vt ēlūdere, prōpulsāre.
parsimonious adj parcus.
parsimoniously adv parcē.
parsimony n parsimōnia f, frūgālitās f.
part n pars f; (play) partēs fpl, persōna f; (duty) officium nt; **~s** loca ntpl; (ability) ingenium nt; **for my ~** equidem; **for the most ~** māximam partem; **on the ~ of** ab; **act the ~ of** persōnam sustinēre, partēs agere; **have no ~ in** expers esse (gen); **in ~** partim; **it is the ~ of a wise man** sapientis est; **play one's ~** officiō satisfacere; **take ~ in** interesse (dat), particeps esse (gen); **take in good ~** in bonam partem accipere; **take someone's ~** adesse alicuī, dēfendere aliquem; **from all ~s** undique; **in foreign ~s** peregrē; **in two ~s** bifāriam; (MIL) bipartītō; **in three ~s** trifāriam; (MIL) tripartītō; **of ~s** ingeniōsus ♦ vt dīvidere, sēparāre, dirimere; **~ company** dīversōs discēdere ♦ vi dīgredī, discēdere; (things) dissilīre; **~ with** renūntiāre.
partake vi interesse, particeps esse; **~ of** gustāre.
partial adj (biased) inīquus, studiōsus; (incomplete) mancus; **be ~ to** favēre (dat),

studēre (*dat*); **win a ~ victory** aliquā ex parte vincere.
partiality *n* favor *m*, studium *nt*.
partially *adv* partim, aliquā ex parte.
participant *n* particeps *m/f*.
participate *vi* interesse, particeps esse.
participation *n* societās *f*.
particle *n* particula *f*.
parti-coloured *adj* versicolor, varius.
particular *adj* (*own*) proprius; (*special*) praecipuus; (*exact*) dīligēns, accūrātus; (*fastidious*) fastīdiōsus; **a ~ person** quīdam ♦ *n* rēs *f*; **with full ~s** subtīliter; **give all the ~s** omnia exsequī; **in ~** praesertim.
particularity *n* subtīlitās *f*.
particularize *vt* singula exsequī.
particularly *adv* praecipuē, praesertim, in prīmīs, māximē.
parting *n* dīgressus *m*, discessus *m* ♦ *adj* ultimus.
partisan *n* fautor *m*, studiōsus *m*.
partisanship *n* studium *nt*.
partition *n* (*act*) partītiō *f*; (*wall*) pariēs *m*; (*compartment*) loculāmentum *nt* ♦ *vt* dīvidere.
partly *adv* partim, ex parte.
partner *n* socius *m*; (*in office*) collēga *f*.
partnership *n* societās *f*; **form a ~** societātem inīre.
partridge *n* perdīx *m/f*.
parturition *n* partus *m*.
party *n* (*POL*) factiō *f*, partēs *fpl*; (*entertainment*) convīvium *nt*; (*MIL*) manus *f*; (*individual*) homō *m/f*; (*associate*) socius *m*, cōnscius *m*.
party spirit *n* studium *nt*.
parvenu *n* novus homō *m*.
pass *n* (*hill*) saltus *m*; (*narrow*) angustiae *fpl*, faucēs *fpl*; (*crisis*) discrīmen *nt*; (*document*) diplōma *nt*; (*fighting*) petītiō *f*; **things have come to such a ~** in eum locum ventum est, adeō rēs rediit ♦ *vi* īre, praeterīre; (*time*) trānsīre; (*property*) pervenīre; **~ away** abīre; (*die*) morī, perīre; (*fig*) dēfluere; **~ by** praeterīre; **~ for** haberī prō (*abl*); **~ on** abīre; **~ over** trānsīre; **come to ~** fierī, ēvenīre; **let ~** intermittere, praetermittere ♦ *vt* praeterīre; (*riding*) praetervehī; (*by hand*) trādere; (*law*) iubēre; (*limit*) excēdere; (*sentence*) interpōnere, dīcere; (*test*) satisfacere (*dat*); (*time*) dēgere, agere; **~ accounts** ratiōnēs ratās habēre; **~ the day** diem cōnsūmere; **~ a law** lēgem ferre; **~ a decree** dēcernere; **~ off** ferre; **~ over** praeterīre, mittere; (*fault*) ignōscere (*dat*); **~ round** trādere; **~ through** trānsīre.
passable *adj* (*place*) pervius; (*standard*) mediocris.
passably *adv* mediocriter.
passage *n* iter *nt*, cursus *m*; (*land*) trānsitus *m*; (*sea*) trānsmissiō *f*; (*book*) locus *m*; **of ~** (*bird*) advena.
passenger *n* vector *m*.
passer-by *n* praeteriēns *m*.

passing *n* obitus *m* ♦ *adj* admodum.
passion *n* animī mōtus *m*, permōtiō *f*, ārdor *m*; (*anger*) īra *f*; (*lust*) libīdō *f*.
passionate *adj* ārdēns, impotēns, ācer; īrācundus.
passionately *adv* vehementer, ārdenter; īrācundē; **be ~ in love** amōre ārdēre.
passive *adj* iners.
passiveness *n* inertia *f*, patientia *f*.
passport *n* diplōma *nt*.
password *n* tessera *f*.
past *adj* praeteritus; (*recent*) proximus ♦ *n* praeterita *ntpl* ♦ *prep* praeter (*acc*); (*beyond*) ultrā (*acc*).
paste *n* glūten *nt* ♦ *vt* glūtināre.
pastime *n* lūdus *m*, oblectāmentum *nt*.
pastoral *adj* pastōrālis; (*poem*) būcolicus.
pastry *n* crustum *nt*.
pasture *n* pāstus *m*, pāscuum *nt* ♦ *vt* pāscere.
pat *vt* dēmulcēre ♦ *adj* opportūnus.
patch *n* pannus *m* ♦ *vt* resarcīre.
patchwork *n* centō *m*.
pate *n* caput *nt*.
patent *adj* apertus, manifestus ♦ *n* prīvilēgium *nt*.
patently *adv* manifestō.
paternal *adj* paternus.
path *n* sēmita *f*, trāmes *m*.
pathetic *adj* miserābilis.
pathetically *adv* miserābiliter.
pathfinder *n* explorātor *m*.
pathless *adj* āvius.
pathos *n* misericordia *f*; (*RHET*) dolor *m*.
pathway *n* sēmita *f*.
patience *n* patientia *f*.
patient *adj* patiēns ♦ *n* aeger *m*.
patiently *adv* patienter, aequō animō.
patois *n* sermō *m*.
patrician *adj* patricius ♦ *n* patricius *m*.
patrimony *n* patrimōnium *nt*.
patriot *n* amāns patriae *m*.
patriotic *adj* pius, amāns patriae.
patriotically *adv* prō patriā.
patriotism *n* amor patriae *m*.
patrol *n* excubiae *fpl* ♦ *vi* circumīre.
patron *n* patrōnus *m*, fautor *m*.
patronage *n* patrōcinium *nt*.
patroness *n* patrōna *f*, fautrīx *f*.
patronize *vt* favēre (*dat*), fovēre.
patronymic *n* nōmen *nt*.
patter *vi* crepitāre ♦ *n* crepitus *m*.
pattern *n* exemplar *nt*, exemplum *nt*, nōrma *f*; (*ideal*) specimen *nt*; (*design*) figūra *f*.
paucity *n* paucitās *f*.
paunch *n* abdōmen *nt*, venter *m*.
pauper *n* pauper *m*.
pause *n* mora *f*, intervallum *nt* ♦ *vi* īnsistere, intermittere.
pave *vt* sternere; **~ the way** (*fig*) viam mūnīre.
pavement *n* pavīmentum *nt*.
pavilion *n* tentōrium *nt*.
paw *n* pēs *m* ♦ *vt* pede pulsāre.
pawn *n* (*chess*) latrunculus *m*; (*COMM*) pignus *nt*,

fīdūcia f ♦ vt oppignerāre.
pawnbroker n pignerātor m.
pay n mercēs f; (MIL) stīpendium nt; (workman)
manupretium nt ♦ vt solvere, pendere; (debt)
exsolvere; (in full) persolvere; (honour)
persolvere; (MIL) stīpendium numerāre (dat);
(penalty) dare, luere; ~ **down** numerāre; ~ **for**
condūcere; ~ **off** dissolvere, exsolvere; ~ **out**
expendere; (publicly) ērogāre; ~ **up**
dēpendere; ~ **a compliment to** laudāre; ~
respects to salūtāre ♦ vi respondēre; **it ~s**
expedit.
payable adj solvendus.
paymaster n (MIL) tribūnus aerārius m.
payment n solūtiō f; (money) pēnsiō f.
pea n pīsum n; **like as two ~s** tam similis quam
lac lactī est.
peace n pāx f; ~ **and quiet** ōtium nt; **breach of
the ~** vīs f; **establish ~** pācem conciliāre; **hold
one's ~** reticēre; **sue for ~** pācem petere.
peaceable adj imbellis, placidus.
peaceably adv placidē.
peaceful adj tranquillus, placidus, pācātus.
peacefully adv tranquillē.
peacemaker n pācificus m.
peace-offering n piāculum nt.
peach n Persicum nt.
peacock n pāvō m.
peak n apex m, vertex m.
peal n (bell) sonitus m; (thunder) fragor m ♦ vi
sonāre.
pear n pirum nt; (tree) pirus f.
pearl n margarīta f.
pearly adj gemmeus; (colour) candidus.
peasant n agricola m, colōnus m.
peasantry n agricolae mpl.
pebble n calculus m.
pebbly adj lapidōsus.
peccadillo n culpa f.
peck n (measure) modius m ♦ vt vellicāre.
peculate vi pecūlārī.
peculation n pecūlātus m.
peculiar adj (to one) proprius; (strange)
singulāris.
peculiarity n proprietās f, nota f.
peculiarly adv praecipuē, praesertim.
pecuniary adj pecūniārius.
pedagogue n magister m.
pedant n scholasticus m.
pedantic adj nimis dīligenter.
pedantically adv dīligentior.
pedantry n nimia dīligentia f.
peddle vt circumferre.
pedestal n basis f.
pedestrian adj pedester ♦ n pedes m.
pedigree n stirps f, stemma nt ♦ adj generōsus.
pediment n fastīgium nt.
pedlar n īnstitor m, circumforāneus m.
peel n cortex m ♦ vt glūbere.
peep n dīspicere ♦ n aspectus m; **at ~ of day**
prīmā lūce.
peer vi: ~ **at** intuērī ♦ n pār m; (rank) patricius
m.

peerless adj ūnicus, ēgregius.
peevish adj stomachōsus, mōrōsus.
peevishly adv stomachōsē, mōrōsē.
peevishness n stomachus m, mōrōsitās f.
peg n clāvus m; **put a round ~ in a square hole**
bovī clītellās impōnere ♦ vt clāvīs dēfīgere.
pelf n lucrum nt.
pellet n globulus m.
pell-mell adv prōmiscuē, turbātē.
pellucid adj perlūcidus.
pelt n pellis f ♦ vt petere ♦ vi violenter cadere.
pen n calamus m, stilus m; (cattle) saeptum nt ♦
vt scrībere.
penal adj poenālis.
penalize vt poenā adficere, multāre.
penalty n poena f, damnum nt; (fine) multa f;
pay the ~ poenās dare.
penance n supplicium nt.
pencil n graphis f.
pending adj sub iūdice ♦ prep inter (acc).
penetrable adj pervius.
penetrate vt penetrāre.
penetrating adj ācer, acūtus; (mind)
perspicāx.
penetration n (mind) acūmen nt.
peninsula n paenīnsula f.
penitence n paenitentia f.
penitent adj: **I am ~** mē paenitet.
penknife n scalpellum nt.
penmanship n scrīptiō f, manus f.
pennant n vexillum nt.
penny n dēnārius m.
pension n annua ntpl.
pensioner n ēmeritus m.
pensive adj attentus.
pensiveness n cōgitātiō f.
pent adj inclūsus.
penthouse n (MIL) vīnea f.
penurious adj parcus, avārus, tenāx.
penuriousness n parsimōnia f, tenācitās f.
penury n egestās f, inopia f.
people n hominēs mpl; (nation) populus m, gēns
f; **common ~** plēbs f ♦ vt frequentāre.
peopled adj frequēns.
pepper n piper nt.
peradventure adv fortasse.
perambulate vi spatiārī, inambulāre.
perceive vt sentīre, percipere, intellegere.
perceptible adj: **be ~** sentīrī posse, audīrī
posse.
perception n sēnsus m.
perch n (bird's) pertica f; (fish) perca f ♦ vi
īnsidēre.
perchance adv fortasse, forsitan (subj).
percolate vi permānāre.
percussion n ictus m.
perdition n exitium nt.
peregrinate vi peregrīnārī.
peregrination n peregrīnātiō f.
peremptorily adv praecīsē, prō imperiō.
peremptory adj imperiōsus.
perennial adj perennis.
perfect adj perfectus, absolūtus; (entire)

integer; (*faultless*) ēmendātus ♦ *vt* perficere, absolvere.
perfection *n* perfectiō *f*, absolūtiō *f*.
perfectly *adv* perfectē, ēmendātē; (*quite*) plānē.
perfidious *adj* perfidus, perfidiōsus.
perfidiously *adv* perfidiōsē.
perfidy *n* perfidia *f*.
perforate *vt* perforāre, terebrāre.
perforation *n* forāmen *nt*.
perforce *adv* per vim, necessāriō.
perform *vt* perficere, peragere; (*duty*) exsequī, fungī (*abl*); (*play*) agere.
performance *n* (*process*) exsecūtiō *f*, fūnctiō *f*; (*deed*) factum *nt*; (*stage*) fābula *f*.
performer *n* āctor *m*; (*music*) tībīcen *m*, fidicen *m*; (*stage*) histriō *m*.
perfume *n* odor *m*, unguentum *nt* ♦ *vt* odōrāre.
perfumer *n* unguentārius *m*.
perfumery *n* unguenta *ntpl*.
perfunctorily *adv* neglegenter.
perfunctory *adj* neglegēns.
perhaps *adv* fortasse, forsitan (*subj*), nesciō an (*subj*); (*tentative*) vel; (*interrog*) an.
peril *n* perīculum *m*, discrīmen *nt*.
perilous *adj* perīculōsus.
perilously *adv* perīculōsē.
perimeter *n* ambitus *m*.
period *n* tempus *nt*, spatium *nt*; (*history*) aetās *f*; (*end*) terminus *m*; (*sentence*) complexiō *f*, ambitus *m*.
periodic *adj* (*style*) circumscrīptus.
periodical *adj* status.
periodically *adv* certīs temporibus, identidem.
peripatetic *adj* vagus; (*sect*) peripatēticus.
periphery *n* ambitus *m*.
periphrasis *n* circuitus *m*.
perish *vi* perīre, interīre.
perishable *adj* cadūcus, fragilis, mortālis.
peristyle *n* peristȳlium *nt*.
perjure *vi*: ~ o.s. pēierāre.
perjured *adj* periūrus.
perjurer *n* periūrus *m*.
perjury *n* periūrium *nt*; **commit** ~ pēierāre.
permanence *n* cōnstantia *f*, stabilitās *f*.
permanent *adj* stabilis, diūturnus, perpetuus.
permanently *adv* perpetuō.
permeable *adj* penetrābilis.
permeate *vt* penetrāre ♦ *vi* permānāre.
permissible *adj* licitus, concessus; **it is** ~ licet.
permission *n* potestās *f*; **ask** ~ veniam petere; **give** ~ veniam dare, potestātem facere; **by** ~ of permissū (*gen*); **with your kind** ~ bonā tuā veniā; **without your** ~ tē invītō.
permit *vt* sinere, permittere (*dat*); **I am ~ted** licet mihī.
pernicious *adj* perniciōsus, exitiōsus.
perorate *vi* perōrāre.
peroration *n* perōrātiō *f*, epilogus *m*.
perpendicular *adj* dīrēctus.
perpendicularly *adv* ad perpendiculum, ad līneam.

perpetrate *vt* facere, admittere.
perpetual *adj* perpetuus, perennis, sempiternus.
perpetually *adv* perpetuō.
perpetuate *vt* continuāre, perpetuāre.
perpetuity *n* perpetuitās *f*.
perplex *vt* sollicitāre, cōnfundere.
perplexing *adj* ambiguus, perplexus.
perplexity *n* haesitātiō *f*.
perquisite *n* pecūlium *nt*.
persecute *vt* īnsectārī, exagitāre; persequi.
persecution *n* īnsectātiō *f*.
persecutor *n* īnsectātor *m*.
perseverance *n* peseverāntia *f*, cōnstantia *f*.
persevere *vi* perseverāre, perstāre; ~ **in** tenēre.
Persian *n* Persa *m*.
persist *vt* īnstāre, perstāre, perseverāre.
persistence, persistency *n* pertinācia *f*, perseverāntia *f*.
persistent *adj* pertināx.
persistently *adv* pertināciter, perseveranter.
person *n* homō *m/f*; (*counted*) caput *nt*; (*character*) persōna *f*; (*body*) corpus *nt*; **in** ~ ipse praesēns.
personage *n* vir *m*.
personal *adj* prīvātus, suus.
personality *n* nātūra *f*; (*person*) vir ēgregius *m*.
personally *adv* ipse, cōram.
personal property *n* pecūlium *nt*.
personate *vt* persōnam gerere (*gen*).
personification *n* prosōpopoeia *f*.
personify *vt* hūmānam nātūram tribuere (*dat*).
personnel *n* membra *ntpl*, sociī *mpl*.
perspective *n* scaenographia *f*.
perspicacious *adj* perspicāx, acūtus.
perspicacity *n* perspicācitās *f*, acūmen *nt*.
perspicuity *n* perspicuitās *f*.
perspicuous *adj* perspicuus.
perspiration *n* sūdor *m*.
perspire *vi* sūdāre.
persuade *vt* persuādēre (*dat*); (*by entreaty*) exōrāre.
persuasion *n* persuāsiō *f*.
persuasive *adj* blandus.
persuasively *adv* blandē.
pert *adj* procāx, protervus.
pertain *vi* pertinēre, attinēre.
pertinacious *adj* pertināx.
pertinaciously *adv* pertināciter.
pertinacity *n* pertinācia *f*.
pertinent *adj* appositus; **be** ~ ad rem pertinēre.
pertinently *adv* appositē.
pertly *adv* procāciter, protervē.
perturb *vt* perturbāre.
perturbation *n* animī perturbātiō *f*, trepidātiō *f*.
peruke *n* capillāmentum *nt*.
perusal *n* perlēctiō *f*.
peruse *vt* perlegere; (*book*) ēvolvere.

pervade *vt* permānāre per, complēre; (*emotion*) perfundere.
pervasive *adj* crēber.
perverse *adj* perversus, prāvus.
perversely *adv* perversē.
perversion *n* dēprāvātiō *f*.
perversity *n* perversitās *f*.
pervert *vt* dēprāvāre; (*words*) dētorquēre; (*person*) corrumpere.
perverter *n* corruptor *m*.
pessimism *n* dēspērātiō *f*.
pest *n* pestis *f*.
pester *vt* sollicitāre.
pestilence *n* pestilentia *f*, pestis *f*.
pestilential *adj* pestilēns, nocēns.
pestle *n* pistillum *nt*.
pet *n* dēliciae *fpl* ♦ *vt* in dēliciīs habēre, dēlēnīre.
petard *n*: **be hoist with his own ~** suō sibī gladiō iugulārī.
petition *n* precēs *fpl*; (*POL*) libellus *m* ♦ *vt* ōrāre.
petrify *vt* (*fig*) dēfīgere; **be petrified** stupēre, obstupēscere.
pettifogger *n* lēgulēius *m*.
pettiness *n* levitās *f*.
pettish *adj* stomachōsus.
petty *adj* levis, minūtus.
petulance *n* protervitās *f*.
petulant *adj* protervus, petulāns.
petulantly *adv* petulanter.
pew *n* subsellium *nt*.
phalanx *n* phalanx *f*.
phantasy *n* commentīcia *ntpl*.
phantom *n* simulacrum *nt*, īdōlon *nt*.
phases *npl* vicēs *fpl*.
pheasant *n* phāsiānus *m*.
phenomenal *adj* eximius, singulāris.
phenomenon *n* rēs *f*, novum *nt*, spectāculum *nt*.
philander *vi* lascīvīre.
philanthropic *adj* hūmānus, beneficus.
philanthropically *adv* hūmānē.
philanthropy *n* hūmānitās *f*, beneficia *ntpl*.
Philippic *n* Philippica *f*.
philologist *n* grammaticus *m*.
philology *n* grammatica *ntpl*.
philosopher *n* philosophus *m*, sapiēns *m*.
philosophical *adj* philosophus; (*temperament*) aequābilis.
philosophize *vi* philosophārī.
philosophy *n* philosophia *f*, sapientia *f*.
philtre *n* philtrum *nt*.
phlegm *n* pituīta *f*; (*temper*) lentitūdō *f*.
phlegmatic *adj* lentus.
phoenix *n* phoenīx *m*.
phrase *n* locūtiō *f*; (*GRAM*) incīsum *nt*.
phraseology *n* verba *ntpl*, ōrātiō *f*.
physic *n* medicāmentum *nt*; **~s** *pl* physica *ntpl*.
physical *adj* physicus; (*of body*) corporis.
physician *n* medicus *m*.
physicist *n* physicus *m*.
physique *n* corpus *nt*, vīrēs *fpl*.

piazza *n* forum *nt*.
pick *n* (*tool*) dolabra *f*; (*best part*) lēctī *mpl*, flōs *m* ♦ *vt* (*choose*) legere, dēligere; (*pluck*) carpere; **~ out** ēligere, excerpere; **~ up** colligere.
pickaxe *n* dolabra *f*.
picked *adj* ēlēctus, dēlēctus.
picket *n* (*MIL*) statiō *f*.
pickle *n* muria *f* ♦ *vt* condīre.
picture *n* pictūra *f*, tabula *f* ♦ *vt* dēpingere; (*to oneself*) ante oculōs pōnere.
picturesque *adj* (*scenery*) amoenus.
pie *n* crustum *nt*.
piebald *adj* bicolor, varius.
piece *n* pars *f*; (*broken off*) fragmentum *nt*; (*food*) frustum *nt*; (*coin*) nummus *m*; (*play*) fābula *f*; **break in ~s** comminuere; **fall to ~s** dīlābī; **take to ~s** dissolvere; **tear in ~s** dīlaniāre.
piecemeal *adv* membrātim, minūtātim.
pied *adj* maculōsus.
pier *n* mōlēs *f*.
pierce *vt* perfodere, trānsfīgere; (*bore*) perforāre; (*fig*) pungere.
piercing *adj* acūtus.
piety *n* pietās *f*, religiō *f*.
pig *n* porcus *m*, sūs *m/f*; **buy a ~ in a poke** spem pretiō emere; **~'s** suillus.
pigeon *n* columba *f*; **wood ~** palumbēs *f*.
pig-headed *adj* pervicāx.
pigment *n* pigmentum *nt*.
pigsty *n* hara *f*.
pike *n* dolō *m*, hasta *f*.
pikeman *n* hastātus *m*.
pile *n* acervus *m*, cumulus *m*; (*funeral*) rogus *m*; (*building*) mōlēs *f*; (*post*) sublica *f* ♦ *vt* cumulāre, congerere; **~ up** exstruere, adcumulāre, coacervāre.
pile-driver *n* fistūca *f*.
pilfer *vt* fūrārī, surripere.
pilferer *n* fūr *m*, fūrunculus *m*.
pilgrim *n* peregrīnātor *m*.
pilgrimage *n* peregrīnātiō *f*.
pill *n* pilula *f*.
pillage *n* rapīna *f*, dēpopulātiō *f*, expīlātiō *f* ♦ *vt* dīripere, dēpopulārī, expīlāre.
pillager *n* expīlātor *m*, praedātor *m*.
pillar *n* columen *nt*, columna *f*.
pillory *n* furca *f*.
pillow *n* pulvīnus *m*, culcita *f*.
pilot *n* gubernātor *m*, ductor *m* ♦ *vt* regere, gubernāre.
pimp *n* lēnō *m*.
pimple *n* pustula *f*.
pin *n* acus *f* ♦ *vt* adfīgere.
pincers *n* forceps *m/f*.
pinch *vt* pervellere, vellicāre; (*shoe*) ūrere; (*for room*) coartāre.
pine *n* pīnus *f* ♦ *vi* tābēscere; **~ away** intābēscere; **~ for** dēsīderāre.
pinion *n* penna *f*.
pink *adj* rubicundus.
pinnace *n* lembus *m*.

pinnacle *n* fastīgium *nt*.
pint *n* sextārius *m*.
pioneer *n* antecursor *m*.
pious *adj* pius, religiōsus.
piously *adv* piē, religiōsē.
pip *n* grānum *nt*.
pipe *n* (*music*) fistula *f*, tībia *f*; (*water*) canālis *m*
♦ *vi* fistulā canere.
piper *n* tībīcen *m*.
pipkin *n* olla *f*.
piquancy *n* sāl *m*, vīs *f*.
piquant *adj* salsus, argūtus.
pique *n* offēnsio *f*, dolor *m* ♦ *vt* offendere.
piracy *n* latrōcinium *nt*.
pirate *n* pīrāta *m* praedō *m*.
piratical *adj* pīrāticus.
piscatorial *adj* piscātōrius.
piston *n* embolus *m*.
pit *n* fovea *f*, fossa *f*; (*THEAT*) cavea *f*.
pitch *n* pix *f*; (*sound*) sonus *m* ♦ *vt* (*camp*)
pōnere; (*tent*) tendere; (*missile*) conicere.
pitch-black *adj* piceus.
pitched battle *n* proelium iustum *nt*.
pitcher *n* hydria *f*.
pitchfork *n* furca *f*.
pitch pine *n* picea *f*.
piteous *adj* miserābilis, flēbilis.
piteously *adv* miserābiliter.
pitfall *n* fovea *f*.
pith *n* medulla *f*.
pithy *adj* (*style*) dēnsus; ~ **saying** sententia *f*.
pitiable *adj* miserandus.
pitiful *adj* miser, miserābilis; misericors.
pitifully *adv* miserē, miserābiliter.
pitiless *adj* immisericors, immītis.
pitilessly *adv* crūdēliter.
pittance *n* (*food*) dēmēnsum *nt*; (*money*) stips
f.
pity *n* misericordia *f*; **take ~ on** miserērī (*+acc
of person, gen of things*); **it is a ~ that** male
accidit quod ♦ *vt* miserērī (*gen*); **I ~ mē**
miseret (*gen*).
pivot *n* cardō *m*.
placability *n* plācābilitās *f*.
placable *adj* plācābilis.
placard *n* libellus *m*.
placate *vt* plācāre.
place *n* locus *m*; **in another ~** alibī; **in the first ~**
prīmum; **in ~ of** locō (*gen*), pro (*+ abl*); **to this
~** hūc; **out of ~** intempestīvus; **give ~ to**
cēdere (*dat*); **take ~** fierī, accidere; **take the ~**
of in locum (*gen*) succēdere ♦ *vt* pōnere,
locāre, collocāre; **~ beside** adpōnere; **~ over**
(*in charge*) praepōnere; **~ round** circumdare;
~ upon impōnere.
placid *adj* placidus, tranquillus, quiētus.
placidity *n* tranquillitās *f*, sedātus animus *m*.
placidly *adv* placidē, quiētē.
plagiarism *n* fūrtum *nt*.
plagiarize *vt* fūrārī.
plague *n* pestilentia *f*, pestis *f*.
plain *adj* (*lucid*) clārus, perspicuus;
(*unadorned*) subtīlis, simplex; (*frank*)
sincērus; (*ugly*) invenustus ♦ *n* campus *m*,

plānitiēs *f*; **of the ~** campester.
plainly *adv* perspicuē; simpliciter, sincērē.
plainness *n* perspicuitās *f*; simplicitās *f*.
plaint *n* querella *f*.
plaintiff *n* petītor *m*.
plaintive *adj* flēbilis, queribundus.
plaintively *adv* flēbiliter.
plait *vt* implicāre, nectere.
plan *n* cōnsilium *nt*; (*of a work*) fōrma *f*,
dēsignātiō *f*; (*of living*) ratiō *f*; (*intent*)
prōpositum *nt*; (*drawing*) dēscrīptiō *f* ♦ *vt* (*a
work*) dēsignāre, dēscrībere; (*intent*)
cōgitāre, meditārī; cōnsilium capere *or*
inīre; (*with verb*) in animō habēre (*inf*).
plane *n* (*surface*) plānitiēs *f*; (*tree*) platanus *f*;
(*tool*) runcīna *f* ♦ *adj* aequus, plānus ♦ *vt*
runcīnāre.
planet *n* stēlla errāns *f*.
plank *n* tabula *f*.
plant *n* herba *f*, planta *f* ♦ *vt* (*tree*) serere; (*field*)
cōnserere; (*colony*) dēdūcere; (*feet*) pōnere;
~ firmly īnfīgere.
plantation *n* arbustum *nt*.
planter *n* sator *m*, colōnus *m*.
plaque *n* tabula *f*.
plaster *n* albārium *nt*, tectōrium *nt*; (*MED*)
emplastrum *nt*; **~ of Paris** gypsum *nt* ♦ *vt*
dealbāre.
plasterer *n* albārius *m*.
plastic *adj* ductilis, fūsilis.
plate *n* (*dish*) catillus *m*; (*silver*) argentum *nt*;
(*layer*) lāmina *f* ♦ *vt* indūcere.
platform *n* suggestus *m*; rōstrum *nt*, tribūnal
nt.
platitude *n* trīta sententia *f*.
platter *n* patella *f*, lanx *f*.
plaudit *n* plausus *m*.
plausibility *n* vērīsimilitūdō *f*.
plausible *adj* speciōsus, vērī similis.
play *n* lūdus *m*; (*THEAT*) fābula *f*; (*voice*)
inclīnātiō *f*; (*scope*) campus *m*; (*hands*) gestus
m; **~ on words** agnōminātiō *f*; **fair ~** aequum et
bonum ♦ *vi* lūdere; (*fountain*) scatēre ♦ *vt*
(*music*) canere; (*instrument*) canere (*abl*);
(*game*) lūdere (*abl*); (*part*) agere; **~ the part of**
agere; **~ a trick on** lūdificārī, impōnere (*dat*).
playbill *n* ēdictum *nt*.
player *n* lūsor *m*; (*at dice*) āleātor *m*; (*on flute*)
tībīcen *m*; (*on lyre*) fidicen *m*; (*on stage*)
histriō *m*.
playful *adj* lascīvus; (*words*) facētus.
playfully *adv* per lūdum, per iocum.
playfulness *n* lascīvia *f*; facētiae *fpl*.
playground *n* ārea *f*.
playmate *n* collūsor *m*.
playwright *n* fābulārum scrīptor *m*.
plea *n* causa *f*; (*in defence*) dēfēnsiō *f*, excūsātiō
f.
plead *vi* causam agere, causam ōrāre, causam
dīcere; (*in excuse*) dēprecārī, excūsāre; **~
with** obsecrāre.
pleader *n* āctor *m*, causidicus *m*.
pleasant *adj* iūcundus, dulcis, grātus; (*place*)

amoenus.
pleasantly *adv* iūcundē, suāviter.
pleasantry *n* facētiae *fpl*, iocus *m*.
please *vt* placēre (*dat*), dēlectāre; **try to ~**
īnservīre (*dat*); **just as you ~** quod
commodum est; **if you ~** sīs; **~d with**
contentus (*abl*); **be ~d with oneself** sibī
placēre ♦ *adv* amābō.
pleasing *adj* grātus, iūcundus, amoenus; **be ~**
to cordī esse (*dat*).
pleasurable *adj* iūcundus.
pleasure *n* voluptās *f*; (*decision*) arbitrium *nt*; **it**
is my ~ libet; **derive ~** voluptātem capere
♦ *vt* grātificārī (*dat*).
pleasure grounds *n* hortī *mpl*.
pleasure-loving *adj* dēlicātus.
plebeian *adj* plēbēius ♦ *n*: **the ~s** plēbs *f*.
plebiscite *n* suffrāgium *nt*.
plectrum *n* plēctrum *nt*.
pledge *n* pignus *nt* ♦ *vt* obligāre; **~ oneself**
prōmittere, spondēre; **~ one's word** fidem
obligāre, fidem interpōnere.
Pleiads *n* Plēiadēs *fpl*.
plenary *adj* īnfīnītus.
plenipotentiary *n* lēgātus *m*.
plenitude *n* cōpia *f*, mātūritās *f*.
plentiful *adj* cōpiōsus, largus.
plentifully *adv* cōpiōsē, largē.
plenty *n* cōpia *f*, abundantia *f*; (*enough*) satis.
pleonasm *n* redundantia *f*.
pleurisy *n* lateris dolor *m*.
pliable *adj* flexibilis, mollis, lentus.
pliant *adj* flexibilis, mollis, lentus.
pliers *n* forceps *m/f*.
plight *n* habitus *m*, discrīmen *nt* ♦ *vt* spondēre.
plod *vi* labōrāre, operam īnsūmere.
plot *n* coniūrātiō *f*, īnsidiae *fpl*; (*land*) agellus *m*;
(*play*) argūmentum *nt* ♦ *vi* coniūrāre, mōlīrī.
plotter *n* coniūrātus *m*.
plough *n* arātrum *nt* ♦ *vt* arāre; (*sea*) sulcāre; **~**
up exarāre.
ploughing *n* arātiō *f*.
ploughman *n* arātor *m*.
ploughshare *n* vōmer *m*.
pluck *n* fortitūdō *f* ♦ *vt* carpere, legere; **~ out**
ēvellere; **~ up courage** animum recipere,
animō adesse.
plucky *adj* fortis.
plug *n* obtūrāmentum *nt* ♦ *vt* obtūrāre.
plum *n* prūnum *nt*; (*tree*) prūnus *f*.
plumage *n* plūmae *fpl*.
plumb *n* perpendiculum *nt* ♦ *adj* dīrēctus ♦ *adv*
ad perpendiculum ♦ *vt* (*building*) ad
perpendiculum exigere; (*depth*) scrūtārī.
plumber *n* artifex plumbārius *m*.
plumb line *n* līnea *f*, perpendiculum *nt*.
plume *n* crista *f* ♦ *vt*: **~ oneself on** iactāre, prae
sē ferre.
plummet *n* perpendiculum *nt*.
plump *adj* pinguis.
plumpness *n* nitor *m*.
plunder *n* (*act*) rapīna *f*; (*booty*) praeda *f* ♦ *vi*
praedārī ♦ *vt* dīripere, expīlāre.

plunderer *n* praedātor *m*, spoliātor *m*.
plundering *n* rapīna *f* ♦ *adj* praedābundus.
plunge *vt* mergere, dēmergere; (*weapon*)
dēmittere ♦ *vi* mergī, sē dēmergere.
plural *adj* plūrālis.
plurality *n* multitūdō *f*, plūrēs *pl*.
ply *vt* exercēre.
poach *vt* surripere.
pocket *n* sinus *m*.
pocket money *n* pecūlium *nt*.
pod *n* siliqua *f*.
poem *n* poēma *nt*, carmen *nt*.
poesy *n* poēsis *f*.
poet *n* poēta *m*.
poetess *n* poētria *f*.
poetic *adj* poēticus.
poetical *adj* = **poetic**.
poetically *adv* poēticē.
poetry *n* (*art*) poētica *f*; (*poems*) poēmata *ntpl*,
carmina *ntpl*.
poignancy *n* acerbitās *f*.
poignant *adj* acerbus, acūtus.
poignantly *adv* acerbē, acūtē.
point *n* (*dot*) pūnctum *nt*; (*place*) locus *m*;
(*item*) caput *nt*; (*sharp end*) aciēs *f*; (*of sword*)
mucrō *m*; (*of epigram*) aculeī *mpl*; **~ of honour**
officium *nt*; **beside the ~** ab rē; **to the ~** ad
rem; **from this ~** hinc; **to that ~** eō; **up to this**
~ hāctenus, adhūc; **without ~** īnsulsus; **in ~ of**
fact nempe; **make a ~ of doing** consultō
facere; **on the ~ of death** moritūrus; **on**
the ~ of happening inibī; **I was on the ~ of**
saying in eō erat ut dīcerem; **matters have**
reached such a ~ eō rēs recidit; **come to the**
~ ad rem redīre; **the ~ at issue is** illud
quaeritur; **the main ~** cardō *m*, caput *nt*;
turning ~ articulus temporis *m* ♦ *vt* acuere,
exacuere; (*aim*) intendere; (*punctuate*)
distinguere; **~ out** indicāre, dēmōnstrāre;
ostendere.
point-blank *adj* simplex ♦ *adv* praecīsē.
pointed *adj* acūtus; (*criticism*) acūleātus; (*wit*)
salsus.
pointedly *adv* apertē, dīlūcidē.
pointer *n* index *m*.
pointless *adj* īnsulsus, frīgidus.
pointlessly *adv* īnsulsē.
point of view *n* iūdicium *nt*, sententia *f*.
poise *n* lībrāmen *nt*; (*fig*) urbānitās *f* ♦ *vt*
lībrāre.
poison *n* venēnum *nt* ♦ *vt* venēnō necāre; (*fig*)
īnficere.
poisoned *adj* venēnātus.
poisoner *n* venēficus *m*.
poisoning *n* venēficium *nt*.
poisonous *adj* noxius.
poke *vt* trūdere, fodicāre.
polar *adj* septentriōnālis.
pole *n* asser *m*, contus *m*; (ASTRO) polus *m*.
poleaxe *n* bipennis *f*.
polemic *n* contrōversia *f*.
police *n* lictōrēs *mpl*; (*night*) vigilēs *mpl*.
policy *n* ratiō *f*, cōnsilium *nt*; **honesty is the**

best ~ ea māximē condūcunt quae sunt rēctissima.
polish n (*appearance*) nitor m; (*character*) urbānitās f; (*LIT*) līma f ♦ vt polīre; (*fig*) expolīre.
polished adj polītus, mundus; (*person*) excultus, urbānus; (*style*) līmātus.
polite adj urbānus, hūmānus, cōmis.
politely adv urbānē, cōmiter.
politeness n urbānitās f, hūmānitās f, cōmitās f.
politic adj prūdēns, circumspectus.
political adj cīvīlis, pūblicus; ~ **life** rēs pūblica f.
politician n magistrātus m.
politics n rēs pūblica f; **take up** ~ ad rem pūblicam accēdere.
polity n reī pūblicae fōrma f.
poll n caput nt; (*voting*) comitia ntpl ♦ vi suffrāgia inīre.
poll tax n tribūtum nt in singula capita impositum.
pollute vt inquināre, contāmināre.
pollution n corruptēla f.
poltroon n ignāvus m.
pomegranate n mālum Pūnicum nt.
pomp n adparātus m.
pomposity n māgnificentia f, glōria f.
pompous adj māgnificus, glōriōsus.
pompously adv māgnificē, glōriōsē.
pompousness n māgnificentia f.
pond n stagnum nt, lacūna f.
ponder vi sēcum reputāre ♦ vt animō volūtāre, in mente agitāre.
ponderous adj gravis, ponderōsus.
ponderously adv graviter.
poniard n pugiō m.
pontiff n pontifex m.
pontifical adj pontificālis, pontificius.
pontoon n pontō m.
pony n mannus m.
pooh-pooh vt dērīdēre.
pool n lacūna f, stagnum nt ♦ vt cōnferre.
poop n puppis f.
poor adj pauper, inops; (*meagre*) exīlis; (*inferior*) improbus; (*pitiable*) miser; ~ **little** misellus.
poorly adj aeger, aegrōtus ♦ adv parum, tenuiter.
pop n crepitus m ♦ vi ēmicāre.
pope n pāpa m.
poplar n pōpulus f.
poppy n papāver nt.
populace n vulgus nt, plēbs f.
popular adj grātus, grātiōsus; (*party*) populāris.
popularity n populī favor m, studium nt.
popularly adv vulgō.
populate vt frequentāre.
population n populus m, cīvēs mpl.
populous adj frequēns.
porcelain n fictilia ntpl.
porch n vestibulum nt.

porcupine n hystrīx f.
pore n forāmen nt ♦ vi: ~ **over** scrūtārī, incumbere in (*acc*).
pork n porcīna f.
porous adj rārus.
porridge n puls f.
port n portus m ♦ adj (*side*) laevus, sinister.
portage n vectūra f.
portal n porta f.
portcullis n cataracta f.
portend vt portendere.
portent n mōnstrum nt, portentum nt.
portentous adj mōnstruōsus.
porter n iānitor m; (*carrier*) bāiulus m.
portico n porticus f.
portion n pars f; (*marriage*) dōs f; (*lot*) sors f.
portliness n amplitūdō f.
portly adj amplus, opīmus.
portrait n imāgō f, effigiēs f.
portray vt dēpingere, exprimere, effingere.
pose n status m, habitus m ♦ vt pōnere ♦ vi habitum sūmere.
poser n nōdus m.
posit vt pōnere.
position n (*GEOG*) situs m (*body*) status m, gestus m; (*rank*) dignitās f; (*office*) honōs m; (*MIL*) locus m; **be in a ~ to** habēre (*inf*); **take up a ~** (*MIL*) locum capere.
positive adj certus; **be ~ about** adfirmāre.
positively adv certō, adfirmātē, rē vērā.
posse n manus f.
possess vt possidēre, habēre; (*take*) occupāre, potīrī (*abl*).
possession n possessiō f; **~s** pl bona ntpl, fortūnae fpl; **take ~ of** potīrī (*abl*), occupāre, manum inicere (*dat*); (*inheritance*) obīre; (*emotion*) invādere, incēdere (*dat*); **gain ~ of** potior (+ *abl*).
possessor n possessor m, dominus m.
possibility n facultās f; **there is a ~** fierī potest.
possible adj: **it is ~** fierī potest; **as big as ~** quam māximus.
possibly adv fortasse.
post n pālus m; (*MIL*) statiō f; (*office*) mūnus nt; (*courier*) tabellārius m; **leave one's ~** locō cēdere, signa relinquere ♦ vt (*troops*) locāre, collocāre; (*at intervals*) dispōnere; (*letter*) dare, tabellāriō dare; (*entry*) in cōdicem referre; **be ~ed** (*MIL*) in statiōne esse.
postage n vectūra f.
poster n libellus m.
posterior adj posterior.
posterity n posterī mpl; (*time*) posteritās f.
postern n postīcum nt.
posthaste adv summā celeritāte.
posthumous adj postumus.
posthumously adv (*born*) patre mortuō; (*published*) auctōre mortuō.
postpone vt differre, prōferre.
postponement n dīlātiō f.
postscript n: **add a ~** adscrībere, subicere.
postulate vt sūmere ♦ n sūmptiō f.
posture n gestus m, status m.

pot n olla f, matella f.
pot-bellied adj ventriōsus.
potency n vīs f.
potent adj efficāx, valēns.
potentate n dynastēs m, tyrannus m.
potential adj futūrus.
potentiality n facultās f.
potentially adv ut fierī posse vidētur; ~ **an emperor** capāx imperiī.
potently adv efficienter.
potion n pōtiō f.
pot-pourri n farrāgō f.
potsherd n testa f.
pottage n iūs nt.
potter n figulus m; ~'s figulāris.
pottery n fictilia ntpl.
pouch n pēra f, sacculus m.
poultice n fōmentum nt, emplastrum nt.
poultry n gallīnae fpl.
pounce vi involāre, īnsilīre.
pound n lībra f; **five ~s** (weight) **of gold** aurī quīnque pondo ♦ vt conterere; pulsāre.
pour vt fundere; ~ **forth** effundere; ~ **in** īnfundere; ~ **on** superfundere; ~ **out** effundere ♦ vi fundī, fluere; ~ **down** ruere, sē praecipitāre.
pouring adj (rain) effūsus.
poverty n paupertās f, egestās f, inopia f; (style) iēiūnitās f.
powder n pulvis m.
powdery adj pulvereus.
power n potestās f; (strength) vīrēs fpl; (excessive) potentia f; (supreme) imperium nt; (divine) nūmen nt; (legal) auctōritās f; (of father) manus f; **as far as is in my ~** quantum in mē est; **have great ~** multum valēre, posse; **have of ~ attorney** cognitōrem esse; **it is still in my ~ to** integrum est mihī (inf).
powerful adj validus, potēns.
powerfully adv valdē.
powerless adj impotēns, imbēcillus; **be ~** nihil valēre.
powerlessness n imbēcillitas f.
practicable adj in apertō; **be ~** fierī posse.
practical adj (person) habilis.
practical joke n lūdus m.
practical knowledge n ūsus m.
practically adv ferē, paene.
practice n ūsus m, exercitātiō f; (RHET) meditātiō f; (habit) consuētūdō f, mōs m; **corrupt ~s** malae artēs.
practise vt (occupation) exercēre, facere; (custom) factitāre; (RHET) meditārī ♦ vi (MED) medicīnam exercēre; (law) causās agere.
practised adj exercitātus, perītus.
practitioner n (MED) medicus m.
praetor n praetor nt; ~'s praetōrius.
praetorian adj praetōrius.
praetorian guards npl praetōriānī mpl.
praetorship n praetūra f.
praise n laus f ♦ vt laudāre.
praiser n laudātor m.
praiseworthy adj laudābilis, laude dignus.

prance vi exsultāre.
prank n lūdus m.
prate vi garrīre.
prating adj garrulus.
pray vi deōs precārī, deōs venerārī ♦ vt precārī, ōrāre; ~ **for** petere, precārī; ~ **to** adōrāre.
prayer(s) n precēs fpl.
prayerful adj supplex.
preach vt, vi docēre, praedicāre.
preacher n ōrātor m.
preamble n exōrdium nt.
prearranged adj cōnstitūtus.
precarious adj dubius, perīculōsus.
precariousness n discrīmen nt.
precaution n cautiō f, prōvidentia f; **take ~s** cavēre, praecavēre.
precede vt praeīre (dat), anteīre (dat), antecēdere.
precedence n prīmārius locus m; **give ~ to** cēdere (dat); **take ~** (thing) antīquius esse; (person) prīmās agere.
precedent n exemplum nt; (law) praeiūdicium nt; **breach of ~** īnsolentia f; **in defiance of ~** īnsolenter.
preceding adj prior, superior.
precept n praeceptum nt.
preceptor n doctor m, magister m.
precinct n terminus m, templum nt.
precious adj cārus; pretiōsus; (style) pūtidus.
precious stone n gemma f.
precipice n locus praeceps m, rūpēs f.
precipitancy n festīnātiō f.
precipitate vt praecipitāre ♦ adj praeceps; praeproperus.
precipitation n festīnātiō f.
precipitous adj dēruptus, praeceps, praeruptus.
precise adj certus, subtīlis; (person) accūrātus.
precisely adv dēmum.
precision n cūra f.
preclude vt exclūdere, prohibēre.
precocious adj praecox.
precocity n festīnāta mātūritās f.
preconceive vt praecipere; ~**d idea** praeiūdicāta opīniō f.
preconception n praeceptiō f.
preconcerted adj ex compositō factus.
precursor n praenūntius m.
predatory adj praedātōrius.
predecessor n dēcessor m; **my ~** cuī succēdō.
predestination n fātum nt, necessitās f.
predestine vt dēvovēre.
predetermine vt praefīnīre.
predicament n angustiae fpl, discrīmen nt.
predicate n attribūtum nt.
predict vt praedīcere, augurārī.
prediction n praedictiō f.
predilection n amor m, studium nt.
predispose vt inclīnāre, praeparāre.
predisposition n inclīnātiō f.
predominance n potentia f, praestantia f.

predominant *adj* praepotēns, praecipuus.
predominantly *adv* plērumque.
predominate *vi* pollēre, dominārī.
pre-eminence *n* praestantia *f*.
pre-eminent *adj* ēgregius, praecipuus, excellēns.
pre-eminently *adv* ēgregiē, praecipuē, excellenter.
preface *n* prooemium *nt*, praefātiō *f* ♦ *vi* praefārī.
prefect *n* praefectus *m*.
prefecture *n* praefectūra *f*.
prefer *vt* (*charge*) dēferre; (*to office*) anteferre; (*choice*) antepōnere (*acc and dat*), posthabēre (*dat and acc*); (*with verb*) mālle.
preferable *adj* potior.
preferably *adv* potius.
preference *n* favor *m*; **give ~ to** antepōnere, praeoptāre; **in ~ to** potius quam.
preferment *n* honōs *m*, dignitās *f*.
prefix *vt* praetendere ♦ *n* praepositiō *f*.
pregnancy *n* graviditās *f*.
pregnant *adj* gravida.
prejudge *vt* praeiūdicāre.
prejudice *n* praeiūdicāta opīniō *f*; (*harmful*) invidia *f*, incommodum *nt*; **without ~** cum bonā veniā ♦ *vt* obesse (*dat*); **be ~d against** invidēre (*dat*), male opīnārī dē (*abl*).
prejudicial *adj* damnōsus; **be ~ to** obesse (*dat*), nocēre (*dat*), officere (*dat*), dētrīmentō esse (*dat*).
preliminaries *npl* praecurrentia *ntpl*.
preliminary *adj* prīmus ♦ *n* prōlūsiō *f*.
prelude *n* prooemium *nt*.
premature *adj* immātūrus; (*birth*) abortīvus.
prematurely *adv* ante tempus.
premeditate *vt* praecōgitāre, praemeditārī.
premeditated *adj* praemeditātus.
premier *adj* prīnceps, praecipuus.
premise *n* (*major*) prōpositiō *f*; (*minor*) adsūmptiō *f*; **~s** *pl* aedēs *fpl*, domus *f*.
premium *n* praemium *nt*; **be at a ~** male emī.
premonition *n* monitus *m*.
preoccupation *n* sollicitūdō *f*.
preoccupied *adj* sollicitus, districtus.
preordain *vt* praefīnīre.
preparation *n* (*process*) adparātiō *f*, comparātiō *f*; (*product*) adparātus *m*; (*of speech*) meditātiō *f*; **make ~s for** īnstruere, exōrnāre, comparāre.
prepare *vt* parāre, adparāre, comparāre; (*speech*) meditārī; (*with verb*) parāre; **~d for** parātus ad (*+ acc*).
preponderance *n* praestantia *f*.
preponderate *vi* praepollēre, vincere.
preposition *n* praepositiō *f*.
prepossess *vt* commendāre (*dat and acc*), praeoccupāre.
prepossessing *adj* suāvis, iūcundus.
prepossession *n* favor *m*.
preposterous *adj* absurdus.
prerogative *n* iūs *nt*.
presage *n* ōmen *nt* ♦ *vt* ōminārī, portendere.

prescience *n* prōvidentia *f*.
prescient *adj* prōvidus.
prescribe *vt* imperāre; (*MED*) praescrībere; (*limit*) fīnīre.
prescription *n* (*MED*) compositiō *f*; (*right*) ūsus *m*.
presence *n* praesentia *f*; (*appearance*) aspectus *m*; **~ of mind** praesēns animus *m*; **in the ~ of** cōram (*abl*); apud (*abl*); **in my ~** mē praesente.
present *adj* praesēns, īnstāns; **be ~** adesse; **be ~ at** interesse (*dat*) ♦ *n* praesēns tempus *nt*; (*gift*) dōnum *nt*; **at ~** in praesentī, nunc; **for the ~** in praesēns ♦ *vt* dōnāre, offerre; (*on stage*) indūcere; (*in court*) sistere; **~ itself** occurrere.
presentable *adj* spectābilis.
presentation *n* dōnātiō *f*.
presentiment *n* augurium *nt*.
presently *adv* mox.
preservation *n* cōnservātiō *f*.
preserve *vt* cōnservāre, tuērī; (*food*) condīre.
preside *vi* praesidēre (*dat*).
presidency *n* praefectūra *f*.
president *n* praefectus *m*.
press *n* prēlum *nt* ♦ *vt* premere; (*crowd*) stīpāre; (*urge*) īnstāre (*dat*); **~ for** flāgitāre; **~ hard** (*pursuit*) īnsequī, īnstāre (*dat*), īnsistere (*dat*); **~ out** exprimere; **~ together** comprimere.
pressing *adj* īnstāns, gravis.
pressure *n* pressiō *f*, nīsus *m*.
prestige *n* auctōritās *f*, opīniō *f*.
presumably *adv* sānē.
presume *vt* sūmere, conicere ♦ *vi* audēre, confīdere; **I ~** opīnor, crēdō.
presuming *adj* adrogāns.
presumption *n* coniectūra *f*; (*arrogance*) adrogantia *f*, licentia *f*.
presumptuous *adj* adrogāns, audāx.
presumptuously *adv* adroganter, audacter.
presuppose *vt* praesūmere.
pretence *n* simulātiō *f*, speciēs *f*; **under ~ of** per speciem (*gen*); **under false ~s** dolō malō.
pretend *vt* simulāre, fingere; **~ that ... not** dissimulāre.
pretender *n* captātor *m*.
pretension *n* postulātum *nt*; **make ~s to** adfectāre, sibī adrogāre.
pretentious *adj* adrogāns, glōriōsus.
pretext *n* speciēs *f*; **under ~ of** per speciem (*gen*); **on the ~ that** quod + *subj*.
prettily *adv* pulchrē, bellē.
prettiness *n* pulchritūdō *f*, lepōs *m*.
pretty *adj* formōsus, pulcher, bellus ♦ *adv* admodum, satis.
prevail *vi* vincere; (*custom*) tenēre, obtinēre; **~ upon** persuādēre (*dat*); (*by entreaty*) exōrāre.
prevailing *adj* vulgātus.
prevalent *adj* vulgātus; **be ~** obtinēre; **become ~** incrēbrēscere.
prevaricate *vi* tergiversārī.

prevarication n tergiversātiō f.
prevaricator n veterātor m.
prevent vt impedīre (+ quōminus/quīn and subj), prohibēre (+ acc and infin).
prevention n impedītiō f.
previous adj prior, superior.
previously adv anteā, antehāc.
prevision n prōvidentia f.
prey n praeda f ♦ vi: ~ **upon** īnsectārī; (fig) vexāre, carpere.
price n pretium nt; (of corn) annōna f; **at a high** ~ māgnī; **at a low** ~ parvī ♦ vt pretium cōnstituere (gen).
priceless adj inaestimābilis.
prick vt pungere; (goad) stimulāre; ~ **up the ears** aurēs adrigere.
prickle n acūleus m.
prickly adj aculeātus, horridus.
pride n superbia f, fastus m; (boasting) glōria f; (object) decus nt; (best part) flōs m ♦ vt: ~ **oneself on** iactāre, prae sē ferre.
priest n sacerdōs m; (especial) flāmen m; **high** ~ pontifex m, antistēs m.
priestess n sacerdōs f; **high** ~ antistita f.
priesthood n sacerdōtium nt, flāminium nt.
prig n homō fastīdiōsus m.
priggish adj fastīdiōsus.
prim adj modestior.
primarily adv prīncipiō, praecipuē.
primary adj prīmus, praecipuus.
prime adj prīmus, ēgregius; ~ **mover** auctor m ♦ n flōs m; **in one's** ~ flōrēns ♦ vt īnstruere, ērudīre.
primeval adj prīscus.
primitive adj prīstinus, incultus.
primordial adj prīscus.
prince n rēgulus m; rēgis fīlius m; prīnceps m.
princely adj rēgālis.
princess n rēgis fīlia f.
principal adj praecipuus, prīnceps, māximus ♦ n (person) prīnceps m/f; (money) sors f.
principally adv in prīmīs, māximē, māximam partem.
principle n prīncipium nt; (rule) fōrmula f, ratiō f; (character) fidēs f; ~**s** pl īnstitūta ntpl, disciplīna f; **first** ~**s** elementa ntpl, initia ntpl.
print n nota f, signum nt; (foot) vestīgium nt ♦ vt imprimere.
prior adj prior, potior.
priority n: **give** ~ **to** praevertere (dat).
prise vt sublevāre; ~ **open** vectī refringere.
prison n carcer m, vincula ntpl; **put in** ~ in vincula conicere.
prisoner n reus m; (for debt) nexus m; (of war) captīvus m; ~ **at the bar** reus m, rea f; **take** ~ capere.
pristine adj prīscus, prīstinus, vetus.
privacy n sēcrētum nt.
private adj (individual) prīvātus; (home) domesticus; (secluded) sēcrētus ♦ n (MIL) gregārius mīles m.
privately adv clam, sēcrētō.
private property n res familiāris f.
privation n inopia f, egestās f.

privet n ligustrum nt.
privilege n iūs nt, immūnitās f.
privileged adj immūnis.
privy adj sēcrētus; ~ **to** cōnscius (gen).
prize n praemium nt; (captured) praeda f; ~ **money** manubiae fpl ♦ vt māgnī aestimāre.
pro-Athenian adj rērum Athēniēnsium studiōsus.
probability n vērī similitūdō f.
probable adj vērī similis; **more** ~ vērō propior.
probably adv fortasse.
probation n probātiō f.
probationer n tīrō m.
probe vt īnspicere, scrūtārī.
probity n honestās f, integritās f.
problem n quaestiō f; **the** ~ **is** illud quaeritur.
problematical adj dubius, anceps.
procedure n ratiō f, modus m; (law) fōrmula f.
proceed vi pergere, prōcēdere, prōgredī; (narrative) īnsequi; ~ **against** persequī, lītem intendere (dat); ~ **from** orīrī, proficīscī ex.
proceedings n ācta ntpl.
proceeds n fructus m, reditus m.
process n ratiō f; (law) āctiō f; **in the** ~ **of time** post aliquod tempus.
procession n pompa f; (fig) agmen nt.
proclaim vt ēdīcere, prōnūntiāre, praedicāre, dēclārāre; ~ **war against** bellum indīcere + dat.
proclamation n ēdictum nt.
proclivity n prōpēnsiō f.
proconsul n prōcōnsul m.
proconsular adj prōcōnsulāris.
proconsulship n prōcōnsulātus m.
procrastinate vt differre, prōferre ♦ vi cunctārī.
procrastination n prōcrāstinātiō f, mora f.
procreate vt generāre, prōcreāre.
procreation n prōcreātiō f.
procreator n generātor m.
procumbent adj prōnus.
procurator n prōcūrātor m.
procure vt parāre, adipīscī, adquīrere; (by request) impetrāre.
procurer n lēnō m.
prod vt stimulāre.
prodigal adj prōdigus ♦ n nepōs m.
prodigality n effūsiō f.
prodigally adv effūsē.
prodigious adj ingēns, immānis.
prodigy n prōdigium nt, portentum nt; (fig) mīrāculum nt.
produce vt ēdere; (young) parere; (crops) ferre; (play) dare, docēre; (line) prōdūcere; (in court) sistere; (into view) prōferre; (from store) prōmere, dēprōmere ♦ n fructus m; (of earth) frūgēs fpl; (in money) reditus m.
product n opus nt; ~ **of** fructus (gen).
production n opus nt.
productive adj fēcundus, ferāx, fructuōsus.
productivity n fēcunditās f, ūbertās f.
profanation n violātiō f.
profane adj profānus, impius ♦ vt violāre, polluere.

profanely *adv* impiē.
profanity *n* impietās *f.*
profess *vt* profitērī, prae sē ferre; ~ **to be** profitērī sē.
profession *n* professiō *f*; (*occupation*) ars *f*, haeresis *f.*
professor *n* doctor *m.*
proffer *vt* offerre, pollicērī.
proficiency *n* prōgressus *m*, perītia *f*; **attain ~** prōficere.
proficient *adj* perītus.
profile *n* ōris līneāmenta *ntpl*; (*portrait*) oblīqua imāgō *f.*
profit *n* lucrum *nt*, ēmolumentum *nt*, fructus *m*; **make a ~ out of** quaestuī habēre ♦ *vt* prōdesse (*dat*) ♦ *vi*: ~ **by** fruī (*abl*), ūtī (*abl*); (*opportunity*) arripere.
profitable *adj* fructuōsus, ūtilis.
profitably *adv* ūtiliter.
profligacy *n* flāgitium *nt*, perditī mōrēs *mpl.*
profligate *adj* perditus, dissolūtus ♦ *n* nepōs *m.*
profound *adj* altus; (*discussion*) abstrūsus.
profoundly *adv* penitus.
profundity *n* altitūdō *f.*
profuse *adj* prōdigus, effūsus.
profusely *adv* effūsē.
profusion *n* abundantia *f*, adfluentia *f*; **in ~** abundē.
progenitor *n* auctor *m.*
progeny *n* prōgeniēs *f*, prōlēs *f.*
prognostic *n* signum *nt.*
prognosticate *vt* ōminārī, augurārī, praedīcere.
prognostication *n* ōmen *nt*, praedictiō *f.*
programme *n* libellus *m.*
progress *n* prōgressus *m*; **make ~** prōficere ♦ *vi* prōgredī.
progression *n* prōgressus *m.*
progressively *adv* gradātim.
prohibit *vt* vetāre, interdīcere (*dat*).
prohibition *n* interdictum *nt.*
project *n* prōpositum *nt* ♦ *vi* ēminēre, exstāre; (*land*) excurrere ♦ *vt* prōicere.
projectile *n* tēlum *nt.*
projecting *adj* ēminēns.
projection *n* ēminentia *f.*
proletarian *adj* plēbēius.
proletariat *n* plēbs *f.*
prolific *adj* fēcundus.
prolix *adj* verbōsus, longus.
prolixity *n* redundantia *f.*
prologue *n* prologus *m.*
prolong *vt* dūcere, prōdūcere; (*office*) prōrogāre.
prolongation *n* (*time*) propāgātiō *f*; (*office*) prōrogātiō *f.*
promenade *n* ambulātiō *f* ♦ *vi* inambulāre, spatiārī.
prominence *n* ēminentia *f.*
prominent *adj* ēminēns, īnsignis; **be ~** ēminēre.
promiscuous *adj* prōmiscuus.

promiscuously *adv* prōmiscuē.
promise *n* prōmissum *nt*; **break a ~** fidem fallere; **keep a ~** fidem praestāre; **make a ~** fidem dare; **a youth of great ~** summae speī adulēscēns ♦ *vt* prōmittere, pollicērī; (*in marriage*) dēspondēre; ~ **in return** reprōmittere ♦ *vi*: ~ **well** bonam spem ostendere.
promising *adj* bonae speī.
promissory note *n* syngrapha *f.*
promontory *n* prōmunturium *nt.*
promote *vt* favēre (*dat*); (*growth*) alere; (*in rank*) prōdūcere.
promoter *n* auctor *m*, fautor *m.*
promotion *n* dignitās *f.*
prompt *adj* alacer, prōmptus ♦ *vt* incitāre, commovēre; (*speaker*) subicere.
prompter *n* monitor *m.*
promptitude *n* alacritās *f*, celeritās *f.*
promptly *adv* extemplō, citō.
promulgate *vt* prōmulgāre, palam facere.
promulgation *n* prōmulgātiō *f.*
prone *adj* prōnus; (*mind*) inclīnātus.
prong *n* dēns *m.*
pronounce *vt* ēloquī, appellāre; (*oath*) interpōnere; (*sentence*) dīcere, prōnūntiāre.
pronounced *adj* manifestus, īnsignis.
pronouncement *n* ōrātiō *f*, adfirmātiō *f.*
pronunciation *n* appellātiō *f.*
proof *n* documentum *nt*, argūmentum *nt*; (*test*) probātiō *f* ♦ *adj* immōtus, impenetrābilis.
prop *n* adminiculum *nt*, firmāmentum *nt* ♦ *vt* fulcīre.
propaganda *n* documenta *ntpl.*
propagate *vt* propāgāre.
propagation *n* propāgātiō *f.*
propel *vt* incitāre, prōpellere.
propensity *n* inclīnātiō *f.*
proper *adj* idōneus, decēns, decōrus; rēctus; **it is ~** decet.
properly *adv* decōrē; rēctē.
property *n* rēs *f*, rēs mancipī, bona *ntpl*; (*estate*) praedium *nt*; (*attribute*) proprium *nt*; (*slave's*) pecūlium *nt.*
prophecy *n* vāticinium *nt*, praedictiō *f.*
prophesy *vt* vāticinārī, praedīcere.
prophet *n* vātēs *m*, fātidicus *m.*
prophetess *n* vātēs *f.*
prophetic *adj* dīvīnus, fātidicus.
prophetically *adv* dīvīnitus.
propinquity *n* (*place*) vīcīnitās *f*; (*kin*) propinquitās *f.*
propitiate *vt* plācāre.
propitiation *n* plācātiō *f*, litātiō *f.*
propitious *adj* fēlīx, faustus; (*god*) praesēns.
proportion *n* mēnsūra *f*; **in ~** prō portiōne, prō ratā parte; **in ~ to** prō (*abl*).
proportionately *adv* prō portiōne, prō ratā parte.
proposal *n* condiciō *f.*
propose *vt* prōpōnere; (*motion*) ferre, rogāre; (*penalty*) inrogāre; (*candidate*) rogāre

magistrātum.
proposer *n* auctor *m*, lātor *m*.
proposition *n* (*offer*) condiciō *f*; (*plan*)
cōnsilium *nt*, prōpositum *nt*; (*logic*)
prōnūntiātum *nt*.
propound *vt* expōnere, in medium prōferre.
propraetor *n* prōpraetor *m*.
proprietor *n* dominus *m*.
propriety *n* decōrum *nt*; (*conduct*) modestia *f*;
with ~ decenter.
propulsion *n* impulsus *m*.
prorogation *n* prōrogātiō *f*.
prorogue *vt* prōrogāre.
prosaic *adj* pedester.
proscribe *vt* prōscrībere.
proscription *n* prōscrīptiō *f*.
prose *n* ōrātiō *f*, ōrātiō solūta *f*.
prosecute *vt* (*task*) exsequī, gerere; (*at law*)
accūsāre, lītem intendere (*dat*).
prosecution *n* exsecūtiō *f*; (*at law*) accūsātiō *f*;
(*party*) accūsātor *m*.
prosecutor *n* accūsātor *m*.
prosody *n* numerī *mpl*.
prospect *n* prōspectus *m*; (*fig*) spēs *f* ♦ *vi*
explōrāre.
prospective *adj* futūrus, spērātus.
prosper *vi* flōrēre, bonā fortūnā ūtī ♦ *vt*
fortūnāre.
prosperity *n* fortūna *f*, rēs secundae *fpl*,
fēlīcitās *f*.
prosperous *adj* fēlix, fortūnātus, secundus.
prosperously *adv* prosperē.
prostrate *adj* prōstrātus, adflīctus; **lie ~** iacēre
♦ *vt* prōsternere, dēicere; **~ oneself**
prōcumbere, sē prōicere.
prostration *n* frāctus animus *m*.
prosy *adj* longus.
protagonist *n* prīmārum partium āctor *m*.
protect *vt* tuērī, dēfendere, custōdīre,
prōtegere.
protection *n* tūtēla *f*, praesidium *nt*; (*law*)
patrōcinium *nt*; (*POL*) fidēs *f*; **put oneself under**
the ~ of in fidem venīre (*gen*); **take under**
one's ~ in fidem recipere.
protector *n* patrōnus *m*, dēfēnsor *m*, custōs *m*.
protectress *n* patrōna *f*.
protégé *n* cliēns *m*.
protest *n* obtestātiō *f*; (*POL*) intercessiō *f* ♦ *vi*
obtestārī, reclāmāre; (*POL*) intercēdere.
protestation *n* adsevērātiō *f*.
prototype *n* archetypum *nt*.
protract *vt* dūcere, prōdūcere.
protrude *vi* prōminēre.
protruding *adj* exsertus.
protuberance *n* ēminentia *f*, tūber *nt*.
protuberant *adj* ēminēns, turgidus.
proud *adj* superbus, adrogāns, īnsolēns; **be ~**
superbīre; **be ~ of** iactāre.
proudly *adv* superbē.
prove *vt* dēmōnstrāre, arguere, probāre; (*test*)
experīrī ♦ *vi* (*person*) se praebēre; (*event*)
ēvādere; **~ oneself** sē praebēre, sē praestāre;
not ~n nōn liquet.

proved *adj* expertus.
provenance *n* orīgō *f*.
provender *n* pābulum *nt*.
proverb *n* prōverbium *nt*.
proverbial *adj* trītus; **become ~ in** prōverbium
venīre.
provide *vt* parāre, praebēre; **~ for** prōvidēre
(*dat*); **the law ~s** lēx iubet; **~ against**
praecavēre.
provided that *conj* dum, dummodo (+ *subj*).
providence *n* prōvidentia *f*; Deus *m*.
provident *adj* prōvidus, cautus.
providential *adj* dīvīnus; secundus.
providentially *adv* dīvīnitus.
providently *adv* cautē.
providing *conj* dum, dummodo.
province *n* prōvincia *f*.
provincial *adj* prōvinciālis; (*contemptuous*)
oppidānus, mūnicipālis.
provision *n* parātus *m*; **make ~ for** prōvidēre
(*dat*); **make ~** cavēre.
provisionally *adv* ad tempus.
provisions *n* cibus *m*, commeātus *m*, rēs
frūmentāria *f*.
proviso *n* condiciō *f*; **with this ~** hāc lēge.
provocation *n* inrītāmentum *nt*, offēnsiō *f*.
provocative *adj* (*language*) molestus,
invidiōsus.
provoke *vt* inrītāre, lacessere; (*to action*)
excitāre.
provoking *adj* odiōsus, molestus.
provost *n* praefectus *m*.
prow *n* prōra *f*.
prowess *n* virtūs *f*.
prowl *vi* grassārī, vagārī.
proximate *adj* proximus.
proximity *n* propinquitās *f*, vīcīnia *f*.
proxy *n* vicārius *m*.
prude *n* fastīdiōsa *f*.
prudence *n* prūdentia *f*.
prudent *adj* prūdēns, cautus, sagāx.
prudently *adv* prūdenter, cautē.
prudery *n* fastīdiōsa quaedam pudīcitia *f*.
prudish *adj* fastīdiōsus.
prune *vt* amputāre.
pruner *n* putātor *m*.
pruning hook *n* falx *f*.
pry *vi* inquīrere; **~ into** scrūtārī.
pseudonym *n* falsum nōmen *nt*.
psychology *n* animī ratiō *f*.
Ptolemy *n* Ptolemaeus *m*.
puberty *n* pūbertās *f*.
public *adj* pūblicus; (*speech*) forēnsis; **~ life** rēs
pūblica *f*, forum *nt*; **in ~** forīs; **appear in ~** in
medium prōdīre; **make ~** in mediō pōnere,
forās perferre; **make a ~ case of** in medium
vocāre; **act for the ~ good** in medium
cōnsulere; **be a ~ figure** in lūce versārī,
digitō mōnstrārī ♦ *n* vulgus *nt*, hominēs *mpl*.
publican *n* (*taxes*) pūblicānus *m*; (*inn*) caupō *m*.
publication *n* ēditiō *f*, prōmulgātiō *f*; (*book*)
liber *m*.
publicity *n* lūx *f*, celebritās *f*.

publicly *adv* palam; (*by the state*) pūblicē.
public opinion *n* fāma *f*.
publish *vt* vulgāre, dīvulgāre; (*book*) ēdere.
pucker *vt* corrūgāre.
puerile *adj* puerīlis.
puerility *n* ineptiae *fpl*.
puff *n* aura *f* ♦ *vt* īnflāre ♦ *vi* anhēlāre.
puffed up *adj* īnflātus, tumidus.
pugilism *n* pugilātus *m*.
pugilist *n* pugil *m*.
pugnacious *adj* pugnāx.
pugnacity *n* ferōcitās *f*.
puissance *n* potentia *f*, vīrēs *fpl*.
puissant *adj* potēns.
pull *n* tractus *m*; (*of gravity*) contentiō *f* ♦ *vt* trahere, tractāre; ~ **apart** distrahere; ~ **at** vellicāre; ~ **away** āvellere; ~ **back** retrahere; ~ **down** dēripere, dētrahere; (*building*) dēmōlīrī; ~ **off** āvellere; ~ **out** ēvellere, extrahere; ~ **through** *vi* pervincere; (*illness*) convalēscere; ~ **up** (*plant*) ēruere; (*movement*) coercēre; ~ **to pieces** dīlaniāre.
pullet *n* pullus gallīnāceus *m*.
pulley *n* trochlea *f*.
pulmonary *adj* pulmōneus.
pulp *n* carō *f*.
pulpit *n* suggestus *m*.
pulsate *vi* palpitāre, micāre.
pulse *n* (*plant*) legūmen *nt*; (*of blood*) vēnae *fpl*; **feel the** ~ vēnās temptāre.
pulverize *vt* contundere.
pumice stone *n* pūmex *m*.
pummel *vt* verberāre.
pump *n* antlia *f* ♦ *vt* haurīre; ~ **out** exhaurīre.
pumpkin *n* cucurbita *f*.
pun *n* agnōminātiō *f*.
punch *n* ictus *m* ♦ *vt* pertundere, percutere.
punctilious *adj* riligiōsus.
punctiliousness *n* riligiō *f*.
punctual *adj* accūrātus, dīligēns.
punctuality *n* dīligentia *f*.
punctually *adv* ad hōram, ad tempus.
punctuate *vt* distinguere.
punctuation *n* interpūnctiō *f*.
puncture *n* pūnctiō *f* ♦ *vt* pungere.
pundit *n* scholasticus *m*.
pungency *n* ācrimōnia *f*; (*in debate*) acūleī *mpl*.
pungent *adj* ācer, mordāx.
punish *vt* pūnīre, animadvertere in (*acc*); poenam sūmere dē (+ *abl*); **be ~ed** poenās dare.
punishable *adj* poenā dignus.
punisher *n* vindex *m*, ultor *m*.
punishment *n* poena *f*, supplicium *nt*; (*censors'*) animadversiō *f*; **capital** ~ capitis supplicium *nt*; **corporal** ~ verbera *ntpl*; **inflict** ~ **on** poenā adficere, poenam capere dē (*abl*), supplicium sūmere dē (*abl*); **submit to** ~ poenam subīre; **undergo** ~ poenās dare, pendere, solvere.
punitive *adj* ulcīscendī causā.
punt *n* pontō *m*.
puny *adj* pusillus.

pup *n* catulus *m* ♦ *vi* parere.
pupil *n* discipulus *m*, discipula *f*; (*eye*) aciēs *f*, pūpula *f*.
pupillage *n* tūtēla *f*.
puppet *n* pūpa *f*.
puppy *n* catulus *m*.
purblind *adj* luscus.
purchase *n* emptiō *f*; (*formal*) mancipium *nt* ♦ *vt* emere.
purchaser *n* emptor *m*; (*at auction*) manceps *m*.
pure *adj* pūrus, integer; (*morally*) castus; (*mere*) merus.
purely *adv* pūrē, integrē; (*solely*) sōlum, nīl nisi; (*quite*) omnīnō, plānē.
purgation *n* pūrgātiō *f*.
purge *vt* pūrgāre, expūrgāre.
purification *n* lūstrātiō *f*, pūrgātiō *f*.
purify *vt* pūrgāre, expūrgāre.
purist *n* fastīdiōsus *m*.
purity *n* integritās *f*, castitās *f*.
purloin *vt* surripere, fūrārī.
purple *n* purpura *f* ♦ *adj* purpureus.
purport *n* sententia *f*; (*of words*) vīs *f*; **what is the** ~ **of?** quō spectat?, quid vult? ♦ *vt* velle spectāre ad.
purpose *n* prōpositum *nt*, cōnsilium *nt*, mēns *f*; **for that** ~ eō; **for the** ~ **of** ad (*acc*), ut (*subj*), eā mente ut, eō cōnsiliō ut (*subj*); **on** ~ cōnsultō, dē industriā; **to the** ~ ad rem; **to what** ~? quō?, quōrsum?; **to no** ~ frustrā, nēquīquam; **without achieving one's** ~ rē īnfectā ♦ *vt* in animō habēre, velle.
purposeful *adj* intentus.
purposeless *adj* inānis.
purposely *adv* cōnsultō, dē industriā.
purr *n* murmur *nt* ♦ *vi* murmurāre.
purse *n* marsupium *nt*, crumēna *f*; **privy** ~ fiscus *m* ♦ *vt* adstringere.
pursuance *n* exsecūtiō *f*; **in** ~ **of** secundum (*acc*).
pursue *vt* īnsequī, īnsectārī, persequī; (*closely*) īnstāre (*dat*), īnsistere (*dat*); (*aim*) petere; (*course*) īnsistere.
pursuer *n* īnsequēns *m*; (*law*) accūsātor *m*.
pursuit *n* īnsectātiō *f*; (*hunt*) vēnātiō *f*; (*ambition*) studium *nt*.
purvey *vt* parāre; (*food*) obsōnāre.
purveyance *n* prōcūrātiō *f*.
purveyor *n* obsōnātor *m*.
purview *n* prōvincia *f*.
pus *n* pūs *nt*.
push *n* pulsus *m*, impetus *m* ♦ *vt* impellere, trūdere, urgēre; ~ **away** āmovēre; ~ **back** repellere; ~ **down** dēprimere, dētrūdere; ~ **forward** prōpellere; ~ **in** intrūdere; ~ **on** incitāre; ~ **through** perrumpere.
pushing *adj* cōnfīdēns.
pusillanimity *n* ignāvia *f*, timor *m*.
pusillanimous *adj* ignāvus, timidus.
pustule *n* pustula *f*.
put *vt* (*in a state*) dare; (*in a position*) pōnere; (*in words*) reddere; (*argument*) pōnere; (*spur*) subdere; (*to some use*) adhibēre; ~ **an end to**

fīnem facere (*dat*); ~ **a question to** interrogāre; ~ **against** adpōnere; ~ **among** intericere; ~ **aside** sēpōnere; ~ **away** pōnere, dēmovēre; (*store*) repōnere; ~ **back** repōnere; repellere; ~ **beside** adpōnere; ~ **between** interpōnere; ~ **by** condere; ~ **down** dēpōnere; (*revolt*) opprimere; ~ **forth** extendere; (*growth*) mittere; ~ **forward** ostentāre; (*plea*) adferre; ~ **in** immittere, īnserere; (*ship*) adpellere; ~ **off** differre; ~ **on** impōnere; (*clothes*) induere; (*play*) dare; ~ **out** ēicere; (*eye*) effodere; (*fire*) exstinguere; (*money*) pōnere; (*tongue*) exserere; ~ **out of the way** dēmovēre; ~ **out to sea** in altum ēvehi, solvere; ~ **over** superimpōnere; ~ **to** adpōnere; (*flight*) dare in (*acc*), fugāre, prōflīgāre; in fugam conicere; (*sea*) solvere; ~ **together** cōnferre; ~ **under** subicere; ~ **up** (*for sale*) prōpōnere; (*lodge*) dēvertere, dēversārī apud; ~ **up with** ferre, patī; ~ **upon** impōnere.

putrefaction *n* pūtor *m*.
putrefy *vi* putrēscere.
putrid *adj* putridus.
puzzle *n* nōdus *m* ♦ *vt* impedīre, sollicitāre; **be ~d** haerēre.
puzzling *adj* ambiguus, perplexus.
pygmy *n* pygmaeus *m*.
pyramid *n* pȳramis *f*.
pyramidal *adj* pȳramidātus.
pyre *n* rogus *m*.
Pyrenees *npl* Pyrenaeī (montēs) *mpl*.
python *n* pȳthōn *m*.

Q, q

quack *n* (*doctor*) circulātor *m* ♦ *vi* tetrinnīre.
quadrangle *n* ārea *f*.
quadruped *n* quadrupēs *m/f*.
quadruple *adj* quadruplex.
quaestor *n* quaestor *m*; ~**'s** quaestōrius.
quaestorship *n* quaestūra *f*.
quaff *vt* ēpōtāre, haurīre.
quagmire *n* palūs *f*.
quail *n* (*bird*) coturnīx *f* ♦ *vi* pāvēscere, trepidāre.
quaint *adj* novus, īnsolitus.
quaintness *n* īnsolentia *f*.
quake *vi* horrēre, horrēscere ♦ *n* (*earth*) mōtus *m*.
quaking *n* horror *m*, tremor *m* ♦ *adj* tremulus.
qualification *n* condiciō *f*; (*limitation*) exceptiō *f*.
qualified *adj* (*for*) aptus, idōneus, dignus; (*in*) perītus, doctus.

qualify *vi* prōficere ♦ *vt* temperāre, mītigāre.
qualities *npl* ingenium *nt*.
quality *n* nātūra *f*, vīs *f*; indolēs *f*; (*rank*) locus *m*, genus *nt*; **I know the ~ of** sciō quālis sit.
qualm *n* riligiō *f*, scrūpulus *m*.
quandary *n* angustiae *fpl*; **be in a ~** haerēre.
quantity *n* cōpia *f*, numerus *m*; (*metre*) vōcum mēnsiō *f*; **a large ~** multum *nt*, plūrimum *nt*; **a small ~** aliquantulum *nt*.
quarrel *n* dissēnsiō *f*, contrōversia *f*; (*violent*) rixa *f*, iūrgium *nt* ♦ *vi* rixārī, altercārī.
quarrelsome *adj* pugnāx, lītigiōsus.
quarry *n* lapicīdinae *fpl*, metallum *nt*; (*prey*) praeda *f* ♦ *vt* excīdere.
quart *n* duō sextāriī *mpl*.
quartan *n* (*fever*) quartāna *f*.
quarter *n* quarta pars *f*, quadrāns *m*; (*sector*) regiō *f*; (*direction*) pars *f*, regiō *f*; (*respite*) missiō *f*; ~**s** castra *ntpl*; (*billet*) hospitium *nt*; **come to close ~s** manum cōnserere; (*armies*) signa cōnferre; **winter ~s** hīberna *ntpl* ♦ *vt* quadrifidam dīvidere; (*troops*) in hospitia dīvidere.
quarterdeck *n* puppis *f*.
quarterly *adj* trimestris ♦ *adv* quartō quōque mēnse.
quartermaster *n* (*navy*) gubernātor *m*; (*army*) castrōrum praefectus *m*.
quarterstaff *n* rudis *f*.
quash *vt* comprimere; (*decision*) rescindere.
quatrain *n* tetrastichon *nt*.
quaver *n* tremor *m* ♦ *vi* tremere.
quavering *adj* tremebundus.
quay *n* crepīdō *f*.
queasy *adj* fastīdiōsus.
queen *n* rēgīna *f*; (*bee*) rēx *m*.
queer *adj* īnsolēns, rīdiculus.
quell *vt* opprimere, domāre, dēbellāre.
quench *vt* exstinguere, restinguere; (*thirst*) sēdāre, explēre.
querulous *adj* querulus, queribundus.
query *n* interrogātiō *f* ♦ *vt* in dubium vocāre ♦ *vi* rogāre.
quest *n* investīgātiō *f*; **go in ~ of** investīgāre, anquīrere.
question *n* interrogātiō *f*; (*at issue*) quaestiō *f*, rēs *f*; (*in doubt*) dubium *nt*; **ask a ~** rogāre, quaerere, scīscitārī, percontārī; **call in ~** in dubium vocāre, addubitāre; **out of the ~** indignus; **be out of the ~** improbārī, fierī nōn posse; **the ~ is** illud quaeritur; **there is no ~ that** nōn dubium est quīn (*subj*); **without ~** sine dubiō ♦ *vt* interrogāre; (*closely*) percontārī; (*doubt*) in dubium vocāre ♦ *vi* dubitāre.
questionable *adj* incertus, dubius.
questioner *n* percontātor *m*.
questioning *n* interrogātiō *f*.
queue *n* agmen *nt*.
quibble *n* captiō *f* ♦ *vi* cavillārī.
quibbler *n* cavillātor *m*.
quibbling *adj* captiōsus.
quick *adj* (*speed*) celer, vēlōx, citus; (*to act*)

alacer, impiger; (*to perceive*) sagāx; (*with hands*) facilis; (*living*) vīvus; **be ~** properāre, festīnāre; **cut to the ~** ad vīvum resecāre; (*fig*) mordēre.
quicken *vt* adcelerāre; (*with life*) animāre.
quickening *adj* vītālis.
quickly *adv* celeriter, citō; (*haste*) properē; (*mind*) acūtē; **as ~ as possible** quam celerrimē.
quickness *n* celeritās *f*, vēlōcitās *f*; (*to act*) alacritās *f*; (*to perceive*) sagācitās *f*, sollertia *f*.
quicksand *n* syrtis *f*.
quick-tempered *adj* īrācundus.
quick-witted *adj* acūtus, sagāx, perspicāx.
quiescence *n* inertia *f*, ōtium *nt*.
quiescent *adj* iners, ōtiōsus.
quiet *adj* tranquillus, quiētus, placidus; (*silent*) tacitus; **be ~** quiēscere; silēre ♦ *n* quiēs *f*, tranquillitās *f*; silentium *nt*; (*peace*) pāx *f* ♦ *vt* pācāre, compōnere.
quietly *adv* tranquillē, quiētē; tacitē, per silentium; aequō animō.
quietness *n* tranquillitās *f*; silentium *nt*.
quill *n* penna *f*.
quince *n* cydōnium *nt*.
quinquennial *adj* quinquennālis.
quinquereme *n* quinquerēmis *f*.
quintessence *n* flōs *m*, vīs *f*.
quip *n* sāl *m*, facētiae *fpl*.
quirk *n* captiuncula *f*; **~s** *pl* trīcae *fpl*.
quit *vt* relinquere ♦ *adj* līber, solūtus.
quite *adv* admodum, plānē, prōrsus; **not ~** minus, parum; (*time*) nōndum.
quits *n* parēs *mpl*.
quiver *n* pharetra *f* ♦ *vi* tremere, contremere.
quivering *adj* tremebundus, tremulus.
quoit *n* discus *m*.
quota *n* pars *f*, rata pars *f*.
quotation *n* (*act*) commemorātiō *f*; (*passage*) locus *m*.
quote *vt* prōferre, commemorāre.
quoth *vt* inquit.

R, r

rabbit *n* cunīculus *m*.
rabble *n* turba *f*; (*class*) vulgus *nt*, plēbēcula *f*.
rabid *adj* rabidus.
rabidly *adv* rabidē.
race *n* (*descent*) genus *nt*, stirps *f*; (*people*) gēns *f*, nōmen *nt*; (*contest*) certāmen *nt*; (*fig*) cursus *m*, curriculum *nt*; (*water*) flūmen *nt*; **run a ~** cursū certāre; **run the ~** (*fig*) spatium dēcurrere ♦ *vi* certāre, contendere.
racecourse *n* (*foot*) stadium *nt*; (*horse*)

spatium *nt*.
racer *n* cursor *m*.
racial *adj* gentīlis.
rack *n* (*torture*) tormentum *nt*; (*shelf*) pluteus *m*; **be on the ~** (*fig*) cruciāri ♦ *vt* torquēre, cruciāre; **~ off** (*wine*) diffundere.
racket *n* (*noise*) strepitus *m*.
racy *adj* (*style*) salsus.
radiance *n* splendor *m*, fulgor *m*.
radiant *adj* splendidus, nitidus.
radiantly *adv* splendidē.
radiate *vi* fulgēre; (*direction*) dīversōs tendere ♦ *vt* ēmittere.
radical *adj* īnsitus, innātus; (*thorough*) tōtus ♦ *n* novārum rērum cupidus *m*.
radically *adv* omnīnō, penitus, funditus.
radish *n* rādīx *f*.
radius *n* radius *m*.
raffish *adj* dissolūtus.
raffle *n* ālea *f* ♦ *vt* āleā vēndere.
raft *n* ratis *f*.
rafter *n* trabs *f*, tignum *nt*.
rag *n* pannus *m*.
rage *n* īra *f*, furor *m*; **be all the ~** in ōre omnium esse; **spend one's ~** exsaevīre ♦ *vi* furere, saevīre; (*furiously*) dēbacchārī.
ragged *adj* pannōsus.
raid *n* excursiō *f*, incursiō *f*, impressiō *f*; **make a ~** excurrere ♦ *vt* incursiōnem facere in (*acc*).
rail *n* longurius *m* ♦ *vt* saepīre ♦ *vi*: **~ at** maledīcere (*dat*), convīcia facere (*dat*).
railing *n* saepēs *f*, cancellī *mpl*.
raillery *n* cavillātiō *f*.
raiment *n* vestis *f*.
rain *n* pluvia *f*, imber *m* ♦ *vi* pluere; **it is raining** pluit.
rainbow *n* arcus *m*.
rainstorm *n* imber *m*.
rainy *adj* pluvius.
raise *vt* tollere, ēlevāre; (*army*) cōgere, cōnscrībere; (*children*) ēducāre; (*cry*) tollere; (*from dead*) excitāre; (*laugh*) movēre; (*money*) cōnflāre; (*price*) augēre; (*siege*) exsolvere; (*structure*) exstruere; (*to higher rank*) ēvehere; **~ up** ērigere, sublevāre.
raisin *n* astaphis *f*.
rajah *n* dynastēs *m*.
rake *n* rastrum *nt*; (*person*) nepōs *m* ♦ *vt* rādere; **~ in** conrādere; **~ up** (*fig*) ēruere.
rakish *adj* dissolūtus.
rally *n* conventus *m* ♦ *vt* (*troops*) in ōrdinem revocāre; (*with words*) hortārī; (*banter*) cavillārī ♦ *vi* sē colligere.
ram *n* ariēs *m*; (*battering*) ariēs *m* ♦ *vt*: **~ down** fistūcāre; **~ home** (*fact*) inculcāre.
ramble *n* errātiō *f* ♦ *vi* vagārī, errāre.
rambling *adj* vagus; (*plant*) errāticus; (*speech*) fluēns.
ramification *n* rāmus *m*.
rammer *n* fistūca *f*.
rampage *vi* saevīre.
rampant *adj* ferōx.

rampart n agger m, vallum nt.
ranch n lātifundium nt.
rancid adj pūtidus.
rancour n odium nt, acerbitās f, invidia f.
random adj fortuītus; **at ~** temerē.
range n ōrdō m, seriēs f; (mountain) iugum nt;
(of weapon) iactus m; **within ~** intrā tēlī
iactum; **come within ~** sub ictum venīre ♦ vt
ōrdināre ♦ vi ēvagārī, pervagārī; (in speech)
excurrere.
rank n (line) ōrdō m; (class) ōrdō m; (position)
locus m, dignitās f; **~ and file** gregāriī mīlitēs
mpl; **keep the ~s** ōrdinēs observāre; **the ~s**
(MIL) aciēs, aciēī f; **leave the ~s** ōrdine ēgredī,
ab signīs discēdere; **reduce to the ~s** in
ōrdinem redigere ♦ vt numerāre ♦ vi in
numerō habērī.
rank adj luxuriōsus; (smell) gravis, foetidus.
rankle vi exulcerāre.
rankness n luxuriēs f.
ransack vt dīripere, spoliāre.
ransom n redemptiō f, pretium nt ♦ vt
redimere.
rant vi latrāre.
ranter n rabula m, latrātor m.
rap n ictus m ♦ vt ferīre.
rapacious adj rapāx, avidus.
rapaciously adv avidē.
rapacity n rapācitās f, aviditās f.
rape n raptus m.
rapid adj rapidus, vēlōx, citus, incitātus.
rapidity n celeritās f, vēlōcitās f, incitātiō f.
rapidly adv rapidē, vēlōciter, citō.
rapine n rapīna f.
rapt adj intentus.
rapture n laetitia f, alacritās f.
rare adj rārus; (occurrence) īnfrequēns;
(quality) singulāris.
rarefy vt extenuāre.
rarely adv rārō.
rarity n rāritās f; (thing) rēs īnsolita f.
rascal n furcifer m, scelestus m.
rascally adj improbus.
rash adj temerārius, audāx, incōnsultus;
praeceps.
rashly adv temerē, incōnsultē.
rashness n temeritās f, audācia f.
rat n mūs m/f.
rate n (cost) pretium nt; (standard) nōrma f;
(tax) vectīgal nt; (speed) celeritās f; **at any ~**
(concessive) utique, saltem; (adversative)
quamquam, tamen ♦ vt (value) aestimāre;
(scold) increpāre, obiūrgāre.
rather adv potius, satius; (somewhat)
aliquantum; (with comp) aliquantō; (with
verbs) mālō; (correcting) immo; **~** tristior;
I would ~ mālō; **I ~ think** haud sciō an; **~ than**
magis quam, potius quam.
ratification n (formal) sānctiō f.
ratify vt ratum facere, sancīre; (law) iubēre.
rating n taxātiō f, aestimātiō f; (navy) nauta m;
(scolding) obiūrgātiō f.
ratiocinate vi ratiōcinārī.

ratiocination n ratiōcinātiō f.
ration n dēmēnsum nt.
rational adj animō praeditus; **be ~** sapere.
rationality n ratiō f.
rationally adv ratiōne.
rations npl cibāria ntpl, diāria ntpl.
rattle n crepitus m; (toy) crotalum nt ♦ vi
crepitāre, increpāre.
raucous adj raucus.
ravage vt dēpopulārī, vastāre, dīripere.
rave vi furere, īnsānīre; (fig) bacchārī,
saevīre.
raven n cornīx f.
ravenous adj rapāx, vorāx.
ravenously adv avidē.
ravine n faucēs fpl, hiātus m.
raving adj furiōsus, īnsānus ♦ n furor m.
ravish vt rapere; (joy) efferre.
raw adj crūdus; (person) rudis, agrestis.
ray n radius m; **the first ~ of hope appeared**
prīma spēs adfulsit.
raze vt excīdere, solō aequāre.
razor n novācula f.
reach n (space) spatium nt; (mind) captus m;
(weapon) ictus m; **out of ~ of** extrā (acc);
within ~ ad manum ♦ vt advenīre ad (+ acc);
attingere; (space) pertinēre ad; (journey)
pervenīre ad.
react vi adficī; **~ to** ferre.
reaction n: **what was his ~ to?** quō animō
tulit?
read vt legere; (a book) ēvolvere; (aloud)
recitāre; **~ over** perlegere.
reader n lēctor m.
readily adv facile, libenter, ultrō.
readiness n facilitās f; **in ~** ad manum, in
prōmptū, in expedītō.
reading n lēctiō f.
readjust vt dēnuō accommodāre.
ready adj parātus, prōmptus; (manner) facilis;
(money) praesēns; **get, make ~** parāre,
expedīre, adōrnāre.
reaffirm vt iterum adfirmāre.
real adj vērus, germānus.
real estate n fundus m, solum nt.
realism n vēritās f.
realistic adj vērī similis.
reality n rēs f, rēs ipsa f, vērum nt; **in ~** rēvērā.
realize vt intellegere, animadvertere; (aim)
efficere, peragere; (money) redigere.
really adv vērē, rēvērā, profectō; **~?** itane
vērō?
realm n rēgnum nt.
reap vt metere; **~ the reward of** fructum
percipere ex.
reaper n messor m.
reappear vi revenīre.
rear vt alere, ēducāre; (structure) exstruere ♦
vi sē ērigere ♦ n tergum nt; (MIL) novissima
aciēs f, novissimum agmen nt; **in the ~** ā
tergō; **bring up the ~** agmen claudere, agmen
cōgere ♦ adj postrēmus, novissimus.
rearguard n novissimum agmen nt,

novissimī *mpl*.
rearrange *vt* ōrdinem mūtāre (*gen*).
reason *n* (*faculty*) mēns *f*, animus *m*, ratiō *f*;
(*sanity*) sānitās *f*; (*argument*) ratiō *f*; (*cause*)
causa *f*; (*moderation*) modus *m*; **by ~ of**
propter (*acc*); **for this ~** idcircō, ideō,
proptereā; **in ~** aequus, modicus; **with good
~** iūre; **without ~** temerē, sine causā; **without
good ~** frustrā, iniūriā; **give a ~ for** ratiōnem
adferre (*gen*); **I know the ~ for** sciō cūr,
quamobrem (*subj*); **there is no ~ for** nōn est
cūr, nihil est quod (*subj*); **lose one's ~**
īnsānīre ♦ *vi* ratiōcinārī, disserere.
reasonable *adj* aequus, iūstus; (*person*)
modestus; (*amount*) modicus.
reasonably *adv* ratiōne, iūstē; modicē.
reasoning *n* ratiō *f*, ratiōcinātiō *f*.
reassemble *vt* colligere, cōgere.
reassert *vt* iterāre.
reassume *vt* recipere.
reassure *vt* firmāre, cōnfirmāre.
rebate *vt* dēdūcere.
rebel *n* rebellis *m* ♦ *adj* sēditiōsus ♦ *vi*
rebelliōnem facere, rebellāre, dēscīscere.
rebellion *n* sēditiō *f*, mōtus *m*.
rebellious *adj* sēditiōsus.
rebound *vi* resilīre.
rebuff *n* repulsa *f* ♦ *vt* repellere, āversārī.
rebuild *vt* renovāre, restaurāre.
rebuke *n* reprehēnsiō *f*, obiūrgātiō *f* ♦ *vt*
reprehendere, obiūrgāre, increpāre.
rebut *vt* refūtāre, redarguere.
recalcitrant *adj* invītus.
recall *n* revocātiō *f*, reditus *m* ♦ *vt* revocāre;
(*from exile*) redūcere; (*to mind*) reminīscī
(*gen*), recordārī (*gen*).
recant *vt* retractāre.
recantation *n* receptus *m*.
recapitulate *vt* repetere, summātim dīcere.
recapitulation *n* ēnumerātiō *f*.
recapture *vt* recipere.
recast *vt* reficere, retractāre.
recede *vi* recēdere.
receipt *n* (*act*) acceptiō *f*; (*money*) acceptum *nt*;
(*written*) apocha *f*.
receive *vt* accipere, capere; (*in turn*) excipere.
receiver *n* receptor *m*.
recent *adj* recēns.
recently *adv* nūper, recēns.
receptacle *n* receptāculum *nt*.
reception *n* aditus *m*, hospitium *nt*.
receptive *adj* docilis.
recess *n* recessus *m*, angulus *m*; (*holiday*)
fēriae *fpl*.
recharge *vt* replēre.
recipe *n* compositiō *f*.
recipient *n* quī accipit.
reciprocal *adj* mūtuus.
reciprocally *adv* mūtuō, inter sē.
reciprocate *vt* referre, reddere.
reciprocity *n* mūtuum *nt*.
recital *n* nārrātiō *f*, ēnumerātiō *f*; (*LIT*) recitātiō
f.

recitation *n* recitātiō *f*.
recite *vt* recitāre; (*details*) ēnumerāre.
reciter *n* recitātor *m*.
reck *vt* ratiōnem habēre (*gen*).
reckless *adj* temerārius, incautus, praeceps.
recklessly *adv* incautē, temerē.
recklessness *n* temeritās *f*, neglegentia *f*.
reckon *vt* (*count*) computāre, numerāre;
(*think*) cēnsēre, dūcere; (*estimate*) aestimāre;
~ on cōnfīdere (*dat*); **~ up** dīnumerāre; (*cost*)
aestimāre; **~ with** contendere cum.
reckoning *n* ratiō *f*.
reclaim *vt* repetere; (*from error*) revocāre.
recline *vi* recumbere; (*at table*) accumbere;
(*plur*) discumbere.
recluse *n* homō sōlitārius *m*.
recognition *n* cognitiō *f*.
recognizance *n* vadimōnium *nt*.
recognize *vt* agnōscere; (*approve*) accipere;
(*admit*) fatērī.
recoil *vi* resilīre; **~ from** refugere; **~ upon**
recidere in (*acc*).
recollect *vt* reminīscī (*gen*).
recollection *n* memoria *f*, recordātiō *f*.
recommence *vt* renovāre, redintegrāre.
recommend *vt* commendāre; (*advise*)
suādēre (*dat*).
recommendation *n* commendātiō *f*; (*advice*)
cōnsilium *nt*; **letter of ~** litterae
commendātīciae.
recompense *vt* remūnerārī, grātiam referre
(*dat*) ♦ *n* praemium *nt*, remūnerātiō *f*.
reconcile *vt* compōnere, reconciliāre; **be ~d**
grātiam redīre.
reconciliation *n* reconciliātiō *f*, grātia *f*.
recondite *adj* reconditus, abstrūsus.
recondition *vt* reficere.
reconnaissance *n* explōrātiō *f*.
reconnoitre *vt, vi* explōrāre; **without
reconnoitring** inexplōrātō.
reconquer *vt* recipere.
reconsider *vt* reputāre, retractāre.
reconstruct *vt* restituere, renovāre.
reconstruction *n* renovātiō *f*.
record *n* monumentum *nt*; (*LIT*) commentārius
m; **~s** *pl* tabulae *fpl*, fāstī *mpl*, ācta *ntpl*; **break
the ~** priōrēs omnēs superāre ♦ *vt* in
commentārium referre; (*history*)
perscrībere, nārrāre.
recount *vt* nārrāre, commemorāre.
recourse *n*: **have ~ to** (*for safety*) cōnfugere ad;
(*as expedient*) dēcurrere ad.
recover *vt* recipere, recuperāre; (*loss*)
reparāre; **~ oneself** sē colligere; **~ one's
senses** ad sānitātem revertī ♦ *vi*
convalēscere.
recovery *n* recuperātiō *f*; (*from illness*) salūs *f*.
recreate *vt* recreāre.
recreation *n* requiēs *f*, remissiō *f*, lūdus *m*.
recriminate *vi* in vicem accūsāre.
recrimination *n* mūtua accūsātiō *f*.
recruit *n* tīrō *m* ♦ *vt* (*MIL*) cōnscrībere;
(*strength*) reficere.

recruiting officer n conquīsītor m.
rectify vt corrigere, ēmendāre.
rectitude n probitās f.
recumbent adj supīnus.
recuperate vi convalēscere.
recur vi recurrere, redīre.
recurrence n reditus m, reversiō f.
recurrent adj adsiduus.
red adj ruber.
redden vi ērubēscere ♦ vt rutilāre.
reddish adj subrūfus.
redeem vt redimere, līberāre.
redeemer n līberātor m.
redemption n redemptiō f.
red-haired adj rūfus.
red-handed adj: **catch ~ in** manifestō scelere
    dēprehendere.
red-hot adj fervēns.
red lead n minium nt.
redness n rubor m.
redolent adj: **be ~ of** redolēre.
redouble vt ingemināre.
redoubt n prōpugnāculum nt.
redoubtable adj īnfestus, formīdolōsus.
redound vi redundāre; **it ~s to my credit** mihī
    honōrī est.
redress n remedium nt; **demand ~** rēs
    repetere ♦ vt restituere.
reduce vt minuere, attenuāre; (to a condition)
    redigere, dēdūcere; (MIL) expugnāre; **~ to the
    ranks** in ōrdinem cōgere.
reduction n imminūtiō f; (MIL) expugnātiō f.
redundancy n redundantia f.
redundant adj redundāns; **be ~** redundāre.
reduplication n gemīnātiō f.
re-echo vt reddere, referre ♦ vi resonāre.
reed n harundō f.
reedy adj harundineus.
reef n saxa ntpl ♦ vt (sail) subnectere.
reek n fūmus m ♦ vi fūmāre.
reel vi vacillāre, titubāre.
re-enlist vt rescrībere.
re-establish vt restituere.
refashion vt reficere.
refer vt (person) dēlēgāre; (matter) rēicere,
    remittere ♦ vi: **~ to** spectāre ad; (in speech)
    attingere, perstringere.
referee n arbiter m.
reference n ratiō f; (in book) locus m.
refine vt excolere, expolīre; (metal)
    excoquere.
refined adj hūmānus, urbānus, polītus.
refinement n hūmānitās f, cultus m, ēlegantia
    f.
refit vt reficere.
reflect vt reddere, repercutere ♦ vi meditārī; **~
    upon** cōnsīderāre, sēcum reputāre; (blame)
    reprehendere.
reflection n (of light) repercussus m; (image)
    imāgō f; (thought) meditātiō f, cōgitātiō f;
    (blame) reprehēnsiō f; **cast ~s on** maculīs
    aspergere, vitiō vertere; **with due ~**
    cōnsīderātē; **without ~** incōnsultē.

reflux n recessus m.
reform n ēmendātiō f ♦ vt (lines) restituere;
    (error) corrigere, ēmendāre, meliōrem
    facere ♦ vi sē corrigere.
reformation n corrēctiō f.
reformer n corrēctor m, ēmendātor m.
refract vt īnfringere.
refractory adj contumāx.
refrain vi temperāre, abstinēre (dat),
    supersedēre (inf).
refresh vt recreāre, renovāre, reficere; (mind)
    integrāre.
refreshed adj requiētus.
refreshing adj dulcis, iūcundus.
refreshment n cibus m.
refuge n perfugium nt; (secret) latebra f; **take ~
    with** perfugere ad (acc); **take ~ in** confugere.
refugee n profugus m.
refulgence n splendor m.
refulgent adj splendidus.
refund vt reddere.
refusal n recūsātiō f, dētrectātiō f.
refuse n pūrgāmenta ntpl; (fig) faex f ♦ vt
    (request) dēnegāre; (offer) dētrectāre,
    recūsāre; (with verb) nōlle.
refutation n refūtātiō f, reprehēnsiō f.
refute vt refellere, redarguere, revincere.
regain vt recipere.
regal adj rēgius, rēgālis.
regale vt excipere, dēlectāre; **~ oneself**
    epulārī.
regalia n īnsignia ntpl.
regally adv rēgāliter.
regard n respectus m, ratiō f; (esteem) grātia f;
    with ~ to ad (acc), quod attinet ad ♦ vt (look)
    intuērī, spectāre; (deem) habēre, dūcere;
    send ~s to salūtem dīcere (dat).
regarding prep dē (abl).
regardless adj neglegēns, immemor.
regency n interrēgnum nt.
regent n interrēx m.
regicide n (person) rēgis interfector m; (act)
    rēgis caedēs f.
regime n administrātiō f.
regimen n vīctus m.
regiment n legiō f.
region n regiō f, tractus m.
register n tabulae fpl, album nt ♦ vt in tabulās
    referre, perscrībere; (emotion) ostendere,
    sūmere.
registrar n tabulārius m.
registry n tabulārium nt.
regret n dolor m; (for past) dēsīderium nt; (for
    fault) paenitentia f ♦ vt dolēre; **I ~** mē
    paenitet, mē piget (gen).
regretful adj maestus.
regretfully adv dolenter.
regrettable adj īnfēlīx, īnfortūnātus.
regular adj (consistent) cōnstāns; (orderly)
    ōrdinātus; (habitual) solitus, adsiduus;
    (proper) iūstus, rēctus.
regularity n moderātiō f, ōrdō m; (consistency)
    cōnstantia f.

regularly *adv* ōrdine; cōnstanter; iūstē, rēctē.
regulate *vt* ōrdināre, dīrigere; (*control*)
moderārī.
regulation *n* lēx *f*, dēcrētum *nt*.
rehabilitate *vt* restituere.
rehearsal *n* meditātiō *f*.
rehearse *vt* meditārī.
reign *n* rēgnum *nt*; (*emperor's*) prīncipātus *m*;
in the ~ of Numa rēgnante Numā ♦ *vi*
rēgnāre; (*fig*) dominārī.
reimburse *vt* rependere.
rein *n* habēna *f*; give full ~ to habēnās
immittere ♦ *vt* īnfrēnāre.
reindeer *n* rēnō *m*.
reinforce *vt* firmāre, cōnfirmāre.
reinforcement *n* subsidium *nt*; ~s *pl* novae
cōpiae *fpl*.
reinstate *vt* restituere, redūcere.
reinstatement *n* restitūtiō *f*, reductiō *f*; (*to
legal privileges*) postlīminium *nt*.
reinvigorate *vt* recreāre.
reiterate *vt* dictitāre, iterāre.
reiteration *n* iterātiō *f*.
reject *vt* rēicere; (*with scorn*) respuere,
aspernārī, repudiāre.
rejection *n* rēiectiō *f*, repulsa *f*.
rejoice *vi* gaudēre, laetārī ♦ *vt* dēlectāre.
rejoicing *n* gaudium *nt*.
rejoin *vt* redīre ad ♦ *vi* respondēre.
rejoinder *n* respōnsum *nt*.
rejuvenate *vt*: be ~d repuerāscere.
rekindle *vt* suscitāre.
relapse *vi* recidere.
relate *vt* (*tell*) nārrāre, commemorāre,
expōnere; (*compare*) cōnferre ♦ *vi*
pertinēre.
related *adj* propinquus; (*by birth*) cognātus; (*by
marriage*) adfīnis; (*fig*) fīnitimus.
relation *n* (*tale*) nārrātiō *f*; (*connection*) ratiō *f*;
(*kin*) necessārius *m*, cognātus *m*, adfīnis *m*.
relationship *n* necessitūdō *f*; (*by birth*)
cognātiō *f*; (*by marriage*) adfīnitās *f*;
(*connection*) vīcīnitās *f*.
relative *adj* cum cēterīs comparātus ♦ *n*
propinquus *m*, cognātus *m*, adfīnis *m*,
necessārius *m*.
relatively *adv* ex comparātiōne.
relax *vt* laxāre, remittere ♦ *vi* languēscere.
relaxation *n* remissiō *f*, requiēs *f*, lūdus *m*.
relay *n*: ~s of horses dispositī equī *mpl*.
release *vt* solvere, exsolvere, līberāre,
expedīre; (*law*) absolvere ♦ *n* missiō *f*,
līberātiō *f*.
relegate *vt* relēgāre.
relent *vi* concēdere, plācārī, flectī.
relentless *adj* immisericors, inexōrābilis;
(*things*) improbus.
relevant *adj* ad rem.
reliability *n* fīdūcia *f*.
reliable *adj* fīdus.
reliance *n* fīdūcia *f*, fidēs *f*.
reliant *adj* frētus.
relic *n* rēliquiae *fpl*.

relief *n* levātiō *f*, levāmen *nt*, adlevāmentum *nt*;
(*aid*) subsidium *nt*; (*turn of duty*) vicēs *fpl*; (*art*)
ēminentia *f*; (*sculpture*) toreuma *nt*; bas ~
anaglypta *ntpl*; in ~ ēminēns, expressus;
throw into ~ exprimere, distinguere.
relieve *vt* levāre, sublevāre; (*aid*) subvenīre
(*dat*); (*duty*) succēdere (*dat*), excipere; (*art*)
distinguere.
religion *n* religiō *f*, deōrum cultus *m*.
religious *adj* religiōsus, pius; ~ feeling religiō
f.
religiously *adv* religiōsē.
relinquish *vt* relinquere; (*office*) sē abdicāre
(*abl*).
relish *n* sapor *m*; (*sauce*) condīmentum *nt*; (*zest*)
studium *nt* ♦ *vt* dēlectārī (*abl*).
reluctance *n*: with ~ invītus.
reluctant *adj* invītus.
reluctantly *adv* invītus, gravātē.
rely *vi* fīdere (*dat*), cōnfīdere (*dat*).
relying *adj* frētus (*abl*).
remain *vi* manēre, morārī; (*left over*) restāre,
superesse.
remainder *n* reliquum *nt*.
remaining *adj* reliquus; the ~ cēterī *pl*.
remains *n* rēliquiae *fpl*.
remand *vt* (*law*) ampliāre.
remark *n* dictum *nt* ♦ *vt* dīcere; (*note*)
observāre.
remarkable *adj* īnsignis, ēgregius,
memorābilis.
remarkably *adv* īnsignītē, ēgregiē.
remediable *adj* sānābilis.
remedy *n* remedium *nt* ♦ *vt* medērī (*dat*),
sānāre.
remember *vt* meminisse (*gen*); (*recall*)
recordārī (*gen*), reminīscī (*gen*).
remembrance *n* memoria *f*, recordātiō *f*.
remind *vt* admonēre, commonefacere.
reminder *n* admonitiō *f*, admonitum *nt*.
reminiscence *n* recordātiō *f*.
remiss *adj* dissolūtus, neglegēns.
remission *n* venia *f*.
remissness *n* neglegentia *f*.
remit *vt* remittere; (*fault*) ignōscere (*dat*);
(*debt*) dōnāre; (*punishment*) condōnāre;
(*question*) referre.
remittance *n* pecūnia *f*.
remnant *n* fragmentum *nt*; ~s *pl* rēliquiae *fpl*.
remonstrance *n* obtestātiō *f*, obiūrgātiō *f*.
remonstrate *vi* reclāmāre; ~ with obiūrgāre;
~ about expostulāre.
remorse *n* paenitentia *f*, cōnscientia *f*.
remorseless *adj* immisericors.
remote *adj* remōtus, reconditus.
remotely *adv* procul.
remoteness *n* longinquitās *f*.
removal *n* āmōtiō *f*; (*going*) migrātiō *f*.
remove *vt* āmovēre, dēmere, eximere,
removēre; (*out of the way*) dēmovēre ♦ *vi*
migrāre, dēmigrāre.
remunerate *vt* remūnerārī.
remuneration *n* mercēs *f*, praemium *nt*.

rend *vt* scindere, dīvellere.
render *vt* reddere; (*music*) interpretārī; (*translation*) vertere; (*thanks*) referre.
rendering *n* interpretātiō *f*.
rendez-vous *n* cōnstitūtum *nt*.
renegade *n* dēsertor *m*.
renew *vt* renovāre, integrāre, īnstaurāre, redintegrāre.
renewal *n* renovātiō *f*; (*ceremony*) īnstaurātiō *f*.
renounce *vt* renūntiāre, mittere, repudiāre.
renovate *vt* renovāre, reficere.
renown *n* fāma *f*, glōria *f*.
renowned *adj* praeclārus, īnsignis, nōtus.
rent *n* (*tear*) fissum *nt*; (*pay*) mercēs *f* ♦ *vt* (*hire*) condūcere; (*lease*) locāre.
renunciation *n* cessiō *f*, repudiātiō *f*.
repair *vt* reficere, sarcīre ♦ *vi* sē recipere ♦ *n*: **keep in good ~** tuērī; **in bad ~** ruīnōsus.
reparable *adj* ēmendābilis.
reparation *n* satisfactiō *f*.
repartee *n* facētiae *fpl*, salēs *mpl*.
repast *n* cēna *f*, cibus *m*.
repay *vt* remūnerārī, grātiam referre (*dat*); (*money*) repōnere.
repayment *n* solūtiō *f*.
repeal *vt* abrogāre ♦ *n* abrogātiō *f*.
repeat *vt* iterāre; (*lesson*) reddere; (*ceremony*) īnstaurāre; (*performance*) referre.
repeatedly *adv* identidem, etiam atque etiam.
repel *vt* repellere, dēfendere.
repellent *adj* iniūcundus.
repent *vi*: **I ~** mē paenitet (+ *gen of thing*).
repentance *n* paenitentia *f*.
repentant *adj* paenitēns.
repercussion *n* ēventus *m*.
repertory *n* thēsaurus *m*.
repetition *n* iterātiō *f*.
repine *vi* conquerī.
replace *vt* repōnere, restituere; **~ by** substituere.
replacement *n* supplēmentum *nt*.
replenish *vt* replēre, supplēre.
replete *adj* plēnus.
repletion *n* satietās *f*.
replica *n* apographon *nt*.
reply *vi* respondēre ♦ *n* respōnsum *nt*.
report *n* (*talk*) fāma *f*, rūmor *m*; (*repute*) opīniō *f*; (*account*) renūntiātiō *f*, litterae *fpl*; (*noise*) fragor *m*; **make a ~** renūntiāre ♦ *vt* referre, dēferre, renūntiāre.
repose *n* quiēs *f*, requiēs *f* ♦ *vt* repōnere, pōnere ♦ *vi* quiēscere.
repository *n* horreum *nt*.
reprehend *vt* reprehendere, culpāre.
reprehensible *adj* accūsābilis, improbus.
reprehension *n* reprehēnsiō *f*, culpa *f*.
represent *vt* dēscrībere, effingere, exprimere, imitārī; (*character*) partēs agere (*gen*), persōnam gerere (*gen*); (*case*) prōpōnere; (*substitute for*) vicārium esse (*gen*).
representation *n* imāgō *f*, imitātiō *f*; **make ~s to** admonēre.

representative *n* lēgātus *m*.
repress *vt* reprimere, cohibēre.
repression *n* coercitiō *f*.
reprieve *n* mora *f*, venia *f* ♦ *vt* veniam dare (*dat*).
reprimand *vt* reprehendere, increpāre ♦ *n* reprehēnsiō *f*.
reprisals *n* ultiō *f*.
reproach *vt* exprobāre, obicere (*dat*) ♦ *n* exprobrātiō *f*, probrum *nt*; (*cause*) opprobrium *nt*.
reproachful *adj* contumēliōsus.
reprobate *adj* perditus.
reproduce *vt* propāgāre; (*likeness*) referre.
reproduction *n* prōcreātiō *f*; (*likeness*) imāgō *f*.
reproductive *adj* genitālis.
reproof *n* reprehēnsiō *f*, obiūrgātiō *f*.
reprove *vt* reprehendere, increpāre, obiūrgāre.
reptile *n* serpēns *f*.
republic *n* lībera rēspūblica *f*, cīvitās populāris *f*.
republican *adj* populāris.
repudiate *vt* repudiāre.
repudiation *n* repudiātiō *f*.
repugnance *n* fastīdium *nt*, odium *nt*.
repugnant *adj* invīsus, adversus.
repulse *n* dēpulsiō *f*; (*at election*) repulsa *f* ♦ *vt* repellere, āversārī, prōpulsāre.
repulsion *n* repugnantia *f*.
repulsive *adj* odiōsus, foedus.
reputable *adj* honestus.
reputation *n* fāma *f*, existimātiō *f*; (*for something*) opīniō *f* (*gen*); **have a ~** nōmen habēre.
repute *n* fāma *f*, existimātiō *f*; **bad ~** īnfāmia *f*.
reputed *adj*: **I am ~ to be** dīcor esse.
request *n* rogātiō *f*, postulātum *nt*; **obtain a ~** impetrāre ♦ *vt* rogāre, petere; (*urgently*) dēposcere.
require *vt* (*demand*) imperāre, postulāre; (*need*) egēre (*abl*); (*call for*) requīrere.
requirement *n* postulātum *nt*, necessārium *nt*.
requisite *adj* necessārius.
requisition *n* postulātiō *f* ♦ *vt* imperāre.
requital *n* grātia *f*, vicēs *fpl*.
requite *vt* grātiam referre (*dat*), remūnerārī.
rescind *vt* rescindere, abrogāre.
rescript *n* rescrīptum *nt*.
rescue *vt* ēripere, expedīre, servāre ♦ *n* salūs *f*; **come to the ~ of** subvenīre (*dat*).
research *n* investīgātiō *f*.
resemblance *n* similitūdō *f*, imāgō *f*, īnstar *nt*.
resemble *vt* similem esse (*dat*), referre.
resent *vt* aegrē ferre, indignārī.
resentful *adj* īrācundus.
resentment *n* dolor *m*, indignātiō *f*.
reservation *n* (*proviso*) exceptiō *f*.
reserve *vt* servāre; (*store*) recondere; (*in a deal*) excipere ♦ *nt* (*MIL*) subsidium *nt*; (*disposition*) pudor *m*, reticentia *f*; (*caution*) cautiō *f*; **in ~** in succenturiātus; **without ~**

palam.
reserved *adj* (*place*) adsignātus; (*disposition*) taciturnus, tēctus.
reservedly *adv* circumspectē.
reserves *npl* subsidia *ntpl*.
reservoir *n* lacus *m*.
reside *vi* habitāre; **~ in** incolere.
residence *n* domicilium *nt*, domus *f*.
resident *n* incola *m/f*.
residual *adj* reliquus.
residue, residuum *n* reliqua pars *f*.
resign *vt* cēdere; (*office*) abdicāre mē, tē *etc* dē (+ *abl*); **~ oneself** acquiēscere ♦ *vi* sē abdicāre.
resignation *n* abdicātiō *f*; (*state of mind*) patientia *f*, aequus animus *m*.
resigned *adj* patiēns; **be ~ to** aequō animō ferre.
resilience *n* mollitia *f*.
resilient *adj* mollis.
resist *vt* resistere (*dat*), adversārī (*dat*), repugnāre (*dat*).
resistance *n* repugnantia *f*; **offer ~** obsistere (*dat*).
resistless *adj* invictus.
resolute *adj* fortis, cōnstāns.
resolutely *adv* fortiter, cōnstanter.
resolution *n* (*conduct*) fortitūdō *f*, cōnstantia *f*; (*decision*) dēcrētum *nt*, sententia *f*; (*into parts*) sēcrētiō *f*.
resolve *n* fortitūdō *f*, cōnstantia *f* ♦ *vt* dēcernere, cōnstituere; (*into parts*) dissolvere; **the senate ~s** placet senātuī.
resonance *n* sonus *m*.
resonant *adj* canōrus.
resort *n* locus celeber *m*; **last ~** ultimum auxilium *nt* ♦ *vi* frequentāre, ventitāre; (*have recourse*) dēcurrere, dēscendere, cōnfugere.
resound *vi* resonāre, personāre.
resource *n* subsidium *nt*; (*means*) modus *m*; **~s** *pl* opēs *fpl*, cōpiae *fpl*.
resourceful *adj* versūtus, callidus.
resourcefulness *n* calliditās *f*, versūtus animus *m*.
respect *n* (*esteem*) honōs *m*, observantia *f*; (*reference*) ratiō *f*; **out of ~** honōris causā; **pay one's ~s to** salūtāre; **show ~ for** observāre; **in every ~** ex omnī parte, in omnī genere; **in ~ of** ad (*acc*), ab (*abl*) ♦ *vt* honōrāre, observāre, verērī.
respectability *n* honestās *f*.
respectable *adj* honestus, līberālis, frūgī.
respectably *adv* honēstē.
respectful *adj* observāns.
respectfully *adv* reverenter.
respectfulness *n* observantia *f*.
respective *adj* suus (*with* quisque).
respectively *adv* alius ... alius.
respiration *n* respīrātiō *f*, spīritus *m*.
respire *vi* respīrāre.
respite *n* requiēs *f*, intercapēdō *f*, intermissiō *f*.
resplendence *n* splendor *m*.

resplendent *adj* splendidus, illūstris.
resplendently *adv* splendidē.
respond *vi* respondēre.
response *n* respōnsum *nt*.
responsibility *n* auctōritās *f*, cūra *f*.
responsible *adj* reus; (*witness*) locuplēs; **be ~ for** praestāre.
responsive *adj* (*pupil*) docilis; (*character*) facilis.
rest *n* quiēs *f*, ōtium *nt*; (*after toil*) requiēs *f*; (*remainder*) reliqua pars *f*; **be at ~** requiēscere; **set at ~** tranquillāre; **the ~ of** reliquī ♦ *vi* requiēscere, acquiēscere; **~ on** nītī (*abl*), innītī in (*abl*) ♦ *vt* (*hope*) pōnere in (*abl*).
rest *n* cēterī *mpl*.
resting place *n* cubīle *nt*, sēdēs *f*.
restitution *n* satisfactiō *f*; **make ~** restituere; **demand ~** rēs repetere.
restive *adj* contumāx.
restless *adj* inquiētus, sollicitus; **be ~** fluctuārī.
restlessness *n* sollicitūdō *f*.
restoration *n* renovātiō *f*; (*of king*) reductiō *f*.
restore *vt* reddere, restituere; (*to health*) recreāre; (*to power*) redūcere; (*damage*) reficere, redintegrāre.
restorer *n* restitūtor *m*.
restrain *vt* coercēre, comprimere, cohibēre.
restraint *n* moderātiō *f*, temperantia *f*, frēnī *mpl*; **with ~** abstinenter.
restrict *vt* continēre, circumscrībere.
restricted *adj* artus; **~ to** proprius (*gen*).
restriction *n* modus *m*, fīnis *m*; (*limitation*) exceptiō *f*.
result *n* ēventus *m*, ēventum *nt*, exitus *m*; **the ~ is that** quō fit ut ♦ *vi* ēvenīre, ēvādere.
resultant *adj* cōnsequēns.
resume *vt* repetere.
resuscitate *vt* excitāre, suscitāre.
retail *vt* dīvēndere, vēndere.
retailer *n* caupō *m*.
retain *vt* retinēre, tenēre, cōnservāre.
retainer *n* satelles *m*.
retake *vt* recipere.
retaliate *vi* ulcīscī.
retaliation *n* ultiō *f*.
retard *vt* retardāre, remorārī.
retention *n* cōnservātiō *f*.
retentive *adj* tenāx.
reticence *n* taciturnitās *f*.
reticent *adj* taciturnus.
reticulated *adj* rēticulātus.
retinue *n* satellitēs *mpl*, comitātus *m*.
retire *vi* recēdere, abscēdere; (*from office*) abīre; (*from province*) dēcēdere; (MIL) pedem referre, sē recipere.
retired *adj* ēmeritus; (*place*) remōtus.
retirement *n* (*act*) recessus *m*, dēcessus *m*; (*state*) sōlitūdō *f*, ōtium *nt*; **life of ~** vīta prīvāta.
retiring *adj* modestus, verēcundus.
retort *vt* respondēre, referre ♦ *n*

respōnsum *nt.*
retouch *vt* retractāre.
retrace *vt* repetere, iterāre.
retract *vt* revocāre, renūntiāre.
retreat *n* (MIL) receptus *m*; (*place*) recessus *m*, sēcessus *m*; **sound the ~** receptuī canere ♦ *vi* sē recipere, pedem referre; regredī.
retrench *vt* minuere, recīdere.
retrenchment *n* parsimōnia *f.*
retribution *n* poena *f.*
retributive *adj* ultor, ultrīx.
retrieve *vt* reparāre, recipere.
retrograde *adj* (*fig*) dēterior.
retrogression *n* regressus *m.*
retrospect *n*: **in ~** respicientī.
retrospective *adj*: **be ~** retrōrsum sē referre.
retrospectively *adv* retrō.
return *n* reditus *m*; (*pay*) remūnerātiō *f*; (*profit*) frūctus *m*, pretium *nt*; (*statement*) professiō *f*; **make a ~ of** profitērī; **in ~ for** prō (+ *abl*); **in ~** in vicem, vicissim ♦ *vt* reddere, restituere, referre ♦ *vi* redīre, revenīre, revertī; (*from province*) dēcēdere.
reunion *n* convīvium *nt.*
reunite *vt* reconciliāre.
reveal *vt* aperīre, patefacere.
revel *n* cōmissātiō *f*, bacchātiō *f*; **~s** *pl* orgia *ntpl* ♦ *vi* cōmissārī, bacchārī; **~ in** luxuriārī.
revelation *n* patefactiō *f.*
reveller *n* cōmissātor *m.*
revelry *n* cōmissātiō *f.*
revenge *n* ultiō *f*; **take ~ on** vindicāre in (*acc*) ♦ *vt* ulcīscī.
revengeful *adj* ulcīscendī cupidus.
revenue *n* frūctus *m*, reditus *m*, vectīgālia *ntpl.*
reverberate *vi* resonāre.
reverberation *n* repercussus *m.*
revere *vt* venerārī, colere.
reverence *n* venerātiō *f*; (*feeling*) religiō *f*; reverentia *f.*
reverent *adj* religiōsus, pius.
reverently *adv* religiōsē.
reverie *n* meditātiō *f*, somnium *nt.*
reversal *n* abrogātiō *f.*
reverse *adj* contrārius ♦ *n* contrārium *nt*; (MIL) clādēs *f* ♦ *vt* invertere; (*decision*) rescindere.
reversion *n* reditus *m.*
revert *vi* redīre, revertī.
review *n* recognitiō *f*, recēnsiō *f* ♦ *vt* (MIL) recēnsēre.
revile *vt* maledīcere (*dat*).
revise *vt* recognōscere, corrigere; (LIT) līmāre.
revision *n* ēmendātiō *f*; (LIT) līma *f.*
revisit *vt* revīsere.
revival *n* renovātiō *f.*
revive *vt* recreāre, excitāre ♦ *vi* revīvīscere, renāscī.
revocation *n* revocātiō *f.*
revoke *vt* renūntiāre, īnfectum reddere.
revolt *n* sēditiō *f*, dēfectiō *f* ♦ *vi* dēficere, rebellāre.
revolting *adj* taeter, obscēnus.
revolution *n* (*movement*) conversiō *f*; (*change*)

rēs novae *fpl*; (*revolt*) mōtus *m*; **effect a ~** rēs novāre.
revolutionary *adj* sēditiōsus, novārum rērum cupidus.
revolve *vi* volvī, versārī, convertī ♦ *vt* (*in mind*) volūtāre.
revulsion *n* mūtātiō *f.*
reward *n* praemium *nt*, mercēs *f* ♦ *vt* remūnerārī, compēnsāre.
rhapsody *n* carmen *nt*; (*epic*) rhapsōdia *f.*
rhetoric *n* rhētorica *f*; **of ~** rhētoricus; **exercise in ~** dēclāmātiō *f*; **practise ~** dēclāmāre; **teacher of ~** rhētōr *m.*
rhetorical *adj* rhētoricus, dēclāmātōrius.
rhetorically *adv* rhētoricē.
rhetorician *n* rhētōr *m*, dēclāmātor *m.*
rhinoceros *n* rhīnocerōs *m.*
rhyme *n* homoeoteleuton *nt*; **without ~ or reason** temerē.
rhythm *n* numerus *m*, modus *m.*
rhythmical *adj* numerōsus.
rib *n* costa *f.*
ribald *adj* obscēnus.
ribaldry *n* obscēnitās *f.*
ribbon *n* īnfula *f.*
rice *n* oryza *f.*
rich *adj* dīves, locuplēs; opulentus; (*fertile*) ūber, opīmus; (*food*) pinguis.
riches *n* dīvitiae *fpl*, opēs *fpl.*
richly *adv* opulentē, largē, lautē.
richness *n* ūbertās *f*, cōpia *f.*
rid *vt* līberāre; **get ~ of** dēpōnere, dēmovēre, exuere.
riddle *n* aenigma *nt*; (*sieve*) cribrum *nt* ♦ *vt* (*with wounds*) cōnfodere.
ride *vi* equitāre, vehī; **~ a horse** in equō vehī; **~ at anchor** stāre; **~ away** abequitāre, āvehī; **~ back** revehī; **~ between** interequitāre; **~ down** dēvehī; **~ into** invehī; **~ off** āvehī; **~ out** ēvehī; **~ past** praetervehī; **~ round** circumvehī (*dat*), circumequitāre; **~ up and down** perequitāre; **~ up to** adequitāre ad, advehī ad.
rider *n* eques *m.*
ridge *n* iugum *nt.*
ridicule *n* lūdibrium *nt*, irrīsus *m* ♦ *vt* irrīdēre, illūdere, lūdibriō habēre.
ridiculous *adj* rīdiculus, dērīdiculus.
ridiculously *adv* rīdiculē.
riding *n* equitātiō *f.*
rife *adj* frequēns.
riff-raff *n* faex populī *f.*
rifle *vt* expīlāre, spoliāre.
rift *n* rīma *f.*
rig *vt* (*ship*) armāre, ōrnāre ♦ *n* habitus *m.*
rigging *n* rudentēs *mpl.*
right *adj* rēctus; (*just*) aequus, iūstus; (*true*) rēctus, vērus; (*proper*) lēgitimus, fās; (*hand*) dexter; **it is ~** decet (+ *acc and infin*); **it is not ~** dēdecet (+ *acc and infin*); **you are ~** vēra dīcis; **if I am ~** nisi fallor; **in the ~ place** in locō; **at the ~ time** ad tempus; **at ~ angles** ad parēs angulōs; **on the ~** ā dextrā ♦ *adv* rēctē, bene,

probē; (*justifiably*) iūre; ~ **up to** usque ad
(+ *acc*); ~ **on** rēctā ♦ *n* (*legal*) iūs *nt*; (*moral*) fās
nt ♦ *vt* (*replace*) restituere; (*correct*)
corrigere; (*avenge*) ulcīscī.
righteous *adj* iūstus, sanctus, pius.
righteously *adv* iūstē, sanctē, piē.
righteousness *n* sanctitās *f*, pietās *f*.
rightful *adj* iūstus, lēgitimus.
rightfully *adv* iūstē, lēgitimē.
right hand *n* dextra *f*.
right-hand *adj* dexter; ~ **man** comes *m*.
rightly *adv* rēctē, bene; iūre.
right-minded *adj* sānus.
rigid *adj* rigidus.
rigidity *n* rigor *m*; (*strictness*) sevēritās *f*.
rigidly *adv* rigidē, sevērē.
rigmarole *n* ambāgēs *fpl*.
rigorous *adj* dūrus; (*strict*) sevērus.
rigorously *adv* dūriter, sevērē.
rigour *n* dūritia *f*; sevēritās *f*.
rile *vt* inrītāre, stomachum movēre (*dat*).
rill *n* rīvulus *m*.
rim *n* labrum *nt*.
rime *n* pruīna *f*.
rind *n* cortex *m*.
ring *n* ānulus *m*; (*circle*) orbis *m*; (*of people*)
corōna *f*; (*motion*) gȳrus *m* ♦ *vt* circumdare;
(*bell*) movēre ♦ *vi* tinnīre, sonāre.
ringing *n* tinnītus *m* ♦ *adj* canōrus.
ringleader *n* caput *nt*, dux *m*.
ringlet *n* cincinnus *m*.
rinse *vt* colluere.
riot *n* tumultus *m*, rixa *f*; **run** ~ exsultāre,
luxuriārī, tumultuārī, turbās efficere; (*revel*)
bacchārī.
rioter *n* cōmissātor *m*.
riotous *adj* tumultuōsus, sēditiōsus;
(*debauched*) dissolūtus; ~ **living** cōmissātiō *f*,
luxuria *f*.
riotously *adv* tumultuōsē; luxuriōsē.
rip *vt* scindere.
ripe *adj* mātūrus; **of** ~ **judgment** animī
mātūrus.
ripen *vt* mātūrāre ♦ *vi* mātūrēscere.
ripeness *n* mātūritās *f*.
ripple *n* unda *f* ♦ *vi* trepidāre.
rise *vi* orīrī, surgere; (*hill*) ascendere; (*wind*)
cōnsurgere; (*passion*) tumēscere; (*voice*)
tollī; (*in size*) crēscere; (*in rank*) ascendere;
(*in revolt*) coorīrī, arma capere; ~ **and fall**
(*tide*) reciprocāre; ~ **above** superāre; ~ **again**
resurgere; ~ **in** (*river*) orīrī ex (*abl*); ~ **out**
ēmergere; ~ **up** exsurgere ♦ *n* ascēnsus *m*;
(*slope*) clīvus *m*; (*increase*) incrēmentum *nt*;
(*start*) ortus *m*; **give** ~ **to** parere.
rising *n* (*sun*) ortus *m*; (*revolt*) mōtus *m* ♦ *adj*
(*ground*) ēditus.
risk *n* perīculum *nt*; **run a** ~ perīculum subīre,
ingredī ♦ *vt* perīclitārī, in āleam dare.
risky *adj* perīculōsus.
rite *n* rītus *m*.
ritual *n* caerimōnia *f*.
rival *adj* aemulus ♦ *n* aemulus *m*, rīvālis *m* ♦ *vt*

aemulārī.
rivalry *n* aemulātiō *f*.
river *n* flūmen *nt*, fluvius *m* ♦ *adj* fluviātilis.
riverbed *n* alveus *m*.
riverside *n* rīpa *f*.
rivet *n* clāvus *m* ♦ *vt* (*attention*) dēfīgere.
rivulet *n* rīvulus *m*, rīvus *m*.
road *n* via *f*, iter *nt*; **on the** ~ in itinere, ex
itinere; **off the** ~ dēvius; **make a** ~ viam
mūnīre.
roadstead *n* statiō *f*.
roam *vi* errāre, vagārī; ~ **at large** ēvagārī.
roar *n* fremitus *m* ♦ *vi* fremere.
roast *vt* torrēre ♦ *adj* āssus ♦ *n* āssum *nt*.
rob *vt* spoliāre, exspoliāre, expīlāre; (*of hope*)
dēicere dē.
robber *n* latrō *m*, fūr *m*; (*highway*) grassātor *m*.
robbery *n* latrōcinium *nt*.
robe *n* vestis *f*; (*woman's*) stola *f*; (*of state*)
trabea *f* ♦ *vt* vestīre.
robust *adj* rōbustus, fortis.
robustness *n* rōbur *nt*, firmitās *f*.
rock *n* saxum *nt*; (*steep*) rūpēs *f*, scopulus *m* ♦ *vt*
agitāre ♦ *vi* agitārī, vacillāre.
rocky *adj* saxōsus, scopulōsus.
rod *n* virga *f*; (*fishing*) harundō *f*.
roe *n* (*deer*) capreolus *m*, caprea *f*; (*fish*) ōva *ntpl*.
rogue *n* veterātor *m*.
roguery *n* nēquitia *f*, scelus *nt*.
roguish *adj* improbus, malus.
role *n* partēs *fpl*.
roll *n* (*book*) volūmen *nt*; (*movement*) gȳrus *m*;
(*register*) album *nt*; **call the** ~ **of** legere;
answer the ~ **call** ad nōmen respondēre ♦ *vt*
volvere ♦ *vi* volvī, volūtārī; ~ **down** *vt*
dēvolvere ♦ *vi* dēfluere; ~ **over** *vt* prōvolvere
♦ *vi* prōlābī; ~ **up** *vt* convolvere.
roller *n* (*AGR*) cylindrus *m*; (*for moving*)
phalangae *fpl*; (*in book*) umbilīcus *m*.
rollicking *adj* hilaris.
rolling *adj* volūbilis.
Roman *adj* Rōmānus ♦ *n*: **the** ~**s** Rōmānī *mpl*.
romance *n* fābula *f*; amor *m*.
romantic *adj* fābulōsus; amātōrius.
Rome *n* Rōma *f*; **at** ~ Rōmae; **from** ~ Rōmā; **to** ~
Rōmam.
romp *vi* lūdere.
roof *n* tēctum *nt*; (*of mouth*) palātum *nt* ♦ *vt*
tegere, integere.
rook *n* corvus *m*.
room *n* conclāve *nt*; camera *f*; (*small*) cella *f*;
(*bed*) cubiculum *nt*; (*dining*) cēnāculum *nt*;
(*dressing*) apodytērium *nt*; (*space*) locus *m*;
make ~ **for** locum dare (*dat*), cēdere (*dat*).
roominess *n* laxitās *f*.
roomy *adj* capāx.
roost *vi* stabulārī.
rooster *n* gallus gallīnāceus *m*.
root *n* rādīx *f*; **take** ~ coalēscere ♦ *vt*: ~ **out**
ērādīcāre.
rooted *adj* (*fig*) dēfixus; **deeply** ~ (*custom*)
inveterātus; **be** ~ **in** īnsidēre (*dat*); **become**
deeply ~ inveterāscere.

rope n fūnis m; (thin) restis f; (ship's) rudēns m; **know the ~s** perītum esse.
rose n rosa f.
rosemary n rōs marīnus m.
rostrum n rōstra ntpl, suggestus m.
rosy adj roseus, purpureus.
rot n tābēs f ♦ vi putrēscere, pūtēscere ♦ vt putrefacere.
rotate vi volvī, sē convertere.
rotation n conversiō f; (succession) ōrdō m, vicissitūdō f; **in ~** ōrdine; **move in ~** in orbem īre.
rote n: **by ~** memoriter.
rotten adj putridus.
rotund adj rotundus.
rotundity n rotunditās f.
rouge n fūcus m ♦ vt fūcāre.
rough adj asper; (art) incultus, rudis; (manners) agrestis, inurbānus; (stone) impolītus; (treatment) dūrus, sevērus; (weather) atrōx, procellōsus ♦ vi: **~ it** dūram vītam vīvere.
rough-and-ready adj fortuītus.
rough draft n (LIT) silva f.
roughen vt asperāre, exasperāre.
rough-hew vt dolāre.
roughly adv asperē, dūriter; (with numbers) circiter.
roughness n asperitās f.
round adj rotundus; (spherical) globōsus; (cylindrical) teres ♦ n (circle) orbis m; (motion) gȳrus m; (series) ambitus m; **go the ~s** (MIL) vigiliās circumīre ♦ vt (shape) superāre; **~ off** rotundāre; (sentence) concludere; **~ up** compellere ♦ adv circum, circā; **go ~** ambīre ♦ prep circum (acc), circā (acc).
roundabout adj: **~ story** ambāgēs fpl; **~ route** circuitus m, ānfrāctus m.
roundly adv (speak) apertē, līberē.
rouse vt excīre, excitāre; (courage) adrigere.
rousing adj vehemēns.
rout n fuga f; (crowd) turba f ♦ vt fugāre, fundere; in fugam conicere; prōflīgāre.
route n cursus m, iter nt.
routine n ūsus m, ōrdō m.
rove vi errāre, vagārī.
rover n vagus m; (sea) pīrāta m.
row n (line) ōrdō m; (noise) turba f, rixa f ♦ vi (boat) rēmigāre ♦ vt rēmīs incitāre.
rowdy adj turbulentus.
rower n rēmex m.
rowing n rēmigium nt.
royal adj rēgius, rēgālis.
royally adv rēgiē, rēgāliter.
royalty n (power) rēgnum nt; (persons) rēgēs mpl, domus rēgia f.
rub vt fricāre, terere; **~ away** conterere; **~ hard** dēfricāre; **~ off** dētergēre; **~ out** dēlēre; **~ up** expolīre.
rubbing n trītus m.
rubbish n quisquiliae fpl; (talk) nūgae fpl.
rubble n rūdus nt.
rubicund adj rubicundus.

rudder n gubernāculum nt, clāvus m.
ruddy adj rubicundus, rutilus.
rude adj (uncivilized) barbarus, dūrus, inurbānus; (insolent) asper, importūnus.
rudely adv horridē, rusticē; petulanter.
rudeness n barbariēs f; petulantia f, importūnitās f.
rudiment n elementum nt, initium nt.
rudimentary adj prīmus, incohātus.
rue n (herb) rūta f ♦ vt: **I ~** mē paenitet (gen).
rueful adj maestus.
ruffian n grassātor m.
ruffle vt agitāre; (temper) sollicitāre, commovēre.
rug n strāgulum nt.
rugged adj horridus, asper.
ruggedness n asperitās f.
ruin n ruīna f; (fig) exitium nt, perniciēs f; **go to ~** pessum īre, dīlābī ♦ vt perdere, dēperdere, pessum dare; (moral) corrumpere, dēprāvāre; **be ~ed** perīre.
ruined adj ruīnōsus.
ruinous adj exitiōsus, damnōsus.
rule n (instrument) rēgula f, amussis f; (principle) nōrma f, lēx f, praeceptum nt; (government) dominātiō f, imperium nt; **ten-foot ~** decempeda f; **as a ~** ferē; **lay down ~s** praecipere; **make it a ~ to** īnstituere (inf); **~ of thumb** ūsus m ♦ vt regere, moderārī ♦ vi rēgnāre, dominārī; (judge) ēdīcere; (custom) obtinēre; **~ over** imperāre (dat).
ruler n (instrument) rēgula f; (person) dominus m, rēctor m.
ruling n ēdictum nt.
rumble vi mūgīre.
rumbling n mūgītus m.
ruminate vi rūminārī.
rummage vi: **~ through** rīmārī.
rumour n fāma f, rūmor m.
rump n clūnis f.
run vi currere; (fluid) fluere, mānāre; (road) ferre; (time) lābī ♦ n cursus m; **~ about** discurrere, cursāre; **~ across** incidere in (acc); **~ after** sectārī; **~ aground** offendere; **~ away** aufugere, terga vertere; (from) fugere, dēfugere; **~ down** dēcurrere, dēfluere ♦ vt (in words) obtrectāre; **~ high** (fig) glīscere; **~ into** incurrere in (acc), īnfluere in (acc); **~ off with** abripere, abdūcere; **~ on** pergere; **~ out** (land) excurrere; (time) exīre; (supplies) dēficere; **~ over** vt (with car) obterere; (details) percurrere; **~ riot** luxuriārī; **~ through** (course) dēcurrere; (money) disperdere; **~ short** dēficere; **~ up to** adcurrere ad; **~ up against** incurrere in (acc); **~ wild** lascīvīre ♦ vt gerere, administrāre.
runaway adj fugitīvus.
rung n gradus m.
runner n cursor m.
running n cursus m ♦ adj (water) vīvus.
rupture n (fig) dissidium nt ♦ vt dīrumpere.
rural adj rūsticus, agrestis.

ruse n fraus f, dolus m.
rush n (*plant*) cārex f, iuncus m; (*movement*)
impetus m ♦ vi currere, sē incitāre, ruere; ~
forward sē prōripere; prōruere; ~ in inruere,
incurrere; ~ out ēvolāre, sē effundere ♦ adj
iunceus.
russet adj flāvus.
rust n (*iron*) ferrūgō f; (*copper*) aerūgō f ♦ vi
rōbīginem trahere.
rustic adj rūsticus, agrestis.
rusticate vi rūsticārī ♦ vt relēgāre.
rusticity n mōrēs rūsticī mpl.
rustle vi increpāre, crepitāre ♦ n crepitus m.
rusty adj rōbīginōsus.
rut n orbita f.
ruthless adj inexōrābilis, crūdēlis.
ruthlessly adv crūdēliter.
rye n secāle nt.

S, s

sabbath n sabbata ntpl.
sable adj āter, niger.
sabre n acīnacēs m.
sacerdotal adj sacerdōtālis.
sack n saccus m; (*MIL*) dīreptiō f ♦ vt dīripere,
expīlāre; spoliāre.
sackcloth n cilicium nt.
sacred adj sacer, sanctus.
sacredly adv sanctē.
sacredness n sanctitās f.
sacrifice n sacrificium nt, sacrum nt; (*act*)
immolātiō f; (*victim*) hostia f; (*fig*) iactūra f ♦
vt immolāre, sacrificāre, mactāre; (*fig*)
dēvovēre, addīcere ♦ vi sacra facere; (*give
up*) prōicere.
sacrificer n immolātor m.
sacrilege n sacrilegium nt.
sacrilegious adj sacrilegus.
sacristan n aedituus m.
sacrosanct adj sacrōsanctus.
sad adj maestus, tristis; (*thing*) tristis.
sadden vt dolōre adficere.
saddle n strātum nt ♦ vt sternere; (*fig*)
impōnere.
saddlebags n clītellae fpl.
sadly adv maestē.
sadness n tristitia f, maestitia f.
safe adj tūtus; (*out of danger*) incolumis,
salvus; (*to trust*) fīdus. ~ and sound salvus ♦
n armārium nt.
safe-conduct n fidēs pūblica f.
safeguard n cautiō f, prōpugnāculum nt ♦ vt
dēfendere.
safely adv tūtō, impūne.
safety n salūs f, incolumitās f;

seek ~ in flight salutem fugā petere.
saffron n crocus m ♦ adj croceus.
sag vi dēmittī.
sagacious adj prūdēns, sagāx, acūtus.
sagaciously adv prūdenter, sagāciter.
sagacity n prūdentia f, sagācitās f.
sage n sapiēns m; (*herb*) salvia f ♦ adj sapiēns.
sagely adv sapienter.
sail n vēlum nt; set ~ vēla dare, nāvem solvere;
shorten ~ vēla contrahere ♦ vi nāvigāre; ~
past legere, praetervehī.
sailing n nāvigātiō f.
sailor n nauta m.
sail yard n antenna f.
saint n vir sanctus m.
sainted adj beātus.
saintly adj sanctus.
sake n: for the ~ of grātiā (*gen*), causā (*gen*),
propter (*acc*); (*behalf*) prō (*abl*).
salacious adj salāx.
salad n morētum nt.
salamander n salamandra f.
salary n mercēs f.
sale n vēnditiō f; (*formal*) mancipium nt;
(*auction*) hasta f; for ~ vēnālis; be for ~
prōstāre; offer for ~ vēnum dare.
saleable adj vēndibilis.
salient adj ēminēns; ~ points capita ntpl.
saline adj salsus.
saliva n salīva f.
sallow adj pallidus.
sally n ēruptiō f; (*wit*) facētiae fpl ♦ vi
ērumpere, excurrere.
salmon n salmō m.
salon n ātrium nt.
salt n sal m ♦ adj salsus.
saltcellar n salīnum nt.
saltpetre n nitrum nt.
salt-pits n salīnae fpl.
salty adj salsus.
salubrious adj salūbris.
salubriously adv salūbriter.
salubriousness n salūbritās f.
salutary adj salūtāris, ūtilis.
salutation n salūs f.
salute vt salūtāre.
salvage vt servāre, ēripere.
salvation n salūs f.
salve n unguentum nt.
salver n scutella f.
same adj īdem; ~ as īdem ac; all the ~
nihilōminus; one and the ~ūnus et īdem;
from the ~ place indidem; in the ~ place
ibīdem; to the ~ place eōdem; at the ~ time
simul, eōdem tempore; (*adversative*) tamen;
it is all the ~ to me meā nōn interest.
Samnites n Samnītēs, Samnītium mpl.
sample n exemplum nt, specimen nt ♦ vt
gustāre.
sanctify vt cōnsecrāre.
sanctimony n falsa rēligiō f.
sanction n comprobātiō f, auctōritās f ♦ vt
ratum facere.

sanctity n sanctitās f.
sanctuary n fānum nt, dēlubrum nt; (for men)
asȳlum nt.
sand n harēna f.
sandal n (outdoors) crepida f; (indoors) solea f.
sandalled adj crepidātus, soleātus.
sandpit n harēnāria f.
sandstone n tōfus m.
sandy adj harēnōsus; (colour) flāvus.
sane adj sānus.
sangfroid n aequus animus m.
sanguinary adj cruentus.
sanguine adj laetus.
sanitary adj salūbris.
sanity n mēns sāna f.
sap n sūcus m ♦ vt subruere.
sapience n sapientia f.
sapient adj sapiēns.
sapling n surculus m.
sapper n cunīculārius m.
sapphire n sapphīrus f.
sarcasm n aculeī mpl, dicācitās f.
sarcastic adj dicāx, acūleātus.
sardonic adj amārus.
sash n cingulum nt.
satchel n loculus m.
sate vt explēre, satiāre.
satellite n satelles m.
satiate vt explēre, satiāre, saturāre.
satiety n satietās f.
satire n satura f; (pl, of Horace) sermōnēs mpl.
satirical adj acerbus.
satirist n saturārum scrīptor m.
satirize vt perstringere, notāre.
satisfaction n (act) explētiō f; (feeling)
voluptās f; (penalty) poena f; **demand** ~ rēs
repetere.
satisfactorily adv ex sententiā.
satisfactory adj idōneus, grātus.
satisfied adj: **be** ~ satis habēre, contentum
esse.
satisfy vt satisfacere (dat); (desire) explēre.
satrap n satrapēs m.
saturate vt imbuere.
satyr n satyrus m.
sauce n condīmentum nt; (fish) garum nt.
saucer n patella f.
saucily adv petulanter.
saucy adj petulāns.
saunter vi ambulāre.
sausage n tomāculum nt, hīllae fpl.
savage adj ferus, efferātus; (cruel) atrōx,
inhūmānus; saevus.
savagely adv ferōciter, inhūmānē.
savagery n ferōcitās f, inhūmānitās f.
savant n vir doctus m.
save vt servāre; ~ **up** reservāre ♦ prep praeter
(acc).
saving adj parcus; ~ **clause** exceptiō f ♦ n
compendium nt; ~**s** pl peculium nt.
saviour n līberātor m.
savory n thymbra f.
savour n sapor m; (of cooking) nīdor m ♦ vi

sapere; ~ **of** olēre, redolēre.
savoury adj condītus.
saw n (tool) serra f; (saying) prōverbium nt ♦ vt
serrā secāre.
sawdust n scobis f.
say vt dīcere; ~ **that ... not** negāre; ~ **no**
negāre; **he** ~**s** (quoting) inquit; **he** ~**s yes** āit;
they ~ ferunt (+ acc and infin).
saying n dictum nt.
scab n (disease) scabiēs f; (over wound) crusta
f.
scabbard n vāgīna f.
scabby adj scaber.
scaffold, scaffolding n fala f.
scald vt ūrere.
scale n (balance) lanx f; (fish, etc) squāma f;
(gradation) gradūs mpl; (music) diagramma nt
♦ vt scālīs ascendere.
scallop n pecten m.
scalp n capitis cutis f.
scalpel n scalpellum nt.
scamp n verberō m.
scamper vi currere.
scan vt contemplārī; (verse) mētīrī.
scandal n īnfāmia f, opprobrium nt; (talk)
calumnia f.
scandalize vt offendere.
scandalous adj flāgitiōsus, turpis.
scansion n syllabārum ēnārrātiō f.
scant adj exiguus, parvus.
scantily adv exiguē, tenuiter.
scantiness n exiguitās f.
scanty adj exiguus, tenuis, exīlis; (number)
paucus.
scapegoat n piāculum nt.
scar n cicātrīx f.
scarce adj rārus; **make oneself** ~ sē āmovēre,
dē mediō recēdere ♦ adv vix, aegrē.
scarcely adv vix, aegrē; ~ **anyone** nēmō ferē.
scarcity n inopia f, angustiae fpl.
scare n formīdō f ♦ vt terrēre; ~ **away**
absterrēre.
scarecrow n formīdō f.
scarf n fōcāle nt.
scarlet n coccum nt ♦ adj coccinus.
scarp n rūpēs f.
scathe n damnum nt.
scatter vt spargere; dispergere, dissipāre;
(violently) disicere ♦ vi diffugere.
scatterbrained adj dēsipiēns.
scattered adj rārus.
scene n spectāculum nt; (place) theātrum nt.
scenery n locī faciēs f, speciēs f; (beautiful)
amoenitās f.
scent n odor m; (sense) odōrātus m; **keen** ~
sagācitās f ♦ vt odōrārī; (perfume) odōribus
perfundere.
scented adj odōrātus.
sceptic n Pyrrhōnēus m.
sceptical adj incrēdulus.
sceptre n scēptrum nt.
schedule n tabulae fpl, ratiō f.
scheme n cōnsilium nt, ratiō f ♦ vt māchinārī,

mōlīrī.
schemer *n* māchinātor *m.*
schism *n* discidium *nt*, sēcessiō *f.*
scholar *n* vir doctus *m*, litterātus *m*; (*pupil*)
  discipulus *m.*
scholarly *adj* doctus, litterātus.
scholarship *n* litterae *fpl*, doctrīna *f.*
scholastic *adj* umbrātilis.
school *n* (*elementary*) lūdus *m*; (*advanced*)
  schola *f*; (*high*) gymnasium *nt*; (*sect*) secta *f*,
  domus *f* ♦ *vt* īnstituere.
schoolboy *n* discipulus *m.*
schoolmaster *n* magister *m.*
schoolmistress *n* magistra *f.*
science *n* doctrīna *f*, disciplīna *f*, ars *f.*
scimitar *n* acīnacēs *m.*
scintillate *vi* scintillāre.
scion *n* prōgeniēs *f.*
Scipio *n* Scīpiō, Scipiōnis *m.*
scissors *n* forfex *f.*
scoff *vi* irrīdēre; ~ **at** dērīdēre.
scoffer *n* irrīsor *m.*
scold *vt* increpāre, obiūrgāre.
scolding *n* obiūrgātiō *f.*
scoop *n* trulla *f* ♦ *vt*: ~ **out** excavāre.
scope *n* (*aim*) fīnis *m*; (*room*) locus *m*, campus
  m; **ample** ~ laxus locus.
scorch *vt* exūrere, torrēre.
scorched *adj* torridus.
score *n* (*mark*) nota *f*; (*total*) summa *f*;
  (*reckoning*) ratiō *f*; (*number*) vīgintī ♦ *vt*
  notāre ♦ *vi* vincere.
scorn *n* contemptiō *f* ♦ *vt* contemnere,
  spernere.
scorner *n* contemptor *m.*
scornful *adj* fastīdiōsus.
scornfully *adv* contemptim.
scorpion *n* scorpiō *m*, nepa *f.*
scot-free *adj* immūnis, impūnītus.
scoundrel *n* furcifer *m.*
scour *vt* (*clean*) tergēre; (*range*) percurrere.
scourge *n* flagellum *nt*; (*fig*) pestis *f* ♦ *vt*
  verberāre, virgīs caedere.
scout *n* explōrātor *m*, speculātor *m* ♦ *vi*
  explōrāre, speculārī ♦ *vt* spernere,
  repudiāre.
scowl *n* frontis contractiō *f* ♦ *vi* frontem
  contrahere.
scraggy *adj* strigōsus.
scramble *vi*: ~ **for** certātim captāre; ~ **up**
  scandere.
scrap *n* frūstum *nt.*
scrape *vt* rādere, scabere; ~ **off** abrādere.
scraper *n* strigilis *f.*
scratch *vt* rādere; (*head*) perfricāre; ~ **out**
  exsculpere, ērādere.
scream *n* clāmor *m*, ululātus *m* ♦ *vi* clāmāre,
  ululāre.
screech *n* ululātus *m* ♦ *vi* ululāre.
screen *n* obex *m/f*; (*from sun*) umbra *f*; (*fig*)
  vēlāmentum *nt* ♦ *vt* tegere.
screw *n* clāvus *m*; (*of winepress*) cochlea *f.*
scribble *vt* properē scrībere.

scribe *n* scrība *m.*
script *n* scrīptum *nt*; (*handwriting*) manus *f.*
scroll *n* volūmen *nt.*
scrub *vt* dētergēre, dēfricāre.
scruple *n* rēligiō *f*, scrūpulus *m.*
scrupulous *adj* rēligiōsus; (*careful*) dīligēns.
scrupulously *adv* rēligiōsē, dīligenter.
scrupulousness *n* rēligiō *f*; dīligentia *f.*
scrutinize *vt* scrūtārī, intrōspicere in (*acc*),
  excutere.
scrutiny *n* scrūtātiō *f.*
scud *vi* volāre.
scuffle *n* rixa *f.*
scull *n* calvāria *f*; (*oar*) rēmus *m.*
scullery *n* culīna *f.*
sculptor *n* fictor *m*, sculptor *m.*
sculpture *n* ars fingendī *f*; (*product*) statuae *fpl*
  ♦ *vt* sculpere.
scum *n* spūma *f.*
scurf *n* porrīgō *f.*
scurrility *n* maledicta *ntpl.*
scurrilous *adj* maledicus.
scurvy *adj* (*fig*) turpis, improbus.
scythe *n* falx *f.*
sea *n* mare *nt*; aequor *nt*; **open** ~ altum *nt*; **put to**
  ~ solvere; **be at** ~ nāvigāre; (*fig*) in errōre
  versārī ♦ *adj* marīnus; (*coast*) maritimus.
seaboard *n* lītus *nt.*
seafaring *adj* maritimus, nauticus.
seafight *n* nāvāle proelium *nt.*
seagull *n* larus *m.*
seal *n* (*animal*) phōca *f*; (*stamp*) signum *nt* ♦ *vt*
  signāre; ~ **up** obsignāre.
seam *n* sūtūra *f.*
seaman *n* nauta *m.*
seamanship *n* scientia et ūsus nauticārum
  rērum.
seaport *n* portus *m.*
sear *vt* adūrere, torrēre.
search *n* investigātiō *f* ♦ *vi* investīgāre,
  explōrāre ♦ *vt* excutere, scrūtārī; **in ~ of**
  causa (+ *gen*); ~ **for** quaerere, exquīrere,
  investīgāre; ~ **into** inquīrere, anquīrere; ~
  out explōrāre, indāgāre.
searcher *n* inquīsītor *m.*
searching *adj* acūtus, dīligēns.
seashore *n* litus *nt.*
seasick *adj*: **be** ~ nauseāre.
seasickness *n* nausea *f.*
seaside *n* mare *nt.*
season *n* annī tempus *nt*, tempestās *f*; (*right
  time*) tempus *nt*, opportūnitās *f*; **in** ~
  tempestīvē ♦ *vt* condīre.
seasonable *adj* tempestīvus.
seasonably *adv* tempestīvē.
seasoned *adj* (*food*) condītus; (*wood*) dūrātus.
seasoning *n* condīmentum *nt.*
seat *n* sēdēs *f*; (*chair*) sedīle *nt*; (*home*) domus *f*,
  domicilium *nt*; **keep one's** ~ (*riding*) in equō
  haerēre ♦ *vt* collocāre; ~ **oneself** īnsidēre.
seated *adj*: **be** ~ sedēre.
seaweed *n* alga *f.*
seaworthy *adj* ad nāvigandum ūtilis.

secede *vi* sēcēdere.
secession *n* sēcessiō *f*.
seclude *vt* sēclūdere, abstrūdere.
secluded *adj* sēcrētus, remōtus.
seclusion *n* sōlitūdō *f*, sēcrētum *nt*.
second *adj* secundus, alter; **a ~ time** iterum ♦
n temporis pūnctum *nt*; (*person*) fautor *m*; **~**
sight hariolātiō *f* ♦ *vt* favēre (*dat*), adesse
(*dat*).
secondary *adj* īnferior, dēterior.
seconder *n* fautor *m*.
second-hand *adj* aliēnus, trītus.
secondly *adv* deinde.
secrecy *n* sēcrētum *nt*, silentium *nt*.
secret *adj* secretus; occultus, arcānus;
(*stealth*) fūrtīvus ♦ *n* arcānum *nt*; **keep ~**
dissimulāre, cēlāre; **in ~** clam; **be ~** latēre.
secretary *n* scrība *m*, ab epistolīs, ā manū.
secrete *vt* cēlāre, abdere.
secretive *adj* tēctus.
secretly *adv* clam, occultē, sēcrētō.
sect *n* secta *f*, schola *f*, domus *f*.
section *n* pars *f*.
sector *n* regiō *f*.
secular *adj* profānus.
secure *adj* tūtus ♦ *vt* (*MIL*) fīrmāre, ēmūnīre;
(*fasten*) religāre; (*obtain*) parāre, nancīscī.
securely *adj* tūtō.
security *n* salūs *f*, impūnitās *f*; (*money*) cautiō
f, pignus *nt*, spōnsiō *f*; **sense of ~** sēcūritās *f*;
give good ~ satis dare; **on good ~** (*loan*)
nōminibus rēctis cautus; **stand ~ for**
praedem esse prō (*abl*).
sedan *n* lectīca *f*.
sedate *adj* placidus, temperātus, gravis.
sedately *adv* placidē.
sedateness *n* gravitās *f*.
sedge *n* ulva *f*.
sediment *n* faex *f*.
sedition *n* sēditiō *f*, mōtus *m*.
seditious *adj* sēditiōsus.
seditiously *adv* sēditiōsē.
seduce *vt* illicere, pellicere.
seducer *n* corruptor *m*.
seduction *n* corruptēla *f*.
seductive *adj* blandus.
seductively *adv* blandē.
sedulity *n* dīligentia *f*.
sedulous *adj* dīligēns, sēdulus.
sedulously *adv* dīligenter, sēdulō.
see *vt* vidēre, cernere; (*suddenly*) cōnspicārī;
(*performance*) spectāre; (*with mind*)
intellegere; **go and ~** vīsere, invīsere; **~ to**
vidēre, cōnsulere (*dat*); curāre (+ *acc and*
gerundive); (*through*) dīspicere; **~ that you**
are vidē ut sīs, fac sīs; **~ that you are not** vidē
nē sīs, cavē sīs.
seed *n* sēmen *nt*; (*in a plant*) grānum *nt*; (*in fruit*)
acinum *nt*; (*fig*) stirps *f*, prōgeniēs *f*.
seedling *n* surculus *m*.
seed-time *n* sēmentis *f*.
seeing that *conj* quōniam, siquidem.
seek *vt* petere, quaerere.

seeker *n* indāgātor *m*.
seem *vi* vidērī.
seeming *adj* speciōsus ♦ *n* speciēs *f*.
seemingly *adv* ut vidētur.
seemly *adj* decēns, decōrus; **it is ~** decet.
seep *vi* mānāre, percōlārī.
seer *n* vātēs *m/f*.
seethe *vi* fervēre.
segregate *vt* sēcernere, sēgregāre.
segregation *n* sēparātiō *f*.
seize *vt* rapere, corripere, adripere,
prehendere; (*MIL*) occupāre; (*illness*) adficere;
(*emotion*) invādere, occupāre.
seizure *n* ēreptiō *f*, occupātiō *f*.
seldom *adv* rārō.
select *vt* ēligere, excerpere, dēligere ♦ *adj*
lēctus, ēlēctus.
selection *n* ēlēctiō *f*, dēlēctus *m*; (*LIT*) ecloga *f*.
self *n* ipse; (*reflexive*) sē; **a second ~** alter īdem.
self-centred *adj* glōriōsus.
self-confidence *n* cōnfīdentia *f*, fīdūcia *f*.
self-confident *adj* cōnfīdēns.
self-conscious *adj* pudibundus.
self-control *n* temperantia *f*.
self-denial *n* abstinentia *f*.
self-evident *adj* manifestus; **it is ~** ante pedēs
positum est.
self-governing *adj* līber.
self-government *n* lībertās *f*.
self-important *adj* adrogāns.
self-interest *n* ambitiō *f*.
selfish *adj* inhūmānus, avārus; **be ~** suā causā
facere.
selfishly *adv* inhūmānē, avārē.
selfishness *n* inhūmānitās *f*, incontinentia *f*,
avāritia *f*.
self-made *adj* (*man*) novus.
self-possessed *adj* aequō animō.
self-possession *n* aequus animus *m*.
self-reliant *adj* cōnfīdēns.
self-respect *n* pudor *m*.
self-restraint *n* modestia *f*.
self-sacrifice *n* dēvōtiō *f*.
selfsame *adj* ūnus et īdem.
sell *vt* vēndere; (*in lots*) dīvēndere; **be sold**
vēnīre.
seller *n* vēnditor *m*.
selvage *n* limbus *m*.
semblance *n* speciēs *f*, imāgō *f*.
semicircle *n* hēmicyclium *nt*.
senate *n* senātus *m*; **hold a meeting of the ~**
senātum habēre; **decree of the ~** senātus
cōnsultum *nt*.
senate house *n* cūria *f*.
senator *n* senātor *m*; (*provincial*) decuriō *m*; **~s**
pl patrēs *mpl*.
senatorial *adj* senātōrius.
send *vt* mittere; **~ across** trānsmittere; **~**
ahead praemittere; **~ away** dīmittere; **~ back**
remittere; **~ for** accersere; (*doctor*) adhibēre;
~ for accersere; **~ forth** ēmittere; **~ forward**
praemittere; **~ in** immittere, intrōmittere; **~**
out ēmittere; (*in different directions*)

dīmittere; ~ **out of the way** ablēgāre; ~ **up** submittere.
senile *adj* senīlis.
senility *n* senium *nt*.
senior *adj* nātū māior; (*thing*) prior.
sensation *n* sēnsus *m*; (*event*) rēs nova *f*; **lose ~** obtorpēscere; **create a ~** hominēs obstupefacere.
sensational *adj* novus, prōdigiōsus.
sense *n* (*faculty*) sēnsus *m*; (*wisdom*) prūdentia *f*; (*meaning*) vis *f*, sententia *f*; **common ~** prūdentia *f*; **be in one's ~s** apud sē esse, mentis suae esse; **out of one's ~s** dēmēns; **recover one's ~s** resipīscere; **what is the ~ of** quid sibī vult? ♦ *vt* sentīre.
senseless *adj* absurdus, ineptus, īnsipiēns.
senselessly *adv* īnsipienter.
senselessness *n* īnsipientia *f*.
sensibility *n* sēnsus *m*.
sensible *adj* prūdēns, sapiēns.
sensibly *adv* prūdenter, sapienter.
sensitive *adj* mollis, irrītābilis, patibilis.
sensitiveness *n* mollitia *f*.
sensual *adj* libīdinōsus.
sensuality *n* libīdō *f*, voluptās *f*.
sensually *adv* libīdinōsē.
sentence *n* (*judge*) iūdicium *nt*, sententia *f*; (*GRAM*) sententia *f*; **pass ~** iūdicāre; **execute ~** lēge agere ♦ *vt* damnāre; **~ to death** capitis damnāre.
sententious *adj* sententiōsus.
sententiously *adv* sententiōsē.
sentient *adj* patibilis.
sentiment *n* (*feeling*) sēnsus *m*; (*opinion*) sententia *f*; (*emotion*) mollitia *f*.
sentimental *adj* mollis, flēbilis.
sentimentality *n* mollitia *f*.
sentimentally *adv* molliter.
sentries *npl* statiōnēs *fpl*, excubiae *fpl*.
sentry *n* custōs *m*, vigil *m*; **be on ~ duty** in statiōne esse.
separable *adj* dīviduus, sēparābilis.
separate *vt* sēparāre, dīvidere, disiungere; (*forcibly*) dīrimere, dīvellere ♦ *vi* dīgredī ♦ *adj* sēparātus, sēcrētus.
separately *adv* sēparātim, seōrsum.
separation *n* sēparātiō *f*; (*violent*) discidium *nt*.
September *n* mēnsis September *m*; **of ~** September.
sepulchral *adj* fūnebris.
sepulchre *n* sepulcrum *nt*.
sepulture *n* sepultūra *f*.
sequel *n* exitus *m*, quae sequuntur.
sequence *n* seriēs *f*, ōrdō *m*.
sequestered *adj* sēcrētus.
serenade *vt* occentāre.
serene *adj* tranquillus, sēcūrus.
serenely *adv* tranquillē.
serenity *n* sēcūritās *f*.
serf *n* servus *m*.
serfdom *n* servitūs *f*.
sergeant *n* signifer *m*.

series *n* seriēs *f*, ōrdō *m*.
serious *adj* gravis, sērius, sevērus.
seriously *adv* graviter, sēriō, sevērē.
seriousness *n* gravitās *f*.
sermon *n* ōrātiō *f*.
serpent *n* serpēns *f*.
serpentine *adj* tortuōsus.
serrated *adj* serrātus.
serried *adj* cōnfertus.
servant *n* (*domestic*) famulus *m*, famula *f*; (*public*) minister *m*, ministra *f*; **family ~s** familia *f*.
servant maid *n* ancilla *f*.
serve *vt* servīre (*dat*); (*food*) ministrāre, adpōnere; (*interest*) condūcere (*dat*) ♦ *vi* (*MIL*) stīpendia merēre, mīlitāre; (*suffice*) sufficere; **~ as** esse prō (*abl*); **~ in the cavalry** equō merēre; **~ in the infantry** pedibus merēre; **having ~d one's time** ēmeritus; **~ a sentence** poenam subīre; **~ well** bene merērī dē (*abl*).
service *n* (*status*) servitium *nt*, famulātus *m*; (*work*) ministerium *nt*; (*help*) opera *f*; (*by an equal*) meritum *nt*, beneficium *nt*; (*MIL*) mīlitia *f*, stīpendia *ntpl*; **be of ~ to** prōdesse (*dat*), bene merērī dē; **I am at your ~** adsum tibī; **complete one's ~** stīpendia ēmerērī.
serviceable *adj* ūtilis.
servile *adj* servīlis; (*fig*) abiectus, humilis.
servility *n* adūlātiō *f*.
servitude *n* servitūs *f*.
session *n* conventus *m*; **be in ~** sedēre.
sesterce *n* sēstertius *m*; **10 ~s** decem sēstertiī; **10,000 ~s** dēna sēstertia *ntpl*; **1,000,000 ~s** deciēs sēstertium.
set *vt* pōnere, locāre, statuere, sistere; (*bone*) condere; (*course*) dīrigere; (*example*) dare; (*limit*) impōnere; (*mind*) intendere; (*music*) modulārī; (*sail*) dare; (*sentries*) dispōnere; (*table*) īnstruere; (*trap*) parāre ♦ *vi* (*ASTRO*) occidere; **~ about** incipere; **~ against** oppōnere; **~ apart** sēpōnere; **~ aside** sēpōnere; **~ down** (*writing*) perscrībere; **~ eyes on** cōnspicere; **~ foot on** ingredī; **~ forth** expōnere, ēdere; **~ free** līberāre; **~ in motion** movēre; **~ in order** compōnere, dispōnere; **~ off** (*decoration*) distinguere; (*art*) illūmināre; **~ on** (*to attack*) immittere; **~ on foot** īnstituere; **~ on fire** incendere; **~ one's heart on** exoptāre; **~ out** *vi* proficīscī; **~ over** praeficere, impōnere; **~ up** statuere; (*fig*) cōnstituere.
set *adj* (*arrangement*) status; (*purpose*) certus; (*rule*) praescrīptus; (*speech*) compositus; **of ~ purpose** cōnsultō ♦ *n* (*persons*) numerus *m*; (*things*) congeriēs *f*; (*current*) cursus *m*.
setback *n* repulsa *f*.
settee *n* lectulus *m*.
setting *n* (*ASTRO*) occāsus *m*; (*event*) locus *m*.
settle *n* sella *f* ♦ *vt* statuere; (*annuity*) praestāre; (*business*) trānsigere; (*colony*) dēdūcere; (*debt*) exsolvere; (*decision*) cōnstituere; (*dispute*) dēcīdere, compōnere

♦ vi (abode) cōnsīdere; (agreement)
cōnstituere, convenīre; (sediment) dēsīdere;
~ in īnsidēre (dat).

settled adj certus, explōrātus.

settlement n (of a colony) dēductiō f; (colony)
colōnia f; (of dispute) dēcīsiō f, compositiō f;
(to wife) dōs f.

settler n colōnus m.

set to n pugna f.

seven num septem; ~ **each** septēnī; ~ **times**
septiēns.

seven hundred num septingentī.

seven hundredth adj septingentēsimus.

seventeen num septendecim.

seventeenth adj septimus decimus.

seventh adj septimus; **for the** ~ **time**
septimum.

seventieth adj septuāgēsimus.

seventy num septuāgintā; ~ **each** septuāgēnī; ~
times septuāgiēns.

sever vt incīdere, sēparāre, dīvidere.

several adj complūrēs, aliquot.

severally adv singulī.

severe adj gravis, sevērus, dūrus; (style)
austērus; (weather) asper; (pain) ācer,
gravis.

severely adv graviter, sevērē.

severity n gravitās f, asperitās f, sevēritās f.

sew vt suere; ~ **up** cōnsuere; ~ **up in** īnsuere in
(acc).

sewer n cloāca f.

sex n sexus m.

shabbily adv sordidē.

shabbiness n sordēs fpl.

shabby adj sordidus.

shackle n compēs f, vinculum nt ♦ vt impedīre,
vincīre.

shade n umbra f; (colour) color m; ~s pl mānēs
mpl; **put in the** ~ officere (dat) ♦ vt opācāre,
umbram adferre (dat).

shadow n umbra f.

shadowy adj obscūrus; (fig) inānis.

shady adj umbrōsus, opācus.

shaft n (missile) tēlum nt, sagitta f; (of spear)
hastīle nt; (of cart) tēmō m; (of light) radius m;
(excavation) puteus m.

shaggy adj hirsūtus.

shake vt quatere, agitāre; (structure)
labefacere, labefactāre; (belief) īnfīrmāre;
(resolution) labefactāre, commovēre; ~
hands with dextram dare (dat) ♦ vi quatī,
agitārī, tremere, horrēscere; ~ **off** dēcutere,
excutere; ~ **out** excutere.

shaking n tremor m.

shaky adj īnstābilis, tremebundus.

shall aux vb = fut indic.

shallot n caepa Ascalōnia f.

shallow adj brevis, vadōsus; (fig) levis.

shallowness n vada ntpl; (fig) levitās f.

shallows n brevia ntpl, vada ntpl.

sham adj fictus, falsus, fūcōsus ♦ n simulātiō f,
speciēs f ♦ vt simulāre.

shambles n laniēna f.

shame n (feeling) pudor m; (cause) dēdecus nt,
ignōminia f; **it** ~**s** pudet (+ acc of person, gen of
thing); **it is a** ~ flāgitium est ♦ vt rubōrem
incutere (dat) ♦ interj prō pudor!

shamefaced adj verēcundus.

shameful adj ignōminiōsus, turpis.

shamefully adv turpiter.

shameless adj impudēns.

shamelessly adv impudenter.

shamelessness n impudentia f.

shank n crūs nt.

shape n fōrma f, figūra f ♦ vt fōrmāre, fingere;
(fig) īnfōrmāre ♦ vi: ~ **well** prōficere.

shapeless adj īnfōrmis, dēfōrmis.

shapelessness n dēfōrmitās f.

shapeliness n fōrma f.

shapely adj fōrmōsus.

shard n testa f.

share n pars f; (plough) vōmer m; **go** ~**s with**
inter sē partīrī ♦ vt (give) partīrī, impertīre;
(have) commūnicāre, participem esse (gen).

sharer n particeps m/f, socius m.

shark n volpēs marīna f.

sharp adj acūtus; (fig) ācer, acūtus; (bitter)
amarus.

sharpen vt acuere; (fig) exacuere.

sharply adv ācriter, acūtē.

sharpness n aciēs f; (mind) acūmen nt,
argūtiae fpl; (temper) acerbitās f.

shatter vt quassāre, perfringere, adflīgere;
(fig) frangere.

shave vt rādere; ~ **off** abrādere.

shavings n rāmenta ntpl.

she pron haec, ea, illa.

sheaf n manipulus m.

shear vt tondēre, dētondēre.

shears n forficēs fpl.

sheath n vāgīna f.

sheathe vt recondere.

shed vt fundere; (blood) effundere; (one's
own) profundere; (tears) effundere;
(covering) exuere; ~ **light on** (fig) lūmen
adhibēre (dat).

sheen n nitor m.

sheep n ovis f; (flock) pecus nt.

sheepfold n ovīle nt.

sheepish adj pudibundus.

sheepishly adv pudenter.

sheer adj (absolute) merus; (steep) praeruptus.

sheet n (cloth) linteum nt; (metal) lāmina f;
(paper) carta f, scheda f; (sail) pēs m; (water)
aequor nt.

shelf n pluteus m, pēgma nt.

shell n concha f; (egg) putāmen nt; (tortoise)
testa f.

shellfish n conchȳlium nt.

shelter n suffugium nt, tegmen nt; (refuge)
perfugium nt, asȳlum nt; (lodging) hospitium
nt; (fig) umbra f ♦ vt tegere, dēfendere;
(refugee) excipere ♦ vi latēre; ~ **behind** (fig)
dēlitēscere in (abl).

sheltered adj (life) umbrātilis.

shelve vt differre ♦ vi sē dēmittere.

shelving *adj* dēclīvis.
shepherd *n* pastor *m*.
shield *n* scūtum *nt*; clipeus *m*; (*small*) parma *f*; (*fig*) praesidium *nt* ♦ *vt* prōtegere, dēfendere.
shift *n* (*change*) mūtātiō *f*; (*expedient*) ars *f*, dolus *m*; **make ~ to** efficere ut; **in ~s** per vicēs ♦ *vt* mūtāre; (*move*) movēre ♦ *vi* mūtārī; discēdere.
shiftless *adj* iners, inops.
shifty *adj* vafer, versūtus.
shilling *n* solidus *m*.
shimmer *vi* micāre ♦ *n* tremulum lūmen *nt*.
shin *n* tībia *f*.
shine *vi* lūcēre, fulgēre; (*reflecting*) nitēre; (*fig*) ēminēre; **~ forth** ēlūcēre, ēnitēre; effulgēre; **~ upon** adfulgēre (*dat*) ♦ *n* nitor *m*.
shingle *n* lapillī *mpl*, glārea *f*.
shining *adj* lūcidus, splendidus; (*fig*) illūstris.
shiny *adj* nitidus.
ship *n* nāvis *f*; **admiral's ~** nāvis praetōria; **decked ~** nāvis tēcta, nāvis cōnstrāta ♦ *vt* (*cargo*) impōnere; (*to a place*) nāvī invehere.
shipowner *n* nāviculārius *m*.
shipping *n* nāvēs *fpl*.
shipwreck *n* naufragium *nt*; **suffer ~** naufragium facere.
shipwrecked *adj* naufragus.
shirk *vt* dēfugere, dētrectāre.
shirt *n* subūcula *f*.
shiver *n* horror *m* ♦ *vi* horrēre, tremere ♦ *vt* perfringere, comminuere.
shivering *n* horror *m*.
shoal *n* (*fish*) exāmen *nt*; (*water*) vadum *nt*; **~s** *pl* brevia *ntpl*.
shock *n* impulsus *m*; (*battle*) concursus *m*, cōnflīctus *m*; (*hair*) caesariēs *f*; (*mind*) offēnsiō *f* ♦ *vt* percutere, offendere.
shocking *adj* atrōx, dētestābilis, flāgitiōsus.
shoddy *adj* vīlis.
shoe *n* calceus *m*.
shoemaker *n* sūtor *m*.
shoot *n* surculus *m*; (*vine*) pampinus *m* ♦ *vi* frondēscere; (*movement*) volāre; **~ up** ēmicāre ♦ *vt* (*missile*) conicere, iaculārī; (*person*) iaculārī, trānsfīgere.
shop *n* taberna *f*.
shore *n* lītus *nt*, ōra *f* ♦ *vt* fulcīre.
short *adj* brevis; (*broken*) curtus; (*amount*) exiguus; **for a ~ time** parumper, paulisper; **~ of** (*number*) intrā (*acc*); **be ~ of** indigēre (*abl*); **cut ~** interpellāre; **in ~** ad summam, dēnique; **very ~** perbrevis; **fall ~ of** nōn pervenīre ad, abesse ab; **run ~** dēficere; **to cut a long story ~** nē multīs morer, nē multa.
shortage *n* inopia *f*.
shortcoming *n* dēlictum *nt*, culpa *f*.
short cut *n* via compendiāria *f*.
shorten *vt* curtāre, imminuere, contrahere; (*sail*) legere.
shorthand *n* notae *fpl*.
shorthand writer *n* āctuārius *m*.
short-lived *adj* brevis.

shortly *adv* (*time*) brevī; (*speak*) breviter; **~ after** paulō post, nec multō post.
shortness *n* brevitās *f*, exiguitās *f*; (*difficulty*) angustiae *fpl*.
short-sighted *adj* (*fig*) imprōvidus, imprūdēns.
short-sightedness *n* imprūdentia *f*.
short-tempered *adj* īrācundus.
shot *n* ictus *m*; (*range*) iactus *m*.
should *vi* (*duty*) dēbēre.
shoulder *n* umerus *m*; (*animal*) armus *m* ♦ *vt* (*burden*) suscipere.
shout *n* clāmor *m*, adclāmātiō *f* ♦ *vt*, *vi* clāmāre, vōciferārī; **~ down** obstrepere (*dat*); **~ out** exclāmāre.
shove *vt* trūdere, impellere.
shovel *n* rutrum *nt*.
show *n* speciēs *f*; (*entertainment*) lūdī *mpl*, spectāculum *nt*; (*stage*) lūdicrum *nt*; **for ~ in** speciem; **put on a ~** spectācula dare ♦ *vt* mōnstrāre, indicāre, ostendere, ostentāre; (*point out*) dēmōnstrāre; (*qualities*) praestāre; **~ off** *vi* sē iactāre ♦ *vt* ostentāre.
shower *n* imber *m* ♦ *vt* fundere, conicere.
showery *adj* pluvius.
showiness *n* ostentātiō *f*.
showing off *n* iactātiō *f*.
showy *adj* speciōsus.
shred *n* fragmentum *nt*; **in ~s** minūtātim; **tear to ~s** dīlaniāre ♦ *vt* concīdere.
shrew *n* virāgō *f*.
shrewd *adj* acūtus, ācer, sagāx.
shrewdly *adv* acūtē, sagāciter.
shrewdness *n* acūmen *nt*, sagācitās *f*.
shriek *n* ululātus *m* ♦ *vi* ululāre.
shrill *adj* acūtus, argūtus.
shrine *n* fānum *nt*, dēlubrum *nt*.
shrink *vt* contrahere ♦ *vi* contrahī; **~ from** abhorrēre ab, refugere ab, dētrectāre.
shrivel *vt* corrūgāre ♦ *vi* exārēscere.
shroud *n* integumentum *nt*; **~s** *pl* rudentēs *mpl* ♦ *vt* involvere.
shrub *n* frutex *m*.
shrubbery *n* fruticētum *nt*.
shudder *n* horror *m* ♦ *vi* exhorrēscere; **~ at** horrēre.
shuffle *vt* miscēre ♦ *vi* claudicāre; (*fig*) tergiversārī.
shun *vt* vītāre, ēvītāre, dēfugere.
shut *vt* claudere; (*with cover*) operīre; (*hand*) comprimere; **~ in** inclūdere; **~ off** interclūdere; **~ out** exclūdere; **~ up** inclūdere.
shutter *n* foricula *f*, lūmināre *nt*.
shuttle *n* radius *m*.
shy *adj* timidus, pudibundus, verēcundus.
shyly *adv* timidē, verēcundē.
shyness *n* verēcundia *f*.
sibyl *n* sibylla *f*.
sick *adj* aeger, aegrōtus; **be ~** aegrōtāre; **feel ~** nauseāre; **I am ~ of** mē taedet (*gen*).
sicken *vt* fastīdium movēre (*dat*) ♦ *vi* nauseāre, aegrōtāre.

ickle n falx f.

ickly adj invalidus.

ickness n nausea f; (illness) morbus m, aegritūdō f.

ide n latus nt; (direction) pars f; (faction) partēs fpl; (kin) genus nt; **on all ~s** undique; **on both ~s** utrimque; **on one ~** unā ex parte; **on our ~** ā nōbis; **be on the ~ of** stāre ab, sentīre cum; **on the far ~ of** ultrā (acc); **on this ~** hīnc; **on this ~ of** cis (acc), citrā (acc) ♦ vi: **~ with** stāre ab, facere cum.

ideboard n abacus m.

idelong adj oblīquus.

ideways adv oblīquē, in oblīquum.

idle vi oblīquō corpore incēdere.

iege n obsidiō f, oppugnātiō f; **lay ~ to** obsidēre.

iege works n opera ntpl.

iesta n merīdiātiō f; **take a ~** merīdiāre.

ieve n crībrum nt.

igh n suspīrium nt; (loud) gemitus m ♦ vi suspīrāre, gemere.

ight n (sense) vīsus m; (process) aspectus m; (range) cōnspectus m; (thing seen) spectāculum nt, speciēs f; **at ~** ex tempore; **at first ~** prīmō aspectū; **in ~** in cōnspectū; **come into ~** in cōnspectum sē dare; **in the ~ of** in oculīs (gen); **catch ~ of** cōnspicere; **lose ~ of** ē cōnspectū āmittere; (fig) oblīvīscī (gen) ♦ vt cōnspicārī.

ightless adj caecus.

ightly adj decōrus.

ign n signum nt, indicium nt; (distinction) īnsigne nt; (mark) nota f; (trace) vestīgium nt; (proof) documentum nt; (portent) ōmen nt; (Zodiac) signum nt; **give a ~** innuere ♦ vi signum dare, innuere ♦ vt subscrībere (dat); (as witness) obsignāre.

ignal n signum nt; **give the ~ for retreat** receptuī canere ♦ vi signum dare ♦ adj īnsignis, ēgregius.

ignalize vt nōbilitāre.

ignally adv ēgregiē.

ignature n nōmen nt, manus f, chīrographum nt.

ignet n signum nt.

ignet ring n anulus m.

ignificance n interpretātiō f, significātiō f, vīs f; (importance) pondus nt.

ignificant adj gravis, clārus.

ignification n significātiō f.

ignify vt significāre, velle; (omen) portendere; **it does not ~** nōn interest.

ilence n silentium nt; **in ~** per silentium ♦ vt comprimere; (argument) refūtāre.

ilent adj tacitus; (habit) taciturnus; **be ~** silēre, tacēre; **be ~ about** silēre, tacēre; **become ~** conticēscere.

ilently adv tacitē.

ilhouette n adumbrātiō f.

ilk n bombȳx m; (clothes) sērica ntpl ♦ adj bombȳcinus, sēricus.

ilken adj bombȳcinus.

sill n līmen nt.

silliness n stultitia f, ineptiae fpl.

silly adj fatuus, ineptus; stultus; **be ~** dēsipere.

silt n līmus m.

silver n argentum nt ♦ adj argenteus.

silver mine n argentāria f.

silver plate n argentum nt.

silver-plated adj argentātus.

silvery adj argenteus.

similar adj similis.

similarity n similitūdō f.

similarly adv similiter.

simile n similitūdō f.

simmer vi lēniter fervēre.

simper vi molliter subrīdēre.

simple adj simplex; (mind) fatuus; (task) facilis.

simpleton n homō ineptus m.

simplicity n simplicitās f; (mind) stultitia f.

simplify vt faciliōrem reddere.

simply adv simpliciter; (merely) sōlum, tantum.

simulate vt simulāre.

simulation n simulātiō f.

simultaneously adv simul, ūnā, eōdem tempore.

sin n peccātum nt, nefās nt, dēlictum nt ♦ vi peccāre.

since adv abhinc; **long ~** iamdūdum ♦ conj (time) ex quō tempore, postquam; (reason) cum (+ subj), quōniam; **~ he** quippe quī ♦ prep ab (abl), ex (abl), post (acc); **ever ~** usque ab.

sincere adj sincērus, simplex, apertus.

sincerely adv sincērē, ex animō.

sincerity n fidēs f, simplicitās f.

sinew n nervus m.

sinewy adj nervōsus.

sinful adj improbus, impius, incestus.

sinfully adv improbē, impiē.

sing vt canere, cantāre; **~ of** canere.

singe vt adūrere.

singer n cantor m.

singing n cantus m ♦ adj canōrus.

single adj ūnus, sōlus, ūnicus; (unmarried) caelebs ♦ vt: **~ out** ēligere, excerpere.

single-handed adj ūnus.

singly adv singillātim, singulī.

singular adj singulāris; (strange) novus.

singularly adv singulāriter, praecipuē.

sinister adj īnfaustus, malevolus.

sink vi dēsīdere; (in water) dēmergī; **~ in** inlābī, īnsīdere ♦ vt dēprimere, mergere; (well) fodere; (fig) dēmergere.

sinless adj integer, innocēns, castus.

sinner n peccātor m.

sinuous adj sinuōsus.

sip vt gustāre, lībāre.

siphon n siphō m.

sir n (to master) ere; (to equal) vir optime; (title) eques m.

sire n pater m.

siren n sīrēn f.

sirocco n Auster m.
sister n soror f; ~'s sorōrius.
sisterhood n germānitās f; (*society*) sorōrum societās f.
sister-in-law n glōs f.
sisterly adj sorōrius.
sit vi sedēre; ~ **beside** adsidēre (*dat*); ~ **down** cōnsīdere; ~ **on** īnsidēre (*dat*); (*eggs*) incubāre; ~ **at table** accumbere; ~ **up** (*at night*) vigilāre.
site n situs m, locus m; (*for building*) ārea f.
sitting n sessiō f.
situated adj situs.
situation n situs m; (*CIRCS*) status m, condiciō f.
six num sex; ~ **each** sēnī; ~ **or seven** sex septem; ~ **times** sexiēns.
six hundred num sēscentī; ~ **each** sēscēnī; ~ **times** sēscentiēns.
six hundredth adj sēscentēsimus.
sixteen num sēdecim; ~ **each** sēnī dēnī; ~ **times** sēdeciēns.
sixteenth adj sextus decimus.
sixth adj sextus; **for the** ~ **time** sextum.
sixtieth adj sexāgēsimus.
sixty num sexāgintā; ~ **each** sexāgēnī; ~ **times** sexāgiēns.
size n māgnitūdō f, amplitūdō f; (*measure*) mēnsūra f, fōrma f.
skate vi per glaciem lābī; ~ **on thin ice** (*fig*) incēdere per ignēs suppositōs cinerī dolōsō.
skein n glomus nt.
skeleton n ossa ntpl.
sketch n adumbrātiō f, dēscrīptiō f ♦ vt adumbrāre, īnfōrmāre.
skewer n verū nt.
skiff n scapha f, lēnunculus m.
skilful adj perītus, doctus, scītus; (*with hands*) habilis.
skilfully adv perītē, doctē; habiliter.
skill n ars f, perītia f, sollertia f.
skilled adj perītus, doctus; ~ **in** perītus (+ *gen*).
skim vt dēspūmāre; ~ **over** (*fig*) legere, perstringere.
skin n cutis f; (*animal*) pellis f ♦ vt pellem dētrahere (*dat*).
skinflint n avārus m.
skinny adj macer.
skip vi exsultāre ♦ vt praeterīre.
skipper n magister m.
skirmish n leve proelium nt ♦ vi vēlitārī.
skirmisher n vēles m, excursor m.
skirt n īnstita f; (*border*) limbus m ♦ vt contingere (*dat*); (*motion*) legere.
skittish adj lascīvus.
skulk vi latēre, dēlitēscere.
skull n caput nt.
sky n caelum nt; **of the** ~ caelestis.
skylark n alauda f.
slab n tabula f.
slack adj remissus, laxus; (*work*) piger, neglegēns.
slacken vt remittere, dētendere ♦ vi laxārī.
slackness n remissiō f; pigritia f.

slag n scōria f.
slake vt restinguere, sēdāre.
slam vt adflīgere.
slander n maledicta ntpl, obtrectātiō f; (*law*) calumnia f ♦ vt maledīcere (*dat*), īnfāmāre, obtrectāre (*dat*).
slanderer n obtrectātor m.
slanderous adj maledicus.
slang n vulgāria verba ntpl.
slant vi in trānsversum īre.
slanting adj oblīquus, trānsversus.
slantingly adv oblīquē, ex trānsversō.
slap n alapa f ♦ vt palmā ferīre.
slapdash adj praeceps, temerārius.
slash vt caedere ♦ n ictus m.
slate n (*roof*) tēgula f; (*writing*) tabula f ♦ vt increpāre.
slatternly adj sordidus, incōmptus.
slaughter n caedēs f, strāgēs f ♦ vt trucīdāre.
slaughterhouse n laniēna f.
slave n servus m; (*domestic*) famulus m; (*home born*) verna m; **be a** ~ **to** īnservīre (*dat*); **household** ~**s** familia f.
slave girl n ancilla f.
slavery n servitūs f.
slavish adj servīlis.
slavishly adv servīliter.
slay vt interficere, occīdere.
slayer n interfector m.
sleek adj nitidus, pinguis.
sleep n somnus m; **go to** ~ obdormīscere ♦ vi dormīre; ~ **off** vt ēdormīre.
sleeper n dormītor m.
sleepiness n sopor m.
sleepless adj īnsomnis, vigil.
sleeplessness n īnsomnia f.
sleepy adj somniculōsus; **be** ~ dormītāre.
sleeve n manica f.
sleight of hand n praestīgiae fpl.
slender adj gracilis, exīlis.
slenderness n gracilitās f.
slice n frūstum nt ♦ vt secāre.
slide n lāpsus m ♦ vi lābī.
slight adj levis, exiguus, parvus ♦ n neglegentia f ♦ vt neglegere, offendere.
slightingly adv contemptim.
slightly adv leviter, paululum.
slightness n levitās f.
slim adj gracilis.
slime n līmus m.
slimness n gracilitās f.
slimy adj līmōsus, mūcōsus.
sling n funda f ♦ vt mittere, iaculārī.
slinger n funditor m.
slink vi sē subdūcere.
slip n lāpsus m; (*mistake*) offēnsiuncula f; (*plant*) surculus m ♦ vi lābī; ~ **away** ēlābī, dīlābī; ~ **out** ēlābī; (*word*) excidere; **give the** ~ **to** ēlūdere; **let** ~ āmittere, ēmittere; (*opportunity*) ōmittere; **there's many a** ~ **twixt the cup and the lip** inter ōs et offam multa interveniunt.
slipper n solea f.

lippery *adj* lūbricus.
lipshod *adj* neglegēns.
lit *n* rīma *f* ♦ *vt* findere, incīdere.
loe *n* spīnus *m*.
lope *n* dēclīve *nt*, clīvus *m*; (*steep*) dēiectus *m*
♦ *vi* sē dēmittere, vergere.
loping *adj* dēclīvis, dēvexus; (*up*) adclīvis.
lot *n* rīma *f*.
loth *n* inertia *f*, segnitia *f*, dēsidia *f*, ignāvia *f*.
lothful *adj* ignāvus, iners, segnis.
lothfully *adv* ignāvē, segniter.
louch *vi* languidē incēdere.
lough *n* (*skin*) exuviae *fpl*; (*bog*) palūs *f*.
lovenliness *n* ignāvia *f*, sordēs *fpl*.
lovenly *adj* ignāvus, sordidus.
low *adj* tardus, lentus; (*mind*) hebes.
lowly *adv* tardē, lentē.
lowness *n* tarditās *f*.
ludge *n* līmus *m*.
lug *n* līmāx *f*.
luggard *n* homō ignāvus *m*.
luggish *adj* piger, segnis; (*mind*) hebes.
luggishly *adv* pigrē, segniter.
luggishness *n* pigritia *f*, inertia *f*.
luice *n* cataracta *f*.
lumber *n* somnus *m*, sopor *m* ♦ *vi* dormīre.
lump *n* vīlis annōna *f*.
lur *n* nota *f*; **cast ~ on** dētrectāre ♦ *vt*: **~ words**
balbūtīre.
y *adj* astūtus, vafer, callidus; **on the ~** ex
opīnātō.
yly *adv* astūtē, callidē.
yness *n* astūtia *f*.
mack *n* (*blow*) ictus *m*; (*with hand*) alapa *f*;
(*boat*) lēnunculus *m*; (*taste*) sapor *m* ♦ *vt*
ferīre ♦ *vi*: **~ of** olēre, redolēre.
mall *adj* parvus, exiguus; **how ~** quantulus,
quantillus; **so ~** tantulus; **very ~** perexiguus,
minimus; **a ~ meeting of** īnfrequēns.
maller *adj* minor.
mallest *adj* minimus.
mallness *n* exiguitās *f*, brevitās *f*.
mall talk *n* sermunculus *m*.
mart *adj* (*action*) ācer, alacer; (*dress*)
concinnus, nitidus; (*pace*) vēlōx; (*wit*)
facētus, salsus ♦ *n* dolor *m* ♦ *vi* dolēre; (*fig*)
ūrī, mordērī.
martly *adv* ācriter; nitidē; vēlōciter; facētē.
martness *n* alacritās *f*; (*dress*) nitor *m*; (*wit*)
facētiae *fpl*, sollertia *f*.
mash *n* ruīna *f* ♦ *vt* frangere, comminuere.
mattering *n*: **get a ~ of** odōrārī, prīmīs labrīs
attingere; **with a ~ of** imbūtus (*abl*).
mear *vt* oblinere, ungere.
mell *n* (*sense*) odōrātus *m*; (*odour*) odor *m*; (*of
cooking*) nīdor *m* ♦ *vt* olfacere, odōrārī ♦ *vi*
olēre.
melly *adj* olidus.
melt *vt* fundere.
mile *n* rīsus *m* ♦ *vi* subrīdēre; **~ at** adrīdēre
(*dat*); **~ upon** rīdēre ad; (*fig*) secundum esse
(*dat*).
miling *adj* laetus.

smirk *vi* subrīdēre.
smith *n* faber *m*.
smithy *n* fabrica *f*.
smock *n* tunica *f*.
smoke *n* fūmus *m* ♦ *vi* fūmāre.
smoky *adj* fūmōsus.
smooth *adj* lēvis; (*skin*) glaber; (*talk*) blandus;
(*sea*) placidus; (*temper*) aequus; (*voice*) lēvis,
teres ♦ *vt* sternere, līmāre.
smoothly *adv* lēviter, lēniter.
smoothness *n* lēvitās *f*, lēnitās *f*.
smother *vt* opprimere, suffocāre.
smoulder *vi* fūmāre.
smudge *n* macula *f*.
smug *adj* suī contentus.
smuggle *vt* fūrtim importāre.
smugness *n* amor suī *m*.
smut *n* fūlīgō *f*.
snack *n* cēnula *f*; **take a ~** gustāre.
snag *n* impedīmentum *nt*, scrūpulus *m*.
snail *n* cochlea *f*.
snake *n* anguis *m*, serpēns *f*.
snaky *adj* vīpereus.
snap *vt* rumpere, praerumpere; **~ the fingers**
digitīs concrepāre ♦ *vi* rumpī, dissilīre; **~ at**
mordēre; **~ up** corripere.
snare *n* laqueus *m*, plaga *f*, pedica *f* ♦ *vt* inrētīre.
snarl *n* gannītus *m* ♦ *vi* gannīre.
snatch *vt* rapere, ēripere, adripere,
corripere; **~ at** captāre.
sneak *n* perfidus *m* ♦ *vi* conrēpere; **~ in** sē
īnsinuāre; **~ out** ēlābī.
sneaking *adj* humilis, fūrtīvus.
sneer *n* irrīsiō *f* ♦ *vi* irrīdēre, dērīdēre.
sneeze *n* sternūtāmentum *nt* ♦ *vi* sternuere.
sniff *vt* odōrārī.
snip *vt* praecīdere, secāre.
snob *n* homō ambitiōsus *m*.
snood *n* mitra *f*.
snooze *vi* dormītāre.
snore *vi* stertere.
snoring *n* rhoncus *m*.
snort *n* fremitus *m* ♦ *vi* fremere.
snout *n* rōstrum *nt*.
snow *n* nix *f* ♦ *vi* ningere; **~ed under** nive
obrutus; **it is ~ing** ningit.
snowy *adj* nivālis; (*colour*) niveus.
snub *vt* neglegere, praeterīre.
snub-nosed *adj* sīmus.
snuff *n* (*candle*) fungus *m*.
snug *adj* commodus.
snugly *adv* commodē.
so *adv* (*referring back*) sīc; (*referring forward*) ita;
(*with adj and adv*) tam; (*with verb*) adeō;
(*consequence*) ergō, itaque, igitur; **and ~**
itaque; **~ great** tantus; **so-so** sīc; **~ as to** ut; **~
be it** estō; **~ big** tantus; **~ far** usque adeō,
adhūc; **~ far as** quod; **~ far from** adeō nōn; **~
little** tantillus; **~ long as** dum; **~ many** tot; **~
much** *adj* tantus ♦ *adv* tantum; (*with compar*)
tantō; **~ often** totiēns; **~ that** ut (+ *subj*); **~ that
... not** (*purpose*) nē; (*result*) ut nōn; **and ~ on**
deinceps; **not ~ very** haud ita; **say ~** id dīcere.

soak *vt* imbuere, madefacere.
soaking *adj* madidus.
soap *n* sapō *m*.
soar *vi* in sublīme ferrī, subvolāre; ~ **above**
superāre.
sob *n* singultus *m* ♦ *vi* singultāre.
sober *adj* sobrius; (*conduct*) modestus; (*mind*)
sānus.
soberly *adv* sobriē, modestē.
sobriety *n* modestia *f*, continentia *f*.
so-called *adj* quī dīcitur.
sociability *n* facilitās *f*.
sociable *adj* facilis, cōmis.
sociably *adv* faciliter, cōmiter.
social *adj* sociālis, commūnis.
socialism *n* populāris ratiō *f*.
socialist *n* homō populāris *m/f*.
society *n* societās *f*; (*class*) optimātēs *mpl*;
(*being with*) convīctus *m*; **cultivate the ~ of**
adsectārī; **secret ~** sodālitās *f*.
sod *n* caespes *m*, glaeba *f*.
soda *n* nitrum *nt*.
sodden *adj* madidus.
soever *adv* -cumque.
sofa *n* lectus *m*.
soft *adj* mollis; (*fruit*) mītis; (*voice*) submissus;
(*character*) dēlicātus; (*words*) blandus.
soften *vt* mollīre; (*body*) ēnervāre; (*emotion*)
lēnīre, mītigāre ♦ *vi* mollēscere, mītēscere.
soft-hearted *adj* misericors.
softly *adv* molliter, lēniter; blandē.
softness *n* mollitia *f*, mollitiēs *f*.
soil *n* sōlum *nt*, humus *f* ♦ *vt* inquināre,
foedāre.
sojourn *n* commorātiō *f*, mānsiō *f* ♦ *vi*
commorārī.
sojourner *n* hospes *m*, hospita *f*.
solace *n* sōlātium *nt*, levātiō *f* ♦ *vt* sōlārī,
cōnsōlārī.
solar *adj* sōlis.
solder *n* ferrūmen *nt* ♦ *vt* ferrūmināre.
soldier *n* mīles *m*; **be a ~** mīlitāre; **common ~**
manipulāris *m*, gregārius mīles *m*; **fellow ~**
commīlitō *m*; **foot ~** pedes *m*; **old ~** veterānus
m ♦ *vi* mīlitāre.
soldierly *adj* mīlitāris.
soldiery *n* mīles *m*.
sole *adj* sōlus, ūnus, ūnicus ♦ *n* (*foot*) planta *f*;
(*fish*) solea *f*.
solecism *n* soloecismus *m*.
solely *adv* sōlum, tantum, modō.
solemn *adj* gravis; (*religion*) sanctus.
solemnity *n* gravitās *f*; sanctitās *f*.
solemnize *vt* agere.
solemnly *adv* graviter; rītē.
solicit *vt* flāgitāre, obsecrāre.
solicitation *n* flāgitātiō *f*.
solicitor *n* advocātus *m*.
solicitous *adj* anxius, trepidus.
solicitously *adv* anxiē, trepidē.
solicitude *n* cūra *f*, anxietās *f*.
solid *adj* solidus; (*metal*) pūrus; (*food*) firmus;
(*argument*) firmus; (*character*) cōnstāns,
spectātus; **become ~** concrēscere; **make ~**
cōgere.
solidarity *n* societās *f*.
solidify *vt* cōgere ♦ *vi* concrēscere.
solidity *n* soliditās *f*.
solidly *adv* firmē, cōnstanter.
soliloquize *vi* sēcum loquī.
soliloquy *n* ūnīus ōrātiō *f*.
solitary *adj* sōlus, sōlitārius; (*instance*) ūnicus
(*place*) dēsertus.
solitude *n* sōlitūdō *f*.
solo *n* canticum *nt*.
solstice *n* (*summer*) sōlstitium *nt*; (*winter*)
brūma *f*.
solstitial *adj* sōlstitiālis, brūmālis.
soluble *adj* dissolūbilis.
solution *n* (*of puzzle*) ēnōdātiō *f*.
solve *vt* ēnōdāre, explicāre.
solvency *n* solvendī facultās *f*.
solvent *adj*: **be ~** solvendō esse.
sombre *adj* obscūrus; (*fig*) tristis.
some *adj* aliquī; (*pl*) nonnūllī, aliquot; **~ peopl**
sunt quī (+ *subj*); **~ ... other** alius ... alius; **fo**
~ time aliquamdiū; **with ~ reason** nōn sine
causā ♦ *pron* aliquis; (*pl*) nonnūllī, sunt quī
(*subj*), erant quī (*subj*).
somebody *pron* aliquis; **~ or other** nescioquis
somehow *adv* quōdammodō, nescio
quōmodō.
someone *pron* aliquis; (*negative*) quisquam; **~**
or other nescioquis; **~ else** alius.
something *pron* aliquid; **~ or other** nescioqui
~ else aliud.
sometime *adv* aliquandō; (*past*) quondam.
sometimes *adv* interdum, nonnumquam; **~ ..**
~ modo ... modo.
somewhat *adv* aliquantum, nōnnihil, paulum
(*with compar*) paulō, aliquantō.
somewhere *adv* alicubi; (*to*) aliquō; **~ else**
alibī; (*to*) aliō; **from ~** alicunde; **from ~ else**
aliunde.
somnolence *n* somnus *m*.
somnolent *adj* sēmisomnus.
son *n* fīlius *m*; **small ~** fīliolus *m*.
song *n* carmen *nt*, cantus *m*.
son-in-law *n* gener *m*.
sonorous *adj* sonōrus, canōrus.
soon *adv* mox, brevī, citō; **as ~ as** ut prīmum,
cum prīmum (+ *fut perf*), simul āc/atque (+
perf indic); **as ~ as possible** quam prīmum;
too ~ praemātūrē, ante tempus.
sooner *adv* prius, mātūrius; (*preference*)
libentius, potius; **~ or later** sērius ōcius; **no ~**
said than done dictum factum.
soonest *adv* mātūrissimē.
soot *n* fūlīgō *f*.
soothe *vt* dēlēnīre, permulcēre.
soothing *adj* lēnis, blandus.
soothingly *adv* blandē.
soothsayer *n* hariolus *m*, vātēs *m/f*, haruspex
m.
sooty *adj* fūmōsus.
sop *n* offa *f*; (*fig*) dēlēnīmentum *nt*.

sophism n captiō f.
sophist n sophistēs m.
sophistical adj acūleātus, captiōsus.
sophisticated adj lepidus, urbānus.
sophistry n captiō f.
soporific adj sopōrifer, somnifer.
soprano adj acūtus.
sorcerer n veneficus m.
sorceress n venefica f, saga f.
sorcery n venēficium nt; (*means*) venēna ntpl, carmina ntpl.
sordid adj sordidus; (*conduct*) illīberālis.
sordidly adv sordidē.
sordidness n sordēs fpl; illīberālitās f.
sore adj molestus, gravis, acerbus; **feel ~** dolēre ♦ n ulcus nt.
sorely adv graviter, vehementer.
sorrel n lapathus f, lapathum nt.
sorrow n dolor m, aegritūdō f; (*outward*) maeror m; (*for death*) lūctus m ♦ vi dolēre, maerere, lūgēre.
sorrowful adj maestus, tristis.
sorrowfully adv maestē.
sorry adj paenitēns; (*poor*) miser; **I am ~ for** (*remorse*) mē paenitet, mē piget (*gen*); (*pity*) mē miseret (*gen*).
sort n genus nt; **a ~ of** quīdam; **all ~s of** omnēs; **the ~ of** tālis; **this ~ of** huiusmodī; **the common ~** plēbs f; **I am not the ~ of man to** nōn is sum quī (+ *subj*); **I am out of ~s** mihī displiceō ♦ vt dīgerere, compōnere; (*votes*) diribēre.
sortie n excursiō f, excursus m, ēruptiō f; **make a ~** ērumpere, excurrere.
sot n ēbriōsus m.
sottish adj ēbriōsus, tēmulentus.
sottishness n vīnolentia f.
soul n anima f, animus m; (*essence*) vīs f; (*person*) caput nt; **not a ~** nēmō ūnus; **the ~ of** (*fig*) medulla f.
soulless adj caecus, dūrus.
sound n sonitus m, sonus m; (*articulate*) vōx f; (*confused*) strepitus m; (*loud*) fragor m; (*strait*) fretum nt ♦ vt (*signal*) canere; (*instrument*) īnflāre; (*depth*) scrūtārī, temptāre; (*person*) animum temptāre (*gen*) ♦ vi canere, sonāre; (*seem*) vidērī; **~ a retreat** receptuī canere ♦ adj sānus, salūbris; (*health*) firmus; (*sleep*) artus; (*judgment*) exquīsītus; (*argument*) vērus; **safe and ~** salvus, incolumis.
soundly adv (*beat*) vehementer; (*sleep*) artē; (*study*) penitus, dīligenter.
soundness n sānitās f, integritās f.
soup n iūs nt.
sour adj acerbus, amārus, acidus; **turn ~** acēscere; (*fig*) coacēscere ♦ vt (*fig*) exacerbāre.
source n fōns m; (*river*) caput nt; (*fig*) fōns m, orīgō f; **have its ~ in** orīrī ex; (*fig*) proficīscī ex.
sourness n acerbitās f; (*temper*) mōrōsitās f.
souse vt immergere.

south n merīdiēs f ♦ adj austrālis ♦ adv ad merīdiem.
south-east adv inter sōlis ortum et merīdiem.
southerly adj ad merīdiem versus.
southern adj austrālis.
south-west adv inter occāsum sōlis et merīdiem.
south wind n auster m.
souvenir n monumentum nt.
sovereign n rēx m, rēgīna f ♦ adj prīnceps, summus.
sovereignty n rēgnum nt, imperium nt, prīncipātus m; (*of the people*) māiestās f.
sow n scrōfa f, sūs f.
sow vt serere; (*field*) cōnserere ♦ vi sementem facere.
sower n sator m.
sowing n sēmentis f.
spa n aquae fpl.
space n (*extension*) spatium nt; (*not matter*) ināne nt; (*room*) locus m; (*distance*) intervallum nt; (*time*) spatium nt; **open ~** ārea f; **leave a ~ of** intermittere ♦ vt: **~ out** dispōnere.
spacious adj amplus, capāx.
spaciousness n amplitūdō f.
spade n pāla f, rūtrum nt.
span n (*measure*) palmus m; (*extent*) spatium nt ♦ vt iungere.
spangle n bractea f.
spangled adj distinctus.
spar n tignum nt.
spare vt parcere (*dat*); (*to give*) suppeditāre; **~ time for** vacāre (*dat*) ♦ adj exīlis; (*extra*) subsecīvus.
sparing adj parcus.
sparingly adv parcē.
spark n scintilla f; (*fig*) igniculus m.
sparkle vi scintillāre, nitēre, micāre.
sparrow n passer m.
sparse adj rārus.
spasm n convulsiō f.
spasmodically adv interdum.
spatter vt aspergere.
spawn n ōva ntpl.
speak vt, vi loquī; (*make speech*) dīcere, contiōnārī, ōrātiōnem habēre; **~ out** ēloquī; **~ to** adloquī; (*converse*) colloquī cum; **~ well of** bene dīcere (*dat*); **it ~s for itself** rēs ipsa loquitur.
speaker n ōrātor m.
speaking n: **art of ~** dīcendī ars f; **practise public ~** dēclāmāre ♦ adj: **likeness ~** vīvida imāgō.
spear n hasta f.
spearman n hastātus m.
special adj praecipuus, proprius.
speciality n proprium nt.
specially adv praecipuē, praesertim.
species n genus nt.
specific adj certus.
specification n dēsignātiō f.
specify vt dēnotāre, dēsignāre.

specimen *n* exemplar *nt*, exemplum *nt*.
specious *adj* speciōsus.
speciously *adv* speciōsē.
speciousness *n* speciēs *f*.
speck *n* macula *f*.
speckled *adj* maculīs distinctus.
spectacle *n* spectāculum *nt*.
spectacular *adj* spectābilis.
spectator *n* spectātor *m*.
spectral *adj* larvālis.
spectre *n* larva *f*.
speculate *vi* cōgitāre, coniectūrās facere; (*comm*) forō ūtī.
speculation *n* cōgitātiō *f*, coniectūra *f*; (*comm*) ālea *f*.
speculator *n* contemplātor *m*; (*comm*) āleātor *m*.
speech *n* ōrātiō *f*; (*language*) sermō *m*, lingua *f*; (*to people or troops*) cōntiō *f*; **make a ~** ōrātiōnem/cōntiōnem habēre.
speechless *adj* ēlinguis, mūtus.
speed *n* celeritās *f*, cursus *m*, vēlōcitās *f*; **with all ~** summa celeritate; **at full ~** māgnō cursū, incitātus; (*riding*) citātō equō ♦ *vt* adcelerāre, mātūrāre ♦ *vi* properāre, festīnāre.
speedily *adv* celeriter, citō.
speedy *adj* celer, vēlōx, citus.
spell *n* carmen *nt*.
spellbound *adj*: **be ~** obstipēscere.
spelt *n* far *nt*.
spend *vt* impendere, īnsūmere; (*public money*) ērogāre; (*time*) agere, cōnsūmere, terere; (*strength*) effundere; **~ itself** (*storm*) dēsaevīre; **~ on** īnsūmere (*acc* & *dat*).
spendthrift *n* nepōs *m*, prōdigus *m*.
sphere *n* globus *m*; (*of action*) prōvincia *f*.
spherical *adj* globōsus.
sphinx *n* sphinx *f*.
spice *n* condīmentum *nt*; **~s** *pl* odōrēs *mpl* ♦ *vt* condīre.
spicy *adj* odōrātus; (*wit*) salsus.
spider *n* arānea *f*; **~'s web** arāneum *nt*.
spike *n* dēns *m*, clāvus *m*.
spikenard *n* nardus *m*.
spill *vt* fundere, profundere ♦ *vi* redundāre.
spin *vt* (*thread*) nēre, dēdūcere; (*top*) versāre; **~ out** (*story*) prōdūcere ♦ *vi* circumagī, versārī.
spindle *n* fūsus *m*.
spine *n* spīna *f*.
spineless *adj* ēnervātus.
spinster *n* virgō *f*.
spiral *adj* intortus ♦ *n* spīra *f*.
spire *n* cōnus *m*.
spirit *n* (*life*) anima *f*; (*intelligence*) mēns *f*; (*soul*) animus *m*; (*vivacity*) spīritus *m*, vigor *m*, vīs *f*; (*character*) ingenium *nt*; (*intention*) voluntās *f*; (*of an age*) mōrēs *mpl*; (*ghost*) anima *f*; **~s** *pl* mānēs *mpl*; **full of ~** alacer, animōsus.
spirited *adj* animōsus, ācer.
spiritless *adj* iners, frāctus, timidus.
spiritual *adj* animī.

spit *n* verū *nt* ♦ *vi* spuere, spūtāre; **~ on** cōnspūtāre; **~ out** exspuere.
spite *n* invidia *f*, malevolentia *f*, līvor *m*; **in ~ of me** mē invītō; **in ~ of the difficulties** in his angustiīs ♦ *vt* incommodāre, offendere.
spiteful *adj* malevolus, malignus, invidus.
spitefully *adv* malevolē, malignē.
spitefulness *n* malevolentia *f*.
spittle *n* spūtum *nt*.
splash *n* fragor *m* ♦ *vt* aspergere.
spleen *n* splēn *m*; (*fig*) stomachus *m*.
splendid *adj* splendidus, lūculentus; īnsignis; (*person*) amplus.
splendidly *adv* splendidē, optimē.
splendour *n* splendor *m*, fulgor *m*; (*fig*) lautitia *f*, adparātus *m*.
splenetic *adj* stomachōsus.
splice *vt* iungere.
splint *n* ferula *f*.
splinter *n* fragmentum *nt*, assula *f* ♦ *vt* findere.
split *vt* findere ♦ *vi* dissilīre ♦ *adj* fissus ♦ *n* fissum *nt*; (*fig*) dissidium *nt*.
splutter *vi* balbūtīre.
spoil *n* praeda *f* ♦ *vt* (*rob*) spoliāre; (*mar*) corrumpere ♦ *vi* corrumpī.
spoiler *n* spoliātor *m*; corruptor *m*.
spoils *npl* spolia *ntpl*, exuviae *fpl*.
spoke *n* radius *m*; **put a ~ in one's wheel** inicere scrūpulum (*dat*).
spokesman *n* interpres *m*, ōrātor *m*.
spoliation *n* spoliātiō *f*, dīreptiō *f*.
spondee *n* spondēus *m*.
sponge *n* spongia *f*.
sponsor *n* spōnsor *m*; (*fig*) auctor *m*.
spontaneity *n* impulsus *m*, voluntās *f*.
spontaneous *adj* voluntārius.
spontaneously *adv* suā sponte, ultrō.
spoon *n* cochlear *nt*.
sporadic *adj* rārus.
sporadically *adv* passim.
sport *n* lūdus *m*; (*in Rome*) campus *m*; (*fun*) iocus *m*; (*ridicule*) lūdibrium *nt*; **make ~ of** illūdere (*dat*) ♦ *vi* lūdere.
sportive *adj* lascīvus.
sportiveness *n* lascīvia *f*.
sportsman *n* vēnātor *m*.
sportsmanlike *adj* honestus, generōsus.
spot *n* macula *f*; (*place*) locus *m*; (*dice*) pūnctum *nt*; **on the ~** īlicō ♦ *vt* maculāre; (*see*) animadvertere.
spotless *adj* integer, pūrus; (*character*) castus.
spotted *adj* maculōsus.
spouse *n* coniunx *m/f*.
spout *n* (*of jug*) ōs *nt*; (*pipe*) canālis *m* ♦ *vi* ēmicāre.
sprain *vt* intorquēre.
sprawl *vi* sē fundere.
sprawling *adj* fūsus.
spray *n* aspergō *f* ♦ *vt* aspergere.
spread *vt* pandere, extendere; (*news*) dīvulgāre; (*infection*) vulgāre ♦ *vi* patēre; (*rumour*) mānāre, incrēbrēscere; (*feeling*) glīscere.

spreadeagle *vt* dispandere.
spreading *adj* (*tree*) patulus.
spree *n* cōmissātiō *f.*
sprig *n* virga *f.*
sprightliness *n* alacritās *f.*
sprightly *adj* alacer, hilaris.
spring *n* (*season*) vēr *nt*; (*water*) fōns *m*; (*leap*)
saltus *m* ♦ *vi* (*grow*) crēscere, ēnāscī; (*leap*)
salīre; ~ **from** orirī ex, proficīscī ex; ~ **on to**
īnsilīre in (*acc*); ~ **up** exorīrī, exsilīre ♦ *vt*: ~
a leak rīmās agere; ~ **a surprise on**
admīrātiōnem movēre (*dat*) ♦ *adj* vērnus.
springe *n* laqueus *m.*
sprinkle *vt* aspergere; ~ **on** īnspergere (*dat*).
sprint *vi* currere.
sprout *n* surculus *m* ♦ *vi* fruticārī.
spruce *adj* nitidus, concinnus.
sprung *adj* ortus, oriundus.
spume *n* spūma *f.*
spur *n* calcar *nt*; ~ **of a hill** prōminēns collis; **on
the ~ of the moment** ex tempore ♦ *vt*
incitāre; ~ **the willing horse** currentem
incitāre; ~ **on** concitāre.
spurious *adj* falsus, fūcōsus, fictus.
spurn *vt* spernere, aspernārī, respuere.
spurt *vi* ēmicāre; (*run*) sē incitāre ♦ *n* impetus
m.
spy *n* speculātor *m*, explōrātor *m* ♦ *vi* speculārī
♦ *vt* cōnspicere; ~ **out** explōrāre.
squabble *n* iūrgium *nt* ♦ *vi* rixārī.
squad *n* (*MIL*) decuria *f.*
squadron *n* (*cavalry*) āla *f*, turma *f*; (*ships*)
classis *f.*
squalid *adj* sordidus, dēfōrmis.
squall *n* procella *f.*
squally *adj* procellōsus.
squalor *n* sordēs *fpl*, squālor *m.*
squander *vt* dissipāre, disperdere, effundere.
squanderer *n* prōdigus *m.*
square *n* quadrātum *nt*; (*town*) ārea *f* ♦ *vt*
quadrāre; (*account*) subdūcere ♦ *vi* cōnstāre,
congruere ♦ *adj* quadrātus.
squash *vt* conterere, contundere.
squat *vi* subsīdere ♦ *adj* brevis atque obēsus.
squatter *n* (*on land*) agripeta *m.*
squawk *vi* crōcīre.
squeak *n* strīdor *m* ♦ *vi* strīdēre.
squeal *n* vāgītus *m* ♦ *vi* vāgīre.
squeamish *adj* fastīdiōsus; **feel** ~ nauseāre,
fastīdīre.
squeamishness *n* fastīdium *nt*, nausea *f.*
squeeze *vt* premere, comprimere; ~ **out**
exprimere.
squint *adj* perversus ♦ *n*: **person with a** ~
strabō *m* ♦ *vi* strabō esse.
squinter *n* strabō *m.*
squinting *adj* paetus.
squire *n* armiger *m*; (*landed*) dominus *m.*
squirm *vi* volūtārī.
squirrel *n* sciūrus *m.*
squirt *vt* ēicere, effundere ♦ *vi* ēmicāre.
stab *n* ictus *m*, vulnus *nt* ♦ *vt* fodere, ferīre,
percutere.

stability *n* stabilitās *f*, firmitās *f*, cōnstantia *f.*
stabilize *vt* stabilīre, firmāre.
stable *adj* firmus, stabilis ♦ *n* stabulum *nt*,
equīle *nt*; **shut the ~ door after the horse is
stolen** clipeum post vulnera sūmere.
stack *n* acervus *m* ♦ *vt* congerere, cumulāre.
stadium *n* spatium *nt.*
staff *n* scīpiō *m*, virga *f*; (*augur's*) lituus *m*;
(*officers*) contubernālēs *mpl.*
stag *n* cervus *m.*
stage *n* pulpitum *nt*, proscēnium *nt*; (*theatre*)
scēna *f*, theātrum *nt*; (*scene of action*) campus
m; (*of journey*) iter *nt*; (*of progress*) gradus *m* ♦
adj scēnicus ♦ *vt* (*play*) dare, docēre.
stage fright *n* horror *m.*
stagger *vi* titubāre ♦ *vt* obstupefacere.
stagnant *adj* iners.
stagnate *vi* (*fig*) cessāre, refrīgēscere.
stagnation *n* cessātiō *f*, torpor *m.*
stagy *adj* scēnicus.
staid *adj* sevērus, gravis.
stain *n* macula *f*, lābēs *f*; (*fig*) dēdecus *nt*,
ignōminia *f* ♦ *vt* maculāre, foedāre,
contāmināre; ~ **with** īnficere (*abl*).
stainless *adj* pūrus, integer.
stair *n* scālae *fpl*, gradus *mpl.*
staircase *n* scālae *fpl.*
stake *n* pālus *m*, stīpes *m*; (*pledge*) pignus *nt*; **be
at** ~ agī, in discrīmine esse ♦ *vt* (*wager*)
dēpōnere.
stale *adj* obsolētus, effētus; (*wine*) vapidus.
stalemate *n*: **reach a** ~ ad incitās redigī.
stalk *n* (*corn*) calamus *m*; (*plant*) stīpes *m* ♦ *vi*
incēdere ♦ *vt* vēnārī, īnsidiārī (*dat*).
stall *n* (*animal*) stabulum *nt*; (*seat*) subsellium
nt; (*shop*) taberna *f* ♦ *vt* stabulāre.
stallion *n* equus *m.*
stalwart *adj* ingēns, rōbustus, fortis.
stamina *n* patientia *f.*
stammer *n* haesitātiō *f* ♦ *vi* balbūtīre.
stammering *adj* balbus.
stamp *n* fōrma *f*; (*mark*) nota *f*, signum *nt*; (*of
feet*) supplōsiō *f* ♦ *vt* imprimere; (*coin*) ferīre,
signāre; (*fig*) inūrere; ~ **one's feet** pedem
supplōdere; ~ **out** exstinguere.
stampede *n* discursus *m*; (*fig*) pavor *m* ♦ *vi*
discurrere; (*fig*) expavēscere.
stance *n* status *m.*
stanchion *n* columna *f.*
stand *n* (*position*) statiō *f*; (*platform*) suggestus
m; **make a** ~ resistere, restāre ♦ *vi* stāre;
(*remain*) manēre; (*matters*) sē habēre ♦ *vt*
statuere; (*tolerate*) ferre, tolerāre; ~ **against**
resistere (*dat*); ~ **aloof** abstāre; ~ **by** adsistere
(*dat*); (*friend*) adesse (*dat*); (*promise*)
praestāre; ~ **convicted** manifestum tenērī; ~
down concēdere; ~ **fast** cōnsistere; ~ **one's
ground** in locō perstāre; ~ **for** (*office*) petere;
(*meaning*) significāre; (*policy*) postulāre; ~ **in
awe of** in metū habēre; ~ **in need of** indigēre
(*abl*); ~ **on** īnsistere in (*abl*); ~ **on end**
horrēre; ~ **on one's dignity** gravitātem suam
tuērī; ~ **out** ēminēre, exstāre; (*against*)

resistere (*dat*); (*to sea*) in altum prōvehī; ~
out of the way of dēcēdere (*dat*); ~ **over**
(*case*) ampliāre; ~ **still** cōnsistere, īnsistere;
~ **to reason** sequī; ~ **trial** reum fierī; ~ **up**
surgere, cōnsurgere; ~ **up for** dēfendere,
adesse (*dat*); ~ **up to** respōnsāre (*dat*).
standard n (*MIL*) signum nt; (*measure*) nōrma f;
~ **author** scrīptor classicus m; **up to** ~ iūstus;
judge by the ~ **of** referre ad.
standard-bearer n signifer m.
standing adj perpetuus ♦ n status m; (*social*)
locus m, ōrdō m; **of long** ~ inveterātus; **be of**
long ~ inveterāscere.
stand-offish adj tēctus.
standstill n: **be at a** ~ haerēre, frīgēre; **bring**
to a ~ ad incitās redigere; **come to a** ~
īnsistere.
stanza n tetrastichon nt.
staple n uncus m ♦ adj praecipuus.
star n stēlla f, astrum nt; sīdus nt; **shooting ~s**
acontiae fpl.
starboard adj dexter.
starch n amylum nt.
stare n obtūtus m ♦ vi intentīs oculīs intuērī,
stupēre; ~ **at** contemplārī.
stark adj rigidus; simplex ♦ adv plānē, omnīnō.
starling n sturnus m.
starry adj stēllātus.
start n initium nt; (*movement*) saltus m;
(*journey*) profectiō f; **by fits and ~s** carptim;
have a day's ~ **on** diē antecēdere ♦ vt
incipere, īnstituere; (*game*) excitāre;
(*process*) movēre ♦ vi (*with fright*) resilīre;
(*journey*) proficīscī; ~ **up** exsilīre.
starting place n carcerēs mpl.
startle vt excitāre, terrēre.
starvation n fāmes f.
starve vi fāme cōnficī; (*cold*) frīgēre ♦ vt fāme
ēnecāre.
starveling n fāmēlicus m.
state n (*condition*) status m, condiciō f; (*pomp*)
adparātus m; (*POL*) cīvitās f, rēs pūblica f; **the**
~ **of affairs is** ita sē rēs habet; **I know the** ~ **of**
affairs quō in locō rēs sit sciō; **of the** ~
pūblicus ♦ adj pūblicus ♦ vt adfirmāre,
expōnere, profitērī; ~ **one's case** causam
dīcere.
stateliness n māiestās f, gravitās f.
stately adj gravis, grandis, nōbilis.
statement n adfirmātiō f, dictum nt; (*witness*)
testimōnium nt.
state of health n valētūdō f.
state of mind n adfectiō f.
statesman n vir reī pūblicae gerendae
perītus m, cōnsilī pūblicī auctor m.
statesmanlike adj prūdēns.
statesmanship n cīvīlis prūdentia f.
static adj stabilis.
station n locus m; (*MIL*) statiō f; (*social*) locus m,
ōrdō m ♦ vt collocāre, pōnere; (*in different*
places) dispōnere.
stationary adj immōtus, statārius, stabilis.
statistics n cēnsus m.

statuary n fictor m.
statute n statua f, signum nt, imāgō f.
statuette n sigillum nt.
stature n fōrma f, statūra f.
status n locus m.
status quo n: **restore the** ~ ad integrum
restituere.
statutable adj lēgitimus.
statute n lēx f.
staunch vt (*blood*) sistere ♦ adj fīdus,
cōnstāns.
stave vt perrumpere, perfringere; ~ **off**
arcēre.
stay n firmāmentum nt; (*fig*) columen nt;
(*sojourn*) mānsiō f, commorātiō f ♦ vt (*prop*)
fulcīre; (*stop*) dētinēre, dēmorārī ♦ vi
manēre, commorārī.
stead n locus m; **stand one in good** ~ prōdesse
(*dat*).
steadfast adj firmus, stabilis, cōnstāns; ~ **at**
home tenēre sē domī.
steadfastly adv cōnstanter.
steadfastness n firmitās f, cōnstantia f.
steadily adv firmē, cōnstanter.
steadiness n stabilitās f; (*fig*) cōnstantia f.
steady adj stabilis, firmus; (*fig*) gravis,
cōnstāns.
steak n offa f.
steal vt surripere, fūrārī ♦ vi: ~ **away** sē
subdūcere; ~ **over** subrēpere (*dat*); ~ **into** sē
īnsinuāre in (*acc*); ~ **a march on** occupāre.
stealing n fūrtum nt.
stealth n fūrtum nt; **by** ~ fūrtim, clam.
stealthily adv fūrtim, clam.
stealthy adj fūrtīvus, clandestīnus.
steam n aquae vapor m, fūmus m ♦ vi fūmāre.
steed n equus m.
steel n ferrum nt, chalybs m ♦ adj ferreus ♦ vt
dūrāre; ~ **oneself** obdūrēscere.
steely adj ferreus.
steelyard n statēra f.
steep adj arduus, praeceps, praeruptus;
(*slope*) dēclīvis ♦ vt imbuere.
steeple n turris f.
steepness n arduum nt.
steer vi gubernāre, regere, dīrigere ♦ n
iuvencus m.
steering n gubernātiō f.
steersman n gubernātor m; rector m.
stellar adj stēllārum.
stem n stīpes m, truncus m; (*ship*) prōra f ♦ vt
adversārī (*dat*); ~ **the tide of** (*fig*) obsistere
(*dat*).
stench n foetor m.
stenographer n exceptor m, āctuārius m.
stenography n notae fpl.
stentorian adj (*voice*) ingēns.
step n gradus m; (*track*) vestīgium nt; (*of stair*)
gradus m; ~ **by** ~ gradātim; **flight of ~s**
gradus mpl; **take a** ~ gradum facere; **take ~s**
to ratiōnem inīre ut, vidēre ut; **march in** ~ in
numerum īre; **out of** ~ extrā numerum ♦ vi
gradī, incēdere; ~ **aside** dēcēdere; ~ **back**

regredī; **~ forward** prōdīre; **~ on** insistere (*dat*).
stepdaughter n prīvīgna f.
stepfather n vītricus m.
stepmother n noverca f.
stepson n prīvīgnus m.
stereotyped adj trītus.
sterile adj sterilis.
sterility n sterilitās f.
sterling adj integer, probus, gravis.
stern adj dūrus, sevērus; (*look*) torvus ♦ n puppis f.
sternly adv sevērē, dūriter.
sternness n sevēritās f.
stew vt coquere.
steward n prōcūrātor m; (*of estate*) vīlicus m.
stewardship n prōcūrātiō f.
stick n (*for beating*) fūstis m; (*for walking*) baculum nt ♦ vi haerēre; **~ at nothing** ad omnia dēscendere; **~ fast in** inhaerēre (*dat*), inhaerēscere in (*abl*); **~ out** ēminēre; **~ to** adhaerēre (*dat*); **~ up** ēminēre; **~ up for** dēfendere ♦ vt (*with glue*) conglūtināre; (*with point*) fīgere; **~ into** īnfīgere; **~ top on** praefīgere.
stickler n dīligēns (*gen*).
sticky adj lentus, tenāx.
stiff adj rigidus; (*difficult*) difficilis; **be ~** rigēre.
stiffen vt rigidum facere ♦ vi rigēre.
stiffly adv rigidē.
stiff-necked adj obstinātus.
stiffness n rigor m.
stifle vt suffocāre; (*fig*) opprimere, restinguere.
stigma n nota f.
stigmatize vt notāre.
stile n saepēs f.
still adj immōtus, tranquillus, quiētus; tacitus ♦ vt lēnīre, sēdāre ♦ adv etiam, adhūc, etiamnum; (*past*) etiam tum; (*with compar*) etiam; (*adversative*) tamen, nihilōminus.
stillness n quiēs f; silentium nt.
stilly adj tacitus.
stilted adj (*language*) īnflātus.
stilts n grallae fpl.
stimulant n stimulus m.
stimulate vt stimulāre, acuere, exacuere, excitāre.
stimulus n stimulus m.
sting n aculeus m; (*wound*) ictus m; (*fig*) aculeus m, morsus m ♦ vt pungere, mordēre.
stingily adv sordidē.
stinginess n avāritia f, sordēs fpl, tenācitās f.
stinging adj (*words*) aculeātus, mordāx.
stingy adj sordidus, tenāx.
stink n foetor m ♦ vi foetere; **~ of** olēre.
stinking adj foetidus.
stint n modus m; **without ~** abundē ♦ vt circumscrībere.
stipend n mercēs f.
stipulate vt pacīscī, stipulārī.
stipulation n condiciō f, pactum nt.
stir n tumultus m ♦ vt movēre, agitāre; (*fig*)

commovēre; **~ up** excitāre, incitāre ♦ vi movērī.
stirring adj impiger, tumultuōsus; (*speech*) ārdēns.
stitch vt suere ♦ n sūtūra f; (*in side*) dolor m.
stock n stirps f, genus nt, gēns f; (*equipment*) īnstrūmenta ntpl; (*supply*) cōpia f; (*investment*) pecūniae fpl; **live~** rēs pecuāria f ♦ vt īnstruere ♦ adj commūnis, trītus.
stockade n vallum nt.
stock dove n palumbēs m/f.
stock in trade n instrūmenta ntpl.
stocks n (*ship*) nāvālia ntpl; (*torture*) compedēs fpl.
stock-still adj plānē immōtus.
stocky adj brevis atque obēsus.
stodgy adj crūdus, īnsulsus.
stoic n Stōicus m ♦ adj Stōicus.
stoical adj dūrus, patiēns.
stoically adv patienter.
stoicism n Stōicōrum ratiō f, Stōicōrum disciplīna f.
stoke vt agitāre.
stole n stola f.
stolid adj stolidus.
stolidity n īnsulsitās f.
stolidly adv stolidē.
stomach n stomachus m; venter m ♦ vt patī, tolerāre.
stone n lapis m, saxum nt; (*precious*) gemma f, lapillus m; (*of fruit*) acinum nt; **leave no ~ unturned** omnia experīrī; **kill two birds with one ~** ūnō saltū duōs aprōs capere; **hewn ~** saxum quadrātum; **unhewn ~** caementum nt ♦ vt lapidibus percutere ♦ adj lapideus; **~ blind** plānē caecus; **~ deaf** plānē surdus.
stonecutter n lapicīda m.
stony adj (*soil*) lapidōsus; (*path*) scrūpōsus; (*feeling*) dūrus, ferreus.
stool n sēdēcula f.
stoop vi sē dēmittere; **~ to** dēscendere in (*acc*).
stop n mora f; (*punctuation*) pūnctum nt; **come to a ~** īnsistere; **put a ~ to** comprimere, dirimere ♦ vt sistere, inhibēre, fīnīre; (*restrain*) cohibēre; (*hole*) obtūrāre; **~ up** occlūdere, interclūdere ♦ vi dēsinere, dēsistere; (*motion*) īnsistere.
stopgap n tībīcen m.
stoppage n interclūsiō f, impedīmentum nt.
stopper n obtūrāmentum nt.
store n cōpia f; (*place*) horreum nt; (*for wine*) apothēca f; **be in ~ for** manēre; **set great ~ by** māgnī aestimāre ♦ vt condere, repōnere; **~ away** recondere; **~ up** repōnere, congerere.
storehouse n (*fig*) thēsaurus m.
storekeeper n cellārius m.
storeship n nāvis frūmentāria f.
storey n tabulātum nt.
stork n cicōnia f.
storm n tempestās f, procella f; **take by ~** expugnāre ♦ vt (*MIL*) expugnāre ♦ vi saevīre; **~ at** īnsectārī, invehī in (*acc*).

stormbound *adj* tempestāte dētentus.
stormer *n* expugnātor *m*.
storming *n* expugnātiō *f*.
stormy *adj* turbidus, procellōsus; (*fig*)
turbulentus.
story *n* fābula *f*, nārrātiō *f*; (*short*) fābella *f*;
(*untrue*) mendācium *nt*.
storyteller *n* nārrātor *m*; (*liar*) mendāx *m*.
stout *adj* pinguis; (*brave*) fortis; (*strong*)
validus, rōbustus; (*material*) firmus.
stouthearted *adj* māgnanimus.
stoutly *adv* fortiter.
stove *n* camīnus *m*, fornāx *f*.
stow *vt* repōnere, condere; **~ away** *vi* in nāvī
dēlitēscere.
straddle *vi* vāricāre.
straggle *vi* deerrāre, pālārī.
straggler *n* pālāns *m*.
straggling *adj* dispersus, rārus.
straight *adj* rēctus, dīrēctus; (*fig*) apertus,
vērāx; **in a ~ line** rēctā, ē regiōne; **set ~**
dīrigere ♦ *adv* dīrēctō, rēctā.
straighten *vt* corrigere, extendere.
straightforward *adj* simplex, dīrēctus; (*easy*)
facilis.
straightforwardness *n* simplicitās *f*.
straightness *n* (*fig*) integritās *f*.
straightway *adv* statim, extemplō.
strain *n* contentiō *f*; (*effort*) labor *m*; (*music*)
modī *mpl*; (*breed*) genus *nt* ♦ *vt* intendere,
contendere; (*injure*) nimiā contentiōne
dēbilitāre; (*liquid*) dēliquāre, percōlāre ♦ *vi*
ēnītī, vīrēs contendere.
strained *adj* (*language*) arcessītus.
strainer *n* cōlum *nt*.
strait *adj* angustus ♦ *n* fretum *nt*; **~s** *pl*
angustiae *fpl*.
straiten *vt* coartāre, contrahere; **~ed**
circumstances angustiae *fpl*.
strait-laced *adj* tristis, sevērus.
strand *n* lītus *nt*; (*of rope*) fīlum *nt* ♦ *vt* (*ship*)
ēicere.
strange *adj* novus, īnsolitus; (*foreign*)
peregrīnus; (*another's*) aliēnus; (*ignorant*)
rudis, expers.
strangely *adv* mīrē, mīrum in modum.
strangeness *n* novitās *f*, īnsolentia *f*.
stranger *n* (*from abroad*) advena *f*; peregrīnus
m; (*visiting*) hospes *m*, hospita *f*; (*not of the
family*) externus *m*; (*unknown*) ignōtus *m*.
strangle *vt* strangulāre, laqueō gulam
frangere.
strap *n* lōrum *nt*, habēna *f*.
strapping *adj* grandis.
stratagem *n* cōnsilium *nt*, fallācia *f*.
strategic *adj* (*action*) prūdēns; (*position*)
idōneus.
strategist *n* artis bellicae perītus *m*.
strategy *n* ars imperātōria *f*; cōnsilia *ntpl*.
straw *n* (*stalk*) culmus *m*; (*collective*)
strāmentum *nt*; **not care a ~ for** floccī nōn
facere ♦ *adj* strāmenticius.
strawberry *n* frāgum *nt*.

strawberry tree *n* arbutus *m*.
stray *vt* aberrāre, deerrāre; vagārī ♦ *adj*
errābundus.
streak *n* līnea *f*, macula *f*; (*light*) radius *m*;
(*character*) vēna *f* ♦ *vt* maculāre.
stream *n* flūmen *nt*, fluvius *m*; **down ~** secundō
flūmine; **up ~** adversō flūmine ♦ *vi* fluere, sē
effundere; **~ into** īnfluere in (*acc*).
streamlet *n* rīvus *m*, rīvulus *m*.
street *n* via *f*, platea *f*.
strength *n* vīrēs *fpl*; (*of material*) firmitās *f*; (*fig*)
rōbur *nt*, nervī *mpl*; (*MIL*) numerus *m*; **know
the enemy's ~** quot sint hostēs scīre; **on the ~
of** frētus (*abl*).
strengthen *vt* firmāre, corrōborāre; (*position*)
mūnīre.
strenuous *adj* impiger, strēnuus, sēdulus.
strenuously *adv* impigrē, strēnuē.
strenuousness *n* industria *f*.
stress *n* (*words*) ictus *m*; (*meaning*) vīs *f*;
(*importance*) mōmentum *nt*; (*difficulty*) labor
m; **lay great ~ on** in māgnō discrīmine pōnere
♦ *vt* exprimere.
stretch *n* spatium *nt*, tractus *m*; **at a ~** sine ullā
intermissiōne ♦ *vt* tendere, intendere;
(*length*) prōdūcere, extendere; (*facts*) in
māius crēdere; **~ a point** indulgēre; **~ before**
obtendere; **~ forth** porrigere; **~ oneself** (*on
ground*) sternī; **~ out** porrigere, extendere ♦
vi extendī, patēscere.
strew *vt* (*things*) sternere; (*place*) cōnsternere.
stricken *adj* saucius.
strict *adj* (*defined*) ipse, certus; (*severe*)
sevērus, rigidus; (*accurate*) dīligēns.
strictly *adv* sevērē; dīligenter; **~ speaking**
scīlicet, immo.
strictness *n* sevēritās *f*; dīligentia *f*.
stricture *n* vītuperātiō *f*.
stride *n* passus *m*; **make great ~s** (*fig*) multum
prōficere ♦ *vi* incēdere, ingentēs gradūs
ferre.
strident *adj* asper.
strife *n* discordia *f*, pugna *f*.
strike *vt* ferīre, percutere; (*instrument*)
pellere, pulsāre; (*sail*) subdūcere; (*tent*)
dētendere; (*mind*) venīre in (*acc*); (*camp*)
movēre; (*fear into*) incutere in (*acc*); **~ against**
offendere; **~ out** dēlēre; **~ up** (*music*)
incipere; **~ a bargain** pacīscī; **be struck**
vāpulāre ♦ *vi* (*work*) cessāre.
striking *adj* īnsignis, īnsignītus, ēgregius.
strikingly *adv* īnsignītē.
string *n* (*cord*) resticula *f*; (*succession*) seriēs *f*;
(*instrument*) nervus *m*; (*bow*) nervus *m*; **have
two ~s to one's bow** duplicī spē ūtī ♦ *vt* (*bow*)
intendere; (*together*) coniungere.
stringency *n* sevēritās *f*.
stringent *adj* sevērus.
strip *vt* nūdāre, spoliāre, dēnūdāre; **~ off**
exuere; (*leaves*) stringere, dēstringere ♦ *n*
lacinia *f*.
stripe *n* virga *f*; (*on tunic*) clāvus *m*; **~s** *pl*
verbera *ntpl*.

striped *adj* virgātus.
stripling *n* adulescentulus *m*.
strive *vi* nītī, ēnītī, contendere; (*contend*)
certāre.
stroke *n* ictus *m*; (*lightning*) fulmen *nt*; (*oar*)
pulsus *m*; (*pen*) līnea *f*; ~ **of luck** fortūna
secunda *f* ♦ *vt* mulcēre, dēmulcēre.
stroll *vi* deambulāre, spatiārī.
strong *adj* fortis, validus; (*health*) rōbustus,
firmus; (*material*) firmus; (*smell*) gravis;
(*resources*) pollēns, potēns; (*feeling*) ācer,
māgnus; (*language*) vehemēns, probrōsus; **be**
~ valēre; **be twenty** ~ vīgintī esse numerō.
strongbox *n* arca *f*.
stronghold *n* arx *f*.
strongly *adv* validē, vehementer, fortiter,
ācriter, graviter.
strong-minded *adj* pertināx, cōnstans.
strophe *n* stropha *f*.
structure *n* aedificium *nt*; (*form*) structūra *f*;
(*arrangement*) compositiō *f*.
struggle *n* (*effort*) cōnātus *m*; (*fight*) pugna *f*,
certāmen *nt* ♦ *vi* nītī; certāre, contendere;
(*fight*) luctārī; ~ **upwards** ēnītī.
strut *vi* māgnificē incēdere.
stubble *n* stipula *f*.
stubborn *adj* pertināx, pervicāx.
stubbornly *adv* pertināciter, pervicāciter.
stubbornness *n* pertinācia *f*, pervicācia *f*.
stucco *n* gypsum *nt*.
stud *n* clāvus *m*; (*horses*) equī *mpl*.
studded *adj* distinctus.
student *n* discipulus *m*; **be a** ~ **of** studēre (*dat*).
studied *adj* meditātus, accūrātus; (*language*)
exquīsītus.
studio *n* officīna *f*.
studious *adj* litterīs dēditus, litterārum
studiōsus; (*careful*) attentus.
studiously *adv* dē industriā.
study *vt* studēre (*dat*); (*prepare*) meditārī; ~
under audīre ♦ *n* studium *nt*; (*room*)
bibliothēca *f*.
stuff *n* māteria *f*; (*cloth*) textile *nt* ♦ *vt* farcīre,
refercīre; (*with food*) sagīnāre.
stuffing *n* sagina *f*; (*of cushion*) tōmentum *nt*.
stultify *vt* ad inritum redigere.
stumble *vi* offendere; ~ **upon** incidere in
(*acc*), offendere.
stumbling block *n* offēnsiō *f*.
stump *n* stīpes *m*.
stun *vt* stupefacere; (*fig*) obstupefacere,
cōnfundere.
stunned *adj* attonitus.
stunt *vt* corporis auctum inhibēre.
stunted *adj* curtus.
stupefaction *n* stupor *m*.
stupefied *adj*: **be** ~ stupēre, obstupefacere.
stupefy *vt* obstupefacere.
stupendous *adj* mīrus, mīrificus.
stupid *adj* stultus, hebes, ineptus.
stupidity *n* stultitia *f*.
stupidly *adv* stultē, ineptē.
stupor *n* stupor *m*.

sturdily *adv* fortiter.
sturdiness *n* rōbur *nt*, firmitās *f*.
sturdy *adj* fortis, rōbustus.
sturgeon *n* acipēnser *m*.
stutter *vi* balbūtire.
stuttering *adj* balbus.
sty *n* hara *f*.
style *n* (*kind*) genus *nt*, ratiō *f*; (*of dress*) habitus
m; (*of prose*) ēlocūtiō *f*, ōrātiō *f*; (*pen*) stilus *m*
♦ *vt* appellāre.
stylish *adj* ēlegāns, lautus, expolītus.
stylishly *adv* ēleganter.
suasion *n* suāsiō *f*.
suave *adj* blandus, urbānus.
suavity *n* urbānitās *f*.
subaltern *n* succenturiō *m*.
subdivide *vt* dīvidere.
subdivision *n* pars *f*, mōmentum *nt*.
subdue *vt* subigere, dēvincere, redigere,
domāre; (*fig*) cohibēre.
subdued *adj* dēmissus, summissus.
subject *n* (*person*) cīvis *m/f*; (*matter*) rēs *f*;
(*theme*) locus *m*, argūmentum *nt* ♦ *adj*
subiectus; ~ **to** obnoxius (*dat*) ♦ *vt* subicere;
obnoxium reddere.
subjection *n* servitūs *f*.
subjective *adj* proprius.
subject matter *n* māteria *f*.
subjoin *vt* subicere, subiungere.
subjugate *vt* subigere, dēbellāre, domāre.
sublime *adj* sublīmis, ēlātus, excelsus.
sublimely *adv* excelsē.
sublimity *n* altitūdō *f*, ēlātiō *f*.
submarine *adj* submersus.
submerge *vt* dēmergere; (*flood*) inundāre ♦ *vi*
sē dēmergere.
submersed *adj* submersus.
submission *n* obsequium *nt*, servitium *nt*; (*fig*)
patientia *f*.
submissive *adj* submissus, docilis,
obtemperāns.
submissively *adv* submissē, oboedienter,
patienter.
submit *vi* sē dēdere; ~ **to** pārēre (*dat*),
obtemperāre (*dat*), patī, subīre ♦ *vt*
(*proposal*) referre.
subordinate *adj* subiectus, secundus ♦ *vt*
subiungere, subicere.
suborn *vt* subicere, subōrnāre.
subpoena *vt* testimōnium dēnūntiāre (*dat*).
subscribe *vt* (*name*) subscrībere; (*money*)
cōnferre.
subscription *n* collātiō *f*.
subsequent *adj* sequēns, posterior.
subsequently *adv* posteā, mox.
subserve *vt* subvenīre (*dat*), commodāre.
subservience *n* obsequium *nt*.
subservient *adj* obsequēns; (*thing*) ūtilis,
commodus.
subside *vi* dēsīdere, resīdere; (*fever*)
dēcēdere; (*wind*) cadere; (*passion*)
dēfervēscere.
subsidence *n* lābēs *f*.

subsidiary *adj* subiectus, secundus.
subsidize *vt* pecūniās suppeditāre (*dat*).
subsidy *n* pecūniae *fpl*, vectīgal *nt*.
subsist *vi* cōnstāre, sustentārī.
subsistence *n* vīctus *m*.
substance *n* (*matter*) rēs *f*, corpus *nt*; (*essence*) nātūra *f*; (*gist*) summa *f*; (*reality*) rēs *f*; (*wealth*) opēs *fpl*.
substantial *adj* solidus; (*real*) vērus; (*important*) gravis; (*rich*) opulentus, dīves.
substantially *adv* rē; māgnā ex parte.
substantiate *vt* cōnfirmāre.
substitute *vt* subicere, repōnere, substituere ♦ *n* vicārius *m*.
substratum *n* fundāmentum *nt*.
subterfuge *n* latebra *f*, perfugium *nt*.
subterranean *adj* subterrāneus.
subtle *adj* (*fine*) subtīlis; (*shrewd*) acūtus, astūtus.
subtlety *n* subtīlitās *f*; acūmen *nt*, astūtia *f*.
subtly *adv* subtīliter; acūtē, astūte.
subtract *vt* dētrahere, dēmere; (*money*) dēdūcere.
subtraction *n* dētractiō *f*, dēductiō *f*.
suburb *n* suburbium *nt*.
suburban *adj* suburbānus.
subvention *n* pecūniae *fpl*.
subversion *n* ēversiō *f*, ruīna *f*.
subversive *adj* sēditiōsus.
subvert *vt* ēvertere, subruere.
subverter *n* ēversor *m*.
succeed *vi* (*person*) rem bene gerere; (*activity*) prosperē ēvenīre; ~ in obtaining impetrāre ♦ *vt* īnsequī, excipere, succēdere (*dat*).
success *n* bonus ēventus *m*, rēs bene gesta *f*.
successful *adj* fēlīx; (*thing*) secundus; be ~ rem bene gerere; (*play*) stāre.
successfully *adv* fēlīciter, prosperē, bene.
succession *n* (*coming next*) successiō *f*; (*line*) seriēs *f*, ōrdō *m*; alternate ~ vicissitūdō *f*; in ~ deinceps, ex ōrdine.
successive *adj* continuus, perpetuus.
successively *adv* deinceps, ex ōrdine; (*alternately*) vicissim.
successor *n* successor *m*.
succinct *adj* brevis, pressus.
succinctly *adv* breviter, pressē.
succour *n* auxilium *nt*, subsidium *nt* ♦ *vt* subvenīre (*dat*), succurrere (*dat*), opem ferre (*dat*).
succulence *n* sūcus *m*.
succulent *adj* sūcidus.
succumb *vi* succumbere, dēficere.
such *adj* tālis, ēiusmodī, hūiusmodī; (*size*) tantus; at ~ a time id temporis; ~ great tantus.
suchlike *adj* hūiusmodī, ēiusdem generis.
suck *vt* sūgere; ~ in sorbēre; ~ up exsorbēre, ēbibere.
sucker *n* surculus *m*.
sucking *adj* (*child*) lactēns.
suckle *vt* nūtrīcārī, mammam dare (*dat*).
suckling *n* lactēns *m/f*.

sudden *adj* subitus, repentīnus.
suddenly *adv* subitō, repente.
sue *vt* in iūs vocāre, lītem intendere (*dat*); ~ for rogāre, petere, ōrāre.
suffer *vt* patī, ferre, tolerāre; (*injury*) accipere; (*loss*) facere; (*permit*) patī, sinere ♦ *vi* dolōre adficī; ~ defeat cladem accipere; ~ from labōrāre ex, adficī (*abl*); ~ for poenās dare (*gen*).
sufferable *adj* tolerābilis.
sufferance *n* patientia *f*, tolerantia *f*.
suffering *n* dolor *m*.
suffice *vi* sufficere, suppetere.
sufficiency *n* satis.
sufficient *adj* idōneus, satis (*gen*).
sufficiently *adv* satis.
suffocate *vt* suffocāre.
suffrage *n* suffrāgium *nt*.
suffuse *vt* suffundere.
sugar *n* saccharon *nt*.
suggest *vt* admonēre, inicere, subicere; ~ itself occurrere.
suggestion *n* admonitiō *f*; at the ~ of admonitū (*gen*); at my ~ mē auctōre.
suicidal *adj* fūnestus.
suicide *n* mors voluntāria *f*; commit ~ mortem sibī cōnscīscere.
suit *n* (*law*) līs *f*, āctiō *f*; (*clothes*) vestītus *m* ♦ *vt* convenīre (*dat*), congruere (*dat*); (*dress*) sedēre (*dat*), decēre; it ~s decet; to ~ me dē meā sententiā.
suitability *n* convenientia *f*.
suitable *adj* aptus (+ *acc*), idōneus (+ *acc*).
suitably *adv* aptē, decenter.
suite *n* comitēs *mpl*, comitātus *m*.
suitor *n* procus *m*, amāns *m*.
sulk *vi* aegrē ferre, mōrōsum esse.
sulky *adj* mōrōsus, tristis.
sullen *adj* tristis, mōrōsus.
sullenness *n* mōrōsitās *f*.
sully *vt* īnfuscāre, contāmināre.
sulphur *n* sulfur *nt*.
sultriness *n* aestus *m*.
sultry *adj* aestuōsus.
sum *n* summa *f*; ~ of money pecūnia *f* ♦ *vt* subdūcere, computāre; ~ up summātim dēscrībere; to ~ up ūnō verbō, quid plūra?
summarily *adv* strictim, summātim; sine morā.
summarize *vt* summātim dēscrībere.
summary *n* summārium *nt*, epitomē *f* ♦ *adj* subitus, praesēns.
summer *n* aestās *f* ♦ *adj* aestīvus; of ~ aestīvus.
summit *n* vertex *m*, culmen *nt*; (*fig*) fastīgium *nt*; the ~ of summus.
summon *vt* arcessere; (*meeting*) convocāre; (*witness*) citāre; ~ up courage animum sūmere.
summons *n* (*law*) vocātiō *f* ♦ *vt* in iūs vocāre, diem dīcere (*dat*).
sumptuary *adj* sūmptuārius.
sumptuous *adj* sūmptuōsus, adparātus,

mägnificus, lautus.
sumptuously _adv_ sūmptuōsē, mägnificē.
sun _n_ sōl _m_ ♦ _vt:_ ~ **oneself** aprīcārī.
sunbeam _n_ radius _m._
sunburnt _adj_ adūstus.
sunder _vt_ sēparāre, dīvidere.
sundial _n_ sōlārium _nt._
sundry _adj_ dīversī, complūrēs.
sunlight _n_ sōl _m._
sunlit _adj_ aprīcus.
sunny _adj_ aprīcus, serēnus.
sunrise _n_ sōlis ortus _m._
sunset _n_ sōlis occāsus _m._
sunshade _n_ umbella _f._
sunshine _n_ sōl _m._
sup _vi_ cēnāre.
superabundance _n_ abundantia _f._
superabundant _adj_ nimius.
superabundantly _adv_ satis superque.
superannuated _adj_ ēmeritus.
superb _adj_ mägnificus.
superbly _adv_ mägnificē.
supercilious _adj_ adrogāns, superbus.
superciliously _adv_ adroganter, superbē.
superciliousness _n_ adrogantia _f_, fastus _m._
supererogation _n: of_ ~ ultrō factus.
superficial _adj_ levis; **acquire a ~ knowledge of**
  prīmīs labrīs gustare.
superficiality _n_ levitās _f._
superficially _adv_ leviter, strictim.
superfluity _n_ abundantia _f._
superfluous _adj_ supervacāneus, nimius; **be ~**
  redundāre.
superhuman _adj_ dīvīnus, hūmānō māior.
superimpose _vt_ superimpōnere.
superintend _vt_ prōcūrāre, praeesse (_dat_).
superintendence _n_ cūra _f._
superintendent _n_ cūrātor _m_, praefectus _m._
superior _adj_ melior, amplior; **be ~** praestāre,
  superāre ♦ _n_ prīnceps _m_, praefectus _m._
superiority _n_ praestantia _f_; **have the ~**
  superāre; (_in numbers_) plūrēs esse.
superlative _adj_ ēgregius, optimus.
supernatural _adj_ dīvīnus.
supernaturally _adv_ dīvīnitus.
supernumerary _adj_ adscrīptīcius; **~ soldiers**
  accēnsī _mpl._
superscription _n_ titulus _m._
supersede _vt_ succēdere (_dat_), in locum
  succēdere (_gen_); **~ gold with silver** prō aurō
  argentum suppōnere.
superstition _n_ rēligiō _f_, superstitiō _f._
superstitious _adj_ rēligiōsus, superstitiōsus.
supervene _vi_ īnsequī, succēdere.
supervise _vt_ prōcūrāre.
supervision _n_ cūra _f._
supervisor _n_ cūrātor _m._
supine _adj_ supīnus; (_fig_) neglegēns, segnis.
supinely _adv_ segniter.
supper _n_ cēna _f_; **after ~** cēnātus.
supperless _adj_ iēiūnus.
supplant _vt_ praevertere.
supple _adj_ flexibilis, mollis.

supplement _n_ appendix _f_ ♦ _vt_ amplificāre.
supplementary _adj_ additus.
suppleness _n_ mollitia _f._
suppliant _n_ supplex _m/f._
supplicate _vt_ supplicāre, obsecrāre.
supplication _n_ precēs _fpl._
supplies _npl_ commeātus _m._
supply _n_ cōpia _f_ ♦ _vt_ suppeditāre, praebēre;
  (_loss_) supplēre.
support _n_ firmāmentum _nt_; (_help_) subsidium _nt_,
  adiūmentum _nt_; (_food_) alimenta _ntpl_; (_of party_)
  favor _m_; (_of needy_) patrōcinium _nt_; **I ~** subsidiō
  sum (_dat_); **lend ~ to rumours** alimenta
  rūmōribus addere ♦ _vt_ fulcīre; (_living_)
  sustinēre, sustentāre; (_with help_) adiuvāre,
  opem ferre (_dat_); (_at law_) adesse (_dat_).
supportable _adj_ tolerābilis.
supporter _n_ fautor _m_; (_at trial_) advocātus _m_; (_of
  proposal_) auctor _m._
supporting cast _n_ adiūtōrēs _mpl._
suppose _vi_ (_assume_) pōnere; (_think_)
  existimāre, opīnārī, crēdere; **~ it is true** fac
  vērum esse.
supposedly _adv_ ut fāma est.
supposing _conj_ sī; (_for the sake of argument_) sī
  iam.
supposition _n_ opīniō _f_; **on this ~** hōc positō.
supposititious _adj_ subditus, subditīvus.
suppress _vt_ opprimere, comprimere;
  (_knowledge_) cēlāre, reticēre; (_feelings_)
  coercēre, reprimere.
suppression _n_ (_of fact_) reticentia _f._
supremacy _n_ imperium _nt_, dominātus _m_,
  prīncipātus _m._
supreme _adj_ summus; **be ~** dominārī; **~
  command** imperium _nt._
supremely _adv_ ūnicē, plānē.
sure _adj_ certus; (_fact_) explōrātus; (_friend_) fīdus;
  be ~ of compertum habēre; **feel ~** persuāsum
  habēre, haud scīre an; pro certō habēre;
  make ~ of (_fact_) comperīre; (_action_) efficere
  ut; **to be ~** quidem; **~ enough** rē vērā.
surely _adv_ certō, certē, nonne; (_tentative_)
  scīlicet, sānē; **~ you do not think?** num
  putās?; **~ not** num.
surety _n_ (_person_) vās _m_, praes _m_, spōnsor _m_;
  (_deposit_) fīdūcia _f_; **be ~ for** spondēre prō.
surf _n_ fluctus _m._
surface _n_ superficiēs _f_; **~ of the water** summa
  aqua.
surfeit _n_ satietās _f_ ♦ _vt_ satiāre, explēre.
surge _n_ aestus _m_, fluctus _m_ ♦ _vi_ tumēscere.
surgeon _n_ chīrūrgus _m._
surgery _n_ chīrūrgia _f._
surlily _adv_ mōrōsē.
surliness _n_ mōrōsitās _f._
surly _adj_ mōrōsus, difficilis.
surmise _n_ coniectūra _f_ ♦ _vi_ suspicārī,
  conicere, augurārī.
surmount _vt_ superāre.
surmountable _adj_ superābilis.
surname _n_ cognōmen _nt._
surpass _vt_ excellere, exsuperāre, antecēdere.

surpassing *adj* excellēns.
surplus *n* reliquum *nt*; (*money*) pecūniae residuae *fpl*.
surprise *n* admīrātiō *f*; (*cause*) rēs inopīnāta *f*; **take by** ~ dēprehendere ♦ *adj* subitus ♦ *vt* dēprehendere; (*MIL*) opprimere; **be ~d** dēmīrārī; **be ~d at** admīrārī.
surprising *adj* mīrus, mīrābilis.
surprisingly *adv* mīrē, mīrābiliter.
surrender *vt* dēdere, trādere, concēdere ♦ *vi* sē dēdere; ~ **unconditionally** to sē suaque omnia potestāti permittere (*gen*) ♦ *n* dēditiō *f*; (*legal*) cessiō *f*; **unconditional** ~ permissiō *f*.
surreptitious *adj* fūrtīvus.
surreptitiously *adv* fūrtim, clam; **get in** ~ inrēpere in (*acc*).
surround *vt* circumdare, cingere, circumvenīre, circumfundere.
surrounding *adj* circumiectus; **~s** *n* vīcīnia *f*.
survey *vt* contemplārī, cōnsīderāre; (*land*) mētārī ♦ *n* contemplātiō *f*; (*land*) mēnsūra *f*.
surveyor *n* fīnītor *m*, agrīmēnsor *m*, mētātor *m*.
survival *n* salūs *f*.
survive *vt* superāre ♦ *vt* superesse (*dat*).
survivor *n* superstes *m/f*.
susceptibility *n* mollitia *f*.
susceptible *adj* mollis.
suspect *vt* suspicārī; **be ~ed** in suspiciōnem venīre.
suspend *vt* suspendere; (*activity*) differre; (*person*) locō movēre; **be ~ed** pendēre.
suspense *n* dubitātiō *f*; **be in** ~ animī pendēre, haerēre.
suspicion *n* suspiciō *f*; **direct** ~ **to** suspiciōnem adiungere ad.
suspicious *adj* (*suspecting*) suspiciōsus; (*suspected*) dubius, anceps.
sustain *vt* (*weight*) sustinēre; (*life*) alere, sustentāre; (*hardship*) ferre, sustinēre; (*the part of*) agere.
sustenance *n* alimentum *nt*, vīctus *m*.
sutler *n* lixa *m*.
suzerain *n* dominus *m*.
swaddling clothes *n* incūnābula *ntpl*.
swagger *vi* sē iactāre.
swaggerer *n* homō glōriōsus *m*.
swallow *n* hirundō *f* ♦ *vt* dēvorāre; ~ **up** absorbēre.
swamp *n* palūs *f* ♦ *vt* opprimere.
swampy *adj* ūlīginōsus.
swan *n* cycnus *m*; ~'**s** cycnēus.
swank *vi* sē iactāre.
sward *n* caespes *m*.
swarm *n* exāmen *nt*; (*fig*) nūbēs *f* ♦ *vi*: ~ **round** circumfundī.
swarthy *adj* fuscus, aquilus.
swathe *vt* conligāre.
sway *n* dīciō *f*, imperium *nt*; **bring under one's** ~ suae dīciōnis facere ♦ *vt* regere ♦ *vi* vacillāre.
swear *vi* iūrāre; ~ **allegiance to** iūrāre in verba (*gen*).

sweat *n* sūdor *m* ♦ *vi* sūdāre.
sweep *vt* verrere; ~ **away** rapere; ~ **out** ēverrere.
sweet *adj* dulcis, suāvis.
sweeten *vt* dulcem reddere.
sweetheart *n* dēliciae *fpl*.
sweetly *adv* dulciter, suāviter.
sweetness *n* dulcitūdō *f*, suāvitās *f*.
sweet-tempered *adj* suāvis, cōmis.
swell *n* tumor *m* ♦ *vi* tumēre, tumēscere; (*fig*) glīscere ♦ *vt* īnflāre.
swelling *adj* tumidus ♦ *n* tumor *m*.
swelter *vi* aestū labōrāre.
swerve *vi* dēclīnāre, dēvertere ♦ *n* dēclīnātiō *f*.
swift *adj* celer, vēlōx, incitātus.
swiftly *adv* celeriter, vēlōciter.
swiftness *n* celeritās *f*, vēlōcitās *f*.
swill *vt* (*rinse*) colluere; (*drink*) ēpōtāre.
swim *vi* nāre, innāre; (*place*) natāre; ~ **across** trānāre; ~ **ashore** ēnāre; ~ **to** adnāre.
swimming *n* natātiō *f*.
swindle *vt* circumvenīre, verba dare (*dat*) ♦ *n* fraus *f*.
swine *n* sūs *m/f*.
swineherd *n* subulcus *m*.
swing *n* (*motion*) oscillātiō *f* ♦ *vi* oscillāre ♦ *vt* lībrāre.
swinish *adj* obscēnus.
swirl *n* vertex *m* ♦ *vi* volūtārī.
switch *n* virga *f* ♦ *vt* flectere, torquēre.
swivel *n* cardō *f*.
swollen *adj* tumidus, turgidus, īnflātus.
swoon *n* dēfectiō *f* ♦ *vi* intermorī.
swoop *n* impetus *m* ♦ *vi* lābī; ~ **down on** involāre in (*acc*).
sword *n* gladius *m*; **put to the** ~ occīdere; **with fire and** ~ ferrō ignīque.
swordsman *n* gladiātor *m*.
sworn *adj* iūrātus.
sybarite *n* dēlicātus *m*.
sycophancy *n* adsentātiō *f*, adūlātiō *f*.
sycophant *n* adsentātor *m*, adūlātor *m*.
syllable *n* syllaba *f*.
syllogism *n* ratiōcinātiō *f*.
sylvan *adj* silvestris.
symbol *n* signum *nt*, īnsigne *nt*.
symmetrical *adj* concinnus, aequus.
symmetry *n* concinnitās *f*, aequitās *f*.
sympathetic *adj* concors, misericors.
sympathetically *adv* misericorditer.
sympathize *vi* cōnsentīre; ~ **with** miserērī (*gen*).
sympathy *n* concordia *f*, cōnsēnsus *m*; misericordia *f*.
symphony *n* concentus *m*.
symptom *n* signum *nt*, indicium *nt*.
syndicate *n* societās *f*.
synonym *n* verbum idem dēclārāns *nt*.
synonymous *adj* idem dēclārāns.
synopsis *n* summārium *nt*.
syringe *n* clystēr *m*.
system *n* ratiō *f*, fōrmula *f*; (*PHILOS*) disciplīna *f*.

systematic *adj* ōrdinātus, cōnstāns.
systematically *adv* ratiōne, ōrdine.
systematize *vt* in ōrdinem redigere.

T, t

tabernacle *n* tabernāculum *nt.*
table *n* mēnsa *f;* (*inscribed*) tabula *f;* (*list*) index *m;* **at ~** inter cēnam; **turn the ~s on** pār parī referre.
tablet *n* tabula *f,* tabella *f.*
taboo *n* rēligiō *f.*
tabulate *vt* in ōrdinem redigere.
tacit *adj* tacitus.
tacitly *adv* tacitē.
taciturn *adj* taciturnus.
taciturnity *n* taciturnitās *f.*
tack *n* clāvulus *m;* (*of sail*) pēs *m* ♦ *vt:* **~ on** adsuere ♦ *vi* (*ship*) reciprocārī, nāvem flectere.
tackle *n* armāmenta *ntpl* ♦ *vt* adgredī.
tact *n* iūdicium *nt,* commūnis sēnsus *m,* hūmānitās *f.*
tactful *adj* prūdēns, hūmānus.
tactfully *adv* prūdenter, hūmāniter.
tactician *n* reī mīlitāris perītus *m.*
tactics *n* rēs mīlitāris *f,* bellī ratiō *f.*
tactless *adj* ineptus.
tactlessly *adv* ineptē.
tadpole *n* rānunculus *m.*
tag *n* appendicula *f.*
tail *n* cauda *f;* **turn ~** terga vertere.
tailor *n* vestītor *m.*
taint *n* lābēs *f,* vitium *nt* ♦ *vt* inquināre, contāmināre, īnficere.
take *vt* capere, sūmere; (*auspices*) habēre; (*disease*) contrahere; (*experience*) ferre; (*fire*) concipere; (*meaning*) accipere, interpretārī; (*in the act*) dēprehendere; (*person*) dūcere; **~ after** similem esse (*dat, gen*); **~ across** trānsportāre; **~ arms** arma sūmere; **~ away** dēmere, auferre, adimere, abdūcere; **~ back** recipere; **~ by storm** expugnāre; **~ care that** curāre ut/ne (+ *subj*); **~ down** dētrahere; (*in writing*) exscrībere; **~ for** habēre prō; **~ hold of** prehendere; **~ in** (*as guest*) recipere; (*information*) percipere, comprehendere; (*with deceit*) dēcipere; **~ in hand** incipere, suscipere; **~ off** dēmere; (*clothes*) exuere; **~ on** suscipere; **~ out** eximere, extrahere; (*from store*) prōmere; **~ over** excipere; **~ place** fierī, accidere; **~ prisoner** capere; **~ refuge in** cōnfugere ad (+ *infin*); **~ the field** in aciem dēscendere; **~ to** sē dēdere (*dat*), amāre; **~ to oneself** suscipere; **~ up** sūmere, tollere; (*task*) incipere, adgredī ad; (*in turn*) excipere; (*room*) occupāre; **~ upon oneself** recipere, sibī sūmere.
taking *adj* grātus ♦ *n* (*MIL*) expugnātiō *f.*
tale *n* fābula *f,* fābella *f.*
talent *n* (*money*) talentum *nt;* (*ability*) ingenium *nt,* indolēs *f.*
talented *adj* ingeniōsus.
talk *n* sermō *m;* (*with another*) colloquium *nt;* **common ~** fāma *f;* **be the ~ of the town** in ōre omnium esse ♦ *vi* loquī; (*to one*) colloquī cum; **~ down to** ad intellectum audientis dēscendere; **~ over** cōnferre, disserere dē.
talkative *adj* loquāx.
talkativeness *n* loquācitās *f.*
tall *adj* prōcērus, grandis.
tallness *n* prōcēritās *f.*
tallow *n* sēbum *nt.*
tally *n* tessera *f* ♦ *vi* congruere.
talon *n* unguis *m.*
tamarisk *n* myrīca *f.*
tambourine *n* tympanum *nt.*
tame *vt* domāre, mānsuēfacere ♦ *adj* mānsuētus; (*character*) ignāvus; (*language*) īnsulsus, frīgidus.
tamely *adv* ignāvē, lentē.
tameness *n* mānsuētūdō *f;* (*fig*) lentitūdō *f.*
tamer *n* domitor *m.*
tamper *vi:* **~ with** (*person*) sollicitāre; (*writing*) interpolāre.
tan *vt* imbuere.
tang *n* sapor *m.*
tangible *adj* tāctilis.
tangle *n* nōdus *m* ♦ *vt* implicāre.
tank *n* lacus *m.*
tanned *adj* (*by sun*) adūstus.
tanner *n* coriārius *m.*
tantalize *vt* lūdere.
tantamount *adj* pār, īdem.
tantrum *n* īra *f.*
tap *n* epitonium *nt;* (*touch*) plāga *f* ♦ *vt* (*cask*) relinere; (*hit*) ferīre.
tape *n* taenia *f.*
taper *n* cēreus *m* ♦ *vi* fastīgārī.
tapestry *n* aulaea *ntpl.*
tar *n* pix *f.*
tardily *adv* tardē, lentē.
tardiness *n* tarditās *f,* segnitia *f.*
tardy *adj* tardus, lentus.
tare *n* lolium *nt.*
targe *n* parma *f.*
target *n* scopus *m.*
tariff *n* portōrium *nt.*
tarn *n* lacus *m.*
tarnish *vt* īnfuscāre, inquināre ♦ *vi* īnfuscārī.
tarry *vi* morārī, commorārī, cunctārī.
tart *adj* acidus, asper ♦ *n* scriblīta *f.*
tartly *adv* acerbē.
tartness *n* asperitās *f.*
task *n* pēnsum *nt,* opus *nt,* negōtium *nt;* **take to ~** obiūrgāre.
taskmaster *n* dominus *m.*
tassel *n* fimbriae *fpl.*

taste n (*sense*) gustātus m; (*flavour*) sapor m; (*artistic*) iūdicium nt, ēlegantia f; (*for rhetoric*) aurēs fpl; **of ~** doctus; **in good ~** ēlegāns ♦ vt gustāre, dēgustāre ♦ vi sapere; **~ of** resipere.
tasteful adj ēlegāns.
tastefully adv ēleganter.
tastefulness n ēlegantia f.
tasteless adj īnsulsus, inēlegāns.
tastelessly adv īnsulsē, inēleganter.
tastelessness n īnsulsitās f.
taster n praegustātor m.
tasty adj dulcis.
tattered adj pannōsus.
tatters n pannī mpl.
tattoo vt compungere.
taunt n convīcium nt, probrum nt ♦ vt exprobrāre, obicere (*dat of pers, acc of charge*).
taunting adj contumēliōsus.
tauntingly adv contumēliōsē.
taut adj intentus; **draw ~** addūcere.
tavern n taberna f, hospitium nt.
tawdry adj vīlis.
tawny adj fulvus.
tax n vectīgal nt, tribūtum nt; **a 5 per cent ~** vīcēsima f; **free from ~** immūnis ♦ vt vectīgal impōnere (*dat*); (*strength*) contendere; **~ with** (*charge*) obicere (*acc & dat*), īnsimulāre.
taxable adj vectīgālis.
taxation n vectīgālia ntpl.
tax collector n exāctor m.
tax farmer n pūblicānus m.
taxpayer n assiduus m.
teach vt docēre, ērudīre, īnstituere; (*thoroughly*) ēdocēre; (*pass*) discere; **~ your grandmother** sūs Minervam.
teachable adj docilis.
teacher n magister m, magistra f, doctor m; (PHILOS) praeceptor m; (*of literature*) grammaticus m; (*of rhetoric*) rhētor m.
teaching n doctrīna f, disciplīna f.
team n (*animals*) iugum nt.
tear n lacrima f; **shed ~s** lacrimās effundere ♦ vt scindere; **~ down** revellere; **~ in pieces** dīlaniāre, discerpere, lacerāre; **~ off** abscindere, dēripere; **~ open** rescindere; **~ out** ēvellere; **~ up** convellere.
tearful adj flēbilis.
tease vt lūdere, inrītāre.
teat n mamma f.
technical adj (*term*) proprius.
technique n ars f.
tedious adj longus, lentus, odiōsus.
tediously adv molestē.
tedium n taedium nt, molestia f.
teem vi abundāre.
teeming adj fēcundus, refertus.
teens n: **in one's ~** adulescentulus.
teethe vi dentīre.
tell vt (*story*) nārrāre; (*person*) dīcere (*dat*); (*number*) ēnumerāre; (*inform*) certiōrem facere; (*difference*) intellegere; (*order*) iubēre (+ *acc and infin*), imperāre (+ **ut/ne** *and subj*);

~ the truth vēra dīcere; **~ lies** mentior ♦ vi valēre; **~ the difference between** discernere; **I cannot ~** nesciō.
telling adj validus.
temerity n temeritās f.
temper n animus m, ingenium nt; (*bad*) īra f, īrācundia f; (*of metal*) temperātiō f ♦ vt temperāre; (*fig*) moderārī (*dat*).
temperament n animī habitus m, animus m.
temperamental adj incōnstāns.
temperance n temperantia f, continentia f.
temperate adj temperātus, moderātus, sobrius.
temperately adv moderātē.
temperature n calor m, frīgus nt; **mild ~** temperiēs f.
tempest n tempestās f, procella f.
tempestuous adj procellōsus.
temple n templum nt, aedēs f; (*head*) tempus nt.
temporal adj hūmānus, profānus.
temporarily adv ad tempus.
temporary adj brevis.
temporize vi temporis causā facere, tergiversārī.
tempt vt sollicitāre, pellicere, invītāre.
temptation n illecebra f.
tempter n impulsor m.
ten num decem; **~ each** dēnī; **~ times** deciēns.
tenable adj inexpugnābilis, stabilis, certus.
tenacious adj tenāx, firmus.
tenaciously adv tenāciter.
tenacity n tenācitās f.
tenant n inquilīnus m, habitātor m; (*on land*) colōnus m.
tenantry n colōnī mpl.
tend vi spectāre, pertinēre ♦ vt cūrāre, colere.
tendency n inclīnātiō f, voluntās f.
tender adj tener, mollis ♦ vt dēferre, offerre.
tenderhearted adj misericors.
tenderly adv indulgenter.
tenderness n indulgentia f, mollitia f.
tendon n nervus m.
tendril n clāviculus m.
tenement n habitātiō f; **block of ~s** īnsula f.
tenet n dogma nt, dēcrētum nt.
tennis court n sphaeristērium nt.
tenor n (*course*) tenor m; (*purport*) sententia f.
tense adj intentus ♦ n tempus nt.
tension n intentiō f.
tent n tabernāculum nt; (*general's*) praetōrium nt.
tentacle n bracchium nt.
tentatively adv experiendō.
tenterhooks n: **on ~** animī suspēnsus.
tenth adj decimus; **for the ~ time** decimum; **men of the ~ legion** decumānī mpl.
tenuous adj rārus.
tenure n possessiō f.
tepid adj tepidus; **be ~** tepēre.
tergiversation n tergiversātiō f.
term n (*limit*) terminus m; (*period*) spatium nt; (*word*) verbum nt ♦ vt appellāre, nuncupāre.

terminate *vt* termināre, fīnīre ♦ *vi* dēsinere; (*words*) cadere.
termination *n* fīnis *m*, terminus *m*.
terminology *n* vocābula *ntpl*.
terms *npl* condiciō *f*, lēx *f*; **propose ~** condiciōnem ferre; **be on good ~** in grātiā esse; **we come to ~** inter nōs convenit.
terrain *n* ager *m*.
terrestrial *adj* terrestris.
terrible *adj* terribilis, horribilis, horrendus.
terribly *adv* horrendum in modum.
terrific *adj* formīdolōsus; vehemēns.
terrify *vt* terrēre, perterrēre, exterrēre.
terrifying *adj* formīdolōsus.
territory *n* ager *m*, fīnēs *mpl*.
terror *n* terror *m*, formīdō *f*, pavor *m*; **object of ~** terror *m*; **be a ~ to** terrōrī esse (*dat*).
terrorize *vt* metum inicere (*dat*).
terse *adj* pressus, brevis.
tersely *adv* pressē.
terseness *n* brevitās *f*.
tessellated *adj* tessellātus.
test *n* experīmentum *nt*, probātiō *f*; (*standard*) obrussa *f*; **put to the ~** experīrī, perīclitārī; **stand the ~** spectārī ♦ *vt* experīrī, probāre, spectāre.
testament *n* testāmentum *nt*.
testamentary *adj* testāmentārius.
testator *n* testātor *m*.
testify *vt* testificārī.
testifying *n* testificātiō *f*.
testily *adv* stomachōsē.
testimonial *n* laudātiō *f*.
testimony *n* testimōnium *nt*.
testy *adj* difficilis, stomachōsus.
tether *n* retināculum *nt*, vinculum *nt* ♦ *vt* religāre.
tetrarch *n* tetrarchēs *m*.
tetrarchy *n* tetrarchia *f*.
text *n* verba *ntpl*.
textbook *n* ars *f*.
textile *adj* textilis.
textual *adj* verbōrum.
texture *n* textus *m*.
than *conj* quam *abl*; **other ~** alius ac.
thank *vt* grātiās agere (*dat*); **~ you** bene facis; **no, ~ you** benīgnē.
thankful *adj* grātus.
thankfully *adv* grātē.
thankfulness *n* grātia *f*.
thankless *adj* ingrātus.
thanklessly *adv* ingrātē.
thanks *n* grātiae *fpl*, grātēs *fpl*; **return ~** grātiās agere, grātēs persolvere; **~ to you** operā tuā, beneficiō tuō; **it is ~ to sb that ... not** per aliquem stat quominus (+ *subj*).
thanksgiving *n* grātulātiō *f*; (*public*) supplicātiō *f*.
that *pron* (*demonstrative*) ille; (*relat*) quī ♦ *conj* (*statement*) *acc* & *infin*; (*command, purpose, result*) ut; (*fearing*) nē; (*emotion*) quod; **oh ~** utinam.
thatch *n* culmus *m*, strāmenta *ntpl* ♦ *vt* tegere,

integere.
thaw *vt* dissolvere ♦ *vi* liquēscere, tabēscere.
the *art not expressed*; (*emphatic*) ille; (*with compar*) quō ... eō.
theatre *n* theātrum *nt*.
theatrical *adj* scēnicus.
theft *n* fūrtum *nt*.
their *adj* eōrum; (*ref to subject*) suus.
theme *n* māteria *f*, argūmentum *nt*.
themselves *pron* ipsī; (*reflexive*) sē.
then *adv* (*time*) tum, tunc; (*succession*) deinde, tum, posteā; (*consequence*) igitur, ergō; **now and ~** interdum; **only ~** tum dēmum.
thence *adv* inde.
thenceforth *adv* inde, posteā, ex eō tempore.
theologian *n* theologus *m*.
theology *n* theologia *f*.
theorem *n* prōpositum *nt*.
theoretical *adj* contemplātīvus.
theory *n* ratiō *f*; **~ and practice** ratiō atque ūsus.
there *adv* ibī, illīc; (*thither*) eō, illūc; **from ~** inde, illinc; **here and ~** passim; **~ is** est; (*interj*) ecce.
thereabout(s) *adv* circā, circiter, prope.
thereafter *adv* deinde, posteā.
thereby *adv* eā rē, hōc factō.
therefore *adv* itaque, igitur, ergō, idcircō.
therein *adv* inibī, in eō.
thereof *adv* ēius, ēius reī.
thereon *adv* īnsuper, in eō.
thereupon *adv* deinde, statim, inde, quo facto.
therewith *adv* cum eō.
thesis *n* prōpositum *nt*.
thews *n* nervī *mpl*.
they *pron* iī, hī, illī.
thick *adj* dēnsus; (*air*) crassus.
thicken *vt* dēnsāre ♦ *vi* concrēscere.
thickening *n* concrētiō *f*.
thicket *n* dūmētum *nt*.
thickheaded *adj* stupidus, hebes.
thickly *adv* dēnsē; **~ populated** frequēns.
thickness *n* crassitūdō *f*.
thickset *adj* brevis atque obēsus.
thick-skinned *adj*: **be ~** callēre; **become ~** occallēscere.
thief *n* fūr *m*.
thieve *vt* fūrārī, surripere.
thievery *n* fūrtum *nt*.
thievish *adj* fūrāx.
thigh *n* femur *nt*.
thin *adj* exīlis, gracilis, tenuis; (*attendance*) īnfrequēns ♦ *vt* attenuāre, extenuāre; **~ out** rārefacere; **~ down** dīluere.
thine *adj* tuus.
thing *n* rēs *f*; **as ~s are** nunc, cum haec ita sint.
think *vi* cōgitāre; (*opinion*) putāre, existimāre, arbitrārī, rērī, crēdere; **as I ~** meā sententiā; **~ about** cōgitāre dē; **~ highly of** māgnī aestimāre; **~ nothing of** nihilī facere; **~ out** excōgitāre; **~ over** reputāre, in mente agitāre.
thinker *n* philosophus *m*.

thinking _adj_ sapiēns ♦ _n_ cōgitātiō _f_; ~ **that** ratus, arbitratus.

thinly _adv_ exīliter, tenuiter; rārē.

thinness _n_ exīlitās _f_, gracilitās _f_; (_person_) maciēs _f_; (_number_) exiguitās _f_, īnfrequentia _f_; (_air_) tenuitās _f_.

thin-skinned _adj_ inrītābilis.

third _adj_ tertius; **for the ~ time** tertium ♦ _n_ tertia pars _f_, triēns _m_; **two ~s** duae partēs, bēs _m_.

thirdly _adv_ tertiō.

thirst _n_ sitis _f_ ♦ _vi_ sitīre; ~ **for** sitīre.

thirstily _adv_ sitienter.

thirsty _adj_ sitiēns.

thirteen _num_ tredecim; ~ **each** ternī dēnī; ~ **times** terdeciēns.

thirteenth _adj_ tertius decimus.

thirtieth _adj_ trīcēsimus.

thirty _num_ trīgintā; ~ **each** trīcēnī; ~ **times** trīciēns.

this _pron_ hīc.

thistle _n_ carduus _m_.

thither _adv_ eō, illūc.

thole _n_ scalmus _nt_.

thong _n_ lōrum _nt_, habēna _f_.

thorn _n_ spīna _f_, sentis _m_.

thorny _adj_ spīnōsus.

thorough _adj_ absolūtus, germānus; (_work_) accūrātus.

thoroughbred _adj_ generōsus.

thoroughfare _n_ via _f_.

thoroughly _adv_ penitus, omnīnō, funditus.

thoroughness _n_ cūra _f_, diligentia _f_.

thou _pron_ tū.

though _conj_ etsī, etiamsī, quamvīs (+ _subj_), quamquam all (+ _indic_).

thought _n_ (_faculty_) cōgitātiō _f_, mēns _f_, animus _m_; (_an idea_) cōgitātum _nt_, nōtiō _f_; (_design_) cōnsilium _nt_, prōpositum _nt_; (_expressed_) sententia _f_; (_heed_) cautiō _f_, prōvidentia _f_; (_RHET_) inventiō _f_; **second ~s** posteriōrēs cōgitātiōnēs.

thoughtful _adj_ cōgitābundus; prōvidus.

thoughtfully _adv_ prōvidē.

thoughtless _adj_ incōnsīderātus, incōnsultus, imprōvidus, immemor.

thoughtlessly _adv_ temerē, incōnsultē.

thoughtlessness _n_ incōnsīderantia _f_, imprūdentia _f_.

thousand _num_ mīlle; ~**s** _pl_ mīlia (+ _gen_) _ntpl_; ~ **each** mīllēnī; ~ **times** mīlliēns; **three** ~ tria mīlia.

thousandth _adj_ mīllēsimus.

thrall _n_ servus _m_.

thraldom _n_ servitūs _f_.

thrash _vt_ verberāre.

thrashing _n_ verbera _ntpl_.

thread _n_ fīlum _nt_; **hang by a** ~ (_fig_) fīlō pendēre ♦ _vt_: ~ **one's way** sē īnsinuāre.

threadbare _adj_ trītus, obsolētus.

threat _n_ minae _fpl_, minātiō _f_.

threaten _vt_ minārī (_dat of pers_), dēnūntiāre ♦ _vi_ imminēre, impendēre.

threatening _adj_ mināx, imminēns.

threateningly _adv_ mināciter.

three _num_ trēs; ~ **each** ternī; ~ **times** ter; ~ **days** triduum _nt_; ~ **years** triennium _nt_; ~ **quarters** trēs partēs _fpl_, dōdrāns _m_.

three-cornered _adj_ triangulus, triquetrus.

threefold _adj_ triplex.

three hundred _num_ trecentī; ~ **each** trecēnī; ~ **times** trecentiēns.

three hundredth _adj_ trecentēsimus.

three-legged _adj_ tripēs.

three-quarters _n_ dōdrāns _m_, trēs partēs _fpl_.

thresh _vt_ terere, exterere.

threshing floor _n_ ārea _f_.

threshold _n_ līmen _nt_.

thrice _adv_ ter.

thrift _n_ frūgālitās _f_, parsimōnia _f_.

thriftily _adv_ frūgāliter.

thrifty _adj_ parcus, frūgī.

thrill _n_ horror _m_ ♦ _vt_ percellere, percutere ♦ _vi_ trepidāre.

thrilling _adj_ mīrābilis.

thrive _vi_ vigēre, valēre, crēscere.

thriving _adj_ valēns, vegetus; (_crops_) laetus.

throat _n_ faucēs _fpl_, guttur _nt_; **cut the ~ of** iugulāre.

throaty _adj_ gravis, raucus.

throb _vi_ palpitāre, micāre ♦ _n_ pulsus _m_.

throe _n_ dolor _m_; **be in the ~s of** labōrāre ex.

throne _n_ solium _nt_; (_power_) rēgnum _nt_.

throng _n_ multitūdō _f_, frequentia _f_ ♦ _vt_ celebrāre; ~ **round** stīpāre, circumfundī (_dat_).

throttle _vt_ strangulāre.

through _prep_ per (_acc_); (_cause_) propter (_acc_), _abl_ ♦ _adv_: ~ **and** ~ penitus; **carry** ~ exsequī, peragere; **go** ~ trānsīre; **run** ~ percurrere; **be** ~ **with** perfūnctum esse (_abl_).

throughout _adv_ penitus, omnīnō ♦ _prep_ per (_acc_).

throw _n_ iactus _m_, coniectus _m_ ♦ _vt_ iacere, conicere; ~ **about** iactāre; ~ **across** trāicere; ~ **away** abicere; (_something precious_) prōicere; ~ **back** rēicere; ~ **down** dēturbāre, dēicere; ~ **into** inicere; ~ **into confusion** perturbāre; ~ **off** excutere, exsolvere; ~ **open** patefacere; ~ **out** ēicere, prōicere; ~ **over** inicere; (_fig_) dēstituere; ~ **overboard** iactūram facere (_gen_); ~ **to** (_danger_) obicere; ~ **up** ēicere; (_building_) exstruere; ~ **a bridge over** pontem inicere (_dat_), pontem faciendum cūrāre in (_abl_); ~ **light on** (_fig_) lūmen adhibēre (_dat_); ~ **a rider** equitem excutere.

throwing _n_ coniectiō _f_, iactus _m_.

thrum _n_ līcium _nt_.

thrush _n_ turdus _m_.

thrust _vt_ trūdere, pellere, impingere; ~ **at** petere; ~ **away** dētrūdere; ~ **forward** prōtrūdere; ~ **home** dēfīgere; ~ **into** īnfīgere, impingere; ~ **out** extrūdere.

thud _n_ gravis sonitus _m_.

thug _n_ percussor _m_, sīcārius _m_.

thumb n pollex m; **have under one's** ~ in potestāte suā habēre.

thump n plāga f ♦ vt tundere, pulsāre.

thunder n tonitrus m ♦ vi tonāre, intonāre; **it ~s** tonāt.

thunderbolt n fulmen nt.

thunderer n tonāns m.

thunderstruck adj attonitus.

thus adv (referring back) sīc; (referring forward) ita; ~ **far** hāctenus.

thwack vt verberāre.

thwart vt obstāre (dat), officere (dat), remorārī, frustrārī ♦ n (boat's) trānstrum nt.

thy adj tuus.

thyme n thymum nt; (wild) serpyllum nt.

tiara n diadēma nt.

ticket n tessera f.

tickle vt titillāre.

tickling n titillātiō f.

ticklish adj lūbricus.

tidal adj: ~ **waters** aestuārium nt.

tide n aestus m; (time) tempus nt; **ebb** ~ aestūs recessus m; **flood** ~ aestūs accessus m; **turn of the** ~ commūtātiō aestūs; **the** ~ **will turn** (fig) circumagētur hīc orbis.

tidily adv concinnē, mundē.

tidiness n concinnitās f, munditia f.

tidings n nūntius m.

tidy adj concinnus, mundus.

tie n (bond) vinculum nt, cōpula f; (kin) necessitūdō f ♦ vt ligāre; (knot) nectere; ~ **fast** dēvincīre, cōnstringere; ~ **on** illigāre; ~ **to** adligāre; ~ **together** colligāre; ~ **up** adligāre; (wound) obligāre.

tier n ōrdō m.

tiff n dissēnsiō f.

tiger n tigris m, more usu f.

tight adj strictus, astrictus, intentus; (close) artus; **draw** ~ intendere, addūcere.

tighten vt adstringere, contendere.

tightly adv artē, angustē.

tightrope n extentus fūnis; ~ **walker** n fūnambulus m.

tigress n tigris f.

tile n tegula f, imbrex f, later nt.

till conj dum, dōnec ♦ prep usque ad (acc), in (acc); **not** ~ dēmum ♦ n arca f ♦ vt colere.

tillage n cultus m.

tiller n (AGR) cultor m; (ship) clāvus m, gubernāculum nt.

tilt vt inclīnāre.

tilth n cultus m, arvum nt.

timber n (for building) māteria f; (firewood) lignum nt.

timbrel n tympanum nt.

time n tempus nt; (lifetime) aetās f; (interval) intervallum nt, spatium nt; (of day) hōra f; (leisure) ōtium nt; (rhythm) numerus m; **another** ~ aliās; **at** ~**s** aliquandō, interdum; **at all** ~**s** semper; **at any** ~ umquam; **at one** ~ ... **at another** aliās ... aliās; **at that** ~ tunc, id temporis; **at the right** ~ ad tempus, mātūrē, tempestīvē; **at the same** ~ simul; tamen; **at**

the wrong ~ intempestīvē; **beating** ~ percussiō f; **convenient** ~ opportūnitās f; **for a** ~ aliquantisper, parumper; **for a long** ~ diū; **for some** ~ aliquamdiū; **for the** ~ **being** ad tempus; **from** ~ **to** ~ interdum, identidem; **have a good** ~ geniō indulgēre; **have** ~ **for** vacāre (dat); **in** ~ ad tempus, tempore; **in a short** ~ brevī; **in good** ~ tempestīvus; **in the** ~ **of** apud (acc); **keep** ~ (marching) gradum cōnferre; (music) modulārī; **many** ~**s** saepe, saepenumerō; **pass, spend** ~ tempus sūmere, dēgere; **several** ~**s** aliquotiēns; **some** ~ aliquandō; **waste** ~ tempus terere; **what is the** ~? quota hōra est?; ~ **expired** ēmeritus.

time-honoured adj antīquus.

timeliness n opportūnitās f.

timely adj opportūnus, tempestīvus, mātūrus.

timid adj timidus.

timidity n timiditās f.

timidly adv timidē.

timorous adj timidus.

timorously adv timidē.

tin n stannum nt, plumbum album nt ♦ adj stanneus.

tincture n color m, sapor m ♦ vt īnficere.

tinder n fōmes m.

tinge vt imbuere, īnficere, tingere.

tingle vi horrēre.

tingling n horror m.

tinkle vi tinnīre ♦ n tinnītus m.

tinsel n bractea f; (fig) speciēs f, fūcus m.

tint n color m ♦ vt colōrāre.

tiny adj minūtus, pusillus, perexiguus.

tip n apex m, cacūmen nt, extrēmum nt; **the** ~ **of** prīmus, extrēmus ♦ vt praefīgere; ~ **over** invertere.

tipple vi pōtāre.

tippler n pōtor m, ēbrius m.

tipsy adj tēmulentus.

tiptoes n: **on** ~ suspēnsō gradū.

tirade n obiūrgātiō f, dēclāmātiō f.

tire vt fatīgāre; ~ **out** dēfatīgāre ♦ vi dēfetīscī, fatīgārī; **I** ~ **of** mē taedet (gen); **it** ~**s** taedet (+ acc of person, gen of thing).

tired adj (dē)fessus, lassus; ~ **out** dēfessus; **I am** ~ **of** mē taedet.

tiresome adj molestus, difficilis.

tiring adj labōriōsus, operōsus.

tiro n tīrō m, rudis m.

tissue n textus m.

tit n: **give** ~ **for tat** pār parī respondēre.

Titan n Tītān m.

titanic adj immānis.

titbit n cuppēdium nt.

tithe n decuma f.

tithe gatherer n decumānus m.

titillate vt titillāre.

titillation n titillātiō f.

title n (book) īnscrīptiō f, index m; (inscription) titulus m; (person) nōmen nt, appellātiō f; (claim) iūs nt, vindiciae fpl; **assert one's** ~ **to** vindicāre; **give a** ~ **to** īnscrībere.

titled adj nōbilis.

title deed n auctōritās f.
titter n rīsus m ♦ vi rīdēre.
tittle-tattle n sermunculus m.
titular adj nōmine.
to prep ad (acc), in (acc); (attitude) ergā (acc);
(giving) dat; (towns, small islands, domus, rūs)
acc ♦ conj (purpose) ut ♦ adv: **come** ~ animum
recipere; ~ **and fro** hūc illūc.
toad n būfō m.
toady n adsentātor m, parasītus m ♦ vt
adsentārī (dat).
toadyism n adsentātiō f.
toast n: **drink a** ~ propīnāre ♦ vt torrēre; (drink)
propīnāre (dat).
today adv hodiē; ~**'s** hodiernus.
toe n digitus m; **big** ~ pollex m.
toga n toga f.
together adv ūnā, simul; **bring** ~ cōgere,
congerere; **come** ~ convenīre, congregārī;
put ~ cōnferre, compōnere.
toil n labor m; (snare) rēte nt ♦ vi labōrāre; ~ **at**
ēlabōrāre in (abl).
toilet n (lady's) cultus m.
toilsome adj labōriōsus, operōsus.
toil-worn adj labōre cōnfectus.
token n īnsigne nt, signum nt, indicium nt.
tolerable adj tolerābilis, patibilis; (quality)
mediocris; (size) modicus.
tolerably adv satis, mediocriter.
tolerance n patientia f, tolerantia f.
tolerant adj indulgēns, tolerāns.
tolerantly adv indulgenter.
tolerate vt tolerāre, ferre, indulgēre (dat).
toleration n patientia f; (freedom) lībertās f.
toll n vectīgal nt; (harbour) portōrium nt.
toll collector n exāctor m; portitor m.
tomb n sepulcrum nt.
tombstone n lapis m.
tome n liber m.
tomorrow adv crās; ~**'s** crāstinus; **the day
after** ~ perendiē; **put off till** ~ in crāstinum
differre.
tone n sonus m, vōx f; (painting) color m.
tongs n forceps m/f.
tongue n lingua f; (shoe) ligula f; **on the tip of
one's** ~ in prīmōribus labrīs.
tongue-tied adj ēlinguis, īnfāns.
tonnage n amphorae fpl.
tonsils n tōnsillae fpl.
tonsure n rāsūra f.
too adv (also) etiam, īnsuper, quoque; (excess)
nimis ♦ compar adj: ~ **far** extrā modum; ~
much nimium; ~ **long** nimium diū; ~ **great to**
māior quam quī (subj); ~ **late** sērius; ~ **little**
parum (+ gen).
tool n īnstrūmentum nt; (AGR) ferrāmentum nt;
(person) minister m.
tooth n dēns m; ~ **and nail** tōtō corpore atque
omnibus unguīs; **cast in one's teeth**
exprobrāre, obicere; **cut teeth** dentīre; **in the
teeth of** obviam (dat), adversus (acc); **with
the teeth** mordicus.
toothache n dentium dolor m.

toothed adj dentātus.
toothless adj ēdentulus.
toothpick n dentiscalpium nt.
toothsome adj suāvis, dulcis.
top n vertex m, fastīgium nt; (tree) cacūmen nt;
(toy) turbō m; **from** ~ **to toe** ab īmīs unguibus
usque ad verticem summum; **the** ~ **of**
summus ♦ vt exsuperāre; ~ **up** supplēre ♦ adj
superior, summus.
tope vi pōtāre.
toper n pōtor m.
topiary adj topiārius. ♦ n topiārium opus nt.
topic n rēs f; (RHET) locus m; ~ **of conversation**
sermō m.
topical adj hodiernus.
topmost adj summus.
topography n dēscrīptiō f.
topple vi titubāre; ~ **over** prōlābī.
topsail n dolō m.
topsyturvy adv praeposterē; **turn** ~ sūrsum
deōrsum versāre, permiscēre.
tor n mōns m.
torch n fax f, lampas f.
torment n cruciātus m; (mind) angor m ♦ vt
cruciāre; (mind) discruciāre, excruciāre,
angere.
tormentor n tortor m.
tornado n turbō m.
torpid adj torpēns; **be** ~ torpēre; **grow** ~
obtorpēscere.
torpor n torpor m, inertia f.
torrent n torrēns m.
torrid adj torridus.
torsion n tortus m.
torso n truncus m.
tortoise n testūdō f.
tortoiseshell n testūdō f.
tortuous adj flexuōsus.
torture n cruciātus m, supplicium nt;
instrument of ~ tormentum nt ♦ vt torquēre,
cruciāre, excruciāre.
torturer n tortor m, carnifex m.
toss n iactus m ♦ vt iactāre, excutere; ~ **about**
agitāre; **be** ~**ed** (at sea) fluitāre.
total adj tōtus, ūniversus ♦ n summa f.
totality n ūniversitās f.
totally adv omnīnō, plānē.
totter vi lābāre, titubāre; **make** ~ labefactāre.
tottering n titubātiō f.
touch n tāctus m; **a** ~ **of** aliquantulum (gen);
finishing ~ manus extrēma f ♦ vt tangere,
attingere; (feelings) movēre, tangere ♦ vi
inter sē contingere; ~ **at** nāvem appellere ad;
~ **on** (topic) attingere, perstringere; ~ **up**
expolīre.
touch-and-go adj anceps ♦ n discrīmen nt.
touching adj (place) contiguus; (emotion)
flexanimus ♦ prep quod attinet ad (acc).
touchstone n (fig) obrussa f.
touchy adj inrītābilis, stomachōsus.
tough adj dūrus.
toughen vt dūrāre.
toughness n dūritia f.

tour n iter nt; (abroad) peregrīnātiō f.
tourist n viātor m, peregrīnātor m.
tournament n certāmen nt.
tow n stuppa f; **of ~** stuppeus ♦ vt adnexum trahere, remulcō trahere.
toward(s) prep ad (acc), versus (after noun, acc); (feelings) in (acc), ergā (acc); (time) sub (acc).
towel n mantēle nt.
tower n turris f ♦ vi ēminēre.
towered adj turrītus.
town n urbs f, oppidum nt; **country ~** mūnicipium nt ♦ adj urbānus.
town councillor n decuriō m.
townsman n oppidānus m.
townspeople npl oppidānī mpl.
towrope n remulcum nt.
toy n crepundia ntpl ♦ vi lūdere.
trace n vestīgium nt, indicium nt ♦ vt investīgāre; (draw) dēscrībere; **~ out** dēsignāre.
track n (mark) vestīgium nt; (path) callis m, sēmita f; (of wheel) orbita f; (of ship) cursus m ♦ vt investīgāre, indāgāre.
trackless adj invius.
tract n (country) tractus m, regiō f; (book) libellus m.
tractable adj tractābilis, facilis, docilis.
trade n mercātūra f, mercātus m; (a business) ars f, quaestus m; **freedom of ~** commercium nt ♦ vi mercātūrās facere, negōtiārī; **~ in** vēndere, vēnditāre.
trader n mercātor m, negōtiātor m.
tradesman n opifex m.
tradition n fāma f, mōs māiōrum m, memoria f.
traditional adj ā māiōribus trāditus, patrius.
traditionally adv mōre māiōrum.
traduce vt calumniārī, obtrectāre (dat).
traducer n calumniātor m, obtrectātor m.
traffic n commercium nt; (on road) vehicula ntpl ♦ vi mercātūrās facere; **~ in** vēndere, vēnditāre.
tragedian n (author) tragoedus m; (actor) āctor tragicus m.
tragedy n tragoedia f; (fig) calamitās f, malum nt.
tragic adj tragicus; (fig) tristis.
tragically adv tragicē; male.
tragicomedy n tragicocōmoedia f.
trail n vestīgia ntpl ♦ vt trahere ♦ vi trahī.
train n (line) agmen nt, ōrdō m; (of dress) īnstita f; (army) impedīmenta ntpl; (followers) comitēs mpl, satellitēs mpl, cohors f ♦ vt īnstituere, īnstruere, docēre, adsuēfacere; exercēre; (weapon) dīrigere.
trainer n (sport) lanista m, aliptēs m.
training n disciplīna f, īnstitūtiō f; (practice) exercitātiō f.
trait n līneāmentum nt.
traitor n prōditor m.
traitorous adj perfidus, perfidiōsus.
traitorously adv perfidiōsē.

trammel vt impedīre.
tramp n (man) planus m; (of feet) pulsus m ♦ vi gradī.
trample vi: **~ on** obterere, prōterere, prōculcāre.
trance n stupor m; (prophetic) furor m.
tranquil adj tranquillus, placidus, quiētus, sēdātus.
tranquility n tranquillitās f, quiēs f, pāx f.
tranquillize vt pācāre, sēdāre.
tranquilly adv tranquillē, placidē, tranquillō animō.
transact vt agere, gerere, trānsigere.
transaction n rēs f, negōtium nt.
transactor n āctor m.
transalpine adj trānsalpīnus.
transcend vt superāre, excēdere.
transcendence n praestantia f.
transcendent adj eximius, ēgregius, excellēns.
transcendental adj dīvīnus.
transcendentally adv eximiē, ēgregiē, ūnicē.
transcribe vt dēscrībere, trānscrībere.
transcriber n librārius m.
transcript n exemplar nt, exemplum nt.
transfer n trānslātiō f; (of property) aliēnātiō f ♦ vt trānsferre; (troops) trādūcere; (property) abaliēnāre; (duty) dēlēgāre.
transference n trānslātiō f.
transfigure vt trānsfōrmāre.
transfix vt trānsfīgere, trāicere, trānsfodere; (mind) obstupefacere; **be ~ed** stupēre, stupēscere.
transform vt commūtāre, vertere.
transformation n commūtātiō f.
transgress vt violāre, perfringere ♦ vi dēlinquere.
transgression n dēlictum nt.
transgressor n violātor m.
transience n brevitās f.
transient adj fluxus, cadūcus, brevis.
transit n trānsitus m.
transition n mūtātiō f; (speech) trānsitus m.
transitory adj brevis, fluxus.
translate vt vertere, reddere; **~ into Latin** Latīnē reddere.
translation n: **a Latin ~ of Homer** Latīnē redditus Homērus.
translator n interpres m.
translucent adj perlūcidus.
transmarine adj trānsmarīnus.
transmission n missiō f.
transmit vt mittere; (legacy) trādere, prōdere.
transmutable adj mūtābilis.
transmutation n mūtātiō f.
transmute vt mūtāre, commūtāre.
transom n trabs f.
transparency n perlūcida nātūra f.
transparent adj perlūcidus; (fig) perspicuus.
transparently adv perspicuē.
transpire vi (get known) ēmānāre, dīvulgārī; (happen) ēvenīre.
transplant vt trānsferre.

transport n vectūra f; (_ship_) nāvis onerāria f; (_emotion_) ēlātiō f, summa laetitia f ♦ vt trānsportāre, trānsvehere, trānsmittere; **be ~ed** (_fig_) efferrī, gestīre.
transportation n vectūra f.
transpose vt invertere; (_words_) trāicere.
transposition n (_words_) trāiectiō f.
transverse adj trānsversus, oblīquus.
transversely adv in trānsversum, oblīquē.
trap n laqueus m; (_fig_) īnsidiae fpl ♦ vt dēcipere, excipere; (_fig_) inlaqueāre.
trappings n ōrnāmenta ntpl, īnsignia ntpl; (_horse's_) phalerae fpl.
trash n nūgae fpl.
trashy adj vīlis.
Trasimene n Trasimēnus m.
travail n labor m, sūdor m; (_woman's_) puerperium nt ♦ vi labōrāre, sūdāre; parturīre.
travel n itinera ntpl; (_foreign_) peregrīnātiō f ♦ vi iter facere; (_abroad_) peregrīnārī; **~ through** peragrāre; **~ to** contendere ad, in (_acc_), proficīscī in (_acc_).
traveller n viātor m; (_abroad_) peregrīnātor m.
traverse vt peragrāre, lūstrāre; **~ a great distance** multa mīlia passuum iter facere.
travesty n perversa imitātiō f ♦ vt perversē imitārī.
tray n ferculum nt.
treacherous adj perfidus, perfidiōsus; (_ground_) lūbricus.
treacherously adv perfidiōsē.
treachery n perfidia f.
tread vi incēdere, ingredī; **~ on** īnsistere (_dat_) ♦ n gradus m, incessus m.
treadle n (_loom_) īnsilia ntpl.
treadmill n pistrīnum nt.
treason n māiestās f, perduelliō f; **be charged with ~** māiestātis accūsārī; **be guilty of high ~ against** māiestātem minuere, laedere (_gen_).
treasonable adj perfidus, perfidiōsus.
treasure n gāza f, thēsaurus m; (_person_) dēliciae fpl ♦ vt māximī aestimāre, dīligere, fovēre; **~ up** condere, congerere.
treasure house n thēsaurus m.
treasurer n aerārī praefectus m; (_royal_) dioecētēs m.
treasury n aerārium nt; (_emperor's_) fiscus m.
treat n convīvium nt; dēlectātiō f ♦ vt (_in any way_) ūtī (_abl_), habēre, tractāre, accipere; (_patient_) cūrāre; (_topic_) tractāre; (_with hospitality_) invītāre; **~ with** agere cum; **~ as a friend** amīcī locō habēre.
treatise n liber m.
treatment n tractātiō f; (_MED_) cūrātiō f.
treaty n foedus nt; **make a ~** foedus ferīre.
treble adj triplus; (_voice_) acūtus ♦ n acūtus sonus m ♦ vt triplicāre.
tree n arbor f.
trek vi migrāre ♦ n migrātiō f.
trellis n cancellī mpl.
tremble vi tremere, horrēre.

trembling n tremor m, horror m ♦ adj tremulus.
tremendous adj immānis, ingēns, vastus.
tremendously adv immāne quantum.
tremor n tremor m.
tremulous adj tremulus.
trench n fossa f.
trenchant adj ācer.
trenchantly adv ācriter.
trend n inclīnātiō f ♦ vi vergere.
trepidation n trepidātiō f.
trespass n dēlictum nt ♦ vi dēlinquere; **~ on** (_property_) invādere in (_acc_); (_patience, time, etc_) abūtī (_abl_).
trespasser n quī iniussū dominī ingreditur.
tress n crīnis m.
trial n (_essay_) experientia f; (_test_) probātiō f; (_law_) iūdicium nt, quaestiō f; (_trouble_) labor m, aerumna f; **make ~ of** experīrī, perīculum facere (_gen_); **be brought to ~** in iūdicium venīre; **put on ~** in iūdicium vocāre; **hold a ~ on** quaestiōnem habēre dē (_abl_).
triangle n triangulum nt.
triangular adj triangulus, triquetrus.
tribe n tribus m; gēns f; (_barbarian_) nātiō f.
tribulation n aerumna f.
tribunal n iūdicium nt.
tribune n tribūnus m; (_platform_) rōstra ntpl.
tribuneship, tribunate n tribūnātus m.
tribunician adj tribūnicius.
tributary adj vectīgālis ♦ n: **be a ~ of** (_river_) īnfluere in (_acc_).
tribute n tribūtum nt, vectīgal nt; (_verbal_) laudātiō f; **pay a ~ to** laudāre.
trice n: **in a ~** mōmentō temporis.
trick n dolus m, fallācia f, fraus f, īnsidiae fpl, ars f; (_conjurer's_) praestīgiae fpl; (_habit_) mōs m ♦ vt fallere, dēcipere, ēlūdere; (_with words_) verba dare (_dat_); **~ out** ōrnāre, distinguere.
trickery n dolus m, fraus f, fallāciae fpl.
trickle n guttae fpl ♦ vi mānāre, dēstillāre.
trickster n fraudātor m, veterātor m.
tricky adj lūbricus, difficilis.
trident n tridēns m, fuscina f.
tried adj probātus, spectātus.
triennial adj trietēricus.
triennially adv quartō quōque annō.
trifle n nūgae fpl, paululum nt ♦ vi lūdere, nūgārī; **~ with** lūdere.
trifling adj levis, exiguus.
triflingly adv leviter.
trig adj lepidus, concinnus.
trigger n manulea f.
trim adj nitidus, concinnus ♦ vt putāre, tondēre; (_lamp_) oleum īnstillāre (_dat_) ♦ vi temporibus servīre.
trimly adv concinnē.
trimness n nitor, munditia f.
trinket n crepundia ntpl.
trip n iter nt ♦ vt supplantāre ♦ vi lābī, titubāre; **~ along** currere; **~ over** incurrere in (_acc_).
tripartite adj tripartītus.

tripe n omāsum nt.

triple adj triplex, triplus ♦ vt triplicāre.

triply adv trifāriam.

tripod n tripus m.

trireme n trirēmis f.

trite adj trītus.

triumph n triumphus m; (victory) victōria f ♦ vi triumphāre; vincere; ~ **over** dēvincere.

triumphal adj triumphālis.

triumphant adj victor; laetus.

triumvir n triumvir m.

triumvirate n triumvirātus m.

trivial adj levis, tenuis.

triviality n nūgae fpl.

trochaic adj trochaicus.

trochee n trochaeus m.

Trojan n Trōiānus m.

troop n grex f, caterva f; (cavalry) turma f ♦ vi cōnfluere, congregārī.

trooper n eques m.

troops npl cōpiae fpl.

trope n figūra f, trānslātiō f.

trophy n tropaeum nt; **set up a** ~ tropaeum pōnere.

tropic n sōlstitiālis orbis m; ~**s** pl loca fervida ntpl.

tropical adj tropicus.

trot vi tolūtim īre.

troth n fidēs f.

trouble n incommodum nt, malum nt, molestia f, labor m; (effort) opera f, negōtium nt; (disturbance) turba f, tumultus m; **take the** ~ **to** operam dare ut; **be worth the** ~ operae pretium esse ♦ vt (disturb) turbāre; (make uneasy) sollicitāre, exagitāre; (annoy) incommodāre, molestiam exhibēre (dat); ~ **oneself about** cūrāre, respicere; **be ~d with** labōrāre ex.

troubler n turbātor m.

troublesome adj molestus, incommodus, difficilis.

troublesomeness n molestia f.

troublous adj turbidus, turbulentus.

trough n alveus m.

trounce vt castīgāre.

troupe n grex f, caterva f.

trousered adj brācātus.

trousers n brācae fpl.

trow vi opīnārī.

truant adj tardus ♦ n cessātor m; **play** ~ cessāre, nōn compārēre.

truce n indutiae fpl.

truck n carrus m; **have no** ~ **with** nihil commercī habēre cum.

truckle vi adsentārī.

truculence n ferōcia f, asperitās f.

truculent adj truculentus, ferōx.

truculently adv ferōciter.

trudge vi rēpere, pedibus incēdere.

true adj vērus; (genuine) germānus, vērus; (loyal) fīdus, fidēlis; (exact) rēctus, iūstus.

truism n verbum trītum nt.

truly adv rēvērā, profectō, vērē.

trumpery n nūgae fpl ♦ adj vīlis.

trumpet n tuba f, būcina f.

trumpeter n būcinātor m, tubicen m.

trump up vt ēmentīrī, cōnfingere.

truncate vt praecīdere.

truncheon n fustis m, scīpiō m.

trundle vt volvere.

trunk n truncus m; (elephant's) manus f; (box) cista f.

truss n fascia f ♦ vt colligāre.

trust n fidēs f, fīdūcia f; **breach of** ~ mala fidēs; **held in** ~ fīdūciārius; **put** ~ **in** fidem habēre (dat) ♦ vt cōnfīdere (dat), crēdere (dat); (entrust) committere, concrēdere.

trustee n tūtor m.

trusteeship n tūtēla f.

trustful adj crēdulus, fīdēns.

trustfully adv fīdenter.

trustily adv fidēliter.

trustiness n fidēs f, fidēlitās f.

trusting adj fīdēns.

trustingly adv fīdenter.

trustworthily adv fidēliter.

trustworthiness n fidēs f, integritās f.

trustworthy adj fīdus, certus; (witness) locuplēs; (authority) certus, bonus.

trusty adj fīdus, fidēlis.

truth n vēritās f, vērum nt; **in** ~ rē vērā.

truthful adj vērāx.

truthfully adv vērē.

truthfulness n fidēs f.

try vt (attempt) cōnārī; (test) experīrī, temptāre; (harass) exercēre; (judge) iūdicāre, cognōscere; ~ **for** petere, quaerere.

trying adj molestus.

tub n alveus m, cūpa f.

tubby adj obēsus.

tube n fistula f.

tufa n tōfus m.

tuft n crista f.

tug vt trahere, tractāre.

tuition n īnstitūtiō f.

tumble vi concidere, corruere, prōlābī ♦ n cāsus m.

tumbledown adj ruīnōsus.

tumbler n pōculum nt.

tumid adj tumidus, īnflātus.

tumour n tūber nt.

tumult n tumultus m, turba f; (fig) perturbātiō f.

tumultuous adj tumultuōsus, turbidus.

tumultuously adv tumultuōsē.

tumulus n tumulus m.

tun n dolium nt.

tune n modī mpl, carmen nt; **keep in** ~ concentum servāre; **out of** ~ absonus, dissonus; (strings) incontentus ♦ vt (strings) intendere.

tuneful adj canōrus.

tunefully adv numerōsē.

tunic n tunica f; **wearing a** ~ tunicātus.

tunnel n cunīculus m.

tunny n thunnus m.

turban *n* mitra *f*, mitella *f*.
turbid *adj* turbidus.
turbot *n* rhombus *m*.
turbulence *n* tumultus *m*.
turbulent *adj* turbulentus, turbidus.
turbulently *adv* turbulentē, turbidē.
turf *n* caespes *m*.
turgid *adj* turgidus, īnflātus.
turgidity *n* (*RHET*) ampullae *fpl*.
turgidly *adv* īnflātē.
turmoil *n* turba *f*, tumultus *m*; (*mind*)
perturbātiō *f*.
turn *n* (*motion*) conversiō *f*; (*bend*) flexus *m*,
ānfrāctus *m*; (*change*) commūtātiō *f*,
vicissitūdō *f*; (*walk*) spatium *nt*; (*of mind*)
adfectus *m*; (*of language*) sententia *f*,
cōnfōrmātiō *f*; ~ **of events** mutātiō rērum *f*;
bad ~ iniūria *f*; **good** ~ beneficium *nt*; ~ **of the
scale** mōmentum *nt*; **take a ~ for the worse** in
pēiōrem partem vertī; **in ~s** invicem,
vicissim, alternī; **in one's** ~ locō ōrdine ♦ *vt*
vertere, convertere, flectere; (*change*)
vertere, mūtāre; (*direct*) intendere, dīrigere;
(*translate*) vertere, reddere; (*on a lathe*)
tornāre; ~ **the edge of** retundere; ~ **the head**
mentem exturbāre; ~ **the laugh against**
rīsum convertere in (*acc*); ~ **the scale** (*fig*)
mōmentum habēre; ~ **the stomach** nauseam
facere; ~ **to account** ūtī (*abl*), in rem suam
convertere ♦ *vi* versārī, circumagī; (*change*)
vertere, mūtārī; (*crisis*) pendēre; (*direction*)
convertī; (*scale*) prōpendēre; ~ **king's/
queen's evidence** indicium profitērī; ~
against *vt* aliēnāre ab ♦ *vi* dēscīscere ab; ~
around (se) circumvertere; ~ **aside** *vt*
dēflectere, dēclīnāre ♦ *vi* dēvertere, sē
dēclīnāre; ~ **away** *vt* āvertere, dēpellere ♦ *vi*
āversārī, discēdere; ~ **back** *vi* revertī; ~
down *vt* invertere; (*proposal*) rēicere; ~ **into**
vi vertere in (*acc*), mūtārī in (*acc*); ~ **out** *vt*
ēicere, expellere ♦ *vi* cadere, ēvenīre,
ēvādere; ~ **outside in** excutere; ~ **over** *vt*
ēvertere; (*book*) ēvolvere; (*in mind*) volūtāre,
agitāre; ~ **round** vt circumagere ♦ *vi*
convertī; ~ **up** *vt* retorquēre; (*earth*) versāre;
(*nose*) corrūgāre ♦ *vi* adesse, intervenīre; ~
upside down invertere.
turncoat *n* trānsfuga *m*.
turning *n* flexus *m*, ānfrāctus *m*.
turning point *n* discrīmen *nt*, mēta *f*.
turnip *n* rāpum *nt*.
turpitude *n* turpitūdō *f*.
turquoise *n* callais *f* ♦ *adj* callainus.
turret *n* turris *f*.
turreted *adj* turrītus.
turtle *n* testūdō *f*; **turn ~** invertī.
turtle dove *n* turtur *m*.
tusk *n* dēns *m*.
tussle *n* luctātiō *f* ♦ *vi* luctārī.
tutelage *n* tūtēla *f*.
tutelary *adj* praeses.
tutor *n* praeceptor *m*, magister *m* ♦ *vt* docēre,
praecipere (*dat*).

tutorship *n* tūtēla *f*.
twaddle *n* nūgae *fpl*.
twang *n* sonus *m* ♦ *vi* increpāre.
tweak *vi* vellicāre.
tweezers *n* forceps *m/f*, volsella *f*.
twelfth *adj* duodecimus ♦ *n* duodecima pars *f*,
ūncia *f*; **eleven ~s** deūnx *m*; **five ~s** quīncūnx
m; **seven ~s** septūnx *m*.
twelve *num* duodecim; ~ **each** duodēnī; ~ **times**
duodeciēns.
twelvemonth *n* annus *m*.
twentieth *adj* vīcēsimus ♦ *n* vīcēsima pars *f*;
(*tax*) vīcēsima *f*.
twenty *num* vīgintī; ~ **each** vīcēnī; ~ **times**
vīciēns.
twice *adv* bis; ~ **as much** duplus, bis tantō; ~ **a
day** bis diē, bis in diē.
twig *n* virga *f*, rāmulus *m*.
twilight *n* (*morning*) dīlūculum *nt*; (*evening*)
crepusculum *nt*.
twin *adj* geminus ♦ *n* geminus *m*, gemina *f*.
twine *n* resticula *f* ♦ *vt* nectere, implicāre,
contexere ♦ *vi* sē implicāre; ~ **round**
complectī.
twinge *n* dolor *m*.
twinkle *vi* micāre.
twirl *vt* intorquēre, contorquēre ♦ *vi*
circumagī.
twist *vt* torquēre, intorquēre ♦ *vi* torquērī.
twit *vt* obicere (*dat*).
twitch *vt* vellicāre ♦ *vi* micāre.
twitter *vi* pīpilāre.
two *num* duo; ~ **each** bīnī; ~ **days** biduum *nt*; ~
years biennium *nt*; ~ **years old** bīmus; ~ **by** ~
bīnī; ~ **feet long** bipedālis; **in** ~ **parts**
bifāriam, bipartītō.
two-coloured *adj* bicolor.
two-edged *adj* anceps.
twofold *adj* duplex, anceps.
two-footed *adj* bipēs.
two-headed *adj* biceps.
two-horned *adj* bicornis.
two hundred *num* ducentī; ~ **each** ducēnī; ~
times ducentiēns.
two hundredth *adj* ducentēsimus.
two-oared *adj* birēmis.
two-pronged *adj* bidēns, bifurcus.
two-way *adj* bivius.
type *n* (*pattern*) exemplar *nt*; (*kind*) genus
nt.
typhoon *n* turbō *m*.
typical *adj* proprius, solitus.
typically *adv* dē mōre, ut mōs est.
typify *vt* exprimere.
tyrannical *adj* superbus, crūdēlis.
tyrannically *adv* superbē, crūdēliter.
tyrannize *vi* dominārī, rēgnāre.
tyrannous *adj see* **tyrannical**
tyrannously *adv see* **tyrannically**.
tyranny *n* dominātiō *f*, rēgnum *nt*.
tyrant *n* rēx *m*, crūdēlis dominus *m*; (*Greek*)
tyrannus *m*.
tyro *n* tīrō *m*, rudis *m*.

U, u

ubiquitous adj omnibus locīs praesēns.
ubiquity n ūniversa praesentia f.
udder n über nt.
ugliness n foeditās f, dēfōrmitās f, turpitūdō f.
ugly adj foedus, dēfōrmis, turpis.
ulcer n ulcus nt, vomica f.
ulcerate vi ulcerārī.
ulcerous adj ulcerōsus.
ulterior adj ulterior.
ultimate adj ultimus, extrēmus.
ultimately adv tandem, ad ultimum.
umbrage n offēnsiō f; **take ~ at** indignē ferre, patī.
umbrageous adj umbrōsus.
umbrella n umbella f.
umpire n arbiter m, disceptātor m.
unabashed adj intrepidus, impudēns.
unabated adj integer.
unable adj impotēns; **be ~** nōn posse, nequīre.
unacceptable adj ingrātus.
unaccompanied adj sōlus.
unaccomplished adj īnfectus, imperfectus; (person) indoctus.
unaccountable adj inexplicābilis.
unaccountably adv sine causā, repentē.
unaccustomed adj īnsuētus, īnsolitus.
unacquainted adj ignārus (gen), imperītus (gen).
unadorned adj inōrnātus, incōmptus; (speech) nūdus, ēnucleātus.
unadulterated adj sincērus, integer.
unadvisedly adv imprūdenter, incōnsultē.
unaffected adj simplex, candidus.
unaffectedly adv simpliciter.
unaided adj sine auxiliō, nūdus.
unalienable adj proprius.
unalloyed adj pūrus.
unalterable adj immūtābilis.
unaltered adj immūtātus.
unambiguous adj apertus, certus.
unambitious adj humilis, modestus.
unanimity n cōnsēnsiō f, ūnanimitās f.
unanimous adj concors, ūnanimus; **be ~** idem omnēs sentīre.
unanimously adv ūnā vōce, omnium cōnsēnsū.
unanswerable adj necessārius.
unanswerably adv sine contrōversiā.
unappreciative adj ingrātus.
unapproachable adj inaccessus; (person) difficilis.
unarmed adj inermis.
unasked adj ultrō, suā sponte.
unassailable adj inexpugnābilis.
unassailed adj intāctus, incolumis.

unassuming adj modestus, dēmissus; **~ manners** modestia f.
unassumingly adv modestē.
unattached adj līber.
unattempted adj intentātus; **leave ~** praetermittere.
unattended adj sōlus, sine comitibus.
unattractive adj invenustus.
unauthentic adj incertō auctōre.
unavailing adj inūtilis, inānis.
unavenged adj inultus.
unavoidable adj necessārius.
unavoidably adv necessāriō.
unaware adj īnscius, ignārus.
unawares adv inopīnātō, dē imprōvīsō; incautus.
unbalanced adj turbātus.
unbar vt reserāre.
unbearable adj intolerābilis, intolerandus.
unbearably adv intoleranter.
unbeaten adj invictus.
unbecoming adj indecōrus, inhonestus; **it is ~** dēdecet.
unbeknown adj ignōtus.
unbelief n diffīdentia f.
unbelievable adj incrēdibilis.
unbelievably adv incrēdibiliter.
unbelieving adj incrēdulus.
unbend vt remittere, laxāre ♦ vi animum remittere, aliquid dē sevēritāte remittere.
unbending adj inexōrābilis, sevērus.
unbiassed adj integer, incorruptus, aequus.
unbidden adj ultrō, sponte.
unbind vt solvere, resolvere.
unblemished adj pūrus, integer.
unblushing adj impudēns.
unblushingly adv impudenter.
unbolt vt reserāre.
unborn adj nōndum nātus.
unbosom vt patefacere, effundere.
unbound adj solūtus.
unbounded adj īnfīnītus, immēnsus.
unbridled adj īnfrēnātus; (fig) effrēnātus, indomitus, impotēns.
unbroken adj integer; (animal) intractātus; (friendship) inviolātus; (series) perpetuus, continuus.
unburden vt exonerāre; **~ oneself of** aperīre, patefacere.
unburied adj inhumātus, īnsepultus.
unbusinesslike adj iners.
uncalled-for adj supervacāneus.
uncanny adj mīrus, mōnstruōsus.
uncared-for adj neglectus.
unceasing adj perpetuus, adsiduus.
unceasingly adv perpetuō, adsiduē.
unceremonious adj agrestis, inurbānus.
unceremoniously adv inurbānē.
uncertain adj incertus, dubius, anceps; **be ~** dubitāre, pendēre.
uncertainly adv incertē, dubitanter.
uncertainty n incertum nt; (state) dubitātiō f.
unchangeable adj immūtābilis; (person)

cōnstāns.
unchanged *adj* immūtātus, īdem; **remain ~**
permanēre.
uncharitable *adj* inhūmānus, malignus.
uncharitableness *n* inhūmānitās *f*.
uncharitably *adv* inhūmānē, malignē.
unchaste *adj* impudīcus, libīdinōsus.
unchastely *adv* impudīcē.
unchastity *n* incestus *m*, libīdō *f*.
unchecked *adj* līber, indomitus.
uncivil *adj* inurbānus, importūnus,
inhūmānus.
uncivilized *adj* barbarus, incultus, ferus.
uncivilly *adv* inurbānē.
uncle *n* (*paternal*) patruus *m*; (*maternal*)
avunculus *m*.
unclean *adj* immundus; (*fig*) impūrus,
obscēnus.
uncleanly *adv* impūrē.
uncleanness *n* sordēs *fpl*; (*fig*) impūritās *f*,
obscēnitās *f*.
unclose *vt* aperīre.
unclothe *vt* nūdāre, vestem dētrahere (*dat*).
unclothed *adj* nūdus.
unclouded *adj* serēnus.
uncoil *vt* explicāre, ēvolvere.
uncomely *adj* dēfōrmis, turpis.
uncomfortable *adj* incommodus, molestus.
uncomfortably *adv* incommodē.
uncommitted *adj* vacuus.
uncommon *adj* rārus, īnsolitus, inūsitātus;
(*eminent*) ēgregius, singulāris, eximius.
uncommonly *adv* rārō; ēgregiē, ūnicē.
uncommonness *n* īnsolentia *f*.
uncommunicative *adj* tēctus, taciturnus.
uncomplaining *adj* patiēns.
uncompleted *adj* imperfectus.
uncompromising *adj* dūrus, rigidus.
unconcern *n* sēcūritās *f*.
unconcerned *adj* sēcūrus, ōtiōsus.
unconcernedly *adv* lentē.
uncondemned *adj* indemnātus.
unconditional *adj* absolūtus.
unconditionally *adv* nullā condiciōne.
uncongenial *adj* ingrātus.
unconnected *adj* sēparātus, disiūnctus;
(*style*) dissolūtus.
unconquerable *adj* invictus.
unconquered *adj* invictus.
unconscionable *adj* improbus.
unconscionably *adv* improbē.
unconscious *adj*: **~ of** īnscius (*gen*), ignārus
(*gen*); **become ~** sōpīrī, animō linquī.
unconsciousness *n* sopor *m*.
unconsecrated *adj* profānus.
unconsidered *adj* neglectus.
unconstitutional *adj* illicitus.
unconstitutionally *adv* contrā lēgēs, contrā
rem pūblicam.
uncontaminated *adj* pūrus, incorruptus,
integer.
uncontrollable *adj* impotēns, effrēnātus.
uncontrollably *adv* effrēnātē.

uncontrolled *adj* līber, solūtus.
unconventional *adj* īnsolitus, solūtus.
unconvicted *adj* indemnātus.
unconvincing *adj* incrēdibilis, nōn vērī
similis.
uncooked *adj* crūdus.
uncorrupted *adj* incorruptus, integer.
uncouple *vt* disiungere.
uncouth *adj* horridus, agrestis, inurbānus.
uncouthly *adv* inurbānē.
uncouthness *n* inhūmānitās *f*, rūsticitās *f*.
uncover *vt* dētegere, aperīre, nūdāre.
uncritical *adj* indoctus, crēdulus.
uncultivated *adj* incultus; (*fig*) agrestis,
rūsticus, impolītus.
uncultured *adj* agrestis, rudis.
uncut *adj* intōnsus.
undamaged *adj* integer, inviolātus.
undaunted *adj* intrepidus, fortis.
undecayed *adj* incorruptus.
undeceive *vt* errōrem tollere (*dat*), errōrem
ēripere (*dat*).
undecided *adj* dubius, anceps; (*case*) integer.
undecked *adj* (*ship*) apertus.
undefended *adj* indēfēnsus, nūdus.
undefiled *adj* integer, incontāminātus.
undemonstrative *adj* taciturnus.
undeniable *adj* certus.
undeniably *adv* sīne dubiō.
undependable *adj* inconstāns, mōbilis.
under *adv* īnfrā, subter ♦ *prep* sub (*abl*), īnfrā
(*acc*); (*number*) intrā (*acc*); (*motion*) sub (*acc*);
~ arms in armīs; **~ colour** (pretext of) speciē
(*gen*), per speciem (*gen*); **~ my leadership** mē
duce; **~ the circumstances** cum haec ita sint;
labour ~ labōrāre ex; **~ the eyes of** in
cōnspectū (+ *gen*); **~ the leadership of** *abl* +
duce.
underage *adj* impūbēs.
undercurrent *n*: **an ~ of** lātens.
underestimate *vt* minōris aestimāre.
undergarment *n* subūcula *f*.
undergo *vt* subīre, patī, ferre.
underground *adj* subterrāneus ♦ *adv* sub
terrā.
undergrowth *n* virgulta *ntpl*.
underhand *adj* clandestīnus, fūrtīvus ♦ *adv*
clam, fūrtim.
underline *vt* subscrībere.
underling *n* minister *m*, satelles *m/f*.
undermine *vt* subruere; (*fig*) labefacere,
labefactāre.
undermost *adj* īnfimus.
underneath *adv* īnfrā ♦ *prep* sub (*abl*), īnfrā
(*acc*); (*motion*) sub (*acc*).
underprop *vt* fulcīre.
underrate *vt* obtrectāre, extenuāre, minōris
aestimāre.
understand *vt* intellegere, comprehendere;
(*be told*) accipere, comperīre; (*in a sense*)
interpretārī; **~ Latin** Latīnē scīre.
understandable *adj* crēdibilis.
understanding *adj* sapiēns, perītus ♦ *n*

intellegentia f; (faculty) mēns f, intellectus m; (agreement) cōnsēnsus m; (condition) condiciō f.
undertake vt suscipere, sūmere, adīre ad; (business) condūcere; (case) agere, dēfendere; (promise) recipere, spondēre.
undertaker n dissignātor m.
undertaking n inceptum nt, inceptiō f.
undervalue vt minōris aestimāre.
underwood n virgulta ntpl.
underworld n īnferī mpl.
undeserved adj immeritus, iniūstus.
undeservedly adv immeritō, indignē.
undeserving adj indignus.
undesigned adj fortuītus.
undesignedly adv fortuītō, temerē.
undesirable adj odiōsus, ingrātus.
undeterred adj immōtus.
undeveloped adj immātūrus.
undeviating adj dīrēctus.
undigested adj crūdus.
undignified adj levis, inhonestus.
undiminished adj integer.
undiscernible adj invīsus, obscūrus.
undisciplined adj lascīvus, immoderātus; (MIL) inexercitātus.
undiscovered adj ignōtus.
undisguised adj apertus.
undisguisedly adv palam, apertē.
undismayed adj impavidus, intrepidus.
undisputed adj certus.
undistinguished adj ignōbilis, inglōrius.
undisturbed adj tranquillus, placidus.
undo vt (knot) expedīre, resolvere; (sewing) dissuere; (fig) īnfectum reddere.
undoing n ruīna f.
undone adj infectus; (ruined) perditus; **be ~** perīre, disperīre; **hopelessly ~** dēperditus.
undoubted adj certus.
undoubtedly adv sine dubiō, plānē.
undress vt exuere, vestem dētrahere (dat).
undressed adj nūdus.
undue adj nimius, immoderātus, inīquus.
undulate vi fluctuāre.
undulation n spīra f.
unduly adv nimis, plūs aequō.
undutiful adj impius.
undutifully adv impiē.
undutifulness n impietās f.
undying adj immortālis, aeternus.
unearth vt ēruere, dētegere.
unearthly adj mōnstruōsus, dīvīnus, hūmānō māior.
uneasily adv aegrē.
uneasiness n sollicitūdō f, perturbātiō f.
uneasy adj sollicitus, anxius, inquiētus.
uneducated adj illitterātus, indoctus, rudis; **be ~** litterās nescīre.
unemployed adj ōtiōsus.
unemployment n cessātiō f.
unencumbered adj expedītus, līber.
unending adj perpetuus, sempiternus.
unendowed adj indōtātus.

unendurable adj intolerandus, intolerābilis.
unenjoyable adj iniūcundus, molestus.
unenlightened adj rudis, inērudītus.
unenterprising adj iners.
unenviable adj nōn invidendus.
unequal adj impār, dispār.
unequalled adj ūnicus, singulāris.
unequally adv inaequāliter, inīquē.
unequivocal adj apertus, plānus.
unerring adj certus.
unerringly adv certē.
unessential adj adventīcius, supervacāneus.
uneven adj impār; (surface) asper, inīquus, inaequābilis.
unevenly adv inīquē, inaequāliter.
unevenness n inīquitās f, asperitās f.
unexamined adj (case) incognitus.
unexampled adj inaudītus, ūnicus, singulāris.
unexceptionable adj ēmendātus; (authority) certissimus.
unexpected adj imprōvīsus, inopīnātus, īnsperātus.
unexpectedly adv dē imprōvīsō, ex īnspērātō, inopīnātō, necopīnātō.
unexplored adj inexplōrātus.
unfading adj perennis, vīvus.
unfailing adj perennis, certus, perpetuus.
unfailingly adv semper.
unfair adj inīquus, iniūstus.
unfairly adv inīquē, iniūstē.
unfairness n inīquitās f, iniūstitia f.
unfaithful adj īnfidēlis, īnfīdus, perfidus.
unfaithfully adv īnfidēliter.
unfaithfulness n īnfidēlitās f.
unfamiliar adj novus, ignōtus, īnsolēns; (sight) invīsitātus.
unfamiliarity n īnsolentia f.
unfashionable adj obsolētus.
unfasten vt solvere, refīgere.
unfathomable adj īnfīnītus, profundus.
unfavourable adj inīquus, adversus, importūnus.
unfavourably adv inīquē, male; **be ~ disposed** āversō animō esse.
unfed adj ieiūnus.
unfeeling adj dūrus, crūdēlis, ferreus.
unfeelingly adv crūdēliter.
unfeigned adj sincērus, vērus, simplex.
unfeignedly adv sincērē, vērē.
unfilial adj impius.
unfinished adj īnfectus, imperfectus.
unfit adj inūtilis, incommodus, aliēnus.
unfix vt refīgere.
unflinching adj impavidus, firmus.
unfold vt explicāre, ēvolvere; (story) expōnere, ēnārrāre.
unfolding n explicātiō f.
unforeseen adj imprōvīsus.
unforgettable adj memorābilis.
unforgiving adj implācābilis.
unformed adj īnfōrmis.
unfortified adj immūnītus, nūdus.

unfortunate *adj* īnfēlīx, īnfortūnātus.
unfortunately *adv* īnfēlīciter, male; ~ **you did
not come** male accidit quod nōn vēnistī.
unfounded *adj* inānis, vānus.
unfrequented *adj* dēsertus.
unfriendliness *n* inimīcitia *f.*
unfriendly *adj* inimīcus, malevolus; **in an ~
manner** inimīcē.
unfruitful *adj* sterilis; (*fig*) inānis, vānus.
unfruitfulness *n* sterilitās *f.*
unfulfilled *adj* īnfectus, inritus.
unfurl *vt* explicāre, pandere.
unfurnished *adj* nūdus.
ungainly *adj* agrestis, rūsticus.
ungallant *adj* inurbānus, parum cōmis.
ungenerous *adj* illīberālis; ~ **conduct**
illīberālitās *f.*
ungentlemanly *adj* illīberālis.
ungirt *adj* discinctus.
ungodliness *n* impietās *f.*
ungodly *adj* impius.
ungovernable *adj* impotēns, indomitus.
ungovernableness *n* impotentia *f.*
ungraceful *adj* inconcinnus, inēlegāns.
ungracefully *adv* inēleganter.
ungracious *adj* inhūmānus, petulāns,
importūnus.
ungraciously *adv* acerbē.
ungrammatical *adj* barbarus; **be ~**
soloecismum facere.
ungrateful *adj* ingrātus.
ungrudging *adj* largus, nōn invītus.
ungrudgingly *adv* sine invidiā.
unguarded *adj* intūtus; (*word*) incautus,
incōnsultus.
unguardedly *adv* temerē, incōnsultē.
unguent *n* unguentum *nt.*
unhallowed *adj* profānus, impius.
unhand *vt* mittere.
unhandy *adj* inhabilis.
unhappily *adv* īnfēlīciter, miserē.
unhappiness *n* miseria *f*, tristitia *f*, maestitia
f.
unhappy *adj* īnfēlix, miser, tristis.
unharmed *adj* incolumis, integer, salvus.
unharness *vt* disiungere.
unhealthiness *n* valētūdō *f*; (*climate*) gravitās
f.
unhealthy *adj* invalidus, aeger; (*climate*)
gravis, pestilens.
unheard *adj* inaudītus; (*law*) indictā causā.
unheard-of *adj* inaudītus.
unheeded *adj* neglectus.
unheeding *adj* immemor, sēcūrus.
unhelpful *adj* difficilis, invītus.
unhesitating *adj* audāx, prōmptus.
unhesitatingly *adv* sine dubitātiōne.
unhewn *adj* rudis.
unhindered *adj* expedītus.
unhinged *adj* mente captus.
unhistorical *adj* fictus, commentīcius.
unholiness *n* impietās *f.*
unholy *adj* impius.

unhonoured *adj* inhonōrātus.
unhoped-for *adj* īnspērātus.
unhorse *vt* excutere, equō dēicere.
unhurt *adj* integer, incolumis.
unicorn *n* monocerōs *m.*
uniform *adj* aequābilis, aequālis; ♦ *n* īnsignia
ntpl; (*MIL*) sagum *nt*; **in ~** sagātus; **put on ~** saga
sūmere.
uniformity *n* aequābilitās *f*, cōnstantia *f.*
uniformly *adv* aequābiliter, ūnō tenōre.
unify *vt* coniungere.
unimaginative *adj* hebes, stolidus.
unimpaired *adj* integer, incolumis, illībātus.
unimpeachable *adj* (*character*) integer; (*style*)
ēmendātus.
unimportant *adj* levis, nullīus mōmentī.
uninformed *adj* indoctus, ignārus.
uninhabitable *adj* inhabitābilis.
uninhabited *adj* dēsertus.
uninitiated *adj* profānus; (*fig*) rudis.
uninjured *adj* integer, incolumis.
unintelligent *adj* īnsipiēns, tardus, excors.
unintelligible *adj* obscūrus.
unintelligibly *adv* obscūrē.
unintentionally *adv* imprūdēns, temerē.
uninteresting *adj* frīgidus, āridus.
uninterrupted *adj* continuus, perpetuus.
uninterruptedly *adv* continenter, sine ullā
intermissiōne.
uninvited *adj* invocātus; ~ **guest** umbra *f.*
uninviting *adj* iniūcundus, invenustus.
union *n* coniūnctiō *f*; (*social*) cōnsociātiō *f*,
societās *f*; (*POL*) foederātae cīvitātēs *fpl*;
(*agreement*) concordia *f*, cōnsēnsus *m*;
(*marriage*) coniugium *nt.*
unique *adj* ūnicus, ēgregius, singulāris.
unison *n* concentus *m*; (*fig*) concordia *f*,
cōnsēnsus *m.*
unit *n* ūniō *f.*
unite *vt* coniungere, cōnsociāre, cōpulāre; ♦ *vi*
coīre; cōnsentīre; cōnspīrāre; (*rivers*)
cōnfluere.
unity *n* (*concord*) concordia *f*, cōnsēnsus *m.*
universal *adj* ūniversus, commūnis.
universally *adv* ūniversus, omnis; (*place*)
ubīque.
universe *n* mundus *m*, rērum nātūra *f.*
university *n* acadēmia *f.*
unjust *adj* iniūstus, inīquus.
unjustifiable *adj* indignus, inexcūsābilis.
unjustly *adv* iniūstē, iniūriā.
unkempt *adj* horridus.
unkind *adj* inhūmānus, inīquus.
unkindly *adv* inhūmānē, asperē.
unkindness *n* inhūmānitās *f.*
unknowingly *adv* imprūdēns, īnscius.
unknown *adj* ignōtus, incognitus; (*fame*)
obscūrus.
unlawful *adj* vetitus, iniūriōsus.
unlawfully *adv* iniūriōsē, iniūriā.
unlearn *vt* dēdiscere.
unlearned *adj* indoctus, inēruditus.
unless *conj* nisī.

unlettered *adj* illitterātus.
unlike *adj* dissimilis (+ *gen or dat*), dispār.
unlikely *adj* nōn vērīsimilis.
unlimited *adj* īnfīnītus, immēnsus.
unload *vt* exonerāre, deonerāre; (*from ship*)
  expōnere.
unlock *vt* reserāre, reclūdere.
unlooked-for *adj* īnspērātus, inexpectātus.
unloose *vt* solvere, exsolvere.
unlovely *adj* invenustus.
unluckily *adv* īnfēlīciter.
unlucky *adj* īnfēlīx, īnfortūnātus; (*day*) āter.
unmake *vt* īnfectum reddere.
unman *vt* mollīre, frangere, dēbilitāre.
unmanageable *adj* inhabilis.
unmanly *adj* mollis, ēnervātus, muliebris.
unmanneriness *n* importūnitās *f*,
  inhūmānitās *f*.
unmannerly *adj* importūnus, inhūmānus.
unmarried *adj* (*man*) caelebs; (*woman*) vidua.
unmask *vt* nūdāre, dētegere.
unmatched *adj* ūnicus, singulāris.
unmeaning *adj* inānis.
unmeasured *adj* īnfīnītus, immoderātus.
unmeet *adj* parum idōneus.
unmelodious *adj* absonus, absurdus.
unmentionable *adj* īnfandus.
unmentioned *adj* indictus; **leave ~** ōmittere.
unmerciful *adj* immisericors, inclēmēns.
unmercifully *adv* inclēmenter.
unmerited *adj* immeritus, indignus.
unmindful *adj* immemor.
unmistakable *adj* certus, manifestus.
unmistakably *adv* sine dubiō, certē.
unmitigated *adj* merus.
unmixed *adj* pūrus.
unmolested *adj* intāctus.
unmoor *vt* solvere.
unmoved *adj* immōtus.
unmusical *adj* absonus, absurdus.
unmutilated *adj* integer.
unnatural *adj* (*event*) mōnstruōsus; (*feelings*)
  impius, inhūmānus; (*style*) arcessītus,
  pūtidus.
unnaturally *adv* contrā nātūram; impiē,
  inhūmānē; pūtidē.
unnavigable *adj* innāvigābilis.
unnecessarily *adv* nimis.
unnecessary *adj* inūtilis, supervacāneus.
unnerve *vt* dēbilitāre, frangere.
unnoticed *adj*: **be ~** latēre, fallere.
unnumbered *adj* innumerus.
unobjectionable *adj* honestus, culpae expers.
unobservant *adj* tardus.
unobserved *adj*: **be ~** latēre, fallere.
unobstructed *adj* apertus, pūrus.
unobtrusive *adj* verēcundus; **be ~** fallere.
unobtrusiveness *n* verēcundia *f*.
unoccupied *adj* vacuus, ōtiōsus.
unoffending *adj* innocēns.
unofficial *adj* prīvātus.
unorthodox *adj* abnōrmis.
unostentatious *adj* modestus, verēcundus.

unostentatiously *adv* nullā iactātiōne.
unpaid *adj* (*services*) grātuītus; (*money*)
  dēbitus.
unpalatable *adj* amārus; (*fig*) iniūcundus,
  īnsuāvis.
unparalleled *adj* ūnicus, inaudītus.
unpardonable *adj* inexcūsābilis.
unpatriotic *adj* impius.
unpitying *adj* immisericors, ferreus.
unpleasant *adj* iniūcundus, ingrātus,
  īnsuāvis, gravis, molestus.
unpleasantly *adv* iniūcundē, ingrātē,
  graviter.
unpleasantness *n* iniūcunditās *f*, molestia *f*.
unpleasing *adj* ingrātus, invenustus.
unploughed *adj* inarātus.
unpoetical *adj* pedester.
unpolished *adj* impolītus; (*person*) incultus,
  agrestis, inurbānus; (*style*) inconditus, rudis.
unpopular *adj* invidiōsus, invīsus.
unpopularity *n* invidia *f*, odium *nt*.
unpractised *adj* inexercitātus, imperītus.
unprecedented *adj* īnsolēns, novus,
  inaudītus.
unprejudiced *adj* integer, aequus.
unpremeditated *adj* repentīnus, subitus.
unprepared *adj* imparātus.
unprepossessing *adj* invenustus, illepidus.
unpretentious *adj* modestus, verēcundus.
unprincipled *adj* improbus, levis, prāvus.
unproductive *adj* infēcundus, sterilis.
unprofitable *adj* inūtilis, vānus.
unprofitably *adv* frustrā, ab rē.
unpropitious *adj* īnfēlīx, adversus.
unpropitiously *adv* malīs ōminibus.
unprotected *adj* indēfēnsus, intūtus, nūdus.
unprovoked *adj* ultrō (*adv*).
unpunished *adj* impūnītus ♦ *adv* impūne.
unqualified *adj* nōn idōneus; (*unrestricted*)
  absolūtus.
unquestionable *adj* certus.
unquestionably *adv* facile, certē.
unquestioning *adj* crēdulus.
unravel *vt* retexere; (*fig*) ēnōdāre, explicāre.
unready *adj* imparātus.
unreal *adj* falsus, vānus.
unreality *n* vānitās *f*.
unreasonable *adj* inīquus, importūnus.
unreasonableness *n* inīquitās *f*.
unreasonably *adv* inīquē.
unreasoning *adj* stolidus, temerārius.
unreclaimed *adj* (*land*) incultus.
unrefined *adj* impolītus, inurbānus, rudis.
unregistered *adj* incēnsus.
unrelated *adj* aliēnus.
unrelenting *adj* implācābilis, inexōrābilis.
unreliable *adj* incertus, levis.
unreliably *adv* leviter.
unrelieved *adj* perpetuus, adsiduus.
unremitting *adj* adsiduus.
unrequited *adj* inultus, inānis.
unreservedly *adv* apertē, sine ullā
  exceptiōne.

unresponsive *adj* hebes.
unrest *n* inquiēs *f*, sollicitūdō *f*.
unrestrained *adj* līber, impotēns, effrēnātus, immoderātus.
unrestricted *adj* līber, absolūtus.
unrevenged *adj* inultus.
unrewarded *adj* inhonōrātus.
unrewarding *adj* ingrātus, vānus.
unrighteous *adj* iniūstus, impius.
unrighteously *adv* iniūstē, impiē.
unrighteousness *n* impietās *f*.
unripe *adj* immātūrus, crūdus.
unrivalled *adj* ēgregius, singulāris, ūnicus.
unroll *vt* ēvolvere, explicāre.
unromantic *adj* pedester.
unruffled *adj* immōtus, tranquillus.
unruliness *n* licentia *f*, impotentia *f*.
unruly *adj* effrēnātus, impotēns, immoderātus.
unsafe *adj* perīculōsus, dubius; (*structure*) īnstābilis.
unsaid *adj* indictus.
unsatisfactorily *adv* nōn ex sententiā, male.
unsatisfactory *adj* parum idōneus, malus.
unsatisfied *adj* parum contentus.
unsavoury *adj* īnsuāvis, taeter.
unscathed *adj* incolumis, integer.
unschooled *adj* indoctus, inērudītus.
unscrupulous *adj* improbus, impudēns.
unscrupulously *adv* improbē, impudenter.
unscrupulousness *n* improbitās *f*, impudentia *f*.
unseal *vt* resignāre, solvere.
unseasonable *adj* intempestīvus, importūnus.
unseasonableness *n* incommoditās *f*.
unseasonably *adv* intempestīvē, importūnē.
unseasoned *adj* (*food*) nōn condītus; (*wood*) viridis.
unseat *vt* (*rider*) excutere.
unseaworthy *adj* īnfirmus.
unseeing *adj* caecus.
unseemly *adj* indecōrus.
unseen *adj* invīsus; (*ever before*) invīsitātus.
unselfish *adj* innocēns, probus, līberālis.
unselfishly *adv* līberāliter.
unselfishness *n* innocentia *f*, līberālitās *f*.
unserviceable *adj* inūtilis.
unsettle *vt* ad incertum revocāre, turbāre, sollicitāre.
unsettled *adj* incertus, dubius; (*mind*) sollicitus, suspēnsus; (*times*) turbidus.
unsew *vt* dissuere.
unshackle *vt* expedīre, solvere.
unshaken *adj* immōtus, firmus, stabilis.
unshapely *adj* dēfōrmis.
unshaven *adj* intōnsus.
unsheathe *vt* dēstringere, stringere.
unshod *adj* nūdis pedibus.
unshorn *adj* intōnsus.
unsightliness *n* dēfōrmitās *f*, turpitūdō *f*.
unsightly *adj* foedus, dēfōrmis.
unskilful *adj* indoctus, īnscītus, incallidus.

unskilfully *adv* indoctē, īnscītē, incallide.
unskilfulness *n* īnscītia *f*, imperītia *f*.
unskilled *adj* imperītus, indoctus; ~ **in** imperitus (+ *gen*).
unslaked *adj* (*lime*) vīvus; (*thirst*) inexplētus.
unsociable *adj* īnsociābilis, difficilis.
unsoiled *adj* integer, pūrus.
unsolicited *adj* voluntārius ♦ *adv* ultrō.
unsophisticated *adj* simplex, ingenuus.
unsound *adj* īnfirmus; (*mind*) īnsānus; (*opinion*) falsus, perversus.
unsoundness *n* īnfirmitās *f*; īnsānitās *f*; prāvitās *f*.
unsparing *adj* inclēmēns, immisericors; (*lavish*) prōdigus.
unsparingly *adv* inclēmenter; prōdigē.
unspeakable *adj* īnfandus, incrēdibilis.
unspeakably *adv* incrēdibiliter.
unspoilt *adj* integer.
unspoken *adj* indictus, tacitus.
unspotted *adj* integer, pūrus.
unstable *adj* īnstabilis; (*fig*) incōnstāns, levis.
unstained *adj* pūrus, incorruptus, integer.
unstatesmanlike *adj* illīberālis.
unsteadily *adv* incōnstanter; **walk** ~ titubāre.
unsteadiness *n* (*fig*) incōnstantia *f*.
unsteady *adj* īnstabilis; (*fig*) incōnstāns.
unstitch *vt* dissuere.
unstring *vt* retendere.
unstudied *adj* simplex.
unsubdued *adj* invictus.
unsubstantial *adj* levis, inānis.
unsuccessful *adj* īnfēlīx; (*effort*) inritus; **be** ~ offendere; **I am** ~ mihī nōn succēdit.
unsuccessfully *adv* īnfēlīciter, rē īnfectā.
unsuitable *adj* incommodus, aliēnus, importūnus; **it is** ~ dēdecet.
unsuitableness *n* incommoditās *f*.
unsuitably *adv* incommodē, ineptē.
unsuited *adj* parum idōneus.
unsullied *adj* pūrus, incorruptus.
unsure *adj* incertus, dubius.
unsurpassable *adj* inexsuperābilis.
unsurpassed *adj* ūnicus, singulāris.
unsuspected *adj* latēns, nōn suspectus; **be** ~ latēre, in suspiciōnem nōn venīre.
unsuspecting *adj* imprōvidus, imprūdēns.
unsuspicious *adj* nōn suspicāx, crēdulus.
unswerving *adj* cōnstāns.
unsworn *adj* iniūrātus.
unsymmetrical *adj* inaequālis.
untainted *adj* incorruptus, integer.
untamable *adj* indomitus.
untamed *adj* indomitus, ferus.
untaught *adj* indoctus, rudis.
unteach *vt* dēdocēre.
unteachable *adj* indocilis.
untenable *adj* inānis, īnfirmus.
unthankful *adj* ingrātus.
unthankfully *adv* ingrātē.
unthankfulness *n* ingrātus animus *m*.
unthinkable *adj* incrēdibilis.
unthinking *adj* incōnsīderātus, imprōvidus.

unthriftily adv prōdigē.
unthrifty adj prōdigus, profūsus.
untidily adv neglegenter.
untidiness n neglegentia f.
untidy adj neglegēns, inconcinnus, squālidus.
untie vt solvere.
until conj dum, dōnec ♦ prep usque ad (acc), in (acc); ~ **now** adhūc.
untilled adj incultus.
untimely adj intempestīvus, immātūrus, importūnus.
untiring adj impiger; (effort) adsiduus.
unto prep ad (acc), in (acc).
untold adj innumerus.
untouched adj intāctus, integer.
untoward adj adversus, malus.
untrained adj inexercitātus, imperītus, rudis.
untried adj intemptātus, inexpertus; (trial) incognitus.
untrodden adj āvius.
untroubled adj tranquillus, placidus, quiētus; (mind) sēcūrus.
untrue adj falsus, fictus; (disloyal) īnfīdus, īnfidēlis.
untrustworthy adj īnfīdus, mōbilis.
untruth n mendācium nt, falsum nt.
untruthful adj mendāx, falsus.
untruthfully adv falsō, falsē.
untuneful adj absonus.
unturned adj: **leave no stone** ~ nihil intemptātum relinquere, omnia experīrī.
untutored adj indoctus, incultus.
unused adj (person) īnsuētus, īnsolitus; (thing) integer.
unusual adj īnsolitus, inūsitātus, īnsolēns, novus.
unusually adv īnsolenter, praeter cōnsuētūdinem.
unusualness n īnsolentia f, novitās f.
unutterable adj īnfandus, inēnārrābilis.
unvarnished adj (fig) simplex, nūdus.
unveil vt (fig) aperīre, patefacere.
unversed adj ignārus (gen), imperītus (gen).
unwanted adj supervacāneus.
unwarily adv imprudenter, incautē, incōnsultē.
unwariness n imprūdentia f.
unwarlike adj imbellis.
unwarrantable adj inīquus, iniūstus.
unwarrantably adv iniūriā.
unwary adj imprūdēns, incautus, incōnsultus.
unwavering adj stabilis, immōtus.
unwearied, unwearying adj indēfessus, adsiduus.
unweave vt retexere.
unwedded adj (man) caelebs; (woman) vidua.
unwelcome adj ingrātus.
unwell adj aeger, aegrōtus.
unwept adj indēflētus.
unwholesome adj pestilēns, gravis.
unwieldy adj inhabilis.
unwilling adj invītus; **be** ~ nolle.
unwillingly adv invītus.

unwind vt ēvolvere, retexere.
unwise adj stultus, īnsipiēns, imprūdēns.
unwisely adv īnsipienter, imprūdenter.
unwittingly adv imprūdēns, īnsciēns.
unwonted adj īnsolitus, inūsitātus.
unworthily adv indignē.
unworthiness n indignitās f.
unworthy adj indignus (+ abl).
unwounded adj intāctus, integer.
unwrap vt ēvolvere, explicāre.
unwritten adj nōn scrīptus; ~ **law** mōs m.
unwrought adj īnfectus, rudis.
unyielding adj dūrus, firmus, inexōrābilis.
unyoke vt disiungere.
up adv sūrsum; ~ **and down** sūrsum deōrsum; ~ **to** usque ad (acc), tenus (abl, after noun); **bring** ~ subvehere; (child) ēducāre; **climb** ~ ēscendere; **come** ~ **to** aequāre; **lift** ~ ērigere, sublevāre; **from childhood** ~ ā puerō; **it is all** ~ **with** āctum est dē; **well** ~ **in** gnārus (gen), perītus (gen); **what is he** ~ **to?** quid struit? ♦ prep (motion) in (acc) ♦ n: ~**s and downs** (fig) vicissitūdinēs fpl.
upbraid vt exprobrāre (dat pers, acc charge); obicere (dat and acc), increpāre, castīgāre.
upbringing n ēducātiō f.
upheaval n ēversiō f.
upheave vt ēvertere.
uphill adj acclīvis ♦ adv adversō colle, in adversum collem.
uphold vt sustinēre, tuērī, servāre.
upholstery n supellex f.
upkeep n impēnsa f.
upland adj montānus.
uplift vt extollere, sublevāre.
upon prep in (abl), super (abl); (motion) in (acc), super (acc); (dependence) ex (abl); ~ **this** quō factō.
upper adj superior; **gain the** ~ **hand** superāre, vincere.
uppermost adj suprēmus, summus.
uppish adj superbus.
upright adj rēctus, ērēctus; (character) integer, probus, honestus.
uprightly adv rēctē; integrē.
uprightness n integritās f.
upriver adj, adv adversō flūmine.
uproar n tumultus m; clāmor m.
uproarious adj tumultuōsus.
uproariously adv tumultuōsē.
uproot vt ērādīcāre, exstirpāre, ēruere.
upset vt ēvertere, invertere, subvertere; ~ **the apple cart** plaustrum percellere ♦ adj (fig) perturbātus.
upshot n ēventus m.
upside-down adv: **turn** ~ ēvertere, invertere; (fig) miscēre.
upstart n novus homō m ♦ adj repentīnus.
upstream adj, adv adversō flūmine.
upward(s) adv sūrsum; ~ **of** (number) amplius.
urban adj urbānus, oppidānus.
urbane adj urbānus, cōmis.
urbanely adv urbānē, cōmiter.

V, v

urbanity n urbānitās f.

urchin n (boy) puerulus m; (animal) echīnus m.

urge vt urgēre, impellere; (speech) hortārī, incitāre; (advice) suādēre; (request) sollicitāre; ~ **on** incitāre ♦ n impulsus m; dēsīderium nt.

urgency n necessitās f.

urgent adj praesēns, gravis; **be** ~ instāre.

urgently adv graviter.

urn n urna f.

usage n mōs m, īnstitūtum nt, ūsus m.

use n ūsus m; (custom) mōs m, cōnsuētūdō f; **be of** ~ ūsuī esse, prōdesse, condūcere; **out of** ~ desuētus; **go out of** ~ exolēscere; **in common** ~ ūsitātus; **it's no** ~ nīl agis, nīl agimus ♦ vt ūtī (abl); (improperly) abūtī; (for a purpose) adhibēre; (word) ūsurpāre; ~ **up** cōnsūmere, exhaurīre; **~d to** adsuētus (dat); solēre (+ infin); **I ~d to do** faciebam.

useful adj ūtilis; **be** ~ ūsuī esse.

usefully adv ūtiliter.

usefulness n ūtilitās f.

useless adj inūtilis; (thing) inānis, inritus; **be** ~ nihil valēre.

uselessly adv inūtiliter, frustrā.

uselessness n inānitās f.

usher n (court) apparitor m; (theatre) dēsīgnātor m ♦ vt: ~ **in** indūcere, intrōdūcere.

usual adj ūsitātus, solitus; **as** ~ ut adsolet, ut fert cōnsuētūdō, ex cōnsuētūdine; **out of the** ~ īnsolitus, extrā ōrdinem.

usually adv ferē, plērumque; **he** ~ **comes** venīre solet.

usufruct n ūsus et fructus m.

usurer n faenerātor m.

usurp vt occupāre, invādere in (acc), ūsurpāre.

usurpation n occupātō f.

usury n faenerātiō f, ūsūra f; **practise** ~ faenerārī.

utensil n īnstrūmentum nt, vās nt.

utility n ūtilitās f, commodum nt.

utilize vt ūtī (abl); (for a purpose) adhibēre.

utmost adj extrēmus, summus; **at the** ~ summum; **do one's** ~ omnibus vīribus contendere.

utter adj tōtus, extrēmus, summus ♦ vt ēmittere, ēdere, ēloquī, prōnūntiāre.

utterance n dictum nt; (process) prōnūntiātiō f.

utterly adv funditus, omnīnō, penitus.

uttermost adj extrēmus, ultimus.

vacancy n inānitās f; (office) vacuitās f; **there is a** ~ locus vacat; **elect to fill a** ~ sufficere.

vacant adj inānis, vacuus; **be** ~ vacāre.

vacate vt vacuum facere.

vacation n fēriae fpl.

vacillate vi vacillāre, dubitāre.

vacillation n dubitātiō f.

vacuity n inānitās f.

vacuous adj vacuus.

vacuum n ināne nt.

vagabond n grassātor m ♦ adj vagus.

vagary n libīdō f.

vagrancy n errātiō f.

vagrant n grassātor m, vagus m.

vague adj incertus, dubius.

vaguely adv incertē.

vain n vānus, inānis, inritus; (person) glōriōsus; **in** ~ frustrā.

vainglorious adj glōriōsus.

vainglory n glōria f, iactantia f.

vainly adv frustrā, nēquīquam.

vale n vallis f.

valet n cubiculārius m.

valiant adj fortis, ācer.

valiantly adv fortiter, ācriter.

valid adj ratus; (argument) gravis, firmus.

validity n vīs f, auctōritās f.

valley n vallis f.

valorous adj fortis.

valour n virtūs f.

valuable adj pretiōsus.

valuation n aestimātiō f.

value n pretium nt; (fig) vīs f, honor m ♦ vt aestimāre; (esteem) dīligere; ~ **highly** māgnī aestimāre; ~ **little** parvī aestimāre, parvī facere.

valueless adj vīlis, minimī pretī.

valuer n aestimātor m.

van n (in battle) prīma aciēs f; (on march) prīmum agmen nt.

vanguard n prīmum agmen nt.

vanish vi diffugere, ēvānēscere, dīlābī.

vanity n (unreality) vānitās f; (conceit) glōria f.

vanquish vt vincere, superāre, dēvincere.

vanquisher n victor m.

vantage n (ground) locus superior m.

vapid adj vapidus, īnsulsus.

vapidly adv īnsulsē.

vaporous adj nebulōsus.

vapour n vapor m, nebula f; (from earth) exhālātiō f.

variable adj varius, mūtābilis.

variableness n mūtābilitās f, incōnstantia f.

variance n discordia f, dissēnsiō f, discrepantia f; **at** ~ discors; **be at** ~ dissidēre,

inter sē discrepāre; **set at ~** aliēnāre.
variant *adj* varius.
variation *n* varietās *f*, vicissitūdō *f*.
variegate *vt* variāre.
variegated *adj* varius.
variety *n* varietās *f*; (*number*) multitūdō *f*;
(*kind*) genus *nt*; **a ~ of** dīversī.
various *adj* varius, dīversus.
variously *adv* variē.
varlet *n* verberō *m*.
varnish *n* pigmentum *nt*; (*fig*) fūcus *m*.
varnished *adj* (*fig*) fūcātus.
vary *vt* variāre, mūtāre; (*decorate*) distinguere
♦ *vi* mūtārī.
vase *n* vās *nt*.
vassal *n* ambāctus *m*; (*fig*) cliēns *m*.
vast *adj* vastus, immānis, ingēns, immēnsus.
vastly *adv* valdē.
vastness *n* māgnitūdō *f*, immēnsitās *f*.
vat *n* cūpa *f*.
vault *n* (ARCH) fornix *f*; (*jump*) saltus *m* ♦ *vi*
salīre.
vaulted *adj* fornicātus.
vaunt *vt* iactāre, ostentāre ♦ *vi* sē iactāre,
glōriārī.
vaunting *n* ostentātiō *f*, glōria *f* ♦ *adj*
glōriōsus.
veal *n* vitulīna *f*.
vedette *n* excursor *m*.
veer *vi* sē vertere, flectī.
vegetable *n* holus *nt*.
vehemence *n* vīs *f*, violentia *f*; (*passion*) ārdor
m, impetus *m*.
vehement *adj* vehemēns, violentus, ācer.
vehemently *adv* vehementer, ācriter.
vehicle *n* vehiculum *nt*.
Veii *n* Veiī, Vēiōrum *mpl*.
veil *n* rīca *f*; (*bridal*) flammeum *nt*; (*fig*)
integumentum *nt* ♦ *vt* vēlāre, tegere.
vein *n* vēna *f*.
vellum *n* membrāna *f*.
velocity *n* celeritās *f*, vēlōcitās *f*.
venal *adj* vēnālis.
vend *vt* vēndere.
vendetta *n* simultās *f*.
vendor *n* caupō *m*.
veneer *n* (*fig*) speciēs *f*, fūcus *m*.
venerable *adj* gravis, augustus.
venerate *vt* colere, venerārī.
veneration *n* venerātiō *f*, cultus *m*.
venerator *n* cultor *m*.
vengeance *n* ultiō *f*, poena *f*; **take ~ on** ulcīscī,
vindicāre in (*acc*); **take ~ for** ulcīscī,
vindicāre.
vengeful *adj* ultor.
venial *adj* ignōscendus.
venison *n* dāma *f*, ferīna *f*.
venom *n* venēnum *nt*; (*fig*) vīrus *nt*.
venomous *adj* venēnātus.
vent *n* spīrāculum *nt*; (*outlet*) exitus *m*; **give ~
to** profundere, ēmittere ♦ *vt* ēmittere;
(*feelings on*) profundere in (*acc*), ērumpere
in (*acc*).

ventilate *vt* perflāre; (*opinion*) in medium
prōferre, vulgāre.
ventilation *n* perflāre.
venture *n* perīculum *nt*; (*gamble*) ālea *f*; **at a ~**
temerē ♦ *vi* audēre ♦ *vt* perīclitārī, in āleam
dare.
venturesome *adj* audāx, temerārius.
venturesomeness *n* audācia *f*, temeritās *f*.
veracious *adj* vērāx, vēridicus.
veracity *n* vēritās *f*, fidēs *f*.
verb *n* verbum *nt*.
verbally *adv* per colloquia; (*translate*) ad
verbum, verbum prō verbō.
verbatim *adv* ad verbum, totidem verbīs.
verbiage *n* verba *ntpl*.
verbose *adj* verbōsus.
verbosity *n* loquendī prōfluentia *f*.
verdant *adj* viridis.
verdict *n* sententia *f*, iūdicium *nt*; **deliver a ~**
sententiam prōnūntiāre; **give a ~ in favour of**
causam adiūdicāre (*dat*).
verdigris *n* aerūgō *f*.
verdure *n* viriditās *f*.
verge *n* ōra *f*; **the ~ of** extrēmus; **on the ~ of**
(*fig*) prope (*acc*) ♦ *vi* vergere.
verification *n* cōnfirmātiō *f*.
verify *vt* cōnfirmāre, comprobāre.
verily *adv* profectō, certē.
verisimilitude *n* vērī similitūdō *f*.
veritable *adj* vērus.
veritably *adv* vērē.
verity *n* vēritās *f*.
vermilion *n* sandīx *f*.
vermin *n* bestiolae *fpl*.
vernacular *adj* patrius ♦ *n* patrius sermō *m*.
vernal *adj* vērnus.
versatile *adj* versūtus, varius.
versatility *n* versātile ingenium *nt*.
verse *n* (*line*) versus *m*; (*poetry*) versus *mpl*,
carmina *ntpl*.
versed *adj* īnstructus, perītus, exercitātus.
versification *n* ars versūs faciendī.
versify *vt* versū inclūdere ♦ *vi* versūs facere.
version *n* (*of story*) fōrma *f*; **give a Latin ~ of**
Latīnē reddere.
vertex *n* vertex *m*, fastīgium *nt*.
vertical *adj* rēctus, dīrēctus.
vertically *adv* ad līneam, rēctā līneā, ad
perpendiculum.
vertigo *n* vertīgō *f*.
vervain *n* verbēna *f*.
verve *n* ācrimōnia *f*.
very *adj* ipse ♦ *adv* admodum, valdē,
vehementer ♦ *superl*: **at that ~ moment** tum
māximē; **not ~** nōn ita.
vessel *n* (*receptacle*) vās *nt*; (*ship*) nāvigium *nt*.
vest *n* subūcula *f* ♦ *vt*: **~ power in** imperium
dēferre (*dat*); **~ed interests** nummī locātī *mpl*.
vestal *adj* vestālis ♦ *n* virgō vestālis *f*.
vestibule *n* vestibulum *nt*.
vestige *n* vestīgium *nt*, indicium *nt*.
vestment *n* vestīmentum *nt*.
vesture *n* vestis *f*.

vetch n vicia f.
veteran adj veterānus ♦ n (MIL) veterānus m; (fig) veterātor m.
veto n interdictum nt; (tribune's) intercessiō f ♦ vt interdīcere (dat); (tribune) intercēdere (dat).
vex vt vexāre, sollicitāre, stomachum movēre (dat); **be ~ed** aegrē ferre, stomachārī.
vexation n (caused) molestia f; (felt) dolor m, stomachus m.
vexatious adj odiōsus, molestus.
vexatiously adv molestē.
vexed adj īrātus; (question) anceps.
via prep per (acc).
viaduct n pōns m.
viands n cibus m.
vibrate vi vībrāre, tremere.
vibration n tremor m.
vicarious adj vicārius.
vice n (general) prāvitās f, perditī mōrēs mpl; (particular) vitium nt, flāgitium nt; (clamp) fībula f.
viceroy n prōcūrātor m.
vicinity n vīcīnia f, vīcīnitās f.
vicious adj prāvus, vitiōsus, flāgitiōsus; (temper) contumāx.
viciously adv flāgitiōsē; contumāciter.
vicissitude n vicissitūdō f; **~s** pl vicēs fpl.
victim n victima f, hostia f; (fig) piāculum m; (exploited) praeda f; **be the ~ of** labōrāre ex; **fall a ~ to** morī (abl); (trickery) circumvenīrī (abl).
victimize vt nocēre (dat), circumvenīre.
victor n victor m.
victorious adj victor m, victrīx f; **be ~** vincere.
victory n victōria f; **win a ~** victōriam reportāre; **win a ~ over** vincere, superāre.
victory message n laureātae litterae fpl.
victory parade n triumphus m.
victual vt rem frūmentāriam suppeditāre (dat).
victualler n caupō m; (MIL) frūmentārius m.
victuals n cibus m; (MIL) frūmentum nt, commeātus m.
vie vi certāre, contendere; **~ with** aemulārī.
view n cōnspectus m; (from far) prōspectus m; (from high) dēspectus m; (opinion) sententia f; **exposed to ~** in mediō; **entertain a ~** sentīre; **in ~ of** propter (acc); **in my ~** meā sententiā, meō iūdiciō; **end in ~** prōpositum nt; **have in ~** spectāre; **point of ~** iūdicium nt; **with a ~ to** eō cōnsiliō ut ♦ vt īnspicere, spectāre, intuērī.
vigil n pervigilium nt; **keep a ~** vigilāre.
vigilance n vigilantia f, dīligentia f.
vigilant adj vigilāns, dīligēns.
vigilantly adv vigilanter, dīligenter.
vigorous adj ācer, vegetus, integer; (style) nervōsus.
vigorously adv ācriter, strēnuē.
vigour n vīs f, nervī mpl, integritās f.
vile adj turpis, impūrus, abiectus.
vilely adv turpiter, impūrē.

vileness n turpitūdō f, impūritās f.
vilification n obtrectātiō f, calumnia f.
vilify vt obtrectāre, calumniārī, maledīcere (dat).
villa n vīlla f.
village n pāgus m, vīcus m; **in every ~** pāgātim.
villager n pāgānus m, vīcānus m.
villain n furcifer m, scelerātus m.
villainous adj scelestus, scelerātus, nēquam.
villainously adv scelestē.
villainy n scelus nt, nēquitia f.
vindicate vt (right) vindicāre; (action) pūrgāre; (belief) arguere; (person) dēfendere, prōpugnāre prō (abl).
vindication n dēfēnsiō f, pūrgātiō f.
vindicator n dēfēnsor m, prōpugnātor m.
vindictive adj ultor, ulcīscendī cupidus.
vine n vītis f; **wild ~** labrusca f.
vinedresser n vīnitor m.
vinegar n acētum nt.
vineyard n vīnea f, vīnētum nt.
vintage n vindēmia f.
vintner n vīnārius m.
violate vt violāre.
violation n violātiō f.
violator n violātor m.
violence n violentia f, vīs f, iniūria f; **do ~ to** violāre; **offer ~ to** vim īnferre (dat).
violent adj violentus, vehemēns; (passion) ācer, impotēns; **~ death** nex f.
violently adv vehementer, per vim.
violet n viola f.
viper n vīpera f.
viperous adj (fig) malignus.
virgin n virgō f ♦ adj virginālis.
virginity n virginitās f.
virile adj virīlis.
virility n virtūs f.
virtually adv rē vērā, ferē.
virtue n virtūs f, honestum nt; (woman's) pudīcitia f; (power) vīs f, potestās f; **by ~ of** ex (abl).
virtuous adj honestus, probus, integer.
virtuously adv honestē.
virulence n vīs f, vīrus nt.
virulent adj acerbus.
virus n vīrus m.
visage n ōs n, faciēs f.
vis-à-vis prep exadversus (acc).
viscosity n lentor m.
viscous adj lentus, tenāx.
visible adj ēvidēns, cōnspicuus, manifestus; **be ~** appārēre.
visibly adv manifestō.
vision n (sense) vīsus m; (power) aspectus m; (apparition) vīsum nt, vīsiō f; (whim) somnium nt.
visionary adj vānus ♦ n somniāns m.
visit n adventus m; (formal) salūtātiō f; (long) commorātiō f; **pay a ~ to** invīsere ♦ vt vīsere; **~ occasionally** intervīsere; **go to ~** invīsere.
visitation n (to inspect) recēnsiō f; (to punish) animadversiō f.

visitor n hospes m, hospita f; (formal) salūtātor m.

visor n buccula f.

vista n prōspectus m.

visual adj oculōrum.

visualize vt animō cernere, ante oculōs pōnere.

visually adv oculīs.

vital adj (of life) vītālis; (essential) necessārius, māximī mōmentī.

vitality n vīs f; (style) sanguis m.

vitally adv praecipuē, imprīmīs.

vitals n viscera ntpl.

vitiate vt corrumpere, vitiāre.

vitreous adj vitreus.

vitrify vt in vitrum excoquere.

vituperate vt vituperāre, obiūrgāre.

vituperation n vituperātiō f, maledicta ntpl.

vituperative adj maledicus.

vivacious adj alacer, vegetus, hilaris.

vivaciously adv hilare.

vivacity n alacritās f, hilaritās f.

vivid adj vīvidus, ācer.

vividly adv ācriter.

vivify vt animāre.

vixen n vulpēs f.

vocabulary n verbōrum cōpia f.

vocal adj: ~ music vōcis cantus m.

vocation n officium nt, mūnus nt.

vociferate vt, vi vōciferārī, clāmāre.

vociferation n vōciferātiō f, clāmor m.

vociferous adj vōciferāns.

vociferously adv māgnīs clāmōribus.

vogue n mōs m; **be in ~** flōrēre, in honōre esse.

voice n vōx f ♦ vt exprimere, ēloquī.

void adj inānis, vacuus; **~ of** expers (gen); **null and ~** irritus ♦ n ināne nt ♦ vt ēvomere, ēmittere.

volatile adj levis, mōbilis.

volatility n levitās f.

volition n voluntās f.

volley n imber m.

volubility n volūbilitās f.

voluble adj volūbilis.

volume n (book) liber m; (mass) mōlēs f; (of sound) māgnitūdō f.

voluminous adj cōpiōsus.

voluntarily adv ultrō, suā sponte.

voluntary adj voluntārius; (unpaid) grātuītus.

volunteer n (MIL) ēvocātus m ♦ vt ultrō offerre ♦ vi (MIL) nōmen dare.

voluptuary n dēlicātus m, homō voluptārius m.

voluptuous adj voluptārius, mollis, dēlicātus, luxuriōsus.

voluptuously adv molliter, dēlicātē, luxuriōsē.

voluptuousness n luxuria f, libīdō f.

vomit vt vomere, ēvomere; **~ up** ēvomere.

voracious adj vorāx, edāx.

voraciously adv avidē.

voracity n edācitās f, gula f.

vortex n vertex m, turbō m.

votary n cultor m.

vote n suffrāgium nt; (opinion) sententia f; **~ for** (candidate) suffrāgārī (dat); (senator's motion) discēdere in sententiam (gen) ♦ vi (election) suffrāgium ferre; (judge) sententiam ferre; (senator) cēnsēre; **take a ~** (senate) discessiōnem facere ♦ vt (senate) dēcernere; **~ against** (bill) antīquāre.

voter n suffrāgātor m.

votive adj vōtīvus.

vouch vi spondēre; **~ for** praestāre, testificārī.

voucher n (person) auctor m; (document) auctōritās f.

vouchsafe vt concēdere.

vow n vōtum nt; (promise) fidēs f ♦ vt vovēre; (promise) spondēre.

vowel n vōcālis f.

voyage n nāvigātiō f, cursus m ♦ vi nāvigāre.

vulgar adj (common) vulgāris; (low) plēbēius, sordidus, īnsulsus.

vulgarity n sordēs fpl, īnsulsitās f.

vulgarly adv vulgō; īnsulsē.

vulnerable adj nūdus; (fig) obnoxius; **be ~** vulnerārī posse.

vulture n vultur m; (fig) vulturius m.

W, w

wad n massa f.

wade vi per vada īre; **~ across** vadō trānsīre.

waft vt ferre, vehere.

wag n facētus homō m, ioculātor m ♦ vt movēre, mōtāre, agitāre ♦ vi movērī, agitārī.

wage n mercēs f; (pl) mercēs f, manupretium nt; (fig) pretium nt, praemium nt ♦ vt gerere; **~ war** on bellum īnferre (dat)/gerere.

wager n spōnsiō f ♦ vi spōnsiōnem facere ♦ vt dēpōnere, oppōnere.

waggery n facētiae fpl.

waggish adj facētus, rīdiculus.

waggle vt agitāre, mōtāre.

wagon n plaustrum nt, carrus m.

waif n inops m/f.

wail n ēiulātus m ♦ vi ēiulāre, dēplōrāre, lāmentārī.

wailing n plōrātus m, lāmentātiō f.

waist n medium corpus nt; **hold by the ~** medium tenēre.

wait n: **have a long ~** diū exspectāre; **lie in ~** īnsidiārī ♦ vi manēre, opperīrī, exspectāre; **~ for** exspectāre; **~ upon** (accompany) adsectārī, dēdūcere; (serve) famulārī (dat); (visit) salūtāre.

waiter n famulus m, minister m.

waive _vt_ dēpōnere, remittere.
wake _vt_ excitāre, suscitāre ♦ _vi_ expergīscī.
wake _n_ vestīgia _ntpl_; **in the ~** pōne, ā tergō;
follow in the ~ of vestīgiīs instāre (_gen_).
wakeful _adj_ vigil.
wakefulness _n_ vigilantia _f_.
waken _vt_ excitāre ♦ _vi_ expergīscī.
walk _n_ (_act_) ambulātiō _f_, deambulātiō _f_; (_gait_)
incessus _m_; (_place_) ambulātiō _f_, xystus _m_; **~ of
life** status _m_; **go for a ~** spatiārī, deambulāre
♦ _vi_ ambulāre, īre, gradī; (_with dignity_)
incēdere; **~ about** inambulāre; **~ out** ēgredī.
wall _n_ mūrus _m_; (_indoors_) pariēs _m_; (_afield_)
māceria _f_; **~s** _pl_ (_of town_) moenia _ntpl_ ♦ _vt_
mūnīre, saepīre; **~ up** inaedificāre.
wallet _n_ pēra _f_.
wallow _vi_ volūtārī.
walnut _n_ iūglāns _f_.
wan _adj_ pallidus.
wand _n_ virga _f_.
wander _vi_ errāre, vagārī; (_in mind_) ālūcinārī;
~ over pervagārī.
wanderer _n_ errō _m_, vagus _m_.
wandering _adj_ errābundus, vagus ♦ _n_ errātiō
_f_, error _m_.
wane _vi_ dēcrēscere, senēscere.
want _n_ inopia _f_, indigentia _f_, egestās _f_, pēnūria
_f_; (_craving_) dēsīderium _nt_; **in ~** inops; **be in ~**
egēre ♦ _vt_ (_lack_) carēre (_abl_), egēre (_abl_),
indigēre (_abl_); (_miss_) dēsīderāre; (_wish_)
velle.
wanting _adj_ (_missing_) absēns; (_defective_)
vitiōsus, parum idōneus; **be ~** deesse,
dēficere ♦ _prep_ sine (_abl_).
wanton _adj_ lascīvus, libīdinōsus ♦ _vi_
lascīvīre.
wantonly _adv_ lascīvē, libīdinōsē.
war _n_ bellum _nt_; **regular ~** iūstum bellum;
fortunes of ~ fortūna bellī; **outbreak of ~**
exortum bellum; **be at ~ with** bellum gerere
cum; **declare ~** bellum indīcere; **discontinue
~** bellum dēpōnere; **end ~** (_by agreement_)
compōnere; (_by victory_) cōnficere; **enter ~**
bellum suscipere; **give the command of a ~**
bellum mandāre; **make ~** bellum īnferre;
prolong a ~ bellum trahere; **provoke ~**
bellum movēre; **wage ~** bellum gerere;
wage ~ on bellum īnferre (_dat_) ♦ _vi_ bellāre.
warble _vi_ canere, cantāre.
warbling _adj_ garrulus, canōrus ♦ _n_ cantus _m_.
war cry _n_ clāmor _m_.
ward _n_ custōdia _f_; (_person_) pupillus _m_, pupilla
_f_; (_of town_) regiō _f_ ♦ _vt_: **~ off** arcēre,
dēfendere, prōpulsāre.
warden _n_ praefectus _m_.
warder _n_ custōs _m_.
wardrobe _n_ vestiārium _nt_.
wardship _n_ tūtēla _f_.
warehouse _n_ apothēca _f_.
wares _n_ merx _f_, merces _fpl_.
warfare _n_ bellum _nt_.
warily _adv_ prōvidenter, cautē.
wariness _n_ circumspectiō _f_, cautiō _f_.

warlike _adj_ ferōx, bellicōsus.
warm _adj_ calidus; (_fig_) ācer, studiōsus; **be ~**
calēre; **become ~** calefierī, incalēscere; **keep
~ fovēre**; **~ baths** thermae _fpl_ ♦ _vt_ calefacere,
tepefacere, fovēre ♦ _vi_ calefierī.
warmly _adv_ (_fig_) ferventer, studiōsē.
warmth _n_ calor _m_.
warn _vt_ monēre, admonēre.
warning _n_ (_act_) monitiō _f_; (_particular_) monitum
_nt_; (_lesson_) documentum _nt_, exemplum _nt_.
warp _n_ stāmina _ntpl_ ♦ _vt_ dēprāvāre, īnflectere.
warped _adj_ (_fig_) prāvus.
warrant _n_ auctōritās _f_ ♦ _vt_ praestāre.
warranty _n_ cautiō _f_.
warrior _n_ bellātor _m_, bellatrīx _f_, mīles _m_.
warship _n_ nāvis longa _f_.
wart _n_ verrūca _f_.
wary _adj_ prōvidus, cautus, prūdēns.
wash _vt_ lavāre; (_of rivers, sea_) adluere; **~ away**
dīluere; **~ clean** abluere; **~ out** (_fig_) ēluere ♦
_vi_ lavārī.
washbasin _n_ aquālis _m_.
washing _n_ lavātiō _f_.
wasp _n_ vespa _f_.
waspish _adj_ acerbus, stomachōsus.
waste _n_ dētrīmentum _nt_, intertrīmentum _nt_;
(_extravagance_) effūsiō _f_; (_of time_) iactūra _f_;
(_land_) sōlitūdō _f_, vastitās _f_ ♦ _adj_ dēsertus,
vastus; **lay ~** vastāre, populārī ♦ _vt_
cōnsūmere, perdere, dissipāre; (_time_)
terere, absūmere; (_with disease_) absūmere ♦
_vi_: **~ away** tābēscere, intābēscere.
wasteful _adj_ prōdigus, profūsus; (_destructive_)
damnōsus, perniciōsus.
wastefully _adv_ prōdigē.
wasting _n_ tābēs _f_.
wastrel _n_ nebulō _m_.
watch _n_ (_being awake_) vigilia _f_; (_sentry_) statiō _f_,
excubiae _fpl_; **keep ~** excubāre; **keep ~ on,
over** custōdīre, invigilāre (_dat_); **set ~** vigiliās
dispōnere; **at the third ~** ad tertiam būcinam
♦ _vt_ (_guard_) custōdīre; (_observe_) intuērī,
observāre, spectāre ad (+ _acc_); **~ for**
observāre, exspectāre; (_enemy_) īnsidiārī
(_dat_); **~ closely** adservāre.
watcher _n_ custōs _m_.
watchful _adj_ vigilāns.
watchfully _adv_ vigilanter.
watchfulness _n_ vigilantia _f_.
watchman _n_ custōs _m_, vigil _m_.
watchtower _n_ specula _f_.
watchword _n_ tessera _f_, signum _nt_.
water _n_ aqua _f_; **deep ~** gurges _m_; **fresh ~** aqua
dulcis; **high ~** māximus aestus; **running ~**
aqua prōfluēns; **still ~** stagnum _nt_; **fetch ~**
aquārī; **fetching ~** aquātiō _f_; **cold ~** frīgida _f_;
hot ~ calida _f_; **troubled ~s** (_fig_) turbidae rēs ♦
_vt_ (_land_) inrigāre; (_animal_) adaquāre.
water carrier _n_ aquātor _m_; (_Zodiac_) Aquārius
_m_.
water clock _n_ clepsydra _f_.
waterfall _n_ cataracta _f_.
watering _n_ aquātiō _f_; **~ place** _n_ (_spa_) aquae _fpl_.

water pipe n fistula f.
watershed n aquārum dīvortium nt.
water snake n hydrus m.
water spout n prēstēr m.
watery adj aquōsus, ūmidus.
wattle n crātēs f.
wave n unda f, fluctus m ♦ vt agitāre, iactāre ♦ vi fluctuāre.
waver vi dubitāre, fluctuārī, nūtāre, vacillāre, labāre, inclīnāre.
wavering adj dubius, incōnstāns ♦ n dubitātiō f, fluctuātiō f.
wavy adj undātus; (hair) crispus.
wax n cēra f ♦ vt cērāre ♦ vi crēscere.
waxen adj cēreus.
waxy adj cērōsus.
way n via f; (route) iter nt; (method) modus m, ratiō f; (habit) mōs m; (ship's) impetus m; **all the ~ to, from** usque ad, ab; **by the ~** (parenthesis) etenim; **get in the ~ of** intervenīre (dat), impedīre; **get under ~** nāvem solvere; **give ~** (structure) labāre; (MIL) cēdere; **give ~ to** indulgēre (dat); **go out of one's ~ to do** ultrō facere; **have one's ~** imperāre; **in a ~** quōdam modō; **in this ~** ad hunc modum; **it is not my ~ to** nōn meum est (infin); **lose one's ~** deerrāre; **make ~** dē viā dēcēdere; **make ~ for** cēdere (dat); **make one's ~ into** sē īnsinuāre in (acc); **on the ~** inter viam, in itinere; **out of the ~** āvius, dēvius; (fig) reconditus; **pave the ~ for** praeparāre; **put out of the ~** tollere; **right of ~** iter; **stand in the ~ of** obstāre (dat); **that ~** illāc; **this ~** hāc; **~s and means** opēs fpl, reditūs mpl.
wayfarer n viātor m.
waylay vt īnsidiārī (dat).
wayward adj protervus, incōnstāns, levis.
waywardness n libīdō f, levitās f.
we pron nōs.
weak adj dēbilis, īnfirmus, imbēcillus; (health) invalidus; (argument) levis, tenuis; (senses) hebes.
weaken vt dēbilitāre, īnfirmāre; (resistance) frangere, labefactāre ♦ vi imminuī, labāre.
weakling n imbēcillus m.
weakly adj invalidus, aeger ♦ adv īnfirmē.
weak-minded adj mollis.
weakness n dēbilitās f, īnfirmitās f; (of argument) levitās f; (of mind) mollitia f, imbēcillitās f; (flaw) vitium nt; **have a ~ for** delectārī (abl).
weal n salūs f, rēs f; (mark of blow) vībex f; **the common ~** rēs pūblica f.
wealth n dīvitiae fpl, opēs fpl; **a ~ of** cōpia f, abundantia f.
wealthy adj dīves, opulentus, locuplēs, beātus; **make ~** locuplētāre, dītāre; **very ~** praedīves.
wean vt lacte dēpellere; (fig) dēdocēre.
weapon n tēlum nt.
wear n (dress) habitus m; **~ and tear** intertrīmentum nt ♦ vt gerere, gestāre; (rub)

terere, conterere; **~ out** cōnficere ♦ vi dūrāre; **~ off** minuī.
wearily adv cum lassitūdine, languidē.
weariness n fatīgātiō f, lassitūdō f; (of) taedium nt.
wearisome adj molestus, operōsus, labōriōsus.
weary adj lassus, fessus, dēfessus, fatīgātus ♦ vt fatīgāre; **I am weary of** me taedet (+ gen).
weasel n mustēla f.
weather n tempestās f, caelum nt; **fine ~** serēnitās f ♦ vt superāre.
weather-beaten adj tempestāte dūrātus.
weave vt texere.
weaver n textor m, textrix f.
web n (on loom) tēla f; (spider's) arāneum nt.
wed vt (a wife) dūcere; (a husband) nūbere (dat).
wedding n nūptiae fpl.
wedge n cuneus m ♦ vt cuneāre.
wedlock n mātrimōnium nt.
weed n inūtilis herba f ♦ vt runcāre.
weedy adj exīlis.
week n hebdomas f.
ween vt arbitrārī, putāre.
weep vi flēre, lacrimārī; **~ for** dēflēre, dēplōrāre.
weeping n flētus m, lacrimae fpl.
weevil n curculiō m.
weft n subtēmen nt; (web) tēla f.
weigh vt pendere, exāmināre; (anchor) tollere; (thought) ponderāre; **~ down** dēgravāre, opprimere; **~ out** expendere ♦ vi pendere.
weight n pondus nt; (influence) auctōritās f, mōmentum nt; (burden) onus nt; **have great ~** (fig) multum valēre; **he is worth his ~ in gold** aurō contrā cōnstat.
weightily adv graviter.
weightiness n gravitās f.
weighty adj gravis.
weir n mōlēs f.
weird adj mōnstruōsus ♦ n fātum nt.
welcome adj grātus, exspectātus, acceptus ♦ n salūtātiō f ♦ vt excipere, salvēre iubēre ♦ interj salvē, salvēte.
welfare n salūs f.
well n puteus m; (spring) fōns m ♦ vi scatēre ♦ adj salvus, sānus, valēns; **be ~** valēre ♦ adv bene, probē; (transition) age ♦ interj (concession) estō; (surprise) heia; **~ and good** estō; **~ begun is half done** dīmidium factī quī coepit habet; **~ done!** probē!; **~ met** opportūnē venis; **~ on in years** aetāte prōvectus; **all is ~** bene habet; **as ~** etiam; **as ~ as** cum … tum, et … et; **let ~ alone** quiēta nōn movēre; **take ~** in bonam partem accipere; **wish ~** favēre (dat); **you may ~ say** iūre dīcis; **you might as ~ say** illud potius dīcās.
well-advised adj prūdēns.
well-behaved adj modestus.
wellbeing n salūs f.
well-bred adj generōsus, līberālis.

well-disposed _adj_ benevolus, amīcus.
well-informed _adj_ ērudītus.
well-judged _adj_ ēlegāns.
well-knit _adj_ dēnsus.
well-known _adj_ nōtus, nōbilis; (_saying_) trītus.
well-nigh _adv_ paene.
well-off _adj_ beātus, fortūnātus; **you are ~** bene est tibī.
well-read _adj_ litterātus.
well-timed _adj_ opportūnus.
well-to-do _adj_ beātus, dīves.
well-tried _adj_ probātus.
well-turned _adj_ rotundus.
well-versed _adj_ perītus, expertus.
well-wisher _n_ amīcus _m_, benevolēns _m_.
well-worn _adj_ trītus.
welter _n_ turba _f_ ♦ _vi_ miscērī, turbārī; (_wallow_) volūtārī.
wench _n_ muliercula _f_.
wend _vt_: **~ one's way** īre, sē ferre.
west _n_ occidēns _m_, sōlis occāsus _m_ ♦ _adj_ occidentālis.
westerly, western _adj_ occidentālis.
westwards _adv_ ad occidentem.
west wind _n_ Favōnius _m_.
wet _adj_ ūmidus, madidus; **be ~** madēre; **~ weather** pluvia _f_ ♦ _vt_ madefacere.
wether _n_ vervēx _m_.
wet nurse _n_ nūtrīx _f_.
whack _n_ ictus _m_, plāga _f_ ♦ _vt_ pulsāre, verberāre.
whale _n_ bālaena _f_.
wharf _n_ crepīdō _f_.
what _pron_ (_interrog_) quid; (_adj_) quī; (_relat_) id quod, ea quae; **~ kind of?** quālis.
whatever, whatsoever _pron_ quidquid, quodcumque; (_adj_) quīcumque.
wheat _n_ trīticum _nt_.
wheaten _adj_ trīticeus.
wheedle _vt_ blandīrī, pellicere.
wheedling _adj_ blandus ♦ _n_ blanditiae _fpl_.
wheel _n_ rota _f_ ♦ _vt_ flectere, circumagere ♦ _vi_ sē flectere, circumagī.
wheelbarrow _n_ pabō _m_.
wheeze _vi_ anhēlāre.
whelm _vt_ obruere.
whelp _n_ catulus _m_.
when _adv_ (_interrog_) quandō, quō tempore ♦ _conj_ (_time_) cum (+ _subj_), ubī (+ _indic_).
whence _adv_ unde.
whenever _conj_ quotiēns, utcumque, quandocumque, cum (+ _perf/pluperf indic_); (_as soon as_) simul āc.
where _adv_ ubī; (_to_) quō; **~ ... from** unde; **~ to** quo (_interrog and relat_).
whereabouts _n_ locus _m_; **your ~** quō in locō sīs.
whereas _conj_ quōniam; (_contrast_) _not expressed_.
whereby _adv_ quō pāctō, quō.
wherefore _adv_ (_interrog_) quārē, cūr; (_relat_) quamobrem, quāpropter.
wherein _adv_ in quō, in quā.
whereof _adv_ cūius, cūius reī.

whereon _adv_ in quō, in quā.
whereupon _adv_ quō factō.
wherever _conj_ ubiubī, quācumque.
wherewith _adv_ quī, cum quō.
wherry _n_ linter _f_.
whet _vt_ acuere; (_fig_) exacuere.
whether _conj_ (_interrog_) utrum; (_single question_) num; (_condition_) sīve, seu; **~ ... or** utrum ... an (_in indir question_); (_in cond clauses_) seu (sive) ... seu (sive); **~ ... not** utrum ... necne (_in indir question_).
whetstone _n_ cōs _f_.
whey _n_ serum _nt_.
which _pron_ (_interrog_) quis; (_of two_) uter; (_relat_) quī ♦ _adj_ quī; (_of two_) uter.
whichever _pron_ quisquis, quīcumque; (_of two_) utercumque.
whiff _n_ odor _m_.
while _n_ spatium _nt_, tempus _nt_; **for a ~** parumper; **a little ~** paulisper; **a long ~** diū; **it is worth ~** expedit, operae pretium est; **once in a ~** interdum ♦ _conj_ dum + _pres indic_ (= _during the time that_); + _imperf indic_ (= _all the time that_) ♦ _vt_: **~ away** dēgere, fallere.
whilst _conj_ dum.
whim _n_ libīdō _f_, arbitrium _nt_.
whimper _n_ vāgītus _m_ ♦ _vi_ vāgīre.
whimsical _adj_ facētus, īnsolēns.
whimsically _adv_ facētē.
whimsy _n_ dēliciae _fpl_, facētiae _fpl_.
whine _n_ quīritātiō _f_ ♦ _vi_ quīritāre.
whinny _n_ hinnītus _m_ ♦ _vi_ hinnīre.
whip _n_ flagellum _nt_, flagrum _nt_ ♦ _vt_ flagellāre, verberare.
whirl _n_ turbō _m_ ♦ _vt_ intorquēre contorquēre ♦ _vi_ contorquērī.
whirlpool _n_ vertex _m_, vōragō _f_.
whirlwind _n_ turbō _m_.
whisper _n_ susurrus _m_ ♦ _vt, vi_ susurrāre, īnsusurrāre; **~ to** ad aurem admonēre, in aurem dīcere.
whistle _n_ (_instrument_) fistula _f_; (_sound_) sībilus _m_ ♦ _vi_ sībilāre.
white _adj_ albus; (_shining_) candidus; (_complexion_) pallidus; (_hair_) cānus; **turn ~** exalbēscere ♦ _n_ album _nt_; (_egg_) albūmen _nt_.
white-hot _adj_: **to be ~** excandēscere.
whiten _vt_ dealbāre ♦ _vi_ albēscere.
whiteness _n_ candor _m_.
whitewash _n_ albārium _nt_ ♦ _vt_ dealbāre.
whither _adv_ quō; **~soever** quōcumque.
whitish _adj_ albulus.
whizz _n_ strīdor _m_ ♦ _vi_ strīdere, increpāre.
who _pron_ quis; (_relat_) quī.
whoever _pron_ quisquis, quīcumque.
whole _adj_ tōtus, cūnctus; (_unhurt_) integer, incolumis; (_healthy_) sānus ♦ _n_ tōtum _nt_, summa _f_, ūniversitās _f_; **on the ~** plērumque.
wholehearted _adj_ studiōsissimus.
wholeheartedly _adv_ ex animō.
wholesale _adj_ māgnus, cōpiōsus; **~ business** negōtiātiō _f_; **~ dealer** mercātor _m_, negōtiātor _m_.

wholesome *adj* salūtāris, salūbris.
wholesomeness *n* salūbritās *f*.
wholly *adv* omnīnō, tōtus.
whoop *n* ululātus *m* ♦ *vi* ululāre.
whose *pron* cūius.
why *adv* cūr, quārē, quamobrem, qua de causa.
wick *n* mergulus *m*.
wicked *adj* improbus, scelestus; (*to gods, kin, country*) impius.
wickedly *adv* improbē, scelestē, impiē.
wickedness *n* improbitās *f*, scelus *nt*, impietās *f*.
wicker *adj* vīmineus ♦ *n* vīmen *nt*.
wide *adj* lātus, amplus; **be ~ of** aberrāre ab ♦ *adv* lātē; **far and ~** longē lātēque.
widely *adv* lātē; (*among people*) vulgō.
widen *vt* laxāre, dilātāre.
widespread *adj* effūsus, vulgātus.
widow *n* vidua *f*.
widowed *adj* viduus, orbus.
widower *n* viduus *m*.
widowhood *n* viduitās *f*.
width *n* lātitūdō *f*, amplitūdō *f*.
wield *vt* tractāre, gestāre, ūtī (*abl*).
wife *n* uxor *f*.
wifely *adj* uxōrius.
wig *n* capillāmentum *nt*.
wild *adj* ferus, indomitus, saevus; (*plant*) agrestis; (*land*) incultus; (*temper*) furibundus, impotens, āmēns; (*shot*) temerārius; **~ state** feritās *f*.
wild beast *n* fera *f*.
wilderness *n* sōlitūdō *f*, loca dēserta *ntpl*.
wildly *adv* saevē.
wildness *n* feritās *f*.
wile *n* dolus *m*, ars *f*, fraus *f*.
wilful *adj* pervicāx, contumāx; (*action*) cōnsultus.
wilfully *adv* contumāciter; cōnsultō.
wilfulness *n* pervicācia *f*, libīdō *f*.
wilily *adv* astūtē, vafrē.
wiliness *n* astūtia *f*.
will *n* (*faculty*) voluntās *f*, animus *m*; (*intent*) cōnsilium *nt*; (*decision*) arbitrium *nt*; (*of gods*) nūtus *m*; (*document*) testāmentum *nt*; **~ and pleasure** libīdō *f*; **against one's ~** invītus; **at ~** ad libīdinem suam; **good ~** studium *nt*; **ill ~** invidia *f*; **with a ~** summō studiō; **without making a ~** intestātus, intestātō ♦ *vt* velle, *fut*; (*legacy*) lēgāre; **as you ~** ut libet.
willing *adj* libēns, parātus; **be ~** velle; **not be ~** nōlle.
willingly *adv* libenter.
willingness *n* voluntās *f*.
willow *n* salix *f* ♦ *adj* salignus.
willowy *adj* gracilis.
wilt *vi* flaccēscere.
wily *adj* astūtus, vafer, callidus.
wimple *n* mitra *f*.
win *vt* ferre, obtinēre, adipisci; (*after effort*) auferre; (*victory*) reportāre; (*fame*) cōnsequī, adsequī; (*friends*) sibī conciliāre; **~ the day**

vincere; **~ over** dēlēnire, conciliāre ♦ *vi* vincere.
wince *vi* resilīre.
winch *n* māchina *f*, sucula *f*.
wind *n* ventus *m*; (*north*) aquilō *m*; (*south*) auster *m*; (*east*) eurus *m*; (*west*) favōnius *m*; **I get ~ of** subolet mihī; **run before the ~** vento sē dare; **take the ~ out of one's sails** suō sibī gladiō iugulāre; **there is something in the ~** nescioquid olet; **which way the ~ blows** quōmodo sē rēs habeat.
wind *vt* torquēre; **~ round** intorquēre ♦ *vi* flectī, sinuāre; **~ up** (*speech*) perōrāre.
windbag *n* verbōsus *m*.
winded *adj* anhēlāns.
windfall *n* repentīnum bonum *nt*.
winding *adj* flexuōsus, tortuōsus ♦ *n* flexiō *f*, flexus *m*; **~s** *pl* (*speech*) ambāgēs *fpl*.
windlass *n* māchina *f*, sucula *f*.
window *n* fenestra *f*.
windpipe *n* aspera artēria *f*.
windward *adj* ad ventum conversus ♦ *adv*: **to ~** ventum versus.
windy *adj* ventōsus.
wine *n* vīnum *nt*; (*new*) mustum *nt*; (*undiluted*) merum *nt*.
winebibber *n* vīnōsus *m*.
wine cellar *n* apothēca *f*.
wine merchant *n* vīnārius *m*.
wine press *n* prēlum *nt*.
wing *n* āla *f*; (*MIL*) cornū *nt*, āla *f*; (*of bird*) penna *f*; **take ~** ēvolāre; **take under one's ~** patrōnus fierī (*gen*), clientem habēre, in custōdiam recipere.
winged *adj* ālātus, pennātus, volucer.
wink *n* nictus *m* ♦ *vi* nictāre; **~ at** cōnīvēre (*dat*).
winner *n* victor *m*.
winning *adj* blandus, iūcundus.
winningly *adv* blandē, iūcundē.
winning post *n* mēta *f*.
winnings *n* lucra *ntpl*.
winnow *vt* ventilāre; (*fig*) excutere.
winnowing-fan *n* vannus *f*.
winsome *adj* blandus, suāvis.
winter *n* hiems *f*; (*mid*) brūma *f* ♦ *adj* hiemālis, hībernus ♦ *vi* hībernāre.
winter quarters *n* hīberna *ntpl*.
wintry *adj* hiemālis, hībernus.
wipe *vt* dētergēre; **~ away** abstergēre; **~ dry** siccāre; **~ off** dētergēre; **~ out** dēlēre; **~ the nose** ēmungere.
wire *n* fīlum aēneum *nt*.
wiry *adj* nervōsus.
wisdom *n* sapientia *f*; (*in action*) prūdentia *f*; (*in judgment*) cōnsilium *nt*.
wise *adj* sapiēns, prūdēns.
wisely *adv* sapienter, prūdenter.
wish *n* optātum *nt*, vōtum *nt*; (*for something missing*) dēsīderium *nt*; **~es** *pl* (*greeting*) salūs *f* ♦ *vt* optāre, cupere, velle; **~ for** exoptāre, expetere, dēsīderāre; **~ good-day** salvēre iubēre; **as you ~** ut libet; **I ~ I could** utinam

possim.
wishful *adj* cupidus.
wishing *n* optātiō *f.*
wisp *n* manipulus *m.*
wistful *adj* dēsīderī plenus.
wistfully *adv* cum dēsīderiō.
wistfulness *n* dēsīderium *nt.*
wit *n* (*humour*) facētiae *fpl,* salēs *mpl;* (*intellect*)
argūtiae *fpl,* ingenium *nt;* **caustic** ~ dicācitās
f; **be at one's wits' end** valdē haerēre; **be out
of one's ~s** dēlīrāre; **have one's ~s about one**
prūdens esse; **to** ~ nempe, dīcō.
witch *n* sāga *f,* strīga *f.*
witchcraft *n* veneficium *nt,* magicae artēs *fpl.*
with *prep* (*person*) cum (*abl*); (*thing*) abl; (*in
company*) apud (*acc*); (*fight*) cum (*abl*), contrā
(*acc*); **be angry** ~ īrāscī (*dat*); **begin** ~ incipere
ab; **rest** ~ esse penes (*acc*); **end** ~ dēsinere in
(*acc*); **what do you want** ~ **me?** quid mē vis?
withdraw *vt* dēdūcere, dētrahere; (*fig*)
āvocāre; (*words*) retractāre ♦ *vi* discēdere,
abscēdere, sē recipere, sē subdūcere.
withdrawal *n* (*MIL*) receptus *m.*
wither *vt* torrēre ♦ *vi* dēflōrēscere.
withered *adj* marcidus.
withhold *vt* abstinēre, retinēre, supprimere.
within *adv* intus, intrā; (*motion*) intrō ♦ *prep*
intrā (*acc*), in (*abl*).
without *adv* extrā, forīs; **from** ~ extrīnsecus;
be ~ vacāre (*abl*), carēre (*abl*) ♦ *prep* sine
(*abl*), expers (*gen*); **I admire** ~ **fearing** ita
laudō ut nōn timeam; ~ **breaking the law**
salvīs lēgibus; **you cannot see** ~ **admiring**
vidēre nōn potes quīn laudēs; **you cannot
appreciate** ~ **seeing for yourself** aestimāre
nōn potes nisī ipse vīderis; ~ **doubt** sine
dubio; ~ **the order of** iniūssū (*gen*); ~ **striking
a blow** rē integrā.
withstand *vt* resistere (*dat*), obsistere (*dat*);
(*attack*) ferre, sustinēre.
withy *n* vīmen *nt.*
witless *adj* excors, ineptus, stultus.
witness *n* (*person*) testis *m/f;* (*to a document*)
obsignātor *m;* (*spectator*) arbiter *m;* (*evidence*)
testimōnium *nt;* **call as** ~ antestārī; **bear** ~
testificārī; **call to** ~ testārī ♦ *vt* testificārī;
(*see*) vidēre, intuērī.
witnessing *n* testificātiō *f.*
witticism *n* dictum *nt;* ~**s** *pl* facētiae *fpl.*
wittily *adv* facētē, salsē.
wittingly *adv* sciēns.
witty *adj* facētus, argūtus, salsus; (*caustic*)
dicāx.
wizard *n* magus *m,* veneficus *m.*
wizardry *n* magicae artēs *fpl.*
wizened *adj* marcidus.
woad *n* vitrum *nt.*
wobble *vi* titubāre; (*structure*) labāre.
woe *n* luctus *m,* dolor *m,* aerumna *f;* ~**s** *pl* mala
ntpl, calamitātēs *fpl;* ~ **to** vae (*dat*).
woeful *adj* tristis, maestus, aerumnōsus.
woefully *adv* triste, miserē.
wolf *n* lupus *m,* lupa *f;* ~**'s** lupīnus.

woman *n* fēmina *f,* mulier *f;* **old** ~ anus *f;*
married ~ mātrōna *f;* ~**'s** muliebris.
womanish *adj* muliebris, effēminātus.
womanly *adj* muliebris.
womb *n* uterus *m.*
wonder *n* admīrātiō *f;* (*of a thing*)
admīrābilitās *f;* (*thing*) mīrāculum *nt,* mīrum
nt, portentum *nt* ♦ *vi* mīrārī; ~ **at** admīrārī,
dēmīrārī.
wonderful *adj* mīrus, mīrābilis, admīrābilis; ~
to relate mīrābile dictu.
wonderfully *adv* mīrē, mīrābiliter, mīrum
quantum.
wonderfulness *n* admīrābilitās *f.*
wondering *adj* mīrābundus.
wonderment *n* admīrātiō *f.*
wondrous *adj* mīrus, mīrābilis.
wont *n* mōs *m,* cōnsuētūdō *f.*
wonted *adj* solitus.
woo *vt* petere.
wood *n* silva *f,* nemus *nt;* (*material*) lignum *nt;*
gather ~ lignārī; **touch** ~! absit verbō invidia
♦ *adj* ligneus.
woodcutter *n* lignātor *m.*
wooded *adj* silvestris, saltuōsus.
wooden *adj* ligneus.
woodland *n* silvae *fpl* ♦ *adj* silvestris.
woodman *n* lignātor *m.*
wood nymph *n* dryas *f.*
woodpecker *n* pīcus *m.*
wood pigeon *n* palumbēs *m/f.*
woodwork *n* tigna *ntpl.*
woodworker *n* faber tignārius *m.*
woody *adj* silvestris, silvōsus.
wooer *n* procus *m.*
woof *n* subtēmen *nt.*
wool *n* lāna *f.*
woollen *adj* lāneus.
woolly *adj* lānātus.
word *n* verbum *nt;* (*spoken*) vōx *f;* (*message*)
nūntius *m;* (*promise*) fidēs *f;* (*term*)
vocābulum *nt;* ~ **for** ~ ad verbum, verbum ē
verbō; **a** ~ **with you!** paucīs tē volō!; **break
one's** ~ fidem fallere; **bring back** ~
renūntiāre; **by** ~ **of mouth** ōre; **fair ~s**
blanditiae *fpl;* **give one's** ~ fidem dare; **have a**
~ **with** colloquī cum; **have ~s with** iūrgāre
cum; **have a good** ~ **for** laudāre; **in a** ~ ūnō
verbō, dēnique; **keep one's** ~ fidem
praestāre; **of few ~s** taciturnus; **take at one's**
~ crēdere (*dat*).
wording *n* verba *ntpl.*
wordy *adj* verbōsus.
work *n* (*energy*) labor *m,* opera *f;* (*task*) opus *nt;*
(*thing done*) opus *nt;* (*book*) liber *m;* (*trouble*)
negōtium *nt;* ~**s** (*MIL*) opera *ntpl;* (*mechanism*)
māchinātiō *f;* (*place*) officīna *f* ♦ *vi* labōrāre ♦
vt (*men*) exercēre; (*metal*) fabricārī; (*soil*)
subigere; (*results*) efficere; ~ **at** ēlabōrāre; ~
in admiscēre; ~ **off** exhaurīre; ~ **out**
ēlabōrāre; ~ **up** (*emotion*) efferre; ~ **one's
way up** prōficere ♦ *vi* gerī.
workaday *adj* cottīdiānus.

workhouse n ergastulum nt.
working n (mechanism) māchinātiō f; (soil) cultus m.
workman n (unskilled) operārius m; (skilled) opifex m, faber m; **workmen** operae fpl.
workmanship n ars f, artificium nt.
workshop n fabrica f, officīna f.
world n (universe) mundus m; (earth) orbis terrārum m; (nature) rērum nātūra f; (mankind) hominēs mpl; (masses) vulgus nt; **of the ~** mundānus; **man of the ~** homō urbānus m; **best in the ~** rērum optimus, omnium optimus; **where in the ~** ubī gentium.
worldliness n quaestūs studium nt.
worldly adj quaestuī dēditus.
worm n vermis m ♦ vi: **~ one's way sē** īnsinuāre.
worm-eaten adj vermiculōsus.
wormwood n absinthium nt.
worn adj trītus.
worried adj sollicitus, anxius.
worry n cūra f, sollicitūdō f ♦ vi sollicitārī ♦ vt vexāre, sollicitāre; (of dogs) lacerāre.
worse adj pēior, dēterior; **grow ~** ingravēscere; **make matters ~** rem exasperāre ♦ adv pēius, dēterius.
worsen vi ingravēscere, dēteriōr fierī.
worship n venerātiō f, deōrum cultus m; (rite) sacra ntpl, rēs dīvīnae fpl ♦ vt adōrāre, venerārī, colere.
worst adj pessimus, dēterrimus; **~ enemy** inimīcissimus m; **endure the ~** ultima patī; vincere.
worsted n lāna f.
worth n (value) pretium nt; (moral) dignitās f, frūgālitās f, virtūs f; (prestige) auctōritās f ♦ adj dignus; **for all one's ~** prō virīlī parte; **how much is it ~?** quanti vēnit?; **it is ~ a lot** multum valet; **it is ~ doing** operae pretium est.
worthily adv dignē, meritō.
worthiness n dignitās f.
worthless adj (person) nēquam; (thing) vīlis, inānis.
worthlessness n levitās f, nēquitia f; vīlitās f.
worthy adj dignus; (person) frūgī, honestus; **~ of** dignus (abl).
wound n vulnus nt ♦ vt vulnerāre; (feelings) offendere.
wounded adj saucius.
wrangle n iūrgium nt, rixa f ♦ vi iūrgāre, rixārī, altercārī.
wrap vt involvere, obvolvere; **~ round** intorquēre; **~ up** involvere.
wrapper n involucrum nt.
wrapping n integumentum nt.
wrath n īra f, īrācundia f.
wrathful adj īrātus.
wrathfully adv īrācundē.
wreak vt: **~ vengeance on** saevīre in (acc), ulcīscī.
wreath n corōna f, sertum nt.
wreathe vt (garland) torquēre; (object) corōnāre.
wreck n naufragium nt ♦ vt frangere; (fig) perdere; **be ~ed** naufragium facere.
wreckage n fragmenta ntpl.
wrecked adj (person) naufragus; (ship) frāctus.
wrecker n perditor m.
wren n rēgulus m.
wrench vt intorquēre, extorquēre; **~ away** ēripere; **~ open** effringere.
wrest vt extorquēre.
wrestle vi luctārī.
wrestler n luctātor m, athlēta m.
wrestling n luctātiō f.
wretch n scelerātus m, nēquam homō m; **poor ~** miser homō m.
wretched adj īnfēlīx, miser; (pitiful) flēbilis.
wretchedly adv miserē.
wretchedness n miseria f; maestitia f.
wriggle vi sē torquēre.
wriggling adj sinuōsus.
wright n faber m.
wring vt torquēre; **~ from** extorquēre.
wrinkle n rūga f ♦ vt corrūgāre.
wrinkled adj rūgōsus.
wrist n prīma palmae pars f.
writ n (legal) auctōritās f.
write vt scrībere; (book) cōnscrībere; **~ off** indūcere; **~ on** īnscrībere (dat); **~ out** exscrībere, dēscrībere; **~ out in full** perscrībere.
writer n (Lit) scrīptor m, auctor m; (clerk) scrība m.
writhe vi torquērī.
writing n (act) scrīptiō f; (result) scrīptum nt.
wrong adj falsus, perversus, prāvus; (unjust) iniūstus, inīquus; **be ~, go ~** errāre ♦ n iniūria f, culpa f, noxa f, malum nt; **do ~** peccāre, dēlinquere; **right and ~** (moral) honesta ac turpia ntpl ♦ vt laedere, nocēre (dat); (by deceit) fraudāre.
wrongdoer n, maleficus m, scelerātus m.
wrongdoing n scelus nt.
wrongful adj iniūstus, iniūriosus, inīquus.
wrongfully adv iniūriā, iniūstē, inīquē.
wrong-headed adj perversus.
wrong-headedness n perversitās f.
wrongly adv falsō, dēprāvātē, male, perperam.
wroth adj īrātus.
wrought adj factus.
wry adj dētortus; **make a ~ face** ōs dūcere.
wryness n prāvitās f.

Y, y

yacht _n_ phasēlus _m_.
yard _n_ (_court_) ārea _f_; (_measure_) trēs pedēs.
yardarm _n_ antenna _f_.
yarn _n_ fīlum _nt_; (_story_) fābula _f_.
yawn _n_ hiātus _m_ ♦ _vi_ hiāre, ōscitāre; (_chasm_) dehiscere.
ye _pron_ vōs.
yean _vt_ parere.
year _n_ annus _m_; **every** ~ quotannīs; **for a** ~ in annum; **half** ~ sēmēstre spatium _nt_; **this** ~'s hōrnus; **twice a** ~ bis annō; **two** ~s biennium _nt_; **three** ~s triennium _nt_; **four** ~s quadriennium _nt_; **five** ~s quinquennium _nt_.
yearly _adj_ annuus, anniversārius ♦ _adv_ quotar.nīs.
yearn _vi_: ~ **for** dēsīderāre, exoptāre.
yearning _n_ dēsīderium _nt_.
yeast _n_ fermentum _nt_.
yell _n_ clāmor _m_; (_of pain_) ēiulātiō _f_ ♦ _vi_ clāmāre, eiulāre.
yellow _adj_ flāvus; (_pale_) gilvus; (_deep_) fulvus; (_gold_) luteus; (_saffron_) croceus.
yelp _n_ gannītus _m_ ♦ _vi_ gannīre.
yeoman _n_ colōnus _m_.
yes _adv_ ita verō (est), māximē; (_correcting_) immo.
yesterday _adv_ herī ♦ _n_ hesternus diēs _m_; ~'s hesternus; **the day before** ~ nudius tertius.
yet _adv_ (_contrast_) tamen, nihilōminus, attamen; (_time_) adhūc, etiam; (_with compar_) etiam; **and** ~ atquī, quamquam; **as** ~ adhūc; **not** ~ nōndum.
yew _n_ taxus _f_.
yield _n_ fructus _m_ ♦ _vt_ (_crops_) ferre, efferre; (_pleasure_) adferre; (_concession_) dare, concēdere; (_surrender_) dēdere ♦ _vi_ cēdere; (_surrender_) sē dēdere, sē trādere; ~ **to the**

wishes of mōrem gerere (_dat_), obsequī (_dat_).
yielding _adj_ (_person_) facilis, obsequēns; (_thing_) mollis ♦ _n_ cessio _f_; dēditiō _f_.
yoke _n_ iugum _nt_ ♦ _vt_ iungere, coniungere.
yokel _n_ agrestis _m_.
yolk _n_ vitellus _m_.
yonder _adv_ illīc ♦ _adj_ ille, iste.
yore _n_: **of** ~ quondam, ōlim.
you _pron_ tū, vōs.
young _adj_ iuvenis, adulēscēns; (_child_) parvus; ~**er** iūnior, nātū minor; ~**est** nātū minimus ♦ _n_ fētus _m_, pullus _m_, catulus _m_.
young man _n_ iuvenis _m_; adulēscēns _m_.
youngster _n_ puer _m_.
your _adj_ tuus, vester.
yourself _pron_ ipse.
youth _n_ (_age_) iuventūs _f_, adulescentia _f_; (_person_) iuvenis _m_, adulēscēns _m_; (_collective_) iuventūs _f_.
youthful _adj_ iuvenīlis, puerīlis.
youthfully _adv_ iuvenīliter.

Z, z

zeal _n_ studium _nt_, ārdor _m_.
zealot _n_ studiōsus _m_, fautor _m_.
zealous _adj_ studiōsus, ārdēns.
zealously _adv_ studiōsē, ārdenter.
zenith _n_ vertex _m_.
zephyr _n_ Favōnius _m_.
zero _n_ nihil _nt_.
zest _n_ (_taste_) sapor _m_; (_fig_) gustātus _m_, impetus _m_.
zigzag _n_ ānfrāctus _m_ ♦ _adj_ tortuōsus.
zither _n_ cithara _f_.
zodiac _n_ signifer orbis _m_.
zone _n_ cingulus _m_.

LATIN PHRASES USED IN ENGLISH

What follows is a list of some of the Latin phrases used in English today.

ab initio	from the beginning.
ab ovo	(lit: from the egg) from the beginning.
absit omen	(lit: may the (evil) omen be absent) may the presentiment not become real or take place.
ab urbe condita	(used in dates) from the foundation of the city (*i.e. from the foundation of Rome in 753 B.C.*).
A.D.	abbr for **anno Domini**.
ad hoc	(lit: for this) for a particular purpose only: **an ad hoc committee; an ad hoc decision.**
ad hominem	(lit: according to the person) 1 directed against a person rather than against his or her arguments. 2 based on or appealing to emotion rather than reason.
ad infinitum	without end; endlessly; to infinity.
ad interim	for the meantime; for the present: **ad interim measures.**
ad-lib	(abbr for **ad libitum**) ♦ *adj* improvised; impromptu ♦ *adv* without restraint; freely; as one pleases ♦ *vb* to improvise and deliver without preparation.
ad libitum	(lit: according to pleasure) as one pleases.
ad majorem Dei gloriam	for the greater glory of God (*the Jesuit motto*).
ad nauseam	(lit: to (the point of) nausea) to a disgusting extent.
ad rem	(lit: to the matter) to the point; without digression: **to reply ad rem; an ad rem discussion.**
advocatus diaboli	devil's advocate.
ad valorem	(lit: according to value) in proportion to the estimated value of the goods taxed.
aet.	(abbr for **aetatis**) at the age of.
Agnus Dei	Lamb of God.
alma mater	(lit: nurturing mother) one's former university, college or school.
alter ego	(lit: other self) 1 a second self. 2 a very close and intimate friend.
a.m.	abbr for **ante meridiem**.
AMDG	abbr for **ad majorem Dei gloriam**.
amor patriae	love of one's country; patriotism.
an.	(abbr for **anno**) in the year.
anno Domini	in the year of our Lord.
anno urbis conditae	in the year of the foundation of the city (*i.e. of Rome in 753 B.C., used in dates*)
anno regni	in the year of the reign (of).

annus mirabilis	(lit: wonderful year) a year of wonders.
antebellum	(lit: before the war) of or during the period before a war, especially the American Civil War.
ante meridiem	before noon.
ante-mortem	before death (*esp in legal or medical contexts*).
a.p.	(abbr for **ante prandium**) before a meal (*in prescriptions*).
apparatus criticus	(lit: critical apparatus) textual notes (*list of variant readings, etc., relating to a document, especially in a scholarly edition of a text*).
aq.	abbr for **aqua**.
aqua vitae	(lit: water of life) brandy.
a.r.	abbr for **anno regni**.
arbiter elegantiae *or* **elegantiarum**	judge in a matter of taste.
arcus senilis	(lit: senile bow) opaque circle around the cornea of the eye (*often seen in elderly people*).
argumentum ad hominem	(lit: argument according to the person: Logic) **1** fallacious argument that attacks not an opponent's beliefs but his motives or character. **2** argument that shows an opponent's statement to be inconsistent with his other beliefs.
ars longa vita brevis	art is long, life is short.
AUC	abbr for: **1 ab urbe condita. 2 anno urbis conditae.**
aut vincere aut mori	death or victory.
aurora australis	the southern lights.
aurora borealis	the northern lights.
ave	**1** hail! **2** farewell!
ave atque vale	hail and farewell!
Ave Maria	Hail Mary.
beatae memoriae	of blessed memory.
Beata Virgo	the Blessed Virgin.
Beata Virgo Maria	the Blessed Virgin Mary.
b.i.d	(abbr for **bis in die**) twice a day (*in prescriptions*).
bis dat, qui cito dat	the person who gives promptly gives twice.
BV	abbr for **Beata Virgo**.
c, ca	abbr for **circa**.
camera obscura	(lit: dark chamber) camera obscura.
carpe diem	(lit: seize the day) enjoy the pleasures of the moment, without concern for the future.
casus belli	(lit: occasion of war) **1** an event or act used to justify a war. **2** the immediate cause of a quarrel.
caveat emptor	let the buyer beware.
cetera desunt	the rest is missing.

ceteris paribus	other things being equal.
circa	around.
Codex Juris Canonici	(lit: book of canon law) the official code of canon law (*in the Roman Catholic Church*).
cogito, ergo sum	I think, therefore I am (*the basis of Descartes' philosophy*).
compos mentis	of sound mind; sane.
coram populo	in the presence of the people; openly.
corpus delicti	(lit: the body of the crime: *LAW*) the body of facts that constitute an offence.
Corpus Juris Canonici	(lit: body of canon law) the official compilation of canon law (*in the Roman Catholic Church*).
Corpus Juris Civilis	(lit: body of civil law) the body of Roman or civil law.
corrigenda	things to be corrected.
corpus vile	(lit: worthless body) person or thing fit only to be the object of an experiment.
culpa	**1** (*LAW*) an act of neglect. **2** (*gen*) a fault; sin; guilt.
cum grano salis	with a grain of salt; not too literally.
cum laude	(*chiefly US*) with praise (*the lowest of three designations for above-average achievement in examinations*).
curriculum vitae	(lit: the course of one's life) curriculum vitae.
de facto	*adv* in fact ♦ *adj* existing in fact.
de gustibus non est disputandem	there is no arguing about tastes.
de jure	according to law; by right; legally.
de mortuis nil nisi bonum	say nothing but good of the dead.
de novo	anew.
Deo gratias	thanks be to God.
Deo Optimo Maximo	to God, the best, the Greatest.
Deo volente	God willing.
de profundis	out of the depths of misery or dejection.
deus ex machina	(lit: the god from the machine) **1** (*in ancient Greek and Roman drama*) a god introduced into a play to resolve the plot. **2** any unlikely or artificial device serving this purpose.
Dies Irae	(lit: the day of wrath) **1** a famous Latin hymn of the 13th century, describing the Last Judgment. It is used in the Mass for the dead. **2** a musical setting of this hymn, usually part of a setting of the Requiem.
disjecta membra	the scattered remains.
DOM	abbr for **Deo Optimo Maximo**.
dramatis personae	(lit: the persons of the drama) the list of characters in a drama.

Ecce Homo   behold the man (*the words of Pontius Pilate to Christ's accusers* [*John 19:5*]).

editio princeps   (lit: the first edition) the first printed edition of a work.

e.g., eg   abbr for **exempli gratia**.

emeritus   retired from office.

e pluribus unum   one out of many (*motto of USA*).

ER   1 (abbr for **Elizabeth Regina**) Queen Elizabeth; 2 (abbr for **Eduardus Rex**) King Edward.

errare est humanum   to err is human.

erratum (*pl* **errata**)   error.

et seq.   (abbr for **et sequens**) and the following.

et seqq.   (abbr for **et sequentia**) and those that follow.

ex   (lit: out of, from) 1 (*FINANCE*) not participating in; excluding; without: **ex bonus; ex dividend; ex rights.** 2 (*COMMERCE*) without charge to the buyer until removed from: **ex quay; ex ship; ex works**.

ex cathedra   (lit: from the chair) 1 with authority. 2 defined by the pope as infallibly true, to be accepted by all Roman Catholics.

exeat   (lit: let him or her go out) formal leave of absence.

exempli gratia   for example.

exeunt   they go out (*used as a stage direction*).

exeunt omnes   they all go out (*used as a stage direction*).

exit   he or she goes out (*used as a stage direction*).

ex libris   (lit: from the books (of)) from the collection or library of.

ex officio   by right of position or office.

ex parte   (*LAW*) on behalf of one side or party only (*of an application in a judicial proceeding*): **an ex parte injunction**.

ex post facto   having retrospective effect: **an ex post facto law**.

ex silentio   (lit: from silence) based on a lack of evidence to the contrary (*of a theory, assumption etc*).

extempore   (lit: instantaneously) without planning or preparation; impromptu.

ex voto   *adv, adj* in accordance with a vow ♦ *n* offering made in fulfilment of a vow.

facile princeps   (lit: easily first) an obvious leader.

fecit (*abbr* **fec**)   (he or she) made it (*used formerly on works of art next to the artist's name*).

felo de se   suicide.

festina lente   more haste, less speed.

fiat lux   let there be light.

Fidei Defensor   defender of the faith.

fidus Achates	(lit: faithful Achates) faithful friend or companion (*the name of the faithful companion of Aeneas in Virgil's Aeneid*).
floruit	(he or she) flourished (*used to indicate the period when a historical figure, whose birth and death dates are unknown, was most active*).
fons et origo	the source and origin.
genius loci	(lit: genius of the place) **1** the guardian spirit of a place. **2** the special atmosphere of a particular place.
Gloria in Excelsis Deo	(lit: glory to God in the highest) **1** the Greater Doxology, beginning in Latin with these words. **2** a musical setting of this.
Gloria Patri	(lit: glory to the father) **1** the Lesser Doxology, beginning in Latin with these words. **2** a musical setting of this.
hinc illae lacrimae	hence those tears.
HJ	(abbr for **hic jacet**) here lies (*on gravestones*).
HJS	(abbr for **hic jacet sepultus**) here lies buried (*on gravestones*).
horrible dictu	horrible to relate.
ibid.	abbr for **ibidem**.
ibidem	in the same place (*in annotations, bibliographies, etc., when referring to a book, article, chapter, or page previously cited*).
id est	that is (to say); in other words.
idem	the same (*used to refer to an article, chapter, etc., previously cited*).
i.e.	abbr for **id est**.
ign.	abbr for **ignotus**.
ignoratio elenchi	(lit: an ignorance of proof: *Logic*) **1** a purported refutation of a proposition that does not in fact prove it false but merely establishes a related but strictly irrelevant proposition. **2** the fallacy of arguing in this way.
ignotum per ignotius	(lit: the unknown by means of the more unknown) an explanation that is obscurer than the thing to be explained.
ignotus	unknown.
ignis fatuus	will o' the wisp.
Imp.	**1** (abbr for **Imperator**) Emperor; **2** (abbr for **Imperatrix**) Empress.
in absentia	in one's absence; in the absence of: **he was condemned in absentia.**
in aeternum	forever; eternally.
in articulo mortis	at the point of death.

in camera	(lit: in the chamber) in private.
in extenso	at full length.
in extremis	(lit: in the furthest reaches) **1** in extremity; in dire straits. **2** at the point of death.
infra	below.
infra dig	(abbr for **infra dignitatem**) beneath one's dignity.
in loco parentis	in place of a parent (*said of a person acting in a parental capacity*).
in medias res	(lit: into the midst of things) in or into the middle of events or a narrative.
in memoriam	in memory of; as a memorial to (*used in obituaries, epitaphs etc*).
in perpetuum	for ever.
in personam	(lit: against the person) directed against a specific person or persons (*LAW: of a judicial act*).
in propria persona	in person; personally.
in rem	(lit: against the matter) directed against property rather than against a specific person (*LAW: of a judicial act*).
in rerum natura	in the nature of things.
INRI	(lit: Jesus of Nazareth, King of the Jews) abbr for **Iesus Nazarenus Rex Iudaeorum** (*the inscription placed over Christ's head during the Crucifixion*).
in situ	(lit: in position) in the natural, original, or appropriate position.
inter alia	among other things.
inter alios	among other people.
inter vivos	(*LAW*) between living people: **an inter vivos gift**.
in toto	totally; entirely; completely.
in utero	within the womb.
in vacuo	in a vacuum.
in vino veritas	in wine there is truth.
in vitro	(lit: in glass) made to occur outside the body of the organism in an artificial environment (*of biological processes or reactions*): **in vitro fertilization**.
in vivo	(lit: in a living (thing)) occurring or carried out in the living organism (*of biological processes or experiments*).
ipse dixit	(lit: he himself said it) an arbitrary and unsupported assertion.
ipsissima verba	the very words.
ipso facto	by the fact itself.
i.q.	(lit: the same as) abbr for **idem quod**.
lapsus linguae	a slip of the tongue.
lc	(abbr for **(in) loco citato**) in the place cited.

ex loci	the law of the place.
ex non scripta	the unwritten law; common law.
ex scripta	the written law; statute law.
ex talionis	the law of revenge or retaliation.
oc. cit.	(abbr for **(in) loco citato**) in the place cited (*in textual annotation*).
magna cum laude	(chiefly US) with great praise (*the second of three designations for above-average achievement in examinations*).
magnum opus	a great work of art or literature (*especially the greatest single work of an artist*).
mala fide	undertaken in bad faith.
mare clausum	(lit: closed sea: LAW) a sea coming under the jurisdiction of one nation and closed to all others.
mare liberum	(lit: free sea: LAW) a sea open to navigation by shipping of all nations.
mare nostrum	(lit: our sea) the Mediterranean.
mater	mother (*often used facetiously*).
mater dolorosa	(lit: sorrowful mother) the Virgin Mary sorrowing for the dead Christ (*especially as depicted in art*).
materfamilias	(lit: mother of family) the mother of a family or the female head of a family.
materia medica	(lit: medical matter) **1** the branch of medical science concerned with the study of drugs used in the treatment of disease. **2** the drugs used in the treatment of disease.
mea culpa	(lit: my fault) an acknowledgement of guilt.
memento mori	(lit: remember you must die) an object, such as a skull, intended to remind people of the inevitability of death.
mens sana in corpore sano	a healthy mind in a healthy body.
mens rea	(lit: guilty mind: LAW) a criminal intention or knowledge that an act is wrong.
miles gloriosus	a braggart soldier (*especially as a stock figure in comedy*).
mirabile dictu	wonderful to relate.
mittimus	(lit: we send) a warrant of commitment to prison or a command to a jailer directing him to hold someone in prison.
modus operandi	procedure; method of operating; manner of working.
modus ponens	(lit: mood that affirms) the principle that whenever a conditional statement and its antecedent are given to be true its consequent may be validly inferred.

modus tollens	(lit: mood that denies) the principle that whenever a conditional statement and the negation of its consequent are given to be true, the negation of its antecedent may be validly inferred.
modus vivendi	(lit: way of living) a working arrangement between conflicting interests; practical compromise.
motu proprio	(lit: of his own accord) an administrative papal bull.
multum in parvo	much in a small space.
mutatis mutandis	with the necessary changes.
NB, N.B., nb, n.b.	(abbr for **nota bene**) note well.
nem. con.	(abbr for **nemine contradicente**) no-one contradicting; unanimously.
nemo me impune lacessit	no-one provokes me with impunity.
ne plus ultra	(lit: not more beyond) the extreme or perfect point or state.
nihil	nil; nothing.
nihil obstat	there is no obstacle.
nil desperandum	(lit: nothing to be despaired of) never despair.
nisi prius	(lit: unless previously) **1** *in England* (a) a direction that a case be brought up to Westminster for trial before a single judge and jury. (b) the writ giving this direction. **2** *in the US* a court where civil actions are tried by a single judge sitting with a jury as distinguished from an appellate court.
nolens volens	whether willing or unwilling.
noli me tangere	(lit: do not touch me) a warning against interfering with or against touching a person or thing.
nolle prosequi	(lit: do not pursue) an entry made on the court record when the plaintiff in a civil suit or prosecutor in a criminal prosecution undertakes not to continue the action or prosecution.
nolo contendere	(lit: I do not wish to contend) a plea made by a defendant to a criminal charge having the same effect in those proceedings as a plea of guilty but not precluding him from denying the charge in a subsequent action.
non compos mentis	(lit: not in control of one's mind) mentally incapable of managing one's own affairs; of unsound mind; insane.
non prosequitur	(lit: he does not proceed) a judgment in favour of a defendant when the plaintiff failed to take the necessary steps in an action within the time allowed.
non sequitur	(lit: it does not follow) **1** (*gen*) a statement having little or no relevance to what preceded it. **2** (*Logic*) a conclusion that does not follow from the premises.
nulli secundus	second to none.

umen	(lit: divine power) **1** (*especially in ancient Roman religion*) a deity or spirit presiding over a thing or place. **2** a guiding principle, force, or spirit.
unc Dimittis	(lit: now let depart) **1** the Canticle of Simeon (*Luke 2:29-32*). **2** a musical setting of this.
b.	**1** abbr for **obiit**. **2** (abbr for **obiter**) incidentally; in passing.
biit	he or she died (*on gravestones*).
biter dictum	(lit: something said in passing) **1** (*LAW*) an observation by a judge on some point of law not directly in issue in the case before him and thus neither requiring his decision nor serving as a precedent, but nevertheless of persuasive authority. **2** any comment, remark, or observation made in passing.
bscurum per obscurius	(lit: the obscure by means of the more obscure) an explanation that is obscurer than the thing to be explained.
mnium-gatherum	(often facetious) a miscellaneous collection; assortment.
nus probandi	(*LAW*) the burden of proof.
p. cit.	(abbr of **opere citato**) in the work cited.
pus anglicanum	(lit: English work) fine embroidery (*especially of church vestments*).
ra pro nobis	pray for us.
tempora! O mores!	oh the times! oh the customs!
a.	abbr of **per annum**.
ace	by leave of; with due deference to (*used to acknowledge politely someone who disagrees with the speaker or writer*).
ari passu	with equal speed or progress; equably (*often used to refer to the right of creditors to receive assets from the same source without one taking precedence*).
assim	here and there; throughout (*used to indicate that what is referred to occurs frequently in the work cited*).
aterfamilias	(lit: father of the family) **1** the male head of a household. **2** the head of a household having authority over its members.
ax vobiscum	peace be with you.
eccavi	(lit: I have sinned) a confession of guilt.
eculium	(lit: property) property that a father or master allowed his child or slave to hold as his own.
er annum	every year; year by year.
er ardua ad astra	through difficulties to the stars (*motto of the RAF*).
er capita	(lit: according to heads) of or for each person.
er contra	on the contrary.

per diem	(lit: for the day) **1** every day; by the day. **2** an allowance for daily expenses, usually those incurred while working.
per mensem	every month; by the month.
per pro	(abbr for **per procurationem**) by delegation to; through the agency of (*used when signing documents on behalf of someone else*).
persona grata	an acceptable person (*especially a diplomat acceptable to the government of the country to which he is sent*).
persona non grata	unacceptable or unwelcome person.
petitio principii	(lit: an assumption at the beginning: *Logic*) a form of fallacious reasoning in which the conclusion has been assumed in the premises; begging the question.
pia mater	(lit: pious mother) the innermost of the three membranes that cover the brain and spinal cord.
pinxit	(he or she) painted this (*used formerly on works of art next to the artist's name*).
p.m., P.M., pm, PM	abbr. for **1** post meridiem **2** postmortem.
post-bellum	(lit: after war) of or during the period after a war, especially the American Civil War.
post hoc	(lit: after this: *Logic*) the fallacy of assuming that temporal succession is evidence of causal relation.
post hoc, ergo propter hoc	after this, therefore because of this (*a fallacy of reasoning*).
post meridiem	after noon.
postmortem	(lit: after death) *n* **1** dissection and examination of a dead body to determine the cause of death. **2** analysis or study of a recently completed event ♦ *adj* occurring after death.
pp	abbr for **1** per pro. **2** post prandium after a meal (*in prescriptions*).
PPS	(lit: after postscript; abbr for **post postscriptum**) additional postscript.
pr	(abbr for: **per rectum**) through the rectum (*in prescriptions*).
prima facie	at a first view.
primum mobile	(lit: first moving (thing)) prime mover.
primus inter pares	first among equals.
prn	(abbr for **pro re nata**) as the situation demands, as needed (*in prescriptions*).
pro forma	(lit: for form's sake) **1** prescribing a set form or procedure. **2** performed in a set manner.
pro patria	for one's country.
pro rata	in proportion.
pro tempore	for the time being.
proxime accessit	(lit: he or she came next) the runner-up.

q.e.	(abbr for **quod est**) which is.
QED	abbr for **quod erat demonstrandum**.
QEF	abbr for **quod erat faciendum**.
quid pro quo	(lit: something for something) **1** a reciprocal exchange. **2** something given in compensation, especially an advantage or object given in exchange for another.
quis custodiet ipsos custodes?	who will guard the guards?
q.l.	(abbr for **quantum libet**) as much as you please (*in prescriptions*).
qm	(abbr for **quaque mane**) every morning (*in prescriptions*).
qn	(abbr for **quaque nocte**) every night (*in prescriptions*).
quod erat demonstrandum	which was to be proved.
quod erat faciendum	which was to be done.
quot homines, tot sententiæ	there are as many opinions as there are people.
quo vadis?	whither goest thou?
qqv	(abbr for **quae vide**) which (*words, items etc*) see (*denoting a cross reference to more than one item*).
qs	(abbr for **quantum sufficit**) as much as will suffice (*in prescriptions*).
qv	(abbr for **quod vide**) which (*word, item etc*) see (*denoting a cross reference*).
rara avis	(lit: rare bird) an unusual, uncommon or exceptional person or thing.
reductio ad absurdum	(lit: reduction to the absurd) **1** a method of disproving a proposition by showing that its inevitable consequences would be absurd. **2** a method of indirectly proving a proposition by assuming its negation to be true and showing that this leads to an absurdity. **3** application of a principle or a proposed principle to an instance in which it is absurd.
requiescat	(lit: may he or she rest) a prayer for the repose of the souls of the dead.
requiescat in pace	may he or she rest in peace.
res gestae	(lit: things done) **1** things done or accomplished; achievements. **2** (*LAW*) incidental facts and circumstances that are admissible in evidence because they introduce or explain the matter in issue.
res ipsa loquitur	(*LAW*) the thing or matter speaks for itself.
res judicata	(*LAW*) a matter already adjudicated upon that cannot be raised again.
res publica	(lit: the public thing) the state, republic, or commonwealth.

resurgam	I shall rise again.
RI	**1** (abbr for **Regina et Imperatrix**) Queen and Empress. **2** (abbr for **Rex et Imperator**) King and Emperor.
rigor mortis	(lit: rigidity of death) the stiffness of joints and muscular rigidity of a dead body.
RIP	abbr for **requiescat** or **requiescant in pace**.
risus sardonicus	(lit: sardonic laugh) fixed contraction of the facial muscles resulting in a peculiar distorted grin, caused especially by tetanus.
sanctum sanctorum	(lit: holy of holies) **1** (*Bible*) the holy of holies. **2** (*often facetious*) an especially private place.
sartor resartus	the tailor patched.
schola cantorum	(lit: school of singers) a choir or choir school maintained by a church.
scire facias	(lit: cause (him) to know) **1** (*LAW, rare*) a judicial writ founded upon some record, such as a judgement, letters patent, etc., requiring the person against whom it is brought to show cause why the record should not be enforced or annulled. **2** a proceeding begun by the issue of such a writ.
semper fidelis	always faithful.
semper idem	always the same.
seq.	(abbr for **sequens**) the following (one).
seqq.	(abbr for **sequentia**) the following (ones).
seriatim	in order.
sic	thus (*often used to call attention to some quoted mistake*).
sic itur ad astra	such is the way to the stars.
sic transit gloria mundi	so passes the glory of the world.
si monumentum requiris, circumspice	if you seek (his) monument, look around you (*inscription on the architect Sir Christopher Wren's tomb in St Paul's Cathedral*).
sine die	without a day.
sine prole	(*LAW*) without issue.
sine qua non	(lit: without which not) an indispensable condition or requirement.
sl	(abbr for **sine loco**) without place (*of publication*).
sp	abbr for **sine prole**.
spiritus asper	rough breathing.
spiritus lenis	smooth breathing.
SPQR	(abbr for **Senatus Populusque Romanus**) the Senate and People of Rome.
sq.	(abbr for **sequens**) the following (one).
sqq.	(abbr for **sequentia**) the following (ones).

Stabat Mater	(lit: the mother was standing) **1** a Latin hymn, probably of the 13th century, commemorating the sorrows of the Virgin Mary at the crucifixion and used in the Mass and various other services. **2** a musical setting of this hymn.
status quo	(lit: the state in which) the existing state of affairs.
stet	let it stand.
sub judice	before a court of law or a judge; under judicial consideration.
sub rosa	(lit: under the rose) secretly.
sub voce	under the word.
sui generis	(lit: of its own kind) unique.
sui juris	(lit: of one's own right) (*LAW*) of full age and not under disability; legally competent to manage one's own affairs; independent.
summa cum laude	(*chiefly U.S.*) with the utmost praise (*the highest of three designations for above-average achievement in examinations. In Britain it is sometimes used to designate a first-class honours degree*).
summum bonum	the principle of goodness in which all moral values are included or from which they are derived; highest or supreme good.
suo jure	(*chiefly LAW*) in one's own right.
suo loco	(*chiefly LAW*) in a person or thing's own or rightful place.
supra	above.
sursum corda	lift up your hearts (to God).
SV	abbr for **sub voce**.
tabula rasa	(lit: a scraped tablet) **1** the mind in its uninformed original state. **2** an opportunity for a fresh start; clean slate.
taedium vitae	(lit: weariness of life) the feeling that life is boring and dull.
Te Deum	(lit: Thee, God) **1** an ancient Latin hymn in rhythmic prose, sung or recited at matins in the Roman Catholic Church and in English translation at morning prayer in the Church of England and used by both churches as an expression of thanksgiving on special occasions. **2** a musical setting of this hymn. **3** a service of thanksgiving in which the recital of this hymn forms a central part.
te igitur	(lit: Thee, therefore: *Roman Catholic Church*) the first prayer of the canon of the Mass.
tempore	in the time of.
tempus fugit	time flies.
terminus ad quem	(lit: the end to which) the aim or terminal point.
terminus a quo	(lit: the end from which) the starting point; beginning.

terra firma	the solid earth; firm ground.
terra incognita	an unexplored or unknown land, region or area for study.
tertium quid	a third something.
t.i.d.	(abbr for **ter in die**) three times a day (*in prescriptions*).
tu quoque	you likewise (*a retort made by a person accused of a crime implying that the accuser is also guilty of the same crime*).
uberrima fides	utmost good faith.
ubique	everywhere.
ubi supra	where (mentioned or cited) above.
ultima Thule	(lit: the most distant Thule) **1** the utmost boundary or limit. **2** a remote goal or aim.
ultra vires	beyond one's powers.
una voce	with one voice.
urbi et orbi	(*Roman Catholic Church*) to the city and the world (*a phrase qualifying the solemn papal blessing*).
ut dict.	(abbr for **ut dictum**) as directed.
ut infra	as below.
ut supra	as above.
v.	abbr for **1 verso**. **2 versus**. **3 vide**.
vade in pace	go in peace.
vade mecum	(lit: go with me) a handbook or other aid carried on the person for immediate use when needed.
væe victis	woe to the conquered!
vale	farewell!
veni, vidi, vici	I came, I saw, I conquered.
venire facias	(lit: you must make come: *LAW*) a writ directing a sheriff to summon suitable persons to form a jury.
verbatim et litteratim	word for word and letter for letter.
verb. sap.	(abbr for **verbum sapienti sat est**) a word is enough to the wise.
verso	**1** the back of a sheet of printed paper. **2** the side of a coin opposite to the obverse; reverse.
versus	**1** against; in opposition to. **2** as opposed to; in contrast with.
via	by way of.
via media	a middle course.
vice	in the place of; instead of; as a substitute for.
vice versa	the other way round.
vide	see.
videlicet	namely; to wit.

vi et armis	(lit: by force and arms) a kind of trespass accompanied by force and violence.
VIR	(abbr for **Victoria Imperatrix Regina**) Victoria, Empress and Queen.
virginibus puerisque	for maidens and youths.
vis inertiæ	the power of inertia.
viva voce	(lit: with living voice) *adv, adj* by word of mouth ♦ *n* an oral examination.
viz.	abbr for **videlicet**.
vl	(abbr for **varia lecto**) variant reading.
vollente Deo	God willing.
vox populi	the voice of the people; popular or public opinion.
vox populi, vox Dei	the voice of the people is the voice of God.
VR	(abbr for **Victoria Regina**) Queen Queen Victoria.
VRI	(abbr for **Victoria Regina et Imperatrix**) Victoria, Queen and Empress.